Random House

mammoth

CROSSWORD PUZZLE
OMNIBUS

Edited by Stanley Newman

Random House
Puzzles & Games

ISBN: 0-8129-3394-X

Random House Puzzles & Games Web site address:
www.puzzlesatrandom.com

Page design and typography by North Market Street Graphics
Manufactured in the United States of America

4   6   8   9   7   5   3

First Edition

SPECIAL SALES
Random House Puzzles & Games books are available at special discounts for bulk purchases for sales promotions or premiums. Special editions, including personalized covers, excerpts of existing books, and corporate imprints, can be created in large quantities for special needs.
For more information, contact Random House Special Markets at 800-800-3246

1 FRUITFUL by Shirley Soloway

ACROSS
1 Alaskan island
5 Leading player
9 Set in
14 Bridle control
15 Have a drink
16 __ Loa
17 Strong brews
18 Felt sorry about
19 Stacked (up)
20 Fats Domino tune
23 Separated
24 Fortune-teller
25 Part of TGIF
28 Tie __ (cravat pins)
30 More costly
32 Traffic snarl
35 Kind of clam
38 "Put __ on it!"
40 Marsupial, for short
41 Matures
42 Application item
47 Matched pieces
48 Actor Estevez
49 1995, e.g.
51 Family pet
52 Cup edges
55 Notched, as a leaf
58 IBM competitor
62 __ Pass (Uris novel)
64 Spanish surrealist
65 Plantation of fiction
66 Fisherman's milieu
67 King or Young
68 Sponsorship
69 Pains in the neck
70 Singer k.d.
71 Like the Mariana Trench

DOWN
1 Jordanian, e.g.
2 "I cannot __ lie"
3 See 32 Across
4 Put out of office
5 Elongate
6 Guided trip
7 Imitators
8 Change color again
9 Realms
10 Post
11 Pond inhabitants
12 Chemical suffix
13 June celebrant
21 Bric-a-__
22 Actress Lamarr
26 Taylor of The Nanny
27 "__ my case"
29 Resident of Belgrade
31 __ glance
32 World-weary
33 Budget rival
34 Makes less severe
36 Louis XVI, e.g.
37 Actor Calhoun
39 Neighbor of Penna.
43 Crankcase parts
44 Silver wrap
45 Precipitating heavily
46 Heavenly instrument
50 Beat easily
53 Go by bike
54 La __ Opera House
56 Phase
57 Spooky
59 Land map
60 Luise Rainer role
61 Grating sound
62 Floor cleaner
63 Winter hazard

2 RADIO DAYS by Patrick Jordan

ACROSS
1 Love Story author
6 Ward off
11 Lincoln son
14 "__, all ye faithful . . ."
15 Allan-__
16 Exist
17 Classic radio skit
19 Sundial numeral
20 Prairie home material
21 Head tops
22 Poppies artist
24 Linguist Chomsky et al.
26 With skill
27 Baryshnikov, in '74
29 Import fee
31 Blew one's stack
32 Reindeer name
33 Purpose
36 Feel sore
37 Cut into cubes
38 Hitch
39 Prepared
40 Beds of a sort
41 32 Across' owner
42 Forest clearings
44 Altered
45 Hands __ the Table (Lombard film)
47 Honey bunch?
48 Shoots the breeze
49 One of four for Hepburn
51 Jefferson Davis' nation: Abbr.
54 __-tac-toe
55 He spoke for Charlie
58 Actor Wallach
59 Oklahoma city
60 War-horse
61 Yahtzee cube
62 Unquestioning followers
63 Abounds (with)

DOWN
1 Lays seed
2 Canyon sound
3 Exit line for Ms. Allen
4 Mornings, briefly
5 Spotted cat
6 Balsa vehicles
7 Singer Adams
8 Course goals
9 Chicago railways
10 Big Bad Wolf's order
11 Molly's rejoinder to Fibber
12 Disney mermaid
13 Divine character
18 Reputation
23 Awry
25 Architectural double curve
26 __ Scott decision
27 Geological periods
28 Spiked club
29 Pillow casings
30 Logging-camp tools
32 Hollywood crosser
34 Stuff to the gills
35 Archaic "Oh, my!"
37 Flops
38 Coal-rich German basin
40 Low-slung hounds
41 Most meager
43 Real-estate unit
44 Cotton-tipped cleaner
45 Behaved
46 Tex-Mex dish
47 Iron or book leader
49 Stare at
50 Manuscript encl.
52 Appear
53 "No ifs, __ or buts"
56 "That was dumb of me!"
57 Short highway?

3 DANCE FEVER by Gregory E. Paul

ACROSS
1 IRS employees
5 Clean a chimney
10 Dogie
14 Gap
15 Pet rocks, e.g.
16 Russian city
17 Whit
18 Amber or mastic
19 Casa __ Orchestra
20 '20s dance
22 Actor Sharif
23 Porridge grain
24 Treat with carbon dioxide
26 Kind of drum
30 Colonist William
32 Forster title start
33 '40s dance
38 Ponce de __
39 Sport shirts
40 Sharpen
41 Lively dance
43 United rival
44 Gasp
45 Silver-tongued speaker
46 Part of AWOL
50 Harem room
51 Great Northern diver
52 Ragtime dance
59 Churchill Downs denizen
60 Needle cases
61 Unctuous
62 MA's motto start
63 Breathing sounds
64 Boo-boo
65 Bring up
66 "__ Lady" (Tom Jones song)
67 Gin flavor

DOWN
1 Cartoonist Young
2 Word of disparagement
3 Neighbor of Mont.
4 Char
5 Something very funny
6 Take by force
7 Bridge position
8 Singer Pinza
9 Stadium souvenirs
10 Silver or gold
11 Scent
12 Paul of *Melvin and Howard*
13 Emergency signal
21 Pend
25 Buffalo-to-Rochester dir.
26 #1 on the Mohs scale
27 Chocolate cookie
28 Debatable
29 Nobelist Morrison
30 Oven light
31 Thames town
33 Merge
34 Big bird
35 *A Man for All Seasons* playwright
36 Golden Rule word
37 Accoutrements
39 "The Great Pretender" group
42 ANA member
43 Cart
45 Black Sea port
46 Modify
47 Wilderness Road warrior
48 March man
49 Sign up for
50 Steinbeck characters
53 The 45th state
54 Hold sway
55 Easy throw
56 Lunar trench
57 Mélange
58 Input data, perhaps

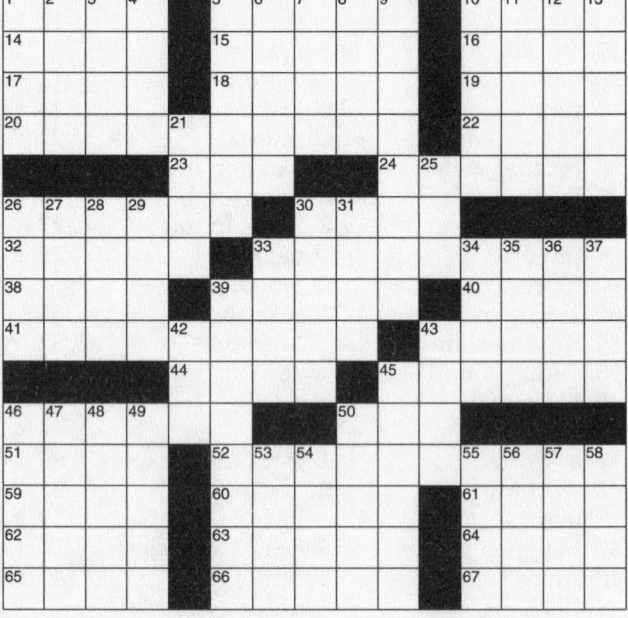

4 PLAY BALL! by Rich Norris

ACROSS
1 Cook a soufflé
5 Singer Lanza
10 Strike, in a way
14 Pub quaffs
15 Maine town
16 Dream
17 Hawker's talk
19 A long time
20 Prank player
21 Memorable time
22 Unreconciled
23 Jackal relatives
25 LPGA members
27 Discard
29 RR stop
32 Bed part
35 Slips up
36 Hue and cry
37 A bit: Mus.
38 Hurts badly
40 Gas and oil
41 St. crosser
42 Show's partner
43 They may be loose
44 Classical beginning
45 Place for valuables
49 Word in golf-ball names
51 Stumped
55 Composer Berg
57 Cameroon neighbor
59 Erase, as a computer file
60 Wild pig
61 1978 Jane Fonda film
63 Get some rays
64 Actress Papas
65 In a while
66 Summer drinks
67 Units of force
68 Honeyed drink

DOWN
1 Computer language
2 Texas mission
3 Water spirit
4 Compass dir.
5 Cleaner, at times
6 Songlike passage
7 Campus mil. recruiters
8 Kind of caterpillar
9 Sound of awe
10 Mold
11 1976 sci-fi film
12 Little, for one
13 Kid brother, perhaps
18 Son of Adam
22 Qtys.
24 NFL Hall-of-Famer Graham
26 What we share
28 "Pirate Jenny" composer
30 __ the line (conformed)
31 Leatherworkers' tools
32 Thumb-to-pinky distance
33 Tennis term
34 "The Sign" singers
38 Vegan's no-no
39 *Pilgrim's Progress*, e.g.
40 Sense
42 Exact match
46 Texas/Louisiana lake
47 Makes up (for)
48 Canine feature
50 Songbirds
52 Layer of note
53 Pago Pago locale
54 Use up
55 Palindromic rock group
56 Significant quantity
58 Last word
61 El __ (national hero of Spain)
62 Breakfast side dish

5 HI SIGNS by Dean Niles

ACROSS

1 Nibble
5 "__, Joy of Man's Desiring"
9 Muslim priests
14 __ Beauty apple
15 Harbinger
16 __ game (pitcher's dream)
17 Object of reverence
18 '50s TV phenomenon
20 Countermelody
22 Tic-tac-toe win
23 Passes, informally
24 Had
26 __ de plume
28 In a neat manner
31 Chernenko's predecessor
36 Speeds
37 Family chart
38 Speaking part
39 Economist Smith
40 Fraud
41 English actress Gwyn
42 '50s sitcom
43 Schubert song
44 Pusillanimous
45 Salty twists
47 Daily event
48 Species division
49 Sound of a plucked string
51 Books expert: Abbr.
54 __ room
56 Studio
60 Jerry Herman musical
63 __ la Douce
64 Ms. Lauder
65 Stare
66 Not masc. or fem.
67 Animated characters
68 Fresh talk
69 To be, to Brutus

DOWN

1 System of coordinates
2 Junction point
3 Famous cookie-maker
4 They may be underfoot
5 Actor Depp
6 Ooze feeling
7 Put in stitches
8 Cancel
9 Like modern plumbing
10 Speak with a Jersey accent?
11 ". . . __ time in the old . . ."
12 South of France
13 Underworld river
19 Over there
21 Shoemaker's tools
25 Most murky
27 Early odds
28 Chaplin persona
29 *M*A*S*H* character
30 *Veni*
32 Exigency
33 Odes and idylls
34 Fran's colleague
35 Grassland
37 Follow
40 Worked a muscle
44 Adjust, as a motor
46 Nonentities
47 Woodland deities
50 Cambria, now
51 Guitarist Atkins
52 Mexican money
53 Certain sax
55 Filches
57 Angers
58 Australian birds
59 Merit
61 Dawson or Cariou
62 Meadow

6 WOOD WORK by Shirley Soloway

ACROSS

1 Twofold
5 Photo session
10 Plumbing problem
14 __ way (not at all)
15 Spouse of Pocahontas
16 Folklore monster
17 Car feature
19 Arizona river
20 Mythical giant
21 Prov. of Canada
22 Is wearing
23 Underwater exploratorium
25 Energy type
27 Tub
29 Other name
32 Do some stretching
37 Walk unsteadily
39 At any time
40 Actor Stacy
42 Sewing-machine inventor
43 Flavorful seed
45 Originating (from)
47 More logical
48 __ Lanka
49 Play groups
52 Grab
57 Reporter Lesley
60 Actor Stephen
62 Author Calvino
63 __ avail (useless)
64 Dolly Levi, e.g.
66 Baseball manager Felipe
67 __ With Judy
68 Show the way
69 Not straight
70 Seamstress Ross
71 Art Deco artist

DOWN

1 Territorial divs.
2 Loosen, as a shoe
3 Loos or Louise
4 In the neighborhood
5 Last year's jrs.
6 Santa sounds
7 Lena and Ken
8 "We're __ See the Wizard"
9 Asian holiday
10 Math exponent
11 Sponsorship
12 Woody's son
13 19th-century actor Edmund
18 Varlet
22 Angelic topper
24 Carnival employees
26 Soaps up
28 Calendar abbr.
30 *"Toujours __"* (always yours)
31 Hemmed
32 Bandleader Brown
33 Burl or Charles
34 Western elevation
35 Expand, as a business
36 __ de deux
38 __ U.S. Pat. Off.
41 Pts. of a dollar
44 Repast
46 Small amount
50 Commerce
51 Attack
53 ". . . thereby hangs __"
54 Greedy sort
55 Sport shoe feature
56 Big crowd
57 Attempt
58 Enameled metal
59 Of unknown authorship: Abbr.
61 Pretends
64 Queen of the fairies
65 "__ There" (*Pajama Game* song)

ANIMATED AVIARY by Patrick Jordan

ACROSS

1 Singer Lane
5 Lincoln's in-laws
10 "Be quiet!"
14 __ *Yesterday*
15 Expect
16 Atop
17 Warners toon
19 Actress Rehan et al.
20 Pay to play
21 Like spring buds
23 Wilder or Guinness
25 Small dam
26 Having no doubt
28 Pitch __-hitter
31 Climbing plant
34 Tops
35 Sudden insight
37 Exists
38 Lantz toon
41 USPS delivery
42 Writer
43 Chops down
44 More reserved
46 123-45-6789 grp.
47 Church service
48 Limerick resident
50 Lion's home
52 Coupon clipper's need
56 Bits of grass
60 Burt's ex
61 Disney toon
63 Russian river
64 See the J.P. on the Q.T.
65 Spanish compass point
66 Count (on)
67 Drainage ditch
68 Load cargo

DOWN

1 Magician's intro?
2 Royal favor
3 Babysitter's bane
4 Won over
5 Brownish gray
6 Hold title to
7 Bohr or Borge
8 *Carpe* __ (seize the day)
9 Scatter
10 Philadelphia sandwich
11 Tackles, as a project
12 Ollie's foil
13 Multitude
18 Hoyle datum
22 Variety show
24 Some fowl
26 Speak the __ (make a prediction)
27 Imitative
29 Ultrabright colors
30 Painful experience
32 Ships' workers
33 That woman's
34 Leather punches
35 Reverence
36 Lifesaving initials
39 WWI battle town
40 Party pastime
45 Hands-down
47 Temperate
49 49er holdings
51 More competent
52 Speak unclearly
53 Essence
54 Actor's quest
55 Ply with flattery
57 Do a cleaning chore
58 Word form for "outer"
59 Bias, as results
62 Simian

THAT'S LIFE by Randolph Ross

ACROSS

1 Silly look
5 Done in
10 Medium for Marsalis
14 Gold deposit
15 From bad to __
16 Double reed
17 Life, in song
20 Sweet treats
21 Cast off from the body
22 Money rolls
23 Mrs. Cleaver
25 Clunkers
28 Roll-call response
29 New Deal initials
32 You must remember this
33 Fill up
34 *Mask* star
35 Life, to Longfellow
38 First place
39 Facsimile
40 Moon valley
41 Conducted
42 1953-59 French president
43 Smile, in a way
44 Author Grey
45 Humorist Barry
46 Figuring everything
49 Peppy one
53 Life, to Gump
56 "__ Rhythm"
57 Boring tool
58 Air outlet
59 Columbia's parent company
60 Urges
61 911 respondents: Abbr.

DOWN

1 Hefty rival
2 Morning wear
3 Wedding vows
4 Sawyer or Stahl
5 Tarot suit
6 Hits a lazy fly
7 Circle sections
8 Sort-of suffix
9 Social Register word
10 Novelist Amado
11 Rose lover of Broadway
12 Caldwell et al.
13 Love for life
18 Get help from
19 First name of 42 Across
23 Pier
24 Nobel chemist
25 Tag
26 Duck
27 Captured the king
28 On cloud nine
29 Whipper-snapper
30 *Power of Positive Thinking* author
31 Military supplier
33 Struck down
34 Police concern
36 Keynes subj.
37 Nonsense
42 Pasture eater
43 Enjoys every drop
44 Polish currency
45 Prepared potatoes
46 Heron cousin
47 Called off
48 Nerve fiber
49 Corporate identifier
50 Gossiper's nugget
51 Monthly payment
52 Ballpark figs.
54 Put the lid on
55 *Ben-*__

WHAT A MESS! by Gregory E. Paul

ACROSS

1 Attacked
6 Actress Celeste
10 Video medium
14 Caribbean isle
15 Square footage
16 Iroquois Indian
17 Gotten up
18 *Sanford and Son* producer
19 Tick off
20 "We have __ the enemy . . ."
21 Eagles coach, 1941-50
24 Lock brand
26 Greek island
27 Writing pads
30 Marathon trophy
34 Author Dahl
35 "Stormy Weather" singer
38 1969 Peace Prize grp.
39 '40s baseballer Vaughan
40 *I, Claudius* character
41 Off-campus building

42 Sault __ Marie
43 Family member
44 Same
45 Paul Newman role
47 Hose attachment
49 Where to find Aconcagua
52 Court ritual
53 Chicago blues great
57 Alias letters
60 Something unique
61 Genghis' domain
62 Italy's Detroit
64 Karnak's river
65 Monopoly fee
66 Like a lady of song
67 Mayberry citizen
68 Service club
69 Demurely

DOWN

1 Damage
2 Auto racer Luyendyk
3 Manager of the Giants

4 Actor Vigoda
5 Like some hair
6 Hearty's partner
7 Mountain nymph
8 Charter
9 Crabcake country
10 Singer Brewer
11 Diva's tune
12 Prescription unit
13 Shoe width
22 On a pension: Abbr.
23 Zero
25 Actress Sheedy
27 Riffraff
28 It comes from the heart
29 Doff
31 Eastwood role
32 Make joyful
33 Tesla invention
36 Fort __, CA
37 Campanella and Clark
40 Nuts and bolts
41 Product of 62 Across

43 Gainsay
44 Extreme
46 National Leaguers
48 __ favor
50 Studio stand
51 Reek
53 Part of MSG

54 Part of BTU
55 Pickle palace
56 Hash-house sign
58 German city
59 Capp of the comics
63 Card game

JAIL BREAK by Chuck Deodene

ACROSS

1 Croquet spots
6 Culture medium
10 Masticate
14 Toulouse ta-ta
15 Bad habit
16 Oral histories
17 Ruthless safecrackers?
20 Deli bread
21 Potion container
22 Hold contents
23 Pepper with pebbles
24 Arias
25 Poetry plagiarist?
30 Point of view
32 __ snag (get stuck)
33 Roman eggs
34 Sentry's yell
35 Exchanges
37 Tsar name
38 __ Got a Secret
39 Catch wind of
40 Skunk's weapon
41 Fast-food pilferer?
45 Does lunch

46 Ballet by 44 Down
47 Reagan daughter
49 Swear
50 Big-leaguer
53 Speedy thief?
56 Clinton cabinet member
57 __ tetra (fish)
58 Major artery
59 Inspired wonder
60 Smart-alecky remarks
61 Terse

DOWN

1 *Wizard of Oz* actor
2 *Queen for __*
3 Telegram
4 Composer Rorem
5 Undermine
6 Work in the cockpit
7 Critic Brendan
8 Becker blast
9 Troops at Lexington
10 Reverend, e.g.

11 *Dukes of Hazzard*'s Boss
12 Therefore
13 *Swamp Thing* director Craven
18 Monet's medium
19 Conference site of 1945
23 Bottled (up)
24 Barbershop sound
25 Parker
26 Harry Belafonte's girl
27 Shack
28 Indiana senator Bayh
29 Unleash a diatribe
30 Mail out
31 Hot rock
35 Pulls apart an orange
36 Conflicts
37 "__ See Clearly Now"
39 Hotel management name
40 Mountain topper

42 Foursome
43 Experts
44 Composer Stravinsky
47 Sigh of relief
48 Top-of-the-line
49 Teapot tempests

50 Left at sea
51 *Goodbye, Columbus* author
52 Approve
53 Hot tub
54 New Deal agcy.
55 French monarch

11   FIGHTIN' WORDS by Gerald R. Ferguson

ACROSS
1 Dear __ (columnist)
5 Fellow
9 Affix a cutting
14 *Damn Yankees* vamp
15 Polynesian dance
16 *Cosby Show* actor Hyman
17 Flapjack franchise
18 Ripening agent
19 Certain tanker
20 Stitch
21 Disassembled
23 Striped cats
25 Roast beef au __
26 Holler
27 Risk-filled, for short
29 D.C. lobby
32 Picasso or Casals
34 Overflowing
36 City in Norway
37 U __ of the UN
38 Not fooled by
39 Post-workout activity
41 Hatfield foe
42 Cut
43 Finished
44 Yup's kin
45 Tango requirement
46 Wood basecoats
49 Attempt
54 Mathers' costar
55 Toward the back
56 "__ Me" (Roger Miller tune)
57 Wry look
58 McCarthy's trunkmate
59 Otherwise
60 Artful dodge
61 Some camcorders
62 Sight or over ender
63 "__ aside!" ("Gangway")

DOWN
1 Favored roster
2 Black tea
3 Detailed, as a description
4 Beat one's gums
5 Designer Coco
6 Sci-fi awards
7 A Baldwin brother
8 Picnic place
9 Large clam
10 Onslaughts
11 Singer Guthrie
12 Aviated
13 Petrel cousin
21 Metric measure
22 VCR button
24 Word after "look out"
27 Classic Ladd film
28 Early video game
29 Ended the workday
30 Range above tenor
31 Become tiresome
32 Deluxe
33 Arthur of tennis
34 Vandyke site
35 __ point (center of attention)
37 Scout group
40 Eight kings of England
41 Potatoes partner
44 Test pilot Chuck
45 Visibly upset
46 Perceive
47 Awaken
48 Do the floors
49 Former Moscow Agency
50 Cartoonist Peter
51 Sharp-witted
52 Some poems
53 Curly cabbage
57 Bride's title: Abbr.

---

12   LUCKY DAY by Nancy Salomon

ACROSS
1 Emulate Bonnie Blair
6 Afrikaner
10 Co-__ (condo kin)
13 Alphabetical guide
14 Singer Lena
15 Informer
16 Achieve an upset
18 Mimic
19 Sun. talk
20 Canoer's need
21 Showy display
23 Honey
25 Comic Carvey
27 Find the mother lode
32 Packaging need
34 Actor Beatty
35 Silents actress Negri
36 Low point
37 Baby bloomer
38 Erie, for one
39 Actor Mischa
40 Posed
41 Algerian seaport
42 Win it all
46 Keep on one's __ (be alert)
47 Makes a choice
50 Drones on and on and on and on and . . .
53 Slugger Canseco
54 To the rear
56 First wife
57 Pick multiple winners
61 Midmorning
62 Eat away
63 One who volunteers, perhaps
64 Comic Carney
65 Evaluate
66 Antidrug advice

DOWN
1 Family members
2 Jabbed with a joint
3 "Not on __!" ("No way!")
4 Asian holiday
5 Blackmailer
6 Unhappy fans' cries
7 Fort __, CA
8 Pass catcher
9 Take umbrage at
10 Evangelist Roberts
11 Daddy
12 Undo a dele
14 "__ go again!"
17 Manes
22 Places for Bentleys
24 Say "Ha"
25 Title document
26 Lend a hand to
28 Coach Rockne
29 New York college
30 *The ___ of the Cave Bear*
31 Actor Holbrook
32 Word form for "bull"
33 "Zip-__-Doo-Dah"
36 Catch in the act
37 Snorts of disgust
38 Backgrounds
40 Sault __ Marie
43 Legit
44 Paladin portrayer
45 Church recess
48 Kitschy
49 All the time
50 Alpha follower
51 Start for look or see
52 Take an apartment
53 Green stone
55 Poi source
58 Lyricist Gershwin
59 Infant
60 Travel grp.

13 CLERICAL WORK by Gregory E. Paul

ACROSS
1 "Get __ of this!"
6 Throws
11 Burst a bubble
14 Oater prop
15 Actor Davis
16 Top card
17 *Life Is Worth Living* host
19 Furrow
20 Ceremony
21 Bridal path
23 Aïda's love
27 Arm art
29 Donizetti works
30 Person from Pago Pago
31 Mental whiz
32 Librarian's device
33 Joker
36 __ Raton, FL
37 Black-magic women
38 Richard of *First Knight*
39 __-Cat (Vail vehicle)
40 First state's capital
41 El Greco's birthplace
42 Required
44 Eton's river
45 Cat's __ (living end)
47 Karen of *Little House on the Prairie*
48 Love, to Luigi
49 Appearance
50 Noted diarist
51 *Taxi* character
58 Elephant ending
59 Mattel rival
60 Writer Jong
61 Comic Bill's nickname
62 Books
63 Potsdam pistol

DOWN
1 Eur. country
2 My __, Vietnam
3 CIA forerunner
4 Light gray
5 Hotel employee
6 Sells for
7 '75 Wimbledon winner
8 NNW opposite
9 Cravat
10 Boxer, for one
11 George Washington biographer
12 Word form for "eye"
13 "For __ sake!"
18 Diner display
22 Call __ day
23 Former first family of Virginia
24 Cook's attire
25 Football Hall-of-Famer
26 Domingo solo
27 Spud
28 Mass ending
30 Accumulated
32 Peaceniks
34 Soviet co-op
35 Silly ones
37 Musical conclusion
38 Mardi __
40 Bad mark
41 Wide strait
43 Musical sense
44 Genealogy chart
45 Hysteria
46 Organic acid
47 Young women
49 Veal or venison
52 Dutch city
53 Get one's goat
54 Joanne of films
55 Lively dance
56 Frozen dessert
57 Spoil

14 FIND THE ANSWERS by Dean Niles

ACROSS
1 Singer Falana
5 Follow
9 Apple types
13 Baseball manager Felipe
14 To say nothing of
15 The __ (uneasiness)
17 Clothing catalog
20 Consecrate
21 Evergreen
22 Draftable
23 Singing style
25 Bistro
27 *What's My Line?* highlight
32 Rice-A-__
33 Bubbles over
34 Hooligan, in Britain
37 Draw forth
39 Ember, later
40 Stocking shade
42 Smidgen
43 "__ Romantic?"
46 Harris honorific
47 *Dallas* spinoff
49 Hemingway of *Central Park West*
52 Party with poi
53 "Put __ on it!"
54 NATO counterpart
57 #2 on the hit parade?
61 Trial tactic
64 Medieval strings
65 Actor O'Neal
66 Greek peak
67 "And here it is!"
68 March time
69 Italian painter

DOWN
1 Flowing rock
2 Actor Ken
3 Bonkers
4 Like Hoffman in *Rain Man*
5 Steak style
6 Poetic pugilist
7 "What'd __" (Charles tune)
8 Get the worst of it
9 Beatles' award: Abbr.
10 *Little Women* writer
11 Chili con __
12 Unmitigated
16 Sojourn
18 Fairy-tale beginning
19 Thoughtful
24 Autocrat
26 Aide: Abbr.
27 Vocal horse
28 Skywalker's teacher
29 Cold-shoulder
30 Wind measures
31 Like some battles
34 Cosmonaut Gagarin
35 Welcoming
36 Ice mass
38 __ kleine *Nachtmusik*
41 Paris, vis-à-vis Helen
44 Wise one
45 Firms up
47 Joshed
48 Votes against
49 Teen's hangout
50 Certain Alaskan
51 Western rope
55 Start for culture
56 Area meas.
58 Seine feeder
59 Petty officer
60 __ B'rith
62 "Rose __ rose . . ."
63 Abu Dhabi's federation: Abbr.

15 ON K-P by Mary E. Brindamour

ACROSS

1 Summer place
5 Decline again
10 Lhasa __
14 Wings
15 Treat badly
16 Annoying one
17 Aunts, uncles, etc.
19 Tom Joad, e.g.
20 Recreate imaginatively
21 __-do-well
22 NASA vehicles
23 Challenges the establishment
25 Makes off with
27 Plenty, to poets
29 Client for Darrow
32 Poses a query
35 Part of a sentence
38 Storm center
39 "If a body __ body . . ."
41 Cereal grain
42 Bowling score
44 French spirit
45 Bounded
48 Supplements, with "out"
49 Water-loving animals
51 Sky show
53 Cup partner
56 Assign new actors
60 Snarl
62 Birds, to Brutus
64 Lone Ranger's sidekick
65 Do yard work
66 Dip
68 So be it
69 Buffet patron
70 *Around the Fish* painter
71 Army meal
72 Like Kilimanjaro
73 Fax, perhaps

DOWN

1 Hardened
2 Still in the game
3 __ *La Mancha*
4 Most annoying
5 Tommy Chong's daughter
6 Black, poetically
7 Patsies
8 Little land in the ocean
9 Titled lady
10 Opponent for Rocky
11 Colorado mountain
12 Svelte
13 Bravo relatives
18 Hammer part
24 Soak (up)
26 Holes in one
28 "Hold it!"
30 Brontë heroine
31 Gets it
32 Asian nursemaid
33 Type of truck
34 Mementos
36 Blame, so to speak
37 "__ o'clock scholar"
40 Baseball brother
43 Proud birds
46 Houdini happenings
47 Golden: Fr.
50 ( )( )( )( )
52 Turn down
54 Perrier rival
55 Right-hand page
57 Bracelet site
58 *Merry Company* painter
59 Schlepped
60 A little bit of weight
61 Appellation
63 Veer off course
67 Be nosy

16 VEGETARIAN by Lee Weaver

ACROSS

1 Big name in fairy tales
6 Yule poem starter
10 Edinburgh native
14 Cowboy competition
15 Beatles movie
16 Tempo
17 Ten-percenter
18 Scat queen
19 Greek war god
20 Toy weapons
23 Mouse kin
24 Many min.
25 Conclude
26 Sir Isaac's family
28 Public disturbance
30 Tavern missile
31 Sounds of glee
35 Lode load
36 Barbecue location
39 Surmounting
40 Chutzpah
43 Small opening
44 Shop tool
46 Sea, in Savoie
47 Shadowbox
48 Fruit seeds
50 Former Iranian VIP
52 Wearing away
55 "How was __ know?"
56 Pat gently
59 Vintner's need
60 MacArthur trademark
63 Arkin of *Chicago Hope*
65 Genuine
66 Chicago gridders
67 Actress Naldi
68 Icicle site
69 Ford or Pyle
70 Santa's laundry problem
71 Rural roads: Abbr.
72 Process ore

DOWN

1 Pie chart, e.g.
2 Pilot's affirmative
3 Brainstorms
4 Haberdashery department
5 May honoree
6 Eleanor's uncle
7 Shoe strip
8 Tim of *Home Improvement*
9 Let off easy
10 Whirlpool bath
11 Redhead
12 Indian or Arctic
13 Tries out
21 Burger topper
22 Make a trade
27 Ensnares
29 School semesters
31 *2001* computer
32 One thing __ time
33 Risky problem
34 Plant pest
37 Keogh relative
38 Above, poetically
41 Autos, buses, etc.
42 Muse of lyric poetry
45 Grist for DeMille
49 Night noisemaker
51 *Calvin and __* (comic strip)
52 Linda or Dale
53 Ham's equipment
54 Super-duper
56 Sawyer of TV news
57 "__ in Paris"
58 Attack
61 Church part
62 Salon offering
64 Wrestler's surface

17 BODY LANGUAGE by Diane C. Baldwin

ACROSS

1 Very important
6 Sunscreen number: Abbr.
9 Meal plan
13 In the know
14 Passed the word
16 Uncomfortable
17 Cut the lawn
18 Jai __
19 Uris or Spinks
20 Priestly vestment
21 Vigorous labor
24 Big birds
26 Corrode
27 Like some showers
29 Computer insert
34 Some graduate exams
35 Strong suit
36 Coffee holder
37 Erie or Huron
38 Inlets
39 Determination
40 Freezer cubes
41 Went rowing
42 Midler or Davis
43 Cargo lifters
45 Waterproof coating
46 Deer relative
47 Wall Street unit
48 Hilarious tale
53 NCAA rival
56 English noble
57 Director Kazan
58 Statement of beliefs
60 Where Moses floated
61 Force
62 Sam or Remus
63 Iditarod vehicle
64 Golf-bag item
65 Makes custard

DOWN

1 Doll word
2 Army offense
3 Hard candy
4 Mine bonanza
5 Turns in, as coupons
6 Wild guesses
7 Sport for Prince Charles
8 Imperfection
9 Use an eraser
10 Notion
11 Conceits
12 Daly of *Cagney & Lacey*
15 Abridgments
22 Put down carpeting
23 Pronged tool
25 Robust
27 Three-D
28 Vestige
29 Cote denizens
30 Angered
31 Kind of shirt
32 Old hat
33 Computer key
35 Split in the road
38 Laughed shrilly
39 Machine part
41 Certain paintings
42 Little grizzly
44 Staggered
45 "__ Loves You" (Beatles tune)
47 Sudden outburst
48 Understandings
49 Catch in the act
50 Gardner of mystery
51 Came to rest
52 Yearn (for)
54 Eric of Monty Python
55 ". . . and bells on her __"
59 Genetic factor

18 MATERIALISM by Norma Steinberg

ACROSS

1 Lazarus or Samms
5 Kiddie-lit elephant
10 Group of wolves
14 Musical Diamond
15 "Now, Pablo!"
16 Monster
17 Barbie, e.g.
18 Do a double-take
19 Spare
20 Daydreaming
23 Like Princeton, as of 1969
24 Behaves
25 Slugger's turn
28 Strainer
31 Sediment
32 Get even for
34 Skiers' meccas: Abbr.
37 Bunny-trail traveler
40 Some coll. students
41 Juan's friends
42 Brown shade
43 Statement of belief
44 Bet acceptor
45 Mule, e.g.
47 Not of the clergy
49 Quarterback great
55 Advise
56 Mrs. Kramden
57 She loved Narcissus
59 Skin-cream ingredient
60 Macpherson or Moss
61 Was sorry for
62 Actress Rowlands
63 Göteborg native
64 Hied

DOWN

1 *Howards* __
2 Feline sound
3 *Venus de* __
4 Set aside
5 Cleo's craft
6 In front
7 Gravy holder
8 Eyebrow shape
9 Assess
10 Part of NYPD
11 Go-between
12 Rocky peaks
13 Actor Olin
21 Piece of real estate
22 Poe bird
25 Snakes
26 Row of seats
27 Certain sandwiches
28 "Ready, __!"
29 Long-division word
30 Strong personalities
32 Wile E. Coyote's supplier
33 Vacuum
34 Truck manufacturer
35 Flag
36 Aspersion
38 More unusual
39 Faculty members
43 Eye part
44 "__ the season . . ."
45 Trite
46 Wading bird
47 Spiked
48 Fred Astaire's sister
50 Root vegetables
51 __ hot and cold (waver)
52 Catch a bus
53 ". . . __ of kindness yet"
54 "This is fun!"
55 Droll wit
58 Bet in roulette

19 NONSENSE by Eileen Lexau

ACROSS

1 Church feature
5 Author Carr
10 Way off
14 Mortgage, e.g.
15 End of a Stein line
16 Swing around
17 Nonsense
19 Confessed to the cops
20 Provided
21 Remodels
23 Small bird
24 Egg-shaped
25 Sir Lancelot rode one
27 Driver's dread
30 Triad, for one
31 Nearsighted toon
32 1/100 of a krone
33 Haws' companions
34 "Close, but no __!"
35 Norse god
36 Clod
37 Dress smartly
38 Some slippers
39 Body's building blocks
41 Passé
42 Unseats
43 Muggy
44 Hoi __
46 Jumbo planes
50 Scott Turow book
51 British nonsense
53 To be, in Nice
54 Old calculators
55 Turner of films
56 __ in the Attic (Hellman play)
57 Tangy fruit
58 Part of CBS

DOWN

1 Duke of __ (Portugal conqueror)
2 Chanteuse Edith
3 Women's mag
4 Benefactors
5 Asked for ID
6 Lauder rival
7 Heavy weight
8 Curve
9 Actions
10 Have at
11 Nonsense
12 Polly or Em
13 Rules: Abbr.
18 Bobbled the ball
22 Dimwit
24 Bach's instrument
25 Gather wool
26 Nonsense
27 Green plums
28 Sobbed
29 Barbie's beau et al.
30 Meat cut
31 Bearings
34 Prone to carp
35 Gets a better response than
37 Colombian coin
38 Venomous snake
40 Brides' fabrics
41 He rode the Beagle
43 Canned-music club
44 Yeats or Keats
45 Aware of
46 Fall guy?
47 "You __ me!"
48 Long, long time
49 Little squabble
52 Brit. decoration

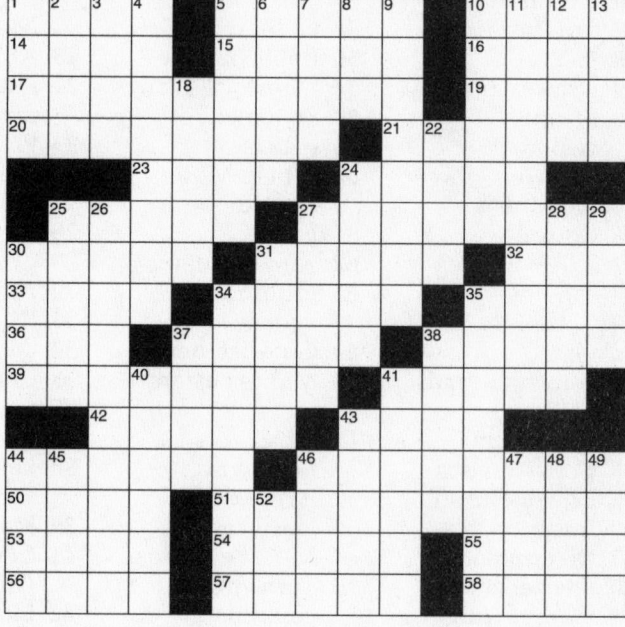

20 PUZZLE OF TODAY by Gregory E. Paul

ACROSS

1 Alger's starting point
5 200 milligrams
10 Green Mansions hero
14 Mashie, e.g.
15 Puccini product
16 Ram or rooster
17 Thin one
19 Otherwise
20 More like molasses
21 Outstanding
23 Four-time Indy champ
26 Singer Pinza
27 Transfer
30 Golfer Ernie
32 Decathlete Johnson
35 Writer Hunter
36 Nova __
38 Polly Holliday role
39 Ecru
40 Ella Wheeler Wilcox, e.g.
41 Pixie
42 Tokyo's ex-name
43 Overcoat
44 Ontario Indian
45 Allude (to)
47 Somme seasoning
48 Veld settlers
49 Bemoan
51 "Blowin' in the Wind" singer
53 Scuba diver
56 Cantankerous
60 Holliman or Hines
61 Something easy
64 "Ma, He's Making Eyes __"
65 "__ we all?"
66 Pan's opposite
67 Miss Durbeyfield
68 Inquisitive
69 Plaintiff

DOWN

1 Barbecue entrée
2 Asian sea
3 Dance style
4 Winter creation
5 US Army attack helicopter
6 GI address
7 Stimpy's pal
8 Greek Mars
9 Personal preference
10 Ms. Bloomer
11 Dynamo
12 Lohengrin's wife
13 Impolite look
18 Have a hunch
22 Pound et al.
24 School break
25 Like some spoons
27 Discourage
28 Sidestep
29 Trouble
31 Like some stares
33 Bugs chaser
34 Rodeo needs
36 Fa follower
37 Neighbor of Syr.
40 Hebrew festival
44 The Rifleman star
46 NFL team
48 Roseanne, née __
50 Jacob's father-in-law
52 Towering
53 Achievement
54 Part of APR
55 Detective Wolfe
57 Birthright seller
58 Dijon dream
59 Belgian river
62 __ Plaines, IL
63 A Chorus Line song

ALLEY OOP by Bob Lubbers

ACROSS

1 Spielberg film
5 Gushes
11 Distress letters
14 Distress words
15 Electrical unit
16 In favor of
17 Sweet treat
19 __ Tin Tin
20 Barbecue bit
21 Golf-hole complement
23 Tire city
26 *Jeanne d'__*
27 Breathing sound
28 Unity
30 In the center of
32 Boyfriend of Barbie
33 Medicine-chest bottle
36 Work stopper
41 Radio adjuncts
42 Anger
44 Read from memory
47 Facial feature
50 The Bard of __

51 Wrestlers' surface
53 Get up
54 Set free
57 Top card
58 Rock producer Brian
59 Show mercy
64 Rep.'s counterpart
65 Most certain
66 Area
67 Make an attempt
68 Trudges
69 Genesis name

DOWN

1 Chore
2 "I see!"
3 Placed first
4 Actress Stone
5 Swedish auto
6 Afternoons: Abbr.
7 Top berth
8 Fossil, e.g.
9 H.S. math
10 Clockmaker Thomas

11 Widen
12 Bay windows
13 Shakespearean product
18 Workday start for many
22 Singer Lopez
23 NASA affirmative
24 Understood
25 Italian painter
26 Very, in music
29 "__ bleu!"
30 __-craftsy
31 Former russian space station
34 School grp.
35 Dot of land
37 Singer Cleo
38 Investigator: Abbr.
39 Opera star __ Te Kanawa
40 Love god
43 Lea beast
44 Hardest to find
45 More level

46 Ant group
48 Apiece
49 Mild wind
51 Stiller's partner
52 Relevant, as an argument

55 Aide: Abbr.
56 Railroad siding
57 Legal reps.
60 Sixth sense
61 Director Howard
62 Yoko __
63 __ Moines, IA

GEOMETRIC by Eugene W. Sard

ACROSS

1 Australian marsupial
6 *Veni*
11 French noble
14 '50s Ford
15 Pitching great Ryan
16 Educational basics?
17 Folk craft
19 Psyche part
20 Ancient France
21 German city
23 Rhode Island resort
27 Composer of *La Mer*
29 Sparta rival
30 Mideast tongue
31 Midwest airport
32 Fierce look
33 Tax org.
36 LeBlanc of *Friends*
37 Shiny fabric
38 At no cost
39 Elected pols
40 Early evening
41 Hiding place

42 Composer Gustav
44 Romantic song
45 Electricity source
47 Makes ill
48 Swiss mathematician
49 Luke Skywalker, for one
50 Prefix for center
51 Sum-thing special in arithmetic
58 Cub-scout unit
59 Representative
60 Inappropriate or excessive
61 Bishop's jurisdiction
62 Sign gases
63 Sea duck

DOWN

1 Barbie's friend
2 Lyric poem
3 Enzyme ending
4 Was ahead
5 Eaten up
6 Computer fodder

7 __ *Hand Luke*
8 Boxer né Clay
9 Game piece
10 Ugandan city
11 Opera-house section
12 Natural impulses
13 Pal
18 "Lend me your __"
22 __ generis (unique)
23 Wynonna's mom
24 Allen or Frome
25 Classic TV game show
26 Saucy
27 Plumbing outlet
28 Be entitled to
30 Change
32 Mallet kin
34 Actress Ada
35 Tournament placements
37 Auction off
38 Arkin's *In-Laws* costar
40 Union general
41 West Indian chief

43 Service winner
44 Offerings
45 *Mr. __ Goes to Town*
46 Indian currency
47 Religious groups
49 Islamic spirit
52 Era

53 Word form for "earth"
54 Verse starter?
55 Mix in
56 Regret
57 Occupational suffix

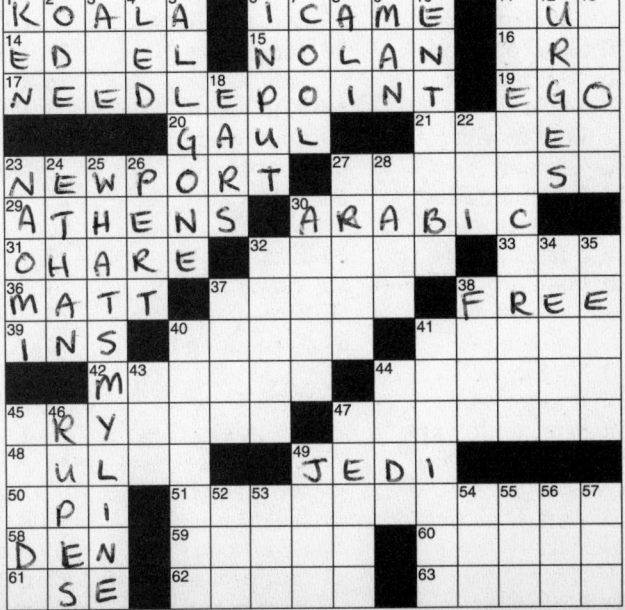

23   CHURCHGOING by Dean Niles

ACROSS
1 Reference book
6 Pancake chain
10 False god
14 Slump down
15 Neck area
16 Actor Lincoln
17 American plant
20 Heights of the Mideast
21 Walks heavily
22 __ City, NV
26 TV talker Ricki
28 "__ You Glad You're You?"
29 Hockey great Gretzky
31 Dollop
34 Try again
35 Thin gruel
36 Swiss city
38 With mutual misunderstanding
41 Roof material
42 Not professional
43 Skewed
44 Sucker
45 Become narrower
47 Brink
48 Coyote sound
49 Fish-tank need
50 Fabled fellow
53 Foul-smelling
56 Insanity
62 Phrase of comprehension
63 Lay __ the line
64 Exxon vessel
65 Lean
66 Skunk Le Pew
67 Terminates

DOWN
1 Pt. of speech
2 Syllable to sing
3 __ cit. (footnote abbr.)
4 NASA affirmative
5 Water tap
6 Part of 6 Across
7 Sounds of glee
8 Without shame
9 Zest
10 Ball participant
11 KalKan rival
12 In between
13 Plenty
18 __ compos mentis
19 Maintenance
22 Diamond measures
23 Queen of Soul
24 Porter
25 Harsh sound
27 Full of wrath
29 "We __ robbed!"
30 Delicious, for one
31 Hot spot
32 Settle a score
33 Roasting accessory
35 "Fiddlesticks!"
37 Dynamite inventor
39 Diver's neighbors
40 Former Mideast union: Abbr.
46 Missouri River feeder
47 Rental fare
48 Washed off, in a way
49 Small whopper
50 Wait __ (slow down)
51 Leisure
52 Submachine gun
54 Cut up
55 Painter Magritte
57 __ and tuck
58 Illumined
59 Showman Ziegfeld
60 House mem.
61 Many mos.

24   GOTHAMITES by Gregory E. Paul

ACROSS
1 Ritz, e.g.
6 Early explorer
10 Secluded valley
14 *Nixon in China*, for one
15 Puerto __
16 Status
17 NYC-born novelist
19 Snorkel's dog
20 Neighbor of Mich.
21 Waif model Kate
22 German
24 Croupier's tool
25 Kestrels and tercels
26 Leatherneck
29 __ Lawrence College
30 "Wellaway!"
31 Budget part
33 Prize endower
37 Remote button
38 Golf great
40 Tom, Dick or Harry
41 Hoard
43 Food shop
44 __ mater
45 Mary I, e.g.
47 Graham's address
49 Pittsburgh gridder
52 Tailless cat
53 Cinema offering
54 Nastase nemesis
55 Sch. auxiliary
58 Limerick's locale
59 NYC-born composer
62 *Ja* opposite
63 Allows to mature
64 Flax fabric
65 Very, in Vichy
66 Time past
67 Something bet

DOWN
1 Sounds of cheer
2 Type of tournament
3 Field house?
4 Be human
5 Nonprofessional
6 Remove
7 Tire mounts
8 Curling surface
9 Name below the title
10 NYC-born comedian
11 Numbers game
12 First name in rock
13 Inert gases
18 Wags
23 Panache
24 NYC-born singer
25 __ *Attraction*
26 Family member
27 Grad
28 Pro __
29 Look of disdain
32 Witch's home
34 Salve
35 Admiral Zumwalt
36 *A Passage to India* director
39 Remove the warhead
42 *Enterprise* navigator
46 Dance club employee
48 Marx colleague
49 Exhausted
50 City on the Moselle
51 Weird
52 Elk kin
54 Remus title
55 Member of the Clinton cabinet
56 Expedition
57 Elizabeth I's mother
60 Alter follower
61 Caboodle's partner

25 SIDEBAR by A.J. Santora

ACROSS

1 Caution color
6 *Exodus* hero et al.
10 Abba of Israel
14 See old friends
15 Agreeable
16 __ Pompilius (a king of Rome)
17 *Little Women* surname
18 Baez or Jett
19 Sassy one
20 23 Across' instructions to the jury?
23 Theme of this puzzle
24 Buggy place?
25 [Not my error]
26 Hgt.
27 Furthermore
28 Denomination
29 *The Merry Widow* composer
33 Western Amerind
34 "Harper Valley __"
35 Make tracks
37 Feast-famine link
38 Less furnished
40 Make (one's way)
41 Distorted
42 Family member
44 Fez, for one
45 GIs' clubs
46 23 Across' favorite excuse?
50 23 Across' vocabulary?
51 Czech river
52 Whine
53 Icicle area
56 Matured
57 *Vous* __ (you are: Fr.)
58 What the tired take
59 Word before hall or kit
60 Beatty film
61 N. Ireland port

DOWN

1 Crosspiece
2 "Give __ break!"
3 Overwhelm, as with work
4 Disguise, as a message
5 Second the emotion?
6 *The Grifters* name
7 Parents' reading, perhaps
8 Corporate Carl
9 New York lake
10 In a series: Fr.
11 Ring-shaped cake
12 Buddy, in Barcelona
13 Neck area
21 Harry
22 Set
23 Coup group
24 Spatter
28 Stretch out
30 In any way
31 Pointer
32 Glimmerings
35 Cold
36 Get __ rut (be stuck)
39 *This Is Your Life* host
40 Pivoted
43 Natty
45 Put on view
46 Waffle
47 S-shaped arches
48 Fry lightly
49 Work with dough
50 Some soil
54 Attention
55 Hovel

26 WEAPONRY by Shirley Soloway

ACROSS

1 Shade of brown
6 Forbidden
10 Chatter
13 Is in first place
14 Memo abbr.
15 Hindu mentor
16 Sinclair Lewis novel
18 Author Bagnold
19 Jacqueline of *The Deep*
20 Another plate of food
22 Understand
23 Southeast Asian
25 Sluggish
26 Bar mixer
29 "My Gal __"
32 Just okay
35 Complaint
36 Trunk item
38 Eiffel's pride
40 Amtrak and B&O: Abbr.
41 Implied
42 Lyric poem
43 Pledge
45 Card game
46 Ukr., formerly
47 California jurist
50 "Let's __" (Porter tune)
52 Post- opposite
53 A Stooge
56 Workplaces
59 Anesthetics
61 Get closer to, with "on"
62 Leading forces
65 Danger
66 Riding gait
67 Banks or Ford
68 Ordinal ending
69 "Auld Lang __"
70 American Beauties, e.g.

DOWN

1 Large chunks
2 Ghostlike
3 Describe grammatically
4 Marriage vows
5 In addition
6 Highlander's hat
7 "__ was saying . . ."
8 Cave creatures
9 Supported
10 Burlap bag
11 Dry as a bone
12 Young blooms
15 School subj.
17 Sportscaster Rusty
21 Shoreline
24 *Wuthering Heights* star
26 For men and women
27 Ice block
28 Out __ (not in synch)
30 Operatic solo
31 Riga resident
32 Fr. exalted women
33 "Clumsy me!"
34 Dish from the sea
37 El __, TX
39 Memento
44 The boss, at times
48 Eniwetok events
49 Restraint
51 Sty cry
53 Wherewithal
54 Do-__ (all-out)
55 Plural makers
56 Folklore villain
57 __ *accompli*
58 Agile
60 Medal winner
63 Long time
64 Took nourishment

27 MEAT MARKET by Richard Silvestri

ACROSS
1 Name in Ohio politics
5 Stand-up guy?
10 Map out
14 Concept
15 Mrs. Gorbachev
16 Swiss river
17 Opponent's program
19 Hook's henchman
20 Disseminate
21 Mine find
22 Aspen transport
23 Play the flute
25 Cross the threshold
27 Second-rank execs
29 Drenching rain
32 Woods inhabitants?
35 Everly Brothers song
37 Have a late bite
38 Penitent person
39 Garden shelter
40 Teen trauma
41 Before, to bards
42 Packing a rod
43 Puff on a pipe
44 Equivocate
46 Discharge from the RAF
48 Here's Howe!
50 Powerfully built
53 Scottish upland
55 Dance step?
57 Longing
59 Old-fashioned learning method
60 Mako kin
62 One of the Waughs
63 Barbecue leftover
64 Oklahoma city
65 Phoenician seaport
66 Lower oneself
67 Carvey or Wynter

DOWN
1 Tumbles, with "over"
2 Take for oneself
3 Word form for "iron"
4 Assume control
5 Treetop rocker
6 Dinghy adjunct
7 Joan of art
8 River to the Rhone
9 Its days are numbered
10 Prom-dress color
11 Red wine
12 Square footage
13 __-do-well
18 1990 Oscar actress Kathy
24 Derby site
26 Williams or Turner
28 Did some planting
30 Greasy thick stuff
31 Fencer's blade
32 Make stout
33 Surrounding glow
34 Yeoman of the guard
36 Matzo meal
39 Violated
40 Attacked from hiding
42 "Thrilla in Manila" victor
43 Clearheaded
45 Wool coat
47 Contemporary
49 Ignominy
51 City in Tuscany
52 Bridal sweeper
53 Army kid
54 __-poly
56 Prefix for "both"
58 Icelandic work
61 Actress Ryan

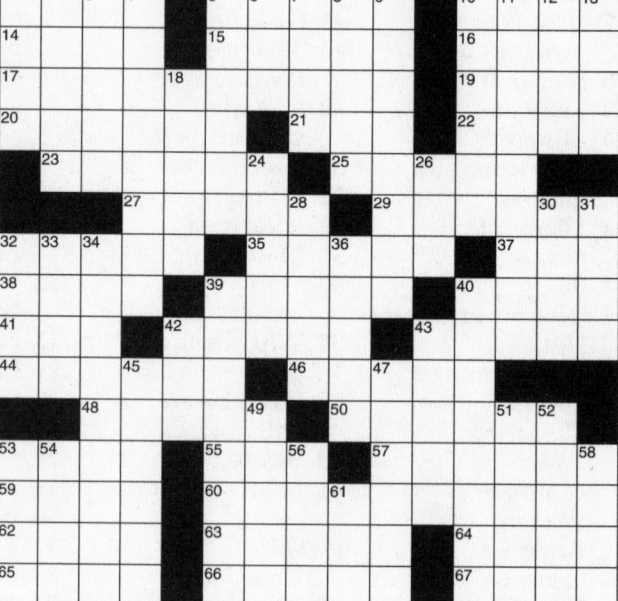

28 BY TH' NUMBERS by Bob Lubbers

ACROSS
1 Sounds of satisfaction
4 Normandy city
8 Permit
13 French head
15 Mishmash
16 Hotelier Helmsley
17 __ of approval
18 Semis
19 Slangy farewell
20 Last minute
23 In Nod
24 Rip
25 Film buff's cable choice
28 Stuck-up one
30 Ben or Jerry
32 Pigpen
35 Bridal-notice word
37 Background babble
38 Jinxed visitor
43 Fight site
44 Dead or Red
45 Comedian Louis
46 Easy-chair occupant
49 Cartoonist Peter
52 Actor Danson
53 Brainstorm
55 Strain
59 Shakespearean comedy
61 Gene Tierney role
64 Shaver brand
65 Triple-decker cookie
66 Prose commentary
67 Honk
68 Close by
69 Insurrectionist Daniel
70 Finishes
71 Give it a shot

DOWN
1 Perplexed
2 Bounders
3 Madame de __
4 Jubilation T. __ (Capp character)
5 Landed
6 Number on a black ball
7 Snacks
8 Attractive
9 Jet manufacturer
10 Home site
11 It's next to nothing
12 Conflict
14 North Pole workers
21 Poetic contraction
22 Nag nibble
25 Man from Mars
26 Unkempt
27 Greek island
29 Spelling contest
31 Singer Rawls
32 Incite
33 "__ Little Words"
34 Give way
36 USN rank
39 Gene material
40 Airport areas
41 Iced drink
42 Construction workers
47 Dutch commune
48 Compare
50 Sister
51 Heavenly hunter
54 Burns river
56 Plumed fisher
57 Harvest wool
58 Yarn
59 Food server
60 Walked on
61 Brown or Paul
62 Hardwood tree
63 "Made in the __"

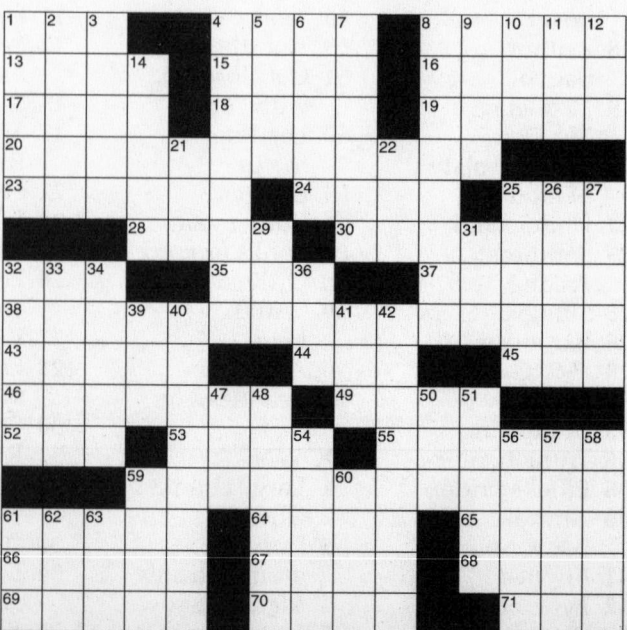

29 GETTING WARMER by Lee Weaver

ACROSS
1 Boxer's bane
6 Droops
10 Seeks information
14 Flexible
15 Spanish river
16 Lab vessel
17 Aisle escort
18 Jockey's strap
19 Chair or bench
20 Western featuring Elvis
23 Blvd. crosser
24 Marshy land
25 Shoebox letters
26 Raged
28 Actor Astin
30 Jai __
31 Huck's transport
35 Heredity factor
36 Turkish currency
39 Pierre's love
40 Mixes
43 Go it alone
44 Reads, with "over"
46 Ayres or Alcindor
47 Actress Markey
48 Suffix denoting smallness
50 Name for a Dalmatian
52 Vermont-inn sitcom
55 Onassis' nickname
56 Plant pouch
59 Numero __
60 Exodus sign
63 Campus building
65 Poker hand
66 Actress Verdugo
67 Nevada city
68 Fork prong
69 Less civil
70 Reply-requested encl.
71 Rosebud, e.g.
72 Tarot users

DOWN
1 Pat the pillow
2 Cotton thread
3 Patriot Allen
4 "Excuse me!"
5 Regular TV show
6 Bilko's rank
7 Vigoda and Burrows
8 Macon breakfast
9 The *Moonlight*, for one
10 DDE's opponent
11 Pressing need
12 Tart thief
13 Overfilled
21 Necessities
22 Parker House or kaiser
27 Employee's goal
29 Hard stuff
31 Modern music style
32 Latin verb
33 July 4th display
34 Saw parts
37 Boxing great
38 Lawn piece
41 Mended
42 Pledged by oath
45 Try
49 Spews forth
51 Detroit sluggers
52 Subjects for Rubens
53 __ *Gay*
54 Forest path
56 Napped leather
57 Emmy-winner Ed
58 Burns slightly
61 Highest digit
62 *NYPD* __
64 Shemp's brother

30 FILM UPDATES by Robert H. Wolfe

ACROSS
1 High-school safety org.
5 Alexander was one
9 Businesses: Abbr.
12 "It's __ point!"
14 Deeds: Lat.
15 Ganges garb
16 Turmoil and struggle: 1939
19 Rich guy gets generous: 1938
20 Card game
21 Film composer Schifrin
22 Govt. security
23 Actress Sommer
24 "Oy!"
26 Fish tales
29 Laid ceramic squares
31 Ad follower
34 Negev adjective
35 Actress Berry
36 Toll road
37 __ *Galahad* (Presley film)
38 Ball girl
39 Abused a pledge
40 17 Down, e.g.
41 Work hard
43 Bert and family
46 Distort
47 NATO member
50 Turmoil and struggle: 1961
54 Rich guy gets generous: 1980
55 Make tracks?
56 *Picnic* playwright
57 Dame Ashcroft
58 Compass pt.
59 Former news agency
60 Dates

DOWN
1 Peg Bundy portrayer
2 Chevron rival
3 "Tiny Bubbles" singer
4 Activist
5 Squealer
6 Dolt
7 "__ boy!"
8 Stadium sounds
9 Illinois town
10 Whether __
11 Move like a crab
13 Suit fabrics
15 Exemplars of grace
17 Writer Dinesen
18 Outward
23 Extremity
24 German folk dance
25 Director Grant
26 Cow kin
27 Meyers of *Kate & Allie*
28 Disencumber
30 Feeling off
31 Hollywood nickname
32 Tina's ex
33 Where some bloomers rest
35 Lady lobster
36 Chum
38 Some singers
39 '90s music style
40 Initiative
42 Word form for "straight"
43 Light sources
44 Vicinities
45 Split
46 First Oscar-winning film
47 Habitude
48 Billow
49 Devine and Rooney
51 Acronym pt.
52 Barrie dog
53 Woolly ones

FIRING LINES by Gerald R. Ferguson

ACROSS

1 Manipulated one
5 Hurry-up initials
9 Flounder stuffing, often
13 Language quirk
15 Oscar-winner as Pasteur
16 Plant no roots
17 NBA Hall-of-Famer Maravich
19 Lyric poems
20 Pick a jury
21 Parroters
23 Prop for Player
24 Big beasts, briefly
25 Where hackles are raised
28 Cereal grain
29 Utah lily
30 Merlin, for one
35 Act rashly
39 Ethical path
40 Standard
41 California fort
42 French cup
44 Agnes' *Bewitched* role
47 "Ready, __, fire!"
48 Televised faux pas
49 Germ-free
54 Stravinsky ballet
55 Indisputable evidence
57 __ Fein (IRA political arm)
58 London gallery
59 Dictation taker
60 ". . . banjo on my __"
61 Winter drifter
62 Marie *et* Jeanne: Abbr.

DOWN

1 Plumbing unit
2 Take __ view of
3 Gossamer bit
4 "__ creature was stirring . . ."
5 More than adequate
6 "A Boy Named __"
7 Foyer
8 Circular graph
9 Warble like Bing
10 Western show
11 Affirms
12 Myerson or Truman
14 Italian peak
18 Meriwether and Majors
22 Tour of duty
25 Soft drink brand
26 Het up
27 Master Christopher's friend
29 "Hush!"
30 Instant lawn
31 Shelley's twilights
32 Greek letters
33 De Valera's land
34 Tach. reading
36 Scout bunch
37 Gump and son
38 Guy with a scope
42 South American monkey
43 Solemn assents
44 Marbles benefactor
45 Not a soul
46 Metaphysical poet
47 Out of whack
48 Lie poolside
50 Mil. grps.
51 "__ Ideas" (1951 song)
52 "*Clair de* __"
53 Son in Genesis
56 Word form for "ear"

PIANO FORTE by Ann Seidel

ACROSS

1 Lofty
5 Narrow cuts
10 Listen up
14 Lot measure
15 German philosopher
16 Jessye Norman role
17 Scam
18 Love, to Luigi
19 Study all night
20 Miller or Landers
21 Largo and West
23 Let the water out of
25 JFK predecessor
26 Didn't participate
28 Religious quarters
33 Embellish
34 Spanish desserts
35 Actor Kilmer
36 Crying shame
37 North Carolina fort
38 Flowing robe
39 "__ Believer" (Monkees tune)
40 Chairs
41 Nervous
42 Canned brand
44 __ *Playing Our Song*
45 Likely
46 Arrow product
47 One on the sidelines
52 Sphere
55 Stench
56 Some spreads
57 Off base, in a way
58 Nickname for Hemingway
59 Egg-shaped
60 Trial recording
61 Hoskins role
62 Evans and Carnegie
63 Sketched

DOWN

1 Sounds of laughter
2 Revered figure
3 Bottom line
4 Put a spell on
5 Reviewer Gene
6 Auto turkey
7 Composer Stravinsky
8 Hatcher of *Lois & Clark*
9 Downhill travel of a sort
10 Computer fanatic
11 Land of Tara
12 Call it __ (quit)
13 St. Louis team
21 Goat-man
22 Fusses
24 Actor Calhoun
26 Palatable
27 Stop on __
28 Home base
29 From __ to riches
30 Academic's perch
31 Gung-ho
32 *Susan* __ (Connie Stevens film)
34 Greek group
37 Rocker type
38 Layer
40 Frosh, next year
41 Humming sound
43 Actor Gordon
44 Dissertations
46 Struck down
47 Clobbers
48 Round cheese
49 "Fat chance!"
50 Thomas __ Edison
51 True-to-life
53 Vatican venue
54 What winds do
57 Tack on

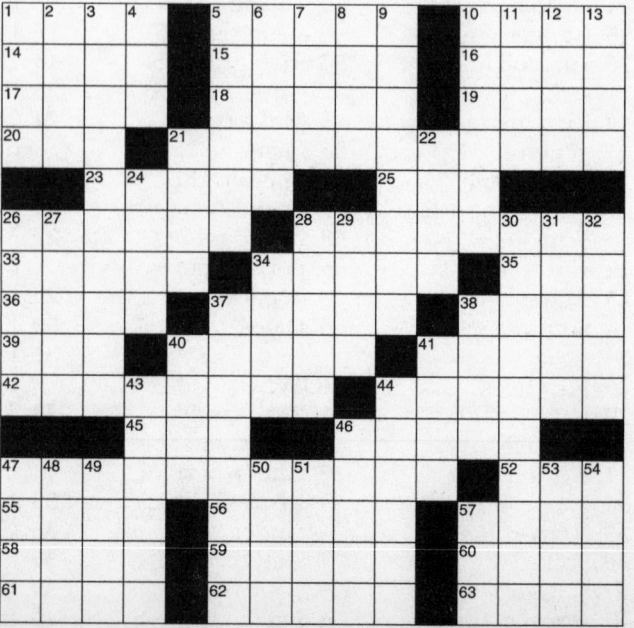

TRIM-A-TREE by Diane C. Baldwin

ACROSS

1 Big brass
6 *Amadeus* star
11 Jethro's uncle
14 Small egg
15 Sandwich treats
16 __ Miss
17 *Who's the Boss?* star
19 Peeples of *Courthouse*
20 Like the gray mare
21 Horseshoe pitch
22 More unnatural
24 Be significant
26 Deuce beater
27 Went quickly
28 Appear once again
32 Weaving frames
34 Toe tormentors
35 Sort
36 "__ well that . . ."
37 U of the UN
38 Patch location, perhaps
39 Blanc or Brooks
40 Perjurers
41 Behind bars
42 Doesn't buy
44 Belafonte tune
45 Coat parts
46 Tart apple
49 Pageboy, e.g.
52 Pumice, before cooling
53 TV schedule abbr.
54 Smarts stats
55 *Easter Parade* star
58 Rev, as an engine
59 Grenoble's river
60 Was brave
61 Millinery item
62 Gangster Lansky
63 Apologetic

DOWN

1 WWII Japanese general's family
2 It separates the tonsils
3 "Peggy Sue" rocker
4 Three-time boxing champ
5 Comes to rest
6 *The Planets* composer
7 Author Leon
8 Chair part
9 Logically consistent
10 Respects
11 James or Mitchell
12 Author Wiesel
13 Letter starter
18 Where the "Boyz" are?
23 Cereal grain
25 Uses the crosshairs
26 Aquatic birds
28 Laughs loudly
29 "You're Sixteen" singer
30 Jubilant mirth
31 Stretched the supply
32 Barnyard bleater
33 Sub in a tub
34 Shoots the breeze
37 Tufted songbird
38 *The Court Jester* cutup
40 Conrad novel of 1900
41 False stories
43 Diner or smoker
44 Battle, for one
46 Take the odds
47 Dogpatch denizen
48 Rice field
49 Elevated
50 Greenish blue
51 Ain't proper?
52 Orpheus' instrument
56 Susan of *L.A. Law*
57 7-faced film doctor

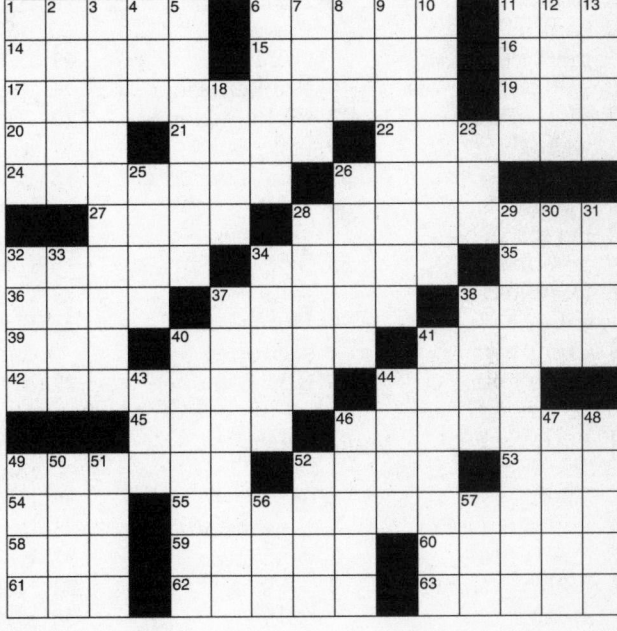

REGULAR GUYS by Bob Lubbers

ACROSS

1 State
5 Sp. miss
9 Vanquishes
14 Voir __ (jury examination)
15 Moss or Lorenz
16 Brazilian state
17 Walcott
19 Like a brook's bottom
20 Attended to
22 Match segments
23 Milquetoast
26 Cloudy gems
28 Extreme
29 Write down
31 Disney characters
32 Double agents
33 *Elle*
36 Aleutian island
37 More angry
38 Tyrannical ruler
39 Guided
40 Texas shrine
41 Bayou cuisine
42 Some autos
44 Actress Dorothy
45 Challenges
46 Baseboard fixtures
47 BLT topper
48 Danish cheese
51 __ Joe (Twain character)
53 DiMaggio
57 Teacake
58 __ breve
59 Projecting point
60 Disreputable
61 Caster's spool
62 Portent

DOWN

1 Pt. of speech
2 Contend
3 Bruin of fame
4 Mideast area
5 Most likely to secede?
6 Indian royal
7 Sulky race
8 Suit to __
9 Small ammo
10 Corrodes
11 Jackson
12 Hues
13 Simon __
18 Gray and Moran
21 Overdoer of a sort
23 Capital of Rio Grande do Norte
24 Wear away
25 Namath
27 __ de deux
29 Models
30 Emulsified spread
32 Gripe
34 Favorite place
35 Flying fishers
37 Trudge in the muck
38 Convince of
40 Ripen
41 Saguaros, e.g.
43 In the neighborhood
44 Ungodlike
45 Bunny hug, for one
46 Room: Fr.
47 Overlook
49 Slightly open
50 Mouse relative
52 *Mrs. Miniver* actor Richard
54 Slim or Diamond follower
55 Single
56 Nighttime, in poems

BOX TOPS by Diane C. Baldwin

ACROSS
1 __ *Las Vegas* (Elvis film)
5 Smears on
10 __ chi
13 Muslim cleric
14 Have the role of
15 Hole makers
16 BOX
19 Samuel's mentor
20 Della or Pee Wee
21 Man of many words
22 Madagascar mammals
24 Person or personality
26 Double-digit column
27 Computer command
28 So far
31 Portable boat
33 '95 Open loser to Graf
34 Pothole patch
35 Poet's hue
36 BOX __ (stable area)

37 Terpsichore's instrument
38 Mischievous fairy
39 Dessert holders
40 A bit cold
41 Court divider
42 Vein bonanzas
43 *Nota* __
44 Forearm stiffeners
46 Rubbernecker
48 Bit of evidence
50 Jest
52 Island welcome
54 BOX
57 Troubles
58 Swordsman's sally
59 Honeycomb section
60 Curly slapper
61 Of bygone times
62 Gaelic

DOWN
1 Certain squad's purview
2 "__ ears!" ("Do tell!")

3 BOX
4 Doctors' grp.
5 Library stamps
6 Workout souvenirs
7 Plains Indians
8 Little League purchase
9 Atl. flier
10 BOX
11 Lotion ingredient
12 "Small world, __ it?"
15 Like __ of bricks
17 Limb holder
18 Dodge car
23 Ornery
25 First name in daredeviltry
27 BOX __ (stadium offerings)
29 Dodge City marshal
30 Deck member
31 Peachy
32 Up to the job
33 Nerve-racking
36 FDR's mother

37 It's on the cuff
39 Co-op alternative
40 Small amphibians
43 Fruitless
45 Bruce and Harper
46 Overcharge
47 Angling gear

48 Take off the top
49 Niihau neighbor
51 Walden, for one
53 Emerald __
55 Mr. Ziegfeld
56 Surface for the Devils

TO A LESSER DEGREE by Norma Steinberg

ACROSS
1 Masticate
5 Reach across
9 Here, in Arles
12 Emanations
14 Shut
15 Negative prefix
16 Football team's option
18 Pampering, initially
19 Go by
20 Mets' stadium
21 Breadth
24 DC group
26 Husbands and wives
28 Magician's illusions
31 Sentry's cry
32 Skyrocket
35 Eastern European
36 Fort __, CA
37 Miserable
39 Mrs. Lennon's maiden name
40 Davis of *The Client*
42 Skillful

43 In addition
44 Start a journey
46 Dolt
48 Discount store
51 Brings up
52 Traffic components
54 Cicero, e.g.
56 Second Mrs. Sinatra
57 Inflation control plan
62 Apparatus
63 Hanks' *Apollo 13* costar
64 Comic DeGeneres
65 He served after HST
66 "Too bad!"
67 Run across

DOWN
1 Scoundrel
2 *Ben-*__
3 Pitcher's stat
4 Wac colleague
5 Feeds the pigs
6 Aplomb
7 Upward climb

8 Born: Fr.
9 Incarcerated
10 Natalie or Old King
11 Early Peruvian
13 Stages
14 Half a dance?
17 John of Monty Python
20 Recipe instruction
21 Scanty
22 Summer place for furs
23 Umpire's call
25 Part of the foot
26 Chases away
27 Auctioneer's call
29 Dorothy's home
30 Rose
33 Brewer's product
34 Musical motif
37 Weight
38 __ India (famous gem)
41 Promissory notes
43 "Now it's clear to me!"

45 Covered with blossoms
47 __ Haute, IN
49 Susan Lucci role
50 Mexican sandwiches
52 Part of a hand
53 Zealous

55 Decimal system base
57 Earl Anthony's org.
58 Leprechaun
59 Inventor Whitney
60 Buddhist sect
61 Conclude

OASES by Bob Lubbers

ACROSS

1 Fixed period
5 Coarse file
9 Gives (out)
14 Lotion ingredient
15 Singer Adams
16 Turn away
17 . . . in Florida?
19 Lachrymose
20 "Open __!"
21 Nebbish
23 Blue-pencil
26 Actress Susan
28 Shrill cry
31 Like some tables
33 Animal track
34 Angry
36 Ruby or Sandra
37 Competition
38 Swerves
39 Rich source
40 Gold: Sp.
41 Caravan stop
42 Oven feature
43 Less fresh
45 Mulled over

47 Helps in a crime
48 Bridge coup
49 Lauder of cosmetics
51 Braking rockets
56 "__ We Dance?"
58 . . . in Israel?
61 Desi's daughter
62 Scary giant
63 Later
64 Else
65 Actor Coward
66 Nailed a stud

DOWN

1 Emulates Gregory Hines
2 Gen. Robt. __
3 Ely and Howard
4 Butte kin
5 Ebb
6 Fuss
7 __ vous plaît
8 Moss material

9 Afternoon show
10 Turns inside out
11 . . . in Wyoming?
12 Goof
13 Eye sore
18 Arab chief
22 Desires
24 Less friendly
25 Clothing
27 Required
28 Lysander's homeland
29 . . . in Florida?
30 Fish eggs
32 Antlered animal
33 Signs of stage success: Abbr.
35 The Little Mermaid
38 Metrical writing
39 Ignited
41 Pioneer, perhaps
42 Trains, as lions

44 Howard or Uggams
46 "Roll Out the __"
50 Black
52 __ Girl ('60s sitcom)
53 "The Biggest Little City"

54 Woodwind
55 Beach surface
56 __-mo
57 Quarterback's call
59 Self
60 Before, poetically

MATERIAL THINGS by Gregory E. Paul

ACROSS

1 Avert, with "off"
5 Whitefish
9 Coal slide
14 Inter __
15 Protagonist
16 Cliff dwelling
17 Skating place
18 Part of AKA
19 UMW member
20 Colonial clergyman
23 Patriot Allen
24 Toast starter
28 Dentist's command
32 Bacon serving
33 Colorful pet
37 Big rig
38 Coach Parseghian
39 Beseech
42 Medical aide: Abbr.
43 Ship off
45 Mel Tormé's nickname, with "The"
47 Enrages
50 Patriot Silas

51 Bile acid, e.g.
53 Warren or Joyce Carol
57 Billy Joel album, with The
61 Topic for McLuhan
64 Palindromic time
65 Swenson of Benson
66 Moon of Uranus
67 Spiffy
68 Earth's inheritors?
69 Equals
70 Countertenor
71 Rochester's beloved

DOWN

1 Mockery
2 Mr. Ness
3 Last inning, usually
4 '60s TV adventure
5 Role for Oland
6 Tiller
7 Bear in the air
8 Stall

9 Tool for Eisenstaedt
10 One with will power
11 Coffeepot
12 Father's Day gift
13 Mountain ending
21 Assured of success
22 That girl
25 Knickknacks' place
26 Cadence
27 Shuttle gasket
29 "Smoking or __?"
30 One-time John Candy series
31 Golden-__ corn
33 Homes: Sp.
34 "__ We All" (1929 song)
35 Hope of Hollywood
36 Marketing start
40 Actress Gardner
41 Domingo, e.g.
44 __ cri
46 British break

48 American Leaguers
49 Part of RSVP
52 Shalala or Summer
54 US Chief Justice, 1836-64
55 Alps peak
56 Plumber's aid

58 Yuletide
59 Application of paint
60 Biblical preposition
61 Glove-box item
62 Before
63 Tool's partner

SMALL TALK by Dean Niles

ACROSS
1 __ avis
5 Russian port
9 Modify
14 Straw in the wind
15 Flag holder
16 10:1, e.g.
17 W.C. Fields' foil
19 Construction-site sight
20 Somebody
21 "We __ Family" (Sister Sledge)
22 Break
24 Fish story
27 Cycle starter
28 "__ De-Lovely" (Porter tune)
29 Bemoaned
34 Moisten the meat
37 Actress Rogers
38 Desiccated
39 "__ a Song Go Out of My Heart"
40 Confronted
41 Former aide Alexander

42 Go out for a strike?
43 Warts and all
44 Annoys, in a way
45 Egg style
47 __ for the course
48 Take first
49 Do recon work
54 Comebacks
58 Excluding none
59 Far from SSW
60 "What's in __?"
61 Albee play
64 Customs
65 On the summit of
66 "__ See Clearly Now"
67 Skew
68 Jonson and Johnson
69 __ up (enlivens)

DOWN
1 Mechanical man
2 Range name
3 Nonconformist

4 Whichever
5 Donizetti works
6 Brown mushroom
7 __-pitch softball
8 Crucial determinants
9 Esoteric
10 *Comic Relief* comic
11 State, in France
12 Nonet count
13 Active guy
18 Coffeehouse choice
23 Dank
25 Winona Ryder movie
26 Brings forth
30 Crooner Ed
31 Hardwood
32 Great Lake
33 BA and MSW
34 Lettuce type
35 Ointment ingredient
36 Attached, in a way
37 Not fem.
40 Hardly audible

44 Zahn of TV
46 Most severe
47 Some jellyfish
50 Church law
51 Like some lager
52 Open, perhaps
53 High schoolers

54 Butts
55 Hydroxyl compound
56 O'Hara's estate
57 Attempt
62 Geologist's suffix
63 Backtalk

HIT FOR THE CYCLE by Ray Hamel

ACROSS
1 Ed Norton's workplace
6 Rubber-duck ritual
10 Revered name in baseball
14 __ *of Two Cities*
15 Film critic James
16 Playwright Novello
17 Blender setting
18 National park?
19 Mideast region
20 By oneself
23 Aluminum coin
24 Cut pizza
28 Mex. matron
31 Leave room for corrections
35 Remain open
37 Nursery-rhyme dieter
38 Fall start
39 Say it's so
40 Put down, in slang
41 French verb
42 San __, Italy

43 Poke fun from the dais
45 Falls to pieces
46 Horse-racing accomplishment
49 Hoop hanger
50 Humiliated
51 Physicist's concern
53 1911 World Series hero
60 Deli spread
63 Lines of admiration
64 Giraffe cousin
65 Skip
66 Quill pen points
67 Attended a banquet
68 Frat jewelry
69 Letter opener
70 Director of *The Deep*

DOWN
1 Weakens
2 Small case
3 Alert
4 "Adonais," e.g.

5 Was sent spinning
6 Shindig
7 Turkish officer
8 Promgoer
9 DJ's need
10 7-star constellation
11 Palindromic Gardner
12 Dickens alias
13 The Big Band __
21 Seth begat him
22 High rails
25 Milk holder
26 Card game
27 Find abominable
28 Athens rival
29 Studio effect
30 Hemoglobin deficiency
32 "What's __?"
33 Pipe material
34 Lariat
36 Soft tennis hits
43 Oregon resort
44 Smaller than queen
47 Composer Delibes

48 "__ Does It Better"
52 '70s police series
54 Gunn's gal
55 Country-music superstar McEntire
56 Ex-UN member

57 Founder of critical realism
58 One-on-one sport
59 Frees (of)
60 Cleaning implement
61 *Bon* follower
62 Yang's counterpart

SPRING FEVER by Gerald R. Ferguson

ACROSS

1 __ in (collapsed)
6 Startling success
10 Athlete, slangily
14 Give __ berth to (avoid)
15 *Born Free* beast
16 Wrinkled fruit
17 Romantic precipice
19 Stew ingredient
20 Certain shirts
21 French physicist
23 Telegenic jurist
24 "__ clear as mud!"
25 Big parties
29 Imitative
32 __ nothing (extreme alternatives)
33 Restaurant
37 Flier's stunt
38 Darken
39 Revolutionary War general
40 Kind of drilling or shipping
42 Type of mattress
43 Consumed
44 Songbird
45 Total anew
48 Sonny's sibling
49 Gladdens
51 Enchantresses
56 Ruler before Galba
57 Attack, as a cat
59 "Help!," to Henri
60 Pittypat or Polly
61 Playwright Bernard
62 Dryer dust
63 Small band
64 To the point

DOWN

1 Young yak
2 Court-martial candidate
3 __ *Zapata!*
4 Anthony or Barbara
5 __ cri (latest fashion)
6 Casals' instrument
7 Flamenco accolades
8 Dos Passos trilogy
9 Bear with a hard bed
10 Go before "go!"
11 Double-curve moldings
12 Bow or Barton
13 Wind-powered toys
18 Tennis units
22 Failed attempt
25 Hairless
26 Spiny plant
27 Plumlike fruit
28 Got going
29 *Enoch __* (Tennyson opus)
30 Twosome
31 Doctrine
33 __ noire
34 Pro __
35 Inventor Sikorsky
36 Counting-out word
38 Cricket tool
41 Walk in water
42 Like a race winner
44 Initials for G.W.B.
45 Of the kidneys
46 Resin used as incense
47 Duelist Burr
48 __ Domingo
50 Falling-out
51 Kind of bond, for short
52 Hold sway
53 On __ with (equal to)
54 Pea holders
55 Old blade
58 __ *Town* (Wilder play)

WYES GUYS by Bob Lubbers

ACROSS

1 Hard work, so to speak
6 Murray or West
9 Aristocratic
14 Poet's Muse
15 Sprite
16 Zodiac sign
17 Carved tree
18 NBA official
19 Missile housings
20 First-stringers
21 Barrymore or Merman
23 Absorbent material
27 AMEX rival
30 Chin whiskers
31 NEA member
32 Fall mo.
35 Part of BTU
36 *Inter* __
37 Ford or Close
39 Haul
41 Goes out of focus
42 Venice resort
43 Small shark
45 Busy insect
46 Finishes
47 Nile beetle
49 Scottish terrier
50 Melee
55 Uncouth one
57 "__ got me" ("I give up")
58 OCS grad
60 __ Mahal
63 Polish city
64 "__, I saw, . . ."
65 Lyric poem
66 Preface, for short
67 Concise
68 "It's __ the pale moon . . ."
69 Aeries

DOWN

1 Attack
2 Penned
3 Diner patron
4 "I did not think to shed __": Shak.
5 Gangster's weapon
6 *Mal de* __
7 Pale brew
8 Decadent
9 Poet Ogden
10 Eastern
11 Cudgel
12 Zodiac sign
13 Double curve
22 Common title starter
24 Against
25 Café au __
26 Footstool
28 English county
29 Wipe clean
32 Eyes
33 Toast sound
34 Cuddly toy
38 Pesty bugs
40 Give the alert
41 Hair holder
44 Actress Kendall
47 '60s campus org.
48 Weevil feed
51 TV honcho Arledge
52 Gives the boot
53 In the open
54 Bingo-like games
56 Suit to __
58 Ignited
59 Ade cooler
61 Tumult
62 Nozzle stream

FLOWERY LANGUAGE by Gregory E. Paul

ACROSS

1 Landlocked Asian country
5 Name for a police dog
9 Part of CNN
14 *The Four Seasons* star
15 Raced
16 *The Life of __*
17 Become exhausted, with "out"
18 Jane of fiction
19 Entertain
20 New Hampshire's state flower
23 Curvy letter
24 Barbara and Nathan
25 Pallet
27 Prairie wolf
30 Seedless raisin
33 Tell a whopper
34 Wipe out
37 __ *Frome*
38 __ breve
40 Winter rain
42 Actor Ken
43 Auctions off
45 Peruvian peaks
47 __ de la Cité
48 Nutrition-label listing
50 Quagmire
52 Prosperity
53 Easy __ (simple)
55 Tolstoy topic
57 Loren/Quinn film, with *The*
62 Wear away
64 Thickening agent
65 Verdi villain
66 Borden mascot
67 Singer James
68 Piscator's place
69 *Dead __ Society*
70 Lively dance
71 Art Deco designer

DOWN

1 Reindeer herder
2 Manager Felipe
3 Aroma
4 Greek poetess
5 NFL team
6 Rules man
7 "To __ human . . ."
8 Compost item
9 Cereal sound
10 Prepare to fire
11 With *The*, Raymond Chandler screenplay
12 Subtraction word
13 Peepers
21 Dilatory
22 Tempe sch.
26 "Sock __ me!"
27 Necklace feature
28 Edmonton skater
29 Texas flower of song
30 Acorn, e.g.
31 Exemplars of toughness
32 Meara and Murray
35 First name of 14 Across
36 D.C. legislator
39 "*Der __*" (Adenauer)
41 Secular
44 *The Fighting __* (Wayne film)
46 Evian evening
49 Land of Lincoln: Abbr.
51 Cookbook entry
53 Severe
54 Use a rink
55 Emulate Niobe
56 "Alice's Restaurant" singer
58 Ripening agent
59 Rapunzel's pride
60 "__ Around" (Beach Boys song)
61 Painter Gustave
63 Dah alternative

HANKIE PANKY by Patrick Jordan

ACROSS

1 Ye __ Tea Shoppe
5 Festivals
10 Spheres
14 Early bird's prize
15 Swiftly
16 Breathing sound
17 Codefendant of Leopold
18 Attach, in a way
19 Trojan War hero
20 Quarterback Bart
22 Swiss river
23 Its cover has a red border
24 American game birds
27 Trombone part
28 __ Lingus
29 Jerusalem shrine
33 Former Chinese chairman
36 Print-shop needs
37 Wheat bristle
38 Gull relative
39 Whillikers preceder
40 It's regrettable
44 Haggard heroine
45 Pulls down
46 Riverbank tree
52 Wheel shaft
53 Part of UAR
54 Lake in the Sierras
57 Make angry
58 Cleric's quarters
60 Mah-jongg piece
61 Answered the charges
62 Brought to a halt
63 Flair
64 Helms and Hatch: Abbr.
65 Prepare for the anthem
66 Challenge

DOWN

1 Fly-by-night group
2 Bandit's booty
3 Fantastical
4 Involves in strife
5 Hiatus
6 Beelike
7 Maui porch
8 Squash variety
9 Westernmost African nation
10 Public speaker
11 Indira's son
12 Culpability
13 Genders
21 Designer Gernreich
25 Animated Chihuahua
26 Tierra __ Fuego
27 Fully marbled?
29 Part of Harpo's outfit
30 Brightly colored
31 Gen. Pershing's conflict
32 Abby's sister
33 Transitional word
34 Provides weaponry to
35 Half of 11?
38 Ruby-__ hummingbird
40 Phi follower
41 Changes the title
42 Toothpaste form
43 Popeye or Ahab
44 Exceeds the limit
46 Distorts
47 Napoleon's fate
48 Burstyn or Barkin
49 Bestow
50 *Happy Birthday, __ June* (Vonnegut novel)
51 *Ghosts* playwright
55 Patron saint of Norway
56 Counting-rhyme opener
59 Teacher's deg.

GLOBAL PALETTE by Jim Page

ACROSS

1 Part of 3 Down
7 Hit beginning
11 *Masqué* dance
14 "Now!"
15 Budget rival
16 *Wheel of Fortune* purchase
17 *River Wild* star
18 Uprising
19 Nondrinkers: Abbr.
20 Dominican resort
22 Black gold
23 Deluge
24 Grimm opener, often
25 Spasmodic movements
28 It's not free of charge
29 Done
31 __ *pro nobis*
32 Scottish novelist
34 Japanese surname
37 Stockings style
39 Confiscate
41 Continental competitor, once
42 As __ the hills
44 ITT rival
45 Seagoing stockade
47 Branch of math.
48 Zillions of years
49 Lotsa money
51 Held in high esteem
54 Santa __, CA
55 African nation
59 Bit of wordplay
60 Danish physicist
61 Net game
62 Fly ball's path
63 Novelist Hunter
64 Groups of three
65 Meadow
66 Word heard January 1
67 Ancient ascetic

DOWN

1 Coarse file
2 Aleutian island
3 Org. founded by James Farmer
4 Neon and argon
5 Word form for "vinegar"
6 Hare-related
7 "Lili __"
8 Water source
9 Florentine painter
10 Screen dog
11 Southern capital
12 Caper
13 Cotton thread
21 See 14 Across
24 Wine opener?
25 Soy product
26 Writer Murdoch
27 Exotic city
30 Hotshots
32 Cross letters
33 Edged
35 "Do __ others . . ."
36 He became Avon
38 Bring on board
40 Belgian painter
43 Penny Marshall role
46 Cool, once
48 A fine figure of a man?
49 Like a Vatican edict
50 Become accustomed
52 Allen or Frome
53 Civil rights activist Medgar
55 U.K. decorations
56 Tavern, old-style
57 Nicole's "nada"
58 Existence: Lat.

HALF-BAKED by Lee Weaver

ACROSS

1 Speak roughly
5 A wife of Henry VIII
9 Anka or Newman
13 Commedia dell'__
14 *Kate & __*
15 Ingrid, in *Casablanca*
16 Sissies
18 Nights before
19 Musician's gift
20 Provide weapons to
21 Small table on wheels
23 Forceful person
25 Wise one
26 Yuletide visitor
29 Andy of *60 Minutes*
33 *Psycho* character
36 Norse explorer
38 Golfer's warning
39 Turkish title
40 Ford of *Murphy Brown*
41 Ade alternative
42 Regrets
43 Sir __ Guinness
44 More stable
45 Spreading tree
47 Knee-ankle connector
49 Comments from Sandy
51 Private Bailey
55 Handel work
58 Nautical "yes"
59 Easter meat
60 Memo notation
61 Luxurious automobile
64 Rajah's consort
65 Eastern Indians
66 Hemsley sitcom
67 Salad veggie, for short
68 Understands
69 Funny Foxx

DOWN

1 Ran at Indy
2 Place in order
3 Ship's rear
4 Shooter or coat opener
5 Jack Horner's prize
6 TV alien
7 Crevices
8 Lab activity
9 "No problem!"
10 Thomas __ Edison
11 PC owner
12 Endure
14 Kitchen cover-up
17 Half of a '60s singing group
22 "Long __ and Far Away"
24 Quite simple
27 Freshwater duck
28 Zodiac ram
30 Lunchtime, often
31 Perry's creator
32 Tenth of a decade
33 Fishhook
34 Water, in Madrid
35 At that time
37 Scratching reason
40 Trumpet flourishes
44 Curl the lip
46 *Exodus* hero
48 Bottomless chasm
50 Singer Dinah
52 Chef's herb
53 Intertwined
54 Make corrections to
55 Cleopatra's beau
56 Twin to Jacob
57 Plummeted
58 Pub brews
62 Fib
63 Skiff accessory

COLD SPELLS by Bob Lubbers

ACROSS

1 First year of the 15th century
5 __ avis
9 Pixieish
14 Shore bird
15 Solemn response
16 __ Haute, IN
17 Bribe money
19 Diaphanous
20 Conference site of 1945
22 Repair
23 Mrs. Smith's rival
26 Mystify
28 Eaten away
29 Food shortage
31 Court cloaks
32 Type type
33 "Kiss my grits" character
36 Applications
37 Tender spots
38 "__ This Moment On"
39 *Mal de* __
40 Diamond data
41 Unconcerned
42 Atlas and company
44 Sailors
45 Following
46 Malicious ones
47 Taj Mahal site
48 Ingredient
51 Early strings
53 Summer cooler
57 Commercial cow
58 __ of paradise
59 Stash
60 Bristles
61 Collections
62 Muscle quality

DOWN

1 Hood and St. Helens
2 Animation unit
3 Actress Joanne
4 To the utmost
5 Emulated Finn
6 Entertain
7 Rip apart
8 "__ partridge in . . ."
9 UFO pilots
10 Shearson's former partner
11 VCR button
12 Singer Cara
13 Dweeb
18 Sinks, as a putt
21 __ *Family* (Vicki Lawrence sitcom)
23 Antitoxin
24 Got up
25 "Birches" poet
27 60 secs.
29 Ticonderoga and Wayne
30 Ed, Nancy or Leon
32 Colorful horse
34 Also-ran
35 Signs
37 Long look
38 Most level
40 *Jeanne d'Arc*, for one: Abbr.
41 Essence
43 Where *Roma* is
44 Uses cash
45 Nimble
46 Clever
47 St. crossers
49 Tennis shots
50 Canal to Buffalo
52 Notice
54 "How was __ know?"
55 Scam
56 Meadow mom

FLORA AND FAUNA by Shirley Soloway

ACROSS

1 Dawber or Shriver
4 Computer input
8 Actor Lorenzo
13 Winglike
15 Burden
16 "Mighty Lak' __"
17 Spotted flower
19 *Niña*'s sister ship
20 Israeli city
21 Even
23 Short play
24 Open, in a way
26 Shoe soles
28 Yeltsin's domain
31 Battleship shade
32 Shore bird
33 "Santa Claus Is Coming __"
37 WA clock setting
40 Bigotry
41 Sports-car part
42 Crowd sound
43 Pose a question
44 Opera giant
45 Border
46 Ornamental case
48 Formal
50 Shock
52 Pesto ingredient
54 Male moose
55 Plant starter
57 Lamp inhabitant
61 Verbal exams
63 Lawn bane
65 Taylor of *The Nanny*
66 San __, Italy
67 River residue
68 Tropical fish
69 Southwestern Indians
70 Marvin or Majors

DOWN

1 Country walkway
2 *Inter* __
3 Yuletide trio
4 Pt. of a fiver
5 Vocalist Baker
6 Spring blossom
7 "__ sow, so shall . . ."
8 Toddler's perch
9 Grain bristle
10 Tropical trees
11 Moving about
12 Theater units
14 Says "No!"
18 Hindu noblewoman
22 Suburban trees
25 Marsh plants
27 Covered vase
28 Singer McEntire
29 *QB VII* author
30 Window-sill flora
34 __ *Town* (Wilder play)
35 Capote, to pals
36 Some MDs
38 Droops
39 Low card
42 Barn dancers
44 __-de-sac
47 More statuesque
49 Diana of *Mystery!*
50 Scrub a mission
51 Baby food
52 *Chapeau*
53 "There Is Nothing Like __"
56 Light tan
58 Toolbox item
59 Resort spot
60 Spanish compass point
62 Coral or Red
64 Derek and Jackson

RHYME SCHEME by Dean Niles

ACROSS
1 Join, in a way
4 False steps
10 Fight decisions
14 He defeated Spinks
15 Dry gulch
16 "Big Island" port
17 "No __ is an island"
18 Slept noisily
19 Mexican mineral
20 Move back and forth
22 Magical Henning
24 Soon
25 Twelve
27 Dutch airline
30 Music genre
33 Zilch
34 Tic-tac-toe win
35 More drenched
37 Ballroom dance
39 Beat
42 Madison County curiosities

44 Tolerate
45 Shock to the system
47 Imprison
48 Nothing but
50 Family member
54 Math. course
55 Actor Delon
57 Synagogue scroll
58 Pigeon
60 Monotonous
63 Off base?
65 Medicinal legume
67 Usurer's charge, for short
68 Mass. neighbor
69 Hooky player
70 Wriggly fish
71 Forum wear
72 Regarded to be
73 Compass dir.

DOWN
1 Chinese boat
2 Tennyson character
3 Separate

4 Pant
5 Cartoonist Peter
6 Fern leaf
7 Done without
8 Take a gander at
9 Soaked through
10 "__ Swell" (Rodgers & Hart song)
11 Big ape
12 Beer nickname
13 Chicago team
21 Nibbled (on)
23 Former
26 __ the Greek
28 Opera box
29 Cow calls
31 Chromosome description
32 Handy abbr.
36 Tropical fish
38 Modifies
39 War photographer Robert
40 First shepherd
41 Chime sound
43 Term of a show

46 Order a second printing of
49 Picks, as a major
51 Horse feet
52 Banks and Kovacs
53 Move a finger
56 Hebrew month

59 Forearm bone
61 Designer Ricci
62 Hoods' weapons
63 Play a role
64 It may be pitched
66 "We __ Family" (Sister Sledge tune)

IN A RUSH by Manny Nosowsky

ACROSS
1 Huntley or Atkins
5 Start of Caesar's boast
10 Big mouths
14 __ avis
15 Mythical friend
16 "L' __, c'est moi"
17 Exclamations of discovery
18 Steak choice
19 Soprano Ponselle
20 Some salespersons
23 Pinning surface
24 What the prepared may have
25 __ Bet Your Life
26 Chemical suffix
27 Lots of feet
28 Firms: Abbr.
30 "__ tov!"
32 The old college cry
33 Lead source
34 Toon sheriff
40 Dr. No name

41 Legal thing
42 Milton who succeeded Idi
43 "My Gal __"
44 M*A*S*H transporters
49 Wine holder
50 Is: Fr.
52 Hotel job
54 "It's __-win situation"
55 Constitution subject
57 Scissorhands portrayer
59 Chain mail?
60 "Take __ from me"
61 Intestinal divisions
62 Atta Troll author
63 Deluxe
64 Part of CBS
65 Scribblings
66 Dos follower

DOWN
1 Sly
2 Laughs
3 Crossword tool

4 Sampled
5 GI's neckwear
6 San Francisco climber
7 One way to run
8 Pecuniary sums
9 Invierno month
10 "__ out!" (ump's call)
11 Perfume sprayer
12 Rose Bowl site
13 Governor's concern
21 NFL scores
22 Poisonous plant
29 Pal Joey playwright
31 HS math course
32 Cereal stat.
33 Baseball execs.
34 Novel set in ancient Rome
35 In a suave manner
36 Elemental relatives
37 __ and run (flee)
38 Pastoral and Twittering Machine

39 Hardly rare
43 Multimedia option
44 Stick out
45 Caught up
46 Publishing employee

47 Laud
48 Graceful women
51 Hall-of-Fame pitcher Warren
53 Actor Lew
56 Give off
58 Boone or Benatar

ACROSS

1 Mutual of __
6 NBA officials
10 Donaldson of ABC News
13 Falana and Albright
14 "I __ Song Coming On"
15 Arafat's grp.
16 Acts
17 Cancel
18 Football filler
19 Glenn Miller tune
22 Nile snake
25 Tipplers
26 Party-game animal
27 First-rate
29 Endowment source
30 Historic Manhattan nightspot
33 Indian princess
37 One who carries
38 Dearie
39 Hayes or Reddy
40 Short drive
41 Bail out of a plane
43 Farm yield
45 At a discount
46 More showy
49 Boa, e.g.
51 Isr. neighbor
52 Daydreamed
55 Fuss
56 Take __ (travel)
57 Bread part
61 Scout Carson
62 Brawls
63 Couric of *Today*
64 Nav. rank
65 Indulge, with "on"
66 Back of a boat

DOWN

1 Ancient
2 A Stooge
3 Pub quaff
4 Muslim pilgrimage
5 Rater
6 Auberjonois and Russo
7 Counting-out word
8 Baloney
9 Wild West oasis
10 Punish, perhaps
11 Wonderland visitor
12 Comic Amsterdam
14 Skip meals
20 Colorful horse
21 Disrobe
22 Savings and checking: Abbr.
23 Sailing vessel
24 Page of music
28 Letterer's aid
29 *Candid Camera* man
31 Poker item
32 Land parcel
34 Assumed name
35 Nice __ (prig)
36 Cartoonist's helper
39 Nags
41 Author Alger
42 Frost
44 Esteem
46 Conscious
47 *The Thinker* sculptor
48 Honks
49 Flag color
50 Agents, for short
53 Fox __ (dance)
54 "Egad!"
58 Western Indian
59 Knight's title
60 Middle of the morning

ACROSS

1 Gooey globule
5 Culinary mavens
10 Rude kid
14 Othello's tormentor
15 "Sweet __ O'Grady"
16 Not on tape
17 Capital on a fjord
18 Appliance maker
19 Congregational response
20 Brother of Ham
21 Be oneself again
23 Diplomatic HQ
25 Costa del __, Spain
26 Stung
30 Sphere of action
34 Tibetan priests
35 "Phooey!"
38 Bone __ (study)
40 Infamous Idi
41 Aboveboard
42 Identification
43 Building add-on
44 Unseal
45 Actress Moorehead
46 Rose-colored dye
48 Side by side
50 __ Aviv
52 P.O. itinerary
53 Agassi offering
59 Quite the style
63 Anne Nichols hero
64 Lake near Donner Pass
65 Courtroom ritual
66 For fear that
67 Keep clear of
68 Mother of Zeus
69 Graph lines
70 Musical pauses
71 Clammy

DOWN

1 Life stories, for short
2 Eye neighbor
3 Stare at
4 Backfires
5 Flash Gordon portrayer Buster
6 __ *sapiens*
7 Biblical barterer
8 Some Lapps
9 Shore
10 Talk out of turn
11 Terza __ (verse form)
12 With: Fr.
13 10,000 meters, for short
22 Freddy's street
24 Rockies and Catskills: Abbr.
26 Popular side order
27 '50s First Lady
28 __ acid (organic compound)
29 Tiresome one
31 Elastic strap
32 '40s toothpaste
33 Mighty volumes
36 Duffer's dream
37 Actress Louise
39 Hawk's home
41 Texas symbol
45 Klees and Dalis
47 Conglomerate inits.
49 AKC classifications
51 Go
53 ". . . to be jolly, __ . . ."
54 Goat with curved horns
55 Shine's partner
56 Hardens
57 Greek letters
58 Sporting-goods name
60 "That's funny!"
61 Agenda part
62 Old boy

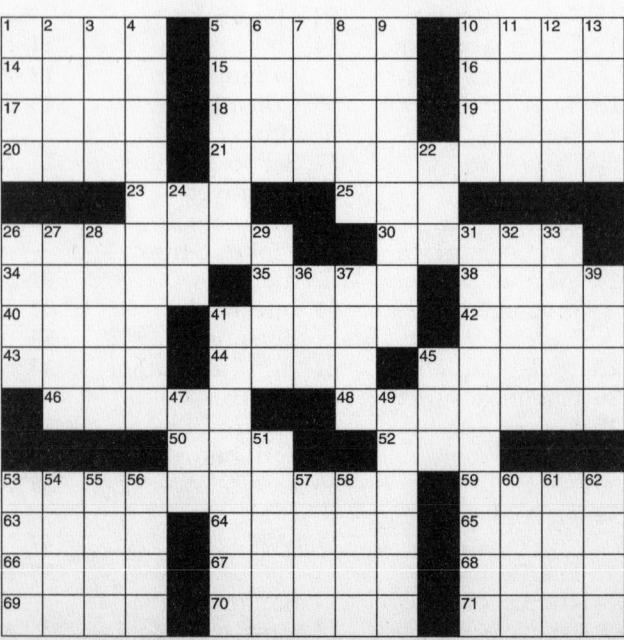

CROSS-WORD PUZZLE by Randolph Ross

ACROSS
1 Element #5
6 Bench pieces
11 Marked a ballot
14 Budget rival
15 Loggers' competition
16 Actress Charlotte
17 Baby Boomer successors
19 Genesis boat
20 Potter's need
21 Jamaican sectist
22 Computer on-line magazine
23 Preceding night
25 Audience cries
27 Baby noodles
31 Nicholas Gage book
32 Sapporo sash
33 Lana Turner film
35 Observed
38 Milk-cap collectible
39 Med. test
40 Hard water?
41 William, to Charles

42 That certain something
46 You can dig it
47 Unfamiliar
49 Rejected
51 Bested
53 Red Zinger is one
54 Military insects
55 Boxer Griffith
59 Gangster's date
63 PTA interest
64 *Midnight Cowboy*, for one
66 Percent finish
67 Vertical number line
68 Like some gases
69 Gender
70 Pizzeria order
71 Claire of *Little Women*

DOWN
1 Luggage
2 Spread in a tub
3 Punjab princess
4 Brunch serving
5 Hide-hair connector

6 *Mlle.* of Madrid
7 Clark's coworker
8 Mucho
9 Readily explained
10 AL cap letters
11 Superman talent
12 Have an __ the ground
13 Fakes out a goalie
18 Ring or rink site
22 Proscribe
24 Vigor's partner
26 Reviewer Reed
27 Ice-cream creations
28 Peek finish
29 Document instruction
30 TV commercial maker
31 Issues forth
34 Parabolic path
36 Land unit
37 Unwanted plant
42 Noon, to Nero?
43 Part of FICA
44 Made a pick

45 Regret
48 Mormons: Abbr.
50 Loretta Young film of '36
51 Desert relief
52 "I give up!"
56 Long dress

57 Adjectival suffix
58 __ majesty
60 Hot spot
61 Turin cash
62 Allows
64 Some chromosomes
65 Ctr.

THRILLERS by Jim Page

ACROSS
1 Colombian city
5 Fir variety
11 Elopers' helpers: Abbr.
14 Sharif or Bradley
15 Salad need
16 Wash. neighbor
17 Racing writer
19 With it
20 Skids
21 Repeal
22 Say "wheee!"
25 Soup grain
27 "That's __ excuse!" ("I don't buy it!")
28 Nautical spike
31 Class break
33 Placed carpet
34 EMT skill
37 Machine-gun sound
38 Optics prop
40 Exist
41 Ordinal ending
42 Paint badly
43 Arts supporter
46 Apathy

49 Succeeded as a siren
50 Sock pattern
52 Cashes in
54 Craze
55 Meanders
57 Former news initials
58 Ian Fleming's successor
63 Port storage spot
64 Twenty hundredweight
65 Competent
66 Paid notices
67 Relay-race props
68 Candied __

DOWN
1 *The Bride Came __*
2 Chartres chum
3 Body of *eau*
4 Vexatious
5 __ acid (antiseptic)
6 Garland
7 Designer wares
8 Assns.

9 Black bird
10 Short papers
11 George Smiley is one of his people
12 Joy's partner
13 1850s rebel
18 Takes wing
21 Samovar
22 __ aves
23 Vote for
24 *The Eagle Has Landed* author
25 Goodyear vehicle
26 Assist
29 Legal excuse
30 __ al Khaima (Arabian Gulf state)
32 Bowler's pickup
35 Introduction
36 Rips
39 Furrow
42 Actress Dolores __ Rio
44 Birch
45 *Mardi*, in Montana
47 Carrie or Louis

48 Zaragoza's province
50 Curaçao neighbor
51 Part of BART
53 Dame Edith
55 Hone
56 Word form for "within"

58 Exemplar of patience
59 "Coming in __ wing . . ."
60 Dr. J's org.
61 Shade tree
62 Where you live: Abbr.

55 PICK-ME-UP by Dean Niles

ACROSS
1 "Let it stand"
5 Political faction
9 Poet Sylvia
14 Fritz's brother
15 *Green Mansions* girl
16 Coin of Calcutta
17 Chicken partner
18 START OF A QUIP
20 Worldwide workers grp.
21 Charge
22 Identifier
23 PART 2 OF QUIP
26 Iced infusion
29 Pay the tab
30 Ref relative
31 Defeats decisively
33 Roman historian
36 The E in Q.E.D.
37 PART 3 OF QUIP
40 PART 4 OF QUIP
42 Sunscreen ingredient
43 Loner's dismissal
47 Plant places
49 Stir
50 Like most roofs
54 Actor Wallach
55 PART 5 OF QUIP
58 James Dean movie
60 __ de plume
61 *Have __ Will Travel*
62 END OF QUIP
65 Jerk's serving
66 Tiki relative
67 Utters
68 __ of March
69 Looks
70 *A __ Grows in Brooklyn*
71 It has been

DOWN
1 It may be short
2 Altering pro
3 Repeat
4 Literary monogram
5 Pithy
6 Animated
7 Gosh preceder
8 Puss pleasers
9 Johns Hopkins curriculum
10 Come-on
11 Opening
12 X
13 __ up (angered)
19 Ashen
21 Like some flaws
24 Offhand
25 Aussie bird
27 Israeli Abba
28 Concerning
32 Divulge
34 The "bad" cholesterol
35 Longest article
37 __ *dixit*
38 Complain
39 Commit legally
41 Nautical adverb
44 Otologist's exam
45 6-pointers
46 Freshwater fish
48 Twitches
51 Fish on *Fish*
52 Chopin pieces
53 Hereditary ruler
56 Music producer Brian
57 Some Scandinavians
59 Particular
62 Lbs. and oz.
63 Gardening tool
64 Dict. abbr.
65 Use a straw

56 HOUSEWORK by Bob Lubbers

ACROSS
1 ERA, e.g.
5 Awful movie
9 Selects
14 Actress Negri
15 Reverend Roberts
16 Little bird
17 Lou Gehrig's nickname
19 Teeny-__
20 Fruit-and-nut candy
21 *Candid __*
23 Estuary
25 Special abilities
28 Calmly
33 Lowest minor league
34 Occupied
35 Shoestrings
37 Guitarist Montgomery
38 Chore
39 Rob and Chad
40 Obtains
41 Quantity: Abbr.
42 Hemmed, perhaps
43 Dodger Pee Wee
44 Spurn
46 Dismantled tents
48 Ski runs
50 Daystar
51 Life's work
53 Lassos
58 Adam of *Chicago Hope*
60 Cover up
62 Play unit
63 Congers
64 New York canal
65 Overfilled
66 Depend (on)
67 Blocker and Rather

DOWN
1 Twirl
2 *Corrida* charger
3 Felipe of baseball
4 Sharp flavor
5 Baby shoe
6 Bruin great
7 Fem. opposite
8 Sheepish cry
9 Eleanor and Jane
10 "If __ Carpenter"
11 Sports wipeout
12 Barbie's beau
13 Hog wallow
18 Author Bret
22 Spiked clubs
24 Permit
26 Feared fly
27 Talked back to
28 Instruments for Shankar
29 Shiny paint
30 Book's cover
31 Inquire
32 Went off course
36 Yields
39 "__ Entertain You"
40 Precious stone
42 Derided
43 Princess of India
45 *Seinfeld* role
47 Barbie's bow
49 Underground duct
52 Former South Korean president Syngman
54 Transfixed
55 O'Hara mansion
56 A __ "apple"
57 __ *Gotta Have It* (Spike Lee film)
58 Buffoon
59 Co. founded by Sarnoff
61 Unwell

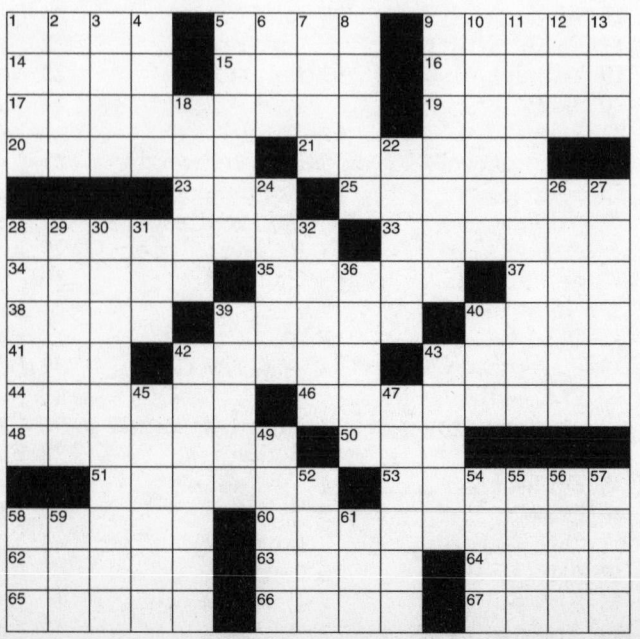

57 GO WEST by Dean Niles

ACROSS

1 __ 1 (the speed of sound)
5 Covers snugly
10 Zig end
13 She loved Narcissus
14 Harriet's husband
15 "Take __ your leader"
16 Streetcar
17 Ross or Rigg
18 __ Three Lives
19 Tranquil
21 Corrective
23 Old Greek coin
25 Really sore
26 Site of the Alhambra
29 Start of Hamlet
31 For fear that
32 Cuban dance
34 Blossomed
38 "Zounds!" is one
39 __ box (TV)
40 Burrow
41 French cheese
42 Grassland
43 Road charge
44 Felt sorrow over
46 Brought to office
48 Coffee choice
51 Blood-component word form
52 Pecuniary
56 Miming a crow
60 Dross
61 Missouri River city
63 Élan
64 Singer Smith
65 Pedestrian
66 Meal for Mister Ed
67 Blvds.
68 Reek
69 Slangy affirmative

DOWN

1 New York team
2 Farmland division
3 Singe
4 Traditional tune
5 Beverly Hills address
6 Submachine gun
7 Corporate VIP
8 Cows, old-style
9 Junction
10 Woody Allen film
11 "I Cried __" (LaVern Baker song)
12 Pious
15 Voight/ Hoffman film
20 Hoops org.
22 Break a fast
24 Extolled
26 Whipped-cream measure
27 Bring up
28 __ spumante
29 Where we live
30 Open audition
33 Wire width
35 Plant anchor
36 Fashion mag
37 Fuse metal
45 Flying cigar, e.g.
47 Time period
48 Office furniture
49 Showy display
50 Winter wear
53 Rowdy groups
54 Mosque priest
55 Sugar source
57 "Dies __"
58 Actress Naldi
59 "How about that!'"
62 2001 computer

58 SEE 60 ACROSS by Kenneth Lurye

ACROSS

1 Give it __ (take five)
6 It brought Hope to war zones
9 Word form for "wing"
14 "__ Thro' the Rye"
15 Swabbie's need
16 Went ballistic
17 Like a Brubeck tune's meter
19 Chemical compound
20 Remove
21 Eye drop
22 Eyeshade
23 Type of equation
26 Waylay
29 Certain Japanese resident
33 Showed again
34 Marine fossil
37 Coach Parseghian
38 Soup server
39 Calendar abbr.
40 Like most legislatures
43 Coeur d'__, ID
45 Word on an LP
46 Lighter-complected
47 Follower of John Biddle
51 Lost Horizon actress
54 "Unto us __ is given"
55 Singer Brickell
59 Afternoon of __
60 Theme of this puzzle
62 Instrumental effect
63 Wayfarer's stop
64 Muggy
65 GMA rival
66 Hall-of-Famer Williams
67 Some tourneys

DOWN

1 Obtained: Abbr.
2 Dissolute one
3 Actor Jannings
4 __ non (essential)
5 Explosive initials
6 Worked the plate
7 Word before wind or power
8 Porgy and Bess, e.g.
9 Restriction
10 Checker product
11 Auspices
12 Furnish anew
13 Swiss river
18 NBA team
24 Mil. branch
25 Painted metal
26 Some Middle Easterners
27 Deserve
28 Support
30 Baseball great Ralph
31 Make amends (for)
32 Defiant cry
34 Pavement material
35 Dietary data: Abbr.
36 Midwestern st.
38 Fifth-century Pope
41 Leafy vegetable
42 Stag
43 Car club
44 In a row
46 Huck or Mickey
48 Implied
49 Together
50 Drink order
51 Marshal Dillon
52 Hair style
53 Foray
56 Capitol topper
57 Victory cry
58 Remnants
61 Nevertheless, for short

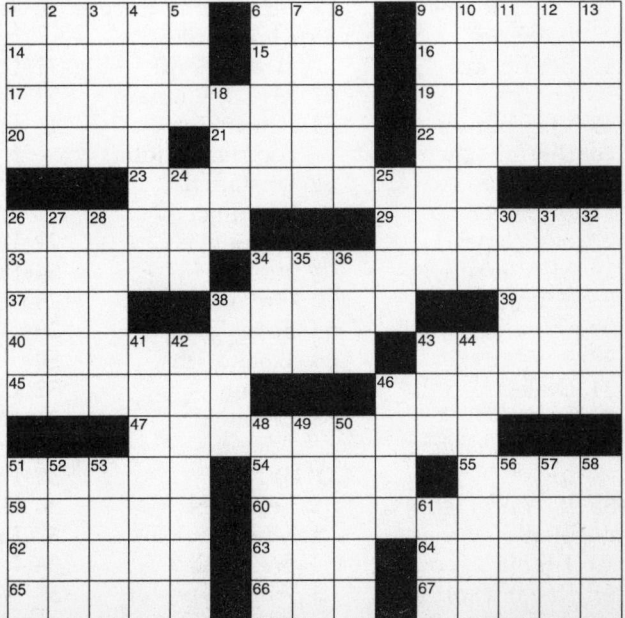

59 ON THE MAP by Gregory E. Paul

ACROSS
1 __ house (spy's retreat)
5 __ house (eatery)
9 Garden burrowers
14 Sub
15 Geometry calculation
16 Kicking's companion
17 War god
18 Dock
19 Crazy Horse's home
20 __ Tin Tin
21 City south of Provo
23 Dicta
25 Second sequel suffix
26 Auto part
27 Character for Camus or Heinlein
32 Western Starr
34 Akron products
35 Tokyo's old name
36 Gallic girlfriend
37 Marketing group
38 The Magi, e.g.
39 Pen brand
40 Applause
41 Sleigh puller
42 Bear State
44 "There once __ man . . ."
45 Toy ammo
46 White veggie
49 Arizona town
54 Golf-club part
55 Gave a hoot
56 Viva voce
57 Cap's partner
58 Quickly
59 Long ago
60 Goose relative
61 Dubbed
62 Elk or wapiti
63 Actress Sten

DOWN
1 Archaeologist's find
2 Home on high
3 Indiana town
4 Greek Aurora
5 Come to pass
6 Nobelist Oscar __ Sanchez
7 Caught, perhaps
8 Dutch spy
9 Olympic decathlete
10 Synthetic fiber
11 Chinese poet
12 Perpetually
13 Play a kids' game
21 Desiccated
22 Paddock parents
24 Playbill listing
27 Grain buildings
28 Vichy "very"
29 Philadelphia section
30 Adams or McClurg
31 46 Across, e.g.
32 Rum cake
33 Muslim prince
34 Exclamation of success
37 Author Sontag
38 Hurl
40 Prepared dough
41 Olds output
43 Per capita
44 "Honeysuckle Rose" writer
46 Follow the leader?
47 Herbert Hoover, for one
48 Neighbor of Del.
49 "__ See Clearly Now"
50 California wine valley
51 Apothecary's weight
52 Termite's meal
53 Seabird
57 Govt. purchasing org.

60 AS YOU LIKE IT by Chuck Deodene

ACROSS
1 *Beetle Bailey* NCO
6 Lessen
11 Box-office smash
14 Rusty-hinge noise
15 Folklore
16 Quick tennis point
17 Boot-camp arrivals
19 VCR button
20 Rhyme scheme
21 Stallone character
22 Hooch need
23 Meat turnovers
25 Young'un
27 Bummed out
28 Iowa city
31 Dialect
33 Liquefy
34 Write a policy for
35 Ill-conceived plan
40 Titania's spouse
41 Radar's soft drink
42 Appalachian or Chisholm
43 Identical
44 Russian ex-orbiter
47 Texas oil town
50 Look up to
52 Celeb's reps.
53 Mrs. Henry Luce
56 *Murder, She Wrote* sheriff
57 My __, Vietnam
58 Reason for congratulations
60 Unstaffed banking ctr.
61 Spinning about
62 Fire work?
63 Born: Fr.
64 Thick with cattails
65 Intended

DOWN
1 Leftovers
2 Mideast peninsula
3 Wanted-poster word
4 Reclusive actress
5 Scrape (out)
6 Shaver brand
7 Oz creator
8 He'll back you up
9 Grand __ National Park
10 Serpentine curve
11 Diatribe
12 Winter weather
13 High or Georgia follower
18 __ War (1850s conflict)
22 Wetland
24 Frolics about
26 Took a shine to
29 Deer's kin
30 Tommy guns
32 Undershirt
34 *Moby Dick* narrator
35 Popular
36 Declare null
37 Prep period
38 Fast-food order
39 Anti-narcotics org.
44 Champagne cocktail
45 Clothing decal
46 Take badly
48 Cross the plate
49 *Three Tall Women* playwright
51 Managua mom
52 Actor Arkin
54 Bowled over
55 Bank (on)
58 Jostle
59 Flight from the law

ACROSS

1 Sly look
5 Have a snack
10 Clarinet relative
14 At rest
15 Musical drama
16 Ship's jail
17 Military medal
19 Tart taste
20 Movie ad
21 British business abbr.
22 Issues an invitation
23 Riveter of note
25 Towel inscription
26 Rim
30 Stir-fry pan
31 Chanted prayer
34 Simba's relatives
36 Sired
38 Have the flu
39 Absent with permission
41 Use over again
43 Word form for "foot"
44 Explorer Polo
46 Backpacker, e.g.
47 Phonograph inventor
49 IRS month
51 Attention-getter
52 Airport info
53 Soak, as tea
55 Sardonic response
57 Ave. crossers
58 Medium's medium
63 Like Bush's office
64 Southern snake
66 Football arena
67 Be of use
68 Saharan
69 Possesses
70 Stair post
71 Like Ichabod Crane

DOWN

1 Tilt, as a ship
2 Singer Adams
3 Scat-singing queen
4 Guns the engine
5 Rob of *Quiz Show*
6 Package delivery org.
7 Resembling mesh
8 Packing box
9 Inflexible
10 Acquire
11 Essentials
12 Farm sound
13 Hen's outlay
18 Poetic adverb
24 Serious
25 Sub door
26 Run away to marry
27 Supped in style
28 *Private Benjamin* star
29 Compass pt.
31 West of Hollywood
32 Makes angry
33 Paying attention
35 Mead's study site
37 Feel one's way
40 Family vehicle
42 Songwriter Harburg
45 Tool
48 Stable areas
50 Vend again
53 Kitchen cooker
54 Each
55 King of the road
56 State firmly
57 Read quickly
59 Melville captain
60 Pianist Peter
61 Eve's oldest
62 Whirlpool
65 Dessert choice

ACROSS

1 Sign gas
5 Packaged paper
9 This could be a stretch
13 Raison d'__
14 Five-sided
16 Runner of rhyme
18 Walkers
19 __-mo
20 Conducted
23 *Krazy* __
24 Attempts
26 Gusted
28 Feudal farmers
32 Wind up
33 Garfield or Garner
35 Kukla's pal
37 Sleeper of rhyme
42 Good: Sp.
43 Carter and Gwyn
45 Composer's deg.
47 Solemn words
50 Noted surrealist
51 Live's partner
53 Alias indicator
55 "King" Cole
56 "__ Were King of the Forest"
57 Adolescent
62 Dickens character
67 Hunts for data
68 Rabbit cousin
69 "¿Cómo __ usted?"
70 Competed
71 Seer's vision

DOWN

1 Unused
2 Summer, in Paris
3 Mined matter
4 Ex-speaker's nickname
5 Tell
6 Actress Markey
7 Suit to __
8 Bryn __, PA
9 Chaney or Nol
10 Does a cartoonist's job
11 Posted
12 Butter subs
14 Court bargains
15 General idea
17 Vex
20 He preceded RMN
21 Airline to Israel
22 Bruce's ex
25 Tottered
27 Den installation
29 Automaton
30 Waitress at Mel's
31 Like a fox
34 R-V fillers
36 __ Saud
38 Gorcey or Durocher
39 *Bambi* deer
40 __ Bator
41 Actress Joyce of *Roc*
44 Pose
45 Stands up to
46 Small-town addr.
48 Extreme dislike
49 Antarctic birds
51 British quart
52 Actress Talbot
54 Paintings and sculpture
58 US missile
59 First year of the 22nd century
60 Yearn
61 Reverberation
63 Vote for
64 Emoter
65 Anger
66 Hamilton's bill

HOT STOVE LEAGUE by Norma Steinberg

ACROSS
1 French-poodle name
5 Heidi's home
9 "Casey __ Bat"
14 Poems
15 Stock-exchange membership
16 Vocal ensemble
17 Paniagua's capital
18 Preserve
19 Henna, e.g.
20 Description of Janus?
23 Mason's aide
24 Slalom
25 Bonkers
29 Thpeak like thith
31 Regal home
33 Deal in
36 Hall's partner
39 Fish eggs
40 Janitorial job?
44 Pie __ mode
45 *Norma* or *Carmen*
46 Rabbit __ (antenna)
47 Metal fasteners
49 Disney sci-fi film
52 Intuit

53 "C'__ la vie!"
56 Financially beset
60 Sale to a quilt maker?
63 __ grabs (available)
66 No-cholesterol spread
67 Run in neutral
68 Abolitionist author
69 Olfactory clue
70 "__ from New York, it's . . ."
71 Tortilla-chip dip
72 Ballpoints
73 Black and Red

DOWN
1 Goes under
2 Knucklehead
3 Thigh bone
4 Christopher's sponsor
5 Balance-sheet figure
6 Jacob's first wife
7 Uses macadam
8 Chuck, e.g.

9 Land measurement
10 All-you-can-eat portion
11 Bon __ (fashionable)
12 "__ Eye Is on the Sparrow"
13 Before
21 Floral offering
22 Chops
26 Rooms in Pompeii
27 Stun
28 Adolescent years
30 Karol Wojtyla's title
32 "Do __ say, not . . ."
33 Muffler
34 J.R.'s mom
35 Take off
37 Loan info: Abbr.
38 Precisely
41 ". . . __ even a mouse"
42 Overturned
43 Vine parts
48 Nudges
50 Difficulties

51 Yoko __
54 Crouch
55 Spanish diacritical mark
57 Carrie's dad
58 Author __ Plain
59 Forest components

61 Vicinity
62 Lighting gas
63 Destroyer's monogram
64 Harper Valley org.
65 Coming next: Abbr.

MEET THE SIMPSONS by Dean Niles

ACROSS
1 Collect
6 Engine part, for short
10 West and Murray
14 Renaissance fiddle
15 Fragrance
16 To be, to Babette
17 Beatle surname
18 "__ Said" (Shirelles song)
19 Balsam or birch
20 Bret's TV brother
23 Greek T
26 Bonds
27 WWII vessels
28 Facet
30 *Antony and Cleopatra* role
31 *Knots Landing* star
34 '60s protest grp.
37 Baltic feeder
38 ". . . and __ sacred honor"

39 Portico
40 Tennis obstacle
41 Reds' ex-owner
45 __ *Dick*
46 Actress Mills
47 Booty
50 Pleased
52 Mess up
53 Seascape painter
56 Poker ritual
57 Back
58 Wanderer
62 "Like __ not!"
63 Road turn
64 Guy Williams role
65 Cloth surfaces
66 Jacuzzis
67 Flaming

DOWN
1 MGM motto start
2 Encountered
3 Attorneys' org.
4 Certain Slav
5 Where to start from

6 French title
7 __ apple
8 "Arrivederci, __"
9 Display of daring
10 Urban areas
11 Lighted courtyards
12 Upright
13 Tries to obtain
21 Comic Rudner
22 Abba of Israel
23 Toucan's toenail
24 In reserve
25 Tummy trouble
29 Attention
30 Hungarian leader Nagy
32 Actor Calhoun
33 Jerk
34 Mink piece
35 Indulgent one
36 Man-goat
39 Unforthcoming
41 Flanders of fiction
42 Soaks in
43 Counterfeit

44 Fancy musical flourish
45 Tightwads
47 Country lad
48 Historic ship
49 Winner's position

50 Gold Coast, today
51 Ladies' companions
54 Cry
55 Housetop
59 CAT scan cousin
60 Timetable abbr.
61 Female deer

ACROSS

1 South Sea island group
6 Sharp strike
10 Use a Singer
13 "His word burned like __": Eccles.
14 Mah-jongg piece
15 Suit to __
16 Rhino's kin
17 "So be it!"
18 Relief org.
19 Start of an epigram
22 Baker's amt.
25 Photo
26 New Jersey town
27 Cup holder
28 Out-of-doors
31 Decorates
33 More of epigram
38 Leg tendons, for short
39 __ nous
41 Economist Smith
42 More of epigram
44 "__ evil . . ."
45 Fergie's younger daughter
48 More of epigram
49 __ from Walla Walla (Canova film)
53 Nabokov novel
54 Fly's back?
55 End of epigram
59 Actor Estrada
60 Metrical foot
61 Johnson's partner
65 Shea team
66 Coffee, Tea, __?
67 Bushed
68 Bradley and Sullivan
69 Stingy
70 1995 US Open finalist

DOWN

1 Met in session
2 Like
3 AAA handout
4 Leave out
5 Fitting
6 Golfer's concern
7 Star's car
8 Kim's ex
9 Small cutter
10 CBS News surname
11 Strange
12 Teary-eyed
15 CPA
20 Kenyan runner Keino
21 Luminous surrounding
22 Hebrew letters
23 Miles or Purcell
24 First-rate
29 Dame preceder
30 Chad's cont.
32 E. Lansing coll.
34 Last name in mortgages?
35 Expert
36 Grandmas
37 Struck down
39 Drawing out of information
40 Electron's chg.
43 Show a preference
44 Manatees
46 Cop, at times
47 Director Lupino
49 Musical motif
50 Took on
51 Spews forth
52 Chinese cookers
56 __ Krishna
57 Samms or Thompson
58 Around the Fish painter
62 Maglie of the mound
63 Before, in verse
64 Gov. Pataki's domain

ACROSS

1 Sugar source
5 Hairdresser's need
9 Ol' Blue __ (Sinatra)
13 Computer language
14 Killer whale
15 Ward of Sisters
16 1984 Prince film
18 Family group
19 Direct path
20 "Love __ Simple Thing"
22 Inc., in England
23 Beach souvenir
25 Angel toppers
27 Dove call
28 Donkey call
30 Life: Ger.
33 Singer Lovett
34 Russian ruler
37 The whole enchilada
38 Alan or Kathy
39 Clean-air org.
40 Sticky stuff
42 Feel sore
43 Bunch of bees
45 Namesake, perhaps
47 Evil laugh
48 Tie again
50 More grimy
54 Altar constellation
55 Musical sense
57 Faint light
59 Baseball great Willie
61 1981 Fonda film locale
63 Pour __ (try hard)
64 Author Wiesel
65 French heads
66 Essence
67 Noticed
68 Smelters' materials

DOWN

1 Hints
2 Concur (with)
3 "There's __ like home"
4 Invisible Man author Ralph
5 Jazzman Chick
6 "Are you a man __ mouse?"
7 Cato's 1102
8 Wailing spirits
9 Computer key
10 China-Korea separator
11 Make happy
12 __ of Iwo Jima
13 Police call: Abbr.
17 Word form for "within"
21 Satisfied sound
24 Musical beats
26 Longitude opposite: Abbr.
29 Gen. Robt. __
30 Be a slowpoke
31 House add-on
32 1977 Linda Ronstadt song
33 Like some curtains
35 Tax mo.
36 Aries
38 First-aid kit contents
41 Center starter
43 Mounted, as a stone
44 Plaintive cry
46 Unified
47 Donut feature
48 Harold of SCTV
49 Muse of poetry
51 Nash of poetry
52 Overact
53 Philosopher Descartes et al.
56 Acting job
58 Hwys.
60 NBC show since 1975
62 Prevaricate

67 EQUITATION by Gerald R. Ferguson

ACROSS

1 Truman opponent
6 Pant
10 Right-angle shape
13 Earthy color
14 Church platform
16 Day, to Dolores
17 Dilutes
18 Gaucho's rope
19 *Platoon* setting
20 Guzzler
21 1917 tune, with "The"
24 Spooky
26 Bill's companion
27 Close by
29 Cliburn, e.g.
33 Snapshot
34 Doughboys
35 Balloon filler
37 Misreckons
38 Swiss capital
39 Arsenal stock
40 Brillo rival
41 John Barth's __ Goat-Boy
42 More morose
43 Happens to
45 Servant's garb
46 Latin I word
47 Actor George
48 Mail service of 1860
53 Stars and Bars initials
56 Sundial number
57 Attach (to)
58 Cries of derision
60 Set a price
61 Relents, with "up"
62 Hardy's nickname
63 Service charge
64 Newshound's need?
65 Aquarium favorite

DOWN

1 Ellipsis elements
2 Yodeler's playback
3 Yukon Territory capital
4 Direction ender
5 "Make up your mind!"
6 Avant-__
7 "Shake __!"
8 Leading player
9 Infant's game
10 Author Ferber
11 Fact twister
12 Weak, as an excuse
15 Some synthetic fabrics
22 Cover
23 Me, to Mimi
25 Consumes
27 Acts like
28 Pulsate
29 Peels
30 Quaint hotels
31 Revolver inventor
32 Microwave feature
34 Holler
36 Actor Calhoun
38 Jeff Davis, in the 1880s
39 Part of T.A.E.
41 Specialized cell
42 Top banana
44 Actress Wray
45 Guitarist Paul
47 Rationality
48 Chanteuse Edith
49 Belgian river
50 Reebok competitor
51 100 centavos
52 Old World stags
54 Move a little
55 Sailing
59 Flamenco accolade

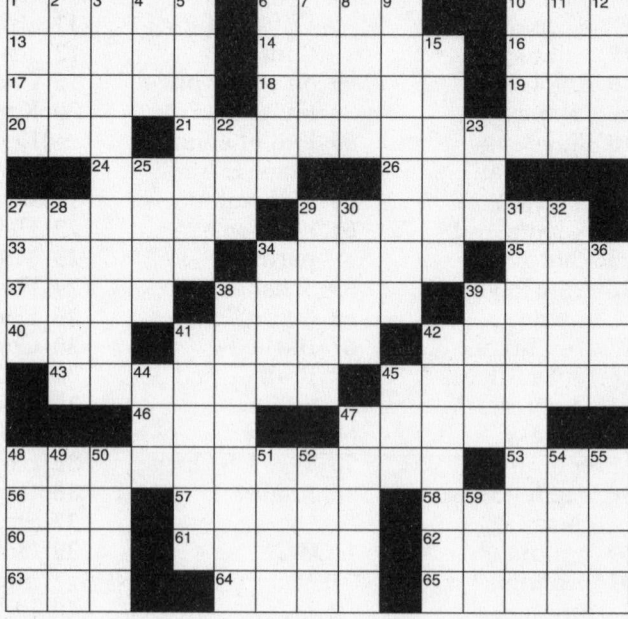

68 THEY GOT LEGS by Bob Lubbers

ACROSS

1 Toddler
4 Intoned
11 Harrison or Reed
14 Gershwin brother
15 Change the form of
16 First lady
17 *Rhoda* mother
19 Ate
20 Earthquake __ (Dogpatch tough)
21 Really weird
23 Marty or Steve
24 Sashes
26 Flowing rock
29 Requirement
30 Give __ for one's money
31 Exhausted
32 General Bradley
33 Prejudiced
34 Gravel-voiced actor
38 Broncos' turf
39 Ripped
40 Come in
41 French city
42 "Phooey!"
46 Kick
47 Trail shelter
48 Briquette rack
49 Turkish bigwig
51 Singer Yearwood
52 Every one
54 Hollywood columnist
57 Yellow or Black
58 Abrasives
59 WSW opposite
60 Islet
61 Strips
62 June honoree

DOWN

1 Jack Haley role
2 Seer of a sort
3 Hair trouble
4 Have a shoulder to __
5 Felled by an ax
6 Simile center
7 Lemieux's league
8 Alter, perhaps
9 Fencing swords
10 Author Earl __ Biggers
11 Practice
12 Actress Le Gallienne
13 Marked a ballot
18 Like some dorms
22 Homeric epic
24 Kind of exam
25 *Resurrection* actress
27 Swerve
28 Sum (up)
30 Part of USA
31 Fork prong
32 Singular person
33 Silo neighbor
34 Carson replacer
35 Bring __ (make use of)
36 __ Culp Hobby
37 Honk
38 Society newcomer
41 Heavy
42 Faucet fault
43 Grated
44 Goddess of wisdom
45 Wept
47 Central idea
48 Icky
50 Drop fur
51 *Of __ I Sing*
52 Inquire
53 Golf star Trevino
55 *Red River* actress
56 Assist

PRIZE PLAYS by Dean Niles

ACROSS

1 "Deck the Halls" finish
5 Cambodian language
10 Saintly image
14 Baseballer Felipe
15 Savoir-__
16 __ contendere
17 Wasserstein play, with *The*
20 Varnish ingredient
21 Alienate
22 Auto pioneer
25 Reaction to a rat
26 Ernie Els' grp.
29 Field
31 Queue after Q
36 Hasty flight
37 Interlace
39 Smash ending
40 Hansberry play
44 *Leave __ Me*
45 *Parade* composer
46 Play a part
47 Stuff
50 Dickens character
51 Questioning grunts
52 Cross letters
54 Stagger
56 Bibliophile's holder
61 Used the microwave
65 Kushner play
68 Jazz guitarist Charlie
69 __ of the trade
70 Heavy metal
71 Former spouses
72 Kicks in
73 Actress Merrill

DOWN

1 Cowardly Lion portrayer
2 Nautical adverb
3 Hi's wife
4 Sound portion
5 Fast-food co.
6 Hoo-__ (to-do)
7 Swampy land
8 Uneven
9 Tenant
10 Old Peruvian
11 City in *Deutschland*
12 Designer Cassini
13 It can really smell
18 Acquired family
19 Annoys
23 *Zwei* follower
24 Connery and O'Casey
26 Braid hair
27 Singer Brooks
28 Stradivari's teacher
30 For the birds
32 Golf peg
33 Bears: Lat.
34 Certify, with "for"
35 Inclinations
38 Computer key
41 Charged atom
42 Mah-jongg piece
43 Author Hanff
48 "The __ From Ipanema"
49 California peak
53 Offspring
55 Like pulp fiction
56 Ruth's nickname
57 Figurine mineral
58 Storybook villain
59 Some gym shoes
60 Chignon
62 __ Te Kanawa
63 A social sci.
64 Actress Delany
66 Frothy brew
67 Bks. in progress

CONTRADICTIONS by Diane C. Baldwin

ACROSS

1 Deception
5 Seles rival
9 Fledgling pigeon
14 Derby winner __ Ridge
15 Actress Hartman
16 Pucker
17 Watchful care/Error
19 Vogues
20 Great numbers
21 Be amused by
23 Assay sample
24 Raccoon relative
25 Game opener?
28 Golden calf, e.g.
30 Gas up
34 Bring together
36 Paper quantity
38 Seagirt real estate
39 Friend of Dennis the Menace
40 Scrutinizes/ Glances over
41 Roof feature
42 "The heat __!"
43 Etna output
44 Trimming device
45 Ostentatious
47 RR sched. data
49 Hesitation sounds
50 Math preposition
52 Gen. Lee's nation
54 Cooked, in a way
57 Summer refresher
61 Timber wolves
62 Inflexible/ Relaxing
64 Skirt style
65 Ripken and Peete
66 Prepare to publish
67 Reward, in a way
68 Checks out
69 Beatty film

DOWN

1 Starting
2 Roman historian
3 Declare with conviction
4 Video-game hero
5 Skated
6 Fits (out)
7 Blonde shade
8 DeLuise film
9 Coke alternative
10 Eligible/Limited
11 Spur
12 On the briny
13 Outwit
18 Attire in Agra
22 Schoolteachers of yore
24 Adheres/Splits
25 Like Jack's beans
26 Mennonite sect
27 Asian capital
29 Willy or Shamu
31 Accepted procedure
32 Young conger
33 Impolite looks
35 Approbations/ Interventions
37 Med. sch. course
40 Lowlifes
44 Ruhr Valley city
46 Snake sounds
48 Get to
51 Bring out
53 Abacus user
54 Spill the beans
55 Barrel maneuver
56 Rose's beau
57 Adjectival suffix
58 Time's impatient partner
59 Author Bagnold
60 G-men
63 Word of protest

71 TIME SHARING by Bob Lubbers

ACROSS
1 Accord
5 Food thickener
9 Pie nut
14 Actor Jannings
15 Arizona city
16 Make amends
17 Lillian Hellman play
20 Pigpen
21 Ambiance
22 Thumbed (through)
23 Legal penalty
24 R.I. neighbor
25 Declare
28 In awe
29 Poetic dusk
32 Arise
33 Hunters' prey
34 Rights org.
35 Leroy Anderson tune, with "The"
38 Comic Johnson
39 Son of Eve
40 *Kate & __*
41 Cow comment
42 Mr. Rogers
43 Goes over the limit
44 Twitches
45 Sailor's greeting
46 Singer Nina
49 Brio
50 Beatnik's home
53 Slim-waisted shape
56 One at __ (individually)
57 Jane's dog
58 Prayer end
59 Challenger
60 Short trips
61 Tiff

DOWN
1 Church seating
2 "I __ my wits' end!"
3 Metropolis
4 RN's offering
5 Quantity
6 Art style
7 Nick and Nora's pooch
8 Stadium sound
9 Mom or Dad
10 Allen or Frome
11 Stylist's forte
12 Charles' sister
13 Require
18 See 11 Down
19 Ran off to wed
23 Pasture divider
24 Dromedary
25 State of India
26 Prefix for foam
27 __ Domingo
28 Evaluated
29 French school
30 Spanish hero
31 Uses the microwave
33 Comic Kaplan et al.
34 Bowler's site
36 Package
37 Golfer Donna
42 Identify, slangily
43 Elevator passageways
44 Singer Mel
45 Columnist Joseph
46 Roe source
47 Smidgen
48 American naturalist
49 Phil of hockey, familiarly
50 Bailer's tool
51 Zone
52 Small amount of progress
54 Ember dust
55 Car fuel

72 FRUCTIFEROUS by Gregory E. Paul

ACROSS
1 Dance unit
5 Doone's love
9 Singer Khan
14 Trim
15 Incense output
16 Person
17 Austen's Woodhouse
18 Belafonte song "locale"
20 Cochise, e.g.
22 "Amo, __, I love a lass"
23 Sault __ Marie
24 Bacon portions
26 Regarding
28 Solti's stick
30 Brightly colored shawl
34 Separately
37 Moniker
39 "I've Got __ in Kalamazoo"
40 Director Wertmuller
41 Enjoy the taste of
42 Fishing gear
43 Short jacket
44 Drain section
45 See eye-to-eye
46 Taper
48 Mantel
50 26 fortnights plus
52 Bedroom furniture
56 Horned viper
59 Love god
61 Discerning
62 Firecracker
65 "No man __ island"
66 Marsh bird
67 Pianist Gilels
68 Matador's need
69 Papal bull, e.g.
70 Gainsay
71 Leg joint

DOWN
1 Harpoon
2 Cigar city
3 Bombeck et al.
4 After-dinner drink
5 *Rules of Order* guy
6 Crete peak
7 Spanish woman
8 Inge forte
9 Pure
10 Airline transfer point
11 Freeman Gosden role
12 Pitcher Jim
13 Poker stake
19 Sadat's predecessor
21 Preliminary race
25 Sub's tracker
27 Manicurist's device
29 Maritime
31 "Ain't She Sweet" songwriter
32 Cracker spread
33 Otherwise
34 Actor Baldwin
35 Gyro bread
36 Before long
38 Scooter
41 R-rated, perhaps
45 Ice and Iron
47 Memorized
49 In a lackluster way
51 Clothed
53 Singer Anton
54 Military encampment
55 Actress Taylor
56 Aspirin target
57 Molt
58 Beautiful girl
60 *Picket Fences* town
63 Fox sitcom of the '90s
64 Andy Gump's wife

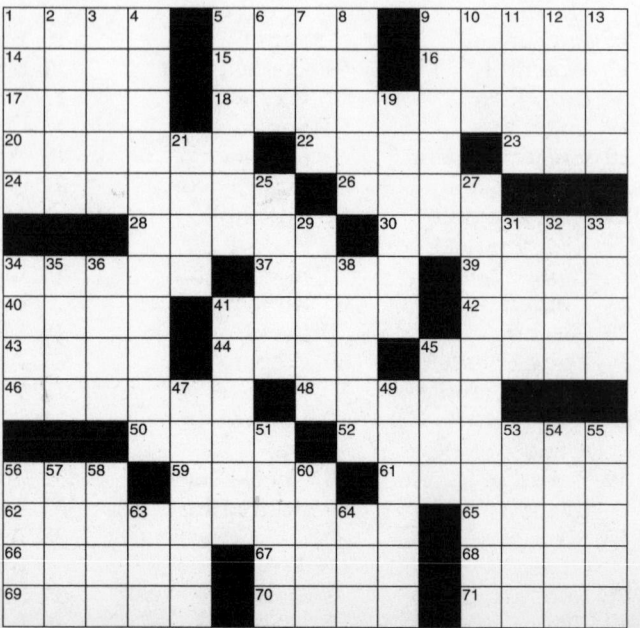

NO MORE by Eileen Lexau

ACROSS

1 __ steer (bad advice)
4 Word of praise
8 Tend the turkey
13 Cartoonist Peter
14 Actress Raines
15 Tailor
16 Kind of deed
18 Scandinavian toast
19 *Wait __ Dark*
20 Sports no-no
22 Cathedral feature
23 Went to Wendy's
25 Chicken, in Chihuahua
27 __-foot oil
30 Far-out person
33 *Time* founder Henry
36 No-good
38 Morse unit
39 Newspaper page
40 Sot
41 Fast time

42 One __ time
43 Spanish bread
44 Therefore
45 Tile artwork
47 Moisten again
49 Candice's dad
51 Fabric sample
55 Bean curd
57 Most August babies
60 Jetson kid
61 Old Roman official
63 Football play
65 Categorizes
66 Sweetie
67 Get close to
68 Hank of hair
69 Chatters
70 Sea bird

DOWN

1 Main impact
2 Get together
3 Made a gesture
4 Toothpaste type
5 Patron saint of Scandinavia
6 Hodgepodge

7 Keep pent
8 __-relief
9 Acid neutralizer
10 Instruction to a broker
11 Afternoon parties
12 Agatha contemporary
13 Bluish green
17 Board game
21 Nonintellectuals
24 Battlefront adjective
26 Rocket expert Willy
28 Disney sci-fi film
29 Fantastic
31 Small dent
32 Comic-strip dog
33 Soil of a sort
34 Capable of
35 Truce
37 Insignificant
41 Not to mention
43 Understand
46 Grownups

48 Vase-shaped jug
50 Oboelike
52 More faithful
53 Role for Arnold
54 Word form for "water"

55 Trial
56 Reputation
58 __-Day vitamins
59 Minn. neighbor
62 Curve shape
64 Part of MGM's motto

BEDTIME by Randolph Ross

ACROSS

1 Gyro ingredient
5 __ acid
10 Dangerous snakes
14 Concert halls
15 Baseball great Paul
16 Bernard, once of CNN
17 Party pooper
19 Mexican moolah
20 Terns and erns
21 Regarding this point
23 Tramp's mate
24 Gentle hit
25 Poe family
28 Cash in
29 Standard and __
30 Rock drummer Helm
31 Good times
34 Makes lace
35 Do studio work
36 Cruising
37 Signs off on
38 He played Wyatt and Eliot

39 Sardonic look
40 Ready the VCR
42 Fills the shelves
43 Poem part
45 Llama land
46 Nixon daughter
47 Windfalls
51 Standing
52 Spousal secrets
54 Advantage
55 Kuwaiti royal
56 Quaker pronoun
57 Adam or Rebecca
58 Rider's prods
59 Fairy-tale opener

DOWN

1 Financial-page info
2 "Zip-__-Doo-Dah"
3 Prefix for physics
4 Nonsense spouters
5 Tony and Edgar
6 Actor Patinkin

7 Signs
8 Maiden-name indicator
9 Conforming to a doctrine
10 On __ (binging)
11 Note paper?
12 Trattoria selection
13 Eagle's maneuver
18 Tale tellers
22 Balanced
24 *Sliver* author
25 Until
26 Drench
27 Arkansas resort
28 Pay the bill
30 Flood preventer
32 Fringe benefit
33 5th Avenue store
35 Molds differently
36 Become
38 De Gaulle's cap

39 Proverbial back breaker
41 Pyrotechnic device
42 Men of La Mancha
43 Spread
44 Exchange
45 Gondola worker

47 Cordon __
48 Newswoman Paula
49 Pianist Templeton
50 __-ball (arcade game)
53 Troublesome tyke

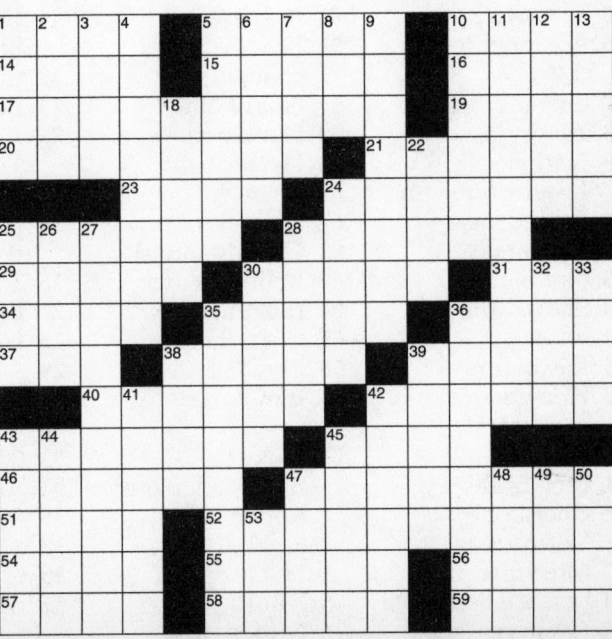

ACROSS

1 Puts the kibosh on
6 Car flaw
10 Wood wedge
14 *Middlemarch* author
15 "Well, Did You __?" (Porter tune)
16 NBC host
17 "Baseball is __ of inches"
18 ACTOR
20 Hard cheese
22 Check the numbers
23 Many mos.
24 Tenderfoot, e.g.
27 Young birds of prey
31 Tropical blooms
35 Inveigled
36 Partridge family?
38 Tennis obstacle
39 *"Dies __"*
40 Theme of this puzzle
41 Jazz jargon
42 Tic-__-toe
43 Solitary type
44 Hollywood nickname
45 Expressing sorrow
47 Small ledge
49 Boleyn and Bancroft
51 As needed, on prescriptions
52 Pianist Glenn
55 Utter frankly
60 FOOTBALLER
63 Keep one's __ the ground
64 __-do-well
65 Related
66 Diversionary tactics
67 Life of Riley
68 Surrealism cousin
69 Some Swiss paintings

DOWN

1 Pile
2 Bit of sea life
3 "Pants on fire" guy
4 ACTOR
5 Navigated
6 __ vu
7 Novak's former fellow pundit
8 *Platoon* setting
9 Longest article
10 Gumshoe
11 Noggin
12 Cross letters
13 Shed feathers
19 Pert
21 Mach topper
25 Secretive
26 Gold sources
27 Cream of the crop
28 Otic
29 ACTRESS
30 Candle bracket
32 ARCHITECT
33 Season, as eggs
34 Frisky horse
37 Somebody
40 Jett or Lunden
41 NAVAL HERO
43 *"Cielito __"*
44 Out of control
46 To spare
48 Choose
50 Unwavering
52 Kelly or Barry
53 Music halls
54 Colorado Indians
56 Forearm bone
57 Scottish Gaelic
58 To __ (exactly)
59 Headphone brand
61 Minute amount
62 Alias: Abbr.

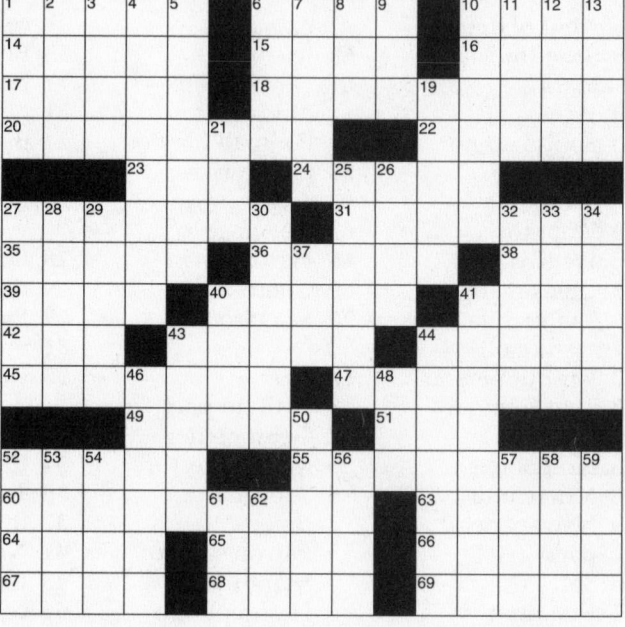

ACROSS

1 Postal codes
5 Davis or Standish
10 "Memory" musical
14 Lone Star State sch.
15 *Let's Make __*
16 "I cannot tell __"
17 Singer Horne
18 Annoy
19 National League quorum
20 Footed vase
21 Ship area
23 Not mine
25 Shows (the way)
26 Jolson tune
28 Horseman's mount
30 Nervous
31 Rich Little, e.g.
32 Cheese city
36 Skillfulness
37 Most meddling
40 *__ Got a Secret*
41 Reviewer Rex
43 African grassland
44 Confirm as true
46 Epitome
48 *Fawlty Towers* star
49 Food merchant
52 Rose feature
53 Kid-TV channel
56 Out of tune
59 Double curve
60 Hersey bell town
61 Diabolic
62 Ghostly sound
63 Bolivian boys
64 Russian river
65 Coastal birds
66 Plow man
67 Bunch

DOWN

1 Bantu language
2 Route: Lat.
3 Small-time
4 Hot tub
5 Adult
6 Notions
7 Sitcom producer Norman
8 Sunrise direction
9 Certain train cars
10 Voltaire novel
11 Green-card holder
12 Colored
13 Looks for
21 Anne, Mary, or Victoria
22 Fish delicacy
24 Light-switch positions
26 Top-billed one
27 Existed
28 Upset
29 __ off (angry)
31 Riding the waves
33 Cheap literature
34 Alamo rival
35 Apportion
38 __ Park, KS
39 Claw
42 *Oliver Twist* author
45 German article
47 Actress Ruby
48 Select
49 Folklore creature
50 Austerity
51 Arctic, for one
52 Corelli or Domingo
54 Garfield's canine pal
55 Jutlander
57 Not quite a half-dozen
58 Imperfection
61 Nav. rank

THE ENVELOPE, PLEASE by Gerald R. Ferguson

ACROSS

1 Ridiculed
6 Health farms
10 Funny one
14 Bolt together?
15 Prepare dinner
16 Matty or Felipe of baseball
17 Kind of boom
18 Green Gables girl
19 Shipshape
20 It requires a signature
23 Ice-cream portion
24 Time period
25 Horse rope
29 Bears witness (to)
33 Bread spread
34 City on the Allegheny
35 __ tree (stuck)
37 Vocalized message
41 CPR expert
42 Permanent location?
43 Pro's opposite
44 Tuxedo accessories
46 Acted autocratic
48 The lot
49 It. island
50 '62 tune
59 Istanbul native
60 "Yes __?"
61 Bright signs
62 Racer Luyendyk
63 Contort
64 "See the point?"
65 Sow's mate
66 Louis and Carrie
67 Tiffs

DOWN

1 Pianist Dame Myra
2 Out of kilter
3 ZIP code's predecessor
4 Grand-scale
5 Agree (on)
6 Sell tickets illegally
7 Watering hole
8 Top-of-the-line
9 Bony
10 Jib material
11 Nautical term
12 Hearty laugh
13 Import tax
21 Football filler
22 Dunne or Papas
25 Gardener's need
26 Out on __ (at risk)
27 Slow, in music
28 Get dressed, with "out"
29 Countertenors
30 High schooler
31 Rotations
32 Outpouring
34 Stare at
36 In the course of
38 Basketry fiber
39 Establish conclusively
40 Chevron offering
45 Pedestrian
46 "Fie!"
47 Primates, for short
49 Organ parts
50 Brief effort
51 Continental prefix
52 *Rigoletto* rendition
53 Fay of *King Kong*
54 Regarding
55 Don't sell
56 Kappa preceder
57 Fit of anger
58 Jet-setters' jets

GRIDDLE-ISMS by Bob Lubbers

ACROSS

1 Deprivation
5 Bagel relative
10 Droops
14 Buck ending
15 *Rocky IV* villain
16 Capri, e.g.
17 Hedge
20 Candidate list
21 Raw, as copy
22 Corn spikes
25 Twosome
26 Make a drop-flat landing
32 __ Faithful
33 Obey
34 1 to 10, for one
36 "Now __ this!"
38 Hogwash
41 Govt. agent
42 Craze
44 Binge
46 JFK posting
47 Honor, as a best man
51 Take to court
52 Judge Roy __
53 Aches and pains
58 Cable network
62 Dawdle
65 "So be it"
66 __ trip (travel)
67 Give off
68 Gun-sight segments
69 Willow twig
70 Derides

DOWN

1 Senate concerns
2 Kind of hygiene
3 Couch
4 Butter up
5 Ike's monogram
6 Spanish gold
7 Mork utterance
8 East African state
9 Work the muscles
10 Juan's emphatic agreement
11 CEO's aide
12 Stickum
13 Begonia-to-be
18 Expert on the rich and famous
19 Role models
23 Charlotte's kin
24 Slant
26 Dress fold
27 Bell town
28 Mrs. Bunker
29 Behave
30 Identified
31 Gladden
32 Resistance unit
35 Disney deer
37 Inlet
39 Leopold's partner
40 Stud site
43 Resource
45 Comics cop
48 Find, as a radio signal
49 Aquarium fish
50 Foot part
53 At a distance
54 *My Friend __*
55 Fibbed
56 Rockies, e.g.: Abbr.
57 Short-story author
59 Western Indian
60 Expatriate of 8 Down
61 Profits
63 Tiny
64 Swiss river

OUCH! by Shirley Soloway

ACROSS
1 Strongman Charles
6 Fourposters
10 Oversize hairdo
14 Destroy
15 Make changes to
16 Songbird
17 Bay city
18 Minuscule
19 Fontanne's partner
20 STRIKE
23 Skater Midori
24 Padre, for short
25 Most loyal
27 European region
30 Broadway eatery
33 Caesar's 401
34 Canadian native
37 Scandinavian
38 Math. subject
39 WHACK
41 Under the weather
42 Varnish ingredient
44 Director Kazan
45 Teachers' org.
46 Believes in
48 CD units
51 Beats badly
54 Wire measure
55 Tie holder
57 PINCH
62 Bauxite and galena
64 Entreaty
65 Pluralizers
66 Get up
67 Aromatic veggie
68 Devise a new plat
69 *Atlantis* group
70 Spanish compass point
71 Sports data

DOWN
1 One of the Aleutians
2 Mine car
3 Light source
4 Hope for, with "to"
5 Generous one
6 Casino activity
7 Decree
8 Bahrain money
9 Cutting tool
10 Hole maker
11 PUNCH
12 *La Bohème*, updated
13 Not fooled by
21 Put out
22 Stood (against)
26 Theater notice: Abbr.
27 Lazybones
28 HIT
29 Commedia dell'__
31 The Bahamas, e.g.
32 Actress Ward
33 Market wagon
35 Moray
36 Send forth
39 Pot starters
40 Ohio city
43 Haifa's loc.
47 Demo
49 Target seekers
50 Clothes holder
52 Bucks and toms
53 Winter hazard
55 Having divided loyalties
56 Diva's specialty
58 Trout source
59 U.S. Grant's alma mater
60 Orderly
61 Baking amts.
63 Vast amount

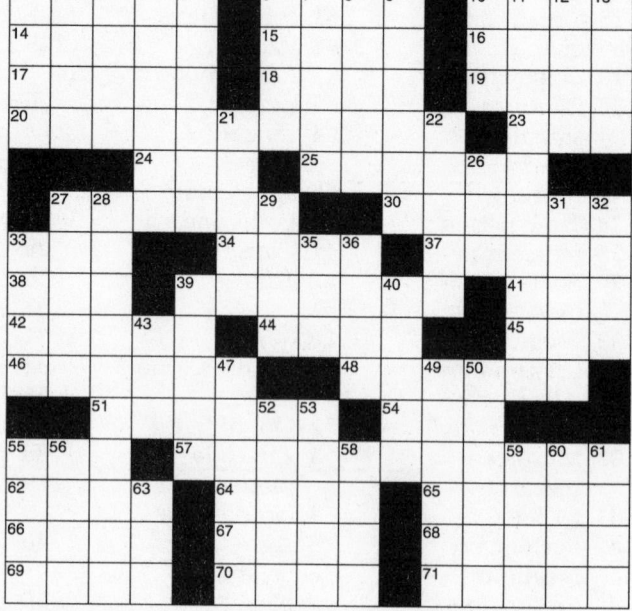

WHAT'S YOUR SIGN? by Randolph Ross

ACROSS
1 Word of woe
5 Like a *Fantasia* mountain
9 Bird, to Brutus
13 Tab
14 "Aha!"
15 Monthly payments
17 Sign at a dance studio?
20 *The Sound of Music* setting
21 Celebratory
22 Writer Amy
23 Bandleader Lanin
24 Sign at a nuclear power plant?
30 Divided
31 Envelope abbr.
32 Cinematic ants
36 Depict by drawing
37 Sort
38 Diamond or chest preceder
39 Notes
40 Co-owned, maybe
41 Natasha's partner
42 Sign at NASA?
44 Skip
48 Pulver, e.g.: Abbr.
49 Clipping, perhaps
51 Vernon Castle portrayer
55 Sign at a dressmaker's shop?
57 Bizarre
58 1/2, e.g.
59 Nod off
60 Thes. entries
61 Similar
62 Snow toy

DOWN
1 "Fernando" foursome
2 Stead
3 Vestments
4 Untidy types
5 Small suit
6 Home to billions
7 Dawson or Cariou
8 Fall on __ ears
9 Gotten up
10 Suit slits
11 Eskimo language
12 Martin or Lawrence
16 Hip ending
18 Fashion
19 Juicy fruits
24 Guys' dates
25 Ronny Howard role
26 Dub
27 Port-__ cheese
28 Ignite
29 "__ Easy" (Ronstadt song)
32 Large cast size
33 Beeper
34 DeMille genre
35 Coordinate
37 Pair
41 African language group
42 Cries of pain
43 Reduce
44 Tempo
45 Van Gogh hangout
46 Account
47 College protest
50 Icelandic tale
51 Con
52 Matinée __
53 Tear down
54 Ogled
56 Veneer variety

81 ATTACHMENTS by Bob Lubbers

ACROSS

1 Ocean
4 Old hat
9 Anecdotes
14 Picnic pest
15 E.T., e.g.
16 Combat zone
17 "Am __ understand that . . ."
18 Lost color
19 Zoo structures
20 Long-necked bird
23 Morning hrs.
24 Necks of the woods
25 Clark or Rogers
26 Ascot
27 Tree home
28 Took a risk
31 Mooring
32 Plane starter
33 Oppose openly
34 Emergency device
38 "__ Day's Night"
40 Eisenhower and Turner
41 Penny
42 Add-on
44 Info
48 __-Magnon man
49 One: Fr.
50 Western elevations
51 Poet's "above"
52 Kids' game
56 Condition
58 Gossip fodder
59 Ring cheer
60 Indonesian island
61 Arab chief
62 Ely or Howard
63 Confidence games
64 Fop
65 Hesitant syllables

DOWN

1 Pacific island
2 Complete
3 Makes amends
4 Mamas' mates
5 Jai __
6 Threshold
7 Planter's purchase
8 Stand the test of time
9 Crass
10 Coach Parseghian
11 Diplomatic staff
12 Foes
13 Back-talkers
21 Tit for __
22 How some pkgs. arrive
28 "Agnus __"
29 Circle segment
30 Batman's sidekick
31 Major leaguer
32 Also
33 Dollar fractions: Abbr.
34 Broad view
35 School class
36 Guitar relative
37 Ritter or Beneke
38 Greets rudely
39 Dissenter
42 Landers or Reinking
43 Approached
44 Morning condensation
45 On land
46 Clothes alterer
47 Poplars
49 Computer owners
50 Cheerful
53 Cougar
54 Federal agents
55 Tilled
57 Male turkey

82 LITERARY LOCATIONS by Dean Niles

ACROSS

1 *Six Degrees of Separation* playwright
6 Belt relative
10 Actress Andersson
14 Expropriate
15 Walesa, e.g.
16 Above, in Berlin
17 Postal buy
18 __ about (around)
19 Casino city
20 Cherry stone
21 Keillor location
24 __-pitch softball
25 Mine find
26 Lyricist Gershwin
27 Waller location
34 __ away (passed pleasantly)
36 Subtracting
37 Want-ad initials
38 Unclear
39 Japanese vegetable
40 Taj Mahal site
41 Part of 49 Across
42 Comfort
44 Author Norman
46 Kantor location
49 Marker
50 Novel ending
51 Tax pro
54 Metalious location
59 Highest-rated
60 D-Day beach
61 Finish off
62 SWAT team actions
64 Symbol of recalcitrance
65 __ out (supplemented)
66 *Sesame Street* character
67 Water extension
68 Halting colors
69 Dancers painter

DOWN

1 Sounds of fright
2 Up to
3 Examined closely
4 Sleep stage: Abbr.
5 Go off
6 Wheel radii
7 Top-drawer
8 Torpid
9 Flamboyant behavior
10 Part of FBI
11 "__ to differ"
12 "Let there __ mistake"
13 Golf club
22 Soulless
23 Warners or Smiths: Abbr.
28 __ Khan
29 Bygone
30 Prefix meaning "new"
31 Passing over
32 Ripped up
33 1066 or 1492
34 It'll hold your horses
35 Goldie of the screen
39 R&R site
40 Feel feverish
42 Switch ending
43 To shreds
44 Catchall category: Abbr.
45 Transmogrified
47 Choice word
48 Delicacies
52 Where conductors stand
53 Church recesses
54 Bicycle-tire inflator
55 Needle case
56 New Haven school
57 Jab
58 Schubert song
63 "We __ Family" (Sister Sledge song)

83 PICTURE THIS by Jim Page

ACROSS

1 Knife handles
6 Ark passenger
10 Culture medium
14 Bee-related
15 Musical motif
16 Pianist Peter
17 '70s nightspot
18 Canter control
19 Melee
20 Versatile one
23 Hit with a ray gun
24 Royal caretaker
25 Ghostly toon
29 Great __ (Bahamian island)
31 German river
32 Arizona river
34 Superior
38 *Magic Flute* character
41 Word with sixth or common
42 Type assortment
43 Trig term
44 Collar holders
46 Enthusiastic about
48 Little swine
51 It's on the edge
52 Ruler of nursery songs
59 Fused: Fr.
60 Part of UAR
61 Ibis' cousin
62 Greek conflict
63 Container allowance
64 Fix
65 Mailed away
66 *Cleopatra*, for one
67 Reeboks alternatives

DOWN

1 Trip to Mecca
2 Samoan port
3 Royal treasury
4 Board nail
5 Grab some Z's
6 Thong
7 Bread endpiece
8 Olympian Zátopek
9 Hindu incantation
10 Adversary
11 Decorative stone
12 Lauder competitor
13 Perch
21 Wells' partner
22 Scout about, for short
25 French roosters
26 Together: Mus.
27 Called, at poker
28 Media contact
29 Marian Anderson et al.
30 German road
33 Not definite
35 Week-ending initials
36 "This can't be!"
37 Word form for "wing"
39 Tidy: It.
40 Set of values
45 __ would have it (by chance)
47 Certain Midwesterner
48 Gull-like birds
49 Turning point
50 Salad ingredient
51 Fiddle precursor
53 Skeet's starting point
54 Last name in espionage
55 Sweet beginning
56 Arduous journey
57 Solitary
58 Winds up

84 FOR THE BIRDS by Fred Piscop

ACROSS

1 Wall Street figure
7 Meat in a can
11 Auto part
14 February plea
15 Narrow way
16 "I __ Rock"
17 Cures meat
18 Relievers' stats
19 Took the gold
20 Avian markers?
22 Blended
23 Beard
24 Sports legend Zaharias
25 Aah's partner
28 Decade parts: Abbr.
29 *Flash Gordon*, e.g.
31 Half a train?
33 __ around (gridiron play)
35 Binge
36 *Car 54* character
38 Drawer or shelf preceder
40 Nasty
43 Tailless amphibian
45 Angular lead-in
47 Was aware of
48 Victor of filmdom
50 Well contents
52 "Wow!"
53 Evangelist Roberts
54 Lorraine of *GoodFellas*
57 *Platoon* setting
58 Avian snack food?
63 Author Levin
64 Annapolis sch.
65 *Breathless* actor
66 __ Tech
67 Egyptian goddess
68 Hospital solution
69 Munched on
70 Actress Daly
71 Intertwine

DOWN

1 1/2 fl. oz.
2 San __, Italy
3 One way to run
4 Dam kin
5 Zing
6 Evaluate anew
7 Winter forecast
8 "Gay" city
9 Three-syllable foot
10 Boot-camp chow
11 Avian phone feature?
12 Pond denizen
13 Howie of *St. Elsewhere*
21 Lacks
24 Jack Palance series of '75
25 Columbus Day mo.
26 Taunting cry
27 Avian spicy dish?
30 Dawn goddess
32 Hall of Famer Lefty
34 Tiny circle
37 Agile
39 Thorn mishap
41 Poor grade
42 Ram's dam
44 *La Mer* composer
46 Tick off
48 Steffi rival
49 Biblical mount
51 Person from Pusan
55 Arrested
56 __ of mistaken identity
58 Knock it off
59 Crystallize
60 __ Minor
61 Not diluted: Abbr.
62 Wounded __, SD

TAKE A STANCE by Ray Hamel

ACROSS

1 Wolfgang Puck, for one
5 Williams role
9 Finish-line prop
13 Opening night line-up?
15 Above, to Schultz
16 Physical, e.g.
17 Watchful
18 Stage extra, for short
19 Luau neckwear
20 Start of a Thurber quote
23 Poetic pugilist
24 ASAP in the ER
25 Part 2 of quote
32 Unc's kid
33 Sandhurst carbine
34 Whine
35 Glee clubber
37 Hoo-ha
40 Sicilian peak
41 Legal claim
42 Onetime Mexican president

44 Batter
45 Part 3 of quote
50 Bluefin, e.g.
51 Diminutive suffix
52 End of quote
59 Bird encountered by Alice
60 "Why Do I Love You?" composer
61 Unearthly
62 Hemsley sitcom
63 Ready for publication
64 Hit off the tee
65 *Pretty Woman* star
66 Fuller creation
67 Sharp smack

DOWN

1 Pottery material
2 Hawaiian port
3 Cassowary lookalike
4 Type of dance
5 Spew
6 Be next to
7 Feast

8 Magic word
9 Obsolete newsroom machine
10 Rink jump
11 Lunch holder
12 Dash lengths
14 Calms
21 Birthday offerings
22 Colorless
25 Courtly Spanish dance
26 Stone-calendar maker
27 Find a tenant for
28 Battery part
29 Bizarre
30 Wrist nerve
31 Paper package
32 Leg part
36 Kind of correspondence
38 Fjord kin
39 Frenzied
43 Exhausted
46 "__ Wiedersehen!"
47 Twisted

48 City on the Inter-American Highway
49 Bride and groom
52 Voluminous volume
53 Czech river
54 Fedora feature
55 Latin preposition
56 Seed covering
57 Racehorse __ Ridge
58 Thought-provoking
59 Honored name in UN history

MEAT MARKET by Lee Weaver

ACROSS

1 Falls (behind)
5 Black Sea port
11 Outlaw
14 Neutral color
15 Gasped
16 *All About __*
17 Small change
19 Poetic eternity
20 Word link
21 On the __ (fleeing)
22 Bushy hairdo
23 Mountainous nation
25 Bullring cheer
26 Calf catcher
30 CD-__ (computer adjunct)
31 Beach hut
34 Overhead
36 Future flowers
38 "You're it" game
39 Confuse
41 Ancient Greek warship
43 Inquire
44 Statue of Liberty prop
46 Alarm sound

47 Data summary
49 Director Spike
51 Attention-getter
52 Slippery, perhaps
53 Type of lily
55 Help a felon
57 Sushi sauce
58 Monet or Rubens
63 Scrooge's comment
64 Old-style side whiskers
66 Bikini part
67 Narrated anew
68 Spin like __
69 Summer hrs. in Delaware
70 Easels, e.g.
71 Makes lace

DOWN

1 Nobelist Walesa
2 "__ Breaky Heart"
3 Clutch
4 Of that kind
5 First game
6 Newsman Rather
7 Kindle

8 Rob
9 Appear to be
10 Say more
11 Tower of London guards
12 Declare positively
13 Pianist Peter
18 Barbie's beau
22 Priest's vestment
24 Tough question
25 Desert refuge
26 *M*A*S*H* clerk
27 Too big
28 Soft, flat-crowned topper
29 Actress Gabor
31 Naval rank: Abbr.
32 Designates
33 Representative
35 Index listing
37 Lucy's sidekick
40 Earned
42 Tear
45 Lone Ranger portrayer Moore

48 Halloween mo.
50 African antelopes
53 Terra __
54 Trajectory path
55 Singer Lane
56 Shakespearean epithet
57 Lard kin
59 Not this
60 Small amount
61 Dalmatian's name
62 Cookbook abbr.
64 __ *Doubtfire*
65 Antiquated

ELEVATING by Bob Lubbers

ACROSS
1 Old hat
6 Singer Brooks
11 Health resort
14 Ski resort
15 Hawaiian "hi"
16 Tic-__-toe
17 Stylish home feature
20 Take on
21 Architect, e.g.
22 Mr. Onassis
23 "__ was saying . . ."
24 Prepares flour
28 Attack
30 Docile
34 __ five (rest)
35 Numero __
37 Kin
39 Thicke film of '92
41 Belgian capital
43 Mess up
44 Homer's kid
45 Regimen
47 Global specks
51 Sociologist Hite
53 __ Khan
55 Model Carol
56 Copy
60 __-European
61 Path to success
65 Vast vessel
66 Oven gadget
67 Reagan appointee
68 Sound of disapproval
69 Double curves
70 Roles

DOWN
1 Titled Turks
2 Seek, with "after"
3 Morale
4 Dry
5 *Bambi* aunt
6 Like Victorian houses
7 Canadian prov.
8 Colorful horse
9 Wispy
10 Rabbit relatives
11 RR depot
12 __ de deux
13 High card
18 '60s records
19 Beasts, so to speak
23 Baxter and Rice
25 Not swarthy
26 Ring win: Abbr.
27 DC VIP
29 Exceed
31 Got up
32 *A Few Good __*
33 Threat ender
36 Newspaper page
38 Lofty lobbies
39 Certain
40 1051, to Caesar
41 Kid's ammo
42 Stadium sound
46 Spuds
48 Plane, at trip's end
49 Firstborn
50 Stashes
52 Overact
54 Toothpaste type
57 Eye part
58 Flat hats
59 Suit to __
60 Brainstorm
61 Urban transport
62 Spanish gold
63 *King Kong* studio
64 Elec. unit

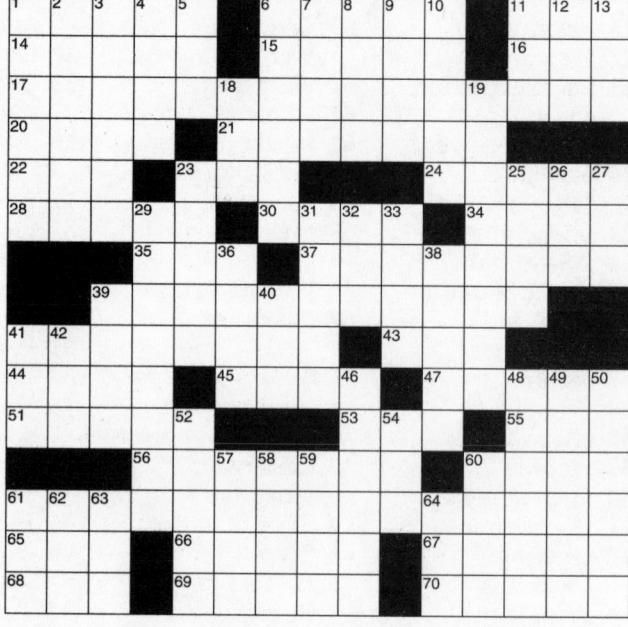

TIED UP by Rich Norris

ACROSS
1 Family member
4 Bribable
9 IOU
13 Once again
15 Appliance name
16 Wine: Pref.
17 Sound producers
19 Extreme anger
20 Plea
21 Swapped
23 Notwithstanding
24 Foppish one
25 Mellow, maybe
26 Hit the mall
27 Little rascal
30 Last inning, usually
33 Docks
34 Actress Peeples
35 Words of dread
36 Filled
37 Abe's coin
38 Prosecutors: Abbr.
39 Incurred, as a bill
40 "Wake Up, Little __"
41 GA summer setting
42 Is in debt
43 Rocky peak
44 Lineage
46 Kander/Ebb musical
50 Drunk
52 One of these days
53 Breathe heavily
54 In trouble
56 Jason's ship
57 Kilmer poem
58 Flat fee
59 Coarse file
60 "He __ got a clue!"
61 Byways: Abbr.

DOWN
1 Held onto
2 "__ ear and out . . ."
3 Religious groups
4 Leave the premises
5 Ham it up
6 Not any
7 Also
8 Arguer's desire
9 Reef material
10 Column toppers
11 *Picnic* playwright
12 Word after open or pigeon
14 On the __ (angry)
18 Actress Jennifer Jason
22 Account execs
24 Docile ones
26 Legal locale
28 Skirt length
29 Appetizer choice
30 Stocking shade
31 "If __ a Hammer"
32 Richard Rodgers musical
33 Window sections
36 Part of a serrated edge
37 Museum worker
39 Chess piece
40 Solemn
43 Least wild
45 Winning
46 Comic Myron
47 Not as green
48 Fix
49 Tries out
50 Warm up with Tyson
51 Scarlett's home
52 Fr. holy women
55 Powerful DC lobby

DICTIONARY VIPS by Patrick Jordan

ACROSS

1 Lucie's dad
5 Water-balloon sound
10 Keep __ (persist)
14 Part of QED
15 Singer Abdul
16 Flicka, e.g.
17 Mae West
19 School grps.
20 Stoical type
21 Carries through
23 Octopus defenses
25 List of names
26 Wood-shaping tool
28 Nightmarish street
31 Minds
34 Plant a bug
35 "Don't move!"
37 Bathwater tester
38 John Hancock
41 Actress Hagen
42 Went a-wandering
43 Brown brews
44 Baseball star Puckett

46 MGM mascot
47 Cal. abbr.
48 Ticks off
50 Say "Yay" at Shea
52 Giving freely
56 Couplings
60 Fancy
61 Annie Oakley
63 Foreman's weapon
64 Banded gemstone
65 Neighborhood
66 Hart's former ET cohost
67 Mazatlán mister
68 Godiva, for one

DOWN

1 Salami shop
2 Clapton or Idle
3 Not out
4 Lists deductions
5 Punish, perhaps
6 Lobbying grp.
7 Biblical physician
8 Swoosie, on *Sisters*

9 Colloquial tuber
10 Medicine vial
11 Playground fink
12 *Dies* follower
13 Hardy girl
18 Tarzan's mate
22 Songwriter Leonard
24 Soap, e.g.
26 "__ a stinker?": Bugs Bunny
27 Dismal state
29 "__ Entertain You"
30 Shower component
32 Taj Mahal features
33 Meets, as a bet
34 *The Winds of War* novelist
35 Back
36 Londoner's last letter
39 More ironic
40 Seafaring
45 Puff of wind

47 Author Morrison
49 Living-room items
51 *The __ Limits*
52 Present
53 Adams or McClurg

54 Egg on
55 Playwright O'Casey
57 Gumbo green
58 Requirement
59 Collar rib
62 Ike's WWII command

CAPITAL TOUR by Dean Niles

ACROSS

1 __ clean (owned up)
5 Word form for "outer"
9 Regarding
14 Winged
15 Actress __ Flynn Boyle
16 *The Most Happy* __
17 French sponges?
19 Yes-man
20 Sound of passing time
21 Unrefined guys
22 Biblical ending
23 Voiced
24 Outpouring
28 Jedi teacher
30 Computer types
34 Hullabaloo
36 Actor Voight
37 __ vera
38 Age following Bronze
39 Learned
41 Tepee
42 Filmmaker Riefenstahl

43 It clings and climbs
44 Cook too much
46 They hold you up
47 Lake in Scotland
49 __ Martin (auto)
50 Loses zip
52 Label
54 Like Brie
57 Diamond cut
62 Actress Palmer
63 Stressed in Switzerland?
64 Elaborate display
65 Flintstones' digs
66 Cooking pot
67 Untended to, in a way
68 Outlined
69 Liquefy

DOWN

1 Picard's rank: Abbr.
2 Jai __
3 Artist Chagall
4 Composer Satie
5 *Middlemarch* author

6 Like some tunes
7 Hard journey
8 W. Hemisphere alliance
9 Actors' union
10 Korean confidantes?
11 Fizzless
12 Like a shoppe?
13 Sunshine
18 Gird
21 Director of *One-Eyed Jacks*
23 Bouquet
24 Like some waters
25 Osterizer setting
26 In the midst of
27 North African lunch?
29 "Love Train" group
31 State of readiness
32 Retiree residence
33 American saint
35 Whatchama-callit
40 Nights before
45 Imprecise
48 Treat a fever, proverbially

51 Good will
53 '70s veep
54 Ball of thread
55 *Taltos* novelist
56 *Vogue* competitor
57 Pessimist on stocks

58 Brother of Jacob
59 Enameled metalware
60 Jethro __ (rock group)
61 French state
63 A-E link

91 TRAIN RIDE by Bob Lubbers

ACROSS

1 Olympian Paavo
6 Take __ (travel)
11 GI address
14 Ryan or Tatum
15 Hunt goddess
16 Statesman Hammarskjöld
17 House covering
19 __ Abner
20 "__ boy!"
21 Afternoon parties
22 Missouri tribe
24 Haberdashery items
26 Hair band
30 "Bali __"
31 Comic singer Sherman
32 Cad
35 Light fog
39 Boxer's move
42 Word form for "huge"
43 Pot base
44 Mongolian mountains
45 Posed
47 G-man Ness et al.
48 Kind of knife
54 Jewelry weight
55 Indian princess
56 Backtalk
60 Ripen
61 Some LPs
64 Author Deighton
65 Tube descriptor
66 Own up
67 Before, poetically
68 Rope loop
69 Encounters

DOWN

1 Exploding star
2 Part of BTU
3 Lease
4 Yucatán Indians
5 Ailing
6 Arles aloha
7 Word before wave or basin
8 Mrs. Gorbachev
9 Lodging place
10 Chinese temple
11 Governor Stevenson
12 Pitcher Satchel
13 Leers at
18 Greek portico
23 Reaction provokers
24 Discover
25 Syngman of Korea
26 Raise crops
27 Hand-lotion additive
28 Fake coin
29 Rummy game
32 Reagan or Howard
33 Unconscious
34 Employ
36 A fan of
37 "Vamoose!"
38 The one here
40 "What __ God wrought?"
41 Ashen
46 Joins the cast of
47 Blue-pencil
48 Minimum wage
49 Bet
50 Dunne or Papas
51 Psychologist Bettelheim
52 Bowling alleys
53 Conductor Previn
56 "Smooth Operator" singer
57 Top
58 Revue bit
59 JFK arrivals
62 Yoko __
63 St. Louis gridder

92 SHOW OF HANDS by Gerald R. Ferguson

ACROSS

1 Grassy plain of Argentina
6 Towel word
10 "Phooey!"
14 Forcefully
15 Genesis name
16 Skip over
17 Shabby
18 Arizona Amerind
19 NYC art center
20 High-tech defense initials
21 Billy Joel, e.g.
24 Bumblers
26 15 Across, to Eve
27 A sorry bunch?
28 Abyssinia, today
33 Bad to the extreme
34 Gigi star
35 Cuba, e.g.: Abbr.
36 Sponsorship
37 Tear up
38 Word form for "eight"
39 Traffic behemoth
40 Dickens title start
41 Tarsal joint
42 Pioneers
44 Cherry, e.g.
45 Above, to Keats
46 1923 loser to Dempsey
47 Baseball award
52 Mainframe brain: Abbr.
55 Miffed
56 Mideast carrier
57 Benefits
59 Embossed emblem
60 Auctioneer's last word
61 Yonder
62 Fervent wish
63 "Terrible" age
64 Completely satisfied

DOWN

1 Tablets
2 In the course of
3 Nails expert
4 Greedy one
5 "__ in a storm"
6 Belly laughs
7 Black, in poesy
8 Bank takeover?
9 Sloppy
10 Pizza cheese
11 Chinese island seaport
12 Fourth dimension
13 Lead player
22 Freudian concerns
23 T-bone's locale
25 Subtraction word
27 Rascal
28 Noble chaps
29 Shade source
30 Urban crook
31 Basketry fiber
32 Popular houseplant
33 Entanglements
34 Burn slightly
37 Most stringent
38 "Movin' __" (The Jeffersons theme)
40 Skipper's word
41 Runs in
43 Walk unsteadily
44 Arith. process
46 Throws in one's cards
47 Lillian or Dorothy
48 Creme-filled cookie
49 Adjective for 1996
50 Aura
51 French composer
53 French papa
54 Pre-owned
58 "That's it!"

93 TEN HUT! by Gregory E. Paul

ACROSS
1 Diving duck
5 James __ Garfield
10 Eating plan
14 Vagabond
15 Blackmore heroine
16 Fairy-tale opener
17 Daredevil Knievel
18 Actor Davis
19 To be, to Satie
20 Bush conveyance
23 Work smoothly
24 Eye part
25 Cubbyhole
27 Clearheaded
30 Safari sights
33 Trig, e.g.
36 Hideout
38 Soprano Lucine
39 "__ du lieber!"
40 Mansion worker
42 Family vehicle
43 Singer Bonnie
45 *Nautilus* man
46 Computer unit
47 Eastwood costar of '95
49 Postpone
51 Coped (with)
53 Feudal vassals
57 Evian, e.g.
59 Devil dogs' tune
62 Dumbbell move
64 Sinful city
65 *My Friend* __
66 Shells and such
67 Garry or Dudley
68 Swerve
69 2-time NL MVP
70 "... man, __, a canal ..."
71 Villa d'__

DOWN
1 Harvest wool
2 In-flight entertainment
3 1975 Pulitzer winner
4 Rapacious
5 Cute
6 Pear variety
7 Bouquet favorite
8 Charged atom
9 Eenie follower
10 Female goat
11 Village People song
12 Beige
13 Abound
21 Lennon's lady
22 Showy display
26 Easter dish
28 Deserve
29 Rosie's pin
31 "Confound it!"
32 Levelheaded
33 Hershey rival
34 One-__ (ball game)
35 Patton's command
37 "__ Lama Ding Dong"
40 Power source
41 Blue bloods
44 Golf gizmo
46 High hairdo
48 Blood fluid
50 Fleur-de-__
52 Cavalry unit
54 Circles
55 Ant
56 Trap
57 Con game
58 Cougar
60 Graven image
61 Director Ephron
63 Part of UCLA

94 NASAL PASSAGES by Chuck Deodene

ACROSS
1 Platter
5 Certain Peruvian
10 *Rent-*__ (Reynolds film)
14 Funny bone neighbor
15 Minnesota city
16 Govern
17 Concert ender
18 Defensive lineman
20 Of an eye part
22 Discharge
23 Drum site
24 Vietnamese waterway
28 Yale students
29 Last Supper setting
33 Pendant
36 Sprat's diet
38 Film __
39 Narc's pooch
44 "La __ Bonita" (Madonna tune)
45 Comic Jay
46 "It's __-win situation!"
47 University unit
51 Entr'__
53 New Age treatment
58 Flabbergast
61 Horned vipers
62 Country-music guitar
63 1980 J. Geils Band song
67 Swiped
68 Kinnear of *Sabrina*
69 Spinning about
70 Mothballed
71 Nautical prefix
72 Ferraro's nickname
73 Clamp shapes

DOWN
1 Found via research
2 __ *Lucy*
3 Condescending expression
4 Burgundy vessel
5 Actor Cariou
6 Nuptial phrase
7 Tightwad
8 Lacking pep
9 Inhabitant
10 Curved path
11 Salad slice, for short
12 Stewpot
13 Social equal
19 "... a __ o'clock scholar"
21 Respites
25 Demeanor
26 *La Bamba* actor Morales
27 Used the phone
30 Sonata ending
31 Androcles' friend
32 Thus
33 Depositor's protector: Abbr.
34 "... __ I've been told"
35 Pamplona hazard
37 Tagliabue's org.
40 Wingding
41 Accomplishment
42 Ruler marking
43 Renowned
48 Geological periods
49 Attend without a date
50 Domain
52 Like Henry Miller's novels
54 Seven-Emmy winner
55 Habitation
56 Wage earner, in Britain
57 Ox collars
58 Marine life
59 Was clad in
60 At any time
64 Self-esteem
65 Plunk or flooey lead-in
66 Crafty

OUT OF ORDER by Shirley Soloway

ACROSS
1 Buckets
6 Zhivago's love
10 Police alerts: Abbr.
14 Work for eight
15 Remove wrinkles
16 __ avis
17 START OF A QUIP
20 Mexican wrap
21 Lions and leopards
22 Shade tree
24 All possible
25 PART 2 OF QUIP
32 Talked wildly
33 Bargains
34 Tennis pro Shriver
37 Winglike
38 Conditions
39 *Mondo Cane* theme
40 Urge
41 Discontinue
42 Loman goal
43 PART 3 OF QUIP
45 Musical Count
48 High __ kite
49 Collects
52 Rubs out
57 END OF QUIP
60 Globes
61 *Dick Tracy* heavy
62 Allen's ex-partner
63 In order
64 Observed
65 Token takers

DOWN
1 Some vessels
2 Yearning
3 Roman road
4 Moon of Jupiter
5 Payment
6 Ignited
7 *Exodus* hero
8 Housetop
9 Actress Jackson
10 Make the scene
11 Pop singer Freda
12 Pipe type
13 Impudent
18 Honeycomb part
19 Baldwin et al.
23 Term of affection
25 Platter
26 Robust
27 Author Hunter
28 Above, poetically
29 As such
30 California town
31 Pacino and Smith
34 Flag support
35 War god
36 Army meal
38 Casual shirt
39 Kind of apple
41 Board game
42 They say "boo!"
43 Most sensible
44 Consumer
45 Shakespeare contemporary
46 Love: It.
47 Xavier Cugat specialty
50 Recedes
51 Desertlike
53 GI offense
54 Just okay
55 Prefix for while
56 Winter gear
58 Adversary
59 Personal

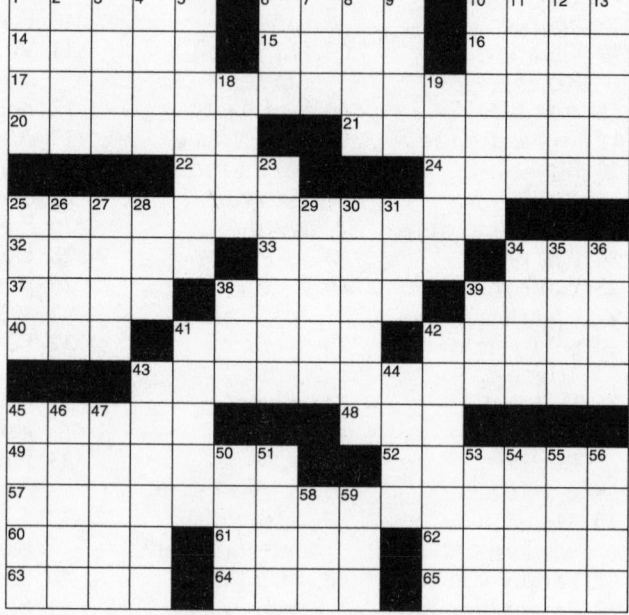

UP IN THE AIR by Diane C. Baldwin

ACROSS
1 Enthralled
5 Spanish houses
10 Winter vehicle
14 Hodgepodge
15 "Remember the __"
16 Garr or Hatcher
17 Ripening agent
18 California county
19 Gloomy forecast
20 Pocket-watch feature
22 Fencing sword
23 Dole's group
24 School assignment
26 Challenges
29 "...a __ every purpose under heaven"
32 Army officer
35 British noblewomen
37 Feel poorly
38 Musical work
39 Groucho prop
40 Canadian Indian
41 Sleep activity: Abbr.
42 Word before space or limits
43 Cowboy gear
44 __ de corps
46 "Shoo!"
48 Spicy sauce
50 Foist (on)
54 Guinness or Templeton
56 Safety-deposit sites
59 Drench
60 As __ (generally)
61 Louver
62 Feed the kitty
63 Telegraph operator
64 Ireland
65 Nuisance
66 Certain joints
67 Fortune-teller

DOWN
1 Strays
2 Pond plants
3 __ the sky (illusory hope)
4 Twisters
5 RV
6 Winglike
7 Agra attire
8 Chemical compound
9 Glee-club member
10 Small river
11 1996 and 2000
12 Part of HOMES
13 Enjoy a banquet
21 Play the lead
25 __ boom bah
27 Prepare to publish
28 Wise ones
30 Neckwear
31 Bread spread
32 Extra
33 Zoo favorites
34 Checker-cab items
36 Artist Chagall
39 Trims
40 University areas
42 Olive product
43 Tibetan monk
45 Clamor
47 TV talker Joan
49 Brother of Moses
51 Hardy's nickname
52 Stunned reaction
53 Fragrant compound
54 Quickly, briefly
55 __ Star State (Texas)
57 Stocking shade
58 Swiss painter

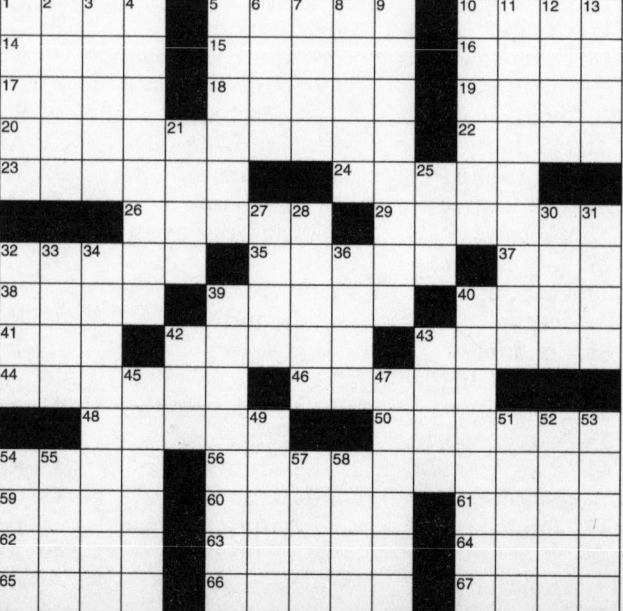

ACROSS
1 Fancy dance
5 Soda-shop order
9 Mends
14 Gen. Robert __
15 Garfield's nemesis
16 Some collars
17 Moola
19 Fire: Ger.
20 4:00 china
21 __ 17 (Holden film)
23 A Bobbsey twin
25 Hid
28 Blabbered
33 Campout cook's can
34 Rave-review excerpt
35 Gay __
37 Bachelor's last words
38 "A __ plan, . . ."
39 TV reporter Shriver
40 Norse god
41 Rile
42 Parts
43 Alla __ (musical direction)
44 Required
46 Avers
48 Kind of bass
50 Sp. lady
51 Mark of *St. Elsewhere*
53 Manor
58 Tolerate
60 Diaper catch
62 Auctions, e.g.
63 HoJo rival
64 Tear
65 Desert trees
66 Badgers
67 Keats works

DOWN
1 Waist cincher
2 Lotion additive
3 Melodious Horne
4 Diamond's moniker
5 Hod load
6 Summer drink
7 Reclines
8 Circus structures
9 Let the air out of
10 Relaxed
11 One of Teddy's troopers
12 Compass dir.
13 Lith., once
18 Playwright Jean
22 Befuddled
24 Himalayan kingdom
26 Salad veggie
27 Lorna's kin
28 Street urchins
29 Turkish inn
30 1775 battle
31 Eagles' grp.
32 Challenged
36 Stands up
39 Computer adjunct
40 Mouths: Lat.
42 Keep down
43 Detonation
45 Royal
47 Obnoxious ones
49 Contents of a hand-drying bag
52 Okinawa capital
54 Novice
55 Imitated
56 Fork part
57 Finishes
58 Nile cobra
59 Sheepish remark

ACROSS
1 Charles' princedom
6 Two together
10 Can. province
14 Separated
15 Nautical adverb
16 Richard of *A Summer Place*
17 Air sign
18 Actress Patricia
19 __ it (amen)
20 Papal name
21 Top-rank
24 Loverboy
26 Opal, e.g.
27 Slat
29 Play thing
34 *Roots* Emmy winner
35 *Les __-Unis*
36 Dander
37 Recipe verb
38 Designer Simpson
39 Word on a penny
40 Racer Fabi
41 Perfect person
42 Novelist Puzo
43 Chanteur
45 Desolate
46 Whopper
47 Tropical fish
48 CNN round table, with *The*
53 Naval noncom
56 Wilma's hubby
57 Shade of blue
58 Scarlett's mother
60 Monster
61 Monstrous
62 Newsboy's concern
63 Mean-spirited
64 Upset
65 Serious

DOWN
1 Stock-exchange street
2 Cap-__ (head to toe)
3 American Federation of Teachers, e.g.
4 Be human
5 Speak hesitatingly
6 "Dueling" instrument
7 Butterine
8 Wear's partner
9 New York City waterway
10 Ali Baba word
11 Spellbound
12 The Elephant Boy
13 Place for a pad
22 Atmospheric word form
23 Diagnostic tests, for short
25 Walkie-talkie word
27 Shoe forms
28 Path starter
29 Guide the ride
30 Like some tales
31 Environmental group
32 "Mr. Cub" Banks
33 River in Montana
35 Precipice
38 UC-Irvine student
39 Dray
41 __ were (so to speak)
42 Crèche items
44 Porch swing
45 Outlaw
47 *Atlantic City* director
48 Corp. VIPs
49 Southern constellation
50 Llama land
51 Jeans name
52 Inventor Borden
54 Senator Domenici
55 Beaut
59 Card game

SNOOPY BRITS by Dean Niles

ACROSS
1 Embark on a tirade
5 *The Seven Year Itch* star
10 Despot
14 Baseball manager Felipe
15 *West Side Story* role
16 Nevada city
17 Linseed-oil source
18 Computer command
19 Vocal range
20 Doyle snoop
23 The Belmonts' lead singer
24 Leavening
25 Long awning
28 HBO medium
31 "Farewell!"
32 Wood wedge
33 "__ bodkins!"
36 Sayers snoop
40 Word form for "equal"
41 Springiness
42 Taj __

43 Key material
45 Bogie costar
46 Orange Bowl locale
49 Flowing robe
50 Dexter snoop
56 Wine valley
57 Biblical mount
58 Muck or mire
60 Unique fellow
61 Where the action is
62 Film genre
63 Tenant's requirement
64 Clarabell colleague
65 Cognizant of

DOWN
1 UK fleet
2 "__ fair in love . . ."
3 Big name in lexicography
4 In black tie
5 Take on
6 LBJ's __ Poverty
7 Leif's dad

8 Unite
9 Wood strip
10 County Kerry seat
11 Alabama city
12 Contributes
13 Perch
21 Shred
22 Olive of comics
25 Colombian city
26 Fusses
27 Robert De __
28 Chase the comic
29 Million suffix
30 Upscale wheels
32 Rile
33 Workplace agcy.
34 "It's agreed!"
35 Word part: Abbr.
37 I: Lat.
38 Adult insect
39 Word in "Yankee Doodle"
43 Bestow

44 Contend
45 Indian port
46 Unimportant
47 Ludicrous
48 Trembling poplar
49 General course

51 African nation
52 Lawn-mower brand
53 Layered cookie
54 Any day now
55 Basso Pinza
59 Sea bird

CITY SHIFTS by Rich Norris

ACROSS
1 Treats
5 Doctrine
8 Manipulates
14 Arkin or Bede
15 Miler Sebastian
16 Get one's attention from afar
17 Mississippi city
19 Georgia city
20 Lead-in for center or gram
21 Current units
22 Spanish queens
23 New York cut, e.g.
25 River in Britain
27 Tranquillity
29 Witness' promise
33 Tennessee city
36 Filing aid
39 River inlet
40 Gets unruly
41 Skimpy
43 Reading room
44 Architect I.M.
46 California city
47 Aide: Abbr.

49 Bartender's need
51 Eskimo homes
54 Famous fabulist
58 Albéniz opus
61 "How about __!"
63 Partner of cry
64 Delaware city
65 Indiana city
67 Tease
68 Above, poetically
69 Aggressive whale
70 Burden
71 Dehumidified
72 Outer covering

DOWN
1 Awaits delivery?
2 Take as one's own
3 Eli
4 Dallas coll.
5 Part of the US arsenal

6 "Dinner's ready!"
7 Kids' rooms, at times
8 Frighten
9 Czech coin
10 Pigmentless plant
11 Map out
12 Sicilian spouter
13 Bean sauces
18 Reconciles
24 Boats of refuge
26 Animal doc
28 Vatican leader
30 Jason's vessel
31 Stadium section
32 Challenging
33 Tune of 1918
34 Poker pair
35 Shipping units: Abbr.
37 Frenzied
38 Not worthy of
42 Farm unit
45 Metric starter
46 Restaurant employee

48 Diatribe
50 Racing car
52 Brownies, e.g.
53 Victoria and George
55 Vacation destination
56 Small quantity
57 Piano device

58 Roadside stopovers
59 Borscht need
60 Pitcher
62 __ *in the Dark* (Streep film)
66 Floor cleaner

101 OVEN-FRESH by Bob Lubbers

ACROSS

1 Very short putt
6 LL.B. holders
10 Train unit
13 Korean, e.g.
14 Chart
16 '20s auto
17 Wise one
19 Coach Parseghian
20 "Wait __ the sun shines . . ."
21 Domain: Abbr.
22 Spanish hero El __
23 From Libya, perhaps
27 Second film versions
29 Life story, for short
30 Time periods
32 One of two teams
33 __ Well That Ends Well
35 Biblical garden spot
37 __ firma
40 Boxing prop
41 Against the clock
43 Open a little
44 Top floor, maybe
46 Latvian capital
47 Alight
48 Arabian sultanate
50 Manor worker
52 Corp. boss
53 Like some shirts
56 Skater Hans
58 Append
59 Scull needs
61 Three __ match
62 Actress West
63 Wage earner
68 Nav. rank
69 Barrel slat
70 Oak fruit
71 Korean soldier
72 Portent
73 Ancient instruments

DOWN

1 Auto fuel
2 Doctrine
3 Actress Farrow
4 Cuban patriot José
5 Lure
6 In the past
7 Horse's gait
8 Customer
9 Church tops
10 A-one
11 Lofty lair
12 Auto paths
15 Recluse
18 Red wine
23 Addis __
24 Boned fish
25 Nostalgic furniture
26 Low point
28 Let's Make __
31 Big trucks
34 Ghostbusters goo
36 Mideast desert
38 Indian princess
39 Passion
42 Scopes' attorney
45 Chocolate substitutes
49 Close by
51 Lampshade ornament
53 More docile
54 Hersey town
55 Night vision?
57 Sinatra or Reagan
60 Store (up)
64 Hideaway
65 "Neither rain __ snow . . ."
66 Before, poetically
67 TLC providers

102 UP A TREE by Gregory E. Paul

ACROSS

1 Actor Baldwin
5 Senate staffer
9 Summarize
14 PBS program
15 Pub pints
16 Aïda, e.g.
17 Give off
18 Envy, pride, etc.
19 Nasser's successor
20 Little House town
23 Actor Vigoda
24 Make up (for)
25 "Believe __ not!"
27 Coddle
30 Sony rival
33 Oklahoma city
34 Dark fur
37 Pale
38 Lassie's offspring
40 Former women's magazine
42 Camping need
43 Everything, to Ernst
45 Viper
47 "Sprechen __ Deutsch?"
48 Pittsburgh gridder
50 Country singer Tex
52 Health clubs
53 __ Carta
55 Ron of Tarzan
57 Howard Hughes' flying boat
62 Singer Vaughan
64 __ mater
65 Footnote abbr.
66 Entertain
67 High schooler
68 A few
69 Berth option
70 Helper: Abbr.
71 Chicken chow __

DOWN

1 Freshly
2 __ Linda, CA
3 Devilish
4 Forty winks
5 Rustic
6 Straighten
7 Art category
8 Exxon, formerly
9 __ stone (famous inscribed slab)
10 Fed. ecology group
11 Fragrant box
12 Arafat, for one
13 Top of the head
21 Western Indians
22 Seneca's seven
26 Hops kiln
27 Actress Irene
28 Grownup
29 Vermont product
30 Grazing group
31 Skater Sonja
32 Prefix for mural
35 Stock pessimist
36 Little shaver
39 Ooze
41 Pepper or York
44 Horror-film heavy
46 Dempsey's domain
49 Sixth sense: Abbr.
51 Chinese religion
53 Stubborn ones
54 Summits
55 Rebekah's son
56 Genie's abode
58 Pro __ (proportionately)
59 Orchestra reed
60 __ Valley, CA
61 Actress Barbara
63 Peer Gynt's mother

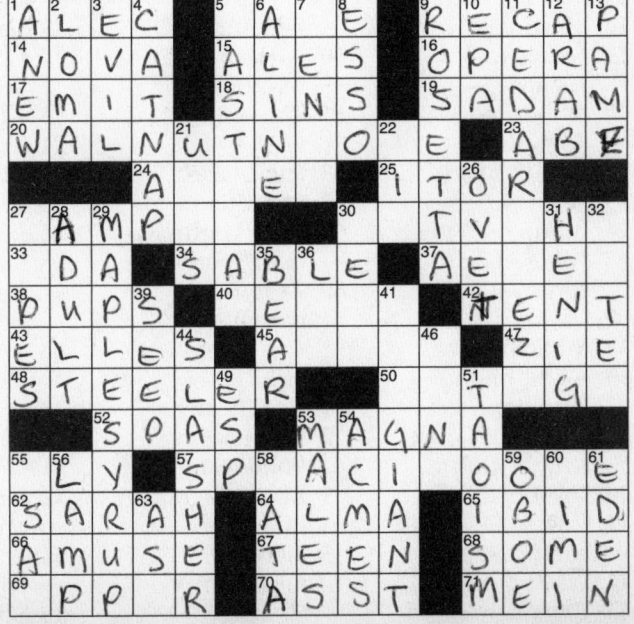

103 ANIMAL ACTS by Mark Diehl

ACROSS
1 Branch
5 ". . . __ man with seven wives"
10 Baloney
14 Draft rating
15 Southern accent
16 Choir member
17 Ballroom dance
19 *Dr. Zhivago* director
20 An archangel
21 Farewell appearance
23 Ignites
26 Solo performance
27 Actor Calhoun
29 Mennonite sect
33 Double curve
36 Taos tie
37 Eaves dropper
38 '60s dance
41 Built __ (durable)
42 Actor Arkin
43 Gridiron stats: Abbr.
44 Off the cuff
45 Czech, for one
46 Source
48 Gets together (with)
54 Novelty dance
58 Muskie's state
59 Buffalo's water
60 Soldier's strides
63 Turns brown
64 One with big eyes
65 Single apartment
66 Rathskeller offerings
67 "__ Dawn" (Reddy song)
68 Hand, across the border

DOWN
1 Yoga position
2 Adapt (to)
3 Raise reason
4 Makes cakes
5 Charley Weaver's Mount __
6 *The A-Team* star
7 Corn units
8 Like Dick Tracy's wrist radio
9 Place of worship
10 Vinegar variety
11 Bread spread
12 Mr. Musial
13 __ Kong
18 "Evil Woman" band, for short
22 A B vitamin
24 Weather system
25 Music genre
28 Blue-blooded
30 Distasteful
31 *Citizen Kane* prop
32 Some turkeys
33 Sundance's girl
34 Wearing loafers
35 Bearish order
36 Cafeteria worker
37 "__ a dream": King
39 Impartiality
40 *B.C.* buck
45 Moe or Larry
47 George Burns film
49 Els' followers
50 Ryan's daughter
51 Tuscany town
52 Let one's hair down, perhaps
53 Pasta sauce
54 VHS alternative
55 River to the Caspian Sea
56 75% of a dozen
57 Harris undertaking
61 Salon job
62 Time period

104 SOLITARY SOLVING by Patrick Jordan

ACROSS
1 Give off vapors
5 Fate
10 Lie next to
14 Orwell alma mater
15 Regular order
16 Welles role
17 Mickey's maker
18 Martini partner
19 Netman Nastase
20 "I'm Into Something Good" band
23 Feel off
24 Bump on a log
25 Alleged Garbo comment
33 Cadre
34 Malicious
35 Addl. phone
37 Pâté de __ gras
38 Dayan of Israel
39 Knight club
40 "You bet!"
41 Curry component
42 Like Cheerios
43 TV tuners
46 Nabokov novel
47 Electrical unit
48 *Quiz Show* locale
56 PBS series
57 Non-studio film, for short
58 Hoop star O'Neal, in headlines
60 African republic
61 *The Way __ Flesh*
62 Icicle base
63 Sanctified
64 "The Highway-man" poet
65 At love, perhaps

DOWN
1 Hardly any
2 Promontory Point state
3 Double agent
4 Infatuate
5 Network newsman Charles
6 ". . . unto us __ is born"
7 Bandleader Columbo
8 Livestock feed
9 Make an enemy of
10 With hands on hips
11 Java neighbor
12 College course section
13 Kicker's props
21 Tiny bit
22 Manageable
25 Questionable
26 He comes a-courtin'
27 Join the rebellion
28 "__, All Ye Faithful"
29 __ *Instinct*
30 Cultural prefix
31 "Peachy keen!"
32 Distinguish oneself
36 Addition column
38 Sci-fi creature
39 Small monkey
41 Fugue ending
42 Roman emperor
44 Affliction
45 Annual prizes
48 Move a little
49 London area
50 Racetrack shape
51 Data
52 Singer Anita
53 Khartoum's river
54 Bangkok citizen
55 Dine on
59 Proof abbr.

GREEK WISDOM by Dean Niles

ACROSS
1 Diarist Frank
5 Complaint
9 Fields' vaudeville partner
14 Ember
15 Spike, as punch
16 Piece for Van Cliburn
17 Author of the quote
19 Glaringly vivid
20 Avoids
21 Wood strips
23 I, in Essen
24 Something in the air
25 Arise (from)
28 FIRST HALF OF A QUOTE
34 Wine cask
35 Angers
36 "__ we all?"
37 Supplemental material
39 Depends on
41 River's end
42 Great __
43 Fumble
44 SECOND HALF OF QUOTE
47 Minute particle
48 Coll. mil. grp.
49 Viper
51 Ill-fated vessel
55 Fast tempo
59 Stow securely
60 Source of quote
62 Mystical poems
63 Nobelist Wiesel
64 Gridder Collingsworth
65 __ directed (medicine instruction)
66 Inoperative
67 Forearm bone

DOWN
1 Dull pain
2 Turndowns
3 Bust organizer
4 Old Testament word
5 Loudmouth
6 Consumes
7 Old French coin
8 Come clean
9 Quite cognizant
10 Needle case
11 Scorch
12 Correct copy
13 Beatty film
18 Xmas time
22 Expert
24 Capp and Gore
25 Letter necessity
26 English royal house
27 Assume
29 Meadow
30 Sea bird
31 Adjust the VCR
32 Preface
33 Cloudburst
35 Working, in a way
38 And so forth: Abbr.
39 T, to 17 Across
40 Like some nuts
42 Mr. Severinsen
45 King of France
46 Had a hankering
47 Quick glance
50 __-pitch softball
51 By way of
52 Debt memos
53 Ditty
54 Sailing
55 __ Minor
56 "The __ From Ipanema"
57 Curb
58 Greek peak
61 __ de France

FELINITY by Gregory E. Paul

ACROSS
1 Medicinal amount
5 Irving hero
9 Gridder Brian's kin
14 Admired one
15 Vicinity
16 Exchange
17 Nick's mate
18 "__ Be Cruel"
19 Clinton defense secretary
20 Senior activist
23 Wind up
24 Catch
25 Pete of tennis
27 McMurtry's __ Dove
32 Fragment
33 Imitate
34 Shoe material
36 Cacophony
39 __ Valley, CA
41 Babel structure
43 ". . . and children of all __!"
44 Kind of shoes
46 Metal strands
48 Dine
49 Choral voice
51 Chopin work
53 Stress
56 A: Ger.
57 Building add-on
58 Wonderland grinner
64 Move furtively
66 Hgt.
67 Part of T.A.E.
68 Sierra __
69 Scale starters
70 Caught in the act
71 Lou Grant portrayer
72 Diary capacity
73 Andrew's dukedom

DOWN
1 Doorbell sound
2 Aroma
3 Marsh bird
4 Comic Boosler
5 Wanderer
6 Elvis __ Presley
7 Monthly payment
8 Walkways
9 Jeff Bridges film
10 DC tax org.
11 Deceptively weak one
12 Minneapolis suburb
13 Transmits
21 Refuse to bid
22 "The Raven" monogram
26 Malay outrigger
27 Eye protector
28 Mayberry moppet
29 Victim of Hercules' first labor
30 Feline sound
31 Newsman Newman
35 Finnish architect Saarinen
37 O'Casey or Penn
38 Villa d'__
40 Troubles
42 Phone piece
45 Decal
47 Recipe direction
50 Aah's partner
52 On pins and needles
53 Inventor Nikola
54 French pronoun
55 Hard up
59 Gin flavor
60 Greek Juno
61 Singer Laine
62 Affirm
63 Army vehicle
65 Compass dir.

MS. PRESIDENT by Lee Weaver

ACROSS

1 Raced
5 Former Iranian ruler
9 Sax range
13 Cod and Hatteras
15 Nero's robe
16 Prejudice
17 Tropical spot
18 Bring up
19 Poet Pound
20 *Designing Women* star
23 Dress (up)
24 Sushi sauce
25 Actor Wallach
26 Dubai, e.g.
28 Bowler's targets
30 Remain
31 Mongolian desert
35 Quagmire
36 Goose egg
39 Yemen port
40 Search, in a way
43 Fly like an eagle
44 Do a double take
46 Way off
47 Goofs
48 Atmosphere
50 __ *Here to Eternity*
52 Wine holders
55 Santa __ winds
56 Big fuss
59 Burning
60 *Charlie's Angels* star
63 Pallid
65 Rescue
66 Some beneficiaries
67 Swing around
68 Ukraine capital
69 '50s tune, e.g.
70 Sea swallow
71 Part of A.D.
72 Annoyance

DOWN

1 Oodles
2 Place to lounge
3 Industrial glue
4 Salami emporium
5 Kitchen device
6 Gardener, at times
7 Playing marble
8 Seraglios
9 Tad's dad
10 Cleopatra to Burton's Antony
11 Seer's deck
12 Inedible orange
14 Snooze
21 *Cheers* mailman
22 Paris hotel
27 Poker ploy
29 Show disdain
31 Needlefish
32 Lyric poem
33 One of *The Golden Girls*
34 Become liable for
37 Elevator compartment
38 Many mins.
41 Bosnian city
42 Monetary unit of Iceland
45 Expedition
49 "Seward's Folly"
51 He-manly
52 Wild party
53 Pews divider
54 Washday worry
56 Stage whisper
57 Day or Duke
58 Beginning
61 Tied up
62 Kind of seaweed
64 Hankering

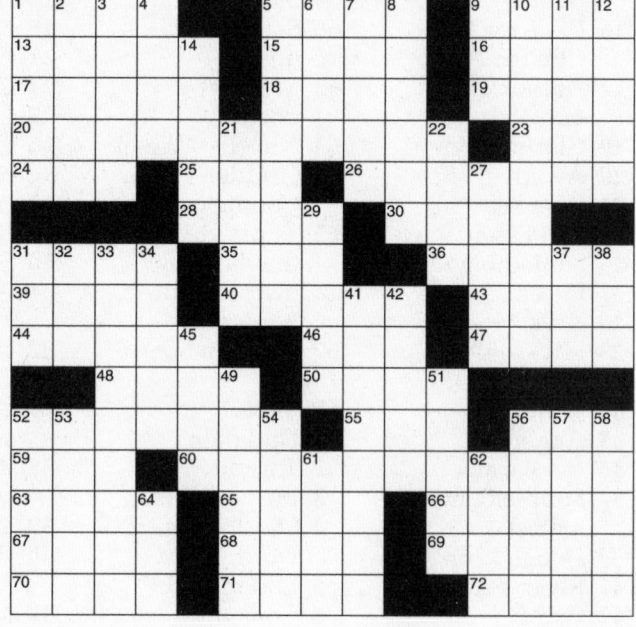

SLEEPY TOWNS by Bob Lubbers

ACROSS

1 Sups
6 "__ girl!"
10 Flu shots, e.g.
14 Astaire's sister
15 Canadian bird
16 Oklahoma city
17 __, MA
19 OTB postings
20 Party pro
21 Give out
23 Ike's command: Abbr.
24 Ooze
26 Antipasto items
29 __ Xiaoping
31 Library tool
34 Big barrel
35 Conger
38 Tardy
40 __, ME
43 Immense
44 Collector's goal
45 Seine sight
46 Film award
48 Con game
52 __ *on Sunday*
54 City on the Wailuku
57 Airline to Tokyo
58 Proficient
61 Graduate course
63 Against
65 __, NJ
67 Swag
68 Netman Nastase
69 Non-studio movie, for short
70 Flubs
71 Guide
72 Position

DOWN

1 Cakewalked
2 Conceive
3 Wayne or Isaac
4 Dresden river
5 Crystal-ball gazers
6 Lord Tennyson
7 Also
8 Spelling the actress
9 "No ifs, __, or buts!"
10 Korean capital
11 Exert oneself
12 Disencumber
13 TV spots
18 Actress Ruby
22 Abrasion
25 __, KY
27 Trading center
28 Pigpen
30 Actress Rowlands
32 Can material
33 Wapitis
36 Audience demand
37 Allows
39 Young 'uns
40 Cabbage kin
41 One way up
42 Paper Mate rival
43 Rummy game
47 Chanced
49 Alberta's home
50 Bayer rival
51 Identified
53 Oversees copy
55 General at Gettysburg
56 All: Lat.
59 *Murphy Brown* barkeep
60 Fib
62 Lacks existence
63 Pub serving
64 Negative connector
66 OSS successor

IT'S ACADEMIC by Gerald R. Ferguson

ACROSS

1 Diamond corner
5 Newsman Huntley
9 Lawful volunteers
14 Unsuitable for farming
15 Sci-fi award
16 Hippodrome
17 Students' sports grp.
18 "Rush it" letters
19 Nobelist Pauling
20 Generally accepted facts
23 Ottoman ruler
24 Egg layer
25 Lacey's partner
29 Lookouts, e.g.
34 Arch types
35 Abner's adjective
36 Nanki-__
37 Disputed point
42 Took the bait
43 Black cuckoo
44 Actress Mills
45 Winter hiking need
48 Vocation
49 "Adam and Eve __ raft!"
50 Cry of surprise
51 Ideological belief
60 Painter Veronese
61 Choir member
62 Jocularity
63 Castaway's spot
64 Pro-shop buy
65 Byron poem
66 Wee
67 Mary or Gary
68 Midmonth day

DOWN

1 French bench
2 Exxon rival
3 Famous twins' home
4 Wax-covered cheese
5 Quasimodo portrayer
6 Dog of the Yukon
7 Former Alaska governor
8 "__ the morning!"
9 Warehouse platform
10 Direct (toward)
11 __ packing (evict)
12 Comfy
13 Slacken
21 Very heavy
22 Pup
25 Searches thoroughly
26 Once more
27 Reach
28 Hoop skirt?
29 Caine role
30 Thumbnail sketch
31 Express oneself
32 Arledge of ABC
33 Naval acronym
38 1992 Indy winner
39 Beatle bride
40 Pocatello's state
41 Hide-hair connector
46 Bulky cloth
47 Snobbish
48 Show partner
50 Weasel relative
51 __ and polish
52 Docket entry
53 Mender's target
54 Courtroom ritual
55 Word before collar or market
56 Wrinkled fruit
57 Hefty rival
58 At this place
59 Afternoon receptions

PICKY PICKY by Dean Niles

ACROSS

1 "If __" (Beatles tune)
6 ASCAP rival
9 Cougar
13 North Atlantic island group
14 Tear apart
16 *Ghostbusters* character
17 Backyard seat
18 Folkie Guthrie
19 Cantata part
20 Book-club procedure
23 "Oh dear!"
24 Cobbler's tool
25 Storm hdg.
28 Tom Cruise movie
34 Succeeded
36 Cowboy's agreement
37 Land of Tara
38 Like some walls
39 Title for Curie: Abbr.
40 German spa
41 Composer Edouard
42 __ good deed
43 Roman poet
44 Campaign climax
47 Holy folk: Abbr.
48 Stimpy's pal
49 Yen
51 Test type
58 Come to life
59 __ up (enliven)
60 Collection of treasures
62 Windstorm
63 Salinger title name
64 Sri Lanka language
65 "__ Can't Be Love"
66 Utter
67 Like some minds

DOWN

1 Suppositions
2 Young deer
3 Cleveland's lake
4 *Ars __, vita brevis*
5 Free advice of a sort
6 Sauté and simmer
7 Game-show mogul Griffin
8 Conspiring (with)
9 __ moss
10 Type of tangelo
11 Lorre role
12 By and by
15 A cappella singing style
21 Sculptor Lorado
22 Arafat grp.
25 Rousseau romance
26 Part of USNA
27 Roman magistrate
29 *Johnny Belinda* star
30 Pricey
31 Exemplar of greed
32 Not supine
33 Hawaiian geese
35 Nondiscrimination agcy.
39 Like a cloudy night
40 Doesn't patronize
42 French seaport
43 "Hell __ no fury . . ."
45 Numerical prefix
46 Author of *Deliverance*
50 Distiller Walker
51 Bilko's rank: Abbr.
52 Beehive State
53 Caron film
54 Very, in Versailles
55 Writer Bombeck
56 Crichton-directed film
57 Nefarious
61 Building extension

ON THE GRIDIRON by Bob Lubbers

ACROSS
1 Cotton variety
5 Nearly all
9 Obligations
14 Eye part
15 Blues singer James
16 *Kate & __*
17 Angler's carryall
19 Actress Massey
20 Afternoon china
21 Greek dialect
23 I love: Lat.
25 Remain loyal to
28 Grows severe
33 Indian tent
34 Interest gouging
35 Farm buildings
37 Hole piercer
38 Coal boxes
39 Hoagies
40 Russian river
41 DC summer setting

42 Gluts
43 __ nous
44 Repair a shoe
46 Arrayed, as for battle
48 Dreaded flies
50 "My Gal __"
51 Actor Omar
53 Redeems, with "in"
58 '30s bandleader Jones
60 Motorcycle actuator
62 Witchlike woman
63 Possess
64 Opera solo
65 Elias and Julia
66 Agitate
67 Yin and __

DOWN
1 *12 Monkeys* costar
2 *"Dies __"*
3 Shiny mineral
4 Inquires
5 __ *in St. Louis*

6 Pony-players' place: Abbr.
7 Ancient colonnade
8 Levies
9 Some newspapers
10 __ Islands (former name of Tuvalu)
11 Street celebration
12 Can metal
13 Vast expanse
18 WWII admiral
22 Kruger and Preminger
24 Beginning
26 Take warning
27 Hollered
28 Lyndon's veep
29 Stage whispers
30 Be boss
31 Jrs., next year
32 Begat
36 Finishes last
39 Healthier
40 One, to Pedro

42 Oil sources
43 Fitzgerald et al.
45 Fuel gas
47 Green Bay player
49 Sect of India
52 Decree
54 Remain

55 __ kiri
56 Actress Moran
57 Male deer
58 *"__ bin ein Berliner"*
59 Broadway hit sign: Abbr.
61 106, to Nero

UNREAL ZOOLOGY by Patrick Jordan

ACROSS
1 Indian honcho
6 Fracas
11 Barker and Bell
14 Calgary iceman
15 Former talk-show host Hamilton
16 Benevolent brother
17 Toni Tennille's partner
19 Slugger's stat
20 Overly formal
21 __ in (collapsed)
23 Brief raids
27 Alleges
29 Preparing to drive
30 __ T. Washington
31 Asian ape
32 Not as good
33 Potsdam pronoun
36 Abounding (with)
37 Mingles
38 '60s hairstyle
39 Slangy agreement

40 Penalized a speeder
41 Stereo systems, for short
42 Stockpiles
44 Clothes hater
45 Life's little jokes
47 Bemoans
48 Translucent
49 Verdi opera
50 Actor Chaney
51 Howling deejay
58 Amin of Uganda
59 Torch's crime
60 Numbers game
61 Peace, to Petrarch
62 Letter closing
63 Long time

DOWN
1 Postal abbr.
2 Miss. neighbor
3 Preserves preserver
4 Grant of gospel
5 Dinner portion
6 Indian wraps
7 __ up (stay quiet)

8 Joplin tune
9 Pitch __-hitter
10 Flapjack
11 Game-show magnate
12 *Seascape* playwright
13 Slides on ice
18 Small remnant
22 Exist
23 Tale
24 Eagle's nest
25 *SpaceCamp* actor
26 Toe the __ (obey)
27 Hollowed apples
28 One of Ben's boys
30 Takes on Tyson
32 *The __ of War*
34 Critic Judith
35 Multitudes
37 Deep mud
38 Assistant
40 Approach to the green
41 Word preceding "possible"
43 Undivided

44 Nothing, in slang
45 Long Island town
46 Role for Valerie
47 Describes precisely
49 Get an __ effort
52 Coronado quest

53 Baton Rouge inst.
54 Regular guy
55 One __ time (singly)
56 Midpt.
57 Puts flat on the canvas

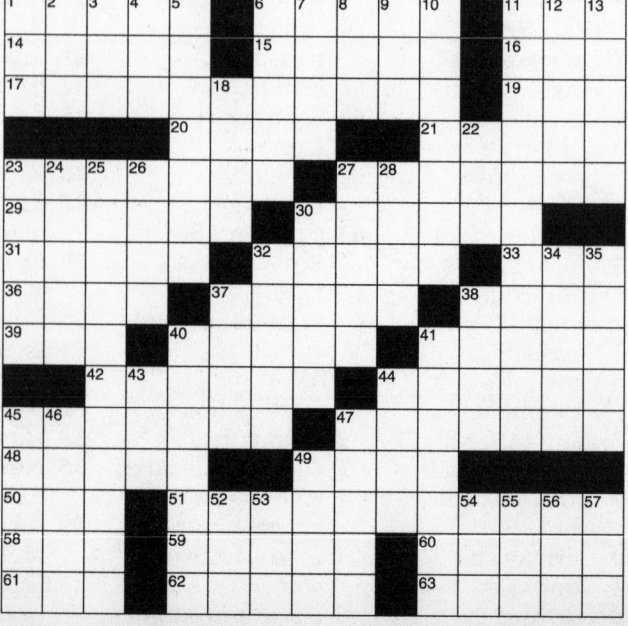

113 LITTERARY by Dean Niles

ACROSS
1 Chanteuse Edith
5 Life, in La Paz
9 Large parrot
14 Word form for "height"
15 Culture medium
16 Mistreatment
17 First infatuation
19 Wearing a toga
20 Word on Irish coins
21 Spills the beans, with "out"
22 Monopoly props
26 7-Up rival
28 Took a breath
30 __ Tin Tin
31 Scoreboard nos.
34 Marks to retain
35 Rubber gasket
37 Sound of discovery
38 Kin
39 Didn't move
40 Chicago paper, for short
41 Grounded bird
42 __-France
43 Learner
44 Reading room
45 It may be the word
46 Part of some acts
48 Pants protector
51 Rue
52 Regardless
54 Give __ for one's money
56 Irish dramatist Brendan
57 Wright place at the right time
62 Bring forth
63 With: Fr.
64 Parrot or ape
65 Boutonniere site
66 Hart's ex-cohost
67 "Cool it!"

DOWN
1 Baby food
2 *ER* location
3 Dadaist Hans
4 Dandy
5 Luggage piece
6 Marty Feldman role
7 Barry and Brubeck
8 *You __ There*
9 Fertilizing, in a way
10 *All __ Eve*
11 Jimmy Olsen, e.g.
12 "I'd hate to break up __"
13 Brings together
18 Rebel cries
21 Seawater
22 Greeted the villain
23 Promptly
24 1952 Ray Anthony tune
25 Gobbles up
27 Holds dear
29 Money
32 Filch
33 "Amen!"
36 Serling or Steiger
39 Changeable
40 __ oil (varnish agent)
42 Seat the jury
43 Really small
47 Forked support
49 Conscious
50 Ingenuous
52 First second son
53 Leningrad river
55 Hwys.
57 *Krazy __*
58 "__ a Rebel"
59 Go through the motions
60 One of the 5 W's
61 Keystone officer

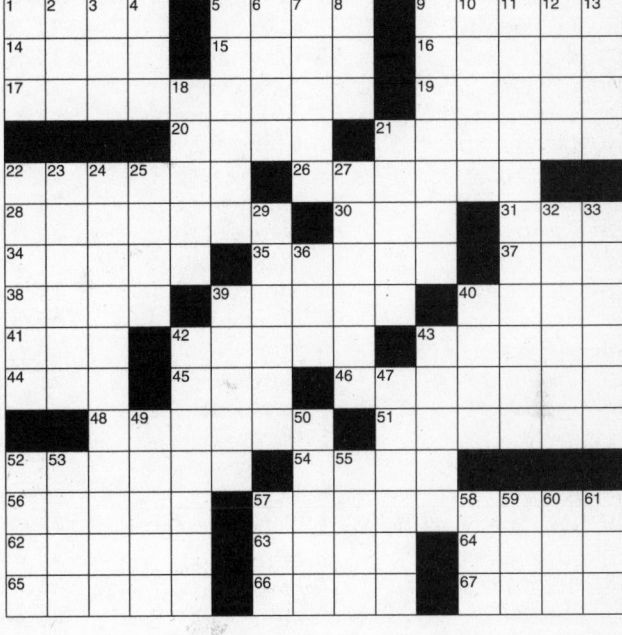

114 MOVIE MISTERS by Gregory E. Paul

ACROSS
1 Weather systems
5 Pair of mules
9 Like Batman
14 "Uh-huh"
15 Windex target
16 Fred's sister
17 Writer Waugh
18 Not fooled by
19 Flower feature
20 Mr. Chips
23 Compass pt.
24 Poet Thomas
25 Talk show pioneer
27 City on the Willamette
30 Meara's partner
33 Genetic abbr.
34 Rival of Coco
37 Rope loop
38 Broadcasts
40 *The Crucible* locale
42 56 Down designer
43 Panache
45 Gold weight
47 Clergyman: Abbr.
48 Jailbreaker
50 Poser's word
52 Mayberry lad
53 Son of Jacob
55 Fuss
57 Mr. Belvedere
62 Red Cloud's residence
64 Traipse
65 Birth of a notion
66 Marlin's milieu
67 Baseballer Manny
68 Actress Naldi
69 Malory's *Le __ d'Arthur*
70 ". . . __ o'clock scholar"
71 Make tight

DOWN
1 Dissembler
2 European capital
3 Football coach Ewbank
4 Withdraw
5 Squeaky-clean
6 World Wildlife Fund symbol
7 Dramatist Chekhov
8 Sign gas
9 Queeg, for one
10 Summer drink
11 Mr. Moto
12 Zest
13 Editor's marking
21 Sandberg of baseball
22 Likely
26 Succulent plant
27 Clear the board
28 Army outfits
29 Mr. Deeds
30 Nostradamus, e.g.
31 Adlai's running mate
32 Town officer
35 Seize
36 Old scale note
39 Open-hand blow
41 Village People song
44 Unisex
46 "And next . . ."
49 Sniggler's catch
51 Rommel et al.
53 Going on
54 Opine
55 Bohr's bit
56 Art __
58 Cookbook author Rombauer
59 Singer Adams
60 Key letter
61 False god
63 Munch

115 MY ACHING FEET! by Fred Piscop

ACROSS

1 Sash inserts
6 Browse the Internet
10 Garr or Hatcher
14 Actress Massey
15 Role for Ronny
16 Part of GE
17 Lumberjack with aching feet?
19 Edward G. Robinson role
20 Rack partner
21 Judge of Israel
23 Route components
26 Legal claims
27 Shells, e.g.
30 Nuke, perhaps
33 It's put on
34 Captive of opera
36 "¿Cómo __ usted?"
40 Marionette with aching feet?
43 Silver producer
44 Mocker
45 City on the Danube
46 Vandyke relative
48 In a strange way
50 Campaign tactic
53 Contemptible one
55 Incantation
57 Asian belief
61 __-European
62 Composer with aching feet?
66 Nasty look
67 Name of three English rivers
68 Mountain home
69 Pianist Duchin
70 Marvin Gardens payment
71 Play

DOWN

1 Gehrig replaced him
2 Jai __
3 Subject, often
4 Volunteer
5 Torpedo, perhaps
6 Biff, to Willy
7 News org.
8 Former capital city
9 Boggy lands
10 Home wreckers
11 "Für __"
12 Scout's job
13 Windows symbols
18 Numero __
22 Mobile's st.
24 Radio button
25 They're usually armed
27 Hair producer
28 Soreness
29 Swizzle
31 Talmudic language
32 Fashion mag
35 Indian bigshot
37 Card game
38 Spill the beans
39 Mule team?
41 Worthless
42 Dope
47 Former Nebraska governor
49 Auto-store buy
50 Funt's order
51 Like a horse
52 Put a stop to
54 Belief
56 Not quite shut
58 Author Ephron
59 In shape
60 Draftable
63 Forbidden-fruit eater
64 Cuban rum
65 NY neighbor

116 BREAD BOXES by Lee Weaver

ACROSS

1 Bread spread
5 Hillside, to Burns
9 Desist
13 Field of study
14 "He's __ the coop!"
15 Fill the hold
16 Be a couch potato
18 Presser's need
19 Printer's measures
20 Learning method
21 Movie awards
23 Ringed planet
25 Mall madness
27 Country walkway
29 Flabbergast
33 Like a cirrus cloud
36 Realty unit
38 Herr's mate
39 Not doing much
40 Pigtail
41 Deposited, as eggs
42 Machine part
43 Pulls a heist
44 Breathers for fish
45 Small bag
47 50%
49 Enjoys a book
51 Itsy-bitsy
55 Quantity
58 Wahine's dance
60 Black cuckoo
61 Arrests
62 Walking-race style
65 Horse's gait
66 Linda of Dynasty
67 Pianist Hines
68 Matches a raise
69 __ avis
70 Ran in the wash

DOWN

1 Drake and gander
2 Bakery output
3 Bakery input
4 Lout
5 Ink mishap
6 Libertines
7 Wheat beard
8 Gave approval to
9 Ad vignette
10 O'Hara home
11 Scent
12 Corrals
14 Façade
17 Deck out
22 Complete collection
24 Socially prominent classes
26 County, in Louisiana
28 Stassen or Lloyd
30 Russian river
31 Hammer's target
32 Ineffectual bombs
33 Hairpieces
34 Mind find
35 Blinds part
37 Urban vehicle
40 Rest between exertions
44 Collect slowly
46 Egg layer
48 Map book
50 Harvest wool
52 Dating from birth
53 Night noise
54 Intersection sign
55 Picnic pests
56 Colt's mom
57 Double-reed instrument
59 Forearm bone
63 Gabor or Perón
64 Young lady in society

EN ROUTE by Bob Lubbers

ACROSS
1 Acting jobs
6 Sales pitch
11 Actor Torn
14 Soap __ (TV fare)
15 Sculpt
16 '70s ring champ
17 Broadway production of 1933
19 Ailing
20 Make believe
21 Inter __ (among other things)
22 Sailor's "yes"
25 Yalie
26 Moving aimlessly
28 Frying medium
30 Bridge seat
33 Bandleader Shaw
34 Gripping tool
36 Romantic isle
38 Broadway production of 1994

43 Show scorn
44 Lawrence's turf
45 Carried
48 Challenge
50 Calm
51 Disinclined
53 Atty.'s degree
55 Golfer's prop
56 Breath freshener
57 Bitty bug
61 Part of Q&A
62 Broadway production of 1929
66 Brenda or Peggy
67 Pay the tab
68 Praise
69 Curved letter
70 Shouts
71 Personal log

DOWN
1 Kitchen vessel
2 GI address
3 Confederate soldier
4 Ensnare

5 "__ bleu!"
6 Nova __
7 Peel
8 De-pleat?
9 Circumvent
10 Guided
11 Scold
12 Urbana footballers
13 Pontius __
18 Actress Holm
21 O'Hare posting
22 European range
23 North Korean border river
24 Ireland
27 More scarce
29 Sweet dish
31 Cross the goal line
32 Greek consonant
35 Tears apart
37 Little drama
39 Flower area
40 Border (on)
41 Irk
42 Evans or Carnegie

45 Chili roll
46 Sheep
47 Tightens (up)
49 Armadas
52 __ nous
54 Rode Greyhound
58 Russian city

59 Notary's need
60 1111, to Caesar
62 Pig's digs
63 Greek vowel
64 Neither's partner
65 Tarzan portrayer Ron

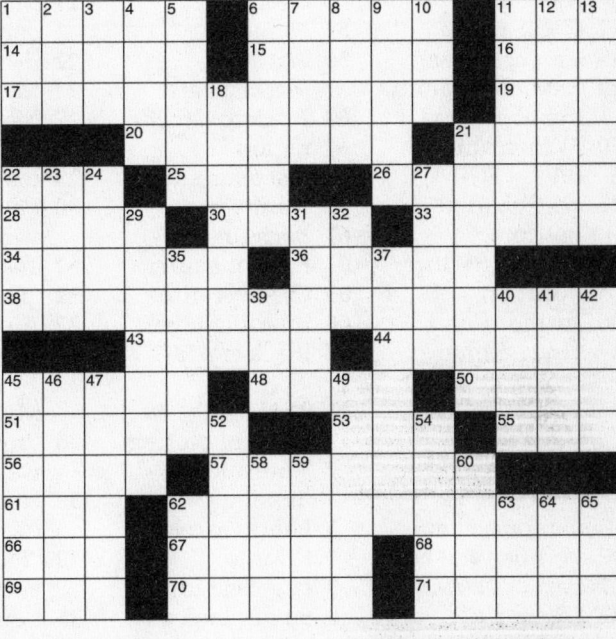

MAKE-UP TEST by Norma Steinberg

ACROSS
1 Send skyward
5 Comic Foxx
9 Mimicked
13 Pittsburgh river
14 Fairy tale's penultimate word
15 Play with crayons
17 Broadway prize
18 Hold the deed to
19 Cord
20 Lamont Cranston
22 "__ care!"
23 Support
24 __ Culp Hobby (Eisenhower cabinet member)
25 Personnel slots
28 "__ Fidelis"
30 Navidad stuffed animal
32 Nosh
33 __-sutra
37 Dilettante
39 Broad-minded

41 The Flintstones' pet
42 The: Ger.
44 Convincing
45 Caught red-handed
48 Org.
49 North Dakota city
51 Layer of paint
53 Trivial
54 Leave out details
59 Follow
60 The Huxtables' youngest
61 Storied bear
62 Military strategy
63 Global speck
64 "The Lord __ shepherd . . ."
65 Luge
66 Bump into
67 Oolong and pekoe

DOWN
1 Mississippi senator
2 Klutz's exclamation

3 Excellent
4 30 Across filling
5 Back-to-normal process
6 Skirts
7 Aficionado
8 Sleuth Nancy
9 In effect
10 Volatile ones
11 Prufrock's creator
12 Actress Reed
16 Like Gen. Schwarzkopf
21 Waste maker
24 Of sight
25 Guitarist Hendrix
26 __ even keel
27 LSU site
29 __ de tête (headache)
30 Hippie digs
31 TV broadcast part
34 Mars' Greek counterpart
35 Jazzman Herbie
36 Computer key
38 Bro., e.g.

40 Dinghies
43 Hermit
46 Saw eye to eye
47 Scribble
49 End of a French film
50 Photographer Adams

52 To date
53 My: Fr.
54 Pessimistic
55 Skip
56 Bouquet container
57 Poet Lazarus
58 Sunbather's quest

119   LEFT FIELD by Dean Niles

ACROSS
1 Small eatery
5 Boot attachment
10 Michael or Susannah
14 Winglike
15 __ ballerina
16 Sea east of the Caspian
17 Cook a cake
18 Career soldier
19 Extended-family member
20 "What Kind of Fool __?"
21 Left-handed patriot
23 Legendary lurer
25 Born: Fr.
26 Author Rand
27 Honest-man seeker
32 For short, for short
35 Ford or Els
36 "__ Como Va" (Santana tune)
37 Left-handed artist
41 Part of NATO
42 Like Seattle
43 Stir-fry pans
44 Oxford preserver
46 He defeated Spinks
48 "__ live and breathe!"
49 Rhoda, e.g.
53 Left-handed outlaw
58 Nemesis
59 The Time Machine race
60 Ancient Greek region
61 List shortener
62 Saint's image
63 Born first
64 Freight hauler
65 OJ substitute
66 Building level
67 Black crystal

DOWN
1 Gang of plotters
2 San Antonio mission
3 Hindu ascetic
4 Prior to
5 Peevish temper
6 Singer Lopez
7 Jazz phrase
8 Part of USA
9 Baseless suspicion
10 Gehrig or Mantle
11 Exam form
12 Rajah's mate
13 Birth of a Nation group
21 Memorable circumnavigator
22 Beersheba locale
24 Merit
27 Male bee
28 __ 500
29 It's verboten
30 Painter Jan van __
31 Twice tres
32 "Dear me!"
33 Alcott "woman"
34 Western tie
35 TV actress McClurg
38 Pretentious, in a way
39 Hen's teeth and blue moons
40 "Heads __, tails you lose"
45 London borough
46 Home for 27 Down
47 Trunk top
49 Mahre, for one
50 Regularly
51 Like the sea
52 Celluloid cat
53 "__ ever so . . ."
54 Actress Chase
55 Goofball
56 Romance novelist Victoria
57 Exo- opposite
61 "__ Beso" ('62 song)

120   JUST A SMATTERING by Manny Nosowsky

ACROSS
1 LBJ son-in-law
5 Glove part
10 Talk too much
14 Land o' lakes?
15 Asian capital
16 It has two gutters
17 Vanity fare?
20 Won __ soup
21 Chooses
22 Cut the mustard
23 The Sons of __ Elder
25 G-men
26 Part of USSR
28 Lead
29 B-F connector
32 Now's partner
33 Pale gray
34 Drag around
35 Of enormous importance
39 $$$ collectors
40 With 7 Down, United States, in France
41 Green Gables name
42 Burns' negative
43 Eye neighbor
44 Came in a flood
46 Like a pittance?
47 Lots of land
48 Sum total
51 Quite a while
52 Water source
55 Objects of Agnew's scorn
58 Knot-tailed flier
59 Yankovic parody
60 Addition column
61 Cookie creator
62 Baby bouncers
63 Borscht base

DOWN
1 Break in relations
2 Storting place
3 Unrhymed poetry
4 Back, with "on"
5 Commodity-market area
6 Poker Flat chronicler
7 See 40 Across
8 Calendar abbr.
9 Generosity symbol
10 Political groups
11 On a __ (romping)
12 The Egg __
13 Top of the line
18 Carry the load
19 Walk like a duck
24 "It __ fair!"
25 Accomplishments
26 Beer holder
27 Scarlett Butler, née __
28 '70s prime minister
29 It's a peach
30 Irene of Cimarron
31 Prodded, with "on"
33 Full moon, e.g.
36 Offenbach's La Belle __
37 Sci-fi phenomenon
38 Hardly seen
44 Collie clues
45 __ Minor
46 Zaps the audio
47 Certain Texas student
48 Singer Paul
49 Hurt badly
50 Sergeant Snorkel's dog
51 Penny, perhaps
53 Busy as __
54 Call to attention?
56 Fleming or McKellen
57 Go for apples

121 BEJEWELED by Patrick Jordan

ACROSS
1 Alan of *Shane*
5 Knocks on a door
9 Candle centers
14 Kampuchea's continent
15 Singer Adams
16 Global speck
17 Haberdashery department
18 Verse
19 A+, for one
20 Circular stain
23 An NCO
24 Gardner of mysteries
25 Runs off (with)
27 Buffalo NHLers
30 From scratch
32 __ Jima
33 Required
35 Science rooms
38 Did stitchery
40 Toddler
41 Coin of the realm
42 At rest
43 Procession
45 Blocker or Rather
46 Shoe part
48 "__ Fideles"
50 Rectories
52 Issue forth
53 HS math subject
54 Where manners are taught
60 Steam
62 Clare Boothe __
63 __ mater
64 Author Zola
65 Biblical brother
66 Tide type
67 Opus for nine
68 Recognizes
69 Eternities

DOWN
1 Mary's pet
2 On a cruise
3 Force
4 Dancer's yokemate
5 Beat back
6 Pueblo material
7 Marina sight
8 Trucker's rig
9 Shimmy
10 Neighbor of Syr.
11 Greet, in a way
12 Small anchor
13 Leaves in, editorially
21 Vogue
22 Dweeb
26 Norway's capital
27 Emphatic Spanish assent
28 Wowed
29 Alley target
30 Revere
31 Greek cheese
34 List ender, for short
36 Trounce
37 "Auld Lang __"
39 Poet's nighttimes
41 Corpsman
43 Elegant
44 Maidens
47 Hush-hush
49 Fuel type
50 Expert
51 San Antonio landmark
52 TV host
55 "Oh, dear!"
56 Cartoonist Goldberg
57 Margarine
58 Arabian gulf
59 Race segments
61 Bullring cheer

122 SPORTING CHANCE by Gregory E. Paul

ACROSS
1 Impudence
5 Primitive
10 Q-Tip, e.g.
14 London gallery
15 Fire-truck rolls
16 Charter
17 Kind of vaccine
18 Occurrence
19 Radiate
20 Baseball event
23 "Phooey!"
24 Registers
25 Lithium, e.g.
27 Dispatch funds
30 Self-effacing
33 Young woman
36 Parched
38 Car accessory
39 Tempe sch.
40 Enliven
42 Frequently, to a poet
43 Flutist
45 Location
46 Chip in a chip
47 Solid alcohol
49 Actor Alain
51 Provide with new troops
53 Inventor Otis
57 Catch
59 Yachting prize
62 Clarinet cousin
64 Patti LuPone role
65 Corn spikes
66 First name in politics
67 Peter and Franco
68 *Glamour* rival
69 Stewpot
70 Italian city
71 "Those Were the __"

DOWN
1 Vermont resort
2 Composer Copland
3 Begin
4 Clouseau portrayer
5 Bishop, for one
6 Meander
7 __-friendly
8 Jeans material
9 Regard
10 That girl
11 Tennis event
12 Sills solo
13 Playwright Henley
21 Dr. of rap
22 Shop
26 Nabokov novel
28 Spring flower
29 Sheepish
31 Prepare flour
32 Schlep
33 Glove-box items
34 "__ bigger than a breadbox?"
35 NFL event
37 Palm fruit
40 Odor
41 Put on the air
44 Poetic palindrome
46 Ouzo flavoring
48 Bewail
50 Slangy suffix
52 Diehard's cry
54 La __ (Milan landmark)
55 __-burly
56 Church nooks
57 It's forbidden
58 Genesis name
60 Laugh: Fr.
61 "Blame __ the Bossa Nova"
63 Greek vowel

WATER LOG by Gerald R. Ferguson

ACROSS

1 Pistol packer of song
5 "Roger __" (radio phrase)
10 Small weight
14 Midmonth date
15 City on the Allegheny
16 Novelist Jaffe
17 Freckles and speckles
18 Established practice
19 Gabs
20 Part of the US/Canada border
22 Levin's namesakes
23 Happened next
24 Atlanta '96 org.
26 Room for Jekyll
27 Racer Mario
32 Cereal center
36 Capek play
37 Ebro y Orinoco
38 Ike's command: Abbr.
39 Whimper
40 TV spots
41 Midwestern capital
45 Sweet finales
47 Dashed (off)
48 Be obliged to
49 Benedict or Tom
53 Defect
56 Masters' __ Anthology
60 Hurry
61 Chan portrayer
62 Half of a Samoan town
63 Coloratura's piece
64 Bind again
65 Handy abbr.
66 Scout's shelter
67 Sample
68 Farmer's place

DOWN

1 Gnat
2 Bedeck
3 Doles out
4 Onslaughts
5 Aspiring
6 Victor Laszlo's wife
7 Plumbing problem
8 Actor Nicolas
9 "Gangway!"
10 Solid carbon dioxide
11 Crowd sound
12 "Lonely Boy" singer
13 Church service
21 Marsh duck
25 Mork's planet
27 Hoopster Gilmore
28 Illumination gas
29 Undeniable
30 Jethro of rock
31 Miffed
32 Metal fastener
33 Details handler
34 Fling
35 Part of CD
39 Walrus, for one
41 Clinch, with "up"
42 Bulk-mail ritual
43 Nobleman of Spain
44 Actor Jamie
46 "Who cares?"
50 Egg-shaped
51 Legitimate
52 Whimsical
53 Sigma Chi, e.g.
54 Tackle-box item
55 G __ "gnaw"
57 Defendant's answer
58 Morsels for mudders
59 "Step __!" ("Hurry!")

SERENITY by Fred Piscop

ACROSS

1 Beethoven's "Für __"
6 Humorist Sahl
10 Vibraphonist Jackson
14 Filled a hold
15 More than
16 Anthem starter
17 COOL
20 Crocodile Dundee et al.
21 A Mouseketeer
22 On Soc. Sec., maybe
23 Pre-Christmas purchase
25 Driller's deg.
26 Wall St.'s locale
27 El __, TX
29 Aachen "alas"
32 Ronny Howard role
35 Actress Moran
37 Raid
39 CALM
42 Carpet fiber
43 Chinese dollar
44 Past due
45 Porker's pad
46 IOU signer
48 Some 45s
50 "__ been had!"
51 Malevolent
53 JFK's predecessor
56 Arête producer
60 Some spuds
62 COLLECTED
64 Words to Brutus
65 Concerning
66 Rich cake
67 Stinger
68 Nasty look
69 Actor Davis

DOWN

1 "Pomp and Circumstance" penner
2 Lash of oaters
3 That is: Lat.
4 Salty seven
5 Thing
6 Archie's dense pal
7 Egg cells
8 McEntire of country
9 Election-night topics
10 Specks
11 Doesn't exist
12 Café au __
13 Little feller
18 Japanese auto model
19 On __ (intermittently)
24 Gastronome
26 Hud star
28 "Diana" singer
29 Oratorio number
30 "I __ Get Started"
31 __ Park, NY
32 Singer Redding
33 Emily of etiquette
34 __-bitty
36 Abbott & Costello costar
38 Hooters
40 10th-century pope
41 Iroquoian language
47 Destructive insect
49 __ a draw (end up tied)
50 Freeze
52 Spiteful sort
53 Active ones
54 Tooth, in combinations
55 First name in cosmetics
56 Cultivated
57 "__ Smile Be Your Umbrella"
58 Bible book
59 Painter Magritte
61 Med. plans
63 Dr. __ (rap star)

SHAPING UP by Chuck Deodene

ACROSS
1 Indy respite
8 Where zlotys are spent
14 Monument
15 Spur love
16 Tree-planting occasion
17 Calcutta Mother
18 Delta of TV
19 Remains unused
21 __ U.S. Pat. Off.
22 Linguistic suffix
23 With caution
26 Quirks
27 Marxist
28 Salt block
29 Plant with two seed leaves
30 Epic tale
31 Lighter fuel
32 Exercise coach
37 Meeting program
38 Stable baby
39 Alone, to Cicero
40 Bike or van lead-in
41 Hosts, for short
44 Complacent
45 Glossy fabrics
47 Wobble, in rocketry
48 Congressional contributor
49 *Mildred Pierce* author
50 Magna __
52 Having a single layer
54 Sameness
57 Washes clean
58 Old timers
59 Parlor purchase
60 At the beach

DOWN
1 Flip through
2 Genetic
3 Fleeced
4 Scatter about
5 Just a pinch
6 __-Locka, FL
7 Concern of 32 Across
8 Nitpicking
9 Individuals
10 __ *familiaris* (household spirit)
11 United rival
12 Rocket tip
13 Hot-rod racer
14 Scottish game pole
20 Kind
24 George Hamilton's ex
25 Latvian capital
26 South American monkey
29 Twin
30 Creates a lawn
31 Egghead
32 Proof of citizenship
33 Dictator's quality
34 Shimmering
35 Comfy
36 Singer Tennille
40 __ tai (cocktail)
41 Innumerable
42 Range rovers
43 Undulates
45 Final word
46 A multitude
49 Role for Liz
51 Others: Lat.
53 L.A. setting
55 "¿__ pasa, amigo?"
56 Actress Merkel

WESTERN OMELET by Bob Lubbers

ACROSS
1 Light ray
5 Wrestling needs
9 Emily and Wiley
14 Taj Mahal locale
15 Latin I word
16 Bizarre
17 Precipitation
18 Nerve
19 Wood finish
20 Western advanceman
23 Hood's weapon
24 Actress Gardner et al.
25 Tommy's ex
27 Hound dog
30 Cavort
32 "__ live and breathe!"
33 Retrieve, as a trout
35 Labor
38 Vetoes
40 __-tac-toe
41 Desist
42 Vane direction
43 *Remington* __
45 100 yrs.
46 More sacred
48 Gibson of tennis
50 Musically unkeyed
52 Brainstorm
53 Also
54 Western footwear
60 __ nous
62 Ranch helper
63 Flapjack franchise letters
64 Guide the wheel
65 Caruso solo
66 Word form for "China"
67 Wrongful acts
68 Waiter's load
69 Nearly all

DOWN
1 Italian seaport
2 Actor Richard
3 Dry as a desert
4 Crazes
5 Tycoon
6 Pile up
7 Powder base
8 Normandy battle site
9 Part of USPS
10 Not at home
11 Western vehicle
12 Test
13 Actress Berger
21 States
22 Atop
26 Microscopic bug
27 Curse
28 Largest continent
29 Western weapon
30 Airman
31 Paddy crop
34 Diminutive suffix
36 "Oh, that's what you mean!"
37 Horne or Olin
39 British school
41 VIP, for short
43 Missile housing
44 Billie Holiday's sobriquet
47 They tie shoes
49 Lao-tzu's teachings
50 Alamogordo event
51 Lone Ranger's sidekick
52 Ancient Greek region
55 Exclamation of disbelief
56 Roseanne's former surname
57 Buckeye State
58 Oodles
59 Dick and Jane's dog
61 On a pension: Abbr.

127 GROUP THERAPY by Norma Steinberg

ACROSS

1 Film spy Matt
5 Merchandise
10 Animal lovers' org.
14 Mayberry moppet
15 Tolerate
16 Plane or rasp
17 Prejudice
18 Desi's daughter
19 Football linemen
20 Step into the strike zone
23 Menageries
24 Wallach and Whitney
25 Under
28 D'Artagnan ally
31 Jai __
32 Something seen
34 Polynesian finger food
37 Create a defense
40 Used to own
41 Goes in
42 Model Macpherson
43 Conductor's prop
44 In the wink of __
45 Consequently
47 Hosiery shade
49 Annual bash
55 Mini-lake
56 *Atlantic City* director
57 "Up, up and __!"
59 *Picnic* playwright
60 Hunter constellation
61 Leslie Caron film
62 Garden site
63 Easel
64 Pace

DOWN

1 Prefix for goblin
2 Of grand scope
3 Perjurer
4 Era of the dinosaurs
5 Ralph __ Emerson
6 Lies adjacent to
7 Like some desserts
8 Adams or Brickell
9 Ooze
10 Filches
11 Loren's husband
12 Encryptions
13 Pacino and Capp
21 "Awesome!"
22 Hotelier Helmsley
25 *Goldberg Variations* composer
26 Director Kazan
27 Frying substance
28 Pale
29 Section of seats
30 "__ the family?"
32 Jacket opening
33 "Sock __ me!"
34 Gdansk native
35 Just
36 Words of understanding
38 Fewest
39 Top brass
43 Weight
44 Oklahoma city
45 Investor's choice
46 Door pivot
47 Synthetic fiber
48 Invert
50 Managed-care grps.
51 Small missile
52 *Inter* __
53 Simpleton
54 New Haven campus
55 Dessert option
58 Lyricist Harburg

128 CATCH OF THE DAY by Gregory E. Paul

ACROSS

1 Miner's tool
5 Elite group
10 Applaud
14 Traditional teachings
15 Shire of *Rocky*
16 Olympic sled
17 Gone fishing
18 Astrologist Sydney
19 Father of Eros
20 Apprehend
21 Vegas dish?
23 Calms down
25 Map features
26 Spinets
28 Newswoman Sawyer
30 L.A. athlete
31 Small gull
32 Telegram "."
36 Epoch
37 The catch of the day
40 Actress Thurman
41 Prepare salad
43 Atop
44 Deeply felt
46 Blender setting
48 Lessee
49 Moon project
52 Wise ones
53 New Orleans dish
56 Use a calculator
59 Succotash ingredient
60 Studio stand
61 Mr. Green's game
62 "Put a lid __!"
63 White poplar
64 Corridor
65 Hamilton's bills
66 Makes a home
67 At rest

DOWN

1 Blueprint
2 Keokuk's state
3 Baltimore dish
4 *Hazel* cartoonist
5 Pacific spots
6 Writer Janowitz et al.
7 Shem's son
8 Broadcasts
9 Walcott opponent
10 School groups
11 Novelist Alison
12 Intermediary
13 Cancún cash
21 Rolling Rock rival
22 Massachusetts cape
24 United
26 Realtor's map
27 1995 role for Kenneth Branagh
28 Crusoe's creator
29 Waffle or pig follower
31 Paper repairer
33 Deli dish
34 Foreshadowing
35 Divide
38 Dane, e.g.
39 Muralist Rivera
42 Wood strips
45 Wind dir.
47 Einstein's birthplace
48 Waiter's charge
49 Cravat kin
50 Brit's blower
51 Hatch of Utah
52 California fish
54 Comic Kaplan
55 Applications
57 Blunt
58 Marginal mark
61 Psi preceder

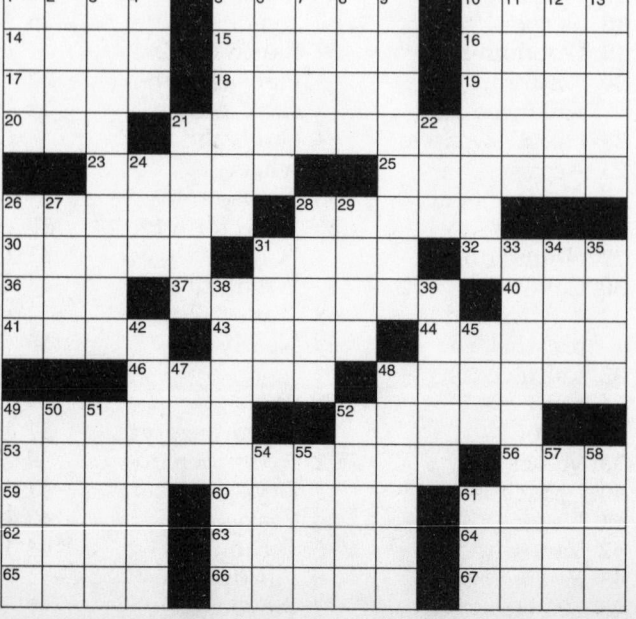

DOWN AND DIRTY by Fred Piscop

ACROSS
1 Stop, at sea
6 "Nothing-but-net" sound
11 Maglie or Mineo
14 Decrees
15 __-surface missile
16 Method
17 Sir, in India
18 Cheap seats
20 Big name in software
22 "Go away!"
23 Bird call
26 Suffolk suffix
28 USAF bigwig
29 "__ want for Christmas . . ."
30 Coffee-and-chat group
33 Nabokov novel
34 Identical
35 "__ bagatelle!"
39 Makes a scene
41 Ant.
42 Used a sordino
43 __ World Turns
44 Speaker of baseball

46 Imbibe, in a way
47 Runner's destination
49 Hawaiian coastal area
50 Ripoff
53 Additional: Abbr.
54 Pencil part
56 Contentious one
58 One drop, roughly
60 No rocket scientist
62 Girl in an Everlys song
66 Writer Harper
67 Brings up
68 Outer, zoologically
69 ". . . __ I saw Elba"
70 Attack
71 Striped stinker

DOWN
1 Circular filler
2 Through

3 Innsbruck interjection
4 Old fogy
5 Verboten
6 Kemo __
7 "Golden Fleece" award presenter
8 Spleen
9 Equilibria
10 Pawn
11 Borg, for one
12 Home-run king
13 Air-freshener brand
19 Big cheese
21 Korean soldiers
23 *Meet John Doe* director
24 Radius neighbors
25 Black or Walker
27 Become involved
31 Taoism founder
32 Engine part
36 Moral nature
37 Come together

38 Mystery award
40 Part of a yen
45 Observed
48 *T.J. Hooker* actor
50 Mercury model
51 Colonial newsman
52 Go along

55 Reacts to yeast
57 Spanish river
59 Part of MIT
61 Some batteries
63 Actor Erwin
64 Scottish John
65 Wapiti

QUICK THINKING by Dean Niles

ACROSS
1 Voodoo spells
6 Good time
10 Crimson rivals
14 Think
15 Forearm bone
16 Hiker's home
17 1993 treaty
18 Actress Patricia
19 Sociologist Hite
20 TV alien
21 Clairvoyance
24 Boor
26 Engraves with acid
27 Grouchy
29 City by a bay
31 Watery meal
32 Robust
33 K-P link
37 Pop-top
38 Endangered cat
41 Euripides drama
42 Winter transport
44 Takes advantage of
45 Bert's buddy

47 Pencil-case item
49 Romantic adventures
50 City on Lake Ontario
53 Writer's rep
54 Dale Arden's love
57 Wool-coat owner
60 Former Soviet press agency
61 On the rocks
62 Sri Lanka language
64 Novel ending
65 And others: Abbr.
66 Novak's one-time partner
67 Exigency
68 Like some losers
69 Thickheaded

DOWN
1 __ Lisa
2 Milky mineral
3 Oil-change place

4 Can. province
5 Conch, e.g.
6 Con game
7 Common spread
8 __ even keel
9 French ill
10 Principled
11 Jamie Lee Curtis' mom
12 Man-moon link
13 Marks to retain
22 Long time
23 Engine additive
25 Pub offering
27 Some NCOs
28 Caspian Sea feeder
29 Come to a point
30 Word of regret
32 Water carrier
34 US missile
35 Film __
36 Small bills
39 Praiseful speeches
40 Mad
43 Prepped the turkey
46 Reagan son

48 "That's gross!"
49 "Long __ and Far Away"
50 Time and again
51 Metamorphic rock
52 Fritter away
53 Mix up

55 Numerical word form
56 Bring up
58 Takes it all
59 Word in an ultimatum
63 "__ Maria"

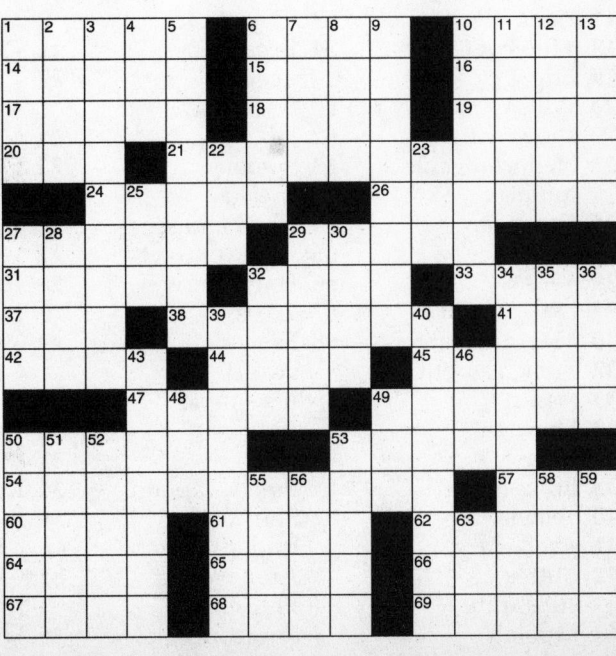

SUITS ME by Rich Norris

ACROSS
1 Charity
5 Not secret
10 Brother of Cain
14 Golfers' props
15 More ashen
16 Cartoonist Walker
17 Playing field
20 Nav. rank
21 Greenish blue
22 Snow bits
23 Fr. holy woman
24 Show remorse
25 France's Mont __
26 Until now
28 "Anything __" (Porter tune)
29 Cut (off)
32 Annoys
34 Enveloping glow
35 Scrooge, e.g.
38 Summer in France
39 Nudge
40 Pathway
41 Rust causer
43 Total
44 H.S. juniors' exam
45 More than enough
49 Hurler Warren
51 Prefix for gram or dermis
52 Suffix for press
53 Load the trunk again
55 Ardor
56 Greek letters
57 Joseph Conrad story
60 Earth: Ger.
61 Walkway material
62 Johnson of *Laugh-In*
63 Pro votes
64 Actress Veronica
65 Hopalong Cassidy portrayer

DOWN
1 Optimally
2 Makeshift shed
3 Goofed (up)
4 Wind dir.
5 Becomes murky
6 Deem important
7 Singer Fitzgerald
8 Eric the __
9 Toys (with)
10 Capital of Jordan
11 Mail-order company
12 Sea eagle
13 Old Ford models
18 Trade
19 Word of woe
25 Not interested
27 Imitated
28 "Understand?"
30 Gold, to Pizarro
31 Fido's foot
33 Lone Star State denizen
34 Old one, in Germany
35 __ *Doubtfire*
36 Marker, for short
37 *The Maltese Falcon* detective
39 Connect, as a chain
41 Wisconsin city
42 Clothes
44 Agreement
46 __ uno
47 Reliable
48 Agreed with
50 Trims the excess
51 Make joyful
53 Actress Perlman
54 Weird
55 Mild cheese
58 Ft. Myers' home
59 Catch, as a felon

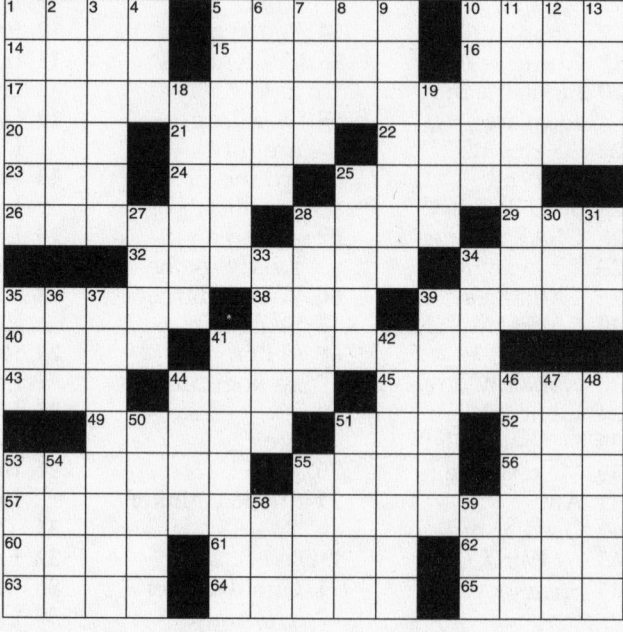

BEASTIE BOYS by Bob Lubbers

ACROSS
1 Taj Mahal site
5 Roe source
9 Upstart
14 Buck Rogers' mentor, Dr. __
15 Relief org.
16 Harden
17 Zone
18 "Too bad!"
19 Edgar __ Poe
20 Wild West showman
23 Hallucinogenic initials
24 European range
25 Yens
27 Do __ (fight)
30 Mexican state
32 French assent
33 Assert
35 Dresden's river
38 Long-limbed
40 Televise
41 Amber, e.g.
42 Butter substitute
43 Moolah
45 Inventor Whitney
46 Turn in
48 Complied with
50 Quarterback Len
52 Bettor's words
53 Classic car
54 Legendary deejay
60 Ascended
62 Jai __
63 Siouan speaker
64 Che's amigo
65 Ink a contract
66 Harvard rival
67 Trials
68 Fencer's sword
69 It's simple

DOWN
1 *Pequod* captain
2 Spiritual leader
3 Atoll barrier
4 PLO chief
5 Surgeon's tool
6 Auras
7 Part of UAR
8 Lucie's dad
9 Theater district
10 Blow up, as a photo: Abbr.
11 WWII admiral
12 Delete
13 __ an ear (listens)
21 Calm
22 Queue
26 Canadian Indian
27 Western tie
28 Fantasy writer Jean
29 1994 Amateur Golfer of the Year
30 Paris divider
31 Monster
34 Den
36 Inclination to anger
37 Oklahoma town
39 Hits the road
41 Spring harbinger
43 Pebbles' pet
44 Lettuce type
47 Dries (off)
49 Delights in
50 Beer category
51 High home
52 Reflection
55 Emit coherent light
56 Toss
57 __ impasse (stuck)
58 Soft drink
59 Retain
61 Collection

133 TO YOUR TASTE by Fred Piscop

ACROSS
1 Casper, for one
6 Da __, Vietnam
10 Highest-rated
14 Oscar de la __
15 Where most people live
16 Role for Shirley
17 Northwestern highway
18 Some vehicles
19 Voyage
20 Fabled fruit
22 Big bag
23 Pittsburgh gridder
24 Cut off
26 Selves
28 __ Rosenkavalier
29 Envelope material
33 Of few words
37 "Whatever __ Wants"
38 Flows slowly
41 Yuletide
42 German autos
44 Noted sitcom couple
46 Summit
48 __ Ifni (Moroccan seaport)
49 Sock-drawer contents
53 Royal homes
58 Told a whopper
59 2/14 word
61 __ the Woods (Sondheim musical)
62 Arcade flub
63 Delegate
64 Wide-eyed
65 __ podrida
66 Parenthetical remark
67 Business partners, at times
68 Smeltery waste
69 Auberjonois et al.

DOWN
1 Tennis surface
2 Ancient serf
3 At the right time
4 Unremitting look
5 Tonsorial woes
6 The Guns of __
7 PDQ
8 Dressed to the __
9 Blotto
10 Diehard's destination?
11 Ballplayer's no-no
12 Strike down
13 Prerecorded
21 Millionaire host
25 Dog doc
27 Looks for
29 Day-__ (fluorescent paint)
30 __-eared (droopy)
31 Pub quaff
32 Vodka drinks
34 Generic defendant
35 Sun Yat-__
36 Golfer Ernie
39 Cost, so to speak
40 Mubarak's predecessor
43 Impresario Hurok
45 Perceive incorrectly
47 Green sauces
49 Alternate identity
50 One of the Fab Four
51 Board, as a bus
52 Hogwash
54 Preterit, e.g.
55 Linda of Alice
56 Chip away at
57 Eye sores
60 Actress Raines

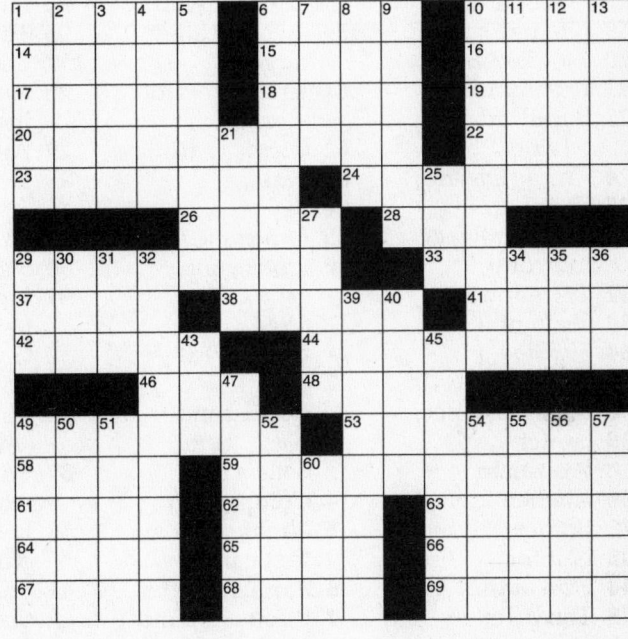

134 3 BY 5'S by Charles Gersch

ACROSS
1 Unkempt
6 Prepare the presents
10 Drain element
14 Faye or Cooper
15 Pants measure
16 Picket Fences town
17 Hardware-store purchases
20 Word form for "strange"
21 __ Jury (Spillane novel)
22 Bit of land
23 Smallest part
25 Main highway
26 Ecstasy actress
29 See 10 Down
31 Squash variety
32 "Your majesty!"
33 Singer Irene
37 Bakery buy
40 Say no to
41 Ship part
42 Avian home
43 Even
44 "__ to grow on!"
45 Clergyman
49 Truffles, e.g.
51 Cast member
52 Confined
53 Cash drawer
57 1995 film, with The
60 Barnum client
61 Peruvian's ancestor
62 Heron's relative
63 Track info
64 Prepares Easter eggs
65 He played Grant

DOWN
1 Tailless feline
2 Nobelist Wiesel
3 Leo, for one
4 Erudite
5 Still
6 Judicial orders
7 Ballpark boundary
8 Tennis great
9 Millie or Socks
10 With 29 Across, custodial account
11 Esther of Good Times
12 Traffic-light color
13 Annoying
18 Münchhausen, for one
19 Charlie Parker's nickname
24 Shoreline flyer
25 Work without __ (take risks)
26 De __ (Marc Connelly character)
27 Soreness
28 Apollo 13's goal
30 Russian river
32 Cage's 1995 costar
33 Those owed
34 Plane-related
35 Showers
36 "Zip-__-Doo-Dah"
38 Running-motor sound
39 Loud sound
43 John Major, for one
44 Lit. collection
45 Cellist Casals
46 Pungent
47 Put up with
48 Lincoln in-laws
50 Fictional Mohican
52 Insignificant
54 Tennis star Lendl
55 What's My __?
56 Villainous look
58 Nod at Sotheby's, perhaps
59 Entertainment conglomerate

135 HIDDEN BIRDS by A. J. Santora

ACROSS
1 "Waterloo" singers
5 Thrash
9 Winter wear
14 Any time now
15 Turner of film
16 Nelligan role
17 Disreputable
19 Niamey's river
20 Monkeyshines
21 Prohibition
23 Bandleader Alvino
24 Comic Olsen
25 Filly, e.g.
27 Acura mileage indicator
32 Turn down
33 Train unit
34 Surplus
35 Urge (on)
36 Mouselike pets
39 Golfer Woosnam
40 Kitchen utensil
42 Bother
43 Not for
44 One of the Three Tenors
48 Cheese dip
49 Swimsuit top
50 Examine closely
52 Mesh
53 Oklahoma Indian
57 *A Town Like __* (Shute novel)
59 Two-pin alley target
61 Underground worker
62 Currier partner
63 Trailing
64 Beeps
65 Flintstone pet
66 Exxon, once

DOWN
1 "__ I cared!"
2 Cher's ex-husband
3 *The __* (1967 Sellers film)
4 Comparison
5 Nightingale's first name
6 Baroness' title
7 Plastic __ Band
8 Clad
9 Boz and Twain
10 Boxing great
11 Wishing undone
12 Low joint
13 Jaunty
18 Edit out
22 I love, to Livy
25 Turned thumbs down
26 *Lois & Clark* heavy
27 Authorized
28 Horticultural activity
29 Patriotic org.
30 Sister of Thalia
31 Indian princess
32 Grape portrayer
36 They're all smiles
37 Witness' response
38 Italian criminologist
41 Prefix for system
43 "__ a day . . ."
45 HST follower
46 Bested
47 S&L offerings
50 Bara persona
51 *London Magazine* essayist
53 Yemeni city
54 "Ah, me!"
55 Catcall
56 Palindromic name
58 Em follower
60 Word form for "egg"

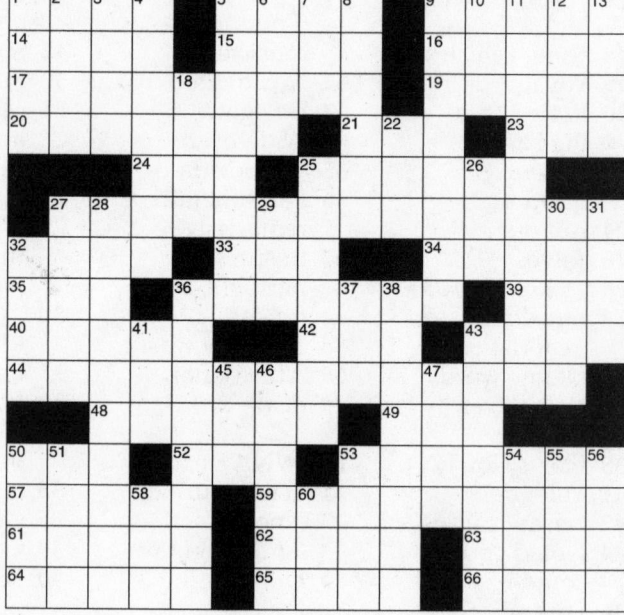

136 HEAVYWEIGHTS by Fred Piscop

ACROSS
1 Covenants
6 Talk like Daffy Duck
10 Party bowlfuls
14 G sharp's alias
15 Director Preminger
16 Singer Guthrie
17 Location
18 Toasty
19 Sweetheart
20 Hallucinations of a sort
23 Arm art
25 Simile center
26 Suburban add-on
27 __ *Town* (Wilder play)
28 Ghost
31 Bad habits
33 *Mmes.*, in Spain
35 Comics cry
36 Spongy ground
37 Doctor's pledge
43 Cuttlefish's defense
44 Buddy
45 Hair maintenance
46 Packing unit
49 Holy book
51 L-P connectors
52 Males
53 Totally
55 Puts forth
57 Far from the truth
61 Salt, chemically
62 Thug
63 The __ Kid (Western hero)
66 Pack (in) tightly
67 Tennis situation
68 Spud
69 Writer Ferber
70 Strong alkalis
71 Slow equines

DOWN
1 Unappetizing food
2 Gridders' grp.
3 Baloney
4 Unspoken
5 Office workers of the past
6 Actor Rob
7 Type style: Abbr.
8 Winning sequence
9 Ostentatious displays
10 "The Aba __ Honeymoon"
11 Peaceful
12 River to the Missouri
13 Guzzlers
21 Fraction of a ruble
22 Devastation
23 Nonsense, to a Brit
24 Word form for "ear"
29 Poet's contraction
30 Giraffelike animal
32 "__ Rhythm"
34 Rotisserie need
36 Soldier's lodging
38 Ryan or Tatum
39 Slot insert
40 Couch parts
41 Dye
42 Medical coverage grps.
46 Likelihood
47 Poster word
48 It's full of garbage
49 __ Mary (drink)
50 Track wager
54 Aboveboard
56 Inventor Howe
58 __ mater
59 Liver: Fr.
60 Landers and Miller
64 Not-so-hot grade
65 Hosp. areas

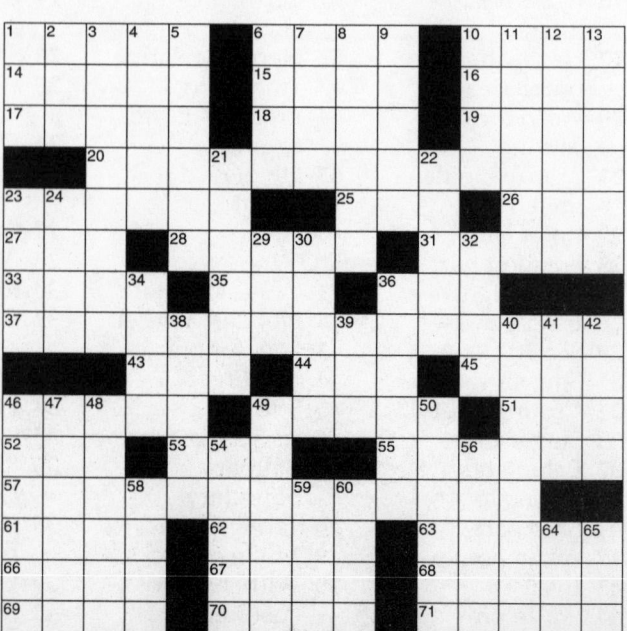

137 SIESTA TIME by Shirley Soloway

ACROSS
1 Pre-Easter season
5 "Oops!"
9 Elec. units
13 Potpourri
14 Beast
15 Rhythm
16 Apollo 11 astronaut
18 Basso Pinza
19 Fruity cooler
20 Boxer Sonny
21 Bible book
22 Promote new undergrowth
24 Biological partitions
26 Crossword fans
29 Penpoint
32 Arizona Indian
35 Shoe width
36 Yours, once
38 Neat as __
39 Handed out cards
42 *A Man __ Woman*
43 Measuring device
45 Clock numeral
46 Antique autos
47 Dispenser candy
48 Steal, in a way
52 Shock
54 African nation
58 Mama's mate
60 Pertaining to milk
63 Hosp. employees
64 Yale students
65 Star shortstop
67 Matures
68 Some tides
69 Ranch mom
70 Letter enclosure: Abbr.
71 Goofs up
72 Son of Seth

DOWN
1 Of a lung area
2 Steer clear of
3 Lawyer Louis
4 From A __
5 Commands: Abbr.
6 Injured
7 Futile
8 Actress Marilu
9 Red as __
10 Stadium level
11 Duet
12 Greek portico
14 Attacked
17 Manager Felipe
23 Express a view
25 CA zone
27 Zuider __
28 Take off
30 __-European (language family)
31 Arthur and Lillie
32 Door fastener
33 Mayberry child
34 Italian food
37 Sultan's pride
40 Columnist Smith
41 States of agitation
44 Tie silk
49 Molly of song
50 Sports jacket
51 Varnish ingredients
53 Out of style
55 Skater Boitano
56 Opening bars
57 Fireplace residue
58 Pod occupants
59 Seaweed
61 Emperor
62 Gratuities
66 Mrs., in Marseilles

138 SCHOOL COLORS by Gregory E. Paul

ACROSS
1 Singer Wooley
5 Stock unit
10 Smile broadly
14 Exude
15 Credo
16 Pasternak heroine
17 Spinner, e.g.
18 Bert's buddy
19 PC operator
20 Syracuse team
22 Golfer Calvin
23 Neighbor of Fla.
24 Scribbles
26 Distrustful
30 Compass part
32 Admiration
34 Neckline style
35 I saw: Lat.
39 Beaver's dad
40 Nautical direction
42 Object of worship
43 Plaintiff
44 Annoy
45 Moon goddess
47 __ Army (links legion)
50 Liability opposite
51 Energize
54 Bruins' #4
56 Heaps
57 Tulane team
63 Musical quality
64 Kicking partner
65 Plow pullers
66 Unique sort
67 Graf nemesis
68 Mixture
69 Capone catcher
70 Rhone feeder
71 Loupe, e.g.

DOWN
1 Fly unaided
2 From 0900 to 1000
3 Poet Pound
4 Existed
5 Gary product
6 Mr. Munster
7 Shakespeare's missus
8 Lapland animal
9 French season
10 Duke team
11 Three-legged stand
12 Alpine ridge
13 __-nest (hoax)
21 "What's Going On" singer
22 Office seeker, for short
25 *Waiting for Lefty* playwright
26 Wallace and Archer
27 Genesis name
28 To be, in Tours
29 Colgate team
31 Draw forth
33 Home of the Black Bears
36 May 15, e.g.
37 Fully cooked
38 "__ a Song Go . . ."
41 Lay's competitor
46 Have coming
48 Campers, for short
49 At all
51 Rocker John
52 Not a soul
53 Bowler's haunt
55 Dodger great
58 Incense
59 New Zealand export
60 Wheel holder
61 Blood vessel
62 NASA chimp
64 "__ live and breathe!"

139   SAY AAH by Dean Niles

ACROSS

1 Loathe
5 Canned meat
9 Kind of fastener
14 Chester __ Arthur
15 "And here it is!"
16 Scarlett's surname
17 Sweet stuff
19 Father Damien's charge
20 Flabbergasts
21 Senator Simon trademark
22 Vitamin-label initials
23 Skirt length
24 Fawn of film
28 Father of 24 Across
30 Salamander
34 Hardens by exposure
36 Like some deals
37 Merriment
38 Sky sight
39 Ohio river
41 Ridicule
42 Ancient Greek city
43 Hem-haw link
44 Wheat component
46 Take it easy
47 Ship mates
49 Board material
50 Cod cousin
52 Not vert.
54 Holds responsible
57 Lives it up
62 Flushed
63 Sweet stuff
64 Expiate, with "for"
65 Roll spread
66 Math course
67 Inclinations
68 Aquatic bird
69 Hops kiln

DOWN

1 Joke response
2 "Dear me!"
3 Sharp on the tongue
4 Word form for "within"
5 Continue in force
6 Bamboo eaters
7 Interjects
8 Merry month
9 Wise one
10 Sweet stuff
11 Absorbed
12 ". . . __ saw Elba"
13 Piece of merchandise
18 Big name in physics
21 Hotshot
23 Term of respect
24 Tour de France entrant
25 Doddering
26 Hushes
27 Aromatic stuff
29 Barter
31 Type type
32 Sociologist Max
33 Really small
35 Clobbers
40 Concerning
41 Ridicule
45 The king, in France
48 Trawler
51 Yellow-fever mosquito
53 Acrylic fiber
54 Gossip
55 Beer choice
56 English river
57 Kid-lit king
58 Until
59 Marsh bird
60 Amer. Anglican
61 Certain NCO
63 Whole bunch

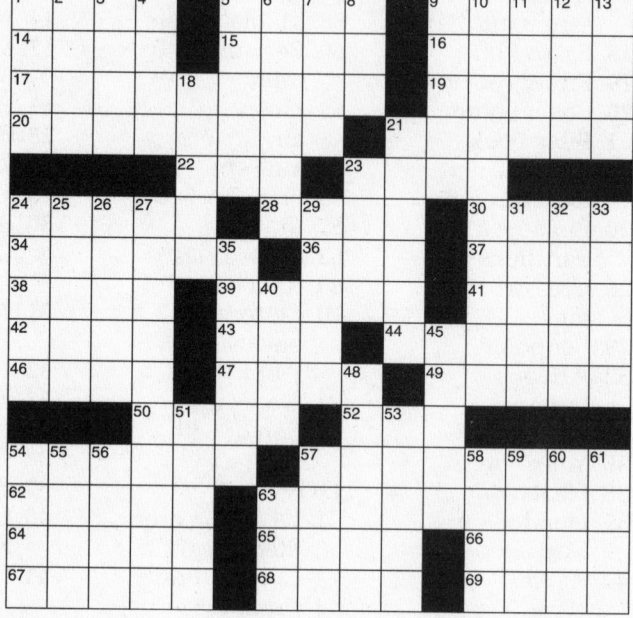

140   CAPITALISM by Bob Lubbers

ACROSS

1 Newsletter
6 Tugboat tow
11 Red or Yellow
14 Pro __
15 Deep concern
16 Shade maker
17 Fourth of July buys?
19 Carpet surface
20 Baked, as eggs
21 Regale
22 Tarzan's neighbor
25 Corn starter
26 Typewriter bar
28 Vainglory
30 Disaster-response grp.
33 Obliterate
34 Inflationary path
36 Up
38 Ship of song?
43 Jim or David
44 Staggered
45 Incited, with "on"
48 Broom mates
50 __ shotgun (protect)
51 Actor McGavin
53 Fall mo.
55 Slalom shape
56 Wallach and Whitney
57 Ethyl, for one
61 CD follower
62 Red Cross inventory?
66 Actor Herbert
67 Perfect
68 Sees
69 UFO crew
70 Scriptures
71 Sting

DOWN

1 Vacationing
2 French king
3 Canine sound
4 Iowa city
5 "Stille __"
6 Pan's creator
7 Winged
8 Marathon, e.g.
9 Ex-srs.
10 River to the North Sea
11 Iroquois tribe
12 Lifts up
13 Current unit
18 Wind-tunnel observation
21 More distant
22 Lhasa __
23 Soft drinks
24 Runner Zátopek
27 "Give __ a Chance"
29 Searchers
31 San __, CA
32 LL.D. holder
35 Dwelling
37 Red course
39 Goal
40 Foe of Bjorn
41 Buntline and Sparks
42 Summer coolers
45 Channel swimmer
46 Foolish one
47 Tale family
49 __ skirt ('50s fashion)
52 Nita of the silents
54 Frog cousins
58 Leopold's partner
59 Furnace fuel
60 Actor Neeson
62 Dinner wear
63 Harper Valley org.
64 Poet's adverb
65 Column finish

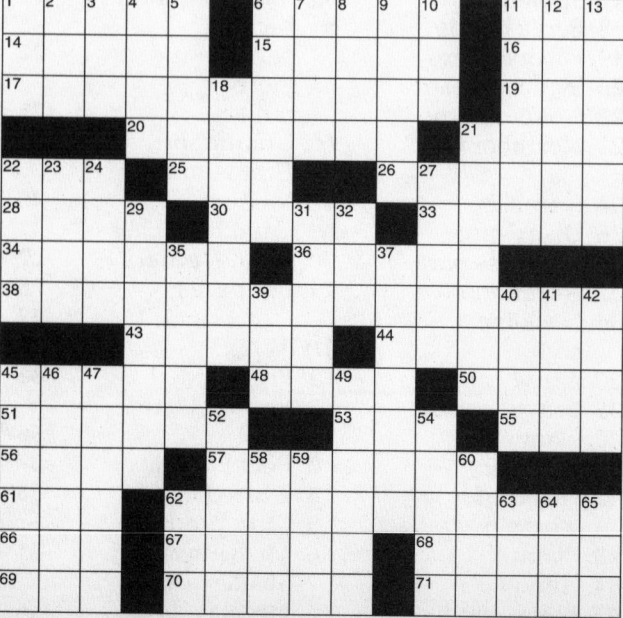

141 THE GAME'S AFOOT by Lee Weaver

ACROSS
1 Wane
4 Headquarters
8 Dip out water
12 Intersection sign
15 Verve
16 Not fooled by
17 One at lunch
18 Donate
19 Face shape
20 Jockey Willie
22 Cash drawer
23 Lucid
24 "Gosh!"
26 Like sateen
30 Gomer of TV
31 Volcano output
32 Hodgepodge
35 Everglades bird
39 Portent
40 Fuss and feathers
41 Redcoat general
42 Bearlike beast
44 Roy Rogers' mate
46 Business-school subj.
47 Cohort
49 Nab
51 Half a Washington city
53 Certain
55 Demonstrate
56 Lifts weights
61 Poi source
62 Vacation option
63 Spiritual advisors
65 Chorus voice
66 Leer at
67 Has to have
68 Necklace component
69 Jury member
70 Match a raise

DOWN
1 Hurricane center
2 Prejudice
3 Sibling of Jo, Amy and Meg
4 Started
5 Share and share __
6 Rescue
7 Pep
8 Rumrunner
9 Blacksmith's shaper
10 Neighbor of France
11 Laze (about)
13 Zodiacal lion
14 Frock or gown
21 Bread spread
25 Flamenco dancer's shout
26 Muck
27 Tibetan monk
28 Cookie cooker
29 Aromatic evergreen
30 Swimming site
33 Godiva, for one
34 Actress Lupino
36 Slalom or regatta
37 Selves
38 Camper's quarters
43 Nothing's alternative
45 "Lend me your __"
48 Portable PC
50 Rule
51 Moby Dick, e.g.
52 Main artery
53 Show pleasure
54 Berth place
55 Wild guess
57 Craving
58 Feel remorse
59 Mine finds
60 Hosiery shade
64 U-turn from NNW

142 MAKING TRACKS by Chuck Deodene

ACROSS
1 Tête-à-tête
5 Painter Chagall
9 Big name in TV talk
14 Fattening
15 On a cruise
16 Mania
17 Tapered sword
18 David Geddes song of 1975
20 Enthusiasm
22 Jethro __ of rock
23 Letters before esses
24 Depth-finding instrument
25 Haphazard
27 Desert beast
29 __ 17 (Holden film)
33 Eschewers of pleasure
36 Frost
37 Illinois city
38 Royal headband
40 French friends
41 "Call it in the air" event
43 Tranquillity
46 Gut feeling
47 Peabrain
49 Blood vessel
53 __ Lingus
56 Fraud
57 Strengthen by tempering
58 1959 Godard film
61 Hammerhead's kin
62 Bring together
63 Faucet problem
64 Gulf of __ (Arabian Sea arm)
65 Copier chemical
66 Dory propellers
67 Pacific goose

DOWN
1 Salad green
2 Zoo heavyweight
3 __ the hole (secret weapon)
4 Jack Jones song of '65
5 Trade center
6 Tempe school: Abbr.
7 Hertz offerings
8 Louisiana cooking style
9 Spotted cat
10 Be too inquisitive
11 __ avis
12 Sky color, in Paris
13 They're fowl
19 Delta 88 maker
21 Angry
25 VCR button
26 '76 Hoffman thriller
28 Cambridge sch.
30 Italian resort
31 Singer Ed
32 Precious stones
33 Not quite shut
34 A number of
35 Remove, as a coupon
38 Uproar
39 Like Cuzco ruins
41 Fantastic dream
42 Unconscious
44 Jane, to Peter
45 Carve in stone
48 Ralph __ Emerson
50 *The Cloister and the Hearth* author
51 Occupied, as a seat
52 Solo
53 Share a border
54 Cube maker Rubik
55 Harness part
57 Nile reptiles
59 Consumed
60 Dubbed title

PUNISHING by Dean Niles

ACROSS
1 First name on jeans
5 Arp's genre
9 Manicotti, e.g.
14 Minute particle
15 Oodles
16 *Laugh-In* name
17 Very sharp
19 Muse of poetry
20 The Big Apple: Abbr.
21 "This __ joke!"
22 __ down the hatches
23 Contemptible one
25 __ *in the Hat*
27 Hodges or Gerard
28 "Put a lid on it!"
29 Curve shape
32 Actress Hayes
35 *Jane* __
36 Guitar device
37 Juice fruits
39 Footrest
41 History

42 "Put __ writing!"
44 Rash
45 Boy or girl ending
46 Genesis site
47 Computer monitor: Abbr.
48 Valentine exchangers
50 Pastoral
54 Chalkboard tool
56 Takes advantage
58 Latin I verb
59 Screened again
60 Befuddled
62 Dial device
63 Not colorful
64 Victorian prime minister
65 Expedite
66 The A in B.A.
67 Paris airport

DOWN
1 Grassy areas
2 Gas additive
3 Tenor or bass

4 Mischievous sprite
5 Distressed one of old films
6 Shepard of NASA
7 Wit Parker
8 ABA member
9 Evangelize
10 Heart line
11 Special forces
12 London gallery
13 Bartlett's abbr.
18 Fabric strengthener
22 Hem in
24 FBI guy
26 A Great Lake
30 Tiff
31 Walkman maker
32 Western Indian
33 Time intervals
34 Cowboy hero
35 Acid + alcohol result
36 Paint layers

38 Diving duck
40 Songbird
43 Narrow-minded
46 Made smooth
47 Fancy pancakes
49 Siouan language
51 Slim down

52 Force on
53 With modesty
54 Work units
55 Gather the crop
57 Shaker contents
60 Warm spot
61 Mil. address

CLUMSY by Bob Lubbers

ACROSS
1 Tease
4 Dollop
7 Alan of *M*A*S*H*
11 Pitcher's stat
12 Fruit trees
16 Boxer Spinks
17 Class outings
19 Deposed Ugandan
20 Soup alternative
21 Last bits
23 Single
24 Plead
26 __ *Even With Dad* (1994 film)
28 Drain
31 Scale pair
33 Sturm __ Drang
34 Winter fall
37 Barber's gear
40 *The Numerals* painter
41 Belgian Congo, once
43 Acting part

44 Factions
46 Wood smoother
48 With it
49 True
50 Tippler
51 Pension payee
54 __ *culpa*
56 Guitarist Montgomery
57 Japanese-American
59 Mule kin
63 Felled
65 Doesn't succeed
67 Bard's river
68 Wrestle
69 Estuary
70 Cat sound
71 Tote (up)
72 Sawbuck

DOWN
1 NBA officials
2 Siepi solo
3 Highlander
4 Shakes
5 Model Carol

6 Hoopster Larry
7 __ carte
8 Candy bits
9 "Nothing __!"
10 Baxter or Boleyn
13 Stately dances?
14 Dueling sword
15 Certain noncom: Abbr.
18 Igor's domain
22 Erwin et al.
25 Saxophonist Stan
27 Mural starter
28 __ *Gotta Have It* (Lee film)
29 Bern's river
30 Acts amorously
32 Emu cousins
35 "__ all hang out!"
36 Sea eagle
38 Butter sub
39 Jaunty
42 Balled cheese

45 Make yarn
47 Glad
51 Actor Christopher
52 Fissure
53 Jacob's brother
55 Fire residue
56 "Kapow!"

58 Rick's love
60 Type
61 Albany-to-Buffalo canal
62 Comic Freberg
64 Wind dir.
66 Vended: Abbr.

145 HERO WORSHIP by Randall J. Hartman

ACROSS

1 Former spouses
5 Sudan neighbor
9 Leaf pores
14 Bullets, e.g.
15 Munich mister
16 Atoll material
17 LOOK!
19 Embryonic sacs
20 *Bambi* aunt
21 Grocery scanning: Abbr.
22 Begin, for one
24 Move slowly
26 Dine
27 Give too much to, perhaps
29 UP IN THE SKY!
34 Violin virtuoso
35 Skirt length
36 Long, long time
37 IT'S A BIRD!
41 I: Lat.
42 Picnic pests
43 Asian woods
44 IT'S A PLANE!
47 *The 39 __*
48 Mining product
49 Middle East currency
51 Get ready
55 Mythical bird
56 Faux __
59 I, __ (Asimov work)
60 IT'S SUPERMAN!
63 Thoroughly saturate
64 Despise
65 Sicilian spewer
66 Jigger and mizzen
67 Was in debt
68 Clothing

DOWN

1 Comfort
2 Fox cartoon heroes
3 Thompson or Samms
4 Weep
5 Oratory
6 As a result
7 Rainbow shape
8 *Vier* minus *eins*
9 Nile beetle
10 Marinara need
11 English Channel feeder
12 Daily delivery
13 Jai __
18 Enticing
23 Font feature
24 Reactor part
25 __ Desert, AZ
27 Jurassic word form
28 *Evita* surname
30 Midmonth day
31 Sum up
32 English-muffin parts
33 Austrian river
34 Product detail
35 Opinion
38 Not as common
39 Sic
40 Nasty look
45 Weak excuse
46 Pounds the pulpit
47 Made noise, in a way
50 Seeing red
51 Proper companion
52 Capital of *Italia*
53 Wanes
54 It may be off the wall
56 Sampras or Rose
57 __ *Karenina*
58 Betelgeuse, e.g.
61 Math rule
62 Frat-party need

146 BED TIME by Bob Lubbers

ACROSS

1 Frolic
5 Volcano flow
9 Prefix for "within"
14 Moa cousin
15 "Oh, sure!"
16 Water duct
17 Top rating
18 Quarterback Starr
19 Dominican Republic neighbor
20 Tennis boo-boo
23 DC lobby
24 Bouncy melody
25 Singer Sheena
27 Fix a shoe
30 Page size
32 Actor Wallach
33 Approximately
35 Filled with fear
38 Script entries
40 God: Lat.
41 Mediterranean island
42 Safecracker
43 Afternoon nap
45 Bled, as dye
46 Triangular sail
48 Loosens forcibly
50 "That's water over __"
52 Uncountable years
53 NFL official
54 Subantarctic bird
60 In reserve
62 Med. school class
63 *The Thin Man* dog
64 Houston gridder, once
65 Medieval weapon
66 They follow effs
67 Fruit skins
68 Pitcher
69 Humorist Bombeck

DOWN

1 Peruse
2 Melville novel
3 Entrée list
4 Colorado city
5 Defamer
6 Toward the stern
7 Actress Miles
8 Aleutian island
9 Hoffman/ Beatty film
10 Teachers' org.
11 World Trade Center, familiarly
12 Braking rocket
13 Suffix for sect
21 Actresses Kedrova and Lee
22 Conduct
26 Headliner
27 Count (on)
28 Writer Wiesel
29 Narrow march formation
30 Elizabeth, e.g.
31 Spanish ones
34 Garfield's pal
36 State: Fr.
37 Lairs
39 Old oath
41 Leslie of *Gigi*
43 Big rig
44 Audio-speaker feature
47 They'll bet
49 Hire
50 Scout group
51 Skater Sonja
52 Quickly
55 Title
56 Chew on, with "at"
57 Employer
58 Gossip tidbit
59 *Discovery* grp.
61 Cartoon unit

FRIGHTFUL by Diane C. Baldwin

ACROSS
1 Snaillike
5 Computer message
10 Burn slightly
14 __ colada
15 Heavenly food
16 The __ Ranger
17 Waker-upper
19 Assns.
20 Ode to joy
21 Menu item
23 In the know
26 For each
27 Lock opening
28 Is of use
30 Life's work
31 Twist or frug
32 Usual routine
33 Conciliatory bribe
36 Adams or Brickell
37 Scamp
38 Bangkok native
39 Part of a min.
40 Ward off
41 Bullwinkle, e.g.
42 Theodore Cleaver
44 Cat, often
45 Dove (in)
47 Auction action
48 Draft org.
49 Roadside eyesore
50 Unbroken
52 Against
53 Cornfield protectors
58 Composer Stravinsky
59 Boring tool
60 Opera highlight
61 Not any
62 Clues of news
63 Fellow

DOWN
1 Fitness center
2 __ Abner
3 "__ Clear Day . . ."
4 Buckle
5 Roast hosts
6 Of the cheek
7 Shortly
8 Corp. name ender
9 Sight from Buffalo
10 Accouter
11 Scary films
12 Play backer
13 Attend again
18 "__ Leaf Rag"
22 Yeltsin turndown
23 Mythical underworld
24 Get away from
25 Alarm activator
27 Afghani capital
29 Drink cooler
30 Basketball player
32 Expected
34 Desert spots
35 Ships' landing places
37 Turnaround
38 Also
40 Violent anger
41 Army corpsman
43 Complete
44 Long-distance runners
45 Without frills
46 Special vocabulary
47 Not amused
50 Epic tale
51 Bummer
54 Pool tool
55 Unrefined metal
56 Come out on top
57 Waited

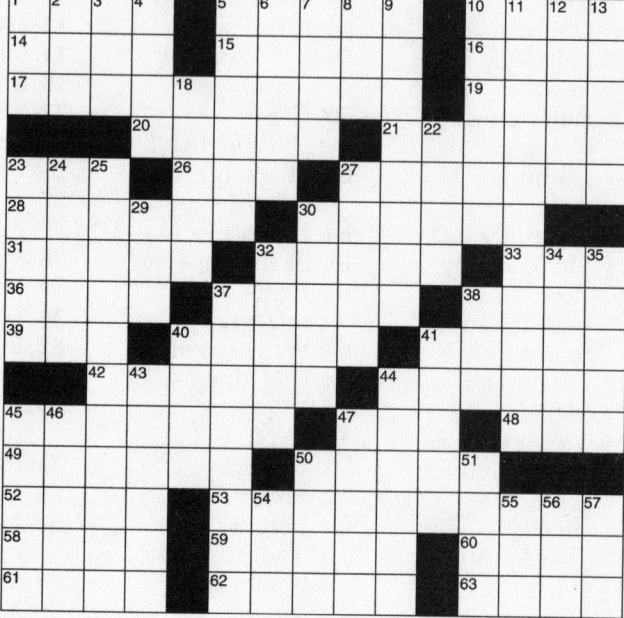

TRUE COLORS by Dean Niles

ACROSS
1 Acreage
5 Wine valley
9 "Arrivederci, __"
13 Sore spot
14 Straws in the wind
16 Vice
17 "Take __ leave it!"
18 Coffee choice
19 Pre-Easter season
20 Hypocritical principle
23 Nightwear
24 __-Mex cuisine
25 Songlike passage
29 Fortune-teller
31 Bake-sale org.
34 Seed pod
35 Great period for business
38 "Deutschland über __"
40 Table part
41 Tall tales
42 Patriotic songs
45 Corporate symbol
46 Rugrat
47 Wing-shaped
48 Hotel name
50 Thimbleful
51 Singing syllable
52 World Series participants
60 __ mater
61 Physicist Marie
62 Kerrigan leap
63 Hairdo
64 Smart __ (wise guy)
65 Actress Lollobrigida
66 Caesarean query
67 Sediment
68 Put away

DOWN
1 Set down
2 Word form for "eight"
3 You, once
4 Certain Slav
5 Rhinoplasty
6 Put together
7 Confined
8 "Diana" singer
9 Take five
10 Concluded
11 Pay attention to
12 Model Carol
15 South Carolina river
21 Pre-CD purchases
22 Irish county seat
25 To the rear, nautically
26 Norse chieftain
27 __ ease (awkward)
28 Designer Cassini
29 Scornful look
30 B&O job
31 '92 candidate
32 Dramatic dance
33 Fiery crime
36 Thomas __ Edison
37 "__ come back now!"
39 Rustic fellow
43 Variety of wool
44 Expresses horror
49 Oddjob's creator
50 Big mess
51 Think __ about (reconsider)
52 Garden area
53 Send forth
54 __ and void
55 Family chart
56 Keeps on one's case
57 Stadium sign
58 Gambling town
59 Deli dish
60 Hotshot aviator

VOCABULARY BUILDER by Norma Steinberg

ACROSS

1 Eye covers
5 Dred Scott, e.g.
10 Bandstand equipment
14 *The King* __
15 Indian spice
16 Yarn
17 Patient's status
20 Chinese sauce
21 United, in France
22 Bird house
23 Club offering?
24 Mamie's predecessor
26 In any way
29 Nautical
33 Poet Teasdale
34 Worries
35 John __ Passos
36 Let one's hair down
40 Geologic period
41 Broadway lights
42 Swiss artist
43 Stocking style
45 Takes five
46 Adjutant
47 Oolong et al.
49 Colonial Quaker
51 Long skirt
52 Buscaglia or Gorcey
55 Protest formally
59 Sheriff Taylor's boy
60 Configuration
61 Matthew's former name
62 Suds
63 Flower part
64 Fellows

DOWN

1 Annie Laurie, for one
2 Long-division word
3 6/6/44
4 Bro or sis
5 Emotional confrontation
6 Desi's daughter
7 Famous cookie maker
8 Sportscaster Scully
9 Movie's last word
10 Warrant
11 "__ oui!"
12 Story line
13 Hatch or Boxer: Abbr.
18 Eye of the storm
19 Stick to one's guns
23 Word before hand or rags
24 Points
25 ". . . __ saw Elba"
26 Long-eared equines
27 California/Nevada lake
28 Madison Square Garden, e.g.
29 Water carriers
30 Role models
31 Contemporary of Degas
32 Curvy letters
34 Picked out
37 Skate style
38 Prerequisite
39 Turner and Eisenhower
44 "Away in a __"
45 Racetrack fence
47 Buccaneers' home
48 Kick out
49 Karol Wojtyla's title
50 Mrs. Ernie Kovacs
51 Castle protector
52 Stead
53 Covetousness
54 Singer Redding
55 Toss
56 Snake
57 Fidel's lieutenant
58 HS math

SOUND REMEDIES by Cathy Millhauser

ACROSS

1 Elegance
6 Jazz accompaniment
10 Actress Corday
14 Outer ear
15 Hurricane of '95
16 Karras of football
17 Cockeyed
18 Dunce cap, e.g.
19 Wheels of fortune?
20 How the aspirin company led a girl astray
23 Gung-ho interest
24 *Awake and Sing* playwright
25 Realm
28 Computer "fail" alternative
31 Chop cut
32 Saying
33 Bradley and Ames
36 How Mrs. Franklin helped in her husband's workshop
40 Balaam's beast
41 Essential
42 __-day (vitamin dose)
43 Evil personified
44 Site for Gorcey and Hall
46 Types
49 Skipper, for short
50 Why the decongestant company got government funds
56 Actor Holliman
57 Scoff
58 Mideast emirate
60 Loyal
61 Comic Johnson
62 Extremist
63 Navajo painting medium
64 Brief holiday?
65 Imperative on a button

DOWN

1 Books pro: Abbr.
2 Table contents
3 Egyptian cross
4 Allergy symptom
5 Lumberman
6 Sung
7 Slithering critter
8 Mare hair
9 Appeal
10 Affliction
11 Albee girl
12 Bill verb
13 Neural appendages
21 Fannie __
22 Bellini opera
25 Designer Schiaparelli
26 Hardness-scale name
27 Diner desserts
28 Meir follower
29 CFO, e.g.
30 Badge metal
32 Southwest feature
33 Sea eagle
34 Beautician's role
35 Do in
37 Disconcert
38 Distillery tank
39 Ruination
43 Molded
44 Acting up
45 Not lucid
46 Leaves in
47 Tara belle
48 *Peanuts* character
49 Restoratives
51 Trojan War hero
52 Skin, in suffixes
53 Botanical bristle
54 Leather finish
55 *Jeanne* __
59 Templeton in *Charlotte's Web*

151 ANTE UP by Bob Lubbers

ACROSS
1 The two
5 Small bite
8 Barter
13 Creme cookie
14 __ Alto, CA
15 Sponsorship
16 Beige
17 "Who __?" (knock response)
18 Limas and soys
19 Rant and rave
22 "__, Brute?"
23 Hockey great Bobby
24 Flightless bird
27 Texaco rival
30 __ worse than death
32 German surname starter
33 Navigation aid
34 Weather-map line
36 Seed covering
37 Wager
38 Theater grp.
39 Landed, as a trout
42 Slammin' Sammy
43 Traveler's stop
44 Actress Radner
46 Confound
47 Army bunk
48 Hair goo
49 Jacob's wife
51 Cruise game
56 Make happy
59 Hurler Hershiser
60 Waikiki party
61 Radio and TV
62 Camera eye
63 Faucet fault
64 Cutlass or épée
65 __ Moines, IA
66 Rational

DOWN
1 Afrikaner
2 Killer whale
3 Garr or Hatcher
4 Doctor's visit
5 New Hampshire city
6 Nastase of tennis
7 Braised beef
8 Type of stool
9 Atoll barrier
10 Turkish official
11 Racket
12 Double curve
14 Brad of *Seven*
20 British prep school
21 "__ take arms against a sea of troubles": Shak.
24 Tied (up)
25 Human
26 Sloppy, like a bed
27 Visigoth king
28 Actress Rita
29 East Asia
31 Devil
35 Climber's grips
37 Wallet
40 Intellectual
41 God: Fr.
42 Swedish car
45 Funt and Drury
50 Morays
51 Agitate
52 Set loose
53 Ambiance
54 April forecast
55 Fool
56 El followers
57 Ayres or Wallace
58 Fuss

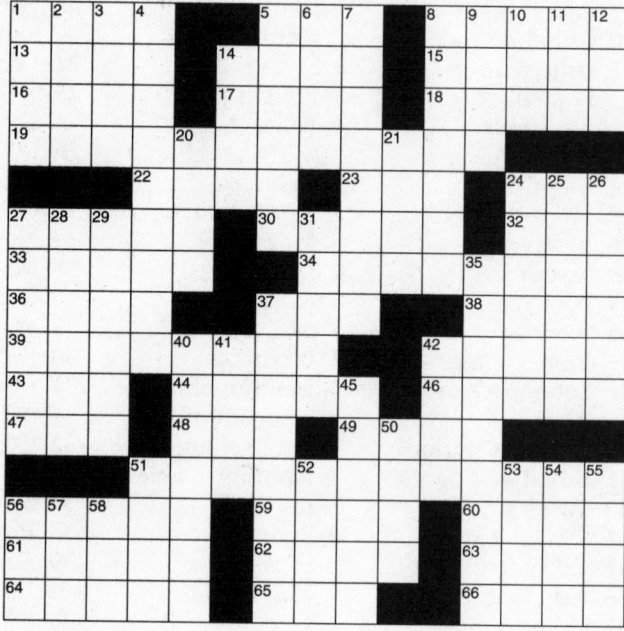

152 LET'S FACE IT by Lee Weaver

ACROSS
1 Stinging insect
5 Shoulder covering
10 __ up (finished)
14 Canyon effect
15 *M*A*S*H* setting
16 *Jane* __ (Brontë book)
17 Intimidated by a bully
19 Uncluttered
20 Comprehend
21 Out of kilter
22 Loses vitality
24 Winter vehicle
25 Sip loudly
26 Hesitate
29 Edinburgh native
30 Mrs. Perón
33 Other name
34 Lasting impressions
35 Silent assent
36 Imitate
37 Beagle or basset
38 Hung on to
39 Naval rank: Abbr.
40 Passed out the cards
41 Blacksmith's furnace
42 Shirt shape
43 Rank above viscount
44 Salad type
45 Enjoys a book
47 Dull sound
48 Reno's locale
50 Bearing
51 Kimono sash
54 Go offstage
55 Indulged in idle gossip
58 Kitchen spice
59 Door part
60 Alternatively
61 Augury
62 Trimmed the lawn
63 Arizona city

DOWN
1 Spider's creations
2 *God's Little* __
3 Foot covering
4 "Wham!" relative
5 Shish kebab need
6 Accumulation
7 Pretentious
8 Like Willie Winkie
9 Rent collector
10 Spanish gent
11 Surprising bits of news
12 Decorate a gift
13 Knicks' rivals
18 Hay units
23 Wagon-wheel paths
24 Remain
25 Meager
26 Aspect
27 Unaccompanied
28 Insincere expression of loyalty
29 Light racing boat
31 Russian river
32 Viper
34 Flies like an eagle
37 Aspirin target
38 Worked in the garden
40 __ duck (goner)
41 Regional animals
44 Masticated
46 Gone from the plate
47 Hint of tint
48 *Nautilus* captain
49 Test
50 Chinese dynasty
51 Leer at
52 Mrs. Truman
53 Concept
56 Stashed away
57 Opal, e.g.

FOWL PLAY by Rich Norris

ACROSS
1 Track circuits
5 Rainbows
9 Aug. and Sept.
12 Thick-pile carpets
14 Letter opener
15 Kick
16 Sign of fear
18 Vicinity
19 Pop's bro
20 Polite refusal
21 Knight wear
22 Coll. hoops tourney
23 Easy mark
25 North Atlantic islands
27 Greek markets
28 Hospital supplies
29 Ventriloquist Lewis
32 Farm enclosure
33 Harassed, in a way
37 __ gratia artis
40 Stadium sounds

41 "Fernando" singing group
45 Employ, as an attorney
47 Morality tales
49 Trifling amount
53 Gore and Capp
54 Sword parts
55 Did a maintenance chore
56 OSS successor
57 Perry's creator
58 Habit-breaking method
60 Rex or Donna
61 "That's clear!"
62 Complaint
63 Lith., once
64 Pre-1959 Hawaii: Abbr.
65 Barney's pal

DOWN
1 Inlets
2 Worry (about)
3 Exam overseer

4 Airline to Stockholm
5 Scorched
6 Send the check
7 Isle in Naples Bay
8 Grads-to-be: Abbr.
9 Speaks low
10 Ball game variant
11 Ringo's real last name
13 Meaning
15 TV announcer Don
17 Wood: Fr.
21 Longhorn rival
24 Stoolie, in Sussex
26 Stadium sound
29 Sauna locale
30 That girl
31 Cooling appliances: Abbr.
34 Estrada and Satie
35 Not any
36 Apply lightly

37 Cupid et al.
38 Employs again
39 Meara's partner
42 More soiled
43 Accept as truth
44 Analyzed, as ore
46 Pretended

47 Stocking fillers
48 Make sense
50 Lasso end
51 Secretary, at times
52 Church figure
58 Townsman, for short
59 Ump's kin

LONG QUINTET by Mary Brindamour

ACROSS
1 __ Beach, FL
5 Insecticides: Abbr.
9 Fashion magazine
13 Enthusiasm
14 Political power
15 Null's partner
16 Oriole's home
17 Small egg
18 Writer Bombeck
19 Quixote's quest
22 Butter quantity
23 Dykstra or Kravitz
24 Flowering plant
27 DDE's opponent
28 Regarding
32 Coral deposit
33 In the past
34 Molecular relative
35 One of a Latin trio
36 __ Haute, IN
38 Marry, for some
39 Golf club

41 Postal Creed word
42 Epithet for Athena
43 Facial contortion
44 NASA assent
45 Not active
46 Dieter's concern
48 Embellish
49 Endorse, in a way
56 Bear's cave
57 Religious worshipers
58 Runner's goal
59 Vocal
60 Sea eagles
61 Sicilian spouter
62 Work monotonously
63 M.B.A. and Ph.D.
64 Finger tip

DOWN
1 Latin I word
2 Basic: Abbr.
3 Coarse file

4 Overjoyed
5 556, in old Rome
6 Gambler's choice
7 Veil materials
8 Dutch painter
9 Sporadically
10 Traditional knowledge
11 Peruvian capital
12 Party cheese
14 Market price
20 Kenny G's instrument
21 Genetic codes: Abbr.
24 Baby buggies
25 Virile type
26 Consumer's option
27 ID information
29 Novelist Zola
30 At no time
31 Something special
33 Took sustenance
34 Comparative suffix

37 Korean soldier
40 Mideast country
44 Looking intently
45 Altar response
47 Twiddled one's thumbs
48 Carter and Vanderbilt

49 Hog feed
50 Hoopster Monroe
51 Luigi's farewell
52 Parisian summers
53 Little bit
54 Atlanta arena
55 Actress Patricia

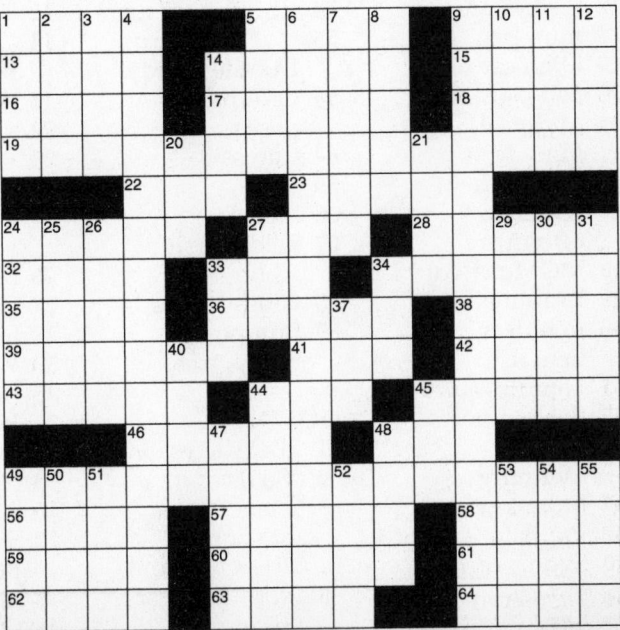

MIDDLING by Dean Niles

ACROSS

1 Christmas figures
5 Come to terms
10 Health retreats
14 '60s NASA name
15 Rove about
16 Pinball boo-boo
17 CAROL
19 Informed about
20 Baserunner's coup
21 Unorthodox
23 Class-standing stat.
25 Earth tone
26 BUTLER
33 Liver complement
34 Director Preminger
35 Network
38 Give the go-ahead
39 Melting snow
41 Boat dock
42 Turk. neighbor
43 Vegan's no-no
44 Short-story master
46 WALDO
48 *60 Minutes* reporter
51 Eliminated, in a way
52 Railroad freebie
56 Enthusiasm
61 Horse breed
62 BERNARD
64 Gambling town
65 Act to excess
66 Farmer's environs
67 Wyo. neighbor
68 Good thinking
69 Lemon and lime treats

DOWN

1 Some mil. men
2 Zillions
3 "What's Going On" singer
4 South American Indian
5 Mil. address
6 Dancer Martha
7 Fixed procedure
8 Jug
9 "Or __!"
10 Impassive ones
11 Bit of salt
12 Religious site
13 Purloined
18 __ Marbles
22 Dorothy's dog
24 Bunch
26 Curries favor with
27 Pitch black
28 Perjurer
29 Actress Myrna
30 Kid
31 *X-Files* subjects
32 Receiving company
35 Takes the pot
36 Architect Saarinen
37 __ Mawr
40 Santa's perch
41 Part of MPG
43 Soda-shop offering
45 Equivocate
46 African antelope
47 Wields
48 *Les Miz* song
49 Pooped
50 Range name
53 Matures
54 "I've Gotta __"
55 Diving flier
57 Meat-grading org.
58 Slough off
59 Yarn
60 Night navigators
63 __-whiz (wondrous)

SUITE TALK by Bob Lubbers

ACROSS

1 Patriot Nathan
5 FDR veep John __ Garner
10 XXV x X
13 "I __ return"
15 Yale or Root
16 __ polloi
17 Restaurant mingler
19 High card
20 Self-esteem
21 Mythical hunter
23 Predicaments
27 La Scala offerings
28 MGM mascot
29 Examination
30 Reindeer herder
31 Flightless bird
32 Belgian port
34 Singer McEntire
37 More kind
39 Prefix for center
40 Sophia of *Two Women*
41 Grey
42 Fix a sandal
44 Pose
45 Bosc or Bartlett
47 "Oh, sure!"
48 Single
49 Scoffs at
51 Mesh material
53 Untrue
54 Rev, as a motor
55 "__ Yankee Doodle Dandy"
56 Grounded pilots
64 Caress
65 "Doe, __ . . ."
66 Weird
67 Sold-out sign: Abbr.
68 Grassy spreads
69 Bumper bump

DOWN

1 FDR successor
2 "So *that's* it!"
3 Science room, for short
4 *Oklahoma!* aunt
5 Word form for "recent"
6 Swiss peak
7 __ in the bud
8 Fidel's pal
9 A moon of Jupiter
10 Committee head
11 Hot chocolate
12 Property claims
14 One who bequeaths
18 Aspirations
22 Printer's copy
23 Big rigs
24 TV junkie
25 Cosmetician Lauder
26 Substitutes (for)
27 Passé
28 Singer Horne
33 Weeper of myth
35 Existence
36 Penny-__ (minor)
38 Starers
40 Salad bed
42 Short Line and B&O
43 Release
46 Of an electrode
49 Quick cuts
50 Up-and-__ (promising one)
52 Signed, slangily
57 Writer LeShan
58 Use a needle and thread
59 Barbie's beau
60 Next year's seniors: Abbr.
61 Before, poetically
62 Yang's partner
63 Tennis unit

157 IN THE MIDDLE by Elizabeth C. Gorski

ACROSS
1 H.S. exam
5 Workmen's __
9 Vowel sound
14 Police calls: Abbr.
15 Confirm
16 Contend
17 Floppy __
18 Billy goat or tomcat
19 Poker ploy
20 E.T.'s transport
21 Hearty ho-hos
23 Social event
25 Enervates
26 Darted
29 Seesaw
33 Destined
35 __ Mongolia
37 News org.
38 Haley or Trebek
39 Carrier
40 "Yes to that!"
41 Distress
42 Kirsten of *Little Women*
43 Clocked
44 President Mandela

46 Birthday frequency
48 Monogram part: Abbr.
50 Tootsie portrayer
53 Overeater's complaint
58 One for Carmen
59 Small: Fr.
60 Land mass
61 251 in old Rome
62 Writer Zola
63 At hand
64 Instruments for Tiny Tim
65 Checked out the joint
66 Willing
67 Spanish direction

DOWN
1 Italian city
2 Spruce (up)
3 Top-selling workout video
4 "Shame on you!"

5 Tourist's takealong
6 Like Bush's office
7 Pell-__ (disorderly)
8 Hunts, with "on"
9 Driver's winter need
10 Contract unit
11 Former Secretary of State
12 Hope
13 Singer Ed
21 Macaw or thrush
22 Not now
24 Top
27 Common lunch hour
28 Brave
30 Diet alternatives
31 Dueler's foil
32 Fruit skin
33 Young deer
34 Medicinal plant
36 Head: Fr.
39 Loose-fitting garment

40 Is unwell
42 Gave (to)
43 Loyal
45 "Sharp as a tack," e.g.
47 Cling (to)
49 Object
51 Small bay

52 Loud sounds
53 Architect's guideline
54 Musical motif
55 Elevator man
56 On the briny
57 Chowder base
61 Pool stick

158 MATCHING PAIRS by Thomas W. Schier

ACROSS
1 Mosque figure
5 Receive enthusiastically
10 Arp's style
14 Sitar music
15 __ acid (organic compound)
16 North Carolina university
17 Children's teaching innovator
20 Stradivari's teacher
21 Carry
22 Top 40 song
23 Cinema canine
26 Cornell locale
28 Fifth Dimension singer
33 Word form for "outer"
34 __ *Arden*
35 Swedish inventor
39 School book
41 Fouled up

43 Surreal artist
44 So far
46 Slugger Hank
48 Squealer
49 Yankees' #7
52 Wrist-related
55 Fifth-century pope
56 Mature
57 Narrow inlets
60 Fibber of old radio
64 *Law & Order* actor
68 *The Time Machine* people
69 Pacific island
70 Green land
71 Give for a bit
72 Detroit player
73 Imitated

DOWN
1 __ *la Douce*
2 Sir's counterpart
3 Taj Mahal city
4 Rum drink
5 On the __ (fleeing)

6 I love: Lat.
7 Quaff quantity
8 "For __ us a child . . ."
9 Of verse
10 __ Plaines, IL
11 Ho's hello
12 Column type
13 Singer Baker
18 Usher's beat
19 Attack
24 Actress Daly
25 Eskimo parka
27 Parka adjunct
28 "I never __ man I . . ."
29 Hatchets
30 Theater name
31 Singer Carmen
32 Ladd or Tiegs
36 Homer's kid
37 Mideast airline
38 Lo-fat
40 Office fill-in
42 Rotunda topper
45 Pageant prop
47 Wynonna's mom

50 Customer
51 Ancient Asia Minor city
52 Bumpy beast
53 Like gymnasts
54 Spy work, for short
58 Jai __

59 Self-satisfied
61 Stagehand
62 French 101 verb
63 Looked at
65 Laid low
66 Boxcar cargo
67 Capek drama

ACROSS

1 Entranced
5 Big name in insurance
10 __ mecum (handbook)
14 Czech river
15 Essays
16 Seed cover
17 1984 movie
19 Actor Neeson
20 Late morning
21 Principles
23 Varnish ingredient
24 Contaminate
27 1981 movie
32 Rotation letters
35 Percolates
36 Concerning
37 Makes true
39 Region of Spain
41 Options list
42 Physicist Nikola
45 French connections
46 1936 movie
50 Component
51 Muggy
55 Holiday rival
58 Adjust the guitar again
59 Declare openly
60 1942 movie
64 Contribute
65 Shiraz native
66 Composer __-Carlo Menotti
67 Put to work
68 Oversized book
69 Laborer of old

DOWN

1 Gallup rival
2 Allan-__
3 Fathers of France
4 Small stuff
5 Notice abbr.
6 Afore
7 Ducat, informally
8 Teachers' grp.
9 St. Francis of __
10 Sweet orange
11 *Fidelio* feature
12 Phone feature, once
13 *Desire Under the __*
18 Forwarded
22 Mr. Severinsen
24 Poet Octavio
25 A person
26 "__ Too Late" (Carole King tune)
28 Victoria de __ Angeles
29 *Picnic* playwright
30 Gait
31 Cravings
32 St. Louis team
33 Guilty or not guilty
34 N. Dak. neighbor
38 Laughed heartily
39 Jolson and Jarreau
40 *Silent Spring* author Carson
42 Cable station
43 Author Umberto
44 *To __ With Love*
47 Groovy
48 Yellow-flowered shrub
49 Power failure
52 Some bonds
53 Ancient Peruvian
54 Colonial diplomat Silas
55 Aunt Millie's rival
56 Rara __
57 Ambulate
58 Baseball stats
61 __ Deco
62 Maglie or Mineo
63 Santa __, CA

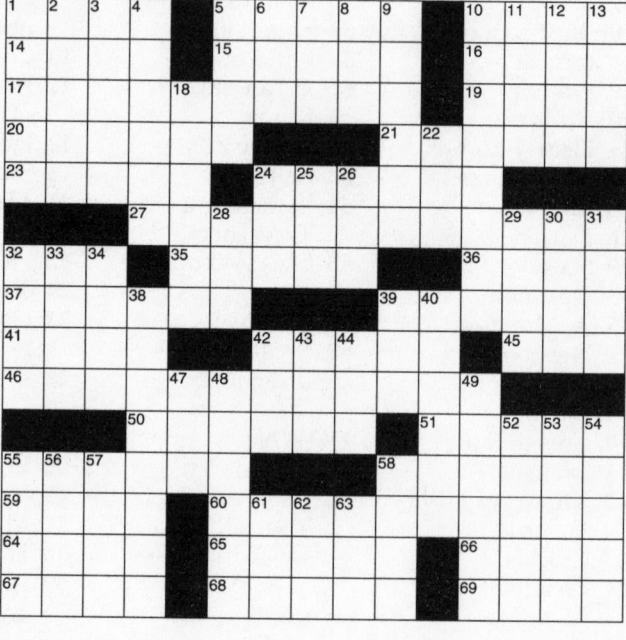

ACROSS

1 Itself: Lat.
5 Artist Holbein
9 Reddish purple
14 Landing place
15 Discharge
16 Singer Baker
17 Workplace agcy.
18 Zip
19 Start
20 Football team that's a laugh?
23 Worthless
24 Malt drinks
25 Gompers' org.
28 Actress Gardner
30 Fight the Hulkster
32 French Oscar
36 Designer Christian
38 Where most people live
39 Football team with pigtails?
42 *The Haj* author
43 Sty cry
44 Not o'er
45 Fortification reinforcement
47 Juliet, to Romeo
49 6-pt. scores
50 Dresden denial
52 Sleep
57 Football team on the highway?
59 Islamic offshoot
62 Radar's soda
63 Claims
64 Dexterous
65 The Bard of __
66 Biblical pronoun
67 Round-topped
68 Run easily
69 Tale

DOWN

1 "__ Care" (1905 song)
2 Pretentious one
3 Neutral vowel sound
4 Initials, maybe
5 Drama by 65 Across
6 Out of control
7 Japanese mercenary
8 Smelting place
9 *Tao te Ching* author
10 Taverns
11 Lily: Fr.
12 Annoyed, with "at"
13 Jazzy guy
21 *Butterfield 8* author
22 Capistrano missionary
25 Totally lost
26 Play the coquette
27 Toto tether
29 Bonus
31 Peter Brook's *Marat/__*
32 Pursue, in a way
33 Like some seals
34 Slip-slides away
35 Additionally
37 Arabic name prefix
40 Prize endower
41 __ Mongolia
46 Set free, perhaps
48 Bearish
51 New, in Peru
53 English meat pie
54 City near Council Bluffs
55 One who spots
56 German manufacturing center
57 Bargain time
58 Flapjack franchise
59 Good, to some
60 Past
61 e.e. cummings play

ACROSS

1 Sport hats
5 Pays attention to
10 Collections
14 Just __ (slightly)
15 Embellish
16 Light tan
17 Mr. __ (Lorre character)
18 Diva Callas
19 Winged
20 *Bye Bye Birdie* song
23 Mexican money
24 Diner patron
25 Backslide
28 "Fuzzy Wuzzy was __"
31 Muslim bigwig
32 Talked monotonously
35 Corn portions
39 Puts up with something
42 Price reduction
43 Get a new tenant
44 Tax preparer: Abbr.
45 Migrating birds
47 Earthy yellow
49 Skirt feature
52 Ashen
54 Is vindicated
61 Ratio phrase
62 Singing sounds
63 "Vamoose!"
64 Sly look
65 Edge (around)
66 Continental prefix
67 Raw metals
68 What the nose knows
69 Molt

DOWN

1 Summer destination
2 __ ben Adhem
3 Actor Brad
4 Bends down
5 Papas' costars
6 Potato variety
7 Nick Charles' wife
8 Faucet defect
9 Break apart
10 Mariner
11 Brilliance
12 Least remnant
13 More certain
21 Must have
22 Affirmative vote
25 Falls behind
26 Taj Mahal city
27 Bucket
28 Court star Agassi
29 Actress Daniels
30 Genesis locale
33 Uncommon
34 Wallet items
36 Writer Sholom
37 Prime for picking
38 Lead player
40 Voiders
41 Coral reef
46 Addis Ababa's country: Abbr.
48 Puts an end to
49 Detective Vance
50 Intense light
51 First name in cosmetics
52 Religious song
53 Confused
55 *Born Free* lioness
56 Home for 55 Down
57 Actor Ray
58 "I don't think so!"
59 Al or Tipper
60 Parka part

ACROSS

1 Coolidge, for short
4 Finish
9 Pay increase
14 River: Sp.
15 String quartet member
16 Stevens of *The Farmer's Daughter*
17 Farm equine
18 Stocking stuffer, perhaps
20 Parasite
22 Color range
23 Suit material
24 Computer unit
25 Loon relative
28 Fire sign
32 Whip
35 String tie
37 Singer O'Day
39 Inert
42 Beach Boy Wilson
43 Hard work
44 Gossipy Barrett
45 Foy or Arcaro
47 "Cool!"
49 Ship's pole
51 Church area
55 Curtail
59 Not the real thing
61 Beyond difficulty
63 Arguer's word
64 Repudiate
65 Aladdin's servant
66 Before
67 In bundles
68 Silvery fish
69 Extremist, informally

DOWN

1 Shellfish
2 Walkway
3 Also-ran
4 One that got away
5 Lake Nasser locale
6 Moody
7 City on the Danube
8 Abner's dad
9 Chuck Connors TV show, with *The*
10 Noun-forming suffix
11 "__ Rhythm"
12 Rush-hour prize
13 Perry's penner
19 Horse fodder
21 Intellectual
24 Triple Crown track
26 Fade away
27 Boxing event
29 Performing well
30 About 2.2 pounds
31 School founded by Henry VI
32 Legal deg.
33 Leeds' river
34 Slip, as on ice
36 Mayberry name
38 __ Khan
40 Lively
41 Slangy suffix
46 Apiece
48 Machine part
50 Keel extensions
52 Rome's river
53 Legend maker
54 Gave a PG to
55 Tiger Hall-of-Famer
56 Eye part
57 Swiss archer
58 Salted cheese
59 Secret writing
60 Pianist Gilels
62 Sewing job

163 ON COURSE by Bob Lubbers

ACROSS
1 Careless
5 Leather band
10 British streetcar
14 Grid great Graham
15 __ facie
16 Aviation word form
17 Thrust
18 Light beam
19 *Kiss Me, __*
20 CADDY
23 Addams cousin
24 Model-train name
28 Hunger pains
31 Some Indonesians
33 __ Jessica Parker
34 Become united
35 Simile center
36 TEE
40 Massachusetts cape
41 Fill
42 High schoolers
43 Atomic piles
46 Ladd classic
47 Close up again
48 '60s ring king
49 TRAP
56 Big brass
59 Hackneyed
60 Run in neutral
61 Software buyer
62 Annoy
63 Beatty and Rorem
64 Jokes
65 Scorches
66 Former Moscow Agency

DOWN
1 Diva Ponselle
2 Aleutian island
3 Right away, in the ER
4 Rail rider
5 Takes off
6 Area
7 Peril
8 "Hallelujah!"
9 Side-by-side
10 Hire
11 Actor Stephen
12 Skilled workmanship
13 A Stooge
21 Darkness
22 1002, to Caesar
25 Spruce up
26 Ancient ascetic
27 Norman and Edward
28 Kansas Indian
29 Fight sites
30 Bobbsey girl
31 __ in (meddles)
32 North Carolina county
33 Bart or Kay
34 Dread
37 Sets apart
38 Moral discipline
39 Midday quaff
44 Lebanese trees
45 Old salt
46 Rains ice
48 __ *Is Born*
50 "*Dies __*"
51 Naldi of the silents
52 Hue
53 Brainstorm
54 Buick rival
55 Nitti nemesis
56 Haul
57 "Born in the __"
58 Beseech

164 RUNNING THE GAMUTS by Dean Niles

ACROSS
1 Heavenly strings
5 Schism
9 Doled (out)
14 USA part
15 Memo words
16 Breathing
17 Burt's ex
18 Sly as __
19 More logical
20 Completely, in the Navy
23 Put into law
24 Traveler's rider
25 "__ *luego*"
28 Hoppers
30 Aggregate
33 .33333 . . .
35 Letter abbr.
36 Tiny insect
37 Across
40 Exhaust
41 Jack of *Barney Miller*
42 *My __ With Andre*
43 Watched Junior
44 Lettuce varieties
46 Tractor name
47 USAF unit
48 Lacking
50 Meteoric rise
57 More than miffed
58 "Three men in __"
59 "I could __ horse"
60 Playing marble
61 Like some horror films
62 French silk center
63 Cotton worker
64 Iowa State home
65 Moistens, in a way

DOWN
1 Equal share
2 Eros
3 Clinton cabinet member
4 Broadcasting period
5 Ranchero's rope
6 Spoil
7 Completely
8 Written material
9 ". . . huddled __ yearning . . ."
10 Thrill
11 Trident feature
12 At all
13 Father-daughter acting name
21 Tie-up
22 Ireland, affectionately
25 Sword holders
26 Open-air malls
27 Underfunded
29 Likely
30 Actress Hasso
31 King Arthur's father
32 Scotland yard?
34 Italian director
36 Area fraught with danger
38 Watch pocket
39 Unencumbered with
44 With less tread
45 Sewing seam
47 Do in
49 Namesakes of a Shakespearean sot
50 Bodybuilder's bane
51 Latvian capital
52 Race track
53 Epic tale
54 Mirthful Martha
55 Put away
56 Summer shades

165 — LOVE NOTE by Dean Niles

ACROSS

1 '50s sitcom
5 Treacherous
10 Current configuration
14 Map out
15 Modern message mode
16 Kid-lit bear
17 Indication
18 Clock sounds
19 "A __ 'clock scholar"
20 START OF A ZELDA FITZGERALD QUOTE
23 Arafat grp.
25 "__ you kidding?"
26 Wrathful
27 Greased up
29 Folkie Baez
32 __ Alamos, NM
33 Satanic
34 Disconcerts
37 MIDDLE OF QUOTE
42 Beg
43 Sport sword
44 Engine additive
47 Transmit
48 Flying Pan
49 Menu
51 JVC product
53 CIA precursor
54 END OF QUOTE
59 Military board game
60 King or queen
61 Rowing musts
64 To __ (exactly)
65 Low-tech calculators
66 Beehive State
67 Pieces' partners
68 Extras
69 Refute

DOWN

1 Army cops
2 He defeated Spinks
3 Fragrant shrub
4 The A in A.D.
5 Big stink
6 Organic compound
7 With frills
8 Hindu sect member
9 Actress Lanchester
10 More appropriate
11 Of the same age
12 Inflicted upon
13 Washing and cleaning, e.g.
21 Michael Jackson song
22 Tendon
23 Sonnet or ode
24 Not taped
28 Word in an ultimatum
29 Wearied
30 Workplace agcy.
31 ". . . __ time in the old town tonight"
34 Commedia dell'__
35 European capital
36 Hoskins role
38 Racing name
39 Current
40 Mediocre grades
41 Towel word
44 Egyptian amulet
45 *Bounty* destination
46 Like some channels
48 Old hand
50 Expropriates
51 Sweater style
52 Evonne contemporary
55 Snag
56 Six-sided solid
57 Winglike
58 Like a Hawaiian shirt
62 Supervised
63 Unforthcoming

166 — DIZZY by Bob Lubbers

ACROSS

1 Saudi, for one
5 Swedish rock group
9 Syrian president
14 Memo
15 Achiever
16 Overly sentimental
17 Pre-CD need
19 Layers
20 Old tar
21 Korean, e.g.
23 Talk like Daffy Duck
26 Barter
28 Irving Berlin song
32 Distant
34 Food plans
35 Homer epic
37 Half a dance
38 __ mater
39 Obdurate
40 Sky twinkler
41 Arafat's org.
42 Moisten, as meat
43 Swiss river
44 Metal worker of a sort
46 Materialized
48 Piano piece
49 Attempt
50 Goods
52 Unseat
57 Organic acid
59 Flighty person
62 Maine bay
63 Top-notch
64 Choir voice
65 Carved pole
66 Howard and Maynard
67 Comprehends

DOWN

1 Picnic pests
2 Dissolute one
3 Shaver brand
4 Road curve
5 Slow tempo
6 Dole or Denver
7 Barbara __ Geddes
8 Vicinity
9 Had hopes
10 Dar es __
11 Press agent, perhaps
12 Imitate
13 Word form for "bad"
18 Bridge fares
22 Wander off
24 Angry moods
25 Jai alai balls
27 Fuel gas
28 Conform
29 Comic Bea
30 Cocktail garnish
31 __ glance (instantly)
33 Like some seals
36 All thumbs
39 Delhi dress
40 __ Na Na
42 Apartment part
43 Revolt
45 Nicety
47 Chaplains
51 Envelope acronym
53 Lindstrom and Zadora
54 Stare at
55 Location
56 Self-images
57 Play segment
58 __ Zedong
60 Garden tool
61 Wayside stopover

GAMES PEOPLE PLAY by Gregory E. Paul

ACROSS
1 Endure
5 Common mineral
9 Banal
14 Wheel holder
15 Russian river
16 Sweltering
17 Children's game
19 Silly
20 Greek H
21 Calendar abbr.
22 Crew member
24 Bagel centers
26 Somewhat: Suff.
27 Counsel
30 New Jersey city
35 Semiconductor, e.g.
36 English composer
37 Emerald Isle
38 Put on board
39 Tiny insects
40 Formulate
41 "__ Dinka Doo" (Durante song)
42 Cuts down
43 French seaport
44 Boston nickname
46 Seeks pests, as a cat
47 __ Plaines, IL
48 Crave
50 Storage spaces
54 Diagnostic aid: Abbr.
55 Not at home
58 Waterproof fabric
59 Sidewalk game
62 South American range
63 Word form for "straight"
64 Farm structure
65 Annoying
66 "__ Little Tenderness"
67 Genesis man

DOWN
1 Army camp
2 Theater sign
3 __ mater
4 Pierce Arrow rival
5 Triceps, e.g.
6 Wrathful
7 Island
8 As well
9 Want for water
10 Backyard game
11 Muslim prayer leader
12 Turner or Louise
13 *Paradise Lost* locale
18 Rope loop
23 Buenos __
24 Kindergarten game
25 Gaunt
27 Wing it
28 Sawyer of ABC News
29 Clear liquor
31 Hill dwellers
32 Miffs
33 Remove
34 Canvas homes
36 Once more
39 "Great Caesar's __!"
43 __ acid (antiseptic)
45 Quite small
46 Actress Mason
49 Needing refueling
50 Express approval
51 Solitary
52 Likelihood
53 Photograph
55 Cornelia __ Skinner
56 Bruins' sch.
57 You, once
60 Hockey great
61 Sugar suffix

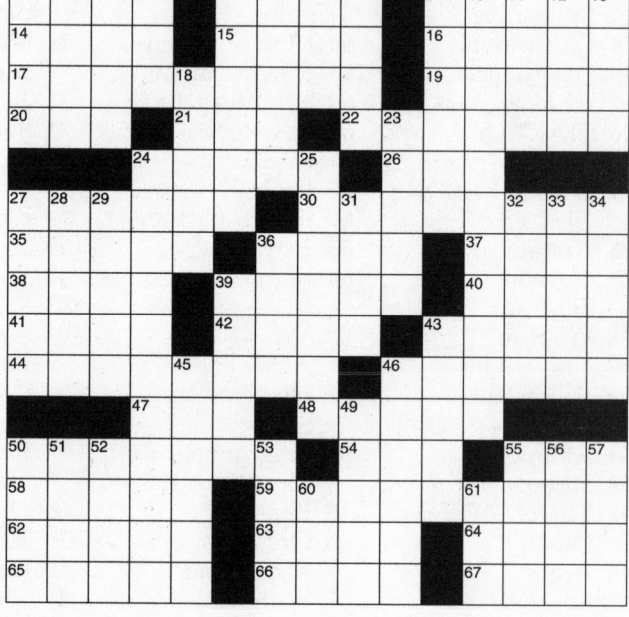

FULL OF BALONEY by Gerald R. Ferguson

ACROSS
1 Locket feature
6 Shooting game
10 Kemo __
14 Ring boundaries
15 Simplify
16 Fearsome dinosaur, briefly
17 Claptrap
19 Yorkshire river
20 Stately home
21 Abandon
23 Navigator's dir.
24 Cable choice
26 Baste a bit
27 Bafflegab
33 Day, in Dijon
36 The Continent: Abbr.
37 Frightening
38 Pluralizers
40 Relig. school
41 Dimwitted
42 Armada
43 "__ to Pieces" (1965 song)
44 Witnessed
45 Symbol of untruth
49 Negative vote
50 Convened
51 Twaddle
54 Sweet treat
58 Verdi opera
60 Julio Iglesias song
61 Gibberish
65 Ruinous thing
66 Gull cousin
67 Indian royalty
68 Queued up
69 Invasion
70 British guns

DOWN
1 French pancake
2 Miller's salesman
3 IBM rival
4 __ good example
5 Hitchcock thriller
6 GM car
7 Dory accessory
8 Hallucinogen
9 Came clean, with "up"
10 Asterisk
11 58 Across solo
12 Aare city
13 Made one's mark
18 He was Friday
22 Jacket material
25 Nutritionist's concern
26 Pulpit orations
27 Plato's tongue
28 "¡Hasta __!"
29 Gaggle group
30 Sarah __ Jewett
31 Seine tributary
32 Sharp
33 Mutt's pal
34 Cold capital
35 Internet patron
39 Office transcriber
46 Temper
47 London lockup
48 Says
51 Aircraft
52 Paar predecessor
53 Jabs
54 Raisin cake
55 General Bradley
56 Taboo
57 Percolate
59 State of France
62 Man-mouse link
63 Cycle start
64 Garden area

NOUN YOU SEE IT by Dean Niles

ACROSS
1 Mexican munchies
6 Noted pediatrician
11 Time-shifting device
14 Disconcert
15 Mr. Television
16 __ mode
17 Time off
19 One of two Chaneys
20 Competed
21 "Tiny" singer
22 Clobber
23 Actor Lahr
25 Righteous Brothers tune
27 Bear
31 __ Khan
32 Baby powder
33 Lake of talk
35 Cut, in a way
38 Everywhere
42 Actress Arthur
43 Startle
44 Part of 64 Across
45 Energy

46 Senior's keepsake
49 Grad-school offering
53 Swiss artist
54 Fuddy-duddy
55 Notwithstanding, informally
57 Sale site
61 High-proof spirit
62 Doohickey
64 Wire service
65 Moore of stew
66 School for Stendhal
67 And like that: Abbr.
68 Reporter's coup
69 Steel rod

DOWN
1 Timothy Hutton movie
2 Help feloniously
3 Mystery writer John Dickson
4 Veal dish
5 Pickup tool
6 Loan agcy.

7 Hit with stones
8 "Live Free __"
9 Get-together
10 Largo or Biscayne
11 "Grease" singer
12 Obscure
13 Extent
18 Geek
22 Porker's pad
24 __ firma
26 Radar spot
27 Pierce
28 Hearty
29 Cooking pot
30 Swank
34 Effrontery
35 __ War (racehorse)
36 Numerical prefix
37 Bubbly bandleader
39 Puffed-up
40 Showing concern
41 Flamboyant pianist

45 Turn, in a way
47 Aquatic organism
48 Pipe tool
49 Metal-mold opening
50 Blow up
51 Ape or parrot

52 Horned mammal
56 Informed (about)
58 "Get __" ('58 tune)
59 __ monster
60 German river
62 6-pt. scores
63 Swindle

BOYS BOOKS by Bob Klahn

ACROSS
1 To boot
5 '74 role for Martin Sheen
11 Tango quorum
14 Creamy, perhaps
15 Ness nemesis
16 Queen Latifah's genre
17 *Jo's Boys* author
20 Barnstorming
21 Certain actions
22 Nautical adverb
24 All to the __
25 *The Burning Boys* author
29 Pop art?
33 Gatling descendant
34 Cathedral recess
35 *Beautiful Girls* star
37 __ disturb
39 Edith __ (Tomlin persona)
41 Gets warmer
42 With 31 Down, Genoese admiral

44 Stable diet
46 Ipanema's city
47 One with will power
48 *Rally 'Round the Flag, Boys* author
51 Nixon aide Krogh
53 Narrative dance
54 Bridge bid
58 Pitchblende part
62 *The Birthday Boys* author
64 Namath's Super Bowl
65 Digs for de Gaulle
66 1937 Tommy Dorsey song
67 Big-game animal
68 Addams uncle
69 Novelist Elinor

DOWN
1 Woody's son
2 He has his pride
3 Bunny tail
4 Dean Martin, e.g.

5 Ferret out
6 Hasty escape
7 "Fire" stone
8 Trip
9 Succinctly
10 Horse of the Year: 1960-64
11 *Star Trek: The Next Generation* role
12 Power unit
13 Chooses
18 Sodium compound
19 Hold close
23 Actress Martinelli
25 Ben-Hur's first name
26 O_3
27 Indian language
28 Tanglewood Festival site
30 Morning rouser
31 See 42 Across
32 He played Potsie on TV
36 Narrow-minded
38 Solar-system model

40 Humorous poet
43 Congenial
45 Mitty's maker
49 Soothes
50 Bill of __
52 Staff leader
54 Stage award

55 Obscure
56 Composer Satie
57 Tilt
59 Poster boy
60 *The __ Duckling*
61 5, to 2 and 8
63 Born: Fr.

GROUND ROUND by Bob Lubbers

ACROSS
1 Mardi __
5 Diplomat Eban
9 Bothersome
14 Actor Calhoun
15 Black: Fr.
16 Ne plus __ (the best)
17 Mosque official
18 Jest
19 Ashcan School painter John
20 Golfer's mecca
23 Ending for beat or peace
24 Unctuous
25 Eightsomes
27 Atom centers
30 Soap ingredient
32 __ *Well That Ends Well*
33 Put on ice
35 Donna and Rex
38 "__ pig's eye!"
39 Ad-hoc baseball field
41 Prefix for wit or pick
42 Apply, as varnish
44 Actor Richard
45 Tommie of baseball
46 Make glad
48 Clown Kelly
50 Indulged one's ego
52 Suit to __
53 Floor covering
54 Small hen
60 Too big
62 Good-deed doer
63 Parcel (out)
64 Deck
65 Prayer ender
66 And others: Abbr.
67 Puts in the mail
68 Durante's famous feature
69 Moist

DOWN
1 Take rudely
2 Italy's capital
3 Mubarak, e.g.
4 Emblems
5 Actress Huston
6 __ prize (loser's award)
7 Kid's vehicle
8 Vicinity
9 Sidewalk fruit stand
10 Building addition
11 English landmark
12 Characteristic
13 Pulls at
21 Untruth
22 Army bunk
26 Mao __-tung
27 Hammer target
28 Arm bone
29 Flying target
30 Hodge partner
31 Cooking pot
34 Singles
36 Weight-loss program
37 Proofreader's word
39 Those with nasty looks
40 Kind of correspondence
43 Used
45 Changed
47 Fuss
49 *Mal de* __
50 College teachers, for short
51 Moscow money
52 Farm land
55 Sleuth Charlie
56 __ Sabe (Tonto's pal)
57 Bit
58 Bridge feat
59 Aid
61 Grass square

ROYAL SUBJECTS by Rich Norris

ACROSS
1 Bounder
4 Show relief
8 Drive-in employee
14 Summer drink
15 Not in port
16 Think
17 "Stand By Me" singer
19 Grownups
20 Food
21 Notice
22 Meek as a __
23 Scram ending
25 Dock
27 Tennis officials
30 Sort
33 Antic
36 Word weaver
37 Dundee denial
38 Topped with ice cream
41 Mottled
43 Sprat's taboo
44 Partner of Crosby and Stills
46 Stadium sections
47 Ending for differ
48 Actually there
51 Swimming-lesson place
53 Account exec
54 Parlor piece
58 Green gem
60 "__ a true story"
62 Visual
65 *Hawaii Five-O* star
66 Develop a liking for
67 To __ (perfectly)
68 Actress Charlotte
69 Unyielding
70 Ancient Persian
71 Part of CBS

DOWN
1 Conspiratorial group
2 __ Rogers St. Johns
3 Jeans fabric
4 Rice drink
5 Has knowledge of
6 Not harsh
7 Witch
8 US spy grp.
9 Tack on
10 Get more out of
11 Tony-winning director
12 Preminger or Klemperer
13 Harasser
18 Badge, e.g.
24 African snake
25 Apple skin
26 Wholly
28 Funny, sort of
29 Unruly group
31 Cowardly Lion actor
32 C Major and A Minor
33 Small restaurant
34 Alda or Thicke
35 Oscar winner as Helen Keller
39 Carvey or Delany
40 Sixth sense
42 Holiday hanging
45 That woman
49 Buyer's enticement
50 Kept apart
52 Donnybrook
55 Aromas
56 Organized assault
57 Chilean mountain range
58 Scribbles (down)
59 Room to swing __
61 __-ball (arcade game)
63 Part of NATO
64 Clark or Orbison
65 Causeway congestion

173 PUNISHMENT by Randolph Ross

ACROSS
1 Islamic priest
5 Charlie Brown expletive
9 Annex
14 Major story
15 Computer symbol
16 Talk idly
17 Kids' cereal
18 Greek colonnade
19 Freak out
20 Symbol of betrayal
23 From __ Z
24 Org. once headed by George Bush
25 Kiss
33 Roman goddesses
34 Large ref. work
35 They're on the books
37 Collar types
38 Shake up
39 Principle
40 Have supper
41 Spanish article
42 __ Rogers St. Johns
43 Ambition
47 Cow-feteria
48 Tokyo, originally
49 Light punishment
57 Aglow
58 Music to a comic
59 German region
61 Woody Allen film
62 State strongly
63 Nautical adverb
64 Little pests
65 Exigency
66 Pier

DOWN
1 Special suffix
2 Grade
3 Opposed to, informally
4 Long dress
5 __ the occasion
6 Director's call
7 Betty Boop, e.g.
8 Grabber
9 Attractiveness
10 Unexciting
11 Actress Wynter
12 Aural
13 Violin part
21 Charlatans
22 Got going
25 Got rid of
26 Recurring theme
27 Rice-__
28 Rattan artisan
29 Salute with drink
30 __ France (Former French province)
31 Expert group
32 Blow up
36 Corset stiffener
38 Swift fellow
39 Little drum
41 Bank attachment
44 Emulates Romeo and Juliet
45 Titter
46 Albert or Arnold
49 Shut loudly
50 Leslie Caron role
51 Busy
52 Shade of purple
53 Retain
54 OPEC member
55 *Enterprise* name
56 "Take __ Train"
60 Alejandro or Fernando

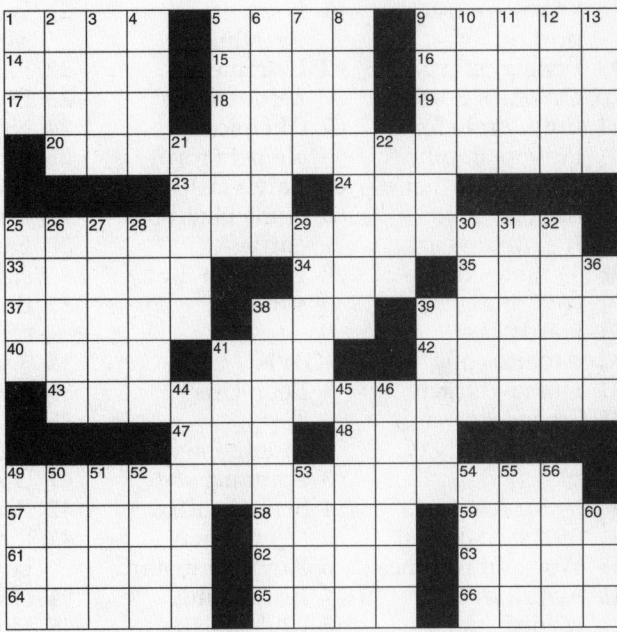

174 SPEAKING XHOSA by Matt Gaffney

ACROSS
1 Stocky marsupial
7 "Harrumph!"
10 Strike callers
14 Shirley, in *Terms of Endearment*
15 Cable choice
16 Do some budget-cutting
17 DC
19 Skating jump
20 Barnaby Jones portrayer
21 Pre-game music
23 Plant swelling
26 Lessen
28 Stadium cousin
29 Ankle-length
30 Caspian feeder
31 Oolong et al.
32 Kurt Waldheim's predecessor
34 Not granted
36 Wet expanse
37 List starter
39 Turn on the charm
40 Obstacle, in a way
43 __ in (heralds)
46 Woodstock companion
48 Concerning
49 Earned
51 Staff marking
52 Available
53 Actress Irving
54 Some e-mail
55 Ladle, e.g.
57 McEnroe's ex
59 Czech Olympian Zátopek
60 Albanian leader, 1944-85
65 Music medium
66 Fission products
67 Threw in the towel
68 Enjoy the snow
69 It's about 80% nitrogen
70 Nervous

DOWN
1 Used to be
2 Arles assent
3 Mystery man
4 Czech region
5 Resort island
6 Vacation by-products
7 Spoil
8 Employ
9 Mock fanfare
10 Cornered
11 '80s cyber-character
12 Adorns (oneself)
13 Alabama River city
18 Antelope playmate
22 Iroquois, e.g.
23 Some cassowaries
24 See
25 Car part
27 Botched
30 *The __ Reader* (literary mag)
33 Pessimist's problem
35 Wine attribute
38 Writer Bombeck
41 Plotting
42 Tournament exemptions
44 Forsook paper clips
45 Russian for "self-boiler"
47 Bob Marley song
48 Muppets drummer
50 A little force
52 *Waiting for Lefty* playwright
54 Naval historian
56 Shah name
58 Thus
61 Coveted NCAA ranking
62 Signed, perhaps
63 Clasp
64 Boor

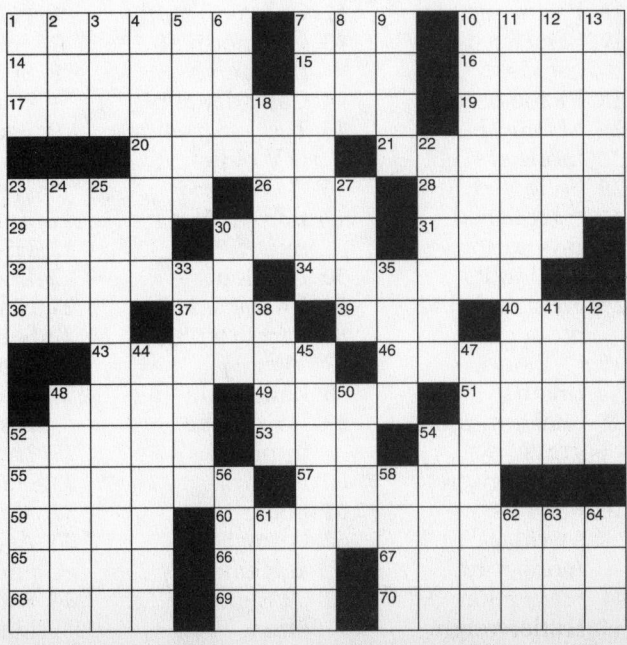

ODE TO JAY by Cathy Millhauser

ACROSS
1 Pinter and Robbins
8 Moving roles
14 Like day
15 Public-school song
17 Williams film
18 Digestive tract portion
19 Pentagon grp.
20 On one's horse
21 Emmy role for Powers Boothe
26 Social reformer's targets
27 It's put on ears
28 __ mater (brain covering)
31 Hardy lass
32 Archies song
37 Heavy ref. set
38 Stevedores' org.
39 Like some NYC plays
40 __ for Africa ('85 music coalition)
43 Workout routines
46 Filmdom's talking pig

49 RFK was one
50 XXIII x XXIV
51 Periods
52 Panama hat
56 One not partaking
60 Org. Bush quit in '95
61 Form of wrestling
62 Extreme nervousness
67 Chemical element form
68 Italy's last king
69 Some blue-book entries
70 Living in the sticks?

DOWN
1 Leon Uris' The __
2 Montgomery sch.
3 Spinning stat.
4 Slangy suffix
5 "__ Goshen!"
6 Kind of mustard
7 Insinuating
8 Chilean lake

9 City near Des Moines
10 __ vu
11 Learned
12 Brooklet
13 Rowing pair
16 Make __ of (botch)
21 Former Celtic MVP White
22 Bjorn rival
23 Darn
24 Nudge
25 It may be spring-loaded
29 Privy to
30 Eagerly expectant
33 Brooklyn, NY sch.
34 Shade sources
35 Make fun of
36 '64 button letters
40 Bruins' school
41 Do without
42 Part of SEATO
43 Ignatius of Loyola's group
44 Hypo, for short
45 Pt. of speech

46 Pooch of '74 film fame
47 Evoke
48 Opry instruments
53 __ Joe (*Tom Sawyer* character)
54 Heyday
55 Frost feet

57 Covered colonnade
58 Spot
59 Wishes undone
63 Deep black
64 *Exodus* role
65 St. Helens is one
66 Soak

READING MATTER by Rich Norris

ACROSS
1 Fellow
5 Mama's mate
9 Bonnie's partner
14 Lofty
15 San __ Obispo, CA
16 Parka parts
17 Sandwich cookie
18 Picnic pests
19 Mythical monsters
20 Followed established procedure
23 Mall units
24 *Treasure Island* monogram
25 __ Paulo, Brazil
28 Snake-in-the-grass
29 Collar insert
30 *The Time Machine* monogram
31 Fiery felony
34 Underweight

35 Part of some phones
36 Detailed information
39 Roman historian
40 Diller's spouse
41 Bumbling
42 Chemical suffix
43 City north of Pittsburgh
44 Calendar abbr.
45 *The __ Squad* (TV oldie)
46 *A Few Good __*
47 Bob Marley's music
50 All along
54 Characteristic
56 Part in a play
57 Vicinity
58 Italian bowling
59 It rings the pupil
60 Exam
61 Looks for
62 Formal agreement
63 CPR givers, often

DOWN
1 Grub
2 Takes on
3 Ten-percenter
4 Duplicate, as a document
5 Game participant
6 Family members
7 Solidity
8 Speaking confidently
9 Persnickety
10 Corporate symbol
11 English county
12 HST follower
13 Double curve
21 Main force
22 Sans spice
26 Acting shocked
27 Nocturnal nestling
29 Ladd western
31 Happy as __
32 African beast
33 Avoided embarrassment
34 Excursion of a kind

35 Malign
37 Actor Zimbalist, Jr.
38 Last sign of summer
43 Overacts
44 Least
47 Dig find
48 Relevant, in legalese

49 Cast out
51 *Casablanca* role
52 Israeli dance
53 Stall sustenance
54 Cable network: Abbr.
55 Fish eggs

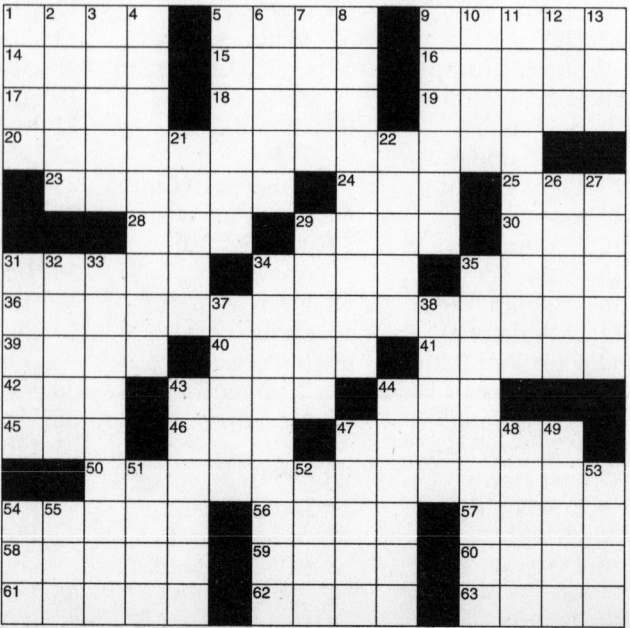

177 BAKER'S HALF-DOZEN by Shirley Soloway

ACROSS

1 Roster
5 Significant
10 Ski lift
14 Ancient Peruvian
15 Cognizant
16 Actress Raines
17 Escape blame
19 Rain heavily
20 Moses crossed it
21 Citrus fruits
23 Promos
24 Mrs., in Madrid
26 Touch down
27 Affect adversely
30 Fraternal order member
33 Actor Rob
36 Dieters' retreats
37 Plymouth colonist
39 Anesthetic
41 N.Y. zone
42 "Mule Train" singer
43 Short stalk
44 Flyer's word form
46 TV interference
47 Call for help
48 Magazine features
51 Astute
53 *Jeanne*, e.g.
54 High __ kite
57 Tusked animal
59 First family of the 1870s
61 Whimper
62 Instigating
65 Jai __
66 Spooky
67 Hosiery shade
68 *The __ the Limit* (Astaire film)
69 Sipper's need
70 Org.

DOWN

1 Zodiac sign
2 "__ Your Love Tonight" (Presley tune)
3 A lot
4 Creates lace
5 George of *Route 66*
6 Fill with fear
7 Food container
8 Vocal
9 Throws off
10 Wyoming range
11 Became part of the group
12 Pub orders
13 St. Louis athlete
18 Pianist John
22 Taj __
25 Charisma
27 Sob
28 Used a light beam
29 Houston team
31 Letterman rival
32 Was aware of
33 Not as much
34 Director Preminger
35 Snatch quickly
38 Highland miss
40 Pass along, as a client
45 Got too big for
49 Burdens
50 Garr or Hatcher
52 New York island
54 Cattle breed
55 Certain buttons
56 Colorado resort city
57 Bubbly bandleader
58 Printer's mark
60 __ *Karenina*
61 Barker and Bell
63 Not perf.
64 Stream

178 CHRISTMAS IN JULY by Dean Niles

ACROSS

1 Smeltery leftover
5 Burden
9 Boat or plane
14 TV actress Williams
15 Hungarian leader Nagy
16 Madagascar primate
17 Paris airport
18 Actress Patricia
19 Yellowish white
20 Food mishap
23 Diverting
24 Passbook abbr.
25 Turns abruptly
30 Time period
32 *Inter* __
34 First one counted
35 Lts.' school
37 Roughly forever
38 Water pipe
39 Vacillate
43 Milky quartz
44 The third degree?
45 Island in a stream
46 Waffle brand
47 Beef concoction
49 Casino city, for short
53 Director Tarantino
55 Record label
57 Model Carol
58 Meringue-top dessert
61 Kids' entertainer
65 Burglar
66 Ski lift
67 Certain postings
68 Pulitzer author Robert __ Butler
69 Soda-shop offering
70 Video-display element
71 Meat-inspecting agcy.
72 Sponsorship

DOWN

1 Derides, with "at"
2 Thrash
3 Actress Dahl
4 "Ain't That Peculiar" singer
5 Bedding
6 Code of silence
7 Breed of horse
8 Grandeur, often
9 Singer Patsy
10 Title for Dr. King
11 Latin lover's verb
12 Sable or mink
13 Essay
21 Exactly nothing
22 African republic
26 Distant
27 Cutlet meat
28 Sooner city
29 Dictionary abbr.
31 __ broil (steak choice)
33 Sales prospects
36 Mrs. Ponti
39 Sauce brand
40 Yen
41 Courteous remark
42 Courteous
43 Et __ (footnote abbr.)
48 Equivocated
50 Blowhard
51 Acid neutralizer
52 Kicks off
54 Treasury offering
56 __ Carta
59 Lampreys
60 "Ma! (He's Making Eyes __)"
61 Agent
62 "Who __ to say?"
63 Office output
64 "Fee, __, foe, fum . . .'"

179 BACK TO WOODSTOCK by Fred Piscop

ACROSS
1 Part of L.A.
4 __ *Three Lives*
8 Antarctic sea
12 Prefix for center
13 "Well, I __!"
15 Musical pace
16 *The Novel of the Future* writer
17 Woodstock wear
19 Does a vet's chore
21 Banishes
22 Artoo Detoo's owner
23 Granular snows
24 Woodstock wear
29 Redact
30 Party
31 Seer's card
33 Sleep phenom.
34 Sculpted form
39 Ebbets Field great
42 Do
43 Woodstock wear
46 Social stratum
47 Ring sites?
48 Shots at the majors
50 Board with a thumbhole
53 Woodstock wear
55 Work unit
56 China name
57 Nine, in combinations
58 __ trade (fashion industry)
59 Parisian parent
60 Williams and Danson
61 Mole, for one

DOWN
1 Do a bank job
2 Role for Ronny
3 Oil company with a dinosaur logo
4 Hurting
5 Margins
6 Spacewalks, to NASA
7 Calendar abbr.
8 Kick out
9 Shadows: Fr.
10 Stage illumination
11 Peruvian coins
14 Coach Auerbach
15 Compose, in a way
18 Smell, e.g.
20 Slowly, on a score
24 Garner
25 Dietary initials
26 Motown founder
27 City on the Meuse
28 Dangerous partner
32 Idiot box
35 Earthy color
36 Revels noisily
37 Francis Drake title
38 Frequently, in poetry
40 Shelley's "__ the West Wind"
41 Really ticked
43 Singer Dayne
44 Wagnerian heroine
45 Hot sauces
46 Fancy flapjack
48 1/2 fl. oz.
49 __-Foy, Que.
50 Corn concoction
51 It may be cheese-filled
52 Like some waffles
54 Blaster's need

180 SAY LA VIE by Bob Lubbers

ACROSS
1 *Tête*wear
6 Asian capital
11 Stomach muscles, for short
14 Vibrant
15 Static
16 Sock part
17 French absurdist
19 "Turn left!"
20 Lowers a kite
21 __ noire
22 Dance, in France
25 Dutch commune
26 Wage-__ (employee)
28 Swelled heads
30 Exxon predecessor
33 Former women's mag
34 Worship
36 Hot drink
38 French short-story writer
43 State of India
44 Ballpark aide
45 Deli offering
48 Pyramid, e.g.
50 Roy Rogers, né __
51 Snoozing
53 Oddjob's creator
55 Erode
56 Mel and Ed of baseball
57 Stove-top pan
61 Zodiac beast
62 French playwright/director
66 Give __ whirl
67 *A votre* __
68 Start of an Irish tune
69 DC title
70 Grant
71 Certain NCOs

DOWN
1 Meadow call
2 Right-angle shape
3 Kid
4 Always
5 Chuckle sound
6 Foot joints
7 Kiwi's extinct kin
8 Puccini heroine
9 Together
10 Prefix for classical
11 Goddess of wisdom
12 Straw hat
13 Seamstresses
18 Cashes in
21 Chicken parts
22 *Titanic* undoer
23 *The African Queen* screenwriter
24 Valentine word
27 Hail, in Hilo
29 Calms
31 Jerk
32 "Alley __!"
35 Charlotte __ (cake)
37 Occult doctrine
39 Bran source
40 Competent
41 Georgetown athlete
42 Novosibirsk "no"
45 Native New Zealanders
46 Social class
47 *Short Cuts* director
49 Did a dairy-farm job
52 "Rats!" relative
54 Salamanders
58 Hawaii coast
59 Verb type: Abbr.
60 Ref's calls
62 Eva's half-sister?
63 Dress up, with "out"
64 Table scrap
65 Owns

GROUND CREW by Lee Weaver

ACROSS
1 Attempt
5 Rugged rock
9 Lima or soy
13 Cougars
15 First-rate
16 Bargain time
17 Leaning
18 Justice __ Bader Ginsburg
19 Singer Guthrie
20 Innovative blues musician
23 Nearly a dozen
24 Realty unit
25 Feeling restless
27 Farewell, in France
30 Sweater material
32 Singer Campbell
33 Poor, as an excuse
35 Black tea
38 Sushi servings
39 Fear
41 Pickling herb
42 Praise highly
44 "Do __ others . . ."
45 Part of a list
46 Frightens
48 Oven gloves
50 Too big
51 Egg layer
52 African antelope
53 *The Hogan Family* star
60 Ventilates
62 Appear
63 Stir up
64 Came to
65 Portent
66 Creepy
67 Leg joint
68 Shows agreement silently
69 Heavy metal

DOWN
1 Canned meat
2 Ballet costume
3 Surrounded by
4 Hairless
5 Diamond weight
6 One-sided fight
7 Start the pot
8 Babe Ruth teammate
9 Troop group: Abbr.
10 Sultry night-club singer
11 Bowling lane
12 Broadway light
14 Panache
21 Was willing to
22 Halt
26 Bank offering
27 *Jeopardy!* host Trebek
28 *Designing Women* star
29 Shoe part
30 Prayer endings
31 Nifty
32 "That's incredible!"
34 Calla-lily family
36 Toreador accolades
37 Shade tree
40 Round-topped
43 Glaswegian girl
47 Motive
49 Accustom
50 Burger topping
51 Sunday songs
52 Stare
54 *Nautilus* captain
55 Monopoly card
56 Christmas carol
57 Treat meat
58 India's location
59 Require
61 Catch sight of

POSTURING by Bob Lubbers

ACROSS
1 Fashionable
5 Terrier of film
9 Of yore
14 Dynamics starter
15 Afternoon socials
16 __ Selassie
17 Unprosperous period
19 DXI x V
20 Ate well
22 Garfield's foil
23 Account subtractions
26 Two-year-old
28 Garden spot
29 Corn unit
32 Deuce topper
33 Bedsheets
35 Euripides tragedy
37 Educ. center
40 __ *Gabler*
41 Actress Gardner
42 Provoke
44 Word form for "equal"
45 Different
47 Harden (to)
48 Moniker
50 Meadow
52 Colorado resort
53 Linksman Lee
56 Shows of contempt
58 Ascend
59 Breathing tube
62 States firmly
64 Kids' game
68 "__ porridge hot . . ."
69 Singular person
70 Ade base
71 Cast about
72 Meeting point
73 Osprey cousin

DOWN
1 Presidential nickname
2 __ *Haw*
3 Lyricist Gershwin
4 Pent up
5 Resting
6 Red and Yellow
7 Sharply flavored
8 Poise, e.g.
9 Electrical unit
10 Pie à __
11 Nothing, slangily
12 J.R.'s mom
13 Not even once
18 Still
21 Indulge, with "on"
23 Indian metropolis
24 Adams and Brickell
25 Talk to tiresomely
27 Window cover
30 Asian nanny
31 Delight (in)
34 Singer Judd
36 Challenge
38 Radium researcher
39 Cads
43 Not capable of sustaining life
46 Circus shelter
49 Opposed
51 On land
53 Golf obstacles
54 Metal connector
55 Bean or Welles
57 Vim
60 __ cost (free)
61 Like some dorms
63 Stitch
65 Atmosphere
66 K followers
67 Bruce or Peggy

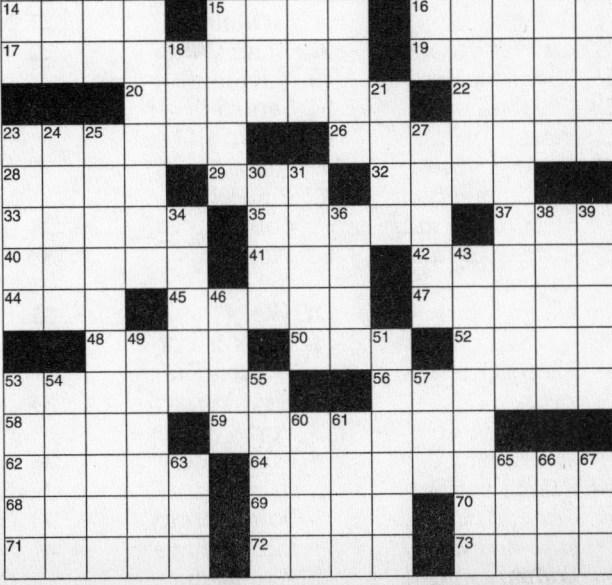

183   FISH OUT OF WATER by Rose White

ACROSS

1 Tax preparer: Abbr.
4 Wave tops
8 Less distant
14 Scene stealer
15 Exclamation of surprise
16 Alert again
17 Cold War phenomenon
19 Kampala's country
20 Stunt sport
22 Lion coiffure
23 Still
24 Taylor's nickname
27 Thin margin
32 Russo of *Outbreak*
33 Part of TGIF
36 Sign of the future
37 Devout
38 Hitchhiker's motto
42 Bottomless pit
43 In __ veritas
44 *The Daughter of Time* novelist
45 Father
46 Grass sign
49 __ Paulo
50 Corn holder
51 Quickly, for short
55 "The Twist" singer
61 Inuit
63 Humidifier output
64 Cotton pest
65 Soft drink
66 Prevaricate
67 Lengthen
68 Baseball manager Felipe
69 Writer Kesey

DOWN

1 Wide fissure
2 Hooded jacket
3 Jordan's capital
4 Treat meat
5 Jezebel's husband
6 Somewhat, musically
7 Where the Mets play
8 Less refined
9 On the level
10 Gulf off Iran
11 Specify
12 Result
13 Cereal-box info: Abbr.
18 Simmer slowly
21 Whiskey grain
25 Occupied
26 Like salsa
28 One of the Cartwrights
29 Mischievous child
30 Bishop's domain
31 Rogue
32 Tease
33 Cardplayer's comment
34 Shinbone
35 Rise rapidly
37 College teacher, casually
39 WNW opposite
40 Kenyan runner Keino
41 Yoko __
46 German spirit
47 Decline
48 True statement
50 Chili spice
52 Slink
53 Eagle's nest
54 Groom
56 Hotbed of activity
57 Village People song
58 Unresponsive
59 City near Mauna Loa
60 Birthright seller
61 Ram's mate

184   VEGGIE ANATOMY by Patrick Jordan

ACROSS

1 '92 rival of Bill and George
5 Pack tightly
9 Descendant
14 "Now __ me down . . ."
15 Breathing sound
16 TV announcer Don
17 Convent room
18 "Self" starter
19 Galahad's getup
20 Boxer feature
23 Undamaged
24 Stuff to the gills
25 Cave-painting subject
28 *No Exit* author
32 Be disputatious
35 He reached his peak
37 Shocking swimmer
38 Feeble notions
42 Track transaction
43 Espied
44 Move obliquely
45 Rough design
48 Begrimes
50 Baldwin of *The Shadow*
52 Most agreeable
56 Translucent stationery
60 Silverstein et al.
61 Galileo's birthplace
62 Actor Calhoun
63 Yes follower
64 Settled down
65 CCII x III
66 Actor James
67 Pinocchio's polygraph
68 Worn out

DOWN

1 Christina of *The Addams Family*
2 New York city
3 Port __ cheese
4 Milk/cider drink
5 Some county fair displays
6 Actor Julia
7 Choir voice
8 Feline lines
9 Conqueror of Athens
10 Profession
11 Mlle. la Douce
12 Olfactory offense
13 Postal Creed word
21 More arctic
22 Went (in) gradually
26 Bee's grandnephew
27 Dressed to the __
29 Sore, with "off"
30 Tangible
31 Other
32 PD alerts
33 Offend the nose
34 Box-office receipts
36 Lottolike game
39 Pale
40 New York town
41 Poker-hand rejects
46 Followed, à la Spade
47 Does the finale
49 Hereditary
51 Where *Booknotes* may be seen
53 Geologic term
54 Electronic mechanism
55 "Have a taste!"
56 Louisville's river
57 Rex's tec
58 Metric unit, briefly
59 Egyptian deity
60 Compass dir.

STARGAZING by Diane C. Baldwin

ACROSS
1 Fed. agent
5 Leftovers dish
9 Animal life
14 Artist Bonheur
15 Marian Anderson, e.g.
16 Group of eight
17 Troop group
19 Dentist's diagnostic aid
20 Curvy array of stars
22 Absolved of sins
23 Footlike part
24 Hideaway
28 Howls
30 Pang
32 Biblical stargazers
35 Sargasso or Sulu
37 Mentor of the Four Horsemen
38 "This __ House" (Clooney tune)
39 '80s tennis star

41 Tupperware top
42 Gaucho's wear
44 Outdo
45 Boxer Willard
46 "Peace!"
47 Storage bldg.
49 Where Bill met Hillary
50 And the like: Abbr.
53 Seuss despot
57 Sky show
60 Basket maker
63 More fidgety
64 Due
65 Chalky mineral
66 Carmaker Ferrari
67 Plaster of Paris
68 Petitions
69 Char the surface of

DOWN
1 Tennis surface
2 Alter an image by computer
3 Up and at 'em
4 African capital

5 1986 visitor
6 "Break __!"
7 Thong
8 Whist whiz
9 '30s slugger Jimmie
10 Kind of paint
11 Actress Hagen
12 One way to vote
13 Words from the sponsor
18 Hot rocks
21 Space science
25 Bracelet locale
26 __ fatuus (eerie glow)
27 Oboes, saxes, etc.
29 Date
31 Tribulation
32 Sibling of Peter Rabbit
33 __ State (Hawaii)
34 Of the cheek
36 Aardvark morsel
39 Conductance unit

40 Run-in
43 Man from Missouri
45 Hines and Kern
48 Very: Ger.
51 Tries out
52 __ vin (chicken dish)
54 String

55 TV host Gibbons
56 Slip
58 Consequently
59 Make a decision
60 Gear part
61 Bedazzle
62 US soldiers

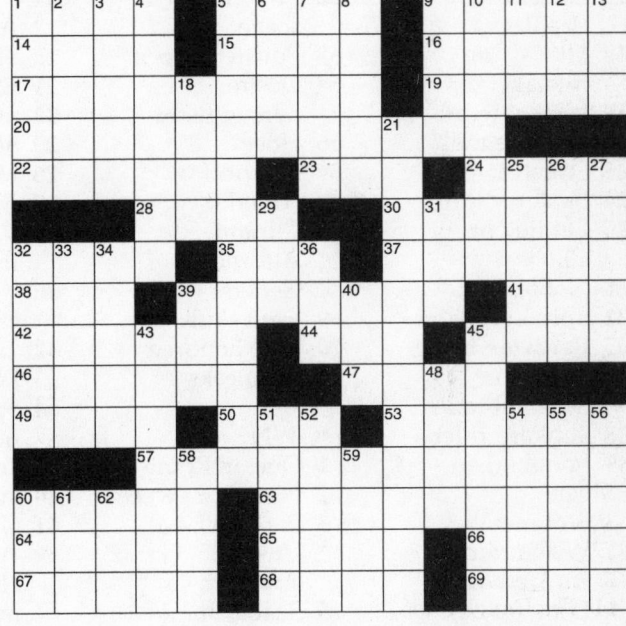

BEASTLY FOLKS by Gerald R. Ferguson

ACROSS
1 Skiing site
6 Show dismay
10 Tumble
14 Safe spot
15 Choir voice
16 Actress Perlman
17 Turn inside out
18 Clarinet adjunct
19 Long, long time
20 Unexpected victor
22 Sawyer or Keaton
23 Confident
24 Gave a nudge
26 High-school dance
29 Tennis unit
30 Not ambitious
31 Greet the day
33 Down in the dumps
37 "Three Bears" name
38 Tendon-bone connection

40 Woody Guthrie's son
41 Eases off
43 Stable partition
44 Bring up
45 High card
47 Thus far
48 Fast tempo
51 Sandwich fish
53 Church crosses
54 Roadside rogue
59 Singer Clapton
60 Alan of M*A*S*H
61 Tropical fruit
62 Roman despot
63 Food shop, for short
64 Modify
65 Once again
66 Utopia
67 The Merry Widow composer

DOWN
1 Cast off
2 Vesuvius output

3 All done
4 Makes java
5 Thrill
6 Artist's room, perhaps
7 Pale brews
8 Church tops
9 Pea holder
10 Timid chap
11 In the future
12 Sierra __
13 Like most highways
21 Lode stuff
22 Get forty winks
25 Indian prince
26 Deli meats
27 Kind of exam
28 Cotton variety
32 One immune from criticism
33 AMA members
34 Cafeteria carrier
35 Vogue rival
36 Clod
38 Smokey or Yogi
39 Opened a scroll

42 Beer holders
43 West African country
45 Reach
46 Director's cry
48 Bout site
49 Actress Sophia

50 France's longest river
52 As __ (generally)
55 Not active
56 Shower alternative
57 Eye feature
58 Teri of Tootsie
60 Lime drink

OOPS! by Gerald R. Ferguson

ACROSS
1 Mil. branch
5 H.S. exam
9 Act stealthily
14 Saint Philip __
15 Doily material
16 Philadelphia gridder
17 General Bradley
18 "It's __ big mistake!"
19 Line of work
20 "Excuse me!"
23 Streetcar
24 Skater Midori
25 Dudley or Clayton
28 Nobleman
31 Spiders' snares
35 Peruvian beast
37 Saint, in Mozambique
38 Tankard filler
39 Spoonerism, e.g.
43 Soft metal
44 Wish undone
45 Sank a basket
46 Look (to be)
48 Some motels
50 Braid of hair
51 *NYPD Blue* network
53 Angelou or Frost
55 Maxwell Smart catchphrase
62 Put on, as a scene
63 Pollster Roper
64 Desire personified
66 Host
67 Nautical adverb
68 Clinton Attorney General
69 Fruit skins
70 June honorees
71 Henpecks

DOWN
1 One, in Rome
2 Prefix for sweet
3 Part of U.A.R.
4 Unsafe structure
5 Beach: Sp.
6 Strauss opera
7 Rights group: Abbr.
8 Rip
9 __ ease (make comfortable)
10 Like AAA shoes
11 "Yikes!"
12 Actor __ Ray
13 Sharp
21 El __ (painter)
22 Steers
25 Ships' poles
26 Hardy, to Stan
27 Express oneself
29 Visibly frightened
30 __ Dawn Chong
32 Tidal flood
33 Jazz form
34 Spring planting need
36 Togo's locale
40 Wine cask
41 Group of eight
42 What "borealis" means
47 Mime Marceau
49 Formed froth
52 Computer units
54 Oklahoma Indians
55 Flow slowly
56 "This one's __!" (treater's phrase)
57 Marathon, e.g.
58 Dewdrop
59 Stewpot
60 Sphere
61 Chinese secret society
65 Brillo alternative

AFTER SEVEN by Bob Lubbers

ACROSS
1 Rec rooms
5 Extra-base hit
11 __ Cob, CT
14 Actress Moran
15 Banks and Ford
16 Choose
17 Desk accessory
19 Actor Christopher
20 Sea hawk
21 *Abbie an' Slats* creator Van Buren
23 Burpee products
24 Part of USA
26 Arabian sultanate
27 Goof
28 Eyed
30 Loren's mate
31 Draft org.
32 Hussein's queen
33 Rectories
34 Gloomy
36 Frasier's ex
39 Train storage area
40 Commerce or Treasury: Abbr.
43 Wane
44 Concur
45 Geologic division
46 Llama land
47 Gator cousin
48 Rise up
50 Plains Indian
52 Fill with fizz
53 Boundary: Abbr.
54 *Oktoberfest* entrée
57 Zetterling of *Quartet*
58 Metalsmith
59 Hiker's home
60 Chemical suffix
61 On land __ (everywhere)
62 Betting line

DOWN
1 Takes testimony
2 Pencil ends
3 Little boys
4 Bergen dummy
5 Moist, in a way
6 Metal container?
7 Word form for "one"
8 Cornell team
9 Hungarian composer
10 Spanish direction
11 Op-Ed pieces
12 Run
13 NASA's __ space center
18 Echo
22 Daniel or Pat
24 Ballplayer Matty
25 __-round
29 Barbarian
30 Exploiter
33 Entangle
34 Bit of exercise
35 DEA agent
36 California city
37 Spaniard, e.g.
38 Wyoming city
40 Argued
41 Make believe
42 God-given gifts
44 About
47 Word before letter or mail
49 Poet's Muse
51 Hammett terrier
52 Incantation start
55 Naval rank: Abbr.
56 Dakota Indian

189 NAME THAT THEME by Frank Longo

ACROSS

1 Mr. Stravinsky
5 Sealing-wax ingredient
8 Paper piece
13 Use a U-Haul
14 Miss. neighbor
15 Actor Everett
16 Haiku, e.g.
17 Cher, to Chastity
18 Kink
19 THEME CLUES
22 Where buoy meets gull
23 Captain's diary
24 Curve shape
25 THEME CLUES
31 Stupefy
32 Preschooler
33 *Exodus* hero
34 Made a choice
37 Chatter
41 Epoch
42 Lend a hand
43 Comedian Philips
44 THEME CLUES
50 Mag execs.
51 Actor Mineo
52 Educators' grp.
53 THE THEME
59 Harsh
60 Calendar abbr.
61 Explorer Heyerdahl
63 Appetite, in psychology
64 CCLI quadrupled
65 Well ventilated
66 Hawk homes
67 SST heading
68 Cape on the Seward Peninsula

DOWN

1 Little pest
2 Mess up
3 Superior to
4 Lax
5 Excoriate
6 Succulent houseplant
7 The Kennedy era
8 Bulgar, e.g.
9 Sharpen
10 City in Wisconsin
11 Join the Navy
12 Microscopic
15 Male deer
20 Get the joke
21 Namath of football
25 Owned
26 Must pay
27 Some genes
28 Coal carrier
29 Buddy
30 Southern constellation
35 Anger
36 Dollop
37 Indy stop
38 Adjusting easily
39 Rhea's look-alike
40 CD follower
42 Martin/Tomlin film
44 Backs at the track
45 Cling
46 Pack animals
47 Install carpeting
48 Ultimate degree
49 Highlander's pattern
54 Teller's cry
55 Cubist painter
56 *Topaz* novelist
57 Mississippi feeder
58 Contemptible person
62 Bagel alternative

190 ALL FOR ALL by Dean Niles

ACROSS

1 Gait
5 Humorist Barry
9 Blend
13 Drink flavor
14 Animated Pepe
15 In __ (lined up)
16 Wash. neighbor
17 Delicious, e.g.
18 Costa __
19 START OF A QUOTE
21 Movie award
22 Heart line
23 MIDDLE OF QUOTE
24 Gregorian form
27 Light carriage
29 *Emma* author
31 Beloved
32 Politico Landon
35 Flying toy
37 Noise
39 Letter from Corinth
40 Gold source
42 Straight man
43 Scads
45 "A House __ a Home"
46 END OF QUOTE
49 Author/ director Barker
51 Freeway exits
52 Author of quotation
56 Noun suffix
57 Popular dance
58 Czar name
59 Apportion
60 Group of eight
61 __ cava
62 Rabbits, to foxes
63 Part of PTA
64 The E in Q.E.D.

DOWN

1 Barge
2 Bull, in La Paz
3 Kind of sch.
4 Certain showcases
5 Where trains stop
6 Give a hand to
7 Grassland
8 She-sheep
9 Like a swamp
10 Author Jong
11 Union group
12 Overshadow
14 Cowardly Lion portrayer
20 Some computers
21 Secret agent
23 Caspian range
24 Java joint
25 Wound
26 Part of SEATO
28 VCR button
30 Not cool
32 Ancient Greek contest
33 Corporate identifier
34 Guitar part
36 Slithery one
38 Abrupt decline
41 Trigonometric ratios
43 Florida bird
44 Catchy phrase
46 Chaplin persona
47 What "phobe" means
48 Ham it up
50 Arrow rival
52 Raincoats
53 Done with
54 Grandma
55 Wee irritant
57 __ fault (excessively)

191 HEADS UP by Bob Lubbers

ACROSS
1 Remove, as a hat
5 Singer Kay
10 Corn holders
14 Mine: Fr.
15 Indian dwelling
16 Opera solo
17 Lunch course
19 Repast
20 Actress Hawn et al.
21 Mattress support
23 Chop (off)
24 Mideast desert
25 __-Powell (Scouts founder)
28 Darlin'
29 Savage
33 Western Indian
34 Bit of barbecue
35 Nabokov novel
36 Bonkers
40 Mixes
41 Psyche parts
42 Twist the truth
43 Eagle's nest
44 One of Mel's waitresses
45 Not cloudy
47 Expert group
49 Onassis, familiarly
50 Visits
53 Prickly shrub
57 Arizona Indian
58 Lanky one
60 Actress Barbara
61 Legal excuse
62 Director Preminger
63 Bell sound
64 Renter's paper
65 "__ only a bird in a . . ."

DOWN
1 "Doggone!"
2 Melville novel
3 Silly one
4 Monkey (with)
5 Exorbitant
6 Thomas Hardy heroine
7 Part of some GI addresses
8 Corned beef and cheese sandwich
9 Fix a floor, perhaps
10 Scottish surname
11 Cookie sandwich
12 Slant
13 Shaker contents
18 Disney's The __ King
22 Crusoe's creator
24 San Francisco neighborhood
25 Good-ol'-boy nickname
26 __ of Two Cities
27 Inhibit
28 __ the books (study)
30 Army arm
31 Lofty hotel lobbies
32 Stratum
34 Med. professionals
35 Weight units: Abbr.
37 Cutting quickly
38 Brainstorms
39 Tokyo, once
44 Condition
45 Rocky cliff
46 Caribbean dances
48 Twangy
49 Golfer Palmer, to fans
50 Lean-to
51 Fuss
52 Unlock
53 Tots' coverings
54 Jo's sister
55 Tardy
56 Seth's son
59 Spanish creek

192 THRU THE RANKS by Elizabeth C. Gorski

ACROSS
1 Afrikaner
5 Pines (for)
10 Uninteresting
14 Leer at
15 Limber
16 Do a yard chore
17 Goldie Hawn film
20 Bering, e.g.
21 55 Across under Reagan
22 Olympian Jesse
23 Catches some rays
24 Took a dive
26 Emphasis
29 Religious group
30 Computer key
33 Prepared baking apples
34 Ship's body
35 Choral voice
36 "Big show," to baseballers
39 Granola ingredient
40 Just
41 West Point student
42 U-turn from SSW
43 Dewey and Louie's brother
44 Apartment workers
45 Wealthy man of verse
46 Domesticated
47 Plowmaker John
50 Pickle juice
52 Oklahoma city
55 Cabinet member
58 Singer Phoebe
59 Lagers
60 Eliot's Adam __
61 Ranch helper
62 Resource
63 Bo Peep hears them

DOWN
1 Smacks in the noggin
2 Meanie
3 Director Kazan
4 Gun the engine
5 Unactualized
6 Double curves
7 Penpoints
8 With great joy
9 Rep.'s colleague
10 Free-for-all
11 Weak, as an excuse
12 Similar
13 Cluckers
18 Plummer of The Fisher King
19 Sudden impact
23 Comes down in buckets
25 Model Macpherson
26 Make happen
27 "Over There" composer
28 Largest Greek isle
29 Like permed hair
30 Give the slip to
31 Direct
32 Prices
34 Apiary residents
35 Wide open
37 Day: Fr.
38 Shrewdness
43 Soil worker
44 Most lucid
45 Mass of people
46 French beast
47 Morse unit
48 Sicilian volcano
49 British school
51 Sandwich breads
52 Vicinity
53 Baby's word
54 Pub pints
56 Hoopster's org.
57 Recede

ACROSS

1 George Ruth
5 Western of '53
10 Scripto rival
13 Roman journey
14 Prestigious prize
15 Sufficient, to Spenser
17 One of a film pair
19 Under control
20 Proof abbr.
21 Bitterly pungent
22 On a cruise
23 Opens
25 Mounts
26 Idyllic place
27 Dorothy's dog
29 Never, in Berlin
30 Belief
33 Algerian port
34 French seasoning
35 Typical situation for 17 Across and 59 Across
40 "Smoking or __?"
41 *Clueless* catchphrase
42 34th Pres.
43 Mao __-tung
44 Keystone __
45 Clothing
49 Waited
51 Flair
54 Adams and others
55 Myanmar's former name
57 Cicero's heart
58 Author Jaffe
59 One of a film pair
61 Litigant
62 Curtain material
63 Gas, e.g.
64 Attempt
65 Goes a round with Foreman
66 Actress Harper

DOWN

1 Cream soup
2 Go to
3 Parish official
4 Sea bird
5 Nosh
6 Office schedule
7 Dugout
8 Have to have
9 Pipe joint
10 Davis or Midler
11 Sort of
12 Some of Shakespeare's plays
16 Equivocators
18 Fond du __, WI
22 Did penance
24 ". . . with a blue ribbon __"
25 Retail booth
27 Dandies
28 Word form for "mouth"
31 Military hats
32 Subatomic particle
35 Pollen holders
36 Barely beat
37 Short gag
38 Actor Torn
39 Big prefix
46 Accumulate
47 Aegean island
48 Emerald and aquamarine
50 Honeybunch
51 Abbey bigwig
52 Agreeing words
53 Slangy denial
55 Radar spot
56 Arm bone
59 Cricket sides
60 To the rear

ACROSS

1 Scruff
5 NYC cultural inst.
9 Pronounce
14 Savings plans
15 Biblical twin
16 Sea eagles
17 Slogan
19 Reds and whites
20 Uses a stylus
21 Fleur-de-__
23 Prime-time hour
24 That girl
25 Door openers
27 Prepared a second draft of
30 Irate
31 Fuss
32 Beloved
34 Leash
38 Social clod
40 Upright
42 Presidents' Day event
43 Likewise
45 Noted naturalist
47 Canterbury can
48 Arrest
50 University of Cincinnati athlete
52 Set of computer commands
56 Japanese drama
57 Part of ABC
58 Service charge
59 Underwater outfits
62 Divided, as a highway
64 '60s game show, with *The*
66 Govt. bill
67 Home to billions
68 Wharton subj.
69 More logical
70 Deion Sanders' nickname
71 Piece of comedy

DOWN

1 Pleasant
2 "I smell __!"
3 Like some quilts
4 Optical illusionist/artist
5 Kitten cries
6 Bolivian bruin
7 Ex-Mrs. Trump
8 IRS work
9 Put in stitches
10 Baubles
11 "Tomorrow" girl
12 Wee
13 Slalom tracks
18 Biblical king
22 Fala was one
25 Regan's dad
26 Charlemagne's realm: Abbr.
27 Punjab princess
28 Perfect place
29 Angry
33 Comment, in computerese
35 Trunkless car
36 Author Kazan
37 Dollars for quarters
39 Unconnected
41 Raise to the third power
44 Unspecified degree
46 Dressing choice
49 Retailer of rhyme
51 Makeup selection
52 Estonians and Latvians
53 RadaRange maker
54 Mortise mate
55 Driver's option
59 Quick read
60 Mine, in Marseilles
61 Posted
63 __ *Spiegel*
65 Uruguayan uncle

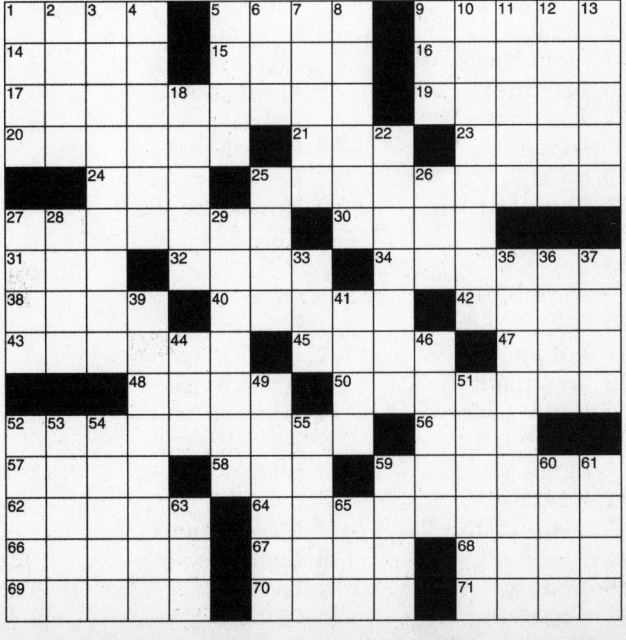

195 SWITCH-ER-OO by Cathy Millhauser

ACROSS
1 Ceiling
6 Settled accounts
10 Pencil puzzle
14 Muscat dweller
15 Sand shade
16 Corporate VIP
17 Hairless reindeer?
19 Rachel's sister
20 Taking a sabbatical
21 Space program
23 Coagulate
24 Shelley's black
25 Fill with cargo
28 Magic-show gleam?
33 They're instrumental
35 Frankfurt's river
36 Diminutive suffix
37 Babble
38 Wallower's spot
39 Renown
41 Snakelike swimmer
42 Shade source
44 Sad: Fr.
45 Riga resident's dive?
48 Clarke and West
49 Guns
50 Ethereal emanation
52 Wool source
55 Attic function
59 Cut the mustard?
60 Nursery rhyme Jack's brother?
63 Close
64 Ballet move
65 Manners
66 Commercial oil source?
67 Wrangle
68 Nail

DOWN
1 TV sheriff
2 Somalian model
3 Teen hangout
4 __ *Proposal* (Redford film)
5 Like some waves
6 Cordovan coin
7 Alas, in lieder
8 Miffed state
9 Built to last
10 Pumpkin kin
11 Lillehammer leap
12 Ardor
13 Sonar signal
18 Declares
22 Waiter, often
24 Pianist Duchin
25 Coat part
26 Mesh
27 Handled, with "with"
29 Famous
30 Arkansas River city
31 Cheer
32 Motel room posting
34 Pet rope
38 Wet septet
40 Ferber book
43 Makes over
44 Memorable abolitionist
46 Heisman, for one
47 South Pacific island
51 Quarters
52 Florence's river
53 Young of rock
54 Enrapt
56 *Three Men __ Baby*
57 Will of *The Waltons*
58 Celtic tongue
61 Gran Paradiso is one
62 Actress Carrere

196 SLUGFEST by Shirley Soloway

ACROSS
1 Sportscaster Albert
5 South African
9 "Splish Splash" singer
14 Opera solo
15 Singer Fitzgerald
16 Remove
17 Hold back
20 Beer mug
21 Aleutian island
22 Solidify
23 Part of a plan
26 Promos
28 Fail completely
36 Give __ whirl
37 Lord's house
38 Top quality
39 Ranee's wrap
41 Half a Latin dance
42 Bestow
43 Seafood fare
44 __-toity
46 Actress Scala
47 Attack unfairly
51 __-mo replay
52 Just fair
53 D'Amato and Gore
56 Actor Arkin
59 Give a speech
63 Do one's best
67 Getz and Musial
68 Icelandic literary work
69 Fraulein's refusal
70 Ghostlike
71 Consider
72 Rowlands of film

DOWN
1 Driver's aids
2 In __ (stuck)
3 Antagonize
4 Suitcase
5 Kingsley or Jonson
6 Grand __ Opry
7 Movie lioness
8 Engrossed
9 Lay bare
10 Circle segment
11 Stadium shouts
12 Words of comprehension
13 Heron's home
18 Prompt
19 Mormon state
24 Greek vowel
25 Sleeveless wrap
27 Look over
28 Larry, ex of CBS
29 Computer name
30 Gold measure
31 "Impossible!"
32 Characteristics
33 Podge preceder
34 How some tuna is packed
35 Inexperienced with
40 Recedes
42 *The __ Laura Mars* (Dunaway film)
45 But, for short
48 Run out
49 Singer Falana
50 Uninteresting
53 Church area
54 Renaissance instrument
55 Night-sky sight
57 Matured
58 Plant protrusion
60 Film critic James
61 Willowy
62 Italian volcano
64 Cycle starter
65 Verse form
66 Hoover, for one

197 BATHDAY PRESENTS by Lee Weaver

ACROSS

1 Man of morals
6 Revolutionary War general
10 Fisherman's maneuver
14 Reduced to fragments
15 Territory
16 Hoarfrost
17 Delete
18 Milky Way part
19 Sign of the future
20 Kitchen meas.
21 Handy wiper-uppers
24 Begins the bidding
26 Cope with
27 Call the strikes
29 Karpov's game
31 Film holder
32 Hula performer
34 Troop group: Abbr.
37 Young ladies
39 Food fish
40 Light racing boat
42 Notable period
43 Hall of Famer Spahn
46 Reed instrument
47 Like some coats
48 Baked bricks
50 Inquiring
53 Hardly huge
54 Light desserts
57 Freudian concept
60 Fabled race loser
61 Places
62 Navajo dwelling
64 *East of __*
65 Finished the cake
66 Spew forth
67 Red and Baltic
68 Scoundrels
69 Alfa __ (car)

DOWN

1 Help with the heist
2 Makes mistakes
3 Daily TV fare
4 Approvals, for short
5 Baby chick, e.g.
6 Sounds of surprise
7 Johnson of *Laugh-In*
8 Machine part
9 Made of baked clay
10 Tiaras, e.g.
11 Pointed (at)
12 Aroma
13 All wound up
22 All over again
23 Caravan stops
25 Medicinal medium
27 Coax
28 Golda of Israel
29 Tonal combination
30 Stay out of sight
33 Realty unit
34 Kid's jaw exerciser
35 Gin flavoring
36 Pub potables
38 Playground item
41 Swell, in the '50s and '90s
44 Heavenly
45 Moniker
47 Sheets and pillowcases
49 Dancer's partner
50 Campfire residue
51 Fictional detective Sam
52 Asian nation
53 Slips on the ice
55 Comedienne Imogene
56 Passed easily
58 Stare with dropped jaw
59 Aware of
63 Conquistador's quest

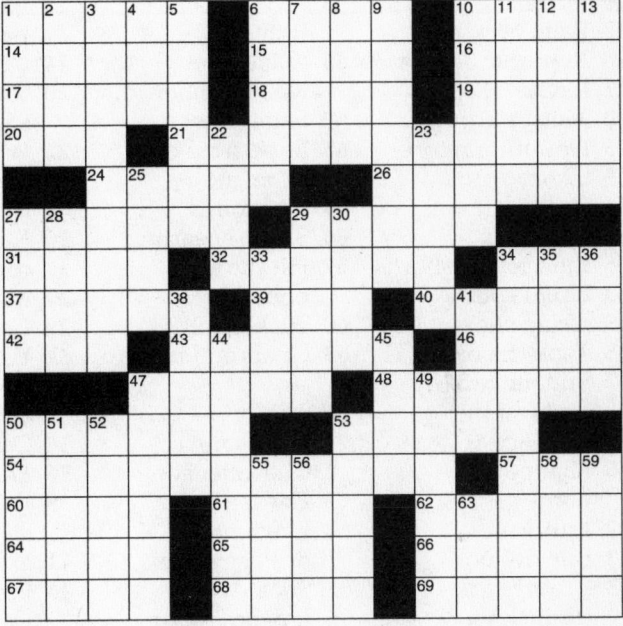

198 BAA-BAA by Bob Lubbers

ACROSS

1 Amoeba, e.g.
5 Way
9 Sp. ladies
13 Mishmash
14 Director Kazan
15 Hokkaido city
16 Thrashed
18 Rising star
19 Electrical unit
20 Lassos
22 "__ De-Lovely"
24 Scythe tracks
26 Bring order to
31 Bargain sign
33 At __ for words
34 Racetrack shapes
36 NT bk.
37 Dull
38 Pitchers
39 Religious image
40 Wager
41 Sidestep
42 Nixon's Secretary of Transportation
43 Guarantee
45 Order
47 On one's back
49 Part of R.S.V.P.
50 Lowest minor league
52 Baked __ (dessert)
57 "__ Whoopee"
59 Stevenson classic
61 Hebrew letters
62 Anthony or Barbara
63 __ off (sore)
64 Impudent
65 Former Haitian president Préval
66 EMK et al.

DOWN

1 Soft drink
2 Actor Jack
3 Sagging
4 Stud site
5 100 centimos
6 Model Carol
7 Layer
8 Mythical underworld
9 Summer ermines
10 Rickety
11 Exist
12 Big __, CA
15 Southern constellation
17 Seed covers
21 MP prey
23 Vermont ski center
25 Sailboats
26 Religious teacher
27 Barkin and Drew
28 European bird
29 Seat, slangily
30 Chris of tennis
32 Ocean fliers
35 *Ars gratia __*
38 Half the digits
39 Charged particle
41 Suffix meaning "believers"
42 Country estate
44 Raise, as spirits
46 Oscar-winner Wiest
48 Sand ridge
51 Helper
53 Urban dwellings: Abbr.
54 *Graf __*
55 Sharp
56 Puts in
57 Chart
58 Hearty brew
60 Playroom

199 SEA IT NOW by Dean Niles

ACROSS

1 Auguries
6 Group symbol
12 Hallway
15 Think
16 They come and go
17 Light carriage
18 __ *volente*
19 Bank acct. plus
20 Reporter Batista
21 Icelandic epic
23 Mets' stadium
25 Doubting retort
28 Clairvoyant ability
30 Shoulder muscle, for short
32 Up to spec
33 Asian sheep
35 Took the part
37 Still, in verse
38 Request in advance
40 Shannon's home
42 Lubricate
43 Buckin' pony
45 __ *Angelicus* (Franck work)
46 Folkloric collections
48 Greek meeting place
49 Letters of urgency
50 Scuba gear
51 Part of TAE
53 Two-person fight
56 "Mack the Knife" singer
59 Fade away
61 Superfund org.
62 Of an artery
64 Embroiled
66 Sheep shearing
67 Hit the high points
68 Tucked in
69 Gnats and brats

DOWN

1 Lead source
2 Chevalier song
3 Garden spots
4 Lawrence Welk or Peggy Lee
5 Sp. lady
6 Japanese soup
7 Rub-__
8 Its capital is Belgrade
9 Billy Ocean tune
10 Resident: Suff.
11 Mystery writer Josephine
12 Yield
13 Newspaper page
14 Certain chicken
20 Monopoly square
22 Without delay
24 Common Market inits.
26 Kate Nelligan role
27 Manages
29 Commoner
31 Word form for "thrice"
33 WWII sub
34 Queen: Sp.
36 *Ed Wood* star
39 __ *longa, vita brevis*
41 *Shane* star
44 Lon of Cambodia
47 Emulated Kerrigan
52 Fosters wrong
54 Pentathlon need
55 Friday's employer: Abbr.
57 Playwright Elmer
58 Chilled
60 Whack
62 Wright-Patterson __, OH
63 __ Miss
64 Keystone comic
65 Belittle, slangily

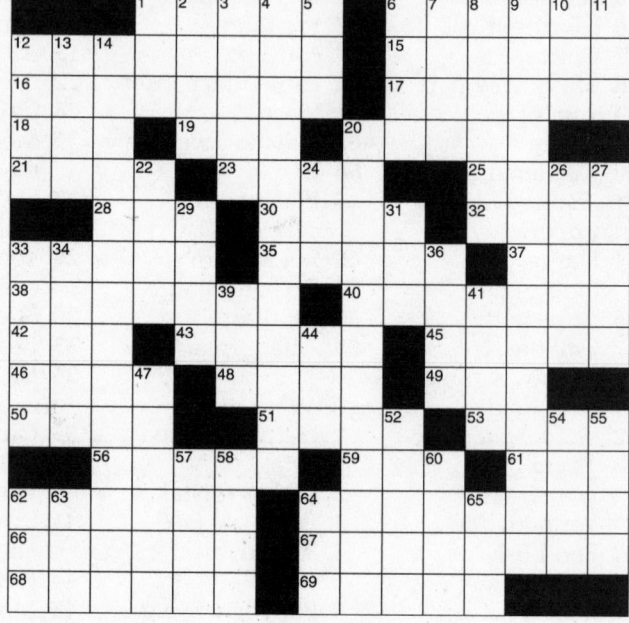

---

200 "OOH-LA-LA!" by Matt Gaffney

ACROSS

1 Strays, mostly
6 SkyDome players, informally
10 Elegant
14 Type of sorcery
15 Jai __
16 Singer Falana
17 Brass-dominated group
19 Balanchine ballet
20 Spots
21 Rainy-day fund
23 Brosnan TV role
24 Judge of Israel
25 Subterfuge
27 Reflexive pronoun
30 Darer's words
32 In __ (hurried)
34 Barents or Laptev
35 Unskilled worker
36 Pep
37 Twain kid
38 Feeling off
39 Impact sound
40 Closed hand
41 Support, in a way
43 Polite refusal
45 Lacking an owner
47 Sandinista Daniel
51 Everest adjective
53 Aromatic herb
54 Pre-deal ritual
55 Chaplin's wife
57 December 25
58 Part of BTU
59 F. Scott's wife
60 Piece of cake
61 Recipe amts.
62 Op-Ed piece

DOWN

1 They might swing
2 *Lusitania* sinker
3 ASU's city
4 Employed a resource
5 Onion kin
6 Rocky hits
7 In the style of
8 New Age musician
9 Fries or slaw
10 __ *Republic*
11 Egg formation
12 Work hard
13 Suspend
18 Listen to
22 Fourth man
24 2 Down creators
26 The Tower of London, once
28 Pre-Easter time
29 Ticket buyer
30 Farmer's place
31 Dark drink
33 Doing
35 Photo
36 Extends
37 Cone homes
39 Brake part
40 City of *Italia*
42 *Aider*
44 London district
46 Some jackets
48 Bad things
49 Hayworth role
50 Put to rest
51 Physicist Bethe
52 Part of
53 Broadway opening of '82
56 Tuck partner

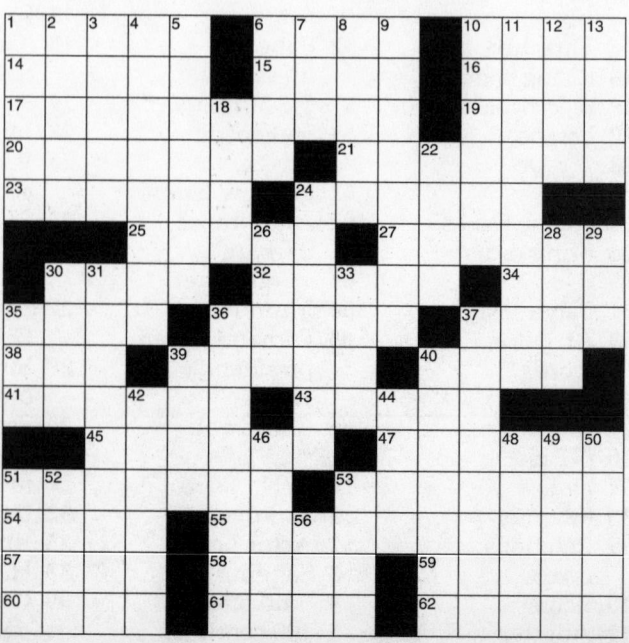

ON THE MOVE by Diane C. Baldwin

ACROSS

1 Work hard
6 Work stint
11 Director Reiner
14 Higher than
15 Asian city
16 Bullring cry
17 Night traveler
19 Fruity quaff
20 Munich mister
21 Chichi
22 Birch kin
24 Faucet problem
26 Dresses up
27 Fish group
30 Part of FBI
32 Indicate, with "at"
33 Beer barrels
34 "Uh-uh!"
37 Advantage
38 Kathy of *Misery*
39 "Do __ others . . ."
40 Morse Code sound
41 Some coastal cities
42 Villain's look
43 Old car
45 California team
46 Main points
48 Chess-game conclusion
49 Hebrew letter
50 Flue dirt
52 Wily subterfuge
56 Little rascal
57 Green cocktail
60 Be in contention
61 National bird
62 TNT center
63 Poet's adverb
64 Chases off
65 Elitists

DOWN

1 Mascara target
2 Competent
3 South African settler
4 Cooked too much
5 House mem.
6 Pointy
7 Sentry's cry
8 Very dark
9 Antagonist
10 Verbal eruptions
11 Cartoon bird
12 Of bygone times
13 Malty drinks
18 Mournful noise
23 Mauna __
25 Disintegrate
26 Large vessels
27 Went lickety-split
28 Musical ending
29 Track athlete
30 Eccentric
31 Takes advantage of
33 Find fault
35 Suit to __
36 __ d'oeuvres
38 Cries of derision
39 Support, as a foundation
41 Promises
42 Took a chair
44 Logger's tool
45 Walkway
46 Novelist Cussler
47 Fabric fiber
48 Painter Grandma __
50 Kind of palm
51 European capital
53 No higher than
54 Eastern European
55 Love god
58 Cheering sound
59 Light-switch positions

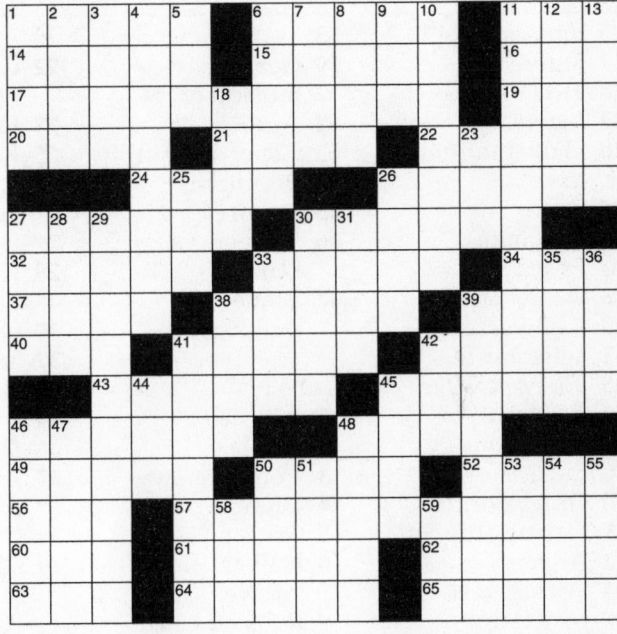

VIRTUOUS by Fred Piscop

ACROSS

1 Nettle
5 Perfecto, e.g.
10 Tough spot
13 You love: Lat.
14 Comfort
15 Environmental prefix
16 Mary Baker Eddy, for one
18 Greek P
19 Diatribe
20 Elephant, e.g.
22 Porters' relatives
23 German city
24 Sock mender
27 Monarch's spouse
30 Do a front-end job
31 Chunk of ice
32 Witch
34 Hold unrealistic expectations
38 Moo __ pork
39 Matterhorn's range
40 Sculptor Auguste
41 Dismays
44 Unruffled
45 Andy's pal
46 Sheriff's badge
47 Eye neighbors
50 Copper coating
53 Bunyan tool
54 Fund-raiser
58 Ms. Caldwell
59 Goddess of witchcraft
60 Rickey flavoring
61 Conclusion
62 Cosmetician Lauder
63 Jack of westerns

DOWN

1 Battle of Britain flyers: Abbr.
2 "Look at me, __ helpless . . ."
3 Secular
4 Alienate
5 '50s dorm denizens
6 Stevedores' grp.
7 "My __ Sal"
8 Colorless solvents
9 Summer TV fare
10 Dweeb
11 Post-workout woe
12 Anchor
14 Like some fabrics
17 Rubinstein of cosmetics
21 __-cone (ice treat)
23 Blessings
24 Morse bits
25 Hawaii "hi"
26 Tear apart
27 Evens the hedges
28 __ Island Red
29 Two-pointer
31 Niagara, e.g.
33 Wilder or Hackman
35 Rainy-day footwear
36 Versailles document
37 Abominable
42 Oom-__
43 Don of *Cocoon*
44 Aver
46 Ill will
47 Lounge around
48 Nerve-cell part
49 Feeder filler
51 Makeshift coat hanger
52 __ mater
55 Play a part
56 Comic Charlotte
57 Apollo component

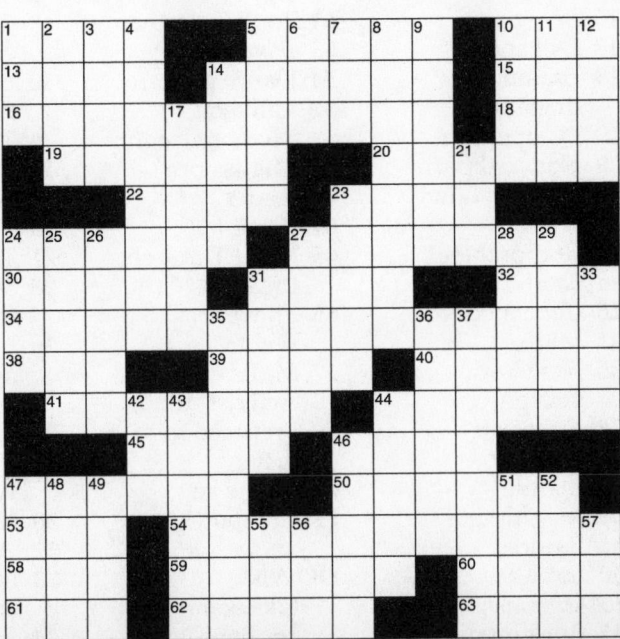

203 REMEMBERING GENE by Bob Lubbers

ACROSS
1 Turkish city
6 '70s ring champ
9 Emoter
12 Grows limp
13 Chaney, Sr. or Jr.
14 Pie __ mode
15 Gene Kelly musical of '49
17 Slopes rig
18 Tina's ex
19 Yearn
20 Show gratitude to
21 Some Balkanites
24 Faded star
26 Winter jacket
28 Well-versed
31 Teherani
35 *The Man in the __ Mask*
36 Gene Kelly musical of '52
40 Greek portico
41 Flapjack flipper
42 Arenas
44 Wickerwork material
48 Uncomfortable position
52 Gettysburg general
53 Mexican money
55 Cop a __
57 Carmine or cherry
58 Tsar name
59 Gene Kelly musical of '44
62 Auto
63 General Amin
64 Brouhaha
65 Inquire
66 "__ Cents a Dance"
67 Tennis rankings

DOWN
1 Aroused
2 Moola
3 Computer key
4 High degree
5 Cruising
6 Hail or farewell
7 Rob and Chad
8 Small hotel
9 Cuban dance
10 Alda or Hale
11 Notch
16 "Tut tut!"
17 Gene Kelly musical of '48
18 *The Heart __ Lonely Hunter*
20 __-Mex cuisine
22 Gene Kelly musical of '54
23 Delhi dress
25 Role for Navarro or Heston
27 Dole's state
29 King, in France
30 Opry network
32 Tang
33 Actress Balin
34 Lwyr.
36 Draft org.
37 Addams' cousin
38 Genesis craft
39 Character actor Jack
43 Part of TGIF
45 Punished severely
46 Fred's sister et al.
47 Actor Beatty
49 Lyric poem
50 Sergeant York
51 Shirt shape
53 12-point type
54 Gabor and Perón
56 Weaponry
59 Op. __ (footnote tag)
60 "Golly!"
61 __ du Diable

204 WATER LOG by Gregory E. Paul

ACROSS
1 Embarrass
6 Smelter leftover
10 Sci-fi creature
14 Ma's instrument
15 Flooring unit
16 Berg opera
17 Evil spirit
18 Ugandan dictator
19 PC operator
20 National park
22 A James Bond school
23 Comprehend
24 Satan's doing
26 Cable network
31 Mideast VIP
35 New York college
36 Dozes off
38 Playing marble
39 Marathoner Zátopek
40 Subway stations
42 Buck heroine
43 Crystal-lined stone
45 Kovacs' wife
46 '52 Olympics site
47 Opry star Tubb
49 Casey Jones, e.g.
51 Tooth's partner
53 *Platoon* locale
54 Dance pattern
57 Jefferson Memorial sight
63 Mississippi feeder
64 Berserk
65 "__ It Through the Rain"
66 Flowerless plant
67 Midevening
68 Activist Abzug
69 Prepared to drive
70 Phone key
71 Computer key

DOWN
1 Like some appliances
2 Suds
3 __ mater
4 Letter drop
5 "No fooling!"
6 Deadlock
7 Succotash bean
8 Similarly
9 Convention city
10 Brooke Shields film, with *The*
11 A deadly sin
12 Grocery buy
13 Be angry
21 Tack-room gear
25 Savings plan, for short
26 Long onslaught
27 Round-tripper
28 Salad add-in
29 "Life in the Woods" locale
30 Horace work
32 Quiz choice
33 Dickens title start
34 Pavarotti, e.g.
37 Regatta sight
41 *Love Story* author
44 Spanish pronoun
48 Giants
50 Drink
52 The sky, perhaps
54 Cushy
55 Quaker pronoun
56 Shamrock isle
58 Lisbon lady
59 Revival shout
60 NaCl
61 Run in place
62 At hand

205 HARD ON THE BARD by Dean Niles

ACROSS

1 Prattles
6 Samarra native
11 Bread spread
14 Of birds
15 Second showing
16 Mine find
17 Pepys on *A Midsummer Night's Dream*
19 The present
20 Everglades-like
21 A Bobbsey twin
22 Flower holder
23 Zoo group
25 Impressed
27 *L.A. Law* role
30 Masonry stone
33 Dry as dust
34 Big name in feet
35 Baedeker feature
38 Shaw on *Antony and Cleopatra*
41 __ Wednesday
42 Futurist's concerns
43 Weight
44 Big party
45 Outspoken
46 Dogpatch creator
49 Vend
51 Imitation
52 One __ customer
55 Roof support
59 Prevaricate
60 Voltaire on *Hamlet*
62 Beethoven's Symphony No. 3 __-flat
63 Prospero's spirit
64 Mysterious
65 Scratched, in a way
66 Overwrought
67 Easter lickings

DOWN

1 Scottish headwear
2 Proclaim
3 Simpson kid
4 Asian capital
5 Ill-tempered
6 Major CPA employer
7 Harness part
8 Prop for *un angelo*
9 Some bets
10 Mich. neighbor
11 Jinx
12 Got out of bed
13 Complained like a kitten
18 TV "Science Guy"
22 TV attachment
24 __ torte
26 Baby powder
27 __ ghanouj
28 Aphrodite's son
29 Apt rhyme for "nearby"
31 Alan Ladd role
32 Multitudes
34 Sacred book
35 Computer display
36 Give __ for one's money
37 "Lend me your ear!"
39 Red sign
40 Like 888 numbers
44 Jazz instrument
45 Swords
46 Tack on
47 "Mule Train" singer
48 To the third power
50 Transgress
53 *thirtysomething* star
54 Long time
56 Irish kings' home
57 Actor Jannings
58 Charlotte et al.
60 Tub for wine
61 Malty drink

206 TABLE SETTING by Rich Norris

ACROSS

1 Baby's word
5 Office item
9 Animal's stomach
13 Monogram part: Abbr.
14 Breathing sound
15 Urbane
16 Exemplar of dullness
18 Lively frolic
19 Lined up
20 Lined up
22 Knock down
24 Skirmish
25 Ticket leftover
27 Wisconsin college
29 Western alliance: Abbr.
30 AT&T rival
32 Most achy
35 Like better
37 "Neat!"
39 Aphrodite's love
41 Prefix for function
42 *Norma* __
43 Go back on one's word
45 Meadowlands team
46 Actor Gregory
49 Boxer's weak spot
52 Surgeon's tools
54 Piranha
57 Southwestern Indians
58 Pamper
60 Up in the air
61 Camp sight
62 Mil. coll.
63 Took off
64 Scraps for Fido
65 Former Ford models

DOWN

1 Conn of *Grease*
2 Has __ with (knows)
3 Freed from error
4 Pulsing
5 Slow speech
6 Dine
7 Jacket part
8 Corn bits
9 Personal preference
10 Less common
11 Oat grass
12 Overgrown, as a lawn
15 Fast flier: Abbr.
17 Amazed shout
21 Tired-looking
23 Japanese sash
25 Absorb, with "up"
26 Scarlett's home
28 Makes angry
30 Biblical graffiti word
31 Shrink away
33 Most outlandish
34 The other one
36 Warehouse device
38 "Sure!"
40 Does business with
41 __ Moines, IA
44 Horror film watcher, at times
45 Cookies quantity
46 Word of disapproval
47 French school
48 Kind of chicken
50 Glaswegians
51 First mo.
53 L.A. zone
55 Gentle curve
56 Author LeShan et al.
59 Ottawa's prov.

207 HAVE IT YOUR WAY by Gerald R. Ferguson

ACROSS
1 Downturn
6 Church event
10 Schmo
14 Word before code or colony
15 Adjoin
16 Spiny houseplant
17 Palm Springs neighbor
18 Actress Miles
19 Kelly or Tunney
20 Boot tip
21 When to get it?
24 Uncle of fiction
26 Actress Gardner
27 Oklahoma Indian
29 Mighty
34 Wading bird
35 Back tooth
36 Cell chemical: Abbr.
37 Levin and Gershwin
38 __ Island (Big Apple resort)
39 Guzzlers
40 Sass
41 Madrid museum
42 Send payment
43 Meetings
45 Midler et al.
46 Med. insurance plan
47 Football coach Bill
48 How to do it?
53 Wriggly fish
56 On the briny
57 Once, old-style
58 Preface, for short
60 Waist cincher
61 Learning method
62 Sign gases
63 Clockmaker Thomas
64 Ship's mast
65 Is wide-eyed

DOWN
1 Shish-kebab need
2 *Tonight Show* host
3 Where to keep it?
4 __ tai (drink)
5 Tillers
6 Gospel singer Staples
7 Genesis name
8 Certain
9 Emulate a no-show
10 Panther kin
11 Util. product
12 Novelist Jaffe
13 Sharp
22 Color
23 Finished
25 Genesis figure
27 Silvers and Foster
28 Eagle's nest
29 Small lakes
30 Toast spread
31 Where to take it?
32 Open a bow
33 Endures
35 Groan's companion
38 Bing's emulators
39 Hardens
41 Egyptian cotton
42 Trusting, with "on"
44 Scabbard
45 Coll. degrees
47 Tend the plants
48 Arrests
49 Savvy reply
50 Ancient Briton
51 Bit of rain
52 This: Sp.
54 Sea eagle
55 Financial setback
59 PBS benefactor

208 HOW MANY MOVIES? by Bob Lubbers

ACROSS
1 Latin dance
6 Sap producer
11 Bruins hero
14 Spin
15 Ring source?
16 Corp. boss
17 Davis/Baxter film of '50
19 Swelled head
20 Shore
21 Dart
22 Gibson or Tillis
25 Aliens, for short
26 Veiled dancer
28 Stage cue
30 Beef or veal
33 In a while
34 Scanty
36 Peres predecessor
38 Sinatra/Martin film of '58
43 Senator Specter
44 Tributary
45 Classic violin
48 Urchin
50 "Whatever __ wants, . . ."
51 Scale start
53 Satire mag
55 Law deg.
56 Barnum singer
57 Singer Cole
61 Anger
62 Cruise/Nicholson film of '92
66 __-relief
67 Weird
68 Gorby's wife
69 Draft org.
70 Croakers
71 Shatter

DOWN
1 RR depot
2 Hole maker
3 Wire measure
4 Bikini tops
5 *Three Tall Women* playwright
6 Fluffy dessert
7 Against
8 Like a noted piper
9 Adores
10 Chemical suffix
11 Spotted cat
12 Government
13 Fan
18 Breakfast choice
21 Napped fabric
22 GI dining room
23 National Leaguer
24 Actor Neeson
27 True up
29 Paid the tab
31 Fight site
32 Sailor
35 Theater drop
37 City near Niagara Falls
39 Small gull
40 Role model, perhaps
41 Singer Carter
42 Alum
45 Improvs
46 Shearer and Kelly
47 *The Thing* star
49 Reflections
52 Surmise
54 Certain fashions
58 Nautical start
59 Tree shoot
60 Waxed cheese
62 Gen. Pershing's command
63 Farrow or Sara
64 Road curve
65 Slangy turndown

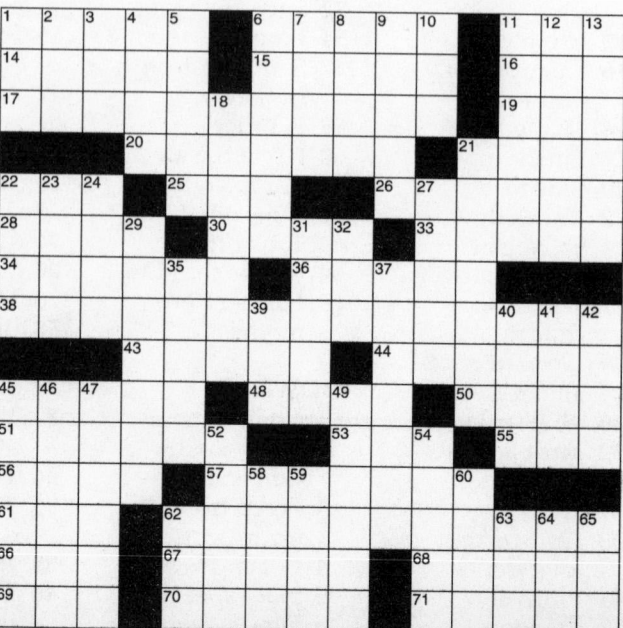

WHO'S COOKIN' by Dean Niles

ACROSS
1 Blind as __
5 __ Buddies (Hanks sitcom)
10 Hideout
14 Biblical verb
15 50 Across' métier
16 Otherwise
17 American Cookery author
19 __ monster
20 Commences
21 Not for kids
23 Cereal sound
24 State formed in 1948
27 Art of Cooking author
32 XLV x X
35 Troubled
36 "Smooth Operator" singer
37 Commotion
39 Fuel choice
41 Cleveland's lake
42 Consumer voice
45 Gal of song
46 Boston Cooking School Cookbook author

50 Soprano Maria
51 Promontory
54 Narrow passages
57 Genie's specialty
59 New York stadium
60 Mastering the Art of French Cooking author
64 Daybreak
65 Out and about
66 __ la Douce
67 M*A*S*H star
68 Baseball great Wagner
69 Pinnacle

DOWN
1 Pts. of speech
2 Cats and canoes
3 The self, in Hinduism
4 British rule in India
5 Hope and Hoskins
6 Uncover, to Keats
7 Big wave

8 Bobby of hockey
9 Colorful weave
10 Brief words
11 Disembarked
12 Gilligan's home
13 Interpret
18 Saul, latterly
22 Salesperson
24 Smarts stats
25 Bring to court
26 Like Sen. Dole
28 Number-cruncher: Abbr.
29 Skip a bid
30 Brainstorm
31 Role for Jodie
32 Kitchen boss
33 Copperfield's first wife
34 Steak cut
38 Liking
39 DC party
40 Peaceful
42 Pro sports org.
43 Top bond rating
44 AMA members

47 "__ Woman" (Reddy tune)
48 Biblical prophet
49 Send again
52 English county
53 City in the news in '65
54 Beliefs

55 Exhibit
56 Hatcher or Garr
57 800-no. rel.
58 Wyo. neighbor
61 USAF headache
62 Screen Chaney
63 Marker

KEEPING CURRENT by Cathy Millhauser

ACROSS
1 Chihuahua "ciao"
6 Revered one
10 They're often checked
14 Dotty
15 Honor, in a way
16 Nabisco nosh
17 What did Mr. Current give his lawyer?
20 Persian poet
21 Hound handle
22 Swedish coin
23 Evangelist McPherson
25 Sellout abbr.
26 What did his trial stem from?
32 Newspaper sections
33 Cannes water
34 Artie's fourth
35 Take out
38 Coleus holder
41 DI doubled
42 Ungainly one
44 Native in The Piano

45 Where was he tried?
50 Natal prefix
51 Well-pitched, à la Ryan
52 Subordinates
55 Helper
56 Ancient Peruvian
60 Why was he happy in confinement?
63 Mashie, e.g.
64 Cancel publication of
65 Like some seals
66 Cartoonist Gross
67 Different
68 Replay option

DOWN
1 Chihuahua chow
2 Ruination
3 Hawkeye State
4 Runner
5 Neighbor of Isr.
6 Less certain
7 Sharpshooter

8 A Ringling brother
9 Voided serve
10 Pulp genre
11 Tuscany river
12 SAT taker
13 Teriyaki sauce source
18 All ___ ('84 film)
19 Soup pod
24 "__ girl!"
25 House of worship
26 Surround
27 Storage site
28 Kind of gun
29 Florida footballer
30 Turn inside out
31 Hindu raiment
32 "The Apostle of the Franks"
36 Gabrielle's nickname
37 Greek cross
39 Mine: Fr.
40 Like some miles
43 Spire toppers

46 Layette recipient
47 Grid judges
48 Take first steps
49 Suspect star
52 Mason's wedge
53 Actress Hatcher
54 USA offense

55 Dye source
57 Pupil of Seneca
58 Role for Red
59 Actor Ray
61 Newsman Pappas
62 Sportscaster's shout

211 CONTAINMENT by Shirley Soloway

ACROSS
1 Composers' org.
6 Greatest amount
10 Brad of *Seven*
14 Norse chieftain
15 Aroma
16 __ about (approximately)
17 WWII sub
18 Horne or Olin
19 Corn dish
20 Is dismissed
23 Actress Peeples
24 New Zealand parrot
25 Put back in office
27 Actor Jason
31 Understands
32 Wedding words
33 Decade parts
36 River to the Rio Grande
39 Schoolbook
41 Sugary
43 Govern
44 Eastern Indians

46 Wash vigorously
48 Pod veggie
49 Short snoozes
51 Window over a door
53 Skin coloring
56 "__ to Pieces" ('65 tune)
57 Goof up
58 Relevant example
64 Dog's wagger
66 Jamie of *M*A*S*H*
67 "The future __!"
68 __ time (never)
69 Sky bear
70 Green sauce
71 Table parts
72 Atl. crossers
73 Senator Kefauver

DOWN
1 Cut __ (dance)
2 "__ it!" ("Amen!")
3 Coagulate

4 *Northern Exposure* state
5 Ceramic ware
6 Underground dweller
7 Commemorative poems
8 Sub detector
9 Vestiges
10 Dad
11 Besotted
12 Pick-me-up
13 Nice surprise
21 Mythological underworld
22 Retain
26 Nasty look
27 Ceremony
28 Czech river
29 Tyson's milieu
30 Wood cutters
34 VCR button
35 Spanish muralist
37 Veggie spread
38 Garment line
40 Mule group
42 City on the Po
45 Architectural detail, for short

47 Scottish instrument
50 Mixups
52 Rope loops
53 Flower part
54 Hot under the collar
55 Peter and Ivan

59 Prefix for while
60 Lyricist Gershwin et al.
61 Part of MIT
62 Short letter
63 Pairs
65 __ Alamos, NM

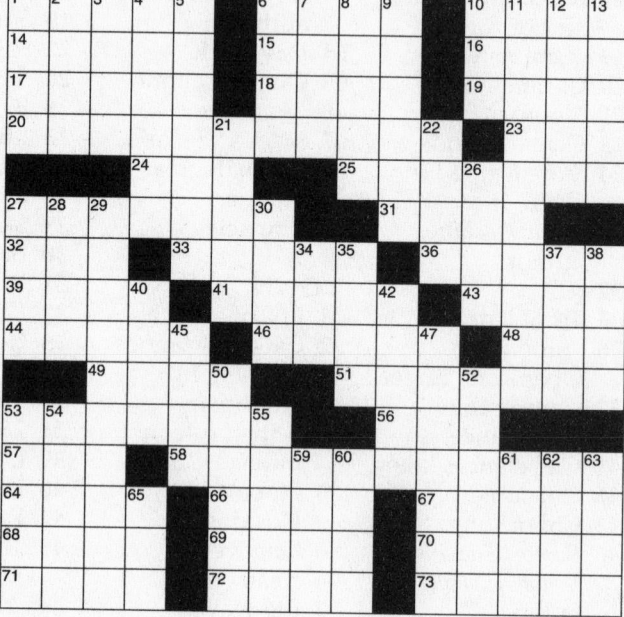

212 KENNEL RATION by Randy Sowell

ACROSS
1 Singer Horne
5 Cowboy rope
10 Rotisserie part
14 "Take __ leave it"
15 Fiery felony
16 Hosiery shade
17 Ill-tempered one
19 Leer at
20 Japanese robe
21 Windflowers
23 Marmalade ingredient
25 Fizzy drink
26 Citadel student
29 Speedy biped
32 Tie type
35 Eros' Roman counterpart
36 Earth, e.g.
38 Certain savings plan: Abbr.
39 Russian jets
40 Ignited again
41 Bathday cake
42 Shade tree

43 Chip ingredient
44 Precious
45 Rent
47 Look at
48 Heston role
49 Eye drop
51 Expensive
53 Possums, for instance
57 Singer Lionel
61 For fear that
62 Dullard
64 Poker fee
65 Greek epic
66 Hence
67 Sit, as for an artist
68 __ Haute, IN
69 Ruin

DOWN
1 Wet an envelope
2 Small case
3 Standard
4 Knight suppliers
5 Dangerous gas
6 Work unit

7 On the ocean
8 Roger Rabbit, e.g.
9 Boleyn and Bancroft
10 Hairnets
11 Combative
12 Not at work
13 Golf props
18 Item
22 Castle protector
24 Strike out
26 Sahara beast
27 Missed by __
28 Doctrine-bound individuals
30 Asian peninsula
31 TWA rival
33 Speak pompously
34 Uses the VCR
36 In favor of
37 WWII command for DDE
41 Burned a bit

43 Garden need
46 Parlor piece
48 Principal
50 Send payment
52 Wear away
53 Applaud
54 Nevada city

55 Have dominion
56 Cooking direction
58 Large sandwich
59 Othello's undoer
60 Esau's country
63 Roof material

SWEET STUFF by Thomas W. Schier

ACROSS
1 Actor Lee J.
5 __ B'rith
9 Notices
13 Atmosphere
14 Start again
15 Pressed (on)
17 Facial ridge
18 Director Reitman
19 Homeric enchantress
20 Candy-shop selections
23 Interject
25 Antediluvian
26 Put together snugly
27 Candy-shop selections
31 Relig. title
32 Take __ (accept risk)
33 Humid
35 Comic Martha
36 Mischievous one
38 Pancake place, initially
42 Former German coin

44 First-century pope
45 Male swan
48 Candy-shop selection
51 Burdens
53 Cable channel
54 Wind dir.
55 Candy-shop selection
59 Clayey
60 Lopez's theme song
61 Matured
64 __ a customer
65 Sign to heed
66 Shoreline recess
67 One-pot meal
68 Split violently
69 Author Wister

DOWN
1 Urban vehicle
2 Sharers' word
3 Cohan's favorite address
4 Cry loudly
5 Pull in
6 The Silver State

7 __ at the Races
8 Charged atoms
9 Achievement
10 Satie and Estrada
11 Marsh birds
12 Hush-hush
16 Since: Sp.
21 Folk tales
22 Tear open
23 Open a bit
24 Baby's word
28 Pitcher Saberhagen
29 Sears rival
30 Around the 30th: Abbr.
34 Wedding-cake feature
36 Move through mud
37 Bus. mogul
39 Slammer
40 Fixes a squeak
41 Carpet asset
43 Was shown up
44 "I __ Song Go . . ."
45 Jazz group

46 Burger toppers
47 Roy Rogers' dog
49 Like some bases
50 Away from the sea
52 Rollerblade

56 __ close to schedule
57 Attend, with "to"
58 Folded food
62 Actress Arden
63 Lair

ON THE RINK by Bob Lubbers

ACROSS
1 Jazzy Washington
6 Satiate
10 Einstein colleague
14 Actress Verdugo
15 Tops
16 __ vera
17 Protest tactic
18 Affable fellow
20 Held onto
21 Bolted
22 Vistas
23 __ avis
25 Confuse
26 Chou's comrade
28 "Ho-hum!"
33 TV alien
34 Norway export
35 USC stats
39 Persevere
42 Oz dog
43 Idle
44 King's employer
45 Soaped up

47 WBA wins
48 Mortar worker
51 __ spumante
53 "__ Fideles"
55 Hockey Hall-of-Famer
57 "__ it rich?"
60 Boxer Walcott
62 Detest
63 Olympian Korbut
64 Citrus skin
65 Rostropovich's instrument
66 Stagger
67 "Zounds!"
68 Use a fitting room

DOWN
1 Rolltop, e.g.
2 Tennis pro Nastase
3 Annual-report stat
4 O'Day or Loos
5 Solo of Star Wars
6 Loopy

7 Lake diver
8 Numero __
9 Danson and Knight
10 Shirred item
11 Chan portrayer
12 Hailey bestseller
13 Della or Pee Wee
19 Lasting impression
21 Drumroll
24 Hazard
26 Sail support
27 Sax range
29 Indolence
30 Dean Martin song topic
31 Gaffe
32 Bend __ (talk too much)
36 In a mischievous manner
37 __ domini
38 Retirees' IDs
40 Huge
41 Norms: Abbr.

46 Chip in
48 Important
49 Designer Simpson
50 Lint collector
52 Rome's river
54 Jane __

55 Wife of Charlie Chaplin
56 Funny Foxx
58 __ contendere
59 Disney sci-fi film
61 Lively dance
62 False front

215 ON TV by A.J. Santora

ACROSS

1 Put into service
4 Long sentence
8 Big hit
13 Business partner, at times
14 Folklore being
16 Noted caravel
17 Tax mo.
18 Like some channels
20 Symbol of authority
22 Eugene's home
23 Put away
24 New Zealand tree
26 Purposeful
27 Accept
28 Political alliance
30 J.P. clientele
32 Walks
34 Khartoum's river
35 It's heard on TV
38 Appear
40 Most watchful
44 Slugger Jose
47 Fake-gold alloys
48 Blackbird
49 Stallone role
51 Renter's document
52 Evenings: Abbr.
53 Pyramid builder
55 Plane letters
56 TV figure
59 Penpoint
61 "It's the end of __!"
62 High home
63 *Bambi* role
64 __ metabolism
65 Aide: Abbr.
66 Emmy-winner Walston

DOWN

1 Cable network
2 Sills or Battle
3 On the way
4 Shirt size: Abbr.
5 China preceder
6 Lowest UHF channel
7 TV personality
8 TV news bias
9 "*O Sole* __"
10 Poe subject
11 Importance
12 Alex and Jack
15 Golfing feat
19 Sweat
21 Shifts, e.g.
24 Spigoted container
25 TV paid programming
29 Robert Morse role
31 Devotions
33 Writer LeShan
36 TV foul-ups
37 Occupational suffix
38 '70s Latin-rock band
39 Isolates
40 Most watchful
41 Lou Grant on TV
42 Verse form
43 Mao __-tung
44 Cambridge student
45 "Three Coins in the Fountain" lyricist
46 The end
50 Black tea
54 *Je ne __ quoi*
57 Malay isthmus
58 PD prober
60 Kind of horse

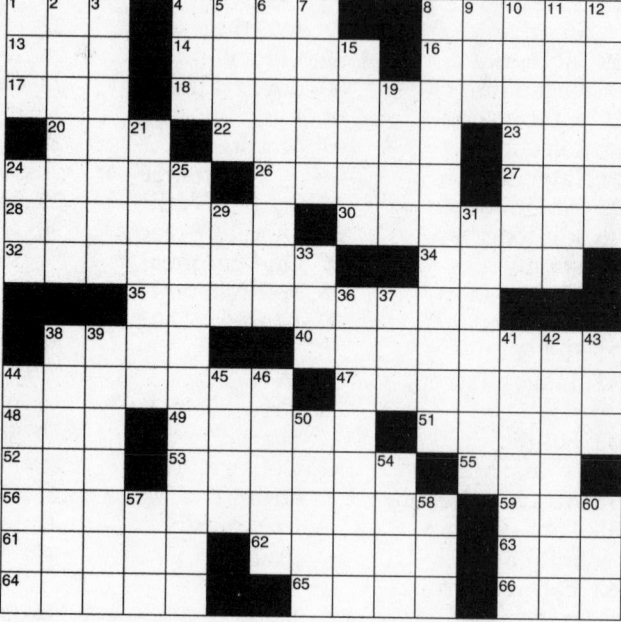

216 FARE IS FOWL by Bob Lubbers

ACROSS

1 Within
5 Stitched line
9 Islamic center
14 Lucid
15 Sailors' saint
16 A Musketeer
17 Nagged
19 Have an opinion
20 Certain paints
22 Top cards
23 Legal adverb
26 Leg part
28 More than some
29 Talk-sing
32 Estimate
35 Blackthorn fruits
37 Requires
39 "It's __ for Me to Say"
40 Wimp
41 __ Aviv
42 Michael Caine role
44 Play part
45 Pours
47 Plow maker
48 __ with (encounter)
50 Droop
52 __-do-well
53 Uses a lasso
55 Awaits
57 Singer __ James
59 Gold-watch recipient
62 Lasso
64 Lamp type
68 Sign of the Ram
69 Cartoonist Peter
70 __ in (collapse)
71 Monica of tennis
72 Mortgage, for example
73 Ireland

DOWN

1 Bat wood
2 Ginnie __
3 Rural hotel
4 Uses up
5 Area
6 Actress Sommer
7 NYSE competitor
8 Fashions
9 Gym pad
10 Allen and Frome
11 Paltry amount
12 Ice-cream holder
13 Inquires
18 Consume
21 Roe source
23 Painter Childe __
24 __ Islands (former name of Tuvalu)
25 Speedboat's wake
27 Syrian president
30 Against
31 Hammer parts
33 Evening party
34 Takes the wheel
36 Waffle topper
38 *Born Free* lioness
43 Mercy
46 Copycat
49 Exactly
51 She played Mrs. Miniver
54 *Love Story* author
56 Honey maker
57 Time periods
58 Whitewall, e.g.
60 Matador's foe
61 New York campus
63 Wild equine
65 Jug handle
66 106, to Caesar
67 Author Kesey

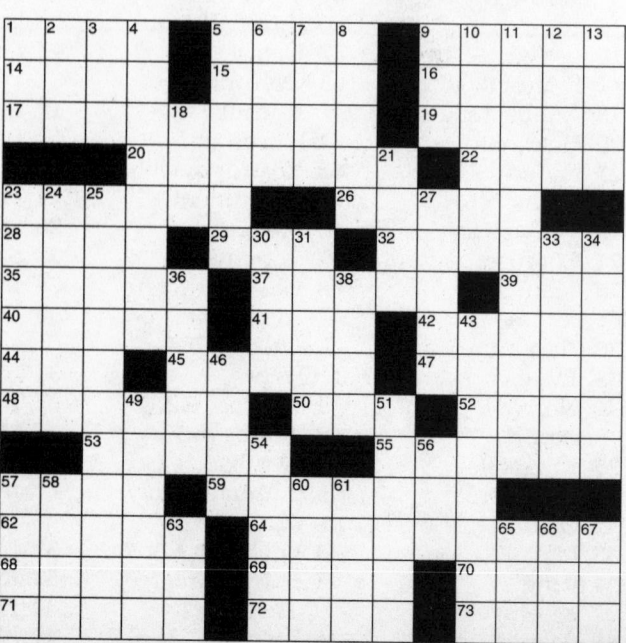

TOPOGRAPHICALS by Gerald R. Ferguson

ACROSS

1 Religious service
5 Lead actor
9 Ugandan exile
13 "*Dies* __"
14 ". . . thereby hangs __"
15 Zilch
16 Singer Carter
17 *Salvador* star
19 Sailing ships
21 Ballroom dances
22 Egg parts
23 Optimistic
24 Say no
26 Xylophones' cousins
30 Top-drawer
31 Thesaurus compiler
32 __ Jima
33 Islands: Fr.
34 VCR input
35 Big family
36 Animator's unit
37 Like O'Brien potatoes
38 Fast dance
39 In a row
41 Participant
42 Like __ of sunshine
43 Muse of poetry
44 Grownups
47 Like some literary endings
50 *Pillow Talk* star
52 Pianist Peter
53 She: Fr.
54 Washer cycle
55 Strong wind
56 Scorch
57 Kitchen conclusion
58 Haughty one

DOWN

1 Flash Gordon's foe
2 Geometric calculation
3 *Norma Rae* star
4 Hit shows
5 Musial and Laurel
6 Scottish caps
7 Pub quaff
8 Puts back
9 Alias
10 Synthesizer creator
11 Subcontinental prefix
12 Famous T-man
14 "Can't you take __?"
18 "__ something I said?"
20 Alternatively
23 Threw a fit
24 Chill again
25 Actress Barkin
26 Acted pouty
27 "Suddenly" singer
28 Alert
29 Submarine finder
31 Prone to showers
34 Pirate's haul
35 Latex layers
37 Onward
38 Outline
40 Mynah or parrot
41 On one's stomach
43 Unevenly notched
44 War god
45 1996 campaign name
46 Bruins' sch.
47 "Ain't," correctly
48 Folk singer Guthrie
49 Leopold's partner
51 Telegraphy sound

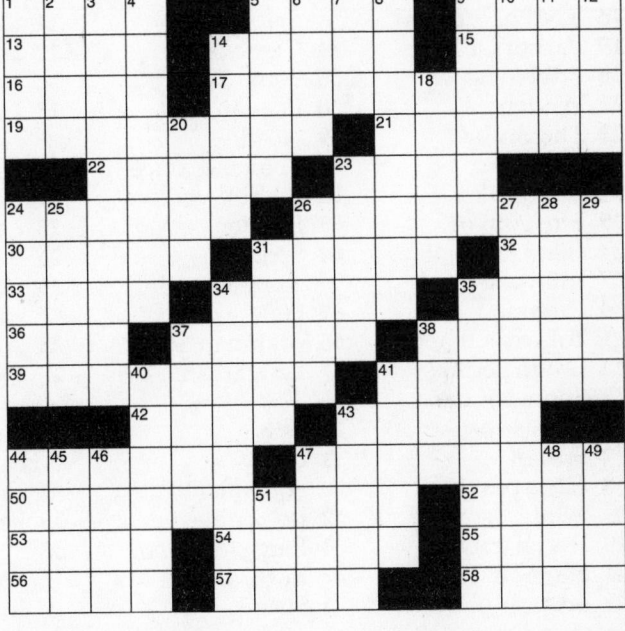

OUTSIDE THE LAW by Diane C. Baldwin

ACROSS

1 Monica of tennis
6 Barber's need
11 Chew the fat
14 Drab hue
15 Deb's crown
16 Time to remember
17 Papillon was one
19 Take first
20 Real lulu
21 Sommer of *The Prize*
22 Jacket material
24 Horsehair
26 Fishhook attachments
27 Ornate style
30 Least vivid
32 Midwest airport
33 Shady recess
34 Bricklayer's tote
37 Location
38 Winter weather
39 Pitchfork poker
40 Whimper
41 Eat well
42 Musical selection
43 Hedger's word
45 Norman or Faldo
46 Tremulous
48 Peacock's pride
49 Easy to tote
50 Boot attachment
52 Verdi masterpiece
56 Feeling off
57 Cat Ballou was one
60 Pie __ mode
61 $10 gold coin
62 Smart __ (wise guy)
63 Neighbor of Isr.
64 Transactions
65 President Bush's state

DOWN

1 Just fair
2 Zest
3 Photo magazine
4 Henceforth
5 Wine-bottle word
6 Old hat
7 Sound of time passing
8 Leaf gatherer
9 Bonanza find
10 Ginger, to Fred
11 The Lone Wolf was one
12 Shakespearean sprite
13 Wizards' sticks
18 Town near Tahoe
23 Hoopster Unseld
25 Flying wonder
26 Pigeonhole
27 Clooney, on *ER*
28 Part of B&O
29 Hudson Hawk was one
30 Fourth Estate
31 Aid a criminal
33 "Ah me!"
35 In the past
36 Antelope's playmate?
38 Kernel
39 Fit for cultivation
41 Moved like a moth
42 Luau food
44 "Nope"
45 Teri of *Tootsie*
46 Felonious handle
47 Future mare
48 Melodies
50 Epic tale
51 Vitamin medium
53 Wild goat
54 Word form for "ten"
55 Torah holders
58 Actress __ Dawn Chong
59 Feedbag bit

PARTY LINES by Dean Niles

ACROSS

1 Breakfast order
5 Basketball player
10 Summer shirts
14 Steak order
15 As __ (usually)
16 Author O'Brien
17 Oil cartel
18 Kind of bug
19 Part of QED
20 Bubble up
22 Wildebeest
23 The Bruins: Abbr.
24 Bird beak
25 Most out of shape
27 Kit's partner
30 Diamond __
31 Tolstoy's Ilyich
32 Dawn goddess
33 Source of the Mississippi
37 Spasm
38 Little pest
39 Winter hazard
40 Dutch uncle
41 Nanook was one

43 "Put __ Happy Face"
44 Peak
45 White House advisory grp.
46 Starter
48 Rural music
52 Tenn. neighbor
53 The __ of Spring
54 Circle part
55 Some T-shirts
58 Persian poet
59 Needle
61 Thailand, once
62 Biblical visitors
63 Hidden
64 Spanish compass point
65 Halt
66 Brahman, e.g.
67 Lamb dish

DOWN

1 Cupid's equivalent
2 Look amazed
3 Party founded in 1874
4 Slice

5 Gumshoe's job
6 Dance or drama
7 Water sounds
8 Actress Verdugo
9 Party founded in 1854
10 Bar order
11 Draw forth
12 Hydroxyl compounds
13 Camp David Accords signatory
21 Cinemax rival
25 Lay an egg
26 Small taste
27 Give as an example
28 Alamo rival
29 Party founded in 1828
34 Party founded in 1901
35 Crooner Perry
36 Pews response
38 "__ Excited" (Pointer Sisters song)

39 1953 Pulitzer playwright
42 Meantime
43 Lubricant holders
44 Graphic references
47 "__ the Walrus"
48 Seniors' events

49 Get in one's sights
50 Put on
51 Field of competition
55 Desiccated
56 Recent
57 Eurasian duck
60 Game, __, match

NON-CENTS by Wayne Robert Williams

ACROSS

1 Cushion
4 Outbuildings
9 Hotel rooms
14 Cool down
15 Marriage
16 Called off
17 Long-running nongame show?
20 Zeus' wife
21 Valletta's nation
22 Ye __ Shoppe
23 Mauna __
25 Md. neighbor
27 Nonhealthy financially?
36 Scandinavians
37 Flooring
38 Congo beast
39 Glaze base
40 Universal soul
41 Roundish
42 Addams relative
43 King of Troy
44 City on the Mohawk
45 Newman nonmovie?

48 Tennis shot
49 Thai's neighbor
50 Beef-rating grp.
53 French river
57 Bank deal
61 Be nongenerous?
64 Consumed
65 Soft down
66 __-en-Provence
67 Accouterments
68 Family member
69 Singer Cole

DOWN

1 Heart of the matter
2 Sore spot
3 Woodlands ruminant
4 Saddle irritant
5 20 Questions category
6 Costa __
7 Christmas
8 Tizzy
9 Stitch
10 Wind out
11 Golden calf
12 Look after

13 Advantage
18 Least colorful
19 Bring down
24 Corrida cheer
26 Goddess of the dawn
27 Not up to it
28 Rob Reiner film of '94
29 Pen
30 Where the toys are?
31 Author of Donovan's Brain
32 Crockett's last stand
33 Actress Linda
34 Quickly
35 Send along
40 Land of sand
41 Star of My Favorite Year
43 Mideast grp.
44 Pulp Fiction name
46 Loud sounds
47 Bent

50 Suckered
51 Box to train
52 Dinner and a movie, maybe
54 Winter glider
55 Director Kazan
56 Comic Foxx

58 __ even keel
59 Where most people live
60 On deck
62 Nav. rank
63 Mind someone else's business

221   WATER PIX by Lee Weaver

ACROSS
1 Amount paid
5 Merry pranks
10 Stinger
14 Fragrance
15 Goddess of peace
16 Hodgepodge
17 Himalayan legend
18 Even
19 Opera box
20 '60 Sinatra film
23 Where girls learn to swim
24 Army chow
25 Tango or twist
28 Mexican money
31 College exam
32 Drip source
34 Go out with
37 '54 Mitchum/ Monroe film
40 Merry month
41 Move swiftly
42 Peddle
43 Farm buildings

44 Woodworking tools
45 Acquire
47 18-wheeler
49 '81 Fonda/ Hepburn film
54 Former West German capital
55 Frightfully strange
56 Wine valley
59 India's location
60 Wed on the run
61 Spirit
62 Film holder
63 Stands up
64 Lease

DOWN
1 Flirtatious
2 Shelley poem
3 "And __ bed"
4 Tot's transportation
5 Pale purple
6 Stadium

7 Guns the engine
8 Leg joint
9 Deal in
10 *Dances With* __
11 African lilies
12 Portents
13 Mystery-story pioneer
21 Woolly one
22 Ham it up
25 Campus building
26 Diva's solo
27 Armada
28 Fourth-down plays
29 Environmental sci.
30 Dried out
32 Out of bounds, in baseball
33 Bushy hairdo
34 Egyptian canal
35 Sea eagle
36 Extremities
38 Horned animal
39 Frozen-food buy

43 Flare, e.g.
44 I love: Lat.
45 Golden-egg layer
46 Sharpshooter Oakley
47 Sandpiper
48 Fencing swords

50 Impolite look
51 Cold-cuts center
52 Aphrodite's child
53 Roy Rogers' wife
54 Saloon
57 Wok
58 Picnic pest

222   BURGER BUDDIES   by Patrick Jordan

ACROSS
1 Make fun of
5 Highest point
9 Around, to a historian
14 Like Bush's office
15 Siren sound
16 Negatively charged atom
17 English essayist
20 Ames and Bradley
21 Tom Joad, for one
22 Midwest capital
23 "__ o'clock scholar"
24 Lotion additive
25 *Clue* character
31 Overactive, for short
32 Symbol of servitude
33 Soup veggie
34 Six-legged colonists
35 Reach home plate

37 Wild revelry
38 Reagan program: Abbr.
39 Course of action
40 Wanted-poster word
41 Buddy's wife on *The Dick Van Dyke Show*
45 Smell awful
46 Type of lily
47 Obliquely
50 Lhasa __
51 Greek letter
54 Clinic founders
57 Ore digger
58 Ship's timber
59 Wood cutters
60 Georgia university
61 Eye irritation
62 General's decoration

DOWN
1 San __, CA
2 Enthusiastic
3 Golfer's goals

4 Santa's helper
5 Heed the alarm
6 Pointed tooth
7 Lab rodents
8 Actor Wallach
9 Train ender
10 Sulking
11 Paddy crop
12 Chef
13 Paquin of *The Piano*
18 Helicopter part
19 N.T. author
23 Medieval quaffs
24 Latin love
25 Singer Lauper
26 Vision-related
27 Film critic Jeffrey
28 Spring month
29 Fit for a queen
30 Dennis and Doris
31 Door fastener
35 Like an icy downpour
36 Wine holder
37 Margarine

39 Fully attended
40 Jargon
42 Seinfeld's neighbor
43 Fish hawk
44 Mend a sandal
47 "Don't look __!"
48 Wood wedge

49 Late-night name
50 Help with a heist
51 Scriptural passage
52 Field of interest
53 Former UN member
55 Signs off on
56 Dines on

URSINE LANGUAGE by Dean Niles

ACROSS
1 Victuals
5 Golfer Ballesteros
9 Pauley of NBC
13 Caribbean resort
14 Sooner city
15 Draft animals
16 Arrives
17 Fairy
18 __ *Three Lives*
19 They're paper-trained
22 Massage area
23 River arm
24 World-carrying figure
28 __ d'oeuvres
29 Authorized
31 "Do __ say . . ."
32 Long-haired cat
35 Compass dir.
36 Some sandwiches
37 Kiddie-lit characters
40 Was indebted to
41 Crude, for one
42 Land of Grieg
43 Colorado Indian
44 Shade source
45 Origin
46 Copier need
48 __ Cologne
50 *Juin* predecessor
53 Dan Haggerty TV role
56 Like some floors
59 "Body and __"
60 Bedding
61 Surmounting
62 Pertaining to
63 "__ Wanna Cry" (Mariah Carey song)
64 Body of a book
65 Start a lawn
66 Transgressions

DOWN
1 Collection
2 Cuban dance
3 Above, in Berlin
4 Of humble parentage
5 Indian soldiers
6 *Diciembre* successor
7 Horowitz, Rubinstein, et al.
8 Peter Gunn's girlfriend
9 Reinforcing beam
10 Rocker Rose
11 Born, in Brest
12 Goal
13 S&L units
20 Shade source
21 Energy dose
25 Former NBC series
26 *Ad __ per aspera*
27 Mama's boy
28 Gardened, maybe
30 Big name in Massachusetts
32 Roughly
33 __ the neighborhood (just moved in)
34 Inexperienced
35 Gal of song
36 Road shoulder
38 Longitudinal division
39 Aurora __
44 Blow it
45 Hoodwinked
47 Land of Thebes
49 Cerulean
50 Massenet opera
51 Agreements, in church
52 "Small world, __ it?"
54 Egyptian goddess
55 Actress Conn
56 Angkor __
57 Broke bread
58 Tic-tac-toe loser

SAY IT AGAIN by Matt Gaffney

ACROSS
1 Roseanne, née __
5 Mediterranean port
9 Land ending
14 "Aha!"
15 Prom wheels
16 Passageways
17 City on the Dnieper
18 Take __ (acknowledge applause)
19 Ahead
20 Theater category
23 Pantsmaker Strauss
24 Hosiery shade
25 Immature insect
28 Hot drink
30 Doctors' grp.
33 Least friendly
35 Defendants: Lat.
36 Pierce
37 Literary genre
40 Kitchen sight
41 Dearie
42 Zodiac sign
43 Morse plea
44 Unauthorized TV greeting
46 Stares at
47 Roll reply
48 North Carolina college
50 Family tree member
56 Panache
57 Diving birds
58 Quaker pronoun
59 Singing cowboy
60 Lose solidity
61 Forever and a day
62 '50s Dodger shortstop
63 Ben & Jerry's rival
64 Ladies

DOWN
1 Denzel Washington role
2 *Clueless* cry
3 Surfing hazard
4 Some arms
5 Former king of Norway
6 Frog sound
7 *Omnia vincit __*
8 "That's logical!"
9 Poorly made
10 "__ talk?": Rivers
11 Utah resort
12 Maneuver
13 Clairvoyant's claim
21 Famine alternative
22 Checks
25 Talks like Cindy Brady
26 Ragweed reaction
27 They're hysterical
29 Maine town
30 Eniwetok, e.g.
31 Runner Sydney
32 Bottomless pit
34 *Grease* garb
36 Makes no progress
38 What the Maple Leafs play in Toronto
39 "Move it!"
44 Crier's cry
45 With deference
47 Legacy recipients
49 Cobbler's forms
50 Stamp feature
51 Have standing
52 Regretted
53 Fulghum book
54 Hawaiian bird
55 Hardy heroine
56 Nowhere near

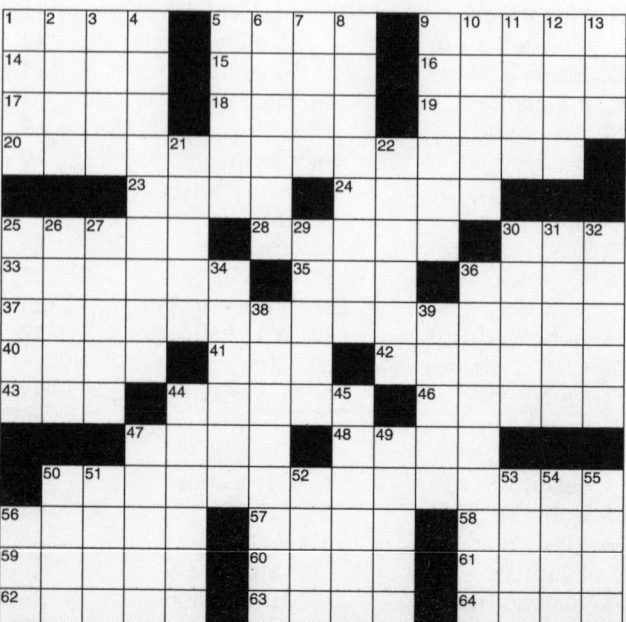

STAR-TREK VOYAGER by Bob Lubbers

ACROSS
1 Cookie man
5 Role for Red
9 Violin maker
14 Solitary
15 O'Neill's daughter
16 Snitches on
17 WITH 22, 48 AND 54 ACROSS, RESEARCH GOAL OF A PROBE TO THE ASTEROID EROS
19 Spike
20 Scrabble piece
21 *Merci!*
22 PART 2 OF GOAL
26 A Major signs
27 Successors of a sort
28 Outmoded
29 Age
30 Biblical kingdom
34 ETO C.O.

35 Martinets
39 Anger
40 River from Uganda
42 Dawber or Tillis
43 Boston airport
45 Tropical climber
47 Lagging
48 PART 3 OF GOAL
51 Fountain treat
52 Waffle name
53 Proportion
54 END OF GOAL
59 Signs
60 Settled down
61 Adidas rival
62 Join forces
63 Playrooms
64 Coming up

DOWN
1 In the style of
2 May honoree
3 Single
4 Hunting dogs
5 __ a cucumber

6 Ore sources
7 Med. specialty
8 Chou contemporary
9 News pro
10 Lethargy
11 Edit
12 Furniture trees
13 Conformers: Suff.
18 More savvy
21 Threesome
22 Uniform color
23 Studio tripod
24 Rising air current
25 Eliel's son
26 Twirl
31 Start eating
32 Red-headed ape
33 Repair
36 Quickly
37 Hand, in Honduras
38 Heavy hammer

41 Running off
44 Buckeyes
46 Force (upon)
47 Bays
48 Baseball inning
49 Critic, often
50 Admit

51 As of
54 Roll of bills
55 __ du Diable
56 Bravo, for one
57 WBA decision
58 Roost mom

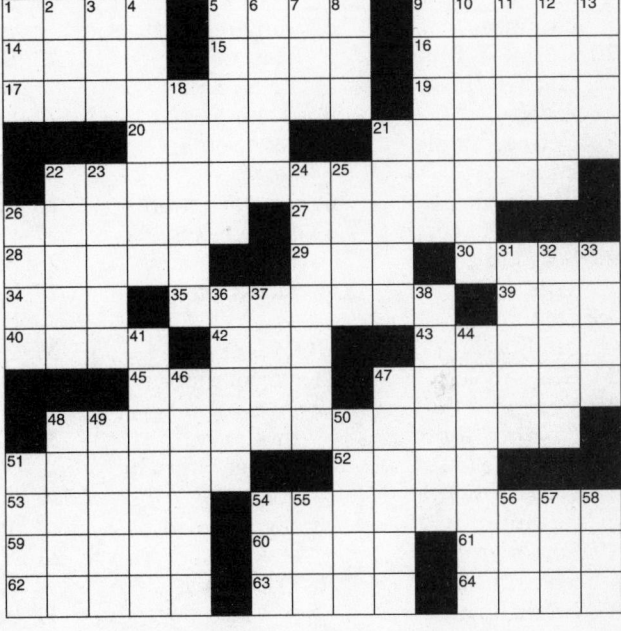

ORDINALITY by Shirley Soloway

ACROSS
1 Fabric surface
5 Kansas Indian
10 Bad reviews
14 Smell __ (be suspicious)
15 ALF or Mork
16 Touched down
17 "To begin with . . ."
20 Youngsters
21 Falk or Boyle
22 Hem or baste
23 Resident's suffix
25 Spanish river
27 Infielder
34 Antiquity
35 Studied, with "over"
36 The __ Lama
38 Bridle strap
40 Alabama city
42 Air strike
43 Change prices
45 States with conviction
47 Campers' vehicles, for short

48 Tune from a Welles film, with "The"
51 Romanian money
52 Sweet potato
53 Seer's gift: Abbr.
56 Sport shoe attachment
60 Ethical
64 Reporters
67 Banned act
68 Mythical giant
69 Author Hunter
70 Not home
71 Trial races
72 Singer Coolidge

DOWN
1 Bide one's time
2 British composer Thomas __
3 Past due
4 Racial
5 Clumsy one
6 Blunder

7 Suffix for million
8 Adventure tale
9 Comes in
10 Buddy
11 "Woe is me!"
12 Pleasant
13 Cook slowly
18 Prevent legally
19 Was nosy
24 Slaughter of baseball
26 Sharif of *Funny Girl*
27 Icy rain
28 Mrs. Bunker
29 Wild fancy
30 Writer Plain
31 Promo producers
32 Warning sound
33 Ingenuous
34 Go awry
37 Psyche parts
39 Hit precisely
41 Pretentious
44 Painter El __
46 Pillow covers
49 Minnesota city

50 Overactor
53 Italian volcano
54 Display
55 Clinton cabinet member
57 New York canal
58 "__ boy!"

59 One of those
61 Sitarist Shankar
62 Rat-__
63 Horne or Olin
65 Vaudevillian Eddie
66 Naval off.

TUTTI-FRUTTI by Fred Piscop

ACROSS
1 Roman robes
6 Muddy
10 *What's My Line?* regular
14 Make excuses
15 Bread spread
16 A Great Lake
17 Single-export countries
20 Aerial sighting
21 Garden flower, for short
22 Periodic-table stats.
23 Phone inventor
24 Cartoon bear
26 Seafood selection
33 Distinctive quality
34 Russian sea
35 Wrath
36 "__ the Mood for Love"
37 Grow toward morning
39 Seth's brother
40 Mythical bird
41 English river
42 Sandberg of baseball
43 South African province
48 Wraps up
49 Golf gadgets
50 Hurler Satchel
53 Composer Bartók
54 Ring ref's call
57 Hair color
61 ERA or RBI
62 Actor Richard
63 Like some seals
64 __ out (ignore)
65 Network junction
66 Has a feast

DOWN
1 Prohibition
2 Norwegian monarch
3 Singer Vannelli
4 Attorneys' org.
5 Big name in sewing
6 Principals
7 __ *Three Lives*
8 Sen.'s counterpart
9 __ *Are There*
10 Boston hoopster
11 Actress Gray
12 Puerto __
13 Actor Parker
18 Comrade
19 Breakfast selection
23 Breakfast selection
24 Long ago
25 __ upswing (rising)
26 Port on the Nile
27 Wit
28 Novelist Jong
29 Spud
30 Benghazi's land
31 Don't exist
32 Donnybrook
37 Fibbed
38 Kennel comments
39 Word after fine or liberal
41 Nixon's first veep
44 Bring to naught
45 Everlasting, old-style
46 Slithery
47 Ocean floor
50 "Hey, you!"
51 Aleutian island
52 Armenia neighbor
53 Actor Pitt
54 Ripped
55 It's above the shin
56 Two to one, e.g.
58 Golfing great Hogan
59 Self-importance
60 Chou En-__

LOW-RENT DISTRICT by Gregory E. Paul

ACROSS
1 "O __ Mio"
5 With 29 Across, jazz pianist
10 Study hard
14 High-school dance
15 Emergency signal
16 Lunar light
17 Pent-up problem
19 Scent
20 Brown brew
21 On the briny
22 Egg stone
24 Odyssey
25 __-Christian ethic
26 Find not guilty
29 See 5 Across
32 Bind (up)
33 *The Price Is Right* shout
34 Cry's partner
35 Glimpse
36 Propelled a gondola
37 Kismet
38 New England cape
39 Folklore being
40 Transparent
41 Conferences
43 Curious George is one
44 "We have met the __ . . ."
45 A gift of the Magi
46 Zen goal
48 Quasimodo's charge
49 Actress Zetterling
52 *Cinco + tres*
53 Hooverville
56 Bible bk.
57 Banks of the Cubs
58 Weirdo
59 Part of D.A.
60 Luster
61 Yet

DOWN
1 Humane org.
2 Ph.D. exam
3 Ear part
4 British record label
5 Counterbalance
6 Glossy
7 Vena __
8 Exist
9 Sent another way
10 Anger
11 Electronics chain
12 Gobs
13 *Utopia* author
18 Nostril
23 Baltic Sea feeder
24 Walrus feature
25 Sparkler
26 Mythical Titan
27 Witch
28 Marine's dwelling
29 Surveys
30 Navel type
31 Impecunious
33 Bonkers
36 Takes an oath
37 The "F" in UNICEF
39 Layer
40 Sucker, for short
42 Snobbish
43 Liquefied
45 Wish granter
46 Drink mixer
47 Word form for "vinegar"
48 Scourge
49 Apollo goal
50 Leatherneck on the lam
51 Black
54 Buckingham initials
55 Ring result: Abbr.

TOWNIES by Bob Lubbers

ACROSS
1 Bottom lines?
5 Bronze and Iron
9 Shiny minerals
14 Mayberry lad
15 Domesticated
16 Texas mission
17 Sup
18 Fedora feature
19 Girls: Sp.
20 English urbanites
23 Ben-__
24 Skater Midori
25 Firstborn
27 Builds
29 Theda of the silents
31 Classic car
32 Flashy fish
33 Reporter Ernie
34 Beginner
35 California urbanites
38 Extremity
41 Regretful sound
42 Key letter
46 "This __ raid!"
47 Burn inside
48 Hardly ever
49 Pancake ingredient
51 Alley of the funnies
52 A Bobbsey twin
53 English urbanites
57 Country estate
58 Sailing
59 Drink garnish
61 Mug
62 Soon
63 Eye drop
64 Sows
65 See 45 Down
66 Greek peak

DOWN
1 Brick carrier
2 Gourmet
3 Mosque tower
4 Espied
5 Diamond statistics
6 Enigmatic star
7 Desert chieftain
8 Truck rig
9 Type of paper
10 Homeric epic
11 Tuna packager
12 Fortune builder
13 "Mayday!"
21 Giant
22 Bridge maven Charles
23 __ up (excited)
26 Also
28 Sole stuffing
29 Club rule
30 Pub draws
33 Soccer great
34 Despot
36 Florida athlete
37 Giraffe cousin
38 Sass
39 Set apart
40 Afternoon performance
43 Cents
44 Blood components
45 With 65 Across, *The Fountainhead* author
47 Boat ends
48 Actor Young of *Topper*
50 Shun
51 Greek theater
54 Carson followed him
55 Pres. Carter's alma mater
56 Marian Anderson, e.g.
57 Editors' concerns: Abbr.
60 Time to remember

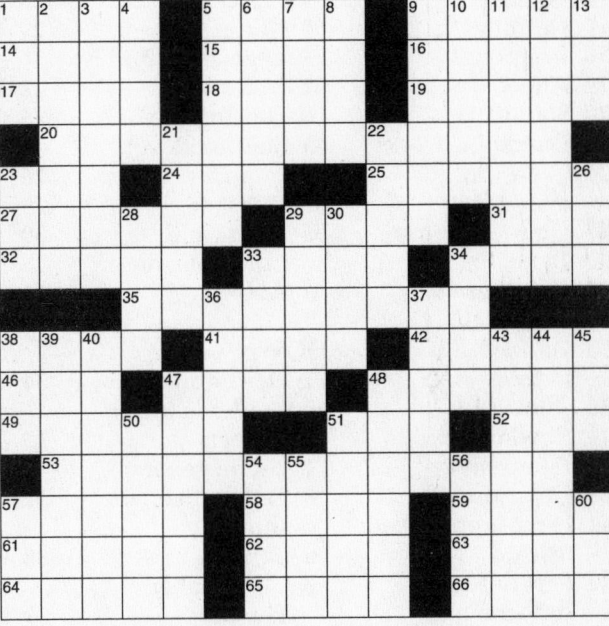

THAT'S LIFE by Dean Niles

ACROSS
1 Brit. money
4 Lam it
8 Oxford adjuncts
13 Word form for "ear"
14 "My times __ thy hand": Psalms
15 Florida city
16 Card game
17 Origins
18 Suggest
19 . . . to Laurens Van der Post
22 Provincial capital
23 Remick or Majors
24 __-relief
27 Fast jets
28 Showtime rival
30 Cheerless
33 . . . to Schiller
35 More pale
40 Sea between Greece and Turkey
41 . . . to Calderón
43 Kerry county seat
44 Composer Rorem
46 Two in a match
50 LAX client
51 Computer monitor
53 Christopher Plummer's daughter
55 . . . to Johnny Mercer
59 Benefit
61 Role for Ethel
62 Sault __ Marie
63 German dessert
64 Marquee times
65 Hoodwink
66 Scuba-suit material
67 Any day now
68 Food scrap

DOWN
1 Psychologist's concerns
2 Prestige
3 English sheep breed
4 Bread style
5 Actor Cobb
6 Unreal image
7 Follow
8 Beef cut
9 High point
10 South American rodent
11 45 inches, in England
12 For example
14 ". . . __ forgive our debtors"
20 Dict. abbr.
21 Use a new hue
25 Elvis __ Presley
26 Isr. neighbor
29 Yawn producer
31 Rule, for short
32 Before
34 Like a bad joke
35 Atmosphere
36 Strongly built
37 *2001* computer
38 Halogen suffix
39 Standing tall
41 A/C unit
42 Actor Banderas
45 Kid in *The Omen*
46 N. or S. follower
47 World education grp.
48 Newspaper title
49 Not actualized
52 __ *Hope* (TV soap)
54 West and Murray
56 Sociologist Shere
57 *Family Ties* kid
58 "Do __ others . . ."
59 Part of NATO
60 US shortwave station

231 BARBERISM by Bob Lubbers

ACROSS
1 Sandwich meat
5 Most contemptible
11 Tam or beret
14 "I cannot tell __"
15 Fatty ester
16 Be in debt
17 Nothing: Sp.
18 Postpones
19 Allow
20 Staunch
23 Diarist Ned
24 __ cri (hot fashion)
27 Ques. response
28 To be: Fr.
32 Hawkins of Dogpatch
33 "Oh, no!" to José
36 Actress Rowlands
37 Like a hive
39 Qatar money
41 Have empathy toward
42 Part of French Indochina
44 Shade trees
45 Equip with guns
48 Fashion zealot
51 Word form for "bone"
53 Separated
57 Actor Wallach
59 Pre-cable need
60 Comic Johnson
61 Legendary bird
62 Actor Depardieu
63 Stadium level
64 Inquire
65 Rubs off
66 Latvia and Lithuania, once: Abbr.

DOWN
1 Dee or Bullock
2 __ words (pun)
3 Helpers
4 Union general
5 Petty officer, for short
6 Landed
7 Clockmaker Thomas
8 Grew less tense
9 Vermont ski center
10 Domingo and Carreras
11 Met head-on
12 Reverence
13 Cat or dog
21 "What __ to say is . . ."
22 Wild donkey
25 German article
26 Actor Stephen
29 Not kosher
30 Actress Martha
31 Jay Leno, e.g.
33 Piña __ (rum drink)
34 Cottonseed pod
35 Like some radios: Abbr.
37 Choose selectively
38 Close, as friends
39 Eng. fliers
40 "__ pig's eye!"
43 Desert "sight"
45 Video-game systems
46 Leaseholder
47 Bill of PBS
49 Range beast
50 __ firma
52 Small fights
54 "Buenos __" (good morning: Sp.)
55 Give a hoot
56 Car pioneer
57 Historical period
58 __ Alamos, NM

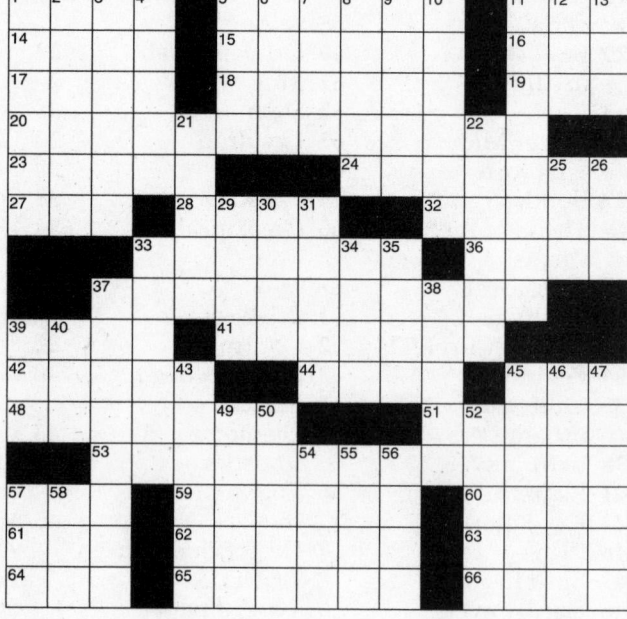

232 CROSSOVERS by Randy Sowell

ACROSS
1 "Thanks __!"
5 Beseech
9 Nebraska city
14 Stun
15 Beans partner
16 Legitimate
17 Clarinet cousin
18 Lamb's pseudonym
19 Sharp
20 Florida beach
23 "I'll say!"
24 Like steppes
25 Big __, CA
27 __ Tin Tin
28 1987 sci-fi film
32 Barbecue residue
35 Dorothy's dog
38 __ Gay (WWII plane)
39 War of 1898
43 Kitchen plastic
44 Part of a list
45 Industrious insect
46 Golfer Lee
48 Corn portion
51 "Am __ understand that . . ."
52 Senator Warner's state
57 Eager
60 Connecticut city
62 __ Open (PGA stop)
64 "Zip-__-Doo-Dah"
65 Fencer's need
66 Type size
67 Connery of The Rock
68 Without: Fr.
69 Garden pests
70 Romance novelist Victoria
71 Waste allowance

DOWN
1 Choose to use
2 Cabinet department
3 Form of oxygen
4 Wobble
5 Forestalls
6 Makes angry
7 Etcher's needs
8 Calendar span
9 Eggs: Lat.
10 Pasta
11 Graduate, for short
12 Author Shere
13 Yemeni port
21 Inventor Whitney
22 Words from Chan
26 Over: Ger.
28 Apple variety
29 Caesar's TV partner
30 The Good Earth heroine
31 Gasp
32 Aide: Abbr.
33 Practice boxing
34 Fabled racer
36 The Buckeye State
37 Make lace
40 Steer the ship
41 Monogram part: Abbr.
42 Rising
47 San Francisco hill
49 Mature
50 Most mature
52 MTV offering
53 Perfect
54 Kind of stock
55 Papas or Dunne
56 Bikini blast
57 Alan Arkin's son
58 Enthusiastic
59 Reverend Roberts
61 Hasty
63 __ Misérables

ACROSS

1 Small particles
6 Therefore
10 Locking device
14 Easygoing gaits
15 Cookout unit
16 Jazzy James
17 Can't be substantiated
20 Gumbo ingredient
21 Bar for a team
22 Listing
23 CEO's PDQ
25 Film connections
27 Gallic witticism
29 Essential part
32 Dusk, to Donne
33 Out on __ (at risk)
35 Like some causes
37 F followers
41 Accelerate
44 Midmonth date
45 Table d'__
46 Made a choice
47 Restorative retreat
49 That woman's
51 Word form for "three"
52 Leak preventers
56 "Oops!"
58 "And we'll have __ good time"
59 Prof. rank
62 Tub parts, at times
65 Faces reality
68 Hard work
69 Nocturnal noise
70 Transactions
71 Sea swoopers
72 Ceases
73 Artist Max

DOWN

1 *Battle Cry* actor Ray
2 Made off with
3 Spy
4 Monument Valley sights
5 Payroll ID no.
6 Bounce back
7 Castle, in chess
8 Beaufort-scale entries
9 Overused, as a joke
10 Intensifying
11 Top story
12 Inscribed stone
13 Labor associate?
18 Kind
19 Fabric texture
24 Prefix for valence
26 Tennis star Sampras
27 Ancient traveling trio
28 Fetid
30 Furthermore
31 Nail's partner
34 Service cafeterias
36 Hook's helper
38 Became troublesome
39 Bakery worker
40 Skywalker was one
42 Where she blows
43 Kid
48 __-mell
50 Campus recruiter: Abbr.
52 Fritter away
53 Knight clothes
54 Welcome, as to one's home
55 Squelched
57 Propose
60 Wearing loafers, perhaps
61 Preps a table
63 Moray and conger
64 Try out
66 That girl
67 Praiseful poem

ACROSS

1 *Masquerade* actor
5 Toolhouse
9 Throw out a line
13 "__ we all?"
15 Shudder at
16 Chinese gelatin
17 Have good penmanship
19 Food fish
20 Rut
21 Tori's dad
22 Flu symptom
24 Outlawed combo
27 Perpetually
29 Yachting
30 Conductor from India
31 Parting words
33 Wood cutter
36 Afore
37 Bangkok haberdashery item
40 Greek letter
41 *Guys & Dolls* name
42 Like cold cream
43 Pass out
45 Ball-__ hammer
47 Punishing rod
48 Plunder a construction site
53 Right-angled extensions
54 Snide remark
55 Camels' cousins
57 Peril
58 Collection of stems
62 Olympic weapon
63 Hors d'oeuvre offering
64 U.S. air-base site in Greenland
65 Shoe strip
66 Mid-sermon interjection
67 Paste

DOWN

1 Bill's future
2 Big-name Bruin
3 Do a dairy job
4 Beg
5 Hindu Trinity member
6 Golf great Walter
7 Neighbor of Som.
8 *NYPD Blue* role
9 Honeydew's relative
10 Forum's Greek counterpart
11 Styling site
12 Vogue
14 Jazzman Macero
18 Sticks up
21 20th-century fabulist
22 *Zapped!* star
23 Record keeper
25 Decked out
26 Actor Morales
28 Sun __-sen
31 Befoul
32 Experience malaise
33 Korean
34 Bikini, for one
35 Lets up
38 Ground breakers
39 Language ending
44 Holiday hangups
45 Mail-carrying vessel
46 Shoe leather
47 Criticism
48 Wood holder
49 Rubbish
50 Studio stand
51 Delight
52 Comic DeGeneres
56 Wyo. setting
58 Steamroom site
59 Hebrides headgear
60 Actor Gulager
61 Beer barrel

235 FOUR OF A KIND by Randall J. Hartman

ACROSS
1 Zagreb resident
5 From
9 Visibly elated
14 Vegas rival
15 Ward of *The Fugitive*
16 Grassy plain
17 THEME ANSWER
19 Phil's wife
20 Delay
21 THEME ANSWER
23 Stout cousin
25 Sci-fi magazine
26 Faux __
29 Type of sch.
32 Idolater
36 Rock-band need
37 Irritates
39 Film scorer Schifrin
40 THE THEME
44 Toledo's water
45 Courtyards
46 Spike or Bruce
47 Tell
50 Religious group
51 Mos. and mos.
52 Blah
54 Rag
56 THEME ANSWER
61 Heat's town
65 Stephen King's home
66 THEME ANSWER
68 Blender setting
69 Slightly open
70 Unable to decide
71 Perlman colleague
72 Catches zzzzzz's
73 Chooses

DOWN
1 Mex. ladies
2 Easter precursor
3 __ *Karenina*
4 "There it is!"
5 Louisville Slugger material
6 Char
7 Spicy stew
8 Multiple Masters champ
9 Chocolate-bar ingredient
10 Spiked flowers
11 Zhivago's love
12 *For Your Eyes* __
13 Courts
18 Queen of mystery
22 "__ Believer" (Monkees tune)
24 Director Kazan
26 Manhandler
27 Love, Italian-style
28 Go bad
30 Joyce of *Roc*
31 Thaws out
33 Comeback
34 Bugs' nemesis
35 "__ of Picardy"
38 Dry
41 Novocaine, e.g.
42 Small notch
43 Mohammed's daughter
48 Soup holder
49 Yale man
53 Miller protagonist
55 "Me, too!"
56 Rascals
57 Seafaring: Abbr.
58 Lose zip
59 Punjab prince
60 Pop's mate
62 Over
63 Mini-mall unit
64 Hostels
67 Many min.

236 SMALL CHANGE by Rand H. Burns

ACROSS
1 Hotelier Helmsley
6 Church platform
11 Egyptian snake
14 Bandleader Desi
15 Baby grand, e.g.
16 Gambler's cube
17 Considerable amount of money
19 "How was __ know?"
20 Slippery swimmers
21 Capital of Jordan
23 Handcuff
27 Assistants
29 Beast
30 Lifestyle writer Stewart
31 Military survey, for short
32 Brief incursion
33 i topper
36 Printer's needs
37 Assigns a value to
38 Got up
39 Keats creation
40 Jaguar and Cougar
41 Hair cutter
42 Moon vehicle
44 Flattens out
45 Scrubbed a mission
47 Award hopeful
48 Wheel spokes
49 Frat party garb
50 Wrath
51 Football VIP
58 In the past
59 Word before berth or class
60 __ *eleison* (Mass section)
61 Trent Lott, e.g.: Abbr.
62 Lauder of perfumes
63 Dilapidated

DOWN
1 Drink like a cat
2 Make mistakes
3 Singleton
4 __ King Cole
5 Pertaining to Montezuma's people
6 Pie fruit
7 "My Bonnie __ over . . ."
8 Catch some rays
9 Landers or Miller
10 Privileged class
11 Very common
12 Instrument for 38 Down
13 Menial workers
18 Holler
22 Speedometer abbr.
23 Cuomo or Puzo
24 Put __ to (stop)
25 Kids' cable-TV network
26 Andy's radio pal
27 Rabbits' kin
28 Historical periods
30 Engine
32 Destined
34 "__ Mio"
35 Short in speech
37 None too polite
38 Musician Shankar
40 Old item
41 Comments
43 *Exodus* hero
44 Theater box
45 Operatic solos
46 Harbor craft
47 *The Hunchback of __ Dame*
49 Spruce or maple
52 FedEx rival
53 Likely
54 "See ya!"
55 "__ we there yet?"
56 El __ (Spanish hero)
57 Door opener

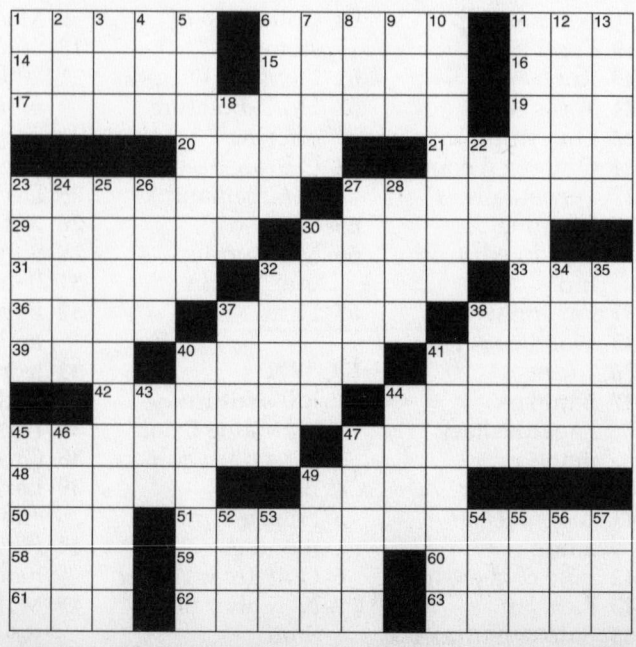

237 LIP SERVICE by Bob Lubbers

ACROSS
1 Inventory entry
5 Gym pad
8 Buccaneers' home
13 Oscar __ Renta
14 Store sign
15 Studio sign
16 Gives up
18 Stickum
19 Waiter's burden
20 Discharges
21 What a glance sometimes does
25 Perpetual, old-style
26 Muscat native
27 Quemoy neighbor
28 Narrow opening
29 Fellow
33 Goof
34 Ghostly image
37 Pitcher's stat.
38 GI hangouts
40 Actress Gardner et al.
41 Computer correspondence
43 German city
45 Slip away
46 Babbles
49 Journalist Bly
50 Palindromic name
51 Famous furrier
52 Gives a false alarm
57 Pub staple
58 American Beauty, e.g.
59 Region
60 Aides: Abbr.
61 Lyric poem
62 Monthly payment

DOWN
1 Driver's licenses, e.g.: Abbr.
2 Afternoon drink
3 TV Tarzan
4 High achievers
5 Thanksgiving Day parade sponsor
6 Totally
7 Golf gizmo
8 Cruise film of '86
9 Listless, in London
10 En __ (together)
11 Actress ZaSu
12 War god
14 Asp, for one
17 Neptune neighbor
20 Gladden
21 Sky sights
22 Word form for "rock"
23 Lava spewer
24 Leaves out
25 Winged walker
28 Lucky number
30 Mounds
31 Come up
32 Wan
35 Out of style
36 Rents again
39 SRO show
42 Legendary racehorse
44 Avoids
45 Cosmetician Lauder
46 Trials
47 Choir voices
48 Harsh sound
49 Shuttle grp.
52 __-Magnon
53 Angler's need
54 Mine load
55 Dawson or Deighton
56 Skim milk's lack

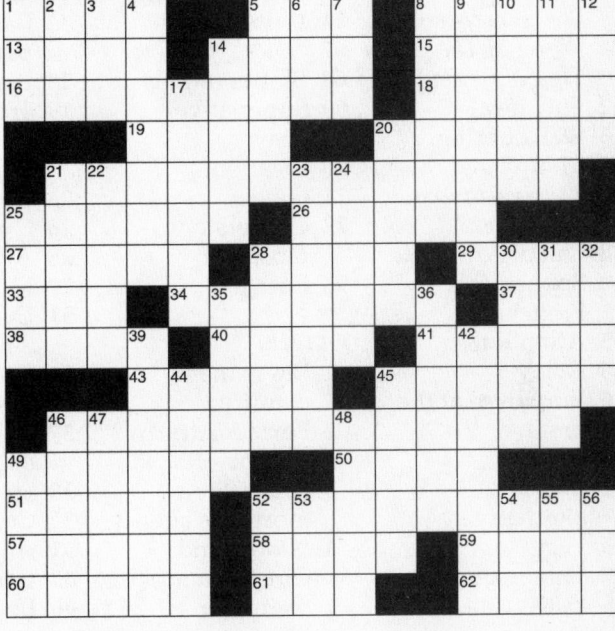

238 HAVE A HEARTH by Lee Weaver

ACROSS
1 Shade trees
5 Make a trade
9 Oddly amusing
14 Money in Teheran
15 *Murphy Brown* barkeep
16 Dashboard device
17 European volcano
18 Long lunch?
19 All thumbs
20 Flue dweller
23 Movie ad
24 Bar crawler
25 AWOL's nemeses
28 Shed tears
31 Singer Brewer
33 Pile up
37 Math-table number
39 The __ Ranger
40 The sun
41 Prepare for a test
42 Gambler's expression
45 Attracting attention
46 Mother's little __
47 Jalopy
49 Lemony quaff
50 Society newcomer
52 Least polite
57 Kitchen device
60 Cowboy contest
63 Alluring
64 Fishline adjunct
65 Write, in a way
66 Vocal
67 Add fringe to
68 Encounters
69 Docile
70 Gardener's purchase

DOWN
1 Straight up
2 Supple
3 Excessive enthusiasm
4 Bridge coups
5 Field of knowledge
6 Miss Muffet's fare
7 Affected mannerisms
8 Farm tools
9 Itinerant
10 Carry on
11 Praiseful poem
12 Golf-hole edge
13 Sodom survivor
21 Fresh information
22 Small amount
25 Montréal's subway
26 Old exclamation
27 Davis or Kaye
29 Famous lioness
30 Asta, for one
32 Well-heeled
33 __ and omega
34 Lowed
35 Place for a bracelet
36 Trickle
38 High spirits
43 Frankfurters
44 Unfettered
45 Sharp projection
48 Sock pattern
51 Infatuate
53 Valleys
54 Piano practice piece
55 Suit fabric
56 Cornered
57 Indian head, e.g.
58 Blood components
59 Final, for one
60 Tach letters
61 Assay specimen
62 Engraved stamp

TWO-FOR-ONE by Wayne Robert Williams

ACROSS
1 Fury
5 Calculating rack
11 Cohort of Fidel
14 Runner Zátopek
15 Turkey part
16 Little shaver
17 First name in crooning
18 Beach Boys song
20 Wong of *The Thief of Bagdad*
22 Fine meal
23 S&L offering
24 Mound stat.
27 Writer Rombauer and others
28 Bauxite or pyrite
30 Sponge cake
33 Frolicked
35 Attention
36 Delay
40 Employee at the first tee
42 Fidgety
44 Butter alternative
45 Peggy or Spike
47 Thin material
48 *Dallas* role

51 Concert box
52 Post fresh troops
55 Port St. Lucie's locale
56 Beloved person
58 Is of use
60 Daughter of Tommy Chong
64 Writer Oates
67 "Dies __"
68 Blotter initials
69 Superlatively achy
70 Wear out
71 Guys
72 Cornerstone tablets
73 Post

DOWN
1 Big name in country
2 Former African despot
3 Federal mortgage agency
4 "Pomp and Circumstance" composer

5 "Fernando" group
6 Ink roller
7 Gas: Pref.
8 Truck compartment
9 Mil. branch
10 Botanist's line
11 Assertion
12 Barbera's partner
13 Best and O'Brien
19 Transfixes
21 *American Buffalo* dramatist
25 White alternative
26 Open a bit
28 Approximately
29 Muslim weight
31 Designer Simpson
32 Rocky ridge
34 Matter-of-fact
37 Celebrated bride of 1994
38 Specialized cell
39 Cry
41 Angler's mecca
43 Burn the end of
46 Building branch

49 Except
50 Singer Julius
52 Hindu title
53 Call to mind
54 Chichén Itz residents
57 Film cuts

59 Highlander
61 "Der __" (Adenauer)
62 Put on guard
63 Yearn for
65 Exist
66 Fam. member

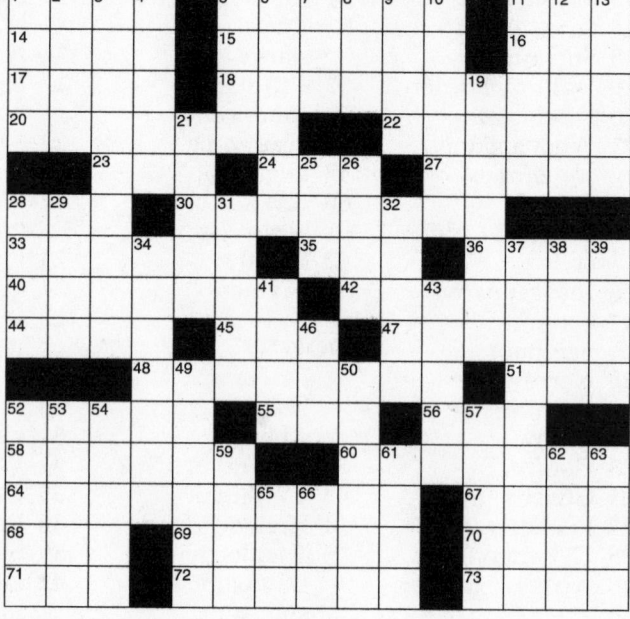

A LITTLE LEARNING by Dean Niles

ACROSS
1 Radner role
5 Donkey __ (video game)
9 Changes course
14 __ kid (prodigy)
15 Part of AARP
16 Have efficacy
17 Skater Katarina
18 With 8 Down, western writer
19 Poet García __
20 Start of a quip
23 Bill partner
24 North China dynasty
25 Virtual
28 "__ Old Cowhand"
31 Ariz. neighbor
35 Decorated vase
36 Attack from the air
38 Offered up
39 Blood-classification system
40 Middle of quip
42 Dailey or Duryea

43 Energy doses
45 Essential
46 Stir
47 Had down
48 Without water
49 Macho guys
51 Cave-dwelling fish
53 Supplicate
54 End of quip
62 Bumbling
63 Official records
64 Wall St. market
66 Free-for-all
67 Like some pickings
68 Voiced
69 Indian lute
70 Fish story
71 Bug

DOWN
1 Part of an Internet address
2 Take __ (sustain injury)
3 Supporting
4 Nahuatl speakers

5 Informal instrument
6 First name in bridge
7 Wild goose
8 See 18 Across
9 Utility
10 Drawing forth
11 Make
12 Puerto __
13 Cabbage concoction
21 Basted
22 Manual holders
25 Postulated particle
26 Civic
27 Battery terminal
28 Actress Papas
29 "__ mia!"
30 In progress
32 Adam's addressee
33 Get around
34 TV tube gas
37 Sparsely
41 A Barrymore
44 Thimble Theatre name
50 Holiday libation

52 Acid-alcohol compound
53 Censure
54 Backus and Brown
55 "The __ Love Belongs to Somebody Else"
56 Mature salmon

57 Hops kiln
58 W. Coast sch.
59 "__ I Kissed You" (Everly Brothers tune)
60 *Jane* __
61 Overlord
65 Horror-film street

241 TWOSOMES by Bob Lubbers

ACROSS

1 Young girls
6 Desist
11 Hit on the head
14 Parcel out
15 Aides: Abbr.
16 Yoko __
17 Uncontestable
19 Actor Kingsley
20 Novelist Bagnold
21 Green stone
23 Fidel's ally
25 Greek letters
27 Ball-__ hammer
28 __-mo replay
29 Nudge
31 1506, to Caesar
34 Magical drink
36 Part of a nation's military might
38 Names of some tsars
39 Goods-and-services meas.
40 __ barrel (lacking choice)
41 Melted down
43 Chicken part
44 Word form for "within"
45 Political refugee
47 Collar shape
48 Farm tools
50 Teachers' org.
51 Koppel or Knight
52 Be manager of
55 Queue
57 Meadow
58 Compromise
63 State leader: Abbr.
64 Happening
65 Knight wear
66 Whichever
67 Richards of tennis
68 Key letter

DOWN

1 __ Tse-tung
2 European mountain
3 __ de France
4 Gift recipient
5 Getz or Kenton
6 Woolen braid
7 Double curve
8 Arthur of tennis
9 Tough puzzle
10 Lauder of cosmetics
11 Box defensively
12 Like Nash's lama
13 Small body of water
18 37th president
22 Eliminate
23 Split, as a hoof
24 Torridly
26 Actor's sub
28 Church topper
29 Ferrer or Greco
30 Rim
32 Well-__ (adept)
33 Quite angry
35 Not alfresco
37 Skin opening
39 Jewel
42 Fidgety
43 Egghead
46 Become more solid
49 Gung-ho
51 Neon fish
52 Olympian Korbut
53 Laborer
54 Tied
56 Bismarck's loc.
59 Wind dir.
60 Current unit
61 Keystone comic
62 Memorable time

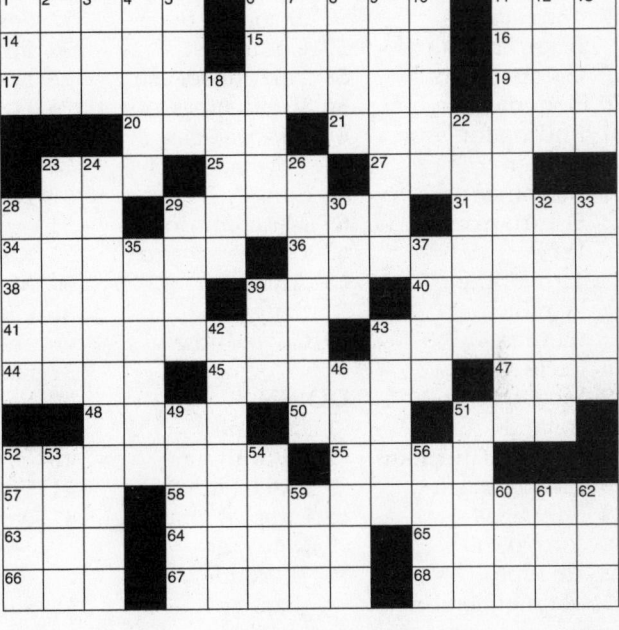

242 EXTREMITIES by Rich Norris

ACROSS

1 Religious group
5 Legend maker
10 "__ girl!"
14 Actress __ Flynn Boyle
15 Kept going
16 Sink alternative
17 Fair
19 Got up
20 Game for a tot
21 Encountering great difficulty
23 "Too bad!"
24 Party offering
25 Onassis, familiarly
26 __ in Terris (papal encyclical)
28 Lord Peter of whodunits
31 Namely
34 Of an orbital intersection
36 Three: It.
37 Word of assent
38 Reveal
39 Ward of *Sisters*
40 Brewed drink
41 Make ready anew, as a ship
42 Computer programmer
43 Low joints
45 Main concern
47 Mauna __
48 NYC radio station
49 Draft org.
52 Calgary's country
55 Boundless
57 Finished
58 Like mountain goats
60 Bearing
61 Burning up
62 Ore source
63 Probability
64 Marshal's group
65 __ about (legal phrase)

DOWN

1 Took a nap
2 Roof overhangs
3 Small stream
4 Army vehicle
5 Semitic language
6 Kitchen tool
7 Take apart
8 Fish eggs
9 *The King* __
10 Teeming
11 Macho
12 Kon-__
13 NYSE counterpart
18 Went after
22 Fingertip cover
26 Brooch, e.g.
27 Dominant theme
28 Pale
29 First name in mysteries
30 Fiscal period
31 "Bye!"
32 Sign of the future
33 Irresolute
35 Morning walkers
38 Bandleader Brown
39 Maritime signal
41 Peruse
42 Novelty
44 Finds out
46 Morning quaff
49 Kind of protest
50 Pool employee of old
51 Passover ritual
52 "It's Impossible" singer
53 Enthusiastic
54 Kin of PDQ
55 Eye part
56 Dodger pitcher Hideo
59 *X-Files* topic

ALLITERATES by Frank Longo

ACROSS

1 Roman date
5 Newswoman Elizabeth
11 Propel a shot
14 Think (over)
15 Asimov et al.
16 *Peer Gynt* character
17 *The Fabulous Baker Boys* star
19 Campaigned
20 Extreme
21 Ending for court or cash
22 Plummer role
23 U-turn from WNW
24 Three-time Wimbledon winner
28 Icicle site
29 Meet a raise
30 Ireland
33 Actress Thurman
35 Astaire's sister
38 *Billy Budd* composer
42 Tie types
43 Magnon lead-in
44 Spanish compass point
45 River island
46 Blues singer James
48 1992 Sullivan Award winner
53 Sine __ non
56 Units of absorbed dose
57 Chou En-__
58 Parts of speech
60 Resident's suffix
61 *Caveman* costar
64 German article
65 San __, TX
66 Maui, for one
67 Dangerous curve
68 Antarctic penguin
69 Cows and ewes

DOWN

1 Saturate
2 Swordfights
3 Make happy
4 Musical marking
5 Man: Lat.
6 "I Wonder __ Wander"
7 Forearm bones
8 Plum varieties
9 Bitter-tasting
10 Conscription org.
11 Talking pets
12 Customary practice
13 Choir member
18 See 62 Down
22 Summer cooler
25 Egg cell
26 Do-fa linkup
27 Actor Morales
28 Commands
30 Retrocede
31 __ Speedwagon
32 Kansans, e.g.
34 Mandela grp.
36 Give the go-ahead
37 Chemical ending
39 Italian wine center
40 La __ Tar Pits
41 French roast
47 Amino acid carrier, for short
48 Shower honoree
49 Hall's partner
50 Spiral-horned antelope
51 Flat boat
52 Defame in print
53 Put down
54 Cry of defeat
55 Fire remnants
59 Kimono sashes
61 Goat's note
62 With 18 Down, *Arabian Nights* persona
63 Salmon-to-be

DE-LIGHTFUL by Dean Niles

ACROSS

1 The bad guys
5 Coop group
9 Friar's superior
14 __ facto
15 Angry
16 Grassy expanse
17 Trendy flier
19 Knight weapon
20 I as in Innsbruck
21 __ Tae Woo
22 Paved, in a way
24 "__ in the bud!"
26 Reaction to a rat
27 Without artifice
30 Goalpost part
34 Rolex rivals
36 "Telephone Line" group
37 Kind of sch.
39 Frosh, next year
40 More competent
42 Rhine feeder
43 Clubs, for instance
44 __ Abner
45 Role for Whitmore or Oldman
47 Russian mystic
50 Expiate
51 In fashion
52 Serta competitor
54 Flippered mammal
58 Egyptian cobra
59 __ Mahal
62 Organic compound
63 Unexpected winner
66 Bedding
67 Commedia dell'__
68 Coral formation
69 Slightest
70 Catty comment
71 Unheeding

DOWN

1 South Pacific island group
2 Oil cartel
3 OT book
4 "__ your old man!"
5 Legally curtail
6 Cathedral style
7 Coll. test
8 Certain Slav
9 WWII winners
10 Anna Sewell novel
11 River border
12 Fairy-tale beginning
13 Three-__ sloth
18 Author Jong
23 Tahoe digs
24 Plant family
25 Latticework
27 One in charge
28 *Hiroshima, Mon __*
29 Photo tint
31 Tijuana cry
32 San Antonio mission
33 Watched the video again
35 Respectful gesture
38 Biblical wall word
41 Bridle piece
46 Mr. Kramden
48 Mighty
49 Close by
53 Crooked
54 Teen hangout
55 Amiens girlfriend
56 Designer Ricci
57 Round cheese
59 Balsam or birch
60 On the bounding main
61 Actor Goldblum
64 "__ we having fun yet?"
65 Fort __, CA

CAPITAL CRITTERS by Patrick Jordan

ACROSS

1 Lumps of dirt
6 Maintain
10 1952 Winter Olympics city
14 Embankment
15 Collection of laws
16 Invoice stamp
17 Related to Mom
18 *Mystery!* host
19 Froze over
20 Game for a White House dog?
23 Who: It.
24 Jovial Johnson
25 "__ was saying . . ."
28 Prepares to shave
32 Working (with)
34 Fleecing victim
35 White House cat's popularity?
38 By way of, briefly
40 Sigh of pleasure
41 Treater's phrase
42 Lunch for a White House dog?
47 Paving goo

48 Claim to be true
49 Electromagnetic particles
51 Luau souvenir
52 Perched upon
55 Imperfect clothing abbr.
56 White House dog's favorite duo?
62 Surrounded by
64 Journalist Chase
65 Perrier rival
66 Have status
67 Champing at the bit
68 Promotional gimmick
69 Phoenix neighbor
70 Gaelic tongue
71 Smooths, in a way

DOWN

1 Pitch symbol
2 Singer Horne
3 Sort of round
4 Separate
5 Stews in one's juices

6 About 4800 square yards
7 "There!"
8 Lawn tool
9 Henley competition
10 Role for Ronny
11 Fort Sutter site
12 Golf-ball position
13 Unmatched
21 Day saver
22 Intense in color
26 Popeye or Bluto
27 Sluggards
28 __ *Weapon*
29 Short time
30 Political issue
31 Large quantity
33 Mil. address
36 Great Plains tribe
37 Transport commercially
39 Employ
43 "I've Got __ in Kalamazoo"
44 Meshy

45 "Pet" that grows on you
46 NBA team
50 Game-show fodder
53 Wayne Gretzky, once
54 Toy dogs
57 Fancy

58 Windmill part
59 Debt security
60 Installed, as carpeting
61 B&Bs, e.g.
62 Fortify
63 W.C. costar

IN THE CARDS by Lee Weaver

ACROSS

1 Unclad
5 Burn a bit
9 Kentucky resource
13 Son of Adam
14 Routine task
15 Forearm bone
16 Go away
18 Take care of
19 Dawn goddess
20 Western marshal of note
21 Inedible oranges
23 Fanciful visions
25 Carpenter's need
27 Ballpark officials
29 Pierces
33 Squander
36 Top-notch
38 Small sailing vessel
39 Sandwich cookie
40 More cunning
41 Algonquian language
42 Donna or Rex
43 Still
44 Room and __

45 Portuguese wine
47 On the briny
49 Second president
51 Short snooze
55 Ski race
58 Scent
60 Balin or Claire
61 Isolated
62 Lower levels, on a ship
65 Ripening agent
66 Carpenter's need
67 Animal skin
68 Knocks for a loop
69 Makes do, with "out"
70 Son of Hera

DOWN

1 Stationed
2 Really detest
3 Exploit again
4 Santa's helper
5 Sonny's ex
6 Basketball targets
7 Canine comment

8 Carry Nation, e.g.
9 Gentleman's formal attire
10 Couturier Cassini
11 Queen Elizabeth's daughter
12 Youngsters
14 Necklace fastening
17 __ fatale
22 Aug. follower
24 Sedan sellers
26 Movies
28 Low bow
30 Zhivago's beloved
31 Water pitcher
32 Luge or toboggan
33 Nightcrawler
34 Field of study
35 Plant-to-be
37 Popeye's Olive
40 Mix up
44 Chef James
46 Wedding promise

48 Threatening look
50 Puzzle out
52 More pleasant
53 Place for a bracelet
54 Subjects of memoirs
55 Deli purchase

56 Company emblem
57 All over again
59 Deer mothers
63 Cartoon exclamation
64 Antipollution agcy.

247 HYDROLOGY by Bob Lubbers

ACROSS
1 German river
5 Fresh talk
9 Anatomical partitions
14 Cairo's river
15 Author Wiesel
16 Enter
17 Health
19 One at __ (singly)
20 Makes use (of)
21 Scams
23 Practice
25 New York canal
26 Proofreader's mark
27 Allegiance
29 Actor Ray
32 Precludes
34 __ Got a Secret
36 Overcooked
38 Consume
39 Mesopotamia region
41 Wind dir.
42 Submit, as homework
45 Legendary loch
46 Evaluate
48 Fem. opposite
50 "__ it!" ("Amen!")
51 Bucolic
55 Say an "h"
58 Kodak product
59 Leighton of *Melrose Place*
60 Stationery imprint
62 French weapons
63 Religious image
64 Western Indian
65 Scruffs
66 Lady's man
67 Slangy noes

DOWN
1 "First __, first . . ."
2 Strainer
3 Islam's Almighty
4 Needs, in a way
5 Is angry
6 Baba or MacGraw
7 Subsequently
8 Utah lily
9 Manatee meal
10 Involve
11 Broadcasting period
12 Voluminous work
13 Pub servings
18 Raucous noise
22 __-do-well
24 Some Dutch paintings
27 Daughter of Muhammad
28 Actor Montand
29 Lincoln's nickname
30 Moon goddess
31 Fancy shoe
33 Naughty
35 Hesitation sounds
37 Pentagon VIPs
40 Rare
43 Cruising
44 Newborn
47 Evening party
49 Polaris, e.g.
51 Tranquillity
52 Lasso
53 Vane pointer
54 Huron and Mead
55 Admiral Shepard
56 Gilbert of *Roseanne*
57 Small branch
61 Heavy weight

248 APPROXIMATIONS by Dean Niles

ACROSS
1 Church seating
5 War photographer Robert
9 *Camille* star
14 Kindergarten thru 12th, briefly
15 Arabic letter
16 "Farewell!"
17 Without __ to stand on
18 Volunteer of 1898
20 View point?
22 Cyclists' gear
23 Media outlets
24 Madras wrap
25 Almost
33 Shack
34 Sauce brand
35 Nobelist Soyinka
36 The A. in B.A.
38 Evade
41 Court order
42 Sgts., e.g.
43 Purina rival
45 Mauna __
46 '80s TV drama
51 Endless times
52 '20s auto
53 Noted tenor
57 Sounded like sleigh bells
61 Brit's carousel
63 Country in West Africa
64 Varnish resin
65 Brew: Ger.
66 Revered figure
67 Exposed
68 Cravings
69 __ kleine *Nachtmusik*

DOWN
1 Top level
2 *Vogue* competitor
3 Curds and __
4 Tourist stops
5 New Mexico caverns site
6 Lotion ingredient
7 More: Mus.
8 Colorful blanket
9 Vampire deterrent
10 Take __ view of
11 Astronaut Sally
12 Red vegetable
13 *Yours, Mine and __*
19 Dagwood sandwich
21 Done with
24 Small apartments
25 Intone
26 Stagger
27 "Great" emperor
28 Actor Tognazzi
29 Wobblies' union: Abbr.
30 Author Maxim
31 Foreigner
32 Label again
37 The Ukraine, once: Abbr.
39 Leg
40 Retiree's title
44 Submachine gun
47 Watched over
48 Body-mind system
49 Highfalutin
50 Thwart, in a way
53 Colorless
54 Chaplin's wife
55 Naturalist John
56 "I've Got the Music __"
57 Evita's husband
58 Venues
59 Painter Schiele
60 Finished
62 Mine find

ACROSS

1 Reindeer herder
5 Lacking
8 Teamster
14 Switch ender
15 Garden sphere
16 Reduced
17 "Wait a minute!"
18 March of '50s TV
19 Shrinks involuntarily
20 September birthstones
23 Reddish purple
24 Intimidate
25 Spanish aunt
27 Bottom line
28 Dumbstruck state
30 Range-hood elements
33 Ness and Lomond
35 Spotter
36 Deep black
37 Author of *Them*
39 List-ending abbr.
43 "Thanks, Jacques"
45 Paris river
46 Wastrel
51 Recycled T-shirt
52 Monkey suit
53 Peer Gynt's mother
54 Surfeited
56 Seed coverings
58 Gutter's outflow
62 Strip of wood
64 U-turn from WSW
65 Spoken
66 French students
67 German article
68 Gear teeth
69 Passover repasts
70 Liquid qty.
71 Baby bouncer

DOWN

1 Take away
2 Greek river
3 Part of a ship
4 Daddy
5 Enigmatic person
6 Home, figuratively
7 Noted drama school
8 "In what way?"
9 Bring to life
10 Annapolis sch.
11 Hiatus
12 Gridiron complement
13 Changes the timer
21 Shades
22 Knucklehead
26 Osiris' wife
28 Arabic name
29 Avoided defeat
31 Up and about
32 Liberate
34 Choir selection
37 Table scraps
38 Rued the aerobics
40 Tool in a trunk
41 Santa __, CA
42 Part of a tour
44 *Lou Grant* star
45 Getz or Kenton
46 Balanced conditions
47 Royal shade
48 Told never to come back
49 Spanish composer
50 Leaflets
55 Author/pediatrician
57 Not prerecorded
59 Change completely
60 Beep
61 Otherwise
63 Double curve

ACROSS

1 Fellow
5 Polynesian kingdom
10 Indistinctness
14 Actress Turturro
15 Cream-colored
16 Screenwriter Hunter
17 START OF A *B.C.* QUESTION
20 Actress Braga
21 Gridder Groza
22 Long chain
23 Those: Sp.
25 Hoopster Archibald
27 Like Welsh rabbit
30 Navy bigwig
33 Peers
34 Tack part
35 "Agnus __"
37 PART 2 OF QUESTION
38 PART 3 OF QUESTION
39 END OF QUESTION
40 Moral wrong
41 Morsels
43 Bloomer girl
45 Artist's board
47 4.5 score
48 Inventor Sikorsky
49 Jug group
50 Talked
53 START OF ANSWER
55 Scheming group
59 END OF ANSWER
62 Verve
63 Furry swimmer
64 Spanish province
65 Anna May of film
66 Internet surfers
67 Handel opera

DOWN

1 Raven racket
2 Ritz rival
3 Former British colony
4 Brain lobe
5 Spasm
6 Track shapes
7 It's forbidden
8 Diamond roller
9 Author Rand
10 Mag founder
11 Voracious
12 Writer Grey
13 Tips
18 Studio stand
19 Have home fare
24 Old oath starter
26 Actress Dolenz
27 RN's expertise
28 Rig
29 Anders of *Easy Rider*
30 Spring up
31 Allan-__ (Robin Hood sidekick)
32 Kosher
36 "Do as __!"
38 Draws
39 Pliant
41 Sire
42 "How was __ know?"
43 Airline to Tokyo
44 Make hash
46 Preference
49 Bundle maker
50 Gush
51 Riding sport
52 *The Good Earth* character
54 Poet Nahum
56 Singer at Woodstock
57 Yves' "yours"
58 O'Brien preceder
60 Evidence of debt
61 *JAMA* readers

SPENDABLES by Shirley Soloway

ACROSS
1 Sunday service
5 Curvy letter
8 Home sites
12 Prom, e.g.
13 Mormon center
15 Concerning
16 Above, with "of"
17 __ Alto, CA
18 British gun
19 Be creative, wordwise
22 Possesses
23 Singer Laine
24 Use up
26 Nutmeg kin
29 Up in __ (irate)
31 __ *a Camera*
32 Gabor et al.
33 Spy's org.
34 Ice-cream servers
37 Denials
38 Alters
40 Teachers' grp.
41 Impious
43 Mrs., in Madrid
44 Rind
45 Actor Wallach
46 Saloon selection
47 Sandberg of baseball
48 __ *Each Other* (Lombard/ Stewart film)
51 Land measure
53 Actress MacGraw
54 Pay (for)
59 Enjoy a meal
61 Ballet bend
62 Pianist Count __
63 In a while
64 Transgressions
65 Making do, with "out"
66 Repair
67 After taxes
68 In the event that

DOWN
1 __' War (racehorse)
2 Against
3 Candle brackets
4 Plant leaf
5 Feeling of elation
6 Leading player
7 Meal starters
8 Fleur-de-__
9 Exactly right
10 Delicacy
11 Logic
12 "What's up, __?"
14 Watering tool
20 Jim-dandy
21 Grand films
25 Asian language
26 Bill of fare
27 River of England
28 Took advantage of
30 Clerical residence
34 Hunt (for)
35 Hammer part
36 Shopper's draw
38 Mountain edge
39 Best of the best
42 Bullring cheer
44 Cook beforehand
46 James of *Hotel*
48 *Call Me* __
49 Skirt design
50 "Sorry about that!"
52 Dissident
55 Fork point
56 Egyptian goddess
57 Fuzz
58 Chicken part
60 Finale

SPREAD THE WORD by Bob Lubbers

ACROSS
1 Newspaper page
5 Nasser of Egypt
10 Story line
14 Evaluate
15 Florida city
16 Ready to pick
17 Gridlock result
19 Director Kazan
20 Prominent
21 Expert: Ger.
23 Fall behind
24 Blood line
25 Less cooked
28 Nav. rank
29 Shoelace end
33 Blackbird
34 Omelet need
35 Arm cover
36 Jazz piano pioneer
40 Inca, e.g.
41 __ Marie Saint
42 Hawaiian instrument, for short
43 Nerves of __
44 Word form for "three"
45 Something of value
47 Pro and con
49 Dallas sch.
50 One past his prime
53 Fork or spoon
57 "__, Brute?"
58 Flatter
60 Sky sight
61 The Little Mermaid
62 Hammer end
63 Crooned
64 Pee Wee or Della
65 18-wheeler

DOWN
1 Table scraps
2 Prefix for psychology
3 List ender: Abbr.
4 Pollute
5 In operation
6 Part of CPA
7 Mil. rank
8 Los __, NM
9 Less valid, as an excuse
10 Seer
11 Light rhythm
12 Mayberry boy
13 Rip
18 Dread
22 Writer Calvino
24 Fishermen
25 Mates of ranis
26 Concerning
27 Author Oscar
28 Psyche part
30 "__ pray"
31 Bring forth
32 Belief
34 Seabird
35 Wee, in Glasgow
37 Virginia town
38 Eli
39 XIV x IV
44 Term of office
45 Part of USA
46 Daybreaks
48 Prohibit
49 Stone marker
50 Dame Myra
51 "__ girl!"
52 Musial or Getz
53 Western Indians
54 *Graf* __
55 List entry
56 Actress Anderson
59 Make knots

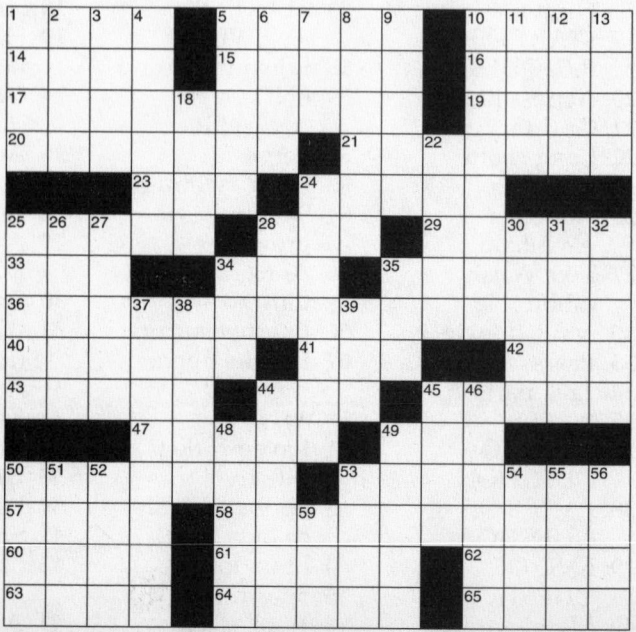

ROCK SPECTRUM by Elizabeth C. Gorski

ACROSS

1 South American range
6 Mascara site
10 Diminutive suffix
14 Comb parts
15 "... sin to tell __"
16 Sense
17 Mideast noble
18 Cape Town cash
19 Columbo portrayer
20 Jazz form
21 "Swamp Ophelia" band
24 Wild cats
26 Yuletide quaff
27 Like a tree farm on 12/26
29 Milker
34 Combat unit
35 Heartbeat
36 Sean Lennon's mom
37 Nile reptiles
38 "Sunshine of Your Love" band

39 Soprano Lily
40 Wire measure
41 Neighbor of Peru
42 Ms. Hawkins
43 Insurance payments
45 Remained
46 Part of D.A.
47 Sour
48 "Astro-Creep 2000" band
53 Moon lander
56 Heckle
57 Say the rosary
58 Actress San Giacomo
60 Switch ending
61 Entreats
62 Occurrence
63 Actor Beatty et al.
64 Breaks ground
65 Bowler's button

DOWN

1 Run up __ (drink on credit)
2 Verne captain
3 "Smoke on the Water" band

4 French season
5 Seafood selections
6 Cooking fats
7 Jai __
8 Warble
9 Pleasure principle
10 Crude image
11 Rip
12 Fabled archer
13 Lodge members
22 Vote against
23 Quayle follower
25 Ballpark figures
27 Rascal
28 __ With Love
29 Some battles
30 Wings: Lat.
31 "A Question of Balance" band, with "The"
32 Comics kid
33 __ around (pried)
35 Proper partner
38 Dershowitz book
39 '50s late-night name

41 Quote
42 Pittsburgh pro
44 Unleavened bread
45 Poli-__
47 Deep chasm
48 Small songbird
49 Fabled racer

50 Designer-shirt name
51 Approximately
52 Earn
54 Sea eagle
55 Helm or Houston
59 "Hail, Caesar!"

DETROIT DEGREES by Bob Frank

ACROSS

1 Dinner holder
5 Portal
9 Daniel or Debby
14 Pennsylvania city
15 Mr. Lugosi
16 Dashes, e.g.
17 "__ chance!"
18 Car's temperature regulator
20 Tense
21 De Valera of Ireland
22 Car's water-pump blade
25 Plays a ukulele
30 Churned
32 Artist's prop
33 Astaire film
36 Part of a cheer
38 Take-out order?
39 Joined, old-style
41 Employed anew
43 Slapstick projectiles

44 __ Dawn Chong
46 Rental papers
47 Farm units
49 Remove a strap
51 Light-plane maker
53 Car's air-blades rotator
57 "The cruellest month"
59 San __, Italy
60 Car coolant
65 Rugged rock
66 Greek isle
67 Arkin or Alda
68 Tennis legend
69 Unmannered
70 Year in the reign of Louis XIV
71 Bog product

DOWN

1 Word form for "tooth"
2 "... wander, anywhere __"
3 Workout bit
4 Car's hot water flex-tubes

5 Approx.
6 Do a shoe repair
7 Less opaque
8 Injure
9 Eyre's creator
10 NATO relative
11 Calendar abbr.
12 Fed. arts sponsor
13 Ultimate suffix
19 11 Down, etc.: Abbr.
23 Advance
24 Bottle size
26 Car's coolant container top
27 Opportunists
28 Riot
29 Rosebud et al.
31 Patriotic org.
33 Rapper Shakur
34 Guaranteed
35 Wharves
37 Hunt of Twister
40 Fam. member
42 Wheelhouse
45 Connecticut town
48 Mixups

50 Le Père Goriot author
52 Auto-loan no.
54 Concise
55 Plains Indian
56 Synonym man
58 Paper quantity

60 Part of CPA
61 "... snow __ rain ..."
62 Song syllable
63 "No __, ands, or buts!"
64 Letter abbr.

STAR PITCHER by Dean Niles

ACROSS

1 Bounder
4 Affirmative action agcy.
8 1970 World's Fair site
13 Finished
15 Melville novel
16 Song and dance
17 Word from the boss
18 Yen
19 *Familia* member
20 Heathcliff creator
22 Western name
24 Black and white
26 Overlord
29 Spirited, to Solti
34 Employ rope
35 __ Romeo
37 Big trucks
38 Walk in water
39 Saxophonist Sonny
41 Cotton cleaners
42 On the ocean
44 On the ocean
45 Long ago
46 Dame Melba
48 Hudson's ship
50 Pamphlets, tickets, etc.
52 Gung-ho type
56 PBS show
60 Budget rival
61 Latin verb
63 Actress Judith
64 Blood part
65 Hollow
66 Give over
67 It'll take you for a ride
68 Sooner city
69 Paper feature

DOWN

1 Hair arranger
2 Maintain
3 Floor model
4 Spread material
5 Paramedic: Abbr.
6 14 Down product
7 Comic Myron
8 Fluid diffusion
9 Jacuzzis
10 Jessye Norman role
11 Street border, in Soho
12 Away from the wind
14 TV pitchperson
21 Spasm
23 Video outlet
25 Mediterranean republic
26 Nile dam
27 Proclamation
28 __ wave
30 14 Down product
31 __ acid
32 Five, to Felipe
33 City north of Cologne
36 Top-drawer operators
40 Able on stage
43 Brook Benton 1962 tune
47 Competent, slangily
49 __ Filippo Lippi
51 Ho preceder
52 Deep cut
53 Sub in a tub
54 *Tootsie* actress
55 Australian runners
57 Peeper part
58 Comic Foxx
59 Takes a gander at
62 He defeated Spinks

KING'S ENGLISH by Bob Lubbers

ACROSS

1 Weaken
4 North star
11 Man in blue
14 I love: Lat.
15 Metrical foot
16 Boxing legend
17 First balcony at the Palladium
19 __-Mex cuisine
20 Journalist Bly
21 Guppy cousin
23 Most Egyptians
24 Selves
26 Oil cartel
29 Withered
30 Ski lift
31 Redden
32 Member of 26 Across
33 Threat ender
34 Adhesive tape at Chelsea Royal Hospital
39 Lake boats
40 Kelly or Disney
41 Choir members
42 Yucatán native
43 Averages
47 Assemble
48 Inlets
49 Sire
50 Staggers
52 Actor Lorne
53 Actress Ullmann
55 Washcloth at Claridge's
58 In the manner of
59 Fragrant
60 4 P.M. drink
61 Hair goo
62 Binds again
63 Wind dir.

DOWN

1 Steam baths
2 Current unit
3 Wispy tree
4 Helen's captor
5 A single time
6 Chou En-__
7 Spring mo.
8 Parish leader
9 Capri and Man
10 Manuscript marking
11 Slingshot at Harrod's
12 "Bravo!" in Barcelona
13 Snapshots, for short
18 Hamburg's river
22 Functions
24 Statesman Abba
25 Aisle at Drury Lane
27 Being: Lat.
28 *Moonstruck* star
30 Speaker of baseball
31 Pesky child
32 Turner and Pappas
33 Pueblo pot
34 Con game
35 Story
36 Intermission at Royal Albert Hall
37 Actor Robert
38 Picks up the check
42 Navy goat, e.g.
43 Hammer part
44 Ten-percenters
45 Actress Adorée et al.
46 Carved pillars
48 Grass unit
49 Copper alloy
51 Get an __ effort
52 Stickum
53 Fall behind
54 __ de France
56 Time period
57 Dandy

PAVING THE WAY by Fred Piscop

ACROSS

1 "Bye!"
5 College mil. group
9 Tourney type
14 Opera solo
15 Cajun-cooking vegetable
16 Baseball great Combs
17 Columnist Charen
18 Lewis novel
20 Unappetizing food
21 Phosphate mineral
22 Spider or mite
25 Central ideas
28 Refusals
29 "__ it Romantic?"
31 Brit. reference work
33 Like tartan
35 Stanford rival
36 __-bodied seaman
37 Malady
39 Southern state
41 Composer Porter
42 Two-syllable foot
44 __ point (hub)
45 Indeed
46 Dope
47 Wine residue
48 As I Lay __ (Faulkner book)
50 Nuance
54 Guilty one
56 Swell, slangily
57 Nostalgic path
60 Bjorn of tennis
61 Without help
62 Golden-__ (senior)
63 The Preakness, for one
64 Paint type
65 T-man Eliot
66 Pervasive quality

DOWN

1 Florida city
2 Tumultuously
3 Music-publishing district
4 Battery type
5 One of Paul's Epistles
6 Giraffe relative
7 Like some chords
8 Is unable to
9 Hoopster Bob
10 __ up (rises on hind legs)
11 Blast-furnace input
12 Pub quaff
13 Encountered
19 Prepare to turn
23 Fictional ship
24 Half a dual personality
26 Caldwell classic
27 39 Across city
30 Thick slice
32 Hand out the cards
33 Type size
34 Comic actor Harold
35 Mil. branch
36 Scrub, to NASA
38 One at a time
40 Way off
43 Dock charge
46 Accustoms
47 Olympic distance measures
49 Symbols
51 Creeping plants
52 Word form for "sleep"
53 Suburbanite's gadget
55 Strategy
57 Publication, for short
58 Right-angled pipe
59 Holstein comment
60 Buddy

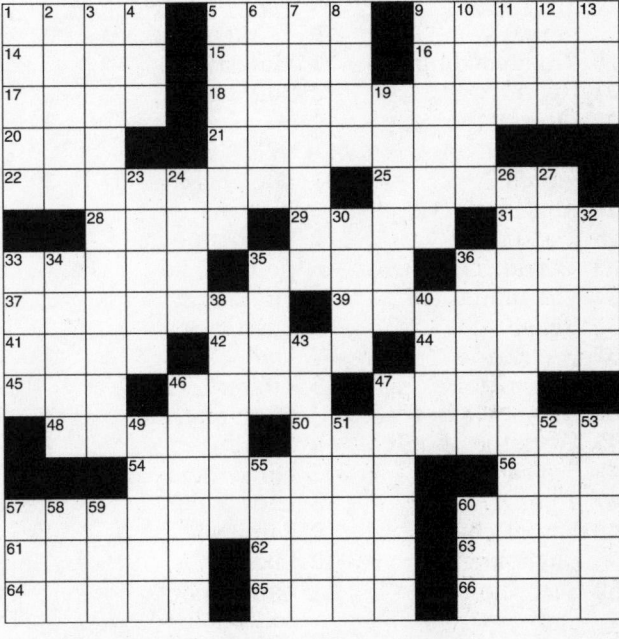

BEASTLY FILMS by Gregory E. Paul

ACROSS

1 Respected one
6 Pierre's father
10 Algerian seaport
14 Toro rival
15 "You said it!"
16 __ Scotia
17 Erect
18 Path
19 Pt. of EMT
20 Spoil
21 1985 Kingsley film
24 Rapunzel's pride
26 Computer correspondence
27 Rogue
30 Grasslands
34 Dishwasher cycle
35 Broad necktie
38 Sturgeon delicacy
39 Can. province
40 Secondary
41 British "bye"
42 62 Across formation
43 Columbus' home
44 Gimlet's kin
45 Misplays
47 Some drums
49 Oater group
52 Person, place, or thing
53 1980 Hopkins film, with The
57 Scrooge portrayer in '51
60 Fuddy-duddy
61 Knee: Lat.
62 Formation fliers
64 Attends, with "to"
65 Gabor et al.
66 Highway hazard
67 Feminine suffix
68 Obi
69 Spring and neap

DOWN

1 Biblical land
2 Singer Horne
3 1978 De Niro film, with The
4 White-tailed bird
5 Ocean pollution
6 Catherine __ (Henry VIII's last wife)
7 Ham it up
8 Domain
9 Strive
10 1936 literature Nobelist
11 "Arrivederci, __"
12 Say it's so
13 Not one
22 Press ending
23 Count calories
25 Looped handle
27 Stalwart
28 Tanker
29 April forecast
31 1944 Hepburn film
32 Clan emblem
33 Mall store
36 __-Cat (Vail vehicle)
37 Paint layer
40 Ouija board output
41 Shearer's skirt
43 David of Rhoda
44 In the thick of
46 Confront
48 "Hooked __ Feeling"
50 Indy champ Tom
51 Lab heaters
53 Nose (out)
54 Canadian bird
55 First place
56 Iditarod cry
58 Words of enlightenment
59 New York nine
63 Samuel's teacher

GIMME A BREAK by Randall J. Hartman

ACROSS

1 Charles' pet
5 Verdure
10 Did great on
14 Singer Vikki
15 Cardinals' stadium
16 Charles' sport
17 Time apart, perhaps
20 Brazilian dance
21 Riis subject
22 Opp. of SSW
23 Not __ many words
26 Med. subject
28 Good shot
33 Corrida cheer
34 *Vier* minus *drei*
35 Relish
37 Feels bad
39 '70s craze
42 Actress Talbot
43 Work the dough
45 Sea eagles
47 Tote
48 Parent-child phenomenon
52 Sean Connery, e.g.
53 Vivacity
54 __ Na Na
57 "__ boy!"
59 Despots
63 1974 Altman film
67 Black Sea arm
68 Orange skins
69 *The __ of Night*
70 Storage unit
71 Hide away
72 Silty soil

DOWN

1 Book before Romans
2 First name in pound cake
3 Fit
4 Lawrence's land
5 Literary monogram
6 Regret
7 Nile vipers
8 Ladderlike
9 Diminished
10 Likely
11 Numismatic collectible
12 Tarheel State college
13 Over
18 Camelot weapon
19 Gather together
24 Mover's platform
25 Former home of the Hawks
27 Fed. agent
28 Stick (to)
29 U.S. Grant foe
30 Balance-sheet item
31 Walled city near Madrid
32 Still sleeping
33 Table wood
36 Scott Joplin's genre
38 Without
40 Newborn's bed
41 __ close to schedule
44 Java order
46 Irritated states
49 Helicopter blades
50 Wear down
51 Mark work
54 Strikebreaker
55 Hard to see
56 Bunches
58 Paquin of *The Piano*
60 Tough-guy actor Ray
61 Latvian port
62 Pipe part
64 "__ Been Working on the Railroad"
65 Dog tags: Abbr.
66 Fire residue

RIPE QUIP by Dean Niles

ACROSS

1 Like some cereals
8 Like Fort Knox
15 Italian town
16 Oregon city
17 START OF A QUIP
18 PART 2 OF QUIP
19 Summer staple
20 Complacent
22 Soaking
23 Pilfer
25 Gossip-column tidbits
28 The worse for wear
32 Bodies of water
36 Sooner city
37 GM car
39 Alaskan tongue
40 Kid's father
43 In the style of
44 Peerage expert
45 Nephew of Donald
46 Squishy orb
48 Check for accuracy
49 They're going for you
51 Some couples
54 After then
56 __ *Can Cook* (PBS show)
57 Mr. Marino
60 Top of the heap
62 Cowboy's attire
66 PART 3 OF QUIP
69 END OF QUIP
71 Put up
72 Midler movie
73 Reels about
74 Griffith films

DOWN

1 Simba's uncle
2 Hankering
3 Will of *The Waltons*
4 Sum total
5 Nancy's hubby
6 Photog. instruction
7 Shift for some
8 A to Z, e.g.
9 Customary ways
10 ABA member
11 Baloney
12 Limned
13 Word on Irish coins
14 Dare, old-style
21 Go-betweens
24 Jordan, once
26 Jordan, once
27 *Enterprise* navigator
28 Indian drum
29 Southwestern farewell
30 Anklebone
31 Zest
33 Chutzpah
34 __ it out (came to blows)
35 Marks to retain
38 Eleanor's mother-in-law
41 "Here __ Love" (Crosby tune)
42 Abominable one
47 One way to cook
50 Grabby type
52 Author Carson
53 Belong by nature
55 Some students
57 Food plan
58 Continental prefix
59 Dacha denial
61 Gobbles up
63 Geological time
64 "Hey, you!"
65 Calls a bet
67 Columbus Day mo.
68 Colorado Indian
70 X

ON THE TABLE by Elizabeth C. Gorski

ACROSS
1 Opera solo
5 Light wood
10 Kooky
14 California city
15 E.T., e.g.
16 Double reed
17 South African
18 Glossy
19 High-schooler
20 Snappy dressers
23 Small horse
24 Center starter
25 Mount an attack
28 Down in the dumps
31 Back-to-health program, for short
35 Mrs. Kramden et al.
37 Time period
39 ". . . man __ mouse?"
40 TV reception enhancers
44 Greek vowel
45 Hither and __
46 Shrewd
47 Feel
50 Singer Cole
52 Shot for, with "at"
53 In the style of
55 Equal: Fr.
57 UFOs
63 Middling grades
64 Duck relative
65 "Bye!"
67 Actor Sean
68 Misplaces
69 All even
70 Concerning
71 Scents
72 Aware of

DOWN
1 Priest's vestment
2 Housetop
3 Concept
4 Atmospheric region
5 Washbowl
6 Bronze and pewter
7 Creditor's claim
8 Drain (into)
9 __-deep (shallow)
10 Country singer West
11 Busy as __
12 Rivals
13 Hamilton's bill
21 Vacation location
22 Spr. month
25 Manuscript enclosures: Abbr.
26 Make happy
27 Giant
29 Met Life competitor
30 Rap star Dr. __
32 Boring
33 Mountain ridge
34 Situated
36 Devious
38 Oklahoma city
41 Charged particle
42 Violinist Stern
43 Short dagger
48 Declines a proposal
49 Inventor Whitney
51 Come-on
54 __-Saxon
56 Estimate
57 Professional charges
58 Fasting period
59 Not bad
60 Not bad
61 Precipitation
62 Editor's note
63 Tax preparer: Abbr.
66 Fuss

ALSO-RANS by Fred Piscop

ACROSS
1 Hindu misters
5 Roy's wife
9 Nez __ Indians
14 Camping need
15 Mephistophelean
16 Rap-sheet datum
17 Goya subject
18 Synagogue scroll
19 Bird homes
20 Also-ran of '68
23 More alluring
24 World Series mo.
25 Also-ran in '28 thru '48
32 Trendy
35 Nikon rival
36 Delete
37 "Pardon me!"
39 Film genre
41 Large quantity
42 Certain flowering plant
44 Discharge
46 Writer Fleming
47 Also-ran of '80
50 Bard's "before"
51 Saudi __
55 Also-ran in '48
59 Smart folks
61 Thermometer type
62 City southeast of New Delhi
63 Staring
64 Pub serving
65 Abound
66 Cantered
67 Batter ingredient
68 London park

DOWN
1 Male deer
2 CSA general
3 Desk feature
4 Have the lead role of
5 Dissuaded
6 State positively
7 Turkish dough
8 Carrier to Tel Aviv
9 Verve
10 Certain college members
11 Get up
12 Jazz player
13 Feminine suffix
21 Earth sci.
22 Fortune
26 Stuck in the mud
27 "Nor iron bars __"
28 Finger-pointer
29 Guinea neighbor
30 On the briny
31 __ up (monopolized)
32 Trip to Mecca
33 B&O part
34 Word in many college names
38 Establish as legal tender
40 Attacks
43 Loitered
45 Pressure unit
48 New: Pref.
49 Super Bowl III hero
52 Bad news for Nicklaus
53 *The Woman __* ('84 film)
54 "There Is Nothin' Like __"
55 Cereal noise
56 Sulk
57 Math subject
58 Put up, as a portrait
59 4 qts.
60 Self

263 VAMPIRE BEWARE by Patrick Jordan

ACROSS
1 Did not exist
6 "Common Sense," for one
11 Truck maker
14 Blood of the gods
15 Ground
16 Stephen of *The Crying Game*
17 George Burns Oscar film
20 Prepares a publication
21 *The Wild Bunch* actor
22 Mystery writer Josephine
23 More nimble
25 Receded
28 Paper
29 Declare one's ownership
31 NFL positions
34 Physicians, familiarly
35 Robert Burns' birthplace
36 Bird-food ingredient
37 Sign, as a contract
38 Trattoria serving
42 In short supply
44 Leaning, at sea
45 In short supply
46 Sault __ Marie, MI
47 Has on
48 Liner lodgings of old
53 In direct opposition
56 Contend (for)
57 Ryan of baseball
58 Sends out
59 Extremity
60 Leggy flier
61 Thickly forested

DOWN
1 Skating star
2 Sore
3 Good name for a herding dog
4 Wine's aroma
5 Board member
6 Ill-humored
7 Cheering words
8 *Exodus* character
9 Whse. box
10 Pythagorean proposition
11 Bizarre works of art
12 Ben's role in *Bugsy*
13 Mama __ Elliot
18 "I __ vacation!"
19 Minnows, worms, etc.
23 Puppeteer Lewis
24 Noted architect
25 Orwell alma mater
26 Deleted, using a keyboard
27 OT parts
28 In an arch way
29 "Star Wars" pgm.
30 Menu, in Marseilles
32 Exhausted
33 Part of MST
36 __ Lanka
38 Actress Greer et al.
39 T or F, on some exams
40 Supply a banquet
41 Censored
43 Singer Vikki
45 Take effect
46 Was terrible
47 Surfer's surface
48 Ship's pole
49 '60 Summer Olympics site
50 M __ "mnemonic"
51 Procures
52 To be: Lat.
54 Barfly
55 Highway warning

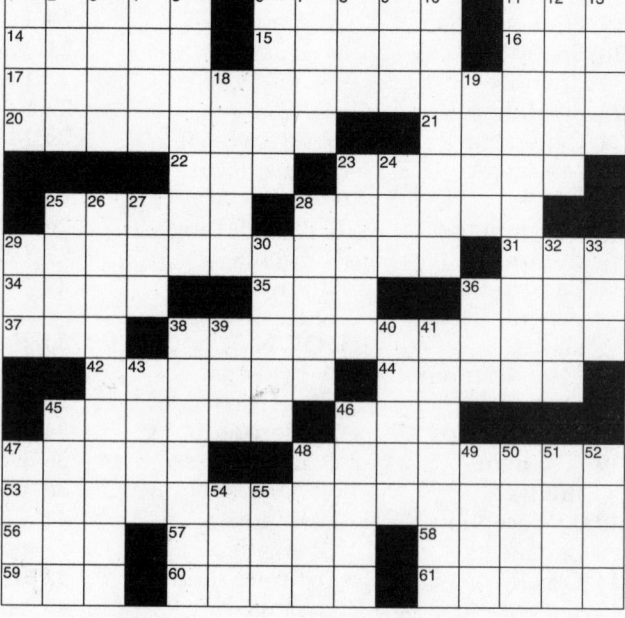

264 ROADSIDE RHYME by Bob Lubbers

ACROSS
1 Bank abbr.
4 Summer drinks
8 NBAer
14 "__ you kidding?"
15 The two
16 Card game
17 Dawson or Deighton
18 START OF A BURMA SHAVE VERSE
20 Stair part
22 Foul up
23 Sugar suffix
24 PART 2 OF VERSE
28 Howl
31 Bandleader Shaw
32 George Burns role
33 Tell a whopper
34 JFK posting
35 __ Lingus
36 *Candid Camera* man
37 PART 3 OF VERSE
41 Actress Moore
42 Teachers' org.
43 Actress Charlotte
44 Sphere
45 Do
46 *Let's Make __*
49 Winged walker
50 PART 4 OF VERSE
54 Studio property
56 Zilch
57 Bridge coup
58 END OF VERSE
63 Latin 101 word
64 Inventor's protection
65 Zilch
66 Made a lap
67 Corrects
68 Ogled
69 Mao __-tung

DOWN
1 Taco topping
2 Singer Franklin
3 Overlay
4 Tummy muscles
5 "What's up, __?"
6 Lucy's pal
7 Seaside
8 Cartoon unit
9 Resounded
10 Asian nation
11 Dependable
12 "__ You or No One"
13 Average grade
19 Toothache soother
21 New York governor
25 Urgent
26 How hero sandwiches may be priced
27 Sisterly
29 __ *Misbehavin'*
30 Still
35 __ rule (usually)
36 *The __ In* (Lamour film)
37 Time in office
38 Walk
39 Wyoming mountains
40 Desert river bed
41 John or Jane
45 Be present
47 Finally
48 Camels' kin
51 Actress Hasso
52 "Crazy Legs" Hirsch
53 Overact
55 Oast
58 Resort
59 Deli choice
60 ACLU concerns
61 Single
62 Marry

265 WHAT'S THE MATTER? by Frank Longo

ACROSS

1 O'Hare abbr.
4 Brillo alternative
7 Rumbles, as thunder
12 Famous fumer
15 Locale of 12 Across
16 Like a lemur
17 Some sheiks
18 ANIMAL
20 Long intro?
21 Hurricane heading: Abbr.
22 Tatum of music
23 Fraternity letter
25 Invests with a name
27 Body
31 Casino sights
33 "Ligeia" author
34 Old hands
35 VEGETABLE
38 Small dog
39 Holm of Hollywood
40 Swivels
41 Quite impressed

42 Louver part
44 Gerundial suffix
45 *Peer Gynt* mother
46 Colorless
48 Greenpeace prefix
51 MINERAL
57 "Where Is Love?" musical
58 They answer back
59 Gunpowder components
60 Follow
61 It'll make your flour grow
62 __ Angelo, TX
63 Novelist Deighton

DOWN

1 Bowl over
2 Less common
3 Elastic
4 Florida city
5 Dairy-section purchases
6 Got high

7 Singer Bonnie
8 Nocturnal, perhaps
9 Headlight
10 Place
11 Falls from grace
13 Negative conjunction
14 Italian peak
15 Most overtalked
19 Cabinet department
24 Improve an edge
26 *Once __ Mattress*
27 Brush off
28 Curaçao flavorer
29 Rolling stone's lack
30 Blonde shade
31 Eject
32 Clipper's need
35 Spring's home
36 More vigorous

37 *Object Lessons* author
43 Selkirk exports
45 Heads-up
47 Beginning
49 __ du jour (menu)
50 Bean of the screen
51 Gaunt

52 Author Wiesel
53 Girl in a Beatles tune
54 Jacques __ Cousteau
55 Lippi's title
56 Gilbert's title

266 UNDER CONTRACT by Norma Steinberg

ACROSS

1 Sailor's call
5 Exchange
9 Cook in the microwave
12 Relocate
13 Female horses
15 Colorless
16 Publicity person
18 Small land mass
19 __ Francisco
20 Chief Exec.
21 Once-a-year
23 Cliques
24 Gator's cousin
25 Flounce about
28 Aggressive experts
32 Pencil pusher
33 Knucklehead
34 Front of the boat
35 Sitarist Shankar
36 Loose-leaf filler
37 She: Fr.
38 Revival meeting cry
39 Roman poet
40 Troll
41 Meat-case item

43 Easter hat
44 Dictionary entry
45 Strong-smelling
46 Hamilton or McGovern
49 Pierre's pop
50 Poem
53 __ mater
54 Accordion
57 Cry
58 Pachyderm teeth
59 "__ lay me down to sleep . . ."
60 Barbie's boyfriend
61 Aide: Abbr.
62 Surface depression

DOWN

1 Rock band equipment
2 Israeli dance
3 Pizzeria appliance
4 "You bet!"
5 __ pants (wise guy)

6 Salary
7 Mars' Greek counterpart
8 Pigsty
9 Actress Pitts
10 __ breve
11 Pare
14 Ignition switch
15 Miser
17 Orate
22 Negatives
23 Supermarket packaging
24 Managed, somehow
25 Tiff
26 San Antonio landmark
27 Cut
28 Music to a hitchhiker's ears
29 Synthetic fiber
30 "My mama done __ . . ."
31 Sugary
33 Solomon's father
36 Lowest-quality

40 Addams family member
42 Fireplace feature
43 Flimsiest
45 Nerds
46 Rubberneck
47 Gen. Robt. __

48 Soothsayer's clue
49 "__ in Boots"
50 Reed-section member
51 Fine feathers
52 Way out
55 Sine __ non
56 Conclude

267 SOLVE WITH E'S by Rand H. Burns

ACROSS
1 German river
5 Tour again
10 *Fresh Prince of __ Air*
13 Unimportant
14 Levels out
15 French father
16 Ego
17 Looks after
18 Actress Russo
19 Become more profound
21 Less chaotic
23 Take five
24 Pince-__
25 Feel annoyed at
28 Guidelines for conduct
33 Comic DeGeneres
34 User charges
35 Flow slowly
36 Night before
37 Stimpy's pal
38 *Uno + due*
39 __ up (concludes)
41 Labor Day mo.
42 Reagan attorney general
44 Perfumes
46 __ up (admitted everything)
47 Alway
48 Not straight
49 Rode a toboggan
53 Cash in
56 Le Moko or Le Pew
57 Went hunting for morays
59 General Robert __
61 Pitcher
62 A.L. city
63 Baseball team since '62
64 B followers
65 Witch, often
66 *Peter Pan* pirate

DOWN
1 Print measures
2 Exploit
3 A Gardner
4 Grid official
5 Student's make-up
6 Occurrence
7 DC title
8 Wraps up
9 Ancient ascetics
10 Happened
11 Sea flier
12 Impolite look
15 Clinton and Coolidge, for short
20 Colonial Quaker
22 __ room
25 Singer Della
26 Santa's helpers
27 Large numbers
28 Sounds from chicks
29 Lease
30 "For __ sake!"
31 None too talkative
32 Bullock movie
34 Yours for the asking
40 Sowing machine
41 Shrill sound
42 Repair
43 Holds in high regard
45 Homer Simpson's neighbor
46 Tributary
48 Alla __
49 Plan detail
50 Indecent
51 Olympic weapon
52 Stet opposite
54 First level of sch.
55 Parcel (out)
58 Superman foe Luthor
60 Ending for legal

268 WEAR ARE THEY NOW by Bob Lubbers

ACROSS
1 Endure
5 Fencer's sword
9 Heathen
14 Singer James
15 H.S. exams
16 Love, in Livorno
17 Infielder
19 Valuated
20 ON BEACH-HEADS
22 Bank abbr.
23 Word form for "one"
24 Student groups
28 Orient
30 Play to __ (require overtime)
32 In the past
33 "Rose __ rose . . ."
36 '20s first family
39 ON TV
42 Biased one
43 Sun Yat-__
44 Provide weapons
45 __ out a living
47 Light punishment
51 Syrian monetary unit
54 Viper
57 Enzyme suffix
58 IN SWAMPS
61 __ ice cap
64 Cut across
65 Warning
66 Food serving
67 Actress Patricia
68 Conical abode
69 Formerly, once
70 Charles' sister

DOWN
1 Nielsen or Howard
2 Goddess of wisdom
3 Ermines
4 Tangy
5 Ruhr valley city
6 Country: Lat.
7 Prince William's school
8 Distinctive
9 Arctic coat
10 Gather up
11 Inherited
12 "Chances __"
13 Actor Beatty
18 Wed-Fri connector
21 Salespeople
25 Warbled
26 Roe
27 Distress signal
29 Pinball goof
31 Feudal lord
34 Hit the slopes
35 Avow
37 Las Vegas cube
38 Lodgings
39 Delhi wrap
40 *My Friend __*
41 Aren't built in a day
42 Baby food
46 Certain seasonal employees
48 Triangular sail
49 Trash holder
50 Mortar mate
52 Frighten
53 Scatter Mel
55 Refine ore
56 __ *favor*
59 Unique person
60 Annapolis initials
61 Sajak or Benatar
62 Bullring cry
63 Race unit

269 ONES OF A KIND by Dean Niles

ACROSS
1 Get ready
5 Senator Thurmond
10 Mata __
14 It may be a stretch
15 __ ballerina
16 God of war
17 Nefarious
18 Smidgens
19 Dart off
20 Food shop
21 Only-child actor
23 Fred Mertz's wife
25 Staggering
26 Nodded off
28 Movie must
32 Moon project
34 Helper
35 __ "Kookie" Byrnes
38 *What's My Line?* host
39 Foolish
41 Role for Liz in '63
42 Chicken __ king
43 Wild swine
44 Hang around
46 Land of C.S. Lewis
48 Book publisher Alfred
49 Internet feature
52 Poet Nash
54 Only-child pianist
58 "A thing of beauty is __ forever"
61 Composer Satie
62 Actress Berger
63 Shoe surface
64 Nick at __
65 __ a hatter
66 "Take __ Train"
67 Zoo favorite
68 Smidgen
69 B&O position

DOWN
1 Beseeched
2 Split
3 Only-child French author
4 With refinement
5 Enliven, in a way
6 Sings in full voice
7 Comic Rudner
8 Poet Khayyám
9 Cher movie
10 Capital of Tasmania
11 Brick structure
12 Lunar trench
13 Chip maker
22 Betray awe
24 The "good" cholesterol: Abbr.
26 Surrealism cousin
27 Iridescent stone
29 Italian isle
30 Shred
31 Pastoral poem
33 Smell
35 Only-child singer
36 Intense
37 Tim Conway character
40 Golfer Woosnam
41 Film fan
43 Fancy dance
45 Authorized
46 Where one might see a buffalo
47 Heart lines
49 Smooths
50 Irving Berlin song
51 Pop singer Baker
53 Chomp
55 Doctrines
56 Bird bill
57 Cancel
59 Designer Cassini
60 Once around the sun

270 WHAT AND Y by Randolph Ross

ACROSS
1 Midsection
6 Boardlike
11 City in Iran
14 Rose oil
15 High house
16 Munched on
17 Peter's age?
19 Juan's aunt
20 Word on an LP
21 Galleys order
22 100%
23 Icelandic tale
25 Some refugees
27 Swiss river
30 Heinrich's exclamation
32 Night before
33 Improper itches?
39 Musical group
40 Have second thoughts about
41 Characteristic
43 Mixed-up safecrackers?
46 Cell acid
47 Enjoy Vail
48 That girl
49 Nursery-rhyme starter
53 Nintendo alternative
56 Mrs. Lennon
57 La __ tar pits
59 Start of a Lazarus poem
63 Photos
64 Early riser?
66 Hot time on the Riviera
67 Joiner's cry
68 Group of three
69 Embarrassed
70 Follow
71 Tommy guns

DOWN
1 They may be civil
2 Rat-__
3 "Let __ Me"
4 Buffalo iceman
5 Heard a case
6 Recite
7 Driver's needs
8 More than sore
9 Relief pitchers
10 Celebration
11 Mideast land
12 With applications
13 Part of the American plan
18 Show created by Sigourney Weaver's father
24 Tart
26 Category
27 Long follower
28 Flight paths
29 Campus mil. org.
31 Lugs
34 "Apostle of California"
35 Ben E. King song
36 Offends, in a way
37 Comedy bits
38 Sound of relief
42 Literary monogram
44 Reagan daughter
45 Artist Rivera
49 Gallup rival
50 Wed
51 Took on Tyson
52 Police patrols
54 They're exchanged in December
55 Head off
58 Not worth __
60 Mrs. Kovacs
61 Average
62 Linemen
65 Stocking stuffer

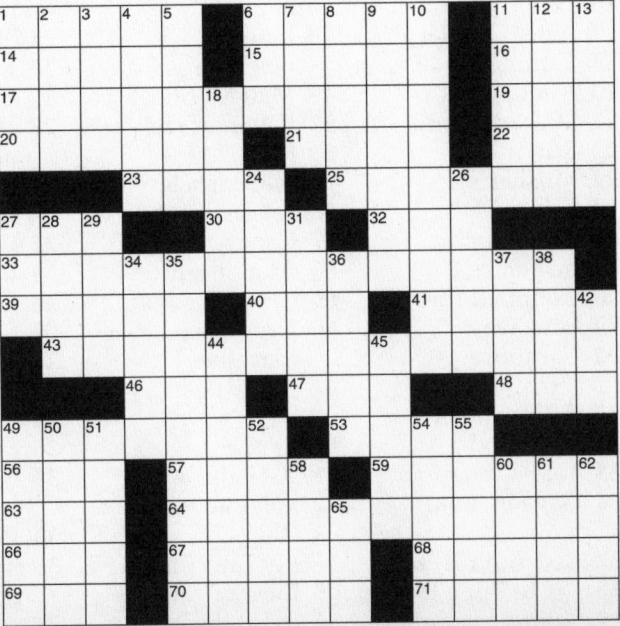

FOOD GROUPS by Randall J. Hartman

ACROSS
1 Musical finale
5 Understand
10 Compass point
14 Norse deity
15 German pistol
16 Ready for picking
17 "__ to Be Wild"
18 January, to Julio
19 Type of exam
20 Café freebies
23 Author Tan
24 Tool and __
25 Fragrant shrubs
29 Retain
31 NBC show since '75
34 Fighting __ (Notre Dame)
35 Author Fleming's namesakes
36 Greek portico
37 Basic foods
40 Letters on the cross
41 Swiss peaks
42 Mends, as socks
43 Your: Fr.
44 Vicinity
45 Texas city
46 Misjudge
47 Heir, often
48 Popular snack
56 Zilch
57 Seer's deck
58 Woodworker's tool
59 PDQ
60 Supply depot
61 Wife of Zeus
62 Window section
63 Like some stadiums
64 Well-groomed

DOWN
1 Actor Lee J.
2 Aroma
3 Desperate
4 __ Karenina
5 Glows
6 Like some noses
7 Matured
8 Eastern European
9 Most gratified
10 Murder, She __
11 The Emerald Isle
12 Practice boxing
13 __ Aviv
21 Russian villa
22 Gratuity
25 Boundary
26 Singer Cara
27 Prevaricators
28 Wine region
29 Fraternity letter
30 Seth's son
31 Mall unit
32 Very much
33 Cowboy's rope
35 Run in neutral
36 Night sight
38 Told the story
39 A Bell for __
44 Noah's ship
45 Pillaged
46 Run off to wed
47 Range
48 __ Verde National Park
49 Shah's domain
50 Org. formed in 1949
51 Apothecary's weight
52 Madeline of Young Frankenstein
53 Notion: Fr.
54 Poet Pound
55 Sofa or stool
56 Ray-gun blast

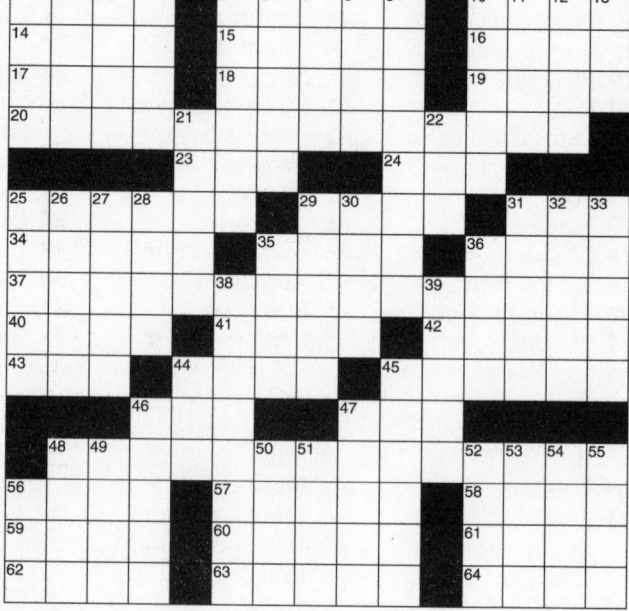

BEDDING by Lee Weaver

ACROSS
1 Seamstress Betsy
5 Summarize
10 Cotton-tipped cleaner
14 Pointed arch
15 Playing marble
16 Water main
17 Artist's tablet
19 Summer coolers
20 Auction suffix
21 Short distance
22 Run in
24 Musher's vehicle
25 Gambling machines
26 Chopped fine
29 Give way
32 Campfire remains
33 Bath adjunct
34 TV brand
35 Told a whopper
36 Gave in, in a way
37 Red and Black
38 "__ to Billie Joe"
39 Solitude seeker
40 Oil-bearing rock
41 Locations
43 Hues
44 Antiquated
45 Black-tongued dog
46 Tibetan mountain climber
48 Huron's neighbor
49 Match a raise
52 Dillon or Helm
53 Magazine's main article
56 Russian river
57 Canary sound
58 At a distance
59 Ceramic square
60 Uses a fax machine
61 Army post

DOWN
1 Took the bus
2 Folklore villain
3 Char
4 Ply a needle
5 Blew off steam
6 __ on (incited)
7 Li'l Abner's creator
8 __ premium (scarce)
9 Went by bike, in Britain
10 Athens' foe
11 Occurring over a vast area
12 Tarzan's friends
13 Most excellent
18 Capri and Man
23 Bread alternative
24 Backyard building
25 Farmer, at times
26 Circles of light
27 Out of the way
28 Tinner's supply
29 Sheltered bays
30 Map feature
31 Smooths the way
33 Piquant
36 Influential acquaintances
37 Author Irwin
39 Talk like Daffy Duck
40 Pumps, loafers, etc.
42 Hard-backed pet
43 Tees and polos
45 Doctrine
46 Plant fungus
47 Mata __
48 __-steven
49 Couch
50 Time periods
51 Rochester's wife
54 Be obligated
55 File-folder projection

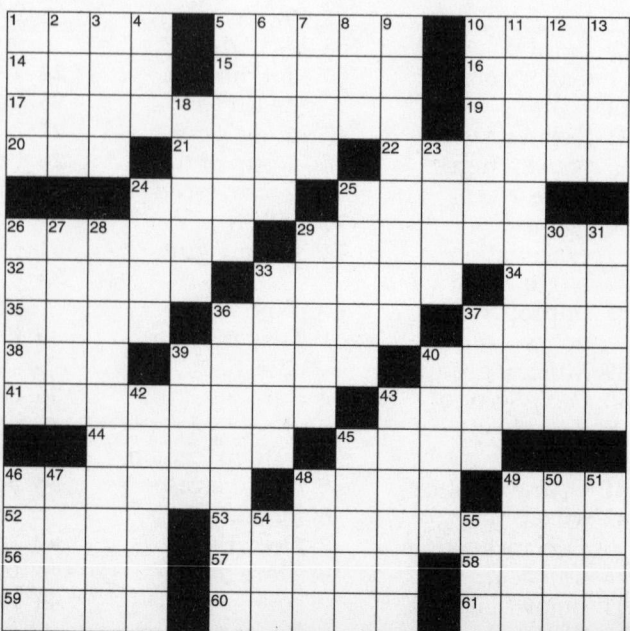

273   FAUNY BUSINESS by Shirley Soloway

ACROSS

1 Guns an engine
5 Flavor enhancer
9 Plotters' group
14 Spew forth
15 Entreaty
16 Demean
17 Verdi work
18 Learn (of)
19 Quench
20 Fashion plate
23 More concise
24 Skater Babilonia
25 Society girl
28 Take it easy
31 Shade of blue
33 Startle
37 Spicy snacks
39 Alan of *M*A*S*H*
40 Newman and Anka
41 Commotions
42 Library habitués
44 Nocturnal mammal
45 Money of India
46 1995 film pig
48 Legal deg. holder
49 Egyptian snake
51 Rubbed out
56 Auto mechanic
59 Montague boy
62 By oneself
63 '96 running-mate
64 French farewell
65 Parade instrument
66 Simba's home
67 Big meal
68 Island group off Ireland
69 Barcelona bravos

DOWN

1 Show feeling
2 Novelist Zola
3 *The Big Parade* director
4 Sports records, for short
5 Orb
6 Foamy brews
7 Jacob's wife
8 Mystical deck
9 Designer Oleg
10 Talented
11 Sheep talk
12 Make a request
13 Actor Majors
21 In this place
22 Banisters
25 Electron tube
26 Urge
27 __ nova
29 *Lion King* villain
30 Hitchhiker's tool
32 6/6/44
33 Israeli native
34 Influence
35 Take on as one's own
36 Leaf gatherer
38 *Casablanca* role
40 Sheriff's band
43 Get full use of
44 Life saver
47 Lament
50 Noodles
52 __-Saxon
53 Swedish toast
54 Ghostly
55 Fabric workers
56 Turns to the right
57 Tart
58 Exile isle
59 Brit. flyers
60 "__ to Joy"
61 Ms. Farrow

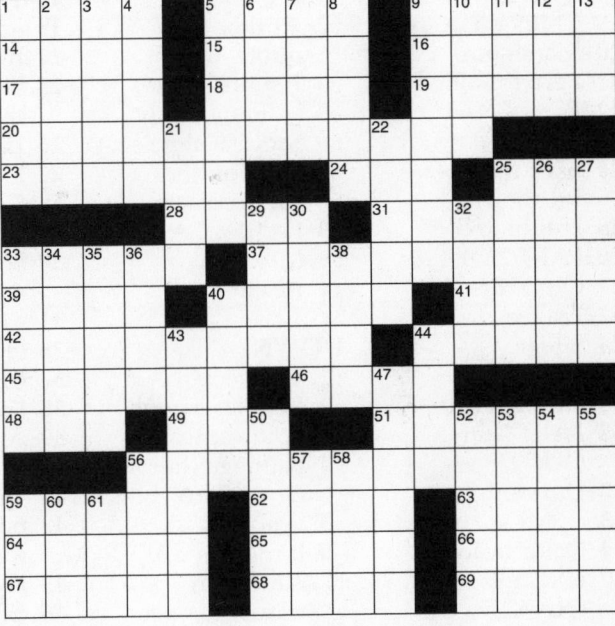

274   HOT TUNES by Bob Lubbers

ACROSS

1 Crew
5 Nanny of Asia
9 La __ opera house
14 Pony (up)
15 Evaluate
16 "__ my wits' end!"
17 Wound memento
18 Mae West tune of 1934
20 With 55 Across, this puzzle's theme
22 Sedative
23 Menlo Park name
25 Disentangle
29 __ Moines, IA
30 Dangerous atmosphere
33 Calamitous
34 Molten material
35 Sierra __
36 The Doors tune of 1967
39 *A Confederacy of Dunces* author
41 Reynolds et al.
42 Once again
43 Less fresh
45 Lamb's wail
48 Insulter
50 Wyoming range
52 Anxiety
55 See 20 Across
56 Glen Gray tune of 1933
60 Mah-jongg piece
61 Broadcaster
62 Buster Brown's dog
63 French summers
64 Cut back
65 Portico for Pericles
66 Playwright Hart

DOWN

1 Sampled
2 Create a cryptogram
3 Some video games
4 Chevy rivals
5 Hammer partner
6 Deli spread
7 On
8 Balloon filler
9 Strains
10 Court dockets
11 Drs.' group
12 On the __ (fleeing)
13 Dug in
19 Actor Andrews
21 Respect
24 Close
26 __-de-camp
27 School learning, so to speak
28 Remick or Grant
31 Qty.
32 Latin dance
34 Brewers' home
35 Clerics' headgear
36 Leopold's partner
37 Actor Brynner
38 Worry
39 Small portion
40 Single
43 Fortune-teller
44 Peculiarities
45 Albacore cousin
46 Fishes
47 Levy
49 Bergen dummy
51 Familial carving
53 Pique
54 Waffle name
56 Gullible one
57 Matthew's *Ferris Bueller* costar
58 Bruins great
59 Vast expanse

275   HEAT-SEEKING MISSIVE by Dean Niles

ACROSS
1 Movie unit
6 Long time
9 Shady recess
14 Harness horse
15 Proclaim
16 Bel __ cheese
17 START OF A QUOTE
19 Chilly quarters
20 Marsh bird
21 Pert. to sailing
22 Part of NATO
23 Weathered
24 Back muscle, for short
25 Hindu god
28 PART 2 OF QUOTE
32 France, once
33 Site of confusion
34 Dupin creator
35 PART 3 OF QUOTE
40 Dance step
43 __ Miss
44 Qatar head
47 END OF QUOTE

52 Sanctuary
53 Soak (up)
54 DDE's command
56 PBS program
57 __ Camera
59 Guess
60 Attorney Melvin
62 Author of quote
64 Astaire's sister
65 __ Remo, Italy
66 Scottish slopes
67 Windows predecessor
68 Fort __, CA
69 Mrs. Steve Allen

DOWN
1 '70s veep
2 Retailer's book
3 Spiny anteater
4 Name in the news, 7/69
5 Seabird
6 It may be real
7 American island
8 Dacha denial
9 Where the bees are
10 Motley
11 Luggage handler
12 Granada grizzly
13 1904 auto
18 Knot on a tree
24 Julia's ex
25 Shapeless mass
26 Pasture plaint
27 Playwright George
29 Schisgal play
30 Montezuma, e.g.
31 Mauna __
36 Hockey area
37 Chicago trains
38 Bound
39 Aussie bird
40 Movie
41 Timber tree
42 Bound, in a way
45 Freezer filler
46 Gotten back

48 Greek god
49 Assemblages
50 "Paper Roses" singer
51 Take off
55 Too big
57 __ facto
58 Not quite shut
59 Koran section
60 Comics sound effect
61 Mag. wheels?
63 Grammatical case: Abbr.

276   SAY WHAT? by Bob Lubbers

ACROSS
1 Store event
5 Unlit
9 Exchange
13 Author Hubbard
14 "Maria __" (Dorsey song)
16 Tennille or Braxton
17 Farming word form
18 Ore deposits
19 Poker payment
20 Muffet's dish
23 Lock insert
24 Chang's twin
25 Eagle nest
29 Skiing surfaces
31 Eve and Enoch
32 Thing of value
35 Like *this*: Abbr.
37 __ off (defer)
38 Warwick asked about it, in a song
42 Singer Zadora
43 Words of discovery

44 Caravan stops
45 National song
48 Quarterback Bradshaw
50 VCR button
51 *Cheers* role for Ted
52 Mil. college
55 Truck stop
60 Hip talk
63 Goose eggs
64 Swabs
65 Finished
66 January: Sp.
67 Gen. Robert __
68 Acquires
69 Group: Abbr.
70 19th-century caricaturist

DOWN
1 Not taut
2 Bicker
3 British truck
4 Oklahoma city
5 Part of FDR
6 Accompanied by
7 Comic Foxx
8 Was aware of
9 Tarried
10 Finished first
11 Picnic pest
12 Dessert choice
15 Hardwood
21 Actress Berger
22 Bowl handle
26 Some taken-back goods
27 Occupied
28 Senator Kefauver
29 Do a tailoring job
30 Ermine in summer
31 __ carte
32 One way to buy bonds
33 Polish
34 Does an usher's job
36 Evaluators
39 November veggie
40 __ *Rae*
41 Leno of late-night
46 Choppers
47 Summer: Fr.

49 Sells out, blamewise
52 String-quartet member
53 Broods
54 Map closeup
56 Verb-forming suffix
57 Actress Rowlands
58 Congressional bill: Abbr.
59 Govt. agents
60 Morning run
61 Common contraction
62 Dog's doc

277 PEOPLE'S CHOICE by Gerald R. Ferguson

ACROSS
1 Ancient Briton
5 Be a bigmouth
9 Great Pyramid, essentially
13 Resound
14 Marquis' inferior
15 Musical work
17 Chime
18 Part of A.D.
19 Complete
20 Some ring wins
23 Notes after dos
24 __-mo replay
25 Change the itinerary
29 __ in the Grass
34 Running wild
35 Spelling or Amos
36 Slugger's stat
37 Viewpoint
41 Word form for "ear"
42 Lord of the Rings creatures
43 Hill openings
44 Jolson tune
47 Brie, e.g.
48 __ de cologne
49 Rock band's initials
50 Nixonian constituency
58 In the sun, poetically
59 Long time
60 We: Fr.
62 Camp craft
63 Brownish purple
64 Fizzy drink
65 Shred
66 Hardens
67 Emcee Trebek

DOWN
1 Vigor
2 Finishes a cake
3 Bloke
4 Bridge fee
5 Defeated
6 Reels in
7 British composer
8 Political group
9 Muss, as hair
10 Choice
11 "Take __ your leader"
12 English gun
16 Letters after cues
21 Beyond peeved
22 New York town
25 Philippines ex-president
26 Poet's Muse
27 Mountain climber's spike
28 Realty unit
29 Easy touch
30 Paid players
31 Go for a spin
32 Clarinets' kin
33 Washer cycle
35 __ avail (fruitless)
38 Contradict
39 Olympian blood
40 Scot's refusal
45 Actor Liam
46 Gave a tug
47 Shuts
49 Discharge
50 USAF unit
51 Construction beam
52 Country byway
53 Atlas contents
54 Fever and chills
55 Peru native
56 Implement
57 Christmas
61 Jazz instrument

278 PINNIPEDIA by Dean Niles

ACROSS
1 Quiver
6 Wall Street traders
10 __ Sutra
14 __-frutti
15 Gold-covered
16 "Right away!"
17 In any quantity
18 Together, musically
19 Fair attraction
20 Lolita author
22 Pitcher's problem
24 Larry and Curly's partner
25 Unexciting
26 Performer's concern
30 Joist
31 A followers
34 Soothing succulents
35 Sailor
36 Pope's topper
38 Cheerful
39 Custom
40 Ritz, e.g.
41 United rival
42 Gentleman
43 Chosen few
44 __ tizzy
45 Soap unit
47 Rouses
48 You, once
49 El-running grp.
50 Arctic traveler
53 '96 Olympics site
58 Marshal of Yugoslavia
59 Geological time
61 City on the Seine
62 For the Boys star
63 German: Abbr.
64 Separate strands of rope
65 Contain
66 Continental prefix
67 Alabama city

DOWN
1 Musial or Getz
2 "__ Little Love in Your Heart"
3 Run __ (pay later)
4 WWII battle site
5 Recent ad feature
6 Century plant
7 Get __ of (lose)
8 Crybaby
9 Stanley Kowalski's cry
10 Churchill photographer
11 Be that __ may
12 Created
13 Mimic
21 "Alley __!"
23 1967 Beatles tune
26 __ Gras
27 Visitor from another planet
28 Qantas mascot
29 MD specialty
30 Big Band leader
31 Method of fabric dyeing
32 Greek island
33 Valleys
35 Booker T. Washington sch.
37 Kansas city
46 Fill with fizz
47 ABA member
48 Govt. security
49 Bel __ (singing style)
50 Longing
51 Parting word
52 And others: Abbr.
54 First-rate
55 Void partner
56 Unite
57 Novelist Seton
60 __ Town (Wilder play)

279 ELEMENTARY by Wayne Robert Williams

ACROSS

1 Throw away
5 Cheers
9 Personification of evil
14 Biblical twin
15 Reverend Roberts
16 Bring joy to
17 Geologists
20 Golfer's mound
21 Ridicule
22 Create lace
23 Acad., e.g.
26 __ fan tutte
28 Passover meals
30 Prickly plant
32 Very wide shoe
33 Top Gun weapon
38 Cut and run
39 Small piece
40 B __ "ball"
41 Olivier film
46 Average scores
47 Transplanter's concern
48 Upper-crust member, in Britain
51 Salinger girl
52 East Coast cape
53 DC title
54 Cotton pod
56 Vex
58 Picnic ammo
64 Writer Rogers St. Johns
65 Creeper
66 Home port in the War of 1812
67 Synthetic fiber
68 "Ah!"
69 Breathe heavily

DOWN

1 Scottish river
2 Olympics chant
3 Calendar abbr.
4 Green stroke
5 German measles
6 Javelin's path
7 Cuba neighbor
8 Large amount
9 Sofas
10 Common Islamic name
11 Refinement
12 Perfume from petals
13 Prepares to lay eggs
18 One hundred: Pref.
19 Second-generation Japanese-American
23 Employee group
24 Spicy dish
25 Employer
27 Vertical fishing nets
29 Process seawater
31 Saturates
32 Smoldering coals
34 Capek play
35 Father of 14 Across
36 Specialized vocabulary
37 Called off
42 High-fiber ingredient
43 Toy-car sound effect
44 Oscar contender
45 Attendees
48 Egyptian dam
49 Fully prepped
50 Chips maker
51 New York island
55 Big name on jeans
57 Stronghold of a castle
59 "Telephone Line" grp.
60 First of a count
61 Memorable time
62 Cacophony
63 Matched outfit

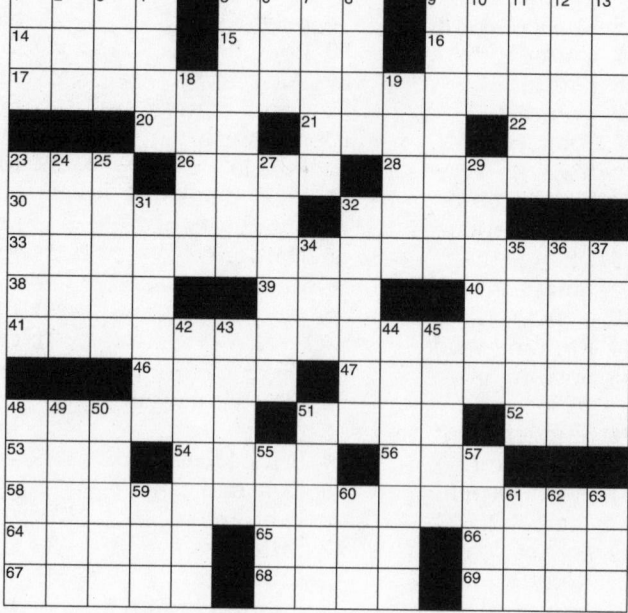

280 NUMERICAL ORDER by Chuck Deodene

ACROSS

1 Teatime treat
6 Completed, in Cannes
10 Arp's movement
14 Conductor Kurt
15 Oft-bruised items
16 Scandinavian name
17 Coherence
18 A Farewell to Arms setting
20 Swarm
21 Lawes' colleagues
22 1996 Olympics squad
27 Overcast
28 Hines or Warren
32 Stipulations
35 Windy City area
36 Faux pas
38 Excommunicator of King John
41 Agree
42 Power unit
43 Gene material
44 Otherwise
45 Install new shingles
47 1/11/70 event
52 Early springs?
55 Prune
57 Movie subtitled "The Final Frontier"
60 Banishment
61 Racer Luyendyk
62 Femur-tibia link
63 1918 Pulitzer writer
64 Turns brown
65 Mythical river
66 Packing

DOWN

1 Plant fungus
2 Made a chair, maybe
3 Willow twig
4 Mace source
5 Mock ending
6 Not many
7 "__ to Rio" (Peter Allen tune)
8 NATO member
9 Faith of about 1 billion
10 Most unstylish
11 Winglike parts
12 "Rats!"
13 Roman bird
19 Soft & __
23 Kate's housemate
24 Io and Europa
25 Animated character
26 Grant authority to
29 Part of 43 Across
30 Wreck
31 Luke's sister
32 __ dixit
33 Stable babe
34 Sutherland/Gould film
36 "Ditto!"
37 Following, perhaps
39 Squalid sights
40 Engine topper, for short
45 Chafe at
46 Bending muscle
48 Final: Abbr.
49 Exec's extras
50 Argot
51 City in France
52 H.S. jr.'s exam
53 Shaver brand
54 Shower
56 __ off (in a huff)
58 Anthem author
59 Confound
60 They monitor PCBs

ESSENCE OF CHANGE by Lee Weaver

ACROSS
1 Hot drink
4 Circus name
10 Feudal servant
14 Med. facilities
15 Provoke
16 "I cannot tell __"
17 Tuck's partner
18 Thin layer of metal
20 High card
21 Prescription amounts
22 Byways
23 Maui porches
25 Apple-pie baker
26 Halt at an exact point
32 Intentions
35 Storytellers
36 Rowboat need
38 Architect Christopher
39 Daffodils' origins
40 Come out second best
41 Ms. Fabray, to friends
42 Carved pin

43 Golden Rule word
44 Gridder who calls the signals
48 "I __ Rhythm"
49 Lyrical
53 E.T., e.g.
56 Part of Iberia
59 Harem room
60 Casual shoe style of the '50s
62 La Brea __ pits
63 Writer Bagnold
64 Llama with valuable wool
65 Cry of discovery
66 Computer input
67 Flew like an eagle
68 Sodom survivor

DOWN
1 Having a key, in music
2 Susan Lucci character
3 Ski resort
4 Robin Hood, for one
5 Opera passage

6 Legendary birds
7 Cook in a microwave
8 Functions
9 Tormé or Tillis
10 Lunchmeat
11 Pizazz
12 Sacred ceremony
13 Lawyer's charges
19 Trudges along
24 Trade group: Abbr.
25 War god
27 Knight's helmet decoration
28 Edmonton hockey player
29 Big shot
30 Landing spot for Neil Armstrong
31 Bridge position
32 Barley beard
33 Mideast land
34 Waiter's offering
37 Antique auto
39 Sheet of cotton
40 *Cool Hand __*
42 Sidekick
45 Planned schedule

46 Each
47 *Lord Jim* author
50 Sum
51 Sun Valley locale
52 Diamond weight
53 Mimicked
54 Melodious Horne

55 "What's __ for me?"
56 Perform without backup
57 Sobriquet for Hemingway
58 A long way off
61 __ Cruces, NM

SOLE SEARCHING by Bob Lubbers

ACROSS
1 Donkey
4 One way to cook beef
9 Skirt features
14 NCAA rival
15 Diplomat
16 Siouan speakers
17 Lyricist Gershwin
18 Going on a date
20 Belief
22 Word form for "blood"
23 Robot relative
26 Run-down place
31 Raid
33 Acting company
34 __ of the Sheik
36 Sign up
38 Sandy's owner
39 Sale stickers
41 French legislature
43 Crisp cookie
44 Type of poplar

46 Chopper blade
48 Electees
49 Customized
51 Generated anew
53 Fancy digs
55 Bridge blunders
58 The Supremes, e.g.
60 Nile dam
61 Showing pride
67 Skater Midori
68 A Chipmunk
69 Wished (for)
70 Ayres or Wallace
71 David's weapon
72 Adolescents
73 Arid

DOWN
1 Singer O'Day
2 Alarm
3 Taking no cards
4 Make like new
5 Canadian prov.
6 St. crosser

7 Frosh, next year
8 Word processor
9 "Ol' Blue Eyes"
10 Sea diary
11 __ Jima
12 Greek cross
13 Supersonic flyer: Abbr.
19 "__ my wits' end!"
21 Fish-eating flier
24 Charged particles
25 Challenger
27 Lots
28 Out of control
29 Bee-related
30 Chick talk
32 Giver
34 Phase
35 Desert stops
37 Slangy farewell
40 Blood fluids
42 "__, or not . . ."
45 Mosquito guard

47 Reagan and Coleman
50 Bruce or Laura
52 Scale notes
54 Vision
56 Chowhound
57 Winter forecast word

59 Western Indian
61 Is no longer
62 100%
63 XIV x IV
64 Relatives
65 Copy
66 Author Deighton

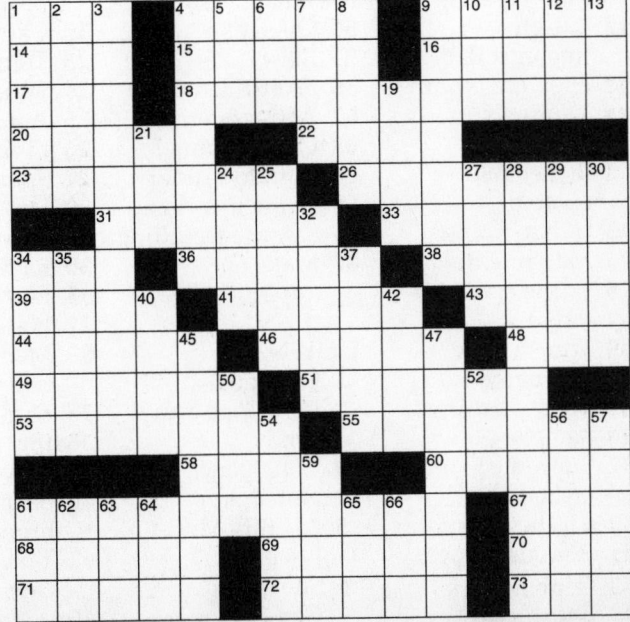

CROSSWORD CLUBS by Fred Piscop

ACROSS
1 Catches
5 Dismal
9 Tito Puente music
14 Doozy
15 Top-quality
16 Like some college walls
17 Vaccine adjective
18 Nabokov novel
19 Tore apart
20 Source of unsolicited advice
23 Streamlined
24 Pouchlike structure
25 Book holders
29 Banquet platforms
34 Sellout sign
37 Tucker of country
39 Hoo-ha
40 Gardening, perhaps
44 __ spumante
45 Vocalist Mel

46 __ Cruces, NM
47 Equilateral figures
50 Cuts into cubes
52 Salad-dressing ingredient
54 Potato holders
58 Undertakings
64 Archie or Dudley
65 Fuzzy fruit
66 Revlon rival
67 Playful mammal
68 Actor Estrada
69 Cheese covering
70 Mexican munchies
71 Ready to serve
72 Cools down

DOWN
1 Mushy masses
2 Of hearing
3 Sugarcoated
4 Moody one
5 Open wide
6 Barrett of gossip
7 Monogram part: Abbr.

8 Makes repairs to
9 Watergate judge
10 Tel __
11 Exist
12 Clairvoyant
13 Tack on
21 Rollerblade, e.g.
22 Swell, slangily
26 Mercury or Saturn
27 Make bootees
28 Church council
30 "How was __ know?"
31 Music genre
32 Author Ferber
33 Redoes the lawn
34 Go a few rounds
35 Go quickly
36 Gridiron great Graham
38 Word form for "farming"
41 *Aladdin* lyricist Rice
42 Cable channel
43 Ebbets Field great
48 Big mistakes

49 Bro's sib
51 "Surfin' __" (Beach Boys tune)
53 Fancied
55 Urban
56 Danish dough
57 E-mails

58 Greek vowel
59 College mil. grp.
60 Hydrox lookalike
61 Robert De __
62 Chang, to Eng
63 Scouting outing
64 Word: Fr.

END OVER END by Patrick Jordan

ACROSS
1 Mountain predator
5 Hikers' stop
9 Witty remarks
14 *Clueless* catchphrase
15 From a distance
16 Hilo greeting
17 Laugh uncontrollably
20 UN Day month
21 Vandenberg, e.g.: Abbr.
22 Sweetened coolers
23 Indian noble
26 Madame de __
28 __ the crack of dawn
29 Ramshackle
34 Pen name
35 Mets' stadium
36 Angelic glows
37 Supreme Court justice
39 Clothes, casually
41 Romance-cover model
42 Rams' mates

43 Chi. summer setting
44 Geraldine's portrayer
47 *Vogue* rival
48 Telegram periods
49 Run in the laundry
50 Wile E.'s supplier
54 Overly
55 Exist
56 Fruit-filled treats
62 Actress Berry
63 Cable channel
64 Buffalo's canal
65 Came to a close
66 Sample recording
67 Make an appointment

DOWN
1 Hole goal
2 Bob Hope tour grp.
3 1/1000 inch
4 Not sinking
5 "__ Buy Me Love"
6 Sternward
7 Gandhi's title

8 Like some housing
9 __ alai
10 Literary lioness
11 Convinced
12 You, to Quakers
13 Impudence
18 Potsdam pronoun
19 Cain's brother
23 Transfer, in a way
24 Situated at the top
25 Actor Derek
26 Litigant
27 Some jets
29 However, in verse
30 Payable
31 Fortune-teller
32 Walk like a duck
33 Made a comfy home
35 Dupes
38 Bite playfully
39 Low cards
40 Barnyard brooder
42 Take up, as a cause
45 __-bitty

46 Ransacked
47 TV news time
49 Fam. member
50 Tummy trouble
51 Martial-arts star Jackie
52 Canasta combo

53 Perry's creator
55 Part of A.D.
57 Mr. Skelton
58 LP abbr.
59 Mesozoic, e.g.
60 Basketball hoop
61 "Get the picture?"

DEVOTIONAL QUOTE by Dean Niles

ACROSS
1 Verdant
5 Darkens, maybe
9 Fumes
14 Mississippi feeder
15 Draft classification
16 Commodore competitor
17 Army leaves
19 __ Cane (1963 movie)
20 START OF A QUOTE
22 Nada
23 Convert atoms
27 Identical to
31 Loses energy
33 Reviewer Reed
34 Mr. Knievel
35 PART 2 OF QUOTE
38 *Glengarry Glen Ross* playwright
40 Uproar
41 "__ pass go . . ."
42 END OF QUOTE

45 Sacred ceremony
46 Thou, at the Sorbonne
47 __-en-scène (setting)
48 Ill will
50 Transported
52 It may move you
53 Author of quote
60 Hot drink
63 Ordeal
64 Shakespearean tale teller
65 Morales of *La Bamba*
66 Blatant
67 Love
68 Ductile metal
69 Stimulus

DOWN
1 Hay area
2 Grunts of disagreement
3 Pop
4 Actress Celeste
5 Florida industry
6 Backer

7 Soda brand
8 Mont. neighbor
9 Hightailed it
10 __ Like Alice (PBS series)
11 Poor review
12 Fort __, CA
13 Cruise port
18 Chaplin's fourth wife
21 Close by
24 Like some endings
25 __-sixty (acceleration standard)
26 Borough of England
27 Phoenician, e.g.
28 '50s teen idol
29 Personal account
30 Hgt.
31 Deprecative
32 __ time (never)
36 Ben & Jerry's rival
37 Sunup
39 Metal pattern
43 Canon competitor

44 Vividly detailed
49 Med. school subject
51 Contemn
52 Salad-bar habitué
54 Don Juan's *madre*
55 Spanish ayes
56 Dirty air

57 Guitar bar
58 Zone
59 Advance
60 Rosemary portrayer
61 Unmatched
62 AFL partner

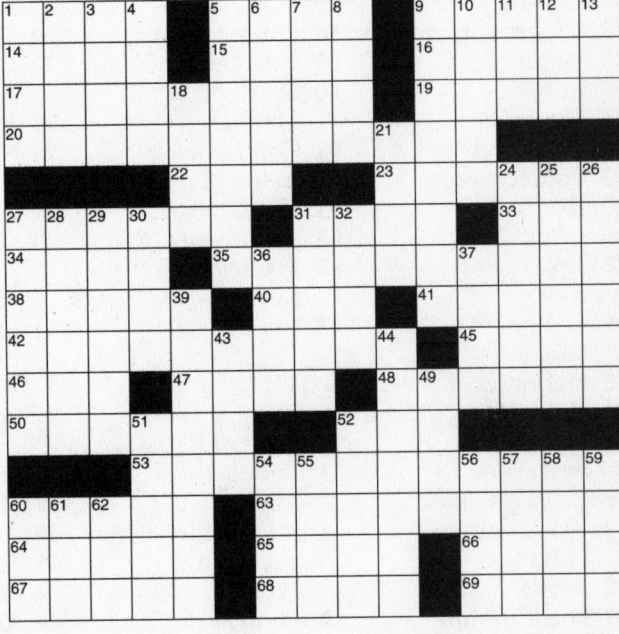

GO FIGURE by Eileen Lexau

ACROSS
1 300, to Caesar
4 Cabinet dept.
7 Noodles
12 Tiresome
13 Overfill
14 Peaks
15 German article
16 Verve
17 "__ all, folks!"
18 Honest one
21 Disapproving sounds
22 Your, Biblically
23 Tic-__-toe
26 Meet the bet
27 Irritates
30 *Idée* __
31 Cub Scout leader
32 __ and dined
33 Area of eerie disappearances
38 Cookie treats
39 Camels' features

40 Honky-__ piano
41 Shrimp dish
43 *Red October* is one
46 Boo or yoo follower
47 Big __, CA
48 Bring into harmony
50 Unpleasant repetition
54 Northern constellation
56 Coagulate
57 Bakery worker
58 Helicopter part
59 *Les États-* __
60 Prying
61 Tableau
62 Gal of song
63 Tax agcy.

DOWN
1 Coterie
2 Danish king
3 Don't play fair
4 Painter Frans
5 Western state

6 Indicate
7 Hamburger unit
8 Sore spot
9 Feeling sore
10 Asian holiday
11 Beast of burden
12 Defeats
13 Boiled
19 Uproar
20 Words of surprise
24 Skater's jump
25 Hand over
28 Neighbor of Fla.
29 Pianist Earl __ Hines
30 Shark features
31 Out of control
32 Elk
33 The two of them
34 Switch ending
35 Overhaul
36 Jamaican beverage

37 Effects
41 __ generis
42 Spring bloomer
43 Aid
44 Weasel word
45 Noah or Wallace
47 Arena posting

49 Singer Lopez
51 Computer symbol
52 Arm bone
53 Farm cover
54 AMA members
55 Mythical bird

287 SHOP TALK by Bob Lubbers

ACROSS
1 Links org.
5 Faucets
9 News summary
14 Armstrong or Simon
15 Vicinity
16 Chou __
17 Office worker
19 Begin
20 Last
21 Errs with a stopwatch
23 Predetermines
25 IBM, e.g.
26 __-bitty
27 Texas border town
29 __ Romeo (auto)
32 Hebrew, e.g.
34 Gold: Sp.
36 Blood vessels
38 __ Vegas, NV
39 Wood cutter
41 Lobe site
42 Spoils
45 Stuck-up one
46 Cause to recall
48 Greek vowels
50 Section of an org.
51 *Guys and Dolls* character
55 Dons, as a holster
58 Praised
59 Warble
60 Craft for Lindbergh
62 Contradict
63 Actress Foch
64 Not now
65 Edited out
66 Tyrolean river
67 Weeps

DOWN
1 Hungry
2 River of Paris
3 Overlays gold
4 Attu resident
5 Innate gifts
6 Exist
7 Salon jobs
8 H.H. Munro
9 Makes as good as new
10 Complete
11 Get tough
12 Swiss river
13 Peach seeds
18 Reviewer: Abbr.
22 "Beat it!"
24 Cornea covering
27 Enumerated
28 Sandwich cookie
29 Blvd. relative
30 Sitcom producer Norman
31 Emergency practice
33 Anthropologist's study
35 Sphere
37 Flecked
40 Attacks
43 Tiny soldiers
44 Astral
47 South African corn
49 "Take __!" (coach's order)
51 Author Nin
52 Moscow's state
53 Star in Cygnus
54 Barbara and Anthony
55 Ship's right side: Abbr.
56 "... a poem lovely as a __"
57 Onetime Atlanta stadium
61 "__ pig's eye!"

288 CHRISTMAS CHARACTERS by Randy Sowell

ACROSS
1 British peeress
5 Horrify
10 Kimono belts
14 Environmental sci.
15 Prepare cheese
16 Hosiery shade
17 "Poetry Man" singer
19 Midmonth day
20 Writer
21 Incidents
23 Art Deco name
25 Panasonic rival
26 Metaphysical poet
29 Turner or Cole
32 Fireplace contents
35 Fracas
36 Tablecloth material
38 Norfolk sch.
39 Pub pints
40 "Walk __ in My Shoes"
41 Minor error
42 Singer Tillis
43 Unwrapped, as gifts
44 Model Macpherson
45 Moved in a curve
47 Actor Chaney
48 Part of MGM
49 Designer Cassini
51 Respond to heat
53 Tall
57 Wiped out
61 Czech or Pole
62 Legendary western outlaw
64 Yorkshire river
65 Computer-bound messages
66 Writer Wiesel
67 Stewart and Steiger
68 Fizzy drinks
69 *Aurora* painter

DOWN
1 *Ed Wood* actor
2 Yearning
3 Phobos, e.g.
4 Basic components
5 Spy
6 Telephonic 7
7 Stamp sheet
8 On
9 Clark's partner
10 Bermuda bulbs
11 "Peggy Sue" singer
12 Notion, in Nantes
13 Meeting of Cong.
18 Unadorned
22 Drench
24 Paint type
26 Play type
27 Crude carrier
28 *Blithe Spirit* playwright
30 Kind of acid
31 Scout's quest
33 Roman official
34 "Swell!"
36 Drop bait lightly
37 But: Lat.
41 Caribbean contents
43 Czech river
46 *École* attenders
48 Damages
50 Agrees
52 Bounders
53 Russian ruler
54 Miscellany
55 Boy of the comics
56 Happy
58 Merchandise mover
59 Ireland
60 *Eins + zwei*
63 __-Fail (Irish coronation stone)

289 IN THE BARNYARD by Wayne Robert Williams

ACROSS

1 Curving courses
5 __ au rhum
9 French Revolution figure
14 Type of salmon
15 Gardner et al.
16 Island in the Antilles
17 Runner Zátopek
18 Stag opposites
20 Boil down
22 Call cost, once
23 Large parrot
24 Tropical porch
25 Olajuwon's nickname
28 Powdered, perhaps
33 Sweetums
34 Not right
36 Butter substitute
37 With 39 Across, John Wayne movie
39 See 37 Across
42 Creative work
43 Catch
45 __ for tat
46 House and grounds
49 Holds close
51 "Amo, amas, I love __"
53 Highway-sign abbr.
54 Mr. Maugham
58 Weather-map line
61 Fowl merchants
63 Prey
64 Loosen wingtips
65 "__ no kick . . ."
66 First governor of Alaska
67 Library stamp
68 Swelled heads
69 First family of Ferrara

DOWN

1 Served perfectly
2 Caesar's home
3 Give up
4 Did it alone
5 Thai cash
6 Roman greeting
7 Small chickens
8 Skiers' mecca
9 Brady daughter
10 Comic Johnson
11 Havoc
12 Aid in crime
13 Soviet news agcy.
19 Med. school class
21 Jewel weight
24 Haunts
25 Pang
26 Basketball targets
27 Scottish uncle
29 High shot
30 Mini-purses
31 Chilling
32 Things to avoid
35 Con games
38 987-65-4321 grp.
40 Sphere
41 Disinfectant's targets
44 Savings
47 More pungent
48 Ultimatum word
50 Orbital point
52 Eagle's nest
54 Potato
55 Geraldine Chaplin's mother
56 Mongrel
57 Nobelist Wiesel
58 Adherents: Suff.
59 *Amo, amas, __*
60 Actor Auberjonois
62 '20s auto

290 SOUNDS OF MUSIC by Ed Julius

ACROSS

1 Man on one knee
9 Delaware Indian
15 Mockery
16 Worships
17 Rock needs
19 Collector's goal
20 Great Lake
21 '60s protest grp.
22 Yank's foe
25 Folk singer Phil
26 Propeller of a sort
27 Nonfielding positions: Abbr.
28 Mass
31 Debate fodder
36 Dress style
37 Electronic instrument
40 "I __ fool!"
41 Central region
42 Us: Sp.
43 "It must be him, __ shall die"
45 Singer Zadora
46 Belgian composer
47 Zambia's official lang.
48 School org.
51 1977 Super Bowl champ
54 Ch. title
55 1967 Lemon Pipers song
61 Assert without proof
62 Mounted attendant
63 Like many plastics
64 Natural numbers

DOWN

1 Media
2 Irked
3 *Waiting for Lefty* playwright
4 Photo
5 Cal. page
6 On: Fr.
7 Hebrew judge
8 __ room
9 Pad activity
10 Piaf and Wharton
11 __ *a Stranger*
12 Sandarac tree
13 Scope starter
14 He: It.
18 Fit condition
22 Antarctic sea
23 Untaxing
24 Ancient Frankish queen
28 Mideast region
29 Draft animals
30 Shuttlecock
31 Govt. agent
32 __ sapiens
33 Ages and ages
34 "When __ a-Dreamin' " (1938 song)
35 Paris when it sizzles
36 Wire measure
38 __ go bragh
39 Unaccompanied
43 California county
44 Was a tenant
46 Run, in a way
48 Austen title word
49 To have: Sp.
50 States positively
51 Old Irish script
52 Singer Guthrie
53 1949 A.L. batting champ
56 "L'état c'est __"
57 Hairstyle
58 Mel of baseball
59 Press ending
60 Offshore apparatus

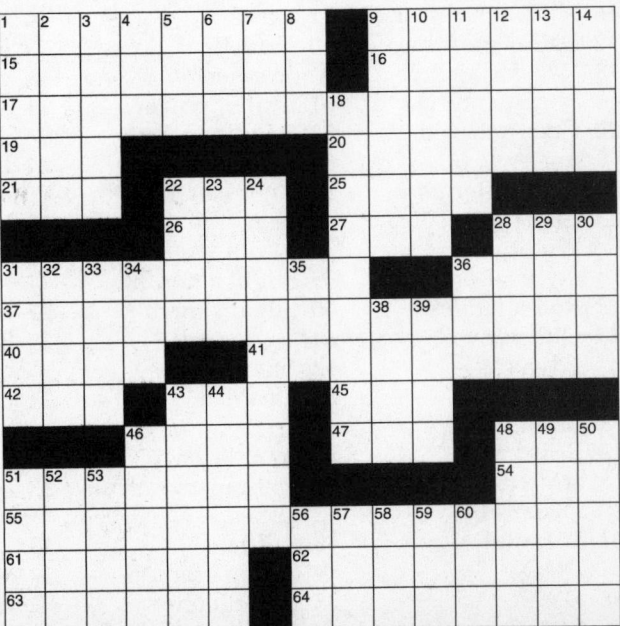

BAGGAGE RACK by Bob Lubbers

ACROSS
1 To the left, at sea
6 Lasting impression
10 Spanish house
14 Finger-pointer
15 Buckeye State
16 Pitcher Hershiser
17 Rifle tubes
19 Mill product
20 Yale student
21 __ *Make a Deal*
22 Earns after taxes
24 Girls
26 Reconnoiter
28 Uriah of fiction
30 Erases
34 Tra-__
37 Pilfer
39 Islands off Sicily
40 Ammonia derivative
42 Conducted
43 Attempted
44 Genesis land
45 Oklahoma city
47 Lodgings
48 Garden tools
50 Fill-in worker
52 Rhythms
54 Igneous rock
58 Generated again
61 Settled (up)
63 Actor Stephen
64 MC Trebek
65 Judicial work
68 Marathon segment
69 Raison d'__
70 Scrub a mission
71 Favorites
72 Betsy or Diana
73 Border flower

DOWN
1 Heavenly being
2 Comic Poundstone
3 Onetime Chrysler cars
4 CSA soldier
5 "Rose of __"
6 Categorize
7 Kasparov's game
8 Feel poorly
9 Gangster's gat
10 Deal (with)
11 Neighborhood
12 Char
13 __ *Well That Ends Well*
18 Alarm button
23 Director Sidney
25 Practices jabs
27 Acknowledgment
29 Most wan
31 Swellheaded
32 Garden spot
33 Caesar's namesakes
34 Final
35 Love god
36 Italian resort
38 Actor Olin
41 Arab chieftain
46 Red-ink entry
49 Bengal soldier
51 Zany
53 Prods
55 Criminal fire
56 Impolite glances
57 Succulent
58 Exitway
59 Author Wiesel
60 Sash
62 War god
66 Western Indian
67 Lawyers' org.

WHO'S ON FIRST by Randolph Ross

ACROSS
1 Hardwood tree
4 Shiny minerals
9 Would-be atty.'s exam
13 Way in
15 Bakery attraction
16 Nobelist Wiesel
17 Lotion additive
18 1994 basketball documentary
20 Goes over old notes
22 Wrench target
23 Capri and Wight
24 Stylus users
25 Roll relatives
27 Director Edwards
28 Tibetan capital
29 Beantown athlete
30 Queens field
34 Part of the DOD
35 David Letterman, e.g.
38 Crew-team member
39 Campaign '96 name
41 NBA team
42 "__ a Parade"
44 Minds
46 Barrel parts
47 Dates
50 "The final frontier"
51 Seat of power
52 Landing site
55 Sing-along
57 Rock star, to a teen
58 __ of Cleves
59 Slight amount
60 Sugar source
61 __-do-well
62 Misanthrope
63 Steamed

DOWN
1 Hebrew month
2 Lone
3 Ruffians
4 Skiing brothers
5 Actor Jeremy
6 Pigeon sounds
7 Current unit
8 Miserable condition
9 Parasites
10 Quench
11 Marksman, at times
12 Trials
14 Pieces maker
19 *Billboard* category
21 Mecca Almighty
24 Immigrant's island
25 Fog up
26 Charlie Chan exclamation
27 Defeats
29 Some dorm occupants
31 Lake Mead adjunct
32 Icicle holder
33 Mars counterpart
36 Tithing amount
37 Moreno and Rudner
40 Playing marble
43 Acid in milk
45 Fish-eating flier
46 More like Mary Lou Retton
47 Allen of Vermont
48 Performed brilliantly
49 Witchlike one
50 From a previous time
52 Gray's subj.
53 NY college
54 Entreated
56 Southern constellation

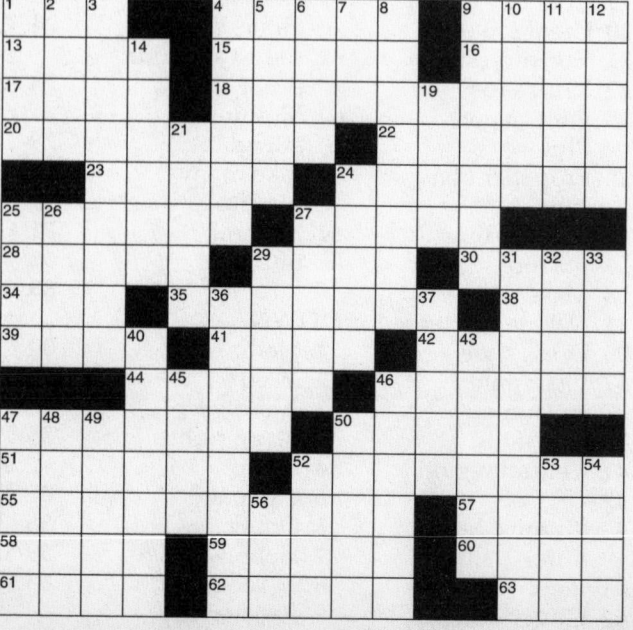

THE PUZZLE by Matt Gaffney

ACROSS

1 Al and Andy
6 Machine parts
10 Visibility blocker
14 High-tech messages
15 Heavenly instrument
16 Hodgepodge
17 Marx work
19 Mountaintop
20 Nahuatl's linguistic family
21 Rink machine
23 Poses anew
24 Ansel Adams photo subject
25 Air holder
26 Italian peak
28 Weight
30 Dirty tactic
34 Treater's words
36 Paris hotel
39 Lucy Van __
40 Hindu texts
41 Archer or Rice
42 In addition

43 Lawyer Dershowitz
44 Stock listing
45 Actor Jannings
47 Protein source
49 Wilbur, in *Charlotte's Web*
51 Brake part
53 Fatty compounds
58 Swimming superhero
60 Unnamed woman
61 Shakespeare staple
62 French fabulist
64 Verdi opera
65 Zodiacal beast
66 For all to hear
67 Cool it
68 Son of Zeus
69 Lithuanians' neighbors

DOWN

1 __ Rapids, IA
2 Blow away
3 Italian menu section

4 Highways
5 Lazybones
6 Beard site
7 Bran source
8 Emulate cows
9 Pool pranks
10 Ancient kingdom
11 1996 Best Picture nominee
12 City south of Florence
13 Poisonous
18 Beyond
22 Astronaut Jemison
24 Fiat
27 December time
29 German wife
30 Watering hole
31 Actor Gibson
32 City near L.A.
33 Molecule part
35 __'War
37 Explosive letters
38 Last letter
40 Odin's home
44 100 kilograms
46 Belief
48 Delicate dessert

49 Potatoes: Sp.
50 Employee's last words
52 Studio sign
54 Norman Vincent __
55 Dostoyevsky character
56 Homer Simpson snack
57 Tournament rankings
59 Quickly: Abbr.
60 Secada and Cryer
63 Anti

BIG SIX by Ed Julius

ACROSS

1 Twig broom
6 "__, Brute"
10 Reach across
14 Famous violin maker
15 So
16 Sea eagle
17 Cole Porter tune
20 Goddess of discord
21 Words of glee
22 He played Grant
23 Opposite of ant.
24 Capital of Yemen
25 Record
26 Aid feloniously
28 Roasting rod
30 Yalie
33 Engaged in conflict
35 James Bond's school
36 Greek letters
37 Gershwin tune
40 Turkish title
41 Pacific palm
42 Up __ (stuck)

43 TV network
44 Ballet skirt
45 Suffer: Scot.
46 Garden tools
48 Cart
50 Hiatus
53 Of bees
55 Ancient kingdom
56 Proofreader's word
57 Statistician's calculations
60 Wings
61 War vehicle
62 Part of a musical piece
63 Watch over
64 Blockheads
65 Nuisances

DOWN

1 __ in Arms
2 Grinding agent
3 Midwest city
4 Singer Redding
5 Max. opposite
6 Actor Hawke
7 Harvard club

8 Musical instrument
9 Exploit
10 Big name in kiddie lit
11 Substitute sovereigns
12 Jackson or Meara
13 __-do-well
18 One of those things
19 Horse's pace
24 Balkan native
25 Flintstones' pet
27 1930s heavyweight champ
29 Silents actress Negri
31 Bar fruit
32 Conversation filler
33 On the briny
34 Pyramid, essentially
35 Redact
36 Tennis pro Sampras
38 Burden

39 Be inconsistent
44 Wide shoe size
45 Rhett's last word
47 Rowed
49 Chessmen
51 Warn
52 Mexican money
53 "I smell __!"
54 Soccer great
55 Son of Isaac
56 Sup
58 Rams' city: Abbr.
59 Durocher's nickname

ARE YOU KIDDING? by Dean Niles

ACROSS
1 Points
5 Red Sea gulf
10 Roosevelt canine
14 Stick in one's __
15 Wall art
16 "Up 'n __!"
17 Bugs' duds?
19 Sitarist Shankar
20 Way out
21 Western dish
23 Canvas cover
25 *The Naked Gun* actress
26 Columbus Day mo.
29 Windy City orch.
30 Course
31 Galsworthy name
33 Court wear
37 Dart about
38 Fuzzy fruit
39 *Appointment in __*
43 Dried up

46 Raise
47 Storm heading
48 Coll. test
49 As, for long
52 Cold War-era weapon
54 Guiding light
55 Northern flier
59 Mogul capital
60 Sold-out shop?
64 Monikers
65 Air layer
66 Color
67 Gen. Robt. __
68 Forest
69 "__ Rebel" (Crystals tune)

DOWN
1 Hungry feeling
2 Levin and Gershwin
3 Artist Chagall
4 Hard work

5 Emily Dickinson's birthplace
6 On the __ vive
7 Flight stat.
8 Flutter
9 Loser
10 Token jiggle?
11 In any way
12 Quay
13 *Jaws* town
18 Disoriented
22 Measure (out)
24 Brooding Baltimorean
25 Letter letters
26 Goes away
27 Popular drink
28 Frills
32 Sight to see?
34 CNN talker
35 Jug
36 Take a taxi
40 Casino city
41 Sky treat
42 Shape of 41 Down

43 North China dynasty
44 Emoluments
45 Ref
49 Slack off
50 Majestic
51 Beetle Bailey's boss

53 Good humor
56 Tom Joad, e.g.
57 Eyepiece
58 R&B singer James
61 Dye group
62 Leaping Australian
63 Conclusion

THE CAPITAL GANG by D.J. DeChristopher

ACROSS
1 Singer Lane
5 Ukrainian city
11 Iota
14 Bench, e.g.
15 Country singer Womack
16 Bullring cheer
17 *Charlie's Angels* actress
19 Curse
20 King's chair
21 Garden activity
23 Low point
25 Friend, out west
26 One of Lear's daughters
29 Asian holiday
31 Impolite look
33 Region of Italy
35 Low digit
37 Ignore
39 Dave's TV rival
40 May birthstone
43 By way of
44 Pinnacle
46 Eggs: Lat.

47 Casino naturals
49 Pack (down)
51 Tax pro: Abbr.
53 Twilled fabric
54 Twosome
56 Fairylike
58 Greets the villain
60 More greasy
63 U.S. soldiers, for short
64 1981 US Open tennis champ
67 Hubbub
68 Magic charm
69 "Step __!"
70 Craving
71 3-D figures
72 Poet Ogden

DOWN
1 Inquire
2 Bushed
3 Immersion
4 Everlasting
5 Chan portrayer
6 Fraud
7 "A mouse!"
8 Waist cincher

9 Pry
10 Strengthen with heat
11 "Annie's Song" singer
12 Designer Cassini
13 John Ritter's dad
18 *Happy Days* daughter
22 Angers
24 Go back over
26 Punjabi prince
27 Solar/lunar year discrepancy
28 TV's Wild Bill Hickok
30 One __ customer
32 Wishing undone
34 I love: Lat.
36 Overhead trains
38 Foundation
41 Actress Gabor
42 Arnaz/Ball studio

45 Aussie birds
48 Deer meat
50 Ziti and vermicelli
52 Became boring
55 Word form for "skin"
57 Proclamations

58 Conceal
59 First king of Israel
61 Italian volcano
62 Reformer Jacob
63 Frolicsome
65 151, to Caesar
66 Ultimate degree

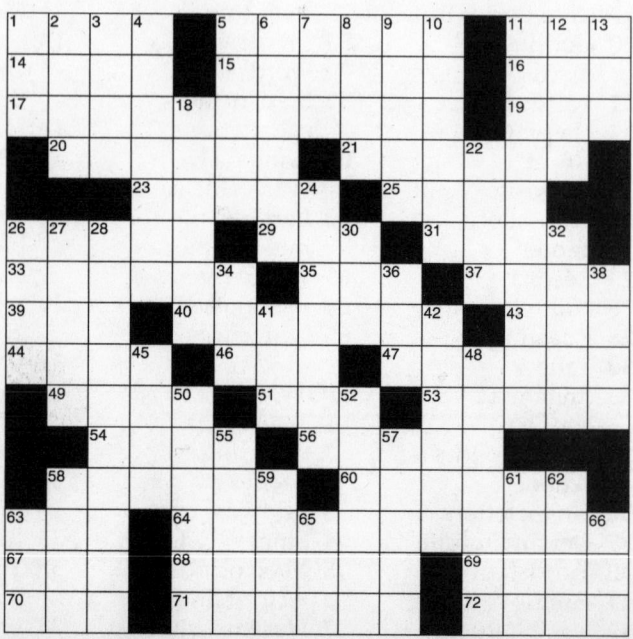

297 TAKE-OUT ORDERS by Bob Lubbers

ACROSS
1 Money
5 Goatee site
9 Brigham Young, e.g.
14 Word form for "eight"
15 Clue
16 Pacific Island group
17 Take-out order
20 __ Lingus
21 Cruising
22 Covers a wall, perhaps
23 Carney's namesakes
24 Letter opener
25 Categories
28 Twosome
29 Salamander
32 Make amends
33 Oven
34 Jai __
35 Take-out order
38 Roof part
39 Diminutive suffix
40 Water mammal
41 __-Cat
42 Golf pegs
43 Rains ice
44 Actress Goldie
45 Relate
46 Polite word
49 Maine river
50 "__ Maria"
53 Take-out order
56 Gladden
57 Midday
58 Comic Johnson
59 Jutlanders
60 Overwhelmed
61 Part of E=mc²

DOWN
1 Caesar's partner
2 Throb
3 Mix
4 Ad __ committee
5 Bureaus
6 Gregory or Earl
7 Ancient Peruvian
8 Highest degree
9 Ascending
10 Drives down
11 Nautical direction
12 Close margin
13 Order members
18 Hoopster Abdul-Jabbar
19 Sedative
23 Golfer Palmer's nickname
24 "If You Knew __ . . ."
25 Neon and oxygen
26 Allen or Frome
27 Vibes player Red
28 Pub game
29 Type size
30 Gem surface
31 Stadium rows
33 Frequently
34 Russian cooperative
36 Shortstop Reese
37 Glob
42 Samples
43 Dueler's aide
44 It makes waste
45 Western resort lake
46 Begged
47 Pop singer Falana
48 Statesman Abba
49 Barge
50 Glow
51 American Legion members
52 Looks at
54 Genetic material
55 American uncle

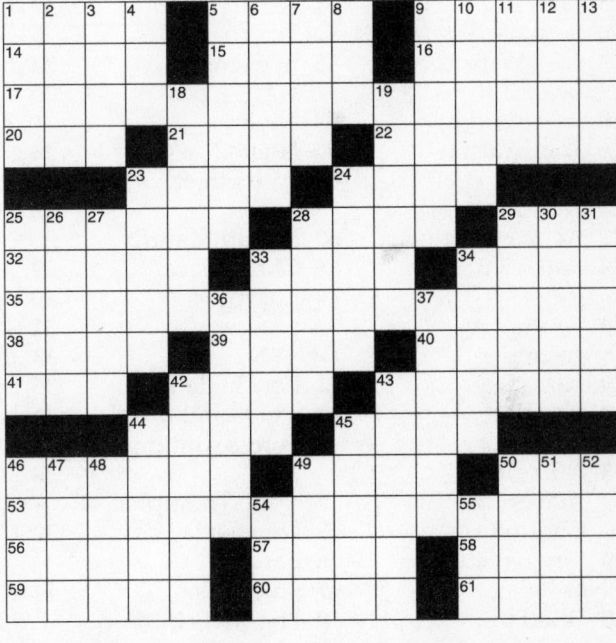

298 SEASON'S GREETINGS by Thomas W. Schier

ACROSS
1 Comic Mabley
5 Somewhat
9 DC org.
12 "The __ See You"
13 Keyboardist John
14 He'll "talk 'til his voice is hoarse"
15 __-Saxon
16 Double curve
17 Dublin's country
18 14 Down, in Paris
20 Dijon dream
21 Actress Black
22 Business news
24 KitchenAid rival
26 Pirandello's country
28 Author Ludwig
29 Slangy assent
31 Kudos
35 Actress Gilbert
37 Mask opening
39 Plumber's tool
40 Entertainer Martha
42 Regretted
43 Golf clubs
45 Base neutralizers
47 Golfer Greg
50 Throws
52 Vicinity
53 14 Down, in Pisa
58 Clammy
59 Vino center
60 Reddish brown
61 Warbler James
62 Sports-page figure
63 Apply gently
64 New Deal agcy.
65 Relaxation
66 Actor Morales

DOWN
1 Stereo alternative
2 Rowdy party
3 14 Down, in Maui
4 Dakota Indian
5 Repent
6 Tropical plant
7 "That's clear"
8 Actress Ritter
9 Norwegian composer
10 Match's outset
11 "Doe, __, a female . . ."
12 USA rank
14 Seasonal greeting
19 Dental photos
23 Gen. Robt. __
24 "Right on!"
25 __ 18 (Uris book)
27 Those chaps
28 Printer's widths
30 Pull down
32 Stentorian
33 Brighton brews
34 Turner of cable
36 Hospital supplies
38 Pine (for)
41 __ a pistol
44 At first, perhaps
46 Rains or Monet
47 1996 candidate
48 Speechify
49 __-car
51 Fuse
54 Court org.
55 Swedish rock group
56 Fifth-century pope
57 Fish-eating bird

299   LONG ALLITERATIVES by Ed Julius

ACROSS
1 M*A*S*H character
6 Biblical brother
10 Nothing else than
14 Greek marketplace
15 Marceau, e.g.
16 Item used by Tom Watson
17 Beautiful
20 Item used by Tom Watson
21 Salary
22 Do housework
23 Actress Virginia
24 Raconteur's forte
26 Southeast Asians
29 Lama, e.g.
32 General Bradley
33 Tanks, etc.
34 Actress Charlotte
36 Strict attention to detail
40 Wind dir.
41 Appraiser
42 Med. school course
43 Nanook et al.
45 Tampico fare
47 Abba of Israel
48 Cross out
49 Pons or Peters
51 Notary need
52 Pea coat?
55 In a cowardly way
59 Neat as __
60 Excited
61 Wall Street action
62 Negative suffix
63 Chess piece
64 Locations

DOWN
1 Lost in delight
2 Chills and fever
3 Ford's running mate
4 __ de Triomphe
5 New Jersey city
6 Pard
7 Spiciness
8 Flightless bird
9 Conducted
10 "__ in G"
11 Greek Cupid
12 Defeat soundly
13 Pulver's rank: Abbr.
18 Sunshine, so to speak
19 Lazybones
23 Painter Chagall
24 Indonesian isle
25 "__ Ben Adhem"
26 Sulk
27 Entertain
28 Bowling establishment
29 Assays
30 Sports site
31 Twangy
33 Illinois city
35 Spanish compass point
37 Of a social unit
38 __ Dancer (ballet film)
39 Questionnaire item
44 Kline and Bacon
45 Ball club
46 Metes
48 Condescend
49 Swindle
50 Egyptian goddess
51 Singer Hank
52 H.S. exam
53 Ye __ Shoppe
54 Works with hair
55 __ Joey
56 Sports circuit
57 Turkish title
58 Swiss canton

300   WHERE'S THE HOOK? by Manny Nosowsky

ACROSS
1 Word form for "dry"
5 Magnificent
10 Ace-high beater
14 Was contrite about
15 Addams butler
16 Actress Sommer
17 Distress signal
18 Bring together
19 Aid in crime
20 1921 song
23 Get rid of
24 Supermarket buys
25 Topper
26 Spell out
28 On one's belly
30 Looked for
35 Toward the mouth
36 "Get lost!"
39 Schoenberg's Moses und __
41 Texas town
42 Rhine joiner at Koblenz
44 Indian figures
49 Bat wood
50 It makes a group unique
55 Yoga posture
56 Dogpatch observance
59 Certain European
60 UNIVAC preceder
61 Little pests
62 Word on Irish coins
63 __ Carlo
64 Caught in the act
65 Hideouts
66 The __ Sanction
67 Go__ (discuss)

DOWN
1 Blue
2 Cheat
3 Prepare leftovers
4 Where Trotsky studied
5 Model stickum
6 Mystical
7 Actress Slezak
8 One with a role to play
9 Pilferage
10 Diamond shape
11 Tuna type
12 Japanese art
13 Did a memo over
21 Bank job
22 Little Orphan Annie character, with "The"
27 Bagful
29 Korean soldier
31 Hilo strings
32 Toothpaste variety
33 Kin of "yuk"
34 "Now hear __!"
36 Mild oath
37 Unnamed person
38 Herbert Hoover, by birth
39 Accumulated
40 Wodehouse opus
43 Black-belt Bruce
45 Francis' home
46 Loons
47 Sore
48 Refuses
51 Main idea
52 Asian capital
53 Due (to)
54 Rollerblade, e.g.
57 Memorable folk singer
58 Cake finisher

ACROSS

1 Theme of this puzzle
5 Nick at Nite offering
10 Leaves town
14 Type like *this*: Abbr.
15 Last Greek letter
16 Springy tune
17 A good way to take bad news
20 Sunday speech: Abbr.
21 What the particular may pick
22 British cattle breed
23 "Zip-__-Doo-Dah"
24 Iowa city
25 Sun worshiper
28 French friends
29 Actor Holbrook
32 Vision-related
33 Struck down, old-style
34 A few
35 Treats casually
38 Moves quickly
39 Suspicious
40 Tilted
41 Commercials, for instance
42 Cindy Crawford ex
43 Colloquial
44 Hostile criticism
45 Tim of *WKRP*
46 *It All Started With Columbus* author
49 *Misery* star
50 Recipe phrase
53 Tropical Asian shrub
56 Take care of
57 Occupied
58 Shatner's best-known role
59 Nintendo rival
60 "A Boy __ Sue"
61 Midmonth day

DOWN

1 Haunches
2 __ *Jury* (Spillane novel)
3 It may be over your head
4 Under the weather
5 More optimistic
6 Overact
7 Sales personnel
8 "That's gross!"
9 Basketball inventor
10 Windshield material
11 Portrait medium
12 High-fashion mag
13 Underworld river
18 Next to bat
19 Stage signals
23 Sheriff Lobo portrayer
24 *Jaws* town
25 Former South African prime minister
26 Plant pest
27 Pigs' digs
28 Love, Italian-style
29 *"Crocodile" Dundee* star
30 In the midst of
31 Southpaw
33 Lewis Carroll beast
34 Golf Hall-of-Famer
36 Does an inaugural job
37 Champaign athletes
42 Substance on stamps
43 Ocean floor
44 Actress Jane
45 Uplift
46 New Testament book
47 '50s president of South Korea
48 Flash Gordon foe
49 Buddy
50 Corrosive chemical
51 Entice
52 Pops the question
54 Aunt in *Bambi*
55 Travel downhill, in a way

ACROSS

1 Like Kojak
5 Prefix for "chute"
9 MacLeod of *Love Boat*
14 Get an __ effort
15 General Bradley
16 In reserve
17 A-one auto
19 Club rule
20 "__ I Know" (Whitney Houston tune)
21 Photographer Ansel
22 Gut busters
25 Legendary engineer Jones
26 Deferred promise
30 Fly high
31 Orient
32 Grade-school grp.
35 Noted middleweight
40 Sellout sign
41 CBer's radio
42 Propagated
43 Lead-pipe cinch
47 Former foe of Ilie and Jimmy
50 Opening remark
51 Sensational
52 Castle feature
57 Match up
58 *Planes, Trains and Automobiles* star
60 From then on
61 Criticism
62 Folksinger Burl
63 All fired up
64 "K-K-K-__"
65 Harp kin

DOWN

1 Big name in baroque music
2 Bushy do
3 Theater magnate Marcus
4 Make a sketch
5 Sturdy fabric
6 Magic charm
7 Brit. fliers
8 Comment from Sandy
9 Revisit
10 Imminently
11 Tennis pro Guillermo
12 Start of Caesar's boast
13 Fit to print
18 Skirt length
23 Apt anagram for THE EYES
24 Close up
26 Decant
27 Shakespearean villain
28 Historic period
29 It's polar to NNW
30 Draft agcy.
32 Boston Common, e.g.
33 Lumber source
34 Figure up
36 Dancer's gang
37 *Norma* __
38 Parisian landmark
39 Celtics' org.
43 Rock artist's name, sometimes
44 Outdated
45 Gofer
46 Dense mixture: Abbr.
47 Apathetic
48 __ Ward Howe
49 Gasket
53 '50s sitcom star Storm
54 Green-eyed monster
55 Frankfurt's river
56 It's at 11 Wall St.
58 Controversial Oliver Stone film
59 Suffix for scram

303   SINGALONG by Mike Miller

ACROSS
1 Soda-shop selections
6 Encourage, in a way
10 A little night music?
14 Into pieces
15 Vaccines
16 Continental prefix
17 WWII novelty song
20 Big collection agcy.
21 Shore amusement area
22 "It's __ Unusual Day"
23 Kind of energy
25 "April Love" singer
28 Publicity, metaphorically
29 Brushing off
33 Chester __ Arthur
36 Supports
37 Alley Oop's land
38 Barbershop-quartet favorite
42 "__ Buttermilk Sky"
43 De-squeaked
44 Turner and Pappas
45 Sea deposit
47 Frequently, poetically
49 Get the better of
50 Blood component
54 Leisurely pace
57 Classical concert halls
59 Magazine staffed by "the usual gang of idiots"
60 Late twenties tune
64 Film swashbuckler Jones, familiarly
65 Munro's pseudonym
66 *Dallas* matriarch
67 Source of Russian news
68 After-school orgs.
69 Guide the ride

DOWN
1 *West Side Story* song
2 Toward the left, at sea
3 Rancher's rope
4 Quadri- preceder
5 Enter
6 Tennis Hall-of-Famer
7 Drinking song
8 Leave the path of righteousness
9 Skater Babilonia
10 Filled to overflowing
11 Insurance category
12 CEO, frequently
13 Kind
18 Clock sound
19 Become invisible
24 Smaller than usual
26 Egg-shaped
27 "Pardon me!"
30 __ *You're OK*
31 Durante claim to fame
32 "Anything __"
33 *Omnia vincit __*
34 Actor Waggoner
35 Showing fear
36 Rice dish
39 Like some toon "Tunes"
40 Urgent
41 She was Gilda
46 *Dynasty* spinoff, with *The*
47 Oil acronym
48 Cereal selection
51 Chaplin song from *Modern Times*
52 Berlin tune of the '20s
53 Viper kin
54 Somewhat
55 Caged talker
56 Roses' home
58 Banquet setup
61 Mentalist's claim
62 Flutter
63 Initial order?

304   TO THE RESCUE by Cathy Millhauser

ACROSS
1 Current figures
5 They may deviate
10 Tiny amount
14 Mitchell mansion
15 *Wait __ Dark*
16 "A loaf of bread . . ." poet
17 The Emerald Isle
18 Big name in shampoo
19 Bad impression?
20 Saloon first aid?
23 Infant
24 Toast topper
25 Whole bunch
26 Put to the test
27 Put a price on
31 Silly goose
34 Whistle sound
36 Clark's *Mogambo* costar
37 Art-gallery first aid?
41 Make mistakes
42 Onetime poet laureate Nahum
43 *Cabin in the Sky* star
44 Top-notch
47 Ursa minor?
48 Charged particle
49 Smeltery trash
51 Waves home
54 Film-set first aid?
59 Forget to remember
60 Hydrox alternatives
61 Toastmaster's platform
62 Secluded spot
63 Prime-time angel portrayer
64 Modern artist
65 Table stake
66 Force units
67 Costner role

DOWN
1 Alamogordo event
2 Singer Lanza
3 Computer command
4 Trolled
5 Economic force
6 Tennis pro John Mc__
7 Word form for "wing"
8 Ceramist's medium
9 Prudential rival
10 See 45 Down
11 Seer's reading
12 Sharp flavor
13 They may be liberal
21 It comes from the heart
22 High ball
26 "Mazel __!"
27 Anecdotal knowledge
28 *Notes on a Cowardly Lion* author
29 Balanced
30 Be bold
31 Cools down
32 Pub projectile
33 Concerning
34 Romanov ruler
35 Giant with 511 homers
38 California school
39 Gorillas
40 Inner ear?
45 With 10 Down, kid from the comics
46 Card game
47 Makes happen
49 Either of two *Wall Street* actors
50 Unrestricted
51 Drum string
52 Sharpens articles
53 Lunkheads
54 Musical postscript
55 Last word of the New Testament
56 Sedimentary soil
57 Die side
58 Port in Yemen

305 SILVER LINING? by Donna J. Stone

ACROSS
1 Mah-jongg tile
4 Awkward one
8 Bead counters?
13 Impetus for a trip
14 Draftable
15 Courtly dance
16 START OF A LAURENCE J. PETER QUOTE
19 Undignified
20 Exercise equipment
21 Dislodge
22 French flapjack
24 Letters before an alias
25 "New York, New York" singer
26 A question of location
27 Frankfurt's river
28 Grand __ Opry
29 Multitude
30 Stirs to action
31 MIDDLE OF QUOTE
34 Lightened up?
37 __ Camera

38 Flow back
41 Wister of westerns
42 All My Children actress
44 Part of BSA
45 Alice's cat, e.g.
46 Alice's cat
47 Heavy breathing?
48 Treasures
50 Billing sharer
51 END OF QUOTE
54 Testimonial host
55 Forbidden act
56 Second name
57 Has an opinion
58 Reagan's Knute Rockne, All American role
59 Bolshevik

DOWN
1 Trouble
2 Trouble, plus
3 Santa __, CA
4 Go for 300
5 Sean Lennon's mother
6 Done, to Donne

7 Todd's profession
8 On the double
9 Crib-sheet user
10 Tropical fruit
11 Did the windows
12 Bawling
17 Cause for revenge?
18 "Omigosh!"
19 Prefix for drama
22 Cameroon neighbor
23 Clone
26 Made one
27 Mine removal
29 Avoided detection
30 Chi Chi and Fuzzy's org.
31 Hands
32 A pop
33 Athos, to Aramis
34 Looking amazed
35 "Wow!"
36 Green stuff
38 Appealing to feeling
39 Chewed out

40 Rabbit of kiddie lit
42 Long ride?
43 Bereft of acclaim
44 Jeopardy! revelation
46 Shortens the galleys
47 __ Canals (Great Lake connectors)

49 K-6 sch.
50 Soybeans, for example
52 French pronoun
53 Macroeconomic stat.

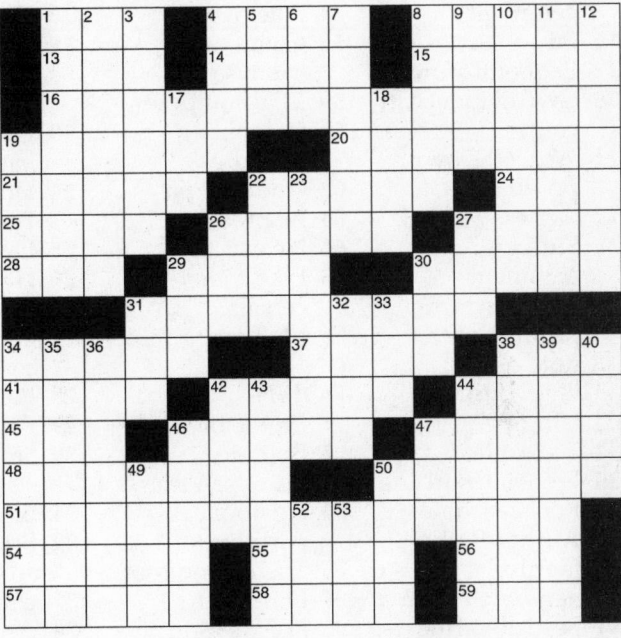

306 ANATOMICALLY CORRECT by Bill Hendricks

ACROSS
1 Bit of gossip
5 Garb for Snoopy, sometimes
10 Resembling, with "to"
14 Word form for "far"
15 Moon-related
16 Attend a banquet
17 Flee
20 Mel of diamond fame
21 Acting part
22 Salespersons' goals
23 Gladys Knight's backup
25 Burger breads
26 Begley Sr. and Jr.
27 Hard journey
28 Beret, for instance
31 Lost
34 Any time now
35 As seen fit
36 Get ready to order a martini
39 Vientiane's land
40 Noisy
41 Too big
42 Part of i.e.

43 Streetcorner sign
44 Miss Piggy, self-referentially
45 "No pain, no __"
46 Unable to leave
50 Start of a Stephen Foster title
53 Treacherous
54 Meadow
55 Tackles et al.
58 Cartwright son
59 Rib
60 Rim
61 Muscle quality
62 Sign up for
63 Gardener's purchase

DOWN
1 Some Like __
2 Saw parts
3 Gladden
4 Garment-tag abbr.
5 Fore-and-aft riggers
6 Shirley Temple trademark
7 Feed the kitty
8 Cheerleader's cry
9 Habituate

10 Pedro's parting word
11 It's worn with a sporran
12 To Live and Die __
13 TV T-man
18 Literary manservant
19 Male model, maybe
24 Banana eaters' garbage
25 Big family
27 Find the sum
28 One of a pair of dice
29 "Oh, woe!"
30 Combustible heap
31 Competent
32 Sri Lankan exports
33 Vegas machine, for short
34 Cereal utensil
35 Left-side entry
37 Final
38 Big to-do
43 Swedish car
44 "The Manassa __" (Jack Dempsey)
45 "Understand?"

46 Small thicket
47 __ France (former province)
48 Brink
49 Lessened
50 "__ first you don't succeed . . ."

51 Behind-the-times type
52 Colorful horse
53 Insipid
56 Actor Cariou
57 Affirmative vote

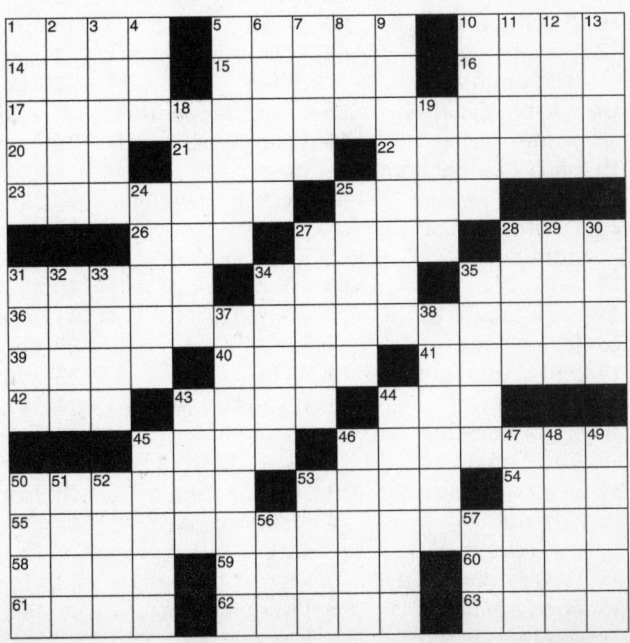

307   ALL BUSINESS by Ed Julius

ACROSS
1 Historical periods
5 Car accessory
10 Soviet news agency
14 Function
15 Parenthetical comment
16 Jai __
17 Economic forces
20 Give evidence in court
21 With 60 Down, popular pet
22 Actress Merkel
23 Suffix for comment
24 Short-term promissory note
33 One __ time (singly)
34 Sea eagles
35 French resort
36 Poet Teasdale
38 Author Philip's family
40 Sandwich shop
41 Seed covering
42 Get ready, for short
43 Was a candidate
44 Software specialists
49 Map abbreviation
50 Corp. bigwig
51 Alleviate
55 Chemical catalyst
59 EDP equipment
61 Colonizing creatures
62 Andes beast
63 Be prevalent
64 Nearly all
65 Like some cereals
66 Mah-jongg piece

DOWN
1 Prefix for while
2 Bounder
3 European range
4 Anatomical partition
5 Traveler on foot
6 Londoner's exclamation
7 Wrestler's goal
8 Teachers' degs.
9 Phone button
10 __ the Bachelor ('57 film)
11 Wings: Lat.
12 __ souci (carefree)
13 Beef quantity
18 One-dimensional figure
19 O.K. Corral battler
24 Houses, in Hermosillo
25 Eared seal
26 Homer hitter Roger
27 Farmer's concern
28 Prefix for mural
29 Pale
30 Seashore structures
31 Brilliant success
32 Bridle attachments
37 Unselfish one
39 Astronaut
45 Coup d'__
46 Prefix for maniac
47 Jump
48 Dairy product
51 Economist Smith
52 __-Japanese War
53 Bilko and York: Abbr.
54 First name in jazz
55 1960 Summer Olympics site
56 Needle case
57 Singer Carter
58 Kilmer poem subject
60 See 21 Across

308   GOING NOWHERE by Lois Sidway

ACROSS
1 Appear to be
5 __ podrida
9 "All kidding __"
14 The O'Hara's home
15 It should be square
16 Act the fink
17 __ happens (incidentally)
18 Nasty, and then some
19 Start of a Dickens title
20 Urban Cowboy device
23 A braid . . .
24 . . . is made of this
25 Intent look
29 Fisherman's boots
33 Velvet pile
36 "__ a Parade"
38 Perched on
39 Spa equipment
43 Shampoo ingredient
44 Bakery enticement
45 Former Cabinet dept.
46 Braced oneself
49 Slow mover
51 Bullring cheers
53 Jefferson portrayer
57 What planes follow to wait
62 Elle competitor
63 Elvis __ Presley
64 "Oh, what a relief __"
65 Shipping centers
66 Do a punch card no-no
67 Onetime Soviet spy grp.
68 Shooter's sport
69 The __ Duckling
70 It smells

DOWN
1 It's licked before use
2 Plate stand
3 Author Jong
4 "Chances Are" singer
5 Sign of the future
6 First name in jeans
7 Not of the cloth
8 God, to Fahd
9 Lawrence's hangout
10 Popular date time
11 Slanted type: Abbr.
12 Cutie pie
13 Compass dir.
21 Storeroom
22 Long-armed entity
26 Larry Holmes' predecessor
27 Singer Julius La __
28 Civil-rights leader Medgar
30 Engrave
31 Romeo or Juliet
32 Gush forth
33 Without ice
34 Wheel connector
35 Unskilled worker
37 Very dark
40 Iron-willed
41 "__ Yankee Doodle dandy . . ."
42 "I __ Say No"
47 Primogeniture beneficiary
48 Agnus __ (mass movement)
50 Rub it in
52 Real confusion
54 Release
55 Game-show giveaways
56 Come next
57 Crook alternative
58 Beastie
59 Sailor's quaff
60 Sample views
61 Mr. Warhol
62 Corp. officers

309   THREE BY FIVES by Matt Gaffney

ACROSS

1 Storyteller's task
9 Bunker's trait
15 San Francisco newspaper
16 Skagway's site
17 Court great
19 *The Price Is Right* prop
20 Seine stuff
21 Ht.
22 Sub in a tub
24 Where students get the brush
28 Outcome
30 Jerome Kern tune
31 Doing
32 Landing area
33 Hesitate verbally
34 Turner et al.
35 Came to a conclusion
38 Bin contents
42 James or Linkletter
43 Acts the bouncer
47 Highway pylon
48 Pool need
49 __ land (unclaimed territory)
51 Earls' girls
54 "There's never __ around . . ."
55 One of Frank's exes
56 A little resistance
57 Golf-club part
58 Teddy Roosevelt received it
64 With candor
65 Told the world
66 Willing victim
67 Acuity

DOWN

1 Parish head
2 Sighs
3 Guinness Book category
4 "__ my brother's keeper?"
5 Las' followers
6 Mendelssohn's *Concerto __ Minor*
7 "Not on your life!"
8 *Jaws* subject
9 Squeal
10 Muslim's Almighty
11 Announce
12 Carbon 14, e.g.
13 Limit, maybe
14 Ticked off
18 Scurried
23 __ *Town*
24 Not fighting
25 Sales attractions
26 Overseas bus. abbr.
27 Inverted flag, e.g.
29 Top
36 First to say "TGIF"?
37 Simon and Garfunkel, e.g.
38 New Deal agcy.
39 *Hollywood Squares* win
40 "Pick __ from one . . ."
41 Indulgent
44 Wee
45 Touchy?
46 Pulls a Van Winkle
50 Bicyclist's choices
52 Score
53 Quizmaster
58 __ de guerre
59 __-Locka, FL
60 Word form for "fire"
61 First wife
62 Puzzler's preference, perhaps
63 Skedaddled

310   SCALE MODEL by Henry Hook

ACROSS

1 RN's sine qua non
4 Cubbies' home, for short
7 Trygve's successor
10 "Fly, fly!"
11 Fish and Bull's neighbor
12 Bat material
13 PART 1 OF A QUOTE
16 PART 2 OF QUOTE
17 Sci-fi author Hubbard
18 Playful swimmer
19 Fast forty?
20 Morgan or Virgil
21 Away, in a way
22 *Señor*'s squiggle
24 "No problem!"
26 To such a point that
28 Turkish viceroy
30 Four ounces
35 Marsh plant
37 Skier's challenge
38 Hero's acquisition
41 Ant.
43 High: Sp.
44 Terrific report card
45 Cabinet department
47 Language suffix
48 END OF QUOTE
51 Speaker of quote
52 Pasture
53 H for a Hellene
54 Graft contributor?
55 Printer's widths
56 Nautilus locale
57 Digs for a DPL

DOWN

1 Consequentially
2 "The __ Love"
3 Understood
4 "__ a River"
5 Tragic flaw, in drama
6 "__ your disposal"
7 Began to develop
8 Glimmering
9 Proxy writer
10 Piece of catcher's equipment
13 *Topper* author Smith
14 Used as a perch
15 Dudley Do-Right's girl
16 Vandalize
17 Security problem
23 Panacea's targets
25 Galileo's birthplace
27 Sting's former rock group
29 Inclination
31 Semaphore specialists
32 Apprehend
33 Author Sinclair
34 Mossy growth
36 Rot
38 Needless violence
39 __ ABC
40 Lorenzo Lamas' mom
42 Lesser match
44 More than enough
46 State of India
49 Designer Cassini
50 Lieutenant Columbo, ostensibly

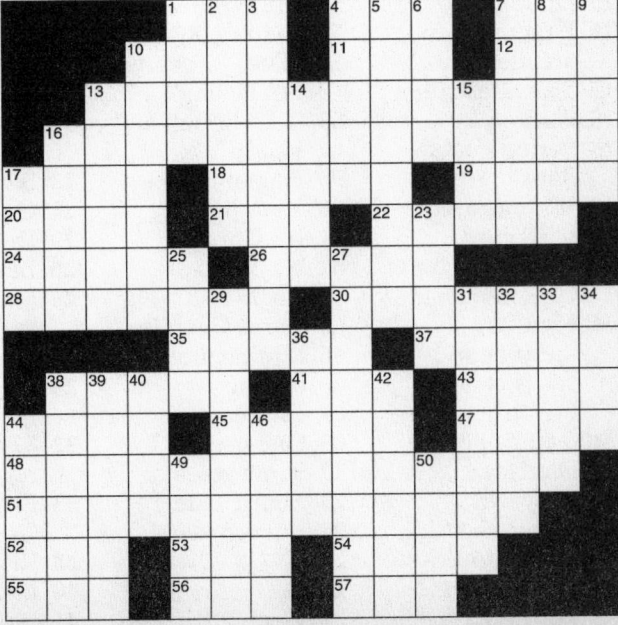

MEN OF THE MONTH by S.N.

ACROSS
1 "I __ Little Prayer"
5 Parisian pals
9 Coffee/chocolate combo
14 Energy source
15 Earth sci.
16 Spheres of interest
17 '80s Big Apple boss
20 Saw wood, so to speak
21 Deeply held
22 Wild blue yonder
23 "__ girl!"
25 The Bee __ (rock group)
27 Giant Hall-of-Famer
31 Annapolis sch.
35 Former ring king
36 High-schooler
37 Magazine exec
39 Melodic
41 P.M. periods
43 "__ you so!"
44 Tied up
46 Agenda component
48 Sugar Loaf Mountain city
49 Split apart
50 Meat magnate
53 Nightclub in a Manilow tune
55 Road attachment
56 May honoree
59 Spartan slave
61 Conductor Sir Georg
65 Clinic founders
68 More mad
69 Appearance
70 __ above the rest (superior)
71 Greek letter
72 Cries of fright
73 "__ a Lady" (Tom Jones tune)

DOWN
1 Antiaircraft weapons: Abbr.
2 __ end (concluded)
3 It has its ups and downs
4 Unscrupulous
5 Sweet 16, e.g.
6 Public-relations people
7 "I would give everything __ . . ."
8 Colloquial
9 The Treasure of the Sierra __
10 Where Mork and Mindy honeymooned
11 Corp. board members
12 Cab driver
13 Pale
18 Give a new name to
19 Singer Della
24 Golf area
26 Work wear
27 Jack and Jill's quest
28 "The Man __" (Gershwin tune)
29 Closet contents
30 Funny business
32 Tale
33 "I'm telling the truth!"
34 Intensity of emotion
38 Least distinct
40 C __ (Pepsi rival)
42 Sci-fi phenomenon
45 Bashful's brother
47 Before, in poems
51 Biblical temptress
52 Honolulu hellos
54 Pal Joey playwright
56 __ Helens, MT
57 Words of dread
58 Nothing more than
60 Off-Broadway award
62 Mr. Walesa
63 Rightful
64 Adherents: Suff.
66 Encountered
67 Light-switch positions

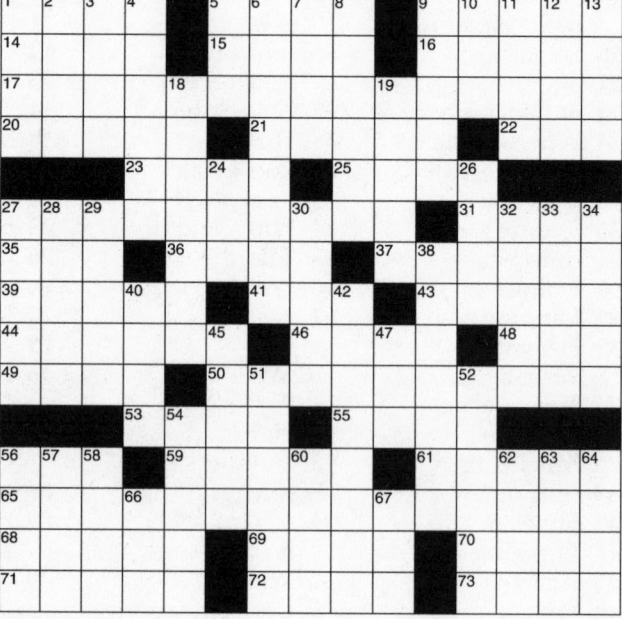

SENSE OF DIRECTION by Frances Hansen

ACROSS
1 Vein content
5 Three-note chord
10 Vending-machine opening
14 Deep black
15 Up high
16 First name in architecture
17 Fish alternative
18 Skirt styles
19 Periodic table datum: Abbr.
20 Midmorning
22 Disregard
24 Spot for a shade
27 Chestnut shade
28 Five-star monogram
30 ". . . sickness __ health"
31 Garage job
34 Director Howard
35 Hungarian dog
36 Snappish
37 Hill builders
39 Feathered talker
42 Synagogue
43 Throw __ From the Train
45 Seize
47 "__ You Lonesome Tonight?"
48 Wholesale
50 Dimensions
51 Aetna's bus.
52 "I've __ Feeling I'm Falling"
53 "Old Rough and Ready"
55 Flag of France
58 Waiting for __
61 Ho Chi __
62 Navratilova rival
65 Dame Chaplin
66 Minimizing ending
67 Take care of
68 One in debt
69 Some votes
70 Matriculate
71 __ even keel

DOWN
1 Went out
2 Mitch Miller's instrument
3 Vaudeville song
4 Chou __
5 Beret kin
6 Slugger's stat
7 Tony Blair's home
8 Tel __
9 Sandy land
10 Liner routes
11 Speak candidly
12 Answer Yes __ (old game show)
13 Swiped
21 Queue before Q
23 Debacle
25 Beat it
26 Smooth of speech
28 Theater fare
29 "__ go gentle . . ."
32 Roadster reversal
33 Ernie and Gomer
38 Kisses
40 Pavarotti piece
41 Blurred
44 In the matter of
46 Neth. neighbor
49 Thy Neighbor's Wife author
54 New-car odometer reading
55 Feds
56 Multitalented Moreno
57 Ceramist's need
59 Draftable
60 Mountain lake
63 U.S. 80, for one
64 Craggy peak

CAPITOL IDEAS by Ed Julius

ACROSS

1 French head
5 Basketball move
10 It may be raised
14 October birthstone
15 One-celled animal
16 '50s song, for instance
17 GOP nightmare
20 Tyrants
21 Tennis-tourney favorite
22 Inventor Whitney
23 Tattoo word
24 House dwellers
33 Make a mistake
34 *Inter* __
35 Actor Waggoner
36 Cornfield pest
38 Undeliverable piece of mail
40 Chicken style
41 First-rate
42 Word of warning
43 Compass pt.
44 '80s name in the news
49 Open TV time slot
50 Ode subject
51 Blackboard adjuncts
55 Silly
59 Party meeting
61 Footnote abbr.
62 Gymnast Comaneci
63 Light source
64 Yield
65 Inexperienced
66 Do in

DOWN

1 Mary __ Lincoln
2 Olympics sword
3 Tasseled toppers
4 Romeo or Juliet
5 Republican supporter, e.g.
6 "__ restless as a willow . . ."
7 Dog doc
8 Newspaper notice
9 Western city
10 Dairy product
11 A weather's opposite
12 French notion
13 __ *Blue*
18 Either of two "Unforgettable" singers
19 Location
24 Newscast segment
25 Diamond bungle
26 Lying flat
27 Omit in pronunciation
28 '50s vice president
29 Tarnish
30 Competing
31 Actress Verdugo
32 Sea complement
37 Jets and Sharks' neighborhood
39 Ancient Italian
45 Skeptic's remark
46 Adventurous
47 Silkworm of India
48 Invalidates
51 *The Odyssey* is one
52 After-bath wear
53 "Put __ on it!"
54 *The Lion King* villain
55 "I cannot tell __"
56 Adjective ending
57 Legendary Roman king
58 Catch sight of
60 Suffix for block

FILM FORAY by Vince Bonzagni

ACROSS

1 Matador's opponent
5 Disable
9 World War I aircraft
14 Crude group
15 Cubemaster Rubik
16 See 1 Down
17 Reagan film
20 Pelé's real first name
21 Walkman maker
22 Abyssal
23 Longhaired dog, for short
25 Decline to bid
27 Character
30 Chocolate flavoring
31 Peer Gynt's mother
34 Protest singer Phil
35 It gets driven
37 Canvas stand
39 '65 Oscar-winner
42 Clint's *Madison County* costar
43 Intl. grp. since '49
44 *Raiders of the Lost Ark* villain
45 Tongue ender?
46 Osiris' wife
48 Loose
50 Top-drawer
51 Kona souvenir
52 Inclination
55 "Oops!"
58 Happen again
62 '54 Oscar-winner
65 *Animal House* brother
66 P.O. bagful
67 Garfield pal
68 Horror-film sound effects
69 Thieves' take
70 Feedbag fill

DOWN

1 With 16 Across and 1 Down, Brooks/Bancroft remake
2 Newspaper page
3 Beatty Oscar film
4 007 film
5 Dues payer: Abbr.
6 Mars equivalent
7 The real dope
8 '62 sci-fi comedy
9 William Holden's last film
10 Provides an incentive
11 __ *of the Thousand Days*
12 Catch 40
13 Telegram word
18 "__ out — make up your mind!"
19 Half of a *Paper Moon* duo
24 Course listing
26 Check
27 Phrase of denial
28 Feels sore
29 "Presto!"
30 Legendary king
31 Very: Mus.
32 Grab
33 '61 Heston film
36 Diane Keaton title role
38 Victim in a '71 film
40 Hodgepodge
41 Vile
47 Kilimanjaro cover
49 Softball brand
50 Pale
52 1968 Taylor/Burton film
53 Obsessed by
54 "__ boy!"
56 Director Preminger
57 Plot participant
59 Song end, perhaps
60 Curriculum section
61 1 and A1A: Abbr.
63 Hesitator's syllables
64 Q-U link

FIRST-PERSON ACCOUNT by Charles E. Gersch

ACROSS

1 Variety-show segment
5 Business end of a drill
8 Runway
13 Soprano Te Kanawa et al.
15 Neighbor of Leb.
16 __ inter pares (firsts among equals)
17 "__ fight no more forever": Chief Joseph
18 4 on a phone
19 Kosher
20 Jackson's home
23 Chess pieces: Abbr.
24 Bandleader's cue
25 "The Great Commoner"
27 Stock-profit levy: Abbr.
28 [Not my error]
30 Illuminated at dusk
34 "The Sweetheart of Sigma __"
35 Sumptuous
36 Boy Scout activity
37 Fair-weather clouds
39 Youngster
41 It "has a thousand eyes"
42 Champaign-Urbana athletes
44 Smug sort
46 __ Way (Sinatra bio)
47 Drops in
48 Drink a little
49 98.6 and 101, to an RN
50 "Like a demigod here __": Shak.
52 Names for female French poodles
54 European auto
57 Children's room fixtures
61 "__ my lamp beside the golden door"
63 City in Serbia
64 It may be tucked in
65 Fruity word form
66 "__ Ruled the World"
67 Basketball shot
68 Nonviolent protest
69 Sermon topic
70 Baker's amts.

DOWN

1 Low-fat milk
2 New Zealander
3 Colleens
4 Semisharp cheese
5 Teddy's proverbial weapon
6 Last of His Tribe biographee
7 Mr. I Magination of early TV
8 Poultry problem
9 Lockheed __-Star
10 Bogie's Casablanca role
11 Not genuine: Abbr.
12 Barbecue areas
14 Open envelopes
21 Spaniard's emphatic affirmative
22 Substantial quality
26 Kon-__ (Heyerdahl book)
27 Hot pepper
29 Fish partner
31 Guidance vessels
32 "__ Good Time" (Browning poem)
33 Archer's objectives: Abbr.
34 LI x IV
35 Cavalry canine of films
38 Turn-of-the-century social reformer
40 Arrives casually
43 Adherents' suffix, in Rome
45 Philippine tree
49 Blockbuster
51 __ fatuus (will-o'-the-wisp)
53 Punch ingredient?
54 Paper Mate rivals
55 1052, to Tiberius
56 Skater Katarina
58 Sound system
59 Stumble
60 RR stops
62 TGIF part

FLOWER POWER by Fred Piscop

ACROSS

1 Small fights
6 City of Light
11 __ Plaines, IL
14 __ once (in unison)
15 One-celled creature
16 Quantity: Abbr.
17 1964 top-10 song
19 Drink cubes
20 Stadium section
21 Confused
23 Year-end singer
27 Passed along
29 Battery terminals
30 __ Abdul-Jabbar
31 Late __ (sleepyhead)
32 1995 NFL MVP Brett
33 Mischievous one
36 AAA recommendations
37 Exposes
38 Muse of history
39 Tie up the phone
40 New __, CT
41 Asks opinions
42 Phonograph inventor
44 Tranquil
45 Animal trainer
47 Encouraged
48 Synthetic fiber
49 Carson predecessor
50 French land mass
51 "Keep it a secret!"
58 G-man
59 Mennonite
60 Until now
61 Unspecified number
62 Ill-natured
63 Lenient one

DOWN

1 Kids' game
2 "Well, __ be!"
3 Dade County state: Abbr.
4 Hula hoop, for one
5 __ Brothers (country band)
6 Less ruddy
7 Latin love
8 Minister, for short
9 "How Can __ Sure" (1967 tune)
10 Pound-cake name
11 Henry James novel
12 Show's host
13 Lieu
18 Fibber's repertoire
22 __ kwon do
23 Tote
24 Singer O'Day
25 Presidential mom
26 Shelley works
27 Poe bird
28 Drops the ball
30 Actress Black
32 Be partial to
34 Pooh's creator
35 Sat, as a model
37 Army post
38 Apple center
40 Mountain dweller
41 Noblewoman
43 Ike's monogram
44 Onetime Iranian ruler
45 Israeli port
46 "Over the Rainbow" composer Harold
47 Noseless comic-strip figure
49 "Hey, you!"
52 Actress Thurman
53 Scale notes
54 Pay court to
55 Inactive
56 Act the stoolie
57 Prohibitionist

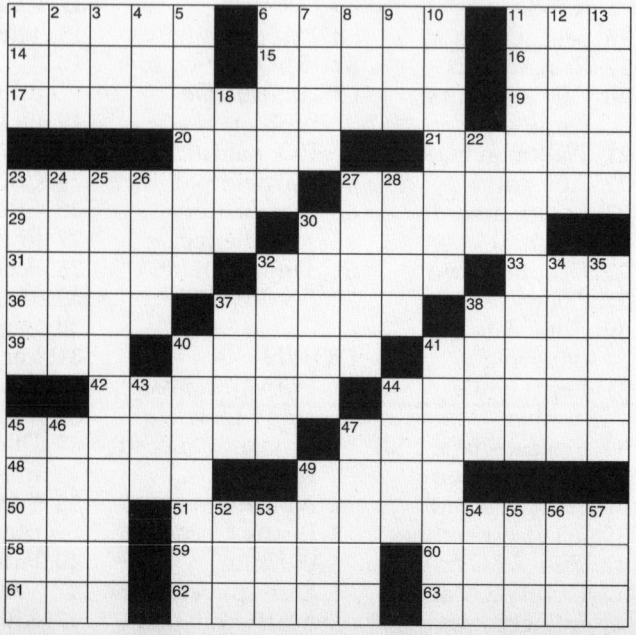

317 MAKING CONTACT by Rich Norris

ACROSS
1 Created
5 Fine rain
9 Type styles
14 October birthstone
15 Wile E. Coyote's supplier
16 __ board (manicurist's need)
17 Reps' check-in area
19 Aphorism
20 Where negotiations stall
22 Crumpets companion
23 Bed-and-breakfast
24 Duster's need
27 Canyon effect
30 Joins, as for a meeting
35 Perry's creator
37 Mad Hatter associate
39 Fishing net
40 Parts of a farewell speech, perhaps
43 Word in Kansas' motto
44 Lady of Spain
45 Get together
46 Consequence
48 Pusher chaser
50 Kildare and Welby: Abbr.
51 "Of course!"
53 __ banana (star comic)
55 Some two-family residences
63 More devious
64 Setting the standard
65 Did a personnel job
66 Make hay?
67 Bone above the ankle
68 Stiff collars
69 Prayer ending
70 Actress Sommer

DOWN
1 Tree-trunk growth
2 Give __ on the back
3 Painter Salvador
4 Put into office
5 Mexican musician
6 Computer symbol
7 Urban health concern
8 Adagio, allegro, etc.
9 NOW's movement
10 Muscat's country
11 Cry at a bakery
12 Baseball Hall-of-Famer Speaker
13 Beethoven work: Abbr.
18 __-ball (arcade game)
21 Switch positions
24 Pave anew
25 Came up
26 Excessive supplies
28 Farm worker
29 Church instrument
31 Jazz or Heat
32 Fathered
33 Signer, slangily
34 Bird houses
36 Light brown
38 Writer Bombeck
41 Hoisting lines, in sailing
42 Extraterrestrial's term of address?
47 Private eye, briefly
49 Farm house?
52 Biblical queen's domain
54 Throb steadily
55 Came down
56 Beginner
57 High schooler
58 Test
59 Wipe out of a manuscript
60 Humorist Mort
61 Estrada of CHiPs
62 "Auld Lang __"
63 That woman

318 BLOW BY BLOW by Bill Swain

ACROSS
1 Hotfooted it
4 Braque's school
10 Advanced degs.
14 Stevedores' grp.
15 Singer Franklin
16 Eye, in Aix
17 Device convenience
19 Stow cargo
20 Mideast ruler
21 Stopped by
23 Nikes, casually
26 More authentic
27 Road goo
28 Greek letter
30 Odd ornaments
33 Tight perm
35 Lizard with adhesive toe pads
36 Sternward
39 "__ Out of Mischief Now"
41 Consume
42 "__ do it, bees . . ."
44 __ Lama
45 Heep and others
47 Catches on to
48 Moving vehicle
51 Caper
53 Actress Kelley of L.A. Law
55 Pedestrian passage
57 Composer Janácek
58 Composer Khachaturian
59 Boxing-match stats
64 Actress Merrill
65 Elicited
66 Language ending
67 Idyllic spot
68 Non-violent demonstrations
69 Le coq __ (Rimsky-Korsakoff opera)

DOWN
1 Most mature
2 Female graduate
3 More likely to pry
4 Driver's compartment
5 S. Amer. nation
6 Wager
7 Addams Family member
8 Jostle
9 Excessively enthusiastic one
10 Tartuffe playwright
11 Dante's love
12 Assistant
13 Winter glider
18 Govt. med. grp.
22 Lazy
24 Appetizer tidbit
25 Painful
26 Wild spree
29 All even
31 River of Orel
32 Drunkard
34 Stack
36 __ Dhabi
37 Evergreen
38 WWI craft
40 Cole and others
43 1990 Neeson film
46 Underhanded characters
48 Saw
49 Dancer Alicia
50 Former Egyptian leader
52 Singer Lauper
54 "Evil Woman" grp.
55 Virginia of tennis
56 Very dry
60 Not at home
61 A fifth of MV
62 Barbie's beau
63 Degree with teeth

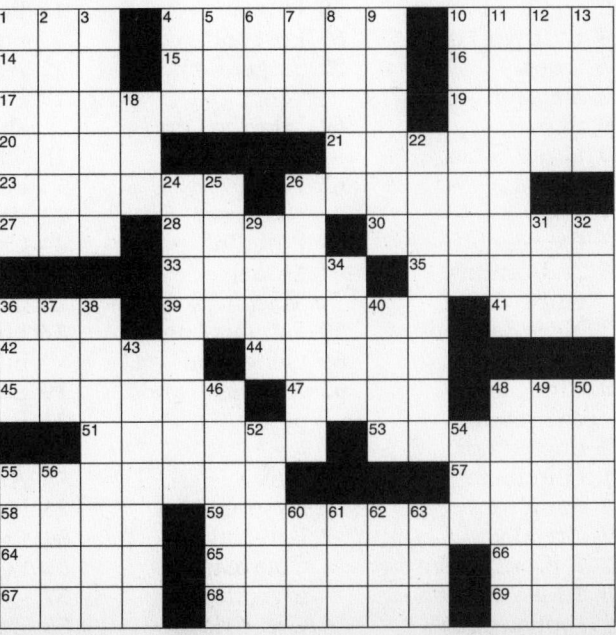

319   SHH! by Randolph Ross

ACROSS
1 Nintendo rival
6 General truth
11 Wharton deg.
14 Erstwhile rock magazine
15 Latin friends
16 Coffee server
17 Cornmeal cakes
19 Staff
20 All __ (attentive)
21 Calf catcher
23 Flea-market item
26 Spy-like
29 Crème de la crème
30 Like some omelets or onions
31 Gdansk residents
32 Fatty substance
33 Big bird
36 Did the same
37 Was partial to, with "with"
38 Deal of a sort
39 Longing
40 Kitchen implement
41 Bacterial trace
42 Wobbles
44 Hatch from Utah
45 Inane
47 Like some missiles
48 Liqueur flavoring
49 Stale humor
50 Grooved on
51 John Ford film
58 Tray content
59 Enjoy immensely
60 Lobster catcher
61 Asian holiday
62 Pumps and flats
63 NAFTA subject

DOWN
1 Teutonic "tsk"
2 Robert Morse role
3 DDE rival
4 Used the microwave
5 Pierces
6 Cartography material
7 Roadie's load
8 Caesar's dozen
9 It's crushed and cubed
10 Lost
11 "It's a secret!"
12 Having moxie
13 Get under one's skin
18 Script conclusion
22 Gore et al.
23 Make good on
24 Emulate Romeo and Juliet
25 December song
26 Arachnids
27 Comes to a point
28 Oklahoma city
30 Hook's opposites
34 Donny's sister
35 Turn over
37 Building spot
38 Track man
40 Whites out
41 Most likely to complain
43 Begley and Bradley
45 Upset with
46 Occupied
47 "There but for fortune __"
49 Recipe units
52 "So there!"
53 WWII theater
54 "¿__ pasa?"
55 She played Rosemary
56 Plus
57 Social-page word

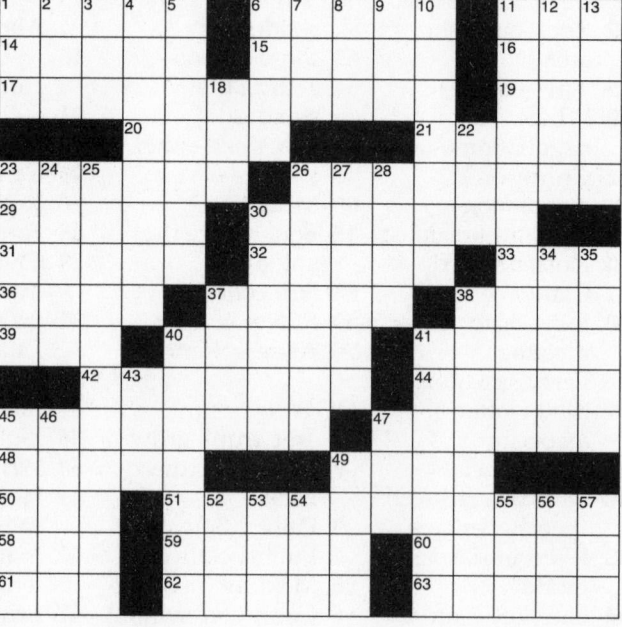

320   SHIP REX by Wayne Robert Williams

ACROSS
1 *Shine* star
5 Speed-of-sound measure
9 ASCII and BASIC
14 Single occurrence
15 __ En-lai
16 Post-workout woes
17 Hats for boaters?
19 Shy
20 Large Greek island
21 T-bar
23 Expressible
25 2nd-century emperor
28 New Zealand parrot
29 Chinese chairman
30 Eng. honor
31 Humiliate
35 Point for Gretzky
37 C.P. or Phoebe
38 Transport some sponsors?
41 Panelist Chase
42 Leopold's cohort
43 Precipitous
44 Fam. member
45 Weight of bricks
46 Paddle
48 Designer Pucci
50 Hitman
55 Lost one's cool
57 Singer Renata
58 "Yep!"
60 Like the *Love Boat?*
62 *Parade* composer
63 Borodin's prince
64 Model Macpherson
65 Fatuous ones
66 Obligation
67 Alejandro and others

DOWN
1 Fragrant bed
2 Full-length
3 Cousteau invention
4 Greek slave
5 __ & Mrs. Miller (Altman film)
6 "So *that's* it!"
7 Stand of trees
8 Outer covering
9 Texas county
10 Biochemist Severo
11 Boat on Wall Street?
12 Auction ending
13 Fast flyer, for short
18 Olduvai anthropologist
22 Author Calvino
24 Coral-reef enclosure
26 Cancel
27 Full of recent info
29 Latin dances
31 Burning
32 City on the Amazon delta
33 Noah's candles?
34 Lady of Sp.
36 Poetic piece
37 __ Na Na
39 Doom's partner
40 Ancient Balkan region
45 Church donations
47 Categorize
49 *Taxi* dispatcher
50 Old saw
51 Sedate
52 Steps over a fence
53 NATO member
54 Fla. State players, to fans
56 Corrosive substance
58 Olympics chant
59 Possesses
61 San Francisco hill

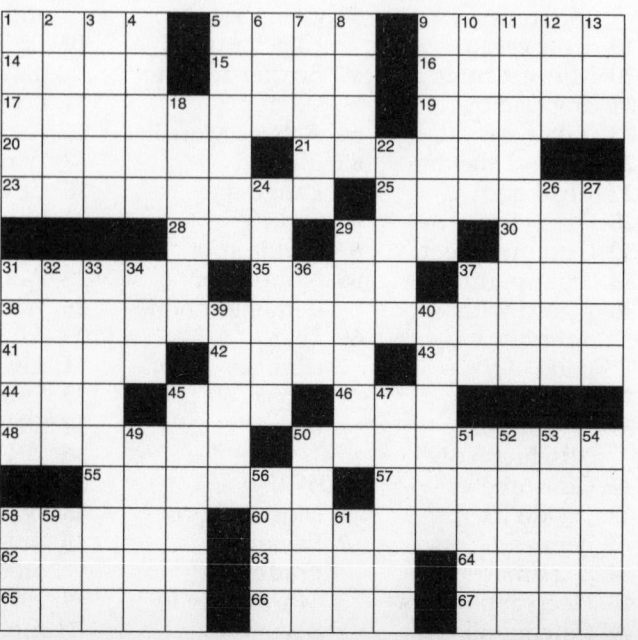

321 PRIZE PACKAGE by Wayne Robert Williams

ACROSS
1 Play part
4 Goes too fast
10 Criminal, to a cop
14 Virgo preceder
15 Hoi __
16 Sea green
17 __ Cruces, NM
18 Lacking recognition
19 Lays (down)
20 1992 Olympics gold-winning lightweight
23 Leavening agent
24 Fish sauce
27 Longtime FBI head
32 Group of rooms
33 Flap lips
36 Makes one
38 Any time now
39 Afore
40 Jerry Mathers' costar
42 U-turn from SSW
43 Louis and Carrie
45 Poetic comparison
46 Stitch
47 Hemp fiber for caulking
49 Military students
51 Listless
53 Monarch's loyal subject
57 *Trio* singer with Parton and Ronstadt
62 Unpaid-debt biz
64 Explanation
65 Breakfast drinks, for short
66 Team in a yoke
67 Have in mind
68 Female rabbit
69 Rocky crags
70 Lads' mates
71 After-dusk time, to a poet

DOWN
1 Combination of metals
2 Come to a halt
3 Puccini opera
4 Gush forth
5 Lake's smaller cousin
6 Otherwise
7 Hebrew month
8 Lady of Spain
9 Eyeful
10 Early paper
11 Math expressions
12 Road track
13 __ de deux
21 Cigar residue
22 W. Hemisphere grp.
25 Make amends
26 Continue a subscription
28 Yoko's family
29 Of wine
30 Former forms of words
31 Made over
33 Italian port
34 Indo-Iranian
35 Honey farmer
37 Shoe part
41 Marshy nesting areas
44 Legal order
48 Demure, in London
50 Knight's address
52 Actor Ritchard
54 Wear away
55 Military doll
56 Ruhr Valley city
58 Singer Horne
59 Cereal grains
60 Employs
61 Sharpen
62 Go bad
63 Word form for "outer"

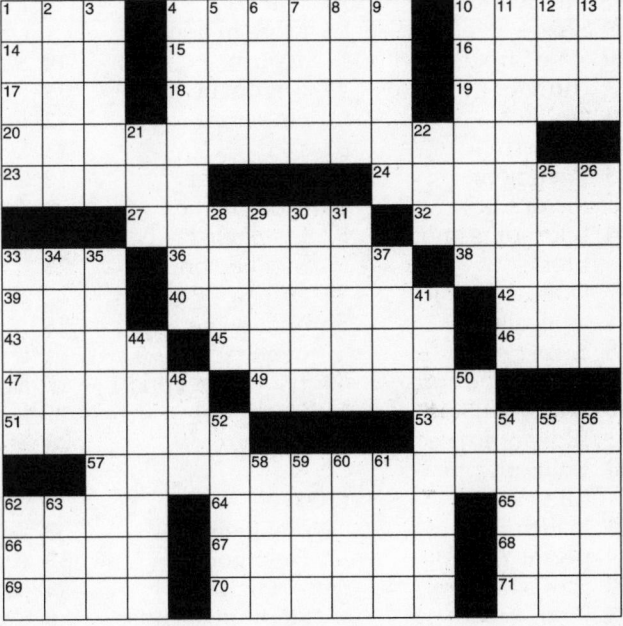

322 DIAMOND CALLS by Rich Norris

ACROSS
1 Hawaiian singer
6 Kids' ball material
10 Does something
14 "So long, Juan!"
15 Track shape
16 Farce
17 Angry tenants' tactic
19 Curbside call
20 Bklyn. campus
21 Superman foe Luthor
22 Pitcher Hershiser
23 Most painful
27 Musical encore
29 #1 Son's dad
30 Madrid Mrs.
32 "Just __" (Nike slogan)
33 Pilaf ingredient
34 Actor LaRue
36 Satisfy completely, as a debt
39 Moose relative
40 Gentle breezes
42 Pal, slangily
43 Paris river
45 Toon skunk Le Pew
46 Tail maneuvers
47 Get close to
49 Cal. neighbor
50 Pub pints
51 Fought for a lower price
54 Brandon of *Shane*
56 __-Romeo (imported auto)
57 Brother of Dopey
59 Spill the beans
60 Support the home team
61 Annual rural event
66 Andrew of *Melrose Place*
67 Card-game fee
68 Ruckus
69 Holbrook and Linden
70 Dennis the Menace, at times
71 Swashbuckler Flynn

DOWN
1 __ es Salaam
2 Poetic tribute
3 Diarist Anaïs
4 Washington-to-Moscow connection
5 Actor Davis
6 Partner of neither
7 Partner of good
8 Suburbanite, in the fall
9 Showed one's muscles
10 Queens community
11 Certain gala dance
12 April concerns for many
13 Happy expression
18 Vigorous fight
23 Farmland units
24 Argentina neighbor
25 Basketball violation
26 Maria Von __
28 Goes like the weasel?
31 Pale
35 Promoted with flair
37 More than suggested
38 Deputized group
40 Enthusiasm
41 Go back (to)
44 Denies the existence of
46 Anticipate the arrival of
48 Depot porter
51 Like Alaskan winters
52 "So long, 1 Across!"
53 *Lorna* __
55 Bruce __ (Batman)
58 Uses a scissors
62 Bottom line
63 Make public
64 Word form for "equal"
65 Family member: Abbr.

323 · AROUND IN CIRCLES by Randolph Ross

ACROSS
1 Summer place
5 Open nuts
10 She: It.
14 Tony relative
15 War hero Murphy
16 __-and-span
17 Movie Mountie
19 Shade
20 1996 Super Bowl runners-up
21 Golfer's concern
23 Pavement materials
24 Like some snow tires
25 Does a chemical analysis
28 Slip
29 Shaves the sod
30 Pine Tree State
31 IRS employee
34 Philanthropist Lilly
35 Halftime performer
37 Scot's topper
38 Penultimate mo.
39 Does a fall clean-up
40 Full of energy
41 Honors groups
43 Dinty and Dudley
45 Connected
47 Xmas gift with wheels
48 More in need of aspirin
49 Ethiopian emperor
53 Wed
54 Helicopter
56 Mont Blanc, e.g.
57 Evangelist McPherson
58 "Break __!"
59 NFL owner Leon
60 1923 Nobel poet
61 Medical measure

DOWN
1 Pen men
2 Help hoods
3 __ High Stadium, Denver
4 They're spent in Spain
5 Furniture artisans
6 Sorry folks
7 Chimes in
8 El __ (Heston role)
9 Pennsylvania adjective
10 State of Mexico
11 Political PR man
12 From then on
13 Did
18 Oil of __
22 Turnip or potato
24 Messes up
25 Last word in church
26 A man from U.N.C.L.E.
27 Elvis' notable features
28 Shows off
30 Ready for broadcast
32 Beep
33 Andy's partner
35 Not novel
36 Canal
40 Sours
42 Frankie and Cleo
43 Paris grands
44 Fine
45 Punjab prince
46 Where to find an *élève*
47 Floppy hat
49 Part of the Earth's crust
50 Farm sight
51 Ticks off
52 Border
55 Get going

324 · UNMARRIED COUPLES by Richard Silvestri

ACROSS
1 Legal group
4 Fiber source
8 "The Happy Warrior"
13 *Time Machine* people
15 Resort near Venice
16 Turkish bigwig
17 Bit of physics
18 __ the finish (competitive to the end)
19 Two-tone treats
20 Mr. and Mrs. of movies
23 Olympus dwellers
24 Kensington quaff
25 Possessive people?
28 Indifferent
33 Mock
34 Collector's suffix
35 Elvis' record label
36 Mr. and Mrs. of literature
40 Ethyl ending
41 Corrida serenade
42 Kiri Te Kanawa, e.g.
43 Did over
46 Hostility
47 Stephen of *Michael Collins*
48 Adorable
49 Mr. and Mrs. of song
56 Where Irving is
57 Sound of pride?
58 Marching-band member
59 Grammy-winner Bonnie
60 Not pro
61 Short cut
62 Unable to sit still
63 Sunday celebration
64 Rider's right

DOWN
1 Ship's width
2 Choir voice
3 Yell from the stands
4 Hunters' hideouts
5 Orange coverings
6 Cain raiser
7 Refuser's words
8 Blighted
9 Wondrous thing
10 "Aha!"
11 Defender of the Aesir
12 Isn't out of
14 Sid's costar
21 Heart line
22 Like some sprays
25 Multiple-choice choice
26 Fort __, IN
27 Some Renoirs
28 Hamstrung
29 Balin and Claire
30 Wrong move
31 Get home safely
32 Flavorful
34 Sitting around
37 Hurler Ryan
38 Old violin
39 Invention protections
44 Picks up the tab
45 Full of foam
46 Arrogance
48 Painters put them on
49 Pastrami preference
50 Leave the scene
51 Sixty grains
52 First name in gossip
53 Choral
54 Stage award
55 Mane site
56 Refrain fragment

325 RIDING THE B&O by Fred Piscop

ACROSS

1 Engineering school, for short
5 Tone down
9 Shirt ruffle
14 Taj Mahal site
15 Andy's pal
16 Tabriz native
17 Expand, as a business
19 Forum duds
20 *Ben-Hur* novelist Wallace
21 English river
22 Times up
23 1996 Olympics site
25 Indian, for one
26 Lose one's temper
28 Louisville Slugger wood
31 Oral-vaccine man
34 Trawler's gear
35 Tic-tac-toe win
36 Poop out
37 Pad holder
39 Succotash bean
40 Small bill
41 Greenspan of the Fed

42 Roger Bannister, for one
43 "Harper Valley __"
44 Lie adjacent to
47 Go-__ (miniature vehicles)
49 Pitch the pigskin
53 Monkey Trial defendant
55 Rocker Hendrix
56 Metric measure
57 *Where's __?* (Segal film)
58 Where to get tickets
60 German autos
61 Related by blood
62 Partook of
63 Religious principle
64 *Buona __, Mrs. Campbell*
65 1990 World Series winners

DOWN

1 Indian drum
2 Everglades bird
3 Poky pace

4 Harrison, in *Star Wars*
5 *H.M.S. Bounty* stopover
6 Indifferent to right or wrong
7 Pout
8 Guinness suffix
9 Nervousness
10 Caribbean resort
11 Insincere flattery
12 "Step __!"
13 Nervous contractions
18 Mass part
22 Vinegar, in combinations
24 Irish Rose lover
25 Pizzeria need
27 Upright
29 A few
30 Winter coating
31 Telegram punctuation
32 "__ Misbehavin' "
33 Get at, in a way
37 Schedule divisions
38 Slanders
39 __-item veto

41 Side by side
42 Recurring theme
45 Panacea
46 Helen Hunt Jackson novel
48 Granny Smith, for one
50 Poker ploy

51 Curved
52 City on 21 Across
53 Difficulty
54 Deal with difficulty
55 One-liner
58 __-relief
59 Beethoven's "__ Elise"

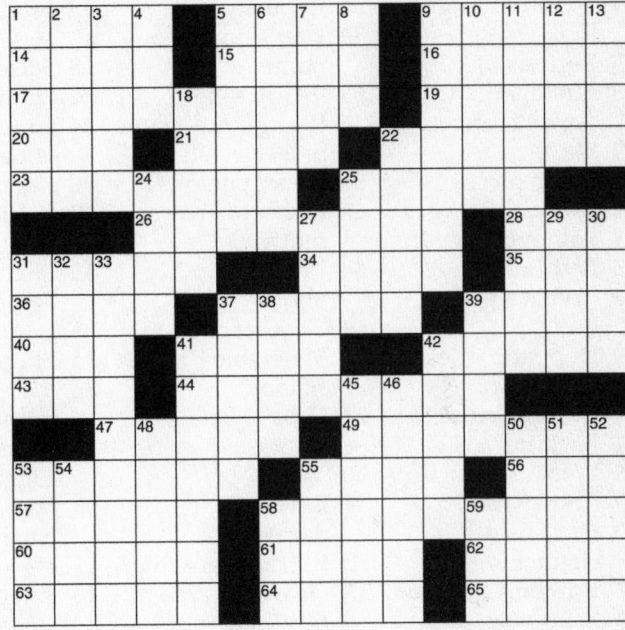

326 DO ME A FLAVOR by S.N.

ACROSS

1 Castle protector
5 Lasting impression
9 Sitcom set in Korea
13 Big name in talk TV
15 Mulligan-stew maker
16 Actress Chase
17 Center of attraction
18 Top draws in poker
19 Profit
20 Toll-house cookie ingredients
23 Krazy __
24 Exerciser's surface
25 Most resolute
29 From a great distance
31 Sound of recognition
34 Verdi specialty
35 Cloudless
36 Steel source
37 Fair-haired one
40 Sushi-bar selections
41 Physicist's tidbit
42 Fudd or Gantry
43 Prefix for long or now

44 CATs do it
45 Punishment personified
46 __ leaf cluster (medal extra)
47 Sup
48 Cake flavoring
56 Actress Moran or Gray
57 Skillful
58 Oldtime anesthetic
60 Clock sound
61 Night, in Normandy
62 Goddess of the moon and the hunt
63 Selections from Shelley
64 Party giver
65 Helen of __

DOWN

1 *Mr. __* (house-husband film)
2 Oil cartel
3 Get one's back up
4 Southwestern snack
5 Commandment verb

6 *Your Show of Shows* costar
7 Help a hood
8 George Clooney's aunt
9 Power
10 Jai __
11 Leap lightly
12 Holbein or Brinker
14 Metal cutter
21 Feedbag bit
22 Traffic component
25 Visit
26 Comparatively competent
27 Actress Oberon
28 Historical periods
29 Composer Copland
30 Unyielding
31 Sweet smell
32 Made sharp
33 Conductor Previn
35 Greek cheese
36 What Pandora unleashed
38 Adverse reaction
39 Color of embarrassment
44 Actor Mineo

45 "Can't Help Lovin' __ Man"
46 Sty's cries
47 Bring to bear
48 Put the kibosh on
49 Much too dry
50 Well-bred

51 Peek-__
52 Connecticut collegians
53 Working hard
54 Treat coal
55 "... a __ 'clock scholar"
59 Bit of sunshine

FAMILIAR QUOTATIONS by David Owens

ACROSS

1 Former Teamsters head
6 Melville South Seas novel
10 Ultra-violet-blocking chemical
14 "__ and hungry look"
15 Refuses to
16 First man
17 Towel fabric
19 Story
20 Piano piece
21 X-ray discoverer
23 Annoying noises
25 Bedtime rituals
26 "What a good boy __"
29 Doorstep drier
30 "Yes, it was spelled wrong!"
31 Backfire
35 Words to Macduff
39 Roman censor
40 Dickens title character
42 Rosebud's owner
43 Bean pole
45 Underwater swimmer
47 Allow
49 $5 bill
50 Hallucinogenic letters
51 Tom and Diane
55 Rushed
57 Grouchy?
59 Iran's former name
63 "Alice's Restaurant" name
64 Sweet snack
66 Sweet person
67 Helen of Troy's mother
68 "Walk __ in My Shoes"
69 Go after flies
70 Venerable British school
71 Tops of heads

DOWN

1 Bowlers and derbies
2 Butter alternative
3 Flowerless plant
4 Electrical unit
5 Whenever
6 Barn bird
7 Othello, for one
8 Winning
9 The "al." in et al.
10 Kids' game
11 Words of wisdom
12 Harvest machine
13 Endings to 25 Across
18 False story
22 Hammer target
24 Autograph hound's quarries
26 Basics
27 Circle of water
28 Little bit
32 Picture-hook device
33 __ compos mentis
34 Blunders
36 "__ come back now, hear?"
37 Cash-drawer compartment
38 Bookworm, maybe
41 Mawkish
44 Singer/actor Howard
46 Patella
48 Extra-base hit
51 An abundance
52 Street-sign shape
53 Half a Washington city's name
54 Shooter's sport
56 Serious show
58 Word form for "inner"
60 Agitated state
61 Doing nothing
62 Roll-call count
65 A Bobbsey

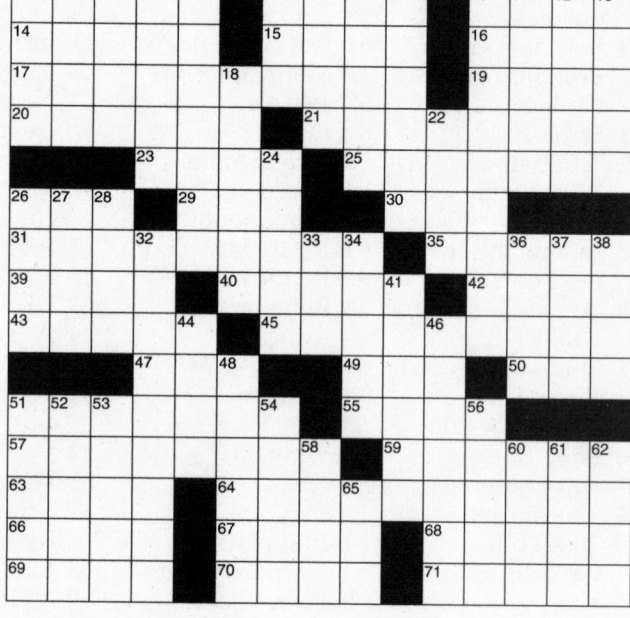

PLACES, EVERYBODY by Mike Miller

ACROSS

1 Tintinnabulation
5 Dog bane
10 Greek cheese
14 Puerto __
15 Restrain
16 Come down hard
17 Exultant
20 Pudding and pie
21 Philadelphia footballers
22 Landing data: Abbr.
23 Makes a choice
24 Cotton-pickin' machines
27 Fortitude
28 Part of a porpoise
31 "You'll Never Walk __"
32 Predisposition
33 __ colada
34 Neither liberal nor conservative
37 Stingers
38 Fill to the max
39 *Voyage to the Center of the Earth* author
40 Rural retreat
41 Hart of Broadway
42 Garden tool
43 The final stroke?
44 Damage
45 Obliterate
48 Part of a nation's jurisdiction
52 Sink maximally
54 Fence feature
55 "__ a Song Comin' On"
56 Words from Caesar
57 Mine find
58 Key people
59 Changes colors

DOWN

1 Urge to action
2 __ kleine Nachtmusik
3 Does something
4 Unfinished business
5 Plant tracts
6 Boxer's blows
7 Grub
8 Hardwood tree
9 Timid
10 Kermit's kin
11 Viscount's superior
12 Board-game piece
13 "No ifs, __ or buts!"
18 Seabird
19 Steam harnesser
23 Stand up and speak
24 Disney deer
25 Horror sci-fi film of '79
26 Outerwear material
27 Stocking stuffers
28 Scandinavian sight
29 Preposterous
30 *Unsafe at Any Speed* author
32 Prideful patter
33 Knocked off the air
35 Abstruse
36 With 41 Down, a lot
41 See 36 Down
42 Sing like the birdies sing
43 Wears a hole in the carpet
44 Outdoorsy type
45 Thus
46 Trepidation
47 Final outcome
48 Scored by serving well
49 *L.A. Law* role
50 Bird house
51 Down-under birds
53 Horse __ different color

329 COST-CUTTING by Ed Stein

ACROSS
1 Paintings and such
4 Frontier
9 Reducing parlor
12 Asian nanny
13 Goosey
14 Actress Anderson
16 Cut-rate polysyllables?
19 With 47 Across, prime-time viewers
20 Echo
21 Men
22 Wait
23 Allurement
26 Venus and Jupiter
27 __ Miniver
30 First course
31 Freudian specialty: Abbr.
32 Bathday cake
33 Cut-rate song?
36 Splicer's need
37 Perfect batting average
38 Put away
39 New Deal org.
40 *Show Boat* songman
41 Sunday paper extra
42 Call's partner
43 *The Nazarene* author
44 Begin home
47 See 19 Across
51 Cost of a cut-rate bionic man?
53 Desqueaks
54 Unadorned
55 *South Pacific* role
56 Leaves to be brewed
57 Seven, in Salerno
58 Shrewd

DOWN
1 "What __ mind reader?"
2 Make a scene
3 Cold spell of long ago
4 One of the Barrymores
5 Wedding-party member
6 DC tract
7 Actress Claire
8 Like Ivan
9 Ski mountain
10 Read intently (over)
11 "All wool __ yard wide"
12 Big name in advice
15 Suffix for a believer
17 El __ (legendary locale)
18 Gets hitched
22 Encouraging word
23 "It's just __ of the times!"
24 Highway man
25 General assemblies
26 Peel it and weep
27 __ Carlo
28 Indy entrant
29 Used up
31 Come to __ (reach a junction)
32 Conchologist's concern
34 Haberdashery display
35 Solver's need
40 Turn (over)
41 "Day __" (Peter, Paul and Mary tune)
42 Raft wood
43 Sit in on a course
44 Roman CL
45 Struck down
46 Anger
47 Med. school course
48 Catch
49 Lobster
50 NC clock setting
52 See 22 Down

330 GOLDWYNISM by A.J. Santora

ACROSS
1 Current unit
4 African capital
9 Glove-compartment stuff
13 Watches
15 In first place
16 Making a crossing
17 START OF A SAM GOLDWYN QUOTE
20 Require
21 Insignificant
22 "__ Gratia Artis"
23 One on the lose?
25 Slow tempo
27 Lots of land
28 Scale notes
31 ". . . __ and hungry look"
32 Got ready to drive
33 Popular cocktail
35 Sum up
36 MIDDLE OF QUOTE
37 Height of fashion?
40 Conspicuous
41 Modern composer John
42 Like __ (possibly)
45 Football scores: Abbr.
46 Musical comedy man?
47 It's often laid down
49 Fine fabric
50 Hot brew
51 Onetime South Korean leader
54 Applications
55 END OF QUOTE
60 State positively
61 Low-pressure system
62 Planetary lap
63 Turner and Weems
64 Scrumptious
65 Calendar column heading

DOWN
1 "__ was saying . . ."
2 Ran into
3 Beset
4 One on the rise
5 T or F, for example
6 List component
7 Ramble
8 *Falstaff,* for one
9 Shortest month, in a way
10 "All the world's __"
11 Where movies are supposed to "play"
12 Victor Mature film role
14 Off one's feet
18 __ out (supplements)
19 Stendhal's *The __ the Black*
23 Statistics
24 Finished the cupcakes
26 "Rumble in the Jungle" winner
28 Unspoken
29 Beset
30 Laurel and Musial
33 1/1000 inch
34 Savings bk. payment
36 St. Peter's cardinal
37 Besets
38 Dairy dozen
39 Like Milquetoast
40 Sun's name
41 Fun fare
42 Besides
43 Gather grain
44 Approached
46 Lowdown
48 Bridge kin
49 Bergen need
52 Spanish 101 verb
53 Baseball Hall-of-Famer Slaughter
56 Monopoly quartet: Abbr.
57 It may be up against the wall
58 Rte. consultant
59 *The A-Team* star

TIME FRAMES by Robert H. Wolfe

ACROSS
1 Gives __ on the back
5 Capital of Bangladesh
10 Reach across
14 Main course
15 How tuna may be packed
16 Military force
17 Rarely
20 Bad weather
21 *Green Mansions* bird-girl
22 One way to cook
23 Pace
24 Deters
26 Cortez's quest
28 Eye makeup
32 Indian noble
37 Triumphant cries
38 Long time
42 Whistle sound
43 Relaxes from work
44 Phases
48 "Can I help you?"
49 Challengees
51 Male turkeys
55 Line of fashion?
58 Casino city
59 Make effervescent
61 Occasionally
64 Soft-drink flavoring
65 Fear
66 Give birth to
67 Trudge
68 Fergie's first name
69 Bullring cheers

DOWN
1 Hubbubs
2 Cream containers
3 British racing site
4 Yonder
5 Rackets
6 Santa __, CA
7 Dangerous snake
8 Eyelash
9 Vassar grad, perhaps
10 Americans' Uncle
11 Univ. title
12 Love: Lat.
13 Manhattan, to the P.O.
18 Article from abroad
19 Packs away
24 Karate school
25 A whole bunch
27 The old college cry
29 *The Man Who Mistook His Wife for __*
30 Comedienne Martha
31 Part of NAACP
32 __ Hari
33 Cookiemaker Wally
34 Skirt shape of yore
35 Started the kitty
36 Astern
39 "Simon __"
40 Waikiki strings
41 In hierarchical sequence
45 Mae's *She Done Him Wrong* co-star
46 Economist's evaluations
47 Spanish woman
50 Crew-team member
52 Word form for "straight"
53 Taj __
54 Canyon of comics
55 Give a leg up
56 Not good
57 Note at the office
59 S __ (green-stamp issuer)
60 Chemical endings
62 Bolshevik's color
63 Highest bond rating

HARD PLACES by S.N.

ACROSS
1 Utters
5 Vigoda and Lincoln
9 Uninteresting
13 Skirt fold
15 Oliver Twist's request
16 Increased
17 Kuklapolitan player
18 Perry Mason portrayer
19 Feel sore
20 Environmental problem
22 Rubberneck
24 MGM's mascot
25 __ *Three Lives*
26 __ facto
27 Gets hitched
29 Get an __ effort
31 Half a pendulum's path
34 "__-daisy!"
36 Farm unit
38 Church instrument
40 Aquarium fish
42 Expert
43 Unknowing
44 "Moving right __ . . ."
45 Game played at and with clubs
47 Radioer on wheels
48 Coop dweller
49 December song
51 Cake finisher
53 Heaven on earth
55 Whitish gem
57 "__ was saying . . ."
60 Elfin
62 Gave a new name to
64 Tide type
65 Blind as __
67 Roadside accommodations
68 War god
69 Junction point
70 Hold responsible
71 Nevada town
72 Way out
73 __ Scott Decision

DOWN
1 Ersatz coffee table
2 *Kate &* __ (sitcom)
3 Old Faithful's home
4 *Je ne* __ *quoi*
5 Mosey
6 National Bureau of Standards headquarters
7 Blow it
8 Musician Mendes
9 Challenges the top gun
10 Symbol of solidity
11 Carolina county
12 It may be Lite or dark
14 Unenthusiastic
21 Ingrid's *Casablanca* role
23 Cook wear
28 Get through hard work
30 Believe
32 Four-star review
33 Singular sensation
34 A Four Corners state
35 Retired soccer star
37 Cashier's workplace
39 Dash, for example
41 Actress Moorehead
46 Italian auto
50 In stock
52 Make an ascent
54 Sot, for short
56 Flying Pan
58 "Why don't you come up and __"
59 Avoided work
60 "I didn't know I had it __"
61 Ground grain
63 Ratted (on)
66 Scare word

ACROSS

1 __ canto (singing style)
4 Baby's word
8 Pipe part
12 Greek war god
14 Speech to the audience
16 Art Deco designer
17 Daytime TV fare
18 Rattled, as 19 Across
19 Board-game equipment
20 1937 Rodgers and Hart musical
23 Slow tempo
24 Do paper work
25 Muscle contraction
29 Jigsaw-puzzle part
33 Cut (off)
36 Daisylike flowers
39 Heartless one
40 1938 Rodgers and Hart musical
43 Bill of fare
44 Nebula shape
45 "By all means!"
46 Dread
48 Sponsorship
50 Act as a judge
53 Make juicier
57 1940 Rodgers and Hart musical
63 Scandinavian capital
64 Like a lot
65 Vicinity
66 "Sacre __!"
67 Hackneyed
68 NBA team
69 Crystal gazer
70 Steak cut
71 By the __ (incidentally)

DOWN

1 Cook's leaves
2 Wear away
3 Gain knowledge
4 Short race
5 Arthur of the court
6 Fancy dress
7 Pueblo material
8 Stirring up discontent
9 Tangential subject, for short?
10 Carve with acid
11 Track competition
13 Fashionable footwear, once
15 Scratched (out) a living
21 Up __ (good as usual)
22 Move with violent speed
26 Dents and all
27 Short distance
28 Radio, TV, etc.
30 Custardlike
31 Algonquian Indian
32 Sniggler's prey
33 Kind of bean
34 Sign of the future
35 Hunger sign
37 Steak order
38 Obstacle
41 Commuting time
42 Culprit's contrivance
47 Ball holder
49 Epic tales
51 Libyan or Iraqi
52 State trooper's tool
54 Small bush
55 Itty-bitty
56 Rub out
57 Goblins
58 Bit of land
59 Cheerfulness
60 Middle-class, to Mitford
61 Apothecaries' unit
62 Beatles film

ACROSS

1 Football-game cheers
5 Suburban development
9 Window sticker
14 Sign over a door
15 Carpet calculation
16 Caribbean resort island
17 Car tune?
20 Liner route
21 Gets on
22 "The Queen of the West"
24 Sample of Keats
25 Bawled
28 Egyptian king
30 Except for
34 On cloud nine
37 Gunk
40 Sheep sound
41 Car tune?
44 Blaster's blast
45 Bambi's family
46 Religious
47 Merit-badge holder
49 New Englander's assent
51 Meadow munchers
52 Man-mouse connector
55 Put off
58 Kid's shoebox project
62 Big bird
66 Car tune?
68 Out of the way
69 Cat's-paw
70 Coffee, Tea, __?
71 Less inane
72 Rural rest stops
73 Despicable one

DOWN

1 Field officials
2 Wheel connector
3 Informal greeting
4 Heel style
5 __ cum laude
6 Zealous
7 Sayer or Durocher
8 Green acres, in estate country
9 Passé
10 Wears down
11 What some irons do
12 Have __ in one's bonnet
13 Thailand neighbor
18 Part of USNA
19 Prefix for classical
23 Kind of doughnut
25 Mae and Rebecca
26 Actress Verdugo
27 Agreements
29 1000 kilograms, to a metricist
31 Strike __ for liberty
32 Prize
33 Bridge positions
35 Leave off
36 ETO initials
38 Unmatched
39 Post- opposite
42 Attention getter
43 Went too far
48 __ combat (out of action)
50 Being
53 Wild one
54 Latin 101 verb
56 Fillies and colts
57 Grandma's order
58 "__ I say, not . . ."
59 Memorable role for Ingrid
60 Valhalla bigwig
61 Some chorus ladies
63 Lawn-equipment maker
64 Poet Lazarus
65 Bamboo, essentially
67 __-Tiki

335 BRIDGE GAME by Karen L. Hodge

ACROSS
1 Otherwise
5 *Waiting for Lefty* writer
10 Lucie's dad
14 Hard to believe
15 Chopper blade
16 __ incline (tilted)
17 Long of Louisiana
18 BRIDGE
20 Rage
21 "¿Qué __?"
22 Cavity filling
23 BRIDGE
27 Soupçon
28 Fought
32 Less risky
35 Creamy quaff
36 What a vein may contain
37 BRIDGE
42 "__ the land of the free . . ."
43 Lemon
44 Between __ and a hard place
45 Part of a castle wall
48 Subjective sensation
50 BRIDGES
55 Put down
58 Prank
59 Sea, in Amsterdam
60 BRIDGE
63 Ramble
64 Green land
65 Viking of comics
66 Not pro
67 Find a place for
68 Rudolf and I.W.
69 Nudnik

DOWN
1 Moral code
2 Gene Tierney mystery film of '44
3 Z's
4 TV's Tarzan
5 Decree
6 *Alice __ Live Here Anymore*
7 Lab heaters
8 Little crawler
9 *Mme.* of Spain
10 __-earth (straightforward)

11 Carbon compound
12 FDR's mom
13 Like a printer's fingers
19 Sound like Sylvester J. Pussycat
21 Teams up
24 Later
25 Pony's purpose, perhaps
26 Bid first
29 Not great
30 Skater Heiden
31 Bridge necessity
32 Organ device
33 Field
34 Klinger portrayer
35 Help
38 Invention inception
39 Noted archbishop
40 Phil Donahue's wife
41 Caspian Sea feeder
46 Missing

47 Hammer part
48 Beast
49 Milk containers
51 Proverb
52 Oxygen variety
53 "The Second Coming" poet
54 Resign
55 A long time
56 Yawn inducer
57 Sills solo
61 __ Na Na
62 Chat
63 Chat

336 BODY DOUBLES by S.N.

ACROSS
1 What you eat
5 Evert of tennis
10 Close-fitting
14 Christie or Karenina
15 Some are dyeing to get it
16 Turnpike payment
17 Consecutive
19 In the matter of
20 Takes the wheel
21 Auto accessories
23 Internalize anger
26 Moreno and Coolidge
27 Three-seaters of a sort
30 Physique, for short
31 Card game
32 Three __ match
33 Reducing salons
35 Grandma's hat
38 Osso __ (Italian entrée)
40 Sheik's home
42 Scotch partner
43 Squanders
45 Thumbs-down answers
47 Drink a bit
48 Device named for its shape
49 Yoko __
50 Assists in crime
52 Swan relative
54 Beach bungalow
56 Who's home?
58 Logical method
62 Heavy metal
63 Kind of combat
66 Come to grips with
67 TV studio sign
68 Passion personified
69 Winter transportation
70 Pace
71 Ltr. enclosure

DOWN
1 Applies lightly
2 __ the finish (competitive to the end)
3 Ending for insist or persist
4 *The Farmer __ Wife* (Henry Fonda's first film)
5 Went for
6 Isr. lang.
7 Cell substance
8 Snuck up slowly
9 Welfare
10 Subway stops
11 Virtually even
12 Extreme
13 Photo finish
18 Lock of hair
22 Singer Guthrie
24 Way up the slopes
25 Praise, in a mass
27 Bawls
28 "Come __!" (invitation of a sort)
29 In person
34 Mas' mates
35 Tournament qualifying exemption
36 Fix sloppy copy
37 "Lights out" music
39 Partial
41 Simp
44 Range player of song
46 Sony competitor
49 Gas rating
51 Big parties
52 Comes out swinging?
53 *Love Story* star
55 Lone Star baseballer
57 Expended
59 Mitchell mansion
60 Monkey in space
61 Store gds.
64 *Platoon* setting
65 Potato-chip partner

337 RHYME TIME by Karen L. Hodge

ACROSS
1 Strong __ ox
5 Frank
9 Tree trunk's cover
13 New pilot's milestone
14 Playwright O'Casey
15 Calcutta cash
16 Ability-based donation
18 Plot twist, perhaps
19 Letters on an urban sign
20 Savoir faire
21 Goes along
22 Oscar de la __
24 Show-off
26 "Fine!"
28 Makes a decision
29 Trendy bunch
32 Goes wrong
33 Decrease
36 Word of regret
37 Martini's wine-making partner
39 Went quickly
40 Cake makings
41 D.C. daily
42 Where to get beer on board
44 Weakens
45 Monterrey money
46 Unreasonable, as prices
48 Adored ones
52 __ cat (fearful one)
54 Verdi opera
56 Deli meat
57 Kemper competitor
58 Wallflower, possibly
60 Like cacti
61 Building wings
62 Face shape
63 Ritzy
64 Ritzy
65 Mousetrap need

DOWN
1 __ as the eye can see
2 Italian wine
3 Man from Mars
4 "__ iron bars a cage"
5 Workplace watchdog grp.
6 Great
7 Keeps an __ the ground
8 Compass pt.
9 Grand Canyon transportation
10 "You're __ and don't know it"
11 Philospher Descartes
12 Props for Captain Kangaroo
15 Arrestee's demand
17 Investment
21 Attribute
23 Play horseshoes
25 Resurfaces roads
27 Progressive decline
29 Jazzmen's session
30 Whitney family patriarch
31 Returns calculation
32 Summer hours in St. Pete
33 Dopey's brother
34 Novelist Levin
35 For every
38 Word form for "bone"
39 Walked on
41 Check time
43 Flu variety
44 Like a beanpole
45 Little bottles
46 "__ Doll" (Ellington tune)
47 Wine giant
49 Butler's wife
50 Polynesian porch
51 Make metal
52 Eat not
53 Payment-misser's risk, for short
55 China piece
58 Get-up-and-go
59 Exemplar of patience

338 "C" AS IN CROSSWORD by Scott Marley

ACROSS
1 River of Arizona
5 Record-store mdse.
8 Motley
14 Jung's specialty: Abbr.
15 C as in climatology
17 C as in chemistry
19 Fly of a sort
20 Hard journey
21 Springsteen's birthplace
22 Negative prefix
24 Criteria
27 GI wear
30 Clock, to Klaus
32 Tossing and turning
36 C as in circles
41 The typical Russian
42 Wimbledon champ, 1975-78
43 Spare
44 C as in composing
47 Group character
48 Bubkes
49 Boulder's zone: Abbr.
50 Bara of silents
54 Kettle and Clampett
56 Blubber
59 Hawk
61 "No bid!"
65 C as in cosmology
69 C as in counting
70 Star Wars heroine
71 Powerful
72 Blow it
73 Catch sight of

DOWN
1 "Surprise!" response
2 California county
3 Word before black or light
4 Book of pictures
5 D divided by II
6 Of sure touch
7 Whiskey gulp
8 Where Sam played piano
9 Turkish title
10 "Scram," to Spot
11 Prohibited
12 Fusses
13 Actress Rowlands
16 Genealogist's work
18 Saint Laurent fragrance
23 Unqualified
25 Burns headwear
26 "Super!"
27 Give your two cents' worth
28 Golfer's hole
29 Secret supply
31 Letters on some letters
33 Mr. T's former group
34 "A thing of beauty . . ." writer
35 Director Lubitsch
37 __ water (troublebound)
38 __ Moines, IA
39 Unwrinkle
40 Just off the bottom, as an anchor
45 Clue for Holmes
46 Beat the air
51 Olympic competition
52 Monopoly prop
53 Conductor Previn
55 Sap spout
56 Corner warning
57 Cry of disappointment
58 Sugar source
60 Agent
62 Iron and Bronze
63 It may come in
64 Visit
66 __ Loves Me ('63 musical)
67 Groaner
68 Dime portrait

339 MONEY WHERE YOUR MOUTH IS by Mike Shenk

ACROSS
1 Late-blooming flower
6 Sportscaster Albert
10 Asterisk
14 Nightclub
15 "I cannot tell __"
16 "Eat your broccoli __ dessert!"
17 Overdo it on expenses?
20 Loser that unseats a winner
21 Nerve center, literally
22 Vicinity
24 Eur. country
25 Reunion attendees
29 Italy's shape
31 Rather boss
34 Solitary
35 Third place, at Pimlico
36 Mao's successor
37 Sure bet
42 "Unaccustomed __ am . . ."
43 It lost to VHS
44 Part of M.A.
45 Sound stage
46 Jai __
47 Scarlett's neighbor
49 From __ Z
50 Early political cartoonist
52 Poker problem
56 "__ Is a Tramp"
61 Result if you 17 Across?
63 Cha-cha or foxtrot
64 Pennsylvania port
65 Put away
66 Variety
67 Author Carnegie
68 Burlesque bits

DOWN
1 Vigoda and Lincoln
2 Bathday cake
3 Notable Yugoslavian
4 Little case
5 Go back to the drawing board
6 Either of two skiing brothers
7 Bath brew
8 Torn and Van Winkle
9 Well done
10 Up to now
11 Journey
12 Powerful crawlers
13 Climbed
18 Actress Garr
19 Kind of punch
23 Avoid voting
25 Robert and Alan
26 Unstructured
27 Dark
28 Tormé or Tillis
30 Expression of surprise
31 Curmudgeon
32 Montana town
33 Stylish
38 That which eases
39 Granted a second mortgage
40 __-Puf
41 Slangy turndown
47 A Forest Hills stadium is named for him
48 Martin and Canyon
49 Proficient
51 Up __ (cornered)
52 Mile's equivalent
53 Concerned with
54 Joke or game ending
55 *Doctor Zhivago* heroine
57 Spill secrets
58 Opposed
59 Four-handed piano piece
60 Longings
62 Small, for short

340 HAIR TODAY, GONE TOMORROW by A.J. Santora

ACROSS
1 Deice
5 Author Alexander
10 Recording speed, initially
13 San __, Italy
14 Chocolate substitute
15 Yale Bowl partisans
17 Household presser
18 Baffle
19 Long hair
20 START OF A QUOTE FROM A LONG-HAIRED ROCK SINGER
23 Mauna __
24 __ Misérables
25 Ink, to Proust
26 D-sharp's alias
28 Tijuana's region
31 Prince or Holbrook
32 Vocal vibrato
35 Snitch
36 MIDDLE OF QUOTE
38 Mind-ful?
40 Pennsylvania town
41 Mule parent
42 "Somebody bet __ bay"
43 Inhibit
47 Passover bread
49 Wire-length unit
51 Born: Fr.
52 END OF QUOTE
57 Peewee
58 Drab hue
59 "__ Buy Me Love"
60 Loft voice
61 Takes the fight out of
62 Peter, Paul and Mary, e.g.
63 Uncommon sense
64 Auctioneer's patter
65 Actress Barbara

DOWN
1 Dally
2 A __ Our Time (Lermontov novel)
3 Qualmless
4 Refuses to
5 Cameo, for example
6 NFL cofounder
7 In __ (stagnating)
8 Predicament
9 Cain's kin
10 Bring in the substitutes
11 Coinmaker's blank
12 "20 Questions" category
16 *Black Beauty* author
21 Extreme
22 Verily
27 "Ma, he's making eyes __"
28 Cabaret
29 What's more
30 Skater Starbuck
33 Actor Richard
34 Card combination
35 Former Russian ruler
36 Moments
37 "I give up!"
38 Maple seed
39 Generally
42 Perfect-game line score, perhaps
44 Private
45 Baddy
46 Fictional town founder
48 Quote author's rock group
49 Expert
50 I.e., for long
53 Coll. training grp.
54 Uninteresting
55 Green bean
56 Entr'__

341 HATS ENTERTAINMENT by Ann W. Masten

ACROSS

1 Works hard
6 Oxford, for example
10 Cartoonist Al
14 Circa
15 From Ger.
16 Small, sweet sandwich
17 Don Carter's six-time title
20 Aquarium performer
21 Publicity piece
22 Poker payment
23 "__ fair in love and war"
24 Eastern European
27 Lose firmness
29 Whistle sound
33 Kiddie colorer
36 Bottle part
39 IV squared
40 "A drop of golden sun"
41 What's left
43 Watering hole
44 GI's hangout
45 Rock tune's attraction
46 Embryonic cell
48 Nota __
50 "I don' wanna!"
52 Was obligated to
53 Wander around
56 PDQ
59 School hymn
62 Thomas Jefferson was one
66 Smashing sport of a sort
68 Champagne bucket
69 Singer/actress Carter
70 Large family
71 What "sic" means
72 Medal metal
73 *Sesame Street* grouch

DOWN

1 File-folder parts
2 One of the winds
3 Corn country
4 A little night music
5 Suds mug
6 Boulders
7 Mag magnate, for short
8 Angry
9 Waters of song
10 Least direct
11 Neighborhood
12 Dinner veggies
13 Read carefully (over)
18 Deteriorate
19 House addition
24 Wash well
25 Undo
26 Polyester partner
28 Actress Ekberg
30 *The __ Incident* (Fonda film)
31 Sort of round
32 Pooped
34 Celestial sphere
35 At birth
37 Slangy relative
38 Crucial
42 California city
47 Errand boys
49 Fielder's bane
51 Prince of the theater
54 *Dynasty* commodity
55 Doing great on
57 DC VIP
58 Increase, as a collection
59 Mine passage
60 Car repairer, for short
61 Big bird
63 Norse explorer
64 Statesman Eban
65 Specialty hairdresser
67 Under the weather

342 QUESTIONNAIRE by Penny A. Roman

ACROSS

1 Roman wear
6 Mix and Selleck
10 Impresses a lot
14 Rub out
15 Smell __ (be suspicious)
16 Tea-time talk
17 Question in a kids' game
19 Carry around
20 Ending for expert
21 Guffaw, à la *Variety*
23 Put in stitches
24 "Ay, __ the rub"
27 Loafer, for instance
29 Least praiseworthy
30 British school of fame
31 Like sushi
32 Distributed, as cards
35 They may be convertible
38 St. __'s Fire
40 Put away for later
42 Pouched bread
43 Like some turkeys
45 Hogs' homes
47 Short Line and B&O
48 Roll of stamps
50 Passes by
52 Rings up
54 Earmark
55 Paw's wife
56 Engineering school, for short
58 Deteriorate
59 Suffix for smash or stink
61 Bugs Bunny's question
66 See 40 Across
67 "Are not!" response
68 Stupendous sales
69 Alter ego of fiction
70 "__-ho and a bottle . . ."
71 Actress Berger

DOWN

1 President pro __
2 Acapulco gold
3 Gangster's gun
4 Comparatively pale
5 Is furious
6 Highlands hat
7 Evangelist Roberts
8 Mexican Amerinds
9 Restrain
10 Play part
11 Lou Costello's question
12 Gone from the plate
13 One-pot dinner
18 __ Pieces (candy)
22 Goes well with
24 ". . . and __ a good night"
25 Start of a tongue-twister question
26 Sports data
28 The lowdown
29 Get ready for a quiz
33 Auctioneer's unit
34 Gave it a whirl
36 ". . . a poem lovely as __"
37 Backtalk
39 Melville novel
41 Specialty fishermen
44 Beer order
46 Enjoys fish and chips
49 Margin for error
51 Chicken dish
52 Fun gathering
53 Fool
55 Interlock
57 Morning side dish
60 Have yet to pay
62 On top of that
63 Put on
64 Baseball great Mel
65 Civil War initials

ACROSS

1 "Yabba __ doo!" (Fred Flintstone's cheer)
6 They may come home
10 Shiny rock
14 So all can hear
15 Considerably
16 Like so: Abbr.
17 Detective of oldtime radio
20 Ten times CLV
21 Bombs on the stage
22 Heart line
23 Hoodwink
25 Uncounted years
27 Former Alabama football coach
31 Bothers
35 Negates
36 What bonds represent
38 Turner of U.S. history
39 Too theatrical
40 Ultimate degree, for some
41 Addis __
43 Mess up
44 "Go," to the chickens
46 We __ Alone (UFO book)
47 Last word of a New Year's song
49 Sci-fi hero
51 Lunch time
53 Play start
54 Plastic wrap
57 Scale starters
59 Actor Beatty
62 Australian film of '86
66 "__ She Sweet"
67 Getting __ years
68 Essence of Mae West's invitation
69 Talks like a kid?
70 Self-images
71 Kovacs or Ford

DOWN

1 Hair-cream application
2 Grad
3 Presumptuous
4 Low-voiced croaker
5 Do sums
6 With wiles
7 Word on some London shop signs
8 Became more difficult
9 R-V link
10 Tropical tree
11 "Take __ leave it!"
12 Isn't up to
13 Filmdom's George Gershwin
18 Air-freshener targets
19 "What a piece of work is __"
24 Minds
26 Wagering hall, initially
27 Urban fleet
28 Way in
29 Give __ (care)
30 Kind of committee
32 Ridiculous
33 Cabinet department
34 Numbers of interest
37 Diviner's deck
40 Lopsided defeat
42 Rookie
45 Cable channel
46 Traveled around?
48 Makes into law
50 Valentine and Black
52 Beatle bride
54 Con game
55 Song for one
56 Author Jaffe
58 Minstrel-show section
60 First place
61 Mrs. Bruce Willis, once
63 Deer daughter
64 Manipulate
65 A foot wide?

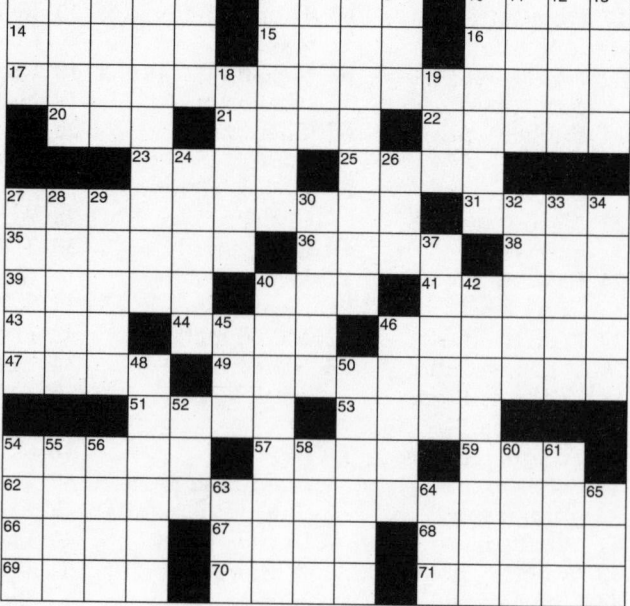

ACROSS

1 Sharp turns
5 Ending for trick and joke
9 Kooky one
14 Slangy suffix
15 Poshness
16 Broadcast
17 EARTH
20 Before
21 Black, in Brittany
22 London art gallery
23 Patsy
25 Night spot
27 The gang
30 Says further
32 One of Bach's instruments
36 Copper head?
37 In __ (in original position)
38 Words of warning
39 MERCURY
42 Home of a Rose of song
43 It may call
44 Pop
45 Elegance
46 An old story
47 Piano pieces
48 Woody's boy
50 Zeus' partner
52 Iowa State city
55 "Eat your vegetables __ dessert!"
57 Put away for a while
61 PLUTO
64 Supplementary
65 __ buco
66 Patsy Cline, for one
67 Vermont resort
68 Russian refusal
69 Spotted

DOWN

1 Comic actress Pitts
2 De-wrinkle
3 __ alone (solo)
4 Spheres, e.g.
5 Road sign
6 Called on
7 World's fair, for short
8 Traces of the past
9 Follower
10 City slob
11 Pavarotti piece
12 Superman's secret identity
13 Penetrating power
18 Bug in the winter
19 Coach Parseghian
24 Satchel of baseball
26 Third point, in tennis
27 Repair-bill line
28 Scrub a mission
29 Wallace running mate
31 Fuddy's follower
33 Forest clearing
34 As plain __
35 Cries out for
37 Show scorn
38 An Enemy __ People
40 Cockeyed
41 Privy
46 Young adherent
47 Auntie Em's home
49 Filmdom's Nora Charles
51 Potential trout
52 Wally of cookie fame
53 Catcher's catcher
54 Audio replay
56 Prying
58 Shiftless
59 Bird house
60 Designer Von Furstenberg
62 Poetic preposition
63 Guzzler

345 HANDIWORK by Trip Payne

ACROSS

1 What pledges pledge
5 Letter opener
9 As of yet
14 "__ Lomond"
15 Depend end
16 Man with a horn
17 South Seas spot
18 Evening, in ads
19 "Have __!" (host's request)
20 Short description
23 Red man?
24 Rudolf and Myra
25 Qum citizens
28 Presidential middle name
30 Actress Jeanette or Kathleen
31 What you can see
32 Pop
36 Punch in the mouth
39 Identical
40 Sushi-bar fare
41 New Haven collegian
42 Unadorned
43 Starts eating, with gusto
44 Gives a start to
48 *Fear of Flying* author
49 Locate
55 Tolerate
56 Icicle spot
57 Teased
58 Send $$
59 Fit to __
60 Give off
61 Utopian spots
62 Not as much
63 Unenviable grades

DOWN

1 Skip about
2 __ Hashanah
3 Rights grp.
4 See 5 Down
5 With 4 Down, Ketcham character
6 Early computer
7 Overture follower
8 Rod attachment
9 Nonplussed
10 Desert stops
11 Stews (over)
12 Quickly
13 Author Philip et al.
21 Precipice
22 Comic Dick
25 Print-shop assortment
26 Barrett of gossip
27 Grad
28 Usher territory
29 Farming fields
31 Deviate
32 Walked arrogantly
33 Some paints
34 XLIII x XIV
35 "Even as __ gathereth her chickens . . .": Matthew
37 New car option
38 Laying an egg
42 Stephen Vincent and William Rose
43 Gift getters
44 Diagonal line, on a bowling score sheet
45 How bouillon is bought
46 "Once upon __ . . ."
47 Thinking man's sculptor
48 Kids
50 Notary's need
51 Clotho, Lachesis, or Athropos
52 Vatican City's surroundings
53 Garfield's pal
54 NBA team

346 REMEMBERING ROCK by Bill Hendricks

ACROSS

1 Science room, for short
4 Michael of tennis
9 Fundamentals
13 "It's Impossible" singer
14 Gulf Coast city
15 Perfume holder
16 Rock Hudson film of '68
19 Rock Hudson film of '51
20 Bandleader Tommy or Jimmy
21 Knight's title
22 *Peer* __
23 Spanish "*chez moi*"
27 Big book
28 Energy
31 Have __ for news
32 Brass-band instrument
33 Panasonic rival
34 Rock Hudson TV series, 1971-76
37 Guys
38 Chopped down
39 Moray catcher
40 Cortés' quest
41 Thumbs-up votes
42 Gets permission for
43 Just __ (minimally)
44 Colonial descendants' grp.
45 Fashion photographer Richard
48 Frequent Rock Hudson costar
53 Hudson film with 48 Across
55 Gait
56 "__ Be There" (Michael Jackson tune)
57 Genesis son
58 Winter glider
59 Party attendee
60 Actress Zadora

DOWN

1 Places
2 Part of AFL
3 Bartlett's cousin
4 Ballparks
5 Spud
6 Fake: Abbr.
7 Navy rank, initially
8 Part of the maintenance staff
9 Stave off
10 Chest protectors
11 Meticulousness
12 Do in
13 Spy org.
17 Mortarboard hanging
18 Sector
22 Spoil
23 Rumba relative
24 Bring down upon oneself
25 Mini-band
26 Warts and all
27 Melodies
28 Magician's word
29 Draw conclusions
30 Fort __, FL
32 Imposed a levy
33 __' Pea (*Popeye* kid)
35 Bomb on stage
36 Actress Dolores
41 Molecule bit
42 "Honest Ed's Auto Land," e.g.
43 Said more
44 Lenient ones
45 Cobras' kin
46 Scallopini need
47 Suffix of action
48 Lavish attention (on)
49 Trade
50 Figure-skater Thomas
51 Land measure
52 Designer monogram
54 __-TURN (highway sign)

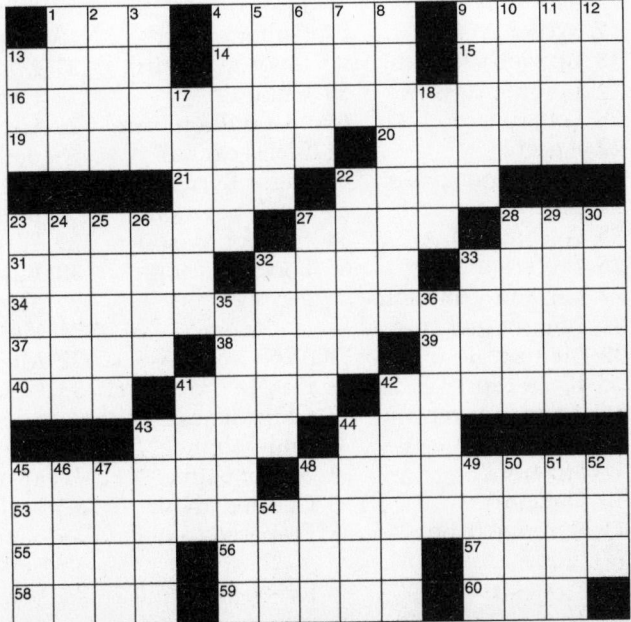

GETTING AROUND by Rich Norris

ACROSS

1 Tiny, in Scotland
4 Rig on the road
8 Shade trees
12 Prom flowers
14 Find innocent
16 Attendance check
17 Black-and-blue mark
18 Region
19 JFK's predecessor
20 Lifts up
21 Basil-based sauce
23 Go no more
25 Part of I.R.S.
27 Video game sites
32 To's opposite
35 Slugger Hank
38 Tabriz native
39 Charge-card system
42 __-trump (bridge bid)
43 Showing no emotion
44 Punch relative
45 Animal that eats tree leaves
47 Model Carol
49 Work the land
51 Put up
55 "Never mind!"
59 Scull propeller
62 Love, to Livy
63 Royal residence
64 Charlie Sheen sitcom
66 Places for bracelets
67 Hides
68 Capone's nemesis
69 Govt. workplace watchdog
70 JFK arrival

DOWN

1 Metal leftovers
2 Bruce Willis' ex-wife
3 1888 van Gogh destination
4 Animal pouch
5 "Zounds!"
6 Pinochle holding
7 Spots of land
8 Prefix with lateral
9 San __ Obispo, CA
10 Vapor
11 Fr. holy women
13 Chair parts
14 More than dislike
15 UFO evidence, to some
22 White House room
24 Ballroom dance
26 Cleveland cager, for short
28 "__ you for real?"
29 Infant's word
30 City west of Tulsa
31 Locale
32 Throat clogger?
33 Actor Santoni
34 "Your turn," to a CBer
36 Chorus platform
37 Canadian province: Abbr.
40 Stop __ dime
41 Bush's org., once
46 Mythological trio
48 Slight indication
50 Rapidly, in music
52 Gives off
53 Pigeon coops
54 Rendezvous
55 Stretch across
56 *Citizen* __
57 Types
58 Good buddies
60 Simians
61 Charlie of country music
65 Powerful D.C. lobby

SPORTS SLIP-UPS by Fred Piscop

ACROSS

1 That guy
4 NBA great Gilmore
9 Tear to shreds
14 Fruit drink
15 Uncouth ones
16 "That's __" (Dean Martin song)
17 Writer Anaïs
18 Bowler's least-favorite dessert?
20 Gauzy fabric
22 Accent
23 Like some glass
24 Salerno sendoff
25 Accomplished
26 Professor's deg.
27 Cow, in Colombia
31 Integra maker
34 Hammock holder
35 Bit of Morse code
36 Tennis player's least-favorite location?
40 Concorde
41 Remove from office
42 "__ a Grecian Urn"
43 Shoemaker McAn
45 Legal matter
46 College sr.'s test
47 Angers
49 Tyrants
53 Tel Aviv greeting
56 Planetary movement
57 Golfer's least-favorite villain?
59 Chou En-__
60 __ a million (rare)
61 Swiss capital
62 Actor Byrnes
63 April payment
64 Jobs for Mason
65 Food coloring, e.g.

DOWN

1 Puts in the closet
2 Chucklehead
3 Brainy bunch
4 Tirana native
5 Gadded about
6 Prepared to play
7 __-Tass
8 Job-application info
9 Dreadlocked one, for short
10 Off-the-cuff comedy
11 Barbershop fixture
12 *Exodus* author
13 Bide-a-Wee adoptions
19 Stage whispers
21 Mideast gulf
24 Deceive
26 Get the wrinkles out
28 Together, musically
29 Wyo. neighbor
30 Business letter abbr.
31 Helper: Abbr.
32 Moolah
33 Golden Rule word
34 Some test answers
37 Scale opening
38 Gives up
39 Skillful
44 Berle's nickname
46 "Buy two, __ free"
48 Colorful horses
49 "Light My Fire" band
50 Like well-maintained machines
51 Yes-man
52 Sarcastic
53 Loch Ness local
54 Mandlikova of tennis
55 High point
56 Actress Perlman
58 *Today* network

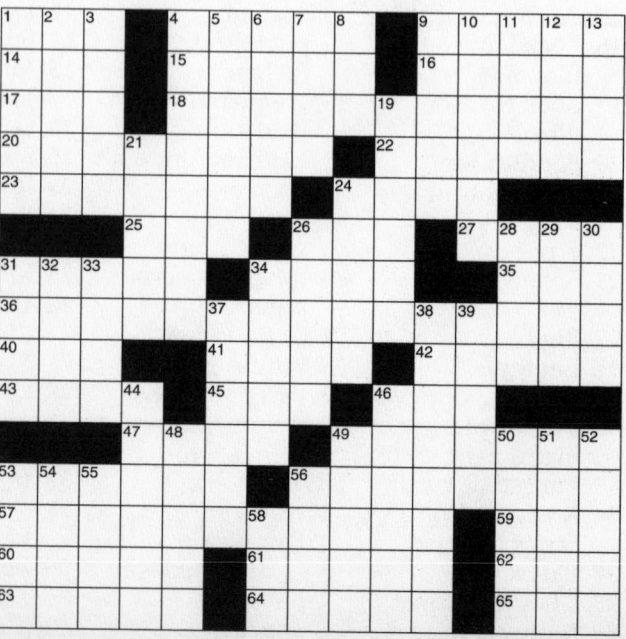

349   SPECIAL DELIVERY by Bill Swain

ACROSS

1 __ es Salaam
4 Eagle's nest
9 Spanish friend
14 Devon river
15 Group of trees
16 Religious grp.
17 Quickly
19 City in Israel
20 Heroine of *The Good Earth*
21 Mrs. Helmsley
23 Nol of Cambodia
24 Conductor Georg
26 Dealer's choice
29 Summer on the Somme
30 Govt. advisory grp.
33 Jay & the Americans song
34 *Kidnapped* author's initials
35 Sphere start
37 Crushable hats
38 Flexible armor
40 Snow White, comparatively

43 Cruise and Conti
44 In addition
47 Capital of Kazakhstan
49 Worldly West
50 Surprising word
51 Cowboy's dread
53 Chambers
55 High crag
56 Midway marks
59 *Inter* __
60 Some collegians
63 Calligrapher's concern
65 Those opposed
66 Closer to reality
67 Bishopric
68 Certain Jamaican
69 Gets out of bed
70 Males

DOWN

1 Ouster
2 Salamander of the Southwest
3 Used purchases
4 Hardwood tree
5 And others: Abbr.

6 Knock down, in London
7 Like a tug's cargo
8 Paradisaical
9 Pt. of speech
10 __ *culpa*
11 Get excited
12 Pull out all the stops
13 Bearse and Plummer
18 Explosive letters
22 Space Camp's home
25 Randomly piled
27 *An American Tragedy* author
28 Icahn or Sagan
31 Golf course employee
32 Friend, in France
36 Que. neighbor
38 Study at the last minute
39 *Mr.* __ (Keaton film)
40 Ferrari, e.g.

41 City in Pennsylvania
42 Turkish inns
44 Do away with
45 Election hopeful
46 Medicinal quantities
48 Grownups
52 Chicago-based critic
54 Paddle
57 Needle case
58 Gang ender
61 Morse unit
62 987-65-4321 grp.
64 Hesitator's sounds

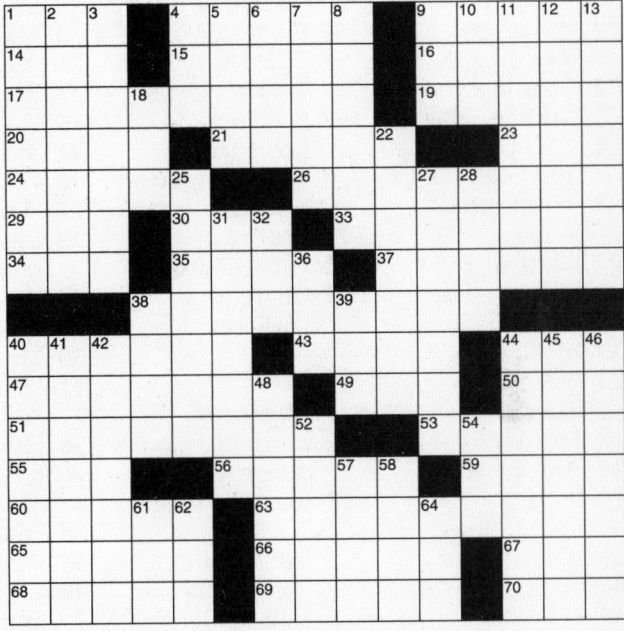

350   TEA FOR TWO by Wayne Robert Williams

ACROSS

1 Smoke residue
5 Unit of capacitance
10 Stanch
14 Taj Mahal site
15 Nina of perfumes
16 Actress Hatcher
17 Neil Simon play
19 Grub
20 Scorers
21 Aerial attacks
23 Western hemisphere
26 San __, Italy
27 One of Regan's sisters
29 Squealer
32 Dinner and a movie, perhaps
36 Carpenter's board
38 Yoked pair
39 Borden's cow
40 Cross letters
41 Double-dealers
43 Smile broadly

44 Pixie
45 Soup holders
48 City on the Oka
50 Inconvenience
55 *Backdraft* extra
58 Spanish dish
59 Social insects
60 Green-and-tan vehicle, e.g.
63 Family plan?
64 John and Lionel's sister
65 Wire spiral
66 Power center
67 Puppeteer Lewis
68 Scenery chewers

DOWN

1 Vertebrae bases
2 Old Irish alphabet
3 Pontificate
4 Thin candle
5 Watercolors on a wall
6 Broadcast
7 New G.I.

8 Top cards
9 Denunciation
10 "__ Heat" (*Pajama Game* song)
11 Half-off sale
12 Art Deco artist
13 Pass over
18 H.S. class
22 Depend (on)
24 Rack element
25 Blows a gasket
28 Pot bumper
30 Identifiable atmosphere
31 Car adornment
32 Act overly fond
33 Eddie, in *Beverly Hills Cop*
34 Batting a thousand, maybe
35 Adjective suffix
37 White lie
39 Takes after
42 List element
46 City in *Italia*

47 Graceful bird
49 Change a timer
51 Nut tree
52 Metals company
53 Miner's stake
54 Malone and Marx
55 Pool legend, familiarly
56 Regarding
57 Eur. kingdom
61 "So *that's* it!"
62 Yukon, for one: Abbr.

TOOT SUITE by Fred Piscop

ACROSS

1 Minor Prophet
5 Rum cakes
10 Actress Ward
14 Actress Virna
15 In plain view
16 Puritan
17 Arthur of tennis
18 TV deputy
20 Japanese beetle, e.g.
22 Clinton's veep
23 Author Follett
24 __ Lopez (chess opening)
25 Bandleader Larry
27 Footballer portrayed by James Caan
33 Musical asset
34 Indonesian island
35 Lux and Ivory
39 And others, in brief
41 Reputations
43 Pianist Peter
44 Spanish mister
46 Is introduced to

48 Burgle
49 Some campaign appearances
52 Computer-screen indicator
55 __ Khan
56 One: Sp.
57 Urgent
60 Ore. peak
64 Pie feature
67 __ la Douce
68 Tropical fruits
69 Sanctum preceder
70 __ off (started golfing)
71 Stair part
72 Hibachi needs
73 Charged particles

DOWN

1 "Too bad!"
2 Catchall category: Abbr.
3 Job-safety org.
4 __ Club (conservation group)
5 Hair holder

6 Actress Gardner
7 Glacier breakaway
8 Florence's river
9 Hi-fi
10 Tanning-lotion letters
11 Soaps star Slezak
12 The Birdman of Alcatraz was one
13 Representative
19 Hollers
21 Mom's sister
26 Hired thug
27 Honey makers
28 Deserve, as a raise
29 Where Farsi is spoken
30 Mosque leaders
31 Hale-Bopp, e.g.
32 Angler's basket
36 Flying word form
37 Stage item
38 Weeps
40 Weather zones
42 Clambake morsels

45 __ Island Red
47 An NCO
50 Of an eye part
51 *Bounty* stop
52 Sleeve ends
53 Dark
54 Khmer __

58 Nevada city
59 Author Ferber
61 Hydrox lookalike
62 Prophetic sign
63 June honorees
65 Recipe meas.
66 Toothpaste type

EXPLETIVES SECRETED by Ann W. Masten

ACROSS

1 Take down __ (demote)
5 "Scramola!"
9 __ Kosher (fit for any rabbi)
14 __ contendere
15 Puerto __
16 Irritate
17 Chances are
20 Dexterity
21 Cheer competitor
22 Sunrise direction
23 Rims
25 Where theories are tested
27 Tinkerbell, e.g.
30 Singer Vikki
31 Dictionary tag: Abbr.
34 *The Good Earth* heroine
35 Blueprint
37 Resource
39 Toon magpies
42 Abdominous
43 Measured amount
44 Narrow in the foot
45 Knight or Kennedy

46 Goatee locale
48 Strawberry of baseball
50 Actress Madlyn
51 Potatoes alternative
52 "I wouldn't do that!"
55 Queue after Q
57 652, to Caesar
61 Some German politicians
64 Woodworker's tool
65 *Omnia vincit* __
66 Greek drink
67 Man of La Mancha
68 Small grid gain
69 Have on

DOWN

1 C __ (cola brand)
2 Unsatisfactory
3 Singer Fitzgerald
4 Tiger Woods' workplace
5 "It's cold!"
6 Shopper's memos
7 It follows Sept. 30
8 Forested areas

9 Main mail bldg.
10 Script elements
11 Light blue
12 Sounds of disapproval
13 Run-through
18 Working hard
19 Cherished
24 __ Le Pew (cartoon skunk)
26 Burns' hillside
27 Not __ (mediocre)
28 First-year cadet
29 Ran
30 Contrapuntal composition
31 Actor Werner
32 Stop, at sea
33 Sneak into second
36 Onetime ballpark promotion
38 Role for Ray Bolger
40 Walesa of Poland
41 Obi-Wan Kenobi, for one
47 Throw hard
49 Like a versatile appliance
50 Big game

51 Bit of gossip
52 Dangerous creepers
53 Bagel middle
54 Open __ of worms
56 Musical motif
58 German physics Nobelist

59 Chichén __
60 "Is You __ Is You Ain't My Baby?"
62 Meteorologist's word form
63 Former fort near Monterey

353 PUZZLER'S PHRASES by Nancy Salomon

ACROSS
1 Bit of a tiff
5 Shade of blond
8 Permanent place?
13 Fashion mag
14 Straight up
16 Commoner
17 Old King
18 Shopaholic's delight
19 Golfer with an army
20 Puzzler's clue remark?
23 Wind dir.
24 __ room (family place)
25 Picked straws
26 Puts under the gun
28 Lyricist Gershwin
31 Fergie's first name
34 List ender: Abbr.
35 Teen fave
36 Puzzler's lament?
40 Rent a garment
41 It may get picked out
42 Track events
43 Storm center
44 Went "boo!"
47 Hood's knife
48 Nancy's hubby
49 Gaming cube
52 Praise, as a puzzler would?
56 Ecclesiastical law
57 Rainbow
58 Shake __ (hurry)
59 Kicking partner
60 Superior, e.g.
61 Unaccompanied
62 Doles (out)
63 Outlaw
64 Very: Fr.

DOWN
1 Religious groups
2 Snow movers
3 Give the nod to
4 Maddened, with "off"
5 *Jeopardy!* revelation
6 Medium meeting
7 Holy headgear
8 Outpourings
9 Robin's weapon
10 Newman's role in *Blaze*
11 Potpourri
12 Maiden-name preceder
15 Takes care of
21 "The Lady __ Tiger?"
22 Upright
26 Reliever's feat
27 "Hollywood Nights" singer
28 Goofing off
29 Big defeat
30 Pub potables
31 Something to build on
32 Sailor's greeting
33 Atypical
35 Chilled the champagne
37 Gone
38 Hardship
39 Change, as a bill
44 Polishes
45 Ruling threesome
46 Let out the belt
47 Hot spot
49 Grief
50 "Goodnight" gal
51 Sidles
52 Chalky white
53 Curriculum division
54 Snatch
55 Poet Whitman
56 Engine part

354 MOVIETOWN by Bill Swain

ACROSS
1 Cathedral service
5 One of the Simpsons
9 __-ski
14 Cooking chamber
15 Hebrew measure
16 South Korean city
17 Eddie Murphy, in an '84 film
20 Double whole notes
21 Military command
22 Captivated
23 Noggin
24 O.T. book
27 Jane or John
28 Olds auto
30 Harebrained
32 Cheech Marin's origin in an '87 film
35 Melville novel
38 12/24 or 12/31
39 O.T. book
40 Michael J. Fox, in a '91 film
45 Ustinov memoir
46 Play about Capote
47 Rocky crag
50 Orch. section
51 The same, on the Seine
54 In
56 Blue mineral
58 1850s war zone
59 Gloria Swanson's address, in a '50 film
62 Make a law
63 Virgin Mary's mother
64 Diminutive ending
65 Taxco cash
66 Afternoon affairs
67 Ride the thermals

DOWN
1 Jam-packed
2 Entrance to Hades
3 Drastic
4 Auto-racer Tom
5 Add support to
6 One of Alcott's girls
7 Betty Ford Clinic's purpose
8 Hackneyed
9 Games host of '96
10 Go by
11 Gate
12 Hot-dog's problem
13 Dine
18 Publishable copy
19 Purchase alternative
25 Delta deposit
26 O.T. woman
29 Like Nash's lama
31 Took advantage of
32 Nobelist of 1922 or 1975
33 Wall growth
34 Witches' brew ingredient
35 Chances
36 French wine
37 Terra-cotta instruments
41 Brunch items
42 On the up-and-up
43 Those with special sight
44 Highly unconventional
47 Popular soup
48 Code of silence
49 Audio-book performer
52 Standing by the plate
53 Sierra __
55 Buzzy places
57 Walgreen's competitor
59 IRA type
60 French one
61 Actress Merkel

COLUMNIZATION by Wayne Robert Williams

ACROSS
1 Tends to the furnace
6 Simple floater
10 Tar's mop
14 Formal proclamation
15 Switch ending
16 Distinctive air
17 Party game
19 Baby bouncer
20 *Uno + due*
21 Stacks
22 Aromatic wood
23 Certain lead
25 Unstructured
27 Burrs, e.g.
29 Burned by the sun
32 Comic Carvey
35 RR stop
36 Well-grounded
38 Draw forth
40 Lady of Sp.
42 Wilted
43 Glacial pinnacles
45 "Evil Woman" rock group
47 War god
48 One way to get to Carnegie Hall
49 Aussie lefty
52 Contain
54 Cattle
58 Actress Irene
60 Painter Rembrandt
62 Spacewalk, to NASA
63 Oodles
64 Marsh bird
66 Flatfish
67 Where most people live
68 Special K rival
69 Clairvoyant
70 *Jurassic Park* actress
71 Dispassionate

DOWN
1 Profundity
2 Worship
3 Molière's Harpagon, e.g.
4 P.D. district
5 "Don't do that!"
6 Ponders
7 Racer Luyendyk
8 Upper deck, briefly
9 Golf-club part
10 "__ alive!"
11 *Kiss Me, Kate* song
12 Neighborhood
13 Boxer Max
18 End of a French film
22 Charges
24 Japanese city
26 Hosp. locales
28 Playwright Capek
30 Model Macpherson
31 Poor grades
32 Lucie's dad
33 State with conviction
34 Top of the world
37 Video-game name
39 Beige shades
41 Certain southerner
44 Distress signal
46 Convex molding
50 Oust
51 Olympics categories
53 Western
55 "Peachy!"
56 French resort
57 Ride in space
58 Football play
59 __ vera
61 Eastern leader
64 Scoundrel
65 Go bad

ENGINEER TALK by S.N.

ACROSS
1 Porous gems
6 Letter carrier's burden
10 Actress Nelligan
14 Ignited again
15 __ close to schedule
16 Israeli airline
17 Digresses
20 Pancake pan
21 Hard rubber
22 Have coming
23 Alphabetic trio
24 One of these
27 Compass reading
29 "A guy walks into __ . . ."
33 Tailor's work
34 Talk like Daffy Duck
36 Miss Molly of song
38 State one's views
41 Little laugh
42 Paris airport
43 Prefix for classical
44 Singer Guthrie
45 Ring result
46 Tree beginning
47 Western Indian
49 Pig of films
52 Pricey spice
56 Hermitic
60 Orderly ideas
62 Dry as a desert
63 Deepest Great Lake
64 Like the Mississippi
65 Unadorned
66 Founded: Abbr.
67 Clockmaker Thomas et al.

DOWN
1 Special-interest grps.
2 Cheat at Hide and Seek
3 Word form for "height"
4 Cotton threads
5 Roman robe
6 Towel asset
7 Termite, essentially
8 Stick together
9 Dobie Gillis' buddy
10 *Show Boat* composer
11 Jai __
12 Mediator's must
13 Actress Sommer
18 Iron: Fr.
19 House crawler
24 Greek letter
25 Witch, often
26 Urge forward
28 Frighten
29 __ Baba
30 "April Love" singer
31 French year
32 Patch up a lawn
34 Gettysburg loser
35 Ending for expert
36 $1,000,000, for short
37 Whichever
39 Greek letter
40 Certified, as a will
45 Choral section
46 Unthreatened
47 Coffee brewer
48 "We're Off __ the Wizard"
50 Wood for bats
51 Simpletons
52 Wild guess
53 Irish expletive
54 Impartial
55 Bona __
57 "__ the sun in the morning . . ."
58 "I wouldn't do that!"
59 Express trains: Abbr.
61 Apropos

BORDERLINE by Rich Norris

ACROSS

1 Polite form of address
5 Opposite of fem.
9 Flower growing areas
13 USC rival
14 Spotted horse
15 Bluish green
16 Amaze
17 *Jeopardy!* contestant, e.g.
18 Ballerina's skirt
19 The Rockies, for one
22 Wee tykes
24 L.A. Lakers' org.
25 Earl Grey or pekoe
26 Landers or Miller
27 Greenish blue
30 Means of approach
32 Carry with effort
34 Theatre district
36 Hypothetical ape-human connection
40 Lawn gadget
41 Fake
44 Show good manners
47 Cook's condiment
50 Be indebted
51 Before, to a poet
52 Feminine word ending
54 Tooth covering
56 Couldn't decide
60 *The Thin Man* dog
61 Western film
62 Phonograph, for short
65 Smell bad
66 Sarcasm
67 Son of Seth
68 Goofs up
69 Watch over
70 Meal plan

DOWN

1 Bandleader's subj.
2 Do something
3 Foil material
4 Lord's land
5 A little fog
6 Singer Paul
7 Beer mug
8 Heavy-handed sentimentalist
9 Shower option
10 Represent as the same
11 Obligations
12 Spa offerings
14 Kind of violet
20 Family member, familiarly
21 Desert plants
22 Scrooge's complaint
23 Santa __, CA
28 Like the Gobi
29 Dressed to the __
31 Partner of pros
33 Kudrow of *Friends*
35 Taj Mahal site
37 Rome's hill complement
38 Makes certain
39 An Ayatollah
42 Great admiration
43 Director Brooks
44 Cautionary word
45 Pencil end
46 *The Scarlet Letter* character
48 Suspicious (of)
49 Former country sta.
53 Stock unit
55 Was sore
57 Acorn sources
58 School on the Thames
59 Ward (off)
63 Enemy
64 Follower: Suff.

GEO-METRICAL by Lee Weaver

ACROSS

1 "And __ goes"
5 Indonesian island
9 Conks on the head
13 German auto
14 Small flutes
15 Fairway hazard
16 London area honoring Lord Nelson
19 Outrageous
20 Intimidate
21 Leave port
24 Vends
26 Make tracks
27 Parasite
31 Neckline shape
32 Made a misplay
35 Sun-dried brick
37 Mysterious region of the Atlantic
43 Project step
44 Washday worry
45 Midwest clock abbr.
47 *Olympia* painter
50 Compete in a slalom
51 Capital of Japan
53 Disliked intensely
56 *Bambi* aunt
57 Like some winds
61 Imaginary line in penguin land
66 Witnessed
67 Decimal fraction
68 Amenable (to)
69 Whirlpool
70 Bath et al.
71 Neighbor of Thailand

DOWN

1 Took a chair
2 __ *Town*
3 Neighbor of Mont.
4 Minor arguments
5 Move like gelatin
6 A long way off
7 Actress Miles
8 Part of YWCA
9 Heat meas.
10 Delphi VIP
11 One way to shorten a sentence
12 Erupts
14 Thresh grain
17 Pie __ mode
18 Milk amounts: Abbr.
21 *Rawhide* actor Wooley
22 Home for Yeats
23 Land area: Abbr.
25 Big happening
28 Devoured
29 Naval off.
30 __ polloi
33 Out of gas, as a tank
34 "That was dumb of me!"
36 Coll. degrees
38 Beaver project
39 Quiet __ mouse
40 Deep cut
41 Enjoy
42 City west of Tulsa
45 Put something over on
46 Emulated Hans Brinker
48 Chooses (to)
49 Brit's flashlight
51 Back-comb hair
52 Above, in verse
54 Poetic pugilist
55 Austrian Alpine region
58 Play parts
59 Short distance
60 Singer Turner
62 Unspecified amount
63 Numbers cruncher: Abbr.
64 July sign
65 Naval off.

FOLD-EROL by Patrick Jordan

ACROSS
1 Used, in a way
5 Alan Ladd classic
10 Baez or Jett
14 He loved an "Irish Rose"
15 Apply, as liniment
16 Wheel shaft
17 FOLD
20 Brief argument
21 Artful Dodger's mentor
22 "I should say __!"
23 Cenozoic or Mesozoic
25 Sunburn soother
27 FOLD
35 That guy
36 Sir, in Stuttgart
37 Admit bluntly
38 Scepter toppers
40 Native American corn
43 Oscar-winner Sorvino
44 Trifling
45 Newcastle export

47 President pro __
48 FOLD
53 Spicy fast-food item
54 Arafat's grp.
55 VCR adjuncts
58 Center of a crowd
61 Allstate rival
65 FOLD
68 Hussein's domain
69 Did in
70 Bison bunch
71 Phobos orbits it
72 Arizona State site
73 Humorist Bombeck

DOWN
1 Funny fellows
2 Clarinet cousin
3 Civil disturbance
4 Genderless
5 Sellout letters
6 Angry mood
7 "Fernando" band
8 Candy bar ingredient
9 Store fodder

10 Brady girl
11 Yoke wearers
12 In addition
13 Hatchling's home
18 Statue of Liberty feature
19 Aware of
24 "May I interrupt?"
26 Mild cheese
27 Bite hard
28 Personnel manager, at times
29 Shadow
30 Coach Parseghian
31 Instant
32 Madonna role
33 Composer Ned
34 Hindu teacher
39 Religious offshoot
41 Leopards are spotted here
42 OK Corral name
46 Purplish shade
49 Pack (down)

50 Most wintry
51 Pamper
52 *Faust* dramatist
55 Physically fit
56 Janet's sister in *Psycho*
57 *The Lion King* villain
59 Thailand, before 1939

60 Stumble
62 Wedding-cake layer
63 *Cheers* character
64 "... __ partridge in ..."
66 Mensa measurements
67 Compass dir.

HIDDEN MUSIC by Wayne Robert Williams

ACROSS
1 *Fort Apache: The Bronx* characters
5 Letter openers?
10 Part of a procedure
14 Roundish shape
15 "__ to you!"
16 Mrs. Nick Charles
17 Rake
18 Baseball great Musial
20 Actress Greene
22 Thin paper
23 Container for personal gear
25 Followed a curved trajectory
29 Monica of tennis
30 Seminole chief
32 Novelist Dostoevski
34 Function
35 Chipper
36 Beattie or Blyth
37 Poseidon alias
40 __ mater

41 Actress Swenson
43 Adversary
44 *Paris __* (Baudelaire work)
46 Tabletop brewers
48 Disenchanted fan
49 Metal fasteners
50 Shopkeeper
53 Request
56 Bigot
57 Book keepers
61 TV handyman
62 Actress McClurg
63 Up to
64 Gymnastic maneuver
65 Utensil
66 ... *Cuckoo's Nest* author
67 Contemporary Irish singer

DOWN
1 Prepared a baked apple
2 Convex moldings

3 '92 presidential candidate
4 Fell, as ice
5 Oohs' partners
6 Siamese fighting fish
7 Golfer Stadler
8 Lions' lairs
9 Approximations, briefly
10 Lip curler
11 Male turkey
12 Time period
13 Woodlands deity
19 '40s DC panel: Abbr.
21 Synthetic fiber
24 Deprived (of)
26 UN goal
27 Beast of Borden
28 Former Israeli defense minister
30 Columbus sch.
31 Detection device
32 Belief
33 Word form for "nine"
34 Western Indian
38 Loc.

39 Time period
42 Garb
45 French port
47 Greek mountain
48 Quarterback Kosar
50 Castles' defenses
51 Nice __ (prig)

52 Refrain syllables
54 Ex-Phillie John
55 Cash penalty
57 Permit
58 Wedding vow
59 H.S. subj.
60 Crafty

361 PLUGGED IN by Rich Norris

ACROSS

1 Sweethearts
5 Conditional phrase
9 Parts of a list
14 Guitarist Clapton
15 Singer Horne
16 Combines, as ingredients
17 Baptism, e.g.
18 Bulletin-board fastener
19 Midler or Davis
20 Running out of time
23 Influential group
24 Spot of paint
25 Brit. fliers
28 Police investigator: Abbr.
29 Make fun of
33 Mystical meeting
35 Splatter catchers
37 Hard to find
38 Means of release for feelings
43 Sitarist Shankar
44 Moves like a mouse
45 Quick drawing
48 Hung on to
49 __ Na Na
52 Always, poetically
53 __ Cruces, NM
55 Rule of conduct
57 Kept up-to-date
62 Threesomes
64 Twist out of shape
65 Therefore
66 Seeps slowly
67 Cupid's Greek counterpart
68 Rich Little, for one
69 Destitute
70 Wet, as morning grass
71 June honorees

DOWN

1 Got the cattle together
2 Baltimore player
3 Dolt
4 Agreeable odor
5 Choir member
6 Do an usher's job
7 Move slowly
8 Made believe
9 Have a drink
10 Stadium level
11 Not from within
12 Bumped into
13 Opposite of NNW
21 Allegro, largo, etc.
22 Existed
26 Land measure
27 Elevation units
30 Gold: Sp.
31 Pros and __
32 Special aptitude
34 They may be liberal
35 Working hard
36 Gin flavoring
38 Gaelic
39 Earn, as money
40 Like some atlases
41 "Alley __!"
42 Say
46 Very stylish
47 Loft material
49 Himalayan guide
50 Like a door
51 Cast members
54 Stitched
56 Tire feature
58 Word after open or pigeon
59 Challenge
60 Boast
61 "__-daisy!"
62 Heavy weight
63 Wade opponent of 1973

362 HOLD EVERYTHING by Norma Steinberg

ACROSS

1 Pants accessory
5 Part of a stair
10 Snakes
14 Opera solo
15 Quitter's word
16 Stubborn beast
17 Nervous wreck
19 Dueling weapon
20 Fall flower
21 Sahara-like
22 Breach of security
23 Vacation spot
25 Corporal's reply
27 Secondhand
29 Nun's garb
32 Liquid conduit
35 Subtlety
39 Keatsian output
40 I: Ger.
41 Office machines
42 Minuscule
43 Gingery drink
44 Words of warning
45 Family group
46 Endures
48 Mexican sandwich
50 Snitch
54 Harass
58 Parts of circles
60 Fifty percent
62 Composer Eubie
63 Source
64 Land near the Mississippi
66 Run in neutral
67 __ a customer
68 Hardens
69 British alphabet enders
70 Troubled
71 Model Macpherson

DOWN

1 Elephant king of kiddie lit
2 Delete
3 Agendas
4 Menu option
5 Boring routine
6 Ancient Peruvian
7 Hair-raising
8 '20s actress Janis
9 Bulrushes
10 Aviatrix Earhart
11 January event
12 Entreaty
13 Car-radio button
18 Goofs
24 Barbershop quartet part
26 "__ only a bird . . ."
28 Hoodwink
30 Think-tank output
31 Numerical ending
32 "Don't touch that __!"
33 Pasadena campus
34 Wintertime woe
36 Feel poorly
37 Finch's home
38 Elite
41 Expenditure
45 Artistic arrangement
47 Samples
49 "The Georgia Peach"
51 Pulsate
52 He sang "High Noon"
53 Santa's helpers
55 Artist's stand
56 Ability
57 High-strung
58 Calif. neighbor
59 Took the escalator
61 Celebration
65 "Baloney!"

363 WOODWORK by Henry Hook

ACROSS

1 Solidarity name
5 Assure
10 Historic baseballer Larry
14 Acapulco eight
15 Singer Lopez
16 Opinion
17 Pavement piece
18 Successful
19 Enjoy the tub
20 Pull down
21 Sapporo stage show
22 Cretan flier
24 Patsy
26 Swearwords
28 Hikes the auction price
30 Mohawk River city
34 With 41 Across, boiled-meat dish
37 Woody Allen book
39 During
41 See 34 Across
42 Split
43 Woody Allen book
46 Hog house
47 Phonograph needles
48 The __ Queene
50 Apprehension
52 Attack verbally
56 Solver's desire
59 Haw preceder
61 Kimono accessory
62 Fizzy refresher
63 Lindbergh's view
65 Androcles' rescuee
66 In any way
67 The pits
68 Come through the cracks
69 "Smooth Operator" singer
70 Beezers
71 Little biter

DOWN

1 Mislays
2 Brilliance
3 Cugat ex
4 What loners won't do
5 Unhearing
6 Inventor Rubik
7 Woody Allen book
8 Numero of note
9 Larklike bird
10 Cataclysm
11 Bloodhound's find
12 Gentleman caller
13 Won't shut up
23 Drink the whole bottle
25 Jazz job
27 Individually
29 Slam-dunks
31 "The Blue Tail Fly" singer
32 Dollar fraction
33 Rooney of 60 Minutes
34 Freebie ticket
35 Fail to discuss
36 Like some sums
38 Health-food stuff
40 Washington's hurdle
44 __ kleine Nachtmusik
45 Actor Alastair
49 Script postscript
51 Out of kneepants
53 Shop steward's charge
54 Legendary Browns placekicker
55 Song for three trios
56 Poker pair
57 Exploding star
58 Citizen Kane prop
60 Sybarite's delight
64 Amorous sound

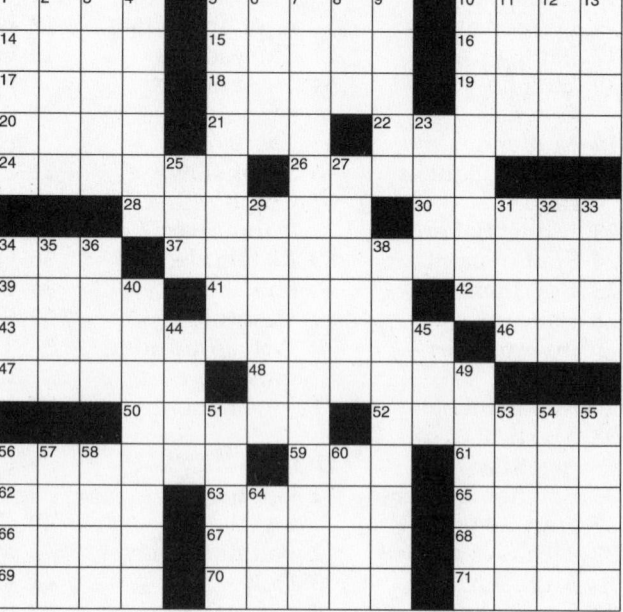

364 FITTING CONCLUSIONS by Wayne Robert Williams

ACROSS

1 Holm and McKellen
5 Recorded
10 Simple floater
14 Sioux tribe
15 Use a soap box
16 New York canal
17 Eternity
20 Decorative bush
21 Ways to go
22 "Das Lied von der __"
25 Prima donna's problem
26 Traditional conclusion of summer
34 Overjoy
35 Dining experiences
36 Afr. nation
37 Actress Virginia
38 Anklebone
39 Storage building
40 Latin 101 word
41 Some hors d'oeuvres
42 Dwight's two-time opponent
43 James Taylor tune
46 Meese and McBain
47 Hearts or diamonds
48 Passover meal
51 __ Juarez, Mexico
56 Creedence Clearwater Revival song
61 Actor Auberjonois
62 "__ and sometimes Y"
63 Lamb's pen name
64 Cater to
65 Leases
66 Depend

DOWN

1 State Fair locale
2 The gamut
3 Writer Ephron
4 Order to a broker
5 Facing
6 Onassis, to pals
7 One way to stand
8 Numerical ending
9 __ volente
10 Captured back
11 Vicinity
12 Discover
13 Turner and Danson
18 Tractor maker
19 Gives arguments for
23 Moynihan colleague
24 Lace targets
25 Cave-dwelling fish
26 Former Air Force bigwig
27 Cottonwood
28 Louisiana backwater
29 Word form for "ear"
30 Wisconsin city
31 M. Zola
32 First name in fastballs
33 Artoo Detoo, e.g.
38 Stops a stealer
39 Star Wars: Abbr.
41 Guerrero of baseball
42 Bandleader Shaw
44 Went off course
45 Triangular shawls
48 Wave action
49 Dueling sword
50 Polonius or Ophelia
52 Over, in Aachen
53 Remove text
54 Indigo dye
55 6/6/44
57 Former Mideast nation: Abbr.
58 Wedding-notice word
59 Cacophony
60 Small child

365 SPENDING SPREE by Patrick Jordan

ACROSS
1 Up to it
5 Mac maker
10 Elegant living
14 Futile
15 Unarmed, in a way
16 Dull pain
17 START OF A QUIP
20 Singer Cassidy
21 Where the Owl and the Pussycat went
22 Crime-lab sample
23 Language suffix
25 Approximately
27 Letter abbr.
30 PART 2 OF QUIP
36 Aquarium process
38 Atlantic food fish
39 Ten C-notes
40 Eye drops
43 Field of interest
44 Lose ground?
46 Wedding service
48 PART 3 OF QUIP

51 Wind dir.
52 Region: Abbr.
53 Actor Wheaton
55 Paragon of patience
58 It's tapped for sap
61 Corporate symbols
65 END OF QUIP
68 Kismet
69 "C'est __!"
70 Casino game
71 Bend
72 Cut quickly
73 Mass agreement

DOWN
1 Alamo rival
2 Chaucer's Wife of __
3 Sax-playing Simpson
4 Come afterward
5 A pip of a card?
6 City map
7 Colombian coin
8 Covers
9 Becomes a contestant

10 Computer memory
11 Topped the tarts
12 At that time
13 Epsilon follower
18 Beginning
19 Saharan sanctuaries
24 Sartre's No __
26 Boxer De La Hoya
27 Pizzeria patron
28 India's first prime minister
29 Sing like Bing
31 Usher's creator
32 Portray
33 Gagarin and Andropov
34 Some tourneys
35 Grammarian's concern
37 Taxpayer's dread
41 Encouraging word
42 Bouillabaisse, e.g.
45 Moriarty, to Holmes
47 *Our Town* girl

49 Drags a net
50 Isolated line of type
54 Certain sponge
55 Daniels of *Trial and Error*
56 Like Bush's office
57 __ noire

59 Matchmaker Dolly
60 Norse mariner
62 Its capital is Agama
63 Grimm creature
64 In a moment
66 Critic Reed
67 "A mouse!"

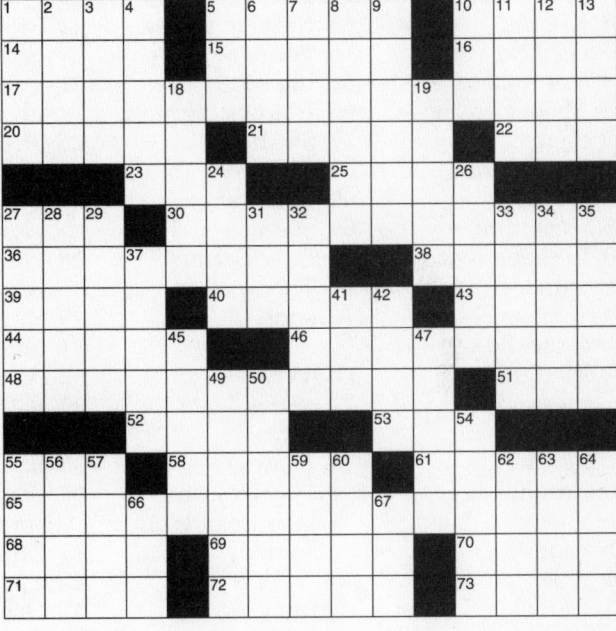

366 GENERALLY SPEAKING by Craig Kasper

ACROSS
1 Nuclear missile's cargo
6 Largest land mass
10 Beside oneself
14 Greyish-brown shade
15 Arctic
16 Silent performer
17 For the most part
19 Not quite round
20 AMA members
21 Detroit footballer
22 New York borough
24 Bandleader Puente
25 Giant-sized
26 Legree et al.
29 Afternoon social event
32 One hundred smackers
33 Schooner's poles
34 Make a knot
35 Permed hairstyle
36 Poetry
37 Talking doll's word

38 Bruce or Pinky
39 Tractor maker John
40 Birthday desserts
41 One's belongings
43 Cathedral cleric
44 Large chasms
45 Like jackhammers
46 Pontius __
48 __ to Five (Jane Fonda film)
49 Dole's grp.
52 Unspoiled place
53 For the most part
56 In addition
57 Demolish
58 Napoleon's fate
59 Actress Harper
60 Related (to)
61 Turn off

DOWN
1 Molecule constituent
2 Musical group
3 Alibis
4 Speedometer letters

5 Direct route
6 "Gesundheit!" preceder
7 In a minute
8 Under the weather
9 Sufficient
10 One-celled animal
11 Approximately
12 Neighbor of Yemen
13 Some toothpastes
18 Funny folk
23 Baseball officials
24 Oz pooch
25 Outlaw James
26 Head part
27 Draw a conclusion
28 Approximately
29 Linger
30 Race statistics
31 Bread ingredient
33 Track competitions
36 Back bone
37 Manor cleaner
39 Sure-handed

40 More nasty
42 Home instruments
43 Frog's hangout
45 Bedsheet fabric
46 Boggy soil
47 Not in use

48 Indiana Jones foe
49 Hold onto
50 Stare at
51 Banana covering
54 Shoot the breeze
55 Lumberjack's need

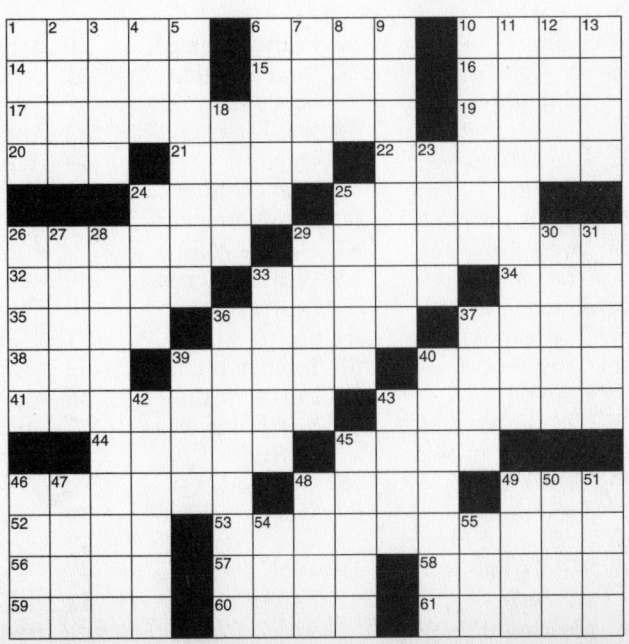

STRETCHING THE TRUTH by Fred Piscop

ACROSS
1 Slot inserts
5 Piglike animal
10 Troubadour
14 Hershey's Syrup rival
15 Ease up
16 Toledo's lake
17 Gaucho's weapon
18 Gogol's __ *Bulba*
19 *Glamour* rival
20 Contrabass
22 Make a crease
23 Sharp instruments
24 Dunces
26 Gets thinner
30 Independence-gainer of 1991
34 __ glance (quickly)
37 Modern messages
39 Advertising lights
40 Brown-bagger's lunch, perhaps
43 Santa __, CA
44 Brazilian dance
45 Daniel __-Lewis

46 Skedaddles
48 Inclined
50 In apple-pie order
52 Grouch
56 Fake coin
59 Ranch sleeping quarters
63 Hired car
64 Russian writer Bonner
65 Big butte
66 It flows through Stratford
67 66 Across, for one
68 Green shot
69 Silents star Theda
70 Bullock film
71 Therapeutic spots

DOWN
1 *Miami Vice* role
2 Circa
3 Tummy
4 Plays for time
5 Jacques of French comedy
6 ". . . no such thing as __ boy"

7 Colleague, out west
8 Novelist Calvino
9 Close the envelope again
10 Meal in a can
11 First name in folk singing
12 Small brook
13 Monopoly card
21 Computer-data identifier
25 Triple-time dance
27 __ *Mine* (George Harrison book)
28 Hitter of 660 homers
29 Rug fiber
31 Null's partner
32 Andean of old
33 Pallid
34 The basics
35 Bath powder
36 Banned apple spray
38 Glittery fabric
41 Citrus drink
42 Hoop grp.

47 Cavalry weapons
49 Outdoes
51 Tiny Tim's favorite flower
53 Exhaust
54 Socialite Perle
55 H.S. juniors' exams

56 Wild guess
57 Vesuvius outflow
58 Wife, in legalese
60 Glacial snow
61 Place for a pants patch
62 Like some cider

ONE-WORD WESTERNS by Rich Norris

ACROSS
1 Give a hoot
5 "Mothers of Invention" name
10 Caron role
14 "That's not __ idea"
15 Ram in the sky
16 Aware of
17 Tidings
18 Spotted horse
19 Bank abbr.
20 Greek capital
22 James Arness western
24 Circus prop
25 Majors or Marvin
26 Actor Chaney
27 Danson of *Cheers*
28 Laugher of Kenya
32 Not whispered
34 Summer cooler
35 DDE's WWII command
36 Partner of fits
37 Will Hutchins western
40 Heading up

43 Damage somewhat
44 Air-rifle ammo
47 Make improvements to
48 Spaghetti
50 Mine find
51 Debussy's "*La __*"
52 Pollution grp.
54 Poet Stephen Vincent __
56 James Garner western
59 Leaseholder
60 Oklahoma city
61 Hint of color
63 With 64 Across, Lestat creator
64 See 63 Across
65 Ten sawbucks
66 Industry VIP
67 Road or poll ending
68 Vagabonds
69 Makes leather

DOWN
1 Card game
2 Aided a felon

3 Clint Eastwood western
4 Auto of '57
5 Nukes
6 Jackie's second
7 Engine noise
8 "Downtown" singer Clark
9 United
10 Actor Neeson
11 Unlike most '50s TV shows
12 Anti-union tactic
13 Has in mind
21 High degree
23 ". . . from __ shining . . ."
29 Safecracker
30 Greek vowel
31 __ *Rae*
33 Long. crosser
36 Alphabetize
37 Fall from grace
38 In the category of
39 Notes after mis
40 Butters
41 "No, seriously!"
42 Restaurant's concern

44 Lorne Greene western
45 *The Real McCoys* star
46 Hunting dogs
48 *City Hall* actor
49 Presidential nickname
53 Hurl

55 Make into law
57 Hesse's river
58 Door opener
59 Starts a golf hole
62 Sports car of song

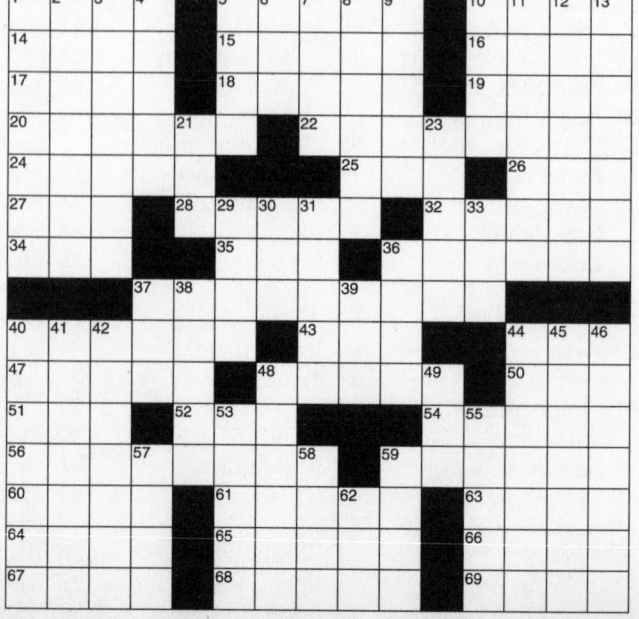

ACROSS

1 Rock and roll Mama
5 Poker variety
9 Implant
14 Hoss' older brother
15 Aaron Spelling's daughter
16 Nary a soul
17 Carry-on bag
18 Western Samoa capital
19 Gators' kin
20 April, as per Eliot
23 That girl
24 Sort
25 Joplin piece
26 Court
28 Streisand role
30 Base's opposite
32 Apprehensive feeling
33 Furniture wood
35 *Nightline* network
36 Tardy
37 1997 John Cleese film
42 Landers' namesakes
43 Corrode
44 Butter serving
45 Division word
46 Compadre
48 Element #54
52 Contemptible
53 Lbs. and ozs.
54 Poetic verb
56 *Xanadu* band
57 Sticky predicaments
61 Rambled
62 Lawn tool
63 Part of TAE
64 Cowboy's transport
65 Tons
66 Cambodian currency
67 Franklin's fifth cousin
68 Sicilian spouter
69 Soccer great

DOWN

1 Easily remembered
2 Actress Renée
3 Titan circles it
4 Hook's toady
5 Stretch, in a way
6 Kansas city
7 *Trinity* author
8 Lengthy denunciation
9 Disguised, for short
10 Norse goddess of fate
11 Sneaks, for example
12 At an early stage
13 Crosses out
21 Perfume flower
22 Impulsively wild
27 Useful metals
29 Statue element
31 Menu
32 Rampal's instrument
34 __ oneself (be secretive)
37 Stop working
38 Be creative
39 Mixed up
40 Poetic pauses
41 It strains
47 Musician's affirmative
49 Journalist Bly
50 Standardized test in Britain
51 Register key
53 Like Chicago
55 Michelangelo work
58 Like some dorms
59 Shaker contents
60 Quibble
61 Queue after Q

ACROSS

1 Antis
5 Summers, for short?
9 Rock singer Khan
14 *The Thrill __ All*
15 Unseat
16 Globetrotter legend
17 Unsatisfactory
18 Bachelor, perhaps
20 START OF AN ART LINKLETTER QUOTE
22 __-mutuel betting
23 PART 2 OF QUOTE
28 Tough to take
29 Blanc of cartoons
30 Strawberry, for one
34 Lesley __ Warren
35 Video format
36 Home on high
37 Mineral spring
38 Sired
39 Kind of cat
40 Ordinal ending
41 Give pleasure to
42 Close rel.
43 Long stepper
45 END OF QUOTE
51 '97 earthquake site
52 Hamlet's kin
53 Dough flattener
57 Time-__-half
58 "Eight Days __"
59 Actress Louise
60 Viewed
61 Hang in the air?
62 Back of a brogan
63 Illustrator Rockwell

DOWN

1 __ plea (bargains, maybe)
2 *The Skin __ Teeth*
3 Mythical weeper
4 Walk like a rooster
5 Farm machinery
6 Associate judge
7 Stubborn sort
8 __ dime (halts quickly)
9 Mild cigars
10 Blood-related
11 "__ to understand that . . ."
12 Decks
13 Termite, e.g.
19 Panama Canal dam
21 __ Island Red
24 Clearly described
25 Symbol of resistance
26 Alloy element
27 Gladden
30 Disney classic
31 Get the facts
32 Whether __
33 Put the kibosh on
35 Ask for alms
37 Toughness
38 Hard rock
40 Allen of Vermont
41 __ retention (optic phenomenon)
43 Perfect pitch
44 Heavenly
46 Helped out the Tin Man
47 Canteen kin
48 Saree wearer
49 Utah city
50 Tried to say
53 Dustcloth
54 Barn dweller
55 Floral greeting
56 Fruit-filled dessert

UNDER CONTRACT by Norma Steinberg

ACROSS
1 Nautical cry
5 Ugly Duckling, eventually
9 Nuke, as leftovers
12 Relocate
13 He hit 61 homers in '61
15 Ashen
16 Spin doctor
18 Wight, for one
19 __ Salvador
20 Chief exec.
21 Once-a-year
23 Cliques
24 Gator's kin
25 Strut
28 Skillful ones
32 Salesperson
33 Jerk
34 Front of a ship
35 Sitarist Shankar
36 Notebook contents
37 Raison d'__
38 Prayer response
39 Roman poet
40 Fairy-tale figure
41 Entrée choice
43 Easter hat
44 Sentence fragment
45 Like venison
46 Hamilton or Harrison
49 French father
50 Poem
53 __ mater
54 Accordion
57 Cry
58 Pachyderm's teeth
59 "__ lay me down to sleep . . ."
60 Barbie's boyfriend
61 Aide: Abbr.
62 Fender flaw

DOWN
1 Bandstand equipment
2 Israeli dance
3 Pizzeria appliance
4 "Uh huh!"
5 Wise guy
6 Salary
7 War god
8 Diarist Anaïs
9 Actress Pitts
10 __ breve
11 Fruit covering
14 Race official
15 Miser
17 Talk
22 Negative votes
23 Plastic packaging
24 Made do
25 Throw out
26 Memorable mission
27 Become separated
28 Words to a hitchhiker
29 English playwright
30 The Velvet Fog
31 Sugary
33 Biblical king
36 Neediest
40 *Addams Family* name
42 Fireplace filler
43 Least adorned
45 Nerds
46 Rubberneck
47 Robt. __
48 Augury
49 "__ in Boots"
50 Woodwind
51 Duck feathers
52 Way out
55 Sine __ non
56 Conclude

HOME SWEET HOME by Rich Norris

ACROSS
1 Performance
5 Auntie of Broadway
9 Snake with a hood
14 Bluefin, for one
15 Not home
16 An archangel
17 Came down
18 Ivy League school
19 Cooking appliance
20 Salad topping
23 Cabbage unit
24 Slip a __ (err)
25 Cheap and showy
28 Bikini part
30 Used needle and thread
34 Figure of speech
35 Diets, with "down"
37 By way of
38 Protest formally
41 Before, to a poet
42 Extends across
43 Pass, as a law
44 Family rooms
46 Also
47 Small bus
48 Railroad unit
50 Biblical trio
51 Milk product
57 Lagoon surrounder
59 Vichyssoise ingredient
60 Theater level
61 Bamboo-eating mammal
62 "¿Que __?"
63 Region
64 Lock of hair
65 Pitcher Hershiser
66 Unpleasant situation

DOWN
1 Sky sight
2 Waikiki dance
3 Getting __ years
4 House guardian
5 Word of distress
6 Oscar or Edgar
7 Oscar or Edgar
8 Peepers
9 Collector's item
10 Bornean apes
11 Harry Lillis Crosby
12 Rule, for short
13 Tap choice
21 Mercury, to the Greeks
22 Troublemaker
25 Like some floors
26 Admire greatly
27 Make broader
28 Fair-haired fellow
29 Canyon borders
31 French spa
32 Flinch
33 Well-dressed
35 Examine carefully
36 Winter vehicle
39 Split up
40 1862 battle site
45 Gives a dressing-down
47 *The Day of the __*
49 Cartographer's project
50 Reagan Cabinet member
51 Ice-cream holder
52 Kal Kan rival
53 Equipment
54 Ireland, to the Irish
55 Goes out with
56 Memorable times
57 Fitting
58 Road covering

ECONOMICS COURSE by Trip Payne

ACROSS
1 Greek vowels
5 Army meal
9 Put into office
14 Scared one's sound
15 "Movin' __" (theme from *The Jeffersons*)
16 Le __, France
17 Pre-World War II period
20 Beatle Ringo
21 Church seat
22 Part of a sock
23 Young goat
25 *Shampoo* Oscar-winner
28 Insecticide
32 __ Paulo, Brazil
33 Prefix for verse or corn
34 Western actor Jack
36 Ridiculous
40 Economic innovation
44 Filch
45 Author Ferber
46 Snakelike fish
47 Leg, slangily
49 Author Steel
52 Make over
56 Byelorussia or Ukraine, once: Abbr.
57 "It's a __-win situation!"
58 Crash into
59 Wipe out
63 Like some modern-day parts
68 Because of
69 __ day (vitamin dosage)
70 __-do-well
71 Wimp
72 Whirlpool
73 Wet, as morning grass

DOWN
1 Soufflé ingredients
2 Small pie
3 On the ocean
4 Fire starters
5 Fashionable, '60s-style
6 WSW's opposite
7 Economic forces
8 Binge
9 Questioning sounds
10 __ Vegas, NV
11 Film about the Peróns
12 Sing like Sinatra
13 Group principle
18 Excursion
19 Some sheep
24 Three: Ger.
26 Author Sheehy
27 Barrett of gossip
28 Roses-to-be
29 Military group
30 United Way request
31 Shampoo ingredient
35 "__ Lisa"
37 Biblical shepherd
38 Caroler's song
39 __ Stanley Gardner
41 Othello's foe
42 Moravian or Croatian
43 Rooting section
48 Chagall of art
50 Phrase of understanding
51 Trip to the grocery, e.g.
52 Refrigerator visits
53 Waiting-in-line feeling
54 Musical symbols
55 Western resort lake
60 Have __ in one's bonnet
61 Whole bunch
62 Like a haunted house
64 Spielberg's aliens
65 Rogers or Acuff
66 Actor Beatty
67 Author Talese

THINK COOL THOUGHTS by Wayne Robert Williams

ACROSS
1 Basics
5 Presidential nickname
8 Soft-drink choice
14 Capital of Okinawa
15 __ Rio, TX
16 Captured back
17 Nomads
19 And others: Lat.
20 More rational
21 *My Little Margie* star
23 *Peter Pan* beast
25 Quatro of *Happy Days*
26 Collegiate cheer
28 Drag behind
30 Attitude
35 Infamous Amin
36 Chair part
38 Man with a hammer
39 Statuesque
41 Sturm und __
43 Hindu teacher
44 Self-confidence
46 Debatable
48 Actor Alastair
49 Henry Moore piece
51 Capek play
52 With it
53 Alternative to 8 Across
55 Track surface
57 Quick pix
62 Toxin or surgeon starter
65 Oval crustacean
66 C&W legend
68 *Friends* character
69 Mineral deposit
70 Graven image
71 Gave lip to
72 Jazz fan
73 Sounds of reproach

DOWN
1 "No ifs, __, or buts!"
2 Theda of silents
3 Squirrellike rodent
4 *60 Minutes* man
5 Lemon drink
6 Ice mass
7 Lanchester and Schiaparelli
8 Stymieing competition
9 Greek wine
10 French state
11 Alone
12 Rope fiber
13 Actor Tamiroff
18 Moves at a quick pace
22 Abner's radio partner
24 Heartless
26 Hayworth and Moreno
27 Change with the times
29 Simple card game
31 Go for the gold
32 Cash for illicit political purposes
33 Spooky
34 Top suit
37 Highland hat
40 Tennis shot
42 Neither's partner
45 Tiny life form
47 Traveler's tote
50 Actor Wallach
54 Kind of committee
56 Meet again
57 Knight's backup
58 Workplace watchdog grp.
59 Playwright Anita
60 Big galoots
61 Actress Gilbert
63 Castle
64 Temple team
67 After expenses

375   SHELLFISH REMARK by Patrick Jordan

ACROSS
1 Unskilled workers
6 Bloodhound's scent
11 Paint daintily
14 Send into ecstasy
15 *Home Improvement* character
16 Sigmund's self
17 START OF A QUIP
19 Altar constellation
20 Abound
21 Layabout
23 Holds in contempt
27 Logged a payment
29 Invested with power
30 Honeycomb parts
31 Rabin's predecessor
32 PART 2 OF QUIP
37 ". . . __ o'clock scholar"
38 T-shirt label abbr.
39 Humorist Bombeck

40 PART 3 OF QUIP
44 Colorado resort
45 "Believe it __!"
46 Haystack hider?
48 Meals, slangily
51 Speech
52 Expedition
53 Baseball surname of fame
54 Greek letter
55 END OF QUIP
62 Valise
63 Actress Adorée
64 Otherworldly
65 Have being
66 Gives the appearance
67 Mead's study site

DOWN
1 Honored architect
2 Tiny toymaker
3 Morsel for Mister Ed
4 Utmost degree
5 Stew in one's own juices
6 Al Bundy's wares
7 Salon offering
8 49 Down product

9 Like some jobs
10 In an amusing way
11 Started the hand
12 Correspond
13 Room's partner
18 Overgrown, perhaps
22 Break an attachment
23 Wallace's '68 running mate
24 ". . . and __ grow on!"
25 Parting word
26 Quisling
27 Educator Bok
28 "Evil Woman" group
30 *Rhumba Is My Life* author
33 *Stand and Deliver* star
34 Profession
35 Jannings et al.
36 Breathing sounds
41 Overdue bills
42 Compass dir.
43 __ the line (last stop)

47 Draws out of
48 Inge dog
49 Middle Eastern sheikdom
50 Grammarian's concern
51 Burn soothers

53 "Up and __!"
56 Actor Horsley
57 Unified
58 Grassland
59 Slot-machine lever
60 "*O Sole __*"
61 Sargasso, for one

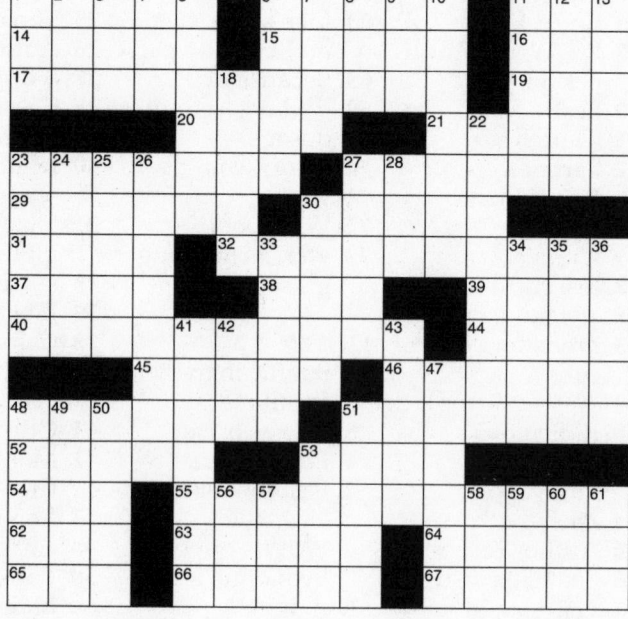

376   MEASURING UP by Lee Weaver

ACROSS
1 Comic Carvey
5 Fragrant wood
10 Long way off
14 Unrefined metals
15 Old saying
16 Bishop of Rome
17 Angler's equipment
19 Work as a model
20 Musical notes
21 One's manner
22 Tried to reduce
24 Hourglass contents
25 Not against the rules
26 Journey
29 Showing respect for
32 Egg-shaped
33 Stair part
34 __ long way (last)
35 Exhaust
36 Hardened
37 Those over there
38 Goal
39 Hopeless case

40 Ownership document
41 One with doubts
43 Suitable for evening wear
44 Licorice-like flavoring
45 Data-speed unit
46 Money in Spain
48 Send a package
49 Yellow Pages entries
52 Singer James
53 Shoelace tie
56 Small bills
57 Showy display
58 Gumbo ingredient
59 __ a one (none)
60 Oscar-winner Field
61 Moby Dick seeker

DOWN
1 Remove, as a hat
2 Diva's big moment
3 Scottish loch
4 Hibachi residue

5 Wolf or fox
6 Trimmed the lawn
7 Repair a sock
8 In the past
9 Blushed
10 Show up
11 Stage illumination
12 Church recess
13 Cattail, e.g.
18 Mirror reflection
23 Composer Stravinsky
24 Fill to the brim
25 Also-ran
26 Took part in the election
27 Sheepish?
28 Railroad superintendent
29 Backpacker, e.g.
30 Yuletide songs
31 Tasting like venison
33 Indian queen
36 Prom-time posies
37 Deadlocked

39 *True __* (Wayne movie)
40 Factually
42 On pins and needles
43 Delicately pretty
45 Run-of-the-mill
46 Unskilled laborer

47 European volcano
48 Teen's hangout
49 Egyptian cross
50 Mrs. Copperfield
51 Wild guess
54 Magnavox competitor
55 Campground initials

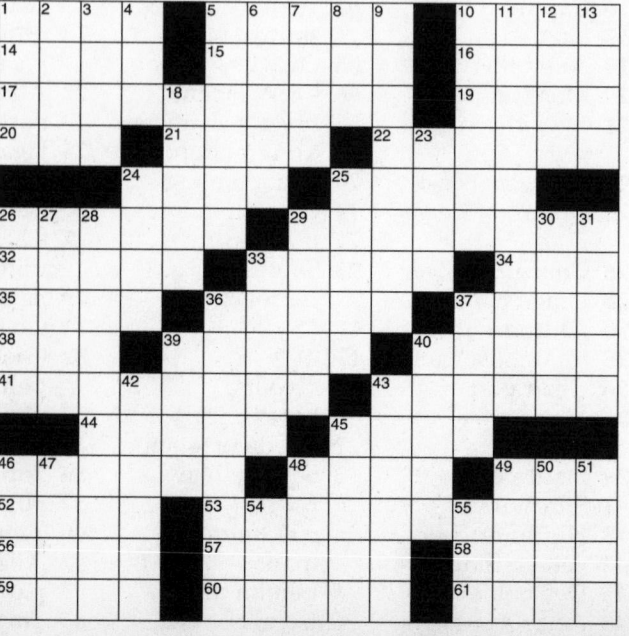

SMALL FRY by Ed Stein

ACROSS

1 Rooting section
5 Old Russian ruler
9 Colors crudely
14 Iridescent gem
15 "Pay __ never-mind!"
16 Arctic structure
17 Give or take a few
18 "Give a __ horse he can ride"
19 Slammin' Sam
20 Juvenile menace of comics
23 Shrewd
24 Give it __ (go for it)
25 *The Hustler* star
29 TV interference
30 Hog home
31 Yoko __
32 Reynolds competitor
35 Canyon effect
37 Hill builders
38 Nightgown wearer of rhyme
41 "No ifs, __, or buts!"

42 Peace Nobelist Wiesel
43 Careless
44 Citizen's suffix
45 "It __ a Very Good Year"
46 Melt
48 Flings
50 Dirty air
51 Set a price
54 He once had a playhouse on TV
57 *10* star
60 Word form for "eye"
61 Until
62 Any way
63 Golden Spike state
64 Gradual
65 Macho
66 Metric pound
67 Cacklers

DOWN

1 See 2 Down
2 With 1 Down, tricksters' big day
3 Snide
4 Pigeonhole

5 "A __ be born . . ."
6 Where flights can be found
7 Irk
8 Path
9 Entertainment conglomerate
10 Nixon's first V.P.
11 Ending for mod or nod
12 Feathery scarf
13 Lay down the lawn
21 Polynesian porch
22 Under protection
26 Order members
27 Legislative opponents
28 Intrusive
29 Scatters seed
30 Steel-mill output
32 Be in store for
33 Slow tempo
34 Gives up
36 XVII x VI
37 From the top
39 Hire
40 P.R. man's concern

45 Like some newspapers
47 Santa's sound
49 Length of time
50 Numerical prefix
51 Adequate
52 Squelched

53 "The Shadow __"
55 *The Winds of War* author
56 Charge
57 Stop up
58 LAX stat
59 Skedaddled

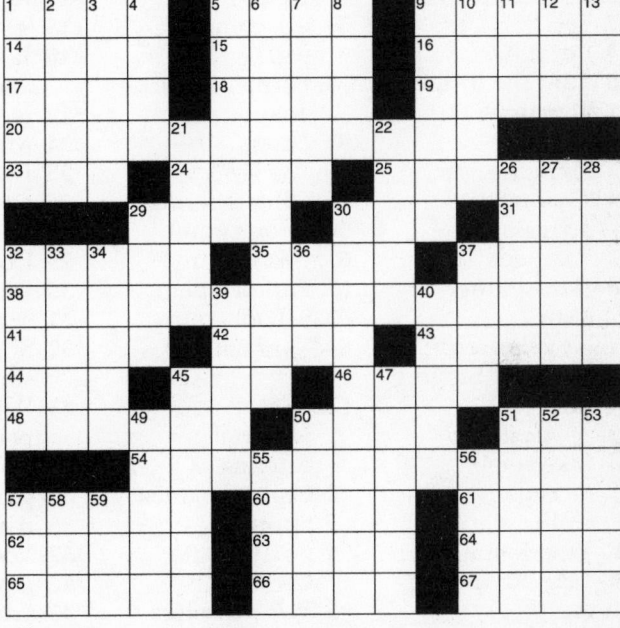

GADGETRY by Fred Piscop

ACROSS

1 Tanning-lotion letters
4 Bungle
9 Broad scarf
14 Kids' card game
15 Glacial ridge
16 Grid coach Don
17 Candle count, perhaps
18 Doodad
20 Actress Stapleton
22 Mythical warrior
23 Like some track meets
24 Prefix for mural
25 Fields of expertise
27 Go hither and thither
31 Hutu foe
34 Perlman of *Pearl*
36 Author Fleming
37 Doodad
41 Elemental suffix
42 Having wings
43 Kid hidden in kids' books

44 On __ (working)
47 Violinist Mischa
49 JFK Interior Secretary
51 Stiff-coated dogs
55 *Doktor Faust* composer
57 Fully attended
58 Doodad
60 Zilch
61 Nostalgic tune
62 Papas of film
63 Parapsychology letters
64 Flaxen-haired
65 Defied
66 Slangy "sure"

DOWN

1 Mystic
2 Unbeliever
3 Psychoanalysis founder
4 Speedy
5 "Rock and Roll __ to Stay"
6 Potato covering
7 Place to relax

8 Piano kin
9 Eritrea's capital
10 Comics exclamation
11 Stephen King beast
12 Actress Lena
13 "You're it!"
19 Ship-to-shore vehicle
21 Cut of meat
24 *Moby Dick* crewman
26 Lake bordering Kazakhstan
28 Comic Cosby
29 Put down, as track
30 Word form for "within"
31 Poke fun at
32 "No way!"
33 Submissive
35 James __ Jones
38 Cuba's capital, to a Cuban
39 Came to
40 Bandleader Lester

45 "This __ . . ." (bulletin intro)
46 Having a scent
48 Danson, on *Cheers*
50 Fatty compound
52 19th-century chief justice

53 Pop up
54 Graceful woman
55 Weevil's meal
56 Reverse
57 Liner's landing place
58 Cos __, CT
59 Song syllable

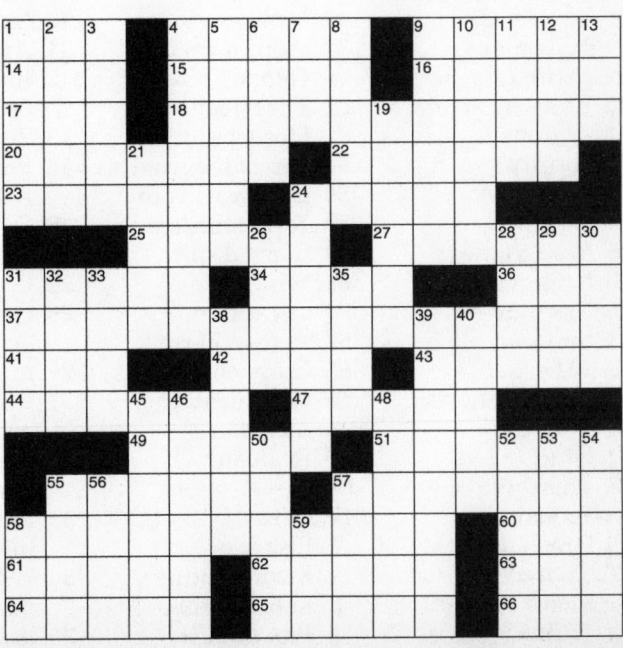

AND JUSTICE FOR ALL by Rich Norris

ACROSS
1 Fare carriers
5 Golfer Julius
10 Carson's predecessor
14 Vicinity
15 "__ America Singing"
16 Fabled meanie
17 *The Trial* author
19 Put down
20 Raid the fridge
21 Dynamic opening
22 Homeric epic
23 *The Client* actress
27 Parched
28 11th-century date
29 Novel essence
31 De Niro/Stone film
33 __ *About You*
36 Like some recruits
37 Golfer's goal
38 Take-home
39 Take advantage of
40 Have
41 Gives an address
43 "Pronto!" to a CEO
44 Boston daily
45 Pen name
46 *Witness* actress
51 Helps a felon
53 e.e. cummings, e.g.
54 Former name of Tokyo
55 Dregs
56 *The Verdict* star
59 Diner offering
60 Strong point
61 "Very funny!"
62 Part of a plan
63 School group
64 __ about

DOWN
1 Sidewalk eateries
2 Chilean pianist
3 Suppresses
4 __ Clemente, CA
5 Two-wheelers
6 Butler's love
7 Social improvements
8 Furniture wood
9 Madrid Mrs.
10 Hoi __
11 What *encore* means
12 Met highlight
13 Tear apart
18 Like Larry, Moe and Curly
22 Jerk
24 Museum fare
25 Dress style
26 Dressed to the __
29 Con's opposite
30 System of rules
31 Mrs. Brady
32 Sheik's home of song
33 Weightlifter, perhaps
34 Comparative phrase
35 Bank acct. entry
37 Voting places
42 Japanese dish
43 Cause distress
44 Greets the day
45 Light meal
46 City in New Hampshire
47 Indianapolis team
48 Hereditary determinants
49 Moscow's state
50 Echolocation acronym
51 Charity
52 Borscht ingredient
56 Cpl.'s subordinate
57 CompuServe rival
58 "__ goes there?"

DOUBLE FEATURE by Wayne Robert Williams

ACROSS
1 Anne Rice novel
7 Loser to Hippomenes
15 Tax figure
16 Zuazo or de Sucre
17 Ava Gardner film of '48
19 Hawaiian goose
20 Rouse to action
21 __ nous
22 Glorify
24 __ Stanley Gardner
26 Synagogue
27 Knight's title
28 Resident of: Suff.
30 "The Gold Bug" author's initials
32 Draft letters
33 The Duke of Brooklyn
35 Israeli dances
37 Character mentioned at 17 or 61 Across
40 High land
42 Work period
44 Numerical prefix
47 Bottom-line figure
48 Color of the Italian sky
49 Monkey suit
50 Word form for "blood"
52 The Green Hornet's aide
54 Top of the head
56 Get away from
58 Top of the head
60 Banned spray
61 Mira Sorvino Oscar film
64 Actress Duse
65 Corn varieties
66 Ornamental melodies
67 Evaluate

DOWN
1 Elsa, e.g.
2 Incorporating new territory
3 Plot outline
4 Monopoly piece
5 Comic Philips
6 Stay in the army
7 Loathe
8 "Ta-ta!"
9 TV E.T.
10 Not on tape
11 Arctic bloom
12 Intervals above octaves
13 Zodiac sign
14 Photographer Adams et al.
18 Canadian Indian
23 Connected
25 Quantity of gossip
29 *Jeopardy!* host
31 Insect's sensory organ
34 Banned spray
35 Presidential initials
36 W.C. Fields persona
38 Isolate
39 Invigorate
40 Acts like
43 Put into words
44 Having a motif
45 Disparage
46 Icons
48 The two
51 For a specific purpose
53 Spanish appetizers
55 Muslim magistrates
57 Sicilian volcano
59 Columnist Bombeck
62 Thither's follower
63 W. Hemisphere grp.

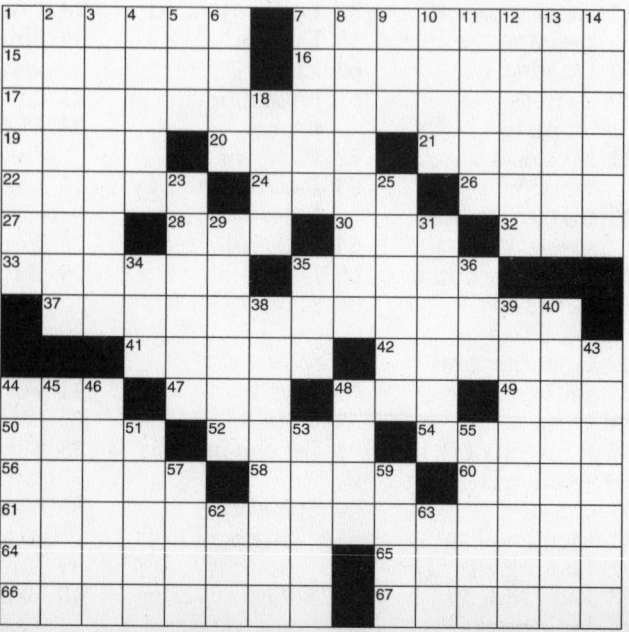

ACROSS

1 Transfixed
5 Biblical king
10 River floater
14 Manipulator
15 Greek-salad item
16 __ Bator, Mongolia
17 Comic Dunn
18 Early evening
19 Actor Brad
20 James Joyce masterpiece
23 Waterfront sight
24 Tinted
25 Shot to pieces
28 Coolly polite
31 *La Bamba* star Morales
32 Perfect embodiment
34 Itsy-bitsy
37 Tropical sitcom
40 *Casablanca* pianist
41 Pure as the driven snow
42 "This shouldn't happen to __!"
43 "It __ Be You"
44 Too big
45 Any minute now
47 Chanteuse Vikki
49 1917 song
55 Solemn ceremony
56 Suspect's excuse
57 Profound
59 Pub orders
60 Half-hearted
61 Actor Sharif
62 Rock singer Joan
63 Act segment
64 Western star Calhoun

DOWN

1 Hosiery snag
2 Ever since
3 Persian fairy
4 Cool as a cucumber
5 Biblical prophet
6 Gray poem
7 Racehorse __ Ridge
8 Major appliance
9 Family rooms
10 Gender-bending singer
11 Identical
12 Predestined
13 Explosive substance
21 Cashew, e.g.
22 Mechanical hums
25 Large barrels
26 Largest continent
27 Tropical tree
28 Poem division
29 __ *Wonderful Life*
30 Colorado ski resort
32 Matured
33 Massive
34 Walk through water
35 Hazzard County deputy
36 Precipice
38 Donald's first
39 Canadian peninsula
43 Straight-shooting
44 Heavenly body
45 Say "cheese"
46 Group of eight
47 Log structure
48 "All kidding __ . . ."
50 Tennis star Wilander
51 Actor Guinness
52 Ready for harvesting
53 Skipper of the *Nautilus*
54 Cherished
55 British rule in India
58 Snoop

ACROSS

1 Mideast gulf
6 Some ballpoints
10 Hit the mall
14 Moons, in Madrid
15 Feel sore
16 Angelic aura
17 Clothes-dryer insert
19 Early automaker
20 Moves toward
22 Be deceitful
23 Goes back to zero
26 Banged into
28 Lodge members
29 Hardy heroine
33 Word form for "earth"
34 British brew
35 Einsteins
36 Copier additive
39 Sebastian Coe, for one
41 PC key
42 Jungian principle
43 Take care of
44 Trolley sound
46 Vietnamese New Year
47 Dancing-shoe attachment
48 Beginner
49 Adam and Hoss, to Ben
50 Bad temper
53 Pageboy, for one
55 Writer Fleming
56 9 to 5, e.g.
60 Greek goddess of victory
62 Crispy snack
66 Mr. Kadiddlehopper
67 Afghanistan neighbor
68 Path
69 Attention getters
70 Coming-out VIPs
71 Barbecue leftover

DOWN

1 Without exception
2 On the __ vive
3 Columnist Landers
4 Enjoys the tub
5 Positive element
6 Poet
7 Cool dessert
8 Restaurant VIP
9 Spanish mister
10 "__ nuff!"
11 High-school sentinel
12 Blast from the past
13 Had portraits taken
18 Social stratum
21 Diverse
23 Lots of paper
24 J.R.'s mother
25 Multidoor opener
27 "Are you putting __?"
30 Make laws
31 Featherbrained
32 Shankar's strings
35 Sought clumsily
37 Make changes
38 *Midnight Cowboy* role
40 List extender
45 Pitcher's dream game
49 *Friends*, for one
50 Piece of cake
51 __ Selassie
52 Fast
54 Ere
57 Olden days
58 Wild attempt
59 Actor Conried
61 Printer's measures
63 Center of activity
64 Descendant: Suff.
65 According to

ON COMMAND by Norma Steinberg

ACROSS

1 West Point: Abbr.
5 Mets' stadium
9 Wash pots
14 Part of a parka
15 Medicinal tablet
16 Name on the Tara deed
17 He played Klinger
18 Gawk at
19 Breathing apparatus
20 Big spender's command
23 "Phooey!"
24 Noah's creation
25 Soft and crumbly
27 Dancer Charisse
29 Tie the knot
32 Brownies and Cadettes
33 Italy's shape
34 Bundle of cotton
35 Irving Berlin command
38 Enter
39 "Do __ others . . ."
40 Dilapidated
41 "We __ not amused!"
42 Greek letter
43 Run after
44 Donkey
46 Hard journey
47 Busman's command
53 To the point
54 Born and __
55 Watch
57 Pungent vegetable
58 Star Wars knight
59 Writer Ferber
60 Take as one's own
61 Chair
62 Takes home

DOWN

1 TV dial marking
2 Take a long bath
3 Oliver Twist's request
4 Fight-or-flight hormone
5 Erratic
6 Some weather systems
7 Pronoun for Françoise
8 Actor Baldwin
9 Of the sun
10 Nugget
11 Tolled
12 Compulsion
13 __-relief
21 Vital sign
22 Was compelled
25 Insignificant
26 Bert's pal
27 Terra __
28 Stringed toy
29 Salary
30 Duck
31 Refuse to admit
32 Head-over-heels
33 Flexed
34 Balance income and outgo
36 Talk-show participant
37 Wedding-party member
43 Attribution
44 Man of morals
45 Paid out
46 Actress Bara
47 Transmit
48 Threesome
49 Parts of sentences: Abbr.
50 Palm, e.g.
51 Adjutant
52 Lease subject
53 Done __ turn
56 Used to be

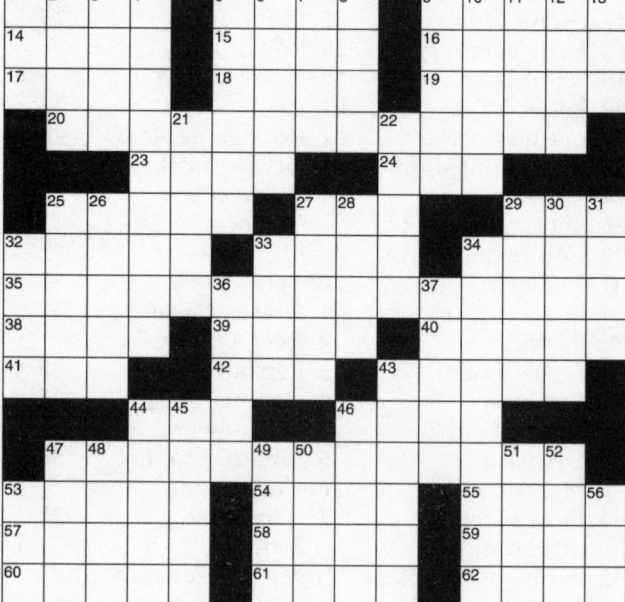

ANIMAL FARE by Robert H. Wolfe

ACROSS

1 __-edged (fancy)
5 In motion
10 "Oh, sure!"
14 Fragrance
15 Paris' river
16 Change the decor
17 Milano money
18 Share equally
19 Therefore
20 How Bambi hangs on?
23 End up with
24 The Man of __ (Superman)
25 Vapors
27 Vapor
30 Printing problems
32 One on the attack
37 Long-distance word form
39 Porridge, beds, etc.?
43 Sugar source
44 Rough stuff
45 Actor Hal
49 Duet quorum
50 Took the act on the road
52 Wild time
57 "Thrilla in Manila" winner
59 Upset a pig?
62 Mideast region
64 Basement appliance
65 "__ brillig . . ."
66 Tied up
67 Roof overhangs
68 In that case
69 Effortless
70 Dictator's assistant
71 Deli display

DOWN

1 Plays 18
2 Simp
3 Casablanca costar
4 Baseball deal
5 Tennis great
6 Scorch
7 Moneyboxes
8 Welcome
9 Double-breasted jacket
10 Infuriation
11 West Side Story composer
12 Brink
13 One of two preceders of "Tootsie"
21 __ marbles (Greek sculptures)
22 Corn portion
26 Photo finish
28 Sussex suds
29 Wine word
31 Sir Guinness
32 Disney network
33 Notary equipment
34 Cleans thoroughly
35 "There __ bad boys": Father Flanagan
36 Gun the engine
38 Compass pt.
40 Pose for pictures
41 Mrs. Pig
42 "When __ You" (Berlin tune)
46 Do Dallas in Danish
47 Deteriorates
48 __ hand (close)
51 Inner motivation
53 Gumshoe Gunn
54 With crudity
55 Wipe out
56 Snaky shapes
57 African Queen screenwriter
58 Running rock
60 High schooler
61 Approximately
63 One or more

385 ELEGANCE by Wayne Robert Williams

ACROSS
1 False move
8 Gets glamorous
15 *Follow the Fleet* star
16 Scrutinize
17 Cattle-ranch overseer
18 Catholic sacrament
19 Glandular word form
20 *Safety Last* star
22 Friday, for one
23 Be overfond
24 Overdo the acting
25 Dream of Delibes
26 Metric land measure
27 Sanctify
28 Less decorated
29 *The Emperor Jones* character
31 High temperatures
32 Painting genre
34 Snowmass attractions

37 Complete and convenient
41 Pink shade
42 Glass-coloring material
43 Actor Alejandro
44 Port on the Mediterranean
45 Foolish
46 Heavenly being: Fr.
47 Half a score
48 Red algae
49 *Let's Make* __
50 Student of Titian
52 1961 Antonioni film
54 Lands, as a fish
55 *Hamlet* character
56 Mamas' boys
57 They're boring

DOWN
1 Layered pavement
2 Dancer Duncan
3 First pope
4 Lyon's river

5 Rookie
6 Segment of history
7 Disorderly
8 Ordnance buildings
9 Type of daisy
10 Find a perch
11 *Little Women* monogram
12 Heartfelt
13 Reveal
14 Wally Cox character
21 New Mexico city
24 Island in New York Bay
25 Lustrous black
27 Palm nut
28 Seem suitable
30 Congress televiser
31 Young mare
33 Welsh seaport
34 Diving ducks
35 German sirens
36 *The Love for Three* __ (Prokofiev opera)

38 Saxophonist Coleman
39 Truth denier
40 __ *in Gaza*
42 Wise lawgivers
45 Port St. __, FL

46 Add beauty to
48 Big name in sitcom history
49 Freshly
51 *Treasure Island* monogram
53 Top-rated

386 ENGLISH 101 by Rich Norris

ACROSS
1 Study feverishly
5 Wood that moths hate
10 Con game
14 Go here and there
15 Angry
16 "Sorry I spilled that!"
17 Ice cream additive
18 Wanderer
19 Hawaiian strings, for short
20 Corporate communication
23 Hunting dog
24 Eye protector
25 Piece of postage
28 Moments of forgetfulness
32 Hydrocarbon suffix
35 "The Red Planet"
37 Proportional expression
38 Believe without questioning
42 __ a customer
43 Wise __ owl

44 Round veggie
45 Brute strength
47 Give encouragement to
50 Eastern European dance
52 Freezes, as a windshield
56 Capone served one
60 One of the Aldas
61 The squiggle in *señor*
62 Portal
63 Warbled
64 Public persona
65 Inventor Rubik
66 Refreshes a stamp pad
67 Frolic
68 Collision consequence

DOWN
1 Seafood selections
2 Scoundrel
3 29 Down, at sea
4 Is deserving of
5 Wide-screen film process

6 Son of Aphrodite
7 River blockers
8 In any way
9 Card-on-the-floor result
10 Lefty
11 Pepsi alternative
12 Mimic
13 SASE enclosures
21 Circus safety device
22 Russian rulers
26 __ Hari
27 Text in paragraphs
29 "Whoa!"
30 Ireland
31 Scotch partner
32 Nuclear-energy source
33 Half of Mork's sign-off
34 Supplements, with "out"
36 Unexpected problem
39 Artist's creations
40 Goes it alone
41 Motorman
46 Sensuous

48 Halloween's mo.
49 Couldn't do without
51 Jungian principle
53 Night noise
54 '95 NCAA women's basketball champs

55 Upstart candidate of '92
56 Make arrangements
57 Military level
58 Mild penalty
59 Barely beat
60 "It's just __ thought!"

387 GONE FISHING by Brendan Emmett Quigley

ACROSS
1 Dutch cheese
5 *Star Wars* character
9 Puppy
14 City in Peru
15 Midterm or final
16 Beach takealong
17 Language learning system
20 "Against a thing," in law
21 Abrasive particles
22 Prefix for picker
23 Halloween attire
26 Stuffed oneself
28 Controversial Presidential option
32 Attorneys' grp.
33 Unaccompanied
34 Moves like the Blob
38 Soil fertilizer
40 *Look Homeward, Angel* author
43 Cancel, as an article
44 Comic Richard
46 Change for a twenty
48 Dead heat
49 Low perspective
53 Legendary siren
56 Information
57 "What a good boy __"
58 Gives a hand to
60 Nonsensical
64 Math-checking procedure
68 Work flour
69 Tickle-Me doll
70 Cereal sound
71 Hole in your head
72 Precisely
73 Antler

DOWN
1 Primary grades, for short
2 Singer Celine
3 Italian love
4 "Don't __ Over" (Warwick tune)
5 A Beverly Hillbilly
6 Prefix meaning "outer"
7 "Phooey!"
8 Ad-lib comedy
9 Corresponded with
10 With 59 Down, *Star Wars* character
11 Minnesota town
12 Permitted by law
13 Correspondence, in Caen
18 Correspondence via computers
19 Bee shelter
24 Put away
25 Gambling game
27 Chess piece
28 Genie's home
29 Girder
30 Not a one
31 Defrosts
35 Tubular pasta
36 Writer Wiesel
37 Did in
39 Actor Rob
41 Farm animals' dinner
42 Irish singer
45 Tums competitor
47 Harden
50 Jockey's brake
51 Reduced-size replica
52 Disappear
53 Doesn't have
54 Certain Arab
55 Gone up
59 See 10 Down
61 Part of A.D.
62 Within reach
63 Sports cable channel
65 Greek letter
66 Thurman of *Batman and Robin*
67 Kiddie

388 TRADE SECRETS by Ed Stein

ACROSS
1 Realizes
5 Was forced
10 Understand
13 Charmer's snake
14 Where Boys Town is
15 Son __ gun
16 Yankee trader?
19 Beethoven specialty
20 Pro __
21 Start the pot
22 Tracy, Hammer, et al.
24 Boy Scout wear
26 Paris hotel
29 Las' followers
31 Trump, at times
35 Word form for "equal"
36 Church tax
38 "__ we all?"
39 Where many trades take place
42 Diversion creator
43 Highway to Fairbanks
44 Kind of shirt
45 Plant part
47 Sellers' *Pink Panther* boss
48 Home for a certain farmer
49 Summer coolers
51 Safe, to a safecracker
53 Float along
56 Catch some rays
58 Sumptuous meal
62 Biblical trade
65 New Jersey fort
66 Take care of
67 No nickname for Hemingway
68 Secrets stealer
69 Made a boo-boo
70 Ending for game or trick

DOWN
1 London neighborhood
2 Scrooge, for short
3 Substitute
4 One way to cook
5 Stolen
6 Latin 101 verb
7 Andersen's countrymen
8 *Make Room for Daddy* star
9 Schlemiel
10 Depressed
11 "__ first you don't . . ."
12 Drop one's jaw
13 Dol. fractions
17 Acid from milk
18 Bogie movie
23 Alaskan town
25 Hall-of-Fame pitcher Warren
26 Orange leftovers
27 "The Best __ to Come"
28 Puccini opera
30 Band location
32 Al __ (pasta specification)
33 Actress Georgia
34 Drum material, maybe
36 Trifled
37 Author Wambaugh, for one
40 Salad need
41 Funt's meal ticket
46 Lower
48 Kick out legally
50 *60 Minutes* reporter
52 Heads, in Le Havre
53 Gum globs
54 "Take __ from me . . ."
55 A bit too clever
57 Memo
59 Tops
60 Swizzle
61 Start of many titles
63 Mao __-tung
64 Mr. Serling

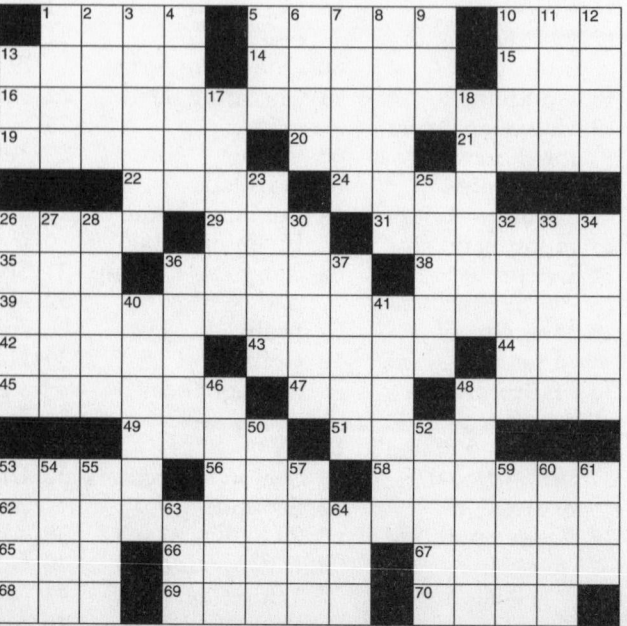

FUNNY MONEY by Patrick Jordan

ACROSS

1 Went down
5 Typing speed: Abbr.
8 Mell Lazarus comic strip
13 Anti-flood device
14 In the style of
15 Make __ of faith
16 One who takes too many courses?
18 Of an earlier time
19 Wealthy *Archie* character
21 Conversational pauses
22 Biblical verb ender
23 Incident
26 Coral formation
28 Daily regimen
30 Bolger or Milland
31 Loathe
34 "How are you?" response
37 Wealthy Disney character
40 Part of P.T.A.
41 Twangy
42 In the past
43 Bingo call
45 '53 Caron film
49 More leonine in color
52 Cola cooler
55 NCAA rival
56 Wealthy *Annie* character
59 Japanese dog breed
61 Cultural groups
62 Singer Shore
63 Singing syllable
64 1969 role for Dustin
65 __-Saxon
66 NBC sketch show
67 Kojak's first name

DOWN

1 Strict in discipline
2 Showing reluctance
3 Actor Franco
4 Nancy Drew's creator
5 Snarling sentry
6 "Not guilty," i.e.
7 Matlin of *Picket Fences*
8 Tuesday, in Toulons
9 Cassini et al.
10 Like overnight success
11 Scratch the surface
12 Mil. mail drop
13 Romeo or Juliet
17 River island
20 The study of light
24 Clammy and humid
25 Needle hole
27 Cabbie's customer
29 Actress Dunne
32 "__ voyage!"
33 Area of accelerated growth
35 Jerry Lewis telethon grp.
36 Completely occupied
37 Heroic story
38 Pressing too closely
39 Out of control
40 Touch gently
44 Secret meetings
46 Foment
47 In this manner
48 "__ Easy" (Ronstadt song)
50 South African province
51 Snake River state
53 Dernier __
54 Critic Roger
57 Showing signs of use
58 51 Down neighbor
59 Oklahoma city
60 Relatives

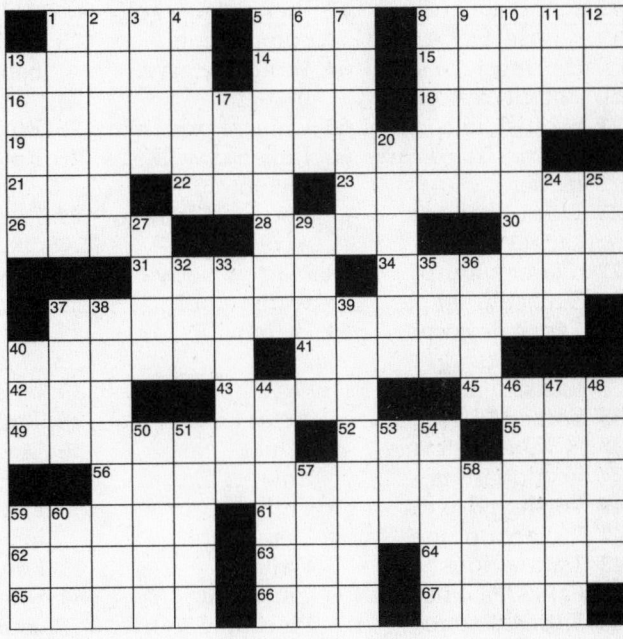

PT 8 by Wayne Robert Williams

ACROSS

1 Gun, as engines
4 Golfer Nick
9 Bamboozled
14 Slangy suffix
15 Actor Navarro
16 French floor
17 West Indian stew
19 Role for Arnold
20 Becomes something new
21 Applies a lacquer
22 Soap opera
23 Early round, for short
25 Champs __
27 Swiss river
30 Run out
33 Betty Grable photo, e.g.
35 __ *Town*
36 Org. of Buccaneers
38 Peer Gynt's mother
39 Actress Gardner
40 Cinderella, compared to her sisters
43 Hotel-door info
45 Life of Riley
46 Meals
48 Fissure
50 Italian sculptor
54 Harangues
56 Singer Pat
57 "__ You Glad You're You?"
58 Judge's concern
60 Boundary marker
61 African republic
62 Pitch __-hitter
63 Organic compound
64 Selling point
65 Playing piece

DOWN

1 Does cowboy work
2 French student
3 Mist
4 Widespread
5 Once in a blue moon
6 Little devils
7 Talk like a baby
8 Way in: Abbr.
9 Transferred design
10 Castles in the air
11 Tropical topper
12 First governor of Alaska
13 Hideouts
18 Ballet movements
21 Christmas-stamp subject
23 World Trade Center architect
24 Scotto or Tebaldi
26 Peevish temper
28 Travel about
29 Greek vowels
30 Easy gait
31 Ambiance
32 Having foresight
34 To the point
37 Glacial snow masses
41 Roman comedy writer
42 Harriet, for one
44 Syrian strongman
47 Coined money
49 Make fit
51 Mr. T's group
52 Granny
53 Playwright Joe
54 Vault
55 C. in C.
56 Kingsley and Cross
58 Law enforcement grp.
59 Scale notes

391   TABLE SETTING by Rich Norris

ACROSS
1 Hive hubbub
5 Relieved sighs
8 Multiplex offerings
14 Dueling sword
15 __ tai (rum cocktail)
16 American Leaguer
17 Pasadena arena
19 "__ the U.S.A." (Springsteen song)
20 Potent explosive
21 Scottish hillside
22 Former Yugoslav leader
23 Extra-terrestrial carrier
27 Skater's jump
30 Stalactite shape
31 Esprit de corps
34 Airline to Jerusalem
35 Some M.I.T. grads
38 NBC's California headquarters
40 Wash-and-wear
42 "__ about time!"
43 Take seriously
45 Fakes, as illness
46 *Silkwood* actress

48 Novgorod negative
49 Stylish dresser
54 Voice above tenor
55 Dinghy needs
56 Music players at weddings
59 Billiard shots
62 Biennial pro golf competition
64 Writes to, via modem
65 Chinese principle
66 Luke Skywalker's mentor
67 Local resident, to a collegian
68 Narrow body of water: Abbr.
69 Extremes

DOWN
1 Actor Lahr
2 "Once __ a time . . ."
3 Enthusiasm
4 Last letter
5 Writer Cleveland __
6 Pineapple source

7 "Hush!"
8 Disorderly group
9 Pizarro's quest
10 Moral excellence
11 Greek column
12 Upper crust
13 Mister, in Madrid
18 Crude-oil unit: Abbr.
23 Bodybuilder's bane
24 __ the lily
25 Winter neckwear
26 Kate's TV companion
27 Prefix meaning "both"
28 Cross off
29 Is mistaken
32 Christine of *Chicago Hope*
33 January, in Spain
35 Tense
36 Sea eagle
37 Part of CBS
39 Penetrating, as insight
41 Long (for)
44 Sends out of the country

46 Sure winner
47 Perform frivolously
49 Diamond surface
50 1836 siege site
51 Sipper's need
52 Intensity
53 Mao __-tung

56 Raid competitor
57 Wynonna or Naomi
58 Health resorts
60 11th-century date
61 U-turn from NNW
63 Pumpernickel alternative

392   THE HARD STUFF by Norma Steinberg

ACROSS
1 Voodoo amulet
5 Rover's pal
9 Very loud, in music
12 Swear
13 Not moving
15 Seethe
16 Bakery buy
18 Stare at
19 Tundra animal
20 __ even keel
21 "We are not __!"
23 Gets free (of)
24 Second son
25 Party handouts
28 Wield
32 Linda Lavin role
33 Nixon chief of staff
34 Author Ferber
35 Bottle part
36 Scouting outings
37 Civil unrest
38 Seize
39 Some poems

40 Put on a pedestal
41 Mightier
43 Covered with metal
44 Drags
45 Part of a hand
46 Meditation phrase
49 Statistics
50 Ring victories
53 Margarine
54 Megalithic monument
57 Flower part
58 Sanctuary
59 Quayle's successor
60 Bricklayer's implement
61 Sash
62 Was obligated to

DOWN
1 Musical Auntie
2 Elliptical
3 Soda-fountain worker

4 Sphere
5 Villains
6 Ancient Peruvians
7 College official
8 Mork's home
9 Mists
10 Arrange alphabetically
11 Ran away
14 Pekoe holders
15 Huge Nevada structure
17 River at Orléans
22 *A Few Good __*
23 Absolute lowest
24 Zodiac sign
25 Dracula's teeth
26 Bright-eyed
27 Clergyman
28 Singer Anita
29 Knucklehead
30 Sleeper's sound
31 Despised
33 Puts out of sight
36 "Baloney!"

40 Koran creator
42 ". . . __ gloom of night . . ."
43 Inventor's protection
45 Committee
46 Slam-dance
47 Voice range

48 Prerequisite
49 Peacenik
50 Have memorized
51 Monster
52 Planter's purchase
55 Typewriter key
56 Sense of self

393 PLAY TIME by Lee Weaver

ACROSS

1 Move swiftly
5 Famous lioness
9 Author Dinesen
13 Government workplace watchdog: Abbr.
14 Place
15 Ramble
16 Bus ancestor
18 *EZ Streets* star Ken
19 Cartoon exclamation
20 Flutist Herbie
21 Mariel Hemingway's grandfather
23 Cattle herder
25 Glacial pinnacle
27 Portland's st.
29 Person seeking sanctuary
33 Recently
36 Deserve
38 Film holder
39 Geological periods
40 Restriction
41 O'Hara home
42 Dismounted
43 Part of YWCA
44 Slugger Hank
45 Instruct over again
47 Mongolian desert
49 Wall hanging
51 Canal city
55 Place for an artist
58 What calories measure
60 "What a piece of work is __"
61 Nickname for 21 Across
62 Baseball game coverage
65 Flexible, electrically
66 Burn slightly
67 Ripening agent
68 Basis
69 Summers on the Riviera
70 Ancient Persian

DOWN

1 Administered medicine
2 Goldenrod relative
3 Drum major's hat
4 Witch, to Shakespeare
5 British prep school
6 Inclines
7 Cul-de-__
8 Supporter
9 Former political barrier
10 Shoe bottom
11 Rara __
12 Superman's alias
14 Frighten
17 Manicurist's material
22 Brit. power
24 It implemented Prohibition
26 Going astray
28 Japanese entertainer
30 First or reverse
31 Architect Saarinen
32 Exuberance
33 Close by
34 Author Gardner
35 Bide one's time
37 Mornings, briefly
40 Game using pouched rackets
44 Assists a felon
46 Onassis' nickname
48 Egg-shaped
50 Gleamed
52 Mirror reflection
53 Surveyed feloniously
54 __ nous
55 Practice punching
56 Tijuana snack
57 Hairstyle
59 Units of energy
63 Cherry stone
64 Machine part

394 WATCH OUT! by Trip Payne

ACROSS

1 Thpeak like thith
5 Perry's secretary
10 Wet weather
14 Longing feeling
15 "__ Your Love Tonight"
16 Failing that
17 Wham! tune of '85
20 Title for some retirees
21 Negated
22 Drops on the grass
23 Metric area measure
24 Pluck
25 Lockheed __-Star
26 Ruby and Sandra
27 P.M. part
30 Hang-glide
33 French city
35 Spooky
37 Inconsideration
40 Deeply felt
41 *Eleanor and Franklin* author
42 Mousers, e.g.
43 Pricey cracker spread
44 Singer Anita
46 "__ Buttermilk Sky"
48 State solemnly
49 Humbling feeling
50 __ *Stoops to Conquer*
53 Up
56 Up
58 Weaving, speeding and the like
60 Busy as __
61 Helena and Mary Kay's rival
62 Nastase of tennis
63 Word for a Will
64 Put up with
65 Doer's suffix

DOWN

1 Sneakered up
2 *Veni*
3 Kate, at first
4 Take a look
5 *The Blue Angel* star
6 Come after
7 -
8 Author Wallace
9 Stick (to)
10 Found another chair
11 Swiss slopes
12 *As __ It* (Getty autobiography)
13 Geek
18 Fabulist
19 Pupils' surroundings
24 Inheritance of a sort
25 Undeniable
26 Stall
27 Milieu
28 It may be shaken
29 Actress Harper
30 Shake up
31 "Say it ain't so!"
32 Start of a Welk intro
34 Attorney __
36 Ending for exist
38 Show subservience
39 Bestowed bountifully
45 Blood recipients
47 Jeansmaker Strauss
48 *You __ for It*
49 Colonial middleman
50 Walking stick?
51 Skater Sonja
52 Garden tool
53 Kuwaiti, for one
54 McEntire of country
55 Bakery finisher
56 Are, to Renaldo
57 Rara __
59 Jet, initially

395 SEVEN SPRINGS by Wayne Robert Williams

ACROSS
1 Bivouac
5 Lock of hair
10 "Beat it!"
14 Barbra's *Funny Girl* costar
15 Sister's clothes
16 Top-rated
17 Spring
19 Planted explosive
20 Motif
21 Mischievous god
22 __ Bator
23 Tax agcy.
25 *Año* starter
27 Spring
32 Iron fishhook
35 Flat fish
36 Hasty retreat
37 Island nation
38 After the style of
39 Spring
41 Resembling: Suff.
42 Drew a breath in shock
44 Music genre
45 Sp. miss
46 Decide to compete
47 Spring
49 Opening bars
51 401(k) relative
52 South American rodent
54 *Yours, Mine and __*
57 Pithy saying
61 Ugandan dictator
62 Spring
64 Campus mil. group
65 Wading bird
66 Ice-hockey position
67 Scottish island
68 Plant starters
69 Fill completely

DOWN
1 Stable youngster
2 Asian nursemaid
3 Manufacture
4 Logical proposition
5 Poetic preposition
6 Actor Julia
7 Spanish river
8 Revolt
9 *Three Lives* author
10 Warrior of old
11 Spring
12 Moffo of opera
13 Adolescent
18 Withered
24 Bar offering
26 Tied: Fr.
27 Missouri river
28 Hale hero
29 Spring
30 For example
31 Three-player card game
33 *Roots* role
34 1952 Masters champ
37 Melanie's mom
39 Impudently bold
40 Motorists' org.
43 Act of devotion
45 Trails
47 Pass time idly
48 Asian sea
50 *The Subject Was __*
52 Golf scores
53 Out of control
55 Infrequently seen
56 Hightailed it
58 Where most live
59 Lady's man
60 Brink
63 Dol. parts

396 WELL-DRESSED by Rich Norris

ACROSS
1 London area
4 More competent
9 __ Bill (legendary cowboy)
14 Bobby of hockey
15 Actress Sonia
16 Precise
17 "__ we there yet?"
18 Vietnam's capital
19 Takes it easy
20 Made bad investments
23 Communion table
24 Sunrise direction
25 Scores in overtime, e.g.
32 Health resort
35 Moran of *Happy Days*
36 Daffy or Donald
37 Bagel filler
38 Great pleasure
42 Speller's competition
43 Oil cartel
45 Cab passenger
46 Program interruptions
47 Not at all sportsmanlike
52 Siamese
53 Clear the blackboard
57 Is boss at home
61 Spin
63 "__ evil, hear . . ."
64 Xenon, e.g.
65 Scary
66 Fielder's misplay
67 Holiday precursor
68 Joyce Kilmer poem
69 Accomplished, old-style
70 Critic Reed

DOWN
1 Australian marsupial
2 Swashbuckling actor Flynn
3 Seize forcibly
4 More than disliked
5 Healthful cereal grain
6 Country byway
7 Selves
8 Brings up, as an issue
9 Cease to exist
10 Made a notable effort
11 __ off (set sail)
12 Fall mo.
13 Holy men: Abbr.
21 Actor Hunter
22 Headgear
26 "Able was I __ . . ."
27 Be indisposed
28 Table setting item
29 Marching band instrument
30 Topped off the cake
31 Squeezes (out), as a living
32 Messy one
33 Poet Alexander
34 Skater's jump
39 Gift of the talkative
40 Charlemagne's reign: Abbr.
41 Move via mental processes
44 Exclusive group
48 Large sea mammals
49 Sailor
50 Showed displeasure publicly
51 Singer's syllable
54 Fury
55 Barrel component
56 English county
57 Telegram
58 Hatcher of *Lois & Clark*
59 Cattle cluster
60 Grandson of Adam
61 Drenched
62 That girl

ACROSS
1 Possessive pronoun
6 Baby's word
10 Lost buoyancy
14 Singer Lena
15 Rara __
16 Pennsylvania port
17 Grand productions
18 With tolerance
20 Graduation keepsakes
22 Employs
23 Ladies' men
27 Disdains
31 Burro
33 Consume
34 Carrying a rifle
35 Architect Saarinen
37 "__ Lama Ding Dong"
38 Outbursts of amusement
41 Small horse
42 "Satin __" (Ellington tune)
43 Della or Pee Wee
44 Actor Wallach
45 At any time, to a poet
46 Card game
47 Alarm button
49 "Hallelujah!"
51 Certain travel costs
57 Cookouts
60 Sandy expanse
62 Fencer's sword
63 Author Ferber
64 Hawaiian veranda
65 Heavy burden
66 Hardens
67 Waxed cheeses

DOWN
1 Common title-starter
2 Jumps on one foot
3 Actor Stoltz
4 Foot division
5 Echoes
6 *Pretty Baby* director
7 States strongly
8 Short skirt
9 B __ "boy"
10 Logic
11 Comic actor Carney
12 Zilch
13 Islet
19 Urges (on)
21 CIA predecessor
24 Less mussed
25 Most docile
26 Ogles, with "at"
27 Demolition expert
28 Spicy cuisine
29 Muscat residents
30 Depend (on)
31 Asian sea
32 Former French coin
35 Get an __ effort
36 Building addition
37 Actress Perlman
39 Lyric poem
40 Winter Olympics site of '68
45 Raison d'__
46 All __ up (steamed)
48 Abated
49 Ten-percenter
50 Some flattops
52 Summer dessert
53 Weekend rancher
54 Heavy metal
55 Turner or Cantrell
56 Con game
57 __ canto (singing style)
58 Mil. address
59 Actor Stephen
61 Part of HRH

ACROSS
1 Foot warmer
5 Eskimo boat
10 Oven for ceramics
14 Norse god
15 Hole __ (ace)
16 Sioux
17 Not any
18 Diacritical mark
19 Put down asphalt
20 Writer Graham
22 Pent up, as a dog
24 Circle dance
26 Hide and __
27 Igor of aircraft fame
31 Okays
35 Playwright Coward
36 One who assesses
38 Numerical prefix
39 Bide-__ Home Association
40 Telegraphy structures
41 German philosopher
42 Store tomatoes
43 Gasps for breath
44 Nastase of tennis
45 Prepares to propose
47 Pounced upon
50 In case
52 Andrew's dukedom
53 Illinois city
57 Campaign event
61 Encourage
62 Completed
64 Island group off Galway
65 Letterman rival
66 Alpine sound
67 Italian lake
68 Eve's domain
69 Plumbing tool
70 Was in on

DOWN
1 Tune
2 Olfactory stimulus
3 Movies: Sp.
4 Desk space
5 Bad-check writers
6 Blackbird
7 Egg center
8 Peru's mountains
9 Alert one's features
10 Russian money
11 Emphatic type: Abbr.
12 Common topic for a 1 Down
13 Requisite
21 Negative conjunction
23 __-do-well
25 Tire center
27 Peanuts or popcorn
28 Hawkeye
29 New Hampshire town
30 1945 conference site
32 Celery unit
33 Ford or Kovacs
34 Located
37 On edge
40 They open many doors
41 Unlawful payment
43 Not guilty, e.g.
46 Maryland city
48 Move like a baby
49 Metric unit
51 Mortise insert
53 Type of cabbage
54 Not up
55 Hawaiian goose
56 Old Norse poetry
58 Elvis' middle name
59 Harmless
60 Plenty, to poets
63 Frightened squeal

PLAYING IN THE HALL by Frank Longo

ACROSS
1 Sitarist Shankar
5 Daredevil Knievel
9 Dieter's dinner
14 *Three Broadway Girls* star
16 Exploratory object
17 Dress-shirt attachment
19 Superabundance
20 Actress Long
21 Dead heat
22 Equi- relative
23 Coach's lecture, often
26 Farm female
28 Cover girl Banks
30 Conductor __- Pekka Salonen
31 Altar in the sky
32 1956 Wimbledon winner
33 Powerful one
37 Unscathed
42 Pad's place, perhaps
43 Ancient Roman marketplaces
44 Novelist Tan

45 Speed-of-sound surpasser
48 Superstar
49 __ *Misérables*
50 Stage managers' listings
54 *Août*'s season
56 Semi
57 Ft. Wayne clock setting
58 Pilot
61 It's spoken in Botswana
65 Comic's prop
66 Art-gallery frequenters
67 Roberts of *Charlie's Angels*
68 Adidas alternative
69 Catch one's breath

DOWN
1 No longer green
2 Strong as __
3 Immunize
4 Roosevelt's Interior Secretary
5 Polishes off
6 Influential one
7 Be off

8 Helmsley of hotels
9 Gives an address
10 It doesn't go straight
11 "Whole __ Love"
12 In a state of excited activity
13 Actor Jacobi
15 Basutoland, today
18 Scrabble piece
23 Suffix with demo or auto
24 Ranted
25 Send-off word
26 Sky swooper
27 Actress Gray
29 "__ said it!"
34 Chess result
35 Wile E. Coyote's preferred brand
36 *Wide Sargasso Sea* author
38 Pianist Myra
39 Installs an outfield
40 __-Magnon
41 Andrew Johnson's birthplace
46 Soul singer __ E.
47 Actress Harper

50 Summit
51 Range of the Rockies
52 Incite
53 Revolutionary War era Allen
55 Less fictional

58 Share paid in advance
59 A long time
60 26 Down's hangout
62 Frequent Powell costar
63 Hilo handout
64 Request, with "for"

BRAINY by Wayne Robert Williams

ACROSS
1 Betting setting
4 Meal
10 Construction piece
14 Tarzan's son
15 Jack Lemmon movie
16 Bond foe
17 Little devil
18 "I haven't got all day!"
20 Cousins of canvasbacks
22 Tossed
23 City on the Ganges
24 Confused mingling
26 Where to see *Arli$$*
29 Differently
31 You, on the Yucatán
33 Leaning
34 Remove from office
35 MIT grad.
38 Runner's ploy
40 Ubiquitous bugs

41 Indicator of impatience
43 Of the sole
45 Solemn promises
46 Desert shrub
50 Mil. installation
51 Pita fiber
53 Way from a man's heart
54 Mazda model
56 Directed to the center
57 *The Spirit of Liberty* writer
61 Silent assent
62 Lot measure
63 Theater district
64 News agcy.
65 Cooking containers
66 Singer Sheena
67 Storm hdg.

DOWN
1 San Luis __, CA
2 Alley denizen
3 Out-of-the-way way
4 Fortified embankment

5 Spacewalks, to NASA
6 Asian nation: Abbr.
7 *Wheel of Fortune* buy
8 Archie's command to Edith
9 Champion's prize
10 Norse goddess
11 Resort on the English Channel
12 Mandela's org.
13 *M*A*S*H* soldier
19 Waiting line
21 Dig up
24 *The __ on the Floss*
25 Of summer
27 Outdo
28 Pindar output
30 Fleeting trace
32 Small singer
34 Removal directive
35 Harrow rival
36 Weather grp.
37 Adams series
39 Venetian honcho

42 Like most people
44 Strand
46 The Colosseum et al.
47 Herschel discovery
48 Razor sharpeners
49 Finnan __
52 Cubic meter

55 Makes angry
56 Involved with
57 Track circuit
58 *The Name of the Rose* author
59 Keeps
60 Hgt.

401 LET ME IN! by Rich Norris

ACROSS
1 High cards
5 Wilkes-__, PA
10 With competence
14 No different
15 Blunted swords
16 Fence attachment
17 Wander aimlessly
19 Comes to a finish
20 Skipped a dance
21 Mattress part
23 Ivan of tennis
24 Shrewd
27 Anonymous John
28 Glass sheet
30 Greek letter
31 Runs easily
34 Spree
35 *Beverly Hillbillies* character
36 Tennis-shirt name
37 Plucky courage
38 Canine command
39 Singer Rawls
40 Roman Empire language
41 Serious
42 Actress Jillian
43 North Carolina county
44 Pub selection
45 Actor Sir __ Hardwicke
47 Warehouse containers
50 Ocean growths
53 Wading birds
55 To-do
57 Informal chat
59 Kid's transport
60 Decorate
61 Actress Spelling
62 March 15th, e.g.
63 Went after
64 Dance component

DOWN
1 Pops a question
2 Artificial waterway
3 Overact
4 Showed support for
5 One of the Fab Four
6 Police alert, briefly
7 Classic cars
8 Enlist again
9 Alienate
10 55 Down employee
11 Extraordinary performance
12 Inc., in Ipswich
13 "Absolutely!"
18 Acclaim
22 "That's clear now!"
25 Unifying idea
26 Type of duck
28 Mischievous elf
29 Has __ with (knows well)
31 Reddish purple
32 Endangered atmospheric layer
33 Dessert choice
34 The two
37 Eyelash makeup
38 Achieves detente
40 Animal's home
41 Atlantic City machines
44 Attendance-book notation
46 Lariats
48 *The Waste Land* poet
49 Mall unit
51 Work at the warehouse
52 Dick and Jane's dog
54 Cut a little
55 Govt. detective agcy.
56 Container cover
58 Madrid Mrs.

402 GONNA FLY NOW by John D. Leavy

ACROSS
1 A Baldwin brother
5 Love god
9 Beseeched
13 Chutzpah
14 Former Egyptian president
16 Civil-rights activist Parks
17 Austen masterpiece
18 Superman's dressing room
20 Not so dull, as clothes
22 Montgomery's WWII foe
23 Chef Graham
24 Co-ed college
25 Coach Knute
28 German greeting
29 Tiger Woods' org.
32 Marsh bird
33 Retail outlet
34 Guitarist Lofgren
35 Spaceman Shepard
36 Wake up
37 Novelist Hunter
38 Fender bender
39 Model Macpherson
40 Took an oath
41 Wind dir.
42 Parimutuel concern
43 Bandleader Lanin
44 Pig's place
45 Bathday cake
46 Actress Andress
50 Inconsistent
54 Superman's home
56 Cougar
57 Electrical connector
58 Make happy
59 Gouda alternative
60 "Auld Lang __"
61 Neck and neck
62 Philosopher Descartes

DOWN
1 Matures
2 Genie's home
3 Ticklish Muppet
4 Superman's secret identity
5 Aim high
6 *Politically Incorrect* host
7 Polecat's defense
8 Took off
9 Spring fling
10 Weaver's need
11 Spanish compass point
12 Author Roald
15 White ant
19 Seethe
21 Nomad's house
24 Poetry
25 Cracks the books
26 Stares at
27 Winch
28 Carries
29 Swivel
30 Menacing look
31 *Lou Grant* star
33 Hackneyed
34 4 Down's workplace
36 Bureaucratic delay
40 Char
42 Ibsen's home
43 Undo, as ropes
45 Ill will
46 Diamond authorities
47 Count (on)
48 Daze
49 Powerful impulse
50 Pole, for instance
51 Guy, in surferese
52 Mrs. David Bowie
53 Showed up
55 Bullring cheer

403 — HOT STUFF by Fred Piscop

ACROSS
1 Play the links
5 "__ bagatelle!"
10 Police alert: Abbr.
13 Laterally, nautically
15 Locker room photo
16 Prevaricate
17 Make a person happy
20 Clothing
21 Yes, to Yvonne
22 Golden Rule preposition
23 Potatoes partner
25 Heartfelt
27 Be an unexpected star
31 "NOW I get it!"
32 Antitoxins
33 1945 conference site
37 Give a hang
39 Scandinavian
42 Chinese money
43 Ceramics ovens
45 School book
47 Writer Anaïs
48 Date someone much younger
52 In a faithful way
55 Watch one's intake
56 Like a bump on __
57 Pick or pack preceder
59 City east of 60 Down
63 Negotiation ultimatum
66 Forbidden-fruit eater
67 Seacoast
68 Simpleton
69 Get __ of (ditch)
70 High-strung
71 Cipher

DOWN
1 Big bash
2 Newspaper notice
3 Remaining
4 Mohammed's daughter
5 Mimic
6 Bit of Japanese cuisine
7 Follows
8 Indonesian money
9 Center starter
10 Skirt style
11 Actress ZaSu
12 Stupefy
14 Types of mushrooms
18 Clean up
19 Stretch at Heathrow
24 "Comin' __ the Rye"
26 Baseball great Campanella
27 Bed, so to speak
28 Malaysian's neighbor
29 Nobleman
30 __ Day (April 22)
34 John of *High Society*
35 Party-game pin-on
36 Green Gables girl
38 Cause to see red
40 Feeder filler
41 Remove
44 Impresario Hurok
46 Rock-boring tool
49 __ *Spirit* (Coward play)
50 Perot, for one
51 Of a throwback
52 By and by
53 Legendary king of Norway
54 Hooked up, as oxen
58 Blows it
60 Betting setting
61 Variety
62 Eye woe
64 Occupational suffix
65 Peggy or Pinky

404 — RUNNING A BIT FAST by Patrick Jordan

ACROSS
1 Hart's former coanchor
5 Reza Pahlavi was the last one
9 Antic
14 Jaunty greeting
15 Combustible heap
16 Speechify
17 Teen suffix
18 Science magazine
19 Hikers' gear
20 Oklahoma
23 Window cleaner's woes
24 Vietnam neighbor
25 Pigpen
26 Husky vegetable?
27 Pie __ mode
30 Wood-shaping machine
33 Atmosphere
34 Spirited style
35 One reason to send one's regrets
38 Storm or Gordon of classic TV
39 Washington's bills
40 Grows
41 "Honest" nickname
42 Jazzman Sims
43 Golf-hole marker
44 Sense
45 Energetic workers
49 Innovative, perhaps
52 Prove useful
53 Roman Empire invader
54 "__ Mommy Kissing Santa Claus"
55 Release
56 Golden Rule word
57 Endangered goose
58 Bloodhound's trail
59 James Bond alma mater
60 Electric-power array

DOWN
1 "__ all, folks!"
2 Black billiard ball's number
3 Like nylons
4 Flicka's footwear
5 Suggestive of the supernatural
6 Sacred songs
7 "Rule Britannia" composer
8 Family treasures
9 Clergyman Mather
10 Zones
11 Gasp
12 Diminutive ending
13 Musical notes
21 Western film
22 Famous restaurateur
26 Hale-Bopp, for one
27 Emcee Trebek
28 Narrow road
29 Pantry pests
30 Nancy Lopez's org.
31 Syrian, e.g.
32 Ceramic square
33 *The Tonight Show* opener
34 Arising (from)
36 Murmured romantically
37 Gemini symbol
42 Fervent supporter
43 Kipling's Kaa, e.g.
44 Pretend
45 "Me, too!"
46 Silas Marner, e.g.
47 Muscat citizen
48 Used needle and thread
49 French preposition
50 Detest
51 Typesetter's selection
52 Jolson and Jarreau

405 FULL-LENGTH VERSIONS by Wayne Robert Williams

ACROSS

1 Fairway shout
5 One of two on the phone
11 Manhandle
14 Hebrew month
15 For each
16 Historic period
17 Full-length computer company
19 Bishopric
20 Friend of Pooh
21 Joined up
23 Gentle one
25 Man of La Mancha
26 Hairy pets
30 Caesar and Waldorf
33 Holly, in *The Piano*
34 Put on a play
36 *Coming of Age in __*
37 Processes leather
39 Massenet opera
41 Group of conspirators
42 Bitter-__ (diehard)
44 Bring joy to
46 Mauna __
47 Replay
49 Glorifiers
51 "__ c'est moi"
53 Vicinity
54 Abu Dhabi and Dubai
57 Gave ten percent
61 Took the prize
62 Full-length rock group
64 Business letter abbr.
65 Ballet star
66 *Green Mansions* girl
67 Collegiate cheer
68 IHOP competitor
69 Dispatch a dragon

DOWN

1 Notoriety
2 Garfield's pal
3 Slightly blue
4 Flynn's namesakes
5 Outward-opening window
6 Mil. address
7 Vivacity
8 Boxer Spinks et al.
9 French schools
10 Eye parts
11 Full-length meat
12 Writer James
13 Garden invader
18 Speak one's mind
22 Word before power or system
24 Astronomer Tycho
26 Couldn't take
27 *A Bell for __*
28 Full-length instrument
29 Head covering
31 Philanthropist
32 Epic tales
35 Crownlet
38 Break off
40 Catches off guard
43 Recorded again
45 Refrain from childhood
48 Like some birds
50 Woodland dwellers of folklore
52 Mortise insertion
54 Water pitcher
55 Angela's mother on *Who's the Boss?*
56 Wiener wrapping
58 Attract a cab
59 Author Bombeck
60 6/6/44
63 Soar

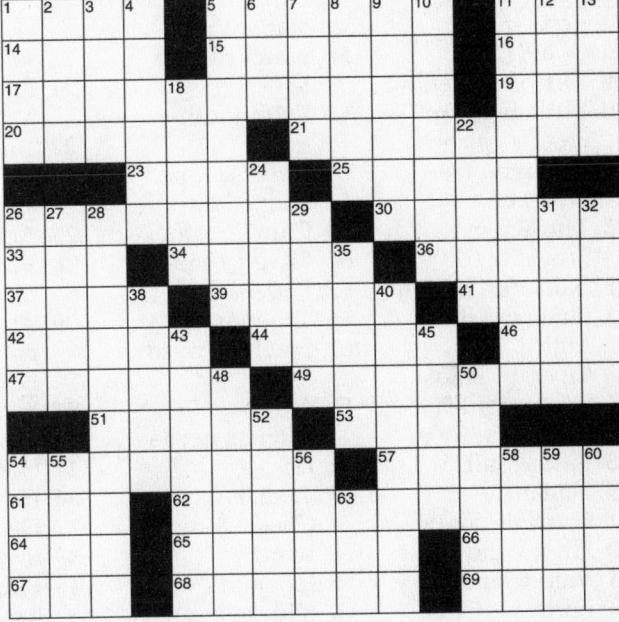

406 WHERE YOU LIVE by Rich Norris

ACROSS

1 CD precursors
4 *__ Gotta Have It* (Spike Lee film)
8 *Yankee Doodle Dandy* Oscar-winner
14 Boxer Muhammad
15 Grotto
16 Used one's key
17 Fellow
18 *Roots* writer Haley
19 Folks like Scrooge
20 Perky 1994 USA skiing medalist
23 Stair segment
24 Have lunch
25 Official proceedings
29 Celebrate with enthusiasm
34 Superficial amounts
37 Lukewarm
38 Mrs. Nixon
39 "Are you a man __ mouse?"
40 Sound of relief
42 Chemical suffix
43 Composer Berg
45 Astronomical events
47 Sanctified condition
50 Yucatán native
51 Wrinkle-nosed dog
52 Singer Diana
56 Dwight Yoakam's field
61 Grownups
64 Buckeye State
65 Altar phrase
66 Phoenician, for one
67 Aug. follower
68 "Hold On Tight" rock group
69 African mammals
70 Return-mail enclosure: Abbr.
71 Account exec

DOWN

1 Reading lights
2 Braid of hair
3 As of
4 Strikebreaker
5 Saintly headgear
6 Nights before
7 Small music groups
8 *The Iceman __*
9 "…baked in __"
10 Be pregnant
11 Pilot's heading: Abbr.
12 Poetic adverb
13 Gridiron distances: Abbr.
21 CEO's calendar entry
22 Tell (on)
26 Manages somehow
27 Strong cord
28 Lake Titicaca's range
30 Show penitence
31 Occupational suffix
32 Powerful D.C. lobby
33 Value system
34 Burst of activity
35 Island near Sicily
36 In check
40 Not this direction: Abbr.
41 In the style of
44 Rather quickly
45 Picnic competition
46 Lima's country
48 Compositions
49 Enjoyment
53 Wickerwork material
54 Move sideways
55 Ice-cream unit
57 Director Preminger
58 Actress Perlman
59 Kennel sounds
60 Dust speck
61 Fireplace residue
62 "*Agnus __*"
63 Ref's cousin

407 THE WILD BUNCH by Lee Weaver

ACROSS
1 Golf-course stats
5 Detective work
9 Big band instruments
14 Actor Guinness
15 Poems of praise
16 Wide awake
17 Space shuttle grp.
18 __ avis
19 Mirror reflection
20 Little Bighorn chief
23 Feel remorse
24 Observe
25 Thrown in a high arc
27 Baltic Sea nation
31 One who flies high
33 Operatic solos
34 Camera filler
35 Swindles
38 Finds fault
39 Hägar the Horrible's wife
40 High wind
41 Vigoda and Fortas
42 Singer Fitzgerald
43 Discussion group
44 Something scarce
46 ". . . far beyond those of __ men"
47 Cried noisily
49 Animation unit
50 July sign
51 *Back to the Future* star
58 Notched, as a leaf
60 Sound from a goose
61 BMW competitor
62 Helped out
63 Cain's brother
64 "I've __ had!"
65 Peevish
66 Too inquisitive
67 Smelting residue

DOWN
1 Kitchen needs
2 Jai __
3 Take it easy
4 Chasing-away word
5 Eye part
6 Old saying
7 Belgrade resident
8 Birthright seller
9 Suit maker
10 Einstein's birthplace
11 Longtime Alabama coach
12 Take the other side
13 War horse
21 Egyptian goddess
22 Andes beast
26 Nonchooser, it's said
27 Actress Turner
28 King Hussein, for one
29 Athlete in the news
30 Feudal tenant
31 Inane
32 Gymnast Korbut
34 Hat material
36 Entreaty
37 Deal in
39 Swiss miss
43 Public-opinion barometer
45 Cure-all
46 Submissively
47 Sheep sound
48 Eagle's nest
49 Walking sticks
52 Sleuth Charlie
53 "King of the road"
54 Fighter's punches
55 Gas or oil
56 Concert halls
57 Word on a school-zone sign
59 Complete collection

408 HOT TUNES by Wayne Robert Williams

ACROSS
1 Nun's garb
6 Corrosive substances
11 Sci. class
14 Author Segal
15 Queensland quart
16 Actress Lupino
17 With 20 Across, Kern tune
19 Obtained
20 See 17 Across
21 Cable channel
22 Brit. fliers
25 Makes lace
26 Relent
28 Yale student
29 *Another 48 __*
30 Hebrew holiday
31 Designated
33 Nada
34 Polar explorer
37 Close by, in poetry
38 Iota
39 Monteverdi opera
40 Equipment
41 __ Paulo, Brazil
42 Consecrate
43 __-gritty
45 Table scrap
46 __ Dawn Chong
47 Skater Ito
49 Singer Paul
50 Conclusion
51 Miscue
52 Bruce Springsteen tune
55 Assam or Darjeeling
56 Elvis tune
60 Blackbird
61 Of seaweed
62 Economist Janeway
63 Author Deighton
64 Smooth: Fr.
65 Relates

DOWN
1 Males
2 Branch
3 Life story, for short
4 Gooey
5 Thomas Tryon novel
6 States of readiness
7 Quotes as an authority
8 Wee
9 Runs out
10 Motion detector
11 The Doors tune
12 Sun-dried brick
13 Seiji's stick
18 Bank employee
22 Mark new prices
23 Coeur d'__, ID
24 James Taylor tune
27 Word form for "filament"
30 Abyss
32 Auto-racer Andretti
33 Disordered situation
35 French historian
36 Was overfond
38 Noisy songbird
39 Progressing goalward
41 Incentives
42 Actor Adam
44 Of the Shawnee or Pawnee
45 Stored, in a way
47 Iron or cobalt
48 Singer Cara
49 Magnani and Moffo
53 Assns.
54 *Vogue* rival
57 Lubricate
58 Encyc. bk.
59 UFO pilots

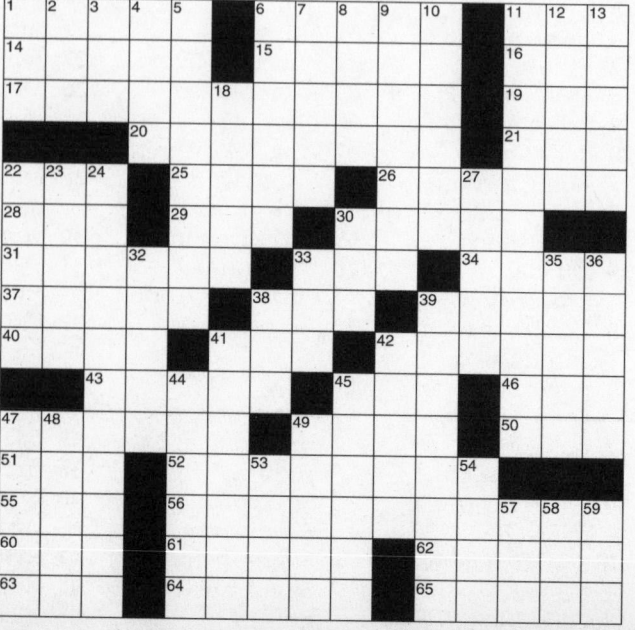

409 INTERNATIONAL CAST by Randolph Ross

ACROSS

1 Sidewalk sight
5 Prefix for "both"
9 Hot spot
14 Barn birds
15 Censure, with "at"
16 Eyebending '60s style
17 Spy on Helsinki citizens?
19 Vile
20 One over *due*
21 Guinness suffix
22 Charlie Parker's instrument
24 Mediterranean arm
27 Cartesian conclusion
28 Reckless Durban driver?
33 Do in
36 Pay to play
37 Miss. neighbor
38 Deli salmon
39 Sports-coverage feature
42 Sound of admonition
43 Top gun
44 Palindrome part
45 "Uh huh!"
46 Warsaw sociologists?
51 "Help!"
52 Deed clause
56 Stuck
60 Corp. officers
61 Card game
62 Light lunch
63 Rob Roy?
66 Make joyful
67 Actor Moses
68 Increase
69 Basted, maybe
70 __ good example
71 Poetic tributes

DOWN

1 Terra __
2 Tony or Edgar
3 Handbill
4 Subj. for immigrants
5 Grain bristle
6 Predatory insect
7 Storage space
8 *Casablanca* role
9 *Die Hard* group
10 Sangfroid
11 Raised platform
12 Humorist Bombeck
13 River of Hades
18 Timidity
23 Like an old sweater
25 Frosty
26 Consecrated cup
29 Once __ while
30 Feedbag filler
31 Otherwise
32 Garden tool
33 Rebuff emphatically
34 Daffy
35 Skating jump
39 Paraphrased
40 Wipe out
41 Favorite
45 Belief
47 Nabob's residence
48 "I __ a thing to wear!"
49 Juan Carlos' home
50 Musical marking
53 Heston role
54 Rope loop
55 Drags around
56 Exploits
57 Without much color
58 "There oughta be __!"
59 Frittata ingredient
64 *Boulevard* kin
65 Box-office sign

410 LOOK BOTH WAYS by Frank Longo

ACROSS

1 Accelerated
7 Jerk's offering
11 Michael Jackson tune of 1972
14 Deep red
15 Gets darker, perhaps
16 Freudian topic
17 Bother Bernhardt
19 Snorkel or Bilko: Abbr.
20 Like some traditions
21 Feather bed?
22 Aquarium fish
24 Tenth mo.
25 Two alternatives to buying
28 Auto agreement
30 Disreputable saloon
31 Small-business mag
33 Entirely
34 Dillydally
35 Doddering cats
39 Recording medium
40 Supermodel Carol
41 About 120 square yards
42 Jeopardize
44 Hoops Hall-of-Famer Dan
48 Hip-hop hater's plea
52 Citrus product
53 Ensnared elvers
54 Name in Beatles history
55 Secluded valley
56 Christina's dad
57 Shy
61 Get the point
62 Brontë governess
63 Compass pointer
64 Lapse
65 Geek
66 Less loose

DOWN

1 Train
2 *Leap of Faith* director
3 Book boo-boos
4 Dash device
5 Letters on some hulls
6 Green stuff
7 Bart or Belle
8 Sculling necessity
9 Trial evidence, sometimes
10 Choreographer Sir Frederick
11 Tower over
12 Chinese appetizers
13 Distinguished
18 Patriotic org.
23 White furs
25 __ Mellal, Morocco
26 Stare at
27 Novelist Cather
29 Plain-dealing
32 Miner's asset
33 Toward the stern
35 One with a silly smile
36 Trellis
37 Palindromic periodical
38 Eye-color area
39 Immunologist's concern
43 Flush
45 They may be made at bars
46 English Channel swimmer
47 Bank, often
49 Participated in crew
50 Shakers founder Lee
51 Indicate, in a way
55 Verdon of *Damn Yankees*
58 Scotch relative
59 Airport abbr.
60 Society-page word

411 FOR CRYIN' OUT LOUD by Norma Steinberg

ACROSS
1 Poisonous snakes
5 Clay brick
10 Fool
14 Bloke
15 Memorize
16 "This can't be!"
17 Cry at the Forum
19 Of low quality
20 Bert's pal
21 Puerto __
22 "Well, __ that special!"
23 Pre-photocopier copies
25 Choose
27 Secondhand
29 Cinders
32 Envelope part
35 Views from the mountain top
39 Tundra animal
40 __ Abner
41 Most submissive
42 Slugger's stat
43 Moray

44 Coordinated
45 __ over heels
46 Don of Get Smart
48 Muscle condition
50 Turned into
54 Dutch flowers
58 Trudge
60 Force
62 Singer Shore
63 Become well
64 Newsboy's cry
66 About
67 Danger
68 Composer Satie
69 Lord's mate
70 Rendezvous
71 Fair to middlin'

DOWN
1 Pined (for)
2 Ventriloquist Lewis
3 Wall covering
4 Separated
5 __ carte
6 Bambi, e.g.
7 Watering hole
8 Reinforce

9 Sign up
10 Agenda items
11 Knock response
12 A part of
13 Legal wrong
18 Corp. heads
24 __ Days in May
26 The Orient
28 Winds down
30 One of Napoleon's homes
31 Slide, as on ice
32 Dog's bane
33 Perjured oneself
34 Conductor's cry
36 The limit, sometimes
37 Bivouac shelter
38 English racing site
41 This and that: Abbr.
45 Spirals

47 Series of songs
49 Hosiery shade
51 Skillful
52 Fraternity party
53 Way in
55 Emcee's speech
56 Helen's abductor
57 Military hat
58 Collins or Silvers
59 Actress Olin
61 Speaker of baseball
65 Height: Abbr.

412 ARTISTIC LICENSE by Patrick Jordan

ACROSS
1 Combine
6 One talking while trucking
10 Colossal, as a film
14 Sound dubber's concern
15 River of Florence
16 Sugar source
17 Create a composition of cushions?
19 Give a job to
20 Lott and colleagues
21 Makes amends
23 ". . . man __ mouse?"
24 Say "Howdy!" to
25 Shutterbug's need
29 Paneled wall lining
32 Aromas
33 Disconcerted
34 Weeder's need
35 Liver secretion
36 Poker pair
37 Singer Minnelli

38 Stop-sign shade
39 Removed, to a proofreader
40 Deals with a dilemma
41 Aegis
43 Hairstyling foam
44 '96 White House aspirant
45 Sigma follower
46 Like the Ark
48 Athenian philosopher
53 Podded vegetable
54 Create a study in soda sippers?
56 Nothing: Fr.
57 Winter Olympics event
58 He bugs Bugs
59 Bird's home
60 Once around the sun
61 Active folks

DOWN
1 Low voice
2 Gospel writer
3 Genesis locale

4 Silent star Naldi
5 Medicos
6 Film director Frank
7 Bikini parts
8 Bring to a halt
9 Prayer beads
10 Radar signals
11 Create a still life with salty snacks?
12 Concerning
13 Middling grades
18 Israeli dance
22 Take care of
24 Looked longingly
25 African snake
26 Parting word
27 Create embryonic fern figurines?
28 Before, to Burns
29 Buffs the floor
30 Moves like molasses
31 Annoy playfully
33 Cut the bones out
36 "After that . . ."
37 Comical Costello

39 Calamitous
40 Went a-wooing
42 Intellectual showoff
43 Some apples
45 Pisa attraction
46 Had on
47 Grapes of Wrath figure
48 Heroic tale
49 Guthrie of folk fame
50 Manageable
51 Water pitcher
52 Estonia and Latvia, before 1991: Abbr.
55 Feel sorry about

413 LIT RE-WRIT by Richard Silvestri

ACROSS

1 Piccadilly pound
5 "Hey, you!"
9 Woody Allen movie
14 Pakistani tongue
15 USC rival
16 Writer Jong
17 Onetime Met Tommie
18 Sir's counterpart
19 Desert wanderer
20 Subtitle of *The Deerslayer*?
23 When DST ends
24 Meteor tail
25 Think the world of
29 Sorrowful sound
31 Flap
34 Hammer parts
35 '40s auto
36 British gun
37 Rags-to-riches story?
40 Actress Russo
41 Legwear
42 Point a finger at
43 Attempt
44 Comic Carvey
45 International socialites
46 Spoil
47 Family nickname
48 Sequel to *Othello*?
56 Disgusted
57 Wheedle
58 Creole vegetable
59 Cordial ingredient
60 Bee flat?
61 Prejudice
62 Dumb mistake
63 Winter vehicle
64 Shrill cry

DOWN

1 Campus area
2 Instinctive impulse
3 Impression
4 Pair piece
5 Volcanic glass
6 In short supply
7 Pole, e.g.
8 Not feral
9 Top
10 Irregular
11 Stretch vehicle
12 Little Engine's words
13 A son of Jacob
21 Derby entrant
22 Late hours
25 Broken up
26 Yield respectfully
27 Spiteful sort
28 About
29 Latin music
30 Small land mass
31 World book
32 *Melvin and Howard* director
33 Beginning
35 Element #10
36 Ice melter
38 Waterfront feature
39 Failing at middle management?
44 Furnace part
45 Under a hex
46 Clock climber
47 *Vino* variety
48 Slots city
49 Norse god
50 Folk singer Phil
51 Stir up
52 __ *Dick*
53 Dust Bowl refugee
54 Viva voce
55 Speak harshly
56 "Terrif!"

414 LETTER CHANGES by Wayne Robert Williams

ACROSS

1 Barracks bed
4 *Hyperprism* composer
10 Actress Ward
14 Botheration
15 Newspaper employee
16 Move laboriously
17 PING
20 Foot control
21 Golf-course features
22 Wish undone
23 Itzhak of Israel
26 Georgia city
29 Actress Taylor
30 Sault __ Marie, Ont.
33 Resting atop
34 Seasonal employees
35 Director Craven
36 PANG
39 Loop loopers
40 Touch emotions
41 Inactive
42 In position
43 Cash drawers
44 Tiny bugs
45 Writer Madame de __
46 "The Greatest"
47 Bicker
50 Included within
54 PONG
58 Rampage
59 Walesa's home
60 Reaction source
61 Dancer Pavlova
62 Performance prizes
63 Mature

DOWN

1 Players
2 Stench
3 Actor Franchot
4 1916 battle site
5 Dancer Astaire
6 Houston university
7 Numerical ending
8 Jack of *Barney Miller*
9 Sounds of hesitation
10 Pitch woo
11 Hebrew month
12 Solitary
13 Annexes
18 Burr et al.
19 Most timid
23 Whodunit writer Ruth
24 Capers
25 Beauty's colleague
26 Ponders
27 Beatles' record label
28 Travel in neutral
29 Fund-raising event
30 Edberg or Wilander
31 Inventor Nikola
32 Curvy letters
34 European capital
37 Hasbro rival
38 Agitating
44 Deluges
45 Above: Lat.
46 Rectify
47 Cinema canine
48 Nîmes nothing
49 Fed
50 Hebrew month
51 Loopy
52 Complacent
53 Head of France
55 Ecology grp.
56 Solemn promise
57 Stevedores' grp.

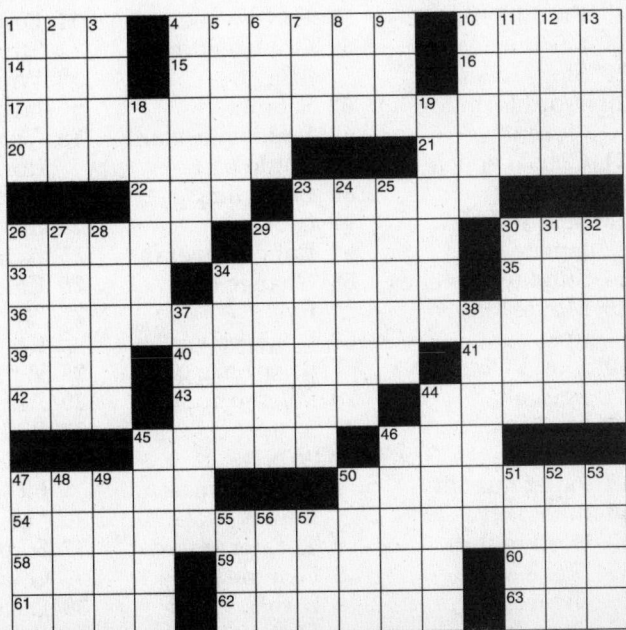

ACROSS
1 Some G-men
6 Loud thud
9 Golf concern
12 Like some plays
14 Tip
16 Roadhouse
17 Book beginning
20 Song beginning
21 Draw out
24 Patty Duke's real first name
25 Lets off
26 Diet Pepsi rival
29 Neighbor of Belg.
30 27 Down, for one
31 Intoxicating
33 Wind dir.
34 Meal beginning
38 Unser, Jr. and Sr.
41 Studio stand
42 Bear in the sky
46 PBS funder
47 Gallery's *raison d'être*
48 WWI soldier's gear
51 Kite and Mix
53 Abba tune of 1976
54 Term-of-office beginning
58 Workout beginning
62 Actress Meyers
63 Singer Braxton
64 Dan Jansen, for one
65 Letters on a food label
66 Alias, for short
67 Nestles

DOWN
1 "__ on your life!"
2 Santa __ winds
3 Antietam soldier
4 Successor of Tiberius
5 Perfumery permeation
6 Burger topping
7 Like two peas in __
8 Choice list
9 Inner surfaces
10 Chants
11 Catch
13 Woolf's __ *Lighthouse*
15 "Generals and Majors" band
18 Most sassy
19 BOS stat
21 Give the go-ahead
22 Word form for "outer"
23 Cpl., for one
26 Pregame picnic site
27 Ax look-alike
28 "Ciao!"
32 It follows *printemps*
35 Pelletlike veggie
36 Norm to Norman
37 Nadia Comaneci, e.g.
38 Like *All Quiet on the Western Front*
39 Movie maven Maltin
40 West Bank district
43 PC capacity letters
44 Fed. funding to individuals
45 Blotter letters
49 Islamic bigwigs
50 Aprons
52 Bottom line
53 Aphorist's offering
55 Belly
56 Second word at storytime
57 Vegas alternative
59 Alphabetic trio
60 Brain-wave readout, for short
61 SAT takers

ACROSS
1 Until now
6 Sandbox accessory
10 Rapid
14 Put up with
15 Writer Bombeck
16 Kal Kan rival
17 Prominent hairline feature
19 Story teller
20 Word form for "recent"
21 Glacial epoch
22 Penny
23 Sold-out sign letters
24 Sunday speeches
26 Movie follow-ups
30 Moral violation
31 Egg cell
32 Medicos
35 Felt sore
39 Paper quantity
40 Inner selves
42 Hard to find
43 "Take a chance!"
45 Orderly
46 Moran of *Happy Days*
47 Put to good use
49 Chambermaid's need
51 Sort of warm
55 Court divider
56 Actress Turner
57 Forty winks
59 Govt. lending org.
62 Satanic
63 Vaudeville stars
65 Bottle part
66 Bestselling cookie
67 Put one over on
68 Change for a five
69 __ majesty (treason, e.g.)
70 Solemn appeals

DOWN
1 Cut down, as a tree
2 Theater award
3 Generic dog's name
4 Fuss
5 Do an electrical job
6 __ Le Pew
7 Regions
8 Public persona
9 L.A. team
10 '80s primetime soap
11 Foreigner
12 Stretches across
13 Wrongful act, in law
18 Gives a dressing-down to
23 World leaders' meetings
25 Actress Farrow
26 Categorize
27 "If __ I Would Leave You"
28 Wharf
29 Any second now
33 Billiards stick
34 Open-handed blow
36 "Listen!"
37 Southernmost Great Lake
38 Disavow
41 Poem part
44 Make lace
48 Small handgun
50 Taken care of
51 Sanctuary
52 *Holiday* __ (skating show)
53 Sleeper's sound
54 Great expectations
56 Carson's successor
58 Bassoon relative
59 State of agitation
60 Johann Sebastian __
61 Poses a question
64 Coach Parseghian

417   BIG BUCKS by Richard Silvestri

ACROSS
1 Spaghetti, e.g.
6 Not us
10 College military grp.
14 The Ram
15 Angel topper
16 Poet Pound
17 Like a rich cobbler?
19 Frog kin
20 Rebel Turner
21 Put on a play
22 Fairy-tale opener
23 Like a rich paver?
26 Pertaining to stars
29 Infant
30 Back-to-health process, for short
31 Significant
34 Summery
37 Tabriz resident
38 Be in debt
39 Too big
41 Quayle or Rather
42 War horse
44 Clinic worker
45 High card
46 Brook
47 Like a rich farmer?
53 Piece of land
54 "Peachy!"
55 Slugger Gehrig
58 Afrikaner
59 Like a rich computer programmer?
62 "This __ outrage!"
63 British carbine
64 Recipient
65 London gallery
66 Bustle
67 Shell out

DOWN
1 Chess piece
2 Vicinity
3 Delta deposit
4 __ Aviv
5 Powdery residue
6 Greek letter
7 Chicago Bears founder
8 Pensive poem
9 California city
10 Verbal zinger
11 Atmospheric layer
12 Smidgen
13 Military student
18 Donkey: Ger.
23 Port of Algiers
24 Fig Newtons name
25 Home of the Blue Jays
26 Like the Negev
27 Vaccines
28 Comparative word
31 A Stooge
32 Wonderment
33 Clampett patriarch
34 At this point
35 Mountain in Thessaly
36 Abound
40 Small town
43 Wimbledon figure
45 Actor Brian
46 Oxford, for one
47 Custom
48 Word form for "twenty"
49 Terrific
50 Fifty past (the hour)
51 Couldn't stand
52 "Culture" word form
55 "I Walk the __" (Cash song)
56 Not decided
57 Secondhand
60 LP successors
61 Dance party

418   DECIMAL SYSTEM by Ray Hamel

ACROSS
1 Defect
5 Con game
9 Poet Angelou
13 Make a decision
14 Radiant ring
15 Engraver Albrecht
16 Sea east of the Caspian
17 Choir voice
18 Nicholas Gage book
19 Biblical code
22 United
23 Soup garnish
24 Loses pounds
27 Nods, maybe
30 "__ Was a Lady" (1932 tune)
31 Lumberjack's tools
32 Pitfall
36 Parlor game
39 Fabric mishap
40 Start of a 1/1 title
41 Muscat resident
42 Makes mittens
43 Yellow-fever carrier
44 Stationary
48 Obstinate sort
49 1980s TV drama
56 Alley button
57 Large wading bird
58 Insist
59 Newsman Garrick
60 Crazy
61 __ avis
62 Clarke and Murray
63 Small fortress
64 *The Dukes of Hazzard* spinoff

DOWN
1 College club
2 Entice
3 Lawyer Dershowitz
4 Greeting warmly
5 Scandal
6 Storm preceder
7 Utah resort
8 Titania or Oberon
9 Hornless cow
10 Football site
11 Streisand film
12 Crop up
15 Floor models
20 Beginning
21 Gown
24 Stage constructions
25 Yard covering
26 Sneaking suspicion
27 River to the Gulf of California
28 Jump for joy
29 Gardening need
32 Split a condo, perhaps
33 Where Kuralt reported from
34 Writer Rice
35 Greek letters
37 __ *Derringer* ('50s TV western)
38 Brown bread
42 __ Hawk, NC
44 Play a guitar
45 Eta follower
46 Pew path
47 Kilmer poem
48 Noted moralist?
50 Chute material
51 Clarinet cousin
52 Bane of the farmer's wife
53 Tennis champ Lendl
54 Pupil of Seneca
55 Mardi __

419 FOUR FOR FOUR by Wayne Robert Williams

ACROSS

1 Fink
4 Under ideal circumstances
10 *Batman* sound effect
14 Novelist Levin
15 Admiral or cabin boy
16 Identifiable atmosphere
17 2 wks. off
18 Do a court sport, perhaps
20 Moves to action
22 Examine, in a way
23 End-table item
24 Worldly
27 Extended gaze
29 Librarian's stamp
30 Skater Babilonia
33 Precolumbian
35 Mil. installation
36 Defraud
37 Goes four for four, maybe
42 Garfield's foil
43 Abu Dhabi, Dubai et al.

44 Price ceiling
45 Khaki shade
46 French clerics
48 Polonius and Laertes
52 EMS devices
54 Dispatched
55 Kerry County seat
58 Peter or Paul, but not Mary
60 Classic saga
63 Faucet
64 Enthusiastic
65 Repayment period
66 Author Umberto
67 Makes one
68 Elapses
69 Home library

DOWN

1 Opposes
2 Biblical mount
3 West Coast port
4 Small vipers
5 Whoppers
6 Showing a preference

7 Tarzan portrayer Ron
8 Sea plea
9 Margarita ingredient
10 Take the odds
11 Green superhero
12 Neighborhood
13 Sail support
19 Close
21 Attempted an overthrow
25 Water supply
26 Sundance Festival state
28 Mischievous creature
30 Muscle spasm
31 Omitting none
32 General nickname
34 Is overcome by guffaws
36 Skip
37 Much utilized
38 Director Lupino
39 Malleable metal
40 '50s AEC chairman

41 Bounder
46 Impersonator
47 Tide targets
49 Trawled
50 Interlock
51 Board
52 Snow-day rides

53 Picard's frontier
55 Return to water
56 Itinerate
57 In the center of
59 Poetic pieces
61 O.T. book
62 __ Cruces, NM

420 BLESS MY SOUL! by Donna J. Stone

ACROSS

1 Breakfast of centurions?
4 Stoneworker
9 Caesarean abbreviation
13 Singer McEntire
15 Intense
16 Act like an ox
17 Olympic imp
18 Minos' realm
19 Botanist Gray et al.
20 START OF A QUIP
23 __ a customer
24 Auto acronym
25 Joanne of *Red River*
27 *Emerald Point* __ (TV oldie)
28 Is it?
32 Humble
34 Kobe robe
36 Geraint's better half
37 SPEAKER OF THE QUIP
41 Wisecrack
42 Jockey giant

43 Set straight
46 What you used to be
47 Bad start?
50 Montana stats
51 Fireworks reaction
53 Ancient problem solvers
55 END OF QUIP
60 Wordless greetings
61 *Macbeth* or *Medea*
62 Sites
63 Pro bono
64 Not as stringent
65 Boring
66 Minus
67 Touch up
68 Pipe fitter's union?

DOWN

1 Astoria site
2 Shakespearean setting
3 Stomachs
4 Medieval weapon

5 Good-sized lot
6 De Lesseps' canal
7 Aquatic mammal
8 Essential
9 Persian bigwig
10 Rose Bowl city
11 Stanza type
12 Literary monogram
14 Short helper?
21 __ so many words
22 Affliction
26 Sturm __ Drang
29 '70s White House kid
30 Spanish etcher
31 Nip
33 Short note
34 Patella's place
35 "That hurts!"
37 Dedicated
38 Soap segments
39 Duncan's denial
40 Super-duper

41 Smidgen
44 Lon of Cambodia
45 Learn to walk
47 Elephant man
48 Eaves dropper?
49 Poetic comparison
52 Walker of whiskey

54 Gritty
56 Takes advantage of
57 __-Coburg
58 Mass communication?
59 Dry-goods measure
60 Punters' org.

421 — UTENSILS FOR YOUR PENCILS by Lee Weaver

ACROSS
1 Delhi dress
5 Like rich soil
10 Three-handed card game
14 Exuberance
15 City or circle preceder
16 Architect Saarinen
17 Male turkeys
18 Meat/vegetable mixtures
19 Lawyer: Abbr.
20 Annual football event
22 __ Park, CO
23 Winnie the Pooh's pal
24 Seed covering
25 Roman sea god
29 Napped leathers
31 Cease, to a sailor
32 Orderly
34 Dutch cheese
36 Brooch
37 Boise's state
38 Feel remorse
39 Reverberate
41 Garr or Hatcher
42 Knocks for a loop
44 Postponed indefinitely
46 West Indies islands
48 __-do-well
49 Bagel filling
50 Confuse
52 Hack novel
58 French Sudan, today
59 Photo tint
60 Inlet
61 Fruit drinks
62 Extraterrestrial
63 Not up yet
64 "Listen!"
65 Skeptical
66 Who's the __? (Danza sitcom)

DOWN
1 Matching groups
2 Baseball manager Felipe
3 Highway exit
4 Skirt panels
5 Capital of Portugal
6 Aware of
7 All over again
8 Kitten sound
9 Many mos.
10 By the shore
11 Large percussion instrument
12 Johnson of Laugh-In
13 Playthings
21 Disastrous defeat
22 Before, poetically
24 Family vehicle
25 Back of the neck
26 Push out
27 Alms seeker
28 Finished
29 Indian title
30 Spa offering
33 A sense organ
35 Army chow
37 Roman road
40 Slender, four-sided pillar
42 "Go away!"
43 City transportation
45 Loser at Gettysburg
47 New York city
50 Asian nursemaid
51 Baby word
52 Brazilian soccer great
53 Role for Ronny Howard
54 Wedding-cake feature
55 Timber wolf
56 Nights before
57 Cincinnati team
59 Gal of song

422 — D DAY by Rich Norris

ACROSS
1 Metered vehicles
6 VCR outlets
9 Milk snake
14 Fight site
15 That guy
16 Concerto instrument
17 Computer component
19 Salad ingredient
20 Trump or Duck
22 Digital watch feature: Abbr.
23 Doohickeys
27 Fox hunter's cry
30 Workers' organizations
31 Sudden police action
32 __ way (not at all)
33 Team swimming game
38 Reading room
39 Wash-and-wear
41 Former Egypt-Syria alliance: Abbr.
42 Hates
44 Palindromic rock group
45 Smell bad
46 Wholesale unit
48 Benefactor, as of a college
51 Genuine
52 Mauna __
53 Poetic device
55 Peter of Easy Rider
58 Desert whirlwind
63 Ancient Peruvian
64 Sharp curve
65 Linda Lavin sitcom
66 Impoverished
67 Porker place
68 Cry of dismay

DOWN
1 Wee bit
2 Jackie's second
3 Signs, in a way
4 Sign
5 Make blue
6 Becomes sparser
7 __ Las Vegas (Presley film)
8 Process, as ore
9 Mil. address
10 Big racket
11 Exacta relative
12 Son of Cain
13 Mozart composition
18 Goes bad
21 Challenger
23 Tour leader
24 Building addition
25 Formal evening gathering
26 Icky stuff
28 NFL Hall-of-Famer Yale __
29 Backtalk
33 Keen perception
34 Imitate
35 Football scores: Abbr.
36 Cabinet department
37 Give an address
39 Made pictures
40 Garden tools
43 Corp. bigshot
44 As simple as __
46 Leave at the altar
47 Eventually
48 Mischievous
49 Nary a soul
50 Carnival attractions
51 Actress Spacek
54 Has to
56 June honoree
57 Some
59 Inventor Whitney
60 Celebrity, initially
61 Wintry hazard
62 Bandleader Brown

423 APT NICKNAMES by Fred Piscop

ACROSS
1 Rum cakes
6 In two
11 Alcott's __ *Boys*
14 Lift up
15 Resiliency
16 Hawaiian instrument
17 Nickname of the boss's driver?
19 Slangy denial
20 Musical form
21 Greek vowel
22 "__ down!" ("Quiet!")
23 Croat's neighbor
25 Humanlike robot
27 Went headlong
31 Portal
32 Tree chopper
33 Long tales
35 Big name in baseball cards
38 Annapolis students, for short
40 Burton of *Star Trek: TNG*
42 On the house
43 "Fiddlesticks!"
45 Like a mosaic
47 __-Locka, FL
48 Airline to Tel Aviv
50 Hero since 1938
52 Baseball star Fisk
55 Boxer Oscar __ Hoya
56 Grand Ole __
57 On the __ vive
59 Videodisc beams
63 Word form for "one"
64 Nickname of the camping-trip leader?
66 TV Chihuahua
67 Knock off work, slangily
68 Run off together
69 License plate
70 Trusty mount
71 Thickheaded

DOWN
1 Mrs. Truman
2 Quartet member
3 Farm structure
4 Resting
5 Some couches
6 Barbecue residue
7 Lotsa cash
8 Novelist Loos
9 Return, as to custody
10 Jefferson's bill
11 Nickname of the dance chaperone?
12 Giraffe's cousin
13 Did some hemming
18 __ *Knowledge* (Nicholson film)
22 Evidence
24 Biblical verb
26 Finish an i
27 Summer retreat
28 WWII enemy
29 Nickname of the misleader?
30 *Jezebel* star
34 "Cheers!"
36 Rap group Salt-N-___
37 Actor Penn
39 Charlie Brown's sister
41 Fights off
44 Angkor __
46 Word on an arrival board
49 Chinese fruit
51 Go to the mat, slangily
52 Wapner's milieu
53 Breathing anomaly
54 Poke in the ribs
58 *Each Dawn __* (Cagney film)
60 007 alma mater
61 Exercise counts
62 *Peter Pan* pirate
64 Air-gun ammo
65 Since 1/1, to a CPA

424 EVERYBODY'S DOING IT by John D. Leavy

ACROSS
1 *The Aeneid*, e.g.
5 Study last-minute
9 Mythical fast friend
14 Western land formation
15 Bugs' home
16 Crème de la crème
17 Coffee vessels
18 First shepherd
19 Spotted pony
20 Pop dance tune
23 Take-home
24 Prosecutors: Abbr.
25 November form
29 Creamy cheese
30 Status __
33 Wall coverings
34 20 Across singers in 1974
36 Voice range
37 Railroad
38 Costa __
39 20 Across singer in 1962
41 Londoner's tube
42 Golfer Ernie
43 Wings
44 Golfer Calvin et al.
45 Moppet
46 Mattress filler
47 20 Across composers
54 Sigourney Weaver thriller
55 John Paul II, e.g.
56 Exile isle
59 Slowly, to Mehta
60 Arab monarch
61 Scorch
62 Mine finds
63 Bawls
64 Time in office

DOWN
1 Australian bird
2 __ capita
3 Proves otherwise
4 Moolah
5 Alpine lodge
6 *Lost in Space* character
7 Sir __ Guinness
8 Serial form
9 Overthrown
10 Came to earth
11 Quant skirt
12 Grid great Graham
13 Element in advertising?
21 Hazzard deputy
22 Down East
25 Good Book
26 Benefit
27 Tilts
28 Just in case
29 Ted Turner employee
30 What bees make?
31 TV spy group
32 Gives the green light
34 Gorillas and chimps
35 Release
37 Jailbird
40 Barrio populace
41 *Mr. Mom* name
44 No humanitarians
46 Off the cuff
47 Chutzpah
48 Toast topping
49 Stumble onto
50 Celebrate
51 Hurler Hideo
52 Cygnet's home
53 Mirth
57 Saloon
58 Provide weapons to

425 EIGHT-LETTER WORDS by Bob Sefick

ACROSS
1 Rent
5 Brillo rival
8 "Phooey!"
13 Skeptic's smell
14 Rock producer Brian
15 Winter months in Mexico
17 The comeback kid?
19 They're essential
20 __ Philip Randolph
21 Start of a Smith title
23 Grammy-winner Bonnie
24 Residents' ends
25 Bavarian souvenirs
27 Fiend
30 Most people
31 1,000,000 preceder
32 Staffordshire river
33 __ at (bug)
36 Have-__ (the needy)
37 Ren and Stimpy
38 18th-century poet laureate
39 UN member since '49
40 Shortwinded
41 Carrier
42 In __ (sort of)
44 Ford press secretary
45 Makes a connection
46 Lapses
47 Lalique et al.
48 Temp skill
50 Born, in Brest
53 Curie and Castle
55 Walks on again
57 Line-score entries
58 Sale-item marking
59 *Antony and Cleopatra* role
60 Start of a '37, '54 and '76 film title
61 WWII spy org.
62 Fair

DOWN
1 Home of ancient Irish kings
2 Rock group
3 Pro __
4 DDE's command
5 Gordon, for one
6 Rare birds
7 Steamed
8 Teachers' grp.
9 Press
10 Hold
11 Commuters' quests
12 What the peeved are out of
16 2707-300, e.g.
18 Quarry *del gato*
22 Dead Sea Scrolls scribe
24 Electra's daughter
26 Some cans
27 Singer Braxton
28 Third-generation member
29 Occupational therapists
30 Came to mind
32 Trunks
34 Fit to __
35 Skimmer relative
37 Encamp
38 Get rid of
40 Small tile
41 Join securely
43 "Eyes have they, but they __"
44 NFL team, in headlines
45 Lucretius' land
46 Predictable ones?
47 __ grass (meadow barley)
49 March movement
50 Student of Seneca
51 Periods
52 It: It.
54 Obsolete geog. term
56 Carol contraction

426 TIME FOR CHANGE by Norma Steinberg

ACROSS
1 Model Macpherson
5 Shoeman McAn
9 *The Trial* author Franz
14 Colorado ski town
15 Angelic corona
16 Prospero's servant
17 Bullets
18 Therefore
19 Monica of tennis
20 *Laverne & Shirley* star
23 Hair goos
24 Owns
25 Shoulder wrap
27 Play about Capote
29 Tachometer abbr.
32 Upper class
33 Minnesota Fats' game
34 Mets' stadium
35 Battle stations
38 Newspaper essay page
39 Boxing match
40 Writer Joyce Carol
41 Ave. crossers
42 Reverence
43 Batters' options
44 Donkey
46 Hourglass filling
47 Argue pettily
53 Devilfish
54 Arkin of *Chicago Hope*
55 Snack
57 Fancy tie
58 Ditka or Wallace
59 Way in
60 Divvy up
61 Congregational response
62 Stick around

DOWN
1 Zsa Zsa's sister
2 Reading light
3 Daiquiri ingredient
4 Stretched
5 "__ never believe me . . ."
6 Does damage to
7 Gymnast Korbut
8 Othello, e.g.
9 Buckwheat groats
10 Vicinities
11 Eat one's __ (have enough)
12 Boat part
13 Gore and D'Amato
21 More recent
22 Former Dolphins coach
25 Caught some z's
26 Dancer Gregory
27 Chef's hat
28 Drive out
29 Scarlett's Butler
30 Former Israeli PM
31 Church service
32 Personalities
33 Turn over earth
34 Sports-page listings
36 Demean
37 Circular
43 Outlaws
44 Cast member
45 Emulate Yamaguchi
46 Plumber's tool
47 Poet Ogden
48 Ancient Peruvian
49 Tibetan leader
50 Take __ view (disapprove)
51 Castle's protection
52 "¿Cómo __ usted?"
53 Advanced degs.
56 "Yo!"

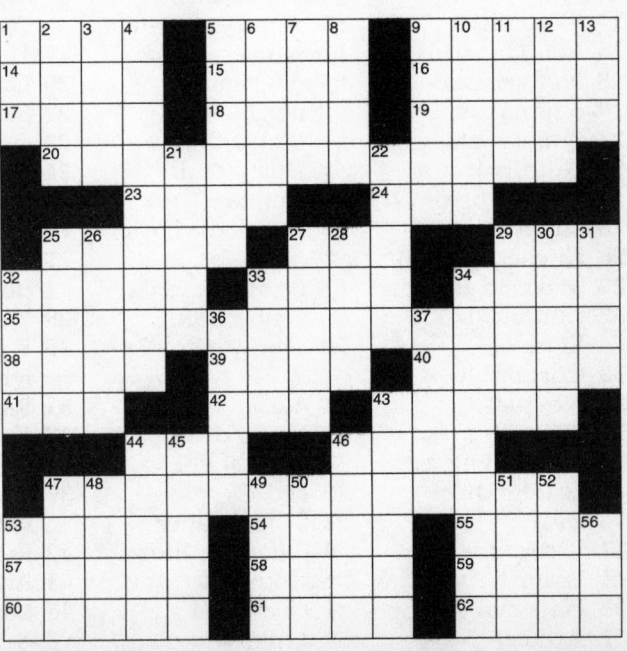

427 ALL AT SEA by Lee Weaver

ACROSS
1 Primary
6 Capp and Capone
9 Halloween disguises
14 Hawaiian "Hi!"
15 Positive vote
16 Be of use
17 More docile
18 Ordinance
19 Cowboy contest
20 Salon offering
23 Dessert choice
24 Agnus __ (Mass movement)
25 GI show sponsor
28 Kuwaiti ruler
31 Tooth covering
36 Helps along temporarily
39 Author Calvino
40 Composer Stravinsky
41 Conceit
42 Change for a five
43 Tennis champ Evert
45 Falsify ore content
48 Agreement
50 Jump
51 Elevator compartment
52 Dawn goddess
54 Segments: Abbr.
56 Subject in a civics class
63 Wickerwork willow
64 Be obligated to
65 Buffet patron
68 Sierra __
69 On a pension: Abbr.
70 Patronize a rink
71 Fur-trading name
72 Many mos.
73 Ice pinnacle

DOWN
1 Dietary component
2 Dockworker's org.
3 Frolic boisterously
4 Part of the herd
5 Lingers awhile
6 *Clan of the Cave Bear* heroine
7 Tilt
8 Made logs
9 007's drink
10 State firmly
11 Actress Thompson
12 Ukraine capital
13 Blackthorn fruit
21 Interoffice note
22 Formerly named
25 New York city
26 Sounds of regret
27 Bakery enticements
29 Currier's partner
30 Fit for a queen
32 Powerful particle
33 Excessively enthusiastic
34 Actress Verdugo
35 Also-ran
37 Canal to Buffalo
38 Part in a play
44 One who scoffs
46 Finish-line feature
47 Suitability
49 Freight weight
53 Fairy tale, e.g.
55 Tent holder
56 Popular soft drink
57 Applications
58 Free-for-all
59 Clinton cabinet member
60 Wash-basin partner
61 Doggie doctors
62 Milky Way part
66 Greek H
67 VCR button

428 THE BLUES by Rich Norris

ACROSS
1 Soprano's pride
6 Every bit
9 Police calls, briefly
13 Passion
14 *The Time Machine* race
15 Floor piece
16 *Clue* character
18 Not very nice
19 Simple tunes
21 __ and outs
22 Adjusted, as a spark plug
26 Slight trace
28 Kitchen cover-up
29 Make an effort
32 Conductor Reiner
33 Coal products
34 Not that
37 Swampy area
38 Sean Young, e.g.
41 Immigrant's subj.
42 Verb suffix
44 Spanish rivers
45 Flavorful
47 Awaits
49 Foot-leg connector
50 Hauled, as trash
52 Team member
53 Superfluous fuss
54 Critically important
58 Some youngsters
60 Nursery need
65 Afghanistan neighbor
66 Makes things up
67 Unaffectedly simple
68 1994 Jodie Foster film
69 Bridge expert Culbertson
70 Throw out

DOWN
1 Easter dish
2 Kind of vb.
3 Mdse.
4 School dance
5 Office furniture
6 Oodles
7 Centers of activity
8 Police artist's drawing, e.g.
9 S&L convenience
10 Illusory prospect
11 *Vin* color
12 Get the feeling
14 Word form for "outer"
17 Help
20 Grand total
22 Social slip-up
23 After, to André
24 King's eldest son
25 Pan partner
27 Suited for a purpose
29 Web site?
30 Fortune-teller's tool
31 Rapunzel feature
35 Yucca fiber
36 More foxy
39 Like some witnesses
40 Rambo portrayer
43 Addl. phone
46 Literary collection
48 Vim
50 Log structure
51 Like a lot
52 Specious talk
55 Ski Hall of Fame site
56 Follow orders
57 Cobb et al.
59 NBC comedy show, for short
61 Grow
62 Chip accompaniment
63 Night time
64 Family mem.

WHO'S SHOUTING? by Patrick Jordan

ACROSS
1 Herringlike fish
6 *Air Force One* star
10 Hurt severely
14 Divination deck
15 Think-tank product
16 Atahualpa's people
17 Thomas Gray work
18 "TALLY-HO!"
20 More meager
22 Like marshland
23 Soprano Jenny
24 1988 Tom Hanks film
26 Most skilled
29 Comes about gradually
34 Much of southern Africa
35 Wharf
36 __ Bator, Mongolia
37 Mild oaths
38 Increases
39 Bible belt?
40 45 Across' city

41 A fathom has six
42 Steakhouse order
43 Frightened suddenly
45 Rubicon crosser
46 Geologic time unit
47 Teri of *Tootsie*
48 Egyptian dam
52 Fun spoilers
56 "EN GARDE!"
59 "Weird Al" Yankovic parody
60 Damage
61 Paris hotel
62 Extent
63 TV award
64 Protein bean
65 Trapshooting target

DOWN
1 Watch part
2 Healthy
3 Field of expertise
4 "MUSH!"
5 Hairdressers
6 Tootled a flute

7 Smell
8 Latin king
9 "Zip-A-Dee-Doo-__"
10 Siderite source
11 Poker opener
12 Topped a torte
13 Mrs. Lincoln
19 Strong motivation
21 Savings acct. rate
24 Beauty's beloved
25 Climbing vine
26 States with conviction
27 Sired
28 Peruvian pack animal
29 Made a fool of
30 "TIMBER!"
31 Hodgepodges
32 City of India
33 Scornful smile
35 Beehive boss
39 Like a cloudy night sky
41 Nickname in Broadway history

44 Watch over
45 Coolidge's nickname
47 Tokyo district
48 Tennis legend
49 Did some laps
50 Despicable one
51 Palmer's followers

52 Girl in a 1918 tune
53 Nebraska native
54 Cry of surprise
55 "Leave it alone," in typesetting
57 Jrs.' dads
58 *"O Sole __"*

430 **OUT OF AFRICA by Randolph Ross**

ACROSS
1 Furnishings
6 Capote's *The Grass __*
10 In __ (on the hot seat)
14 Wide open
15 General Torrijos
16 Cool one's heels, perhaps
17 African colleen?
19 Obote's successor
20 Catches
21 Makes an analogy
23 Raises hackles
24 Unmasks
25 León lady
28 How sarcasts speak
31 Roman encyclopedist
32 8A and 12D
33 Ground breaker
34 Windshield wipers, perhaps
35 Sticks to the ribs?
36 Franklin's mom
37 Feasted on

38 Roquefort receptacle
39 Endangered Hawaiians
40 Boston University athletes
42 Doug of *Melrose Place*
43 *Brave New World* caste
44 PGA nickname
45 Apollo's neighborhood
47 Checked
51 Lateral beginning
52 African ice-cream maker?
54 Mag magnate
55 Look sullen
56 "__ Mio"
57 West et al.
58 Cellini patron
59 Eye sores

DOWN
1 Melba, for one
2 Actor Richard or Eddie

3 Ripken, Sr. and Jr.
4 Views
5 Take a second?
6 Story inconsistencies
7 Oldest prophetic book
8 Operated
9 Cardinals, e.g.
10 Stir
11 African Maverick?
12 Tennis situation
13 Sears section
18 Calculus calculation
22 Saffron's family
24 *L'Arlésienne* composer
25 Nursery-rhyme name
26 Cheer
27 African sidekick?
28 Mountain and touring, for two
29 *El Cid* star
30 Vitamin source
32 Turns
35 Opening

36 Most acute
38 Refer to
39 Hogan dwellers
41 Leans (on)
42 Basted
44 Hobbit's home
45 Martin role

46 Soft tone
47 Bolt connector
48 Schliemann discovery
49 A.A. Fair's real first name
50 Shades
53 Orion's love

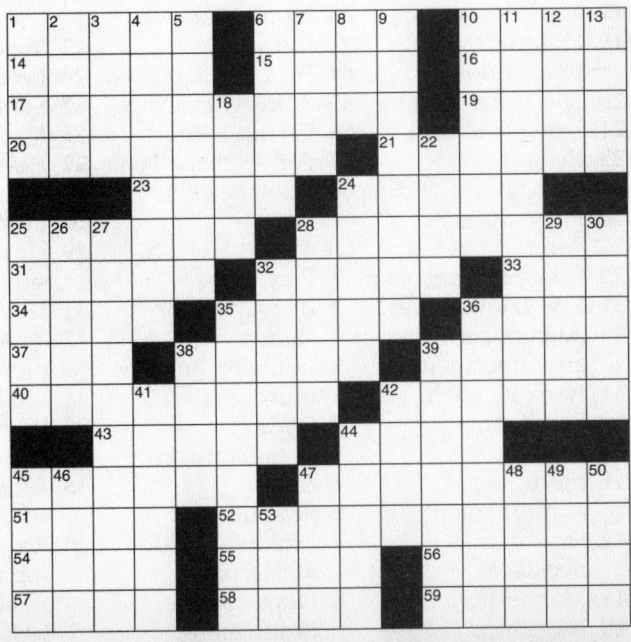

ACROSS
1 Scottish lake
5 Cast member
10 Western writer Grey
14 Taj Mahal site
15 Greene of *Bonanza*
16 "An apple __ ..."
17 Bottomless
18 Pass into law
19 "Encore!"
20 Positive vote
21 Shoe-sole material
23 Encounters
25 Iroquoian Indians
26 Quaking trees
28 Singer Ross
30 Imperfection
31 Joins, as metal
32 Dine
35 Comments from Sandy
36 Small mountains
37 Maneuverable, as a yacht
38 British forces: Abbr.
39 Gyrates
40 Powerful beam
41 Bamboos, e.g.
42 Folkloric woodsman
43 Pay out
45 Winter coat
46 Simple task
49 Resort feature
52 Sea eagle
53 Give up the right to
54 Make a web
55 Min. fractions
56 Gunpowder ingredient
57 Punt, e.g.
58 Singles
59 Winter gliders
60 "Uh huh!"

DOWN
1 Titled woman
2 Pointed arch
3 Pristine used car
4 Prefix for hazard
5 Gives a warning
6 Highway markers
7 Fairway hazard
8 In the past
9 Born-again tires
10 South African country
11 Sun-dried brick
12 Nostrils
13 Ogler
21 Indian Head, e.g.
22 Coffee brewers
24 Wrigglers
26 At a distance
27 Poet Teasdale
28 Forest clearings
29 Troubles
31 Unmanageable
32 Extremely simple
33 Field of study
34 Sea swallow
36 Rural dances
37 Tug sharply
39 Russo of *Tin Cup*
40 Fishline adjunct
41 Niche
42 Bread makers
43 Fire-truck warning
44 Coventry cash
45 Worked on a road
46 Acapulco coin
47 Fall short
48 Refer to
50 12-point type
51 Egyptian cross
54 Upper atmosphere

ACROSS
1 Take __ (travel)
6 Not domesticated
11 FedEx rival
14 Doorbell sound
15 Like beer at a barbecue
16 Total
17 *M*A*S*H* doctor
19 Palindromic preposition
20 *Star Trek* helmsman
21 Universal ideal
22 Region
23 Teenage TV doctor
28 From the U.S.: Abbr.
30 Concert closer, often
31 Like some drives
33 Auctioneer's announcement
34 Rank below lt.
37 Small guns
39 Teaser
41 Paid announcments
42 Hawaiian necklaces
44 Marvelous
45 Iran, once
47 Pond denizens
48 '60s TV doctor
52 Kitchen emanation
53 Psyche parts
54 *On the __* (Kerouac book)
58 Bagel partner
59 '70s TV doctor
63 Numerical word form
64 For a specific purpose
65 Actress MacDowell
66 Go out with
67 Atmospheric layer
68 Take the helm

DOWN
1 Play parts
2 By way of, for short
3 Iranian monetary unit
4 Rude
5 __ talk (pregame ritual)
6 Search, as for food
7 Prohibits legally, as a strike
8 Hope-Crosby destination
9 Ludwig's lament
10 Actor Cariou
11 Computer operators
12 Tomato-sauce ingredient
13 Nasty campaign tactic
18 Ike's WWII command
22 Veneration
24 Baltimore team
25 Subj. for Keynes
26 Made, as a putt
27 Restaurant patron, at first
28 Litmus reddener
29 Unwieldy situation
31 Health resort
32 Paperwork processor
34 Blinds component
35 Precious stones
36 Attempt
38 Affirmative from Alberto
40 Respectfully submissive
43 __ Valley (high-tech region)
45 Each
46 Cite as evidence
48 Unwelcome surprises
49 Cherish
50 Guts
51 Biblical beast
55 Adjective for shoppe
56 Irish Rose's lover
57 Clothing factory employee
59 __ Tse-tung
60 Ax relative
61 Greek letter
62 Used to be

433 SHORT STORIES by Patrick Jordan

ACROSS

1 Bodybuilder's bane
5 Find repugnant
10 Baylor University site
14 Santa __, CA
15 Mild cigar
16 Wrinkle remover
17 Actor Bogosian
18 Great Barrier Reef material
19 __ up (judge)
20 Julia Roberts role
22 Doris and Dennis
23 __ ex machina
24 Business VIP
26 Punish with a fine
29 Behind all the others
34 Outdoor disguise, in Army lingo
35 Some noblemen
36 "Now I understand!"
37 Fairy-tale challenger
41 Wall climber
42 Sit through a second showing
43 *TV Guide* time span
44 Donna Karan, e.g.
46 Mixed drinks
48 Peat digger's place
49 Catamaran canvas
50 Ending for soft or silver
53 Fairy-tale girl
59 Quizmaster Trebek
60 Vietnamese capital
61 Rocker Billy
62 Prizefighter's outerwear
63 Society's crème de la crème
64 Requirement
65 They're split for soup
66 Eminent
67 Festive occasion

DOWN

1 Worry too much
2 Actress Singer
3 P __ "puzzle"
4 Piece of scenery
5 Build up, as interest
6 Shapeless masses
7 Rabbit's kin
8 Type of exam
9 Teacher's daily recitation
10 Solomon's asset
11 Operatic piece
12 Warm and comfortable
13 Wallet fillers
21 Common Market, familiarly
25 While starter
26 Pungent
27 Purple shade
28 58 Down won five of them
29 MPAA employee
30 Shallowest Great Lake
31 Like some furniture
32 Started with fright
33 Sea World structures
35 In __ (basically)
38 Therefore
39 Draw out
40 Bee-sting symptom
45 Wild goats
46 Pampered
47 Commit perjury
49 Struck down
50 Bend out of shape
51 Sunburn soother
52 Musical McEntire
54 Angelic aura
55 Part of BTU
56 Inkling
57 Playwright Coward
58 Alan of *M*A*S*H*

434 CIRCULAR REASONING by A.J. Santora

ACROSS

1 Brando role
7 N.T. book
10 Diminutive suffix
13 Conciliatory
14 Whom: Fr.
15 Role for Edward G.
16 Reversal of fortunes
18 Robt. __
19 *Science and Health* writer
21 __ *See It* (Getty book)
23 Settled
24 Analogize
25 Former CNN anchorman
27 Consumed
28 Cordwood units
29 Phnom __
30 Cartoonist Key
31 Notion
32 Czech river
34 Word form for "flow"
36 Separate
38 __ *volente*
39 Disconcert
43 Hoot's partner
45 Nicklaus' alma mater
46 Frozen sheet
47 Heroic work
48 Hockey position
50 Geological period
51 High-turnover company
54 Stick in the fridge
55 Political press agent
58 Singer Carter
59 Halsey's org.
60 Bone collagen
61 Flour source
62 Mandolin part
63 Natural-history museum souvenirs

DOWN

1 Teen trauma
2 Indonesian island group
3 Paleozoic period
4 O'Neill's Christie
5 Fancy circlet
6 Organic adhesive
7 Associated
8 Devo's music
9 They lie low
10 Irish county
11 Summer quaff
12 "We grope as if we had __": Isaiah
15 Enumerated easily
17 By the way: Lat.
20 Make a new Windsor
21 Shakespearean character
22 What *elle* means
26 Maytag rival
33 Drum material
34 Extend or end a contract
35 #1 tune of '56
36 Attila-era cleric
37 "Mrs. Brown, You've Got __ Daughter"
38 Blair's street
40 Gave notice to
41 Chaotic place
42 Poetic time
43 Frog eaters
44 Guns
49 Cratchits' Christmas dinner
52 __ *dixit*
53 Prefix for pod
56 49 Down, to Thérèse
57 White-hat wearers

ALL OVER THE WORLD by Rand H. Burns

ACROSS
1 Tree labs
9 On the *Golden Hind*
15 Mariner
16 Flat
17 Noted English world traveler
19 Halifax clock setting: Abbr.
20 Ogee's profile
21 Eggy drink
22 __ Cruces, NM
23 Manipulators
25 PC key
27 Knocks off
28 Crescentic
30 Erne
33 Dries timothy
34 Dumbfounds
36 Foot bones
38 Solvent, for short
39 Amenity to change
43 Instant-replay cameras, for short
47 Deplete a region's ichthyofauna
48 Increase
50 State ldrs.
51 Rib
53 Tub-thump
54 Fury
55 __ polloi
57 Layer deposit
59 Mandela's dom.
60 17 Across, in the 1570s
64 Organ rudiment
65 Bargain event
66 Dutch cheese
67 Flushed

DOWN
1 Blitz
2 Print a new edition
3 Attend a tap
4 Away
5 Most unwonted
6 Times to remember
7 Uptight
8 Lob's path
9 Lhasa __
10 City map abbr.
11 Galley slave
12 Comparable things
13 Like autumn leaves
14 Jumpers and muumuus
18 Eats
24 Picture-tube lines
26 Form 1040 ID
27 More grating
29 Zhou __
31 Homecoming group
32 EEC component
35 Rainwear fabric
37 Bark sound
39 Reasoned
40 Piano-key material
41 Boston suburb
42 New Zealand bird
44 Frugal
45 Boot bottom
46 Used a trident
49 Clad
52 *Eau* __ (brandy)
55 Great
56 Sign of things to come
58 Encircle
61 Bounder
62 Loc. of 59 Across
63 *Peer Gynt* role

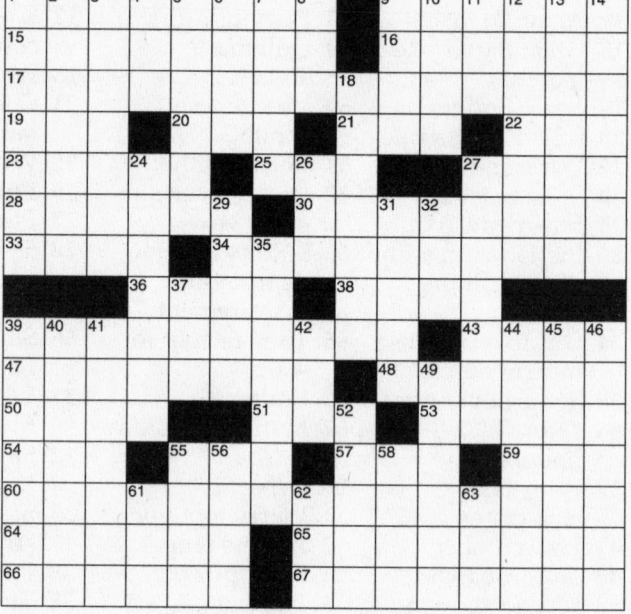

SOUND REASONING by Norma Steinberg

ACROSS
1 Diminishes
5 "__ want is a room somewhere . . ."
9 __-Magnon man
12 Appearance
13 Nary a soul
15 Levin and Gershwin
16 Ali's arena
18 Snack
19 Whichever
20 Automotive pioneer
21 Mistake finder's shout
23 Channel marker
24 Part of the foot
25 Bricklayers
28 Sit-ins, e.g.
32 Choir section
33 Daily delivery
34 Fastener
35 Bridge coup
36 Judge's hammer
37 Pathway
38 Poi ingredient
39 Billfold stuffers
40 Burn slightly
41 Robin Hood's forest
43 Planted clues
44 Willy Loman's son
45 Fried-rice additive
46 Bush Chief of Staff
49 Identical
50 Winter bug
53 Singer Redding
54 45s
57 Desire
58 Fry lightly
59 Zilch
60 That girl
61 Very, in Versailles
62 Partridge's tree

DOWN
1 Napoleon home
2 Blessing
3 Square-shaped
4 Glide
5 Whites, to Chicanos
6 "Oh, my!"
7 Superman's girlfriend
8 Hostel
9 Gator's relative
10 Impetuous
11 DC workplace monitors
14 Chinese appetizer
15 Up the river
17 Parts of speech
22 Autumn mo.
23 Economic extremes
24 The Ram
25 Ship's poles
26 Koran subject
27 Rubberneck
28 Used macadam
29 Perspective
30 Slight coloration
31 Velocity
33 __ *La Mancha*
36 Mistakes
40 Ambulance sound
42 Take the gold
43 Neighborhood friends
45 Sticky stuff
46 Porcine females
47 Brigham Young's destination
48 WXY on a phone
49 Goad
50 Huge ice chunk
51 Actress Olin
52 Computer owner
55 Cereal grain
56 Macroeconomic indicator: Abbr.

437 HARD RAIN by Lee Weaver

ACROSS
1 Movie award
6 Islam holy city
11 Scale starts
14 Swiftly
15 Campfire remains
16 Wise bird
17 Fried cornmeal creations
19 African antelope
20 Not becoming
21 Shoe part
23 Gorilla or chimp
24 Pestle's partner
26 Surfaces of gems
30 Enjoy a favorite book
31 Mountains of Russia
32 Barbecue materials
33 Chromosome component
36 New Jersey NBA team
37 Macbeth's title
38 Ink spot
39 Perfume amount
40 Mountain top
41 Good: Sp.
42 Make happy
44 Soaking wet
45 Boy Scout units
46 James Bond, e.g.
47 Reasoning
48 Putting into office
53 Hole-punching gadget
54 At a diagonal
57 Afternoon social
58 Make happy
59 Nervous
60 Make a mistake
61 Blip producer
62 On the peevish side

DOWN
1 Honolulu's island
2 Whirled
3 Mama __ Elliot
4 Feel sore
5 Does over and over
6 Table wood
7 Catch sight of
8 Tai __ (martial art)
9 Average grade
10 Guarantees
11 Swam in a crouch
12 Deed holder
13 Speak unclearly
18 Refs' counterparts
22 Harper Valley grp.
24 Intended
25 Heraldic border
26 Rainy-day money, e.g.
27 Vicinity
28 Second-story man
29 Overhead trains
30 Friars event
32 Gourmet cooks
34 Not any
35 Like __ of bricks
37 Fall over one's feet
38 Baby bloomer
40 Track official
41 Protest tactic
43 Luau dip
44 Building detail, for short
45 Babel structure
46 More cunning
47 Running behind
48 Sundance's girlfriend
49 Genealogy chart
50 B&Bs
51 Bird's shelter
52 Actor Joel
55 Dockworker's org.
56 Small amount

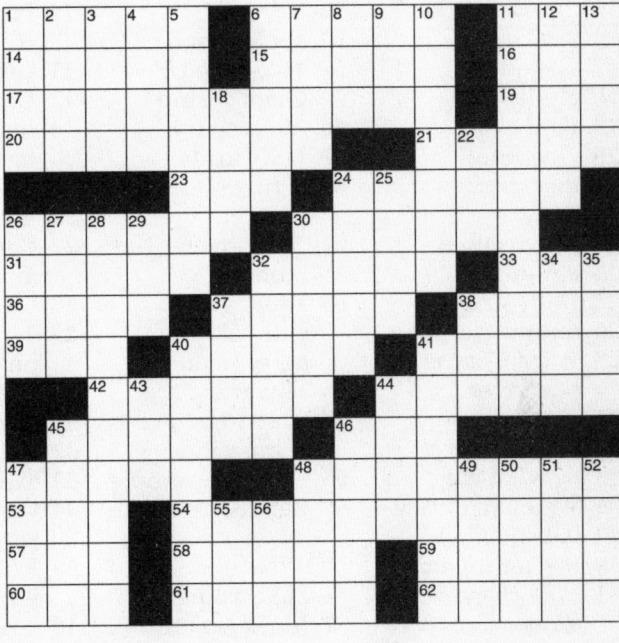

438 MATCHED SETS by Rich Norris

ACROSS
1 Mont Blanc, for one
4 Pundit
9 Openers, in poker
14 Motor vehicle
15 Mortise insert
16 German sub
17 Strong and vigorous
19 Towel off again
20 6 Down, e.g.
21 Flatter, so they say
23 Search for
24 Some NCOs
25 Cockpit features
32 May honoree
35 Wharf
36 Finalize, as a deal
37 Seine sights
39 Gave out cards
42 Astronaut Slayton
43 Thumb-sucker of comics
45 Equal
47 Actor Beatty
48 Long day at Shea
52 Greek Cupid
53 "Catch a Falling Star" singer
56 Rural gathering?
60 Slopes fixture
63 Provide with gear
64 David Lynch TV drama
66 Actress Rene
67 Like The X-Files
68 "O Sole __"
69 Not left over
70 Takes a breather
71 Elected officials

DOWN
1 Playbill heading
2 Estate grounds
3 Ordinary writing
4 Heist
5 Mae or Adam
6 Picnic poopers
7 One of the Stooges
8 Rainbow color
9 Court figures
10 Help a hood
11 Musical ending
12 Go-__ (kid's vehicle)
13 Eye annoyance
18 Nourish
22 Part of a chain: Abbr.
24 Predicaments
26 Help
27 Golfer Elder
28 Beetlike
29 Actor Reginald
30 Gospel writer
31 Went over the limit
32 Balmy
33 Hodgepodge
34 Computer listing
38 Deli offering
40 Grazing area
41 Bill's "excellent" pal
44 Think about, in a way
46 Baker's blueprints
49 Hosp. areas
50 More steamy
51 Actor's quest
54 The Heat's home
55 Next __ (closest relatives)
56 Roll-call response
57 Water color
58 Corrosion
59 Woodshop gadget
60 Letter opener
61 Wrinkle, as one's brow
62 General __ chicken (Chinese fare)
65 Sma

LONE-STAR STARS by Patrick Jordan

ACROSS
1 Slightly open
5 Suffragist Carrie Chapman __
9 Wisecrack
13 Ear lender?
15 Phrase of approximation
16 Charlie Parker's sax
17 Sheeplike
18 __-deucy
19 Ease away (from)
20 Onetime TV detective
23 Weep
24 Unspecified amount
25 Daily grind
26 Summer ermine
28 Ward Cleaver portrayer
32 Nothing more than
35 In what way
36 Vaughan of jazz
37 Part of CEO
38 British streetcars
41 *Wild Horse Mesa* author Grey
42 Checkmarks
44 Dundee declination
45 Vigorous spirit
46 1937 Barbara Stanwyck title role
50 Truce's aftermath
51 Cable TV channel
52 RR stop
55 Took a chair
57 Two-time US Open champ
60 Math course
62 Lode loads
63 Scruggs' C&W partner
64 "The green-eyed monster"
65 Pablo's enthusiastic agreement
66 Thwarts
67 Coleridge composition
68 __ good example
69 Zebras, to lions

DOWN
1 Bakery lure
2 Musk maker
3 Friendliness
4 Talk wildly
5 Literary collaborator
6 Rainbow shapes
7 African menace
8 Imported auto
9 Mandible
10 Preceder of college or vote
11 Get top billing
12 Danza or Dorsett
14 India's first prime minister
21 Word of duty
22 Entre __
27 Causes astonishment
28 Cartoon magpie
29 Term of respect on a safari
30 Grandmother
31 Subsequently
32 NL team
33 Theater sign
34 Open to suggestion
39 Kuala Lumpur is its capital
40 Alabama city
43 Bed board
47 Perpendicular to this answer
48 "So Long __" (*Hello, Dolly!* song)
49 Singer Roy
52 Riser plus tread
53 Royal bestowal
54 Restless
55 52 Down part
56 Italian river
58 "__ la vie!"
59 Feed the pigs
61 Workout locale

BUM STEER by Donna J. Stone

ACROSS
1 Sennett staffers
5 Skip past the ads
8 Far and away
14 Viscount's better
15 High dudgeon
16 Sound uncertain
17 "Clinton's Big Ditch"
18 Ham's surroundings
19 *Sing Along With Mitch* regular
20 START OF AN ADDISON MIZNER QUOTE
23 Impression
24 When the French fry
25 Gayle's sis
26 Plot outline
31 Geologist's suffix
33 Goliath or Glumdalclitch
35 Album selection
36 Smitten
38 MIDDLE OF QUOTE
40 German river
41 Works
43 *Living and Loving* author
45 Mountain of myth
46 Prosecutor's prerogative
48 First name in architecture
50 Actress Zetterling
51 Winner at Actium
54 END OF QUOTE
57 Denver dish
59 *Children __ Lesser God*
60 By herself: Lat.
61 Obsession
62 Family
63 Trunk feature
64 Jacksonian bill
65 Switchboard abbr.
66 Frosty, in Tibet?

DOWN
1 New Hampshire campus
2 Propelled a shell
3 Elite
4 Wintry adjective
5 Mock rock
6 Nordic
7 Pizza handler
8 Parallel
9 Enhance
10 It's a long story
11 Boyar basher
12 Armstrong transport
13 Cen. segments
21 Rat pack
22 College teacher
26 Beezer
27 Almost 120 yards square
28 Cellular ancestor
29 Made secure
30 Prudhomme ingredient
31 *Young Frankenstein* character
32 Surveyor's item
34 Trade letters
37 *Exodus* character
39 *Shampoo* star
42 Front-seat option
44 Lancelot in *Camelot*
47 Unrefined
49 Piece from a Russian composer?
51 Put on
52 Series-to-be, maybe
53 Cremona craftsman
54 __ noire
55 *thirtysomething* star
56 Came to
57 Hardly ne'er
58 Litter sound

441 TAKING UP SPACE by Mary Brindamour

ACROSS
1 Actor Ladd
5 Short swims
9 Walks back and forth
14 Actress Kedrova
15 Buffalo's lake
16 Residence
17 Stargazer's device
19 Too thin
20 Mature
21 Worked with rattan
22 Lab heaters
23 Like some cars
25 Wooden shoe
27 Lend __ (listen)
30 Twilled
33 Dad's brother
36 Scrumptious
38 __-Locka, FL
39 Chime
40 Takes to the pawnshop
41 Was obligated to
42 Aykroyd or Rather
43 __ Island (Big Apple amusement area)
44 Old Norse poems
45 Sage
47 Ancient lute
49 Annuls
51 Not these
55 McQueen of movies
57 Metrical feet
60 Grassy meadow
61 Actress Sophia
62 Astronaut's outfit
64 Disassociated
65 Largest continent
66 Advantage
67 Thaws
68 Fasting time
69 Make one's way

DOWN
1 Mass site
2 Feudal superior
3 *Manhattan* director
4 Aberdeen denial
5 Century component
6 Do a laundry job
7 Plumbing part
8 Garden starters
9 Hair style
10 Nuisance stopper
11 Lift-off preceder
12 Writer Ferber
13 TVs
18 Seascape, for one
24 Like redwoods
26 Performances
28 "This must weigh __!"
29 Indy participant
31 Fencer's sword
32 Most Little League coaches
33 Formal hair style
34 At hand
35 Cape in Florida
37 A terrier
40 Weeded
41 "That hurts!"
43 Law firm's customers
44 Make a new bow
46 Surreptitious
48 Lynx
50 Cordage fiber
52 Circumvent
53 Hold sway
54 Stuffed
55 Shut with a bang
56 Drink to excess
58 Church area
59 Popular street name
63 Stitch

442 TIGHT SPOTS by Rich Norris

ACROSS
1 Caged chirper
7 Calamine target
11 Arafat's org.
14 *Seinfeld* character
15 Scored 100
16 Thompson of *Caroline in the City*
17 Logical propositions
18 Piece of cake, so to speak
20 Very, in Vichy
21 Scout's doing
22 911 responders: Abbr.
23 Toast topping
27 "__ There Eyes"
28 Consumer
30 Mil. fliers' hangout
33 Son of Cain
36 Yankees shortstop Derek
38 Grinning from ear __
40 Ode title opening
41 Paragon
42 Carpentry, e.g.
43 Long-plumed heron
45 ADA member
46 Double Windsor, e.g.
47 Helper: Abbr.
49 Cost increase consequence
56 Brake pad
58 Nephew of Abel
59 Not very busy
60 Sprain treatment
62 Well-pitched
64 Chemical ending
65 Englishman's exclamation
66 Bird attraction
67 CPA's concern
68 __ time (never)
69 Bridge builder's concern

DOWN
1 Boston cagers, for short
2 On one's toes
3 Stool pigeon, e.g.
4 Has in one's sights
5 Genetic info transmitter
6 "Of course!"
7 Bread pro
8 Less receptive
9 Tot's sleep aid?
10 Ames and Wynn
11 Went down dramatically
12 Went away
13 Boors
19 Made fun of
21 Reassign, in a way
24 Cabbie's question
25 Actor Kingsley
26 Karate relative
29 Peruse
30 Lwyr.
31 Road junction
32 Lanky ones
34 Tooth
35 Bother persistently
37 Literary monogram
39 Cherished
44 Title of respect: Abbr.
48 Examiner
50 Magnificent meal
51 Quechua speaker
52 Ginza locale
53 Get away from
54 Sectors
55 Spouted vessels
56 Strikebreaker
57 Toot one's own horn
61 Actress Zadora
62 Conditions
63 Court divider

443 ??? by Patrick Jordan

ACROSS
1 Max who played Jethro
5 Ice-cream server
10 Impudence
14 Speck in the sea
15 Brownish gray
16 Resound
17 Cheetah or Bonzo
19 Carrey, in a '97 film
20 *Route 66* theme composer
22 Canadian capital
25 Sells for
26 *Show Boat* composer
27 Discontinuity
30 Use the crosshairs
31 Bryant or Baker
33 All-time bestselling book
35 Marcus Welby et al.
38 Offers one's hand
41 Dander
42 Jazz giant Art
43 __-one (long odds)
44 Leno of late night
45 Serpentine shape
47 Theater magnate Marcus
48 Montezuma subject
51 Verse
53 Free of charge
58 Speaker of baseball
59 Use matching consonants
63 Reed instrument
64 Fry lightly
65 Admit openly
66 Cartoonist Thomas
67 All in
68 Lion's locks

DOWN
1 PaperMate rival
2 Barbecue residue
3 Whitney or Wallach
4 Odd pieces of carpeting
5 *Hogan's Heroes* setting
6 Cupboard containers
7 Greek liqueur
8 Ready for business
9 Social equal
10 Rarely
11 Litmus-paper reddeners
12 Commandment verb
13 Achy spots
18 Baptist's bench
21 Most arctic
22 Giraffelike creature
23 Choir member
24 Utter nonsense
28 Help with a holdup
29 Arouse, as interest
30 Pub serving
32 Fasten
34 Work shirkers
35 North Dakota city
36 Overly attentive one
37 Like Alpine winters
39 Horse course
40 Wired message
44 Well-heeled travelers
46 Treated maliciously
48 "Flow Gently, Sweet __"
49 Anthony Quinn role
50 Small combos
52 Part of a countdown
54 Bridge position
55 Jai __
56 Defamation
57 Wind-powered toy
60 Glamorous Gardner
61 Freight weight
62 Meadow mama

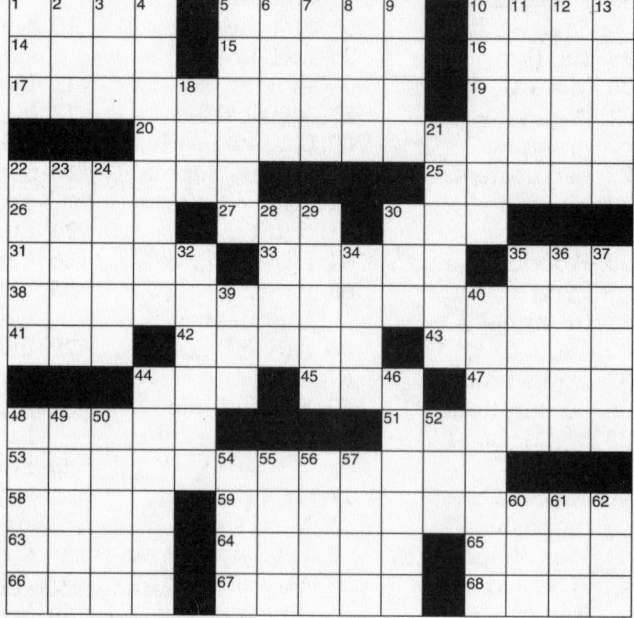

444 GO-BETWEENS by Frank Longo

ACROSS
1 Cuban dance
6 Soaps star Susan
11 Pickle
14 Totally
15 Bountiful resident
16 Clockmaker Terry
17 Atlantic-Pacific go-between
19 NFL stats
20 Platitude
21 Called by conscription
23 One-name supermodel
24 Highway-lane go-between
27 Strikes out, in a way
29 Once called
30 Penny, perhaps
31 Ms. markers
32 Radames' love, in opera
34 Intruded rudely, with "in"
36 Opera-act go-between
38 Sunglasses
41 Nick's wife
42 Maple fluid
45 Arrive
46 Al Bundy's wife
47 Passover bread
49 Governmental go-between
53 1986 World Series winner
54 Funicular, e.g.
55 Glimpses
57 Beauty preceder?
58 Childhood-adulthood go-between
61 Actor/director Stiller
62 Less healthy-looking
63 Fields
64 Speed-of-sound surpasser
65 Performance place
66 Gulls' relatives

DOWN
1 Sea peril
2 Clean, to a cop
3 How-to books
4 Loser to Cleveland
5 Charity
6 Director Jean-__ Godard
7 Actress Hagen
8 Taper, e.g.
9 Flamenco fireball
10 Wedding-party member
11 Going by 64 Across
12 Pasta phrase
13 Transgression
18 Novelist Tan
22 Sudden burst, as of anger
25 *The NeverEnding Story* author
26 Erudite
28 Playing with a full deck
33 "__ My Party"
34 Saddle sticker
35 Comical Sandler
36 Paradigmatic
37 Letterhead imprint
38 Beetle-shaped gems
39 Paeans
40 Encompassing
42 *Gone With the Wind* composer
43 Ancient Mexican culture
44 Hold the title to
46 Illegal secret stipend
48 Electrical unit
50 Barters
51 1978 Peace Nobelist
52 Attorney's thing
56 Jazz vocal
59 Means of support
60 Before, to Byron

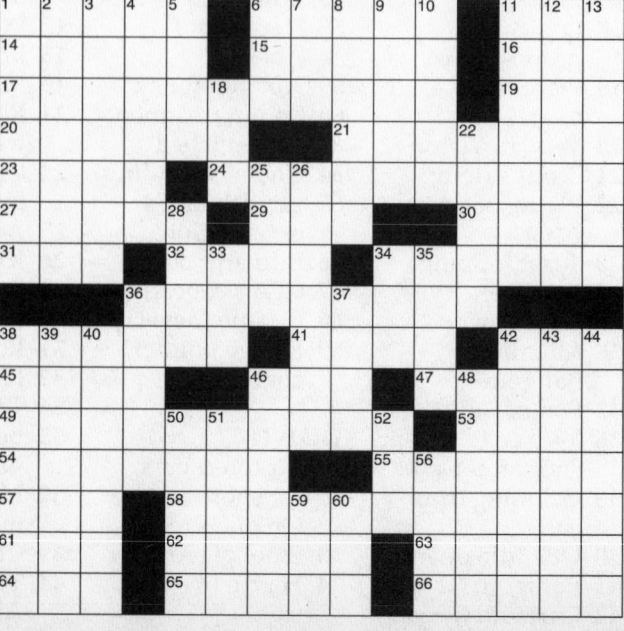

CLOSET BULLY by Cathy Millhauser

ACROSS

1 LP player
5 Dull
10 Shoot
14 *Ghostbusters* role
15 Birling match
16 Poi base
17 What a closet bully might do?
20 Pen fillers
21 Creepy
22 Hawaiian coffee center
23 Jags
24 The ones yonder
28 Goat quote
29 What a closet bully might do?
37 Author Wiesel
38 Refreshes, perhaps
39 Float component
40 What a closet bully might do?
43 Start of MGM's motto
44 Havens
45 They make scents
49 Composer __-Carlo Menotti

52 Stomach soother, for short
53 Graces, e.g.
58 What a closet bully might do?
60 Mayberry youth
61 All-important
62 *Bus Stop* playwright
63 Incline
64 Pernod ingredient
65 Mouser grouse

DOWN

1 Rope source
2 Inventor Sikorsky
3 Centers of attention
4 Pen fillers
5 Actor Kirby
6 *Ready to Wear* star
7 Too-too
8 Hockey Hall-of-Famer Stewart
9 Podium part
10 Advice, so to speak
11 Button material

12 Computer-game industry award
13 They're struck at weddings
18 Keepsake
19 Katmandu's country
23 Fajita dressing
24 Not kosher
25 Bean stack?
26 Irene Cara's '70 award
27 __-ball (arcade game)
28 Heelless slipper
30 They finish eclairs
31 Fling
32 Blast sound
33 Greek peak
34 *"Frère Jacques"* pronoun
35 Pop singer Brickell
36 "Oh, no!"
41 Winter air
42 Music or muscle properties
45 Monks' head

46 Rhetorical device
47 Venom, for one
48 Excited, slangily
49 Armand Assante role
50 Creative seeds
51 Baffle
53 Run fast, clockwise
54 Do a pool-cleaning job
55 Latin preposition
56 Latin conjunction
57 Bouillabaisse, e.g.
59 Actress Bartok

FRANKLY SPEAKING by Norma Steinberg

ACROSS

1 Boo-boo
5 Oranges' coverings
10 Piece of information
14 Make bye-bye
15 Longbow ammo
16 "Now __ me down to sleep . . ."
17 Trend-setting
19 Thpeak like thith
20 Brooch
21 Used to be
22 Newspaper name
24 Add salt to, e.g.
26 '96 presidential candidate
27 Put __ (store)
29 Gloomy
33 Balkan native
36 Average
38 Home of the Dolphins
39 King of the road
40 Map close-up
42 Chuck-wagon food

43 ". . . __ by land . . ."
45 Roman garb
46 Famous Loch
47 London driver's purchase
49 Word form for "sleep"
51 Liberates
53 Head man
57 Pilot
60 Innovative: Ger.
61 Chafe
62 Tubular pasta
63 Mark Twain, e.g.
66 Consumer
67 Perfect
68 Wedding vows
69 Like a poor excuse
70 Office furniture
71 Pierre's dad

DOWN

1 Trades
2 *"C'est __!"*
3 An ex-Mrs. Trump
4 Pigsty

5 Composer for the violin
6 Historical periods
7 Act humanly?
8 Vacation home
9 Attests
10 Expensive steak
11 Dismounted
12 Acting group
13 Use a keyboard
18 Groupings on the ark
23 Kind of lens
25 Social ease
26 Individuals
28 "__ make me laugh!"
30 Unadorned
31 Big birds
32 Barbecue servings
33 Go to the mall
34 Solo
35 Lend a hand, perhaps
37 Prefix for bucks
41 North Carolinians
44 Stronghold

48 Brezhnev of Russia
50 Brilliant move
52 Eat away at
54 Unrefined
55 Drollery
56 Too big
57 Blue, in Baja
58 Passport stamp
59 Line-__ veto
60 Mont. neighbor
64 *"Bonjour, __ amis!"*
65 Backtalk

IT'S ABOUT TIME! by Rich Norris

ACROSS

1 Avoid an F
5 Examine closely
9 Rigatoni, for one
14 General vicinity
15 Lotto relative
16 Freeway fillers
17 *The Time Machine* actor
19 Tread heavily
20 "__ little teapot . . ."
21 Happy-hour order
22 Consumer concerns
23 *A Time to Kill* actress
27 Burgle
28 Handle carelessly
29 Dispensable candy
32 Bird's claw
35 Barbecue accessories
36 Mont. neighbor
37 "Time __, pencils down"
38 Timely words
39 Comedian Wilson

40 Put the kibosh on
41 *Roots* author
42 Losing propositions?
43 Fraternity letter
44 *Der __* (Adenauer)
45 Assistance
46 "Time Is on My Side" group
52 Swallowlike birds
54 Tiebreakers: Abbr.
55 __ Miss
56 More than annoyed
57 *Time* founder
60 In time
61 Creme-filled cookie
62 "It's __ to Tell a Lie"
63 Admits customers
64 Scorecard numbers
65 "Love __" (Beatles song)

DOWN

1 Helen's abductor
2 Scent

3 Family car
4 Took a load off
5 '70s space station
6 Autograph hound's target
7 Pitch __-hitter
8 Postal Creed word
9 Checks the grounds
10 Goldfinger's first name
11 Accumulate
12 Big book
13 Egyptian cobras
18 Moses' brother
22 Mickey's mutt
24 Egg __ soup
25 A whole bunch
26 Congregation
30 Revise copy
31 Uses a ray gun
32 Coloring
33 China's continent
34 Enjoy oneself to the hilt
35 Conductor Sir Georg
38 Shopping meccas
39 Supposed common dog name

41 Summer tops
42 Scatterbrained
45 Houston nine
47 Many times
48 His time has run out
49 Of __ (unavailing)

50 Spanish hero
51 "__ evil, hear . . ."
52 Farm building
53 Prepare a gift
57 School dance
58 Time period
59 Hasty escape

SPECIALTY QUARTET by Alex Vaughn

ACROSS

1 Some mollusks
6 Blue shade
10 Proper partner
14 Rock star Eddie Van __
15 Post-Pablum pronouncement
16 Castor's mom
17 Midwest airport
18 Ooze
19 Baseball manager Felipe
20 Hammer, for one
22 Sidelines sound
23 "The Eighth Wonder of the World"
24 Rate
26 Strigiform structure
30 *Lou Grant* paper
31 Rap-sheet data
32 Fairly recently
36 Scottish caps
37 Business machine
38 Largest of the Tuscan Archipelago
39 Race site

42 Insulated, in a way
44 Fruitless
45 Vitamin A source
46 Evasive tactic
49 Like some foreign adjs.
50 "Tuna, hold the __"
51 *All the President's Men* character
57 Org. cofounded by Jane Addams
58 Composer Bacharach
59 __ *in the Head* (Sinatra film)
60 Literally, "Land of the Aryans"
61 Woody's son
62 French historian
63 Provide pro tem
64 Attendee
65 Senior members

DOWN

1 Cut of lamb
2 "If I Were King of the Forest" singer
3 Jai __

4 Pat and Vanna's boss
5 High-top, e.g.
6 Missing
7 *Caine* captain
8 Manhattan Project participant
9 Turns up
10 Eschews printed notes
11 Arlington autograph
12 Sacred cows
13 Handles badly
21 Sleep poorly
25 Accommodate, as a table
26 Chooses
27 Prepare a present
28 Sour fruit
29 Investigate
30 Impost
32 Nonprofessional
33 Ticklish doll
34 Support sub rosa
35 Nuclear measures
37 Rage
40 *All the King's Men* actress

41 Pompous sort
42 Skip meals
43 Grove
45 Kidnapper
46 Computer message
47 Mother-of-pearl
48 Bob of folk

49 Singer Haggard
52 Continental word form
53 Syngman of Korea
54 Lady Chaplin
55 Admiral Shepard
56 Addition column

VOWELS IN ORDER by Peter Gordon

ACROSS
1 1 Across
5 *Dumb __* (old cartoon)
9 Away from of the wind
13 On
14 Full compass
15 Rink jumps
16 DO BATTLE
18 Most unimportant
19 Floppy-disk holder
20 Squad
22 Coin stamp
23 Trains on *The Bob Newhart Show*
25 Phylum subdivisions
27 Polar
32 Wasp prey
33 "The Jumblies" poet
34 Senator Sam
36 Leaves home?
40 WHERE YOU MAY RAISE A RACKET
43 *The Garden of __* (Dietrich film)
44 Tallow source
45 French cheese
46 Pinochle card
48 Unfriendly sorts
50 Not brand-name
54 Deep-sea gulper
55 "__ Loser" (Beatles tune)
56 Stressed type, for short
58 Disrelish
63 Gounod contemporary
65 JOCULAR
67 Charge, in a way
68 Of all time
69 Retreats
70 Mtg.
71 Mineo et al.
72 About

DOWN
1 Cries of defiance
2 Bibliography abbr.
3 Knock about
4 Foil alternative
5 Article feature
6 "Ear" word form
7 Overwhelm
8 Ancient Mexican
9 Chopper
10 Salesperson's data
11 __ *Venner* (Holmes novel)
12 Opera star Simon
15 *World* book
17 Big name in prints
21 Like
24 Dazes
26 Disco device
27 It's a crock
28 Bell sound
29 Ratchet bar
30 Flowery
31 Listlessness
35 Sonya, to Vanya
37 Kukla's creator
38 Opp. of dup.
39 Fwys., e.g.
41 Escoffier milieu
42 Four-time Super Bowl champs
47 British bubblehead
49 Eclipse, with "out"
50 Football coach Joe
51 Writer Zola
52 *Raiders of the Lost Ark* villains
53 Sidewalk sights, at times
57 The Azores, essentially
59 Sophia Loren role of '53
60 Low digits
61 Reiser's TV costar
62 Sinclair competitor
64 PSAT provider
66 Toon artwork

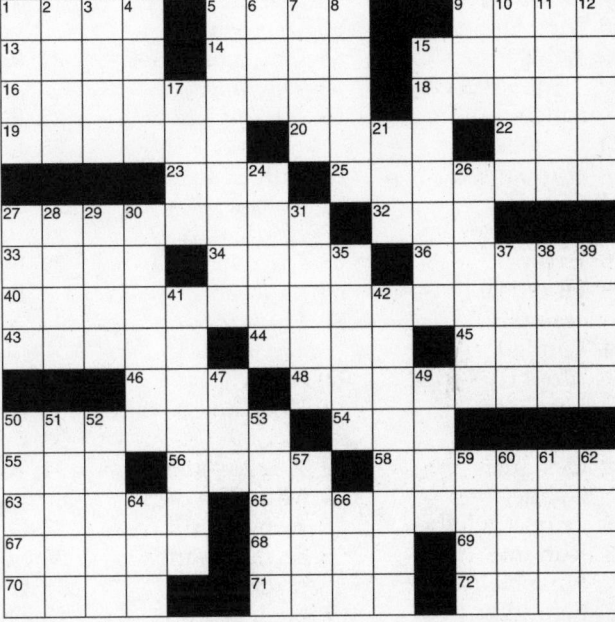

FULL-LENGTH PHRASES by Frank Longo

ACROSS
1 Droll ones
5 Penetrate sharply
9 Bad-news beginner
14 Memo starter
15 Wrong
16 Fleming's *Jeopardy!* announcer
17 Van Gogh offering
19 Guru, e.g.
20 Trap
21 Audits, as a class
22 Not dim
25 Harmless sword
29 Immerses
30 Cowboys' home
33 __ even keel
34 Yonder damsel
37 Probably
40 Perfect number?
41 About 2.2 lbs.
42 Went by windjammer
43 With the pips showing
45 Buffalo Bill
46 WKRP, e.g.
51 1994 Johnny Depp role
52 Attacks, in a way
57 __ ware (Japanese porcelain)
58 Beast in an Ogden Nash verse
60 Was
61 Fraternity letter
62 "Hansel and Gretel" prop
63 They revoke deles
64 Do some arm-twisting
65 Newspaper department

DOWN
1 Hair tuft
2 Protestor, perhaps
3 Abrasive material
4 Starter starter
5 Room, in Rouen
6 Weaves, in a way
7 Pound sound
8 "Ciao!"
9 Agamemnon's daughter
10 Denominations
11 Director Lubitsch
12 Faulkner's Bundren
13 Never-ending song
18 Nizer's field
21 Rope fibers
23 Vigil
24 "*Clair de __*"
25 Mark up, in a way
26 Door section
27 Impetuous ardor
28 Architectural extension
31 Bitter-tasting compounds
32 Made a driving error
34 Recital piece
35 Did a husbandry chore
36 Christian Science founder
38 "__ a Song Go . . ."
39 Latin adverb
43 Broccoli unit
44 Jai-alai ball
46 Works on one's overhead?
47 Let in
48 Part of a seismograph reading
49 Chill out
50 Bando or Maglie
53 Trudge
54 Make regular deposits
55 Iowa State University locale
56 Gas holder
58 Personal quirk
59 Seek to win

451 FORE-SIGHT by Lee Weaver

ACROSS
1 Spider's creations
5 __ McNally
9 Birthday bash
14 All over again
15 Eternally
16 Entertain
17 Outfit for Nero
18 Mrs. Dithers
19 Reb's foes
20 Triple-decker lunch
23 Gretel's companion
24 Org. for hunters
25 Except
28 Hoofbeat sound
31 Landed property
33 Hurry off
37 Casual tops
39 Designer Chanel
40 Impose a levy
41 Run into
42 Financially behind
45 Towel again
46 Black Sea port
47 Neutral color
49 "__ on your life!"
50 Spy org.
52 Houston team
57 Assume responsibility
60 Inexpensive
63 Golda of Israel
64 *The King* __
65 "If You Knew __ . . ."
66 European volcano
67 Bridle part
68 Current style
69 Saucer
70 Hunt for

DOWN
1 Keep an eye on
2 __ *Gay*
3 Already started
4 Mops the deck
5 Bring to mind
6 Shakespeare's river
7 Social misfit
8 Sketched
9 Eschew charge cards
10 Asian nursemaid
11 Seek office
12 Admonisher's sound
13 Thumbs-up vote
21 Religious offshoot
22 Really riles
25 Revealed
26 Complete
27 On the peevish side
29 Director Preminger
30 Author Norman Vincent
32 *Newsweek* rival
33 Offspring
34 Townhouse type
35 Group of eight
36 Sounds of awe
38 CEO, i.e.
43 Flew the coop
44 Head covering
45 Artful dodge
48 Stadium cheers
51 Equipped for battle
53 Skiers' conveyances
54 Indian queen
55 Song from the past
56 Move furtively
57 Eve's oldest
58 Bigfoot cousin
59 Pie pans
60 St. Louis clock setting
61 *Ben-*__
62 U-turn from WNW

452 NEUTRAL CORNERS by Norma Steinberg

ACROSS
1 Ear part
5 Cincinnati team
9 Tick off
13 Pinnacle
14 Memo words
15 Chris of tennis
17 Spouse
18 Spanish custard
19 Unbroken
20 Keep from employment
22 French city
23 Nuthatch's home
24 Bottomless pit
25 Wise person
28 Morsel
30 Officiated at tea
32 Dove call
33 Newspaper page
37 Where to find Turkey
39 Away from the center
41 Theater presentation
42 Part of a circle
44 Group's possessive
45 Stevenson of *M*A*S*H*
48 Vases
49 Young horses
51 Weaving machine
53 Bully
54 Memorable abolitionist
59 Plains formation
60 Author Leon
61 Modeling material
62 Good news for anglers
63 Small insect
64 Unimportant
65 Ripped
66 Annoying one
67 Soldier's place

DOWN
1 Meek one
2 Milky gem
3 Greek letter
4 Pres. or Treas.
5 Hunting weapon
6 Sign up
7 Immoderate
8 Mailed
9 Iron-rich mountain range
10 Self-imposed isolation
11 Cuts down
12 Side order
16 Gridiron scores: Abbr.
21 Leg parts
24 Circa
25 Music genre
26 Halo
27 Intelligence
29 "Inka Dinka __"
30 Vitality
31 TV controls
34 "No __, no gain"
35 Goofs
36 Dental degree: Abbr.
38 "We __ not amused!"
40 Hitchhiker's digit
43 Dieter's measurement
46 *Fawlty Towers* star
47 Part of a perfect-game description
49 Product
50 __ LUNCH (store sign)
52 Beginning
53 Consumer advisory agcy.
54 Checkers move
55 Canadian cops: Abbr.
56 Butter alternative
57 Armed conflicts
58 Sergei's negative

453 FISHING TRIP by Rich Norris

ACROSS
1 Western resort lake
6 Asian music style
10 Grating sound
14 Oneness
15 Netherlands dairy town
16 Choir member
17 Onetime tonsorial symbol
19 Competes
20 Had a bite
21 Roseanne's former surname
22 Rival of ancient Athens
24 Speak with candor
26 Precious stones
29 Sandwich bread
30 Rotational
31 Don of radio
33 Woven fabric
37 Theda Bara, e.g.
38 Director's call
39 Sandwich cookie
40 Equipment for rock bands
41 "Listen!"
42 Uses a lever
43 Make illegal
44 CD divisions
45 Country dance
51 Get one's bearings
52 Animal pouches
53 Pal, slangily
56 Sidewalk eatery
57 No longer responsible
60 ABA members
61 Open to discussion
62 Innocent
63 __ majesty
64 Light on one's feet
65 Like some floors

DOWN
1 "Tubby the __"
2 Med. school subject
3 Take on
4 Handicapper's hangout: Abbr.
5 Look at closely
6 Copy, for short
7 Make pretty
8 Guy's partner
9 February birthstone
10 *Bolero* composer
11 Suspect's story
12 Dutch artist Jan
13 Sheriff's group
18 Sunshine, slangily
23 __ *Haw*
24 Bounds companion
25 Jack locale
26 Coffee, casually
27 Semester ender
28 Ineffectual individual
31 Tabriz native
32 Space station since 1986
33 Point, as of a story
34 Pop musician Clapton
35 Look for
36 Dan Blocker role
38 Apparitions
42 One of the tenses
43 Coal container
44 Pert. to science
45 Outspoken
46 Quite angry
47 Serious disagreements
48 Formation fliers
49 Regarding
50 Shabby, as an old coat
53 One way to cook
54 Wander about
55 Signed off on
58 Vain one
59 "Bali __"

454 HALL OF FLAME by Patrick Jordan

ACROSS
1 Cover with cloth
6 As yet
11 Sodom survivor
14 Type of Greek column
15 Garth's big-screen buddy
16 Gibbon or gorilla
17 Dolly Levi activity
19 Veto
20 Newspaper issues
21 Allstate competitor
23 *Cinco - tres*
24 Evening parties
26 Available for rent
30 Decathlete Bruce
31 The first Mrs. Trump
32 Turns in checkers
33 Magic org.
36 Skeletal
37 Sectors
38 Trojan War hero
39 Wrap up
40 Persian Gulf peninsula
41 Delay by deception
42 Gets the punch line
44 Herman or Reese
45 Eternal
47 Director's directive
48 Shows dejection
49 University of Chile city
54 Jackie's second
55 Chanteuse, perhaps
58 Buddhism branch
59 Violinist Mischa
60 Like Eric the Red
61 Begley and Bradley
62 Symphonic cessations
63 Buzzing pests

DOWN
1 Smallest U.S. coin
2 Trail
3 One opposed
4 Ancient Scot
5 Australian mammal
6 Long-necked waterfowl
7 Adult acorns
8 Murphy Brown's show
9 Author Beattie
10 Wins back
11 Jay Leno feature
12 Offer a thought
13 Michener book
18 Like some points
22 Poetic preposition
24 Separate
25 Binary code digits
26 Intuition, slangily
27 Shakespeare's bardship
28 Bowling variety
29 Unspecified amount
30 Dr. Salk
32 Porch-light circlers
34 Straw unit
35 Wheel shaft
37 Sharp turns
38 Chowed down
40 Galahad, vis-à-vis the Grail
41 Dramatic locale
43 Pub potable
44 Examples of wordplay
45 Stupefy
46 "It depends on whose ox is __"
47 Lyricist Sammy and others
49 Jazz style
50 Part of
51 Taj Mahal site
52 Romantic adventure
53 Mined-over matters?
56 Bullring cheer
57 Realty ad abbr.

JE NE SAIS QUOI by Cathy Millhauser

ACROSS
1 Pampering: Abbr.
4 Da __ (music marking)
8 SKY SHADE
13 Teriyaki ingredient
14 Canvas material
15 *Two Women* star
16 *SCARFACE* ACTRESS
18 Forum wear
19 Tattooed lady of song
20 FINE WOOL
22 SISTER OF EVA AND MAGDA
24 *that thing you do!* setting
25 Stick it in your ear
27 Ancient occultism
32 Giant slugger
35 Composer Copland
37 Beasts of burden
38 NOTED EGG MAKER
40 PARADISAICAL
43 Allison of '50s TV
44 Jibe
46 A spring place
47 Line on a map
50 Rich soil
51 Protuberance
53 "I'VE BEEN THERE" ILLUSION
58 QUADRATIC, E.G.
62 Specified
63 Senate house in old Rome
64 SHARIF ROLE
67 __ Wip (Cool Whip rival)
68 Attendee
69 Literary olios
70 CUSTOMARY
71 They're in orbits
72 Bert Bobbsey's sister

DOWN
1 *Rent* awards
2 Carter of *Wonder Woman*
3 Spanish port
4 Bird word
5 It's pumped
6 Drug experiment control
7 Werner of *Ship of Fools*
8 Tennis pro Gibson
9 Big buzz
10 Drive
11 Parent
12 Start of Massachusetts' motto
13 German seasoning
17 Jackie Bouvier went there
21 [not my mistake]
23 Active, as gossips' tongues
26 Department
28 Cattle genus
29 Gyroscope part
30 Lutz, e.g.
31 Soprano Moffo
32 Extinguishes
33 Turnover cousin
34 One-way lift
36 Seneca student
39 London-to-Ipswich dir.
41 Foremost
42 Aden denizen
45 Inverness valley
48 Necessitate
49 Anjou "you"
52 Shifty move
54 Certain Indonesian
55 Whirlpool competitor
56 Beef eschewer
57 Ginseng-family plants
58 Hosiery shade
59 Part of Q&A
60 Hindu variant
61 Opera slave
65 A bit of sleep?
66 Paycheck abbr.

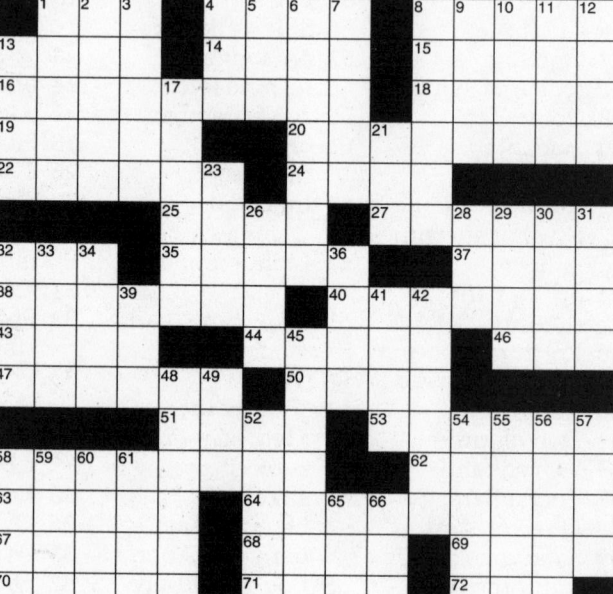

IN THE BALLPARK by Norma Steinberg

ACROSS
1 Sharp taste
5 Severe
10 Bedouin
14 Skin-cream ingredient
15 Carroll heroine
16 Actress Miles
17 No threat
19 Lazily
20 Dumbfound
21 Part of a fork
22 Bible book
23 Desperately
25 Aspiration
27 Actor O'Neal
29 Skeptical one
32 Waller of jazz
35 Newspaperman Greeley
39 Baseball bat wood
40 Lyricist Gershwin
41 Like a pioneer's wagon
42 Actor Gulager
43 Gender
44 Did nothing
45 Consider
46 Was obligated
48 Ump's call
50 Commands
54 Far away
58 *M*A*S*H* star
60 Comic Carvey
62 Nincompoops
63 Omen, e.g.
64 Distances in a kids' game
66 With: Fr.
67 Dramatic whisper
68 Cleveland's lake
69 Pierre's pop
70 Chill out
71 Fathers

DOWN
1 South American appetizers
2 Memorable mission
3 Type of bond
4 Coots
5 Bowler or beret
6 Got down
7 Uncompromising
8 Commotion
9 "__ Johnny!"
10 Bird house
11 '50s scare
12 Woody Guthrie's kid
13 Howls at the moon
18 Depend
24 Boor
26 Frosted
28 __ Scotia
30 Wight, for one
31 Pal
32 Salmon or shad
33 Neighborhood
34 IRS quarry
36 Gridiron arbiter
37 God of war
38 Fragrant wood
41 Lump of earth
45 Took down a peg
47 Hypnotic state
49 Govt. agents
51 __ Allan Poe
52 Salary increase
53 Slow-moving animal
55 *Norma* or *Carmen*
56 Lukewarm
57 Curvy letters
58 Letters on a memo
59 Exist
61 Cost an arm __ leg
65 John Ritter's father

457 UNREAL ATTORNEYS by Rich Norris

ACROSS

1 Locking device
5 Very fast
10 Flower part
14 Concept
15 Love, in Livorno
16 Singing sound
17 Raymond Burr role
19 Mom's sister
20 Confused situation
21 Eastern discipline
22 Debate
23 Entr'__
25 Hothouse plant
26 Gregory Peck role
31 Plaid pattern
32 Birds: Lat.
33 Corp. alias
36 Luau baking pits
37 Wide valleys
39 Drescher of *The Nanny*
40 Golf prop
41 Very, in Vichy
42 Ohio city
44 Susan Dey role
46 Earthy colours
49 Prefix for while
50 Incite, as havoc
51 Christmas tree
53 Down source
57 Terra firma
58 Andy Griffith role
60 Feminine ending
61 Invite to enter
62 Plumb crazy
63 Herbal quaffs
64 Composer Jule
65 Iowa city

DOWN

1 Rose parts
2 Arabian Sea gulf
3 Blood fluids
4 Ice-cream desserts
5 Ewe's mate
6 Astonishes
7 Sit for a photo
8 Fe
9 Reading room
10 Laundry stiffener
11 Leathery
12 Boredom
13 Apportioned
18 New Mexico state flower
22 Circle parts
24 Frozen wastelands
25 Brigadier general's designation
26 Working hard
27 Bring under control
28 With 29 Down, type of test
29 See 28 Down
30 "__ Gotta Be Me"
33 Comic Carey
34 Said, as "farewell"
35 Soon
38 NRC predecessor
39 Small naval unit
41 Arduous journey
43 Beginning
44 Evaluates
45 Exterminator's concern
46 Nocturnal youngster
47 Construction-site sight
48 Salon color
51 Slug or song ending
52 Black
54 Adverse fate
55 Behold, to Brutus
56 Bygone theatres
58 Coll. degrees
59 Chemical ending

458 TWO-WAY NAMES by Matt Gaffney

ACROSS

1 Leg enders
5 Talk-radio name
9 Uneasy state
13 Permit
15 Where most people live
16 One in debt
17 *George & Leo* star
19 Passion
20 Secretariat remarks
21 Grid-system component
22 Talk fondly
23 Sabatini, for short
26 Vietnamese holiday
27 Larry King's channel
30 Clinton cabinet member
33 Big seller in bear markets?
35 Israeli diplomat
38 Congress of Berlin participant
42 Miss Brooks portrayer
43 Greenish blue
44 French philosopher
46 Reporter Donaldson
47 Pavement letters
50 Retinal cells
51 Gridiron div.
54 Prepares to fly
56 Parting words
59 Parting word
60 *Show Boat* star
64 Alan or Robert
65 Lawn treatment
66 Rouen's river
67 Fruit-processing chemicals
68 Is worthwhile
69 Wire ender

DOWN

1 Tide rival
2 Southern school
3 Sight from Dresden
4 Popular mixer
5 Shows team spirit
6 Dos Passos trilogy
7 Letter opener?
8 Medicine __, Alberta
9 Parlor fixture
10 "__ woe and woe I dwell!": Aeschylus
11 Phantasmagorial
12 Take forcibly
14 End of a Gleason catchphrase
18 "__ Sorry Now"
21 Circulatory system
23 Filibusterers
24 Melanin-free one
25 Shropshire sounds
27 USCG off.
28 Treasury offering
29 Teen punishment, perhaps
31 Put forth, with "in"
32 Blind as __
34 Cultivated, maybe
36 Aphrodite's love
37 Recruitment-regulating org.
39 Heraldic furs
40 Dollar-bill word
41 Dutch airline
45 Mock-fanfare phrase
47 Pocket
48 Betraying carelessness
49 Electron-loss result
52 Pine relatives
53 Signs away
55 "Take __ a compliment!"
56 Seasons
57 Whole thing
58 Strange beginning
60 Swiss peak
61 Timetable preposition
62 Curly March
63 Tie material

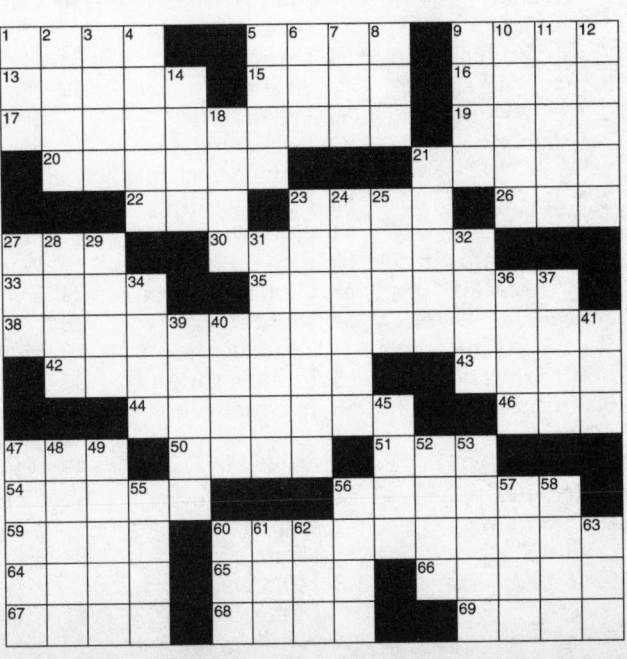

PUNCTUATION FLUCTUATION by Patrick Jordan

ACROSS

1 Somewhat wet
5 Coming-out party honorees
9 Ebenezer's partner
14 Type of exam
15 Branding tool
16 Previously, in poetry
17 Patronize a restaurant
18 Fodder holder
19 "__ bleu!"
20 "CARRY ON!"
23 *Oklahoma!* aunt
24 Meditative discipline
25 Noisy hubbub
28 Wind dir.
29 Brought out
33 Second word in many fairy tales
34 Screenwriter Loos
35 Mimic Pavlov's dogs
36 CARRY-ON
41 Storybook meanies
42 Overused, as a phrase

43 Kane's Rosebud, e.g.
44 For one
46 Damage
49 Pinkerton logo
50 Make a miscue
51 Secret hiding place
53 CARRY ON
58 Still in the game
60 Apprehension
61 Abel parent
62 Invigorating liquid
63 "Nay!" sayer
64 Clementine's dad worked there
65 Dread
66 Choir member
67 Hardens

DOWN

1 Evades
2 Sharon and Durant
3 Cloaklike garment
4 West Point freshman
5 Part of CD
6 *CHiPs* star Estrada
7 Eat rapidly
8 Short sleep

9 Leader of the Argonauts
10 Way over yonder
11 Dog breed
12 NHL legend Bobby
13 Nectar collector
21 Spheres of activity
22 Tie the knot
26 *Let's Make a Deal* selection
27 Just
30 Understand, '60s-style
31 Shoshonean
32 Saguaro and peyote
33 Strong impulse
34 Improved, as wine
35 Abominate
36 Finish second
37 "The __ Duckling"
38 "Aloha" or "Shalom"
39 Have existence
40 *Tic __ Dough*
44 It alit on Ararat
45 Kind of housing
46 Cybill, on *Moonlighting*

47 Oblique
48 Bard's creations
50 Put into office
52 Football factions
54 Hertz rival
55 TV's "Warrior Princess"
56 Broadway record-breaker
57 Flower with droopy petals
58 *One Day __ Time*
59 Actor Chaney

SUBSTITUTIONS by Frank Longo

ACROSS

1 Pillage
5 Palpitate
10 __ *and the Man*
14 Shampoo ingredient
15 19th-century novelist
16 Moolah
17 Roman historian
18 Stage substitute
20 Playwright Burrows
21 Sub
22 Nap-raising device
23 Recipe substitute
26 __ de cacao
27 *Ghosts* playwright
28 Wharton deg.
30 Sound-barrier breaker
31 Author Bellow
32 Reaches
36 Diamond substitute
39 *St. Elsewhere* actor
40 San __, Italy

43 Actress Kendall
46 Not-so-hot grade
47 Conductor Mehta
48 Isfahan inhabitant
50 Manuscript substitute
54 Exorcised entities
56 Frivol
57 Rocker Ocasek
58 Name substitute
60 Major ending
61 Not aweather
62 Rise up
63 Climb, as a tree
64 Monetary equivalents
65 Kitchen fungus
66 Jr.'s exam

DOWN

1 Deli hangings
2 "Open Sesame" sayer
3 Hugger-muggers
4 A minor, for one

5 Comparatively confirmable
6 M. Matisse
7 Radioactive
8 Shelley's "__ to Liberty"
9 Pitcher Blyleven
10 Communion table
11 Stirs
12 Surfing accessories?
13 Sharp-pointed instrument
19 Trig function
21 Harrison, in *Star Wars*
24 Icy
25 Forgo the USPS
29 Memory units
32 Teen trauma
33 Bagdad baddie
34 Everyday article
35 Whey
37 Nobelist Gordimer
38 Spiritual experiences
41 Citizen-soldier group

42 Minimal moolah
43 Abduct
44 Colored ring
45 Whine
47 Nada
49 Central points

51 Oranjestad's island
52 __ *a Horseman*
53 Food fish
55 Chipper
59 *1776* role
60 Parapsychologist's study

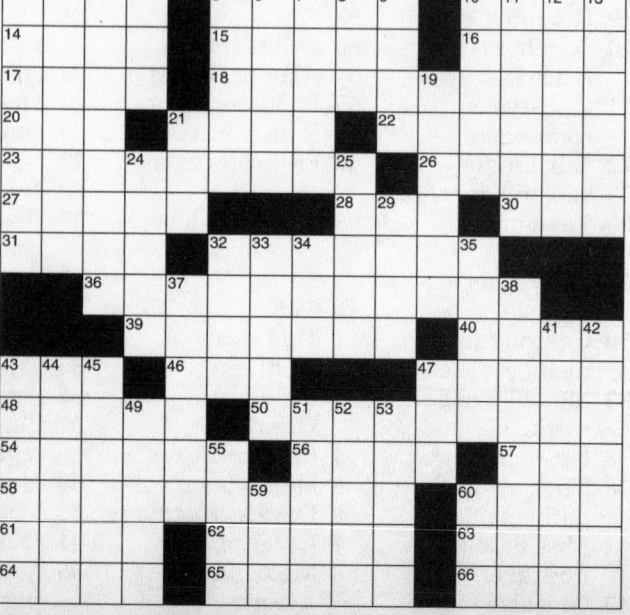

461 ON BOARDS by Bob Lubbers

ACROSS
1 Give off
5 Swimmer Buster
11 Animation unit
14 Teri of *Tootsie*
15 Greetings
16 High card
17 Dinner-table speck
19 A Bobbsey twin
20 Power-broker initials
21 Cruise-ship attendant
23 Buddy of *Barnaby Jones*
26 Mouse menacer
28 Comic Johnson
29 Choral pieces
31 Metal joiner
33 "Made in the __"
34 Alternatively
36 Faction
41 Oregon city
42 Actress Charlotte
44 Lined diagrams

47 Transmit, as from NBC
50 Morays
51 Blockhead
52 Sicily neighbor
53 Swears (to)
56 Smack
57 Edge
58 One way to tie a tie
64 *Bambi* aunt
65 Sports halls
66 "*Dies __*"
67 Actor Duryea
68 Scold
69 Archibald of the NBA

DOWN
1 Omelet need
2 Scratch
3 Lyrical Gershwin
4 Hot-plate holder
5 Use a hatchet
6 Sports judge
7 Capp and Pacino

8 Blowout
9 Metal fastener
10 Princely Italian family
11 Vile rumor
12 Card game
13 Borrower's opposite
18 Actress Foch
22 Hidden kid in picture books
23 French coin
24 Striped fish
25 Piece of cake
26 Poem division
27 Declares
30 Color shades
31 George of *Just Shoot Me*
32 Boat propeller
35 Attempts
37 Discontinuance
38 Suffix of approximation
39 Russian river
40 Done with
43 Greek vowel
44 __ up (got ready)

45 Eye part
46 *Nashville* director
48 Abu Dhabi chief
49 Marsh plant
51 Actor Ed
54 Mop

55 Grow weary
56 Waterer's need
59 Genetic stuff
60 Made a lap
61 New Deal org.
62 Cereal grain
63 Golf prop

462 FAMILY FILMS by Randy Sowell

ACROSS
1 Hillary, to Bill
5 Grain to be ground
10 Clenched hand
14 Farm tools
15 Come back to mind
16 Hammett hound
17 Roz Russell film of '58
19 Sports group
20 Submissions to eds.
21 Bit attachment
22 Area of influence
24 Transmitted
25 German admiral of WWI
26 Splotches
29 Title for Mao
33 Time interval
34 Membership money
35 Vanished
36 Like crazy
37 "__ Johnny!"
38 Probability quote

39 Went quickly
40 Evict
41 Woo
42 Ingress
44 Little ladies
45 Leg joint
46 Paella ingredient
47 Security
50 Physicist Ernst
51 The Buckeyes' sch.
54 __ impasse (stuck)
55 Reagan film of '38
58 "__ Free"
59 Spine-tingling
60 Big name in locks
61 Tube trophy
62 John of rock
63 BPOE members

DOWN
1 Sound of impact
2 Debtors' notes
3 Swampy areas
4 NH clock setting

5 Salad material
6 Send payment
7 "__ do anything better than you"
8 Total
9 Enter unlawfully
10 Cary Grant film of '64
11 Oracle's words
12 Night sky sight
13 Hardly exciting
18 Actress Dunne
23 JFK Library architect
24 Roz Russell film of '46
25 Halloween garb
26 Blackboard
27 Falcon's toenail
28 Left, at sea
29 Gypsy's revenge
30 __ operandi
31 Conductor Previn
32 Avian abodes
34 Tennis tie
37 Busy buzzer
41 Hidden supply

43 *Them!* critter
44 Forest growth
46 Numerical relation
47 Kemo __
48 Energy source
49 Old MacDonald had one

50 Humorist Sahl
51 Spoken
52 Polio fighter
53 Some Sioux
56 Fam. member
57 Bread grain

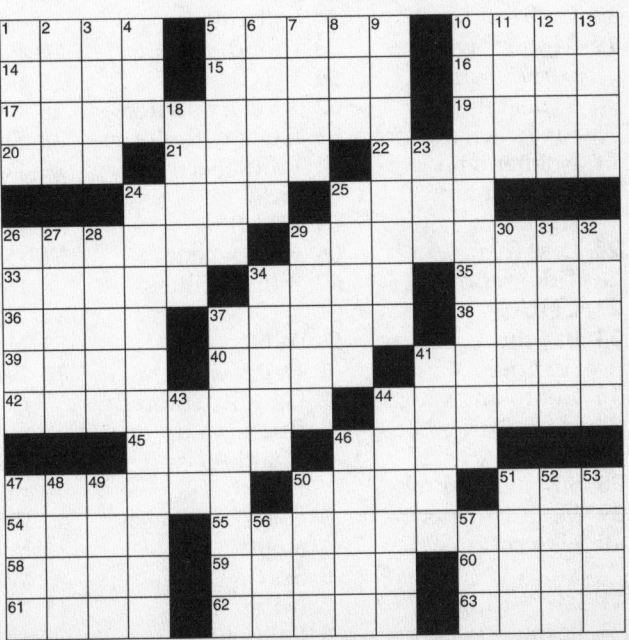

463 DOUBLY DELICIOUS by Mark Moldowsky

ACROSS
1 Doctors' grp.
4 Not as much
8 Nudge
12 67 Across relative
14 Word form for "correct"
16 Square measurement
17 Env. marking
18 Henry and Cassius
19 Track event
20 Sweets on a stick
23 Column order
24 Young horse
25 Deep sleeps
29 Like a lot
33 Burro
36 Pity
39 Wine valley
40 Disc-shaped sweet
43 A Great Lake
44 Human
45 Serpentine curve
46 __ Domingo
48 Judges' attire
50 Annapolis initials
53 Jennifer of *Flashdance*
57 Chocolatey treat
63 Rajah's wife
64 Sub device
65 *Dennis the Menace* girl
66 Not toward land
67 Flat-topped hill
68 Dutch cheese
69 Evergreen trees
70 ". . . and bells on her __"
71 Fathers of Jrs.

DOWN
1 Stradivari's teacher
2 Jealous one's cry
3 __ Martin (007 auto)
4 Focal points
5 Perry's creator
6 General's insignia
7 __ the mark (short)
8 Bull-running city
9 Sandwich cookie
10 Hold on to
11 Breaks a fast
13 Caper
15 Norwegian city
21 Extent
22 Fall behind
26 Suffix for school
27 "Air" word form
28 Bake, as eggs
30 Inevitability
31 Makes a choice
32 Sunbeams
33 Imitates
34 Antitoxins
35 Rotate
37 Aware of
38 Wild guess
41 Funnel-shaped flowers
42 Freshman at 50 Across
47 Columbus sch.
49 Suit material
51 Flight-accident investigators: Abbr.
52 Concerning
54 Amino and lactic
55 Of the moon
56 Sends junk e-mail
57 Meditate
58 Alleviate
59 Once again
60 Golden Rule word
61 London art gallery
62 Very: Fr.

464 HURLY-BURLY by Patrick Jordan

ACROSS
1 Cautious
5 Morocco's capital
10 Coffee
14 Field of study
15 J.R.'s mama
16 River in Russia
17 CAST
19 Monopoly corner square
20 "This Little Piggy" character?
21 Robber's take
22 Without any slack
24 Less fresh
26 Tidal reflux
27 CHUCK
34 Paycheck surprise
36 Get to one's feet
37 Help-wanted ad abbr.
38 Surrounded by
39 Mogul Turner
40 Like cotton candy
41 Larry King's TV home
42 Binding part
44 Foal fathers
45 FLING
48 Feel under the weather
49 Decrease
52 Greatest degrees
55 Tiny crop pest
57 __ Lanka
58 Cloudless
59 PITCH
62 Took a powder
63 Duck with down
64 Emulate cover girls
65 Middling
66 Narrow cuts
67 Billfold fillers

DOWN
1 Drifts lazily
2 Gaudily colored
3 Brushing up on
4 Thanksgiving tuber
5 Seal the sauterne again
6 See 53 Down
7 Ink stain
8 Balloon filler
9 Teachers, at times
10 Jellied candy
11 What the suspicious smell
12 Colorado resort
13 Sheedy of *WarGames*
18 Baldwin et al.
23 Songstress Lane
25 Earsplitting
28 Sheet material
29 Pollster's discovery
30 Lent a hand
31 Denial of freedom
32 Hedonist
33 Hankerings
34 *Brandenburg Concertos* composer
35 Science magazine
40 Orders to attack
42 Yodeler Whitman
43 Royal residences
44 Show contempt
46 Coif
47 Does a tailoring job
50 Clear a floppy disk
51 Frasier's brother
52 Switch positions
53 With 6 Down, California city
54 Makes a sheepshank
55 2501, to Terence
56 "__ a man with seven wives"
60 Squelch a squeak
61 Nav. rank

465   IF THE SHOE FITS . . . by Cathy Millhauser

ACROSS

1 Chevalier tune
5 Elevated state
10 Blueprint
14 Something fishy
15 Hew anew
16 Alma mater of 37 Down
17 After the curfew
18 Greek vowel
19 Hotelier César
20 With 36 Across, subject of a *Shoe* quip
23 Cone, e.g.
24 Clean a pipe
25 Relief from the jeweler
29 Competitor
33 Prefix for goblin
36 See 20 Across
39 Amor alias
41 Oneiromancy subject
42 Comic Freberg
43 Quip, part 1
46 Fitting
47 Kipling's birthplace
48 Linked series
50 Bank take-back
53 April 22 honoree
57 Quip, part 2
62 Platter on Chinese menus
63 Immunization component
64 Hebrew month
65 Insult
66 Bikini, e.g.
67 Lie or rely
68 Evil stuff
69 Mrs. Kurt Weill
70 Word on some diplomas

DOWN

1 Loses a coat
2 Hells Canyon state
3 *Psycho* setting
4 Peaceful
5 Facial feature
6 Apollo vehicles
7 *Body Count* rapper
8 Marilyn, in *Some Like It Hot*
9 Blank look
10 Giza sight
11 Ocelot's spot
12 Model Carol's family
13 __ Percé
21 Party spread
22 Put on guard
26 Ancient Asian
27 Muffs one
28 Cousteau's milieu
30 *Ars longa, __ brevis*
31 P.D.Q.
32 Spring time
33 Front half?
34 Algerian gulf
35 Villain in *Ben-Hur*
37 Revolutionary War spy
38 Wall St. letters
40 Middle-ear bones
44 These, to Caesar
45 Tallow source
49 Sudan neighbor
51 Corolla part
52 Uganda People's Party founder
54 Golf cup provider
55 Breakfast order
56 Smarts
57 Well-stocked
58 1995 hurricane
59 Former Nebraska senator
60 Cunning
61 *To Live and Die* __
62 Pressure meas.

466   LADIES DAY by Bob Lubbers

ACROSS

1 Newborn
5 Thunder god
9 Bacall's mate
14 Bide-__ Home Association
15 Nevada city
16 British nobles
17 Actress Perlman
18 Vicinity
19 Leaning
20 Diagonally
23 Ready
24 City of canals
27 Golf gadget
28 Farrow or Sara
30 Sense of tone
31 Fishing pole
32 Mr. Brezhnev
34 "Uh-oh!"
35 Early yarn machine
39 *Grapes of Wrath* name
40 Prepares broccoli, perhaps
41 Scull seat
42 Before, to a poet
44 Troy, NY campus
45 Boxing victories, for short
48 Actor Lorne
50 Mountainous, in a way
52 Timid one
56 Overture, for short
58 ". . . with a banjo on my __"
59 Energy source
60 Follow behind
61 Summer coolers
62 Camper's need
63 Fibs
64 Olden days
65 Approximately

DOWN

1 Hound, as a dog
2 Once in __ (sometimes)
3 Scarab
4 Irish poet
5 Tire grip
6 Good-deed doer
7 Unique thing
8 Chestnut horse
9 All-purpose check payee
10 Of a grain
11 Football field
12 Ailing
13 Superlative suffix
21 Saudi Arabia neighbor
22 Gabor or Perón
25 Duplicate
26 Asner and Wynn
29 Flavorful herb
30 Lawn tool
32 Cap
33 Bank acct. yield
34 Switch positions
35 Fly high
36 Part of PG
37 Made in Tokyo
38 Writer Zola
39 Trot
42 Signs up
43 Minister: Abbr.
45 Out of __ (awry)
46 Steak topping
47 "Things aren't what they __ be"
49 Spooky
51 Greek philosopher
53 Approve
54 Take apart
55 Fortune-teller
56 Addams Family cousin
57 Gun owners' org.

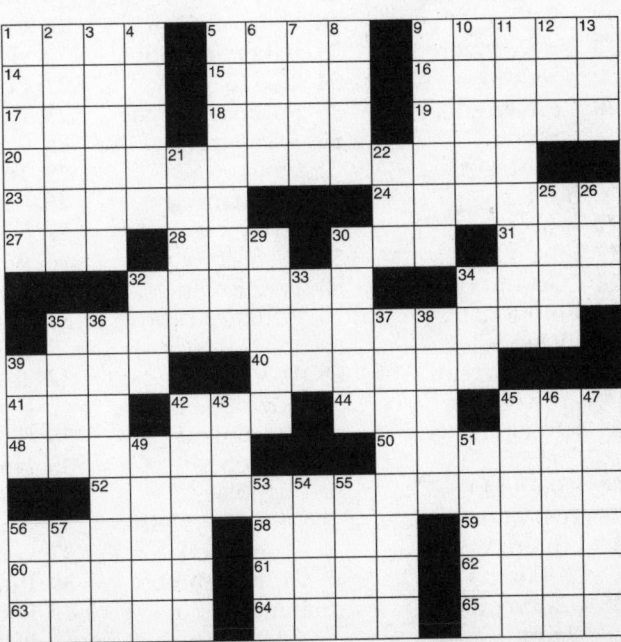

TOPOGRAPHERS by Bob Frank

ACROSS

1 Danson and Koppel
5 File
9 Female honorific
14 Concept
15 Singer Fitzgerald
16 Linda Lavin role
17 Carillon item
18 "Can we talk?" comedienne
20 Part of ILGWU
21 Electrical resistance unit
22 Gladdens
23 Ancient Mideast kingdom
25 Consumed
26 Sports spectator
27 Lens opening
32 Aladdin's helper
35 Like Mozart's music
36 Tony Award relative
37 Collared garment
38 In the dumps
39 Type of pen
41 Closes tightly
42 Not to be consumed
43 Mid.
44 Wriggling fish
45 Bureau sections
49 More limber
53 Opponent
54 Nabisco bestseller
55 *Jury Duty* star
57 Pitcher Hershiser
58 Sandy's owner
59 Tap trouble
60 Medicinal measure
61 Position
62 Meadows
63 Winter vehicle

DOWN

1 Shin bone
2 Barbara and Anthony
3 Shoulder muscles, for short
4 *The Flying Nun* star
5 Unite once again
6 Hawaiian greeting
7 Close abruptly
8 God of woods
9 Padded envelopes
10 Edison's middle name
11 Japanese legislature
12 Land measure
13 Military cafeteria
19 Give a make-up exam
24 __ Dawn Chong
25 Separated
27 Dress style
28 '97 Masters winner
29 USC rival
30 Actor Julia
31 *Desire Under the __*
32 Asian desert
33 Abba of Israel
34 White or Blue river
35 Put on ice
37 Gets serious
40 In one's cups
41 RR depot
43 Obnoxious ones
45 *Andrea __* (ill-fated ship)
46 Swashbuckler Flynn
47 Della or Pee Wee
48 Did a shoe repair
49 Health resorts
50 Huff
51 Mystical symbol
52 Pelvic bones
53 Warning on the links
56 "Good" cholesterol: Abbr.

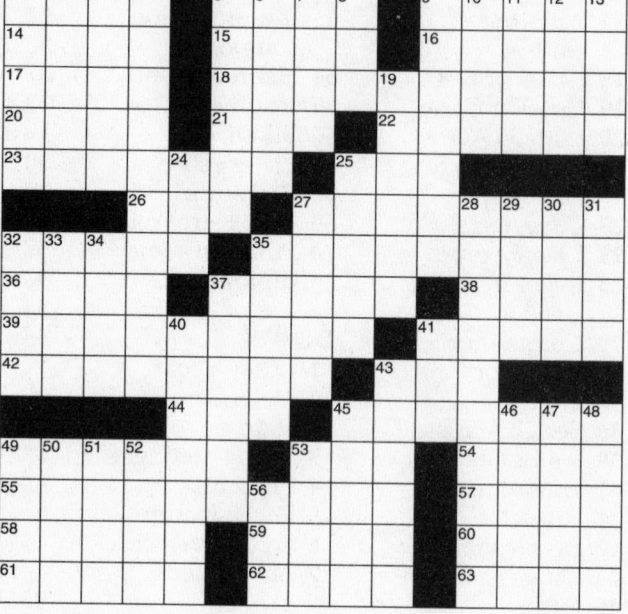

LIKE NIGHT AND DAY by Patrick Jordan

ACROSS

1 Molt
5 Usher's offering
9 Give 10% to the church
14 Comics possum
15 Montreal player
16 Never altared?
17 "Get out of bed!"
19 Undercover operation
20 Converted, as a coupon
21 Candlestick holder
22 Is able to
23 Jolson tune
24 "Get out of bed!"
29 Emotionally distant
30 "It's grrrreat!" growler
31 Jefferson Davis org.
34 Kilted kin
35 Two-door vehicle
37 Limerick or haiku
38 Clairvoyant's claim
39 Freshly cut, as hay
40 Lindsay's *Bionic Woman* role
41 "Go to bed!"
44 Garbage scows
46 Reel's partner
47 Morley or Morse
48 Conic section
53 Bakery output
54 "Go to bed!"
55 Radioactive gas
56 Away from of the wind
57 Assistant
58 Strive vigorously
59 Disorderly heap
60 1992 Robin Williams film

DOWN

1 Cowboy-boot attachment
2 Clinton's birthplace
3 Quaint expletive
4 Completed
5 Crew member
6 Renew, as a subscription
7 Did an impression
8 Male cat
9 Pisa's region
10 Sing
11 Packaging cord
12 Therefore
13 Move slowly
18 Coffee choice, for short
21 Porkers
23 Hit the mall
24 Competition
25 Troubles
26 Laundry need
27 Geologic time unit
28 Daredevil's feat
31 Create a new word
32 Teamster's truck
33 Prayer finale
35 Hale-Bopp, for one
36 Has debts
37 Golfer's goal
39 Itinerant worker
40 Fourth son of Jacob
41 Quivering effect
42 Gives a speech
43 Rich cakes
44 Cleansing agent
45 Residence
47 Seldom encountered
48 Heap
49 Score more than
50 Only state whose flag isn't a rectangle
51 "The __ Is a Tramp"
52 Affirmative votes
54 Easter entree

469   GRID PLAY by Norma Steinberg

ACROSS
1 Part of B.A.
5 Boston sch.
10 "Yeah, sure!"
14 Money in Milan
15 Trump's second
16 Treat leather
17 Undershirt manufacture
19 Fairy tale's second word
20 Avoid
21 Right, on a map
22 Fix
23 Call it a night
25 Salt container
27 On deck
29 Laid up, perhaps
32 Ump's call
35 Separated
39 Eggs
40 Samuel's teacher
41 Keeps
42 Humor
43 Easter prefix
44 Overjoyed
45 Italian menu word
46 Evaluates
48 Uninteresting
50 Bottom-line numbers
54 Leather protector
58 Baby's word
60 Vatican resident
62 __ Carlo
63 Love god
64 Aim at when they've passed
66 Salamander
67 Computer code
68 Change spots
69 Without
70 City on the Aire
71 Wool sources

DOWN
1 Change
2 Hunting gun
3 Freshwater fish
4 Freshwater fish
5 Actress Thurman
6 Spouse
7 Diva's songs
8 Walk in puddles
9 December visitor
10 Intelligence
11 Great serving piece
12 Mineral nutrient
13 __ for oneself (cope)
18 Insignificant
24 Kick out
26 Joshes
28 "Later!" in London
30 Malevolent
31 Facts
32 Transmitted
33 Skin-cream ingredient
34 Gosling's covering
36 Snitch
37 At deuce
38 Become
41 Remainder
45 Sinatra tune
47 Drinks to
49 __ Linda, CA
51 Shock
52 Baggy
53 __ Girls (singing group)
55 Being pulled
56 Comic Martin
57 "__ lookin' at you, kid"
58 Cozy rooms
59 Region
61 Author Bagnold
65 "My country __ of thee . . ."

---

470   NEVER SAY DIET by Henry Hook

ACROSS
1 Man Friday?
5 Conceals
10 *Night Court* cast member
14 "This Is __ Ask" ('58 tune)
15 Livin' quantity?
16 Start of a Cash title
17 Deck
18 *Myra Breckinridge* director
19 "Is this the end of __?"
20 START OF AN ERMA BOMBECK QUOTE
22 PART 2 OF QUOTE
24 Re lyric verse
26 Walker of *Profiler*
27 Wounded Knee event
31 Oscar-winner Tomei
35 Back way
36 River of note?
38 Reagan's old org.
39 Place to eat?
40 PART 3 OF QUOTE
41 Driest Spanish sherry
42 Indivisible
43 Filled in, in a way
44 Harry's cat
45 Dinner
47 Came back in a big way
49 Dance lesson
51 Not a lot of a lot
52 PART 4 OF QUOTE
56 END OF QUOTE
60 *Vaca's* mate
61 Brag
63 Moussaka washdown
64 Cut a picture
65 Plus
66 "It's either you __!"
67 PR hoopla
68 Feminist __ Cottin Pogrebin
69 Despot

DOWN
1 "Now, then, where __?"
2 Raines or Logan
3 '40s French Socialist leader Léon
4 Trademarks of Durante and Farr
5 Pasty coating
6 "So *that's* your game!"
7 Hospital supply
8 Roo's mum
9 Former New York cardinal
10 Becket, e.g.
11 Newspaper article
12 Shy of a full deck
13 Filmdom's Lolita Haze
21 Singer Anita
23 __ Bator
25 "Ribbit!"
27 Considerable
28 Unaccompanied
29 Hypnotist's word
30 WWII reporter Davis
32 Start of a Whitman opus
33 Health: Fr.
34 "What __ boy am I"
37 __ fool of (embarrassed)
40 Gap
41 Hound hand?
43 Ratio part
44 Territory
46 Inclined
48 James Doohan role
50 Porridge ingredient
52 Emulate Urs Graf
53 Chromosome choice
54 Support
55 Turn reddish-brown
57 Mine, in part
58 Baum princess
59 Human dynamo
62 Becker barrier

471 INSTRUMENTAL by Bob Lubbers

ACROSS
1 Brother of Cain
5 Charley horse
9 Buddies
13 Gaucho's device
14 Winter forecast
16 EPA subject
17 "Son of __ !"
18 __ firma
19 Disavow
20 Dabble
23 Golf peg
24 Sea eagle
25 Gladden
29 *Steppenwolf* author
31 Trial balloon
32 Fur magnate
35 Treater's words
37 Word form for "three"
38 Brag
42 Forty winks
43 Like __ of bricks
44 Calms
45 More satanic
48 Yearns (for)
50 Scout's job, for short
51 Menlo Park initials
52 __ carte
55 Feel optimistic
60 Poet Teasdale
63 Singly
64 Low in fat
65 All tied up
66 Ore digger
67 Rescue
68 Rolls of bills
69 Striped fish
70 Part of USA

DOWN
1 Sternward
2 *Maltese Falcon* star's nickname
3 Avoid capture
4 Alight
5 Fall flowers
6 Empties
7 Mister: Ger.
8 Architect Saarinen
9 Sell from a pushcart
10 Expert
11 Actor Chaney
12 Foxy
15 Greek letter
21 Dubious
22 Born: Fr.
26 Female voices
27 Pied-à-__ (second home)
28 Gray and Moran
29 In which way
30 Sign up
31 Not many
32 Daisy Mae's mate
33 Toil
34 Subject
36 Unmodulated voices
39 Boat propeller
40 Mideast desert
41 Owns
46 Ella and Joshua
47 Wind direction: Abbr.
49 Ombudsman Ralph's kin
52 Nautical direction
53 Exit
54 *Roots* Emmy-winner Ed
56 Scottish cap
57 Smooth-talking
58 O'Neill's daughter
59 *Casablanca* heroine
60 Stitch
61 Actress Gardner
62 Cerise or cherry

472 TWO FIRSTS by Norma Steinberg

ACROSS
1 Little wave
7 Undivided
10 "Yuck!"
13 Unscrupulous
14 Income
16 *Seinfeld* actor
18 Mellowed
19 Bad word in pinball
20 John __ Passos
21 "For __ a jolly good fellow"
22 Sty
23 Gridiron scores: Abbr.
25 Hot tub
28 Beethoven opera
30 Ugly Duckling's parent
31 "__ Old Cowhand"
33 Flightless bird
34 Small horse
35 *Babes in Toyland* composer
39 Tirade
40 Chamomile brew
41 Some deer
42 Env. inserts
43 North Carolinian
46 Actress West
47 Leader of the Seven Dwarfs
48 Height: Abbr.
49 IRS employee
52 Russian space station
54 Infield covering
56 Soon
57 Revolutionary War turncoat
60 Canned fish
61 Come to terms
62 Broke a fast
63 British sports cars
64 Prey on one's mind

DOWN
1 Indian ruler
2 Mental picture
3 Affectations
4 Nudge
5 Office-wide computer hookup: Abbr.
6 Walking on air
7 Russian city
8 Subsequently
9 Zsa Zsa's sister
10 Disassemble
11 Unconfident estimation
12 That girl
15 Comes to a finale
17 Out of __ (unruly)
22 Half a quart
24 Gloomy
26 Trousers
27 Some
28 Data
29 Composer of *The Merry Widow*
30 Interval
31 Marla's predecessor
32 Thanksgiving pie choice
36 Director Preminger
37 Combining chemically
38 Borscht ingredient
39 Sleep phenom.
44 Playright Moss
45 City on the Rio Grande
47 __ Scott Decision
49 $100
50 Trend-measuring questions
51 South American peaks
53 About
55 Superior serves
56 Tiny farm animals
57 Explorers' grp.
58 Poorly lit
59 Civil War soldier

473   ROOM SERVICE by Ed Julius

ACROSS

1 *Call Me* __
6 Strike heavily
10 Certain coll. graduates
14 "Ready or not, here __!"
15 Shredded
16 Milan money
17 Genesis event
18 The Emerald Isle
19 "__ o'clock scholar"
20 Carnival-ride inventor
22 Mrs. Yokum
24 Recording milieu
26 First Chief Justice
29 "That hurts!"
30 Hilo neckwear
31 Jai __
33 Depot: Abbr.
34 __ Centauri
38 1960 NBA Rookie of the Year
42 Iron-carbon alloy
43 __ canto
44 Guaranteed
45 Colorado creek
47 Simple
49 Actor Ayres
50 Hotel employee
54 Staubach's sport
55 Few and far between
59 Leslie Caron role
60 Winter need
62 Cloth fold
63 Doll to tickle
64 __ arms (angry)
65 Crème de la crème
66 Org.
67 Dispatched
68 Units of force

DOWN

1 Offend
2 Philippine tree
3 Portal
4 Love, Italian-style
5 Doctor
6 Sault __ Marie, MI
7 Royal-court official
8 Dickens' Heep
9 Friendly
10 Theater handouts
11 Blackjack player's words
12 Glum, in poems
13 Mentally sound
21 "Be quiet!"
23 Do finger-painting
25 Word form for "eight"
26 Peter Benchley thriller
27 Dismounted
28 Ivy League school
32 Repetition
35 Klee or Reiser
36 Take on
37 Once more
39 Scale a peak
40 Gymnastics equipment
41 Lanchester and Maxwell
46 Low-tech calculator
48 Barked like a puppy
50 Spirals
51 Actress Celeste et al.
52 Run off to wed
53 Dawdle
54 Word before market or circus
56 Jockey's controller
57 Gratify fully
58 Are: Fr.
61 Demolition need

---

474   HORNER CORNER by Patrick Jordan

ACROSS

1 Cotton and Gator, for two
6 Opera star
10 Fishhook feature
14 Without restraint
15 Pupil controller
16 Away from the wind
17 Betty Grable ex
19 Hideaway
20 Roy Rogers, né Leonard __
21 Ending for form
22 Under the weather
24 Rex's sleuth
26 Distinctive atmosphere
27 Bebop developer
33 Secondary study
34 Modern recording abbr.
35 Change course, at sea
36 Random amount
37 In the beginning
41 Overtime cause
42 "__ You Babe"
44 Yoo or boo follower
45 Begins admitting customers
47 *Hello, Dolly!* costar
51 Distribute
52 Level
53 Astrologer's chart
56 Make illegal
57 River in a 1957 film
61 Like the Kalahari
62 The A of A&M Records
65 Convent room
66 Satan's specialty
67 Steinway product
68 Sacred
69 All the __ (trendy)
70 Mexican mister

DOWN

1 Outbursts from Scrooge
2 Evangelist Roberts
3 Sinewy and lean
4 Actor Lamas
5 Pig's digs
6 Script lines
7 __ la Douce
8 Compete (for)
9 Military attacks
10 Hot-air balloon stabilizer
11 Jai __
12 Horse controller
13 Peter of *Chicago Hope*
18 Courtroom dozen
23 Anger
25 Old Testament book
26 Having wings
27 Down Under canine
28 "I Believe __" (*How to Succeed . . .* song)
29 Manner of speaking
30 Eucharist plate
31 Cake's crowning touch
32 Supplements with difficulty
33 Weekday delivery
38 Major's predecessor
39 Course cry
40 Ripped
43 With shyness
46 Flat-topped hat
48 Where the buoys are
49 Unchanging
50 Ike's ex
53 Galligan of *Gremlins*
54 Hydrox rival
55 Pickling herb
56 Shipboard lock-up
58 Withdraw (from)
59 *New Yorker* cartoonist
60 *Believe __ Not!*
63 Spacewalk, to NASA
64 33 RPM disks

ACROSS
1 Gospel writer
5 Lugosi and Bartók
10 Saratoga Springs site
13 "Goodness gracious!"
14 *M*A*S*H* procedure
15 Whence some shoot
16 Sheep City?
18 __ for the books
19 Pronoun for George Eliot
20 Made chairs, perhaps
21 Milieux
23 Thorny
24 "Woe __!"
26 Unfeigned
28 How to go woolgathering?
33 Quotable catcher
34 Want-ad inits.
35 Ointment ingredient
36 __ close to schedule
37 Edit
39 Lug around
40 Lucie's dad
41 What's for launch?
42 One who digs heavy metal
43 Ovine agreement?
46 Painter Tanguy
47 Formerly
48 Hardy's partner
50 Treaty town
53 "__ a Nightingale"
55 Name of 13 popes
58 Rowboat accessory
59 Sheep-census question?
62 Pig-poke link
63 Leaving no remainder
64 Dyed-in-the-wool
65 QBs' stats
66 Roseanne's *She-Devil* costar
67 Cookie holders

DOWN
1 Court ploys
2 "Nope!"
3 Baby bouncer
4 1,000,000,000 years
5 *Sayonara* star
6 Green land
7 Words before "the line" or "thick"
8 Generation
9 Halvah, mostly
10 Blackjack dealer's device
11 __ colada
12 Gibbons, e.g.
14 Peter or Paul, but not Mary
17 Gainesville neighbor
22 Nonindependent
23 Popular Ford
25 Lose one's coat
26 Keep up on the issues
27 Jagged
29 "__ say more?"
30 See 50 Down
31 Eye problems
32 Artic Ice, e.g.
33 Presage
37 Larger-than-life
38 Renovated
42 "Skip to __"
44 Country music
45 __ *Do It Every Time*
49 "Love is not __"
50 With 30 Down, solo
51 Bridge holding
52 Dead Ball and Gaslight
54 Say it ain't so
55 Dolly of fiction
56 Gray or Moran
57 At __ (disagreeing)
60 St. crosser
61 One of Bartholomew's 500

ACROSS
1 Waterproof covering
5 Dissention
11 Dentist's deg.
14 Needle case
15 Suit maker
16 Congressman: Abbr.
17 Just in time
19 "__ pig's eye!"
20 '90s music style
21 Attempt
23 Festoon
26 Bikini top
27 Dole (out)
28 Salad-dressing ingredient
30 Dress styles
32 Picnic pest
33 Bernadette's shrine
36 Monroe/Lemmon film of '59
41 Kansas city
42 __ la la
44 "This __ Love"
47 Bellies
50 Hebrew month
51 Overhead railroads
53 Allays
54 Florida Indian
57 Craze
58 "Be Prepared" grp.
59 "Ring-around-the-rosey" ending
64 Lwyr.
65 Nebraska river
66 Pennsylvania port
67 Laugh syllable
68 Talked back
69 Actress Russo

DOWN
1 Midmorning
2 From __ Z
3 Accept the nomination
4 Designer Cardin
5 "Halt!"
6 The way, to Confucius
7 Stair part
8 Actress Massey
9 Nourishment
10 Seabird
11 Highly motivated
12 Designate
13 Extra parts
18 Sharp flavor
22 Pennsylvania sect
23 Actress Gardner
24 Rackets
25 Aware of
26 One way to cook
29 Kate's TV pal
30 Arles farewell
31 Allow
34 Don Ho's instrument
35 Apartment fees
37 Word form for "mother"
38 Recede
39 Elevator inventor
40 Corner, in a way
43 Dunderhead
44 Algiers district
45 "__ Fideles"
46 Quarterback Joe
48 Repast
49 More peeved
51 Raines and Fitzgerald
52 Ring jabs
55 Dozes
56 __ podrida
57 Took off
60 Consumed
61 Mine load
62 Come in first
63 Society-page word

RURAL ROLES by Patrick Jordan

ACROSS

1 Aspiration
5 He stares at stars
10 Halloween costume part
14 Plowing pair
15 Venture a viewpoint
16 Tangelo variety
17 Object to
18 Snake poison
19 Ring out
20 Summer hrs. in St. Pete
21 *Beverly Hillbillies* role
23 Farm machine
25 Fish eggs
26 '40s rural film couple
33 Severe
35 Colosseum site
36 Demonstrate
37 Boater or bowler
38 Imitated a crow
39 Find a purpose for
40 High cards in poker
42 Ready for business
43 Seeks
45 Edgar Bergen dummy
48 WSW opposite
49 Actor Borgnine
52 Old-time radio rural pair
58 Cheer from the bleachers
59 Evangelist Roberts
60 "__ you loud and clear!"
61 Swedish rock group
62 Stare at
63 Type of marble
64 Disney or Whitman
65 Jury member
66 Eminent
67 Looks at

DOWN

1 Greek epic poet
2 Nitrous __
3 Poetic rhythm pattern
4 Gridiron position
5 Oversee the state
6 Imitated
7 Galvanizing element
8 Organic compound
9 Made a comment
10 Jim Henson had a hand in them
11 *A Death in the Family* novelist
12 Thin plank
13 Scot's garb
21 Billie __ King
22 Scowling Stooge
24 Golfer's standard
27 Curtain
28 Energy
29 Congregation's affirmations
30 Ontario city
31 Disoriented
32 Meadow mamas
33 Counterfeit
34 Folded fast food
38 A stand-up guy?
41 Thief
43 Mister, in Munich
44 Coffee vessel
46 Bed-and-breakfast
47 Was obliged (to)
50 Weasel relative
51 "__ all, folks!"
52 Bowknot feature
53 Strong motivation
54 Drake or tom
55 Jason's ship
56 Rhythm
57 NBA Hall-of-Famer Archibald
61 Reverence

MADE TO ORDER by Brendan Emmett Quigley

ACROSS

1 Strong fellows
6 Machine part
9 Lasting impression
13 Newscaster Sawyer
14 Pindar output
15 Deal (with)
16 Hat material
17 Realty division
18 Liqueur flavoring
20 Start of a Ray Charles refrain
23 Elaborate party
24 Sandwich cookies
25 Feel regret for
26 Jackie's second
27 Med. test
28 Wavered
31 "Dinner's ready!"
35 Kilmer poem
36 Pal, in England
37 "Cool!"
41 Elvis tune
44 Small plane
47 Homer Simpson's neighbor
48 Head covering
49 Menu words
50 Sealy competitor
53 Jewels
54 Line from Mark Antony
58 *Star Trek* doctor
59 Genetic material
60 Keeps, as text
62 Word preceding a conclusion
63 Bankbook abbr.
64 Copier need
65 Put in groups
66 CBS logo
67 The Jetsons' dog

DOWN

1 Leaders: Abbr.
2 Choice words
3 Pertaining to the sea
4 Growing outward
5 Small salamander
6 "Kubla Khan" poet
7 Love to pieces
8 "Ditto!"
9 Large number
10 Pt. of speech
11 Bee's home
12 __ *911* (reality TV show)
19 Supplemented, with "out"
21 Antler
22 Aide: Abbr.
23 Actuality
27 Stone worker
29 __ and dined
30 "Do you have two fives for __?"
32 Morays
33 Inedible mouthful
34 Result ultimately (in)
38 Supporter
39 Truck driver, often
40 Bits for Fido
42 Flower holder
43 Rip
44 Serene
45 Decides upon
46 Don Quixote's sidekick
51 Singer Gorme
52 Opie portrayer
53 Cats, to Chavez
55 Ill-humored
56 Popular CD-ROM game
57 "¿Cómo __ usted?"
61 Box-office sign

479   THE WORKS by Alex Vaughn

ACROSS
1 Pooh Bah
5 Leg area
10 Jordanian, e.g.
14 Unceremonious
15 Western range
16 Exploding star
17 Brown brews
18 "Für __"
19 Roast table
20 Got brave?
23 Off the deep end
24 Arthur of TV
25 Bush concern?
34 Product of polymerization
35 Von Bulow portrayer
36 Lieut.'s subordinate
37 Iowa State city
38 X, for one
39 *Stanley & Iris* director
40 Belgian resort
41 Helen, on *Mad About You*
42 Mideast region
43 Marxist logo?
46 Skill
47 Cockney's residence
48 Try to come from behind?
57 Orange cover
58 Pitcher Ryan
59 English-horn kin
60 Draftable
61 Stonehenge worshiper
62 Practice
63 Moist, in a way
64 Botanical uprights
65 Director Buñuel

DOWN
1 Overstuff
2 Michael Caine film of '64
3 Nonpotent potables
4 Phrases anew
5 Sound system
6 Retained
7 Busy
8 Not a big meal
9 Exercise of a sort
10 __ condor (largest flying bird of prey)
11 MGM sound effect
12 Tel __
13 Unrefined
21 Highest point
22 Novel written by Aristophanes?
25 Sweeping motion
26 NFL city
27 '80s prime-time soldiers of fortune
28 Terra __
29 Show the ropes to
30 Improved an edge
31 How to sign
32 Base 8
33 Casual-dress phrase
38 Comes to the aid of the party
39 Chinese restaurant freebie
41 Chowderhead
42 Chowderhead
44 Sea plea
45 Marks and Spencer's receipts
48 Needle
49 Retail grouping
50 All over
51 Suit material
52 Trace
53 *The Lost Boys* actor
54 Palestine prename
55 Jennifer on *WKRP*
56 Rents out

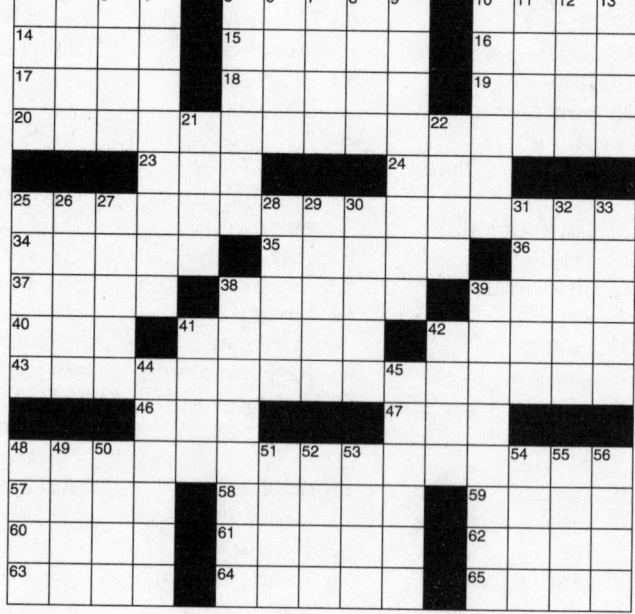

480   NO ONE SPECIAL by Ed Julius

ACROSS
1 Neutered
7 "Surfin' __" (Beach Boys song)
13 Flowery
14 Shaded walk
16 Handyman
19 New Zealand bird
20 High land
21 These: Sp.
22 Plastics ingredient
24 Put in fresh soil
26 Overstuff
27 Washer cycle
29 Coolidge's VP
31 Part of MPH
32 Type of fisherman
34 Most piquant
36 Make __ in (tear)
38 Hwys.
39 Military rifles
43 Added flavor to an ear
47 Western Indian
48 __ on (urged)
50 Irish county
51 Some flies
53 Frightful giants
55 Playwright O'Casey
56 Doddering
58 "Omigosh!"
60 __ rule (generally)
61 Handyman
64 Scholarly
65 Bullfighter
66 Oil source
67 Bridge suit

DOWN
1 Brief stay
2 Rolling grassland
3 Antiquated
4 Wild ox
5 Prep school near London
6 Postpone
7 More pale
8 Model Carol
9 Taxi passenger
10 Collect
11 Bureaucratic delay
12 Forms thoughts
15 State positively
17 Did a Little bit?
18 South American capital
23 Take __ at (try)
25 LSAT and GMAT
28 Weird
30 Porterhouse, e.g.
33 Beatle in the background
35 Man and Capri
37 "Fever" singer
39 Volume
40 They make amends
41 Entourage
42 Letter stroke
44 Picked up the tab
45 Expungement
46 Energetic ones
49 Word form for "ten"
52 Winter Olympics vehicles
54 Cults
57 Assam silkworm
59 Organ part
62 $$ dispenser
63 "Are you a man __ mouse?"

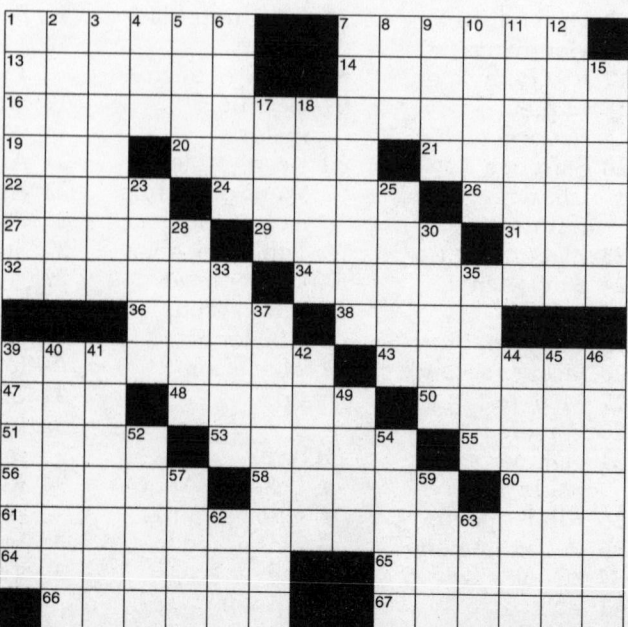

481 WATER LOG by Bob Lubbers

ACROSS
1 Fuel type
4 Master, on safari
9 "__ la vista"
14 Building site
15 Consumed
16 Come in
17 Boston Bruin legend
18 Ride the remote
20 Pile
22 The Emerald Isle
23 Seamen
26 Author Hemingway
30 Listen up
32 Western bar
34 Costa del __
36 Achy spots
38 Tribute
39 __ Called Horse
41 Flower part
43 Go berserk
44 Shoe string
45 Brazilian seaport
47 Change color
48 Topics
51 Enticers
53 Handsome young man
55 Tropical fruits
58 Pub drinks
60 Photographer Adams
61 Door trim
67 Word form for "three"
68 Worship
69 "Mule Train" singer Frankie
70 German article
71 Stairway post
72 Heavens above
73 Actress Ryan

DOWN
1 Shiny finish
2 Blood line
3 Strict
4 Summons
5 Baby's cry
6 One __ time
7 Hawaiian state bird
8 Warbucks' ward
9 Montana's capital
10 Response to a ques.
11 Alphabetic trio
12 Colonizer's holding: Abbr.
13 Barking sound
19 Drops the ball
21 Actor Gulager
24 Classic cars
25 Fire alarm
27 Moose relatives
28 Stereo, e.g.
29 NBC morning show
31 Himalayan kingdom
33 Yup's opposite
34 Popcorn seasoning
35 Nebraska Indian
37 Took notice
40 Verne captain
42 Zhivago's love
46 School glue name
49 Nail polish
50 Missile housing
52 Took off
54 Peddles
56 Condor's nest
57 David's weapon
59 Minn. neighbor
61 Is able to
62 Poetic form
63 Promise
64 Before, to the Bard
65 Square root of IX
66 Wind dir.

482 GRID PLAY by Rich Norris

ACROSS
1 Relative by marriage
6 Mortal
11 Like FDR's Deal
14 Put up with
15 Clear the board
16 Eggs
17 Flirted with
19 Nonsense
20 Gold measure
21 Toll road, for short
22 Most insinuating
26 Privilege loser, often
28 Make available for sale
31 Red-wrapped cheeses
32 Evans' partner
33 Food shop
34 Singer Tucker
36 Oklahoma city
40 Indira Gandhi's father
42 Hackneyed
43 Really enjoyed
46 Stevenson of M*A*S*H
48 Investigates anew, as a case
49 Woeful word
50 "__ Get Started With You"
52 Recyclable item
53 Forced to retreat
59 Circle part
60 Tim or Steve
61 Ruling class
62 Tiny
63 Untended, as a lawn
64 Like some stadiums

DOWN
1 "__ Woman" (Reddy tune)
2 Hoopsters' org.
3 Cover
4 Fruity drink
5 Enervates
6 Fireside setting
7 Sky bear
8 Schooner feature
9 Simile divider
10 Court divider
11 Retailer's guarantee
12 Draw forth
13 Tend the shrubs
18 Gone by
21 Prepare for a kiss
22 Zoomed
23 Art studio subject
24 Type like this: Abbr.
25 Chain reaction pieces
26 Edison's middle name
27 __ constrictor
29 Boredom
30 Lad
34 "Easier said __ done"
35 Covenant holder
37 Nick at __
38 "Blame __ the Bossa Nova"
39 Dict. entries
41 JFK posting
42 Having protrusions, as gears
43 Quick look
44 Nook partner
45 English county
46 Large parrot
47 __ Boothe Luce
50 Do nothing
51 Dorm resident
53 Speak hesitantly
54 Pub pint
55 "Hold On Tight" band
56 Edge
57 Southwestern native
58 Actor Beatty

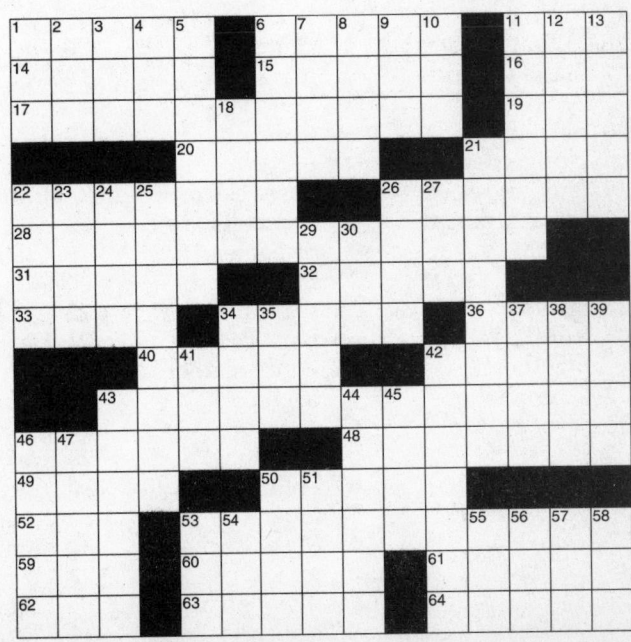

483 ALLOY OOP by Fred Piscop

ACROSS
1 Hay unit
5 Comes to
10 Tell all
14 In the thick of
15 P.R. man's concern
16 Lacoste of tennis
17 __ Beauty (apple variety)
18 Shabby state
19 Poker buy-in
20 Award for heroism
22 Telegram punctuation
23 Aurora's counterpart
24 Justifications
26 Luggage lugger
30 Banned pesticide: Abbr.
31 Like VIP meetings
35 Two below par
39 __ close to schedule
40 Gave the thumbs-down to
42 Greek letters
43 Also-ran in '92 and '96
45 Frontiersmens' garments
47 Quant look
49 French wine region
50 Apollo's twin sister
54 __-night doubleheader
55 Marsh plant
56 Jamaican percussion
62 __ snuff (adequate)
63 Havana's __ Castle
64 Fall birthstone
65 __ Bones (Sleepy Hollow bully)
66 "Halt, salt!"
67 Axis leader
68 Top-of-the-line
69 Twenty Questions replies
70 Negotiations hangup

DOWN
1 Zinger
2 Love personified
3 Star's wheels
4 Biblical paradise
5 Like an unde-fended receiver
6 Out of whack
7 Philosopher Immanuel
8 Actress Samantha
9 Lose one's cool
10 Essentials
11 Slowly, on a score
12 Playwright Chekhov
13 Pager sounds
21 Intensity
25 Lime drink
26 H.S. class
27 Cows, old-style
28 Bela, in *Son of Frankenstein*
29 Egghead
32 Kid-__ (children's shows)
33 Program file suffix
34 Confederate commander
36 Karmann __ (old Volkswagen)
37 *Mod Squad* role
38 Being: Lat.
41 One way to decide
44 The piper's son
46 Lost control on ice
48 Consternation
50 Island off Venezuela
51 Photocopy, for short
52 Grand __ National Park
53 Potbelly, e.g.
54 To the point
57 History chapters
58 Goes bad
59 "__ the Roof" (Drifters song)
60 Goya subject
61 Wade through the surf

484 PEDIATRICKS by Ann W. Masten

ACROSS
1 Wire feature, maybe
5 Make jump
10 Lao-__
13 Software buyer
14 Hawaiian island
15 Main point
16 "What __ say?"
17 Stand up and speak
18 Barrett of Hollywood
19 Shoe style
21 Falsetto singer
23 Disparity
24 Pop fly
25 Speedy
28 Rural get-together
29 Overused
33 Scrooge, for short
34 Power units
36 French friends
37 Ratted
38 "... but is __?"
39 Declines
40 Two words from Caesar
41 In check
42 Elisabeth, in *Leaving Las Vegas*
43 Tearful
45 Droop
46 Leave the trail
47 Cotton machine
49 "Phooey!"
50 Crash the party
53 Bases clearer
57 Football Hall-of-Famer Ewbank
58 Light reading?
60 Balanced
61 Foul-weather friend
62 Crossing medium
63 Followers: Suff.
64 Layer
65 Make tracks on ice
66 "There'll be __ time ..."

DOWN
1 Osso __
2 PDQ
3 Actress Russo
4 Screwball comedy of '38
5 Pleasure boat
6 Prudence
7 Santa __, CA
8 Rickety auto
9 MacDonald's refrain
10 Horseback ride
11 New Mexico Indian
12 Midterm, e.g.
15 Clairvoyance
20 Abe's babe
22 Denials
24 Harp on
25 Darn
26 Let up
27 Board game
28 Traffic tie-up
30 Traffic-light color
31 Sign of fall
32 History homework
34 Through
35 Pigpen
44 Chatter
46 Nunn or Cooke
48 Wheels of fortune?
49 Carried
50 Cashless transaction
51 Singer Carter
52 Hard to hold
53 Miami hoopsters
54 Headstrong
55 Biblical preposition
56 Tree house
59 It's bagged in the supermarket

WHERE IT'S AT by Patrick Jordan

ACROSS

1 Feeds the hogs
6 Watermelon covering
10 Joyce of *Roc*
14 Still in bed
15 Flash of brilliance
16 Having reclined
17 TOP
19 Made one's jaw drop
20 Ma's instrument
21 Hard punches
22 Like harsh language
26 Waiter's handout
27 Kindergarten bottles
28 Dug a hole
32 Fields of interest
33 Paper
34 Prompter's offering
35 USN officer
36 Pulled a lever, perhaps
37 Lingerie designer
38 *Chapeau*, in Chicago
39 Moves like the Blob
40 Bleated
41 Improved in quality
43 Write a crossword clue
44 Perry's creator
45 Photographers
46 Sorrowful poem
48 Dinah or Pauly
50 Alluring
51 BOTTOM
56 Follow closely
57 Chevrolet rival
58 Herbert Hoover, e.g.
59 Poker payment
60 "Terrible" age stage
61 Armored vehicles

DOWN

1 __-cone (summer treat)
2 Bud's comedy cohort
3 Hall-of-Famer Mel
4 Baby seal
5 Biological group
6 Winchester product
7 Golden Calf, e.g.
8 Agrippina's tyrant son
9 Certain blocker
10 Jerry's friend
11 RIGHT
12 Willingly
13 "No ifs, __, or buts!"
18 Guns the engine
21 Group of quail
22 Cochise or Geronimo
23 Mai tai maker
24 LEFT
25 Headliner
26 Gelatin shaper
28 Filled to capacity
29 Goes quickly
30 Oregon city
31 Use novocaine
33 Sleep lightly
36 Sotto __
37 Clumsy fellows
39 Having no siblings
40 Fund-raising event
42 Sock pattern
43 Laura of *Jurassic Park*
45 Washday units
46 "¿Cómo __ usted?"
47 Low in fat
48 Flat-bottomed freighter
49 Long lunch?
51 Frequently, in verse
52 Mauna __
53 Hold the deed to
54 Adult acorn
55 TLC dispensers

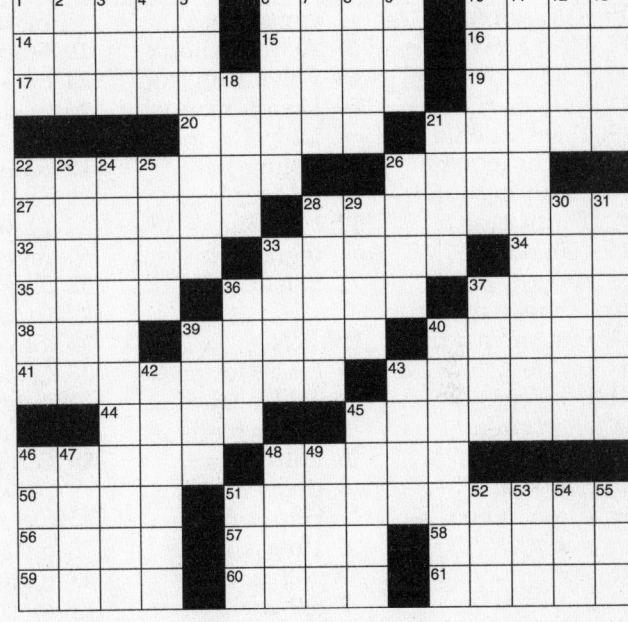

DROPS IN THE BUCKET by Lee Weaver

ACROSS

1 Story
5 Ice-cream utensil
10 German river
14 Felt sorry about
15 Telephone greeting
16 Roman emperor
17 Jason's ship
18 Good-for-nothing
19 Actress Stapleton
20 Atlas item
21 Low walls used as a defense in battle
23 Employers
25 Salary increase
26 Eagle's claws
28 Country gallant
30 Distribute
31 Emerald, essentially
32 Madison's state: Abbr.
35 Weight-loss program
36 Round roofs
37 Julep enhancer
38 Sun. talk
39 First Soviet premier
40 Prom, e.g.
41 Shoe ties
42 Looked for
43 Raccoon's cousin
45 Student of Zeno
46 Suzanne Somers' exercise gadget
49 Very popular
52 New Haven campus
53 In the know
54 Christmas visitors
55 Wharf
56 Exhibited fondness
57 Per __ (daily)
58 Comes to a halt
59 Lots and lots
60 Genealogy chart

DOWN

1 Trolley relative
2 Mystical emanation
3 Practical joker
4 Tokyo, once
5 Prepares eggs by baking
6 Gives up, as territory
7 Pedro's pot
8 Spanish cheers
9 Plays the part of
10 Enforce with authority
11 Sly looks
12 Sedan slower
13 Ages upon ages
21 Proclivity
22 Bemoan
24 Flue fallout
26 Tiny amounts
27 "I cannot tell __"
28 Road rigs
29 Small songbird
31 Fido's reward
32 Fireside seating
33 Part of a foot
34 Undo a dele
36 Topic in arithmetic
37 Hawaiian island
39 Thin slat
40 Entryway
41 Dark brews
42 War horses
43 __-link fence
44 Ended the squeak
45 Scatter (about)
46 Use a keyboard
47 MP's quarry
48 Rescue
50 Curved molding
51 *Newsweek* competitor
54 Summer hrs. in Denver

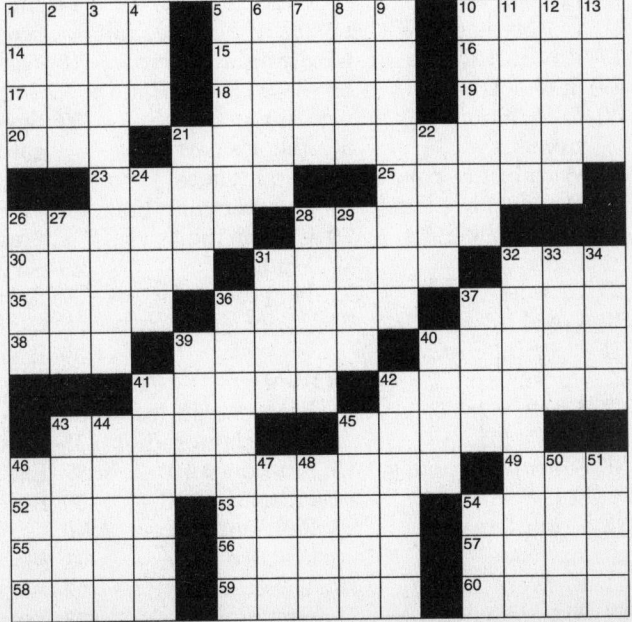

487 AT THE SYMPHONY by Rich Norris

ACROSS

1 Gone by
5 Inky smear
9 Use a razor
14 Leer at
15 Capri coin
16 Stogie
17 Sells successfully
20 Sales-kit item
21 Health farm
22 HST successor
23 Rolaids rival
25 Yale students
27 Weigh-in abbr.
30 Stadium sound
32 Throws out
36 "Uh oh!"
38 Atop
40 Come to terms
41 Engage in self-praise
44 Las Vegas area
45 China item
46 High peaks
47 Star-shaped
49 Diamond of pop music
51 Comedian Louis
52 Hit's opposite
54 Take the lead
56 Former Mideast alliance: Abbr.
58 Short snooze
60 Elevator inventor Otis
64 No __ (without conditions)
67 Actress Anouk
68 Polynesian icon
69 Do a personnel job
70 Bonnie's partner
71 Lip-balm ingredient
72 Son of Seth

DOWN

1 Places for peas
2 Taj Mahal site
3 Urban blight
4 Entice
5 Rodgers and Hart song
6 Hole edge, in golf
7 Spheres
8 Purplish gray
9 High school subj.
10 Second-guessing
11 Matured
12 Still-life subject
13 Hosp. areas
18 Musical phrase mark
19 Store event
24 Socked away
26 __ the Terrible
27 "__ luck!"
28 Rainwear
29 Show off
31 Plastic ingredient
33 Sing like Crosby
34 Towel material
35 Good judgment
37 Used a wok
39 Gift for a sweetheart
42 October birthstone
43 Requiring formal attire
48 Extended
50 Singer's syllables
53 *Ristorante* course
55 Nouveau __
56 Gas or elec.
57 Military group
59 Vessel for Jack and Jill
61 Ankle-knee connector
62 Protagonist
63 Summer drinks
64 Air Force grp.
65 Wedding-page word
66 Ring decision

488 PUZZLE, ANYONE? by Fred Piscop

ACROSS

1 Impresario Ziegfeld
4 Michelangelo masterpiece
9 Cod or Ann
13 Thumbs-up, and then some
15 Pitched in
16 "__ Named Sue"
17 Jim Carrey role
19 Steam up
20 Like many tuxedos
21 With bright colors
23 Bergen's Mortimer
25 Everly Brothers tune
28 Retailer
30 Weed digger
31 "__ Blu, Dipinto di Blu"
32 Greek vowel
33 Dull routine
36 Murphy Brown's son
38 Complete a sentence?
41 Brewers' needs
44 Muslim chief
45 Boned up on
49 Ostrich kin
50 Nine-digit ID
52 __ Park, NJ
54 Ponzi, e.g.
58 Knights-in-training
59 Saint Catherine's city
60 Have a connection
62 Straight __ arrow
63 1980 J. Geils Band song
67 Teller's partner
68 Top invitees
69 Frontiersman Fink
70 City on the Hudson
71 Hereditary factors
72 __ out a living

DOWN

1 Brother's address
2 Varnish ingredient
3 Stuff oneself
4 Huff and puff
5 Pentium maker
6 Practice piece
7 Three times, in prescriptions
8 Slower than andante
9 West Indian
10 Eisenhower Center city
11 Plexiglas, for one
12 Mr. Potato Head part
14 Big name in boxing gear
18 *The NeverEnding Story* author
22 Special Forces soldiers
23 Star Wars initials
24 Word form for "recent"
26 Sweater letter
27 Bridge authority Culbertson
29 Basic education trio
34 Sheeplike
35 President pro __
37 Exactly as spoken
39 Ruhr River city
40 "__ Little Teapot"
41 *Mal de* __
42 Accumulative one
43 Tenor Pavarotti
46 One of Fergie's kids
47 "Chances __"
48 "Bad" word form
51 *Hogan's Heroes* setting
53 Petty quarrel
55 Loggins or Rogers
56 Watergate Senator Sam
57 Ebbets Field great
61 D-Day craft: Abbr.
62 Bldg. unit
64 Grand __ Opry
65 "__-Katy" (1918 song)
66 Go out with

489   GOING NATIVE by Bob Lubbers

ACROSS
1 Long tale
5 It has an eye logo
10 Uttar Pradesh city
14 Musical sign
15 __ bolt from the blue
16 Applaud
17 Certain Scot
19 Record
20 Lanza and Cuomo
21 Stands firm
23 Elite
26 Stash
27 Moorish palace
30 Most lucid
33 Penn or Connery
34 Meddlers
36 GM model
37 Coins in Peru
38 Jazz musician's instrument
39 __ Carlo Menotti

40 Word form for "bird"
41 Hypnotic name
44 Lean
45 Filet __
47 Large snake
49 Oven
50 Influential one
51 Lit
54 Limits
58 Bubble up
59 Certain Belgian
62 "Dies __"
63 Harass
64 ". . . __ a man with seven wives"
65 Transmit
66 Old-time oath
67 Profits

DOWN
1 Con game
2 Canadian prov.
3 Will of *The Waltons*
4 Big-eared elephants
5 Near
6 Storage space
7 Do Aspen
8 Rip
9 Lynn's sister
10 Director's call
11 Certain Scot
12 Engrossed
13 Tarzan's neighbors
18 Campus digs
22 RR depots
24 Neighborhoods
25 Certain Brit
27 State in India
28 Tenth-century Pope
29 Certain Nova Scotian
31 Rise
32 Big name in trucks
35 Singer Marie
39 Gamma __ (antiviral agent)

41 More than half
42 Ugandan city
43 Wood joints
46 Tackled hard
48 Nonchalant
51 Nile wader
52 Author Vidal

53 Vestige
55 Bering Sea port
56 Regimen
57 JFK arrivals
60 Made in the __
61 Crossed out

490   GRAND TOUR by Ed Julius

ACROSS
1 Cold War phone
8 Cut short, as a takeoff
13 Washington character
14 Synagogue scroll
15 Robert Conrad series
19 Part of TWA
20 Iowa State site
21 Dixie: Abbr.
22 March-command words
23 Aged beer
25 Pains
26 Seer's trait
27 Complication
28 Nebraska Indians
30 Pertaining to the wind
34 Fit to be tied
35 Mozart's birthplace
38 '60s style
39 Scrolls site

40 Change the actors
42 Demure
43 __ Kapital
46 Words from Scrooge
47 Gathers in
50 Russian river
51 "__ on parle français"
52 Word on Irish coins
53 Mend
54 Vacationer's goal
58 Approaches
59 Dunk
60 Import
61 Dome or skylight

DOWN
1 "__ deck!"
2 Yellow shades
3 Eastern range
4 Some bowling areas
5 Wading bird
6 Lon of Cambodia
7 Teacher's deg.
8 "Once upon __ . . ."
9 Ravel work
10 Commands: Abbr.
11 Like some deals
12 Rommel arena
16 Witty rogue
17 "Layer" word form
18 End of a Hemingway title
23 Pip
24 Free as __
25 Menu
27 Dole and Byrd: Abbr.
29 Young girl
31 Pound and Stone
32 Epoch
33 Civil rights org.
35 Fruit-derived acid

36 "Do I dare to eat __?"
37 Japanese herbs
41 Judge and jury
44 Loath
45 Lumber-mill worker
48 Uneven

49 WWI group
50 Hawaiian geese
52 Actor Richard
53 Scale pair
55 Once named
56 Kinsman
57 950

491   WEATHER OR NOT by Lee Weaver

ACROSS

1 Former Iranian rulers
6 Wedding promise
9 Talons
14 Biblical prophet
15 '90s music style
16 British quart
17 In pieces
18 "We __ the World"
19 Let free
20 Flute or trumpet
23 __ Lanka
24 Swiss peak
25 Inaccurate
28 Frozen treats
31 Quality of spirit
36 Ball-game ticket stub
39 Took a chance
40 Author __ Stanley Gardner
41 Actress Verdugo
43 Low-lying islands
44 Very tart
46 Fairy-tale heroine
48 Roundabout path
50 Lift for a skier
51 __ Aviv
52 Writer Fleming
54 Domicile: Abbr.
56 President's "theme song"
64 Coiled
65 __ constrictor
66 Nairobi is its capital
67 Yard enclosure
68 __ Abner
69 Gone from one's plate
70 Wickerwork willow
71 Plumber's joint
72 Smelting residue

DOWN

1 Pygmalion playwright
2 Pueblo Indian
3 Wise __ owl
4 Flocks
5 Given to irony
6 Gershwin and Levin
7 Pub missile
8 Carmen, e.g.
9 Walked heavily
10 Bus route
11 Memo abbr.
12 Judicial order
13 Comprehend
21 Place for a statue
22 Einstein's birthplace
25 Greek nymph
26 Foolish show
27 __ mignon
29 Conger and moray
30 Aroma
32 Dashboard dial, for short
33 Characteristic
34 Philippine island
35 '50s Ford model
37 Pianist Peter
38 Door opener
42 In the know
45 Real-estate magnate
47 Destroyed
49 Scoundrel
53 Lordly
55 Clip, as wool
56 Gardener's tools
57 VW cousin
58 Picnic playwright
59 Work hard
60 Foyer
61 Division word
62 Gives a look-see
63 Rooters
64 "__ goes there?"

492   GOING UP by Rich Norris

ACROSS

1 __ Gigio (TV mouse)
5 Pre-meal prayer
10 "Quiet!"
14 Seth's son
15 Berkshire Music Festival site
16 Canton's state
17 Artful deception
20 Royal messenger
21 Plays in the pool
22 Racetrack fence
24 Portion: Abbr.
25 Goddess of plenty
28 Clark's partner
30 Hires a work force
35 Shiny mineral
37 WWII boats
39 Buzzing, as with excitement
40 One way to go out?
43 Auto supercharger
44 28 Across portrayer
45 Choice word
46 Oration
48 Farmer's place, in song
50 Bering or Formosa: Abbr.
51 NRC predecessor
53 Hook's henchman
55 Kitchen appliances
60 Fast gait
64 Eastwood film
66 Lorre role
67 Chew the scenery
68 Composer Charles
69 Part of Q.E.D.
70 Prevent
71 Robin's residence

DOWN

1 Pianist John
2 Treater's phrase
3 Unsatisfactory
4 Actor Werner
5 Plant with sword-shaped leaves
6 Stimpy's pal
7 "No ifs, __, or buts!"
8 Provides at no cost
9 Banishes
10 __ d'oeuvres
11 "Oops!"
12 Royal honorific
13 Dan Blocker role
18 Airline to Haifa
19 Motley
23 Composer Franz
25 Leaves out
26 Photo on the wall
27 Fill with fear
29 Mrs. Peel's partner
31 Qualified
32 Puts one over on
33 Before the rest
34 More cagey
36 French cleric
38 Achy spots
41 Find
42 Multiplex attendee
47 Well-__ (wealthy)
49 Petal
52 Burglary, for one
54 Mischievous
55 Sprinter's concern
56 __ about
57 Boy or girl lead-in
58 Opportunity
59 Nose-in-the-air type
61 Not taped
62 Mine finds
63 Annoying one
65 Greek vowel

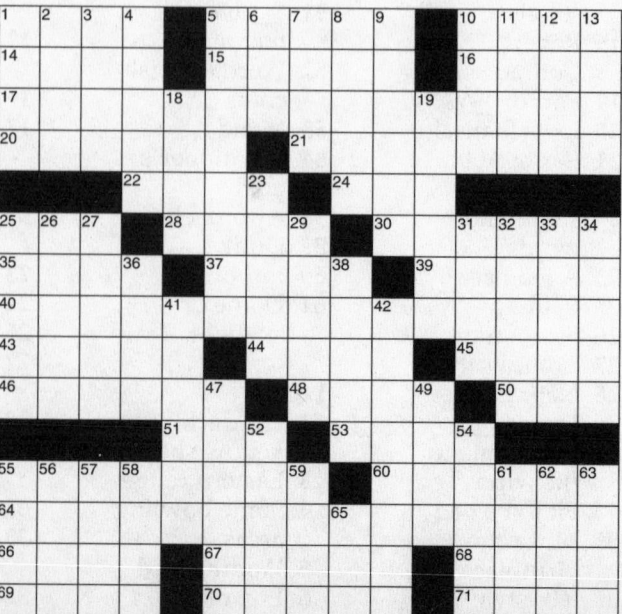

HARD HITTIN' by Fred Piscop

ACROSS
1 Jazz fan
4 Severely hurt
8 200 milligrams
13 Blond shade
14 *Cabaret* director
15 Cornhusker city
16 __ *Stoops to Conquer*
17 Frat letters
18 Tokyo trasher, in film
19 Aaron's nickname
22 Cyberspace memos
23 "That smarts!"
24 Dignitary, for short
27 Sank
31 Expression of sorrow
33 High-tech weapons prog.
34 Do dinner
36 *Ars __, vita brevis*
37 Gehrig's nickname
41 Danish dinero
43 Green Hornet's aide
44 Delta-winged craft
47 Encroach on
49 Get ready to ride again
52 Actress West
53 Classified __
55 Alignment concern
56 Snead's nickname
60 Bologna unit
63 Chill-inducing
64 __ *Mine* (George Harrison book)
65 Viking of the comics
66 Rocket stage
67 Actress Thompson
68 Scrub, NASA-style
69 Tabula __
70 Hockey great Bobby

DOWN
1 They're nuts
2 Guilt-ridden
3 Gershwin tune
4 Anchor
5 Italian wine center
6 "No man __ island"
7 Like fishnets
8 Region of southwest England
9 Crazedly
10 "Awesome!"
11 "Gotcha!"
12 Novelist Amy
14 Pasture land
20 Sch. near Harvard
21 MSN rival
24 Sculpture discovered in 1820
25 Gerundial ending
26 Educators' org.
28 Text scanner: Abbr.
29 *The Caine Mutiny* novelist
30 Without face value
32 Jersey salutation
35 Golfer Tom
38 Santa __, CA
39 Critical warning
40 Discouraging words
41 Model Alexis
42 Genetics abbr.
45 Smaller in girth
46 Decadal
48 Author LeShan
50 *Victory* __ (Rodgers score)
51 __ good deed
54 Microscope sample
56 Lasting impression
57 Prefix for bucks
58 Tees off
59 Historic caravel
60 __ Na Na
61 Retriever, for short
62 "__ to Rio" (Peter Allen song)

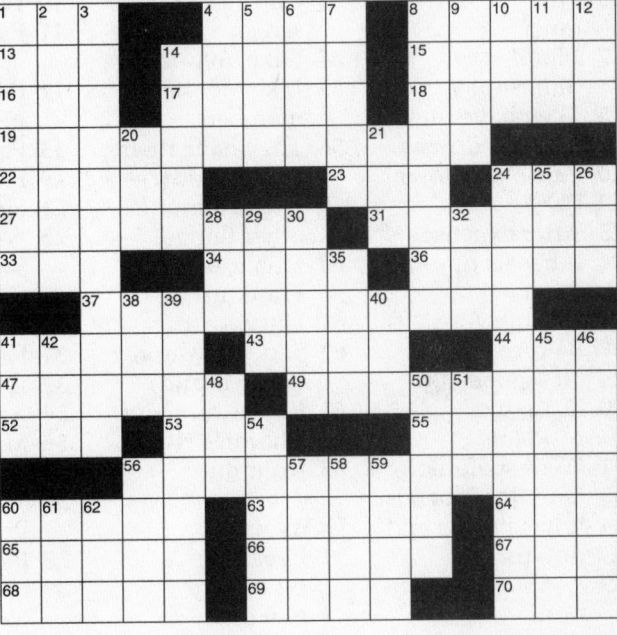

ISN'T IT ROMANTIC by Bob Lubbers

ACROSS
1 BIG APPLE EXCURSION, PART 1
8 Configuration
13 Ostentatiously displaying
14 Bank employee
16 Make over
17 Crude
18 Buck ending
19 Mountain nymph
21 Half a Gabor name
22 Sweet potato
25 Rajiv's mother
27 Go __ tangent (digress)
30 Dentist's deg.
31 *Pequod* captain
34 Dernier __
35 French farewell
37 __ *Gay*
38 WWI army
39 Name of the excursion site
41 ". . . __ of thee"
42 Singer Lenya
44 Rock ledge
45 Cain raiser
46 Writer Seton
47 Sun. talk
48 Deceived
50 Uno, for one
52 Literary miscellany
53 Ring rhymer
55 Misbehave
57 Scout outing
61 Moolah
63 Does battle
66 Hold in custody
67 Award givers
68 Vestige
69 BIG APPLE EXCURSION, PART 3

DOWN
1 Mimicker
2 Fashion name
3 Southwestern gulch
4 Hwy.
5 Estuary
6 Obsessed by
7 BIG APPLE EXCURSION, PART 2
8 Fancy fiddles, for short
9 Spyri book
10 Vestment
11 Landmark near the excursion site
12 Congers
13 Sp. lady
15 Cereal-box info: Abbr.
20 Abide
23 Have __ in the hole
24 Constructed
26 Scurried
27 Florida city
28 Refrigerant
29 Starting street for the excursion
32 Still in play
33 Stationed
36 Enclosure
37 Small and mischievous
40 __ mater
43 Greek cross
47 Brief time
49 African desert
51 Osmond sister
53 Append
54 Big fibs
56 Milne bear
58 Roman way
59 Actor Cameron
60 UFO crew
62 Musical aptitude
64 WSW opposite
65 Soak

UPS AND DOWNS by Frank Longo

ACROSS
1 Thunder sounds
6 Action word
10 Pike or perch
14 Prefix with rocket
15 Canyon comeback
16 With the bow, in music
17 Moral philosophy
18 They have their ups and downs
20 Part of 37 Down
22 PDQ
23 After expenses
24 It has its ups and downs
26 Itsy-bitsy
27 Before
28 "It" game
29 Damascus residents
31 Went spelunking
33 Unrefined metals
34 It has its ups and downs
39 __ Man (Estevez film)
40 Tripoli's locale
41 Thomas Gray, e.g.
45 Head, slangily
46 __ gratia artis
49 Debussy's La __
50 It has its ups and downs
53 Gardner of the screen
54 Lake, to Luigi
55 Like Mensa members
56 They have their ups and downs
59 __ alia (among other things)
60 Finale, in Frankfurt
61 Ditty
62 São __ (a Cape Verde Island)
63 Recipe directive
64 Charon's river
65 Ruhr hub

DOWN
1 Dream up
2 Bit of mail
3 Not out
4 Gussy up
5 Culture-specific
6 Churchillian sign
7 Showy display
8 Lab monkey
9 Flaubert character
10 What gras means
11 Pots, kettles, etc.
12 Résumé reader, perhaps
13 Party thrower
19 Pantomimist
21 Hunger for
25 "Ain't She Sweet" composer
30 Smidgen
31 Drain problem
32 LXV x X
34 Apropos
35 Modus __
36 Sty sound
37 Manhattan Project product
38 Pleasure lover
39 New versions of old films
42 "La __ Bonita" (Madonna song)
43 Kicks off
44 Dress
46 Japanese dogs
47 Back out of a deal
48 Sophie's Choice author
51 Sharp-witted and shrewd
52 Indian princesses
57 Neighbor of Lux.
58 Chromosome determinant

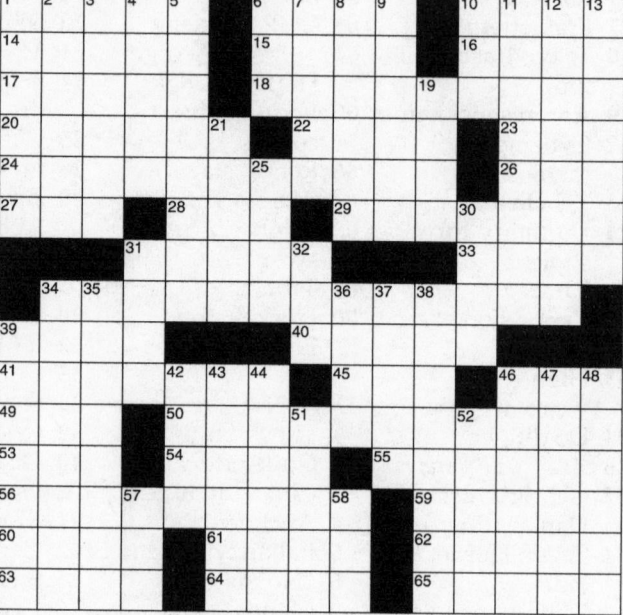

RIGHT DOWN YOUR ALLEY by Norma Steinberg

ACROSS
1 Turkey-stuffing herb
5 Misbehave
10 Scratch
14 Personalities
15 Actress Talia
16 "__ real nowhere man . . ."
17 Lows
18 Burn slightly
19 Terrible czar
20 Small hotel
21 Street urchin
23 Networks
25 Permit
26 Raced along
27 Frigid
32 Sultan's pride
34 Search for weapons
35 Armed conflict
36 Line of rotation
37 Feeds the pigs
38 Knight's wife
39 Sort
40 Navy and lima
41 One Flew Over the Cuckoo's Nest author
42 Oscar-winner for Shampoo
44 Mutt's pal
45 Churl
46 Egyptian stationery
49 Soda-fountain creation
54 Words in a simile
55 Skip
56 Of country life
57 Idi __
58 Actress Russo
59 Overact
60 Give temporarily
61 Leg joint
62 Plied the oars
63 Nervous

DOWN
1 18-wheelers
2 Extreme suffering
3 Stage a walkout
4 Curvy letter
5 Take for granted
6 Vouchers
7 Pale color
8 Cajole
9 Without equal
10 Glazed fabric
11 Son of Jacob
12 Memo letters
13 Diminish
21 Bacterium
22 Pursue
24 Little piggies
27 Facade
28 Torn and Van Winkle
29 Court denial
30 Nominate
31 Actor Joel
32 Sleet relative
33 Rod between wheels
34 Spanish dessert
37 Sailor
38 Stand up to
40 Cereal choice
41 Retained
43 Beard style
44 Incarcerated
46 Blue-__ special
47 Employing
48 Actress Duncan
49 Ill-fated Supreme Court nominee
50 Revival meeting cry
51 Midmorning
52 Japanese wrestling
53 Front of a boat
57 Tavern order

497 CALLING MR. FIX-IT by Lee Weaver

ACROSS
1 Heart of the matter
5 Etch or sketch
9 Shoots the breeze
13 Ancient Peruvian
14 Singer Ross
15 Birthright seller
16 Mouth-shaped garden flower
18 Actress Garr
19 Sportscaster Allen
20 Seine feeder
21 Pour, as wine
23 Delphi VIP
25 Do finger-painting
27 Cincinnati team
29 Put in order
33 Light lunch
36 Bishop of Rome
38 Crotchety one
39 Whitney and Wallach
40 Is willing to
41 Hawaiian wind
42 Mascara's target
43 Comic Johnson
44 Trigonometric functions
45 Most agile
47 Make a web
49 Combustion fluid
51 Hem material
55 Showy shrub
58 Folklore monster
60 Dinghy need
61 Microbe
62 Acrobatics performed to music
65 Sea eagle
66 Talks like Daffy Duck
67 Currency in *Roma*
68 Chimney residue
69 Smooth the way
70 Finished the cake

DOWN
1 Thingamabob
2 More private
3 La __ Opera House
4 Beer-keg adjunct
5 Cape of Good Hope explorer
6 Current crazes
7 Pitch __-hitter
8 Roamed about
9 Begin work
10 Toward the ocean
11 Silo's neighbor
12 Look good on
14 Helped with the dishes
17 Parceled (out)
22 Corn unit
24 Auto racer's headgear
26 Sugar sources
28 Very dapper
30 Lunch time for some
31 Left
32 Greek vowels
33 Do a clerk's job
34 Jai __
35 Santa's reminder
37 Three-strikes result
40 Like drip-dry material
44 __ with (supported)
46 Summer: Fr.
48 Job-related extras
50 Rich soil deposit
52 Greek column type
53 Mother-of-pearl
54 Midas' undoing
55 A long time
56 Zilch
57 Florence's river
59 Stare agog
63 River inlet
64 Poetic pugilist

498 A LITTLE CHANGE by Fred Piscop

ACROSS
1 Colgate competitor
6 Commedia dell'__
10 Astronaut Shepard
14 Silent screen star
15 Copier-paper unit
16 Slaw or fries
17 For the birds?
18 Meat with mint jelly
19 Have no doubts
20 Early movie theater
23 Tram cargo
24 Important time
25 Junior watcher
27 Super, to a Beatles fan
30 Polish partner
33 Collar insert
34 Litmus reddener
36 Peter Fonda role of '97
38 Delhi dough
41 With *The*, 1928 Kurt Weill musical
44 Coupe alternative
45 Catch some z's
46 Joule parts
47 Prefix with China
49 "Arrivederci __"
51 Tosspot
52 Red-pencil
54 Columnist LeShan
56 "Yeah, right!"
57 Woolworth's, e.g.
64 *Like this*: Abbr.
66 Inauguration highlight
67 Sprinters' paths
68 One of a maritime trio
69 Lo-fat
70 Everglades bird
71 "No ifs, __ . . ."
72 Jack of westerns
73 Farm-machinery name

DOWN
1 Biggers sleuth
2 Sitarist Shankar
3 Newsman Sevareid
4 *Thus __ Zarathustra*
5 Copier additives
6 "Alice's Restaurant" name
7 Crack the books
8 Domesticate
9 Carve in relief
10 Solicit responses
11 Desktop publishers' precursors
12 Be gaga over
13 More up-to-date
21 Drink like a dog
22 Explosive liquid
26 Brownish gray
27 Dietary needs
28 Have a yearning
29 Town in Pennsylvania
31 __ *Three Lives*
32 Quality
35 Faculty heads
37 Singer Stuarti
39 *Cogito, __ sum*
40 An NFC division
42 "Till the __ Time"
43 Sheba, today
48 American Leaguer since '54
50 Muddleheaded
52 Long March site
53 Like some kitchens
55 Proverb
58 Rockies resort
59 James of jazz
60 "Beg pardon . . ."
61 Concerning, in legalese
62 '30s pitcher Johnny Vander __
63 Ferrara family name
65 __ Palmas

499   FOWL LANGUAGE by Patrick Jordan

ACROSS
1 Web-site language
5 Prepare tea
10 Dutch town
14 Aid in crime
15 "I cannot __ lie"
16 Guantánamo locale
17 COO
20 Where swine dine and recline
21 Arrests
22 Stirs from sleep
23 Inter __
24 Kane's Rosebud, e.g.
25 HOOT
29 Bo Derek's feature film debut
33 Jeweler's unit
34 Columnist Smith
35 Gather grain
36 Yank
37 Chatter foolishly
39 Make a sheepshank
40 Keats feats
42 __ American Cousin
43 Hall-of-Famer Yogi
45 Silence between notes
46 PEEP
49 Charlie Brown outburst
51 Legendary loch
52 On the train
55 __ on the Side (Goldberg film)
56 Sunblock bottle initials
59 QUACK
62 City map
63 Knee-to-ankle bone
64 Brontë heroine
65 Simon __
66 Went out, as the tide
67 Broke open, in a way

DOWN
1 Traffic bottlenecks
2 Lie next to
3 To the extreme
4 Cash dispenser, for short
5 Run through a sieve
6 It gets into hot water
7 Shade providers
8 "Evil Woman" band
9 Make powerless
10 Peru neighbor
11 Long-shadow time
12 Qualified
13 "The Say Hey Kid"
18 Not yet up?
19 Be in debt
23 __ rule (usually)
24 Business attire
25 Cast member
26 All in the Family spinoff
27 Strong impulses
28 Driving hazard
30 Fashionably nostalgic
31 Africa's largest city
32 Vertically positioned
37 Prepare a check for the future
38 Scoreboard stats
41 They might be dire
43 Cesare Siepi, e.g.
44 Upraised railroads
47 Lack of social standards
48 Calculator feature
50 Circle portion
52 Rock concert needs
53 Horror icon Lugosi
54 Jazz singer Anita
55 Type of lettuce
56 Mythological river
57 Little breather
58 Dino's master
60 Women's __
61 Red, Yellow or Black

500   SHADES OF GLORY by Ray Hamel

ACROSS
1 For __ the Bell Tolls
5 Bug
9 Time to remember
14 Fervent wish
15 1994 NL Manager of the Year
16 Mideast emirate
17 Field of study
18 Turndowns
19 Allotropic oxygen
20 Moon-headed crooner for McDonald's
23 Sleep, so to speak
24 Outcries
25 Punching tool
27 Cheetos-loving cat
34 Parade participant
35 Engine cover
36 "Hail, Caesar!"
37 Hawaii Five-O star
38 Book back
40 Cut down
41 Part of BYOB
42 Congregational conclusion
43 Author of The Cat and the Curmudgeon
44 Battery-powered drumbeater
48 Soaked
49 Cork's place
50 Goat cheese
53 Item worn by 20, 27 and 44 Across
59 Suburbia sights
61 Bewhiskered animal
62 Suffer from poison ivy
63 Out of the way
64 Gallic girlfriend
65 Swiss river
66 Critic Kenneth
67 Cathedral receptacle
68 Filth

DOWN
1 Explosive sound
2 Kibbutz dance
3 Middle East grp.
4 Mike Stivic's nickname
5 Sea goose
6 Plaza Hotel imp
7 Insignificance director
8 Cornmeal product
9 Shogun's capital
10 Something unexplained
11 Double-reed instrument
12 Candy shape
13 Scurries
21 Evict
22 Lake near Carson City
26 Tie the knot
27 Bozo or Krusty
28 Mezzo Marilyn
29 Lorelei's river
30 With: Sp.
31 Genus or species
32 Porky Pig's creator
33 Movie star Lamarr
34 Floating ice
38 NYPD Blue star
39 Dispensed candy
40 Goldie Hawn, in Overboard
42 39, for Jack Benny
43 "__ Lee"
45 Mountain gorilla's country
46 Get back
47 Quarter
50 Tire trouble
51 Simple
52 Romulus or Remus
54 Project Bluebook acronym
55 Nautilus leader
56 Kansas City newspaper
57 Grayish yellow
58 Cast off
60 Rep.'s counterpart

501 HOUSEHOLD HELP by Rich Norris

ACROSS

1 Reasoning
6 Magna __ laude
9 Inventor Nikola
14 Island near Venezuela
15 Genetic letters
16 Peru natives
17 Ticket writer
19 Hart and Matalin
20 Ballroom dance
22 Actor Lugosi
23 Golf score
26 Cigar residue
27 Scenic transport
29 Shocked
31 Pulled suddenly
32 Gear meshers
33 Tremor
34 Fisherman's need
37 Involved with, as a hobby
38 Available money
39 Ready for picking
40 Baseball great Mel
41 Like a defective roof
42 Black bird
43 Flaubert character
45 Errand runners
46 Vacationing traveler
48 Intention
49 *Norma* __
50 Some choristers
51 Riot-squad supply
54 Actress Vera
56 *Terminal* author
60 Episode
61 Brian of rock
62 Wrist bones
63 Pub missiles
64 __ *Rosenkavalier*
65 Made a slip

DOWN

1 On the __ (fleeing)
2 Mine find
3 Abdomen
4 Doubter's words
5 Auto oasis
6 Malfunction, as a computer
7 Military squad
8 Prepared
9 Allen or Conway
10 Give power to
11 Toolbox item
12 Eric Clapton tune
13 Analyze, as ore
18 Nearly all
21 Urban greenery
23 Barbecue site
24 Ten-percenter
25 Scarlett's love
28 Presidential nickname
30 From __ Z
31 Inferior in quality
33 Provided with lodging
35 Wagner work
36 Not too astute
38 Celebratory meal
39 Brit. flying group
41 56, to Caesar
42 Fiction genre
44 East
45 Best Picture of 1958
46 Brought under control
47 Slugger Tony
48 Shaded area
52 Tops
53 Lasting impression
55 Ave. crossers
57 Bobby of hockey
58 Expose, poetically
59 Tease

502 GET LOST! by Patrick Jordan

ACROSS

1 Dirigible
6 Restaurant employee
10 Nile reptiles
14 Sound portion
15 Sitarist Shankar
16 Ostrich relative
17 House type
19 Large cymbal
20 Important
21 Feel antipathy toward
22 Words on a free-sample display
24 Swamp goop
25 Knickknack holder
26 Like a frisky dog's tail
29 Clearly shaped
32 Think the world of
33 Serenity
34 Gleeful shout
35 Animation
36 Fleshy root
37 Church area
38 Zodiac sign
39 Used a crowbar
40 Prickly shrub
41 Excesses
43 Caravan critters
44 Gaucho's weapons
45 Former French coins
46 Calls for
48 Spell of bad luck
49 Keats creation
52 Revered figure
53 Fitzgerald or Tormé
56 Take a shine to
57 Actress Skye
58 Mosaic units
59 Feat
60 Like some dorms
61 Put to use

DOWN

1 Lie in the sun
2 '40s actress Velez
3 Without urgency
4 DI doubled
5 Boulevard blemish
6 Largest Greek island
7 Possess
8 Holiday preceder
9 More soiled
10 Sock pattern
11 Baked molasses treat
12 Sean or William
13 Stuffing herb
18 Shiftless
23 Musical pause
24 Mythical meanie
25 Jumped with fright
26 Ivies climb them
27 "Farewell, François!"
28 Risk everything
29 Dices
30 Painting prop
31 Clothing colorists
33 Resigns
36 Period when dinosaurs appeared
37 Octopus octet
39 Animal skin
40 Aluminum ore
42 "Curses! __ again!"
43 Pros' opposites
45 Located
46 Tame
47 Singer Adams
48 Reformer Addams
49 Leer at
50 Forest foragers
51 Prefix for while
54 Dove sound
55 Veto

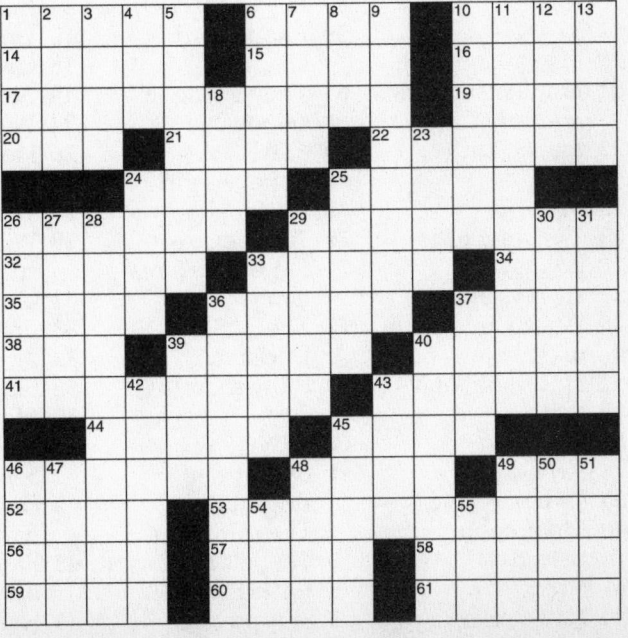

503 EASY AS . . . by Randolph Ross

ACROSS
1 Pastoral deities
6 Sound systems, for short
11 EMT specialty
14 Confess
15 Plant swelling
16 Aussie bounder
17 "Minnie the Moocher" singer
19 Gore and Green
20 Bird perches
21 Scarf down
23 Waiters
24 Municipal
25 French land mass
26 Loose cannon
29 Bloke's buddy
32 Dentist's request
33 Dole's home: Abbr.
34 "There oughta be __!"
35 Like some floors
36 Transmit
37 Clerical garb
38 Napa sights
39 Disguises
40 Labor-saving devices
42 Army VIP
43 Sty sounds
44 Certain fortune-teller
48 X out
50 Plane
51 Pipe joint
52 Oman or Yemen
54 Doctors' grp.
55 The Maids playwright
56 Take care of
57 Hide-hair connector
58 Clio's sister
59 Holy book

DOWN
1 Truisms
2 "Not on __!" ("No way!")
3 Brown shade
4 Mountaintop delight
5 Majestic
6 Pitches in
7 Altar words
8 Just some
9 Fantasized
10 Repeat
11 Maryland treats
12 Survey
13 Lancastrian symbol
18 Folk history
22 Hanks film
24 Gives up
26 Makes angry
27 Mildewy
28 Means justifier
29 Polite address
30 __ breve
31 Button-down alternative
32 Soave and Cabernet
35 Handyman
36 Exodus star
38 Wine datum
39 Shellfish
41 Scoot
42 Dear, to Diego
44 Word form for "icon"
45 Prefix for state
46 Sealy rival
47 Check the fit of
48 College administrator
49 Sailor's saint
50 Help hoods
53 Santa __, CA

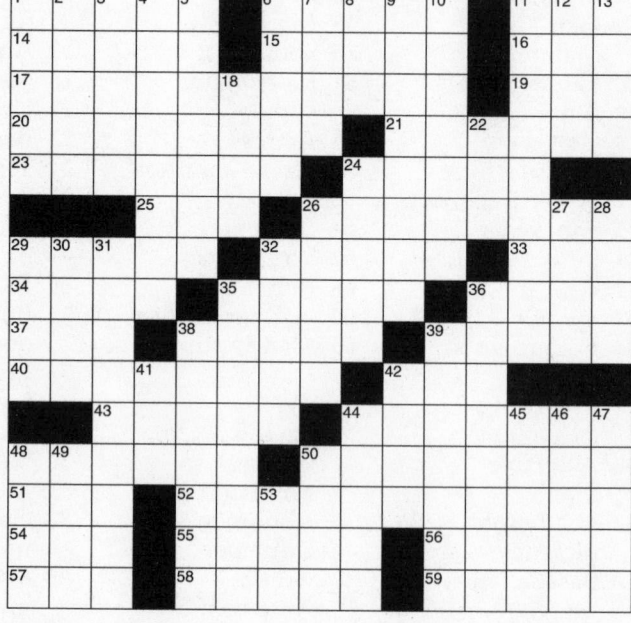

504 ALL-STAR GAME by Ed Stein

ACROSS
1 Itar-__ (Russian news source)
5 Righteous
9 Abandon
14 Rose lover of Broadway
15 Ice house
16 Ruckus
17 STAR
20 Hawaiian hello
21 Frankenstein's assistant
22 Parcel, with "out"
23 Meanie
25 Convergence points
27 A ways away
30 "Pretty maids all in __"
32 Storeroom of a sort
36 Biblical strongman
38 Two of a kind
40 Memorable period
41 STAR
44 Kay chaser
45 Your Erroneous Zones author
46 Glide away
47 Gypsy composer
49 Racetrack prop
51 __-bitty
52 Part of UAR
54 Arkin or Alda
56 In __ (angered)
59 Phone-cord shape
61 They swing in saloons
65 STAR
68 Popeye's girl
69 National flower
70 Tex-Mex treat
71 Superman's real name
72 The __ Scott Decision
73 Plow share?

DOWN
1 Bye-bye, in Brighton
2 The third man
3 The __ 'Clock News
4 Little fish
5 Skippy rival
6 Less pleasant
7 Lava variety
8 Brawny battle
9 Short
10 Perpetrate
11 Prizefighter's wear
12 "There'll be __ time . . ."
13 Undercolored
18 Give in to gravity
19 Box-office sign
24 Went quickly
26 Holiday tune
27 Pompous ones
28 Tennis miscue
29 With room to spare
31 Glass creation
33 Provoke
34 "__ my case!"
35 Singer Mariah
37 Methodize
39 "__ Pretty" (West Side Story tune)
42 Toolhouse hanging
43 Bad news for baseball fans
48 Hardy's returner
50 The Power and the Glory author
53 Unlike this ans.
55 They're often personal
56 Frenziedly
57 Negri of the silents
58 Sinful
60 "Take __ or leave it!"
62 __ upswing (rising)
63 Wealthy, in Juárez
64 Put away
66 Wriggler
67 Bolshevik

505 TOM SWIFTIES by Bob Lubbers

ACROSS
1 Botch
5 Wide ties
11 WWII craft
14 Pro __
15 Examine
16 Geologist's suffix
17 "__," Tom said boldly
19 Conducted
20 Prohibit
21 Anthem word
23 Flowered arch
26 Hula hoop?
27 Newspaper frequency
28 Trinidad rhythm
30 Triads
31 *Bambi* aunt
32 Original Captain Kangaroo
35 "__," Tom said wryly
40 #1 rating in tennis
41 Hidden gold
43 Bottomless pits
46 Singer Patti
49 Cookie filling
50 100%
52 *Law &* __
53 Move
55 ". . . man __ mouse?"
56 Switch positions
57 "__," Tom said flatly
62 Canonized *femme*: Abbr.
63 Composer de Falla
64 Fashion mag
65 Draft org.
66 Part of E=mc^2
67 Noggin

DOWN
1 Part of TGIF
2 Flight
3 Actress Hagen
4 "I'm a __!": Costello
5 Alda or King
6 Distress signal
7 Knot of trees
8 Giraffe cousin
9 Mitchell mansion
10 *The Red and the Black* author
11 Comedienne Bea
12 Brosnan role
13 Roosevelt and Kennedy
18 OK Corral fighter
22 Entrée embellishment
23 Hotshot
24 Carry on
25 Mediocre
26 Loamy deposit
29 Omits
30 Actress Bara
33 French summer
34 Bombard
36 "Who's there?" answer
37 Occasional
38 Pleat
39 Perry's creator
42 Poetic adverb
43 Get __ (explain)
44 Musburger et al.
45 Affirmative votes
47 Caliber
48 Taped over
50 Dress style
51 Monkey cousin
54 Govt. agent
55 Paris airport
58 Wooden pin
59 __-mo
60 Shade tree
61 Sandra or Ruby

506 INEDIBLES by Lee Weaver

ACROSS
1 Spider's creations
5 __ *la Douce*
9 Complain
13 Jai __
14 Kingdom
16 Melville novel
17 Used a doorbell
18 Kismet
19 Musical symbol
20 Oxlike antelope
22 Seaman's coat
24 Has to have
26 Cheer for a bullfighter
27 Less messy
29 Brave deeds
33 Slalom curve
34 Gossiper's tidbit
36 Old-style anesthetic
38 Fret and fume
40 Trivial
42 Explorer Hernando de __
43 Rips
45 Flat-topped lands
47 *Harper Valley* grp.
48 Like some goblets
50 Muppets creator
52 Signal an actor
53 Valuable quality
54 Opaque material used in vases
59 Sound made by taffeta
62 Concert halls
63 Spew forth
65 Canyon effect
66 Couturier Cassini
67 Frightfully strange
68 Leave out
69 Little kid
70 Religious offshoot
71 Recipe amounts: Abbr.

DOWN
1 Ending for soft or dinner
2 Airline to Israel
3 Bicycle part named for its shape
4 Official seal
5 Pique
6 Gathers (crops)
7 Filly's mother
8 __ mater
9 Egos
10 Run __ (go wild)
11 Learning method
12 Burns or Byron
15 Captain's superior
21 Bambi, for one
23 Skin soother
25 Tom-tom or snare
27 Bird's abode
28 __ Park, CO
29 Sharpened
30 Cupid, to the Greeks
31 Easy piano piece
32 Brouhaha
35 Silent performer
37 Colorful horse
39 Tornado aftermath
41 Stadium sounds
44 Self-satisfied
46 Meeting: Abbr.
49 Confused conflict
51 Most up-to-date
53 Savory jelly
54 Beside the point
55 Without purpose
56 Symbol of Wales
57 War god
58 Having no doubt
60 Send off
61 Short journeys
64 Vietnamese festival

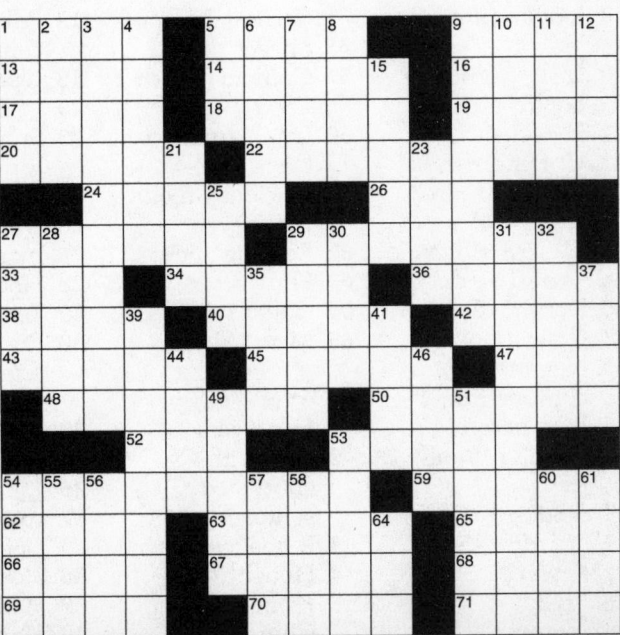

507 DOWN UNDER by Rich Norris

ACROSS
1 Different
6 Less hospitable
11 Bank device: Abbr.
14 Selected
15 From Donegal
16 Golfer's concern
17 Meaningless triumphs
20 Take to court
21 Self-confidence
22 Idiomatic conditions
23 __ brûlée (dessert)
25 Nickname for a sharpshooter
28 Computer peripherals
31 Hardly impartial
32 __ d'oeuvre
33 __ "King" Cole
34 "Gosh, it's cold!"
35 Conclusion
36 Took a chair
38 Corker
41 More, in music
44 Set-to
46 Kid's transport
47 Thoughtful
50 Vehicle with a rumble seat
52 Forcible ejection
54 Turkish coins
55 Cartoonist Peter
56 Noodles
58 Fort Worth sch.
61 Act of desperation
65 WWII command
66 In flames
67 Home on the range
68 President pro __
69 Competed at Indy
70 Approvals

DOWN
1 '60s protest singer Phil
2 Biblical pronoun
3 One of five in stud poker
4 Immigrant's subj.
5 Investigate anew, as a case
6 Coastal resort areas
7 Novelist Leon
8 Cut into cubes
9 N.Y. hours
10 Frat letter
11 Trues up
12 One way to color fabric
13 __ up (erred)
18 Part of NOW
19 *M*A*S*H* character
24 Hosp. employees
26 Recede
27 Broadcast
28 That girl
29 Pro's opposite
30 Super Bowl I MVP
37 Where to find old saws
38 Driving breaks
39 Presidential nickname
40 For every
41 Turn on a point
42 Chemical ending
43 Exclamation of disgust
45 Ralph of *The Waltons*
46 Character-building org.
47 Aspen abode
48 Make bubbly
49 Kidnapper's demand
51 Like an uninsulated room
53 Of the eye
57 Farmland unit
59 Alberta native
60 Southwestern natives
62 Patriotic org. since 1890
63 "__ body meet a body . . ."
64 Charge

508 BEASTLY FILMS by Bob Lubbers

ACROSS
1 Clean air org.
4 Intolerant one
9 Attested
14 Cap with a pompom
15 Studio sign
16 Opposite
17 Hogan film of '86
20 Lost __ (Hilton book)
21 Dweebs
22 Upper crust
23 LP successors
24 Jug handles
27 Musical notes
28 __ and alack
30 Acrylic fiber
31 Collections
33 Negative conjunction
34 Less harsh
35 Fonda film of '65
38 Spates
41 __ culpa
42 Fewer
46 Frisky mammal
47 Dispatched
48 Tennis do-over
49 Necklace unit
50 What SSTs cross
51 Valletta is its capital
53 Good, in Guadalajara
55 Speech
57 Colman film of '29
60 On __-to-know basis
61 Ancient Greek region
62 Driving zone
63 Flip
64 Collar types
65 Mao __-tung

DOWN
1 Engravers
2 One with a shortened sentence
3 Romance writer
4 Hooch
5 French __-China
6 Profit
7 Black gold
8 Vogues
9 Boot jingler
10 Marvelous
11 Sea veteran
12 Comic Charlotte
13 Palindrome center
18 Op. __
19 __ Plaines, IL
23 Sundae topper
25 Caviar
26 Upperclass-man: Abbr.
28 Hill builders
29 Tennis shot
30 Pre-game scoreboard stats
32 Timetables
34 Chair part
36 __ Lingus
37 Author Deighton
38 Steal
39 Had a snack
40 Horse barns
43 Bob of Bob and Ray
44 __ cap for (woo)
45 Aisle occupant
47 Cheap cigar
50 *Wheel of Fortune* buy
51 Stroller wheelers
52 $$ dispenser
54 Baritone Nelson
55 "Answer yes __!"
56 Wreck
57 __-relief
58 Merkel or O'Connor
59 Period

509 UP IN THE AIR by Frank Longo

ACROSS
1 Piquancy
5 Floored it
9 Throw out
14 Choir voice
15 *Casablanca* heroine
16 Water slide
17 Snow remover
18 Largest of the Marianas
19 More mellowed
20 Becoming faulty, as a pipe
23 __-Wan Kenobi
24 Some baby birds
25 Mexican souvenirs
31 Celestial ram
32 Singer Travis
33 Engine part
36 Tumbling surfaces
37 Train support
38 Fruit-juice alternative
39 Sandwich with mayo
40 Kelly of *Chaplin*
41 Actor Quinn
42 Open ocean
44 Spanish royal name
47 Man-mouse link
48 *Annie* exclamation
54 *Seascape* playwright
55 "Puttin' on the __"
56 McNally's partner
58 Fermented-honey beverages
59 Hurler Hershiser
60 Hodgepodge
61 Director Lubitsch
62 Monopoly or marbles
63 Bites gently

DOWN
1 Skip past commercials
2 Architectural annexes
3 "Go no further!"
4 Boat-pulling lines
5 Add one's name to a guest book
6 Stop (up)
7 Morales of movies
8 Rhett Butler's last word
9 Gaunt
10 Puts on ice
11 Calcutta coin
12 Bothered incessantly
13 Exec's extras
21 Wading bird
22 Eggs on
25 Sidepost of a door
26 River to the Caspian Sea
27 Catcher's glove
28 Wheat or corn
29 Puppetmaster Bil
30 Zhou __
33 Musical finale
34 Kirghizian range
35 *The Magic Mountain* author
37 City on the Seine
38 Best Picture of 1931
40 Most glum
41 Taj Mahal locale
42 Two-footed animals
43 Hose end
44 Sweetheart
45 Moray trapper
46 Jacob's father-in-law
49 Diluted rum
50 Milanese money
51 Gossipy tidbit
52 *The Persistence of Memory* painter
53 Use scissors
57 __ and don'ts

510 AUTO SUGGESTION by Patrick Jordan

ACROSS
1 Prepares a present
6 Poker unit
10 Norton, to Kramden
13 Anchorman's summary
14 Pennsylvania port
15 One of the Jackson 5
16 START OF A QUIP
19 Difficult journey
20 Like MacDonald
21 Jimmy's successor
22 Status __
23 Origins
24 Track-and-field item
28 Criticism
29 Boredom
30 Hostile sounds
31 Become a member
35 MIDDLE OF THE QUIP
38 Record a TV program
39 Shopper stopper
40 Supermarket walkway
41 Church feature
42 Froze the pinball machine
43 Rouses to action
47 Actor Chaney
48 Role for Julia
49 Spare hair
50 One of Woods' woods, e.g.
54 END OF THE QUIP
57 Says, in teenspeak
58 Except for
59 Engine knocks
60 Nav. rank
61 Yoked pair
62 Labyrinths

DOWN
1 Judicial document
2 Bring to adulthood
3 Wile E. Coyote's supplier
4 Fill a suitcase
5 Health center
6 "Haven't you been listening?"
7 Desertlike
8 Diarist Anaïs
9 Clean the oven, perhaps
10 Printing measurements
11 __ *of Two Cities*
12 Some Parliament members
15 Daly of *Cagney & Lacey*
17 Gehrig and Costello
18 Jazzman Thelonious
22 Walk out
23 Schoolroom spinner
24 Skillfully executed
25 *To Live and Die* __
26 Crackle's colleague
27 Buttonlike?
28 Ginger Rogers role
30 Orchestra section
31 Monopoly board space
32 Force from office
33 Speck in the ocean
34 Require
36 Steam-brewed coffee
37 Eve's firstborn
41 "__ Misbehavin'"
42 Deli request
43 Yellowish brown
44 Singer John
45 Wise guys
46 Music symbols
47 Sheet or towel
49 "__ Only Just Begun"
50 Pet that grows on you?
51 *Rich Man, Poor Man* actress
52 Incite
53 Porgy's beloved
55 The Grinch's dog
56 Secretarial stat.

HANDYMAN'S SPECIAL by Rich Norris

ACROSS

1 Underground chamber
5 Comic Soupy
10 Queens stadium
14 "Ah, me!"
15 Surrogate
16 Marshal Wyatt
17 Office-supply item
19 French friend
20 Night before
21 Less restrained
22 High points
23 Resolves, as an argument
25 Lake boat
27 Possesses
28 Prepare a present
31 Suit
34 Social group
35 Kimono belt
36 Not "fer"
37 Residences
38 Christmas
39 Tavern
40 Desert mounds
41 Pigeon homes
42 Sufficiency
44 Perfect, at NASA
45 Ninny
46 Jostled, as in a crowd
50 Actress Bo
52 Proportion
54 Eggs
55 Director Kazan
56 Up-front
58 Feels poorly
59 Herculean types
60 Philosopher Descartes
61 Depend (on)
62 Kitchen emanations
63 Picnic crashers

DOWN

1 Sidewalk eateries
2 __ and kicking
3 Manservant
4 Compass reading
5 Germ cells
6 City on the Rhone
7 Metallic deposit
8 Deep knee bends, e.g.
9 Former UAR member
10 Manatee
11 Create with effort, as an agreement
12 Southernmost Great Lake
13 Gorillas and gibbons
18 E natural's alias
22 Poker buy-in
24 Highly diluted
26 PMs
28 Full of spirit
29 Qualified
30 Dessert options
31 __ Wawa (Radner character)
32 Mild oath
33 Safety run-through
34 Caring (about)
37 "Red Scare" grp.
38 __ Ono
40 Dip, as a doughnut
41 Computer language
43 Somewhat anxious
44 Foreigners
46 Anesthetic of old
47 Interlaced
48 Incident
49 Bumpers and Evans
50 Letter opener
51 Nobelist Wiesel
53 Word form for "air"
56 "I see it all now!"
57 Historical period

SUPER EGOS by Patrick Jordan

ACROSS

1 Sheep shelters
6 Pillow coverings
11 June honoree
14 Speechify
15 Hiawatha's craft
16 Playwright Levin
17 Incredible Hulk's alter ego
19 One-fifth of DX
20 Compact
21 Pressman, at times
23 __ Choice (Streep film)
27 Lanky and awkward
28 Waiting lines
29 Angry disposition
31 Absolute
32 Days, in Dijon
33 Football filler
36 Gets one's dander up
37 Bruno of City Slickers
38 Unit of force
39 German article
40 Goes a-wandering
41 Fine rains
42 Segments
44 Play merrily
45 Turn pale
47 1971 Woody Allen film
48 Greene of Bonanza
49 Assimilate
51 Pose a question
52 Wonder Woman's alter ego
58 Last letter
59 Checks text
60 Pepé Le Pew's quest
61 Commit a blunder
62 "__ Pass Go . . ."
63 Military chaplain

DOWN

1 Corn eater's leftover
2 NHL legend Bobby
3 Sigma follower
4 List-ending abbr.
5 More disreputable
6 Reads quickly
7 Skater Brinker
8 Author Rice
9 He liked to harry Larry
10 '40s Saturday movie features
11 Robin's alter ego
12 Disney's Little Mermaid
13 Milk farm
18 Quilting events
22 SSW opposite
23 Tentacled mollusk
24 Unconventional
25 Spider-Man's alter ego
26 Shades
27 Like some horror films
29 Nuclear-reactor centers
30 Major airports
32 Early jazz
34 Within: Pref.
35 Takes a breather
37 People's Court judge, once
38 Prima donna
40 Lost ground
41 Dangerous female
43 Traveler's stop
44 Dogpatch creator
45 Conflagration
46 One finishing second
47 Flaunt one's feats
49 Eve's eldest
50 Aware of
53 Nuptial vow
54 "__ Yankee Doodle Dandy . . ."
55 Show agreement
56 Common canine
57 Before, to Byron

BUSY BEES by Bob Lubbers

ACROSS
1 Saga
5 *Carrie* star
11 Show to a seat, slangily
14 Zhivago's love
15 Yellow paper
16 Sgt., e.g.
17 Overwhelm
19 Sci-fi Doctor
20 "We __ the World"
21 Taken with, with "of"
23 Guam capital
26 Paid player
27 "There Is Nothing Like __"
28 Latino's "Zounds!"
30 Took pot shots
31 Paleozoic, for one
32 Means (to)
35 Tattletales
40 More mountainous
41 Nag's nibble
43 Actress Lombard

46 Make new
49 Coral ensemble?
50 Bale fodder
52 Admit
53 Rubber man
55 Consume
56 Ems' followers
57 Nonsense
62 No longer working: Abbr.
63 __ Belt (constellation portion)
64 Aswan Dam filler
65 Sound of a flat
66 Main course
67 Goldwyn and Nunn

DOWN
1 Pixie
2 Buddy
3 Lyricist Gershwin
4 Beach building
5 Hook's lieutenant
6 Norm
7 Ire

8 '40s Italian foreign minister
9 *Born Free* roarer
10 Nepal's capital
11 Open a gift
12 Plot
13 Like a cobra
18 *Dracula* author Stoker
22 Pindar, for one
23 Hotshot pilot
24 Clothing
25 Russian sea
26 Discussion group
29 Holy book
30 Sleep soundly?
33 Numerical prefix
34 Abrasive substance
36 Get __ of (obtain)
37 *Ode to __* (1976 film)
38 Owl sound
39 Delhi wear
42 Perfect score, perhaps
43 Hoopsters

44 Makes amends
45 Perches
47 Cole __
48 Wyoming range
50 Riding costume
51 Ivied latticework

54 Merit
55 Gaelic
58 Chemical ending
59 Cloak-and-dagger org.
60 Dutch airline
61 "Fine with me!"

STRINGS ATTACHED by Frank Longo

ACROSS
1 Indian seaport
7 Jason's ship
11 __ the Dog (De Niro film)
14 Drill instructor's command
15 Brandy flavor
16 Memorable period
17 Scarlatti's instrument
19 Ring legend
20 Handful for Hingis
22 Dadaist sculptor
25 Post e-mail
26 Cara or Castle
27 Browbeating
29 Looked the other way
31 Furry scarf
32 *The X-Files* character
34 Outdoorsman's accessory
39 Pay to play
40 Vetoes
43 Sailing for sport
48 Swipes

49 Cobwebby place
50 Ayatollah predecessor
52 Do a landscaping chore
53 Rink gear
57 Mauna __
58 Crunchy snack
62 1997 U.S. Open winner
63 Freshly
64 Bookworm
65 Nevertheless
66 Worshipers' seats
67 Cloud layers

DOWN
1 __-jongg
2 *One Day __ Time*
3 Aachen article
4 Spellbound
5 Gets a feeling for
6 Tuna-trapping nets
7 Ladybug's lunch
8 Antique autos
9 *Tootsie* star
10 Confer holy orders on

11 Less potent
12 Francis of *What's My Line?*
13 Trained a horse, in a way
18 Larry King's milieu
21 __-Magnon
22 Madison Ave. output
23 Place to get stuck
24 Lectern figure, for short
28 Yalie
29 *Picnic* playwright
30 Discontinuity
32 Fender nick
33 Hill dweller
35 Solo of *Star Wars*
36 Doing a film shoot
37 Blip on a polygraph
38 It may be oral
41 "Evil Woman" band
42 Wind dir.
43 Cereal plant

44 *Becket* star
45 "Finally!"
46 *Shop __ You Drop*
47 Antarctic covering
48 Dionysian revelers
50 Distorts
51 Guffaw syllable

54 Russo of *Outbreak*
55 Crowd
56 Asterisk
59 Oklahoma city
60 Allow
61 Malay isthmus

ACTING FUEL-ISH by Fred Piscop

ACROSS
1 Testimonial dinner, e.g.
6 Karmann __ ('60s auto)
10 Paint unit
14 Hotpoint rival
15 Reagan and Nessen
16 Pun reaction, perhaps
17 Approach midnight
18 Move slowly
19 Kofi __ Annan
20 Fuel-ish homemade hooch?
22 Androcles' friend
23 French article
24 Turn edible
26 Suds maker
30 Bingo cousin
32 Fix the fairway
33 Detective's device
37 Not __ many words
38 Gets smart, with "up"
39 Shoe saver
40 Smarts
42 Absorb in class
43 Trotter's burden
44 747 alternative
45 Parcels, with "out"
47 Frank holder
48 It may be checkered
49 Make a fuel-ish estimate?
56 Bum's __ (unceremonious ouster)
57 Bump into
58 Ridiculous
59 Gram starter
60 Cartoonist Peter
61 Piano piece
62 Options list
63 High time?
64 Fleur-__

DOWN
1 Dutch portraitist
2 Mideast gulf
3 Thurmond of basketball
4 Draftable
5 Irritated
6 Scenery shifters
7 Use a whetstone
8 Andean of old
9 Car-door fixtures
10 Fuel-ish composer?
11 Navel variety
12 Follow, as advice
13 "More __ You Know"
21 Law or saw ender
25 Beethoven's "Minuet __"
26 Ship's clink
27 Custer colleague
28 One-time Sinclair rival
29 Fuel-ish Shakespearean query?
30 Common cow name
31 Gen. Robert __
33 Coral or rose
34 Fast horse
35 8 Down's land
36 Gossips
38 Tom Jones, for one
41 Take to court
42 Did a '30s dance
44 Word form for "gold"
45 *All in the Family* spinoff
46 Ruhr city
47 Conductor's need
48 Proper's partner
50 Flying start?
51 Founder of Stoicism
52 Poker fee
53 Ancient France
54 *60 Minutes* name
55 Gets the picture

IN THE CARDS by Lee Weaver

ACROSS
1 __ mater
5 Bakery worker
9 Money rolls
13 Canine comment
14 Out of cash
15 At the summit
16 A way over water
18 Painter Magritte
19 Employ
20 Seine feeder
21 __ and groaned
23 Window sills
25 Iron-fisted
27 Ruffles feathers
29 Wearing down
33 Potato coverings
36 Designer Cassini
38 Entreaty
39 "A Bushel __ Peck"
40 Prepare Parmesan
41 Airline to Israel
42 Observed
43 St. Louis landmark
44 Macaroni, e.g.
45 Wrap with bandages
47 Heroic story
49 "I cannot __ lie"
51 Votes in
55 *American __* (Gere film)
58 Mets' stadium
60 Reverence
61 Not "fer"
62 Betraying no emotion
65 Cartoon bear
66 Water pitchers
67 Male deer
68 Guitarist Clapton
69 Cincinnati team
70 Toll road

DOWN
1 Very bad
2 Not tight
3 Sounded like a Guernsey
4 Behind, on a ship
5 Novelist Murdoch
6 Ciphers
7 Heart test, for short
8 Appear again
9 Tolstoy classic
10 "__ o'clock scholar"
11 Finished
12 Went fast
14 Fast
17 Some South Africans
22 Spanish gold
24 Bar order
26 Acquire molars
28 Reddish-brown horse
30 Troubles
31 Orderly
32 Celebration
33 Backtalk
34 Was aware of
35 Brainstorm
37 Varnish ingredient
40 Horse going full tilt
44 Rice dish
46 Neighbor of Penna.
48 Jury members
50 Popped the question
52 Desert plants
53 Pinch playfully
54 Riverbank plant
55 Singer Marvin
56 Composer Stravinsky
57 Role for Caron
59 Towel word
63 Be obligated
64 Viper

517 BED TIME by Rich Norris

ACROSS
1 Type of coffee
6 Actor Baldwin
10 Royal Russian ruler
14 Chan portrayer
15 Influence
16 *Inter* __
17 Military scout's position
20 Stadium cheer
21 Anger
22 Easily bent
23 Not proficient in
26 Beginnings
27 Digger's tool
29 British currency
30 Reed instruments
31 Beatles film
32 Mauna __
35 Stravinsky work
39 Flier out of Stockholm
40 Plant appendages
41 Tripoli's country
42 Cod and May
44 Banquet delicacy
45 Took it easy
48 Reno or Leigh
49 Squared up
50 Always, to a poet
51 End of a British alphabet
54 Fortysomething concern
58 Electric co., e.g.
59 Applaud
60 Main artery
61 Rational
62 Isn't serious
63 In disarray

DOWN
1 Portal
2 Site of a Napoleon exile
3 Money holders
4 Chemical ending
5 HST was his third VP
6 Not connected
7 Guitar relative
8 Inventor Whitney
9 Zoom photos
10 Opened, as a keg
11 Feeds the pigs
12 Bridal path
13 Is valued
18 Tiny bottle
19 Former senator Sam
24 Declare
25 He loved Lucy
26 Takes to the links
27 Fleet fliers
28 "Very funny!"
29 Unskilled workers
31 Cut down
32 Fifths for bridge?
33 Irish New Age singer
34 Ice-cream thickener
36 Cassette player
37 Prepare for the future
38 __ *gauche* (left bank: Fr.)
42 Light source
43 Jump on the ice
44 Motor vehicles
45 Fictional Uncle
46 Madonna role
47 Escorted
48 Versatile vehicles
50 Relative of "Zounds!"
52 Victuals
53 6/6/44
55 __ Baba
56 Actress Dawber
57 44 Across, essentially

518 CELEBRITY TRIVIA by S.E. Wilkinson

ACROSS
1 Indian chief
6 Copacetic
10 Vague form
14 Too big
15 Water pitcher
16 Sean Lennon's mama
17 Actor Delon
18 Actor né Leonard Slye
20 Cozy room
21 Hounds' sounds
23 "__ Diddy Diddy" ('64 tune)
24 Court cry
26 Freight weight
27 VHF selection
29 Collars
33 Actor Villechaize
34 North Pole personnel
36 "__ la la!"
37 *Beverly Hillbillies* daughter
38 Annoy, in a way
39 "We'll tak' a __ kindness yet . . ."
40 AFL's partner
41 On the way
42 Stock descriptor
43 Defers (to)
45 Break down
47 Hosp. areas
48 Hand holders
49 Michener epic
52 "If it __ been for you . . ."
53 Otherwise called: Abbr.
56 Rock singer whose middle name is Hercules
58 Improvise
60 Come into view
61 The duck in *Peter and the Wolf*
62 Take care of
63 Old __, CT
64 Clodhopper
65 English county

DOWN
1 Line on a map
2 Up to
3 First female star on the cover of *Life*
4 "Just __ suspected!"
5 Poisonous plant
6 His film debut was *My Friend Irma*
7 Came around
8 Organ parts
9 Goof
10 Former
11 Cofounder of MGM
12 Stew vegetable
13 "Nonsense!"
19 Bouquets
22 "We __ not amused"
25 Begrudge
26 Arduous voyage
27 Kasparov call
28 Prefix for "sun"
29 Actress once voted the world's most beautiful woman
30 Originator of the Mouse
31 1969 Hitchcock film
32 Coast
35 Author Deighton
38 Pulls along
39 Revolver inventor
41 Bridge maven
42 Ilie of tennis
44 On its way
46 Diarist Anaïs
48 "Whoopee!"
49 Auction off
50 Stratagem
51 Smasher fodder
52 Vagabond
54 High flier
55 "Life is like __ of chocolates"
57 Paragon of patience
59 __ Moines, IA

519   WARREN PIECE by Patrick Jordan

ACROSS

1 Klensch of CNN
5 Was compelled
10 They run with rams and lambs
14 Stop trying
15 Inflate
16 It's fit to be tied
17 Egg on
18 Flintstone's boss
19 Tennis great
20 Prepare to fire
21 Children's party dance
23 Restrained, in a way
25 Got a gold medal
26 Apr. 15 addressee
27 Pirouetted
32 __ acids
35 Lose traction
36 Do an impression
37 Preposterous notion
41 Lodge brother
42 Supplemented, with "out"
43 Clampett portrayer

44 Answering machine holdings
47 Ecol. watchdog
48 In the manner of
49 Leave in one's care
53 Boxer's quick blow
58 Toolshed item
59 Exam type
60 Jay Silverheels role
61 Tarzan's mate
62 Selfish one's exclamation
63 Autumn bloomer
64 Screenwriter James
65 Hipsters' homes
66 Seacoast
67 Ernie's roomie

DOWN

1 Peer
2 Author Alison
3 Rho follower
4 Corroded
5 Chops finely
6 Felt unwell

7 Cheerless
8 Ballerina's skirt
9 Dentist's request
10 Comic Boosler
11 Withstand scrutiny
12 Canyon phenomenon
13 Ooze
21 Pulsate
22 Penultimate mo.
24 Trig function
27 "Blue __" (Berlin tune)
28 Meander
29 Scot's sons
30 Fencing sword
31 Jerry's '50s partner
32 "Pardon me!"
33 Stag-party attendee
34 Gets one's goat
35 Fermented rice beverage
38 Boat races
39 Third dimension
40 Support beam
45 Mink relatives
46 Ring retiree of '79

47 "Sing more!"
49 Go onstage
50 Grammarian's concern
51 Less loony
52 Sing like the birdies sing
53 Light-hearted diversion
54 Soprano solo
55 Halftime marchers
56 Luxurious
57 Golden Rule word
61 Sharp poke

520   NATIVE INTELLIGENCE by Bob Lubbers

ACROSS

1 Albacore armor
6 Pony pace
10 High fashion
13 Like some kitchens
14 Softly, to Solti
15 Color
16 Superb Nairobi native?
18 Dolt
19 Perfectly
20 Left-hand entries
22 Hog's pen
24 Wager
26 Rub-__
27 Taunter's cry
28 Revolving gun mount
30 Blue Eagle org.
32 Realtor's offering
34 Rising
37 Kingly
38 Was in session
39 Taunt
40 Kidnapped
42 Diogenes, for one

43 Picnic pest
44 Barn fledglings
46 Freddy's street
47 Price
49 Dutch commune
50 __ Miniver
51 Grouper group
53 The Longest Day setting
55 __ kwon do
56 Helsinki railway?
62 Comstock load
63 Charged particle
64 Bygone
65 Stir-fryer
66 Tear
67 Bog mosses

DOWN

1 Portion: Abbr.
2 Elevator chamber
3 One __ time
4 Like a dryer trap
5 Word form for "within"
6 Can material
7 "Cry" singer

8 Out, perhaps
9 Muted, with "down"
10 Destructive Bangkok native?
11 Give the boot to
12 Scottish lake
14 Bandleader Duchin
17 Asian capital
21 Jumper's cord
22 Singer Easton
23 Polynesian sass?
25 Spinning-wheel attachment
27 Hockey legend's family
28 Baby powder
29 911 responder: Abbr.
31 Photographer Adams et al.
33 Trumpet signal
35 66 and I-95
36 Tenure
38 Work with thread
41 Emergency phone

42 Broods
45 Newsman Newman
48 As yet
50 Thou, to Thérèse
51 Store aboard
52 Robert Moses biographer

54 Flapjack franchise
57 Delta of Venus author
58 Show assent
59 Cantor or Lupino
60 Profit
61 Nav. rank

521 BRIDAL WEAR by Rich Norris

ACROSS
1 Daunt
5 Press down
9 Soothing ointment
13 Farm animals
14 Banks' storage rooms
15 Words of understanding
16 Immigrant's homeland
18 German philosopher
19 Bandleader Brown
20 Angry
21 Lunar event
23 Golfer Ballesteros
24 Solo of *Star Wars*
25 Yanni et al.
33 Baker or Bryant
34 Walk to and fro
35 Speck
36 *Adam __* (Eliot novel)
37 John Paul and predecessors
39 Thomas __ Edison
40 Mine material
41 Green gem
42 Aviator
43 Worried about another
47 Bed-and-breakfast
48 Do damage to
49 Temporary solution
53 PC panic button
54 Imitate
57 Singer Guthrie
58 Edit
61 Coral formation
62 Golfer Wadkins
63 Beer alternatives
64 Starting with
65 Watched warily
66 Untainted

DOWN
1 Gullible one
2 Wheel holder
3 Brit's last letters
4 Bus. letter abbr.
5 In __ (together)
6 Toward the stern
7 Insignificant
8 Fortune-tellers
9 Two-piece suit of a sort
10 Without delay: Abbr.
11 Camera part
12 Apportion, with "out"
14 Urbane
17 Alpha's opposite
22 Tie, as shoes
23 Fill to excess
25 Wealthy person
26 January, in Juárez
27 More spacious
28 Raised
29 Ms. enclosure
30 Stray from the script
31 Imaginative
32 Fix one's eyes
37 Having collateral value
38 Pindar product
39 Reunion attendee
41 *Fear of Flying* author
42 Compel
44 Swindle
45 Concluding words
46 Unpleasantly grating
49 Poet Teasdale
50 Very, in Vichy
51 Toast topping
52 Broadway production
54 Rights org.
55 Ship's parking place
56 Choice word
59 One, in France
60 Short snooze

522 IN A HURRY by Fred Piscop

ACROSS
1 Train unit
4 Auctioneer's cry
8 Packs down, as dirt
13 Commotions
15 Sloth's home
16 Dizzying design
17 Basketball tactic
19 Newspapers, radio, etc.
20 Store, as grain
21 Fight official
23 Bump into
24 Evening bash
25 Dander
27 Train system
34 Ruth __ Ginsburg
37 Composer Ned
38 Witness' vow
39 Secondhand
40 Filled to the gills
41 Oscar Madison-type
42 __ up (finalize)
43 Singer Blades
44 Ridiculous
45 Cornmeal mush
48 Microscopic
49 Alex Trebek's birthplace
53 Niger neighbor
56 Cheerleader's syllable
59 Wiped out
60 "You __ kidding!"
62 Plaster ingredient
64 One of the Fab Four
65 Celestial bear
66 Author Bellow
67 Wolfed down
68 Resting on
69 Gun owner's org.

DOWN
1 Bistros
2 *A Bell for __*
3 Martini's partner
4 *Silkwood* star
5 Metal-in-the-rough
6 Shakespearean king
7 Fake out, in hockey
8 Comic Arnold
9 Primitive fellows
10 Whipped up
11 __-dieu (kneeling bench)
12 Immediately, to a surgeon
14 Tended the sauce
18 Make indistinct
22 Shot, as a gun
26 Butt into
28 Baseballer Hideki
29 Was excessively fond
30 Tendency
31 Pie-cooling place
32 Worshiped one
33 Shakespeare's Sir __ Belch
34 Florida governor
35 On the briny
36 Morning moistures
40 "Great!"
41 Omens
43 Deli bread
44 Lewis Carroll creature
46 Sudden pain
47 Polar covering
50 Flu variety
51 Voice an objection
52 __ Rogers St. Johns
53 Farmyard female
54 Pavarotti piece
55 Mardi Gras follower
57 Greenish blue
58 Damaged
61 Freight weight
63 "Equal" word form

523 TOP-10 TONES by George Lippold

ACROSS
1 Punjab princess
5 Urge forward
10 *Lion King* baddie
14 The yoke's on them
15 Simoleons
16 Picador's opponent
17 Top-10 tune of 1970
20 Hair style
21 Ferrari or Ford
22 Book boo-boos
23 Sothern and Jillian
24 Per __ (daily)
25 "My kingdom for __!"
28 Actor Sean
29 *Major Barbara* initials
32 __ hand (assist)
33 Humorist Sahl
34 Minimal rain
35 Top-10 tune of 1968
38 Writer Hunter
39 West Point athletes
40 Tokyo shopping district
41 Sleep phenom.
42 *The Grapes of Wrath* character
43 Openness
44 Enrages
45 River border
46 Russian seaport
49 Hem in
50 Tony of *Leave It to Beaver*
53 Top-10 tune of 1966
56 Metallic fabric
57 __ *of Two Cities*
58 Industrious insects
59 Pigeonhole
60 Arabian nation
61 Stocking section

DOWN
1 Plunders
2 Wheel shaft
3 Cleverly effective
4 Bus. abbr.
5 Not susceptible
6 Castle trenches
7 Possum of the comics
8 Inventor Whitney
9 Attack verbally
10 Violent weather
11 Robin Cook bestseller
12 Smell __ (suspect something)
13 Gossipy Barrett
18 One from Wichita
19 Small songbird
23 Miss Brooks portrayer
24 Bat Masterson trademark
25 "Rags to riches" author
26 Ricardo's *Fantasy Island* costar
27 Early hour
28 __ *de terre* (potato: Fr.)
29 Laborious routine
30 Chimp star of the '50s
31 Bit of broccoli
33 '60s slugger Roger
34 Imbibe
36 Subtract
37 Kampala's country
42 Approximately
43 Bizet opera
44 Spot of land
45 Authoritative volume
46 Olive and Castor of comics
47 Do business (in)
48 Fire man?
49 Largest of the Marianas
50 Flintstones' pet
51 Not fooled by
52 Toward 49 Down
54 Fr. holy woman
55 U.K. fliers

524 DANG ME by Bob Lubbers

ACROSS
1 Rose's beau
5 Villa d'__
9 Call up
14 Sent back
16 Barrier-reef material
17 Await the next episode
18 Jargon, e.g.
19 Rich cakes
21 Ancient Peruvian
22 Safely at first
26 Eel
28 Momentarily
29 The whole ball of wax
33 Trolley-bell sound
35 Sheeplike
36 R-V connectors
39 __ *Grows in Brooklyn*
40 Disencumber
41 More pleasant
43 Skelton or Smith
44 One of the senses
46 *Sturm und* __
47 Hardy horse
49 To the sheltered side
50 Receive
53 Enneads
55 Gilbert of *Roseanne*
56 Region of Spain
60 Tendency
62 Backfire
67 Make happy
68 Ink choice
69 Silents actor Novarro
70 Sch. term
71 Ball-__ hammer

DOWN
1 Curved line
2 Barbara __ Geddes
3 "__ Were King of the Forest"
4 Santa's helper
5 Resounds
6 Sheriff's symbol
7 Canvas quarters
8 Lip
9 Desktop products
10 __ up (in hiding)
11 Auburn-haired ape
12 John __ Garner
13 *The Apostles* composer
15 Newts
20 Read a bar code
22 Screendom statuette
23 *Lorenzo's Oil* actor
24 Get on
25 Rice or Heche
27 Upright
30 Actor Buchholz
31 Tony role for Patti
32 Delaware senator
34 Stand
36 Performer's minimum wage
37 Belief
38 Yens
42 Persia, now
45 Hammett hound
47 Intend
48 Folklore beings
50 Fall flower
51 *Cheers* waitress
52 Beat badly
54 Like Nash's lama
57 Hitters' stats
58 Top-notch
59 Deities
61 Family room
63 Clothing flaw
64 Honest __
65 The Mets' div.
66 USAF bigwig

525 NICE COMEBACK by Patrick Jordan

ACROSS
1 Storybook elephant
6 Body of laws
10 Pinnacle
14 Royal supporter
15 Bothersome burden
16 Feathery neckwear
17 START OF A QUIP
20 Gut feeling?
21 Annoy
22 Cone-shaped abode
23 Hamster healer
24 Aristocratic woman
25 Angora fabric
29 U.S.S. Enterprise captain
30 San Antonio landmark
31 "Nay!" sayer
32 FDR's mom
36 MIDDLE OF QUIP
39 Not so much
40 "What a pity!"
41 Gave comfort to
42 Inst. of higher learning
43 Mad feature
44 Presidential advisors
48 Curtain supporter
49 He takes a lot of interest in his work
50 Coffee, so to speak
51 Advertising award
55 END OF QUIP
58 The Larry Sanders Show actor
59 Bar bills
60 Barbershop tool
61 Plains tribesmen
62 Bridge position
63 Gypsy composer

DOWN
1 Radar signal
2 Verdi work
3 Alpine capital
4 Overly eager
5 Gun the engine
6 Cupid's sleighmate
7 Banded quartz
8 Lemon
9 Understood by few
10 Daisy Mae's man
11 Two-door vehicle
12 Spouses
13 Road curves
18 At any time
19 Nerd
23 Stringed instrument
24 ZaSu of films
25 Type of armor
26 Ye __ Antique Shoppe
27 Airplane! star
28 Iowa university town
29 Work dough
31 Musical tone
32 Take the lead
33 Chan's comment
34 Marsh grass
35 Capp of comics
37 Tear
38 Beer foam
42 All over again
43 Limerick or haiku
44 __ the chase (skip the details)
45 Take __ in the dark
46 Pack animal
47 Removes clothes lines
48 Biddy's bed
50 Classified listings
51 Pluto ender
52 Indolent
53 Aware of
54 Foul-tempered fellow
56 Sheep's cry
57 Hosp. sections

526 A MODEST PROPOSAL by Peter Gordon

ACROSS
1 "Shoo!"
6 Went too fast
10 Sharp blow in karate
14 Scarlett of Gone With the Wind
15 Mata __ (infamous spy)
16 Angel topper
17 Large ocean vessel
18 "I cannot tell __"
19 Had a debt
20 It's given when asking 48 Across
23 Sailor's affirmative
24 Auto
25 Grown up
29 Winnie-the-__
31 Actress Thurman
34 Too big, weightwise
35 Flirt's signal
36 Got __ the ground floor
37 Asks 48 Across
40 ". . . lived happily __ after"
41 Musical composition
42 The U of UV
43 Actor Billy __ Williams
44 Poker-pot starter
45 Except
46 Dessert served à la mode
47 Common conjunction
48 Proposal
56 Walk in water
57 __ fide
58 "Old MacDonald" refrain
59 Singer Fitzgerald
60 Israeli submachine guns
61 Spot on clothing
62 Ran in the washing machine
63 Butterfly catchers
64 Bombay garments

DOWN
1 Bottom of a shoe
2 Beard's place
3 Sounded a bell
4 Neighborhood
5 Thatcher of Britain
6 Put to __ (outdo)
7 Fair-skinned
8 Moran of Happy Days
9 Competitor of Tab
10 Church singing group
11 Goldie of Private Benjamin
12 Designer Cassini
13 Pea's home
21 CBS logo
22 Cheerleader's sound
25 Bike that has an engine
26 None of the __
27 Native American home
28 Where Gorbachev ruled: Abbr.
29 Arouse, as interest
30 Burden
31 Join together
32 Secures with cables
33 Karenina et al.
35 Cried
36 "__ be a cold day in July . . ."
38 Sweetheart
39 Woman's summer garment
44 Feel poorly
45 Spanish article
46 Say "Not guilty"
47 Accumulate
48 Room divider
49 Keep the engine running
50 Seep slowly
51 Pound or gallon
52 Moreno or Hayworth
53 1998, for example
54 1003, in old Rome
55 Long periods of time
56 Spider's creation

THREE-RING CIRCUS by Patrick Jordan

ACROSS

1 Heathen
6 The Ugly Duckling, eventually
10 Pedestal part
14 Rub out
15 Quote as an example
16 Crooner Paul
17 First-ring performer
20 "Piece of cake!"
21 Gardener's tool
22 First host of *The Price Is Right*
23 Bumped into
24 Foundation garment of yore
25 Tropical fruit
29 Tony Musante's TV tec
30 Have being
31 Toy with a tail
32 Frying medium
36 Second-ring performer
39 Minus
40 Gaucho's weapon
41 Cartoon adventurer Quest

42 ". . . __ forgive our debtors"
43 Reno and Leigh
44 Megalomaniacs, e.g.
47 Promgoer's rental
48 Beatty of *Reds*
49 Feeling blue
50 Lane of songdom
54 Third-ring performer
57 Declare openly
58 *Return of the Jedi* creature
59 Book of photos
60 Fork-tailed seabird
61 Emulates a seamstress
62 Jury members

DOWN

1 Tennis champ Sampras
2 La Scala solo
3 Comedian's stock-in-trade
4 Very pale
5 After taxes

6 Move along quickly
7 Clean with a rag
8 Enjoyed brunch
9 Rookie
10 Formal dances
11 Foot-leg connector
12 Clay pigeon
13 Work hard for
18 Actress Perlman
19 Angelic atmosphere
23 Legend
24 Terra __ (potting material)
25 Lemon skin
26 Wheel shaft
27 Slapstick movie missiles
28 Egyptian vipers
29 Championship
31 Recognized
32 Simba or Leo
33 Bancroft or Boleyn
34 Tenant's payment
35 Prohibition supporters
37 Attendance-book notations
38 Trojan War hero

42 Prayer response
43 Jujitsu offshoot
44 Purple hue
45 Knight clothing
46 Sketched
47 Fuel receptacles
48 "Huh?"

49 Winter fall
50 Having skill
51 Pig in a '96 film
52 Become indistinct
53 Shade trees
55 Astonishment
56 Short snooze

NOT SO SMART by Fred Piscop

ACROSS

1 Social stratum
6 "Leave it in," editorially
10 Fellow
14 First *Tonight Show* host
15 Prepare for a photo
16 Turner of movies
17 Signs of sorrow
18 *Bonanza* brother
19 Baker's need
20 Hearty bowlful
22 "Phooey!"
23 Hightail it
24 Old-time anesthetics
26 Chopped finely
30 Sound medium
32 Cricket rounds
33 Coll. degrees
34 Piece of parsley
38 __ Cass Elliot
39 Approves
40 Mail away
41 Win by __
43 Branch of Buddhism

44 Yo-Yo Ma's instrument
45 Judean king
47 Puts through a strainer
48 Noggin
51 ABA member
52 Waikiki locale
53 Tailless simian
60 Coal car
61 Lamb pseudonym
62 Auspices
63 Bush had one
64 Pocket fuzz
65 Rain-delay rollouts
66 Singer Anita
67 Wise guy?
68 Clear the tape

DOWN

1 __-nine-tails
2 Karras or Trebek
3 Blinds crosspiece
4 Word form for "trillion"
5 Stores, as grain
6 Spurt of activity

7 Hoo-ha
8 Jacob's twin
9 Filled in at the office
10 Heavy shoe
11 Le __, France
12 Keep __ to the ground
13 Suit part
21 Young fellow
25 Carol contraction
26 NYC art center
27 Lendl of the courts
28 Verne captain
29 Auto test device
30 Tended to the leaves
31 Org.
33 Clown of early TV
35 Function
36 Castaway's locale
37 '70s sporty cars
42 Slithery swimmer
44 Bargain-basement

46 Lee's men
47 School grp.
48 "What's __ like?"
49 Propelled a dinghy
50 Tara surname
51 Taper off

54 *Inter* __ (among others)
55 Foreman's workplace
56 Once around the sun
57 Taj Mahal site
58 Domino spots
59 *In* __ (actually)

ONE TOO MANY by Brian Hulse

ACROSS
1 Morse units
5 Product mention
9 One way to address a lady
13 Step __ (hurry)
14 US : Mary :: Ireland : __
15 Before now, in olden days
16 Nada
17 Yearly record
18 Seasoned pros
19 Macho, macho Stetson?
22 Result
23 Winnow
24 Oath-taking answer
27 Home companion
29 Ark invitees
32 "Who's Sorry __"
33 Ginger on *Gilligan's Island*
36 Fed. gangbusters
37 Big, big rig?
42 *Nautilus* skipper
43 "Out," to an editor
44 Vexation
45 Macon breakfast
47 Glum
49 Double CCV
50 Takes a 1 Down
52 Little kid
54 Bad, bad language?
62 Barge __ (interrupt)
63 Bakery treat, perhaps
64 Milker's prop
65 Savings-protection org.
66 Gin game
67 Extent
68 Brontë heroine
69 Don't move
70 Gusto

DOWN
1 Short sleep
2 "The __ lama, he's a priest"
3 Get bored
4 Countertop heater
5 Hunger message
6 Moon goddess
7 Europe-Asia separators
8 Fast gait
9 Intervening period
10 Shoe part
11 On a cruise
12 __ Helens, WA
14 Order from the people
20 Bus. letter extra
21 Give a speech
24 Traveler's lodging
25 "Nothing __!" ("Forget it!")
26 Store boss
28 Laced up
30 Piece of history?
31 Bergen's dummy
34 Compass hdg.
35 Hole-punching tools
38 Fame
39 Aggregate
40 Sci-fi weapon
41 T follower
46 Broccoli bits
48 Jones' financial partner
51 Vain walk
53 Crystalline gem
54 *Spirit of '76* instrument
55 Spring auto race, familiarly
56 __ dire (jury-selection process)
57 Anti-drug crusader David
58 Small-screen honor
59 Infrequent
60 Bombs on stage
61 Fence piece

WAITING FOR A SIGN by Frank Longo

ACROSS
1 Exterminator's target
5 Have __ to grind
10 King beater
13 Oppositionist
14 *Family Matters* nerd
15 *Dukes of Hazzard* boss
17 It's signed for purchasing power
19 Cherub with a bow
20 Dolphins quarterback, once
21 Multi-vol. lexicon
23 Greek vowel
24 De Mille of dance
25 It's signed for the IRS
28 Capone nemesis
29 Timetable abbr.
30 "Cut that out!"
31 Hank Aaron's 2,211
32 Take the honey and run
33 It's signed before a ceremony
39 *Inter* __ (among others)
40 Santa Claus artist
41 It had a part in the Bible
43 IRA accrual
44 Horner's discovery
48 It's signed at a museum
50 Rhone tributary
51 "Give __ whirl!"
52 Alley follower
53 Waitress on *Mad About You*
54 Penpoints
56 It's signed by a witness
59 12/26 event
60 Wash away
61 Morales of *Bad Boys*
62 Just out
63 Made two-by-fours
64 Miami-__ County

DOWN
1 Arcade classic
2 Incense
3 Boat backs
4 Neatens
5 Prefix with suggestion
6 Atomic energy org.
7 Rap-sheet abbr.
8 Ricoh rival
9 Presbyters
10 "Caught you!"
11 Find by chance
12 Vacations of vanity?
16 Successful financial-aid applicant
18 Those elected
22 Make out
25 High-school math
26 TV Hall of fame
27 Lacquered metalware
29 Attorney's org.
31 __ the occasion (extend oneself)
33 Page peripheries
34 American islander
35 Like a broken horse
36 *The Wiz* star
37 Tall and skinny
38 Ending for hobby or lobby
42 Residences
44 Used rubber cement
45 Creator of Meg and Amy
46 Do a stevedore's job
47 Ogre
49 Puccini piece
50 __ Lanka
53 Put to work
55 Embroider
57 Captured GI
58 Dedicated verse

AROUND THE ROOM by Rich Norris

ACROSS
1 The second Mrs. Trump
6 Tavern
9 Slide on ice
14 Self-evident truth
15 Gold: Sp.
16 __ Gables, FL
17 Very frustrated
20 "For __ a jolly good fellow"
21 Take advantage of
22 "This __ Love" (Rodgers & Hart tune)
23 Immigrant's subj.
24 MGM lion
25 Clobber, as in a contest
34 Part of SEATO
35 Life of __ (ease)
36 Word form for "earth"
37 Military melody
38 Lawn intrusions
39 Charitable offerings
40 Supplement, with out

41 Seven, in Seville
42 Info
43 Causes shame
47 Writer Fleming
48 Scale notes
49 Kidnapper's demand
52 Every
53 Covert WWII org.
56 Bill holders
59 __ Martin (007 auto)
60 Waikiki welcome
61 Put up
62 Shoals
63 Senator Kennedy
64 Charges for use

DOWN
1 Speed-of-sound number
2 Wheel connector
3 Social reformer Jacob
4 Actor Herbert
5 Sneak attack
6 Tibia, for one
7 S.A. country

8 Campus recruiting grp.
9 Stage sets, collectively
10 Act obsequiously
11 Saudi, for one
12 Story
13 Architectural add-on
18 Tropical spot
19 Angels' headgear
23 Greek letters
25 Defeated at chess
26 Japanese city
27 Tom's dad, in the rhyme
28 Turns loose
29 Deceive
30 Like days of yore
31 Dome-shaped hut
32 Metronome setting
33 Gardener, at times
38 Separate grain and chaff
39 Puts in
41 Sprinkles salt, perhaps

44 What "-ish" means
45 Agatha contemporary
46 Merchant
49 Swell, as a river
50 Build the pot
51 Become liquid
52 Zealous

53 Word on a store sign
54 Religious group
55 Fast fliers: Abbr.
56 Kids' card game
57 Born: Fr.
58 Assayer's concern

HANDY by Bob Lubbers

ACROSS
1 Director Howard
4 Fatty
11 Deed
14 I love: Lat.
15 Chooses
16 Funny Charlotte
17 ". . . rain __ sleet . . ."
18 Sign of nerves
20 Search for water
22 Bridge coup
23 Track-and-field contest
24 Very long time
25 Hindsight phrase
27 Pickpocket's assets
33 Hodgepodge
34 EPA concern
35 Flora-filled lobbies
39 Estuary
40 Tours
42 Blow it
43 Fender dings
45 __'War (racehorse)

46 To-do
47 Boxing style of old
50 Previously
53 XIII x IV
54 Achieve
55 Zola novel
59 Movie award
62 Garden experts
65 Coach Parseghian
66 Pub drink
67 Make like new
68 Midmorning
69 Baseballer Cobb et al.
70 Upset with
71 "Dig in!"

DOWN
1 Author Ayn
2 Melville novel
3 From Oslo
4 Agree
5 Morning droplets
6 Seine sights
7 Ring out
8 Word form for "eight"

9 One of the Little Rascals
10 Psychic's sense
11 Composer Harold
12 Sahara beast
13 In a peevish mood
19 "It's __ Unusual Day"
21 London district
26 Monks
27 *Hawaii Five-O* star
28 Nastase of tennis
29 Chemin de __ (casino game)
30 Part of Caesar's boast
31 Kim of *Picnic*
32 Miller or Ford
36 Make a copy of
37 "*Dies __*"
38 Part of B.A.
40 Despot
41 Costello or Gehrig
44 Steak cut

46 Competes in the slalom
48 Tenant
49 Storage space
50 Sired, Biblically
51 Before the deadline
52 Releases

56 Chan rejoinder
57 Party snacks
58 Cookie man Wally
60 Zone
61 Carry on
63 Atomic energy org.
64 Bikini top

GEARING UP by Patrick Jordan

ACROSS

1 Prosecutorial aides: Abbr.
5 *Golden Boy* playwright
10 Pinnacle
14 See 37 Down
15 Physicist from Poland
16 God of thunder
17 Jason's ship
18 Upper crust
19 Orchestral heavyweight
20 Boxer's temporary haven
23 Paint solvent
24 Broad necktie
27 Deuce topper
28 Fast-food store sign
32 Mom's mate
34 Tiny Tim's instrument
35 Appear
36 $$ dispenser
39 *Born Free* beast
42 Maritime message
43 "Get lost!"
45 *Exodus* character
46 Hole's starting point
48 Monopoly property
51 Pesky buzzer
54 Condition
55 Foppish fellows
58 Pauly Shore's specialty
62 Baby bed
64 1996 candidate Alexander
65 Lena of *Havana*
66 Slimy substance
67 Without __ in the world
68 Counterfeit coin
69 Active person
70 Shows flexibility
71 Thick textbook

DOWN

1 Guam's capital
2 Emulate Spielberg
3 Debate-team member
4 Like some spoons
5 Vast quantity
6 Became less keen
7 Guitarist Clapton
8 Onetime Yugoslavian president
9 Fortune hunter?
10 Swears (to)
11 Houses of worship
12 Unruly crowd
13 Memorable period
21 Blue shade
22 Denial in Dundee
25 Bestselling cookie
26 Rolaids rival
29 Like some ancient inscriptions
30 1950s campaign nickname
31 Three-piece suit part
33 Television tuner
36 Egyptian vipers
37 With 14 Across, '60s sitcom
38 Emulate Aesop
40 ". . . man __ mouse?"
41 Sheet-music symbol
44 Fest time in Frankfurt
47 Last on the list
49 Baptist's bench
50 Dancer Villella
52 Danny of *Ruby*
53 Boring quality
56 Farmland measurements
57 Irish dramatist
59 Divulge a secret
60 Competition
61 Arabian sultanate
62 One way to send a pkg.
63 Kanga's kid

DOCTOR OF LETTERS by Jon Delfin

ACROSS

1 Neutralize
6 Aware of
10 Rice wine
14 Tea cake
15 German industrial valley
16 51 qvadrvpled?
17 THE DOCTOR
20 Chemical ending
21 Brazil-born soccer star
22 Down source
23 Canadian prov.
25 Lincoln and Fortas
27 THE DOCTOR'S SPECIALTY
31 Ocean occurrence
35 Bio 101 study
36 Singer Campbell
38 New Deal agcy.
39 Sloppy, as a racetrack
40 Notice
41 G sharp's equivalent
43 Language ending
44 Qualified
46 Predicament
47 Most folks with August birthdays
49 THE DOCTOR'S FAMOUS PATIENT
51 Bloke
53 Symbol for 47 Across
54 Impolite look
57 Moss material
59 Chinese philosophical ideal
62 WHERE THE DOCTOR WAS LAST SEEN
66 Do lobbying
67 "Rule Britannia" composer
68 Size of type
69 "__ giorno!"
70 Turned blue, perhaps
71 High-IQ club

DOWN

1 Cleopatra's undoing
2 Basketball tourn. sponsor
3 "Fish" or "fowl"
4 Gas-pump selection
5 Was winning
6 Tough time
7 Empty, as a set
8 __ *Has Landed* ('77 film)
9 Jazzman Kid __
10 Crystalline rock
11 Corrosive chemical
12 It gets high at the beach
13 Eternally
18 __ point (somewhat)
19 Teeny
24 Tripoli's country
26 Parting word
27 *Road to Morocco* talker
28 Elicit chuckles from
29 Cowboy carnival
30 Double curves
32 One of the spouse's folks
33 Hang (over)
34 Refriger-raider?
37 Acapulco appetizer
40 Hard to handle
42 Land abutting the ocean
45 Costar of Betty and Rue
46 Mean moods
48 Home-movie equipment
50 Overjoyed
52 __ *Haw*
54 Checkbook record
55 O'er
56 Golden Fleece ship
58 Feminizing suffix
60 To __ (unanimously)
61 Picks, with "for"
63 Rogue
64 McTavish's cap
65 Where the buoys are

535 FRUIT MIX by A.J. Santora

ACROSS
1 Thwacked
7 Mayberry boy
11 Miney's follower
14 Block
15 "Hold it!"
16 South end
17 Fruity front-page report?
19 On-__ (bit of gossip)
20 Ivy leaguer
21 Ex-space station
22 More dapper
24 *Our Gang* dog
26 Actor O'Shea
28 Ladd role
29 Be furious
31 Comic Philips
33 Singer James
34 Army unit
38 Annoy
39 Frugal way to dole out fruit?
43 Bach's "Partita __ Minor"
44 Carpet bits
45 Canapé spread
47 Nancy Drew's boyfriend
48 Alabama city
52 Gives off
54 TV rooms
57 Virginia dance
58 Temptress
60 "Caught you!"
62 Santa __, CA
63 Anger
64 Fruity plans?
67 Born: Fr.
68 One of the Jackson 5
69 *Mikrokosmos* composer
70 Both Begleys
71 Take, as advice
72 Sweater material

DOWN
1 Macho pride
2 Charm
3 7-Up rival
4 One of LBJ's beagles
5 Dutch town
6 Jeans fabric
7 Retain
8 Remarkable events
9 *The Music Man* setting
10 Bridge defenders
11 Helps to settle
12 Monopoly avenue
13 Appeal
18 Numerical prefix
23 *Café* alternative
25 All __ (paying attention)
27 Paris paper
30 Rabin's predecessor
32 "Come __!" ("Welcome!")
35 Govt. agents
36 Instant
37 Infants
39 Petroleum pathway
40 Under the spell (of)
41 Pensioners
42 PC owner
46 Midi summer
49 Shed
50 Corporate coach
51 "The Last Frontier"
53 Laziness
55 Humble horse
56 Inge dog
59 Pennsylvania port
61 Palindrome start
65 Silent agreement
66 Work unit

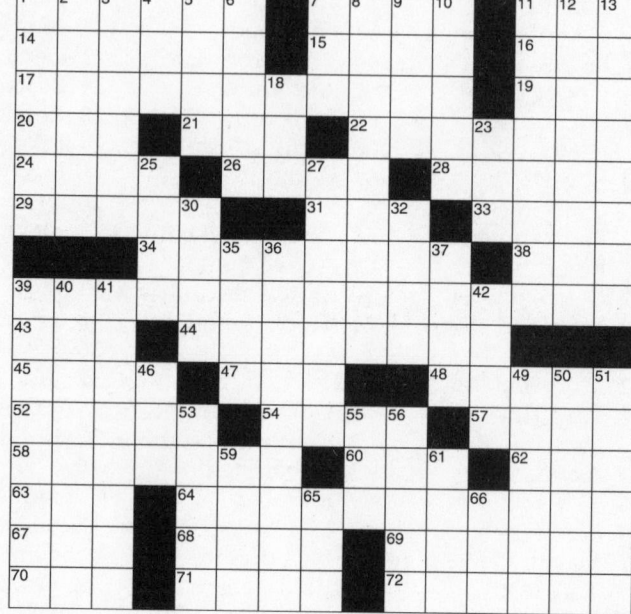

536 CAPITALISTS by Patrick Jordan

ACROSS
1 Deteriorates
5 Got a perfect score on
9 Green sauce
14 Admit openly
15 Ice-cream holder
16 Be of use to
17 New Mexico Indian
18 The item here
19 Told a knee-slapper
20 *Steel Magnolias* costar
23 Actor Stephen
24 Nancy Reagan's son
25 Citrus fruit
26 Swindle
27 Sicilian spouter
28 __ constrictor
31 Chinese, e.g.
34 Fuzzy member of Skywalker's army
35 Drescher of *The Nanny*
36 *From Here to Eternity* costar
39 Bettor's concern
40 Calhoun of filmdom
41 Della or Pee Wee
42 Put into words
43 Baseball gear
44 Wedding attire, for short
45 African nation
46 That girl
47 Boxing stats
50 Paint-dripping artist
54 Explorer __ de Leon
55 *Cheers* character
56 Vicinity
57 Caruso or Domingo
58 Enjoying a cruise
59 Butcher's wares
60 Defeats a dragon
61 Soapmaking substances
62 Source of ruin

DOWN
1 Shaver's need
2 Small egg
3 Skater Harding
4 Do the butterfly
5 Director's command
6 *George M!* subject
7 Writer Bagnold
8 Without a definite purpose
9 *The __ Game* (Doris Day musical)
10 Call forth
11 Munro's pen name
12 Secures a shoelace
13 Ancient
21 Fork feature
22 Closely twisted
26 Some house pets
27 Water pitchers
28 Soft cheese
29 Clumsy sorts
30 Poker payment
31 Andy's radio partner
32 Fizzy quaff
33 500-mile race, for short
34 Appealing to feelings
35 Show off one's biceps
37 Some exams
38 Merciless
43 Pastry purveyors
44 Bush Supreme Court appointee
45 *Star Trek* doctor
46 Shopping binge
47 Divided country
48 Arctic or Indian
49 Ray with winglike fins
50 Rock singer Billy
51 Ballerina Pavlova
52 Overly inquisitive
53 Ewe's child
54 NHL stats

ACROSS
1 LAPD alert
4 Missouri Indian
9 Peel
14 Jack of *Barney Miller*
15 Levies
16 Peter O'__
17 Spanish aunt
18 Leader
20 Ms. Lauder
22 Readied a golf ball
23 Takes umbrage at
26 Tranquilized
31 Anchor setter
33 Lessen the value
34 __ Lanka
36 Fodder storages
38 What IOUs indicate
39 Baby seals
41 Thighbone
43 Jai __
44 Pullman berth
46 Nasser successor
48 Curved shape
49 Actor Keanu
51 Football's "Broadway Joe"
53 Comparatively
55 Countries
58 Business transaction
60 Portable quarters
61 Car-battery hookup
67 Write
68 Actress Stevens
69 Arab chief
70 Asner and Ames
71 Half of a '60s rock foursome
72 Actions
73 Deli bread

DOWN
1 Fall flower
2 Self-possession
3 Sea captain
4 Outrages
5 *To __ With Love*
6 "It's a __-win situation!"
7 Lady's man
8 Senator Kefauver
9 Encrusted
10 2,000 pounds
11 Howard of *American Graffiti*
12 __ du Diable
13 For each
19 Marsh grass
21 Wide shoe
24 End-of-workweek shout
25 Monica of tennis
27 Vicinity
28 Restaurant nuisance
29 Kett and James
30 Arnaz Sr. and Jr.
32 Director Polanski
34 Pony prodders
35 Delhi dollar
37 Khartoum is its capital
40 Golfer Ballesteros
42 Avatar of Vishnu
45 Performs
47 Rags
50 Omen examiner
52 Ascot, e.g.
54 Sped
56 Impoverished
57 Have a feeling
59 Flimsy, as an excuse
61 Conrad's Lord
62 Actress Merkel
63 Movie production giant
64 Little green orb
65 Small buzzer
66 Conducted

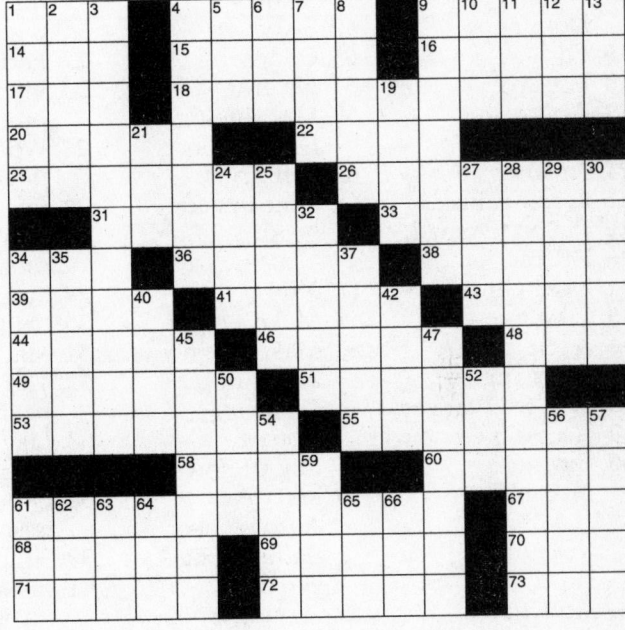

ACROSS
1 *Friends* character
5 Talks back to
11 Dickens nom de plume
14 Waffle name
15 Sends memos by modem
16 "So that's it!"
17 William Conrad role
19 Sought office
20 Nourished
21 Night, in Nîmes
22 Had on
23 Buddy Ebsen role
27 "I Got a Name" singer
29 Goneril's father
30 "All __ Up" (Presley tune)
31 Complains about
36 Perfectly
37 Complete
38 Novelist Jaffe
39 Magicians
41 Discovered
42 La Scala highlight
43 Take flight to unite
44 Tom Selleck role
49 Road warning sign
50 Land on the Caspian Sea
51 Mile High Center architect
54 Mine find
55 James Garner role
59 Dijon disagreement
60 Sign for
61 Pâté, de __ gras
62 Nav. rank
63 Costumes
64 Dog biter

DOWN
1 Actor Bridges
2 Mythical meanie
3 "Zounds!"
4 That, way back then
5 Protected from danger
6 At full speed
7 Annual visitor
8 Transgression
9 "Hold On Tight" rock group
10 Nine-digit ID
11 Element #5
12 Busiest American airport
13 Regions
18 Special skill
22 Hobbyist's space, perhaps
23 Military training site
24 Jazz form
25 Fiscal period
26 Boxer's target
27 Ah follower
28 Jungle warning
30 Map lines: Abbr.
31 Cook clams
32 Fiscal pd.
33 Beginning course
34 Diarist Frank
35 Small amount
37 *Mila 18* author
40 Failed constitutional amendment
41 Score below D
43 Passes, as a law
44 Steakhouse order
45 Iroquois language
46 Portents
47 Buenos __
48 Look for the light switch
51 Mosconi's game
52 City north of Pittsburgh
53 Inspiration
55 Binge
56 Hosp. locale
57 Sprint competitor
58 Dramatically loud, in music

539 TOOL BOXES by S.E. Wilkinson

ACROSS
1 A little night music
5 Cow hand?
9 Double up
13 Frenzied
14 Mr. Magoo's nephew
15 Strain for Domingo
16 FILE
18 Jet-set jet
19 Approx.
20 Excuses
21 Aplenty
23 Lean against
25 Rig on the road
26 DRILL
32 Ocean liner?
35 Vikings
36 A kin
37 Mass appeal
38 First fruit fancier
39 Access method
40 Low-tech propeller
41 __ killing (profited big)
43 Nashville attraction
44 HAMMER
48 Ultraconservative
49 Whatchamacallit
53 Recoil
56 Purchase offers
58 Keogh relative
59 Words of dismay
60 SAW
63 Chops, e.g.
64 Ne'er-do-well
65 Jazz singing
66 Diamond bag
67 Soft drink
68 Hole in your head

DOWN
1 Make a point
2 Make laugh
3 Annie of *Designing Women*
4 Enjoy Snowmass
5 Red deer
6 Auto pioneer
7 Enthusiastic verse
8 Signing crooks
9 Boot-camp command
10 Cookie favorite
11 Yarn spinner
12 Take a risk
14 Meandered
17 Halfway through the day
22 Parisian pal
24 Like some profits
25 Where current flows
27 Eventually
28 Minimum cabaret charge
29 Surmounting
30 Odin's boy
31 Macabre
32 The Munsters' pet monster
33 Like __ of sunshine
34 Popeye Doyle was one
39 Simpleton
41 Instrument inventor
42 Ethereal
45 Significant
46 Kind of snake
47 Unduly interested
50 Dance hall
51 Clamorous
52 Poet Rossetti
53 You may part with it
54 Perlman of *Pearl*
55 Balin and Claire
56 Al's boss, once
57 Abstraction
61 Hubbub
62 Second sight

540 FORUM FILMS by Frank Longo

ACROSS
1 Go by bike
6 Whirlpool outlets
10 Folkie Phil
14 Chopin piece
15 Butter substitute
16 Arraignment offering
17 1990 thriller, to Caesar?
19 Wee
20 Emulate Ebert
21 Change for a five
22 Slip into
23 Metabolism regulator
25 Hebrew, e.g.
28 1970 drama, to Caesar?
31 Sphere start
34 Physician's org.
35 Rewards good service
36 1954 Japanese classic, to Caesar?
40 War god
41 Sega rival, for short
42 *Middletown* author
43 1957 courtroom drama, to Caesar?
47 Baltic state
48 Passed by
53 Hair-styling stuff
54 Is off the mark
56 Ireland's alias
57 A.A. __ (62 Across pen name)
59 1984 teen comedy, to Caesar?
61 Overlay with bacon
62 Perry's creator
63 Field's partner
64 New Haven school
65 Beautician, at times
66 Welcomers

DOWN
1 Lab-dish inventor
2 Frome of fiction
3 Tunes for two
4 Goodbye, to Gabrielle
5 Waikiki wear
6 *Under Fire* actress Cassidy
7 Screen siren Sommer
8 Ball balancers
9 Distress call
10 Medical specialty
11 Workshop giver
12 Clucking mama
13 Articulate
18 Spike Lee's sister
22 Agnus __
24 Ukrainian city
25 Junk e-mail
26 Slightly warm
27 Double curve
29 Pert
30 Singer Sumac
31 Heart chambers
32 Bow's nickname
33 National park in Colorado
37 Swenson of *Benson*
38 Suffix for bombard
39 Wrist-to-elbow bone
40 Rock singer Rose
44 Nothing
45 Mancini collaborator
46 Couturière Schiaparelli
49 Director Almodóvar
50 Fictional Marner
51 Construct
52 Newspaper departments
54 "Climb __ Mountain"
55 Vex
57 Fishing lure
58 Triptik org.
59 Made one's mark
60 Extreme degree

541 VEGETARIAN DIET by Jean Davison

ACROSS
1 Says further
5 "__ Old Cowhand"
9 Puccini opera
14 Urgent
15 Two-wheeled vehicle
16 Corn-oil products
17 Blabbed all
20 Repair videotape
21 Refrigerator-door device
22 Move aimlessly
23 Gear teeth
24 One glued to the tube
29 Bell and Barker
32 Initiation
33 I, to Claudius
34 Wine holder
35 Flabbergast
36 Harness races
38 "All" word form
39 Sharp-tasting
40 Spicy-tasting
41 Used diligently
42 Secret agent
43 Brats' weapons
46 Horse brake
47 Treasury Dept. agency
48 Fluttering trees
51 Unprincipled sort
55 Anne Bancroft film of 1964
59 Chorus member
60 Circus stage
61 Travel randomly
62 Mean-spirited
63 *The __ of Night*
64 Spectacular

DOWN
1 Billboard displays
2 Party spreads
3 Faucet flaw
4 Auction off
5 Martian feature
6 Got by
7 High-school course
8 Ultimate degree
9 Trinidad's partner
10 Designer Cassini et al.
11 Connery or Penn
12 Funnel shape
13 Aide: Abbr.
18 Easy to lift
19 Hams it up
23 Quitter's word
24 Prices
25 Ready to use
26 Loan shark's offense
27 Penny
28 Blows the whistle
29 '50s first lady
30 Lou Grant portrayer
31 Loses traction
34 Big name in guns
36 Religious belief
37 Horse color
41 Deputized group
43 Severe circumstances
44 Looking to add staff
45 Citrus fruit
46 Tend to an overgrown plant
48 Memo abbr.
49 Mets' stadium
50 Signing-ceremony needs
52 Give a hoot
53 On the summit
54 Jeansmaker Strauss
56 Opposite of post-
57 Tease
58 __ room (den)

542 PLAYING THE MARKET by Rich Norris

ACROSS
1 Powerful businessman
5 '97 Marlins, e.g.
11 High-school subj.
14 Pledge
15 NHL team
16 Heavy weight
17 Football strategies
19 Estimated-tax payee
20 Quaint motel
21 *Wheel of Fortune* purchase
22 Pay to play
23 Familiar literary figure
27 Chit
28 Help-wanted abbr.
29 Hungarian composer
30 Miami-__ County
32 Stored up
36 Summit
37 Suitable spot
38 "If __ a Hammer"
42 Physical one
44 Inlet
45 Role player
48 __ Abner
50 Kitten's cry
51 Boatswain or gunner
56 Came down to earth
57 Canoe paddle
58 CD-__
59 Type
60 Slave
65 Kicker's aid
66 Ready to roll
67 Singer Adams
68 Grads-to-be: Abbr.
69 *Seinfeld* character
70 Church passage

DOWN
1 Pigeon English?
2 Use a microwave
3 Disposition
4 Big beast, briefly
5 Debate side
6 Wise, so to speak
7 Islam's Almighty
8 "It don't __ thing . . ."
9 Richard of *Stir Crazy*
10 Former draft org.
11 Tenures
12 Aztec conqueror
13 Magazine filler
18 "__ upon a time, . . ."
22 Like lemon juice
23 Bathday cake
24 Reeves of *Speed*
25 Funny one
26 Pub pint
27 Actress Lupino
31 Take forcibly
33 Ludwig's lament
34 Geological ledge
35 Letter embellishment
39 Like Mom's apple pie
40 Declare
41 Morning condensation
43 "Are you a man __ mouse?"
45 Expects
46 Talk-show participant
47 Kids' wheels
49 Train line to NYC
52 Peter of Herman's Hermits
53 Ballroom dance
54 *Law & __*
55 Commandment word
60 1988 Hanks film
61 Actor's union: Abbr.
62 Palindromic preposition
63 Put the kibosh on
64 Vietnamese New Year

STATE DEPARTMENT by Fred Piscop

ACROSS
1 Tijuana's locale
5 Prepare flour
9 Blackjack-table request
14 Corrida cheers
15 Helen's home
16 Different
17 Some rocket fuel
20 Mount on a surface
21 Be forgiving
22 Marks a ballot
23 Columnist Buchwald
26 Do something
27 Scornful look
29 Bank jobs
34 Tiff
37 Oral or physical
39 Big name in chips
40 "Everything must go" event
43 Put in a vase
44 Send to the bottom
45 Leered at
46 Form a partnership
48 Horace or Pindar
50 Greek consonants
52 Poseidon's domain
53 Rubber-tree yield
56 All-you-can-eat venue
61 Pelvic bones
63 Dizzy Dean and teammates
66 Strong point
67 Chase of theater
68 Ronny Howard role
69 __ Dame
70 Redness typified
71 Grandpa Walton portrayer

DOWN
1 Fenway team, for short
2 Without company
3 Congeals
4 Home to most Turks
5 Indy 500 sponsor
6 Factory-reject tag abbr.
7 Silly one
8 Aggressive personality
9 Dairy cow
10 "__ never work!"
11 Southeast Asian
12 Patch up
13 Art Deco artist
18 Actress Cannon
19 Work with acid
24 Critic Rex
25 Michener novel
27 __ und Drang
28 Sine or cosine
30 Mini-map
31 Admonition to Fido
32 Starter for vision
33 Luge
34 Use a letter opener
35 Knotty wood
36 Blue shade
38 Cares about
41 Overwhelm
42 *Grapes of Wrath* figure
47 Places for pints
49 Encl. for a reply
51 Sir, in India
53 Vista
54 *L.A. Law* character
55 Beeper
56 Kenton of jazz
57 Chan's assent
58 "__ we forget"
59 Golden-__ (senior)
60 Thespian's gig
62 Wide-eyed
64 "Aloha Oe" instrument
65 Served on a jury

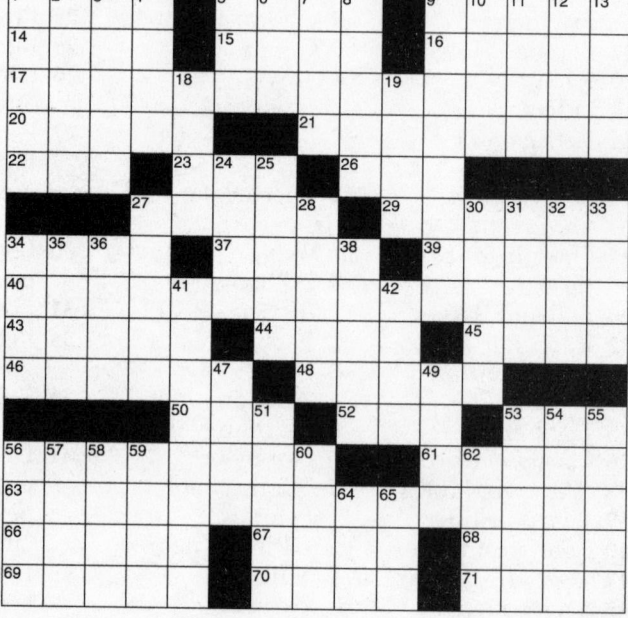

HOE HOE HOE by Nancy Salomon

ACROSS
1 Verbal jab in the ribs
5 Turkish bigwigs
10 Baby's word
14 Suit to __
15 Passed out hands
16 Designer Cassini
17 Dandelion not welcome?
20 Church recess
21 Yonder
22 Moo goo __ pan
23 "The Greatest"
24 Tempe sch.
26 Improve
28 Rosewall of tennis
29 Skedaddled
31 Stratagems
32 Liberal follower
34 Ran first
35 Command to Fido
36 Seed territories well?
41 Attention
42 Original sinner
43 Egg on
45 Command to Fido
48 Barrel-bottom contents
50 Bake-sale grp.
51 Snaps to it
54 66, e.g.: Abbr.
55 Halloween mo.
56 NYC subway
57 Tiny amounts
59 Genie's offering
61 Dig in before it's too late?
65 Baum canine
66 Not up yet
67 Sapphire image
68 Vein contents
69 Rib
70 Desires

DOWN
1 A hand for Lassie
2 Second-story men
3 Permeate
4 Turner and Williams
5 Fruit drink
6 Signer
7 "He that __ clean hands . . .": Psalms
8 *The Sandbox* playwright
9 Stem's opposite
10 Bossy sound
11 Sets right
12 Threaten
13 Texas A&M athletes
18 Rhythm
19 Renowned Yankee
23 Rap sheet abbr.
25 Energy type
27 30 Down et al.
30 '50s make
33 Hard work
35 Caring for, with "on"
37 Pretend
38 Does a foreman's job
39 Directly across from
40 Flyer of opera?
44 Squealer
45 Words on a label
46 Salon
47 Executor's concern
49 Basted, maybe
52 Hide-and-seek words
53 Building material
58 "Fernando" band
60 __-bitsy
62 Denials
63 Offering from Keats
64 Hesitation sounds

545 GAMUTS by Rand H. Burns

ACROSS
1 Racing site
6 18th-century pamphleteer
11 Toothpaste type
14 Willis' ex
15 Emphatic
17 African gamut
19 Bro's sib
20 Stephanie's dad or granddad
21 Women's magazine
22 Road curve
23 Sleep stages
26 Hot sauce
29 Exodus participant
34 Sulk
35 Opp.
36 Met again
37 Weapon gamut
40 Intervene
41 Safari park
42 Gaelic
43 TV and radio
45 Trout basket
46 Pt. of speech
47 Successor of CQD
48 Exploit
52 Word before mail or darter
54 Obscure
57 Pasta gamut
61 Papal pact
62 "The Twelfth of __"
63 Yalie
64 The items yonder
65 Entrap

DOWN
1 Latin 101 word
2 Operatic songs
3 Gear teeth
4 PAC-10 sch.
5 Actress Wright
6 Carson replaced him
7 Flowery gamut
8 Organic compound
9 __ Percé
10 Hurler's stat
11 Taunt
12 Diabolical
13 Frond
16 Copyright relatives: Abbr.
18 Preconditions
22 Legally bars
24 Donkey Kong fighter
25 Flow slowly
26 Muscle movement
27 Main artery
28 Angler's jigs
29 CD add-on
30 German pistols
31 Accustom
32 On tenterhooks
33 Henry Ford II's father
35 He played Grant
38 Sissy
39 Animals, in taxonomy
44 Square-dance call
45 List introducers
47 Be in session
48 Oppose
49 Organic compound
50 Indian guided missile
51 Gumshoe
53 Commedia dell'__
54 Prima donna
55 Brain passage
56 Bog
58 Homesite
59 Initials for Elizabeth
60 Buddhist sect

546 WHERE'S THE ENTRÉE? by Rich Norris

ACROSS
1 Male sheep
4 Current unit
8 Support-group offshoot
14 Latin 101 word
15 Buck add-on
16 Traffic circle
17 Something simple
19 Infant's bed
20 Fireplace flakes
21 Period of youthful inexperience
23 Carter's successor
25 Greek philosopher
26 Massage
28 Process, as film
33 __ homo (behold the man)
37 Chart
39 Dodge
40 Cancels prior increases
44 Fire indicator
45 Title of honor
46 For fear that
47 Homeowner's clearance
50 One of the Dwarfs
52 Stinging insect
54 Sword holder
59 "Nothing to it!"
64 Stan's sidekick
65 Make
66 Personal taste, so to speak
68 Physician, for one
69 Actor Kristofferson
70 Goof up
71 Roy Rogers movies, e.g.
72 Panasonic rival
73 Q-U connection

DOWN
1 Traffic controllers' device
2 Entertain
3 Coffee flavoring
4 Poughkeepsie college
5 Gold: Sp.
6 Gehrig and Costello
7 November birthstone
8 Mysterious
9 Rule, as a kingdom
10 Just __ (not much)
11 Nothing, to Juan
12 Paris airport
13 Louis and Carrie
18 Beer barrel
22 Was in charge of
24 Without sensation
27 Sheep sound
29 Sinful
30 Shoe tie
31 Praiseful poems
32 Annoyer
33 Prefix for while
34 Robin Cook book
35 Backup cause
36 Part of BPOE
38 Mac alternatives: Abbr.
41 Bay-salt source
42 Young goat
43 Paid players
48 Hologram producers
49 Sixth sense, for short
51 Selective
53 Selects
55 Santa subordinate
56 Make changes to
57 Stadium levels
58 Tin Man's desire
59 Canyon phenomenon
60 Locale
61 Do an usher's job
62 Clinton alma mater
63 Continental prefix
67 Sewing-basket item

547   IT'S A PUZZLE by Fred Piscop

ACROSS
1 Train for boxing
5 36 inches
9 Tots up
13 "Gay" city
14 Nobelist Wiesel
15 Romance lang.
16 Deck out
17 King of beasts
18 Actress Foch
19 Intense PR campaign
21 Hoofbeat
22 I love: Lat.
23 *The Pink Panther* star
25 Shouted out
30 Mauna __
31 United
32 Metal sources
34 Immigrant from Japan
38 Irving Berlin tune
42 Aromatic chemical
43 Ward of *Sisters*
44 From __ Z
45 *Platoon* setting
47 __ out (reached a low point)

50 The mold in Brie, e.g.
54 Fortune 500 orgs.
55 *Bonanza* brother
56 Defender/author Alan
62 Tiny parasite
63 "__ Plenty o' Nuttin' "
64 Sierra Nevada lake
65 __ *on the Fourth of July*
66 Walking stick
67 Chan portrayer Warner
68 Leave out
69 Hash-house side order
70 Racetrack quote

DOWN
1 Marquis de __
2 Urge
3 Satellite-dish ancestor
4 Change the title of
5 Cheerleader's routine

6 *Et* __ (and others: Lat.)
7 Runs amok
8 Washington of *Malcolm X*
9 Writer Upton
10 Serving a purpose
11 Lord's home
12 Insults, in a way
13 Actress Dawber
20 Element #5
24 Solo
25 Clinton's birthplace
26 Responsibility
27 Riga resident
28 Valentine's Day figure
29 Star in Cygnus
33 Normandy campaign town
35 Thailand, once
36 Novel suffix
37 Arrow Shirt rival
39 *West Side Story* building
40 Where Farsi is spoken
41 Devise, as an plot
46 *M*A*S*H* figures

48 Excessively affected
49 Ozzie Nelson's real first name
50 Stallone role
51 Distinct style
52 Word form for "father"

53 Fit for a king
57 Gossip queen Barrett
58 Crockpot concoction
59 "If __ a Hammer"
60 A whole bunch
61 Z, to a Brit

548   COUNTRY MUSIC by Ronnie K. Allen

ACROSS
1 Bunco
5 Killer whale
9 Supports
14 Yen
15 Plato's P's
16 Goosey
17 Mrs. David Copperfield
18 With 4 Down, *Evita* song
20 Athenian's enemy
22 Elev.
23 Airport info, initially
24 *Peer Gynt* composer
26 Unit of resistance
28 Words on a film script
31 Georgian and Siberian
36 "__ the body electric"
37 Senator Domenici
38 Struck a blow
39 PDQ, in the OR
40 Coast Guard equipment
41 Old-time tale

42 Singer Tennille
43 Wordsman Webster
44 Alma __
45 Goya or Dali
47 Comparison type
48 "Gimme __!" (start of a Rutgers cheer)
49 Nimble
51 Start of a JFK quote
54 Allow
56 Collide with, perhaps
60 With 27 Down, start of a pageant tune
63 Nastase of tennis
64 Diviner's deck
65 Where Juliet is the sun
66 Christmas candy
67 Moorehead of *Bewitched*
68 Actress Lee
69 Pub stock

DOWN
1 Pub stock
2 Trim photos

3 Taj Mahal site
4 See 18 Across
5 Decree
6 Alps-to-Arles river
7 Pro opposite
8 Hammett hound
9 Maternity stat
10 No matter which
11 Informal eatery
12 Scout creation
13 Vaccines
19 Less distant
21 Branch of math
25 Invasion site in 1983
27 See 60 Across
28 Pugilist's pair
29 Put __ to (halt)
30 Rigg or Ross
32 Salt Lake state
33 Cremona artisan
34 Rathbone colleague Bruce
35 Impolite look
37 Not so hot
40 Entraps
44 __ *18* (Uris novel)

46 Creeks' kin
47 Forty winks, in Juárez
50 Mill fodder
51 "__ girl!"
52 Salon cut
53 *Show Boat* composer

55 __ *Document* (Irving Wallace book)
57 Mideast airline
58 Largest digit
59 Ruby and Sandra
61 Caviar
62 __ de Cologne

SKIMMERS by Bob Lubbers

ACROSS
1 Jerry Herman musical
5 Aerie, e.g.
9 Ravioli or rigatoni
14 Turkey neighbor
15 Bradley or Khayyám
16 Time waster
17 Low-tech calculator
19 Stirs up
20 Threw
21 Line of cliffs
23 Mona __
26 Alamogordo events
29 Overlooks
33 Sonnet ender
34 Oklahoma! aunt
35 Double curves
37 Cell element
38 Exiled Ugandan
39 Aches
40 Boat-deck wood
41 Disencumber
42 Latin beat
43 Dignify
44 Builds
46 Ancient galleys
48 Short races
49 __ good example
50 Cares for deeply
52 Jeans measurement
57 Dudley or Mary Tyler
59 Seaboard
62 Colorado ski center
63 Norse god
64 Mesabi loads
65 Suppose
66 Shoe part
67 Church seats

DOWN
1 Haze
2 Woody's son
3 "__ oui!"
4 Finishes
5 Scandinavian
6 Winged walker
7 Gal of song
8 Very, in Versailles
9 Pittsburgh team
10 Worships
11 Propeller-created wind
12 __ Aviv
13 __ gratia artis (MGM motto)
18 Moray hunter
22 Checks out the joint
24 Filch
25 Helps
27 High-card combo
28 Wooden posts
29 Closed in on
30 New York city
31 Descent path
32 Author Deighton
36 Entrap
39 Outmoded
40 Italian trio
42 Spielberg et al.
43 Bestow
45 Household tasks
47 "__ Fair" (Don Cornell song)
51 Bargelike boat
53 Sty menu
54 Word on Irish currency
55 Over again
56 Disorder
57 GQ or YM
58 Buckeyes' campus: Abbr.
60 Lyric poem
61 Feel poorly

AUTO MOTIVE by Patrick Jordan

ACROSS
1 They're split for soup
5 Night on __ Mountain
9 Lost Horizon director
14 Small brook
15 Field of study
16 Lake containing Saginaw Bay
17 Beetle Bailey dog
18 He's glib with a fib
19 Oneness
20 START OF A QUIP
23 Earthquake
24 Raise one's hackles
25 Tofu ingredient
28 Make a misstep
29 Obliquely
33 FDR's coin
34 Subject of Montezuma
35 Matador's workplace
36 MIDDLE OF QUIP
41 Delon of Is Paris Burning?
42 Blueswoman Bonnie
43 Maintained, as a diary
44 Comet rival
46 Tattletale
49 Alley follower
50 Ventilate
51 One of the Judds
53 END OF QUIP
58 Duvalier's domain, once
60 Got bigger
61 Cutty __ (historic ship)
62 Propelled a lifeboat
63 Mean-tempered fellow
64 Vocal
65 "Near You," to Berle
66 Shows agreement
67 Nabors role

DOWN
1 Dancer Juliet
2 One or the other
3 Bright Northern star
4 One-armed bandit features
5 Healing ointment
6 Solo for Sills
7 Having little fat
8 Evolutionary theorist
9 Big, thick piece
10 Bee, to Opie
11 More puritanical
12 Baloney
13 Whatever amount
21 Wonder Woman, e.g.
22 Tatum or Buchwald
26 Science buff's magazine
27 Affirmative votes
30 Efrem, on 77 Sunset Strip
31 Do-over for Seles
32 Oak source
33 Mild expletive
34 Hard __ (slaving away)
35 Behaving
36 Kind of shark
37 Bogus butter
38 September birthstone
39 Plane regulating grp.
40 Objective
44 Power-drill accessory
45 The Beaver State
46 Prayer beads
47 Lacking ethics
48 Bell sound
50 Remark to the audience
52 Ancient fable spinner
54 Specific
55 Therefore
56 Geek
57 Fills with wonder
58 Highly popular
59 Expression of pleasure

551 MONDAY MORNING QUARTERBACK by Fred Piscop

ACROSS

1 Palindromic address
5 Dad
9 Fresh as a __
14 Bring to ruin
15 Smooth out
16 Word form for "straight"
17 Heed the drill sergeant
20 Do some tailoring
21 Samovars
22 "Common Sense" writer
23 Englander, for short
24 Arthur of tennis
25 Some college offerings
32 Senator Kefauver
33 German article
34 %: Abbr.
35 Slightly
36 Temporary trend
37 Sheet of ice
38 Dernier __ (latest fashion)
39 Raised platform
41 Tabriz native
42 Do a relay-race job
46 Choir voice
47 Evict
48 Ulan __
50 First-rate
51 Actress Charlotte
54 Creative logic
57 Bizarre
58 Bric-a-__
59 First name in fashion
60 Accumulate
61 Letter enc.
62 Like morning grass

DOWN

1 Command to a dog team
2 Heche or Rice
3 West of *Batman*
4 Floor-washing tool
5 Illinois city
6 "Let's go," in Rome
7 Cats and hamsters
8 Industrious insect
9 Former Winfrey rival
10 More bohemian
11 "Put __ writing!"
12 Blackjack dealer's device
13 Over there
18 Bailiwicks, slangily
19 Computer printer maker
23 Teaching deg.
24 Corrosive chemical
25 Fuzzy fruit
26 *Ad __ per aspera* (Kansas motto)
27 Wood coloring
28 Most insignificant
29 Egg-in-the-face sound
30 "Money-saving," in company names
31 Writer Gertrude
36 Inventory-control system, for short
37 College club
39 Actress Del Rio
40 TV workers' union
41 *The Wild Duck* dramatist
43 Receiving-department stamps
44 Uproars
45 Maria Shriver's mom
48 Oz creator
49 "__ boy!"
50 Gillette razor
51 Nettle
52 From square one
53 Like custard
54 Mauna __
55 Scale amts.
56 Flattened

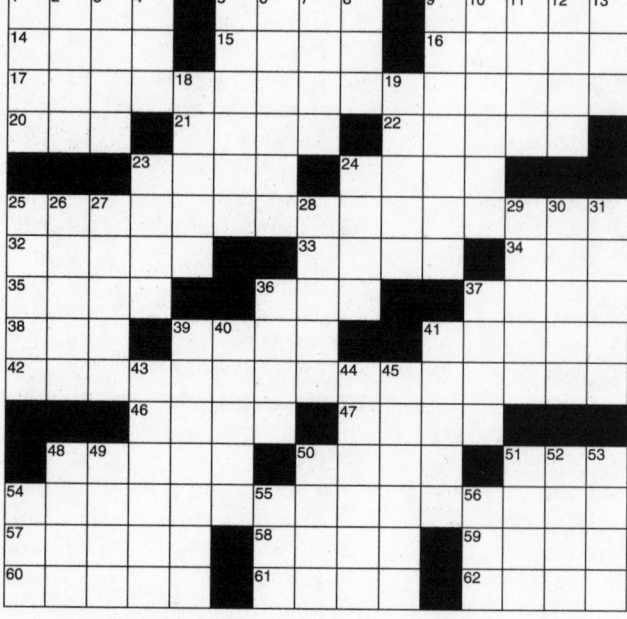

552 CALLING MRS. SPRAT by Lee Weaver

ACROSS

1 Rile up
6 Henhouse
10 Busy bug
13 Comic actor Dudley
14 Fellow who sells space
16 Coffee server
17 Vigorous effort
19 Blaster's initials
20 Capital of the Bahamas
21 Skilled person
23 Goofs up
25 Fit to __
26 Raincoat
29 Country-club fees
31 Like some wits or cheeses
33 Canyon sound
35 Risk taking, for short
37 Set in
39 Biblical queendom
41 100%
42 Like marsh plants
43 Chopped
44 Jacob's wife
46 Take risks
47 Scarecrow stuffing
49 Fly in the ointment
51 Calculator figs.
52 Pueblo Indian
53 Arizona river
55 Tames, as a bronc
58 Arm art
62 Lummox
63 Art-gallery hanging
65 Turkish official
66 Take five
67 Chair builder, i.e.
68 *Krazy* __
69 Steak order
70 Tape over

DOWN

1 Solemn response
2 Vincent Lopez theme
3 Oodles
4 Notched, as a leaf
5 Just deserts
6 Horseless carriage
7 Music halls
8 Bridge expert Sharif
9 Ziti and cannelloni
10 Vegetable variety
11 Sea bird
12 Suffix for differ
15 Nor's partner
18 Spiritual advisors
22 Like some stockings
24 Flower part
26 Interlock
27 __ and pains
28 Have a gabfest
30 Tennis star Monica
32 Peter, in Spain
34 Titania's husband
36 Trolley sound
38 Creates batik
40 Laptop accessory
45 Caribbean republic
48 More cunning
50 Quick look
54 Fragrant oil
55 Head-over-heels
56 Singer Fitzgerald
57 Practice punching
59 Ike Turner's ex
60 Small bills
61 Folklore villain
62 Acorn product
64 Tomahawk

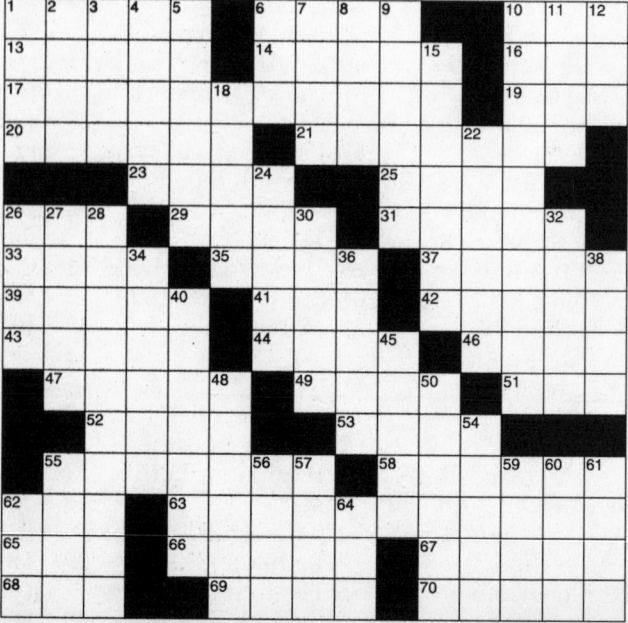

PAGE SETTINGS by Rich Norris

ACROSS

1 Mama of pop music
5 Old Testament bk.
9 Bird houses
14 Epps of *Scream 2*
15 Soft-drink choice
16 Violet lead-in
17 Settle one's bill
19 "__ de Lune"
20 1946 Derby winner
21 Costa del __
23 Cleaning cloth
24 Meadow musings
26 John or Ringo
28 Businessman's concern
33 First course, perhaps
34 Vote against
35 Hosp. employees
38 Architect's detail
39 Pilgrim of Plymouth
41 Car top
43 One __ customer
44 Call to Bo Peep
45 Stiller's mate
46 Marathon at Shea
50 What some scouts seek
53 Schedule opening
54 Three-time heavyweight champ
55 Sharp curve
57 Start of the day
62 Copycat
64 Short putt
66 Madonna role
67 Time past
68 Take a chance
69 Discourage
70 Wide-spouted pitcher
71 Like molasses

DOWN

1 "At the __" (Manilow tune)
2 Latin 101 word
3 Utters
4 *Mlle.*'s Spanish counterpart
5 Leopard's kin
6 Low point
7 In the style of
8 Touches gently
9 Central parts
10 Building addition
11 Square one
12 Court event
13 Certain noncom
18 Summer-forecast word
22 Med. specialty
25 Summer shoes
27 McArdle of *Annie*
28 Letter add-ons: Abbr.
29 Deeply engrossed
30 Butter substitute
31 False front
32 *Norma* __
36 Hope-Crosby title word
37 Upset (at)
39 Borders on
40 Testing site
42 A long way off
45 Montreal's railway
47 Garage capacity
48 Novelist Leonard
49 Dancer, slangily
50 Brought under control
51 Kicking partner
52 Restrict
56 Eye annoyance
58 Consents silently
59 Type of type: Abbr.
60 Evil emperor
61 Expanded
63 Meteor ender
65 Really impress

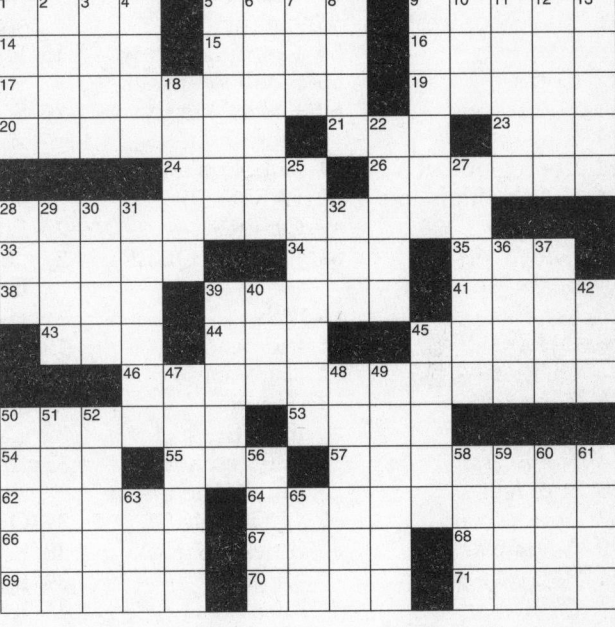

WORD OF MOUTH by Bob Lubbers

ACROSS

1 Biblical lawgiver
6 Choose
9 Recorded
14 Showy display
15 Average grade
16 Tune topic for 34 Across
17 Gives up
19 New Hampshire town
20 Proofreader's mark
21 Unconscious
22 Slept under canvas
23 Native New Zealander
25 California fort
26 Prattles
31 Where opinion is headed
33 One-liner
34 Singer Martin
35 "__ the ramparts . . ."
36 Hockey Hall-of-Famer
39 Light brown
41 French friend
42 Infield cover
44 Poetic adverb
46 Went wrong
48 Means a lot
52 Favorite
53 Low noble
54 Tams
57 Work unit
58 Otherwise
62 Sidestep
63 Gives a false alarm
65 __ *Without a Cause*
66 One-time link
67 Nasser's successor
68 Barter
69 Gym pad
70 Lots

DOWN

1 Jumble
2 One-__ (ball game)
3 Roy Rogers' real name
4 Big name in Rochester
5 Actor Erwin
6 Comes to mind
7 Heavy rainfall
8 Driving need
9 Bet coverers
10 Edited
11 Bard
12 Flying fish eater
13 Title
18 Cubby, e.g.
22 Pacific island group
24 Actor Ray
26 __ Haute, IN
27 Horse morsel
28 Closes in on
29 Identical
30 Oklahoma town
31 Tykes
32 Harvest
37 Takes five
38 Run up an engine
40 *Nautilus* captain
43 Covered a wall
45 Singer Flack
47 Contractual concern
49 Fish holder
50 Lasso
51 Prod
54 Homer's kid
55 Always
56 Musical McEntire
59 Vein bonanza
60 Cabbage creation
61 Newts
63 Machine part
64 Draft org.

555 WOMAN OF LETTERS by Henry Hook

ACROSS
1 START OF A QUERY
8 PART 2 OF QUERY
13 French comic character
14 Hawaii's main industry
16 Like __ of fresh air
17 Court
18 Points
19 Clever
21 Entanglement
22 Guido's high note
23 Square
25 Alley Oop's home
26 Knight spot?
28 PART 3 OF QUERY
31 Classify
33 Grave
34 Nellie et al.
36 Sore feet
37 Condescend
40 As long as
44 PART 4 OF QUERY
46 They get a paste in the mouth
47 Crying noise
48 007 foe
50 Two cents' worth
51 "__ my case!"
54 Heathrow initials, once
55 Round Table knight
56 Fawning fellow
58 Small knapsack
60 Egrets' kin live there
61 Rubber's need
62 PART 5 OF QUERY
63 END OF QUERY

DOWN
1 Rio beach
2 Leg bones
3 Gerunds, infinitives, etc.
4 Belligerent deity
5 Blue Eagle org.
6 "__ People" (Loesser tune)
7 "It don't mean __ . . ."
8 Seek to gain
9 Drones
10 Dr. Seuss' *If __ the Circus*
11 Partridge's relative
12 Third-party payments
14 Met on the sly
15 Financial windfall
20 Some boys of summer
23 *Dinner at Eight* star
24 Pitch
27 "Better is __ than break": Heywood
29 Notorious Henry
30 Rival of Ricki and Maury
32 Galley glitches
35 Apt to take a trip
37 Oriental pooch
38 Personally
39 Bread spread
41 African nation
42 "This Could Be the __ . . ."
43 A good person to know
44 Two-point basket, perhaps
45 Aeschylus output
49 Make a statue
52 Nose-in-air type
53 Pitchfork piece
55 __ one's toes (stay alert)
57 Part of BCE
59 H.S. subj.

556 PLAYING DIRTY by Fred Piscop

ACROSS
1 Mao __-tung
4 Hay units
9 Stick on
14 45 inches
15 Love, in Italy
16 Summa cum __
17 Intention
18 Composer Erik
19 Killer whales
20 Liven up the party, like a dirty baseball player?
23 It's divided by the Urals
24 Actor Liam
27 Go a few rounds
28 Hind part
31 Border
32 Period of history
35 Nasty
37 Wood-shop tool
38 Offer bargains, like a dirty hockey player?
41 Cockpit abbr.
43 Run away from
44 Poodle, e.g.
45 Arguable
47 Word form for "within"
49 Struggle for air
53 Go into a cocoon
55 Boxer Duran
58 Neaten the property, like a dirty football player?
61 Had one's say
63 Senator from North Carolina
64 Cent. parts
65 Computer-file acronym
66 Borden spokescow
67 Director Spike
68 Show as similar
69 Opt
70 Aurora's counterpart

DOWN
1 Picks on
2 Blow it
3 New York city
4 Army posts
5 Cremona violinmaker
6 Mandrake's partner
7 A Great Lake
8 Escape slowly
9 Unaccompanied
10 Mockeries
11 Purplish flowers
12 Wyo. neighbor
13 Failing-paper marks
21 Playwright Capek
22 Pro bono
25 Like an unmatched sock
26 Pince-__ glasses
29 Officiated at Shea
30 Sea: Fr.
33 WWII Brit. flyers
34 Out like a light
36 Cpl., e.g.
38 Faucet
39 Biddy
40 Provoked
41 Hi-fi component
42 Bud's buddy
46 *The Jazz Singer*, notably
48 Threat words
50 Sock style
51 Binaural
52 Sheriffs' helpers
54 Promotional link
56 Of a resistance unit
57 Surrounded
59 Amish pronoun
60 __ to pay (great trouble)
61 "My Gal __"
62 Air-pump letters

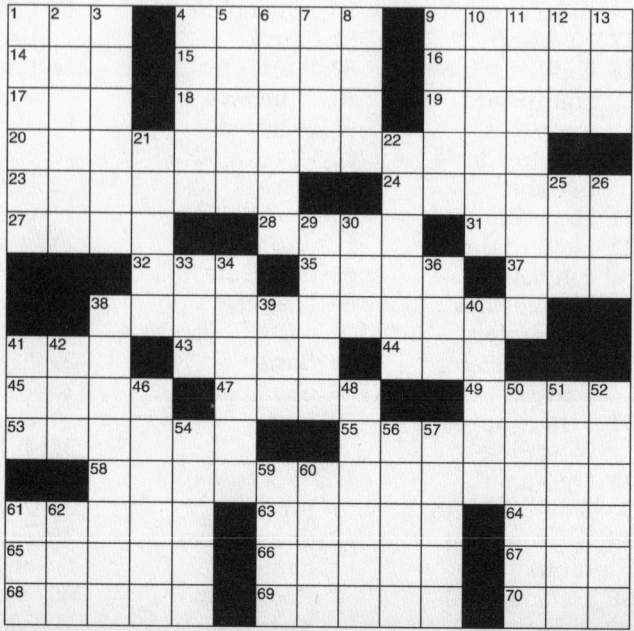

HIGHWAY ALERT by Bob Lubbers

ACROSS
1 Dispense
6 Not that
10 "__ the night before . . ."
14 Knight shirt?
15 "Stop!"
16 Chaplin's wife
17 Lunch-stop alert
19 Russian river
20 Rocks, in a bar
21 Air out
22 Most basic
24 Conveyed title
26 Actor Albert
28 Mideast airline
30 Free time
34 Tiff
37 1996 Tony-winning musical
39 Wander off
40 Bulls, in Barcelona
42 Get it
43 Actress Hasso
44 Northern islander
45 Croat foe
47 Profits
48 Garden bloomer
50 Id
52 Arkin and Alda
54 Daniel and Debby
58 National song
61 Cambridge prep
63 NY summer setting
64 Local knowledge
65 Brake alert
68 Thought
69 "Sorry!"
70 Spooky
71 __ off (angry)
72 Aerie
73 Gave medication

DOWN
1 Tasty
2 Cost
3 TV host
4 "Smoking or __?"
5 Nonsense
6 Comparative word
7 Mary and Gary
8 Seine sight
9 Unvarying
10 Maps alert
11 Eroded
12 Literary collections
13 Old sailor
18 Chest liner
23 Out of kilter
25 Traffic flow alert
27 Changes
29 Abate
31 Prod
32 Carry on
33 "The __ of Texas . . ."
34 RBI, e.g.
35 Gondolier's propeller
36 Zone
38 Born: Fr.
41 Evening wrap
46 Dizzy Gillespie's bag
49 Delilah's wooer
51 Wished (for)
53 Oozes
55 Approaches
56 Comic Murphy
57 Fiery horse
58 Landed
59 Ecliptic intersection
60 Elm or oak
62 Try out
66 First to get socked?
67 Classic Olds

BOND RALLY by Patrick Jordan

ACROSS
1 First Family, 1909-1913
6 Pianist Nat . . .
10 . . . and his genre
14 Remove the paint from
15 Large antelope
16 Subject matter
17 Sports site
18 Leaving stranded
20 "All-Time High" singer (*Octopussy*)
22 Autumn bloomer
23 Mongrel
24 Dishonorable one
27 Bovine gland
30 Lock up tight
32 Klinger portrayer
35 Theater sign
37 Plastic wrap brand
38 __ Bator, Mongolia
39 Memento from the past
41 BBQ option
42 Country star LeAnn
44 Prison division
45 Misplace
46 Striped equines
48 Disreputable
50 New Age musician Brian
51 "__ Clown"
53 Pete and Billy
56 "Licence to Kill" singer
60 The Stooges, e.g.
63 Islamic ruler
64 Lunchtime for some
65 Killer whale
66 "We're off __ the wizard . . ."
67 British boob
68 Like Felix Unger
69 Contest submission

DOWN
1 Bygone Russian despot
2 Places in the heart?
3 Acts the worrywart
4 "GoldenEye" singer
5 __ out (nodded off)
6 Crooner Perry
7 By mouth
8 Sheet music line
9 Mass emigration
10 Mrs. George Jetson
11 Jackie's second hubby
12 __ Buddhism
13 Sharp turn
19 Mythical meanies
21 Waiter's notation
24 Unusual item
25 Most Jordanians
26 Hard to penetrate
28 Corp. official
29 Makes angry
31 "Nobody Does It Better" singer (*The Spy Who Loved Me*)
32 Spiny evergreen shrub
33 Ewok or Klingon
34 Stallone tough guy
36 Scrabble piece
40 Salesperson
43 Luxurious fur
47 Add flavor to
49 Make a contribution
52 Regard lovingly
54 Discharge
55 Transparent, as hosiery
56 Well-behaved chap
57 Village People song
58 Serve as an usher
59 Deuce beater
60 Explosive letters
61 Question of procedure
62 King of France

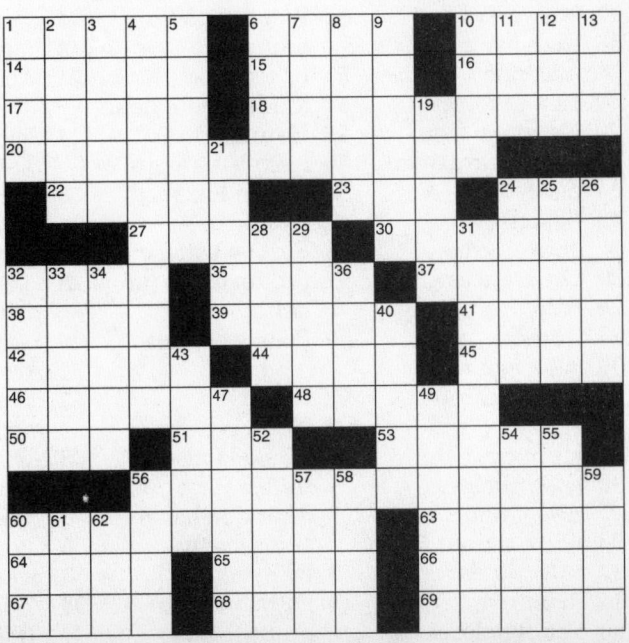

559 FLYING OFF by Norma Steinberg

ACROSS
1 Felix's roommate
6 Israeli leader
11 AMA members
14 Lasso
15 Came up
16 Nonetheless
17 Nursery rhyme bird?
19 Compass reading
20 Strong personalities
21 Seeing red
22 Simile center
23 Royal headgear
26 Composer Legrand
28 Stimpy's friend
29 Parts of a *casa*
33 Snakelike fish
34 Mellow
35 __ trap (dryer part)
36 Coral islands
39 First Christmas visitors
41 Concluded
43 Actress Gilbert
44 One-masted sailboat
46 Soprano Te Kanawa
47 One-liner
48 Couple's pronoun
49 Intuit
51 That's one for Pierre!
52 Miraculous site
55 Facet
57 Ump's call
58 "Quiet!"
60 1977 Richard Harris film
61 Homer Simpson's dad
62 Place to buy a bird?
67 Honorific for McCartney
68 Fielder's goof
69 Beef
70 Decimal system unit
71 Tori, on *90210*
72 Trimmed

DOWN
1 Yoko __
2 Sty female
3 N. Mex. neighbor
4 Out of kilter
5 Rules
6 Tatters
7 Form a parabola
8 Cannon sound
9 World religion
10 Less well-cared for
11 Several teams of birds?
12 Thick-headed
13 Bargain
18 Cash register key
23 Overfills
24 Royal
25 Deserving bird?
27 Hundred dollar bills
30 Golf course
31 Actress MacDowell
32 Demanding
37 100 centimes
38 *Full House* star
40 Promissory notes
42 Relieve of weaponry
45 Forced
50 Get away
52 Cook in the oven
53 Pianist Blake
54 Houston ballplayer
56 Peeled
59 Shofar
60 Gumbo vegetable
63 Director Howard
64 Frat house party container
65 First lady
66 Kennedy or Danson

560 AEROBICS CLASS by Lee Weaver

ACROSS
1 Moolah
5 Rose oil
10 "Don't change," to an editor
14 Be fond of
15 Paris river
16 Bishop of Rome
17 Norse god
18 Uses a fax machine
19 Actor Stoltz
20 Get-up-and-go
21 Final phase of an endeavor
23 Bakery enticements
25 Ore sources
26 AWOL student
28 Run-down
30 Knot again
31 Beat or throb
32 Krazy __
35 Hubbubs
36 Water holes
37 As __ as an owl
38 Week starter: Abbr.
39 Safe places for money
40 Hiding place
41 Louses up
42 Avoided
43 Crevice
45 Sandwich cookies
46 Advanced without going through progressive stages
49 1933 power org.
52 Woodworking tool
53 British peers
54 Made a statement
55 Hammer head
56 Recoils, as a horse
57 Queen Elizabeth's daughter
58 Furtive whisper
59 Producing foamy lather
60 Poems of praise

DOWN
1 Hoofbeat sound
2 White House staffer
3 Abandon hastily and secretly
4 Egg source
5 Distribute into groups
6 Abounds
7 Fork part
8 "No ifs, __, or buts"
9 Unceasingly active
10 __ Gonzales (cartoon character)
11 Nut cake
12 Heroic tales
13 Part of MIT
21 Put an edge on
22 Took the bus
24 Speaker's platform
26 Streetcar, in England
27 Decorate anew
28 Has a case of the pouts
29 House wings
31 Actor Sean
32 It holds the motorcycle up
33 Arthur of tennis
34 __ up (prepared a golf ball)
36 Diner worker
37 Brazos River city
39 Polish
40 Aided an actor
41 Feel contrite
42 Suitable for evening wear
43 Gives up, as territory
44 Emulates a couch potato
45 Gawks at
46 Reindeer herdsman
47 Honolulu's island
48 Grating
50 Climbing plant
51 Summer coolers
54 __ Paulo, Brazil

561   SAY IT WITH MUSIC by Rich Norris

ACROSS
1 Pencil puzzles
6 Deeply engrossed
10 Knee-ankle connector
14 Texas mission
15 Design using acid
16 Corrida competitor
17 Kidnapper's missive
19 Charitable offering
20 Dead heat
21 Abound (with)
22 Brief period of subpar performance
24 *Pygmalion* playwright
25 Hingis rival
26 Toyota model
29 Square dance parties
33 Parting word in Spain
34 Indians or Braves
35 Delta House, e.g.
36 Prevaricator
37 Signals a cab
38 Capital of Peru
39 Kitchen add-on
40 Possessive pronoun
41 Bottle size
42 Dramatic reorganizations
44 Least at risk
45 Choice word
46 *Of __ and Men*
47 Villain's plan
50 Polio vaccine discoverer
51 Historic period
54 Breakfast chain, familiarly
55 Meeting place for the unattached
58 Postal district
59 Arkin of *Chicago Hope*
60 Shouts
61 Water pitcher
62 Loose garment
63 Work hard

DOWN
1 Shopping area
2 Jai __
3 Western writer Grey
4 Printer's measures
5 Gives comfort to
6 Agree to more issues?
7 Tiny particle
8 Interest amt.
9 Statements accepted as fact
10 Bread
11 Ship's area
12 __ *la Douce*
13 Like a busybody
18 One of a daily trio
23 Hula hoops, for one
24 Ball game official
25 Hockey objectives
26 Narratives
27 Archie's spouse
28 Cowboy's rope
29 Will designees
30 Compose, as a letter
31 Identifies
32 Get going
34 Brownish gray
37 Helped out vacationing friends, say
41 Toadies
43 Shade tree
44 Place for a cooling pie
46 Molten rock
47 Shoe box word
48 Eats
49 Improve, as skills
50 Unforeseen problem
51 Competent
52 Festive affair
53 Once, once
56 Altar agreement
57 Alter, as a hem

562   RIGHT AT HOLMES by Patrick Jordan

ACROSS
1 Bambi, at first
5 Laundry
9 Cobra or copperhead
14 Garfield's nemesis
15 Vicinity
16 Gave comfort to
17 One of Judy's daughters
18 Persia, nowadays
19 Has a bawl
20 Sherlock Holmes accessory
23 Word before deck or dial
24 "You, over there!"
25 Flock females
26 Roofer's goo
27 Short Englishman?
28 SST or DC-10
31 Love, in Lyons
34 Ear-to-ear expression
35 It's played in chukkers
36 Sherlock Holmes accessory
39 Old Testament scribe
40 Limp as __ (flaccid)
41 Abbe and Nathan
42 Maiden name indicator
43 Literary figure
44 Affectedly modest
45 Cartoon collectibles
46 Collar type
47 Headed up
50 Sherlock Holmes accessory
54 LBJ, by birth
55 Inning sextet
56 James Bond's school
57 Licorice flavoring
58 Request for help
59 Barbershop call
60 More adorable
61 Pianist Hines
62 Prohibition supporters

DOWN
1 Pleats
2 "Toodle-oo, Toulouse!"
3 Shrink with age
4 Within reach
5 Eatery employee
6 Orderly grouping
7 Aquarium performer
8 Strong desire
9 Confidential matter
10 DEA officers
11 Largest continent
12 Stay fresh
13 Ames and Asner
21 Puppeteer Lewis
22 Hagman role, 1978-91
26 Albacore or bluefin
27 Director De Palma
28 Rivers or Lunden
29 End of a threat
30 Prepare the salad
31 Prayer finale
32 Hedge arrangement, perhaps
33 Foul-tempered fellow
34 Physics lab spinner
35 Stage production
37 Breaks down
38 Cheerlessness
43 *My Fair Lady* lyricist
44 Concerning a catalyst
45 Come to a halt
46 Alma __
47 Metric measure
48 Strong adhesive
49 Fender nicks
50 5 Down's offering
51 Sign over a theater door
52 Luau dance
53 Remain undecided
54 Tic-toe connection

563 SINGING THE BLUES by Richard Silvestri

ACROSS
1 Olympus Mons location
5 Take five
9 Intrinsically
14 Really big
15 Seaman's saint
16 Sweet sandwiches
17 Dog of moviedom
18 TV control
19 Island south of Sicily
20 Song from *The Music Man*?
23 Money player
24 Team transaction
25 Socialist council
28 Typical
32 Lockup
33 Stuffs to the gills
35 Kite type
36 Familiar sound
37 Ply
38 __-mutuel
39 "Hail!"
40 Cut into cubes
41 Swiss city
42 NHL MVP of '90 and '92
44 Completely calm
45 Cookout site
47 Tanner's tub
48 Petula Clark song?
55 Clipped
56 Leaning ltr.
57 "Send for Me" singer
58 Tout's tip
59 Scot's ancestor
60 George or Victoria
61 Ox harnesses
62 Art Deco name
63 Buckinghamshire school

DOWN
1 Headcheese, e.g.
2 Church recess
3 Rudner of comedy
4 Ticket offense
5 Much in demand
6 Newsman Abel
7 He was in C.O.N.T.R.O.L.
8 Stood
9 Hair ointments
10 Schwarzenegger persona
11 Depend
12 __ speak (as it were)
13 Biblical twin
21 Long haul
22 Swing to and fro
25 "Beat it!"
26 Antipasto morsel
27 Tarzan transport
29 Humble
30 Bridge name
31 Napoleon, notably
33 Burnt offering
34 Affirmative on board
37 Mislead
38 Little bit
40 Wiest and Feinstein
41 All in
43 Scattered
44 Gracefully slender
46 Beaver kin
48 Covered with soot
49 Half a train?
50 Part of NYC
51 Stop
52 Zoo trench
53 City on the Humboldt
54 Taken in

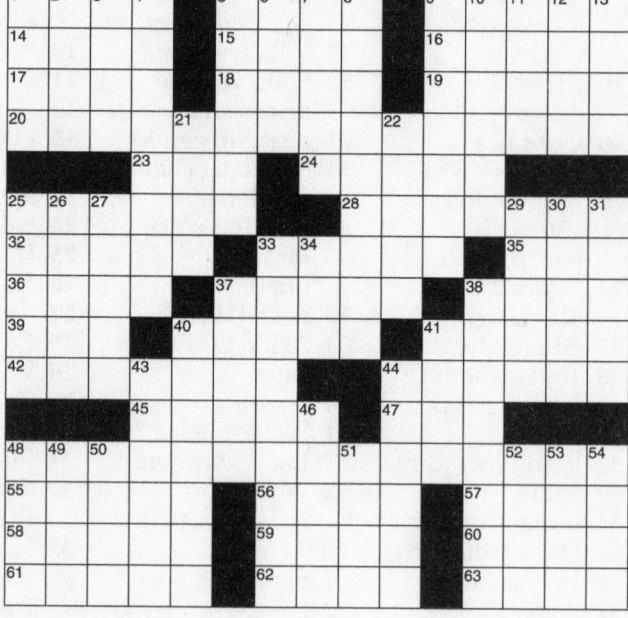

564 FILLING STATION by Frank Longo

ACROSS
1 Dog-collar attachment
6 Family-reunion attendee
11 Form-1040 sender
14 Sales goal
15 Pay for a seat, perhaps
16 Arthur of *The Golden Girls*
17 Sewing lines
18 See 34 Across
20 Seraglios
22 Impulse
23 See 34 Across
27 Word on a wanted poster
28 Come forth
29 See 34 Across
32 *Peter Pan* dog
33 Gathering
34 Theme of this puzzle
41 Arnold __ Schwarzenegger
42 Shipbuilding wood
43 See 34 Across
47 Limericks and sonnets
49 Nary a soul
50 See 34 Across
51 Of some organic compounds
52 Like brine
55 See 34 Across
57 Stallone role
62 WWII New Guinea supply base
63 He keeps things kosher
64 To no __ (useless)
65 Scrabble 3-pointers
66 Use a pencil end
67 Commandeer

DOWN
1 Mensa members' assets
2 Expected
3 *A View __ Kill*
4 S&L device
5 Uneconomical car, perhaps
6 Pola of the silents
7 Concerning
8 Dutch cheese
9 Speeder stoppers
10 Fleecy female
11 Two-nation peninsula
12 He defeated Dukakis
13 Least dangerous
19 Put to sleep
21 Pub potable
23 Tenant's payment
24 Eastern nanny
25 "I came," to Caesar
26 Turkey neighbor
27 Datebook abbr.
29 Golfer Els
30 "Here __ nothing!"
31 Gloomy guy
33 Sticky stuff
35 Strong wind
36 __-mo
37 Western Athletic Conference sch.
38 Regale
39 Actress Felicia
40 "The __ the limit!"
43 Make possible
44 Polite denial
45 Lightweight fabrics
46 Letter abbr.
47 Marker alternative
48 *Lakmé* and the like
50 Mischievous sprite
52 Walk of Fame sight
53 "Waterloo" singers
54 Arcing shots
56 Smeltery need
58 Latin salutation
59 __ tai
60 "That's show __!"
61 Corrida cheer

565 — IN THE NEWS by Rich Norris

ACROSS
1 Earnings
6 Former NYC mayor Ed
10 Drink samples
14 Novelist Brontë
15 Woody's son
16 Put on a tie
17 "The" is the only one
20 JFK arrival
21 Wipe the dishes
22 Causes consternation
23 Hit sign: Abbr.
24 Use a microwave
25 Cat burglar, perhaps
33 Senator Thurmond
34 British prep school
35 Pub pint
36 Hold forth
37 Be sociable
38 Long skirts
40 Public vehicle
41 Writer Morrison
42 Ram of the zodiac
43 Auto-assembly part
47 Bank acct. entry
48 Hood's gun
49 Eroded
53 Crucial
54 __ Schwarz (toy store)
57 Sharp reprimand
60 Caused to go
61 German article
62 Very angry
63 Ben & Jerry's competitor
64 Beef dish
65 Fall bloomer

DOWN
1 Takes a spouse
2 Iowa State University site
3 Birthday purchase
4 Actor Wallach
5 Predictable pattern
6 "K-K-K-__" (1918 song)
7 Mine find
8 Decked out
9 Earth/sky boundary
10 Barely sufficient
11 Ancient Peruvian
12 Roly-__
13 Fr. holy women
18 Press, as a shirt
19 Russian ruler until 1917
23 Dumbarton denizen
25 Pompous gait
26 Clear the board
27 Exorcist's quarry
28 Bite like a bee
29 Poisonous
30 Aphorism
31 Foreigner
32 *The Untouchables* hero
33 Cries openly
38 Kuala Lumpur's country
39 In __ (stuck)
41 Moves with stealth
44 Binding orders
45 Actress Russo
46 S-shaped molding
49 Church section
50 Even, scorewise
51 Counting-out starter
52 "Think nothing __!"
53 Was certain of
54 Binding order
55 Pay to play
56 River to the Baltic Sea
58 Washington's bill
59 __ *Doubtfire*

566 — MESSED-UP MENU by Fred Piscop

ACROSS
1 Walked nervously
6 Hood's knife
10 Big top
14 "It's __ country!"
15 Type size
16 Margarine
17 Sore loser's reaction
19 __ Bator
20 Calendar abbr.
21 Hit broadside
22 Sweet-tasting
24 Raring to go
26 Up to one's ears
28 Caress
29 Group of atoms
33 South Pacific republic
36 Way, way off
38 Trio trebled
39 Like some rural bridges
41 __ ceremony (was a stickler)
43 __ of Two Cities
44 Trumpet accessory
46 Hawaiian coffee center
47 In need of company
49 AT&T rival
51 Cohort of Doc
52 Tournament stage, for short
56 Music-score phrase
59 Caution sign
60 "Not __ bet!"
61 Mata __
62 Last ones in?
66 Sermon subject
67 Follow
68 Iroquois speakers
69 Rock star Jagger
70 Words of approximation
71 __-Coeur (French cathedral)

DOWN
1 Italian dish
2 Run __ of the law
3 Malevolent
4 Poetic adverb
5 Extent
6 Unwanted e-mail
7 Cheer starter
8 Road hazard
9 Feudal bondman
10 Tenacious one
11 Singer Fitzgerald
12 Within reach
13 Actor Curtis
18 Caner's material
23 __ HOOKS (sign on a crate)
25 Cause for crying, perhaps
26 Internists' org.
27 Most awful
30 Nullify
31 Trotsky of Russia
32 Sicilian volcano
33 Young stallion
34 Occupied with
35 Actress Harlow
37 __ fatale
40 Fable creator
42 Philadelphia school
45 Auto reversal, slangily
48 City north of Lisbon
50 Hags
53 Subject for Aristotle
54 Actress Stevens
55 Mosconi maneuver
56 "Beg pardon!"
57 "Rikki-Tikki-__"
58 Comic Idle
59 WWII town
63 Paddle
64 "My country, __ of thee..."
65 Time period

567 — CAESAR'S LAW by Bob Lubbers

ACROSS
1 Stair part
6 Gangster's gal
10 Spree
14 Wipe clean
15 Busy as __
16 Gen. Robert __
17 Discombob-ulating
19 Kelly or Tierney
20 Three __ match
21 Nastase of tennis
22 Use one's noodle
24 Tautened
26 Brief period
28 Lyric poems
30 Partied
34 GI offense
37 Singer McEntire
39 Banish
40 Turkic speaker
42 Flat fish
43 Where Basques live
44 Bishop's headdress
45 Ripening agent
47 Historical periods
48 Temporary fix
50 Raise (up)
52 Emits coherent light
54 Dudley Moore film
58 Bradbury beings
61 Head, in France
63 *A Chorus Line* finale
64 Hex
65 DC suburb
68 Aleutian island
69 Hebrides island
70 Greek writer
71 Olds oldies
72 Appear menacingly
73 British guns

DOWN
1 Transplant a seedling
2 Papas or Dunne
3 Transparent wrap
4 Sixth sense
5 Hinged (on)
6 Dress style
7 Theater awards
8 Author Deighton
9 Stowe villain
10 Trial commentator
11 Pub potations
12 Nevada city
13 Sharp
18 Church leader
23 Sprites
25 Pit of the stomach
27 Bedtime recitation
29 Mexican shawl
31 Truth-twister
32 Director Kazan
33 Family rooms
34 Dol. dispensers
35 Bide one's time
36 Palindromic name
38 Capture
41 Lear's daughter
46 Lasso
49 Set upon
51 Sports sites
53 Pool worker
55 Clydesdale, e.g.
56 Marriage
57 Harvests
58 Slightly open
59 Beer-label word
60 Division word
62 Test
66 Old card game
67 Investigator: Abbr.

568 — OPEN WIDE by Mark Ryder

ACROSS
1 Was first
4 Show host
9 Spoke
13 __ 18 (Uris novel)
14 Highways
15 Annapolis inst.
16 The modern DDS
19 Soda flavor
20 Attention-getter
21 War hero Murphy
22 Having lots of lots
24 Patrol-car attachments
25 Boil
28 The Bulldogs
29 Oil group
30 Walked purposefully
33 Federal purchasing org.
36 DDS's modern tools
39 Would-be lt.'s place
40 Foreign correspondent?
41 A tide
42 Chevron rival
43 Decathlon units
45 "Grin and __"
48 Risk runner
50 Baylor of basketball
51 Director Brooks
52 *The __* (TV action show)
56 Recent inventions for the DDS
59 Sampras of tennis
60 Colander kin
61 Fruity refreshers
62 Small bills
63 Sticks in the mud
64 Former Brit. money

DOWN
1 Fact fudger
2 Lamb's pen name
3 Historic harness-racing horse
4 Before, to Byron
5 Dayan of Israel
6 Looked a joint over
7 Oceanic whirlpool
8 Tip of a tongue?
9 A DDS may tie one on
10 Stage whisper
11 Against moral teachings
12 Sees socially
13 Info for an auto buyer: Abbr.
17 *Solidarnosc* name
18 Carpenter, often
23 Dangerfield's quest
24 Old West merchant
25 London section
26 Monumental
27 Lines of thought?
28 Luke's teacher
31 "A __ 'clock scholar"
32 Salesperson, for short
33 Secluded spot
34 Chair piece
35 African snakes
37 Short run
38 Of a Newtonian concept
42 Gets up
44 Meat treat
45 Italian clown
46 Actress Barkin
47 Playing marble
48 Shelve
49 Still in the game
51 Roman 1102
53 Odds' partners
54 Improved, as champagne
55 Submissions to an ed.
57 Doctrine
58 __ *Misérables*

ACROSS

1 Drip
5 "How unfortunate!"
9 *Carmen* composer
14 Surface measurement
15 Cut out
16 Serviceable
17 Tarzan's transport
18 One of the martial arts
19 Clergyman's quarters
20 START OF A QUIP
23 "Heavens!" to Heinrich
24 Shaft of light
25 Minimal
29 Bathday present?
31 Abundance
34 Gray and Moran
35 San __ Capistrano, CA
36 Guess
37 MIDDLE OF QUIP
40 Unspecified people
41 Light brown
42 Turns over soil
43 Barrie boy
44 "My Way" lyricist
45 Golfer Pavin et al.
46 Candle count
47 Quid pro __
48 END OF QUIP
57 Make amends
58 Scandal suffix
59 Seraph's circle
60 Public performance
61 With 62 Across, graduation hurdle
62 See 61 Across
63 Comes in third
64 Jackson 5's hometown
65 Salt source

DOWN

1 Internet programming language
2 Leif's father
3 City named for a Civil War general
4 Film critic Pauline
5 Hopeless
6 Get the joke
7 Military assistant
8 Walk through mud
9 Erroneous accusation
10 Land of pizzas and piazzas
11 Brass element
12 Klensch of CNN
13 *Saved by the Bell* cast member
21 Calf catcher
22 Turk's neighbor
25 Parker's music
26 Battlefield
27 Become ready to pick
28 Hazzard County deputy
29 Hindu aphorism
30 Pacific island
31 Outdoor wrap
32 Ahead of time
33 Bottomless pit
35 Flat fixer's tool
36 Disturbance
38 Taylor of *The Nanny*
39 Tolerated
44 Concurs
45 In an adorable way
46 Nixon's first veep
47 Mideast nation
48 Denies access to
49 Arches National Park state
50 Matador's foe
51 Highly excited
52 Michelle's rival
53 "May I say something?"
54 Nick-at-Nite sitcom
55 Vigorous spirit
56 Unspecified amount

ACROSS

1 Fencing swords
6 Lifting apparatus
11 JFK arrival
14 Europe's longest river
15 Actress MacDowell
16 Golf goal
17 Oomph
19 Wish one hadn't
20 Chair
21 Bran source
22 Fisherman's net
24 Becomes fatigued
28 Story credits
31 Whitewater carrier
32 Belt holders
33 Partly submerged
37 Marriage vow
38 Weigher's need
40 Victory sign
41 World traveler's need
44 Pacific, e.g.
46 Georgetown athlete
47 WWII vessels
49 Cooking liquid
53 Social misfits
54 Sound from Spot
55 K-P connection
59 Important time
60 Advice to one with a cold
64 104, to Caesar
65 Proverb
66 Statesman Stevenson
67 Crucial
68 Like lions and horses
69 Sneaks a look

DOWN

1 Holiday precursors
2 Mast
3 Where Napoleon was exiled
4 Self-gratifying activity
5 Observed
6 Bother continually
7 __ a customer (sale limit)
8 Actress Lupino
9 Lisa, to Bart
10 Starts a round
11 Parsley unit
12 Spa feature
13 Joyce Kilmer poem
18 No longer there
23 Young newts
25 Young'__ (kids)
26 River to the Caspian Sea
27 Narrative
28 Radar-screen image
29 Luke's teacher
30 Novelist Anita
33 Head cover
34 Part of the eye
35 Tidy
36 Griffey and Kesey
38 Kind of bean
39 Complainer
42 Tool building
43 1945 conference site
44 Kimono sash
45 Be in cahoots
47 Regained strength, with "up"
48 Fashionable Brit
49 Sweater style
50 Like a King novel
51 Open-sandwich topper
52 Jessica of *Tootsie*
56 1,760 yards
57 Minn. neighbor
58 Medical suffix
61 Cereal box abbr.
62 Writer Fleming
63 Once around the track

571 GENE KELLY FILMS by Bob Lubbers

ACROSS
1 Tra follower
5 __ Rabbit (Harris character)
9 Slack-jawed
14 Algerian port
15 Learning method
16 Mideast heights
17 Classic of '41
20 Dig in
21 Columnist Barrett
22 Grammar concerns
23 Filmmaking unit
24 __ Gotta Have It (Spike Lee film)
25 Female honorific
28 Fr. holy women
29 Sounds of understanding
32 Overact
33 Draft drink
34 Pitcher Hershiser
35 Classic of '43
38 Osiris' wife
39 Molecule component
40 Grazing land
41 Average grade
42 "... __ o'clock scholar"
43 Large eel
44 "How sweet __!"
45 Praise
46 "On the double!"
49 Smooch
50 Bandleader Brown
53 Classic of '52
56 Take the helm
57 Center
58 Poet Pound
59 __ Haute, IN
60 Meadow moms
61 Chick's sound

DOWN
1 Earring site
2 Zone
3 Endure
4 Strong insect
5 Shields who played Susan
6 TV honcho Arledge
7 Singer James
8 Boxing off.
9 Nods
10 Ball dresses
11 "Oh, my!"
12 Peel
13 Means justifiers
18 Constitution drafter
19 Different ones
23 Bye-byes
24 Fulton's propellant
25 Army corpsman
26 Entertain
27 The Many Loves of __ Gillis
28 Attach, as a button
29 Red-headed ape
30 Hesitate
31 Trickier
33 Computer storage units
34 Filmdom's first Charlie Chan
36 Parcel out carefully
37 Awaken
42 Garb
43 Processes a check
44 Actress Stevens
45 European quart
46 "Hey, you!"
47 Ceremony
48 Unique thing
49 Be sure of
50 Loll about
51 The Auld Sod
52 Gingery cookie
54 Drink cooler
55 10-percenter

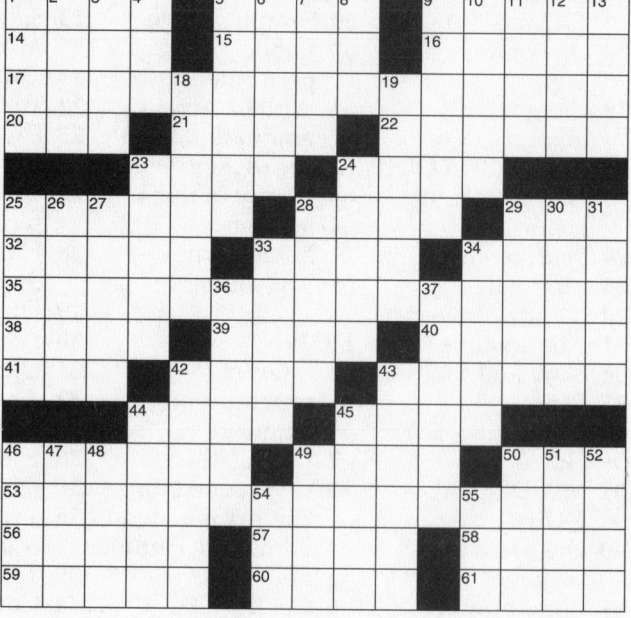

572 ONOMATOPOETIC by Patrick Jordan

ACROSS
1 Gelatin shaper
5 Vaccine developer Jonas
9 Reducing resort
12 Tommie of baseball
13 Inventor's inspiration
14 Sign up for more issues
16 Heightened enforcement
18 Put on cloud nine
19 Daytime drama
20 Left suddenly
22 Profound
24 "And giving __, up the chimney . . ."
25 Motown or Polygram
28 Storch's F Troop role
31 Boxing official
34 Lupino and Tarbell
35 '40s pinup queen Betty
36 Lumberman's need
37 Mover's truck
38 Portable music maker
39 Gerard of Buck Rogers
40 Urge, with "on"
41 United nations
42 Survey
43 Tierra __ Fuego
44 Property claims
45 Enjoys the evening meal
46 Wild way to run?
48 Crystal-ball gazer
50 Felix Unger's quality
54 Rental agreements
58 "Fame" singer Cara
59 Warhol, for one
61 Brutish
62 Wrinkle remover
63 Born Free heroine
64 Fireplace residue
65 Necessity
66 Unkempt sort

DOWN
1 PC alternatives
2 Fairy-tale baddie
3 Sitcom producer Norman
4 Makes a choice
5 Move like a crab
6 Toil and trouble
7 Improper, in a way
8 Citizen __
9 Red-flowered garden plant
10 Folk singer Seeger
11 Filled with reverence
14 Incorporate back into the city
15 Sesame Street cutie
17 Critic Pauline
21 Spain's king
23 Conditional release
25 Dwelt
26 Old saying
27 Asian nation
29 Street urchin
30 Mother superior
32 Force to leave
33 Topples
35 __ the wind (run quickly)
38 Hogwash
42 Seagoing thieves
45 Fawn or stag
47 In pristine condition
49 Spiral-horned antelope
50 "Proud Mary" singer Turner
51 Levin and Gershwin
52 Short drive
53 Miffed
55 Place to cool a pie
56 Exxon, formerly
57 Attempt
60 "The Tell-Tale Heart" author

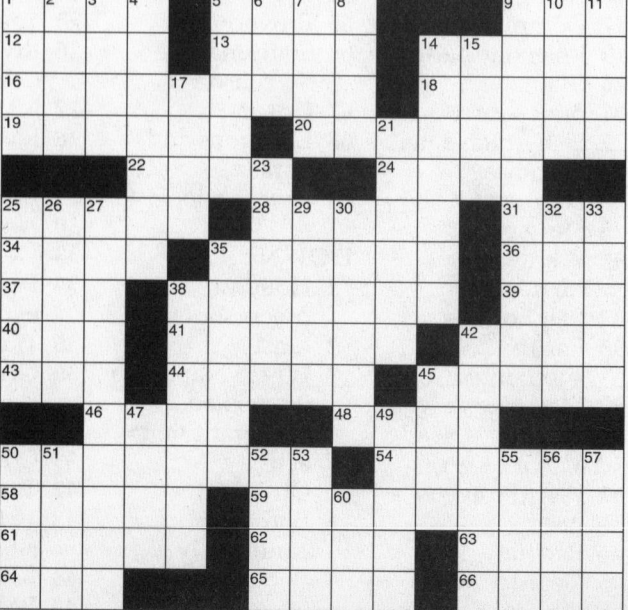

573 MONKEY BUSINESS by Ed Stein

ACROSS
1 More than miffed
6 Blueprint, briefly
10 "Having My Baby" singer
14 Comic modifier
15 It's often held at diners
16 December song
17 Monkey's favorite cookies?
20 Overpriced
21 Capital of Switzerland?
22 Awoke
23 When purchased alone
25 Heavenly strings
26 Lowbrow's love
29 Mustache application
30 Moore poem starter
34 S. Amer. nation
35 Drift
37 Main line of a sort
38 Simian singer?
41 Puccini pieces
42 Top-40 deejay
43 T, to the Trojans
44 Give a little
45 Wetland
46 Maximally mean
48 Scored the same
50 Parcel out
51 Cools one's heels
54 Frat's opp.
55 Part of IRA
59 Monkey author?
62 *Coffee, Tea, __?*
63 One on a one?
64 Pretext
65 Gould/Sutherland film of '74
66 Racer
67 Bruisers

DOWN
1 *The Prophet* author
2 Radar O'Reilly's favorite drink
3 Rum drink
4 Lots of lucre
5 Hoo preceder
6 Boffo hit
7 Butter bits
8 CBS logo
9 Tailbone
10 One who makes Daffy duck
11 Alaskan town
12 Held
13 As well
18 Rake
19 Hardy follower
24 Take the role of
25 "__ Theme" (*Doctor Zhivago* tune)
26 Skewered steak
27 "Why should __ . . ."
28 Shroud site
29 *Femme*, in Flatbush
31 Exhortation from home
32 Earth bearer
33 Port __ cheese
36 Defenseless
37 Word on a ticket
39 Life's downswings
40 "__ dull moment!"
45 Tell all
47 Nautical distance
49 Skater Midori
50 Kid's cry
51 Biblical prophet
52 Aberration
53 West Point footballers
54 Phaser setting
56 *Mary Poppins* song-title word
57 Objective, e.g.
58 Counterfeiter catchers
60 Brian of rock
61 "Disgusting!"

574 A+ by Frank Longo

ACROSS
1 Strikebreakers
6 Circle segments
10 Kukla and Ollie's pal
14 Like some pond growths
15 Trade
16 __ Nui (Easter Island)
17 *Cheers* waitress
18 Actress __ Flynn Boyle
19 Egyptian cobras
20 Everglades, e.g.
22 Basketball-tourney org.
23 Hourglass filler
24 *Silk Stalkings* actress Mitzi
26 Plunder
30 For men only
32 Corridors
33 Runway material
35 Former capital of Japan
37 Warship fleets
39 Musical gourds
44 Kuwaiti or Omani
46 A-flat, enharmonically
47 "That's __!" (director's cry)
51 Ago
53 Utah ski spot
54 Magna __
56 Its cap. is Raleigh
58 Author Janowitz
59 Indian Ocean republic
65 Hexagram
66 In the distance
67 Santa __, CA
68 *Betsy's Wedding* star
69 Granny
70 Jeweler's measure
71 Crate component
72 Run up __ (defer payment)
73 Graceful trumpeters

DOWN
1 Pouchlike parts
2 Talon
3 Taj Mahal locale
4 Soothing lotion
5 Insults
6 Sloping
7 Tanzanian's neighbor
8 Deuce or trey
9 Sudden burst
10 *Lingua* __ (common tongue)
11 Scalawag
12 Horrify
13 Some French speech sounds
21 Indian sailor
25 Overcooks
26 RR stop
27 Kids' card game
28 Phonograph part
29 ABC morning show, for short
31 School of whales
34 Modify
36 Disheveled
38 Maple fluid
40 "Eureka!"
41 Presidential nickname
42 Singer Garfunkel
43 Vacation spot
45 Head scarf
47 Assumes the role of
48 "__ it be?" (bartender's question)
49 Open shelter
50 Where the Ark debarked
52 Sacred Egyptian beetle
55 Maytag competitor
57 Lamb servings
60 ". . . to buy __ pig"
61 Cabbage salad
62 Darling: It.
63 Galway Bay island group
64 "Phooey!"

MIDAS TOUCH by Ronnie K. Allen

ACROSS
1 Finger jewelry
6 Fervent
10 Not this
14 Regional dialect
15 Actress Lollobrigida
16 Matinee idol
17 Fairy-tale trespasser
19 Racetrack fence
20 Shadings
21 More than bad
22 Biased nature
26 Kitchen gadget
27 Made things right
28 Theater district
30 Greek physician
31 Actress Streep
32 Dietary no-no, perhaps
35 Early automaker
36 Downfalls
37 Like a soufflé
38 Silent assent
39 Cools one's heels

40 Barbecue
41 Mrs. Marcos
43 Auto frontpiece
44 South African playwright Athol
46 Cad
47 Slant
48 Cry over __ milk
50 German port
51 James Bond foe
56 To be: Fr.
57 "When I was __ . . ."
58 "Take it easy!"
59 Take it easy
60 Small horse
61 Macho fellows

DOWN
1 Apparatus
2 Bachelor's last words
3 Zilch
4 Olympus figure
5 Infatuated
6 The __ and the Ecstasy
7 Bad habit

8 Printer's supplies
9 German article
10 Neck part
11 Deep-seated benevolence
12 Come about
13 Charlie Chan portrayer Sidney
18 Manor master
21 Water source
22 Have a __ (be drunk)
23 Author Calvino
24 Mercenaries of a sort
25 Change for a five
26 Gulf relatives
28 Oscar de la __
29 Angers
31 Young lady
33 Nimble
34 Mary __ Moore
36 Treadless, as tires
37 Moran of *Happy Days*
39 *The Way We __*

40 Savage
42 Croquet need
43 Tiger Woods' game
44 Charlatan
45 Come together
46 Hen
48 Unaccompanied

49 Make preparations
51 Breach
52 Maiden-name indicator
53 Jewel
54 Seeing organ
55 Turned tail

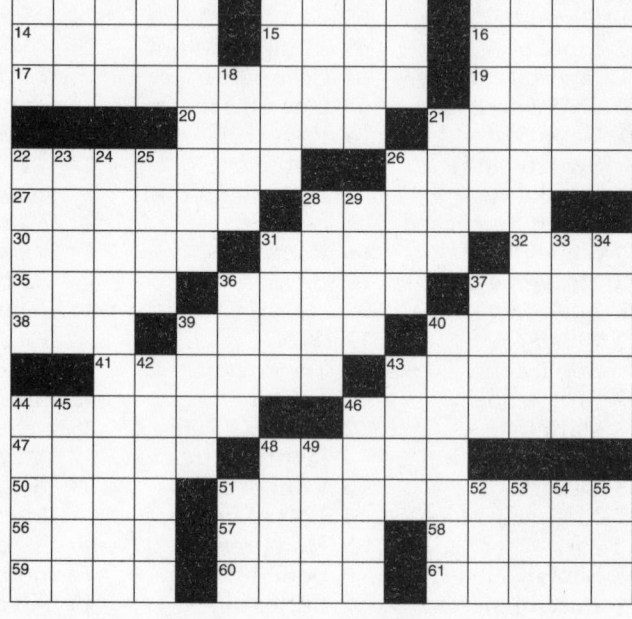

CUT IT OUT by Norma Steinberg

ACROSS
1 Former Iranian ruler
5 House animals
9 Book of the Bible
13 Drab
14 Gen. Robert __
15 Slumber
17 First name in jazz singing
18 Breadth
19 Loren's husband
20 Survey taker's aid
22 Magazine edition
23 Former gas brand
24 Slither
25 Israeli dance
28 Lots
30 Malayan mammals
32 Sound from the pasture
33 Nixon chief of staff
37 Genie's boss
39 Come out even

41 Pastrami source
42 Part of a min.
44 *Simpsons* voice Julie
45 Auto racing org.
48 Germ
49 Fashionably loose
51 Racetrack advisor
53 Mockery
54 Eating implement
59 Driver's reversal
60 Vatican's city
61 DC workplace safety monitors
62 Sci-fi character
63 Valhalla bigwig
64 Skip
65 Snoozes
66 Garden annoyance
67 Use a keyboard

DOWN
1 On __ (experimentally)
2 Corridor

3 "__ want is a room somewhere . . ."
4 Pile
5 Mexican money
6 Texas border town
7 British café
8 Drop in the mailbox
9 Have hopes
10 Narrow escape
11 On edge
12 Organize
16 Dessert choice
21 Chef James
24 Dagger partner
25 Healthy
26 Moonstone
27 Equestrian equipment
29 DMV datum
30 Smidgen
31 Actress Spacek
34 Mrs. Shakespeare
35 Frosted
36 Teut.
38 Vital: Abbr.

40 Stays to the end
43 Part of CRT
46 Spies
47 Apartment sharer
49 Twirler's stick
50 Curaçao's neighbor
52 Overturn

53 Animal hair
54 Boast (about)
55 Whistle sound
56 "The Lord __ shepherd . . ."
57 Poker token
58 Actress Jackson

577 $$$$ by Patrick Jordan

ACROSS

1 Seeger or Sampras
5 Wheat bundle
10 Herringlike fish
14 Chopped down
15 __, Dolly!
16 One-dimensional object
17 Delicious dish
19 "__ boy!"
20 Inventor Whitney
21 Sacred chests
22 Throat feature
24 Unruffled
26 Toadstools and truffles
27 Give new meaning to
30 Autumn chill
33 Pompous people
36 Hollywood Blvd. crosser
37 Taj Mahal site
38 Adams or Kennedy
39 Cobbler's replacements
40 Secluded valley
41 Field of expertise
42 Barely gets by
43 Ranks contestants
44 Highway: Abbr.
45 Laborious effort
47 Seaside cities
49 How Harpo performed
53 Hindu deity
55 Part of a process
57 Status __
58 Singer Paul
59 *The Good Earth* novelist
62 Use a swizzle stick
63 Emulated a siren
64 Expose
65 Sound quality
66 Soaps star Slezak
67 Gravity-powered toy

DOWN

1 Looks inferior by comparison
2 Banish
3 Lukewarm
4 Sullivan and Wynn
5 Had in common
6 Mild oath
7 Antlered animals
8 Pub order
9 Chinese cookie ingredients?
10 Street talk
11 *Billboard* list item
12 Member of the opposition
13 Monty Hall offering
18 British buddies
23 United
25 Gladiator's workplace
26 Least coarse
28 Calls forth
29 Office clerk, sometimes
31 Made angry
32 Reviews unfavorably
33 Slightly open
34 Prepare the laundry
35 Graduate's parchment
37 Ten-percenter
39 Turn 7 into 42
43 Bisque and borscht
45 Directional suffix
46 Ferdinand's wife
48 Chicago hub
50 Social peer
51 "Filthy" money
52 Like some oxen
53 Seemingly limitless
54 Division word
55 Ranee's wrap
56 Arduous journey
60 Pt. of EEC
61 Gun pellets

578 TONIGHT SHOW REUNION by Randolph Ross

ACROSS

1 Managed
4 Halloween choice
9 Poisonous crawlers
13 Busy as __
15 Spartan
16 ASAP, to an MD
17 Corn-meal concoction
19 Scope starter
20 TV listings
21 Theodore's nickname
23 Ate noisily
24 Fail to commit
25 Options between 45s and albums: Abbr.
26 Put one's faith in
29 Singh of the PGA
32 Distributed
33 *Star Trek: Deep Space Nine* character
34 Part of QED
35 Clinks
36 Romantic deity
37 Carefree
38 Sean and William
39 Alpine river
40 Including
42 Cabinet dept.
43 Skating feats
44 Puts in a chip
48 Generous offer
50 Up
51 RC rival
52 Noisy tool
54 Singer Jacques
55 Fred's sister
56 Disagreeable
57 French seas
58 Anniversary gift
59 Infiltrator

DOWN

1 Indian VIPs
2 Percolating
3 Indian VIP
4 Fragrant plants
5 Sped
6 Important times
7 Pose
8 Poe piece
9 "All the world's __ ..."
10 Dock worker
11 Colorless
12 Silver type: Abbr.
14 Beg for
18 Requiring a sweater
22 Correct copy
24 Gets better
26 Controls
27 Telltale sign
28 27 Down sensor
29 Star in Lyra
30 Some savings accts.
31 Careless pedestrian
32 Carvey and Delany
35 Makeshift drinking glass
36 Values highly
38 Appeal
39 Prefix for mural
41 Throws out
42 Creeps (along)
44 Place for a bracelet
45 Greek island
46 Exhaust
47 Matthew of *Friends*
48 Subject of SALT
49 Folk history
50 Italian dessert
53 Ruckus

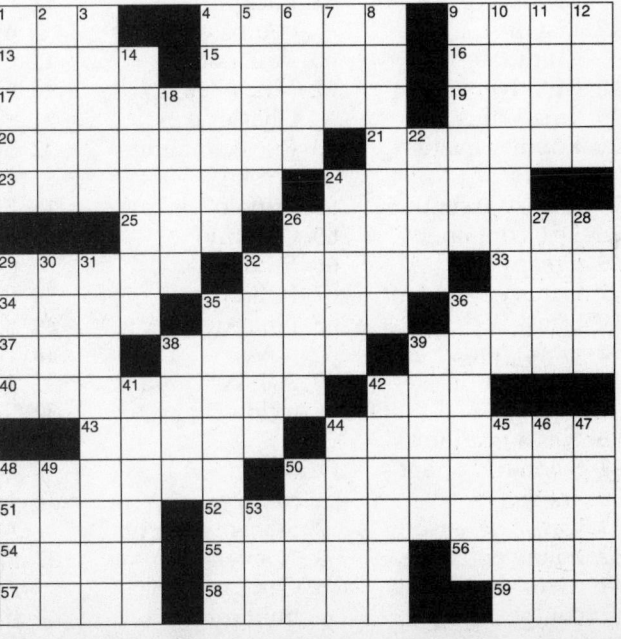

579 THE GAME'S AFOOT by Frank Longo

ACROSS
1 Routes
6 English novelist Barbara
9 Suit part
14 Hasbro rival
15 Actress Thompson
16 Native Alaskan
17 Type of carpentry joint
20 As well as
21 Apr. addressee
22 Worm-__ (rotten)
23 Watch junior
24 Director's cry
25 Swiss canton
26 Actor Vigoda
29 Business owner, perhaps
33 Prevent legally
34 An ex-Trump
35 "Very funny!"
38 Fishhook line
41 Saint Pierre and Miquelon
42 *Hee Haw* host
44 Bake uncovered
46 1982 Stevie Nicks tune
51 Teacher's deg.
52 __ Dawn Chong
53 Actress Scala
54 Fitting
56 Of __ (somewhat)
58 Allow
59 Contend
60 Have fun
64 Out in the open
65 Tripod support
66 *Adam Bede* novelist
67 Can't live without
68 __ Plaines, IL
69 Olympic logo

DOWN
1 Gyro shells
2 Handsome guy
3 Take care of
4 The Bard's witch
5 Floodgates
6 Torso-protecting armor
7 Hankering
8 Fabricated
9 Second-sequel tag
10 Lotion ingredient
11 Concerning newborns
12 Alphabetic trio
13 Sault __ Marie
18 Breaks out
19 Hoffman's girlfriend in *Tootsie*
27 Off-white
28 Precambrian and Paleozoic
30 Inclined
31 *Rigoletto*, for one
32 Lloyd Webber show
35 Putter's target
36 Bowled over
37 Aspirin target
39 *Daddy __* (Fred Astaire film)
40 Gentlemen's partners
43 Hides from view
45 Spread thickly
47 O.K. Corral name
48 Gave another account of
49 Collapse
50 Novel ending
55 Trial balloons
57 Hit the ice
60 Communist leader Béla
61 Suffix of imitiation
62 Formerly called
63 Actor Wallach

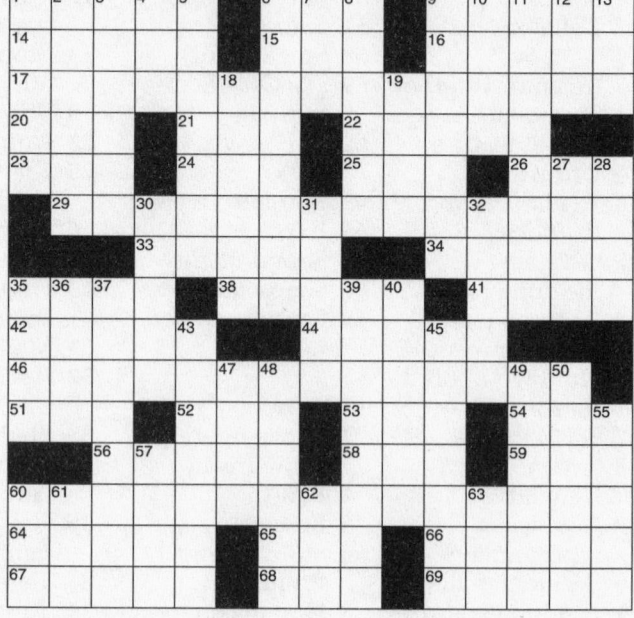

580 THERMOMETRY by Lee Weaver

ACROSS
1 Burn slightly
5 Skier's lift
9 Mimic
13 Baseballer Hank
15 Undercooked
16 Ingrid, in *Casablanca*
17 List of candidates
18 Mil. flyers
19 Small rugs
20 Popular Easter pastry
23 Slangy assent
24 Dye container
25 Creepy
27 Canary sound
30 Straw bed
32 Hang-glide
33 Trumpet or bugle
35 Has a need for
38 Salon treatment
39 Taters
41 Castle defense
42 Allow entrance
44 Med. student's course
45 Ages on end
46 Not up (to)
48 Noblemen
50 Compete in a bee
51 Fort __, CA
52 Sounds of contentment
53 Lacking compassion
60 Pull along
62 Mrs. Nick Charles
63 Rock containing crystal
64 Buffalo's lake
65 Gloomy
66 Eroded
67 Ration out
68 Jane Austen novel
69 Ash Wednesday follower

DOWN
1 Money
2 Symbol of virtue
3 "I smell __!"
4 Campus military org.
5 Have confidence
6 Deep voice
7 Fine horse
8 Gas up the car again
9 Get ready to fire
10 Stay aloof
11 Lauder of cosmetics
12 Coarse file
14 Novocaine target
21 Solemn words
22 Singer/actress Carter
26 Pipe cleaner
27 __ the line (conformed)
28 Jogger's outfit
29 Weasel type
30 Wrinkled fruit
31 Time __ half
32 Resort feature
34 Iridescent gem
36 Topeka's locale: Abbr.
37 Holy men: Abbr.
40 Cubic meter
43 Face-powder ingredient
47 Fair-haired person
49 Wise saying
50 Piece of the pie
51 Scarlett of Tara
52 "Pardon me!"
54 Weaving machine
55 Percussion instrument
56 Not imaginary
57 Carryall
58 Genesis garden site
59 Fender bender
61 Peggy or Spike

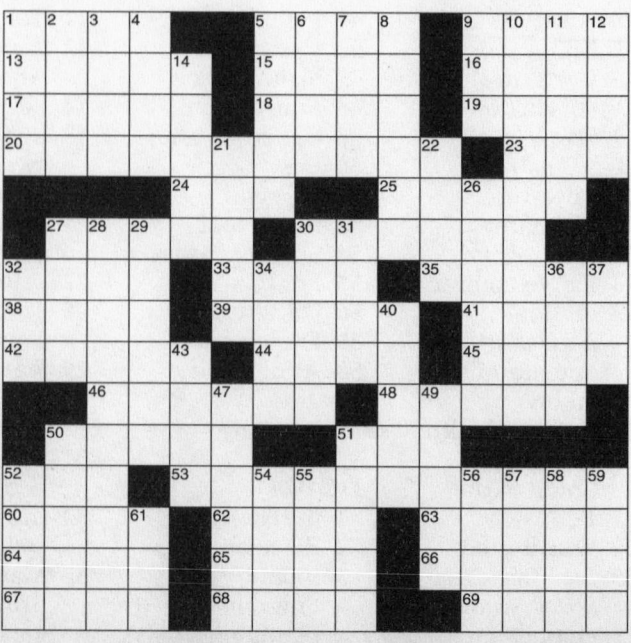

581 — BACK TO SCHOOL by Rich Norris

ACROSS
1 Cookbook meas.
4 Roof overhangs
9 Lhasa's land
14 Female sheep
15 Fissure
16 Frat quarters
17 Exactly what's expected
20 Poet Lazarus
21 Fragrance
22 Tombstone, Arizona's newspaper
26 Holy place
31 Fast flier: Abbr.
32 Unrefined one
34 Despotic ruler
35 Drummed out
37 New Haven collegians
38 Not relevant
42 Workweek-ending utterance
43 Form a queue
44 Make an accusation
47 Require
48 Rotation meas.
51 Derisive shouting
53 Accumulate
55 Medicine holder
57 James of jazz
58 Acted dignified
65 Safe place
66 Make it stick, so to speak
67 Actress Basinger
68 "My word!"
69 Flower part
70 USNA grad

DOWN
1 Conical homes
2 Everglades areas
3 Allow
4 Author Umberto
5 JFK posting
6 Large container
7 Sonic bounce
8 Timetables, briefly
9 Complex, as a predicament
10 Debtor's letters
11 Prickly seed casing
12 Sharp curve
13 Golf gadget
18 Lucrative, as a contract
19 Paint layer
23 Border (on)
24 Ritzy
25 Business-lunch locale
27 Move sneakily
28 After-bath application
29 Brigade
30 Ararat and Everest: Abbr.
33 Varnish ingredient
35 Put up for sale
36 Shore features
38 Look amorously at
39 Put in the archives
40 Borscht ingredient
41 Self-defense method
42 __ Mahal
45 Presumed truths
46 City near Tulsa
48 Shoot the scene again
49 Adds
50 Spurts of activity
52 Shows horror
54 Fam. member
56 Mythology, e.g.
58 "__ Loves You" (Beatles song)
59 Witch, to Shakespeare
60 Eggs
61 Unite in marriage
62 Swabber's need
63 One of the Gabors
64 Animation frame

582 — WING DING by Bob Lubbers

ACROSS
1 Hale or Alda
5 City near Sacramento
9 Farm unit
13 "Arrivederci __"
14 Golf club
15 Bar seat
16 Curved part of a lamp
18 Bagel centers
19 Marked down
20 Rise up
22 Not fem.
25 More ticked
28 Petty quarreler
32 Torrential downpour
33 Son of Jacob
34 __ over (studied)
36 Howard or Reagan
37 Meat cut
38 Jazz pianist Hampton __
39 Mini-play
40 Eng. network
41 Peach __ (dessert)
42 Baseball great Pee Wee
43 '40s actor Jack and kin
45 CARE and CORE
47 Sports centers
48 Greek letters
49 Group of nine
51 Elfin
56 Make amends
58 Keen of sight
61 More factual
62 Gen. Robert __
63 Francis or Murray
64 Vittles
65 __-do-well
66 Low in fat

DOWN
1 Jason's ship
2 Diving bird
3 Famous cookie baker
4 Shuttle group
5 One-dimensional
6 Mine find
7 Disney dwarf
8 Signs, as a contract
9 Musically keyless
10 Abruptly
11 Caviar
12 '97 PGA champ Ernie
15 Didn't hoard
17 Playwright Rice
21 Ocean movements
23 Part of a flower's calyx
24 Lever of a sort
26 Concern for self
27 Edouard's earnings
28 Pacific discoverer
29 Barometric line
30 Lose one's nerve
31 Barbie's boyfriend
35 Attain
38 German author Hermann
39 DC legislator
41 Nastier
42 WWII riveter
44 __ glory (elated)
46 Painter's tool
50 High-schooler
52 Blue shade
53 Actress Daly
54 Olin or Horne
55 Paradise
56 Chowed down
57 Song syllable
59 Pub serving
60 "Golly!"

583   TANDEM TV by Henry Hook

ACROSS
1 One way to run
4 Light-headed?
8 Polite word
12 __ the crack of dawn
14 Put your $.02 in
15 Spanish river
16 Sitcom combo?
19 Intricate interweaving
20 SWAT team accessory
21 Lead-in to swim or pink
24 Lexington sch.
25 Be teammates
28 Water plant
30 Eliot's Macavity, e.g.
33 *Sesame Street* meanie
34 Bit attachments
36 __ Jima
38 WWII western?
41 Schooner's cargo?
42 Get in touch, in a way
43 Served as a cobbler
44 Curvy shape
46 Organic compound
47 "Tough!"
48 "Just __ suspected!"
50 Violinist's accessory
52 Maxwell Smart's partner
56 So far
60 Newsmagazine show on the road?
63 Taj Mahal town
64 Additional
65 Opera star Lily
66 Catcalls
67 Finish third
68 San Diego attraction

DOWN
1 Move quickly
2 Whitish gem
3 Willing
4 An Algonquin wit, familiarly
5 Pick a target
6 Ltr. opener?
7 Germane
8 Measuring system
9 "Nine, ten, __ fat hen"
10 Part of WATS
11 Model Kate
13 Hack
14 *The Bells __ Mary's*
17 Wind-protected garden
18 Candied treat
22 Mark of *Chicago Hope*
23 Powell or Parker
25 *Your Show of Shows* regular
26 "__ Mio"
27 Heights
29 Singer MacKenzie
31 Supermarket section
32 Length of some dashes
35 Musicians' gathering
37 "Somebody bet __ bay"
39 JFK-LBJ time
40 Summarization
45 Seasonal store employees
49 Churchly *femme*: Abbr.
51 Get it all together?
52 League member
53 Aggressive
54 Prefix for dollars or bond
55 Congress of 1980
57 The gamut
58 "A __ 'clock scholar"
59 Former gas name
61 Taunting exclamation
62 Persian plaint

584   RE: PAST REPASTS by Patrick Jordan

ACROSS
1 Vise parts
5 Muckraker Michael
10 Go without grub
14 Author Hunter
15 Tax deadline month
16 Concerning
17 START OF A QUESTION
20 Vacationer's stopover
21 Absolute
22 Military opponent
23 Irregularly notched
25 __ *Got a Secret*
26 Diamond corner
28 PART 2 OF QUESTION
34 European isle
35 Adidas rival
36 "Honest" president
37 Feed the hogs
38 With correctness
40 Underworld river
41 Attention
42 Champagne bucket
43 __ majesty (high crime)
44 PART 3 OF QUESTION
48 Slot-machine features
49 Tissue layer
50 Stuck-up sorts
52 Wild West contest
55 Having hostilities
57 Bake sale grp.
60 END OF QUESTION
63 Hoover Dam's lake
64 Entangle
65 Hera's Roman counterpart
66 Is worth it
67 Fishing holes
68 Stair part

DOWN
1 Luke Skywalker, e.g.
2 Shakespeare's water
3 Town in Georgia
4 __-cone (summer treat)
5 Oscar-winner Tomei
6 Performed first
7 Shamu, for one
8 Omani money
9 Building extension
10 Obsequious one
11 Tennis great Arthur
12 Rose supporter
13 Luxurious
18 E.T.'s vehicle
19 Embankment
24 Harvest
25 Very dark
26 Surrounded
27 Islamic deity
29 Brief beginning?
30 It means nothing
31 Oceanic tornado
32 Deep-bottomed pit
33 Proverbial battlers
38 Troubled by dull pain
39 Cat or canary
40 Smeltery waste
42 Domed Nome home
45 Overturns
46 Toward the sky
47 Large fishing nets
51 Anger
52 Highway exit
53 Top draft ranking
54 6/6/44
55 __ time (never)
56 Compared to
58 Adjust the pitch
59 Perched upon
61 Recipe amt.
62 Record spinners, for short

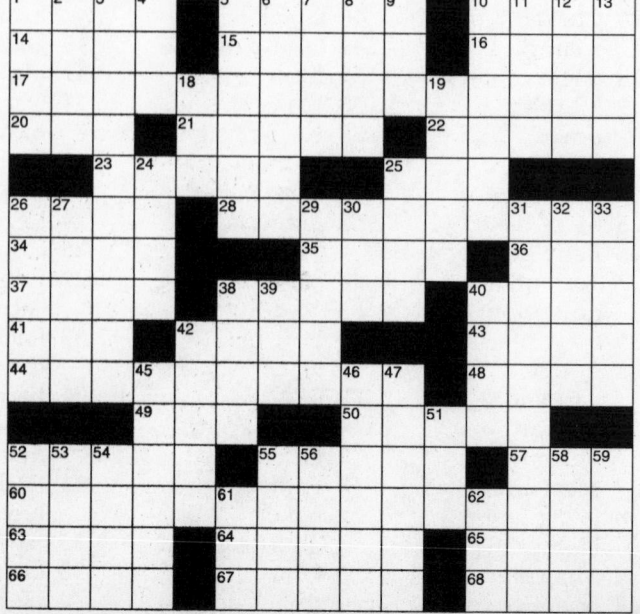

POET'S CORNER by S.E. Wilkinson

ACROSS

1 Profit's opposite
5 Indian prince
9 "Dagburnit!"
14 Foot fraction
15 High point
16 Burn __ in one's pocket
17 Close by
18 Fervor
19 Actress Winona
20 Butt in
22 Tree house
24 Word of wonder
25 Electrical units
27 Abode
29 Plan maker
32 "... blackbirds baked __"
35 Aloof
36 Handyman
39 Pea holders
40 Liq. ingredient
41 To no __ (useless)
42 Speck
43 Garish
45 Piquant
46 Give the once-over
47 Artificial
49 Idle
51 Silvers or Donahue
52 Plant pest
53 Car in a Beach Boys tune
55 Knell
57 Pay before a deal
61 Short summary, for short
63 Trout's breather
65 *Picnic* playwright
66 Accustom
67 Daredevil Knievel
68 Grinder
69 Sat (for)
70 Contradict
71 Revise

DOWN

1 Hookup
2 "Dedicated to the __ Love"
3 Strikebreaker
4 Dry (up)
5 Flashy display
6 Make like
7 Casual pants
8 Hot-rod rod
9 Singer Dolly
10 Timid
11 Mixture
12 Away from the wind
13 *The Way We __*
21 A Smothers brother
23 Vacillate
26 Valuable collection
28 Road guide
29 Weighing device
30 Use crayons
31 Sleight of hand
33 Darlings
34 Adlai's running mate
37 __ in "Able"
38 Illuminated
44 "Zip-A-Dee-Doo-__"
46 Of long standing
48 Overturned, with "over"
50 German article
52 Animated
53 Hold firmly
54 "A __'clock scholar"
56 Matured, as wine
58 Oklahoma city
59 Jamaican citrus fruit
60 Animal skin
62 "Who __ you kidding?"
64 Author Deighton

HOME SWEET HOME by Lee Weaver

ACROSS

1 Puts in stitches
5 Walking speed
9 Long-ago days
13 Chowder ingredient
14 Rolls up, as a flag
16 Turkish official
17 Norway's capital
18 Fabric
19 Opposed to
20 Goes for a stroll
22 Certain raffle reward
24 Greek cheese
26 Prepare to propose, perhaps
27 Soaring aloft
29 Ready for a nap
33 Worldwide workers' grp.
34 Ruffled feathers
37 Bring together
38 Pulls along behind
40 Carpenter's tool
42 Chew like a beaver
43 Fish holder
45 Wealthy one
47 Members of the AMA
48 Section of New York City
50 Trunks
52 Hanger-on
55 Feline remark
56 Nightclub entertainment
60 Prescription amounts
63 Humdinger
64 Boring tool
66 Asian cuisine
67 Help a felon
68 Flat and tasteless
69 Party giver
70 Beer barrels
71 Puts a stop to
72 Tapered sword

DOWN

1 Coal boat
2 Famous lioness
3 Shy person
4 Fire-prevention bear
5 Sgt.'s trainee
6 New Year's Eve word
7 Swindler
8 Rocker John
9 Throughout 2001, e.g.
10 Word form for "all"
11 "Puttin' on the __"
12 Buffalo's lake
15 Tear in little pieces
21 Mix the batter
23 Lima's country
25 Blue dye
27 Plant life
28 Secluded valley
30 Browse from outside
31 Telescope sights
32 Evergreens
33 Desire
35 Zsa Zsa's sister
36 Something owed
39 Causes for SRO signs
41 Weaver's tool
44 Sly look
46 Raised racehorses
49 Scenery around Taos
51 Apply balm to
53 Coal passage
54 Golf great Ben
56 Clamorous criticism
57 Auto-service job
58 Designer Cassini
59 Join, as metals
61 Smooth the way
62 Building location
65 Domicile: Abbr.

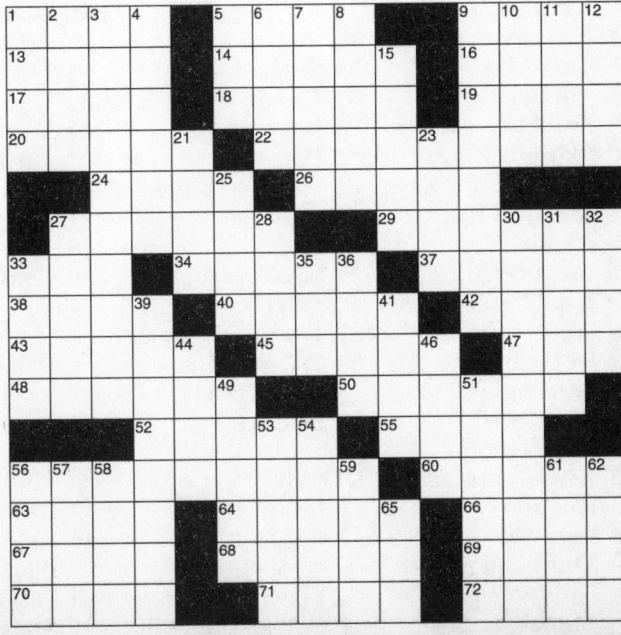

587 NATIONALISM by Fred Piscop

ACROSS
1 Long-tailed parrot
6 Guitarist Atkins
10 "Long, Long __"
13 Lower in prestige
14 Common Market prefix
15 Dry as dust
16 Ballroom dance
18 Church section
19 Villa d'__ (Italian landmark)
20 Congers
21 Ambitionless one
22 Spouse's assent
24 Altar words
25 *Medical Center* star
31 "Me too!"
35 Digs up
36 __ *Jury* (Spillane novel)
37 Bird-feeder filler
39 Two-dimensional measure
40 Most meager
42 Scornful look
43 Place for fine dishes
46 12-mo. periods
47 More easily understood
52 Pizza perimeter
55 Stable newborn
57 "Merry old" king of rhyme
58 Clinton cabinet member
59 Road-sign ad sponsor of yore
61 Getting __ years
62 "Right away" letters
63 Tiny openings
64 Favorite
65 Hair goos
66 *Cabaret* director Bob

DOWN
1 Pal, to a Britisher
2 Treat badly
3 Grocery-store vehicles
4 Popped the question
5 Like Willie Winkie
6 Et __ (and so forth)
7 Toss
8 Cupid, to the Greeks
9 Preschooler
10 Asian inland sea
11 United Way request
12 Frankfurt's river
15 From a tiny European nation
17 Slangy "sure!"
21 Flash of inspiration
23 Environmental prefix
24 Currier's partner
26 Because of
27 Come to a conclusion
28 Raison d'__
29 You, once
30 Pre-1917 autocrat
31 Phonograph record
32 Where to scratch
33 Bangkok resident
34 "Charge of the Light Brigade" poet
37 Parts of mins.
38 Immigrant's course: Abbr.
41 Small pie
42 Fr. holy woman
44 Rascals
45 Scat queen Fitzgerald
48 "Gesundheit!" preceder
49 Crowd noises
50 Santa's subordinates
51 Singer Della
52 Farm yield
53 Philosopher Descartes
54 Condo division
55 Weld
56 Spoken exam
59 Sack
60 Tanning-lotion letters

588 TREES COMPANY by Frank Longo

ACROSS
1 Grouch
5 Tarry
9 Did a service-station job
14 Gardener's need
15 Privy to
16 Make reparations
17 Not in operation
18 Tip or hip follower
19 Stubble remover
20 Skims quickly
23 Actor Chaney
24 Metal-in-the-rough
25 Bigger than med.
26 Air-gun ammo
29 Cop-film line
33 Obstinate equines
34 *Napoli* locale
35 *Return of the Jedi* creature
38 Excavate
40 Third-rail unit
41 Goldwyn or Morse
44 __ Dame
47 Beachwear
51 Break bread
52 Court instructor
53 Assistance
54 "__ the fields we go . . ."
56 Jackie Robinson's mentor
59 Single-file line
62 Not aweather
63 Soprano Ponselle
64 Software buyers
65 "Just the facts, __"
66 Saudi Arabia neighbor
67 Is a breadwinner
68 *The NeverEnding Story* author
69 Dazzles

DOWN
1 Refrigerate
2 Cowboy competitions
3 Like italics
4 Burrito filling
5 Cafés
6 Operating at a loss
7 No couch potato
8 Matriculate
9 Most massive
10 Provo's place
11 Dickens alias
12 Rock producer Brian
13 German article
21 Drenches
22 West Indies citrus fruit
26 Army machete
27 Recipe directive
28 RN's "at once!"
30 Loose rope fiber
31 *Of Thee __* (Gershwin musical)
32 Asylum
35 To be, to Caesar
36 Baba __ (Radner role)
37 Fail to name
39 Caught up, and then some
42 One of Victoria's titles
43 Milanese money
45 Ancient warship
46 Designer Gernreich
48 Generic
49 Indiana University locale
50 Playground fixture
55 __ *Hope* (soap opera)
56 Ruin the roast
57 Rob Roy led one
58 Boast
59 "__ Sera, Sera"
60 Cable network
61 Suffix with chariot

589 LA-LA LEADERS by A.J. Santora

ACROSS
1 At the drop of __
5 Tommy Chong's daughter
8 Smudges
13 Sonora sir
15 Rugged auto: Abbr.
16 Ship deck
17 Volatile liquid
18 Colbert role
20 Groom's reply
21 Knowing
23 Hellion
24 Frank Jr.'s sister
27 Chopper
28 Gibson, in *Lethal Weapon*
29 Spore sacs
31 Onetime Delhi queen
34 Pituitary hormone
36 Discernment
39 Fat substitute
41 Part of Kansas' motto
43 Former Japanese capital
44 In the pink?
46 Biblical twin
47 Bobbsey sister et al.
49 Do-nothing
51 Pack animal?
53 Like some nutrition
58 Conception
60 Alarm hearer
61 Jackie's second
62 Quadrilaterals
64 Bits
66 Stage area
67 Size abbr.
68 Levels off
69 Defensive effort
70 WWII craft
71 __ *plata* (Montana's motto)

DOWN
1 In __ (agitated)
2 Swiss miss
3 Composer Bruckner
4 High rock
5 Petty vehicle
6 Minimally
7 Shotput, for one
8 Jeweler's tool
9 Oman man
10 They're far out
11 Detergent ingredient
12 Outpouring
14 One of Lou Grant's reporters
19 Another: Sp.
22 George Burns trademark
25 Grain appendage
26 The Charles' dog
30 Barracks
31 Certain Asian soldier
32 __ Khan
33 Aquarium fish
35 Valuable property
37 This puzzle's theme
38 French water
40 Singer Braxton
42 Research
45 TV appearances
48 Hitch
50 Strange
51 Moreno and Rudner
52 Expert
54 Memorable bridge guarder
55 Western
56 Word form for "heavens"
57 Fraidy-cat
59 Elvis __ Presley
63 Connecting word
65 *Ab* __ (from the beginning)

---

590 THIS AND THAT by Fred Piscop

ACROSS
1 Highway exit
5 Sweeper
10 False witness
14 __'s Gold (Peter Fonda flick)
15 State Farm rival
16 Against: Pref.
17 Once in a while
19 Egyptian goddess
20 What George couldn't do
21 Be generous
23 Buck's mate
24 Expert
25 Barbecue receptacle
29 Jacques of French comedy
30 Billy __ Williams
33 Not as gregarious
34 Studied carefully, with "over"
35 Bran source
36 Safecracker
37 Latin dog
38 Downs of *20/20*
39 "__-di-dah!"
40 On a scale of one __
41 Name
42 Altar constellation
43 Play parts
44 He swears
45 __-Poo (*The Mikado* character)
47 Six-pack component
48 *Rabbit, Run* author
50 Handcuffed one
55 Scale notes
56 *I Ching* principles
58 Environmental subj.
59 Conjure up
60 Naldi of silents
61 Baseball's "Schoolboy"
62 Units of force
63 Lunkhead

DOWN
1 Litter's smallest
2 Sunburn soother
3 Whimper
4 Bell sound
5 Rotten bunch
6 Secure again
7 Will-__-wisp
8 Undivided
9 Court orders
10 Singer Frankie
11 Fine details
12 Keep __ (persevere)
13 Get up
18 Lowest point
22 *Metamorphosis* poet
24 County north of San Francisco
25 Safe havens
26 Gather some wool
27 Everywhere
28 Cribbage marker
29 Shadings
31 $10 gold piece
32 Old anesthetic
34 Actress LuPone
37 Out of whack
38 That man's
40 Army vehicle
41 In pitch
44 "Bette Davis Eyes" singer Kim
46 Supermarket division
47 Short-billed bird
48 Patron
49 Somewhat, in music
50 Ever and __
51 Lip-__ (mouth the words)
52 Donkey pin-on
53 Word form for "within"
54 Old oath
57 Climbing plant

AVENUES OF SUCCESS by Rich Norris

ACROSS
1 Ear part
5 Without equal
9 Valuable quality
14 Working hard
15 Not carefully considered
16 Blender setting
17 Former Iranian monarch
18 Bear up there
19 Photograph, for one
20 Educational TV show
23 Actress Dunne
24 Solves, in a way
28 Sharp curve
29 Melt
33 Fixes Junior's laces
34 Desert destination
36 One of the Brontës
37 Onetime comic strip
42 Antidrug cop
43 Musical paces
44 Novelist Leonard
47 Per __ (daily)
48 CIA forerunner
51 Quality-control personnel
53 Soak in the tub
55 1949 Joan Crawford film
59 Bizet creation
62 Singer Adams
63 Robin Cook bestseller
64 Former Knicks coach Pat
65 Ash Wednesday starts it
66 Panache
67 Athletic events
68 Vietnam neighbor
69 Reading rooms

DOWN
1 TV dog
2 Additional people
3 Prejudgments
4 Actor Hawke
5 Test answer
6 Galley propellers
7 "Hey, you!"
8 Archaeological fragment
9 Each
10 Aggregate
11 Madrid Mrs.
12 Brain scan: Abbr.
13 Golf gadget
21 Words of agreement
22 Suffix for mountain
25 Eat well
26 Start of a counting-out rhyme
27 Compass dir.
30 *2001* computer
31 __ were (so to speak)
32 Partner of dined
35 Eighteen-wheeler
37 Festive affair
38 Sleeve fillers
39 Having beaten the rap
40 Imitate
41 Backbreaking dance
42 Bottom line
45 Passes along
46 Baseball stat
48 *My Favorite Year* star
49 Tribal magician
50 Family cars
52 Get a whiff of
54 Took a circuitous path
56 Invention beginning
57 El __ (Pacific Ocean current)
58 Obtains
59 Assn.
60 Singer Zadora
61 Shade tree

KNOCKING AROUND by Frances Hansen

ACROSS
1 Break the rules
6 Overcook the meat
10 Svelte
14 *It Happened One Night* director
15 Zeus' consort
16 Toothpaste holder
17 Raps
20 Chest muscle, for short
21 Flying stinger
22 Guarantees a pension
23 Walk in water
24 Does a farm job
26 Peggy Lee song
29 County subdivision
33 Have __ with (know well)
34 Pianist Claudio
35 "All the Things You __"
36 Raps
40 Inhabitant: Suff.
41 Charge
42 Word form for "fire"
43 Riffraff
45 A real hound
47 Organic compound
48 Vaulter's aid
49 "__ woman never yields . . .": Stendhal
52 Cotton cloth
53 Go before the camera
56 Raps
60 Bathday cake
61 Bit of burlesque
62 Erin of *Happy Days*
63 Scot toppers
64 Consecrated
65 Noisy inhalation

DOWN
1 Initials on *Sputnik*
2 __ Krishna
3 Grist for DeMille
4 Give weapons to
5 Seat of the Kuomintang
6 Comic Chevy
7 Second Beatles film
8 Rainbow shape
9 Bowl yell
10 Accent
11 Big galoots
12 "Oh, sure!"
13 Military meal
18 Bubkes, in Barcelona
19 Broad way
23 Decrease
24 Lots of people
25 Man __ (racehorse)
26 Earvin Johnson's nickname
27 Baker or Bryant
28 Phileas Fogg portrayer
29 Vestige
30 '80s Secretary of State and kin
31 Actress Papas
32 Little bird
34 __ *of Divorcement* (Hepburn's first film)
37 Small piano
38 Woody's boy
39 Metalworker's aid
44 __ *Fables*
45 Broadway stinkeroo
46 Causes concern
48 High fidelity?
49 Rt.-hand person
50 "Hold it!"
51 Midmorning
52 Ex-Yankee Rizzuto
53 Flyer's word form
54 Movie mogul
55 Outdoor accommodation
57 Sibilant silencer
58 Ring decision
59 Long time

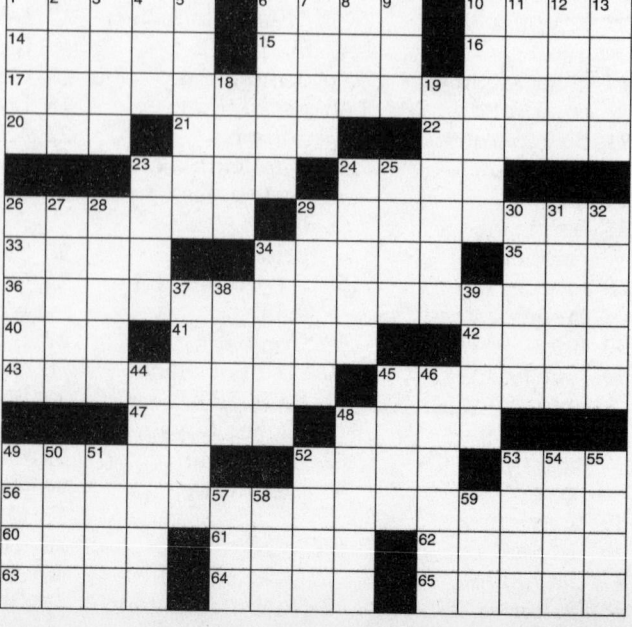

593 GNOME MAN'S LAND by Bob Lubbers

ACROSS
1 Mimicked
5 Jockey's persuader
9 Stage furnishing
13 Raised, as a flag
15 Bee haven
16 Olin or Horne
17 Stuffs
18 Teen ending
19 Yemen port
20 Creature gelling in Tolkien's head?
23 Building addition
24 "__ the ramparts . . ."
25 Artist Neiman
28 Vacillates
31 Transparency
33 Suffix of association
34 Feel under par
35 German name part
36 Meanie's crossing?
40 Former French coin
42 Shoe width
43 Opposition vote
44 Clothes, so to speak
47 Blocked
51 Swami, e.g.
52 Word of disapproval
53 X-ray relative
54 Otherworldly musicmakers?
59 Give off
61 Cloth: Fr.
62 Unbending
63 Mackerel shark
64 The Emerald Isle
65 Drum material
66 Social equal
67 Served perfectly
68 Gaelic

DOWN
1 Bends backward
2 Early release
3 Allow
4 Prefix for struck
5 Abrades
6 Severity
7 More than
8 Salon job
9 Sun orbiter
10 *Georgy Girl* actress
11 Single
12 Give a bad review to
14 Pressure meas.
21 Dried off
22 __ du Diable
26 Western Indian
27 Yearning
29 Title for Elton John
30 From __ Z
31 Tire filler
32 Eastwood's first name
34 Presidential nickname
36 Toll road
37 Brown or Aspin
38 "Night and __"
39 High-school class
40 Ordinal ending
41 "Sweetheart of Sigma __"
45 Newspaper executive
46 Part of WAAC
47 Lathered (up)
48 Vivid describer
49 Ford and Pyle
50 Waste time
52 Trumpet sound
55 "What's the big __?"
56 __ the Red
57 Gen. practitioners
58 Nip
59 Nero, for one: Abbr.
60 West or Murray

---

594 UNDER WRAPS by Frank Longo

ACROSS
1 Pulverize
5 Wingding
9 Footnote abbr.
13 Interests
15 "__ Mio"
16 Attacks, in a way
17 More lenient
18 Undisclosed plan
20 Pindaric poem
21 Tincture
22 Sporty scarfs
26 Here, to Henri
28 *The Addams Family* cousin
29 Opposite of post-
30 Mystery film of '97
35 Clothes-drying frame
36 Forty-niner's find
37 Ancient Greek region
38 Ad phrase
41 Teamwork deterrent
42 Conscription org.
43 Plane's place
44 Largest of the Finger Lakes
46 Driving-exam curve
48 Actress MacGraw
51 Noel Coward comedy
55 King David's father
58 Ever
59 Permit
60 Truman, to Roosevelt
61 Suite section
62 ". . . blackbirds baked in __"
63 Top-flight

DOWN
1 Stallone-esque
2 Plant pest
3 *The Maltese Falcon* sleuth
4 Buffalo bunch
5 Harmonize
6 Estimate
7 Actor's milieu
8 Table d'__
9 Stern with a bow
10 Go a few rounds
11 __ de France
12 Augsburg article
14 Ripen
15 Santa
19 Cager Archibald
23 Theorize
24 Mannerism
25 Actress Ward
26 *New Jack City* star
27 Wine-bottle accessory
28 Fateful March date
30 Feudal vassal
31 Incendiarism
32 Dandies
33 NYC subway
34 Certain conservative
35 Vigoda and Burrows
39 Morales of movies
40 Gist
45 Racetrack town
46 Believe without question
47 *Step by Step* actress Keanan
48 Dispatch boat
49 Slot-machine fruit
50 Rhone feeder
52 Anatomical ducts
53 Caustic compound
54 __ *Wonderful Life*
55 Shake up
56 "Xanadu" group, briefly
57 __-mo

595 GONE FISHIN' by Lee Weaver

ACROSS
1 Onetime Russian ruler
5 Vanquish
9 Yields, as territory
14 Gymnast Korbut
15 Seldom seen
16 Office-communication system
17 Caution
18 Comic Idle
19 Beatles' drummer
20 Deceptive selling method
23 Praiseful poem
24 Valuable quality
25 Frontier
30 Enjoy a favorite book
31 Unrefined metal
32 Wild guess
36 Itsy-bitsy
37 Health resort
38 New York city
39 Therefore
40 Middling grade
41 Stood on a soapbox

42 Water searcher's tool
44 "Shoo!"
47 French holy woman: Abbr.
48 Type of fire engine
54 Long poem division
55 One enjoying the sights
56 Hawaiian guitars, for short
58 Rap talk, i.e.
59 Opposed to
60 English county
61 Princess' headgear
62 Mexican coin
63 Whirlpool

DOWN
1 Travel with a trailer
2 Side of bacon
3 Taj Mahal site
4 Rajah's wife
5 Prepared veal, perhaps
6 Salary receiver

7 Like the Mojave
8 Investigators, slangily
9 Cherry red
10 Gives off
11 Tango or rumba
12 Octopus-leg count
13 School-zone sign
21 NBC morning show
22 Grow faint
25 Tavern fare
26 Portland's st.
27 Nevada city
28 Trots along easily
29 Lyricist Gershwin
30 Mailman's path: Abbr.
32 Milky Way part
33 Former Yugoslav leader
34 Passed easily
35 Awful
37 Work as a tailor
38 Tried to persuade
40 Deep sleep
41 A Great Lake

42 Great Plains Indian
43 Dots in the ocean
44 Puppeteer Lewis
45 Latin American line dance
46 Helicopter blade

49 One of the tides
50 Unit of force
51 British noble
52 Barely got by
53 Rip apart
54 House pet
57 Hog home

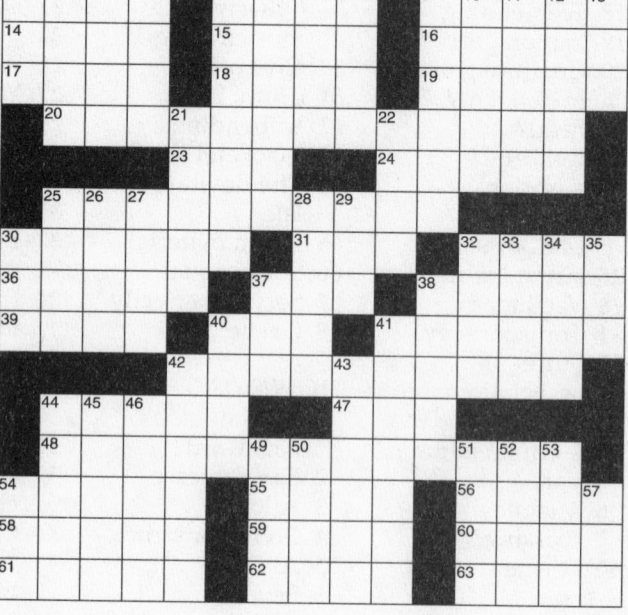

596 REPTILIAN by Rich Norris

ACROSS
1 Balsa vessels
6 La __ (Italian opera house)
11 Used to be
14 D-sharp equivalent
15 Biblical peak
16 Chemical ending
17 Paul Hogan role
20 Fraidy-cat
21 Rapunzel feature
22 Pop the question
24 Inventor Nikola
27 Italian wine region
28 Office furniture
31 Lawyers' grp.
33 Countdown starter
34 Bring into play
36 Gather together
38 Mottled inlay material
42 Some turns
43 Proclaim
45 Acorn source
48 RR stop
49 Brazilian dance

50 Unravel, as rope fiber
52 Walkway material
56 Sort of: Suff.
57 Savage
59 Round the bend too fast
62 Treacherous one
67 Have lunch
68 Societal no-no
69 Choir members
70 Literary monogram
71 Trap
72 Title documents

DOWN
1 VCR function: Abbr.
2 Continent south of Eur.
3 Attends in hordes
4 Tijuana treat
5 Put away
6 Talia of *Rocky*
7 Winter maladies
8 Exist
9 Took command of

10 Border (on)
11 Most sprawling
12 "__ Fideles"
13 Escorts
18 "Can't Help Lovin' __ Man"
19 Powerful D.C. lobby
22 Summer quaff
23 E-mailed
25 Unconvincing, as an excuse
26 Cause embarrassment to
29 Malden or Marx
30 Locations
32 Fireplace flakes
35 Storage areas
36 Beast of burden
37 Flu preventers
39 Type of type: Abbr.
40 Cover with clear plastic
41 Attorneys' degs.
44 Morse code sound
45 Compensate for

46 Playing fields
47 Jujitsu relative
51 Talk too much
53 Role player
54 Sierra Nevada resort lake
55 Poet's preposition

58 __ *Make a Deal*
60 "Zounds!"
61 Perry's creator
63 Scottish John
64 Hoop grp.
65 Turf
66 Former draft org.

597 BIG FOUR by H.R. Lyle

ACROSS
1 Select
5 Insertion mark
10 Man from Dundee
14 Eastern Indian
15 Worship
16 Big book
17 Vaudevillian
20 Unified
21 Ill humor
22 Public
23 Pine Tree State
25 Cupidity
27 Pure
29 Gwyneth's former beau
30 "__ bin ein Berliner"
33 Desi's daughter
34 Torments
35 Road-service agcy.
36 Rock group?
37 __ de menthe
38 Agitated state
39 Scale note
40 Irish county
41 Brit's filament
42 Supplement, with "out"
43 Tries to get elected
44 Noblemen
45 Kind
47 Moses' spy
48 Temporary currency
50 Stable fare
51 Do garden work
54 On a spree
58 Half of M.A.
59 Confused fight
60 Was imitative
61 Amusing Martha
62 Takes a look
63 Military meal

DOWN
1 Monterrey money
2 Mill material
3 Gossip-column subject
4 Beer barrel
5 Popular pet
6 Confuse
7 Took a bus
8 Period
9 Half a score
10 Canyon or Martin
11 Billing for a funnyman
12 Actor Sharif
13 Oasis abode
18 Have __ (nosh)
19 Fordham females
24 Without change
25 Wash problem
26 Appraise
27 Shut up
28 Impresario Sol
29 Max, Buddy and "Bugs"
31 Terrier type
32 Can't stand
34 Ad name
37 Whodunit board game
38 Progenitor
40 Moved slowly
41 Less than faithful
44 Soaks in the tub
46 Dishwasher cycle
47 Feed a party
48 Practice punching
49 Singer Irene
50 Impolite look
52 Is obligated to
53 Where hairs may split
55 Bad boy
56 Born: Fr.
57 Campbell's lid

598 STRIKE UP THE BANDS by Patrick Jordan

ACROSS
1 Quick kiss
5 Healing ointment
9 Peter I or Ivan IV
13 Land area
14 On the *Love Boat*, perhaps
15 Good, in Guadalajara
16 *The Jungle Book* beast
18 Idyllic places
19 Non-academic resident
20 Finds appalling
22 Miscalculates
24 __ d'oeuvres
25 It's set for supper
28 Marsh wader
31 "That's disgusting!"
34 Pitchers' stats
35 Carpentry activity
36 Dove call
37 Hole number?
38 Theme of this puzzle
39 Related group
40 Tidal reflux
41 Witchlike women
42 Hawaii's state bird
43 Pinkerton logo
44 Puts up drapes
45 Small cities
46 Santa's landing strip
48 Mitchell plantation
50 Waterloo loser
54 Foul-smelling
58 "Toodle-oo!" in Honolulu
59 Christmas-tree hanging
61 Bathroom-floor installer
62 Put on the payroll
63 Urges (on)
64 Go to __ (deteriorate)
65 Algerian seaport
66 Search for

DOWN
1 Bygone
2 Canyon phenomenon
3 Deck hands
4 Popcorn pieces
5 Cruller creator
6 Volcano spew
7 Principal role
8 Lion's crowning glory
9 Henry VIII's house
10 Suit fabric
11 Boleyn or Bancroft
12 Henry __ Perot
15 Is a member
17 The Emerald Isle
21 Gives a ring
23 Stone or Gless
25 Conical quarters
26 Sheikdom in an old song
27 Sidewalk symbol
29 Hagman's oilman
30 Most developed
32 On one's way
33 Sharpens
35 Fire upon from above
38 Well-educated person
42 Subtle distinctions
45 Sound like a jackass
47 Expressed delight
49 *Our Miss Brooks* star
50 Turner and Cole
51 "It's a Sin to Tell __"
52 *Siete* follower
53 Neet competitor
55 Nicolas of *Con Air*
56 *Bus Stop* playwright
57 Cubicle furnishing
60 New Deal agcy.

MIXED BREEDS by Cathy Millhauser

ACROSS
1 Chew the greenery
6 Lena of *Havana*
10 Almanac entry
14 Nimbi
15 Lawless role
16 Thumb-twiddling
17 Mixed breed on a spree?
20 Tent pole, e.g.
21 Sudden spate
22 Make stew
23 Borodin opera prince
25 Swift
26 Mixed breed at play?
31 Breathers
32 Columbus sch.
33 Bogus
37 Palindromic Ugandan name
38 Eddie Murphy rescuee in *Metro*
42 Italian author
43 Falafel holder
45 "Pshaw!"
46 "Big Three" conference site
48 Mixed breed in miniature?
52 Wandering
55 Velvety growth
56 Drives off
57 Cantina tidbit
59 Bond or mart start
63 Destructive mixed breed?
66 Ticklish Muppet
67 Treat with milk
68 Poet Doolittle
69 Visits
70 Like paraffin
71 Offspring

DOWN
1 Horror reaction
2 Rhine feeder
3 Slangy suffix
4 Getting a bug, maybe
5 Particularly brief?
6 Ventura County city
7 Endurance, so to speak
8 Creep (along)
9 Dundee denial
10 Richard Simmons' specialty
11 Oft-quoted saying
12 Informed, slangily
13 Towel material
18 Monopoly player's piece
19 Scruff
24 Deep cut
25 Self-pleased
26 Impertinent
27 German carmaker
28 Element
29 __ distance (last)
30 Film-box letters
34 Leadership, figuratively
35 Official proceedings
36 Lamentation
39 Mind
40 Got a load of
41 Peacock-feather features
44 Pertinent
47 As, in the lab
49 Like a no-brainer
50 Paid service
51 Ancient Syrian kingdom
52 *Angela's* __
53 Flaky rock
54 Melodic Mel
57 '97 Miss America __ Dawn Holland
58 Footballer Karras
60 Citrus fruit
61 Overhaul
62 Algerian port
64 Awe
65 Sounds of delight

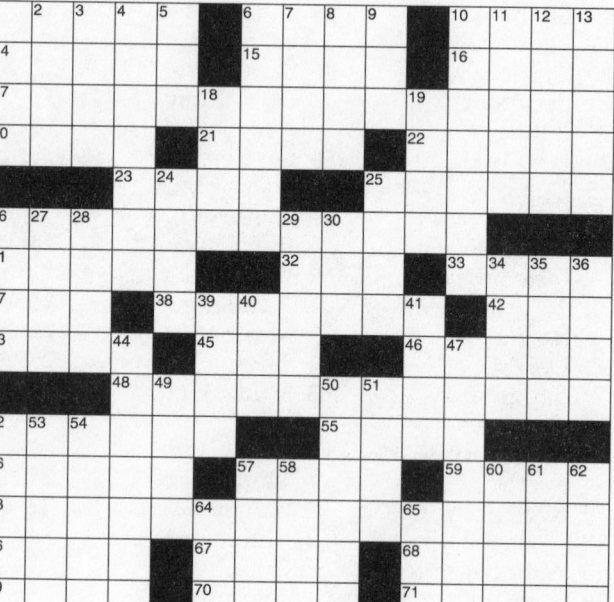

JOINT VENTURE by Mark Moldowsky

ACROSS
1 Misplace
5 Bound grain
10 Droops
14 Does not exist
15 Make fun of
16 Based on fact
17 Whip-cracking motion
20 Spinning toy
21 Carney and Linkletter
22 Moor
23 Shade trees
24 French cheese
26 WWII admiral
29 Lost consciousness
32 Concept
33 Flat-topped hill
34 Cambridge sch.
36 Type of holster
40 Male offspring
41 Space between rows
42 Peruvian Indian
43 Corner chesspieces
45 Openness
47 Animal's hide
48 Sugar source
49 A Musketeer
52 Forced under water
53 Tax expert: Abbr.
56 Be forthright
60 Recreation area
61 Speaker signal
62 Portal
63 Move from side to side
64 College officials
65 Semiprecious stone

DOWN
1 Elevate
2 Norwegian city
3 Insignificant one
4 And so forth: Abbr.
5 Tumultuous
6 Checks the weight
7 Has dinner
8 Fire remnant
9 Licensing charge
10 Paved road
11 Callas solo
12 Blast of wind
13 Clockmaker Thomas
18 Cabbage type
19 Complainer
23 Son of Isaac
24 Bask in the sun
25 Actress Moreno
26 Sound like a snake
27 Kind of committee
28 Hotel magnate Helmsley
29 Rolls up, as a banner
30 Edit
31 *Saturday Night Fever* setting
33 Attack from all sides
35 Onetime Russian ruler
37 Most recent
38 Pickling herb
39 Supreme Court quota
44 Scary
45 Poem parts
46 Egyptian cross
48 Curry ingredient
49 Vipers
50 Melt
51 Israeli dance
52 Soft drink
53 Chinese detective
54 Feel sorry for
55 Summit
57 Temporary fashion
58 Feel sorry about
59 Self

601 IRE EDUCATION by Richard Silvestri

ACROSS

1 Rum cake
5 Manager's special
9 Burns' "sweet" stream
14 Latin 101 word
15 Wicked
16 Newswoman Sawyer
17 Like an angry clockmaker?
19 Rhymester Nash
20 Yoko __
21 Narrow street
22 Get a lungful
23 Like skim milk
25 Turned on again
27 News clipping
29 Caller
33 Take a sip
36 Creative spark
38 Temporary superstar
39 Help in a heist
40 Put right
41 Steffi of tennis
42 Vegetable spread
43 Booty
44 Process ore
45 + & #
47 *Casa* room
49 Inventor Howe
51 Harass
55 __ Island, NY
58 In a bit
60 Log splitter
61 Eyelashes
62 Like an angry ironworker?
64 Rags-to-riches author
65 Designer von Furstenberg
66 Portend
67 All geared up
68 Show flexibility
69 Russian city

DOWN

1 Twirler's tool
2 __ acid (protein component)
3 Breakfast meat
4 Make inquiries
5 Composed
6 Stratford's river
7 Birdman of Alcatraz was one
8 Keebler worker
9 Hunk
10 Like an angry soldier?
11 Fake fanfare
12 "The __ lama . . ."
13 State bird of Hawaii
18 Delight
22 Homeric work
24 Like an angry escape artist?
26 Occurrences
28 Champagne cocktail
30 Ran fast
31 Face shape
32 Huge amount
33 New Mexico town
34 With skill
35 Have the looks of
37 __ *volente*
40 Bushed
44 Jargon
46 Infamous cow owner
48 Teem
50 NCO, familiarly
52 Swamp critter
53 Ooze out
54 Drive back
55 Lasting impression
56 Finish the bathroom
57 Aquatic plant
59 Marshal Kane's deadline
62 Fly catcher
63 Cable network

602 MEET THE BUMSTEADS by Fred Piscop

ACROSS

1 "Voilà!"
5 Hawaiian carving
9 Like many bleacherites
14 Frankenstein's assistant
15 Cassini of fashion
16 Actress Verdugo
17 BLONDIE
20 *Full Metal Jacket* setting
21 Follower of Lao-tzu
22 Ridiculous
26 "Smoking or __?"
27 Watch Junior
30 DAGWOOD
33 Fad disk
34 Pied Piper follower
35 Potato pancake
36 Sit-in participant
40 Word form for "eye"
43 Big goon
44 Bribe
47 COOKIE
52 Yodeler's perch
53 Took the reins
54 Bits of saber-rattling
55 Remove, as a splinter
58 Western treaty grp.
59 ALEXANDER
65 Ain't right?
66 Close at hand
67 Singer Adams
68 *Hollywood Squares* regular
69 Sporty cars of yore
70 Metric prefix

DOWN

1 Soft metal
2 Improve, as beef
3 Tony Blair's street
4 Indo-Europeans
5 *High __* (Anderson play)
6 Kind
7 Retained
8 Galápagos critter
9 Start anew, as a relationship
10 Priestly garb
11 Scrams
12 Bed-and-breakfast
13 Pop
18 Skip over
19 Time for lunch
22 Fuse word
23 __ Canals
24 Infamous emperor
25 Middle of QED
28 "That's gross!"
29 Everyday article
31 Prepare vegetables
32 Armed conflict
36 Arafat's org.
37 Ball game
38 Primer pooch
39 New Age musician John
40 Son-gun link
41 BTU relative
42 A whole bunch of
44 By the shore
45 Horse's tidbit
46 WWII boats
48 Appear to be
49 Shaping wood, in a way
50 Walked on
51 Brought up
56 Proceed along
57 The way out
59 Gal of song
60 Like some humor
61 Freudian topic
62 Some A.L. players
63 Diminutive suffix
64 Mauna __

603 RARE LETTER PAIR by A.J. Santora

ACROSS

1 Checked out
6 Sleep initials
9 NBA hoopster
14 Level
15 Jazzman Kid
16 Dress style
17 TV fare
19 Obligations
20 Clinton appointee
21 Discharge
22 Raring to go
23 Caviar pancakes
25 Hanoi observance
26 Risky baseball play
32 Sing like Bing
33 Foul callers
34 Spanish American
37 Apotheosis
41 Cease
42 Jeweler's weight
43 One liner of the past
48 Pull, as ropes
49 RNA component
50 Runner Rudolph
53 Med. course
54 Painter Chagall
58 More slippery
59 Iraqi foreign minister
61 Saudi VIP
62 Telecommuni-cations org.
63 __ Gay
64 Seabirds
65 These: Fr.
66 Summer Olympics competitor

DOWN

1 N followers
2 Epoxy
3 Reclined
4 Singer Stuarti
5 __ Moines, IA
6 Dorm sharer
7 Actor Stu and kin
8 Aura
9 __ Dog (Terhune book)
10 Hebrew letter
11 Give unsolicited advice
12 Dinner course
13 Furnace button
18 In custody
23 In pairs
24 Pump chamber
26 Coll. or acad.
27 Swiss canton
28 Showy yellow moths
29 Thicket
30 Of sagas
31 Founded: Abbr.
35 Not ritzy
36 Of interest to Wagner
38 Raw material
39 Ring pad
40 Numerical ending
43 Brunch selection
44 More quarrelsome
45 Woolly
46 Ill-fated flier
47 Pasta choice
48 Domino dance
51 Chow __
52 Cumbersome vehicles
54 "The __ Love"
55 Sea of __ (Black Sea arm)
56 Disturb
57 Commissioner's title, maybe
60 Proof letters

604 ALLEN'S ALLEY by Charles E. Gersch

ACROSS

1 Don't Drink __
9 __ New, Pussycat?
14 Frequent Allen costar
15 Asia Minor region
16 In an agitated way
17 Tim Conway sitcom
18 Supreme ruler: Abbr.
19 Word form for "lip"
20 Mideast country, to the French
21 Lucy's mate
23 Love and __
25 __ Mable (WWI humor book)
27 Drench
29 Cartoonist Chast
31 Keep, briefly
32 Brit. medals
34 Locale
35 Helping hand
36 The Purple Rose of __
37 Bit of hair cream
38 Hard candy, in Britain
40 Take the Money __ Run
41 Actor Neeson
43 One way to sit
44 SASE, e.g.
45 Trick ending
46 Yuletide trio
48 Swimmer Diana
50 Rockies resort
52 Old car
56 Tim of WKRP et al.
58 Disney dog
60 Tony-winner Hagen
61 "It's Not for Me "
62 1979 Allen film
64 "Have __ and safe holiday"
65 1978 Allen film
66 Less significant
67 __ Memories

DOWN

1 "__ Kangaroo Down, Sport"
2 Door fasteners
3 Salamander
4 Bemoan
5 Town in Colorado
6 Jeopardy! host
7 Town in Kentucky
8 Train syst.
9 Lean and mean, perhaps
10 Miser's cache
11 1977 Allen film
12 What's Up, __?
13 __ Paulo, Brazil
14 TV equine of yore
20 Photographed
22 "Is You __ Is You Ain't My Baby?"
24 Chicago paper
26 Whirlpool
28 "__ Mio"
30 1983 Allen film
32 Broadway __
33 Allen's onetime employer
34 Play It Again, __
36 French city
37 Radio __
39 Valhalla honcho
42 Gershwin and Levin
46 __ lot (mattered)
47 Hannah __ Sisters
49 Woody's frequent '70s costar
51 Factory
53 Traffic constituents
54 Sudden movement
55 Brinker of fiction
57 Coloring expert
59 Play area
61 Scot's topper
62 Mal- relative
63 God with a day named after him

605 MAKING UP by Rich Norris

ACROSS
1 Baseball, e.g.
6 Dripping sound
10 Bovine baby
14 Filmdom's Phileas Fogg
15 Took the bus
16 Fragrance
17 Cruise ship
19 In widespread use
20 Loud noise
21 Mouth-cooling treats
22 *Waiting for Lefty* playwright
23 Initially
26 Quarry material
29 "I cannot tell __"
30 Uncooked
31 Exxon's former name
33 Big name in small planes
37 Resting on
39 Family-room items
41 Snaillike
42 Fit in
45 Sched. entry
48 Primate
49 Remove, as an outer coating
51 Got there
53 Dessert topping
57 Rabbits' kin
58 Cable
59 Anjou or Bartlett
63 "My word!"
64 Louisiana city
66 Ballerina's attire
67 Make beer
68 Swashbuckling Flynn
69 Ooze
70 Throws in
71 Inexpensive cigar

DOWN
1 Stuck-up one
2 Type of type
3 Bakery fixture
4 Carter's successor
5 Cable home to *WWF Livewire*: Abbr.
6 Most expensive
7 Not the gregarious type
8 Ukrainian seaport
9 __ capita
10 Like cell phones
11 Parting word
12 Some artists' studios
13 Original
18 Picks up
22 Tony Award relative
24 Dead heat
25 RN's specialty
26 Take suddenly
27 Hourly wage
28 GI's offense
32 Eggs
34 Serb or Croat
35 Slangy refusal
36 Highly impressed
38 Appeared
40 Small songbirds
43 Short snoozes
44 College sr.'s test
46 Dress smartly
47 Singing syllable
50 Playwright Albee
52 Bring in from abroad
53 Makes sharper
54 Netherlands city, with "The"
55 Angry
56 Mentioned as a reference
60 Continental prefix
61 Frenzied
62 Bank (on)
64 Bus. school degree
65 Scale notes

606 RINGERS by Bob Lubbers

ACROSS
1 Ore. neighbor
6 Choreographer de Mille
11 WWII craft
14 Spanish province
15 Fortune-tellers
16 "Eureka!"
17 Hotel employee
19 Still
20 Marked with stripes
21 Certain
22 Swiss peak
25 Canoe propeller
26 Tunnel-building soldier
28 Tub toy
30 Gambles
33 Public transports
34 Bela of *Dracula*
36 Edmonton athlete
38 Romantic situation
43 Indian princess
44 Aviator Earhart
45 Beefy bovine
48 Science magazine
50 River blockers
51 Eye layer
53 Explorer Johnson
55 Christmas or New Year's
56 "I __ my wit's end!"
57 Proclaims loudly
61 __ Palmas, NM
62 '70s version of *Amateur Hour*
66 Summer, in Soissons
67 Allude (to)
68 Useful
69 Angler's need
70 Cosmetician Lauder
71 Curvy turns

DOWN
1 Taxi
2 St. crosser
3 __ *Abner*
4 Troubles
5 Ipso __
6 Hope (to)
7 __ load of (notice)
8 Tidy
9 Lake Indians
10 Employee's ID, often
11 Easy baskets
12 Actress North
13 Spuds
18 Fiery steed
21 Showed disdain toward
22 Qualified
23 Vulgarian
24 Geraldine or Patti
27 Off midships
29 Flood
31 Carved pole
32 Knight's title
35 Entrap
37 Connection
39 Zodiac sign
40 Happy
41 Peruvian capital
42 Not very challenging
45 Bluff climber
46 Salad ingredient
47 Wiped away
49 "__ Mr. Nice Guy!"
52 Sore spots
54 Debate
58 Took off
59 Writer James
60 JFK arrivals
62 Three: It.
63 Towel inscription
64 Bullfight cheer
65 Director Craven

607 UNDER PRESSURE by Brendan Emmett Quigley

ACROSS
1 Legal scholar
7 Mythical bird
10 Burn to a crisp
14 Popular record label
15 Yes: Fr.
16 Residence
17 Autumnal door decoration
19 Writer Hunter
20 Close fit
22 Half a dance name
25 6th-century date
26 Wood connector
27 Popular candy bar
32 Hitting the right notes
33 Reagan Secretary of State
34 Satire magazine
37 Kids' cereal
38 Fingerprint part
40 U2 lead singer
41 German article
42 *Grapes of Wrath* name
43 Inert gas

44 Puppy love, perhaps
47 Going on, to Sherlock
50 Ship's heading: Abbr.
51 DiCaprio, to pals
52 Side dish
57 RBI, e.g.
58 Dishes at an Egyptian restaurant
62 Author Morrison
63 Sorority letter
64 New Orleans school
65 State of irritation
66 Do better than
67 Linger

DOWN
1 __ alai
2 Decorative vase
3 Get free (of)
4 "__ bigger than a breadbox?"
5 With solemnity
6 Confuse
7 Carrot, for one

8 Couple's pronoun
9 Five, in France
10 Comic Marin
11 Float in the air
12 Dazzle
13 Extend, as a lease
18 In fashion
21 Ocean rescuers: Abbr.
22 20 fins
23 Painter Matisse
24 Invite to join
28 Nickname for a cowboy
29 '70s sitcom
30 '50s Mideast initials
31 Zip
34 Business biggie
35 Win by __
36 Hawaiian crooner
38 Despair
39 Harrison, in *Star Wars*
40 "It's freezing!"
42 Ballerina's leap
43 Gets the better of
44 Small bird

45 African antelopes
46 Makes into law
47 Aides: Abbr.
48 Thin mattress
49 Man from Muscat
53 Proof of purchase: Abbr.
54 Big Apple neighborhood
55 Funny comment
56 Oahu dance
59 For example
60 Rock producer Brian
61 Lott, for one: Abbr.

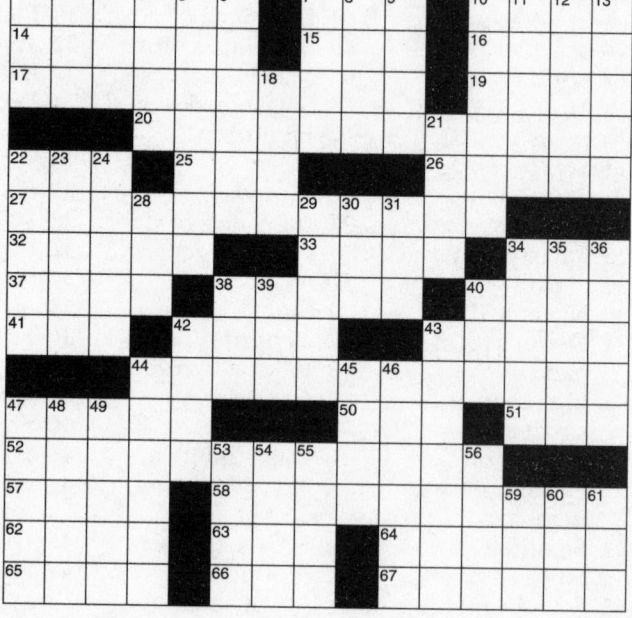

608 HIDDEN GREEKS by Bob Carroll

ACROSS
1 Director Brian De __
6 Is forced to
10 Cabbie
14 Eschewed restaurants
15 Terrier of '30s films
16 Meanie
17 Jargon
18 Pierre's place: Abbr.
19 Complain
20 *The Messiah*, e.g., on cassette
22 Diner delivery
23 Mode
24 Ding-a-__ (airhead)
26 Take potshots
29 "Shut up!"
33 Tel __
37 Vein contents
38 Sandwich extra
39 Trig ratio
40 Dressing type
42 Tied
43 Shoe piece
45 ". . . __ iron bars a cage"

46 Singer Sylvia
47 *Daily Planet* reporter
48 Lose one's cool
50 Loser of 1917
52 "Whole __ Love"
56 Workplace safety org.
59 Project's conclusion
63 Ishmael's superior
64 Arrow Shirt rival
65 Bushel fractions
66 Hard work
67 Painter Magritte
68 Onetime Eastern Indians
69 Seafood choice
70 It was west of Nod
71 NASA brake

DOWN
1 Ardor, in Tin Pan Alley
2 Mythical strongman
3 Tilted
4 Mork's mate

5 AL team
6 Sail support
7 Steak letters
8 Important commodity
9 George of *Star Trek*
10 Anaheim events for 5 Down
11 Eager
12 Rugged cliff
13 Collectible dolls
21 Poe's "rare and radiant maiden"
25 Sgt., e.g.
27 Tax-deferred nest egg
28 Reg. __ Dept. Agr.
30 The Midshipmen
31 Bit of gossip
32 An awful lot
33 Regarding
34 Stringed instrument
35 Rural stopovers
36 Squash, e.g.
38 Make ecstatic
41 Debate side
44 Young '__ (kids)
48 Cherished

49 Statue of Liberty's skin
51 Blazing
53 Yonder
54 Not spoken
55 Game-show host, at times
56 Dobbin's diet
57 "Get lost!"
58 Salute
60 "__ but the brave . . ."
61 Gulf east of the Sinai
62 Gulf Canada rival

609 CROSSING STATE LINES by Thomas W. Schier

ACROSS
1 Karate levels
5 Post-blizzard phenomenon
10 Say "*@&#!"
14 He played Obi-Wan
15 Antique-shop item
16 Resting on
17 State line
20 Engraving instruments
21 Son of Lancelot
22 Anomalistic
23 Next-to-last syllable
24 Dinghy thingie
26 Press on
29 Property encumbrance
31 "Naughty, naughty!"
32 River's beginning
35 Student stumper
37 State line
40 French commune
41 Explosive compound
42 "Attack, dog!"
43 Court statement
45 Help out a borrower
46 Where Mork and Mindy honeymooned
47 Attached, in biology
50 Syr. neighbor
52 Charm
54 Delicate hues
58 State line
60 Journalist Bernstein
61 __ Gay
62 Express copiously
63 Pants part
64 Tackled moguls
65 What a ring lacks

DOWN
1 Honoree's spot
2 Big time
3 State line
4 Burn, in a way
5 Fitzgerald forte
6 Hurler Tiant
7 Large server
8 Beleaguerment
9 Province of China
10 Unceremonious
11 State line
12 Carbonated drink
13 Miner's nail
18 Odysseus nemesis
19 Month after Av
23 Sheet fabric
24 Of the ear
25 "Child's play!"
27 Novelist Jaffe
28 "Where America's day begins"
30 Low point
33 Sheep shelter
34 North Carolina college
36 Pseudo
38 Unfit to eat
39 Somewhat antiquated
44 Architectural pier
48 Highest stages
49 Express appreciation to
51 Mushroom stem
52 Fro
53 Spirit
54 Carpet feature
55 Boarding sch.
56 Praise
57 Gown renters: Abbr.
59 "Li'l ol' me?"

610 WOODY by Norma Steinberg

ACROSS
1 South Sea island
5 Move smoothly
9 Support
14 Strong metal
15 Capital of Peru
16 Enthusiast
17 Point on some wire
18 Hertz rival
19 Tolerate
20 Kvell
23 Committed perjury
24 Author Deighton
25 Attitude
27 Legume
29 Wet earth
32 Works for
33 Conduit
34 Short skirt
35 Be scientific
38 Use a keyboard
39 Chorus voice
40 Ira Gershwin creation
41 "We __ not amused!"
42 Important
43 Actor Willem
44 Fidel's friend
46 Beach toy
47 Organizational offshoot
53 General Powell
54 Sleep like __
55 Prepare a present
57 Together (with)
58 Exist
59 Exxon, once
60 Sill
61 Impolite look
62 Sound hoarse

DOWN
1 Lobster eater's wear
2 Bedouin
3 Folk knowledge
4 Counterpoised
5 Damaged
6 Fit to be tied
7 Skip
8 Launder
9 Sound of trumpets
10 Comic Williams
11 Enthusiastic
12 Yield
13 Before, to a poet
21 Capital of Belarus
22 Dish
25 Half man, half goat
26 Nonsense
27 Glazier's need
28 Resound
29 Word form for "small"
30 Cut free from bonds
31 Round object
32 "¿Cómo __ usted?"
33 Mete (out)
34 It landed at Plymouth
36 Occupied
37 Knack
43 Cloak and __
44 Adhere closely
45 Depend (on)
46 Establish as fact
47 Only
48 Trudge
49 Like some tales
50 Nobelist Wiesel
51 Celestial bear
52 Quarterback's option
53 It's south of Ore.
56 How the weasel goes

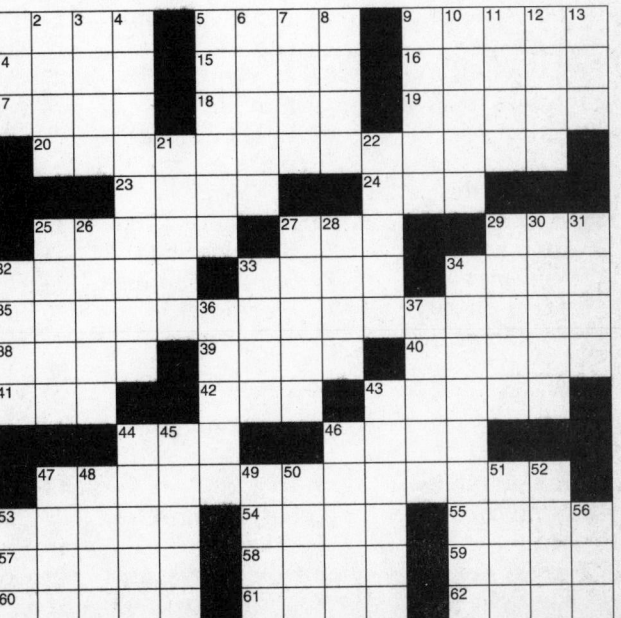

611 GETTING THERE by Rich Norris

ACROSS
1 Glow
5 Metabolism descriptor
10 Walking stick
14 Grouch
15 "__ Entertain You"
16 Some time ago
17 Financial independence, so to speak
19 Banquet, e.g.
20 Reduce drastically, as prices
21 Blocking progress
23 Plastic wrap
26 Actor Mineo
27 Commercially popular
30 That girl
31 Gives an autograph
35 News org.
36 Sgt., for one
38 Home entertainment purchase
39 Politically moderate
43 Lined up
44 Chinese principle
45 Depot: Abbr.
46 Commuter's problem
47 The word, maybe
49 Sea plea
50 Helium, for one
52 Gold or silver
54 *Daily Planet* employee
58 Protuberances
62 Part of MIT
63 Well-traveled route
66 Run away
67 Bert's pal
68 Rubik of cube fame
69 Observer
70 Copter component
71 Stock-exchange membership

DOWN
1 Perfect serves
2 River to the Caspian Sea
3 Tabula __ (clean slate)
4 Bottomless chasm
5 Sandwich initials
6 __ Lingus
7 Beer holder
8 So be it
9 Baltic natives
10 More attractive
11 One more time
12 "Final Four" org.
13 Hard to hang on to
18 Former Iranian ruler
22 Waste maker of adage
24 Continue, as a subscription
25 With the bow, in music
27 Summery forecast
28 State one's case
29 Word before basin or wave
32 Flagrant
33 "Cool!"
34 Fast-food drinks
37 Frequently, in poems
38 Bellow
40 Racing vehicle
41 Faithful
42 Bring under control
48 Educator Horace
51 Curved sword
52 Intended
53 Runs gracefully
54 Animation
55 No more than
56 "Aha!"
57 Infamous emperor
59 Challenge
60 Sicilian spouter
61 Photographed
64 Uncle: Sp.
65 Suffix for mountain

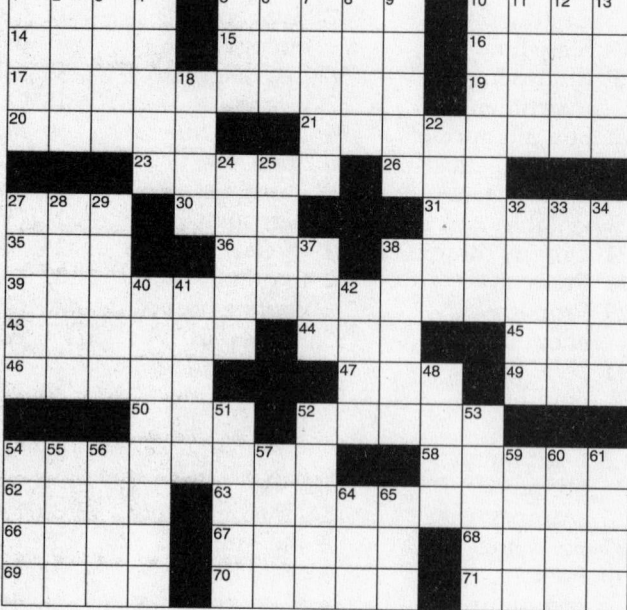

612 LIGHTS OUT by Bob Lubbers

ACROSS
1 Adroit
5 Runyon's women
9 Politico Les
14 Dynamics start
15 "Oh, sure!"
16 Recycling aim
17 Lose one's light, perhaps
19 Latin music
20 Tosses trash
22 Smear
23 Sully
26 Invalidates
28 Enthusiasm
29 June honoree
32 Vincent van __
33 Takes on cargo
35 South Pacific island
37 Writer LeShan
40 Alamogordo event
41 Keogh relative
42 Ninnies
44 Still
45 Artist's prop
47 Pie-fight sound
48 Lyric poems
50 __ semper tyrannis
52 Continental prefix
53 Saskatchewan neighbor
56 Bigger
58 Buddies
59 Pennsylvania city
62 ". . . the bombs bursting __"
64 Lose one's light, perhaps
68 "__ bleu!"
69 Monster
70 Buckeye State
71 Scouting outings
72 Free ticket
73 Sally or Ayn

DOWN
1 Small amount
2 Moray
3 To and __
4 Barge connectors
5 Talented
6 Come up against
7 __ majesty (high crime)
8 Strict
9 __ gratia artis
10 Sailor's tote
11 Lose one's light, perhaps
12 Bring forth
13 Approaches
18 Feel poorly
21 __ lily (Utah state flower)
23 Put off
24 Make happy
25 Lose one's light, perhaps
27 Urges
30 Sale stipulation
31 Is bold
34 Have the helm
36 French Sudan, formerly
38 *The Wreck of the Mary __* (1959 film)
39 Actress Mary
43 "Smooth __" (Sade song)
46 Film terrier
49 Covet
51 Genetic replicas
53 Prone to imitation
54 Sun porch
55 Journalist Joseph
57 In addition
60 Roman garb
61 Yours and mine
63 Musical notes
65 "So that's it!"
66 ATM ID
67 Grass square

DIGITAL READOUT by Mary Brindamour

ACROSS

1 Rudiments
5 Linda of *Dynasty*
10 WWII battle site
14 Chaotic situations
15 Tiny lab tube
16 Ornate pitcher
17 Multifunctional, perhaps
19 Columnist Barrett
20 Frightened squeal
21 Palace of Paris
22 Black, poetically
23 Cuban leader
25 Small liqueur glass
27 __ *Is Enough* ('80s sitcom)
30 Rifled, as book pages
33 Tilter's need
36 Ship of fuels
38 Raw material
39 Cuckoos
40 Spanish hands
41 Tommy of Broadway

42 Traveler's rest stop
43 Prepares ceramic work
44 Added to staff
45 More intense
47 Vegas natural
49 Weight allowance
50 Symbolizes
54 __ gin fizz
56 Husky-voiced
60 New Haven student
61 Vapor
62 Emporium of yore
64 Emanate
65 Taking advantage of
66 Sicilian hot spot
67 Like paraffin
68 *Robert E. Lee* waiting spot
69 Wild pig

DOWN

1 Mexican Indian
2 Chinese tea
3 Wine stoppers
4 Compass pt.
5 Play postscript
6 Ivied, perhaps
7 Mil. addresses
8 Maui goose
9 Church structures
10 Samantha's sister
11 Builder's board
12 Funnyman Jay
13 Algerian port
18 Creepy
24 Sleuths
26 "__ the ramparts . . ."
28 Frost
29 Antler branches
31 Coastal flyer
32 Feat
33 Put down, as tiles
34 Green Gables girl
35 Extended work shift
37 Misplace
40 Happy as a clam
41 Turner or Louise
43 Professional charge

44 Macho types
46 Attractive
48 Countenance
51 Arrive at
52 Skater Valova
53 Iraqi money
54 Kind of duck
55 Succotash bean
57 River of France
58 Tel __
59 Philosopher Descartes
63 Cotillion kid, for short

BOOB TUBE? by Henry Hook

ACROSS

1 Rob Reiner's dad
5 CBer's cousin
8 High land
13 Vaudeville shtick
14 King's crazed canine
15 Ruin the topsoil
16 FORMER COHOST
18 Carries a torch, maybe
19 Eastern
20 They may bounce
22 Bub
24 Gehrig or Groza
25 HALF THE SHOW'S ORIGINAL TITLE
33 Plumed hat
34 Testify
35 Speedwagon letters
36 Director Riefenstahl
37 Fingerpaint
38 Long time
39 ". . . and __ my cap"

40 Prepare eggs, one way
41 Unprocessed
42 THE OTHER HALF OF THE TITLE
45 That woman
46 Exist, to Popeye?
47 Office mate
52 Pancho's pal
56 __ a million
57 THE OTHER COHOST
60 Kid with a cap
61 Indicates it's OK
62 First seagoing vessel, in myth
63 Late bloomer?
64 Swallowed
65 Means' mates

DOWN

1 Runner Sebastian
2 *Rhapsody in Blue* star
3 Hoop edges
4 Central spots
5 "Wha'd'ja say?"
6 "This is __ for Superman!"

7 Poet Van Duyn
8 Mets home
9 Darkness personified
10 Charles' game
11 Actor Wesley
12 Minus
14 Ear area
17 Arthur Murray lesson
21 Cloudiness
23 Universal
25 Churchill's __ *Finest Hour*
26 Pat's partner
27 Take on moguls
28 Mozart medium
29 Sort of white
30 Present your case
31 Cries out for
32 Tablet, perhaps
33 Piece of paper
37 Goldbrick
38 Indiana Jones found it
40 "Ambition should be made of __ stuff"
41 Nightclub performer

43 USDA rating
44 Openers, often
47 "Pas de deux" part
48 Responsibility
49 Left
50 Actress __ May Oliver
51 Someone hysterical
53 Picnic side dish
54 Irene of *Fame*
55 Rowdy party
58 Second file drawer, maybe
59 Decks

615   SPREAD IT AROUND by Lee Weaver

ACROSS
1 Startled sound
5 Plumb crazy
9 Partly open
13 Kal Kan competitor
14 Breakfast meat
15 "So long!"
16 Crowd sound
17 Raw, as diamonds
18 Seer's sign
19 Yellow wildflower
21 Beginning
22 Light beam
23 Genealogy chart
24 Feeling dismay
27 Harsh
29 Sidekick
30 Taj __
32 Tree fluid
34 Repair a rip
35 Changed addresses
36 Leaning Tower town
37 Hot time in Quebec
38 Kitchen utensil
39 African lilies
40 Reply to the captain
42 Cattle identifiers
43 Indonesian island
44 Singer Bonnie
46 Accustom
48 Indecisive person
52 Fender bender
53 Competitor
54 Eye slyly
55 Draw with acid
56 Makes less distinct
57 Playboy
58 Wan
59 Part of a list
60 TV talking horse

DOWN
1 Attire
2 Baseball family name
3 Petty clash
4 Oregon's largest city
5 Knight's weapon
6 Take place
7 Successful accomplishment
8 Toronto's prov.
9 One who makes amends
10 Impromptu jazz performance
11 Fit to __
12 Talk wildly
14 Break open suddenly
20 Simple
21 Evangelist Roberts
23 Frog's relative
24 High point
25 Scacchi of *The Player*
26 Term of endearment
27 Chastity's mom
28 Relieved
30 In greater degree
31 St. crosser
33 Football throw
35 "__ help you?"
36 Place for public discussion
38 Wan
39 Overly pretentious
41 Practical or realistic
42 Monthly payments
44 Las Vegas show
45 Clock function
46 Concept
47 New Jersey NBA team
48 Leave at the altar
49 Composer Stravinsky
50 Swing around
51 Pay attention to
53 Slugger's stat.

616   MASS MEDIA by Trip Payne

ACROSS
1 Find fault
5 Impetuous
9 Historical periods
13 Opera solo
14 Comic DeGeneres
16 Get excited
17 Housing cost
18 Photographer's request
19 Sicilian volcano
20 Ad on the airwaves
23 "Just the Two __"
24 Coral island
25 Farmer's field
28 Plated
32 Confused
34 "Mayday!"
35 __ good example
39 *Sacramento Bee* and *Indianapolis Star*, for two
43 List shortener
44 Actress Arthur
45 Worth
46 Business bigwig
49 So far
50 Scents sense
54 Sassy
56 Sitcoms, news, etc.
63 Just hanging around
64 Tropical fruit
65 Gabor and Perón
66 __-do-well
67 UFO pilot
68 Shaker contents
69 Soviet news agency
70 French blessed ones, for short
71 Big game

DOWN
1 *The Alienist* author
2 Zone
3 Lemon cover
4 Backyard part
5 Save
6 Just about
7 Svelte
8 Steering gear
9 Build
10 3:1, e.g.
11 Part of a chronicle
12 Procrastinate
15 Born: Fr.
21 "In the merry month __"
22 Physicist's unit
25 Fill a hold
26 Coup d'__
27 It's east of the Urals
29 Dam spot
30 __ Alamos, NM
31 Uncommon sense
33 Plumbing joint
35 Mineral bath
36 Hard to hold
37 Undeniable
38 "I'd hate to break up __!"
40 Cagers' grp.
41 Brain-wave chart: Abbr.
42 States
46 1055, to Caesar
47 Orbital extreme
48 Dovetail sections
50 Be frugal
51 Euripedes drama
52 They, to Monet
53 Glances from Groucho
55 Not those
57 "__ Yankee Doodle Dandy"
58 Maglie and Mineo
59 "What's __ for me?"
60 Shape of Bush's office
61 Intersection sign
62 Jet set?

617 SHIP SHAPE by Fred Piscop

ACROSS
1 Open a keg
4 Make suitable
9 Writer Sontag
14 __ Mine (George Harrison book)
15 Guitar with a resonator
16 Set things square
17 __ sequitur
18 Macaroni shape
19 1993 treaty
20 Boxing classification
23 Divination deck
24 Madrid Mrs.
25 "Get the point?"
28 Fox's quality
31 Excellent grade
34 Cashless deal
37 Nick of 48HRS.
38 Underhand pitcher
44 Clock-changing month
45 Weight allowance
46 Made cloudy
48 Most stylish
54 Bank acct. earnings
55 Cut short
58 Lena of Stormy Weather
59 Airborne messenger
64 Olympic ski champ Phil
66 Laundered
67 __-Magnon
68 Construction piece
69 Welcoming word
70 Countdown start
71 Bill of sitcoms
72 Curvy letters
73 Alums.-to-be

DOWN
1 Colors lightly
2 Lacking principles
3 Extreme want
4 "__ Fideles"
5 Kemp's running mate
6 I.e., e.g.
7 Sterns' opposites
8 Minaret, for one
9 Acted the ratfink
10 Provo's state
11 Low-pressure pitch
12 Kitchen intruder
13 Teachers' org.
21 Charged bit
22 Singer Janis
26 Suffix meaning "small"
27 Watchful one
29 Bygone map letters
30 Loretta of M*A*S*H
32 Pig-poke connector
33 Lon of Cambodia
35 Santa __, CA
36 Offender, in copspeak
38 Indian attire
39 Very familiar with
40 Trousers, so to speak
41 A thousand grand
42 Pub selection
43 Nectar gatherer
47 German article
49 Thick-skinned herbivores
50 __ out (dress up)
51 Puts up
52 "SKNXX-X" source
53 Mortise partners
56 Cubbyhole
57 Strikes out
60 Yemeni, e.g.
61 __ Martin (cognac brand)
62 Fam. members
63 White as a sheet
64 Tape-recorder adjunct: Abbr.
65 Blood-classification system

618 RHYME TIME by A.J. Santora

ACROSS
1 Vincent Lopez's theme
5 Built
9 Accept
14 Actress Gray
15 Cain's bane
16 Ownership
17 Wall finish
19 Yoga position
20 Replay type
21 Mahogany star
23 Competent
25 Troop grp.
26 Actress Stevens
29 Gardening need
34 By order of
35 Organic compound
37 Crazed
38 Bruins legend
39 Springsteen sobriquet
42 In the style of
43 Snack treat
45 Social group
46 Whack
47 Relief organization
50 Gallery
52 Mrs. David Duchovny
53 Domingo ditty
54 Gooney bird
59 Sea growth
63 Gun volley
64 Fiasco
66 More real
67 March time
68 The Haj author
69 That is: Lat.
70 Lee of pastry
71 Mexican coin

DOWN
1 Stack role
2 Hurler Hershiser
3 Car with a bar
4 Beast
5 __ de mer
6 Dwelling
7 Lucy's costar
8 Klensch of fashion news
9 "Finally!"
10 Grade schooler's project
11 One of the Ringling brothers
12 Asset
13 Chester Gould girl
18 Stemware item
22 Hoops grp.
24 Lid attachment
26 Hunter's trail
27 __ Haute, IN
28 Flubbed one
29 Armadillos
30 Love god
31 D-Day beach
32 Firm
33 Person, slangily
36 Private eyes, for short
40 Play the lead
41 Ongoing drama
44 Eight-line verses
48 Snappy comeback
49 Crew-team member
51 Draft activity
53 Fall flower
54 __ spumante
55 Enrich
56 Spectrum component
57 Singer Redding
58 Fizzy drink
60 "It's My Party" singer
61 Sale condition
62 Italian pronoun
65 Botanist Gray

GO FIGURE by Patrick Jordan

ACROSS
1 Cambodia neighbor
5 Fury
10 Coral structure
14 About 4050 square meters
15 '30s skating star
16 Jai __
17 START OF A RIDDLE
20 Dr. Ruth's field
21 Wrinkle removers
22 Neat in appearance
23 Stress or worry
24 Rose receptacle
25 END OF RIDDLE
30 Gun owners' grp.
33 Be a bother to
34 Supreme Court complement
35 Youngest Lincoln
36 Devastation
37 Like old St. Nick
39 French film funnyman
40 Jazz band's job
41 Scotch partner
42 Supernatural
43 Biblical verb ending

44 START OF ANSWER
47 At that point
49 April 13th, e.g.
50 Rodeo legend Larry
52 "Stormy Weather" composer
54 Bell and Kettle
57 END OF ANSWER
60 Gin flavoring
61 River near Nottingham
62 Mrs. Cleaver
63 *Bye Bye Birdie* tune
64 Social stratum
65 Maltese comment

DOWN
1 Congressional output
2 Dull pain
3 African antelope
4 *The __-Wolf* (London novel)
5 "... old millstream, __ first met you ..."
6 Seal the wine bottle again
7 Soon, to poets

8 Conway and Allen
9 Up on the latest trends
10 Works for the MPAA
11 Childishly simple
12 Costner role
13 Welterweight's weapon
18 "Eleanor __" (Beatles song)
19 Edict
23 Lo-o-ong time
24 Covered with climbing plants
25 Word on a T-shirt tag
26 Eskimo word for "Eskimo"
27 Galahad's achievement
28 Mosaic, for one
29 Zilch
31 Mathematical proportion
32 Goodbye, in Grenoble
37 Denver or Huston
38 Keats creation
39 Palmer's props
41 Shorthand pro

42 Makes level
45 Like Arbuckle's films
46 Carol start
48 Finds intolerable
50 1985 Cher flick
51 "__ want for Christmas is ..."

52 Taj Mahal site
53 Feels sorry about
54 Pouting expression
55 It flows past Florence
56 Slant
58 Antitrust agcy.
59 Ted Baxter's station

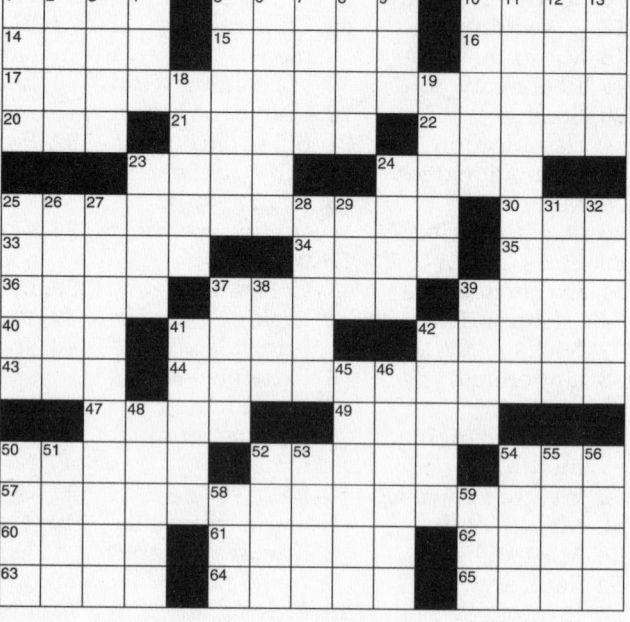

GREENERY by Norma Steinberg

ACROSS
1 Assist
5 Chick's sound
9 Last mo.
12 A Great Lake
13 Moses' brother
15 The two
16 Genealogical chart
18 "Do __ others ..."
19 Recipe abbr.
20 Some verses
21 Turn down
23 Grain husks
24 Carve with acid
25 Rapid
28 Alicia Silverstone film
32 Exhilarating
33 At what time
34 Way out
35 Jason's ship
36 Cease-fire
37 German car
38 Snead's game
39 Lease subject
40 Utah city
41 Fine silver
43 Most faithful

44 Picasso medium
45 Guy
46 Magician's exclamation
49 Perfumer's talent
50 Hawaiian paste
53 Acting part
54 Local, as political support
57 Bank conveniences: Abbr.
58 Sing in the Alps
59 Related (to)
60 "Okay!"
61 Pedestal part
62 Take five

DOWN
1 Weight
2 Time periods
3 Unstarched
4 Kennedy Center architect
5 Wage earners look forward to it
6 Devoured

7 Goofs
8 "The Bells" poet
9 Puts on
10 Caesar's accusation
11 Karate movement
14 Sea god
15 Second-rate
17 "Mercy!"
22 Poker card
23 The easy life
24 Vote into office
25 Thick carpets
26 Presidential candidate of '96
27 National symbol
28 Connie of TV news
29 Give forth
30 Teams
31 Term of employment
33 Small birds
36 Tolkien wrote one

40 Mandate
42 Ignited
43 Go at it
45 Medicinal portions
46 Meditate
47 Fixed routine

48 Shade trees
49 Zilch
50 Nudge
51 Elevator inventor
52 "__ It Romantic?"
55 Filch
56 Sculler's need

621 NATIONAL LEAGUE by Rich Norris

ACROSS
1 In shape
5 Frog's sound
10 Bad habit
14 Actress Russo
15 Mountie's mount
16 Love, to Livy
17 "__ boy!"
18 Glacial ridge
19 Practice pugilism
20 Nashville celebrities
23 High-class
24 Agent: Abbr.
25 Tiebreakers, briefly
27 Banned insecticide
28 Fountain treat
32 Smartly dressed
34 Court challenge
36 1981 Beatty film
37 Teamster, e.g.
40 Have a craving for
42 Parody
43 Lowers in esteem
46 To-do
47 In shape
50 Big __, CA
51 Mineral spring
53 Gull relatives
55 Argues in court
60 Part of a sound system
61 Took steps
62 Don't include
63 Egg cell
64 Land on the Sea of Japan
65 Minus
66 Becomes solid
67 Nor'easter, e.g.
68 Italian noble name

DOWN
1 Made an outline
2 Handed down, as a story
3 Know somehow
4 Stood for
5 Cook, Cajun-style
6 Western actor Calhoun
7 Galena and feldspar
8 Up and about
9 Wailed
10 Still-life subject
11 Not suitable
12 Went downhill, perhaps
13 Mess up
21 Speeds, to Solti
22 Coll. student's concern
26 Some coll. students
29 Mil. address
30 Camera attachment
31 Brings under control
33 Get ready
34 Farm denizens
35 Easter preceder
37 Not like Dickens' Dodger
38 1501, in old Rome
39 Reynolds and Lancaster
40 Used to be
41 Not at all nurturing
44 Superlative suffix
45 Pipes up
47 Optician's wares
48 Give no ground
49 Dangerous fly
52 Broad-ended necktie
54 Where to find an *élève*
56 Prepares to fire
57 Another, in Andalusia
58 Poetic adverb
59 Red-wrapped cheese
60 Be greedy

622 KID STUFF by Trip Payne

ACROSS
1 Thin __ (very skinny)
8 Make good as new
14 Christmas stamp subject
15 Problematic situation
16 Boys Don't Cry song of '86
18 Principal
19 Repent of
20 Five-star nickname
21 Not exactly hard rock?
23 Bleep
26 Mascara applicator
27 Agreement
28 Arthur and Benaderet
31 Terminus
32 Categorize
33 Guys
35 How pros do things
37 Settle
38 Look up to
39 "Smooth Operator" singer
40 Kid's toy
41 "__ Smile Be Your Umbrella"
42 Funny stuff
43 Birthplace of seven Presidents
44 Few and scattered
46 Board material
47 2002 Winter Olympics host
50 French article
51 Keats creations
52 Dungeons and Dragons, e.g.
58 Coined word of a sort
59 Mad
60 Part of ASAP
61 Salad preparers

DOWN
1 "What Kind of Fool __?"
2 Noticed
3 Eden pair
4 Artist Searle
5 Actress Potts
6 __ uproar
7 Chem. classroom
8 Prepares potatoes, perhaps
9 *Xanadu* band
10 Church bench
11 Word form for "both"
12 Phrase in transactional analysis
13 Comic Martha
15 Overawe
17 Put up
21 Say "*&%@#!"
22 *Messiah* composer
23 Actor Elwes
24 Too large
25 Transferred employee's benefit, for short
27 Global extreme
29 Nevertheless
30 __-faire
32 Rein, essentially
33 G-men
34 Rebel of 1857
36 Cats and dogs
37 Fad
39 Sarah Vaughan's nickname
42 Prodigious
43 Alphas' opposites
45 Mel or Steve
46 Boundaries
47 Brutus' bear
48 *The __ of Katie Elder*
49 MacGraw and Baba
51 Aware of
53 Psyche section
54 Arafat's grp.
55 Relative of -arian
56 French sea
57 Bradley and Ames

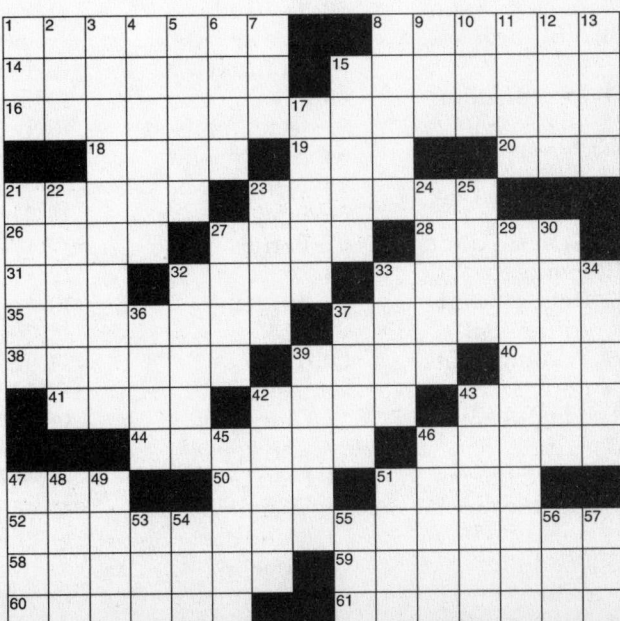

623   SIX OF A KIND by Richard Silvestri

ACROSS
1 "Oh dear!"
5 Footnote abbr.
9 Sound of a wet impact
14 Ring happening
15 Central point
16 Incinerator input
17 VHS rival
18 Hammered on a slant
19 Copland composition
20 WEAPON/COM-MUNICATION/GIRDER
23 Skillet
24 Land's end?
25 College teacher
28 Turned aside
32 Get out of
33 Calls to court
35 Turn left
36 King Cole's request
37 Brownie maker
38 Infuriation
39 Plastic __ Band
40 Sized up
41 Actress Taylor

42 Sinews
44 Sterling
45 Set foot in
47 Honest prez
48 GASKET/DRIVING MANEUVER/COORDINATE-SYSTEM LINE
55 Seed coat
56 Trampled
57 Hatcher of *GoldenEye*
58 Ali's faith
59 Abate
60 Organic compound
61 No longer fresh
62 Coaster
63 Private, e.g.

DOWN
1 "Dancing Queen" group
2 Darrow client
3 Packard, for one
4 Steers out of control?
5 Aim
6 Bust opposite

7 Think-tank output
8 Zealous
9 Bill Murray movie
10 Investigator
11 Fill the hold
12 Out of port
13 Shoemaker McAn
21 Scourge
22 Four-time Wimbledon champ
25 Union Pacific stop
26 Sheeplike
27 Poultry delicacy
29 Clan bigwig
30 Gung-ho
31 Nerdy guy
33 Tape holders
34 Tina's ex
37 Swahili or Zulu
38 Second-time student
40 Sting
41 July birthstone

43 Canine-related
44 Treated icy roads
46 Country
48 Regretful Miss of song
49 What's left

50 Cuba, to Castro
51 Romantic gift
52 Lucy Lawless role
53 Couples' club
54 __ tree (mimosa)

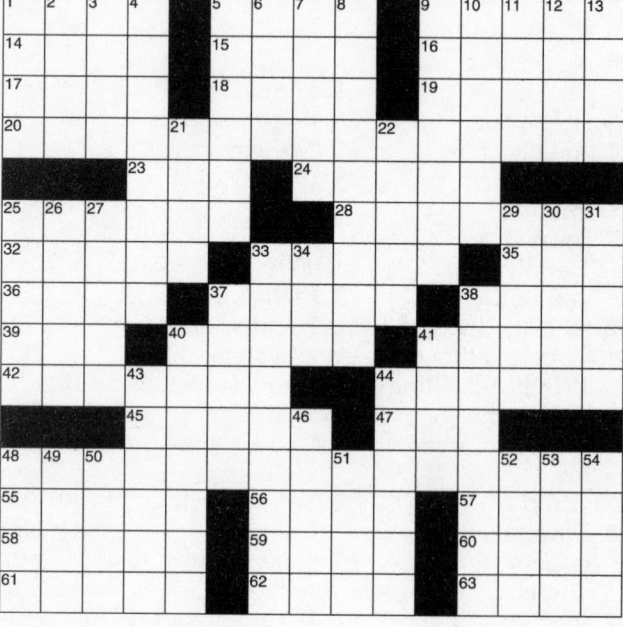

624   IN THE AFFIRMATIVE by Frank Longo

ACROSS
1 Shade provider
4 Vinegary
10 Drop
14 Shemp's brother
15 Thin layer
16 Pianist Peter
17 "Yes!"
19 Interstate sign
20 NBC peacock, e.g.
21 Joule fraction
22 Diarist Nin
24 Thomas Gray work
26 "Yes!"
29 Actress Kidder
31 Smidgen
32 Rock-concert equipment
33 Printing goofs
36 Louver component
37 "Yes!"
41 Holster items
42 Floor leader's milieu
43 Pendulum's path
44 Cable network

46 *Fawlty* __
50 "Yes!"
54 Memorable dieter
55 Like some pretenses
56 Wide of the mark
58 Transude
59 Use an atomizer
60 "Yes!"
63 Jester Johnson
64 Extinguisher
65 __-Magnon
66 Equal
67 Barrels
68 Beast of burden

DOWN
1 Insignia
2 Chicago university
3 Piddling
4 Everybody
5 Made the scene
6 Manicurist's material

7 São __ (Cape Verde island)
8 Country lodge
9 Honeydew relative
10 __ a time (singly)
11 Baja California city
12 Dubliner, e.g.
13 Preschooler
18 Lumberjacks
23 Sparks or Rorem
25 Time past
27 Provo resident
28 Fitting
30 La-la lead-in
34 Analyze
35 Taoism founder Lao-__
36 Olla
37 Guaranteed to work
38 Hardly holy
39 Granola-bar morsel
40 Siouan speakers

41 Schmooze
44 FedEx rival
45 Depletes
47 Beethoven's Third
48 Tonsorial tools
49 Dictation pros

51 Modify
52 Close-fitting hat
53 Serviceable
57 Trough filler
59 Inset, for instance
61 *Alley* __
62 GRE takers

625 SPLIT ENDS by Norma Steinberg

ACROSS
1 Ego
5 Agitates
10 Competent
14 Singer Laine
15 Spike Jones recording
16 Self-absorbed
17 Choir voice
18 Dominion
19 __ Romeo (imported auto)
20 Incrementally
23 Edgar Allan __
24 Lamb's mother
25 Says "grrr"
27 Wander
29 Command in a library
32 Three: Fr.
33 Call __ day (retire)
35 Foot part
37 Approvals
38 Sentiment on a sampler
43 Spigot
44 Girl's pronoun
45 Milk source
46 Vote into office
49 Many feet: Abbr.
51 Send payment
55 Fearful
57 Play on words
59 "__ we having fun yet?"
60 Phone-call type
64 Pieces
65 Birds on Golden Pond
66 Klutz's exclamation
67 "Do __ others . . ."
68 Jessica or Hope
69 Fortune-teller
70 Getz or Laurel
71 Piece of bed linen
72 Annexes

DOWN
1 Tops of heads
2 Mama Cass __
3 Piece of mail
4 __ the bill (pay)
5 Threaded nail
6 Ancient Egyptian city
7 "Now __ me down to sleep . . ."
8 Bagel relative
9 Large trucks
10 Incarnation
11 Place for a cotillion
12 Real-looking
13 Onetime Spanish queen
21 Philippine island
22 Blasting need
26 Draft initials
28 Objective
30 War-horse
31 Farming tool
34 Donkey
36 And so forth: Abbr.
38 One cup
39 *Naughty Marietta*, e.g.
40 Toddler's question
41 Opera star Marilyn
42 Be in debt
43 Chinese drink
47 Leno's predecessor
48 "__ the season . . ."
50 Kitchen item
52 Squished
53 Pressed, as clothing
54 Some male singers
56 Child's playthings
58 Unexpected sports result
61 Lexicographer Webster
62 Muscular condition
63 Civil-rights activist Parks
64 Urban vehicle

626 RH FACTOR by Rich Norris

ACROSS
1 Incline
6 Grabbed onto
10 Composer Khachaturian
14 Decimal fraction
15 Hodgepodge
16 Destiny
17 False clue
19 Old Pontiac models
20 Anger
21 Urban tourist attraction
22 Does a tailor's job
23 Anesthetize
25 Abraham's wife
27 Author Ferber
28 Former draft org.
31 Gary of *Apollo 13*
34 One in a pool
37 Flood control devices
38 Traffic component
41 Traffic hindrance
43 UFO pilots
44 Cause to laugh
46 Followed, as a dog
48 Scenic views
50 Swell, '90s-style
51 Praiseful poems
55 Israeli dances
57 Medical staff member
59 Bounce back
61 __ longue
64 Actress West
65 Sticky stuff
66 Southfork structure
68 Sticky stuff
69 Actress Sommer
70 Less common
71 House's grounds
72 Letter starter
73 Computer operators

DOWN
1 Long step
2 Looked impolitely
3 Like the llama
4 High degree
5 Musical motif
6 __ d'oeuvre
7 Nobelist Wiesel
8 *Peanuts* boy
9 Doctrines
10 Kabul native
11 Price increase
12 Tiny particle
13 Disorderly condition
18 Seeks solace from
24 Paint carefully
26 Chain of hills
29 Former Iranian monarch
30 Passover dinner
32 Collection
33 Curvy letter
35 Toward the back
36 Actress Perlman
38 Cleveland cager, briefly
39 French friend
40 Commuting time
42 Somewhat antiquated
45 Condescended
47 E-mail address element
49 Holy
52 Shy and modest
53 Classroom tool
54 Curls one's lip
56 Layered rock
58 India's first prime minister
59 Like French toast
60 Soft-drink selection
62 "Times of Your Life" singer
63 Bakery employee
67 Western alliance since '48

627 OW! by Lee Weaver

ACROSS
1 Modern music style
4 Congressional contributors
8 Sunbather's goal
11 Morally bad
13 In regard to
15 Artist Salvador
16 Walt Kelly's possum
17 Gossipy
18 CEO, e.g.
19 Not yet paid
21 Keystone Kops comedy
23 Shipshape
25 Slangy refusal
26 Like an overcast night
30 Small scented bag
34 Go one better than
35 Nile dam
37 Steps over a fence
38 Slugger Slaughter
40 Seer's deck
42 Show signs of waking
43 Tight-fisted one
45 The entire range
47 Naval officer: Abbr.
48 Dramatic snippets
50 Women of distinction
52 Assembles a shirt
54 Affectionate
55 Batter's bane
60 Car dud
63 Beef cut
64 Glaringly vivid
66 Ready to be harvested
67 In a tizzy
68 Andes beast
69 Russian autocrat
70 Gym pad
71 Musher's vehicle
72 School-zone sign

DOWN
1 Taken-back car
2 State solemnly
3 Unknown purchase
4 Wok, for example
5 Burrows and Vigoda
6 Monk's hood
7 Brooke Shields TV role
8 Prepare to take off
9 Actor Guinness
10 Shaving mishap
12 Solitude seeker
14 Printer's errors
15 Discovers
20 Festive occasion
22 Mineral springs
24 Give it a try
26 Stair parts
27 Gin's companion
28 Pirate's booty
29 Actress Bernhardt
31 Chancy
32 Leave out in pronunciation
33 Payment conditions
36 Alaskan seaport
39 Somehow aware of
41 Matted earth
44 Offend the nose
46 Saw or hammer
49 Terrific
51 Without energy
53 Spiritual essences
55 Bridge coup
56 Roman robe
57 Laugh-a-minute type
58 Russian river
59 *Newsweek* rival
61 Australian gem
62 Rex's sleuth
65 June honoree

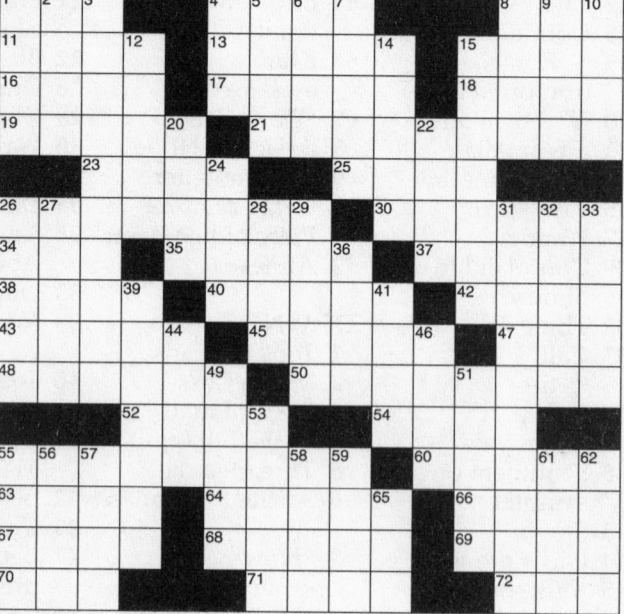

628 JUMBLED GEOGRAPHY by S.N.

ACROSS
1 Dexterity
6 Doing nothing
10 Word form for "height"
14 Part of a TV signal
15 Nitwit
16 "Nope!"
17 Where Robin bought roses?
20 Shade source
21 Purely of abstract interest
22 State-run game
23 Some statuary
25 Muff site
26 "Sic 'em, Spot!"
29 *Our Gang* crooner
33 Marching practice
34 What snobs put on
36 Some MIT grads
37 Formalwear for Mrs. J.R. Ewing?
41 Golf ball's position
42 "Oh, sure!"
43 In reserve
44 Chess situation
47 Starter's words
48 Band aid
49 Theatrical hit
51 Awe
54 Ship part
55 Buffalo water
59 Siamese twins?
62 Caveman's weapon
63 Source
64 Actor Spade
65 Former Japanese P.M.
66 European erupter
67 Town terrorized in *Jaws*

DOWN
1 Part of the movie credits
2 German industrial region
3 "Zip-__-Doo-Dah"
4 Dynamo
5 AAA offering
6 12 inches
7 Doofuses
8 Barn area
9 Capital of Louisiana?
10 Early NASA project
11 IOU
12 Reddish brown
13 "__ be in England ..."
18 Russian city
19 Norwegian royal name
24 The Bruins
25 Alternatively
26 Confound
27 Get ready for a bout
28 Like some floors
29 In __ (routine-bound)
30 Shari or Jerry
31 Equivocator's place
32 Thing of value
34 Singer Lane
35 French spot of land
38 Knucklehead
39 Flees
40 Fleeing
45 Sight on a suburban square
46 Iowa city
47 Celebration
49 Instigate
50 Conductor Zubin
51 Kindergarten basics
52 Actress Powers
53 Juxtapose
54 Interlacement
56 Sitarist Shankar
57 "What's __ for me?"
58 MacDonald's singing partner
60 Madden
61 Author Tarbell

629   ZEES by Fred Piscop

ACROSS

1 Willow relative
7 Calgary native
15 Stir up
16 Part of Western Sahara
17 Snooze
19 Journalist Whitelaw
20 Modify text
21 Go or Go Fish
24 Shea section
26 Indira Gandhi's father
30 Stradivari's mentor
32 Notable periods
34 Mansard, for one
35 Glossy garments
37 Westernmost Aleutian
39 Word form for "recent"
40 Snooze
43 Approximation suffix
45 River to Korea Bay
46 Rang out
49 Shipbuilder's wood
51 Annotate
53 Play the high roller
54 Difficult-to-field kick
56 Quilters' gatherings
58 Takes the plunge
59 Actress Powers
61 Hans Arp genre
63 Snooze
70 Of the Church of England
71 Old-time vendors
72 Newspaper-article header
73 Danish explorer

DOWN

1 Campaign-money source
2 ". . . man __ mouse?"
3 Soup cooker
4 Feminist __ Coffin Mott
5 *A Hard Road to Glory* author
6 Overhaul
7 Timetable abbr.
8 Intelligentsia
9 Hopalong Cassidy portrayer
10 Astronomer Hubble
11 German equestrian
12 Whole lot
13 Two-by-two vessel
14 Turndowns
18 *Garfield* pooch
21 Brake's neighbor
22 Docs' org.
23 *Out to Sea* star
25 Test-paper smudge
27 Puff's home, in song
28 Agile deer
29 Craft in the tabloids
31 Pitch-black
33 Short distance
36 Coal stratum
38 Applications
41 George Wallace, for one
42 Perrier alternative
43 "__ Not Unusual"
44 Et __ (and the following)
47 Wrap up
48 Driller's deg.
50 1993 role for Ford
52 Converse competitor
55 Pesto herb
57 Sir, in India
60 Graph points
62 Leader: It.
63 Go from pillar to post
64 Genetics abbr.
65 FBI worker
66 Compass dir.
67 UK recording label
68 Tokyo tender
69 Chang's twin

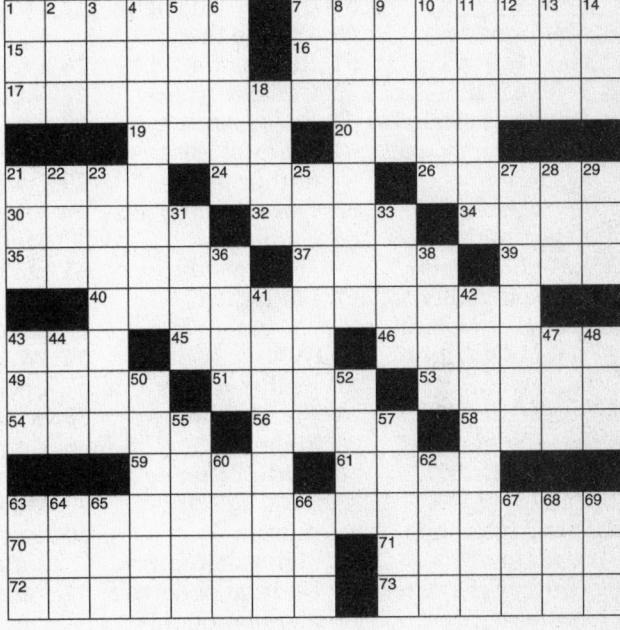

630   COVER STORY by Lee Weaver

ACROSS

1 School subject, for short
5 Oceans
9 Brown shades
13 Jai __
14 Still single
16 Vicinity
17 Score, in pinochle
18 Reduces, in a way
20 Regard as true
22 Narrow cut
23 Encountered
24 Disconcert
26 African desert
28 Mass __ (buses et al.)
31 Singer James
32 Female red deer
33 Simon or Sedaka
35 Contesting teams
39 Play parts
40 Moses' mountain
42 Make over
43 Burglar
45 Gets forty winks
46 Some govt. agents
47 Whitney and Wallach
49 Turning bad, as milk
51 Expressed orally
54 Territory of India
55 Intention
56 Blackthorn fruit
58 Knitted coverlet
62 Wispy hairdo
65 Fence opening
66 Repeated sound
67 Back-comb hair
68 Nights before
69 Bring in the sheaves
70 Bullring cheers
71 Housing fee

DOWN

1 Baby's first word, often
2 Actor Baldwin
3 After-bath powder
4 Children's game
5 Keeps going
6 Business letter abbr.
7 Flooded
8 Deal in
9 Abe Lincoln's youngest
10 Pleasing fragrance
11 More recent
12 12/25 visitor
15 Religious believer
19 Sports numbers
21 Noncommercial TV: Abbr.
25 Rathskeller needs
27 Sensitive firing device
28 Not this
29 Highly caloric
30 Opposed to
31 Pass by, as time
34 One __ million
36 Prefix for "half"
37 Genesis garden
38 Vocal music
41 Sequesters
44 Peach's pulpy portion
48 Cove
50 TV broadcast band
51 Less hazardous
52 Segment
53 Nebraska city
54 Iron-on picture
57 Creme cookie
59 Possess
60 "__ o'clock scholar"
61 Bird's abode
63 Highest part
64 Function

631 GET A HORSE! by Rich Norris

ACROSS
1 Muslim pilgrimage
5 Get in a stew
9 Telegraph inventor
14 A Great Lake
15 Like a poor excuse
16 Madonna role
17 Gaze (at)
18 Send forth
19 Lengthy narratives
20 19th-century mail system
23 "__ been had!"
24 Peggy and Spike
25 Fused, as metal
27 Came together
30 Madrid museum
32 "Hold On Tight" rock group
33 Sordid quality
37 New England's highest peak
41 Café locales
42 Prefix with light or night
43 Thurber character Walter
44 Fine-tune
47 King's seat
50 Baseball family name
51 Amazed exclamation
52 1980 Clint Eastwood film
58 Composed a letter
60 Winnie-the-__
61 Italian farewell
62 Came to a close
63 Razor name
64 *National Velvet* author Bagnold
65 Does a casino job
66 Camera attachment
67 Flu fighters

DOWN
1 Beatles movie
2 Buck add-on
3 Singer Celine
4 Hyde's alter ego
5 Showed some muscle
6 Stairs alternatives
7 Mideast potentate
8 Nantes noggin
9 Interfered with
10 Eggs
11 Uncompromising
12 Barrel part
13 Made more manageable
21 Wide shoe width
22 Hindu religious teacher
26 Protracted
27 Valuable stones
28 *The Time Machine* race
29 Garish, as attire
30 Like Dennis the Menace
31 Stadium sounds
33 Common condiment
34 Words from Caesar
35 Scatters seed
36 Agitated state
38 Verne captain
39 Motel furnishings
40 Dampen the daffodils
44 Pearl City partings
45 Driver's license abbr.
46 Breakfast beverages
47 Did a AAA job
48 Mezzo-soprano Marilyn
49 Valerie Harper role
50 Oak starter
53 October birthstone
54 Musical symbol
55 Queue
56 Animal house
57 Luke Skywalker's teacher
59 __ Aviv

632 TERMS OF ENDEARMENT by Patrick Jordan

ACROSS
1 Litter critters
5 Muscle spasm
10 Nintendo rival
14 "__ sow, so shall . . ."
15 Sound portion
16 Did an impression of
17 Western U.S. cash crop
19 Told a whopper
20 Orchestral gong
21 Delays in progress
23 1960s Tarzan Ron
24 3 on a phone
26 Soybean container
27 Like some peanuts
33 Faint
36 Lessen one's courage
37 Screen siren Gardner
38 Printed material
39 Sheriff's assistants
40 Former spouses
41 Miner matter
42 Be worthy of
43 From Erin
44 Never Land visitor
47 Plus
48 Conclude
49 Prefix for center or cycle
52 Crosses between corners
57 Humidor contents
59 Alda or Thicke
60 1955 song for the Penguins
62 Greater quantity
63 Fix one's shoelaces
64 On the sheltered side
65 Road curve
66 Three Stooges actions
67 Took off

DOWN
1 Fake jewelry
2 Routine
3 Variety of owl
4 Senate position
5 Hacks
6 Regret
7 Fruity refreshers
8 Tiny amount
9 Put off
10 Buffet selections
11 DeMille specialty
12 Socially awkward sort
13 States further
18 Heaviest noble gas
22 Yawl or yacht
25 Felt hat
27 Extremely popular
28 PLO VIP Arafat
29 Sound of wind-blown leaves
30 Danny DeVito vehicle
31 Preceding nights
32 100-yard contest
33 Put into the hold
34 *The Way We __*
35 Draft animals
39 Street vendors
40 Work unit
42 Caged talker
43 Second-most populous country
45 Began to be understood
46 Furlong's 7,920
49 Hole-in-one on a par-3
50 Smooth, as feathers
51 Speck in the sea
52 Door part
53 Lotion ingredient
54 Knitting need
55 Film critic Pauline
56 Sp. maiden
58 Chew away (at)
61 Waiter's reward

633 SMALL TOWNS by Bob Lubbers

ACROSS

1 Least successful
6 Comic Johnson
10 Pairs
14 "Farewell, François"
15 Check
16 Speed test
17 Kingly
18 Copper
19 BC neighbor
20 Clinton's former home
23 &
26 Luau dip
27 Lively
28 Captain's insignia
30 Anti-knock number
33 Beatty of *Deliverance*
34 Pilot
36 Killer whales
38 Burr/Hamilton duel site
42 Hammett detective
43 Leaves port
46 __ Cruces, NM
49 Ate away
52 Entreaty
53 Rise
55 Brown or Paul
57 Ignited
58 Big Apple suburb
62 Irate
63 Rose's boyfriend
64 Desert spots
68 __ the Red
69 Guam, for one: Abbr.
70 Lasso
71 Administrative center
72 Linger
73 Actress Burstyn

DOWN

1 Armed conflict
2 Lyric poem
3 Semi, e.g.
4 Caulk
5 Holland export
6 Watertight boot
7 Country dance
8 Prong
9 Doorway
10 Land area
11 Enter a dwelling
12 Pianist's span
13 Charred
21 As well
22 Oodles
23 Belly muscles
24 Singer Cole
25 Sketched
29 Gets it
31 Hauled
32 Biblical boat
35 Atone
37 PJ fastener
39 Construction workers
40 Fuss
41 Jack's girlfriend
44 Flowery wreath
45 Posed
46 Maidens
47 On land
48 Metal dross
50 Queen of detective fiction
51 __ Moines, IA
54 Build
56 Saw some logs
59 "Oh, sure!"
60 Cassino cash
61 Hoosegow
65 Gal of song
66 Strasbourg summer
67 Japanese honorific

634 UPON REVIEW by A.J. Santora

ACROSS

1 Cartoonist Peter
5 Hunk of meat
9 Complain
13 Low-fat
14 Carol of *Scrooged*
15 Scimitar, e.g.
16 Start of a Tony Pettito quote
18 Clear
19 Swiss city
20 Trite to the max
22 Oklahoma city
23 Part 2 of quote
27 Shea player
28 Health club
29 WWII enlistee
30 Stat for Clemens
31 Lime drinks
33 Like
35 __ over (assisted)
37 Part 3 of quote
41 Spot of land
44 Ingenuity
45 Bouquet
49 Old English letter
50 JFK info
53 "__ De-Lovely"
55 Joanne Woodward role
56 Part 4 of quote
59 Communications abbr.
60 Blight
61 Kathleen Battle's bag
63 Betel palm
64 End of quote
67 Porous, perhaps
68 Ireland
69 S-curve
70 Bollixes
71 *Inter* __
72 Pay attention to

DOWN

1 Country band
2 Went lower
3 Do the commentary
4 Getting __ years
5 Emulate Mahre
6 Fond du __, WI
7 Cookie flavoring
8 Confer (upon)
9 Slugger Rod
10 Feeling shame
11 Work on an old house
12 Opposite of post-
15 Culls
17 Melanie, in *Working Girl*
21 Collective-noun suffix
24 Brightly colored fish
25 Algeria abutter
26 Pathetic
32 USAF unit
34 Comparison words
36 Skater Midori
38 "__ It's Wonderful" (Berlin tune)
39 Cheese treat
40 Jazz singer Jones
41 Notre Dame bench
42 It sticks
43 *Woman of* __
46 Cleanse
47 Direct
48 In the family
51 Also
52 Auto pioneer
54 Pack (away)
57 Capelands
58 Lubricate again
62 Word of contempt
63 Stein filler
65 New Eng. campus
66 Actor Stephen

GOING TO PIECES by Lee Weaver

ACROSS
1 Wedding bands
6 Barney fans
10 James Bond, for one
13 Novelist Brontë
14 Water vehicles
16 Neither's partner
17 Ice-cream treat
19 Beast of burden
20 South American river
21 Argumentative
23 Upper hand
25 Small earring
26 Sun or moon
29 Tennis star Monica
32 Slips up
34 Skin opening
36 Actress Turner
37 Serious play
39 Fruit drinks
40 Ultimate degree
41 Swelled heads
42 "Rich and famous" follower Robin
44 Low, sturdy cart
46 __ on (indulge)
47 Gumbo ingredient
48 Waffle topping
50 Teachers' org.
51 Gloomy
53 Feel sore
55 Uncooked condition
58 Quieted down
62 DC VIP
63 Begin to grin
65 Snow boot
66 Capital of Vietnam
67 Weird
68 You __ There
69 Salamander
70 Feeling of unease

DOWN
1 McEntire of country
2 Muslim leader
3 One of Columbus' ships
4 Pottery finish
5 Church councils
6 Cookbook abbreviation
7 Butterfingers' exclamation
8 Bath powder
9 Blends batter
10 Garden flower
11 Small bouquet
12 Many mos.
15 Declared as fact
18 Treetop ornament
22 Sounded contented
24 Spiral-horned antelopes
26 Milky gem
27 Wild West show
28 Perform acrobatically to music
30 What a ticket provides
31 African desert
33 Struck hard
35 Third-party account
38 On the briny
43 Part of the hip
45 New Mexico state flower
49 __ out (ended gradually)
52 Showed a show again
54 Toon Fudd
55 Bring up
56 Sensible
57 Coal boat
59 Soggy ground
60 Director Kazan
61 Proof of ownership
62 Health resort
64 Tool container

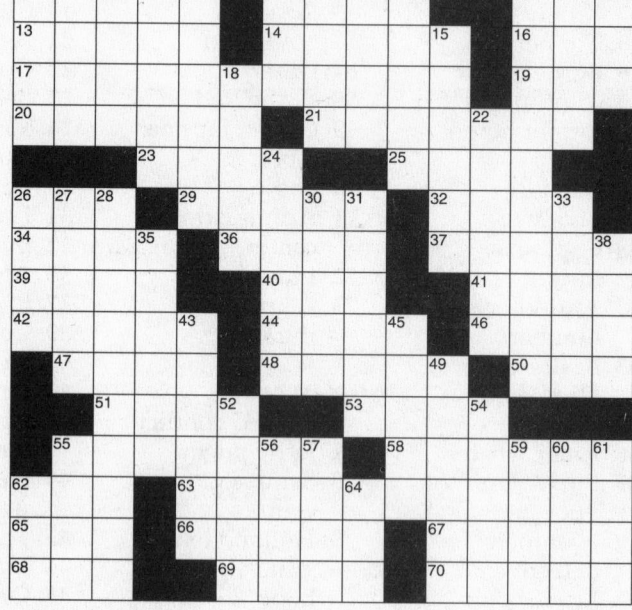

ECHOES by Norma Steinberg

ACROSS
1 Truth twister
5 Term of respect
9 Glaswegian
13 Author Ferber
14 Armbone
15 Location
16 Ophthalmologist's office?
18 Endures
19 Showman Hurok
20 Inquires
21 Soaks in the tub
22 Giggle
24 Ascertain
25 Zeus or Hermes
26 Singer Brewer
27 Kind of tea
30 Bivouac shelters
31 Part of a Web site address
34 Coffee brewers
35 Collide
36 Bloke
37 Prefix for "before"
38 "__ or When"
39 Sharpens
40 Plato's hometown
42 Allen Dulles' org.
43 Unanchored
44 Praying __
47 Restaurant patrons
48 Sharp taste
49 Regret
51 Perfect
52 Stylish Eastern leader?
54 Bumps into
55 Exude slowly
56 Poker buy-in
57 Singer Nelson __
58 One-on-one battle
59 Tennis ranking

DOWN
1 Minus
2 Dingbat
3 Viewpoint
4 "Yay!"
5 Disarranged
6 Identical
7 Picnic pests
8 Actress West
9 Blackboards
10 Piggy bank?
11 Two quartets
12 Mrs. Dick Tracy
15 Dinnerware
17 California/ Nevada lake
21 Bed on a train
23 Personalities
24 Thick
26 Lachrymal drops
27 Baby boxer
28 "To __ is human . . ."
29 Baker's dough?
30 Senator Lott
32 Feedbag bit
33 GI cops
35 Professional cooks
36 Casual talk
38 Rotates
39 Offstage areas
41 Pact
42 Nullify
43 Lent a hand
44 Indian corn
45 Actress Dunne
46 Group of rooms
47 Ten-cent piece
48 Commandments pronoun
50 __ out a living
52 Massachusetts cape
53 Owns

637 LITERARY GENRES by Fred Piscop

ACROSS
1 Cracked open
5 Donaldson of ABC
8 Red Cloud, for one
14 Russian parliament
15 Singer Zadora
16 Like some films
17 Hubbubs
18 Special-interest grp.
19 Be stealthy
20 School-lunch entrée, to kids
23 Young '__ (kids)
24 Tap outflow
25 Writer Loos
27 Recipe meas.
30 -arian relative
32 More smooth-talking
36 Norway's patron saint
38 Asian salt sea
40 Scandinavian coin word
41 Catalan, for one
44 Sunspot center
45 Welles role
46 Neck and neck
47 Bean product
49 "What a dope I am!"
51 Thirsty
52 Winter forecast
54 Musical notes
56 Shriver of tennis
59 Distressing experience
64 Region of Spain
66 French friend
67 Scandinavian chain
68 It's basic
69 "__ overboard!"
70 Pal of Kukla and Ollie
71 Firmly planted
72 Old hand
73 Columbo portrayer

DOWN
1 Edenite
2 Punch's pal
3 Andy's pal
4 Dreadlocked one
5 Pollen source
6 Light as a feather
7 Volcanic outflow
8 Soup ingredient
9 Clamping together, as one's teeth
10 Once around the track
11 Westernmost Aleutian
12 Mr. Trotsky
13 Summer beverages
21 Biblical judge
22 Ethelred I's domain
26 Concerning
27 Donut shape
28 Replay effect
29 Namby-__
31 *Enterprise* fan
33 Interweave
34 Ham-and-__ (oaf)
35 Like a bassoon's sound
37 Works the land
39 Menu words
42 Spackler's target
43 Elementary particle
48 Nikita successor
50 That guy's
53 Chaplin persona
55 Like a stuffed shirt
56 '50s late-night host
57 Folksy Guthrie
58 Great white relative
60 Poet Khayyám
61 Gumbo essential
62 True-to-life
63 Pinstriped player, for short
65 Hood's weapon

638 MINIATURE MUSIC by Ray Hamel

ACROSS
1 Mil. branch
5 Invitation notation
9 Actor Mitchell
14 McEntire of country music
15 Western Samoa's capital
16 Microwave device
17 "My Cup Runneth Over" singer
18 Bridal-gown accessory
19 Iowa commune
20 Top-10 tune of '73
23 Ad __
24 Markers
25 Rhett's rival
27 Forty winks
30 Give an evaluation
32 Work on tires
33 Lure to destruction
36 Theo, to Cliff
37 Spanish appetizers
38 New Deal agcy.
39 Arch pieces
42 Sound of impact
44 Very ambitious
45 Draw squiggles
46 Actress __ Reed Hall
48 Drainage chamber
49 Operate
50 Randy Newman number
56 Broad tie
58 Ardor
59 Peace symbols
60 Mrs. Ethan Frome
61 Fashion
62 Erupter of 1971
63 Foul-up
64 Author Haley
65 Queue after Q

DOWN
1 River to the Caspian
2 __-*Tough* (1977 film)
3 Assist in malfeasance
4 Hungry, perhaps
5 British bash
6 Pours out
7 Clock numeral
8 Become wearisome
9 Doesn't fold, in poker
10 Use a scope
11 *Gypsy* tune
12 Ten-time world skating champion
13 Sheikdom of song
21 Impart
22 Gets clean
26 "__ a Rebel"
27 Wine barrel
28 Lotion additive
29 Elton John song
30 Age
31 MLB stats
33 Levelheaded
34 *Hud* Oscar-winner
35 Toddler protection
37 Actress Feldshuh
40 __ Lanka
41 Old West badge
42 To a degree
43 Hollow bread
45 Rental option
46 Bewilder
47 Hologram creator
48 Gambler's money
51 Baum princess
52 Tangible
53 Cats and canaries
54 Period beginning Ash Wednesday
55 Biblical birthright seller
57 Sean Lennon's mom

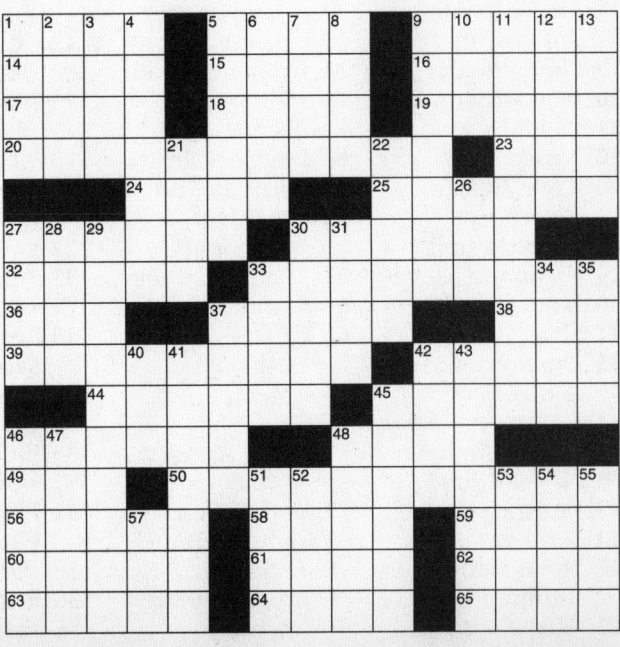

IMPROMPTU by Brendan Emmett Quigley

ACROSS
1 One of seven
5 Union establishment
15 Actress Gershon
16 *Cabaret* basis
17 Impromptu
19 Hurricane dir.
20 Infamous emperor
21 Rapper Tone __
22 Poitier, in a 1967 film
23 Capote nickname
24 Views quickly
28 Thanksgiving guest, perhaps
30 Woods' org.
32 Hook underling
33 Jon Arbuckle's dog
35 Tending to the problem
38 Live
39 Impromptu
42 King of France
43 Overhang
44 Russian river
45 Fender nick
47 Apr. addressee
49 Snooped
52 High schooler's worry
55 Hosp. rooms
57 AFL partner
58 Beer relative
59 Police team
60 Q-U link
61 Impromptu
66 Pay back
67 Film holder
68 Garden flower
69 Memo heading

DOWN
1 1992 Wimbledon winner
2 Participates
3 Meddling
4 Sound of satisfaction
5 Apple drink
6 Thrash
7 Melville work
8 Gullible person
9 Parisian school
10 Actor Willem
11 Hits hard
12 Cynical laugh
13 __ pro nobis
14 Boone or Benatar
18 Mix up, in a way
24 Window part
25 TV, so to speak
26 Eagle's home: Var.
27 Ball holder
29 Hubbub
31 One done for
34 Airport stat.
36 Loan letters
37 Seeks aid from
39 Potter's need
40 Adidas competitor
41 __ Paulo
42 Nutrition stat.
46 Get ready
48 S. African township
50 Disney bigwig
51 Pipe residue
53 Redford, e.g.
54 Direct (to)
56 Japanese noodles
59 Type of hairdo
61 BMOCs, often
62 Cage
63 Actress Thurman
64 Start of a refrain
65 Medical proc.

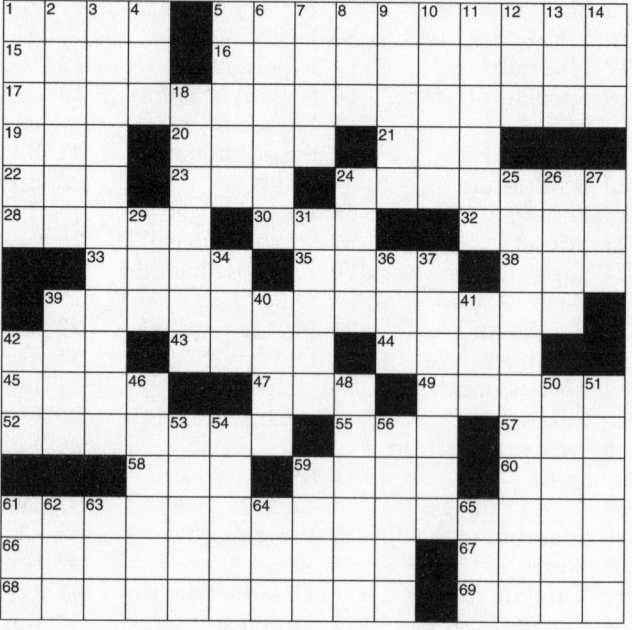

FOR THE AGES by Rich Norris

ACROSS
1 Was slack-jawed
6 New Mexico art colony
10 Widespread
14 Singer Cara
15 Bees' home
16 Messes up
17 One out of touch with reality
19 Gravy holder
20 Dorchester dad
21 Knight's weapon
22 Nuns
26 Corp. treasurer, often
28 Railroad unit
29 Cleopatra's love
30 Like lemon juice
31 Seagoing letters
32 Dumbarton denizens
33 Sensational novel
35 Sober-minded
36 Not sleeping
37 Resting on
40 Symbols
42 Hauls without lifting
43 Airport problem
45 Give a longing look
46 Fixes junior's laces
47 Football filler
48 Snack for a steed
49 Open-mesh fabric
50 __ and dagger
52 Corrects text
54 Don of talk radio
55 Military decoration
60 Long and lean
61 Turnpike rumbler
62 Actor Christopher
63 Means justifiers
64 Summer drinks
65 Coarse wool cloth

DOWN
1 Army recruits: Abbr.
2 Dadaist Jean
3 Shooter ammo
4 SASE, e.g.
5 Becomes more intense
6 __ Entertainment!
7 Assistant
8 Burns, as a steak
9 Collection
10 Country singer McEntire
11 Onetime European barrier
12 Disorderly disturbance
13 Nitrates and phosphates
18 Actor Grant
21 Carefree adventure
22 Give some lip to
23 Ancient Peruvian
24 Like some wheat
25 Venerated symbol
27 Brownish purple
30 Disgrace
33 Suffered in the sun
34 Fifth-largest planet
36 Pond floater
38 S-shaped molding
39 "Hey, you!"
41 Paperback, e.g.
42 Dinner course
43 Easily done
44 J.R. Ewing, for one
46 Pretentious display
49 Conclusion
51 Offers a question
53 Stadium feature
55 Eagles' org.
56 Baste, perhaps
57 Golf gadget
58 "__ Maria"
59 Stop-sign color

AT THE DAIRY by Norma Steinberg

ACROSS
1 Feudal laborer
5 Boutique
9 Turkish leader of old
14 Blue-green color
15 Immaculate
16 French actor Delon
17 Disarrange
18 At a distance
19 Panache
20 Monarchs, e.g.
23 Dairy animal
24 Declare
25 Appreciate a joke
27 Sap
30 Words from the podium
33 And so forth: Abbr.
36 Mortgaged up to here
38 Claudius' adopted son
39 Rulers
41 Historical period
42 Lawyer's work
43 Locale
44 Salad item
46 Lamb's mama
47 Shed
49 Watt's power
51 Butcher's wares
53 Necklace closings
57 Drink like a cat
59 Earth's place
62 Rejoice
64 Ballerina's skirt
65 Trumpet
66 Michael Caine role
67 Bound
68 Comic Idle
69 Put off
70 *Coffee, Tea, __?*
71 Netting

DOWN
1 South American dance
2 Peter Shaffer play
3 Oxidizes
4 Skipped meals
5 No-frills
6 __ and puff
7 Spoken
8 Danger
9 Turn down
10 Model Carol
11 Photographer's request
12 Hawaiian city
13 Again
21 "To __ human . . ."
22 __ *of Eden*
26 Actress Rowlands
28 Brainstorm
29 Square ones
31 Ship's employees
32 Stockings
33 Israeli airline
34 Ripped
35 Choice used car
37 Fisherman's need
40 Aarhus resident
42 Blackboard adjunct
44 Portnoy's creator
45 Sequester
48 Rag
50 Uproar
52 Heated argument
54 Cussed
55 "I Love __"
56 Harmonious relationship
57 Primary role
58 Rod between wheels
60 American naturalist
61 Line-__ veto
63 Be deceitful

FASTENATION by Fred Piscop

ACROSS
1 Stop up
4 Had faith
9 Like two peas in __
13 Author Levin
14 Vestment
15 *Desk Set* star
16 Pitcher's ploy
18 Out of the sack
19 Goya subjects
20 Test answer
22 Patty Hearst's kidnappers
23 Has a crush on
25 Stable adjunct
27 "Get __ Ya-Yas Out" (Stones tune)
28 Greek P
30 Like
31 European airline
33 Dada father
35 "__ Blu Dipinto di Blu"
36 Pamper
40 Recline
41 Madras mister
42 Writer LeShan
44 Best: Sp.
47 "That's obvious!" in teen talk
49 Juilliard subj.
51 *Legends of the Fall* star
54 Bummed out
56 Rail splitter's unit
57 *Middlemarch* author
59 Skate's kin
60 Turn aside
62 Anxious one, perhaps
64 Hockey great Potvin
65 Fragrant compound
66 Norwegian coin
67 __-European
68 Pilot-light spot
69 Nancy Drew's boyfriend

DOWN
1 Alarm
2 Video-game emporia
3 Oregano kin
4 Ship's rope
5 Govt. finance group
6 *"La Vie en Rose"* chanteuse
7 Dazzling effect
8 Perry's aide
9 Uris hero
10 Send along
11 Spotted cat
12 Faraday creation
15 Traveled like Spock
17 Canal site
21 Rare-earth metal
24 Kind of crude
26 Lunar valley
29 Jazz legend Kid __
32 Like some rocket propellants
34 Desktop items, for short
37 Conch cousins
38 Former California fort
39 Saskatchewan River city
43 Tight, budgetwise
44 Part of a Beatles title
45 Established
46 Leftover
48 Guadalajara guy
50 Singed
52 Trident's trio
53 Acclaimed one
55 Ill-fated Heyerdahl craft
58 Bandleader Puente
61 Road-picture destination
63 *My Name Is Asher __*

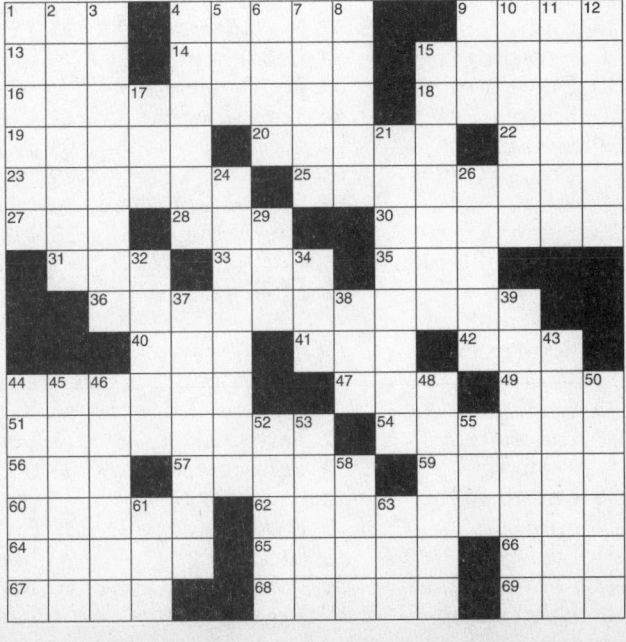

643 — FLOWERY FLICKS by Frank Longo

ACROSS

1 Galena and tinstone
5 Old Glory, e.g.
9 Like sharp cheese
13 Lets off steam
15 Scintilla
16 Volcanic emission
17 Fess up
18 Spoils
19 Bridge coup
20 1955 Magnani/ Lancaster romance
23 Goddess of the dawn
24 Furry foot
25 Boohoo
26 __-mo
29 1959 Loren/ Quinn romance
33 Geologist Sir Charles
34 In the lead
35 Converging points
38 High-fives
41 Distinctive doctrines
42 Pertinent
44 1986 Indy 500 winner
46 1986 Spacek/ Kline romance
51 Santa __, CA
52 Sigma follower
53 Mythical monster
54 Zero
56 1935 Colbert/ MacMurray romance
60 *Charles in Charge* star
62 Toiletry case
63 Worn away
64 Where Farsi is spoken
65 Middle C, for one
66 Unshackled
67 Western author Grey
68 Stowe novel
69 British composer

DOWN

1 Egg-shaped
2 Very controversial
3 Catch, as in a net
4 Hoopla
5 Blaze-resistant partition
6 Spoils
7 Rip into
8 Stomach, in combinations
9 Besides
10 High boots
11 Zsa Zsa's sister
12 Hoover or Roosevelt
14 Visit casually
21 Business owner's concern
22 Supermodel Banks
27 Actor Neeson
28 They may be against you
30 Architect Saarinen
31 Santa __, CA
32 Nip in the air
35 Broad bean
36 Norse god
37 Zagreb resident
39 Did a spoof of
40 Author Hite
43 Apportion
45 Alphabetic beginning
47 Random scrap
48 Plaintiff
49 Consolidator
50 Actress Brennan
55 *Hollywood Squares* regular
57 Fine-tune
58 Mandolin's kin
59 Zhivago's love
60 "That's show __!"
61 Celestial altar

644 — STATUS QUOTE by Richard Silvestri

ACROSS

1 Sting
5 Pursue furtively
10 In-tray item
14 Brown beverage
15 Language of the masses, once
16 Keen
17 Drum sound
18 Ruin a recording
19 Dorothy of Kansas
20 Start of a George Carlin quip
23 Piano part
24 Moon of Jupiter
25 __-cone
27 Foil front
28 Returns letters
31 Thin
33 Spotlight
37 Lancastrian symbol
38 Middle of the quip
41 Pleased
42 Rammed (into)
43 Aden's land
45 Sweetie
46 Irving hero
49 Singer Tillis
50 *Inter* __
54 Eleanor, to Teddy
56 End of the quip
60 *Judge Not* author
61 No longer novel
62 Lhasa holy man
63 Pom's relative
64 Three-tone chord
65 Style
66 Scots Gaelic
67 One of the Corleones
68 Mobile home

DOWN

1 Hollywood reading
2 Barrelmaker
3 Refer indirectly
4 Knight spot
5 It rides on runners
6 Poi base
7 For any reason
8 Hosiery material
9 Work clay
10 Melchior et al.
11 Northwestern University's home
12 Chicken style
13 Lyrical piece
21 Out of this world?
22 Cold and windy
26 Assay specimen
29 Alger beginning
30 Check
32 Like the Kalahari
33 Lose strength
34 Ethan's mate
35 Sign of sensitivity
36 Repeat performance?
38 Scouring powder
39 Swinging beds
40 Red rinse
41 Flimflam
44 "Uh-uh!"
46 Wine and dine
47 O'Neill title "character"
48 Show-off scholar
51 Jousting area
52 Opening bars
53 Over
55 Small bay
57 For whom the bell tolls
58 Celtic group
59 *Ecstasy* name
60 Do an impression of

645 WELL-GROOMED by Lee Weaver

ACROSS
1 Country singer McEntire
5 Story line
9 Grocery-store vehicle
13 Land measure
14 Biblical villain
16 Baseball manager Felipe
17 Guided trip
18 Big name in farm equipment
19 Sound of distress
20 Borden's cow
22 *The Young and the Restless*, e.g.
24 Leader
26 Chases away
27 Cooked beef
30 Parched feeling
34 Overhead trains
35 Melted snow
38 Alaska or Hawaii
39 Silver-tongued
41 Edition
43 Pound the poet
44 Helped out
46 "I cannot __ lie"
48 __ *Town*
49 Looked evilly
51 Word on a dime
53 Makes a sweater
56 Belgrade resident
57 Hangout for bees
61 Pass into law
64 Satanic
65 __ *Gay*
67 Repeated sound
68 Grow faint
69 Incriminate falsely
70 Pelt
71 Do in, as a dragon
72 Bambi's kin
73 Cookbook abbr.

DOWN
1 Tempo
2 Environmental sci.
3 Disregard
4 Homes for hawks
5 Graduate deg.
6 Wine sediment
7 Sandwich cookies
8 Synagogue scroll
9 Place to pitch a tent
10 Skin soother
11 Sound from Simba
12 Albacore, e.g.
15 Railroad terminal
21 Consumes
23 Sounds of awe
25 Pastrami emporium
27 Fit for a queen
28 Kukla's pal
29 Do a cleaning chore
31 Arkansas footballers
32 Walk proudly
33 Visibly upset
36 U-turn from NNW
37 Peanut covering
40 California university city
42 Some Ivy Leaguers
45 Declare untrue
47 Have __ in one's bonnet
50 Chops into cubes
52 Mariel Hemingway's grandpa
54 In good shape
55 Struck down
57 Chops down
58 Egg-shaped
59 Ship of 1492
60 Primary color
62 Dip holder
63 Heavy weights
66 IRS month

646 SOAPDISH by Norma Steinberg

ACROSS
1 Fido's friend
6 Obi
10 Auctioneer's call
14 Singer Baker
15 Director Kazan
16 Singer Laine
17 Part of a wedding vow
18 Satirist Sahl
19 Alan Arkin's son
20 ABC soap
23 Agenda
24 "Positively!"
25 Smith of *Charlie's Angels*
29 Drenched
30 Jai __
31 Soupçon
34 Fools
39 ABC soap
42 Vista
43 Openwork material
44 Donated
45 Devonshire drink
47 Wandered
49 ID documents
53 Roebuck, e.g.
55 ABC soap
59 Thick slice
60 Litter's smallest
61 Conspicuous
64 Muscle quality
65 Low-cholesterol spread
66 Tense, so to speak
67 Washstand pitcher
68 Threaten
69 Feeds the pigs

DOWN
1 Cry from the grandstands
2 Yoko __
3 Italian wine
4 Harrow's rival
5 Seldom
6 Large trucks
7 Overhead
8 Father
9 Actress McDaniel
10 Parboil
11 Nostalgic tune
12 Furlough
13 Like the Capitol
21 Actress Lavin
22 Ready to pour
25 Binges
26 Actor Baldwin
27 Chaplin prop
28 Mortgage, for example
29 "__ on first?"
32 __ mater
33 Girl's pronoun
35 Billboard
36 For men only
37 Roof overhang
38 Winter toy
40 Take another shot
41 Destroy documents
46 Real-estate account
48 Quiver contents
49 Tomato product
50 Permit
51 Runway vehicle
52 Coal remnant
53 Barry Levinson movie
54 Rocker John
56 Maui dance
57 Satan's realm
58 Pianist Peter
62 Salesperson, for short
63 Gridiron scores: Abbr.

647 — IN THE 7-11 by Fred Piscop

ACROSS
1 NHL member
5 The Forbidden City
10 "You're it!"
13 Clearheaded
15 Lets up
16 Be in debt
17 Kids' card game
19 Give no stars to
20 Say it ain't so
21 Isolate
23 Telecom giant
25 Suffix for sonnet
27 Changes the dimensions of
28 Dream-period acronym
29 Slender
31 Double twist
32 Working away
34 DeMille specialty
36 "Who's there?" response
40 Prepare for a fancy party
43 Flip-chart holder
44 Sign gas
45 Restraints, as on spending
46 As well
48 Respond to reveille
50 Deuce, in tennis
51 No-cal fat substitute
55 Jury-__ (improvise)
56 Corn holder
57 Dissolute man
59 Deep cut
61 "What __, chopped liver?"
62 Old-time emporia
66 Beach acquisition
67 City near Venice
68 Euphrates River land
69 Bit of a joule
70 Hits the tarmac
71 Sports channel

DOWN
1 Special attention, for short
2 It's north of Afr.
3 Military schools
4 '50s slugger Johnny
5 Hilo souvenir
6 Macbeth trio
7 Son of Jacob
8 Small sofa
9 Ninja, e.g.
10 Fall birthstone
11 In the know
12 Ladies' men
14 Units of force
18 Lace place
22 Peony part
23 A, as in eggs
24 Numerical prefix
26 Wisconsin college
30 Cut at a 45-degree angle
33 Dangerous fly
35 Loft-y group?
37 Rat finks
38 TV, radio, etc.
39 Ruhr Valley city
41 Suffering from spring fever, maybe
42 Naval rank
47 Frozen-potatoes name
49 "Good grief!"
51 Give a valedictory
52 Politico Alexander
53 Getting with great strain
54 A Chipmunk
58 Put up, as money
60 Eye woe
63 Two-time loser to DDE
64 Tuck's partner
65 __ Fernando Valley

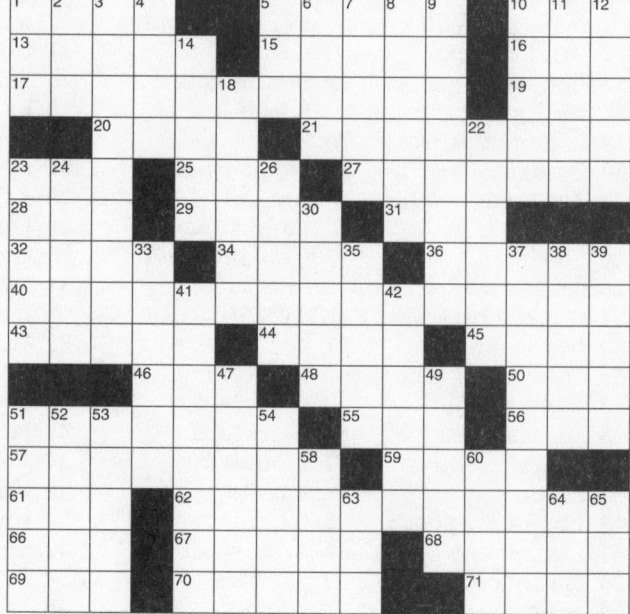

648 — ALL-STAR TEAM by Patrick Jordan

ACROSS
1 Basketball rim
5 Syrup source
8 On a slant
14 Burden
15 Ending for form
16 Different from
17 Rock guitarist Ford
18 Took to one's heels
19 Stock certificates
20 American Revolution heroine
23 Canine coating
24 For each
25 Ram's remark
28 Compass reading
29 *TV Guide*'s first cover girl
33 Church parts
34 Shallowest Great Lake
35 Stinging comments
38 Wallach of *The Misfits*
40 Has a craving for
41 Succulent plant
42 Expect eagerly
44 "Sweet Caroline" crooner
48 Nonspecialized MDs
51 Toothpaste type
52 Come to a close
53 Narrow waterway
55 Seascape painter
58 Mexican rattler
61 "Bravo, bullfighter!"
62 Laboratory animals
63 Shorebird
64 Gas-station freebie
65 All over again
66 Solve a cryptogram
67 __ and don'ts
68 Noted loch

DOWN
1 Rathbone role
2 Liver's partner
3 Black-hat wearer
4 Sacred poem
5 Excess amount
6 Jai __
7 Breathe heavily
8 Harvest measurement
9 Be an essential part of
10 Winglike
11 Title for Galahad
12 __ out a living
13 __ Moines, IA
21 Barks excitedly
22 Klinger's rank: Abbr.
25 Rural structure
26 Came in for a landing
27 Pub beverages
30 So-so grade
31 Middle Eastern faith
32 Apt rhyme for defeat
33 Explorer Tasman
35 Explosive sound
36 Away from the wind
37 Stir turbulently
39 __ Jima
40 Thickness
43 *Jeopardy!* clues
45 Cleared a windshield
46 Evident since birth
47 Newspaper notices
48 Mischievous girl
49 Jigsaw components
50 Scatters
54 Cato, for one
55 Baylor University city
56 Laundry unit
57 Hodgepodge
58 Like Wonderland's Hatter
59 St. crosser
60 Mythical bird

649 FACE THE MUSIC by Brendan Emmett Quigley

ACROSS
1 Unwritten tests
6 Smell
11 Focal pt.
14 Martinique mountain
15 Asian capital
16 Go quickly
17 NHL team
20 Comparative ending
21 Calendar abbr.
22 Prickly plant
23 Partner
25 Sitarist's first name
27 Type of blouse
28 1979 Bob Fosse movie
31 MD's specialty
32 "Auld Lang __"
33 Jeanne d'Arc, e.g.: Abbr.
34 Deli breads
35 Chopped down
38 Singer Brickell
40 Crow's calls
43 Oktoberfest need
45 Horse sound
48 Actress Gardner
49 Escapes punishment
53 Loma __, CA
55 Word with fire and stage
56 Show's partner
57 Rapper Queen __
59 Scotland Yard div.
61 Where the buoys are
62 "Do as you please!"
65 *Wayne's World* word
66 Strand
67 Anatole France opus
68 Box-office sign
69 Consumer
70 Belgian painter James

DOWN
1 Bests
2 Gets better again
3 With eyes open
4 French article
5 Scenery et al.
6 Targeted
7 Fraternity letter
8 Start up
9 Nibble
10 Give meddlesome advice
11 Type of relish
12 Telecomunications link
13 Cuts out
18 *Doctor Zhivago* heroine
19 Tigers' sch.
24 Old lab heaters
26 MTV hosts
29 Put a spell on
30 End of a Cornwall phone book
34 Rent again
36 Squeeze (out)
37 Tie, in horseracing
39 German pronoun
40 Some radio shows
41 Red Baron, e.g.
42 Is game
44 '60s sporty auto
46 Electra's brother
47 Sicilian city
49 Stump
50 Suburban school sport
51 Tom, Dick and Harry
52 Athlete
54 Tire meas.
58 Scope
60 Pull a fast one on
63 12/24, e.g.
64 Rouen refusal

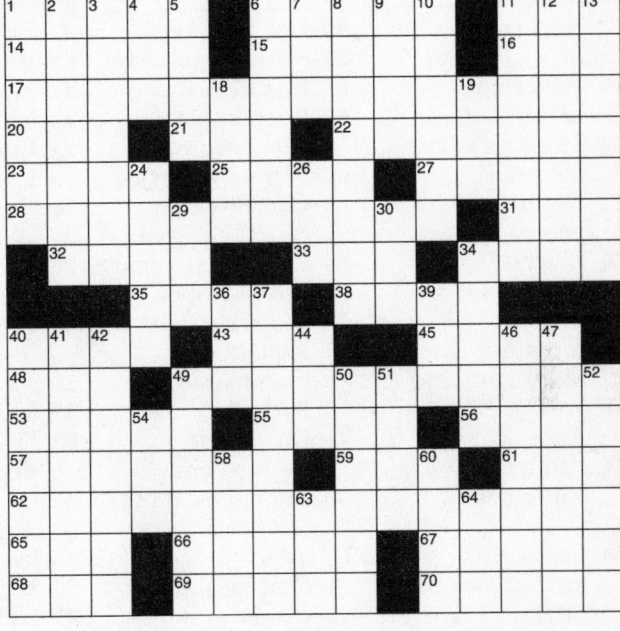

650 ON THE GROUND by Norma Steinberg

ACROSS
1 Miss Longstocking
6 Joe of *GoodFellas*
11 Lummox's remark
14 "Encore!"
15 Astronomical hunter
16 Lyricist Gershwin
17 Unpretentious
19 Preacher's subject
20 Tenure of office
21 Pierre's summer
22 Chinese dynasty
23 Insist
26 Singer Franklin
28 Big bird
29 Profundity
33 German "I"
34 Young man
35 Licentious one
36 Stealer's crime
39 Enumerate
41 African nation
43 Fragrance
44 Moslem's Almighty
46 __ Scotia
47 Fury
48 Drink cooler
49 Frock
51 Magnavox competitor
52 *Green Acres* pig
55 Seasoned
57 Nautical journal
58 Eng. course
60 Jerry Herman musical
61 "__ live and breathe!"
62 Ali, originally
67 __ Tin Tin
68 Diarist Nin
69 Chicago airport
70 Actress Ryan
71 Infield coverings
72 Small amphibians

DOWN
1 Apartment
2 "Here __ again!"
3 Ferret's foot
4 One of Columbus' ships
5 Mean (to)
6 Wordsworth work
7 Historical period
8 Kingly address
9 Terra __
10 Receive by will
11 Gossip
12 Fictional Heep
13 Barbera's partner
18 Commands
23 Actress Reese
24 PC-to-PC communication
25 Lowdown campaigning
27 Sonic bounce
30 Potato unit
31 Henry VIII's house
32 "__ ho!"
37 Coerce
38 Part of a tire
40 Mexican snack
42 Bahamian capital
45 Shrew
50 Biblical strongman
52 Frighten
53 TV host O'Donnell
54 Paul Anka tune
56 Milk, in Managua
59 Onetime Russian ruler
60 Yearn for
63 Nurse a drink
64 Legislation
65 Museum contents
66 "Okay!"

651 THIS BUD'S FOR YOU by Lee Weaver

ACROSS
1 Plant pouches
5 Theater section
9 Pub missile
13 Arthur of tennis
14 Kind of drum
16 Composer Stravinsky
17 Yard parts
18 Mentally acute
19 Governing regulation
20 Third rock from the sun
22 Use flattery to persuade
24 Riverside plant
26 Wander off
27 Reply to the captain
29 Moves upward
33 York or Bilko: Abbr.
34 Painter of ballerinas
37 __ Gay
38 Carson predecessor
40 M*A*S*H clerk
42 U.S. Pacific island
43 Kitchen cover-up
45 Offers a challenge
47 Map abbr.
48 Keep possession of
50 Get back for
52 Speaks unclearly
55 Mix the batter
56 Regrettable conclusion
60 Weighing device
63 Garfield canine
64 Mountain peak
66 Olympic weapon
67 Jury member
68 Church official
69 Aquatic mammal
70 Back talk
71 Decorative evergreens
72 Cookbook abbr.

DOWN
1 Umpire's call
2 On the ocean
3 Fruit pastry
4 Parlor piece
5 Pts. of tons
6 Sounds of awe
7 Chews like a beaver
8 Everglades bird
9 Soiling
10 Water, in Madrid
11 Parker House product
12 Hard journey
15 Musical drama
21 Beer topper
23 Biblical weed
25 Colorist
27 Wide open
28 Archaic exclamation
30 Pretended disdain
31 Make jubilant
32 Identical
33 Practice punching
35 Orthodontist's org.
36 Poet Teasdale
39 Turkey cookers
41 Guns the engine
44 Aswan Dam site
46 Movie locations
49 TLC provider
51 Most pleasant
53 Answer an invitation
54 Derogatory in manner
56 Conks on the head
57 Brainstorm
58 Binds together
59 Sitcom star Carey
61 Vault
62 Sushi serving
65 Hesitation sounds

652 TORCH SONGS by Rich Norris

ACROSS
1 April 1 victims
6 Suit
11 "Now, wait a minute . . ."
14 Da Gama destination
15 African antelope
16 Chemical suffix
17 1962 Corsairs song
19 Shaq org.
20 Wife of Zeus
21 Label word for dieters
22 Not quite shut
23 1990 Bon Jovi song
27 Malicious look
30 Italian car
31 Copenhagen residents
32 Disrespectful acts
36 Scram, oater-style
37 "__ Macabre"
39 Mine find
40 Immense
43 Reef material
45 "__ That a Shame"
46 Willie Mays' birthplace
48 1987 Bryan Adams song
52 Semi feature
53 Give a hoot
54 Map abbrs.
58 Actor Brynner
59 1972 Elvis Presley song
62 Former name of Tokyo
63 Son of Sarah
64 Actress Anouk
65 Part of a match
66 "__ luck!"
67 Bergen alter ego

DOWN
1 Go angling
2 Big spender's phrase
3 Annoying smell
4 Winsome
5 Make a statement
6 British Honduras, today
7 Make happy
8 Hockey openers
9 Female-name ending
10 NFL scores
11 Deliverance instrument
12 Take the bolt off
13 Prone to break down?
18 Be in the game
22 Choir member
24 __ Misérables
25 Drum partner
26 Needlefish
27 Head start
28 Stuck-up
29 Fascinated by
32 Resp.
33 Director Ephron
34 Sussex streetcar
35 Ward of Sisters
37 Slips into
38 Absolute ruler
41 Hard to find
42 Cambridge sch.
43 Jam ingredient?
44 Ohio college
46 Second-largest continent
47 Financial claim
48 President after Grant
49 Radiate
50 Parcel out
51 Grandmas
55 Heavy book
56 At any time
57 Start a lawn
59 Puppeteer Baird
60 Mil. entertainment group
61 Pump product

653 DIFFERENT STROKES by Frank Longo

ACROSS
1 Interfere
7 Mutt's pal
11 Attorney's org.
14 Sergeant's command
15 Gallic girlfriend
16 Stimpy's sidekick
17 Levy legislation
18 Mythical meanie
20 Little green guy
22 *Citizen Kane* actor
23 "__ Now or Never"
25 Jetsons' dog
28 DOS alternative
29 Shutterbug's suggestion
33 Lunchbox treat
34 Electrical unit
35 Superior
42 Whopper teller
43 Leave in a hurry
45 Soar
51 Con __ (vivaciously)
52 German

industrial hub
53 Car-wash option
54 Cascades and Tetons
57 Sudden snag
59 HBO honor, once
62 *Bonanza* star
65 Has the wherewithal
66 Director Kazan
67 Cosmetician Rubinstein
68 Tee preceder
69 Funny Foxx
70 Merchant

DOWN
1 Mr. Masterson
2 Tony-winner Hagen
3 Crude oil
4 Like Wilt Chamberlain
5 Book before Jeremiah
6 Most innovative
7 Pugilistic punch
8 Funnyman Philips

9 Tropical fruits
10 Have a hunch
11 St. Laurent rival
12 Frosh's cap
13 Architectural wing
19 "__ Be Surprised" (Berlin tune)
21 Extreme degree
23 *Sands of __ Jima*
24 Waterproof cover
26 Venerates
27 Old Greek coin
30 __ anglais (English horn)
31 Laid up
32 1 or 66: Abbr.
36 Architectural wing
37 Nero's noon
38 Ice-cream partner
39 Hoopsters' grp.
40 Clock component
41 Actress Raines
44 Animator Avery
45 Brawl

46 Contents of some closets
47 Meditative discipline
48 Blonde shade
49 Corral sounds
50 Dessert preceder
51 Support

55 It'll hold water
56 Mall attraction
58 Spreadsheet unit
60 Unburden oneself
61 Fred, to Pebbles
63 Compass reading
64 Pitcher part

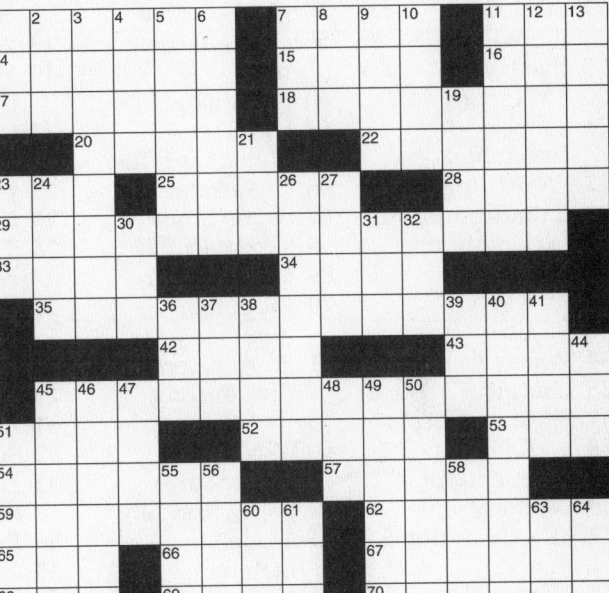

654 LEDGER-DEMAIN by Patrick Jordan

ACROSS
1 Overflows, with "over"
6 Rosebud, for one
10 Mideast region
14 Red River port
15 Became frayed
16 Mountain goat
17 Milo of the movies
18 Sills specialty
19 Robelot or Pauley
20 START OF A RIDDLE
23 More uptight
24 Smooths one's feathers
28 Out of the ordinary
29 __ Tomé
31 Classless newspaper
32 Put a match to
33 MIDDLE OF RIDDLE
36 Mocking comment
39 Butter holder
40 All over again

41 END OF RIDDLE
46 Big Ten sch.
47 Begin to drowse
48 President pro __
49 1105, to Caesar
52 Subside
54 Current unit
56 ANSWER TO RIDDLE
60 Goose egg
63 Composer Stravinsky
64 Morocco's capital
65 Uncontrollably
66 Appoint to an office
67 Condition
68 Purplish red
69 Got taller
70 English county

DOWN
1 __ a seat (usher)
2 Bound with a rope
3 Available
4 Ruth Lilly Prize winners
5 Some cats
6 Stolen goods

7 Singer who's an actress
8 Guitarist Clapton
9 Like Buster Keaton
10 Toy soldier
11 Atty. org.
12 Branch of Buddhism
13 Logging tool
21 Asian inland sea
22 Strong desire
25 Vigorous spirit
26 Reebok rival
27 Simmer slowly
30 Chose
31 Mechanical man
33 One with a nest egg
34 Eat in the evening
35 Welcome item
36 Monopoly square
37 Skilled
38 Buddies
42 Proposer's support
43 Putting on
44 Place in the Senate

45 Submerge
49 Musical Moore and others
50 Bring into existence
51 Junction point
53 Bicycle-wheel feature
55 City maps

57 John of *Fort Apache*
58 Alaskan city
59 Sketched
60 Laser-gun sound effect
61 Flightless fowl
62 Sinbad bird

655 WINGS by S.E. Wilkinson

ACROSS
1 Part of the foot
5 Sobbing
10 Eject strongly
14 Machete's cousin
15 __ Allan Poe
16 Possess
17 Storied pie ingredient
19 Eye layer
20 TV Tarzan Ron
21 Take __ (resemble)
22 Baby bringer
23 Palindromic exclamation
24 Entice
26 Irish river
30 Frolic
34 Waterer's need
35 Gratuity
37 Seismic effect
38 __ T. Firefly (Groucho role)
40 Feathery stole
42 "Ready or not, here __!"
43 Neptune's neighbor
45 ASAP
47 Raw metals
48 __ of Alcatraz
50 Triumph
52 Bravos, old-style
54 NASA affirmative
55 Crickets do it
58 Clemens' pen name
60 Neckline shape
63 Curlicue
64 Flying machine
66 __ Karenina
67 Skater Sonja
68 The Venerable __
69 Letter starter
70 Mountain nymph
71 Word before dive or song

DOWN
1 Singer Lane
2 Bagel, basically
3 Modeling material
4 Ad-__ committee
5 Duck feature
6 Prepare text
7 Wading bird
8 Chaplains
9 Mos. and mos.
10 Badminton prop
11 Peacock constellation
12 At all times
13 Watered-down
18 Otto or Roger
22 Heidi author
23 Birdie, in golf
25 NYSE, i.e.
26 Tree's smaller cousin
27 Dark-eyed damsel
28 __ as (up to)
29 Beak
31 Love, to Luigi
32 Some apples
33 Dime-store magnate
36 Burst open
39 Give a recap
41 TV spots
44 Droop
46 Flinched
49 Infernal
51 Rabbit fur
53 Pigs
55 Attired
56 Whet
57 Hebrides island
59 Opera solo
60 Opinion
61 Das Rheingold role
62 Eve's home
64 Which person
65 Kids' ammo

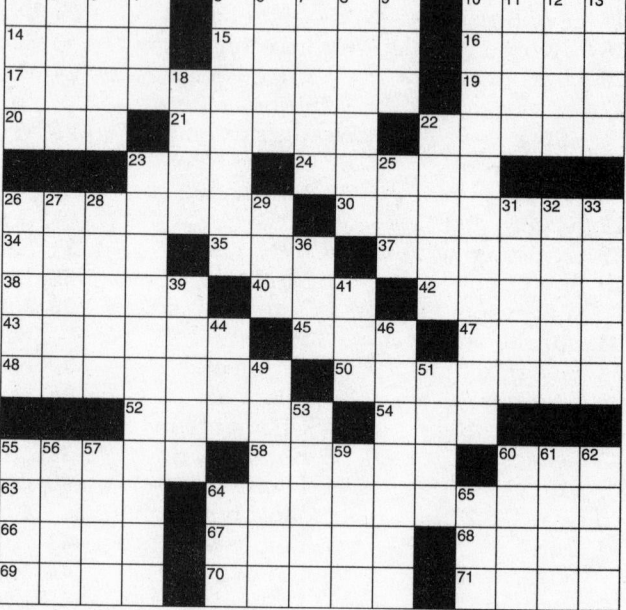

656 IT ALL ADDS UP by Norma Steinberg

ACROSS
1 Skycap's burdens
5 Impertinence
10 Tome
14 Singer Fitzgerald
15 "To err is __ . . ."
16 Rod between wheels
17 Model's asset
19 Impolite look
20 Yoko __
21 French spot of land
22 Mideast nation
24 Part of the forehead
26 Actor McDermott
27 Furlough
29 Dresser-drawer perfumer
33 Bill of fare
36 US/European defense org.
38 Distrustful
39 "Too bad!"
40 Easel, e.g.
42 Large garage
43 Presidential candidate of 1996
45 Location
46 Threat ender
47 Cryptic
49 Poet Federico García __
51 Wherewithal
53 Philip II's fleet
57 Singer Etheridge
60 Cravat
61 __ Tin Tin
62 Microwave, e.g.
63 Marabel Morgan's ideal
66 Stead
67 Author Zola
68 Singer Tennille
69 Lodge members
70 Ate well
71 Aspen, for one

DOWN
1 Had children
2 Without company
3 Doom's partner
4 Blue
5 Santiago natives
6 Immense
7 Big bird
8 Way before the bell
9 Genuflects
10 Gymnastics event
11 Yoked animals
12 No-cholesterol spread
13 Show Boat composer
18 Arrange alphabetically
23 Jezebel's god
25 Margin for error
26 Minutiae
28 Storage containers
30 Get better
31 Goofs
32 Actress Daly
33 Glove-compartment items
34 Gen. Robt. __
35 Antidrug cop
37 Aware of
41 Pushed off the track
44 Football holders
48 Sampled
50 Ship's staff
52 One of the Judds
54 Knight's protection
55 Actress Keaton . . .
56 . . . of __ Hall
57 Double agent
58 Satan's forte
59 Scallion relative
60 Yarn
64 Pewter component
65 New York Giant hero

657 ATTRACTIVE FILMS by Rich Norris

ACROSS
1 Shakespearean epithet
5 Bill of *Maude*
9 __ diem (seize the day)
14 On the briny
15 Shaving-cream ingredient
16 Love, in Livorno
17 "Huh?"
18 Throw the dice
19 Bag carrier
20 1952 Red Skelton film
23 Destroy gradually
24 Stimpy's pal
25 Baseball great Williams
27 Morning moisture
28 Forty winks
31 More eccentric
34 Spoke (up)
36 O. Henry technique
37 1990 Julia Roberts film
40 Hair-raising place?
42 West Coast capital
43 Put together skillfully
46 Solidify
47 Center of activity
50 Porkpie, for one
51 "Cry __ River"
53 Fight site
55 1996 Matt Dillon film
60 Storytellers
61 Fast-food drink
62 Hide's companion
63 Fry lightly
64 Long, long time
65 *In* __ (actually)
66 Al of auto racing
67 ERA, for one
68 Method: Abbr.

DOWN
1 Cried
2 Not 14 Across
3 Make new promises
4 Old-fashioned
5 Peter and Paul's partner
6 Very much
7 Spectrum component
8 Shouted
9 Roman philosopher
10 Out of control
11 Crop-raising technique
12 Twelve-year-old, e.g.
13 Always, in poetry
21 Not strict
22 Lennon's mate
26 Like Chianti
29 Fitting
30 Gerbil or canary
32 Response delay
33 Sussex streetcar
34 Campus VIP
35 Prefix meaning "badly"
37 Tablelands
38 Move one's tail
39 Corrida cry
40 Academy: Abbr.
41 Fine horse
44 Ambulance attendant: Abbr.
45 Cleans the windshield, in a way
47 Joan of Arc's crime
48 Except if
49 Red Riding Hood accessory
52 In progress
54 Goes up
56 Comic Johnson
57 Exploitative one
58 Radius neighbor
59 Cellar dweller's position
60 Shreveport coll.

658 LEGWORK by Fred Piscop

ACROSS
1 Abominable Snowman
5 Finger-pointer
11 Eng. sports cars
14 __ *for All Seasons*
15 Tell
16 High-school course
17 Doing the town, perhaps
19 Needlefish
20 Writer Rand
21 Wood or Cole
23 Ghana's capital
26 Shirt size: Abbr.
28 French movie
29 Afternoon party drink
31 Most current
33 Rocky outcrop
34 Shine brightly
36 Yo-yo stunt
41 Most flexible
42 Dyer's container
44 Chronicles
47 Exhaust tube
50 Exude joy
51 JFK arrival
52 Ancient
53 Rogers partner
56 "Sail __ Ship of State!"
57 Alphabetic trio
58 Carousing
64 Musket end
65 Shrewd
66 Pennsylvania port
67 Ike's monogram
68 *Altered* __
69 Proofreader's mark

DOWN
1 Puppy complaint
2 Ostrich cousin
3 Bar bill
4 __ of (postal phrase)
5 Cereal material
6 Ayres or Wallace
7 100%
8 Memorable ship
9 Sicilian spouter
10 Army unit: Abbr.
11 '50s pitcher
12 Tiny weights
13 Avenue crosser
18 Tatum's dad
22 Played a role
23 Rep.
24 Boast
25 Wax: Lat.
26 Inclines
27 Doodads
30 Threesomes
31 Christine of *Chicago Hope*
32 Partook (of)
35 *Where* __ (1969 film)
37 Andes animal
38 __ Nidre
39 Roman poet
40 Gawk
43 Top score, at times
44 Degraded
45 Like some tables
46 Basic qualities
48 Protracted
49 Cultivated
51 Actress Berger
54 Roth and SEP
55 Corrosion
56 Singles
59 Bolt fastener
60 Ore ending
61 Wrath
62 Like Abner
63 Substandard grade

659 · GET IN by Richard Silvestri

ACROSS
1 Sandwich extra
5 Curtain raiser
9 Mimed "goodbye"
14 Bee flat
15 Masked animal
16 Antipasto morsel
17 In the center of
18 Arthurian lady
19 Piece of the past
20 Doohickey takes off?
23 Yellowstone sight
24 Lod Airport carrier
25 Jump on the ice
27 Longbow wood
30 Crimson rivals
32 Homophony
36 Sci-fi visitor
38 The Alienist author
40 Verne captain
41 Liquor allowance?
44 Discouraging words
45 __ happens (incidentally)
46 Shortstop's asset
47 In __ (intrinsically)
49 Actress Osterwald
51 NATO cousin
52 Part of N.B.
54 Layer
56 "That's tasty!"
59 Plan an attack on cads?
64 Video-game pioneer
66 La Bohème updated
67 Shampoo ingredient
68 Unpretentious instrument
69 Sacramento arena
70 Lots of laughs
71 Glossy surface
72 Look
73 Some tubers

DOWN
1 Layered hairdo
2 Bean town?
3 All fired up
4 Piece of cake
5 Alcohol-based solvent
6 Clashes
7 Plug away
8 Kipling's birthplace
9 Go downhill
10 Brown brew
11 Quite unpleasant
12 Blackhearted
13 Place for a king
21 Nicholas Gage book
22 Outlying area
26 She played Alice on TV
27 New Age musician
28 Thomas Stearns __
29 Cleans off, in a way
31 Master, in Mysore
33 Musical sign
34 Seiko rival
35 Remarks
37 Ruhr Valley city
39 Reserve
42 1993 treaty
43 Fictional clerk
48 Emollient
50 Half of an inning
53 Wall hanging
55 Lachrymose
56 Blabbers
57 Jazz home
58 Rodent's ordeal
60 Sommersby star
61 Lamb of yore
62 Marner's machine
63 Match makers
65 Future fish

660 · DINNER TIME by Robert Walters

ACROSS
1 Roman robe
5 Ponders
10 Propel a boat
13 Copied
14 Mexican fiber
15 Atmosphere
16 Eat like a horse
19 Superman's insignia
20 Newspaper piece
21 Reclines lazily
22 Unusual person
23 Gawks (at)
25 Jacob's first son
28 Upper crust
29 Serf
30 Make amends
31 Lobster __ Diavolo
34 Taunter's remark
38 Pair
39 Mewls
40 "King of the road"
41 Madame de __
42 Head wreath
44 Betrays jealousy
46 Drescher of The Nanny
47 German industrialist
48 Dead heats
49 Baden-Baden, e.g.
52 Dine well
56 Picnic pests
57 Actress Anouk
58 Head-over-heels
59 Wild blue yonder
60 Social equals
61 Aroma

DOWN
1 VCR input
2 Musical work
3 Understands
4 Fuss
5 Fingerless glove
6 Aisle walker
7 Blossom holder
8 Sprite
9 Call on
10 Russian coin
11 Some exams
12 Quipsters
15 Cherish
17 Evening hour
18 Click beetle
22 Heed
23 Plum types
24 Singer Turner
25 Oboe or bassoon
26 Biblical brother
27 "Do __ others . . ."
28 Lucy's pal
30 Celestial ram
31 Supermarket offering
32 Cartoonist Goldberg
33 Nuclear-energy source
35 Multiarmed swimmers
36 Russian river
37 Comparative word
41 Frosh followers
42 Glacial ridges
43 Poet Ogden
44 Guzzled
45 Like a bad road
46 Better, as silver
47 New Zealand parrots
48 Big book
49 Herringlike fish
50 Walt Kelly's possum
51 Culture medium
53 Hiatus
54 Hasten
55 Self

661   EXPLOSIVE by Lee Weaver

ACROSS
1 Sleek jets
5 Pro __ (proportionally)
9 Iowa city
13 Toast topper
14 Gold unit
15 Enameled metal
16 Light classical music performance
18 Fly like a butterfly
19 Prepare to plant
20 Witnessed
21 Chopin pieces
23 Coined money
25 Invalidate
27 Take a break
29 "Sweet __" (quartet tune)
33 Of the moon
36 Hoarfrost
38 Steep, as tea
39 Oil cartel
40 Harder to find
41 Country byway
42 Toil away (at)
43 Cameo shape
44 More stable
45 Sign a check's back
47 Swerves off course
49 Perceives by touch
51 New York and Boston
55 Surrounded by
58 Rotate
60 Singing syllable
61 Poet Teasdale
62 Cosmologist's theory
65 Like a snail's pace
66 Having a roof overhang
67 "I cannot tell __"
68 Nashville is its cap.
69 Prophet
70 Deli loaves

DOWN
1 Some students, for short
2 Single-masted vessel
3 Conical quarters
4 Assn.
5 Marathon, e.g.
6 Sports complex
7 Sailor
8 Person present
9 All the way up, as a boom box
10 Gelatin shaper
11 Nobelist Wiesel
12 Complete collections
14 Leg joints
17 Wickerwork willow
22 Cal. column
24 Sunup
26 To wit
28 Go abroad
30 Persia, today
31 Hawaiian goose
32 Jug
33 Actor Rob
34 "__ my word!"
35 Social misfit
37 Lyricist Gershwin
40 Ornamental ribbons
44 Playground item
46 Scale notes
48 Sharp-tasting
50 Canyon of the comics
52 Boot-shaped country
53 One of the Muppets
54 Wise ones
55 Aide: Abbr.
56 Masculine
57 Bodybuilders pump it
59 Over: Ger.
63 Have, in Scotland
64 Tavern

662   TIGHTENING UP by Fred Piscop

ACROSS
1 Wolf (down)
6 Wrestling officials
10 Healthful spots
14 Repair-bill part
15 One of the Baldwins
16 Give notice
17 Greet the day
18 Robert De __
19 Astronomical bear
20 Publicity person
22 __ May Clampett
23 Blubber
24 Luther's 95
26 Kind of stew
30 Soviet space program
32 Letters at Calvary
33 Head the cast
35 Boost
39 Unfeeling
41 A Gabor
42 Lower in esteem
43 Time being
44 Novelist Jaffe
46 Cooking chamber
47 Overdramatic
49 Bobby-__ ('40s teens)
51 Potter rabbit
54 Corn portion
55 Painter Magritte
56 Philatelist's purchase
63 Blissful state
64 Shopper's bag
65 Nary a soul
66 Getz or Kenton
67 Borodin's Prince
68 Sugar-coated
69 Sacred
70 Snug
71 Annoy, so to speak

DOWN
1 Sharp blow
2 Singer Vikki
3 Irish Rose lover
4 Famous sewer
5 Painting on plaster
6 Long-limbed
7 Author Wiesel
8 Flowerless plant
9 Star Trek engineer
10 Concertina
11 Does some knitting
12 Usher's beat
13 Doesn't fold
21 Liberal pursuits
25 Sinuous dance
26 Hillbilly pronoun
27 Wise about
28 Suffix in accelerator names
29 Tightwad
30 "Stompin' at the __"
31 Mediterranean port
34 Jimmy Carter had one
36 Presented
37 End __ (ultimate customer)
38 Bank items on chains
40 Thumbs-up votes
45 Letters of haste
48 Occult figure
50 New Jersey city
51 Not canned or frozen
52 Caused
53 Star hoopster
54 Manicurist's material
57 Pizza order
58 All-inclusive
59 Joe Hardy's enticer
60 Dory or dinghy
61 Donald Duck, to Dewey
62 Track event

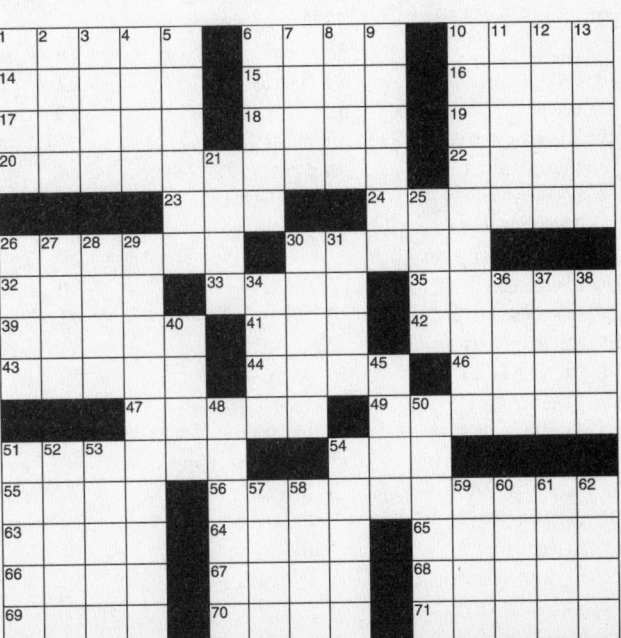

663   PARTIAL POST by Patrick Jordan

ACROSS

1 Imperfections
6 Book-jacket paragraph
11 Puff Daddy's genre
14 Provide with apparatus
15 Actress Blakley
16 Andy Capp beverage
17 Wild West Show originator
19 Yahtzee cube
20 Spice-yielding flowers
21 Less complicated
23 Item on a sales slip
24 Foot soldier's food
25 Pago Pago native
29 Whitman's "Song of __"
30 Shrimplike shellfish
31 Lost color
32 She plays Caroline on TV
35 Otherwise
36 Santa's craftsmen
37 "Daedalus and Icarus," e.g.
38 E-mail address element
39 Curl one's lip
40 City in Tuscany
41 Grid quorum
43 Egyptian beetle
44 Subjects to ridicule
46 Mauna __
47 Ethnic
48 Laborious
53 __ glance (quickly)
54 With precision
56 Chance beginning
57 Fencing swords
58 Birth-related
59 Wrap up
60 College VIPs
61 Wear away

DOWN

1 Attic sights
2 Blue hue
3 Dennis the Menace's dog
4 Petty quarrel
5 Marked by frugality
6 Yankees' home
7 High throws
8 Corn or cycle prefix
9 Turns loose
10 Like some birthday greetings
11 Big name in wagons
12 Sci-fi character
13 Jury members
18 Bank offering
22 __ vous plaît
24 Golf's __ Cup
25 Made haste
26 Patron of Alice's Restaurant
27 Discover competitor
28 Use 27 Down
29 Expert
31 Turns tail
33 Sicilian spewer
34 Captain of the Pequod
36 Award presenter's prop
37 Palermo pronoun
39 Under, perhaps
40 Triangle type
42 Weeks in Augustus' year
43 Washday challenge
44 Cover with cloth
45 Consumed
46 Loamy deposit
48 "In that case . . ."
49 Texas flag symbol
50 A Ringling brother
51 Hoover Dam's lake
52 Creator of Perry and Della
55 The Mad Hatter's beverage

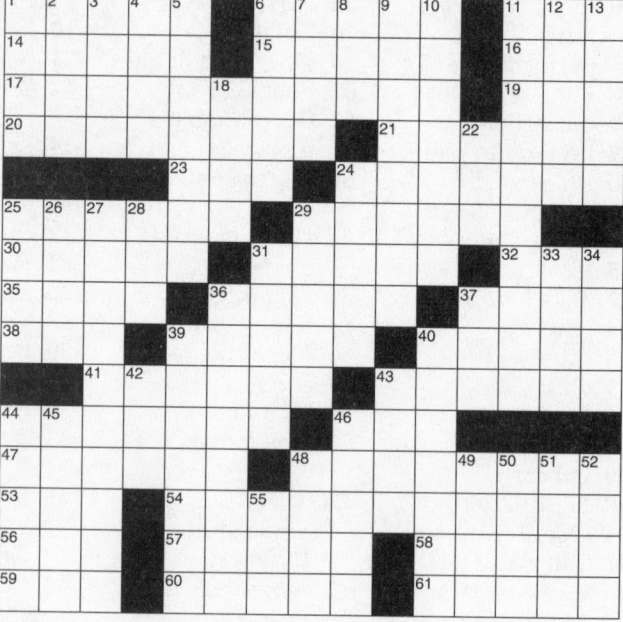

664   NUMERICAL ORDER by A.J. Santora

ACROSS

1 Hangs around
8 Forenoon times
11 Raced ahead
14 For starters
17 Support, in a way
18 Cry of disgust
19 Gunpowder, for one
20 In a strange way
21 River of myth
23 Wallace of E.T.
24 Hostess Maxwell
25 Eastern bigwig
27 Den sets
28 ER network
31 Saucy dances
34 Jacket type
35 "Hold On Tight" group
36 Heady posture
37 After a few
40 Tank filler
41 Botch up
42 Poker winnings
43 Type of engine
45 Headed up
46 Treat leather
47 Listen to
48 Mideast gulf
50 Composer Rorem
51 Makes inquiries
55 Kukla's pal
57 Wriggler
58 Forked letter
59 Time
64 Betrayers
65 Fast flier
66 "Slippery" tree
67 Ballerina's slipper

DOWN

1 Sibilations
2 __ a time
3 Mouse on The Simpsons
4 Poetic conjunction
5 Poetic time
6 P.O. designation
7 Parental employee
8 On the Baltic
9 Rhoda production co.
10 Winds
11 Bombed
12 Earth sci.
13 Withhold
15 '50s South Korean president
16 Some Fords
22 __ out (cancels)
23 Like some hands
24 Sophisticated
26 Ring padding
27 Small amount
29 Uninteresting
30 Penalty
31 Wise one
32 City in India
33 Grease 2 actress
34 Car Wash actor
38 Euripides drama
39 Nay canceler
44 Ret. plan
46 Acquire biters
47 Kohl of Germany
49 Gossip
50 Buzz's capsule-mate
52 "Nothing but net"
53 Japanese city
54 Brains
55 Switch positions
56 Hi's wife
57 Esau's land
60 Corrosive liquid, for short
61 Comic Philips
62 Wind dir.
63 Bro's sib

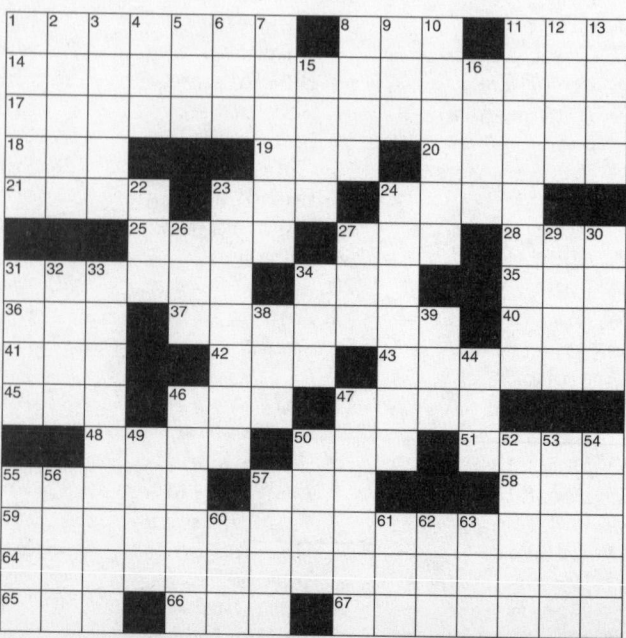

665 — RINGERS by Bob Lubbers

ACROSS

1 Easter entrée
5 Bradley or Sharif
9 Forest clearing
14 Moises of baseball
15 __ Hari
16 Kiboshed
17 Nutmeg St.
18 War god
19 Imitators
20 Chuck Barris creation
23 Western film
24 Roman road
25 Botch
29 First abode
31 Glut
33 __ Moines, IA
36 "Dies __"
38 Singer Skinnay
39 Romantic situation
43 Sunlit lobbies
44 Steering station
45 Collection
46 Church fundraisers
49 __ majesty (high crime)
51 To be: Lat.
52 Texas city
54 Employers
58 Hotel employee
60 Frisky mammal
64 Small glass tube
65 "__ boy!"
66 Lasso
67 Word form for "outer"
68 Deck-planking wood
69 Get satisfaction from
70 Distort
71 Gaelic

DOWN

1 Word form for "milk"
2 Waikiki welcome
3 Painter Claude
4 Stretchy cord
5 Arabian sultanate
6 On the fringe
7 Alamogordo event
8 Spates
9 Chew (on)
10 Sass
11 Hew-man resource?
12 German article
13 Asner and Wynn
21 1st or 2nd, for example
22 "Are you a man __ mouse?"
25 Helsinki native
26 Director Fritz et al.
27 Serviceable
28 Harass
30 Time period
32 Joins forces
33 Mary __ (ill-fated ship)
34 Kett and James
35 Feudal workers
37 Biblical verb suffix
40 Rampant
41 Move to a new home
42 __ du Diable
47 Meadow mom
48 Ointments
50 House and grounds
53 Hit it off
55 Diner patron
56 Moreno et al.
57 Asp or adder
58 Donkey sound
59 Downward, nautically
60 Unrefined metal
61 Can material
62 __ Mahal
63 Ike's command: Abbr.

666 — IN THE ROUND by Rich Norris

ACROSS

1 Applaud
5 Warm up in the ring
9 Burn with water
14 Dan Blocker role
15 Mug for the camera
16 Comedienne Fields
17 ABA member
18 Writer Wiesel
19 Dodge
20 The Lion King song
23 Uproar
24 Hollywood hopeful's hope
28 Ques. response
29 High hairstyle
33 Sluggards
34 Yuletide door hanging
36 Young men
37 Philanthropic event
40 Take a risk
42 Passover dinners
43 Canada's capital
46 Housing cost
47 ACLU concerns: Abbr.
50 SWAT team rescuee
52 Flawless concept
54 Venue for Shakespeare
58 Auto racer Bobby
61 Like Mother Hubbard's cupboard
62 Icy coating
63 India's first prime minister
64 Wicked
65 Golf hazard
66 List components
67 Ed Wood star
68 Cabinet member: Abbr.

DOWN

1 Three-step dance
2 Sunblock, e.g.
3 Houston nine
4 College course, briefly
5 Graf __
6 Palm Beach sport
7 "Yeah, right!"
8 Is unsteady
9 Edberg of tennis
10 Handyman's outfit
11 One __ time (singly)
12 Jar top
13 Poor grade
21 Actress San Giacomo
22 "__ Now or Never"
25 Pushbutton predecessor
26 Ancient
27 Ed.'s concerns
30 According to
31 Table of honor
32 Aquatic mammal
34 Health-food store offering
35 Jekyll's alter ego
37 PC screens
38 Actor Gazzara
39 Bandleader Shaw
40 Homer Simpson expletive
41 From __ Z
44 Marine mammal
45 Past
47 Move to Arizona, maybe
48 Airport surface
49 One of the Dwarfs
51 Went out, as the tide
53 Pub projectiles
55 Roof overhang
56 Vacation excursion
57 1965 Beatles film
58 Word form for "one"
59 Court divider
60 __ Stoops to Conquer

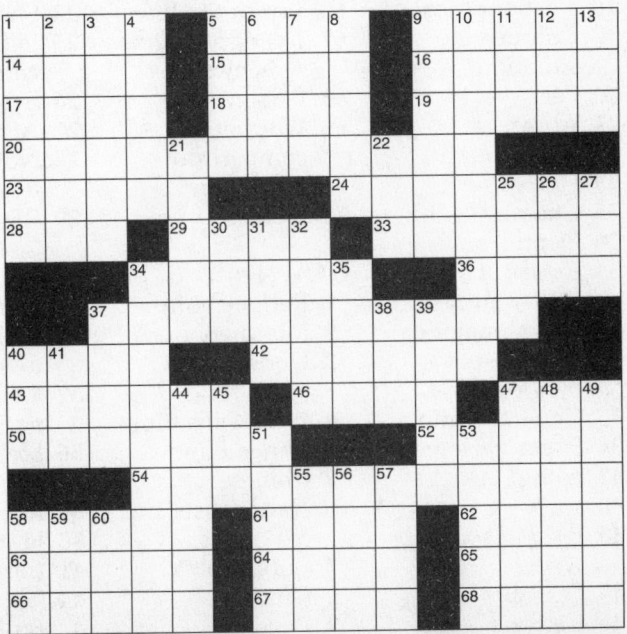

TAKING SIDES by Frances Hansen

ACROSS
1 Implanted
5 Skittish
10 Social reformer Jacob
14 Siamese
15 "You __ mouthful!"
16 Writer Ferber
17 Dry
18 German seaport
19 Barbershop offering
20 Greet the day
22 Grace the place
24 Sanford of *The Jeffersons*
27 Part of QED
28 Fellow
30 Strong wind
31 Author Carson
34 Assn.
35 Nobel Institute site
36 Plow inventor
37 Yegg's target
39 *Amerika* author
42 "Shucks!"
43 Gnawed to a fare-thee-well
45 French actor Jacques
47 Cooling unit: Abbr.
48 French dramatist
50 Role model
51 Aurora alias
52 Property attachment
53 Donahue of *Father Knows Best*
55 Catbird's quaking cousin
58 Greet the day
61 Chesterfield, e.g.
62 Hole __ (ace)
65 Stress, perhaps
66 Printing paper size
67 Madame de __
68 "More __ You Know" (1929 song)
69 Terrier type
70 Warming drink
71 Diminutive suffix

DOWN
1 For men only
2 Czech river
3 Odets play
4 Spider's nest
5 Eliot's monogram
6 Descartes' conclusion
7 Politically moderate
8 Nantes notion
9 One of Santa's reindeer
10 Backtracked
11 Rodgers and Hart musical
12 Monogram pt.
13 Identical
21 Half the name of a Samoan city
23 Toward the mouth
25 Soak up the sun
26 First name in scat
28 Babe in the bulrushes
29 Macaw
32 Muse of poetry
33 "__ pray" (pulpit petition)
38 Ballpark figure
40 Film critic Pauline
41 Abruzzi cathedral town
44 Hebrew eve
46 Hebrides island
49 Sign up
54 Hold forth
55 Recipe amts.
56 Fleece
57 Word form for "within"
59 Usher's offering
60 Sea eagle
63 Actor Beatty
64 Bridge expert Culbertson

III x IV by Brendan Emmett Quigley

ACROSS
1 World: Sp.
6 Dick Tracy's love
10 Bona __
14 Carrier's former name
15 "Summertime," e.g.
16 __ about (near)
17 Confusing situation
20 Per
21 Above
22 Old enough
23 Helper
25 Chemical suffix
26 Depth
33 *Return of the Native* author
34 Lodge member
35 1982 Disney movie
37 General Amin
38 Sugar variety
42 Sound of surprise
43 *Bed Riddance* writer
45 Cal. abbr.
46 Carreras, e.g.
48 Racing coup
52 "Eureka!"
53 1975 Wimbledon champ
54 Above
57 Grub
59 Artificiality
63 "M.T.A." group
66 Top-of-the-line
67 *The African Queen* screenwriter
68 Person
69 Word of comparison
70 Wild thing
71 Increase

DOWN
1 Remote button
2 Job-safety org.
3 Undercover agent
4 1988 Willis film
5 Miner's find
6 Chinese Nationalists' city
7 Cubic Rubik
8 Omen
9 Pouch
10 Throw in the towel
11 Machu Picchu builder
12 George, on *ER*
13 Gaelic
18 Freshwater fish
19 Charged particles
24 Short poem
25 Fills in, as a comic
26 Svelte
27 Attacked
28 Notre Dame team
29 Ran into, with "with"
30 "Hold On Tight" band
31 Maine college town
32 "Absolutely not!"
36 Scandinavian goddess of fate
39 Razor name
40 Frat letter
41 Carve with acid
44 Give heed
47 Built
49 Spicy cuisine
50 Second of two
51 Sinclair rival
54 RBI, e.g.
55 "I'm in trouble!"
56 Clinton cabinet appointee
57 Breakfast waffle
58 On the briny
60 Saharan
61 In perfect condition
62 Walt Kelly comic strip
64 Take
65 Jordan's org.

669 WHO'S LAUGHING NOW? by Patrick Jordan

ACROSS

1 Volcanic material
6 They may hold water
10 Square
14 "Encore!"
15 China setting
16 "I cannot tell __"
17 "Ho, ho, ho!"
20 Get accustomed (to)
21 Invent
22 Rainbow shape
24 Dynamic prefix
27 Hawaiian honkers
28 Brad and William
31 Thick
33 Summer hrs. in NYC
34 Soporific
36 Cause trouble
38 "Nyuk, nyuk, nyuk!"
41 Forbidden practice
42 Catches some Zs
45 __-fi
48 Clairvoyant's cards
50 Clay pigeon
51 Jouster's armful
53 Greek vowels
55 Beam
56 Daniel of Nicaragua
58 Protruding plane parts
61 "Ha-ha-ha-HA-ha!"
66 Radius neighbor
67 Perry's creator
68 Baked-potato garnish
69 House of Lords member
70 Consider
71 Enhanced, as one's muscles

DOWN

1 USA rank
2 In the past
3 Of humongous proportions
4 Like some cheddar
5 Author Seton
6 Carried (off)
7 Take advantage of
8 Mincemeat treat
9 Beach blanket?
10 Trustingly innocent
11 Marilu's *Taxi* role
12 Ran water over
13 Abhor
18 Report-card stat.
19 Most of the Joint Chiefs
22 Mil. address abbr.
23 Storied sleeper
25 Film a second time
26 Aware of
29 Fully stretched
30 Plan
32 Old sayings
35 Exile isle
37 Migration
39 Long ago
40 Native American clothing material
43 It rattles in a whistle
44 Porker's pad
45 Reduce speed
46 Screen legend Lombard
47 Chant
49 One behind the other
52 Chest wood
54 Soak (up)
57 Filled with reverence
59 Zen, e.g.
60 Bounce off the walls
62 Miners dig it
63 Music to a matador's ears
64 Seth's mother
65 San Fernando __ (Skelton character)

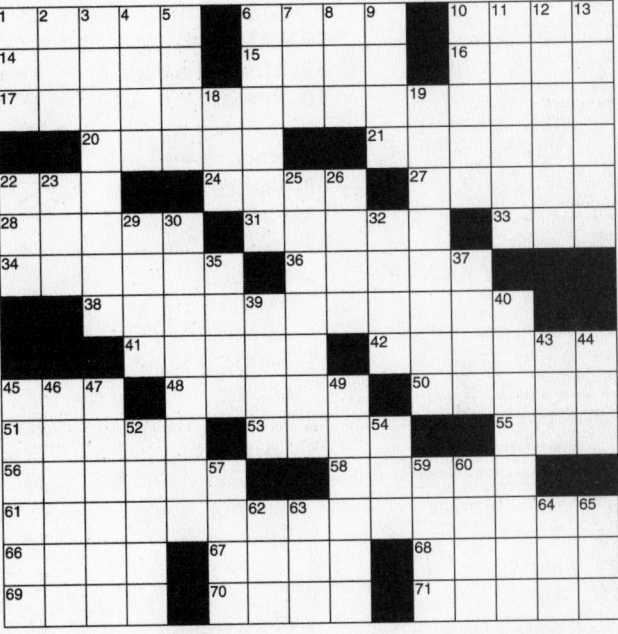

670 RANKINGS by Norma Steinberg

ACROSS

1 Most insignificant
6 Dairy animals
9 Big Apple theater producer Joseph
14 Zeal
15 Ronny Howard role
16 Vicinity
17 Madrid museum
18 Big stringed instrument
19 Blueprint
20 Mets and Mariners
23 Sounds of triumph
24 Paltry
25 Tropical fruit
29 Observe
30 Classroom trial
31 Cheer (for)
34 __ Dame
39 Chaos
42 Cut drastically, as prices
43 Bacterium
44 Actor Hackman
45 __ roll (winning)
47 Holdings
49 Acquiesce
53 Helper: Abbr.
55 Phillips Exeter, e.g.
59 Assess
60 Hemingway's nickname
61 Pier
64 Microwave
65 Swear
66 Come next
67 Finch's home
68 Yearnings
69 Loony

DOWN

1 Track circuit
2 Goof up
3 Actor Arkin
4 Carbonated drink
5 Mythical horse builder
6 Venomous snake
7 Moonstones
8 All-knowing
9 Seed source
10 __ New Guinea
11 City near Marseille
12 Singer Bailey
13 Spring flower
21 *Pal Joey* writer
22 Actress Davis
25 Beseeches
26 Skater's jump
27 Zola heroine
28 Singer Ed
29 Recipe direction
32 Gymnast Korbut
33 Type of poem
35 Grps.
36 Birch or banyan
37 Speak angrily
38 Potato parts
40 Role for Valerie
41 Broadway success
46 Salary-stub phrase
48 Stashed
49 Kitchen covering
50 Long for
51 Quotes
52 Happening
53 Colorado resort
54 Lasting impressions
56 Roof overhang
57 "This can't be!"
58 Endure
62 Boring routine
63 Whimsical

SKY LIGHTS by Bill Leonard

ACROSS

1 Variable star
5 More impolite
10 Charts
14 Incenses
15 Accustom
16 Ancient theaters
17 Check out
18 Astronomers
20 Ceres or Juno
22 Planet discovered in 1781
23 Steak order
24 Celtic sea god
25 Cease
28 Close groups of stars
33 Word for Yorick
34 Actor Kristofferson
35 French pronoun
36 Skating surface
37 Moon lander
38 Close tightly
39 Two-year-old
40 Ooze
41 Head: Fr.

42 Peruvian plant
45 Gazes steadily
47 Pah-pah preceder
48 Practice boxing
49 Navy builder
52 Passerine bird
56 Procyon's constellation
58 Lake city
59 Moslem nation
60 Roman magistrate
61 Narrative
62 Makes a choice
63 Surfeits
64 __ stars (gets bopped)

DOWN

1 Naldi of the silents
2 Metallic rocks
3 Suit part
4 Keyboard symbol
5 Spa
6 Loosen
7 Two
8 Go wrong

9 Leo's brightest star
10 Austrian composer
11 Yemeni seaport
12 South American nation
13 Talk back
19 Mars' alias
21 Ethiopian title
25 Pub game
26 Agent Ness
27 Thanksgiving parade participant
28 Statement of belief
29 Like a wet noodle
30 Old-time anesthetic
31 Highway
32 Locations
34 Painter Paul
38 Young actresses
40 Meanings expressed by morphemes
43 Redbreasts

44 Some deer
45 Bowling marks
46 Roofing material
48 Long scarf
49 I know: Lat.
50 O.K. Corral name
51 Pre-med subj.

52 State of irritation
53 "Dies __"
54 World's longest river
55 Commands to horses
57 Cretan Mount

ON THE GRIDDLE by Bob Lubbers

ACROSS

1 Palermo pelf
5 Addis __
10 Makes mistakes
14 Cain raiser
15 Royal ceremony
17 Equivocate
19 Became skilled in
20 Greek vowel
21 Linguistic suffix
24 Payable
25 Vestige
27 Hang out
29 Prepare for painting
33 Curved shape
34 Some Kenyans
36 Part of RFD
38 Face powder
43 Devil
44 Per __ (yearly)
46 Tint
48 Newspaper sections
51 Subtle atmosphere

52 Gives for a while
54 Tease
56 Came upon
57 Boat propeller
58 Manages
63 Procrastinate
68 Galley worker
69 Nobelist Wiesel
70 Espied
71 Boscs
72 Watered down

DOWN

1 Statute
2 Neighbor of Ore.
3 Churchill's "so few"
4 Letters on a radio
5 Two-pair holding, in poker
6 Field-goal expert, e.g.
7 Rule, Britannia composer
8 Sort of swine

9 __ of Cleves
10 UFO crew
11 Stair parts
12 Itineraries
13 Golf Hall-of-Famer
16 Assists
18 Young feller
21 Shade tree
22 Work up lather
23 Born Free character
26 Western capital
28 Alit
30 Actress Papas
31 Fall bloomer
32 Paleozoic, e.g.
35 Bar rocks
37 Alias letters
39 Latin 101 word
40 Keystone character
41 Word on a quarter
42 Untainted
45 Wrestler's pad
46 Court cry
47 Not pickable
49 Chest part

50 Shankar collection
52 Barn attics
53 Robin and the Seven Hoods characters
55 Actor Turhan
59 Slightest sound

60 Art Deco artist
61 __-tat
62 Hodgepodge
64 Sawbuck
65 Suffix for percent
66 Alice name
67 "It's a mouse!"

BIG REDUCTIONS by Rich Norris

ACROSS
1 Rabbit's foot
4 Island shelter
10 Johnson of *Laugh-In*
14 Barcelona bear
15 West __
16 Brownie, e.g.
17 What retailers pay
20 Mischievous
21 Austrian poet
22 Onion relative
23 Director Craven
26 Casts out
28 Vega's constellation
29 Unable to sit still
31 Work the soil
32 Masked one, maybe
34 Vista
36 Bowl-game entertainment
39 Shirt insert
40 Spock, for one
41 Actor Vigoda
42 Street of fiction
43 "__ brillig . . ."

47 Geometric shape
50 Woosnam of the PGA
51 Hard to find
52 Biker's path
53 Like some well-pitched games
54 Tournament participant
59 Relax, as rules
60 Do a camp project
61 Wedding-page word
62 Fleet fliers
63 Whirling waters
64 Brooklyn ending

DOWN
1 *Dames* star
2 Fictional Wilkes
3 Stereo component
4 Financial claim
5 Nav. rank
6 City south of Tulsa

7 Zero
8 Kicker's aid
9 Fish hawk
10 Well-coordinated
11 Two-wheeled vehicle
12 Forest skyline
13 Golfer Ernie
18 Winsome
19 Trucker's truck
23 Have a yen for
24 Salad vegetable
25 Response creators
27 Go out with
30 Kowalski shout
33 Defunct football grp.
34 __ Na Na
35 Have a handle on
36 Regulars
37 Deviating from the norm
38 Examine in detail
39 Varnish ingredient

42 Erase
44 Waikiki woman
45 Comes up
46 Parlor piece
48 Birthday mail
49 Started a fire
53 Dumbarton denials

54 Montana and Marino: Abbr.
55 Disencumber (of)
56 Catered to
57 First name in Ugandan history
58 TV "science guy"

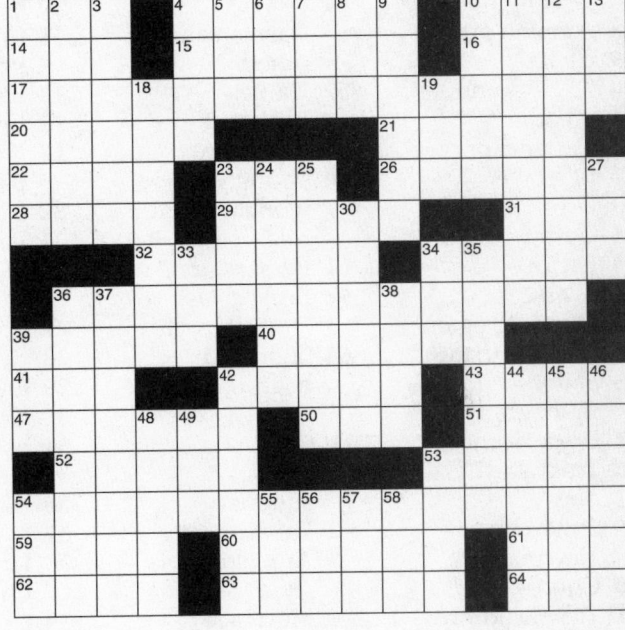

PLAY MONEY by Fred Piscop

ACROSS
1 Fills to the gills
6 "__ Coming" (Laura Nyro song)
10 Edible seaweed
14 Give the slip to
15 Mathematical sets
16 Treat with milk
17 Iraqi credit card?
19 __-Soviet relations
20 Holiday precursor
21 Colorado resort
22 '60s prime minister of Israel
24 Cardinal
26 Manitoba native
27 *Aladdin* character
28 Alice, in *Alice*
32 __ Haute, IN
35 Mrs. Dithers
36 Keg-party locale
37 __ pyrite (fool's gold)
38 Novarro of silents
39 Costa __
40 Margin filler

41 Salty lake
42 Suit-pocket item
43 Nineveh native
45 Mythical piper
46 Puny pup
47 Liked a lot
51 Working, for example
54 Reeve's foster father in *Superman*
55 Jemison of NASA
56 Spirited steed
57 Iranian land?
60 Pianist Gilels
61 Discontinued Dodge
62 Champing at the bit
63 Fill with cargo
64 Samoan port part
65 Beef order

DOWN
1 Ritual repast
2 Full of spirit
3 In perfect pitch
4 Author LeShan
5 Fawning

6 Charlton Heston epic
7 Hang in the hammock
8 Hospital dept.
9 Like some Eskimos
10 French wiener?
11 Composer Satie
12 Late-night host
13 Combine
18 Rani's wraparound
23 Ready to go
25 Russian caveman?
26 December tune
28 Gene Tierney, for one
29 Leprechaun land
30 Base, slangily
31 Hang around
32 Actress Louise
33 Love god
34 Goes bad
35 Gem weight
38 Bit of drizzle
42 Phone part
44 Participate in a 10K

45 Peel
47 Ledger page
48 Adult insect
49 Eroded
50 Farm-machine pioneer
51 Highlander

52 Author Bombeck
53 Midnight fridge visit
54 Long tooth
58 "__ Believer" (Monkees tune)
59 Keyboard word

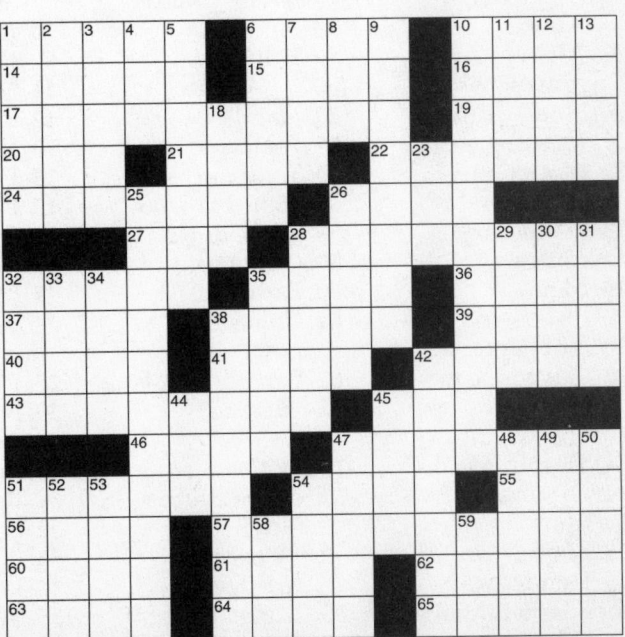

675 SHAPE UP by Norma Steinberg

ACROSS

1 Bring closer, as one's fish
7 *Nova* network
10 Piercing tool
13 Regal fur
14 Acorn source
16 Return to the starting point
18 Arabian gulf
19 Chat
20 "__ live and breathe!"
21 Cat or canary
22 Egg layer
23 Drink like a cat
25 Oath
28 Factory overseer
30 Decorate again
31 Summer fruit
33 Sailors' monogram
34 Press clothes
35 Trustworthy one
39 Simon or Newman
40 Choose
41 Ties the knot
42 Narrow cut
43 Heeds, with "to"
46 Sprite
47 Styling goo
48 Raised railways
49 Hot tub
52 Actress Farrow
54 "Rats!"
56 Caspian and others
57 Daniel Ellsberg's disclosure
60 Young woman's film role
61 Pass, as time
62 Broke a fast
63 __ Plaines, IL
64 Sight and hearing

DOWN

1 Brief summary
2 Eat away at
3 Ant, old-style
4 Mortgage
5 "To be," for example: Abbr.
6 Like "it"
7 Opinion measurer
8 Sharp reaction
9 Move on snow
10 Circle parts
11 Brought, as a parcel
12 Last letter
15 Ensnare
17 Narrow passage
22 Circle dance
24 Part of A.D.
26 Bloodhound's clues
27 Came in first
28 Culpability
29 Obligations
30 Ceremonies
31 Sacred song
32 Gear
36 Acting part
37 Novel's coda
38 Holds the deed on
39 Greek letter
44 Volunteer State: Abbr.
45 Runs off to marry
47 Prize fight's take
49 Oozes
50 Diagram grammatically
51 Donkeys
53 *Bus Stop* playwright
55 Garden tools
56 Stretch across
57 Singer Zadora
58 In addition
59 Pub brew

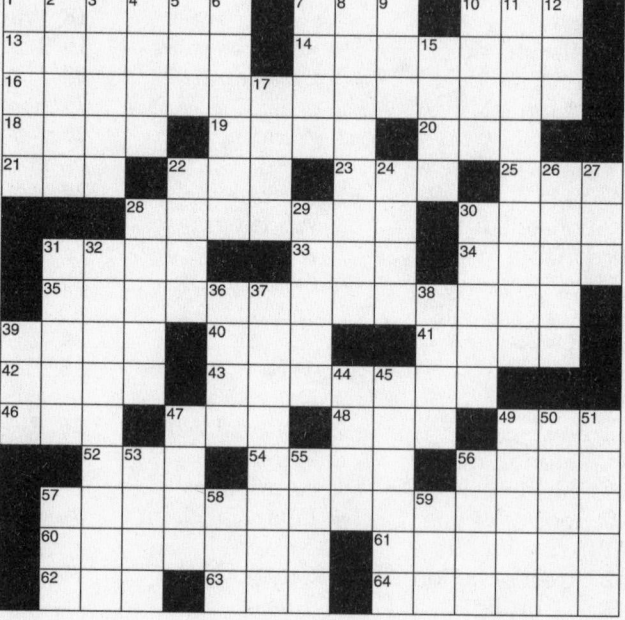

676 SO LONG FILMS by Randall J. Hartman

ACROSS

1 Killer whale
5 At a __ for words
9 Propel a bike
14 Antler
15 Assert
16 Last letter, in Athens
17 Ali MacGraw film of '69
20 Stop __ dime
21 Housing cost
22 Mountain ridges
23 Temporary routes
25 Manuscript directive
26 Not hers
27 Got a hole in one
28 H.S. exam
31 Tibetan monks
34 Disney sci-fi film
35 Markdown
36 Hemingway adaptation of '57
39 Catherine __-Jones of *The Mask of Zorro*
40 Cut, in a way
41 Mighty conflict
42 She-sheep
43 Breakfast cereal
44 Sault __ Marie
45 Networks
46 Belly
50 __ *Weapon*
53 Halt
54 Feathered stole
55 Tony Curtis comedy of '66
58 Strike down
59 Out of control
60 Farm unit
61 Come to a point
62 Party bowlfuls
63 "Buenos __!"

DOWN

1 George Burns film
2 TV exec Arledge
3 Zagreb resident
4 Plus
5 Strata
6 Kilns
7 Religious group
8 Sign at the Bijou
9 Did the honors at tea
10 Irish patriot Robert
11 Money owed
12 Chills and fever
13 Highland girl
18 Fruit flaw
19 Dormant
24 Scarlett of Tara
25 Chew out
27 "Stormy Weather" composer
28 Poet Teasdale
29 Some donations
30 Pianist John
31 Be slothful
32 Some
33 Chess win
34 Lone Star State
35 Witch-trial site
37 Croon
38 Squid relatives
43 Jerry Mathers role
44 Has on hand
45 Author E.B.
46 Razor sharpener
47 Low-tech calculators
48 Hooded snake
49 Helen or Isaac
50 Endure
51 Humorist Bombeck
52 Voyage
53 Road rig
56 Mom's partner
57 Turned, as food

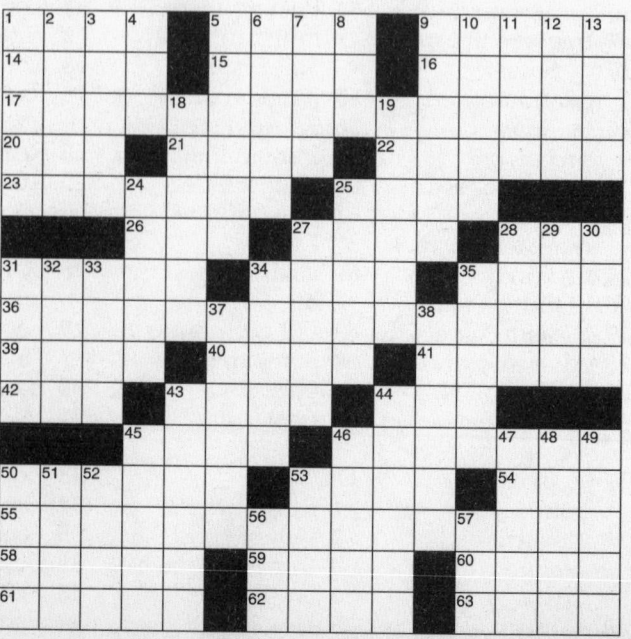

677 IN THE THICK OF THINGS by Fred Piscop

ACROSS
1 "¿Que __?"
5 Walk through water
9 Houston player
14 Construction piece
15 Wide-eyed
16 Actor Cheech
17 It's low on a sports car
20 "Sarabandes" composer
21 Pro's charge
22 High point
23 Pilgrim to Mecca
26 Rhett Butler's last word
28 British wheels
30 Poet Levertov
34 Prefix with metric
37 "__ corny as Kansas . . ."
39 Horse opera
40 Hinterland
44 MacDowell of *Groundhog Day*
45 Char
46 __ tai
47 Loch sighting
49 Insurers incur them
52 Like a sourball
54 Be a drugstore cowboy
57 Allied victory site of 1944
60 Moo goo __ pan
62 Nettles
64 Joseph Conrad novel
68 Upper crust
69 Greek-salad cheese
70 Make bootees
71 Smarts
72 Candied tubers
73 __-serif (type style)

DOWN
1 Paparazzo's wares
2 Crosswise, nautically
3 __ Domingo
4 Virtuoso
5 Children's card game
6 In the past
7 Tip, as a hat
8 Encouraged, with "on"
9 I __ Camera
10 Grassy plain
11 Begin a fall
12 Solemn ceremony
13 Cameo stone
18 Wriggly
19 Crack the books
24 Part of HOMES
25 Notes from the CEO
27 Kitty cry
29 *60 Minutes* man
31 Bit of gossip
32 Antitoxins
33 ". . . __ saw Elba"
34 David Bowie's wife
35 Trig ratio
36 OTB postings
38 Poky critter
41 Twists out of shape
42 *Star Wars* princess
43 About
48 Therefore, to Descartes
50 Spock's boss
51 Brouhahas
53 Chewy candy
55 Actress Verdugo
56 Pine exudation
57 The Beatles' "__ a Woman"
58 Introduction to marketing?
59 Put down
61 Creative spark
63 Some JFK arrivals
65 Golf prop
66 Cash dispenser, for short
67 __ Tafari (Haile Selassie)

678 GRADUATION DAY by Rich Norris

ACROSS
1 VCR insert
5 *Cheers* waitress
10 Summer coolers, briefly
13 Elvis' middle name
14 Shows to be false
15 Slangy term of address
16 Diamond topper
18 One of the Peróns
19 Suitable for the occasion
20 Did as told
21 Use scissors
22 Maple output
23 S. Dak. neighbor
24 Metal refuse
25 Note groupings
27 Like some degrees
30 Mrs. Chaplin
31 Singer Julius
32 Formal wear
36 Makes improvements to
37 Daily records
40 Laments in verse
43 Word before policy or year
45 Clothes holder
46 Cape __, MA
47 Strain, as one's patience
48 Hole-punching tools
49 *1984* author
52 Coffee brewer
53 Do a salon job
54 Intensive interrogation
56 Always, in poetry
57 West __ (Jamaica's home)
58 Bugs on a hill
59 Liquor-free
60 Erato is their Muse
61 Unpleasant situation

DOWN
1 Hot stuff
2 Algonquian language
3 Put off
4 Buffalo-to-Syracuse dir.
5 Hollywood star, for short
6 McBeal on TV
7 Playwright Elmer
8 Heavy metal
9 Horned viper
10 Theban supreme god
11 High-society hors d'oeuvre
12 "Make it __!"
14 Toyland visitors
17 Surety agreement
21 Writes illegibly
24 Not bad
26 Wreaks havoc on
27 Bridge holdings
28 Assns.
29 Seasonal beverage
31 Something to draw or toe
33 Give off
34 Pince-__
35 Chopin work
38 Dingy attics
39 Cunning
40 Got around
41 6 Down, for one
42 Queen of fiction
43 Makes creases
44 Doing nothing
46 Relinquishes
49 Cry of dismay
50 Aptly-named astronaut
51 Legal order
54 Reward for waiting?
55 Leg, in slang

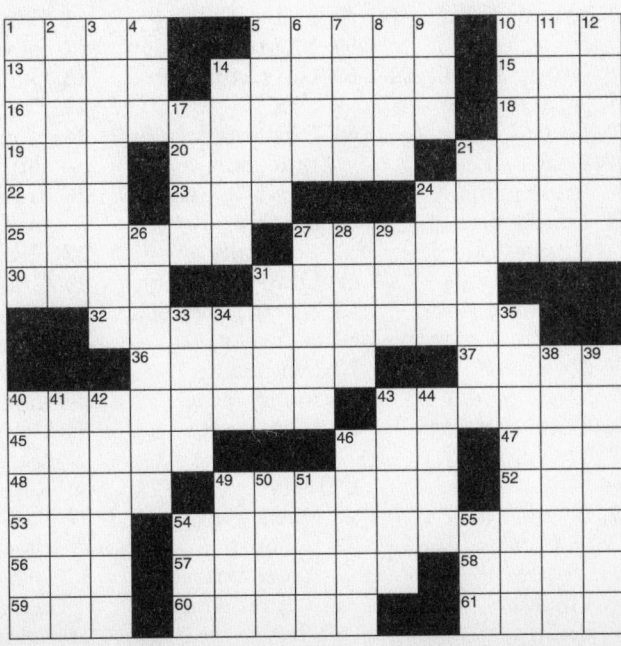

679   JUST FOR U by Bob Lubbers

ACROSS
1 Cruiser direction
4 US intelligence org.
7 Rescue
11 Eastern European
13 Legume
14 Heterogeneous mixtures
16 Honolulu wear
19 Gullet
20 Supplements
22 Masters Tournament locale
25 Hurry up
26 Automobile
27 Mao chum
28 "Keep your __ the ball!"
30 Monetary unit
31 Tuneful tenor
33 Ecuador's capital
35 Rudolph Valentino role
36 Source of feeling, maybe
37 Production component
41 Outmoded jacket
43 Video-game producer
44 Sonar sound
47 Bridge-seat occupants
50 "__ Do That" (*A Chorus Line* song)
51 Missus Lennon, née __
52 Rental unit: Abbr.
53 With laughter
55 *The Last Supper* painter
57 Prudhoe Bay dwelling
58 World view, in Ulm
63 Ms. Evans' pseudonym
64 Diminutive
65 Where Ulupalakua is
66 __ souci
67 Tote up
68 Reduce in intensity

DOWN
1 Vesuvius ejection
2 Southern st.
3 Marble used as a shooter
4 Rest inducer
5 Oceanic route
6 __ Andreas fault
7 Famous magician
8 Shun
9 Citrus fruit
10 Swoop (upon)
12 Cleaning, as a rug
15 African republic
17 Refunders, often
18 Hindu elephant driver
21 Columnist Buchwald
22 Vaudeville spots
23 "Shucks!"
24 Author Vidal
29 Burton film of '77
30 Sequence
32 __ out a living
34 Sp. aunt
36 Potatoes au __
38 Mutual agreement
39 Russian river
40 Minute
42 Music hipsters
44 Whale cluster
45 Full of wonder
46 Ruark works
48 Hauled in
49 Sounded weary
52 Actress Susan
54 Huntsville's home: Abbr.
56 Upper pelvic bones
59 Namibia, until '90: Abbr.
60 Abu Dhabi is its cap.
61 Lump
62 U.K. territory

680   ON THE GRID by Lee Weaver

ACROSS
1 Puts away
6 Ticket ends
11 Guy's date
14 Princess' headgear
15 Comic Kovacs
16 In the past
17 Adam of *Chicago Hope*
18 Group of officers
19 Actress West
20 *Beau* __
21 Deadlocked
22 Daily grinds
23 Letters on a cornerstone
25 Testimonials
27 Fireplace floor
30 Hammer part
31 Sofa parts
32 Gumbo veggie
35 Copier chemical
39 Tree branch
40 Washer cycle
42 Become dim
43 __ *Gay*
45 House, in Tijuana
46 Fed. agent
47 Sty cry
49 Devious plan
51 Surpass in excellence
55 Common article
56 Clamorous criticism
57 Dallas Cowboys emblem
59 Mirror reflection
63 Govt. commerce grp.
64 Customary practice
65 Life of __ (ease)
66 Before, poetically
67 Drapery section
68 Airborne vehicle
69 Squealer
70 Producing foamy lather
71 More crafty

DOWN
1 Doe's mate
2 Exhaust
3 Acorn bearers
4 Author's hang-up
5 Most sensible
6 Religious offshoot
7 Characteristic
8 Road beneath a bridge
9 One under par
10 Match, as a raise
11 Entire range
12 Shooting marble
13 Gardener's soil
22 Really ordinary
24 Norse god of thunder
26 Track transaction
27 Hearty's partner
28 Gray or Moran
29 Snowballs, sometimes
33 It holds a motorcycle up
34 Genetic material: Abbr.
36 Reputation
37 Ball-shaped cheese
38 *Lethal Weapon 4* actress Russo
41 Bridge position
44 Have the flu
48 Capital of the Bahamas
50 Bird sounds
51 Propose
52 Prefix meaning "extremely"
53 Be silent, in music
54 Wise ones
58 Count (on)
60 Jai __
61 Drummer Krupa
62 One looking
64 FedEx rival

681 BUDGET BUSTER by Patrick Jordan

ACROSS
1 Was quietly angry
6 Eye drop
10 Rock singer Joan
14 Repair a wrong
15 Diminish
16 Spiny houseplant
17 Poker player's pack
18 Annoys
19 *Duck Soup* name
20 Words from a 41 Across
23 Brother of Cain and Abel
24 Maiden-name indicator
25 Black Sea peninsula
29 Ave. crossers
30 Contemptible fellow
33 Words from a 41 Across
36 Bullring "Bravo!"
37 News article
38 Kilmer of *The Saint*
39 Movie monster
40 Back talk
41 Nonfrugal sort
45 Morse-code character
46 Took the pennant
47 Does a double take, perhaps
48 Buddy
49 Tumult
51 Words from a 41 Across
59 Brainstorm
60 Paint layer
61 Goosebump-inducing
62 Laugh loudly
63 Director Kazan
64 Jockey's controls
65 Pretentious-looking
66 Barbie or Raggedy Ann
67 Orchard, essentially

DOWN
1 Verifiable statement
2 Beehive State
3 Additional
4 Draws to a close
5 1957 Tracy/Hepburn film
6 Chubby Checker's dance
7 Soil
8 Egyptian cross
9 Takes personally
10 Farr of *M*A*S*H*
11 Western actor Jack
12 Actress Spelling
13 Schoolbook
21 Slangy affirmative
22 For fear that
25 TV chef Julia
26 Mathematical proportion
27 Bumbling
28 *The Wizard of Oz* studio
29 Completely convinced
30 Infant's ailment
31 Up in the air
32 Obligations
34 In equilibrium
35 Has the power to
39 Swimsuit part
41 Persuade
42 Served as a security force for
43 Jazz combo, often
44 President Hoover
48 Arctic explorer Robert
49 Garden mollusk
50 Wreck completely
51 Actress Sorvino
52 Aroma
53 Kin of "Cool!"
54 Flight-school test
55 Express derision
56 Canal completed in 1825
57 Film, in France
58 Thomas Hardy heroine

682 WEAPONRY by Fred Piscop

ACROSS
1 Cowpokes' pals
6 Abbr. in many business names
10 Skater Lipinski
14 Allure
15 __ and file
16 Change for a five
17 Bubble-gum comics character
19 Sitarist Shankar
20 __ and Son (English sitcom)
21 One way to serve beans
23 Barbie's boyfriend
24 Usher's beat
25 Rigatoni relative
28 "What Kind of Fool __?"
31 1-800-FLOWERS rival
32 Oust
34 In any way
36 Pugilists' org.
39 Bullwinkle's colleague
42 Sitcom planet
43 Catty remark
44 Cultured gem
45 Baseball plays: Abbr.
46 *Krazy* __
48 "Power" word form
49 Pentium maker
52 Net holder
54 WWII life jacket
57 Stored fodders
61 __ colada
62 Basketball great Maravich
64 Perpetually
65 Creative spark
66 Thrill to pieces
67 "__ Do It" (Porter tune)
68 Words in print
69 Showed again

DOWN
1 Industrial pollutants
2 At the drop of __
3 Bulldoze
4 Football play
5 Walloped
6 Highlands hillside
7 British rule in India
8 __ close to schedule
9 __-Ball (arcade game)
10 Much more than warm
11 Diarist Nin
12 Party hearty
13 Parenthetical remark
18 Hawaiian coffee center
22 Bully's offering, maybe
25 Centigrade freezing point of water
26 Novello of old films
27 Watch sound
29 Goya's *The Naked* __
30 "No problem!"
31 Winter bug
33 House of worship
35 Pastel shade
36 Fay of *King Kong*
37 Swiss capital
38 Milan's *Teatro __ Scala*
40 "__ the season . . ."
41 Rhode Island's state tree
45 Big name in Scotch
47 Threesome
49 Drive forward
50 Wet behind the ears
51 Ism
53 Less well
55 Kebab holder
56 Rip or neap
57 "Now!" to a surgeon
58 Apparatus
59 Sundance's girlfriend
60 Caught in the act
63 Questionnaire question

BACK AND FORTH by Mark Blakeburn

ACROSS
1 It holds water
4 Parent, back and forth
7 "The bud" preceder, back and forth
12 Edward G.'s *Little Caesar* role
13 Calcutta clothing
14 Parsley-family member
15 Some *Nautilus* Fan Club members, back and forth
17 In force
18 Unproductive
19 Big name in 49 Across
21 Remnant
22 Except for
23 Nonconformists' art movement
27 Condor claws
31 Role for Mae
32 Midmorning
34 Hose material
35 Addams cousin
36 Plane device, back and forth

38 Double CCLI
39 Landing connector
42 Where Ilsa met Rick
44 Guess, in brief
45 Way out
47 Horrifying
49 A soc. sci.
51 Flight-board abbr.
52 Awaken
54 Gad about
58 Baby's complaint
59 Donna's doe, back and forth
61 Tollbooth area
62 Florence's river
63 *Yanks* star
64 Hand over, back and forth
65 __ *Kapital*
66 One of Ernie Keebler's crew

DOWN
1 Japanese legislature
2 High point
3 Tied up, in a way
4 Agatha Christie title
5 "You __ My Sunshine"

6 Some yuppie couples
7 How sailors may move, back and forth
8 How buffoons behave
9 Whole lotta money
10 Wife of Osiris
11 Nancy Drew's beau
12 IV installers
13 Draftee, e.g.
16 Be successful in
20 Scarf down
23 Mark of repetition
24 Praying area
25 Briskness
26 Bit of politesse, back and forth
28 Less fresh
29 Irrelevant data
30 Mean mood
31 Part of Daffy Duck's charm
33 Buddhists' Satan
37 Ball role
40 Detail one's deductions
41 Daytona entrant, back and forth

43 Lee and Teasdale, back and forth
46 Sodom survivor
48 Song section
50 U.S.-Canadian force
52 "King" of jazz
53 King of Norway
54 Counting intervals
55 One of Victoria's prime ministers
56 Villein
57 Before, back and forth
58 EMT technique
60 Century 21 competitor

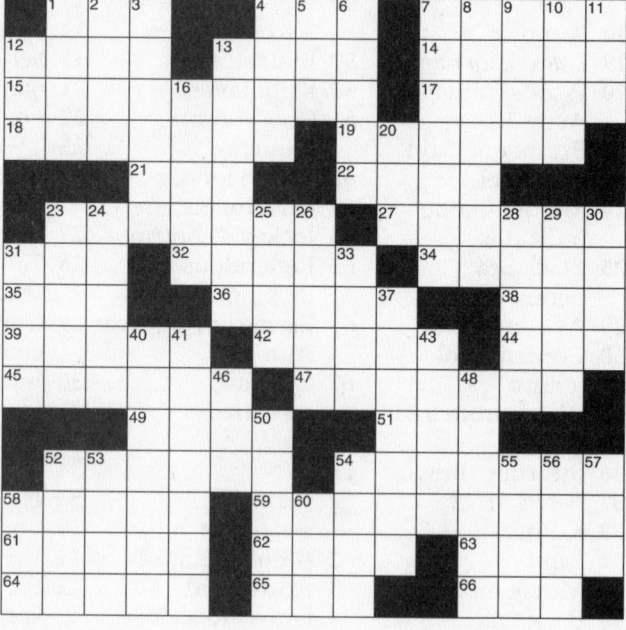

THE COAST IS CLEAR by Frank Longo

ACROSS
1 Bit of buffoonery
6 Brightly colored fish
10 Droops
14 Light brown
15 Barrett or Jaffe
16 Actor Morales
17 Mass migration of 1849
19 Ranch unit
20 Sound system
21 American League team
23 Ho-hum
25 "Shut up!"
26 Beach Boys tune
30 1942 John Wayne film
32 Mrs. Kramden
33 Cass and Michelle, once
35 Microscopic
36 Elated
37 Tiger's roar?
41 Cardiologist's concern
42 Macaroni shape
43 Song by the Eagles

47 Neil Simon play
49 Col. Tibbetts' mother
50 Busily engaged
51 Soul singer of commercials
54 Ibsen works
59 "Leaving on __ Plane"
60 Tune sung by 33 Across
62 Biblical weed
63 Fairy-tale fiend
64 "__ pass Go . . ."
65 They may be inflated
66 Pigeon-__
67 Playwright Zoe

DOWN
1 Essentials
2 Uncluttered
3 Buster Brown's dog
4 Frankenstein's assistant
5 Cause __ (public controversy)
6 Bobby of hockey
7 Joey's safe spot

8 Archaeological handle
9 Taunting cry
10 *Above the Law* star
11 Climb
12 Scampi ingredient
13 Saltillo snooze
18 GI Joe, for one
22 58 Down, e.g.
24 Eritrean capital
26 Stimpy or Felix
27 1996 Olympics flame lighter
28 Rummy variety
29 Like winter roads
30 Affect
31 Parliamentary denial
34 Inclined
36 Ad-__ committee
37 Vaccine target
38 Geisha's sash
39 Go bad
40 She-sheep
41 Jai __
42 *CHiPs* star
43 Goddess of witchcraft

44 Binging
45 Matador
46 Thrills
48 Deputy
50 Netman Agassi
52 Glaswegian
53 Othello's antagonist
55 Frenzied
56 Short skirt
57 Presently
58 Snorkel and Bilko: Abbr.
61 Crimson or carmine

685 SHORT POEMS by Norma Steinberg

ACROSS
1 *Little Women* character
5 Ornamental belt
9 Paid player
12 Aroma
13 Opera songs
15 Clench
16 Illumination in the dark
18 Strong cord
19 Antidrug agcy.
20 Genie's offering
21 Dodged
23 Of sound mind
24 Ugly Duckling, eventually
25 Tuxedo accessory
28 Tabloid fare
32 Extraterrestrial
33 Burn
34 Narrow opening
35 Become weary
36 One of the bases
37 Kind of mug
38 At all
39 Actress Russo
40 Committee
41 Talk about in detail
43 Botch
44 Kudrow of *Friends*
45 Fuse, as metal
46 Articulate
49 Identical
50 Take more than one's share of
53 Pro __ (proportionally)
54 Like Billy Ray Cyrus' heart
57 Actor Sharif
58 Nary a soul
59 Radar-screen light
60 Speedometer letters
61 Pilsner, e.g.
62 Apiary residents

DOWN
1 Connection
2 Mrs. Ernie Kovacs
3 Roman robe
4 Princely monogram
5 Salty
6 Get up
7 Wistful exhalation
8 "Gotcha!"
9 Nudge
10 Ready for harvest
11 Newspaper page
14 Administrator
15 Stadium seating
17 Finn's creator
22 Moving vehicle
23 Stay out of the way
24 Frighten
25 With __ breath
26 Shade of green
27 Telegrams
28 Paris' river
29 Together (with)
30 Malign in print
31 Fashion
33 Biblical queendom
36 Isolde's beloved
40 More ashy
42 __ Tin Tin
43 Constituent
45 Singer Newton
46 Return-address word
47 Lantern
48 Brigham Young's destination
49 Loafer, for one
50 Robust
51 Steinbeck character
52 Swindles
55 Corn on the __
56 Subside

686 RUN-OF-THE-MILL by Rich Norris

ACROSS
1 Crow calls
5 Wife of Zeus
9 Madrid museum
14 Not "fer"
15 Amazed
16 '80s NBC drama
17 Columnist Barrett
18 War, to Sherman
19 Colored like the sky
20 Tax-return category
23 Tune by 63 Across
24 Ballpark beverage
25 Painter's protection
29 Way out
33 Program interruptions
36 Aligns
38 Resting atop
39 November event
43 Without delay, in a memo
44 '60s guru Timothy
45 "__ you serious?"
46 ACLU concerns
49 Get up
51 The Emerald Isle
53 Poetic feet
57 1/2, e.g.
62 Biblical spy
63 Guitarist Clapton
64 Irish folk singer
65 Military chaplain
66 Dole (out)
67 Offend the nose
68 Has __ to the ground
69 Supportive votes
70 Really upset

DOWN
1 Channing of Broadway
2 Greek marketplace
3 Like Chicago
4 Slowpokes
5 "Very funny!"
6 Wide-spouted pitcher
7 Bank (on)
8 Off-the-script comment
9 Locations
10 Hair-salon request
11 Former student, briefly
12 Challenge
13 Have debts
21 Title giver
22 Wedding-page word
26 Eggs
27 Honeycomb part
28 Leg joints
30 Capital of Western Samoa
31 Shoddy in quality
32 Feminine ending
33 Ice-cream thickener
34 He loved Lucy
35 Sweater problem
37 Venetian-blind component
40 Short-lived things
41 Important time
42 Pessimistic type
47 Lumberjack's shout
48 "Sold out" letters
50 Library gadgets
52 Adversary
54 Actor Sal
55 *Gaslight* star
56 Slithery reptile
57 Actor James
58 Shoppe sign word
59 On the loose
60 Comic Rudner
61 King beaters
62 Apr. 15th advisor

MOUSE CALL by Patrick Jordan

ACROSS

1 Skywalker's father
6 Hit the malls
10 Butter servings
14 Puccini genre
15 Frequent song subject
16 With 35 Down, Monty Python member
17 Newton or Hayes
18 PC programmer
19 Mideast bread
20 Cub Scout group
21 He appeared in 10 Disney films
24 Military vehicles
26 Got dirty
27 Isle of Capri attraction
29 Lacerates
31 Weeknightly monologist
32 Head, slangily
34 Lower the lights
37 Paradisiacal places
39 Greedy sort
40 Valerie Harper role
42 Negative votes
43 Kitchen gadget
46 Without siblings
47 Fort __, IN
48 Rouses from slumber
50 Savage
53 Find contemptible
54 She appeared in 4 Disney films
57 Galena or pitchblende
60 Step __ (rush)
61 Longest armbone
62 Composer Erik
64 Well-heeled
65 Sitcom producer Norman
66 Praise greatly
67 Dinner and a movie, maybe
68 Soaks (up)
69 Wren residences

DOWN

1 No longer valid
2 Church area
3 He appeared in 12 Disney films
4 Segment of history
5 Novotna need
6 Speaks indistinctly
7 TV emcee
8 Finished
9 Scrutiny
10 Some sodas
11 Historian Durant
12 Championship
13 Burn with water
22 Second word of many fairy tales
23 More achy
25 School founded by Henry VI
27 Singer Campbell
28 Change the decor
29 Linen fabric
30 Advantage
33 Ready for customers
34 He appeared in 6 Disney films
35 See 16 Across
36 "The Say Hey Kid"
38 "The final frontier"
41 Frost
44 Breathtaking views
45 Tortoise/hare event
47 Squirm
49 Deteriorate
50 Norwegian inlet
51 Ancient Greek region
52 Royal decree
53 Has the lead role
55 Toast topper
56 Simple task
58 Funny one
59 Marine wrigglers
63 Chestnut chopper

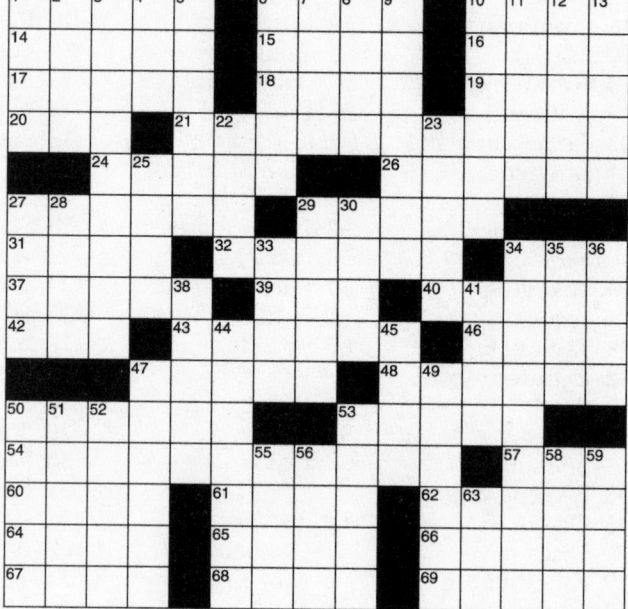

GARDEN VARIETY by Susan Brody

ACROSS

1 Lemon drinks
5 California county
10 Exercise, in a way
14 Wash
15 Skirt type
16 Cancun cash
17 Shocking flow?
20 Dish list
21 Fast runner
22 The buck stops here
23 Materials to assemble
24 Smash into
27 Translucent gem
29 Champagne cocktail
32 Diction student of fiction
35 Joe Tynan portrayer
38 Working hard
39 African republic
40 Make peace?
43 Designer Geoffrey
44 Unstintingly
45 __-bitsy
46 Thin as __
47 Opera star Tebaldi
49 Liquefy
51 Dallas college
52 Remained unused
55 Sal, in the song
57 Important periods
60 Home of the Buccaneers
62 Pants?
66 Former geopolitical initials
67 Endeavored
68 Postpone action
69 Come up short
70 Throng
71 First name in mysteries

DOWN

1 Smart guy?
2 __ Lama
3 Turn outward
4 Faction
5 Scratch the surface
6 "Rope-a-dope" practitioner
7 Buddy of music
8 Early South American
9 Prefix for surgeon
10 Lifesaving course
11 Convertible beacon
12 "Ignorance of the law __ excuse"
13 Make mention of
18 Garr or Hatcher
19 Evangelist's exhortation
25 He loves: Lat.
26 Teresa, e.g.
28 Witt of Cybill
29 Hitchcock film
30 Strainer
31 1896 Olympics site
33 What nodders catch
34 Pretentious
35 Eban of Israel
36 Eye provocatively
37 Like some sleep
41 Old __ (Disney dog)
42 Composer Khachaturian
48 Ballet array
50 Fidelity
52 Fingerpaint
53 Spring time
54 Small sample
55 France, formerly
56 Lhasa __
58 Oversized hairdo
59 Mix up
61 "__ forgive those who trespass against us"
63 Auxiliary verb
64 Actor Buttons
64 Poetic form

689 LETTER OPENERS by Bob Lubbers

ACROSS
1 Gown renters: Abbr.
4 Flower shop svce.
7 Invigorate the brass
14 Tito's predecessor
16 Camden Yards team
17 Some watches
18 Drawing-board staple
19 Triangular houses
20 Poker game
21 Barbra's *A Star Is Born* costar
22 VCR button
24 Moray hunter
28 Not snowed by
30 Hardly vibrant
33 Steak order
34 Rocks
36 First of all
38 Getz's instrument
39 Gender determinant
42 Sound of impact
44 Plan part
45 Second of all
46 Aid in crime
48 First garden
50 Grandson of 36 and 45 Across
53 Olin and Horne
55 Tool shaper
57 Largest dolphin
59 Sloping walk
62 GI meal
64 Centrifuge stresses
67 London section
68 Eddie and Edward
69 Furniture finisher
70 Most daring
71 Best
72 Mao __-tung

DOWN
1 First U.N. General Assembly president
2 Brad of *The Client*
3 ". . . we have seen his __ the east"
4 Gift-card word
5 Woods of fame
6 Put down
7 Decays
8 Formerly, old-style
9 Resentment
10 More garish
11 __ grecque
12 Hawaiian Is., once
13 Compass reading
15 Springy
23 Tight on space
25 Emit coherent light
26 Number for Nomo
27 Latin king
29 Singer Phil
31 Fuss
32 Not refined
35 *The Numerals* painter
37 "Step aside!"
39 Comics heroes
40 UK lexicon
41 Amahl's creator
42 __ Harbour, FL
43 Playwright Burrows
47 Finished a highway
49 Most appropriate
51 Sellers role
52 Quick breads
54 "__ bleu!"
56 Poet's Muse
58 Pianist Previn
60 Shea team
61 "Hey, you!"
63 Memo directive
64 Rap
65 Mrs. Andy Capp
66 Rectangle, e.g.: Abbr.

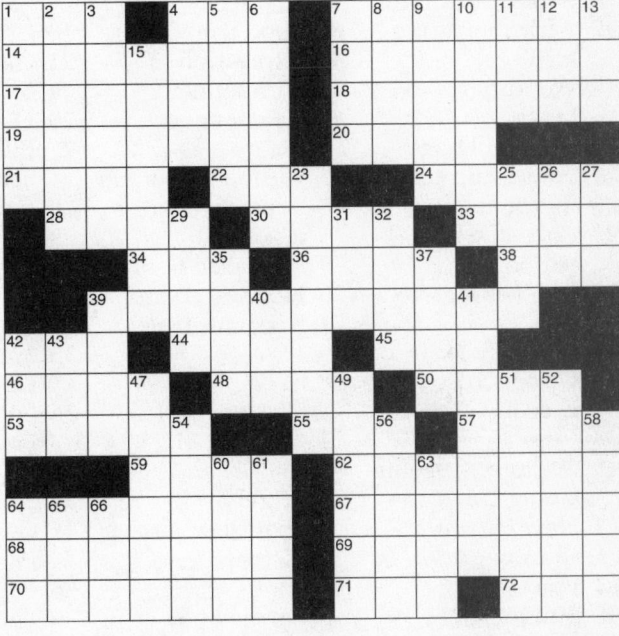

690 A DAY AT THE RACES by Rich Norris

ACROSS
1 Give consent
7 Carbonated drink
11 Soft shoe, for short
14 Got frothy
15 Kojak's first name
16 JFK posting
17 Competitive advantage
19 Bee follower
20 India's first prime minister
21 Subtle quality
22 Boutique
23 PC key
24 Military headquarters
27 Mr. T's TV outfit
29 Mikhail of chess
30 Additional
32 Agricultural business
35 Pack animal
39 *M*A*S*H* star
40 Poke around
42 Carry on
43 Isn't serious
45 Desires
46 Pesky flier
47 Suffix meaning "resident"
49 Helpers
51 Gymnastics event
56 Banking convenience: Abbr.
59 Nastase of tennis
60 Offspring: Abbr.
61 Hidden supply
63 Canadian's "Z"
64 Heckler in the dugout
66 Move irregularly
67 Annapolis sch.
68 Be attached (to)
69 Chemical suffix
70 Night sight
71 Gardening tool

DOWN
1 "__ Romance" (Kern tune)
2 Ice-cream receptacles
3 Banking conveniences
4 Mideast bigwig
5 Figure out
6 Netherlands city
7 Play the banjo
8 *Pal Joey* writer
9 Pour, as wine
10 NASA approval
11 Manly
12 Black-and-white cookies
13 Approached with stealth
18 New York political faction of old
22 Spend wildly
25 Buffoons
26 Apply gently
28 4:00 P.M., perhaps
30 Mil. rank
31 Corrida cry
33 Fish eggs
34 Absolute ruler
36 Searched and messed up
37 Genetic material: Abbr.
38 Baseball great Mel
41 Pitchfork-shaped Greek letters
44 Sault __ Marie, MI
48 Most mature
50 Solve, as a cryptogram
51 Italian pie
52 City on the Allegheny
53 Mosquito-like critter
54 Salon coloring
55 Movie trophy
57 "Who goes __?"
58 Gangster Lansky
62 Sore spot
64 Urban transport
65 Prominent Leno feature

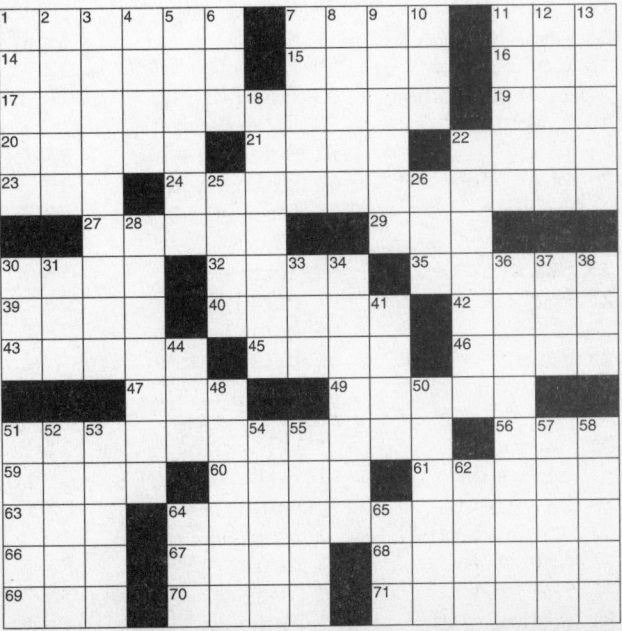

691 HEAVENLY HASH by Patrick Jordan

ACROSS
1 Baby bleater
5 Wizardry
10 Line of fashion?
14 Solo at La Scala
15 Frigidaire competitor
16 Edison's middle name
17 African wading bird
19 Wedding-cake layer
20 Back of a boat
21 Some sculptures
23 Egyptian goddess
26 Pops like a balloon
27 Chicken-hearted sort
32 Whiskey grain
33 Upper crust
34 Disconcerted
38 Russian river
40 "Whole __ Shakin' Going On"
42 New Haven campus
43 Fracas
45 Still in bed
47 Arrest
48 Newborn, so to speak
51 Horrified
54 Actress Conn
55 Stages a Civil War battle, perhaps
58 *Lost in Space* character
62 Food fish
63 Expression of wonderment
66 Celebratory poems
67 Clear a videotape
68 Type of collar or jacket
69 Hawaiian honker
70 Holmes' creator
71 Roof coverings

DOWN
1 Glasgow girl
2 "I smell __!"
3 Mickey and Mighty
4 Spanish-speaking district
5 Sore
6 Parisian pal
7 Runs off at the mouth
8 Monogram pt.
9 Melon variety
10 Matinee time
11 Inventor Howe
12 Ward off
13 Martin and Steenburgen
18 Come next
22 Gang territory
24 "__ do for now"
25 Descendants
27 Fife accompaniment
28 Rochester's love
29 Cutlet meat
30 Preminger and Kahn
31 Made damp
35 Western novelist Grey
36 Spirited quality
37 Financial obligation
39 Beirut citizen
41 German car
44 Film lioness
46 Peter, in Pamplona
49 Drew with acid
50 Rhode Island's state flower
51 Firebug's crime
52 Crystal-lined stone
53 Snger Reddy
56 Matador's foe
57 Do in
59 First Greek consonant
60 Fragrance
61 A lot
64 Designer label initials
65 Golfer's prop

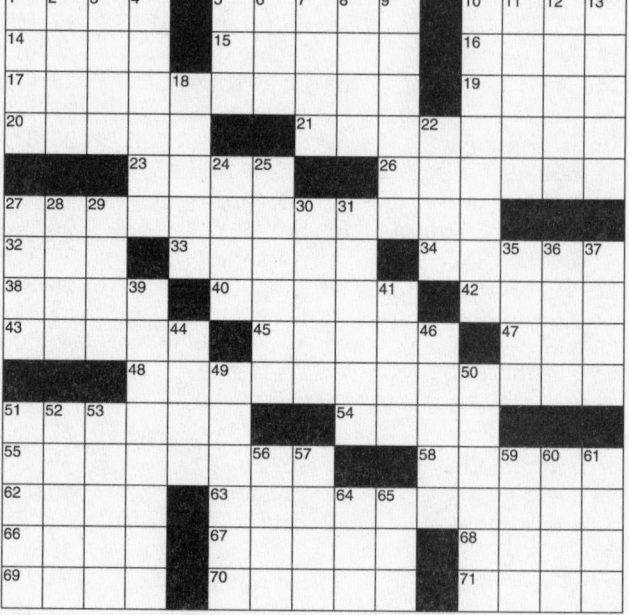

692 UP TO THE MINUTE by Fred Piscop

ACROSS
1 Futuristic literature
6 1040, for one
10 __ Jones' locker
14 Ballpark instrument
15 Draftable
16 Lamb's pseudonym
17 Controller of body rhythms
20 Prepared baby food
21 Hotel-door posting
22 Neighbor of Ga.
23 Sax man Getz
25 Niels Bohr, for one
28 Sentinel's post
34 Ben-Gurion Airport carrier
35 One of the Osmonds
36 I love: Lat.
37 Scotland Yard unit: Abbr.
38 Old Nick
39 Styling stuff
40 Justice Fortas
41 Took notice, in a way
42 Wet blanket
43 Neophyte
46 Intaglio stone
47 Spectrum bands
48 Immigrant's subj.
50 Eloper of rhyme
53 Don't drink
58 Model's shape
61 Sidekick: Abbr.
62 Savings plans, for short
63 Chou __
64 Team that debuted in '62
65 Nada
66 Bath add-ins

DOWN
1 Whimpers
2 Reviewer, for short
3 Frankenstein's flunky
4 Mideast appetizer
5 How tuna may be packed
6 Pâté de __ gras
7 Like most of today's music
8 New Deal agcy.
9 Content starter
10 Presidential middle name
11 Jillions
12 __ versa
13 Ties up the phone
18 Chew (on)
19 Bucket of bolts
23 Tough spot
24 Like a rail
25 Kind of coffee
26 Suspect's story
27 Consumers' crusader
29 Fine fiddles
30 Jazz pianist Art
31 Pioneer's conveyance
32 Manicurist's material
33 Movado rival
38 Fill to the brim
41 Beset by hornets
42 Italian city
44 Bermuda wear
45 Shipwreck site
49 Porcine pads
50 Bogus
51 Sit for a photo
52 Give the boot to
53 Bygone despot
54 Old gas brand
55 Rock band Jethro __
56 "I smell __!"
57 Cruise keepsakes
59 Designer Claiborne
60 "Chances __"

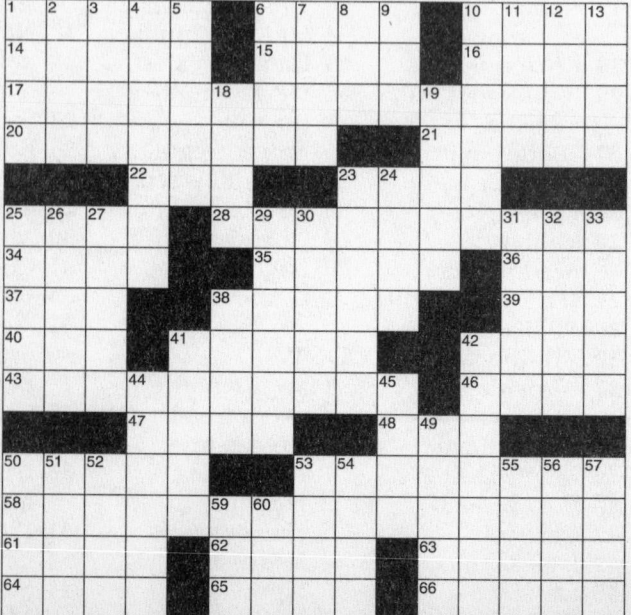

693   JOIN US by Ray Hamel

ACROSS
1 Typing bar
7 Collaborative coalition
11 European airline
14 Professor's goal
15 Pack of pennies
16 Flock leader
17 Horn
18 Drama award
19 Mate of 16 Across
20 Charitable group
23 Quirk
24 Stanley Cup org.
25 Rent anew
27 *Tristia* poet
29 Bring up
32 Calamitous
33 Press conference, sometimes
37 Hush-hush govt. grp.
38 Blackbird
39 Buddy
41 Proposal defeated in 1982
44 Boy George's group
49 Partners of cones
51 Morse clicks
52 With 9 Down, *Havana* actress
53 Howdah occupant, perhaps
55 *Norma* __
57 Highest minor league
58 Rap-music pioneers
63 The Andes, for short
64 Sand ridge
65 *The Blues Brothers* director
67 Term of endearment
68 Sassy
69 Single-minded
70 *48__*
71 "Fine by me!"
72 Zip

DOWN
1 Amtrak loc.
2 Lost in thought
3 Stomach settler
4 Choose the best
5 Hebrew eve
6 Showed again
7 Chicken choice
8 TV sheriff
9 See 52 Across
10 Cloudless
11 Politburo's place
12 *The Practice* figures
13 Mrs., in Marseilles
21 "__ in Manila" (Ali/Frazier bout)
22 Like Mao's book
23 Arnold or Clancy
26 Midday quaff
28 Use a rheostat
30 Finger-pointing
31 River to the Rhine
34 NRC predecessor
35 Rubbish
36 Seek damages
40 CXV x X
41 Need correction
42 Chicken choice
43 Tinkers with
45 Frugal
46 Hero's love
47 Eternal
48 Utterance from 16 Across
50 Lose vigor
54 Silent film star
56 Southfork matriarch
59 Bad smell
60 Queen of the gods
61 *The Journey of Natty __* ('85 film)
62 Start a pot
63 Radar-gun abbr.
66 Porker's place

694   WINGS OF SONG by Bob Lubbers

ACROSS
1 Fowl males
5 Whitewash the facts
9 Resort
12 "Hard __!" (captain's command)
13 Caesar's wardrobe
15 *Family Ties* character
16 Muse count
17 Fatty acid
18 Drop off
19 Warbler's love song?
22 Beast of burden
23 Hound
24 Court rituals
28 Campeche cash
30 Evening reception
31 "Abdulla Bulbul __" (1877 song)
34 Zilch
36 United
37 Chicken's novelty song?
41 __ la la
42 Music to Manolete
43 Ceremonies
44 Store in an etui
47 "Yes __ Bob!"
49 Proportion
50 Agt.
51 Hamster or hound
54 Birdie's love song?
59 Pianist Templeton
62 Big family
63 Blue shade
64 Gouramis, e.g.
65 French room
66 Young dynamo
67 Major appliances
68 Quarter-note line
69 Spots

DOWN
1 Singer Tucker
2 Mishmashes
3 Cartes
4 Fortune-teller
5 Leaf openings
6 Many-sided
7 "__ no kick from champagne . . ."
8 Neet competitor
9 __-mo
10 Dispenser candy
11 Bunyan's load
14 __-fi
15 '50s two-time loser
20 January, in Juarez
21 Old card game
25 Brook catch
26 Therefore
27 Searches for
28 Delt neighbor
29 Gluts
30 Unfortunate
31 Fall flower
32 Oscar Madison's secretary
33 Make into law
35 In demand
38 Usher's creator
39 __ suzette
40 Golf-ball position
45 Gee follower
46 Sty stalwart
48 Cash in
51 Peeve
52 Harden (to)
53 Deck woods
55 UFO crew
56 Swing and Big Band
57 Lean
58 Map lines: Abbr.
59 Sternward
60 Actress Tyler
61 Count ending

695　BENCHWARMERS by Fred Piscop

ACROSS
1 Actress Farrow
4 Sci-fi writer Isaac
10 Vacationer's fill-in
14 D.C. insider
15 "The Raven" maiden
16 Novello of old films
17 Branch office, perhaps
19 Goya subject
20 In any way
21 Twenty-four hours
23 Obstinate
25 TV award
27 The night before
28 Sheds tears
29 Greek letter
30 Cabinet wood
32 __ Cruces, NM
33 Glib quality
35 Former baseball-contract detail
40 Onetime streetcar
41 __ Jima
43 Voice an objection
46 Ancient
47 *Star Wars* villain
49 Inventor Whitney
50 Roof projection
52 Soda-bottle units
53 They roam
55 Sporty Mazda
56 Utah national park
57 Worker seen in 42 Down
62 Bygone gas brand
63 Blotted out
64 Actor Gibson
65 Trimmed of fat
66 Beachgoers' needs
67 Mineo of film

DOWN
1 AWOL chasers
2 Debtor's marker
3 Licia of opera
4 Church platforms
5 Serta rival
6 Worldwide: Abbr.
7 French pronoun
8 Gold, in Guatemala
9 Viper's weapon
10 Marathoner's concern
11 Gave the slip to
12 Western desert
13 Entreaty
18 Stride
22 Lake of southeast Africa
23 Night bird
24 Bring up
25 Getty or Parsons
26 Like egg-roll filling
29 Conditioned-response discoverer
31 Baton Rouge sch.
33 Old hand
34 TV Tarzan Ron
36 R-V link
37 Made a mistake
38 Pistols, perhaps
39 Decorative pitcher
42 Hospital areas: Abbr.
43 1989 Oscar-winner Washington
44 Plaza Hotel heroine
45 Brunch cocktail
47 Delicious dishes
48 Westernmost Aleutian
51 Thing of value
52 Defame in print
54 Soon, poetically
55 Calliope or Clio
58 __-Magnon
59 Like new recruits
60 Bering, for one
61 Right-angle shape

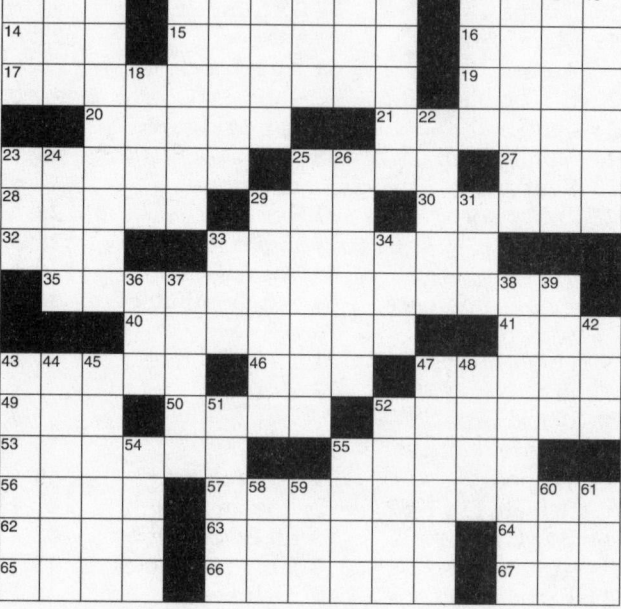

696　HOME SWEET HOME by Lee Weaver

ACROSS
1 Drive headlong into
4 Silent-screen siren
8 More adorable
13 Be inaccurate
14 Writer Wiesel
15 Proceed nonchalantly
16 Calling on
18 Adhere closely
19 Type of potatoes
21 Auctioneer's last word
24 Daystar
25 Difficult duty
26 Corporate newsletter
33 *Nightline* host Koppel
34 Gets forty winks
35 Nemo's creator
36 Most lofty
38 Church officials
40 Utopian
41 Do a clerk's job
42 "__ On a Happy Face"
43 1910s dance
46 Boxer's signal
47 Word form for "bad"
48 Latin being
49 Posh pleasure boat
57 Street crosser
58 Turnpike structure
62 Little laugh
63 Meadow mamas
64 Ironically funny
65 '50s Ford
66 Actress Thompson
67 Soap ingredient

DOWN
1 Gun the engine
2 Nickname for Onassis
3 Bride's title: Abbr.
4 Turn down
5 Dismounted
6 Julep enhancer
7 Winged horse of myth
8 Bossy's offspring
9 Software buyer
10 Asian cuisine
11 Icicle site
12 Deli loaves
15 Public commotion
17 Tops a torte
20 Astronaut Grissom
21 Medieval style of architecture
22 New York lake
23 Prods along
26 Possesses
27 Make a decision
28 Cameo shape
29 VCR button
30 Hunts in the dark
31 Invalidates
32 Cozy up
34 Actress Carter
37 Beanie or beret
38 Neighbor of Penna.
39 Antlered animal
41 Military greetings
44 Host a roast
45 Major conflict
46 Ice mass
49 Zoo enclosure
50 Enthusiastic
51 Pleads
52 *Picnic* playwright
53 __ and void
54 Des Moines' home
55 Musher's vehicle
56 Famous lioness
59 Hole-punching gadget
60 Take a stab at
61 Hurricane center

697   LISTEN CAREFULLY by S.E. Booker

ACROSS
1 Tiny circle
4 Wood strips
9 Police alert: Abbr.
12 Momentous era
15 Disney's "Little Mermaid"
16 Ram's remark
17 Quarter back?
18 Edison town
20 Unornamented
21 One for the book?
22 Global speck
23 Swine
25 One more
27 Ladle, e.g.
30 Ram's remark
31 Off-Broadway award
32 __ *Arabian Nights*
34 Go get
38 Sure thing
39 Reed of sitcomdom
41 Casting slot
42 Unravels
44 Ale holders

45 Horner's surprise
46 Fields' yields
48 Industry publications
50 Facsimile
53 Binge
54 No-cholesterol spread
55 Liquefy
57 Make reparation
61 Really silly
63 Joined cloth
64 "A mouse!"
65 Effective use
66 Out on a limb?
67 Prom attendees: Abbr.
68 Conductor Zubin
69 Uninteresting

DOWN
1 Intense
2 Whitish gem
3 Augustan attire
4 Goosenecks, for instance

5 Milieu
6 BELL
7 Author Hanff
8 Highway warning
9 Embarrass
10 *Ici on __ français*
11 Humorist Russell
13 HORSE
14 *Sun Valley Serenade* star
19 RAIN
24 Electricity distribution system
26 Klutz
27 Tip, as your hat
28 Girder
29 Elite alternative
30 Something extra
33 TUBA
35 Gave away
36 Mystery board game
37 Skirts' outskirts
40 Concerning
43 __ Lanka

47 From C to C
49 Cook one's goose
50 Thorny subjects
51 Aunt in *Oklahoma!*
52 Reaches the top
53 Choreographer Tharp

56 "They have digged __ before me": Psalms
58 Was obliged to
59 __-do-well
60 MacDonald's singing partner
62 Stage show-off

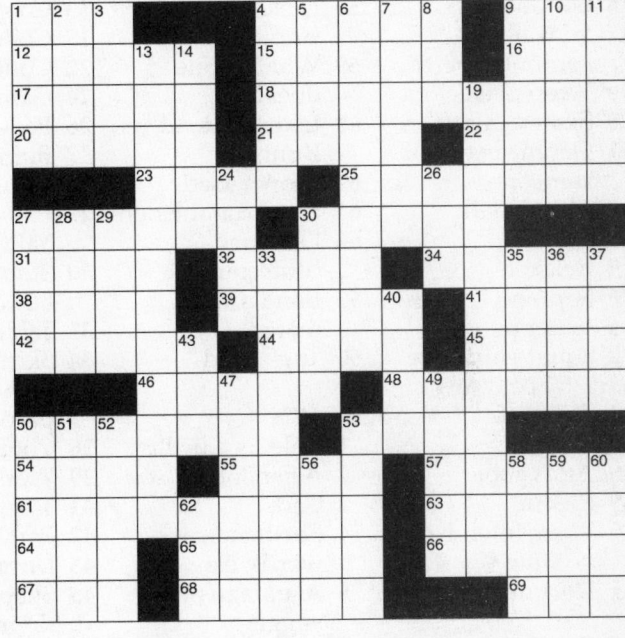

698   FILM TITLES by Bob Lubbers

ACROSS
1 Duchamp's art form
5 Curvy shape
8 Senate gofers
13 Eon segments
14 Defense alliance
15 __ *Gay*
16 Chaplin film of '47
19 Fuss
20 Piglet plea
21 Life sentence?
22 Garson film of '42
26 Hammer end
27 Shark bait
28 Say no to
29 Hockey star and kin
30 Whenever
34 Bridge coup
36 Subdued chuckle
37 Kappa follower
41 Goofs
43 Led to a seat
44 Sty guy

47 "__ the east, and Juliet . . ."
49 Actress Merkel
50 Zero, in tennis
51 Bronson film of '74
55 Ring great
56 Bound
57 First mate
58 MacLaine film of '88
64 Burstyn or Drew
65 High alt. jets
66 Follow
67 Authority
68 Shoebox letters
69 Chooses (to)

DOWN
1 Boulder, e.g.
2 Past
3 Playroom
4 State of India
5 __ de Cologne
6 Endeavored
7 Bolsheviks, later
8 Employment enticement

9 In addition
10 More sticky
11 Escapee
12 They knew all the Angles
14 Illuminating gas
17 General Amin
18 Signs up
22 Butcher's wares
23 Russo of *Outbreak*
24 Roy Rogers' real surname
25 "__ Got Sixpence"
26 Arles apple
31 "Who's __?"
32 Comparative suffix
33 *Carmen* author
35 Open-wide word
38 Very dry, as wine
39 Disclaim
40 Aleutian island
42 German thoroughfare

43 Made in the __
44 Finds fault with
45 "*C'est magnifique!*"
46 With fervor
48 Be ungracious
52 Boxer Willard
53 __ Marie Saint

54 Fistfight
56 K-P filler
59 Loser to DDE
60 Western Indian
61 Nuke
62 Tool set
63 Capp and Pacino

699 YOU SAID IT by Cathy Millhauser

ACROSS
1 Playwright Connelly
5 Reconditioned
9 Accumulated, as bills
14 Slangy suffix
15 Spanish surrealist
16 Summon up
17 Hawaiian computer part?
19 Wrap plastic
20 Skater Valova
21 Get the better of someone, proverbially?
23 From __ Z
25 Relaxed
26 Soprano Upshaw, to her parents?
32 Square measure
33 Isn't colorfast
34 Steamed
37 Quarters
38 Atlas abbr.
39 Rescue
40 Poem intended to be sung
41 Do a microwave task
44 X and Y
45 Car for a model?
47 Span
49 *Danse* step
50 Brownish shopping bag?
54 They may be over your head
58 *Home Improvement* star
59 What a scale does?
61 Like the Road Runner
62 Brown shade
63 Latin conjunction
64 Diamond protectors
65 Bond's alma mater
66 Tug's load

DOWN
1 Role for Lucille
2 Asian inland sea
3 Cad
4 Portmanteau words, e.g.
5 Asparagus-like veggie
6 Biblical king
7 *Lohengrin* role
8 Prie-__ (prayer bench)
9 Runs over
10 "Venus" singer
11 Dunn and Ephron
12 Decree
13 Cooped
18 College major
22 Content
24 Gambling loc.
26 Pedestal part
27 Biting wit
28 Hankering
29 Philanthropist Yale
30 Stopwatch button
31 Table, at meetings
34 Skirt length
35 French preposition
36 Computer spot
39 Wurst
41 Takes umbrage at
42 Part of SEATO
43 Dosage amt.
45 Shepherd of rhyme
46 Filmdom pig
47 Jack-in-the-pulpit cousin
48 Sovereign
50 President from Cincinnati
51 Double curve
52 Savoir-faire
53 Mart start
55 Fed, perhaps
56 Acronymic computer truism
57 Bamboozle
60 Salute element

700 CLOSET CLUTTER by Ed Julius

ACROSS
1 Lhasa __
5 Pack down
9 Sketched
13 Speak unclearly
14 Drink with marshmallows
15 Asian grain
16 Ask for donations
18 Home for Yeats
19 Call __ day
20 Got up
21 Even chance
23 Agree
25 They act
27 Bullring cheers
29 Obtain by effort
33 Perfume application
36 IRS agents
38 Author Dinesen
39 Pirate's plunder
40 Goes up, up and away
41 Painter Magritte
42 Miscellany
43 Nero's robe
44 Sharp-tasting
45 Tiger Woods' tote
47 Spirit
49 Rids of rind
51 Like some salad dressings
55 Wanders off
58 "So long!"
60 Trumped-up story
61 Hawaiian island
62 Rural game
65 Plow pullers
66 Unsuitable
67 Green Gables heroine
68 Main point
69 Seating in church
70 Unwieldy situation

DOWN
1 Tomato jelly
2 Greek philosopher
3 Lucci of soaps
4 Hosp. areas
5 Little piggies
6 Needed liniment
7 Extinct bird
8 Decorative designs
9 Theater area
10 Danish-born journalist
11 Light brown
12 "Read 'em and __!"
14 Routine task
17 In fact
22 Spanish gold
24 Wall covering
26 Musical dramas
28 Larry or Moe or Curly
30 PC owner
31 Punjab princess
32 __ out a living (got by)
33 Make one's way through mud
34 Prince Charles' game
35 Muddy the waters
37 Periodical, for short
40 *USS Enterprise*, e.g.
44 Atmospheres
46 Howl at the moon
48 Group of eight
50 Scarecrow stuffing
52 Unaccompanied
53 Demeanors
54 Votes in favor
55 Air pollution
56 Prepare to take off
57 Feels regret over
59 Nile reptiles
63 Individual
64 Sandwich meat

701 BOWLED OVER by Fred Piscop

ACROSS
1 Sail support
5 Moisten the turkey
10 Shea Stadium player
13 Where vows are exchanged
15 Zones
16 "__ Maria"
17 Unneeded coins
19 Perfect score in gymnastics
20 Top-billing sharer
21 Ship's record
22 Landlord's income
23 Pub brews
25 Returns to a former condition
27 Fulton steamboat
31 "Zip-A-Dee-Doo-__"
32 Yes, to Yves
33 *Gentlemen Prefer Blondes* writer
35 Folger's rival
39 Start conducting
43 Canines and bicuspids
44 Garr or Hatcher
45 New: Pref.
46 Musical acuity
48 Renaissance preceder
51 Male graduate
55 Pigs' places
56 Microscope part
57 Cambridge coll.
59 Jalopy sound
63 "What Kind of Fool __?"
64 Two images on one TV
66 Bon __ (witty saying)
67 Unaccompanied
68 Designer Donna
69 *A Chorus Line* song
70 Hostess Perle
71 Summer-camp site

DOWN
1 Opposite of fem.
2 Purina competitor
3 RR stops
4 Sauce with fish sticks
5 "__, humbug!"
6 Inland Asian sea
7 Sir, in Seville
8 Put a price on
9 Point opposite WNW
10 Alma __
11 Decathlon part
12 Campers' shelters
14 Kingdom
18 New Orleans cuisine
22 Back-to-health program
24 Pig's nose
26 Bouquet holder
27 __-of-living increase
28 Mandolin cousin
29 Irish republic
30 Drank too much
34 Ornamental band
36 Da __, Vietnam
37 Patch place, often
38 Hubbubs
40 List components
41 Genghis __
42 Personnel departments, often
47 Wrinkle up
49 Talent
50 Star-shaped
51 Crockett's last stand
52 Sour fruit
53 Join forces
54 Farm structures
58 Color lightly
60 Trillion: Pref.
61 Dike problem
62 Feminine suffix
64 "I Want You" uncle
65 Drink with crumpets

702 WEE BITS by Bob Lubbers

ACROSS
1 Summer, on the Somme
4 La __ Opera House
9 Foundation
14 Stir
15 Expert group
16 Make joyful
17 Wrath
18 Happening
19 Evaluated
20 Alcott book
23 Gershwin brother
24 Not moving
25 Pub refresher
26 Squeal (on)
27 Fairy-tale monster
28 Mubarak of Egypt
31 Ceremony
32 Diner handout
33 Flower holders
34 Quick work
38 Jazzman Shaw
40 Skirt shape
41 Saucy
42 Stage whisper
44 Nagy of Hungary
48 Golf org.
49 Carney or Linkletter
50 Villainous glare
51 Sup
52 Nickels and dimes
56 Pen name
58 Norman Vincent __
59 Tic follower
60 Long gun
61 Cowboy star Lash
62 Model Carol
63 "__ ain't so!"
64 Bitter-__ (diehard)
65 Bandleader Brown

DOWN
1 Designer Gucci
2 Getting weary
3 Phillips __ Academy
4 Asian wheat
5 Grotto
6 Once again
7 Carson successor
8 *M*A*S*H* director
9 Swiss capital
10 Pie __ mode
11 Jonathan Swift, for one
12 Say repeatedly
13 Calms
21 Three, in Torino
22 New Haven student
28 That girl
29 Prov. of Canada
30 Bar food?
31 Flying Brits
32 A Stooge
33 Nabob, initially
34 Divide into castes
35 Smash
36 Mason's trough
37 Caviar
38 Pops up
39 Royal emblems
42 Pitcher's resource
43 Food basic
44 Buy a pig __ poke
45 In the head
46 Put on a feast
47 Builds
49 Valued property
50 Diaphanous
53 Lanky
54 Frying medium
55 Hint
57 __ Baba

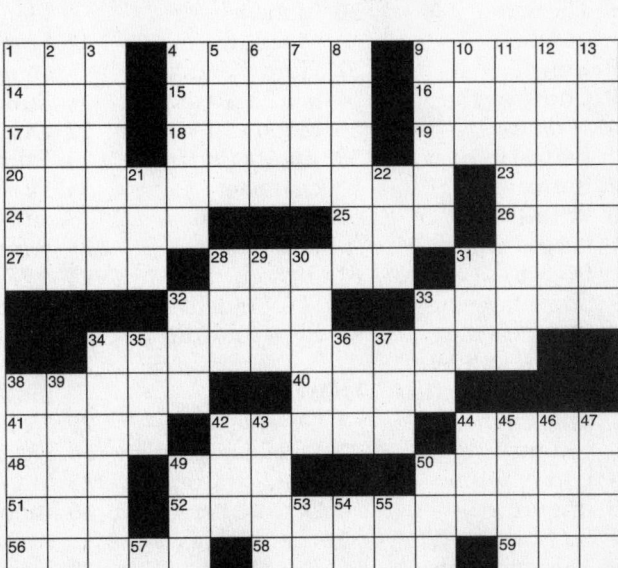

703 BANNED BOXES by Patrick Jordan

ACROSS
1 Kin of "Golly!"
5 Dog caller's word
9 Brazilian dance
14 Succulent plant
15 Actor Stoltz
16 Got nosy
17 Cape __ ('91 De Niro film)
18 Wacky, to Juan
19 Moorehead of Bewitched
20 Unobtainable pleasure
23 Miney follower
24 Adult acorns
25 Like Charlie McCarthy
29 French friends
30 Feedbag morsel
33 Capital of Ghana
34 Apt Biblical rhyme for "hit"
35 __ mater
36 Ness' group
39 Study at the last minute
40 '30s crooner Columbo
41 Move stealthily
42 Biddy
43 Satisfy completely
44 Livestock lineages
45 Cantata composer
46 Visualize
47 Sign at a nuclear power plant
54 Rigg or Ross
55 Correct Time?
56 Afternoon drama
57 More arctic
58 Dudley Do-Right's girl
59 Strike a stance
60 Tortilla-chip dip
61 Chip's chattering chum
62 Underworld river

DOWN
1 Fisherman's handled hook
2 Corn-oil spread
3 Fly high
4 Cardamom or caraway
5 Kept one's grip
6 Wear away
7 Creole cooking staple
8 Nobel Prize category
9 Radioman's nickname
10 100-eyed giant of myth
11 Skirt or series starter
12 Sugar source
13 Newspaper notices
21 "That is to say . . ."
22 Religious belief
25 Observe
26 Earthy hue, in England
27 Indian, e.g.
28 Starr-struck instrument?
29 Entertain
30 Stan's comic foil
31 Change the Constitution
32 Chores
34 Indiana city
35 Sufficiently skilled
37 Bingham of Baywatch
38 Comparable to a 12 Down?
43 World's largest desert
44 Bailey of the funnies
45 Dr. McCoy's nickname
46 Moonshine maker
47 Typesetting unit
48 Stair-climbing aid
49 Brainstorm
50 Nile nippers
51 12 Down, for one
52 Like falling off a log
53 Summit
54 Insult, slangily

704 CHAFING DISH by Henry Hook

ACROSS
1 __-Pei (Asian dog)
5 Projectile scientist
9 Labyrinthine
13 Teensy amount
14 Cuomo or Lanza
15 Rival of Bjorn
16 The entrée in question
19 Run
20 Corby of The Waltons
21 Refuse to raise
22 Entreated
23 With 44 and 55 Across, why the entrée was so named
27 Show tangency
31 On one's toes
32 Terry-cloth term
33 Former Philadelphia Orchestra conductor
34 Part of wpm
35 Immures
37 Rice or Reid
38 This and that
40 WWII espionage film of 1946
41 Nina of fashion
43 __ Wonderful Life
44 See 23 Across
47 The __ Poets (Coleridge and company)
49 Undeleted expletive
50 Mansfield or Meadows
52 Hors d'oeuvres
55 See 23 Across
58 Macintosh owner
59 All My Children character
60 "New Look" designer
61 Restore
62 H.C. Andersen, e.g.
63 Plies a needle

DOWN
1 [As written]
2 Laughter sampling
3 "Take __ from me"
4 Daytona participant
5 The Yankees' #7
6 Tom Thumb composer
7 Grp. once headed by Bush
8 Futile
9 Pond creator
10 Out of the storm
11 City near Waukegan, IL
12 Longing
14 What American Plan includes
17 Frank topper, for short
18 Bullring bravo
22 One of the Everlys
23 Faline's friend
24 Silas Marner author
25 Word on a nickel
26 __ Remember (Eleanor Roosevelt book)
28 Short haircut of the fifties
29 New York city
30 Easily alarmed
35 Maneuvered
36 Tennis great Arthur
39 Hoisting rope
41 Summarize
42 Rubber-stamp partners
45 Probability
46 Safari center
48 Miller or Jillian
50 San __, CA
51 Last word in prayer
52 Make money
53 Ashtabula's water
54 Pack away
55 Bottom line
56 Auto road-debris protector
57 Paternal namesakes: Abbr.

705 WEAR AM I? by S.E. Wilkinson

ACROSS
1 Silly person
6 Washout
10 Big party
14 Traveled a circular path
15 Hitcher's desire
16 Chemistry Nobelist Harold
17 Details
18 Talked to
20 Make a blunder
21 Snake sound
22 Where you live
23 Of interest to John Paul
25 Literary sarcasm
26 Guiding light
28 Horse-donkey offspring
30 Placed in order
31 Pt. of speech
32 Argyle, e.g.
36 Adherent's suffix
37 Excited states
40 Ending for form
41 Arizona city
43 Bee follower
44 Rodin work
46 Reaches across

48 Strands on a Christmas tree
49 Showed interest
51 *10* star
52 Sorrow
53 Lumber
55 Mickey and Minnie
58 On a chase
60 Cleaning chemical
61 Mortgage, for instance
62 "__ It Romantic?"
63 Ready to serve
64 Come back to earth
65 Like Erie
66 Kind of multiple-choice question

DOWN
1 Iron fishhook
2 Evangelist Roberts
3 Lodgers
4 Reversal
5 Mag. execs
6 Not very strong
7 Pots' tops

8 Probability quote
9 According to
10 Dining-room staff
11 Flaming felony
12 Run-down
13 Jekyll's other half
19 Receive interest
21 Analyze racing statistics
24 Ezra Pound's profession
25 Bought bonds
26 Bowler's edge
27 Nonchalance
28 Visibility problems
29 A mean Amin
33 City's periphery
34 One of this puzzle's 78
35 Film critic Pauline
38 Buddhist sect
39 Swizzle
42 Flabbergast
45 Windflower
47 Murmur, as Morris
49 Braga of *The Milagro Beanfield War*

50 Austrian peaks, locally
51 Eccentric
52 Soup flavoring
53 1970 Newman/Woodward film re a radio station
54 Porker's plaint
56 James of *The Godfather*
57 Show, for short
59 Part of RSVP
60 Tarzan's kid

706 YOUR KIND OF MUSIC by Norma Steinberg

ACROSS
1 Homer Simpson's son
5 Slugger's dry spell
10 Mimics
14 Famous cookiemaker
15 Danger
16 Relief pitcher's goal
17 Piece of hose
18 Sri __
19 Cabbage salad
20 Stamp-pad fluid
21 Informal conversations
23 Stuck-up sort
25 "__ the season . . ."
26 Flounder, for one
27 Stuck-up folks
32 Signal light
34 Come in second
35 Expression of wonderment
36 Theater section
37 Adds seasoning to

38 __ *18* (Uris novel)
39 Seth's mother
40 Desi's daughter
41 '30s dance
42 Sweets
44 Ladder step
45 Churl
46 Castro's predecessor
49 Bob Fosse film
54 In the know
55 Milne's bear
56 City on the Nile
57 Pinocchio, often
58 __ Raton, FL
59 Hunter Fudd
60 Bushy hairdo
61 See
62 Loses traction
63 Comic Laurel

DOWN
1 Ellington colleague
2 Surrounded by
3 Popular hymn
4 Sound of disapproval

5 Pool sound
6 Bounded
7 Vases
8 Voice-amplifying device
9 Acetate and cellophane
10 St. Francis' home
11 __ Alto, CA
12 Author Hunter
13 Makes curtains
21 Go up
22 Location
24 Become bored
27 Designer Perry
28 After the bell
29 Midafternoon to midnight stint
30 Snitched
31 Influence
32 Escaped
33 Valentine word
34 Agreement
37 Comes into view
38 Short skirt

40 Jacob's second wife
41 Lipinski feat
43 In order to
44 Shaving equipment
46 Revealed
47 Small crown
48 Kitchen coverup
49 Police alerts: Abbr.
50 Part of a bow
51 Plumb crazy
52 Radio format
53 Guitarist Hendrix
57 __ Vegas, NV

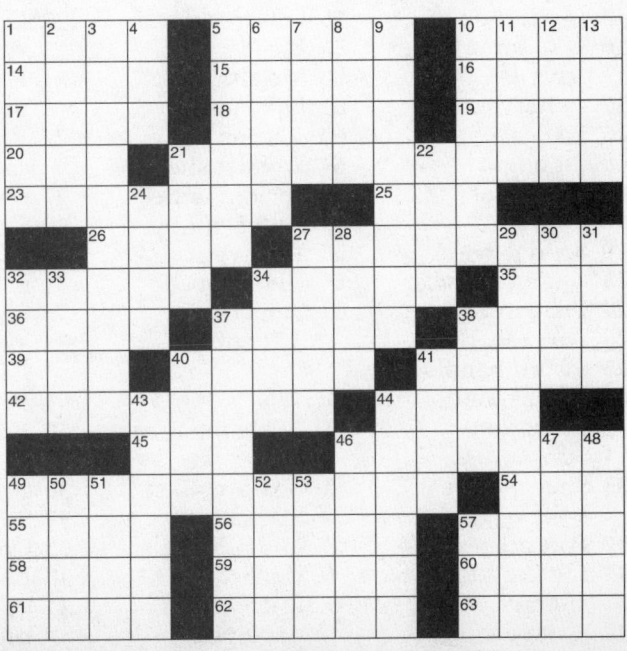

CLEANING UP by Lee Weaver

ACROSS
1 Tater
5 Memo notation
9 Paul and John: Abbr.
12 Fainthearted
14 Western elevations
16 "Eureka!" is one
17 Flatter
19 Director Howard
20 Continue after interruption
21 Freedom of action
23 Tart taste
25 Swift, graceful horse
26 Perfumes, e.g.
30 Acrobatic performance
32 Nautical "yes"
33 Fender benders
35 Turn down
37 Seafood delicacy
39 Baseball stat.
40 Iroquoian Indian
41 Luau dances
43 Smooths wood
46 Put in stitches
47 Type sizes
49 Sauciness
51 Vincent Lopez theme
52 Steak order
53 Indicated a turn
57 Noxious atmosphere
61 "Wham!" relative
62 Post-battle process
64 __ premium (scarce)
65 All thumbs
66 Mortise partner
67 Boxer Baer
68 Matches a raise
69 Gambling site

DOWN
1 Milky Way part
2 Plumbing need
3 Refs' counterparts
4 Make thinner
5 One of a Latin trio
6 Deal in
7 China setting
8 Trattoria courses
9 Hospital worker
10 Walked heavily
11 Since, in Scotland
13 Insist upon
15 Tees and polos
18 Coppers in Coventry
22 Brownish gray
24 Inheritance units
26 Apiece
27 Waffle topping
28 Old-style letter closure
29 Purse handle
31 Makes an effort
34 More sensible
36 Fresh information
38 Pizza topping
42 Pizza topping
44 Type of stage play
45 Exacting
48 Hairdressers' hangouts
50 More tidy
53 Canned meat
54 Tiny amount
55 Olympic weapon
56 Deceive
58 Trig ratio
59 Earth's satellite
60 Part of AD
63 6, for a TD

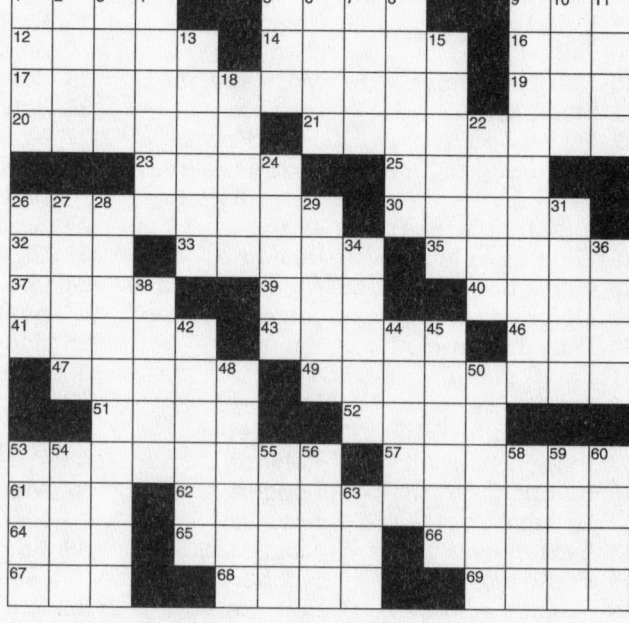

WORKING TOGETHER by Rich Norris

ACROSS
1 Calf catcher, at times
6 "Memories Are Made of __"
10 Desert Storm missile
14 Wagner work
15 In the money
16 Like some old records
17 __ nerve
18 La Scala highlight
19 "Let's not forget . . ."
20 Sci-fi barriers
23 __ Rosenkavalier
24 That, in Toledo
25 Artist Warhol
26 Sword handle
28 River-mouth formations
31 Sires
33 Smallest Great Lake
37 Port opening
38 Ivy League apparel
42 __ noire
43 They make points
44 Something to keep
46 Prevents
50 Awful state
51 Sportscaster Jim
54 Lot of noise
55 O'Hare arrival
56 Bread
60 Metallic rocks
62 Patio turner
63 100 kopecks
64 Wonder site
65 Unadulterated
66 Better equipped
67 Tide type
68 Silver abbr.
69 Can't do without

DOWN
1 Did home-repair work
2 Go up against
3 Glastonbury gas
4 Author Ambler
5 Make tracks
6 Teach employees
7 Added employees
8 In an unfriendly fashion
9 Herringlike fish
10 Tiny, to Burns
11 Loss of confidence
12 Disturb
13 Way out
21 First to the finish line
22 What to call a catamaran
27 Speechless
29 Castle features
30 Author Beattie
31 Showed respect for, maybe
32 Peppermint Patty, to Marcie
34 Part of CPA
35 King Kong studio
36 Syr. neighbor
38 Some radios
39 Come again?
40 List ender
41 Palindromic preposition
45 Curve shape
47 Safe to consume
48 Ransacked
49 Shows disdain
51 Done for
52 In flames
53 Chasing
55 Folk singer Baez
57 Cookbook abbr.
58 Drescher of The Nanny
59 Service-station service
61 Maple output

709 KVETCH'S DELIGHT by Cathy Millhauser

ACROSS
1 Raze
6 Hook's nemesis
10 Burn, in a way
14 Dieter's temptation
15 Frost
16 Rake
17 Condescending
19 The munchies, e.g.
20 Pistol
21 Handel subject
22 Ordered
24 Percussion instrument
25 Exchanges taunts
26 Four of the septuplets
30 Estates and such
31 Dolls, tops, etc.
32 Zeta follower
35 First name in scat
36 Address to a fella
37 Pleasingly tight
38 MCII halved
39 "Zounds!"
41 Visits
43 Psychoanalyst Anna, formally
46 Stirred
48 Den piece
49 Mixes, as companies
50 Pyramid, essentially
51 Hydro
54 Twinge
55 Canola alternative
58 Jean Stein bestseller
59 Sicilian town
60 Had a horse
61 Couple
62 Caribou kin
63 Frill

DOWN
1 "If I Only Had the Nerve" singer
2 Switch attachment
3 Ineffective
4 911 respondent
5 Forks over
6 European crow
7 Agitate
8 Muffin variety
9 Kvetchy kid
10 Like kaiser rolls
11 Sound judgment
12 Boring tool
13 Oboe pair
18 Biting
23 Lennon's in-laws
24 Festive
25 Letters on some invitations
26 Famous neigh-sayer
27 Honeycomb compartment
28 Stockton's home
29 Chopin piece
33 Pavlova outfit part
34 "... in apprehension how like __"
36 Tread-bare
37 Microscopy fluids
39 Cushiness
40 Made a stab
41 Aphorism
42 Unrealistic
44 Like some coasts
45 Weather-map line
46 Whipped up the volume
47 Prep
50 Northumberland river
51 Kind
52 Marina feature
53 *The Four Seasons* director
56 Indivisible
57 Put the kibosh on

710 WAY TO GO by Lee Weaver

ACROSS
1 Hoofbeat sound
5 Moby Dick seeker
9 Clarinet relative
13 Make well
14 Napped leather
15 Red jewel
16 Life of affluence
18 Canal to Buffalo
19 December 24th, for one
20 Frog relative
21 Labeled, as luggage
23 Bother persistently
25 Pool member
27 Was obligated to
29 Literary devices
33 Attempts
36 Anger
38 Ensnare
39 Kudrow of *Friends*
40 Gave up, as land
41 Increase
42 Sir __ Guinness
43 Scent
44 One of the five senses
45 Positioning
47 Calcutta costume
49 Group of eight
51 Selected the choice parts of
55 Collegian's quest
58 Graven image
60 Miner's quest
61 Sailor's saint
62 Nostalgic location
65 Dog pest
66 Primp
67 Surrounded by
68 Take care of
69 Very small amounts
70 Creates batik

DOWN
1 Nestling's noise
2 Head for the exit
3 Caravan stops
4 Cloth layer
5 Atmosphere
6 Obeys
7 Fruit drink
8 Achieved more than
9 Pioneer's way west
10 Small town
11 Theater award
12 Gave the once-over
14 Retailer's spot
17 One-pot dinners
22 Pitch __-hitter
24 Caldwell novel
26 Detroit baseballers
28 Earth remover
30 Part of the eye
31 Compass point
32 WWI German admiral
33 High-five, e.g.
34 Plow the field
35 On the briny
37 Fuss
40 Scorn
44 Very __ yours
46 Winter hazard
48 Squirrel food
50 Used a stopwatch
52 Like some rich soil
53 Comic Kovacs
54 Real-estate documents
55 Skillful
56 Fashion magazine
57 FBI agents
59 Accomplishes
63 Noteworthy time
64 Young boy

ANIMAL ANATOMY by Peter Gordon

ACROSS

1 Hudson, De Soto and La Salle
6 The way you walk
10 Big cheese
14 Dictation pro
15 To boot
16 Northern Norwegian
17 "To Autumn" writer
18 "To Autumn," for one
19 Korea's continent
20 Quaff from Canada
23 IV units
25 Stiff __ board
26 Inconvenience
27 Vent
30 Bled, as colors
31 Hoop coup
32 *Rich Man, Poor Man* author
34 Talks amorously
38 Top with no tie
41 Church area
42 Windmill blade
43 Indian, perhaps
44 Petition
45 Wasn't a buyer
46 Boilermaker, in part
50 It's fit for pigs
52 __ Miniver
53 *M*A*S*H* physician
57 Bassoon relative
58 Hurler Hershiser
59 "Look, ma, no __!"
62 Toll road, for short
63 Green shade
64 Go in
65 Galley notation
66 Snakelike fish
67 Beasts of burden

DOWN

1 Present a poser
2 Western Indian
3 Drivers' union
4 Well aware of
5 Fair
6 Shows astonishment
7 Ho "Hi"
8 What *video* means
9 Cherokee chopper
10 Blurts out
11 Havens
12 Purposeful pitch
13 Bowler's pickup
21 Perched
22 Newsman Rather
23 __ Rica
24 Quite a card
28 Overdue
29 Plumbing joint
30 Hurry up
32 Hitch
33 Farm female
34 Goatee site
35 Balms
36 Mandate
37 Author Turkel
39 *Tout le monde*
40 __ *Stoops to Conquer*
44 Quilting occasion
45 Bar bottle
46 Pork portions
47 Sister's outfit
48 Got up
49 Traps game
50 Time period
51 They may be up against the wall
54 Port in Pennsylvania
55 Perlman of *Cheers*
56 Some recyclables
60 Ruby of *Do the Right Thing*
61 Prom attendees: Abbr.

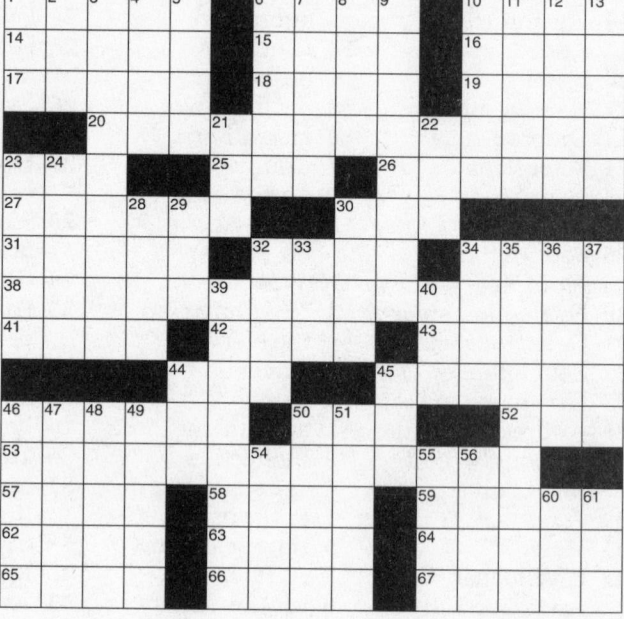

GRIDIRON GROUPS by Rich Norris

ACROSS

1 Sharpens, as skills
6 Dues-paying group
10 Casino unit
14 Gussy up
15 Put on the payroll
16 Superboy's girlfriend
17 Treaty of Versailles creation
20 PC button
21 Ice sheet
22 Canadian trees
23 Eateries
25 Dutch South African
26 Hubbubs
28 Cozumel resident
32 Boston NHLer
34 Son of Seth
35 Mile High Center architect
38 Business meetings of a kind
42 N.Y. or Boston
43 Chilean coin
44 City near Gainesville
45 Curio shelf
48 Long of Louisiana
49 Very dry
51 Cartoonist Goldberg et al.
53 Spouse's kin
55 Kingly address
56 Microsoft rival
59 Assembly-line concept
62 Change one's story?
63 Agreement
64 Kate's TV pal
65 Open fabric
66 Sharp border
67 Give up

DOWN

1 Irwin of the PGA
2 Poems of praise
3 Good-for-nothing
4 Bit of energy
5 Extinguish, with "out"
6 Draw straws, maybe
7 Magazine started in '36
8 Coffee maker
9 Light path
10 Like some bowties
11 Hawaiian non-native
12 *The __ Sanctum*
13 Quarterback's call
18 Kind of sch.
19 Hot sauce
24 *Clueless* remark
26 Basics
27 Rain unit
29 Noble gas
30 Letterhead abbr.
31 Miler Sebastian
33 Family members
35 Not out of the question
36 *Vogue* competitor
37 Brit's exclamation
39 Stephen of *Michael Collins*
40 Superlative suffix
41 Tylenol target
45 Visible spirit
46 Maryland's state bird
47 Home territory
49 Nasty
50 Much-impersonated star
52 Fasten, at sea
53 Bibliography word
54 Show partisanship
55 Unforeseen problem
57 Produce steam
58 '60s TV horse
60 Lge. reference work
61 Actress MacGraw

713 PILGRIMS' PROGRESS by Bob Lubbers

ACROSS
1 Rough it
5 D-Day target town
9 Philippine island
14 Butter alternative
15 Skinny
16 Actress Massey
17 September 16, 1620
20 __ Pan Alley
21 Nautical starter
22 Joins together
23 Federal agents
24 Hook aide
25 Brio
28 Molt
29 One of the Brady daughters
32 Actress Elizabeth et al.
33 Carson predecessor
34 Achy
35 December 26, 1620
38 Sea eagle
39 French moon
40 Single operator
41 WNW opposite
42 __ 'War (famous racehorse)
43 Shuts
44 Yale product
45 Nincompoop
46 Rubens subject
49 Maui beach base
50 Reflux
53 July 30, 1623
56 Ammonia compound
57 Actor Baldwin
58 Stare at
59 Track event
60 Annie Oakley
61 Honey bunch

DOWN
1 Price
2 Jai __
3 "Count __!"
4 Party stalwart
5 Mason's secretary
6 Sticking point
7 Classy wheels
8 __ in a million
9 Inked
10 Jane Curtin role
11 Castle ring
12 Last Stuart queen
13 X-ray units
18 Cause hunger
19 Uno, for one
23 Vestige
24 "Naughty you!"
25 Jollification
26 House of Lords members
27 Silly
28 Refuse
29 Irving and Jay
30 French force
31 Gets close to
33 "Splosh!"
34 Porch steps
36 Puts in context
37 Actress Tracey
42 Fiddle (with)
43 Social science
44 Yorba __, CA
45 Backs up, on a computer
46 Headliner
47 Phrase of resignation
48 Kettle handle
49 Silents star Leeds
50 Nose (out)
51 Cotton bundle
52 Tournament passes
54 Break
55 Swabbie

714 INITIAL APPEARANCES by Patrick Jordan

ACROSS
1 Do drilling
5 Conk out
9 Radioactive gas
14 Highest point
15 Philosopher Descartes
16 Blazing
17 Recipe instruction
18 Historical periods
19 Put a strain on
20 *JFK* star
23 Joshua in *The Ten Commandments*
24 Invoice stamp
25 Briny expanse
28 *M*A*S*H* star
31 Holyfield punch
34 For fear that
35 Rover's pal
36 Freudian practitioner
38 Semi driver, at times
41 Republican from Russell
42 Ladd or Lerner
43 ". . . __ he drove out of sight . . ."
44 *D.O.A.* star
49 *L.A. Law* actress
50 Book before Romans
51 Put back into service
54 *S.O.B.* star
57 Women's rights advocate
60 "That's a new one __!"
61 Scissors sound
62 Reluctant
63 Dundee denizen
64 Europe's tallest active volcano
65 Actress Debra
66 Comic-strip cries
67 Loses buoyancy

DOWN
1 Soak up some sun
2 Made a choice
3 District administrator
4 Become void
5 Howdy Doody features
6 Prefix for space
7 Having trouble
8 Anne Rice vampire
9 Like family films
10 Way over yonder
11 Fort __, NJ
12 Load from a lode
13 Homer's neighbor
21 Nice __ (prig)
22 It's picked by the picky
25 Hotel offering
26 Church official
27 Think the world of
29 Disciple's suffix
30 Switch position
31 World-weary
32 Battery terminal
33 Like the Caribbean climate
37 Pop singer Sayer
38 Camera type, briefly
39 Headgear for food preparers
40 "__ a vacation!"
42 Attendance-book notation
45 Goose egg
46 650, to Caesar
47 Lazy
48 Sips slowly
52 Actress Berger
53 Hagman role
54 Rope fiber
55 One way to run?
56 Health resorts
57 Swiss peak
58 Slithering squeezer
59 Angular turn

MAKING TRACKS by Rich Norris

ACROSS

1 Actor Danson
4 Knocked for a loop
9 Picture holder
14 Large hatchet
15 Making no sense
16 Shockingly intense
17 South Dakota municipality
19 French school
20 Current units
21 *48__*
22 Shatner sci-fi series
23 Do a blacksmith's job
25 AC capacity measure
26 Spotted cat
29 Goalpost part
34 Cargo ship
35 Holy one
36 Pie __ mode
37 Seine sight
38 Procrastinator
40 Understand
41 Teachers' grp.
42 Put up with
43 Three-time Wimbledon champ
45 Equivalence in meaning
47 Land broker's field
48 ADA member
49 Track transactions
50 Written arguments
53 PSAT takers
54 Barely beat
58 "__ luck!"
59 Bog material
61 Collect in abundance
62 Tedium
63 __ *About You*
64 Lean eater of rhyme
65 Feinted, in hockey
66 Porcine pad

DOWN

1 Plantation of fiction
2 Final, for one
3 Scissorhands portrayer
4 Accomplished
5 Network-news VIP
6 Congo, formerly
7 Tolkien tree creatures
8 Actress Susan
9 London newspaper hub
10 Noisy commotion
11 Lined up, poetically
12 __ *18* (Uris book)
13 German river
18 Magazine edition
22 Steak cut
24 Inviolable
26 Signs up with
27 Alvin of dance
28 Gather
29 Golfer's aide
30 Provoke
31 Lox partner
32 Emulate Paul Revere
33 Moth-eaten
35 Go for a dip
39 Immeasurable chasm
44 Still-life subjects
46 Ukrainian port
47 Save from disaster
49 Threshold
50 *Gil* __ (Le Sage novel)
51 Easy victory
52 __-Tass (Russian news agency)
53 When most Geminis are born
55 River blockers
56 Pesky flier
57 Whirling waters
59 Logician's abbr.
60 Young goat

HOLD EVERYTHING by Bob Lubbers

ACROSS

1 Sun-dried brick
6 __-fi
9 Shred, as cheese
14 Secret group
15 Craggy hill
16 Transplant
17 Research institute
19 Representative
20 Snow toy
21 Killer whale
22 Maine national park
23 "No __, Bob!"
25 Make a lap
26 Main/Kilbride film of '49
31 Shrimplike creature
33 Common article
34 Sills solo
35 Fall behind
36 Jack of *Barney Miller*
39 Hole maker
41 Plate scraping
42 Auspices
44 Friar's title
46 Gutter sites
48 Pail passers
52 Anger
53 Relieve of weapons
54 Composer Kodály
57 "Vamoose!"
58 Least bit
62 Goes
63 Cream churn
65 Taylor of *The Nanny*
66 Former ring king
67 "Gloria __" (hymn)
68 Rare birds
69 '60s Chinese chairman
70 Without company

DOWN

1 Deeds
2 Arlene or Roald
3 Off-Broadway award
4 Toothed-belt machine
5 Wapiti
6 Fixed one's eyes
7 Idea
8 Irritate
9 Mrs. George Burns
10 Sailing race
11 Mimicked
12 Singer Braxton
13 Diminutive suffix
18 Ripped
22 Out of whack
24 Fleming and McKellen
26 Legerdemain
27 "Eureka!"
28 Valuable collection
29 Bologna bills
30 Vittles
31 USMA freshman
32 Aunt Millie's rival
37 Frequently
38 Sphere
40 Producer Norman
43 Skip around
45 Pungent salad leaf
47 Navy VIP
49 Deletes
50 *Ab* __ (from the beginning)
51 Int. trade agreement
54 Zilch
55 Draft animals
56 Bit of dialogue
59 Palindromic name
60 Revolve
61 Rose's beau
63 Loud thud
64 Pollution watchdog org.

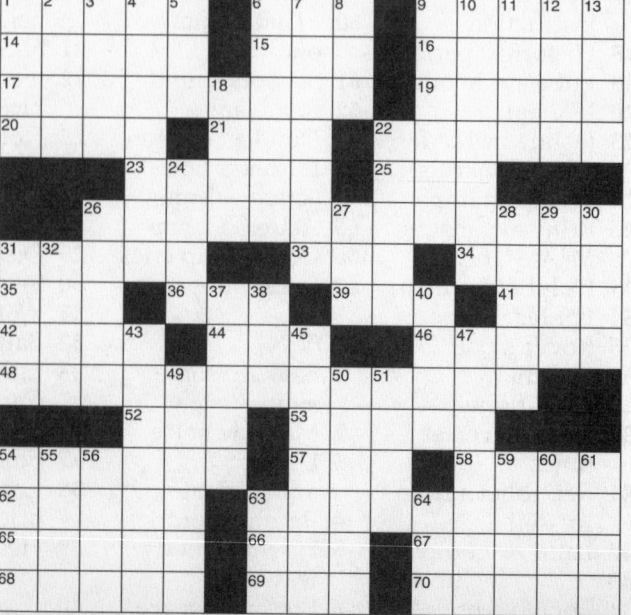

HIT THE DECK by Fred Piscop

ACROSS
1 Auspices
6 Some therapy, for short
11 Old vinyl
14 Sportscaster Musburger
15 Popped up
16 Debtor's letters
17 February sweets
19 Public-house drink
20 Brosnan TV role
21 Fit of pique
22 Spectrum band
23 Social dud
25 As a group
27 Split-off group
30 Intrepid
32 Fuse unit
33 Leb. neighbor
34 Self
35 Nose-in-the-air
38 Not of the cloth
40 __-Cop (Reynolds film)
42 Type of terrier
43 Commotion
45 Seabird
46 MPG raters
47 Pilot's guesstimate: Abbr.
48 Like the Gobi
49 Bellicose Olympian
50 Noxious atmospheres
53 German river
55 Massachusetts cape
56 Depose
58 Overdue payment
62 Like sashimi
63 River crosser, maybe
65 "__ pig's eye!"
66 Gogol's __ Bulba
67 Each companion
68 Relative of -arian
69 Argus-eyed
70 Hockey great Potvin

DOWN
1 First-grade fare
2 QED center
3 Tunney of the ring
4 Start a paragraph
5 Strunk & White concern
6 Actress Charlotte
7 Elizabethan and Big Band
8 Like some toads
9 John of *The Addams Family*
10 Wedding VIP
11 Game played with dollar bills
12 Gondola propellers
13 Napped leather
18 *Babes in Toyland* composer
24 Venetian magistrate
26 Pop singer Tori
27 Delta deposit
28 Genesis twin
29 1850s conflict
31 Solitary soul
35 Flounder cousin
36 Use a keyboard
37 Pro votes
39 Goes AWOL from school
41 The Andrews Sisters, e.g.
44 *Raging Bull* subject
48 Give confidence to
49 Achieve stardom
50 Scientist Curie
51 Nonsensical
52 Of the ear
54 Missed the mark
57 Autocrat of yore
59 Tree of Knowledge site
60 Prefix with culture
61 Actors Alejandro and Fernando
64 Fast way to the UK

A NUMBER OF SHOWS by Frank Longo

ACROSS
1 Syrup source
4 Frosted treat
11 Juice drink
14 Exist
15 Decipher
16 Bowler's target
17 Fred MacMurray series
19 Highlander's hat
20 Theda of the silents
21 Shipped
22 Pedicurist's tool
23 Create a cartoon
26 Countertenors
27 Dick Van Patten series
31 *Crooklyn* director
32 Goofball
33 Up for payment
34 Songwriter Silverstein
37 Woods with a wood
39 Bee __ ("Stayin' Alive" singers)
40 Promoted maj.
41 Featherbrain
42 Wonderment
44 Bonnie Franklin series
48 Wandered
49 Cream-soda flavoring
52 Pizazz
53 Zilch, to Zapata
56 __-do-well
57 Stock option
58 Jack Lord series
61 Pub pint
62 Unspoken language
63 Hosp. sections
64 Failure
65 Homeric epic
66 Louis or Carrie

DOWN
1 Bossa-nova relative
2 Indo-European
3 *The Dick Van Dyke Show* family name
4 Mongrel
5 French article
6 Fix beforehand
7 Instance
8 Shakespeare's river
9 *Daily Planet* reporter
10 Raised railroads
11 Talent
12 Conversation
13 Snarls
18 1976 gold-medalist skater
22 Andy Capp's wife
24 Ripen
25 1982 Pryor/Gleason comedy
26 Up-coming link
28 Metal bar
29 Notice
30 Printing mistakes
34 Board-game need
35 Lei locale
36 Lifted
38 Mrs. McKinley
39 Zodiac sign
41 Pa
43 Take the cake
45 Scouting unit
46 Is of value to
47 Nightly news hour, often
50 Suspicious
51 Got up
53 Aromatic ointment
54 Out of town
55 Speaker's platform
58 Showtime rival
59 __ du Diable
60 Enchanted

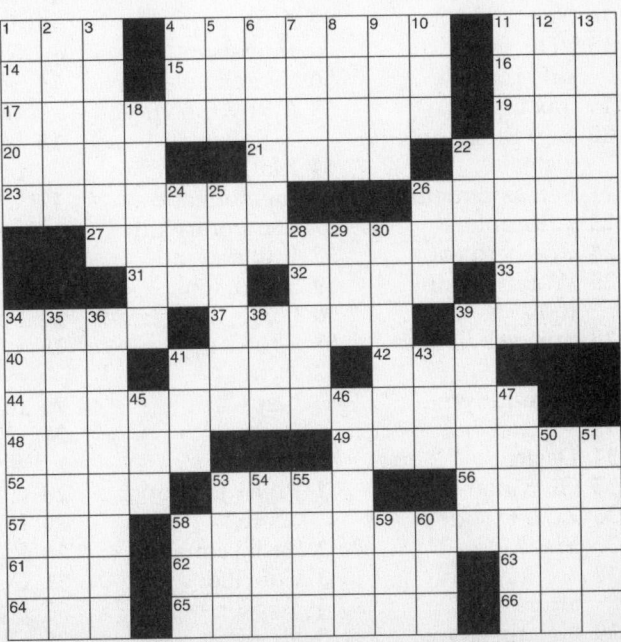

OR REMODELING by Cathy Millhauser

ACROSS
1 Forum doings
5 Bring to a near-boil
10 Assignment
14 Match
15 PGA nickname
16 Concerning
17 How a teacher handled a problem student?
20 Makes boil
21 Helena's home
22 *The Gondoliers* girl
24 Dressy synthetic
25 Roman add-on
28 Spud
31 Peevish
32 They make up periods
34 Java
37 Pledge from a snoop?
40 "Uh-huh!"
41 Ford's namesakes
42 Roman orator
43 Clumsy sort
44 Timber tab
45 Pie-chart lines
48 Krupp Works site
51 Oakland neighbor
54 Bar order
58 Prone gold digger's chain item?
60 Author Hunter
61 Practiced cryonics
62 Leeway
63 City on the Truckee
64 Hauled
65 Sicilian resort

DOWN
1 Church part
2 "High Hopes" lyricist
3 Bank
4 Buzzer part
5 Maintains
6 Mustard-family plant
7 Plus
8 Natasha's husband
9 Art __
10 Horde member
11 Strive
12 Word form for "narrow"
13 Holy book
18 Arch type
19 Riotous state
23 Make mist
25 Glimpse
26 Feeling miffed
27 One-liner
29 Zenith
30 "__ Magic Moment"
32 Shirt shade
33 Bridge, to Brigitte
34 Painter Corot
35 In the know about
36 Thomas Gray ode subject
38 Backup, perhaps
39 "Queen of Country"
43 Peep-Bo's garb
44 Glossary entry
45 Croupier, often
46 Advil rival
47 Six-Day War general
49 Dirty air
50 Filled to the gills
52 Silly
53 Comb home, maybe
55 Get __ the ground floor
56 Gaudy, in a way
57 Cookbook author Rombauer
59 Fortune

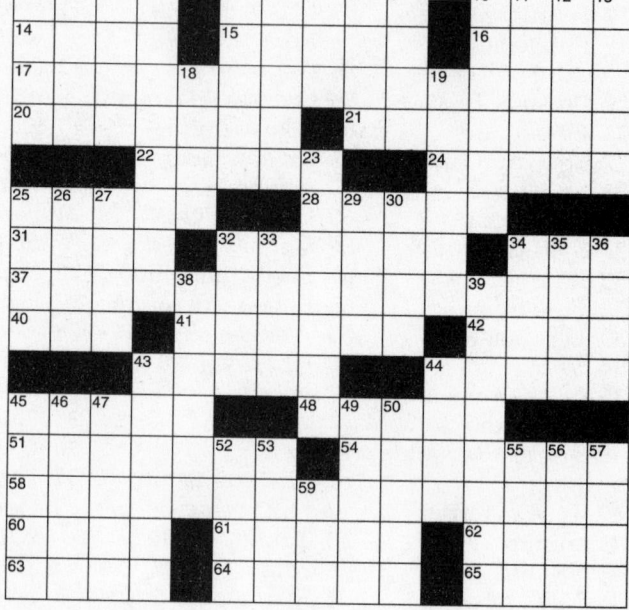

AROUND THE ROOM by Norma Steinberg

ACROSS
1 Mimicked
5 One of the Three Bears
9 Sidekick
12 Diner list
13 Upright
15 Tibia, for one
16 The easy life
18 "Do __ others . . ."
19 Tax org.
20 Bart Simpson's sister
21 Set, as cement
23 Adorable
24 Ready to eat
25 Woodworking tools
28 Spice-shelf choice
32 Pseudonym
33 Agreement
34 Desire
35 Chevalier song
36 Zodiac sign
37 Yield
38 ". . . happily __ after"
39 Gelatin shaper
40 Midas' undoing
41 Tall trees
43 *Beverly Hillbillies* role
44 Responsibility
45 Sharpen
46 Brigham Young follower
49 Mule or moccasin
50 Switch position
53 "Why, the very __!"
54 Math memorization
57 Temporary gift
58 Bull's sound
59 Sullen look
60 Goof
61 Grows up
62 Actress Neuwirth

DOWN
1 Prefix meaning "both"
2 Social equal
3 Concludes
4 Twosome
5 Deserves
6 Got up
7 Southwestern land formation
8 Poker card
9 Golden or Walden
10 Poker stake
11 Trotsky of Russia
14 Some gym-wear
15 Inflexible official
17 Chimney parts
22 Tax mo.
23 Meeting leader
24 Sped
25 Worse, as an excuse
26 In existence
27 Used a stopwatch
28 Coin-toss choice
29 Inexperienced
30 Poet Nash
31 Destitute
33 Nudges
36 Quantities
40 Say "hi" to
42 Lennon's wife
43 Spirits
45 Reporter's question
46 1760 yards
47 Aroma
48 Bring up
49 Dirty air
50 Woodwind
51 Blunder
52 Fancy party
55 Buy a pig __ poke
56 Police announcement: Abbr.

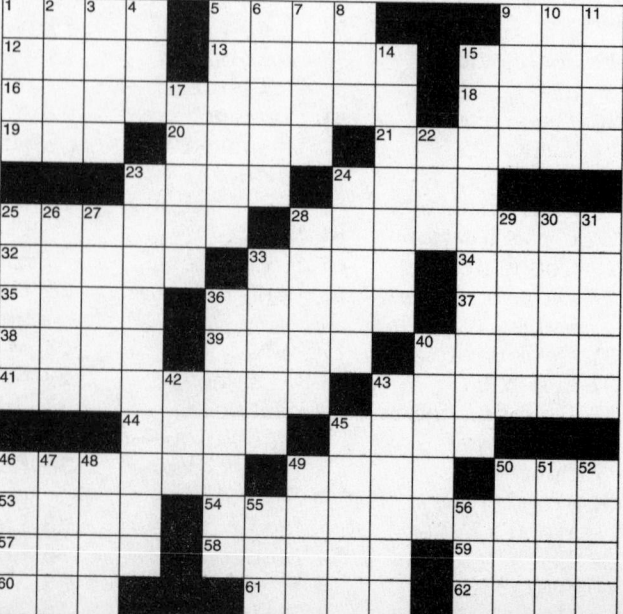

721 THINK BIG by Rich Norris

ACROSS
1 Bundle of papers
6 "__ a Woman" (Beatles tune)
10 Short race
14 Sculptured forms
15 Nobelist Morrison
16 Purina competitor
17 Bred-in-the-bone
19 Toe cover
20 Former draft org.
21 EMT's skill
22 *Seinfeld* role
24 Unaffected by criticism
27 Cow of note
30 Outdoorsman's activity
31 Polaroid product
33 Giraffe feature
34 Precious stone
37 Higher than
38 Onassis' language
40 Open to view
41 Scot's negative
42 Habeas corpus, for one
43 Ad catchphrase
45 Like verse
47 Speechify
48 Extensive in scope
52 *Northern Exposure* setting
53 High school subj.
54 "The Greatest" boxer
57 Chimney passage
58 Comprehensive
62 Camping gear
63 Penitential period
64 *Paper Moon* star
65 *Mlle.*'s Spanish counterpart
66 Preceding periods
67 Off-the-wall

DOWN
1 Norms: Abbr.
2 Does some gardening
3 "__ Tu" (1974 song)
4 African serpent
5 Bobby of chess
6 Laundry additive
7 Like Szechuan food
8 Wind dir.
9 Heroes' helpers
10 Vietnamese seaport
11 French actor Delon
12 Backbone
13 Sank, as a putt
18 Prefix with center
23 Chain part
24 Grandstand section
25 Motion-related
26 __-Ball (arcade game)
27 Subj. for Keynes
28 Volcanic output
29 *Peter Pan* pirate
32 Pleasant
34 Ape, so to speak
35 Part of QED
36 Word on a Biblical wall
39 Comic Rudner
40 Connors rival
42 Operate effectively
44 Archer's tool of yore
45 Spanish coin
46 Deals from the bottom, say
48 Floats on the breeze
49 More under the weather
50 Frighten
51 Like Perot's party: Abbr.
54 "Just __!"
55 Plumbing problem
56 Without hurrying
59 Accelerate, with "up"
60 Individual
61 Santa __, CA

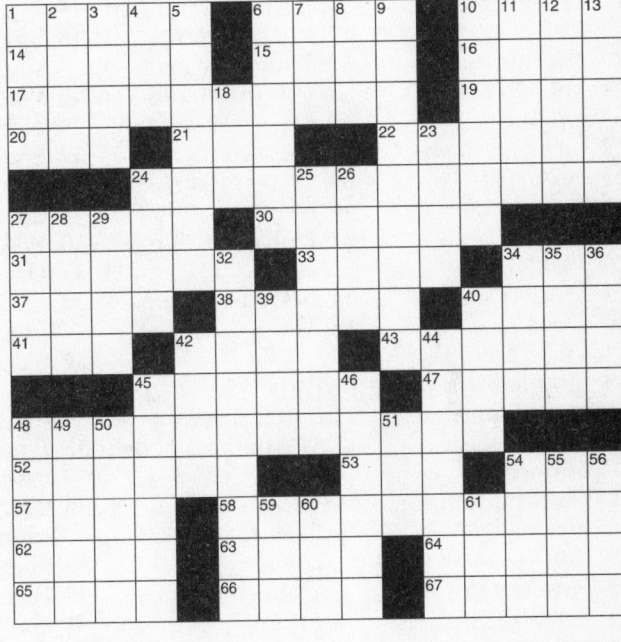

722 HERE'S THE SCOOP by Patrick Jordan

ACROSS
1 Apparatus
5 Entreaties
10 Front of a frigate
14 Wheel shaft
15 Shire of *The Godfather*
16 Boxer's ringside wrap
17 Ice-cream variety
19 Champagne bucket
20 Tiny circus performers
21 E or G, e.g.
22 Terrier type
23 Bacon units
25 She'd rather roughhouse than play house
27 Denial from Yeltsin
29 Dismantle sail supports
32 Hits with a ray gun
35 Bistro server
39 Washington's bill
40 Inventor Whitney
41 Traveling by Airbus
42 Past
43 Musical notes
44 Videotaped over
45 Verses of tribute
46 Moving about
48 Sauce thickener
50 Where some bracelets are worn
54 Removes water, in a way
58 Denominational offshoot
60 Balladeer Burl
62 Think the world of
63 Throbbing pain
64 Ice-cream variety
66 Vibratory sound
67 Up to the time that
68 Speeds along
69 Momentarily
70 Cherry pit
71 Fencing sword

DOWN
1 Iron fishhooks
2 Rejoice
3 Birch relative
4 Wins back
5 Scoreboard nos.
6 Suburban spread
7 George or T.S. of literature
8 __-surface missile
9 Witch-trial venue
10 Alcatraz or Sing Sing
11 Ice-cream variety
12 Do the bidding of
13 Used to be
18 Catch sight of
24 Ed Norton's workplace
26 City
28 British "Bye-bye!"
30 *Come Back, Little Sheba* playwright
31 Metros and Prizms
32 Epsilon follower
33 Baba and MacGraw
34 Ice-cream variety
36 Part of TGIF
37 Wedding-cake layer
38 Create, as a scholarship
41 Quick pull
45 Begin to rust
47 New doctor
49 River to the Caspian Sea
51 Fan of The Great Pumpkin
52 Occurrence
53 Alliance formed in 1954
55 What a poor 35 Across gets
56 Fabled fox's forbidden fruit
57 Have a premonition of
58 Toothed tools
59 Canyon phenomenon
61 Recreational drive
65 Roar for a toreador

723 SILENT TREATMENT by Fred Piscop

ACROSS

1 Suffix with auto or pluto
5 Play's essence
9 Quebec city
14 Verdi heroine
15 Hangover?
16 Taos dwelling
17 Construction tools
20 Psychic attribute
21 Tolkien tree creature
22 Operator's wear
23 Group of attendants
25 Akela's org.
26 "Tsk!"
27 Mound stat
29 Certain undergrad
33 Stopped from squeaking
36 Float like a butterfly
37 Cultural funding grp.
38 Roy G. Biv et al.
42 Nest egg, for short
43 Toledo's lake
44 Like krypton
45 Bit of bickering
47 __ XING
48 "Do __ say, not . . ."
49 GE purchase
51 Biker's wear
55 Filmdom's *Spy Smasher* et al.
59 It may be coddled
60 Ivy Leaguer
61 They may keep you in stitches
64 Dostoyevsky title character
65 Letter after theta
66 Moranis of *SCTV*
67 Unlike a rolling stone?
68 Betty Boop, e.g.
69 Young'uns

DOWN

1 Tartar-sauce morsel
2 Use the finger bowl
3 Masterful
4 Cross shape
5 G.W. Carver concern
6 Coffeehouse order
7 Egg starter
8 Georgia __
9 "__ Theme" (*Doctor Zhivago* tune)
10 Reebok rival
11 Tennessee gridders
12 Up to the task
13 "__ we forget"
18 Spicy Mexican soup
19 War of words
24 News bit
27 Spanish hero
28 Hitchhiker's quest
30 Way back when
31 Use a spyglass
32 ". . . why __ thou forsaken me?"
33 Skip over
34 Calvary inscription
35 Pine needle, essentially
36 Command to a cannoneer
39 Sherpa, perhaps
40 Facial expression
41 Handkerchief ltr.
44 Like krypton
46 Chips choice
48 Cyclades' sea
50 Subtly cruel
51 Slowly, on a score
52 Word form for "sun"
53 Choose
54 Speculators' concerns
55 Take off the top
56 Opposite of ecto-
57 Reformer Jacob
58 Huff
62 Sticky stuff
63 *The 5,000 Fingers of __* (Dr. Seuss movie)

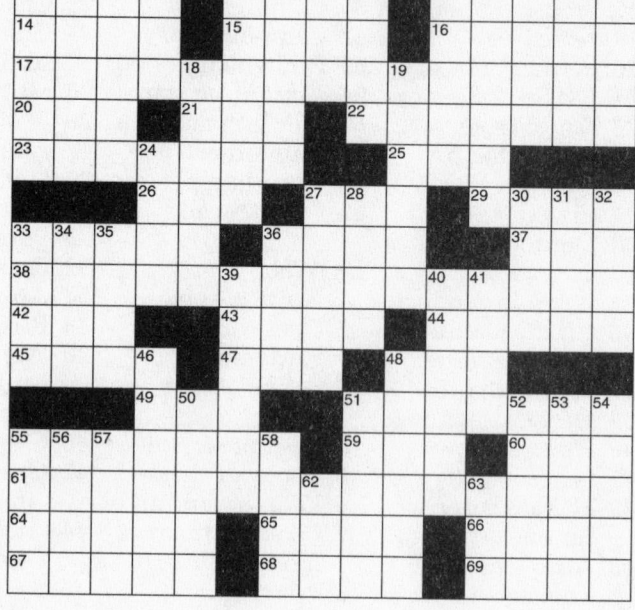

724 NO ONE by S.E. Booker

ACROSS

1 Chitchat
4 Impede
10 Jaunty
14 Hebrew judge
15 Ariel of Israel
16 Butterine
17 Single performance
19 Frolic
20 WWII craft
21 *The Iceman Cometh* playwright
23 Mete out
25 Close to
26 Bake-sale sponsor
27 "Twice have I stood __": Dickinson
29 Utilizes
31 Little fellow
32 Lyrical piece
33 Drove
34 6/6/44
35 Risqué
38 Art __
41 Chap
42 Canonized *femme*, for short
45 Poppycock
49 Round Table knight
51 Pen full of oink
52 Geezer
54 For the __ (free)
55 Ralph and Alice
58 Dialect
59 Florence's river
60 Moore role
62 Some club members
63 Corfu's island group
64 Chang's closest relative
65 Turn tail
66 Added, with "up"
67 Hwy.

DOWN

1 Across-the-board
2 "Open Sesame" sayer
3 Intolerant
4 "Really!"
5 Sounds of surprise
6 Restrain
7 Wernher von __
8 Pined (for)
9 Charm
10 The Bishop of Rome
11 Curved shape
12 One with lots to show you
13 Herbert locale
18 Former White House chief of staff
22 New Deal org.
24 Nil, in Seville
28 Actor Fernando
30 A question of motive
34 Adams or Johnson
35 Mil. unit
36 "__ Lee" (folk song)
37 Big Apple seaside neighborhood
38 Spinning-wheel attachment
39 Captivate
40 Hot stuff
42 Vodka drink
43 Touching
44 Eat too much
46 Cool and refreshing
47 Small bird
48 Informal greeting
50 Orange coat
53 English river
56 Water carrier
57 Aperture
61 Explorer John

ANATOMY 101 by Rich Norris

ACROSS

1 Marsh material
5 Hammer's grabber
9 Obstinate animal
13 Units of current
14 Mystical quality
15 Like Fran Drescher's voice
16 Church instrument
18 Go on all fours
19 Era
20 "__ we there yet?"
21 Specters
23 Sly
25 Give substance to
27 Cry out loud
28 Pitcher Hershiser
29 Casino cube
30 Easy pace
33 Fancy digs
36 House detective's tool
38 Conspire
40 Huck Finn's creator
41 Man-mouse connection

42 At what time
44 Anatomical pouches
48 Hostile relationship
51 On __ (punctually)
53 Like most Theda Bara films
54 __ Lanka
55 Compete
56 Front-running
57 Fine tableware
60 Students' stations
61 Winged Greek god
62 Got 100 on
63 Villa d'__
64 Society newcomers
65 Actress Lamarr

DOWN

1 Vatican rule
2 Political escapee
3 Attractive quality
4 Mao __-tung
5 Tote
6 Winter Olympics event

7 Coach Parseghian
8 Accomplish underhandedly
9 Cattail site
10 National newspaper
11 Court case
12 Architectural add-on
15 Sgts. and cpls.
17 Food grain
22 Montana city
24 Snow unit
25 Worried
26 Shirt shape
28 Bullring cheer
31 Dues payer: Abbr.
32 Tried to cool, in a way
34 Travel on snow
35 Not relaxed
36 Least reputable
37 Have
38 React to a tearjerker
39 Traffic snarlers
43 Environment favoring rapid growth

45 Recommendation
46 Invented, as a phrase
47 Unwavering
49 *M*A*S*H* colonel
50 Watch readouts, briefly
51 Hair lock

52 Sound from the bar?
54 Nose-in-the-air type
56 Summer quaff
58 Assayer's concern
59 "Fat chance!"

ELVIS QUARTET by Ed Julius

ACROSS

1 Tasks
5 Letter on a key
10 Tory opponent
14 Mishmash
15 Buenos __
16 Socks
17 1956 Elvis tune
20 Questionable remedies
21 They stare
22 Luau musicmaker
23 Dumbbell
25 1963 Elvis tune
33 Tusk material
34 Comrade
35 Headlight setting
36 Nick at __
37 Sophia's mate
39 Even
40 Dined
41 Porter or Younger
42 Glistened
43 1958 Elvis tune
47 Disencumbers
48 Jack of *Barney Miller*

49 Celestial hunter
52 Draws
57 1962 Elvis tune
60 Gasoline, e.g.
61 Het up
62 Ticklish Muppet
63 Having oomph
64 Taunted
65 "Break __!"

DOWN

1 Adams or Tyler
2 Margarine
3 Prejudice
4 Do post office work
5 Japanese drama
6 Cadets of Colorado Springs
7 CEO, at times
8 Garden veggie
9 Inquire
10 ". . . it's __ know"
11 Table d'__
12 River to the Elbe

13 Solidifies
18 Very __ yours
19 Like a steeplechase course
23 Gherkin kin
24 1952 Olympics site
25 Singer Washington
26 1996 Madonna role
27 One exercising a franchise
28 Wrath
29 Defied
30 Language peculiarity
31 College in New York
32 German port
37 Like most colleges
38 "Woe is me!"
39 Shortened adverb
41 Cotton fabric
42 Hand-to-hand weapon
44 With humor

45 Asset holdings
46 Like some lines
49 Switch positions
50 Bounder
51 Holly
52 *Pequod* skipper

53 Neighborhood
54 Biology topic
55 Domesticate
56 Component of urban air
58 Hairpiece
59 Cycle starter

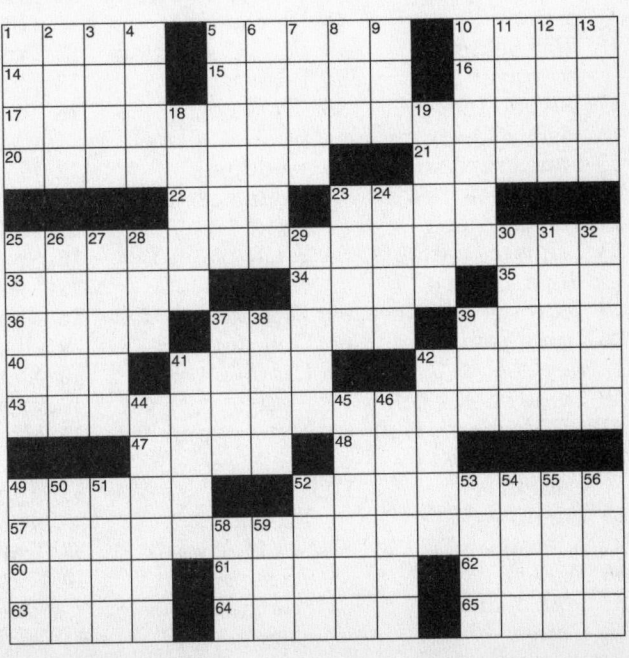

727   SHOPPING SPREE by Bob Lubbers

ACROSS
1 Chair piece
5 Calculating subject
9 Fun's partner
14 Sites
15 Skin-cream ingredient
16 Humiliate
17 Gulf near Yemen
18 Designate
19 Put into service again
20 Store come-on
23 Patriotic org.
24 __ Alamos, NM
25 Exist
28 Stronghold
32 Long-eared equine
35 Less feral
37 Lock holder
38 Talon
39 Store come-on
42 Smirk
43 Perry's creator
44 Let up
45 Three-way joint
46 Challenges
48 Still
49 Deal maker
50 VI x L
52 Store come-on
61 Hibachi residue
62 Doozy
63 Dynamic start
64 Use a plane
65 Cain's brother
66 Agitated mood
67 Abhors
68 Examination
69 Per person

DOWN
1 Cabbage concoction
2 New Jersey town
3 Got a hole in one
4 Having prongs
5 Krishna chant
6 "Oh woe!"
7 Big book
8 Achilles' weak point
9 French waiter
10 Helps a perpetrator
11 Hawaii's "Valley Isle"
12 Exxon's ex-name
13 "As __ on TV!"
21 Buffalo NHLer
22 Steal away with one's intended
25 Skewed
26 Indian princess
27 Alex Trebek, e.g.
29 Ignore one's duties
30 Put off
31 British __
32 Assuage
33 Recipe direction
34 Bonbon, e.g.
36 Go astray
38 Auto for hire
40 Distributed the cards
41 Ethel Mertz portrayer
46 Throws
47 Supernatural
49 Source of annoyance
51 End
52 Whip
53 Workplace oversight agcy.
54 "Huh?"
55 Real-estate map
56 Cartoonist Goldberg
57 Tahiti *et* Martinique
58 __ cava
59 Clapton or Idle
60 *Goodbye, Columbus* author

---

728   GOING TO EXTREMES by Patrick Jordan

ACROSS
1 Piece of land
6 Rainwater pipe
11 *48 __* (Murphy/ Nolte flick)
14 With 2 Down, academic roster
15 A question of purpose
16 1959 Solomon portrayer
17 Beyond the visible spectrum
19 Songstress Zadora
20 More apt to nod off
21 Ten-percenter
23 Bring the curtain down on
24 Blow one's budget
26 Labor-saving device?
30 Some patchwork
31 Like Jabba the Hutt
32 Ditch created by erosion
33 Friendly dog's offering
36 Pesters
37 Male mallard
38 Coffee
39 Greek letter
40 They may be shifted
41 Essayist Francis
42 *The __ Trap* (1998 remake)
44 Sidewalk stuff
45 In opposition to
47 Ill-mannered fellow
48 Kit contents
49 Party decorations
54 Possess
55 "Paper or plastic?" place
58 Wedding-announcement word
59 White-plumed wader
60 *West Side Story* tune
61 Golf pro Ernie
62 Lapping-waves locale
63 Nursery purchase

DOWN
1 Therefore
2 See 14 Across
3 Start a pot
4 Prepare apples for baking
5 Circus swinger
6 Showed fright
7 Inadequate
8 Hooting hunter
9 Get some good out of
10 100 percent
11 Milieu for the *U.S.S. Enterprise*
12 Wishing undone
13 Flintstone's boss
18 Tarzan's transportation
22 Violin-string material
24 Broods silently
25 Heap
26 Roundish projection
27 Lie next to
28 Cheerleaders' cones
29 Obstinate sort
30 Motor-oil measurement
32 Hayes' predecessor
34 Bard of __
35 Crave
37 Moose relative
38 Traffic snarl
40 Barley and rye, for two
41 Nightstand fixture
43 Leatherworker's puncher
44 Windless
45 Do penance (for)
46 Cabana boy's offering
47 A la __ (ordered separately)
49 Drink for Bunker
50 Evangelist Roberts
51 Gumbo ingredient
52 Dresden denial
53 RBI, e.g.
56 Sound of disgust
57 Con's counterpart

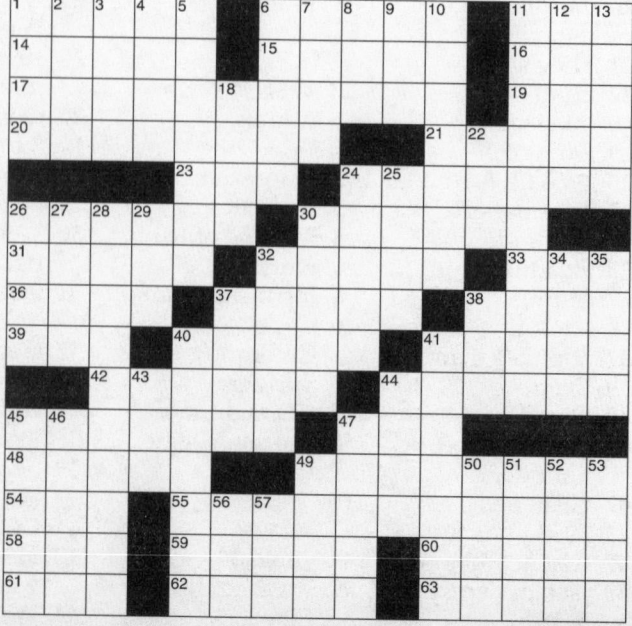

ATHLETES' FEAT by Brenda Pomerance

ACROSS

1 Stinging
5 Aerial support
9 Value system
14 Tennis term
15 Spot
16 Ring, perhaps
17 Tennis quadrille?
19 Steals from
20 Vergilian hero
21 It may be given
23 Tint
24 Grad
26 Conductor Koussevitzky
28 Arcane
32 Energy parcels
35 Wide partner
36 Blood component
38 No philanthropist
39 Fly, for one
41 Memento
43 *Hud* Oscar-winner
44 Extra
46 Hat material
48 Compass pt.
49 Stadiumlike
51 Hit (with)
53 Air-race marker
55 Day saver
56 Pizarro's bounty
58 Hollywood giants
60 High-priced spreads
64 Hypothesize
66 Football UFO?
68 Fuse
69 *Vogue* rival
70 *Advise and Consent* star
71 Full
72 Big name in fruit
73 Germ

DOWN

1 Seaweed
2 Earth's center
3 Rival of Boris and Stefan
4 Trounce
5 Tailor, often
6 African menace
7 Discharge
8 Green ones
9 Hammer neighbor
10 Singing syllable
11 Skating game?
12 Dr. Jones, familiarly
13 Carrier
18 Compares unfavorably
22 Personnel form: Abbr.
25 Entangles
27 Dow rise
28 It's next to D
29 Riyadh resident
30 Hockey vein?
31 Religious groups
33 Nettler
34 *The Green Hat* author
37 Joviality
40 Spooky
42 Astaire/Rogers film
45 Taken out
47 Lighting pro
50 Pursue
52 Exerts no effort
54 Was prying
56 Work
57 Novelist Jaffe
59 Town near Caen
61 Dealing box
62 Fork part
63 Facilitated
65 Mineral suffix
67 Nothing but

ON EDGE by Norma Steinberg

ACROSS

1 Pageantry
5 Amber, originally
10 Ali __
14 Glenn's state
15 __ Cologne
16 *X-Files* sightings
17 Stock-market locale
19 Sharp barks
20 Pitcher's stat
21 Attila the __
22 If all else fails
24 Hostility
26 Steve or Ethan
27 1987 U.S. Open tennis champ
29 New York city
33 "__ Ever Need Is You"
36 Rip
38 Linda of *Alice*
39 Deer foot
40 Circumnavigate from above
42 Fury
43 In the air
45 Defense grp.
46 Nibble
47 Soaked in the tub
49 Indigenous New Zealander
51 Author Loos
53 Crow's-nest cry
57 He played Bunker
60 Food-additive initials
61 Chafe
62 Booze on the *Bounty*
63 "See the USA..." singer
66 Demolish
67 Pierre's school
68 Evils
69 Washstand pitcher
70 Hemmed, perhaps
71 Otherwise

DOWN

1 Energy
2 Name on the Tara deed
3 La Scala city
4 D.C. dealmaker
5 "__ Sender" (Elvis tune)
6 Work for
7 Bring to court
8 Perfect
9 Irk
10 Purchase stocks with credit
11 At a distance
12 Conks
13 Adjutant: Abbr.
18 Brogan, for one
23 In the pink
25 Serial installment's ending
26 "Heart of Dixie"
28 Bruce or Laura
30 First name of 27 Across
31 Latvian capital
32 Again
33 Jezebel's husband
34 *Damn Yankees* heroine
35 Pillager's take
37 Actress Moreno
41 Backyard building
44 Memphis' home: Abbr.
48 Electron tubes
50 Tatters
52 Short time
54 Wry
55 Flings
56 Too big
57 Monster
58 Bird crop
59 Seep
60 Drake or ram
64 Feminist org.
65 Scurry

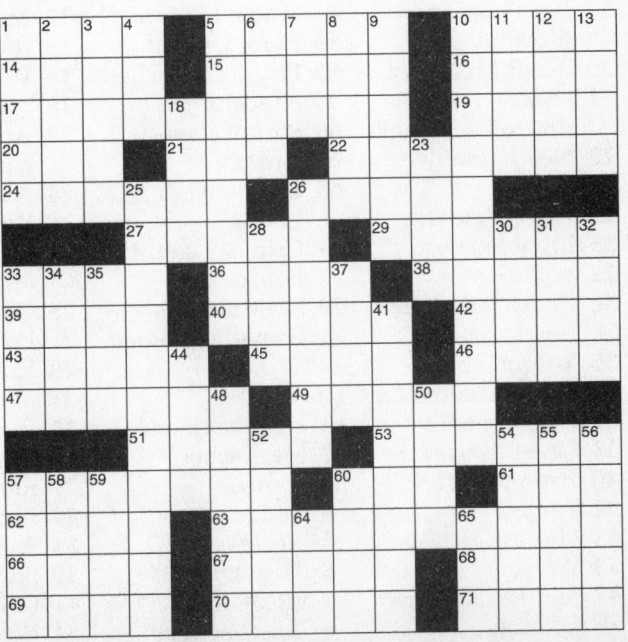

731 GET THE POINT? by Fred Piscop

ACROSS
1 Told a whopper
5 Bean curd
9 Marsh plant
14 Inside: Pref.
15 Off the __ (bizarre)
16 Standard partner
17 Tennis situation
18 Idle of comedy
19 Titicaca's locale
20 Sandwich partner
23 "I didn't know that!"
24 Glossy fabric
25 Snooze takers
27 Thumbs-up votes
30 Parakeet's dinner
31 Yank's foe
34 Oz pooch
36 Four-star review
39 Hard to comprehend
41 Standee's support
42 Punctilious one
43 Sleek, in auto lingo
44 Parcel's partner
45 Put out, one way
46 Ran like the dickens
48 Get Yer __ Out (Rolling Stones album)
52 __ forth (sets out)
55 Horrified
59 Neighbor of Tenn.
60 Indian peace symbol
63 Japanese assassin
65 Escapade
66 Concerning
67 Windshield sticker
68 Poker payment
69 Tiny parasite
70 Bergen dummy
71 Epitome of thinness
72 Organic fuel

DOWN
1 Springs
2 Gunga Din setting
3 Papal bull
4 Democratic Party symbol
5 10-, 11- and 12-year-olds
6 Rowing equipment
7 Go head over heels
8 Worrier's woe, it's said
9 Not at all dense
10 Very long time
11 '60s compact car
12 Garson of filmdom
13 Snaky curves
21 Beauregard's boss
22 He wrote of "sour grapes"
26 Maryland collegian
28 Blues singer James
29 "Pardon me!"
31 Vitamin qty.
32 Brogan width
33 Carter budget director
35 "See ya!"
37 Itinerary word
38 Quiche base
40 Combine, as resources
41 Inside the Third Reich writer
47 Scurrilous
49 Removed, as a tooth
50 Turkish general
51 Scampi need
52 Removes the rough spots
53 From Mars, perhaps
54 Word before battery or wind
56 Palmer's nickname
57 Not exactly, informally
58 Aviary sound
61 Memorable Welles role
62 Art Deco notable
64 Jelly holder

732 POST-DOCTORAL WORK by Manny Nosowsky

ACROSS
1 Painter Chagall
5 Come apart at the seams
9 Vacuum-tube gas
14 __ close to schedule
15 Italian resort
16 __ Haute, IN
17 Physician-turned-dictator
20 Actor McQueen
21 "Eat __ eaten" (law of the jungle)
22 Not __ many words
23 Actor Baldwin
25 Bit of legalese
27 IOU
30 Physician-turned-revolutionary
35 Young fellow
36 Movie-chain name
37 Israeli money
38 Greet the day
40 Even the score
42 Skilled
43 Hid away
45 Workers' rights org.
47 Southeast Asian language
48 Physician-turned-synonymist
50 Sunbeams
51 Seeing things
52 Presidential prerogative
54 Aid in wrongdoing
57 Water, to Juan
59 From Utrecht
63 Physician-turned-educator
66 Sort of stew
67 Aroma
68 Handy bit of Latin
69 Crimean country house
70 Scale starters
71 Something owed

DOWN
1 Kitchen cleaners
2 Med. school course
3 Rodeo prop
4 Neckwear
5 Ziegfeld's nickname
6 Bullet bounce
7 ID info
8 "Leave him alone, __ bully!"
9 __ glance (quickly)
10 No longer worried
11 Look of contentment
12 Metals in the rough
13 Wolfe the detective
18 __ Monte
19 Aphrodite's equivalent
24 Author Umberto
26 Kind of therapy
27 Envelope attachment
28 "Outcasts of Poker Flat" writer
29 Knucklehead
31 Dallas family name
32 Cub-scout leader
33 Satisfy, as a mortgage
34 Some singers
36 Suspicious
39 Sort of sugary
41 Car in a building
44 Wild fancy
46 Hwy.
49 Rhyming newsman Charles
50 Stirred to anger
53 QB's stats
54 In the center of
55 Theda of silent films
56 Leif's pop
58 Bring to naught
60 Big bag
61 Bellyacher
62 To the __ (completely)
64 "Now I get it!"
65 Before, in poems

733 TERMINAL TRIOS by Richard Silvestri

ACROSS
1 Not too hot
5 Pave over
10 "Dancing Queen" group
14 Time to beware
15 Skater Valova
16 __ ball (spongy sphere)
17 Barbershop call
18 Smooth white flower?
20 Swinging Sammy
21 Justice Dept. employee
22 Figure of speech?
23 African nation's former name
25 Religious address
26 Put in a kitty
28 Powerful dogs
33 Einstein's birthplace
34 Come up again
36 __ Gay
37 Taunt
39 Get rid of
41 Makeup, e.g.
42 Force out
44 Prepare to drive
46 Sumac of songdom
47 Threatened to fall
49 Codger
51 Took charge
52 '60s greeting
53 Crown covering
57 Veep before Al
58 Slinger's dish
61 Milky Way area?
63 Mixed bag
64 Shortly
65 Moves like the Blob
66 Long, long time
67 Steady, maybe
68 Yule tunes
69 Galley marking

DOWN
1 Go down
2 Old Greek theaters
3 Character in a NC-17 horror film?
4 Bony
5 Given compensation
6 Tickle pink
7 Passage for a sermon
8 Whichever
9 Father's Day gifts
10 Visitor to Siam
11 Out of shape?
12 Vivacity
13 Way out there
19 Incensed
24 Occupational suffix
25 Charley's Aunt, for one
26 Sound of Washington
27 Pimiento holder
28 Toned down
29 Serpent tail?
30 Sly fanatic?
31 Calgary hockey player
32 Philippine island
35 Called to court
38 Opposite of end-
40 Immensity
43 Fax forerunner
45 Podded plant
48 Trust
50 Sonic returns
52 Judging group
53 "Yikes!"
54 Peter Pan pooch
55 Gobs
56 Lion's pride
57 Catnap
59 Triangle ratio
60 Large number
62 Bronx attraction

734 TO THE LETTER by Frank Longo

ACROSS
1 __ for (picks)
5 Iron clothes
10 Fly in the ointment
14 Touched down
15 Lotto cousin
16 Albacore, e.g.
17 Washington had a memorable one
20 Milwaukee-to-Miami dir.
21 Kazan of Hollywood
22 Colanders
23 Yothers of Family Ties
25 Caesar's septet
27 Serta rival
28 Billy Budd star
31 Love personified
32 Early Christian-ity center
33 __ Jima
36 Video-store offering
38 Church book
40 Carders' requests
41 Former New Jersey governor
45 French 101 verb
46 Chatter
48 Marsh of whodunits
51 Novelist Beattie
52 Dory propellers
53 Bothers incessantly
55 Per-__ allowance
57 It may be slung
59 Exceed accepted limits
62 Permit Me Voyage poet
63 Application
64 Orthodontist's concern
65 Starring role
66 Grinch creator
67 Feed the hogs

DOWN
1 Klutzes
2 Stewed
3 Flat-fixing tools
4 __ Croix, Quebec
5 Seth's brother
6 Went through anew
7 Discomfort
8 __ trial basis
9 Curtain inserts
10 Out of Africa star
11 New, in Madrid
12 Photographer Adams
13 Bombastic
18 Ablactate
19 Daunt
24 Hatchling's home
26 "__ showtime!"
28 Garr or Hatcher
29 Classical temple's center
30 "... who lived in __"
33 Agitated
34 Becomes friendlier with
35 Chihuahua cheers
37 Buoyant
39 Prefix with bit or hit
42 __-Locka, FL
43 17th-century musical form
44 Shea stanzas
46 Angled
47 Not all
48 View from Everest
49 Measure precisely
50 Yachting
54 Consequently
56 12/24 and 12/31
58 Profound
60 Suffix with Brooklyn
61 Lots of oz.

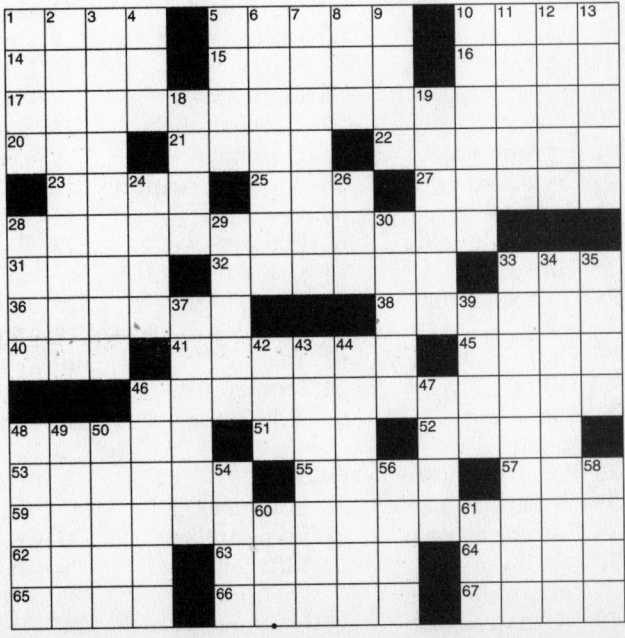

735   SPICE RACK by Rich Norris

ACROSS
1 "__ mia!"
6 50 percent portion
10 Frosh, next year
14 Mr. T's former outfit
15 *Rubáiyát* name
16 Preserve, as meat
17 Mentor's offering
19 66 and others: Abbr.
20 Railroad stop: Abbr.
21 Match the bet
22 Practice pieces
24 Sherlock Holmes portrayer
28 Fry lightly
30 Sequence
31 Moved in a curved path
32 Prefix for sphere
33 Sarasota's st.
36 Garden tool
37 Unrestrained episode
39 Entice
40 Sit-ups strengthen them
41 WWI German admiral
42 Chap
43 Barbershops
45 Customary procedures
46 Perfect shape, to a collector
50 Most frosty
51 Fireplace throw-in
52 Rowboat need
55 Baked dessert
56 Builder's knot
60 Roman god of love
61 Busy place
62 Glacial ridge
63 Cluckers
64 Wine-list datum
65 Newspapers, magazines, etc.

DOWN
1 Church service
2 Rat-__
3 Big money
4 West of Hollywood
5 Piled up
6 Humble dwellings
7 Fifi's friend
8 Varnish ingredient
9 Off hours
10 Uses elbow grease
11 Beat
12 Dress smartly
13 *Steppenwolf* author
18 "Agnus __"
23 Kojak's first name
25 To __ (perfectly)
26 Hit from behind
27 Commedia dell'__
28 Poet Teasdale
29 Yemeni, for one
33 Like a research paper
34 Erie or Huron
35 Graph lines
37 Full of blots and spots
38 Menial laborer
39 Advertising award
41 Baglike structures
42 Mormon leader Young
43 Takes the wheel
44 Coin material
46 Minor Biblical prophet
47 Start of Caesar's boast
48 Ricoh competitor
49 Rhythm keeper, sometimes
53 Play beginning
54 Actress Perlman
57 Tell it like it isn't
58 Egg cells
59 Fury

736   THE A TEAM by Randall J. Hartman

ACROSS
1 On vacation
5 Car lifter
9 Hippie phrase
14 Daytona 500, for one
15 Author Hunter
16 Breathing
17 The yoke's on them
18 Yorkshire river
19 Its capital is Niamey
20 Encountered
21 Tennis star once married to Brooke Shields
23 Hatred
25 Like a debtor's ink
26 Dancer Charisse
27 Wiser companion
30 Likely
33 Raccoon cousin
35 Hokey acting
36 Surface at Vail
37 Northern metropolis
40 Maui necklaces
41 Director Kazan
42 Pays attention to
43 Hallucinogenic initials
44 African antelope
45 Kin: Abbr.
46 U-turn from SSW
47 Harbinger
50 College-football star
56 German article
57 Home of the Dolphins
58 Algerian seaport
59 Perth pal
60 Estuary
61 In the thick of
62 Large flightless birds
63 Tale
64 Numerous
65 Nile nippers

DOWN
1 Bouquet
2 Like candles
3 Vinegar, chemically
4 Craving
5 Informal clothing
6 Gung-ho
7 Chanteuse Vikki
8 Leg joint
9 Peril
10 Homeric epic
11 Jazz dates
12 Currier's partner
13 *Lois & Clark* star Hatcher
21 Sound transmission
22 Sports stadium
24 Ancient stories
27 Florida citrus center
28 Sign on
29 Trepidation
30 Yosemite photographer
31 Dawdling
32 "__ the night before Christmas . . ."
33 Cry out
34 Change for a five
36 Soldier's sword
38 U.S. Grant foe
39 Matthau's bride in *Grumpier Old Men*
44 Hatred
46 Rat, in a way
47 Deft
48 Back off
49 Attire
50 French friends
51 Fabric fuzz
52 Composer Schifrin
53 Wander
54 __ *la Douce*
55 First son
59 "Cry __ River"

737 CHURCHILLIAN TRIO by Fred Piscop

ACROSS

1 One __ kind (unique)
4 Conniving sort
11 Well put
14 Half a diam.
15 Venezuelan river
16 Innovator's prefix
17 Movie violence
20 Go all-out
21 Windbag's output
22 "__ to Your School" (Beach Boys tune)
23 Abrasive particles
25 Schooner filler
26 "No __" (Chinese-restaurant sign)
28 Harper Valley grp.
31 Switch positions
32 Half a dual personality
34 Shuffle
37 Togs for the treadmill
40 Xerox predecessor
43 Dame Hess
47 Cleveland cager
48 Teachers' grp.
49 Anat. or chem.
52 Granola grain
53 Take a header
55 All wound up
57 Trying to be
61 Go __ (rot)
62 Little Anthony and the Imperials song
65 Compass line
66 Looked like a villain
67 Lodge member
68 Tricky turn
69 Make like new
70 Monogram of 32 Across' creator

DOWN

1 Crystal ball, e.g.
2 In a deceptive manner
3 Accepted, as a resolution
4 Element in salt
5 Strains, as one's neck
6 "You're getting warmer," e.g.
7 Wind up
8 Flying insect
9 Canyon sound
10 Lopsided win
11 Yule-log holder
12 Using a magnifying glass
13 Craggy hill
18 Bruin Bobby
19 Racetrack slacker
22 Ebenezer's exclamation
24 Lao-__
27 Persona non __
28 Histories
29 Play about Capote
30 *Exodus* character
33 RI zone
35 Zeta follower
36 PIN requester
38 Attained
39 Nationality ending
40 Agt.'s take
41 __ Ferry, WV
42 Egg containers
44 Tyrolean tunesmith
45 Ann or Andy
46 Grabbed a bite
50 *Sergeant York* star
51 Protected from the elements
54 Pricing word
56 Sinuous swimmer
58 Gorby's realm, once: Abbr.
59 Ready to serve
60 People
61 Novice
62 __ kwon do
63 Ran into
64 Calendar divs.

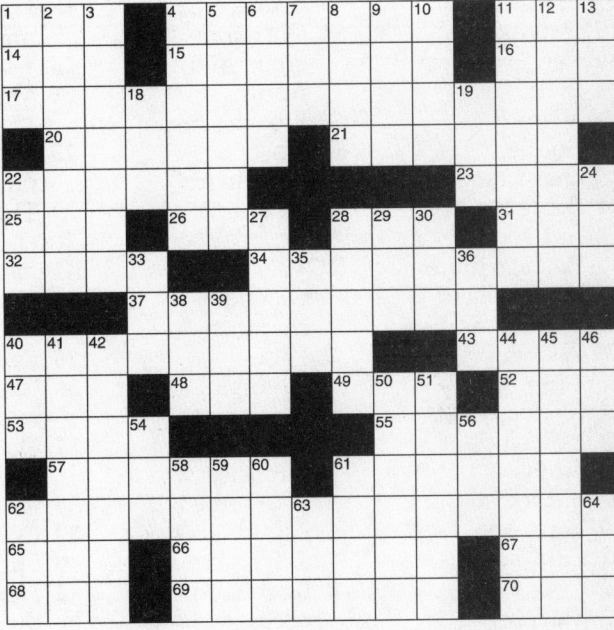

738 POP POP CULTURE by Ray Hamel

ACROSS

1 Jazz form
4 Largest US tribe
10 Fellow
14 Medicinal plant
15 *Wuthering Heights* actress
16 On a __ (winning)
17 Statute
18 Police dispatcher's "signal weak"
19 Global region
20 Robert Conrad TV series
23 Reddish deer
24 White Rabbit's declaration
25 Normans' enemies
28 *Happy Days* character
30 Actress Verdugo
31 Irked
32 Give up
36 Lucy-Desi movie, with *The*
39 Meadows
40 Floor coverings
41 Arbor growth
42 Advice columnist
43 Travolta movie musical
44 Djibouti language
48 Thai currency
49 Wee-hour broadcast
55 Go on and on
56 Christie of mystery
57 Hatchet
58 Stellar bear
59 Tied up, in a way
60 *Crooklyn* director
61 Eye drop
62 Smiles with contempt
63 The final word in movies

DOWN

1 Unruly child
2 Sound of pain
3 Jazzman Fountain
4 Existing only in the mind
5 White poplars
6 Hawks
7 "Pretty maids all in __"
8 Pop singer Mitchell
9 Youngman specialty
10 Swimming stroke
11 Hebrew prophet
12 Tipping
13 China piece
21 Treats unjustly
22 No man's land: Abbr.
25 Get something for
26 Lotion additive
27 TV's "Warrior Princess"
28 Obscured
29 Leftover morsels
31 Turn aside
32 Jungle cats
33 Lamb's pseudonym
34 Low grades
35 Gaelic
37 Certain electrons
38 Space cadets
42 Chicken __ king
43 Assemble
44 Pompous step
45 Chicago landing site
46 Bright bunch
47 Wedding site
48 Soak in the tub
50 Inspiration for *The French Connection*
51 Emit coherent light
52 Strong and healthy
53 Beasts of burden
54 Garden nuisance

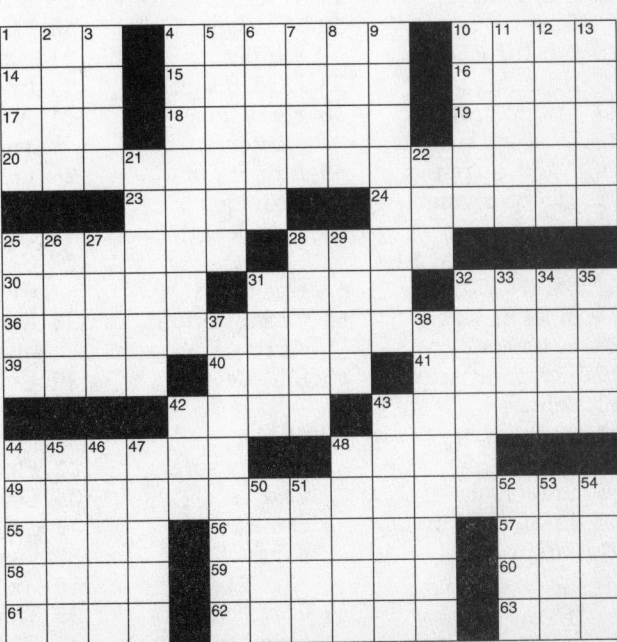

739 BRAINIACS by A.J. Santora

ACROSS

1 Bell town
5 Pack foursome
9 Flu shots
13 Research institutes
16 Petrol org.
17 Egghead
19 Provoke
20 Penpoint
21 Swizzle again
22 Boulle characters
24 Some kind of nut
27 Poetic tribute
28 WWII island
30 Blue Cross system: Abbr.
31 Iowa city
32 Yale student
34 Sirens
37 Strategists
39 Escaped
41 Paris season
42 Goes bad
43 Tie fabric
45 Beginning
49 Mil. address
50 Unprincipled
53 "Bye!"
54 In truth
56 Unsweetened
58 Henpeck
59 Reasoning
63 Circus area
64 Corporate emigration result
65 French seraph
66 Host
67 African iris, for short

DOWN

1 Of a body chamber
2 1912 Olympics hero
3 Gin drink
4 Publicity
5 Like some wit
6 Algiers area
7 Ref. book
8 Biathlete's need
9 Sir Toby Belch et al.
10 Abstracts
11 Dweller
12 Lucci or Leoni
14 Actor Olin
15 Withered
18 Freshly minted
23 T-bones
25 More like a 17 Across
26 Celeste or Ian
29 Threat ender
31 Passionate
33 Skater Midori
35 Recline
36 Golden Rule word
37 On the road, perhaps
38 Of a continent
39 Cockiness
40 Entices
44 Here and there
46 Footwear
47 And others: Lat.
48 Remnant
50 HS subject
51 Abby's initial advice
52 Comic Bruce
55 *Picnic* playwright
57 Atlantic fish
60 Arms lobby: Abbr.
61 Sound perception
62 Part of NATO

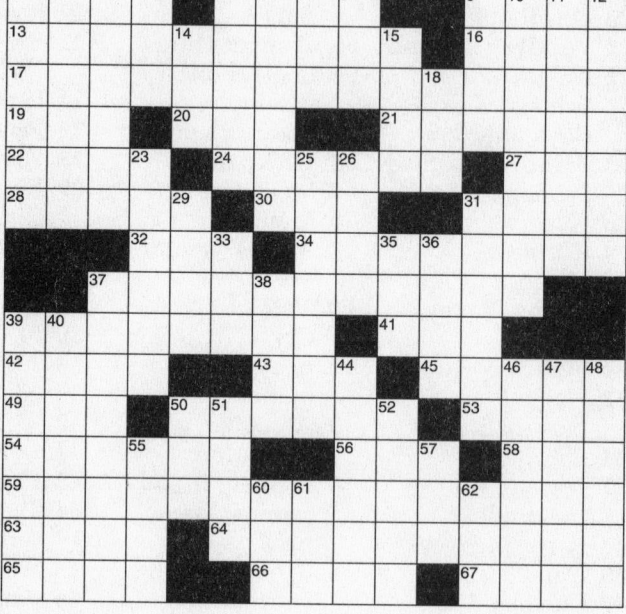

740 ON THE CANVAS by Rich Norris

ACROSS

1 Son of Hera
5 Yucatán denizen
9 Long, narrow inlet
14 Small inlet
15 Land on the Caspian Sea
16 Nocturnal primate
17 Public protest
19 Of some benefit
20 Aged, as paper
21 Placed on an agenda
22 Poorly behaved
23 Baby's word
24 In a fair way
28 __ *Quixote*
29 Sticky situation
33 Belittle
34 Ice mass, for short
35 Universal Studios' former parent co.
36 Sportscaster specialty
40 *Krazy* __
41 Selves
42 Operatic highlights
43 Eye annoyance
45 Reading room
46 Sailors' patron
47 Medical picture
49 Waikiki welcome
50 *High Noon* Oscar-winner
53 Declares guilty
58 Heavenly hunter
59 Elm, for one
60 Crowded
61 Skirt length
62 Locale
63 Cockeyed
64 Organization: Abbr.
65 Still sleeping

DOWN

1 Feeling sore
2 Cad
3 Daredevil Knievel
4 Arctic barker
5 Carnival area
6 Like a rainbow
7 Gridiron unit
8 "__ port in a storm"
9 Liquid
10 Sea debris
11 Leave out
12 Regulation
13 Stowe novel
18 More stately
21 Actress Jessica
23 College quarters
24 Accessories found in trunks
25 *Lusitania* sinker
26 Like some chips
27 General on a Chinese menu
28 Exorcist's quarry
30 Cyberspace letters
31 "Beat it!"
32 Final authority
34 One over par, in golf
37 Furniture wood
38 Indigenous
39 Three, in Turin
44 Public revelation
46 Submit, as an application
48 Extend a subscription
49 Gives temporarily
50 Musical ending
51 Vein pursuits
52 Sty cry
53 Greek letters
54 "__ boy!"
55 Nursery furniture
56 Nantes noggin
57 Flower starter
59 Tiny, in Scotland

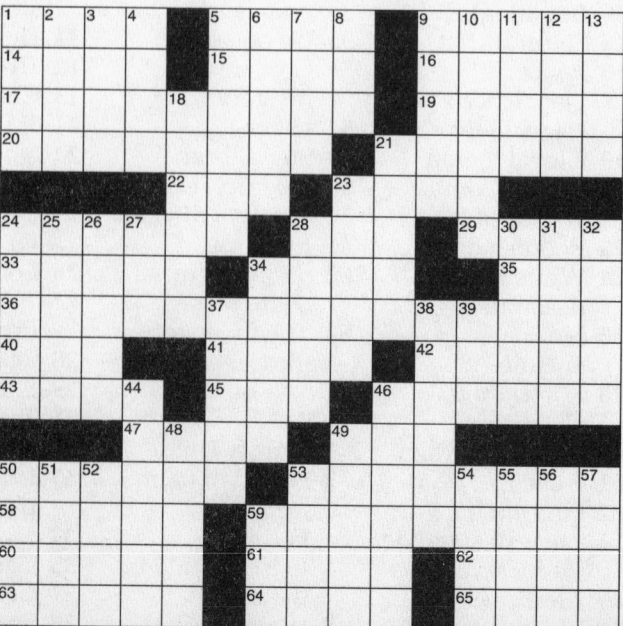

ON THE CANVAS by Norma Steinberg

ACROSS

1 The lion's share
5 Prohibit
8 Opposite of "to"
11 Cartoon "light bulb"
12 Truths
14 Cleansing agent
15 Defeated
18 April 15 addressee
19 ". . . __ suffer the slings and arrows . . ."
20 As a companion
21 Toon Fudd
22 Yellowish-red
23 *Catch-22* author
25 Storage area
26 Racer Andretti
27 Feeling blue
28 "Woe __!"
32 Admit defeat
36 Immense
37 For example
38 Austere
39 Have a bawl

40 Make from scratch
42 South Seas island group
45 Stands in line
46 Establish as fact
47 Assns.
48 __ Vegas
51 Fight unfairly
54 *Mila 18* author
55 Dingbat
56 West Coast sch.
57 Garden tool
58 Cozy room
59 Lanky

DOWN

1 Long skirt
2 Scent
3 Makes clothes
4 Sunbathe
5 Cashless trade
6 Thespian
7 Extreme degree
8 Stumbled upon
9 Lanky

10 Choose
12 "But Not __" (Gershwin tune)
13 Shore
14 Imminently
16 Come next
17 Extended family
21 Prufrock's creator
23 Sounds of laughter
24 Goofs up
25 Ebenezer's exclamation
26 Cable rock station
27 Pigpen
28 Smidgens
29 Police dept. unit
30 Pierre's mom
31 Tundra beast
33 From Tel Aviv
34 No vote
35 African fly
39 Inlet

40 Milk container
41 Correct
42 Hubert's successor
43 Clarinetist Shaw
44 Throngs
45 Exclamation of surprise

48 Polish leader Walesa
49 "__ Ever Need Is You"
50 Ollie's partner
51 "What?"
52 Roulette bet
53 Except for

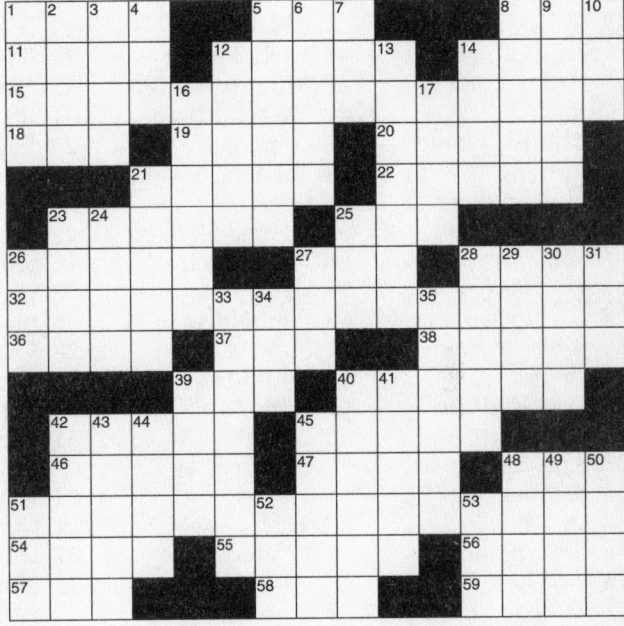

ROCKY IV by Lee Weaver

ACROSS

1 Book of maps
6 School org.
9 Auction action
12 One who cajoles
14 Entered the race
15 Chills and fever
17 The __ State (New York)
18 Got
20 Pueblo Indian art
22 Prefix for hazard
25 Sounds of awe
26 Prudential rival
27 Iroquoians
30 Violin part
32 Elevate
33 Oldest national park
36 Muslim's Almighty
37 Rocker John
41 California golf locale
46 Performing mammal
50 Family chart
51 Rose oil

52 Gold bar
54 Currier's partner
56 Possesses
57 *Dick Tracy* character
61 Dacron or denim
62 Too
66 Ripening agent
67 Citrine cooler
68 More cautious
69 Superman's insignia
70 Color of Santa's suit
71 Protuberances

DOWN

1 High card
2 Selleck or Seaver
3 Race segment
4 Line of rotation
5 Blood components
6 Isaiah, for one
7 Hot sauce
8 Opposed to

9 Fisherman, at times
10 Cause to burn
11 Chaperon in Cádiz
13 Clinton's A.G.
16 Mystery writers' award
19 Santa __, CA
21 Adams and Johnson
22 "Yo!"
23 Carpet calculation
24 Medicinal form
28 House addition
29 Motel freebie
31 Leg joint
34 Sharpen
35 Napoleon's exile isle
38 Vietnamese festival
39 Solemn promise
40 March Madness org.
42 Military unit
43 Cut on a slant
44 Impolite look
45 Slugger's stat.

46 Greek letter
47 Incense
48 Striped stones
49 Romeo and Juliet, e.g.
53 Three times, in a prescription

55 Load cargo
58 Whopper teller
59 Lendl of tennis
60 Architect Saarinen
63 Clear out (of)
64 Loser at Gettysburg
65 Many mos.

POWER PLAY by Patrick Jordan

ACROSS

1 Having a charley horse
5 Blows gently
10 "The Wave" performers
14 "My __ Heaven"
15 Under way
16 Door sign
17 Springfield scamp
18 Sawyer of TV news
19 Thinly layered mineral
20 Hole maker
21 '60s country singer
23 "__ the Top"
25 Gridlock element
26 Vine-covered shelters
28 1994 Redford film
33 Sales of comedy
34 Brother of 57 Down
35 Biblical judge
36 __ d'oeuvres
37 College officials
38 Pet rocks et al.
39 Immigrant's course: Abbr.
40 Air gusts
41 Foster of filmdom
42 They give hair flair
44 Ship's money handler
45 Early P.M.
46 Military student
47 Tie-twiddling comedian
52 Take the wrong way?
55 Actress Hatcher
56 Felt unwell
57 Lawn burrower
58 Pen refills
59 Slow pace
60 Billfold contents
61 Kimono closer
62 Uptight
63 Future fowl

DOWN

1 "Waterloo" group
2 Pincer
3 Uproar
4 To this point
5 Trout fisherman's wear
6 Blazing
7 Infant Appaloosa
8 Author Morrison
9 Lettering tools
10 Thighbones
11 Allies' opponents
12 Shaving mishap
13 Overnight visit
21 Rage
22 Vague, as a recollection
24 Klutzy comment
26 Campfire remains
27 Chicken's resting place
28 Campus areas
29 Grecian vessels
30 Extremely willful
31 '50s tune
32 More sagacious
34 Where Abe faces right
37 Divert
38 Warning from Woods
40 Sophia, to Carlo
41 Punch puncher
43 Extravagant
44 Oar
46 Oarsmen
47 Elevator name
48 Horne or Olin
49 Peeves
50 Give a job to
51 Ladd or Alda
53 Designer Cassini
54 Mrs. Truman
57 Stern-faced Stooge

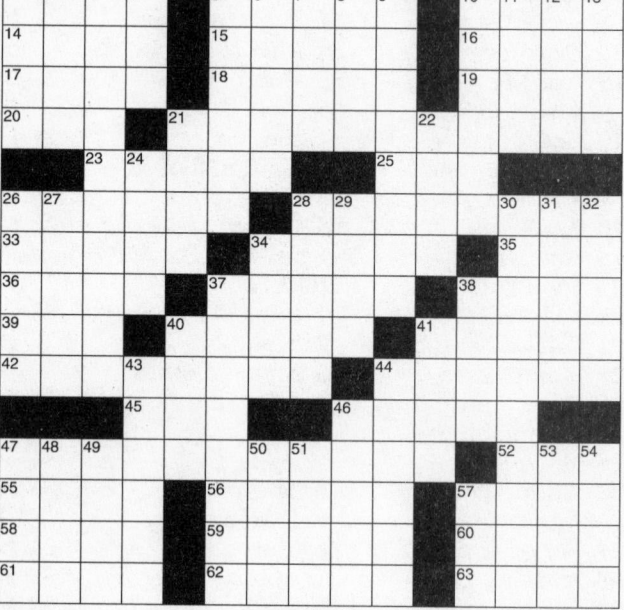

MOVIE PROFILE by Ed Julius

ACROSS

1 Showed fright
7 1965 role for Andrews
12 Start to breathe
13 Passover book
17 *A __ Born*
18 Build castles in the air
19 Taro root
20 Efforts
21 Feel off
22 Give __ (care)
23 Nebraska Indians
24 Shoppe descriptor
25 Bowling site
26 Prohibitionists
27 Clio hopefuls
28 Mrs. Andy Capp
29 Haunted-house sound
30 *Clueless* remark
31 Man with a familiar profile
36 "Self" starter
37 Hoopster Archibald
38 Some deer
39 Ms. Hawkins
41 Aloe __
42 Cocksure
43 Lay __ the line
44 "Bei Mir __ Du Schön"
45 Sheet-music notations
46 *Turandot* girl
47 Trading centers
48 Diploma, e.g.: Abbr.
49 Walk
51 Part of a printing press
53 Even a score
54 Play the market
55 Feared mosquito
56 Noah and Wallace

DOWN

1 USO frequenters
2 Waiting room
3 31 Across film
4 Absolve
5 Thomas Stearns __
6 French preposition
7 31 Across film, with *The*
8 Car accessories
9 James and Tommie
10 Major golf tourneys
11 Intimate
14 31 Across film
15 Nitrogen compound
16 Trojan War name
20 Pentateuch
22 __ Romeo
24 Like "To a Skylark"
26 Knucklehead
27 "... exclaim __ drove out of sight"
29 Ration
30 Official proceedings
32 Devastate
33 Queen of Hearts' specialty
34 __ car (loaner)
35 Tavern inventory
39 Fictional miser
40 "Once upon __ ..."
41 Patience, for one
42 Record protector
44 Bleated
45 Part of a play
47 Fr. miss
50 Actress Hagen
51 White lie
52 ACLU concern

745 RICH FOLKS by Randall J. Hartman

ACROSS
1 Word of regret
5 Air-traffic control device
10 Sleeveless garment
14 Croissant, e.g.
15 Rust, for example
16 Type of exam
17 "Two Tickets to Paradise" singer
19 Call companion
20 Lake lander
21 Up and about
22 Arroz __ pollo
23 Ashen
25 Watchband
28 *The Good Earth* author
33 Stability
34 Prepares text
35 Bert Bobbsey's twin
36 Church niche
37 Chess pieces
38 Qualified
39 *Norma* __
40 WWII correspondent Pyle
41 Author Zola
42 American poet
44 Purple Heart, for one
45 Held on to
46 What ensigns call admirals
47 Michael Caine film
50 Comprehends
55 Serene
56 "A Boy Named Sue" singer
58 Melville captain
59 Turn over
60 Pay to play
61 James Bond foe
62 Greek promenades
63 Require

DOWN
1 Greek god of war
2 Store of ore
3 Actor Alan
4 Book holder
5 Director Polanski
6 Part of a neuron
7 Enjoy a repast
8 Fruity drink
9 Actor Alejandro
10 Spider's creation
11 Region
12 Prepare to travel
13 Screen siren Sommer
18 Wed on the run
21 __ *Well That Ends Well*
23 Showing discomfort, as a look
24 Liberal __
25 Extra
26 November birthstone
27 Step part
28 Oil source
29 Language expert Newman
30 Not invited
31 Marsh plant
32 Show obeisance
37 Stage object
38 United rival
40 Fencing weapon
41 Etiquette authority Post
43 With hands on hips
46 Makes smooth
47 Mil. sch.
48 Cowardly Lion portrayer
49 Custard treat
50 Word form meaning "current"
51 Sicilian commune
52 Western writer Grey
53 Spanish compass point
54 Storage structure
56 Roast beef au __
57 Make a choice

746 POETIC CONCLUSIONS by Fred Piscop

ACROSS
1 Night vision
6 Singer Zadora
9 Reduce, as fears
14 Strike back, e.g.
15 Chapel Hill sch.
16 Mix
17 Backwards
19 Does as told
20 Confined, with "up"
21 "That's amazing!"
22 Poetic preposition
23 *Seinfeld* character
29 Author Ferber
30 Number on the sports page
31 Neither masc. nor fem.
32 Clairvoyance, for short
34 32-card game
36 Highway warning
37 Pawn in another's game
41 Layer
43 In the style of
44 Asterisk
46 A, in Worms
47 Mrs. Nick Charles
49 Left in a hurry
51 ". . . three men in __"
54 Deteriorating condition
57 Possesses
58 Complete a street
59 Trumpeter Al
61 Clear the windshield
64 Meteorologist's device
66 Hold responsible
67 Unusually smart
68 Speak at length
69 Big ship
70 Villain's snort
71 Prone to giving orders

DOWN
1 Faucet problem
2 Go back on one's word
3 Acquired deservedly
4 Varnish ingredients
5 VH-1 alternative
6 Baby foods, at times
7 Flies, e.g.
8 Flying standout
9 Cancel, to NASA
10 Big name in mail order
11 Director Spike
12 Whichever
13 Many ft.
18 Ovum
22 Heir-splitting subject
24 Carpentry tools
25 Former acorns
26 Arboreal abode
27 Natal native
28 Tiny particle
33 Literary device
35 Docket listing
37 Six-pack units
38 Big time
39 Fictional plantation
40 Model persona
42 Unlikely protagonist
45 Bureaucratic hassle
48 Not away
50 Scarcity
52 Hall-of-Fame quarterback Johnny
53 Artists' toppers
55 Raring to go
56 __-Magnon
60 Low card
61 Two-bagger: Abbr.
62 Actor Wallach
63 Summer cooler
64 Exclamation of annoyance
65 Riotous crowd

747 BEDROCK ROLL CALL by Patrick Jordan

ACROSS
1 Dexterous
5 Fall flower
10 OOO, in love letters
14 Fairy-tale fiend
15 Indian corn
16 From the start
17 PBS show host since 1968
19 __ la Douce
20 Service charge
21 Biblical landing place
22 Take a breather
23 Shale features
25 Was a passenger
27 1960 Summer Olympics star
33 Star's brief appearance
36 Sans companions
37 Promissory initials
38 Bullring accolades
39 Prevaricator's penchant
40 Bancroft or Brontë
41 Serpentine squeezer
42 Weeper of myth
43 Kermit colleague
44 *The Feminine Mystique* author
47 Borscht veggie
48 Loosens one's laces
52 Getz of jazz
54 Church structures
58 Actor Gulager
59 Ripken et al.
60 *Andy Griffith Show* character
62 Wheel support
63 Plunders
64 "Put __ on it!"
65 Fail to attend
66 Rob of *Melrose Place*
67 English river

DOWN
1 Tips one's topper
2 Wading bird
3 Less restricted
4 Knight or Nugent
5 Ignorant of right and wrong
6 Heroic tale
7 Stadium level
8 Poet Pound
9 Fixed a tennis racket
10 Pageboy or pompadour
11 Letting out more line
12 Highly prized objects
13 Smack a skeeter
18 Mathematical proportion
24 Inspires reverence
26 Keats creation
28 City leader
29 Defendant's excuse
30 Blakley of *Nashville*
31 First video game
32 One of Donald's nephews
33 Baseball's "Georgia Peach"
34 Skin-soothing stuff
35 Pasta topping of a sort
39 Not too heavy to hoist
40 "__ Misbehavin' "
42 "Science Guy" Bill
43 Mammy Yokum's first name
45 Grammarian's concerns
46 Coercion
49 With aloofness
50 Like Ernie Keebler
51 Napped leather
52 Sting
53 Urban vehicle
55 Cambodia neighbor
56 Moderate gait
57 Poker-pot part
61 Budgetary excess

748 EVERYBODY LOVES RAIMENT by Richard Silvestri

ACROSS
1 Current unit
7 Devil-may-care
11 Bummed out
14 Springlike
15 First name in scat
16 Dog-days drink
17 Valley duds?
19 Pocket-watch adjunct
20 Driving need
21 Like the Mojave
22 Gambling game
23 Memorable shell seller
25 Gardener, in fall
27 Sultry singer
28 Long time
30 Walk-up getup?
32 Opulent
33 Passed the puck to
34 Gained a lap?
35 Jam spot, in L.A.
37 Wither
41 Luau souvenir
42 Pi follower
43 Campbell of *Scream*
44 The Lone Ranger's outfit?
48 Summer pest
49 Fishing spot
50 Balance-sheet entry
52 Demolition compound
53 Fire fodder
54 Like crazy
55 Prefix for puncture
57 *Bambi* aunt
58 Outer garments?
62 Like Gen. Schwarzkopf
63 Support in the stadium
64 Midnight rider
65 Flap
66 "Brillig" preceder
67 Black Sea port

DOWN
1 Pt. of GPA
2 *Lethal Weapon* name
3 False show
4 -trix kin
5 Indy entrant
6 Wright angle?
7 Certain tire
8 "Java" player
9 Football blockers' practice device
10 Isn't out of
11 Veldt jaunt
12 Religious devotee
13 Fillet
18 Memorable Merman role
22 Suitable
23 Personal identity
24 1 to 2, e.g.
26 Catered event
27 Top banana
29 Library locales
31 Where to spend liberty
36 Pay period, often
37 California peak
38 Speculative moves
39 Bayh of Indiana
40 Riga resident
42 Vacation places
44 Eye covering
45 Was pressing
46 Smooth, to Chopin
47 Solidarity name
51 Not live
54 Profess
56 Surrender, in a way
58 Make a decision
59 Backing
60 Sounds of hesitation
61 Grazing ground

749 THEATER BOXES by Julian Ochrymowych

ACROSS
1 Stars, to Seneca
6 Solemn promise
9 Rodeo rope
14 British poet Tate
15 One of Perón's wives
16 Spends time in leisure
17 Start of a quote from a 1946 play review
20 Hand-lotion additive
21 United Federation of Planets member
22 Sharp-tasting
23 Olive __ (army uniforms)
25 Soft as __ cheek
27 California raisin center
29 Copier-cartridge contents
31 Aurora's counterpart
32 Bridal-gown part
34 Dona __ pacem
38 Middle of quote
41 Did in
42 "Eye of newt and __ frog"
43 Chess pieces
44 Ascended
46 Like corduroy
48 Unscrupulous sort
51 Copycat's comment
52 Caesarean phrase
53 Ta-ta, in Tours
56 It may be open
59 End of quote
62 Buenos __
63 __ Hear a Waltz?
64 Tooth type
65 Bel __ (semisoft cheese)
66 "__ Clear Day . . ."
67 Words before "the face" or "the sky"

DOWN
1 Theater org.
2 Humorist Mort
3 Forsyth's __ File
4 Heads of state
5 Camarade
6 Actress Miles et al.
7 Walkie-talkie word
8 Steam-engine developer
9 City "by the sea, oh"
10 Annual Alaskan sled-dog race
11 Preakness winner in '42
12 Lachrymose
13 Aides: Abbr.
18 "A time to __, a time . . ."
19 Compared to
24 Willa Cather heroine
26 Fund-raiser
27 Government agents
28 Muddy up
29 Attach, in a way
30 In the past
33 Pre-deal ritual
35 Hoodwink
36 Conversation filler
37 Glass ingredient
39 Barnum and Bailey's business
40 Destroyed, perhaps
45 Cabbage dish
47 Russian wolfhound
48 Newscast segment
49 Skylit courts
50 Accumulate
51 TV, radio, magazines, etc.
54 Bygone bird
55 Smooth out
57 Jai __
58 Laura of Jurassic Park
60 Wind dir.
61 Strike caller

750 CYCLICAL by Lee Weaver

ACROSS
1 Desert plants
6 Land unit
10 Thailand, once
14 Oak nut
15 Affirmative votes
16 Get rid of a knot
17 On the up-and-up, briefly
18 Born Free lioness
19 TV interference
20 Midcalf-length slacks
23 Fish-eating hawk
25 Ireland
26 Illegal correspondence
30 Suburbanite's concern
31 __ and hearty
32 Shriver of tennis
35 Portland's st.
36 Closes tightly
38 Folk singer Guthrie
39 Wander idly
40 Molecule part
41 Asks for alms
42 Advantageous situation
46 Window frame
49 Quietly composed
50 Press secretary, e.g.
54 Not polluted
55 Queen of Olympus
56 Turn the __ cheek
60 Poker opener
61 Capri or Wight
62 Source of annoyance
63 Three-handed card game
64 Yule song
65 Glacial pinnacle

DOWN
1 Nickname for Coolidge
2 Top blackjack card
3 Gear tooth
4 Losing one's footing
5 Young doctor
6 Reply to the captain
7 Monk's quarters
8 Wood file
9 Jacob's twin
10 Raw-fish dish
11 City or circle preceder
12 Cherish
13 Does a yard chore
21 Costa __ Sol
22 Dried out
23 Pal Joey writer
24 Cut, as wood
26 Drain problem
27 Hitchhiker's digit
28 Make lace
29 Overhead trains
32 Fuss at the mirror
33 Pond organisms
34 Majority
36 RR stop
37 Very popular
38 No-show
40 Feel sore
43 Jerusalem's country
44 Scale notes
45 Loses vitality
46 Grit
47 Main artery
48 Clay-target shooting
50 Baden-Baden and Bath
51 Ankle-knee connector
52 Mexican money
53 Author Gardner
57 That schooner
58 Zsa Zsa's sister
59 VCR button

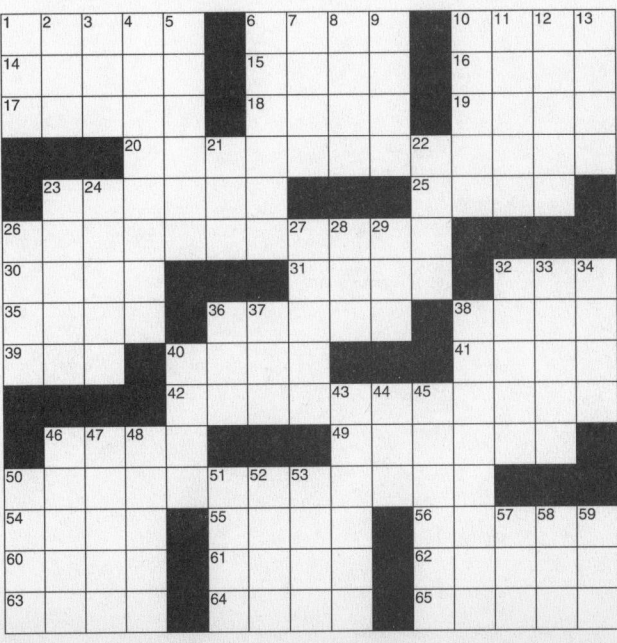

ANSWERS

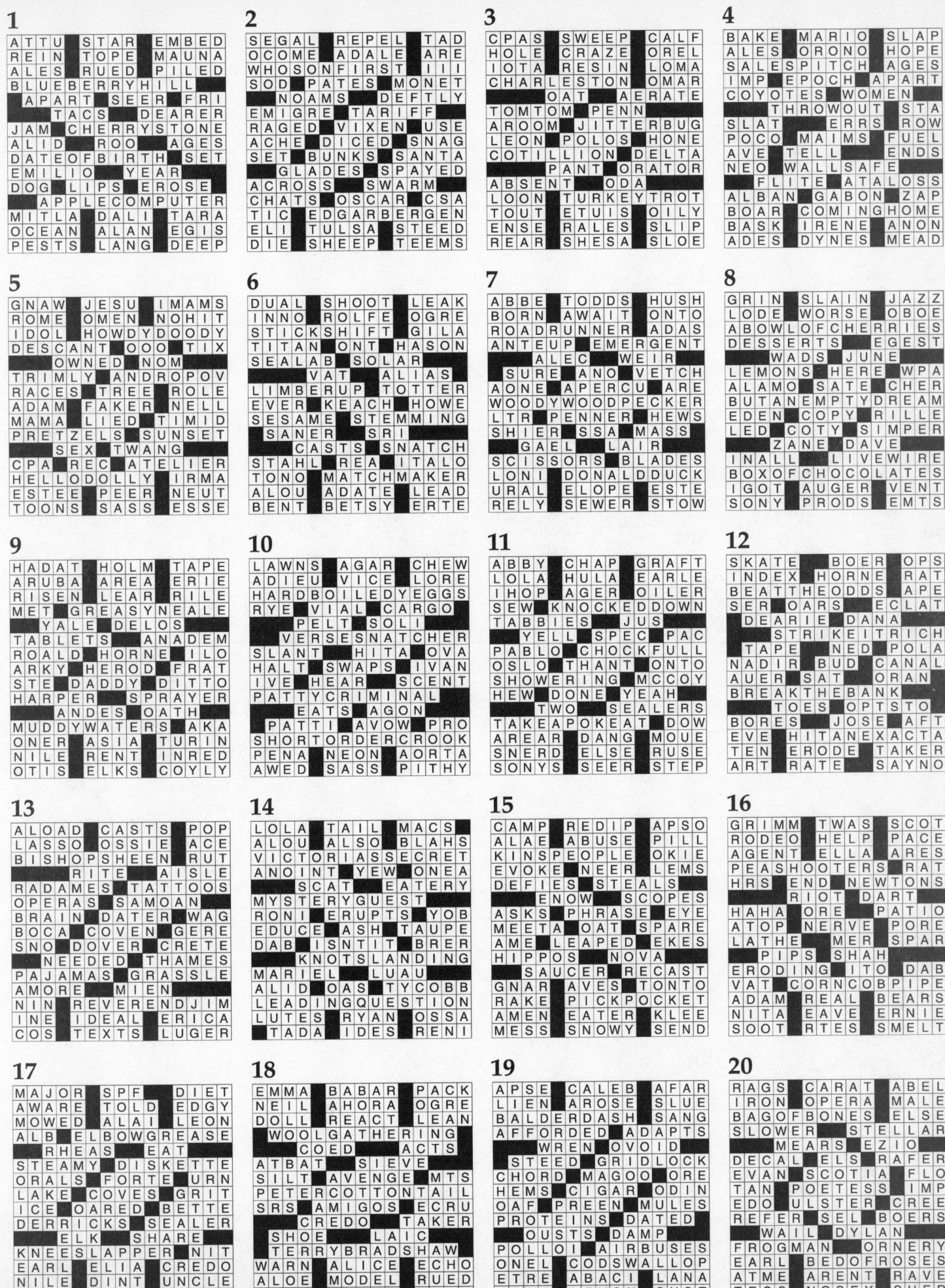

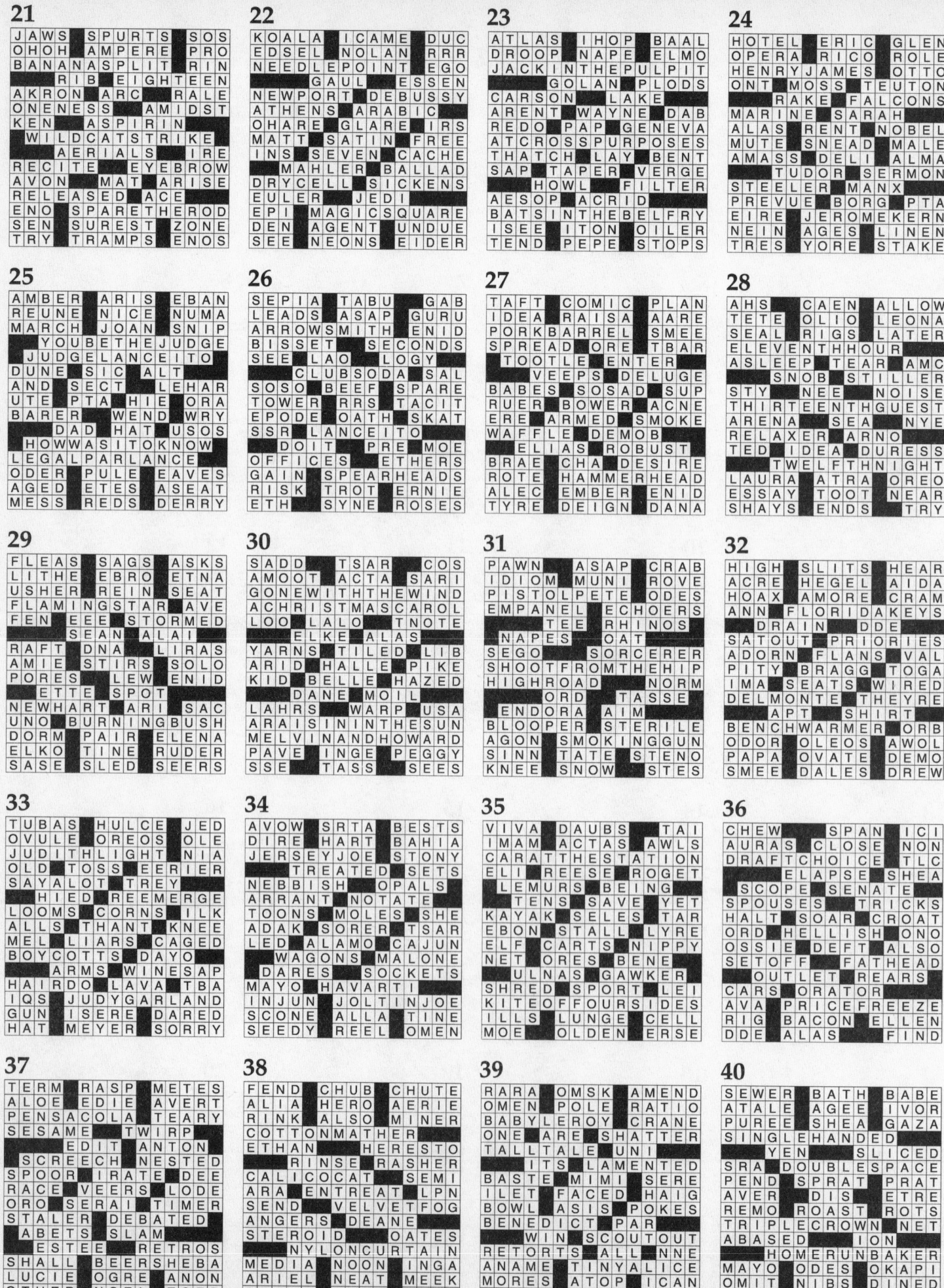

41

```
CAVED COUP JOCK
AWIDE ELSA UGLI
LOVERSLEAP MEAT
FLANNELS AMPERE
ITO ITSAS
BASHES APISH
ALLOR BRASSERIE
LOOP BEDIM GAGE
DEEPWATER FUTON
EATEN CANARY
READD SIS
ELATES MANTRAPS
NERO POUNCEUPON
AMOI AUNT SLADE
LINT TRIO TERSE
```

42

```
SWEAT MAE NOBLE
ERATO ELF ARIES
TOTEM REF SILOS
ATEAM ETHEL
TERRYCLOTH NYSE
GOATEE TCHR
OCT UNIT ALIA
GLENN TOW BLURS
LIDO MAKO BEE
ENDS SCARAB
SKYE DONNYBROOK
BEAST YOUVE
LIEUT TAJ POSEN
ICAME ODE INTRO
TERSE NOT NESTS
```

43

```
LAOS SHEP CABLE
ALDA TORE RILEY
POOP EYRE AMUSE
PURPLELILAC ESS
HALES SKID
COYOTE SULTANA
LIE ERASE ETHAN
ALLA SLEET OLIN
SELLS ANDES ILE
PROTEIN MORASS
WEAL ASPIE
WAR BLACKORCHID
ERODE GUAR IAGO
ELSIE ETTA PIER
POETS REEL ERTE
```

44

```
OLDE GALAS ORBS
WORM APACE RALE
LOEB PINON AJAX
STARR AARE TIME
MOURNINGDOVES
SLIDE AER
WAILINGWALL MAO
INKS AWN TERN
GEE CRYINGSHAME
SHE EARNS
WEEPINGWILLOW
AXLE ARAB TAHOE
RILE MANSE TILE
PLED ENDED ELAN
SENS STAND DEFY
```

45

```
RACIAL MEGA BAL
ATONCE AVIS ANI
STREEP RIOT TTS
PUERTOPLATA OIL
TORRENT ONCE
TICS ION OVER
ORA INNES INOUE
FISHNET IMPOUND
USAIR OLDAS GTE
BRIG ALG AEON
PILE REVERED
ANA COTEDIVOIRE
PUN BOHR TENNIS
ARC EVAN TRINES
LEA SYNE ESSENE
```

46

```
RASP PARR PAUL
ARTE ALLIE ILSA
CREAMPUFFS EVES
EAR ARM TEACART
DYNAMO SAGE
SANTA ROONEY
BATES ERIC FORE
AGHA FAITH COLA
RUES ALEC SANER
BANYAN SHANK
ARFS BEETLE
MESSIAH AYE HAM
ASAP ROLLSROYCE
RANI ERIES AMEN
CUKE SEES REDD
```

47

```
MCDI RARA ELFIN
TERN AMEN TERRE
SLUSHFUND SHEER
POTSDAM MEND
SARALEE AMAZE
ERODED FAMINE
ROBES ROMAN FLO
USES SORES FROM
MER STATS BLASE
TITANS SEAMEN
AFTER SPITERS
AGRA ELEMENT
VIOLS ORANGEICE
ELSIE BIRD STOW
SETAE SETS TONE
```

48

```
PAM DATA LAMAS
ALAR ONUS AROSE
TIGERLILY PINTA
HAIFA TIED SKIT
UNCAP OUTERS
RUSSIA GRAY
ERNE TOTOWN PST
BIAS TURBO ROAR
ASK CARUSO EDGE
ETUI DRESSY
APPALL BASIL
BULL SEED GENIE
ORALS CRABGRASS
RENEE REMO SILT
TETRA UTES LEE
```

49

```
SEW GAFFES TKOS
ALI ARROYO HILO
MAN SNORED ONYX
PINGPONG DOUG
ANON DOZEN KLM
NEWAGE NONE OOO
WETTER TANGO
CADENCE BRIDGES
ABIDE TRAUMA
PEN MERE NEPHEW
ALG ALAIN TORA
DUPE SINGSONG
AWOL CASSIA VIG
CONN TRUANT EEL
TOGA SEENAS SSE
```

50

```
CHET ICAME YAPS
RARA DAMON ETAT
AHAS TBONE ROSA
FASTTALKERS MAT
THEEDGE YOU IDE
YARDS COS MAZEL
RAH GALENA
QUICKDRAWMCGRAW
URSULA RES
OBOTE SAL JEEPS
VAT EST LAUNDRY
ANO SPEEDYTRIAL
DEPP ARMOR ATIP
ILEA HEINE POSH
SYST NOTES TRES
```

51

```
OMAHA REFS SAM
LOLAS FEELA PLO
DEEDS ANNUL AIR
JERSEYBOUNCE
ASP SOTS DONKEY
CLASSA FUND
COTTONCLUB RANI
TOTER HON HELEN
SPIN HITTHESILK
CROP ONSALE
ARTIER WRAP SYR
WOOLGATHERED
ADO ATRIP CRUST
KIT RIOTS KATIE
ENS DOTE STERN
```

52

```
BLOB CHEFS BRAT
IAGO ROSIE LIVE
OSLO AMANA AMEN
SHEM BOUNCEBACK
EMB SOL
SMARTED AMBIT
LAMAS RATS UPON
AMIN LICIT NAME
WING OPEN AGNES
EOSIN ABREAST
TEL RTE
FIRSTSERVE CHIC
ABIE TAHOE OATH
LEST AVOID RHEA
AXES RESTS DAMP
```

53

```
BORON SLATS XED
ALAMO ROLEO RAE
GENERATIONX ARK
SOIL RASTA BYTE
EVE BRAVOS
PASTINA ELENI
OBI MADAMEX SAW
POG MRI ICE
SON XFACTOR ORE
ALIEN SPURNED
OUTDID TEA
ANTS EMILE MOLL
SCH XRATEDMOVIE
ILE YAXIS INERT
SEX SLICE DANES
```

54

```
CALI BALSAM JPS
OMAR ONIONS ORE
DICKFRANCIS HIP
SLIDES UNDO
REJOICE BARLEY
ALAME MARLINE
RECESS LAID CPR
ACK PRISM ARE
ETH DAUB PATRON
INERTIA LURED
ARGYLE REDEEMS
RAGE WEAVES
UPI JOHNGARDNER
BIN ONETON ABLE
ADS BATONS YAMS
```

55

```
STET BLOC PLATH
HANS RIMA RUPEE
RICE IFITWERENT
ILO FEE NAMER
FORCAFFEINE TEA
TREAT UMP DRUBS
SALLUST ERAT
IWOULD HAVENO
PABA LETMEBE
SILLS ADO EAVED
ELI PERSONALITY
GIANT NOM GUN
WHATSOEVER SODA
TOTEM SAYS IDES
SEEMS TREE PAST
```

56

```
STAT BOMB PICKS
POLA ORAL OWLET
IRONHORSE WEENY
NOUGAT CAMERA
RIA TALENTS
SEDATELY CLASSA
INUSE LACES WES
TASK LOWES GETS
AMT SEWED REESE
REJECT DECAMPED
SLALOMS SUN
CAREER REATAS
ARKIN WHITEWASH
SCENE EELS ERIE
SATED RELY DANS
```

57

```
MACH RUCKS ZAG
ECHO OZZIE METO
TRAM DIANA ILED
SERENE REMEDIAL
OBOL ANGRY
GRANADA ACTI
LEST RUMBA GREW
OATH IDIOT HOLE
BRIE VELDT TOLL
RUED ELECTED
DECAF SERO
ECONOMIC CAWING
SLAG OMAHA BRIO
KATE BANAL OATS
STS SMELL YEAH
```

58

```
AREST USO PTERO
COMIN MOP RAGED
QUINTUPLE OXIDE
DELE TEAR VISOR
QUADRATIC
AMBUSH OSAKAN
RERAN TRILOBITE
ARA LADLE NOV
BICAMERAL ALENE
STEREO FAIRER
UNITARIAN
MARGO ASON EDIE
AFAUN COUNTDOWN
TRILL INN HUMID
TODAY TED OPENS
```

59

```
SAFE HASH MOLES
HERO AREA ALIVE
ARES PIER TEPEE
RIN SPANISHFORK
DECREES III
HORN STRANGER
BELLE TIRES EDO
AMIE SALES TRIO
BIC KUDOS COMET
ARKANSAS WASA
PEA PARSNIP
INDIANWELLS TOE
CARED ORAL GOWN
APACE ONCE SWAN
NAMED DEER ANNA
```

60

```
SARGE ABATE HIT
CREAK TALES ACE
RAWRECRUITS REC
ABAB RAMBO MASH
PIROGI INFANT
SAD AMES ARGOT
MELT INSURE
HALFBAKEDSCHEME
OBERON NEHI
TRAIL SAME MIR
ODESSA ADMIRE
AGTS CLARE AMOS
LAI JOBWELLDONE
ATM AREEL ARSON
NEE REEDY MEANT
```

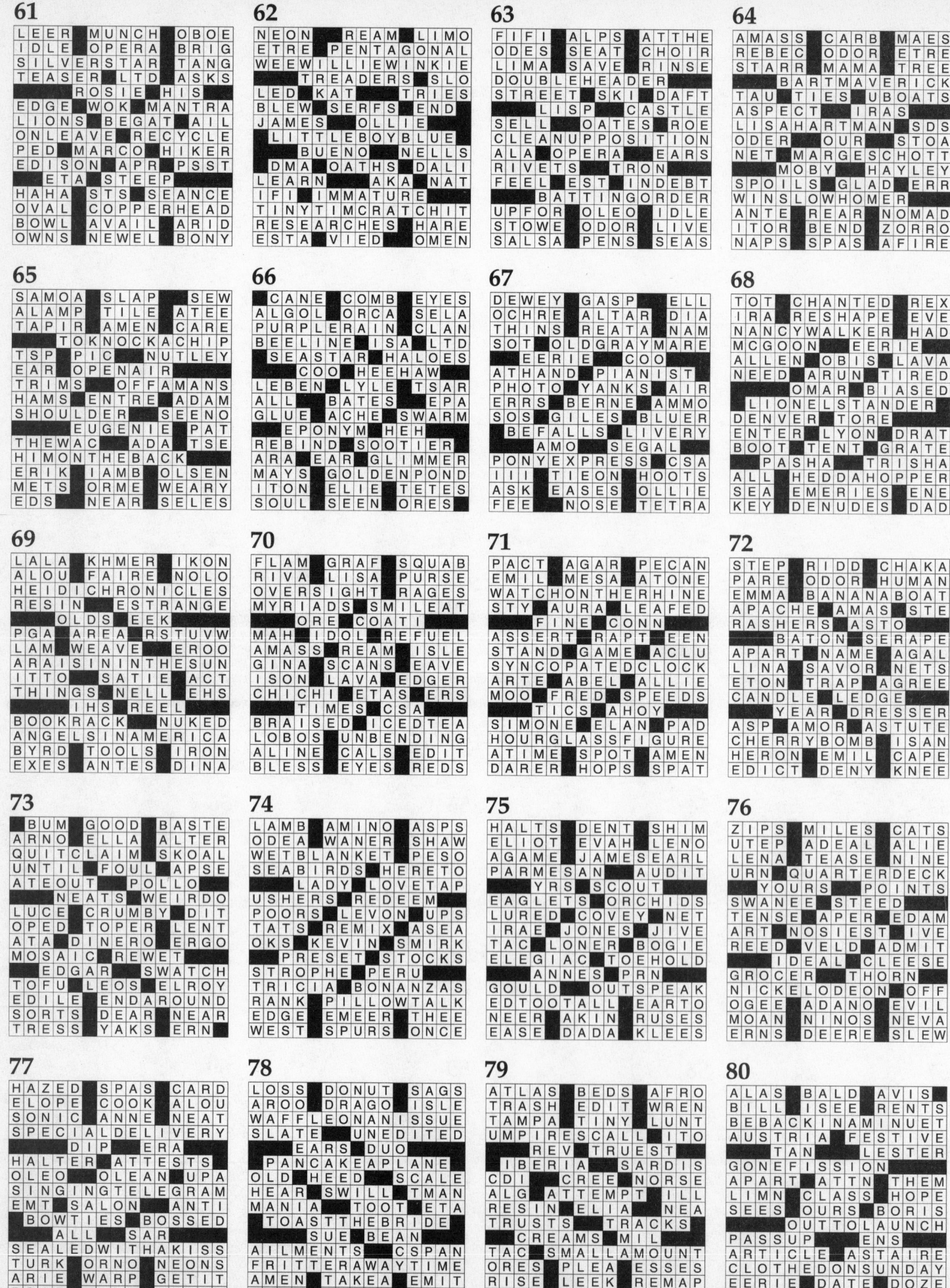

61

```
LEER  MUNCH  OBOE
IDLE  OPERA  BRIG
SILVERSTAR  TANG
TEASER  LTD  ASKS
    ROSIE  HIS
EDGE  WOK  MANTRA
LIONS  BEGAT  AIL
ONLEAVE  RECYCLE
PED  MARCO  HIKER
EDISON  APR  PSST
    ETA  STEEP
HAHA  STS  SEANCE
OVAL  COPPERHEAD
BOWL  AVAIL  ARID
OWNS  NEWEL  BONY
```

62

```
NEON  REAM  LIMO
ETRE  PENTAGONAL
WEEWILLIEWINKIE
TREADERS  SLO
LED  KAT  TRIES
BLEW  SERFS  END
JAMES  OLLIE
LITTLEBOYBLUE
BUENO  NELLS
DMA  OATHS  DALI
LEARN  AKA  NAT
IFI  IMMATURE
TINYTIMCRATCHIT
RESEARCHES  HARE
ESTA  VIED  OMEN
```

63

```
FIFI  ALPS  ATTHE
ODES  SEAT  CHOIR
LIMA  SAVE  RINSE
DOUBLEHEADER
STREET  SKI  DAFT
LISP  CASTLE
SELL  OATES  ROE
CLEANUPPOSITION
ALA  OPERA  EARS
RIVETS  TRON
FEEL  EST  INDEBT
BATTINGORDER
UPFOR  OLEO  IDLE
STOWE  ODOR  LIVE
SALSA  PENS  SEAS
```

64

```
AMASS  CARB  MAES
REBEC  ODOR  ETRE
STARR  MAMA  TREE
BARTMAVERICK
TAU  TIES  UBOATS
ASPECT  IRAS
LISAHARTMAN  SDS
ODER  OUR  STOA
NET  MARGESCHOTT
MOBY  HAYLEY
SPOILS  GLAD  ERR
WINSLOWHOMER
ANTE  REAR  NOMAD
ITOR  BEND  ZORRO
NAPS  SPAS  AFIRE
```

65

```
SAMOA  SLAP  SEW
ALAMP  TILE  ATEE
TAPIR  AMEN  CARE
TOKNOCKACHIP
TSP  PIC  NUTLEY
EAR  OPENAIR
TRIMS  OFFAMANS
HAMS  ENTRE  ADAM
SHOULDER  SEENO
EUGENIE  PAT
THEWAC  ADA  TSE
HIMONTHEBACK
ERIK  IAMB  OLSEN
METS  ORME  WEARY
EDS  NEAR  SELES
```

66

```
CANE  COMB  EYES
ALGOL  ORCA  SELA
PURPLERAIN  CLAN
BEELINE  ISA  LTD
SEASTAR  HALOES
COO  HEEHAW
LEBEN  LYLE  TSAR
ALL  BATES  EPA
GLUE  ACHE  SWARM
EPONYM  HEH
REBIND  SOOTIER
ARA  EAR  GLIMMER
MAYS  GOLDENPOND
ITON  ELIE  TETES
SOUL  SEEN  ORES
```

67

```
DEWEY  GASP  ELL
OCHRE  ALTAR  DIA
THINS  REATA  NAM
SOT  OLDGRAYMARE
EERIE  COO
ATHAND  PIANIST
PHOTO  YANKS  AIR
ERRS  BERNE  AMMO
SOS  GILES  BLUER
BEFALLS  LIVERY
AMO  SEGAL
PONYEXPRESS  CSA
III  TIEON  HOOTS
ASK  EASES  OLLIE
FEE  NOSE  TETRA
```

68

```
TOT  CHANTED  REX
IRA  RESHAPE  EVE
NANCYWALKER  HAD
MCGOON  EERIE
ALLEN  OBIS  LAVA
NEED  ARUN  TIRED
OMAR  BIASED
LIONELSTANDER
DENVER  TORE
ENTER  LYON  DRAT
BOOT  TENT  GRATE
PASHA  TRISHA
ALL  HEDDAHOPPER
SEA  EMERIES  ENE
KEY  DENUDES  DAD
```

69

```
LALA  KHMER  IKON
ALOU  FAIRE  NOLO
HEIDICHRONICLES
RESIN  ESTRANGE
OLDS  EEK
PGA  AREA  RSTUVW
LAM  WEAVE  EROO
ARAISININTHESUN
ITTO  SATIE  ACT
THINGS  NELL  EHS
IHS  REEL
BOOKRACK  NUKED
ANGELSINAMERICA
BYRD  TOOLS  IRON
EXES  ANTES  DINA
```

70

```
FLAM  GRAF  SQUAB
RIVA  LISA  PURSE
OVERSIGHT  RAGES
MYRIADS  SMILEAT
ORE  COATI
MAH  IDOL  REFUEL
AMASS  REAM  ISLE
GINA  SCANS  EAVE
ISON  LAVA  EDGER
CHICHI  ETAS  ERS
TIMES  CSA
BRAISED  ICEDTEA
LOBOS  UNBENDING
ALINE  CALS  EDIT
BLESS  EYES  REDS
```

71

```
PACT  AGAR  PECAN
EMIL  MESA  ATONE
WATCHONTHERHINE
STY  AURA  LEAFED
FINE  CONN
ASSERT  RAPT  EEN
STAND  GAME  ACLU
SYNCOPATEDCLOCK
ARTE  ABEL  ALLIE
MOO  FRED  SPEEDS
TICS  AHOY
SIMONE  ELAN  PAD
HOURGLASSFIGURE
ATIME  SPOT  AMEN
DARER  HOPS  SPAT
```

72

```
STEP  RIDD  CHAKA
PARE  ODOR  HUMAN
EMMA  BANANABOAT
APACHE  AMAS  STE
RASHERS  ASTO
BATON  SERAPE
APART  NAME  AGAL
LINA  SAVOR  NETS
ETON  TRAP  AGREE
CANDLE  LEDGE
YEAR  DRESSER
ASP  AMOR  ASTUTE
CHERRYBOMB  ISAN
HERON  EMIL  CAPE
EDICT  DENY  KNEE
```

73

```
BUM  GOOD  BASTE
ARNO  ELLA  ALTER
QUITCLAIM  SKOAL
UNTIL  FOUL  APSE
ATEOUT  POLLO
NEATS  WEIRDO
LUCE  CRUMBY  DIT
OPED  TOPER  LENT
ATA  DINERO  ERGO
MOSAIC  REWET
EDGAR  SWATCH
TOFU  LEOS  ELROY
EDILE  ENDAROUND
SORTS  DEAR  NEAR
TRESS  YAKS  ERN
```

74

```
LAMB  AMINO  ASPS
ODEA  WANER  SHAW
WETBLANKET  PESO
SEABIRDS  HERETO
LADY  LOVETAP
USHERS  REDEEM
POORS  LEVON  UPS
TATS  REMIX  ASEA
OKS  KEVIN  SMIRK
PRESET  STOCKS
STROPHE  PERU
TRICIA  BONANZAS
RANK  PILLOWTALK
EDGE  EMEER  THEE
WEST  SPURS  ONCE
```

75

```
HALTS  DENT  SHIM
ELIOT  EVAH  LENO
AGAME  JAMESEARL
PARMESAN  AUDIT
YRS  SCOUT
EAGLETS  ORCHIDS
LURED  COVEY  NET
IRAE  JONES  JIVE
TAC  LONER  BOGIE
ELEGIAC  TOEHOLD
ANNES  PRN
GOULD  OUTSPEAK
EDTOOTALL  EARTO
NEER  AKIN  RUSES
EASE  DADA  KLEES
```

76

```
ZIPS  MILES  CATS
UTEP  ADEAL  ALIE
LENA  TEASE  NINE
URN  QUARTERDECK
YOURS  POINTS
SWANEE  STEED
TENSE  APER  EDAM
ART  NOSIEST  IVE
REED  VELD  ADMIT
IDEAL  CLEESE
GROCER  THORN
NICKELODEON  OFF
OGEE  ADANO  EVIL
MOAN  NINOS  NEVA
ERNS  DEERE  SLEW
```

77

```
HAZED  SPAS  CARD
ELOPE  COOK  ALOU
SONIC  ANNE  NEAT
SPECIALDELIVERY
DIP  ERA
HALTER  ATTESTS
OLEO  OLEAN  UPA
SINGINGTELEGRAM
EMT  SALON  ANTI
BOWTIES  BOSSED
ALL  SAR
SEALEDWITHAKISS
TURK  ORNO  NEONS
ARIE  WARP  GETIT
BOAR  NYES  SPATS
```

78

```
LOSS  DONUT  SAGS
AROO  DRAGO  ISLE
WAFFLEONANISSUE
SLATE  UNEDITED
EARS  DUO
PANCAKEAPLANE
OLD  HEED  SCALE
HEAR  SWILL  TMAN
MANIA  TOOT  ETA
TOASTTHEBRIDE
SUE  BEAN
AILMENTS  CSPAN
FRITTERAWAYTIME
AMEN  TAKEA  EMIT
RADS  OSIER  PANS
```

79

```
ATLAS  BEDS  AFRO
TRASH  EDIT  WREN
TAMPA  TINY  LUNT
UMPIRESCALL  ITO
REV  TRUEST
IBERIA  SARDIS
CDI  CREE  NORSE
ALG  ATTEMPT  ILL
RESIN  ELIA  NEA
TRUSTS  TRACKS
CREAMS  MIL
TAC  SMALLAMOUNT
ORES  PLEA  ESSES
RISE  LEEK  REMAP
NASA  ESTE  STATS
```

80

```
ALAS  BALD  AVIS
BILL  ISEE  RENTS
BEBACKINAMINUET
AUSTRIA  FESTIVE
TAN  LESTER
GONEFISSION
APART  ATTN  THEM
LIMN  CLASS  HOPE
SEES  OURS  BORIS
OUTTOLAUNCH
PASSUP  ENS
ARTICLE  ASTAIRE
CLOTHEDONSUNDAY
EERIE  DATE  DOZE
SYNS  AKIN  SLED
```

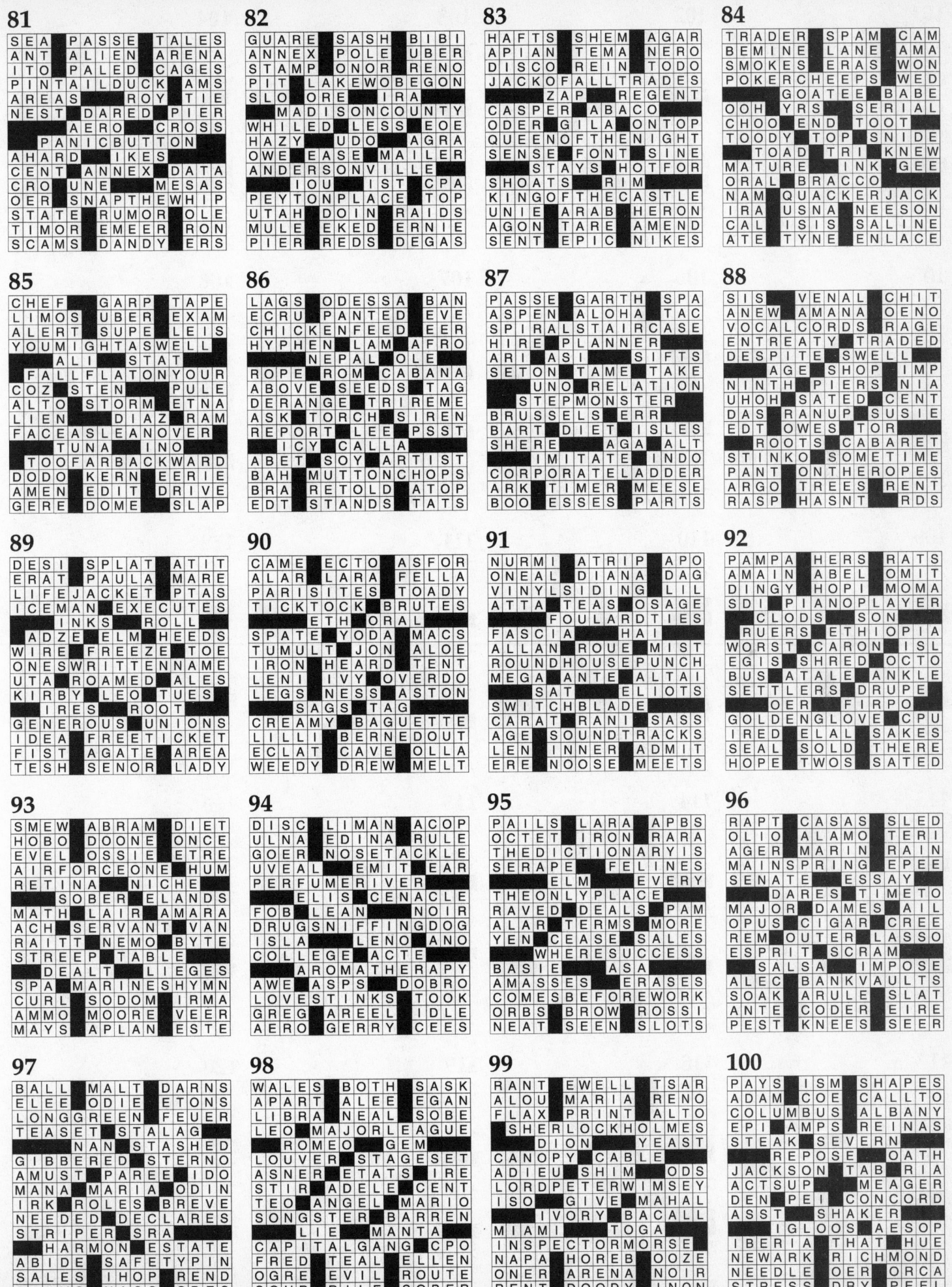

101
GIMME ATTS CAR
ASIAN GRAPH REO
SMARTCOOKIE ARA
TIL TERR CID
AFRICAN REMAKES
BIO ERAS SIDE
ALLS EDEN TERRA
BELL TIMED AJAR
ATTIC RIGA LAND
OMAN SERF CEO
TAPERED BRINKER
ADD OARS ONA
MAE BREADWINNER
ENS STAVE ACORN
ROK OMEN LYRES

102
ALEC PAGE RECAP
NOVA ALES OPERA
EMIT SINS SADAT
WALNUTGROVE ABE
ATONE ITOR
PAMPER HITACHI
ADA SABLE ASHEN
PUPS LEARS TENT
ALLES ADDER SIE
STEELER RITTER
SPAS MAGNA
ELY SPRUCEGOOSE
SARAH ALMA IBID
AMUSE TEEN SOME
UPPER ASST MEIN

103
LIMB IMETA BOSH
ONEA DRAWL ALTO
TURKEYTROT LEAN
URIEL SWANSONG
SETSOFF ARIA
RORY AMISH
ESS BOLO ICICLE
THEFUNKYCHICKEN
TOLAST ALAN YDS
ADLIB SLAV
ROOT MEETSUP
BUNNYHOP MAINE
ERIE GOOSESTEPS
TANS OGLER UNIT
ALES DELTA MANO

104
FUME KARMA ABUT
ETON USUAL KANE
WALT ROSSI ILIE
HERMANSHERMITS
AIL NUB
IWANTTOBEALONE
FORCE CATTY EXT
FOIE MOSHE MACE
YES CUMIN OATEN
REMOTECONTROLS
ADA OHM
ISOLATIONBOOTH
NOVA INDIE SHAQ
CHAD OFALL EAVE
HOLY NOYES TIED

105
ANNE BEEF WEBER
COAL LACE ETUDE
HERODOTUS LURID
ESCHEWS SPLINTS
ICH AURA
STEM ALLPOWERIS
TUN IRES ARENT
ADDENDA TURNSTO
MOUTH DANE ERR
PRECARIOUS ATOM
ROTC ASP
TITANIC ALLEGRO
HOUSE HISTORIES
RUNES ELIE CRIS
USEAS DEAD ULNA

106
DOSE GARP SIPES
IDOL AREA TRADE
NORA DONT ASPIN
GRAYPANTHER END
NAB SAMPRAS
LONESOME PART
APE SUEDE NOISE
SIMI TOWER AGES
HEELS WIRES EAT
ALTO NOCTURNE
TENSION EIN
ELL CHESHIRECAT
SLINK ELEV ALVA
LEONE DORE SEEN
ASNER YEAR YORK

107
SPED SHAH ALTO
CAPES TOGA BIAS
ATOLL REAR EZRA
DIXIECARTER TOG
SOY ELI EMIRATE
PINS STAY
GOBI FEN ZILCH
ADEN FRISK SOAR
REACT FAR ERRS
AURA FROM
BARRELS ANA ADO
LIT KATEJACKSON
ASHY SAVE HEIRS
SLUE KIEV OLDIE
TERN ANNO PEST

108
DINES ATTA SERA
ADELE LOON ENID
NEWBEDFORD ODDS
CATERER ISSUE
ETO SEEP CLAMS
DENG DATER VAT
EEL DILATORY
KENNEBUNKPORT
GALACTIC SET
ILE OSCAR SCAM
NEVER HILO ANA
ADEPT SEMINAR
ANTI HACKENSACK
LOOT ILIE INDIE
ERRS LEAD STAND

109
BASE CHET POSSE
ARID HUGO ARENA
NCAA ASAP LINUS
COMMONKNOWLEDGE
BEY HEN
CAGNEY ABETTORS
OGEES LIL POO
MATTEROFOPINION
BIT ANI DONNA
SNOWSHOE CAREER
ONA OOH
SCHOOLOFTHOUGHT
PAOLO ALTO GLEE
ISLET TEES LARA
TEENY HART IDES

110
IFELL BMI PUMA
FAROE REND EGON
SWING ARLO ALTO
NEGATIVEOPTION
ALAS AWL
ENE AFEWGOODMEN
MADEIT YUP EIRE
IVIED MME BADEN
LALO DOA HORACE
ELECTIONDAY STS
REN ITCH
MULTIPLECHOICE
STIR PERK TROVE
GALE ESME TAMIL
THIS SAY SMALL

111
PIMA MOST DEBTS
IRIS ETTA ALLIE
TACKLEBOX ILONA
TEASET AEOLIC
AMO STICKBY
HARSHENS TEEPEE
USURY SILOS AWL
BINS HEROS URAL
EDT SATES ENTRE
REHEEL DEPLOYED
TSETSES SAL
SHARIF CASHES
ISHAM KICKSTART
CRONE HAVE ARIA
HOWES STIR YANG

112
RAJAH SCRAP MAS
FLAME ALANA ELK
DARYLDRAGON RBI
PRIM CAVED
SALLIES CHARGES
TEEING BOOKER
ORANG WORSE ICH
RIFE MIXES AFRO
YEP FINED HIFIS
HOARDS NUDIST
IRONIES LAMENTS
SHEER AIDA
LON WOLFMANJACK
IDI ARSON LOTTO
PAX YOURS YEARS

113
PIAF VIDA MACAW
ACRO AGAR ABUSE
PUPPYLOVE ROBED
EIRE BLURTS
HOTELS SPRITE
INHALED RIN PTS
STETS ORING OHO
SIBS FROZE TUBE
EMU ILEDE TUTEE
DEN MUM SCENEVI
NAPKIN REGRET
ANYWAY ARUN
BEHAN KITTYHAWK
EVOKE AVEC ECHO
LAPEL TESH STOP

114
LOWS SPAN CAPED
ISEE PANE ADELE
ALEC ONTO PETAL
ROBERTDONAT ENE
DYLAN PAAR
EUGENE STILLER
RNA ESTEE NOOSE
AIRS SALEM ERTE
STYLE KARAT REV
ESCAPEE CHEESE
OPIE ASHER
ADO CLIFTONWEBB
TEPEE ROAM IDEA
OCEAN MOTA NITA
MORTE ATEN SEAL

115
PANES SURF TERI
ILONA OPIE ELEC
PAULBUNION RICO
PINION SAMSON
STOPS LIENS
PASTA REHEAT
ACT GRETEL ESTA
PHINEASTBLISTER
PERU JEERER ULM
GOATEE ODDLY
SMEAR SWINE
MANTRA SHINTO
INDO JEROMECORN
LEER AVON AERIE
EDDY RENT DRAMA

116
MAYO BRAE STOP
AREA FLOWN LADE
LOAFAROUND IRON
EMS ROTE OSCARS
SATURN SPREE
PATH ASTOUND
WISPY ACRE FRAU
IDLE BRAID LAID
GEAR ROBS GILLS
SATCHEL HALF
READS TEENSY
AMOUNT HULA ANI
NABS HEELANDTOE
TROT EVANS EARL
SEES RARA BLED

117
PARTS SPIEL RIP
OPERA CARVE ALI
TOBACCOROAD ILL
PRETEND ALIA
AYE ELI ERRANT
LARD EAST ARTIE
PLIERS CAPRI
SUNSETBOULEVARD
SNEER ARABIA
TOTED DEFY LULL
AVERSE LLB TEE
MINT NOSEEUM
ANS STREETSCENE
LEE TREAT EXTOL
ESS YELLS DIARY

118
LOFT REDD APED
OHIO EVER COLOR
TONY HAVE TWINE
THESHADOW IDONT
ABET OVETA
JOBS SEMPER
PINATA EAT KAMA
AMATEUR LIBERAL
DINO DER COGENT
NAILED ASSN
FARGO COAT
MINOR GLOSSOVER
ENSUE RUDY MAMA
SIEGE ISLE ISMY
SLED MEET TEAS

119
CAFE STRAP YORK
ALAR PRIMA ARAL
BAKE LIFER NANA
AMI BENFRANKLIN
LORELEI NEE
AYN DIOGENES
ABBR ERNIE OYE
LEONARDODAVINCI
ATL RAINY WOKS
SHOETREE ALI
ASI SPINOFF
BILLYTHEKID FOE
ELOI IONIA ETAL
IKON ELDER SEMI
TANG STORY ONYX

120
ROBB THUMB BLAB
ISLE HANOI LANE
FLATTERINGWORDS
TON OPTS HACKIT
KATIE FEDS
SOVIET HEAD CDE
THEN PEARL LUG
EARTHSHATTERING
IRS ETATS ANNE
NAE LASH SURGED
MERE ACRES
AMOUNT AGES TAP
NATTERINGNABOBS
KITE EATIT ONES
AMOS KNEES BEET

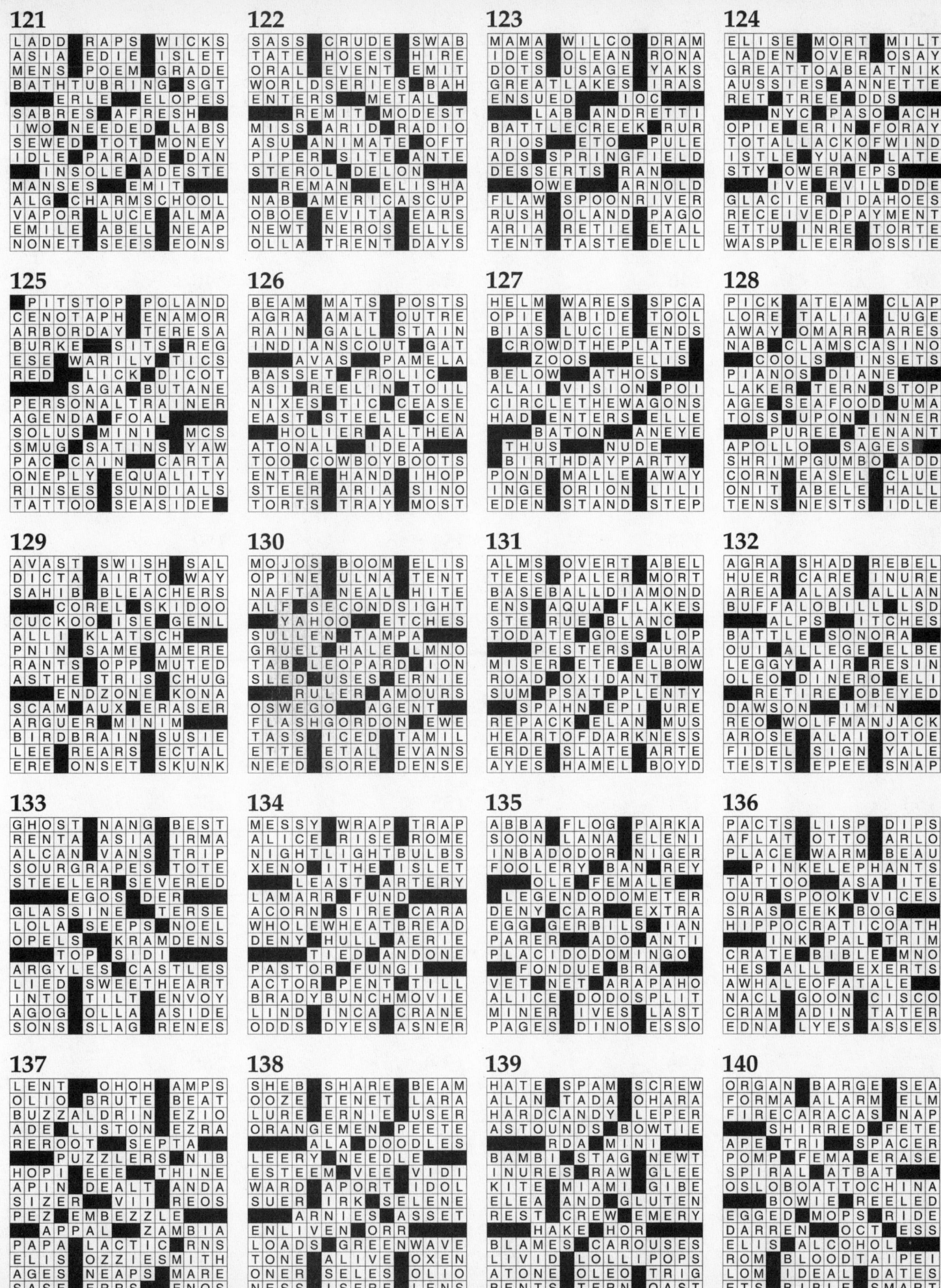

141
```
EBB..BASE.BAIL
YIELD ELAN.ONTO
EATER GIVE.OVAL
.SHOEMAKER TILL
..SANE.GOLLY..
GLOSSY..PYLE..
LAVA.OLIO.EGRET
OMEN.ADO.GAGE
PANDA.DALE.ECON
..ALLY.ARREST
.WALLA.SURE..
SHOW PUMPSIRON
TARO TRIP GURUS
ALTO OGLE NEEDS
BEAD PEER.SEE
```

142
```
CHAT MARC OPRAH
RICH ASEA CRAZE
EPEE RUNJOEYRUN
SPIRIT TULL ARS
SONAR RANDOM..
.CAMEL.STALAG
ASCETICS.RIME
JOLIET.DIADEM
AMIS.COINTOSS
REPOSE HUNCH..
.NITWIT.AORTA
AER.SCAM ANNEAL
BREATHLESS MAKO
UNITE DRIP ADEN
TONER OARS NENE
```

143
```
LEVI DADA PASTA
ATOM ALOT ROWAN
WHIPSMART ERATO
NYC ISNO BATTEN
SLEAZE THECAT
.GIL HUSH ESS
HELEN EYRE CAPO
ORANGES OTTOMAN
PAST ITIN HASTY
ISH EDEN CRT
LOVERS RUSTIC
ERASER USES AMO
RERAN SLAPHAPPY
GAUGE PALE PEEL
SPEED ARTS ORLY
```

144
```
RAG DAB.ALDA
ERA OLIVES LEON
FIELDTRIPS AMIN
SALAD DREGS ONE
.BEG GETTING
SAP REMI.UND
HAILSTONE STROP
ERTE.ZAIRE ROLE
SECTS SANDPAPER
.HIP REAL SOT
RETIREE MEA
WES NISEI ASSES
HEWN FALLSSHORT
AVON TUSSLE RIA
MEOW.ADD TEN
```

145
```
EXES CHAD STOMA
AMMO HERR CORAL
SEMBLANCE AMNIA
ENA UPC ISRAELI
CREEP EAT
SPOIL AIRBORNE
STERN MIDI EON
PEREGRINEFALCON
EGO ANTS TEAKS
CONCORDE STEPS
ORE DINAR
PREPARE ROC PAS
ROBOT CLARKKENT
IMBUE HATE ETNA
MASTS OWED GEAR
```

146
```
ROMP LAVA INTRA
EMEU IBET SEWER
AONE BART HAITI
DOUBLEFAULT NRA
LILT EASTON
RESOLE QUARTO
ELI AROUND AWED
LINES DEO CRETE
YEGG SIESTA RAN
LATEEN WRESTS
THEDAM AEON
REF KINGPENGUIN
ONICE ANAT ASTA
OILER MACE GEES
PEELS EWER ERMA
```

147
```
SLOW EMAIL CHAR
PINA MANNA LONE
ALARMCLOCK ORGS
PAEAN ENTREE
HEP PER KEYHOLE
AVAILS CAREER
DANCE HABIT SOP
EDIE ROGUE THAI
SEC REPEL MOOSE
BEAVER MEOWER
PLUNGED BID SSS
LITTER SOLID
ANTI SCARECROWS
IGOR AUGER ARIA
NONE LEADS GENT
```

148
```
LOTS NAPA ROMA
ACHE OMENS EVIL
ITOR SANKA LENT
DOUBLESTANDARD
PJS TEX
ARIOSO SEER PTA
BOLL BANNERYEAR
ALLES LEG YARNS
FLAGWAVERS LOGO
TOT ALAR HILTON
SIP TRA
PENNANTWINNERS
ALMA CURIE AXEL
COIF ALECK GINA
ETTU LEES STOW
```

149
```
LIDS SLAVE AMPS
ANDI CUMIN TALE
STABLECONDITION
SOY UNIS NEST
GLEE BESS
ATALL MARITIME
SARA CARES DOS
SHEDINHIBITIONS
EON NEONS KLEE
SEAMLESS RESTS
AIDE TEAS
PENN MAXI LEO
LODGEACOMPLAINT
OPIE SHAPE LEVI
BEER PETAL GUYS
```

150
```
CLASS VAMP MARA
PINNA OPAL ALEX
ASKEW CONE LIMO
THEYMADEANACIN
ZEAL ODETS
EMPIRE RETRY
LOIN MAXIM EDS
SHEGAVEBENADRYL
ASS BASIC ONEA
SATAN BOWERY
SORTS CAPN
THEYHADSUDAFED
EARL JEER QATAR
TRUE ARTE ULTRA
SAND XMAS ELECT
```

151
```
BOTH NIP TRADE
OREO PALO AEGIS
ECRU ISIT BEANS
RAISETHEROOF
ETTU ORR EMU
AMOCO AFATE VON
LORAN ISOTHERM
ARIL BET ANTA
REELEDIN SNEAD
INN GILDA ADDLE
COT GEL LEAH
SHUFFLEBOARD
ELATE OREL LUAU
MEDIA LENS DRIP
SWORD DES SANE
```

152
```
WASP SHAWL SEWN
ECHO KOREA EYRE
BROWBEATEN NEAT
SEE AWRY DROOPS
SLED SLURP
FALTER SCOT EVA
ALIAS SCARS NOD
COPY HOUND HELD
ENS DEALT FORGE
TEE EARL CAESAR
READS THUD
NEVADA MIEN OBI
EXIT CHINWAGGED
MACE HINGE ELSE
OMEN EDGED MESA
```

153
```
LAPS ARCS MOS
AGRAS DEAR PUNT
GOOSEBUMPS AREA
UNC NOSIR ARMOR
NIT SITTINGDUCK
AZORES AGORAE
SERA SHARI STY
HENPECKED
ARS ROARS ABBA
RETAIN FABLES
CHICKENFEED ALS
HILTS OILED CIA
ERLE COLDTURKEY
REED ISEE PEEVE
SSR TERR FRED
```

154
```
VERO DDTS ELLE
ELAN CLOUT VOID
NEST OVULE ERMA
IMPOSSIBLEDREAM
PAT LENNY
PHLOX AES ANENT
REEF AGO ISOMER
AMAT TERRE WIVE
MASHIE NOR ALEA
SNEER AOK INERT
WAIST ADD
SECONDTHEMOTION
LAIR LAITY HOME
ORAL ERNES ETNA
PLOD DEGS NAIL
```

155
```
MAGI AGREE SPAS
ALAN PROWL TILT
JOYCEOATES ONTO
STEAL HERETICAL
GPA OCHRE
WILLIAMYEATS
ONIONS OTTO WEB
OKAY SLUSH PIER
SYR MEAT OHENRY
RALPHEMERSON
STAHL XED
TIMETABLE GUSTO
ARAB GEORGESHAW
RENO EMOTE DELL
SDAK SENSE ADES
```

156
```
HALE NANCE CCL
SHALL ELIHU HOI
TABLEHOPPER ACE
EGO ORION
SCRAPES OPERAS
LEO TEST LAPP
EMU OSTEND REBA
NICER EPI LOREN
ASHY RESOLE SIT
PEAR IBET ONE
SCORNS NETTING
NOTSO GUN
IMA DESKJOCKEYS
PET ADEER EERIE
SRO LAWNS DENT
```

157
```
PSAT COMP SCHWA
APBS AVER CLAIM
DISK MALE RAISE
UFO BELLYLAUGHS
AFFAIR SAPS
SPRANG TEETER
FATED OUTER UPI
ALEX TOTER AMEN
WOE DUNST TIMED
NELSON YEARLY
INIT DUSTIN
STOMACHACHE UNO
PETIT ISLE CCLI
EMILE NEAR UKES
CASED GAME ESTE
```

158
```
IMAM LAPUP DADA
RAGA AMINO ELON
MARIAMONTESSORI
AMATI TOTE HIT
ASTA ITHACA
MARILYNMCCOO
EXO ENOCH NOBEL
TEXT ERRED DALI
ASYET AARON RAT
MICKEYMANTLE
CARPAL LEOI
AGE RIAS MCGEE
MICHAELMORIARTY
ELOI NAURU EIRE
LEND TIGER APED
```

159
```
RAPT AETNA VADE
ODER TRIES ARIL
PARISTEXAS LIAM
ELEVEN IDEALS
RESIN POISON
ATLANTICCITY
RPM OOZES INRE
ALIGNS ARAGON
MENU TESLA ETS
SANFRANCISCO
FACTOR HUMID
RAMADA RETUNE
AVOW CASABLANCA
GIVE IRANI GIAN
USED ATLAS ESNE
```

160
```
IPSO HANS LILAC
DOCK EMIT ANITA
OSHA NONE ONSET
NEWYORKJESTS
TRASHY ALES AFL
AVA WRESTLE
CESAR DIOR ASIA
OAKLANDBRAIDERS
URIS OINK NEATH
REDOUBT SUN
TDS NEIN REPOSE
STLOUISRAMPS
BAHAI NEHI SAYS
AGILE AVON THEE
DOMED LOPE YARN
```

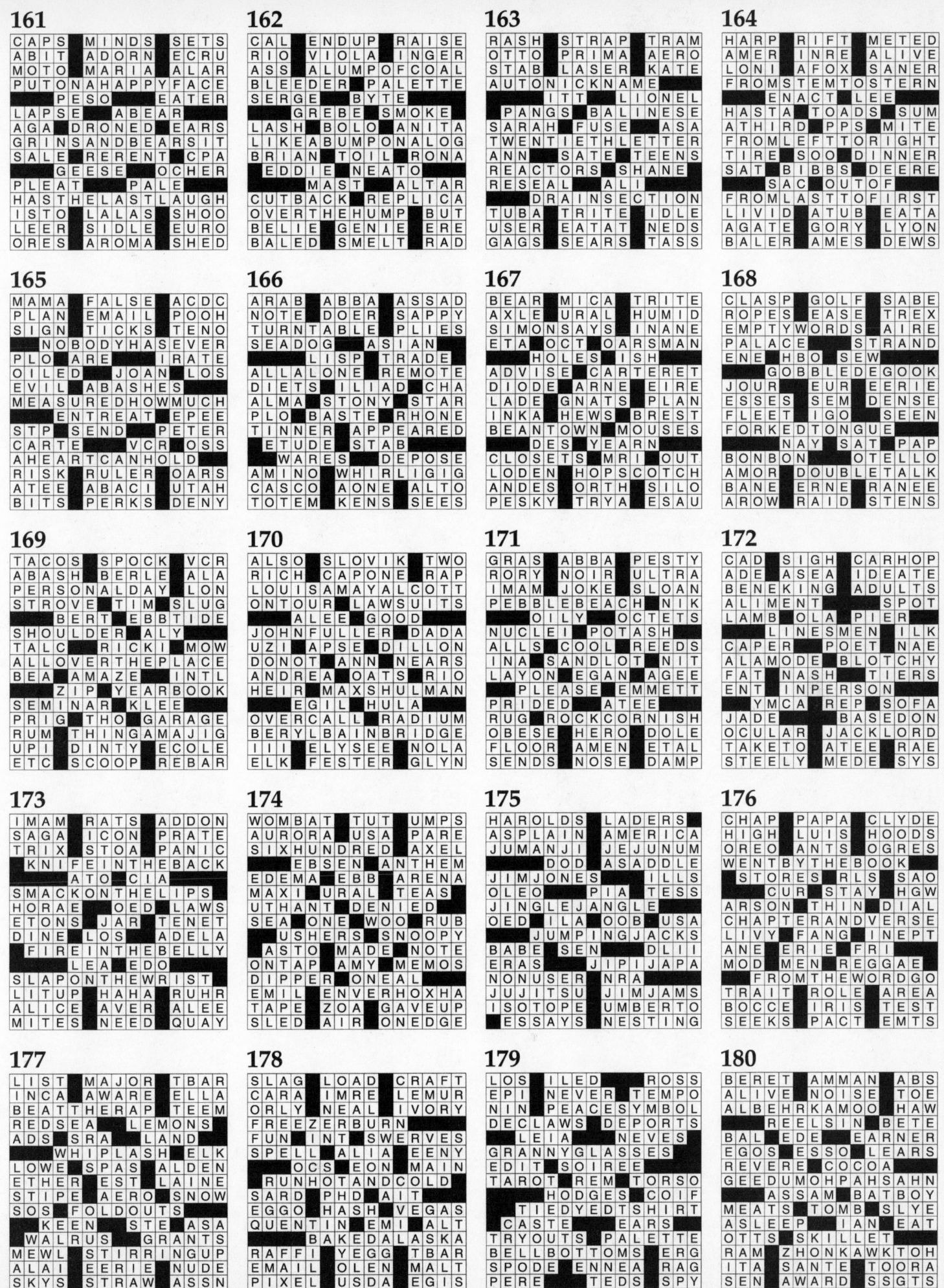

181

S	T	A	B		C	R	A	G		B	E	A	N
P	U	M	A	S		A	O	N	E		S	A	L	E
A	T	I	L	T		R	U	T	H		A	R	L	O
M	U	D	D	Y	W	A	T	E	R	S		T	E	N
			L	O	T				I	T	C	H	Y	
A	D	I	E	U		A	N	G	O	R	A			
G	L	E	N		L	A	M	E		P	E	K	O	E
E	E	L	S		D	R	E	A	D		D	I	L	L
E	X	T	O	L		U	N	T	O		I	T	E	M
			A	L	A	R	M	S		M	I	T	T	S
	O	B	E	S	E				H	E	N			
G	N	U		S	A	N	D	Y	D	U	N	C	A	N
A	I	R	S		S	E	E	M		R	O	U	S	E
W	O	K	E		O	M	E	N		E	E	R	I	E
K	N	E	E		N	O	D	S		L	E	A	D	

182

CHIC ASTA OLDEN
AERO TEAS HAILE
LEANYEARS MMDLV
FEASTED ODIE
DEBITS TODDLER
EDEN EAR TREY
LINEN MEDEA SCH
HEDDA AVA PIQUE
ISO OTHER ENURE
NAME LEA VAIL
TREVINO SPITES
RISE TRACHEA
AVERS STOOPBALL
PEASE ONER LIME
STREW NODE ERNE

183

CPA CAPS CLOSER
HAM UHOH REMIND
ARMSRACE UGANDA
SKATEBOARDING
MANE YET LIZ
WHISKER RENE
ITS OMEN PIOUS
PIKESPEAKORBUST
ABYSS VINO TEY
SIRE KEEPOFF
SAO COB ASAP
CHUBBYCHECKER
ESKIMO MOISTURE
WEEVIL COLA LIE
EXTEND ALOU KEN

184

ROSS CRAM SCION
ILAY RALE PARDO
CELL AUTO ARMOR
CAULIFLOWEREAR
INTACT SATE
BISON SARTRE
ARGUE PIKE EEL
PEABRAINEDIDEAS
BET SEEN SIDLE
SKETCH SOILS
ALEC NICEST
ONIONSKINPAPER
SHELS PISA RORY
SIREE ALIT DCVI
WOODS NOSE SHOT

185

GMAN HASH FAUNA
ROSA ALTO OCTAD
ARTILLERY XRAYS
SPIRALGALAXY
SHROVE PES LAIR
BAYS TWINGE
MAGI SEA ROCKNE
OLE MCENROE LID
PONCHO TOP JESS
SHALOM WHSE
YALE ETC YERTLE
METEORSHOWER
CAGER SQUIRMIER
OWING TALC ENZO
GESSO SUES SEAR

186

SLOPE GASP FALL
HAVEN ALTO RHEA
EVERT REED AEON
DARKHORSE DIANE
SURE PRODDED
HOP SET LAZY
ARISE DEJECTED
MAMA BURSA ARLO
SLACKENS STALL
REAR ACE YET
ALLEGRO TUNA
ROODS LITTERBUG
ERIC ALDA GUAVA
NERO DELI ALTER
ANEW EDEN LEHAR

187

USAF PSAT SNEAK
NERI LACE EAGLE
OMAR ALLA TRADE
IBEGYOURPARDON
TRAM ITO
MOORE EARL WEBS
ALPACA SAO ALE
SLIPOFTHETONGUE
TIN RUE SCORED
SEEM INNS TRESS
ABC POET
SORRYABOUTTHAT
ENACT ELMO EROS
EMCEE ALEE RENO
PEELS DADS NAGS

188

DENS DOUBLE COS
ERIN ERNIES OPT
PAPERWEIGHT LEE
OSPREY RAEBURN
SEEDS AMER OMAN
ERR OGLED PONTI
SSS NOOR MANSES
SATURNINE
LILITH YARD DPT
ABATE AGREE ERA
PERU CROC REBEL
ARAPAHO AERATE
LIM SAUERBRATEN
MAI TINNER TENT
ANE ANDSEA ODDS

189

IGOR LAC SHEET
MOVE ALA SLOANE
POEM MOM TANGLE
FRISBEEJAVELIN
SEA LOG ESS
HORSESHOESPARTY
AWE TOT ARI
DECIDED PALAVER
ERA AID EMO
BASEBALLTANTRUM
EDS SAL PTA
THINGSYOUTHROW
SEVERE FRI THOR
OREXIS MIV AIRY
NESTS ESE NOME

190

STEP DAVE MELD
COLA LEPEW AROW
OREG APPLE RICA
WOMENHOLD OSCAR
AORTA UPHALF
CHANT SURREY
AUSTEN DEAR ALF
FRISBEE CLANGOR
ETA ORES STOOGE
OODLES ISNOT
THESKY CLIVE
RAMPS MAOZEDONG
ATOR TANGO IVAN
METE OCTAD VENA
PREY ASSN ERAT

191

DOFF STARR COBS
AMOI TEPEE ARIA
NOODLESOUP MEAL
GOLDIES BEDPOST
LOP NEGEB
BADEN HON FERAL
UTE RIB LOLITA
BATSINTHEBELFRY
BLENDS IDS LIE
AERIE FLO CLEAR
PANEL ARI
STOPSAT BRAMBLE
HOPI STRINGBEAN
EDEN ALIBI OTTO
DONG LEASE SHES

192

BOER LONGS BLAH
OGLE AGILE RAKE
PRIVATEBENJAMIN
SEA MEESE OWENS
TANS FELL
ACCENT CULT ESC
CORED HULL ALTO
THEMAJORLEAGUES
OATS ONLY CADET
NNE HUEY SUPERS
CORY TAME
DEERE BRINE ADA
ATTORNEYGENERAL
SNOW BEERS BEDE
HAND ASSET BAAS

193

BABE SHANE BIC
ITER NOBEL ENOW
STANLAUREL TAME
QED ACRID ATSEA
UNLOCKS STEEDS
EDEN TOTO NIE
ISM ORAN SEL
ANOTHERFINEMESS
NON ASIF DDE
TSE KOPS GARB
HELDON PANACHE
EDIES BURMA COR
RONA OLLIEHARDY
SUER NINON FUEL
TRY SPARS TESS

194

NAPE MOMA STATE
IRAS ESAU ERNES
CATCHWORD WINES
ETCHES LIS NINE
HER LATCHKEYS
REWROTE SORE
ADO DEAR TETHER
NERD ERECT SALE
INKIND MUIR TIN
STOP BEARCAT
BATCHFILE NOH
AMER FEE SCUBAS
LANED MATCHGAME
TNOTE ASIA ECON
SANER NEON SKIT

195

LIMIT PAID MAZE
OMANI ECRU EXEC
BALDDASHER LEAH
ONLEAVE APOLLO
CLOT EBON
LADE WANDLUSTER
AGENTS ODER ULA
PRATE STY ECLAT
EEL TREE TRISTE
LETTHEADER MAES
REVS AURA
ANGORA STORAGE
REAP MATTHORNER
NIGH PLIE MODES
OLAY SPAR SNARE

196

MARV BOER DARIN
ARIA ELLA ERASE
PULLONESPUNCHES
STEIN ATTU SET
STEP ADS
TAKEITONTHECHIN
ITA MANOR AONE
SAREE CHA ENDOW
CRAB HOITY GIA
HITBELOWTHEBELT
SLO SOSO
ALS ALAN ORATE
PUTUPAGOODFIGHT
STANS EDDA NEIN
EERIE DEEM GENA

197

AESOP GAGE CAST
BROKE AREA RIME
ERASE STAR OMEN
TSP PAPERTOWELS
OPENS HANDLE
UMPIRE CHESS
REEL WAHINE BSA
GIRLS COD SCULL
ERA WARREN OBOE
LINED ADOBES
ASKING SMALL
SPONGECAKES EGO
HARE LOCI HOGAN
EDEN ICED ERUPT
SEAS CADS ROMEO

198

CELL PATH SRAS
OLIO ELIA OTARU
LAMBASTED COMER
AMPERE REATAS
ITS SWATHS
REGULATE ONSALE
ALOSS OVALS COR
BLAH EWERS IKON
BET AVERT VOLPE
INSURE TIDINESS
SUPINE SIL
CLASSA ALASKA
MAKIN KIDNAPPED
ALEFS EDEN TEED
PERT RENE SENS

199

OMENS MASCOT
CORRIDOR IDEATE
EPHEMERA SURREY
DEO INT BOBBI
EDDA SHEA IBET
ESP DELT ABLE
URIAL ACTED EEN
BESPEAK IRELAND
OIL BRONC PANIS
ANAS STOA PDQ
TANK ALVA DUEL
DARIN EBB EPA
AORTIC KNEEDEEP
FLEECE OUTLINED
BEDDED PESTS

200

MUTTS JAYS POSH
OBEAH ALAI LOLA
OOMPAHBAND AGON
DAPPLES NESTEGG
STEELE GIDEON
DODGE ITSELF
DOIT ARUSH SEA
PEON OOMPH FINN
ILL SPLAT FIST
CLOTHE NOSIR
NOONES ORTEGA
HIGHEST CHERVIL
ANTE OONAONEILL
NOEL UNIT ZELDA
SNAP TSPS ESSAY

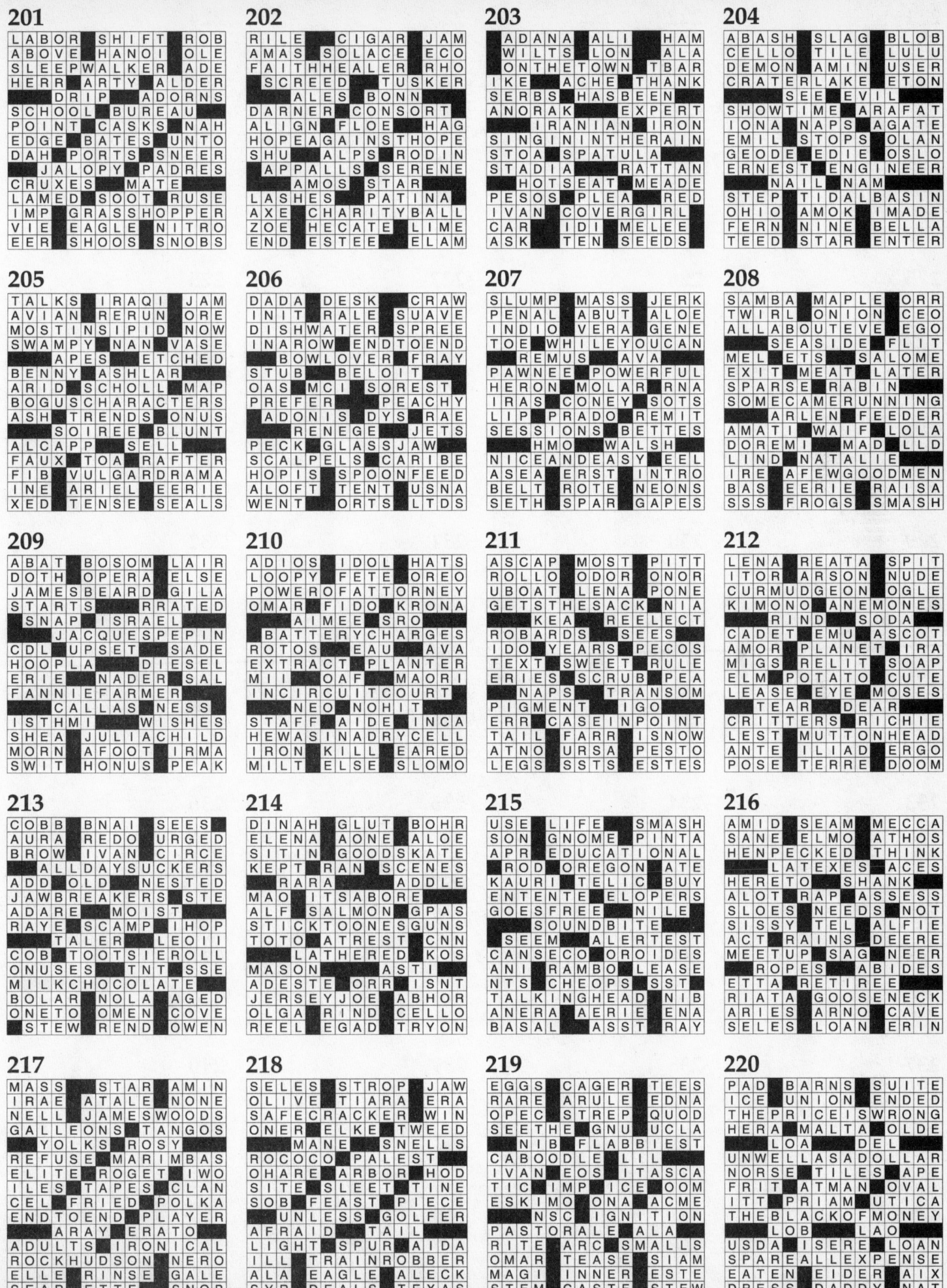

201

```
LABOR■SHIFT■ROB
ABOVE■HANOI■OLE
SLEEPWALKER■ADE
HERR■ARTY■ALDER
■■■DRIP■■ADORNS
SCHOOL■BUREAU■■
POINT■CASKS■NAH
EDGE■BATES■UNTO
DAH■PORTS■SNEER
■■JALOPY■PADRES
CRUXES■■MATE■■■
LAMED■SOOT■RUSE
IMP■GRASSHOPPER
VIE■EAGLE■NITRO
EER■SHOOS■SNOBS
```

202

```
RILE■■CIGAR■JAM
AMAS■SOLACE■ECO
FAITHHEALER■RHO
■SCREED■■TUSKER
■■■ALES■BONN■■■
DARNER■CONSORT■
ALIGN■FLOE■■HAG
HOPEAGAINSTHOPE
SHU■■ALPS■RODIN
■APPALLS■SERENE
■■■AMOS■STAR■■■
LASHES■■PATINA■
AXE■CHARITYBALL
ZOE■HECATE■LIME
END■ESTEE■■ELAM
```

203

```
■ADANA■ALI■■HAM
■WILTS■LON■■ALA
■ONTHETOWN■TBAR
IKE■■ACHE■THANK
SERBS■HASBEEN■■
ANORAK■■■EXPERT
■■■IRANIAN■IRON
SINGININTHERAIN
STOA■SPATULA■■■
STADIA■■■RATTAN
■■HOTSEAT■MEADE
PESOS■PLEA■■RED
IVAN■COVERGIRL■
CAR■■IDI■MELEE■
ASK■■TEN■SEEDS■
```

204

```
ABASH■SLAG■BLOB
CELLO■TILE■LULU
DEMON■AMIN■USER
CRATERLAKE■ETON
■■■■SEE■EVIL■■■
SHOWTIME■ARAFAT
IONA■NAPS■AGATE
EMIL■STOPS■OLAN
GEODE■EDIE■OSLO
ERNEST■ENGINEER
■■■NAIL■NAM■■■■
STEP■TIDALBASIN
OHIO■AMOK■IMADE
FERN■NINE■BELLA
TEED■STAR■ENTER
```

205

```
TALKS■IRAQI■JAM
AVIAN■RERUN■ORE
MOSTINSIPID■NOW
SWAMPY■NAN■VASE
■■■APES■■ETCHED
BENNY■ASHLAR■■■
ARID■SCHOLL■MAP
BOGUSCHARACTERS
ASH■TRENDS■ONUS
■■■SOIREE■BLUNT
ALCAPP■■SELL■■■
FAUX■TOA■RAFTER
FIB■VULGARDRAMA
INE■ARIEL■EERIE
XED■TENSE■SEALS
```

206

```
DADA■DESK■■CRAW
INIT■RALE■SUAVE
DISHWATER■SPREE
INAROW■ENDTOEND
■■BOWLOVER■FRAY
STUB■■BELOIT■■■
OAS■MCI■SOREST■
PREFER■■■PEACHY
■ADONIS■DYS■RAE
■■■RENEGE■■JETS
PECK■GLASSJAW■■
SCALPELS■CARIBE
HOPIS■SPOONFEED
ALOFT■TENT■USNA
WENT■■ORTS■LTDS
```

207

```
SLUMP■MASS■JERK
PENAL■ABUT■ALOE
INDIO■VERA■GENE
TOE■WHILEYOUCAN
■■REMUS■■AVA■■■
PAWNEE■POWERFUL
HERON■MOLAR■RNA
IRAS■CONEY■SOTS
LIP■PRADO■REMIT
SESSIONS■BETTES
■■■HMO■■WALSH■■
NICEANDEASY■EEL
ASEA■ERST■INTRO
BELT■ROTE■NEONS
SETH■SPAR■GAPES
```

208

```
SAMBA■MAPLE■ORR
TWIRL■ONION■CEO
ALLABOUTEVE■EGO
■■■SEASIDE■FLIT
MEL■ETS■■SALOME
EXIT■MEAT■LATER
SPARSE■RABIN■■■
SOMECAMERUNNING
■■■ARLEN■FEEDER
AMATI■WAIF■LOLA
DOREMI■■MAD■LLD
LIND■NATALIE■■■
IRE■AFEWGOODMEN
BAS■EERIE■RAISA
SSS■FROGS■SMASH
```

209

```
ABAT■BOSOM■LAIR
DOTH■OPERA■ELSE
JAMESBEARD■GILA
STARTS■■■RRATED
■SNAP■ISRAEL■■■
■■■JACQUESPEPIN
CDL■UPSET■■SADE
HOOPLA■■■DIESEL
ERIE■■NADER■SAL
FANNIEFARMER■■■
■■■CALLAS■NESS■
ISTHMI■■■WISHES
SHEA■JULIACHILD
MORN■AFOOT■IRMA
SWIT■HONUS■PEAK
```

210

```
ADIOS■IDOL■HATS
LOOPY■FETE■OREO
POWEROFATTORNEY
OMAR■FIDO■KRONA
■■■AIMEE■SRO■■■
■BATTERYCHARGES
ROTOS■■EAU■■AVA
EXTRACT■PLANTER
MII■■OAF■■MAORI
INCIRCUITCOURT■
■■■NEO■NOHIT■■■
STAFF■AIDE■INCA
HEWASINADRYCELL
IRON■KILL■EARED
MILT■ELSE■SLOMO
```

211

```
ASCAP■MOST■PITT
ROLLO■ODOR■ONOR
UBOAT■LENA■PONE
GETSTHESACK■NIA
■■■KEA■■REELECT
ROBARDS■■SEES■■
IDO■YEARS■PECOS
TEXT■SWEET■RULE
ERIES■SCRUB■PEA
■■NAPS■■TRANSOM
PIGMENT■■IGO■■■
ERR■CASEINPOINT
TAIL■FARR■ISNOW
ATNO■URSA■PESTO
LEGS■SSTS■ESTES
```

212

```
LENA■REATA■SPIT
ITOR■ARSON■NUDE
CURMUDGEON■OGLE
KIMONO■ANEMONES
■■■RIND■■SODA■■
CADET■EMU■ASCOT
AMOR■PLANET■IRA
MIGS■RELIT■SOAP
ELM■POTATO■CUTE
LEASE■EYE■MOSES
■■TEAR■■DEAR■■■
CRITTERS■RICHIE
LEST■MUTTONHEAD
ANTE■ILIAD■ERGO
POSE■TERRE■DOOM
```

213

```
COBB■BNAI■SEES■
AURA■REDO■URGED
BROW■IVAN■CIRCE
■■ALLDAYSUCKERS
ADD■OLD■■NESTED
JAWBREAKERS■STE
ADARE■■MOIST■■■
RAYE■SCAMP■IHOP
■■■TALER■■LEOII
COB■TOOTSIEROLL
ONUSES■■TNT■SSE
MILKCHOCOLATE■■
BOLAR■NOLA■AGED
ONETO■OMEN■COVE
■STEW■REND■OWEN
```

214

```
DINAH■GLUT■BOHR
ELENA■AONE■ALOE
SITIN■GOODSKATE
KEPT■RAN■SCENES
■■RARA■■■■ADDLE
MAO■ITSABORE■■■
ALF■SALMON■GPAS
STICKTOONESGUNS
TOTO■ATREST■CNN
■■■LATHERED■KOS
MASON■■■■ASTI■■
ADESTE■ORR■ISNT
JERSEYJOE■ABHOR
OLGA■RIND■CELLO
REEL■EGAD■TRYON
```

215

```
USE■LIFE■■SMASH
SON■GNOME■PINTA
APR■EDUCATIONAL
■ROD■OREGON■ATE
KAURI■TELIC■BUY
ENTENTE■ELOPERS
GOESFREE■■NILE■
■■■SOUNDBITE■■■
■SEEM■■ALERTEST
CANSECO■OROIDES
ANI■RAMBO■LEASE
NTS■CHEOPS■SST■
TALKINGHEAD■NIB
ANERA■AERIE■ENA
BASAL■■ASST■RAY
```

216

```
AMID■SEAM■MECCA
SANE■ELMO■ATHOS
HENPECKED■THINK
■■■LATEXES■ACES
HERETO■■SHANK■■
ALOT■RAP■ASSESS
SLOES■NEEDS■NOT
SISSY■TEL■ALFIE
ACT■RAINS■DEERE
MEETUP■SAG■NEER
■■ROPES■■ABIDES
ETTA■RETIREE■■■
RIATA■GOOSENECK
ARIES■ARNO■CAVE
SELES■LOAN■ERIN
```

217

```
MASS■■STAR■AMIN
IRAE■ATALE■NONE
NELL■JAMESWOODS
GALLEONS■TANGOS
■■YOLKS■ROSY■■■
REFUSE■MARIMBAS
ELITE■ROGET■IWO
ILES■TAPES■CLAN
CEL■FRIED■POLKA
ENDTOEND■PLAYER
■■■ARAY■ERATO■■
ADULTS■IRONICAL
ROCKHUDSON■NERO
ELLE■RINSE■GALE
SEAR■ETTE■■SNOB
```

218

```
SELES■STROP■JAW
OLIVE■TIARA■ERA
SAFECRACKER■WIN
ONER■ELKE■TWEED
■■■MANE■■SNELLS
ROCOCO■PALEST■■
OHARE■ARBOR■HOD
SITE■SLEET■TINE
SOB■FEAST■PIECE
■■UNLESS■GOLFER
AFRAID■■TAIL■■■
LIGHT■SPUR■AIDA
ILL■TRAINROBBER
ALA■EAGLE■ALECK
SYR■DEALS■TEXAS
```

219

```
EGGS■CAGER■TEES
RARE■ARULE■EDNA
OPEC■STREP■QUOD
SEETHE■GNU■UCLA
■■NIB■FLABBIEST
CABOODLE■LIL■■■
IVAN■EOS■ITASCA
TIC■IMP■ICE■OOM
ESKIMO■ONA■ACME
■■■NSC■IGNITION
PASTORALE■ALA■■
RITE■ARC■SMALLS
OMAR■TEASE■SIAM
MAGI■INNER■ESTE
STEM■CASTE■STEW
```

220

```
PAD■BARNS■SUITE
ICE■UNION■ENDED
THEPRICEISWRONG
HERA■MALTA■OLDE
■■■LOA■■■DEL■■■
UNWELLASADOLLAR
NORSE■TILES■APE
FRIT■ATMAN■OVAL
ITT■PRIAM■UTICA
THEBLACKOFMONEY
■■■LOB■■■LAO■■■
USDA■ISERE■LOAN
SPAREALLEXPENSE
EATEN■EIDER■AIX
DRESS■DADDY■NAT
```

221
```
COST  LARKS  WASP
ODOR  IRENE  OLIO
YETI  LEVEL  LOGE
  OCEANSELEVEN
    YWCA    MESS
DANCE      PESOS
ORAL  FAUCET  SEE
RIVEROFNORETURN
MAY  HURTLE  VEND
   SILOS  ADZES
  GAIN    SEMI
  ONGOLDENPOND
BONN  EERIE  NAPA
ASIA  ELOPE  ELAN
REEL  RISES  RENT
```

222
```
JAPE  ACME  CIRCA
OVAL  WAIL  ANION
SIRFRANCISBACON
EDS  OKIE  TOPEKA
   ATEN  ALOE
 COLONELMUSTARD
HYPER  YOKE   PEA
ANTS  SCORE  ORGY
SDI  PLAN  ALIAS
 PICKLESSORRELL
   REEK  SEGO
ASLANT  APSO  TAU
THEMAYOBROTHERS
MINER  KEEL  AXES
EMORY  STYE  STAR
```

223
```
 GRUB  SEVE  JANE
ARUBA  ENID  OXEN
COMES  PERI  ILED
 CUBREPORTERS
SPA  BAYOU  ATLAS
  HORS  OKD  ASI
ANGORA  SSE  BLTS
BERENSTAINBEARS
OWED  OIL  NORWAY
UTE  ELM  GERM
TONER  EAUDE  MAI
  GRIZZLYADAMS
WAXY  SOUL  LINEN
ATOP  INRE  IDONT
TEXT  SEED  SINS
```

224
```
BARR  ORAN  SCAPE
ISEE  LIMO  HALLS
KIEV  ABOW  ONTOP
 OFFOFFBROADWAY
     LEVI  NUDE
LARVA  TODDY  AMA
ICIEST  REI  STAB
SHORTSHORTSTORY
POTS  HON  SCALES
SOS  HIMOM  OGLES
     HERE  ELON
 GREATGREATAUNT
FLAIR  AUKS  THEE
AUTRY  MELT  EONS
REESE  EDYS  SHES
```

225
```
AMOS  CLEM  AMATI
LONE  OONA  NAMES
AMETHODTO  CLEAT
   TILE  THANKS
 KEEPASTEROIDS
SHARPS   HEIRS
PASSE  ERA  EDOM
IKE  RAMRODS  IRE
NILE  PAM  LOGAN
  LIANA  BEHIND
 FROMCOLLIDING
FRAPPE   EGGO
RATIO  WITHEARTH
OMENS  ALIT  NIKE
MERGE  DENS  SOON
```

226
```
WALE  OSAGE  PANS
ARAT  ALIEN  ALIT
INTHEFIRSTPLACE
TEENS  PETER  SEW
   ITE  RIO
 SECONDBASEMAN
ELD  PORED  DALAI
REIN  SELMA  RAID
RETAG  AVERS  RVS
 THIRDMANTHEME
    LEU  YAM
ESP  CLEAT  MORAL
THEFOURTHESTATE
NONO  TITAN  EVAN
AWAY  HEATS  RITA
```

227
```
TOGAS  MIRY  CERF
ALIBI  OLEO  ERIE
BANANAREPUBLICS
UFO  GLAD  ATNOS
   BELL  YOGI
CHERRYSTONECLAM
AURA  ARAL   IRE
IMIN  LATEN  ABEL
ROC  AIRE  RYNE
ORANGEFREESTATE
    ENDS  TEES
PAIGE  BELA  TKO
STRAWBERRYBLOND
STAT  EGAN  EARED
TUNE  NODE  DINES
```

228
```
SOLE  OSCAR  CRAM
PROM  FLARE  HALO
CABINFEVER  ODOR
ALE  ASEA  OOLITE
   TREK  JUDEO
ACQUIT  PETERSON
TRUSS  LOWER  HUE
LOOK  POLED  FATE
ANN  TROLL  LUCID
SESSIONS  MONKEY
   ENEMY  GOLD
SATORI  BELL  MAI
OCHO  SHANTYTOWN
DEUT  ERNIE  KOOK
ATTY  SHEEN  ONLY
```

229
```
HEMS  AGES  MICAS
OPIE  TAME  ALAMO
DINE  BRIM  NINAS
 CANTABRIGIANS
HUR  ITO  OLDEST
ERECTS  BARA  REO
TETRA  PYLE  TYRO
   ANGELENOS
LIMB  ALAS  KAPPA
ISA  STEW  RARELY
POTATO  OOP  NAN
 LIVERPUDLIANS
MANOR  ASEA  LIME
STEIN  ANON  TEAR
SEEDS  RAND  OSSA
```

230
```
LSD  FLEE  LACES
OTO  AREIN  OCALA
WAR  SEEDS  IMPLY
 ITSOWNJOURNEY
QUEBEC  LEE  BAS
SSTS  HBO  DREARY
   ONLYERROR
 ASHIER  AEGEAN
   BUTADREAM
TRALEE  NED  DUEL
UAL  CRT  AMANDA
 WHATYOUMAKEIT
AVAIL  ANNIE  STE
TORTE  NITES  CON
LATEX  SOON  ORT
```

231
```
SPAM  BASEST  CAP
ALIE  OLEATE  OWE
NADA  SITSON  LET
 DYEDINTHEWOOL
ROREM  DERNIER
ANS  ETRE  SADIE
  CARAMBA  GENA
  HONEYCOMBED
RIAL  FEELFOR
ANNAM  ELMS  ARM
FADDIST  OSTEO
 PARTEDCOMPANY
ELI  AERIAL  ARTE
ROC  GERARD  TIER
ASK  ERASES  SSRS
```

232
```
ALOT  PRAY  OMAHA
DAZE  RICE  VALID
OBOE  ELIA  ACUTE
PONTEVEDRA  AMEN
TREELESS   SUR
    RIN  ROBOCOP
ASH  TOTO  ENOLA
SPANISHAMERICAN
SARAN  ITEM   ANT
TREVINO   EAR
   ITO  VIRGINIA
AGOG  BRIDGEPORT
DORAL  ADEE  EPEE
AGATE  SEAN  SANS
MOLES  HOLT  TRET
```

233
```
ATOMS  ERGO  HASP
LOPES  COAL  ETTA
DOESNTHOLDWATER
OKRA  YOKE  ATILT
   ASAP  SPLICES
MOT  MEAT   EEN
ALIMB  LOST  GHIJ
GIVEITSOMEJUICE
IDES  HOTE  OPTED
SPA  HERS  TRI
WASHERS   OHOH
AREAL  ASST  FEET
SMELLSTHECOFFEE
TOIL  HOOT  DEALS
ERNS  ENDS  ERNST
```

234
```
LOWE   SHED  CAST
ARENT  HATE  AGAR
WRITERIGHT  SOLE
  GROOVE  AARON
ACHE  BANNEDBAND
ALWAYS   ASEA
MEHTA  TATA  SAW
ERE  THAITIE  ETA
SKY  OILY  SWOON
   PEEN  FERULE
STEALSTEEL  ELLS
CRACK  LLAMAS
RISK  STALKSTOCK
EPEE  PATE  THULE
WELT  AMEN  SLUG
```

235
```
SLAV  ASOF  AGLOW
RENO  SELA  LLANO
ANNIEHALL  MARLO
STALL  RADIODAYS
     ALE  OMNI
PAS  ELEM  ADORER
AMP  RILES  LALO
WOODYALLENFILMS
ERIE  ATRIA  LEE
RELATE  SECT  YRS
    DULL  KID
INTERIORS  MIAMI
MAINE  MANHATTAN
PUREE  AJAR  TORN
STERN  NAPS  OPTS
```

236
```
LEONA  ALTAR  ASP
ARNAZ  PIANO  DIE
PRETTYPENNY  ITO
    EELS  AMMAN
MANACLE  HELPERS
ANIMAL  MARTHA
RECON  FORAY  DOT
INKS  RATES  ROSE
ODE  AUTOS  RAZOR
  LANDER  LEVELS
ABORTED  NOMINEE
RADII   TOGA
IRE  QUARTERBACK
AGO  UPPER  KYRIE
SEN  ESTEE  SEEDY
```

237
```
ITEM   MAT  TAMPA
DELA  SALE  ONAIR
SAYSUNCLE  PASTE
   TRAY  EGESTS
 SPEAKSVOLUMES
ETERNE   OMANI
MATSU  SLIT  CHAP
ERR  SPECTER  ERA
USOS  AVAS  EMAIL
  ESSEN  ELAPSE
 TALKSNONSENSE
NELLIE   OTTO
ASTOR  CRIESWOLF
STOUT  ROSE  AREA
ASSTS  ODE  RENT
```

238
```
ELMS  SWAP  DROLL
RIAL  PHIL  RADIO
ETNA  HERO  INEPT
 CHIMNEYSWIFT
TEASER  SOT  MPS
   WEEP  TERESA
AMASS  LOGARITHM
LONE  SOL  CRAM
POKERFACE  SHOWY
HELPER   HEAP
ADE  DEB  RUDEST
 CHEESEGRATER
RODEO  SEXY  LURE
PRINT  ORAL  EDGE
MEETS  TAME  SEED
```

239
```
RAGE  ABACUS  CHE
EMIL  BREAST  LAD
BING  BARBARAANN
ANNAMAY   FARINA
IRA  ERA  IRMAS
ORE  MARYJANE
ROMPED  EAR  SLOW
STARTER  RESTIVE
OLEO  LEE  TISSUE
  SUEELLEN  AMP
REMAN  FLA  GEM
AVAILS  RAEDAWN
JOYCECAROL  IRAE
AKA  SOREST  TIRE
HES  STELAE  SEND
```

240
```
WAWA  KONG  VEERS
WHIZ  AMER  AVAIL
WITT  ZANE  LORCA
 THEMOREYOUKNOW
    COO  WEI
QUASI  IMAN  NMEX
URN  STRAFE  GAVE
ABO  THEMORE  DAN
RADS  INMOST  ADO
KNEW  NEAT  HEMEN
   EEL  BEG
 JOKESYOU'LLGET
INEPT  ACTA  NYSE
MELEE  SLIM  ORAL
SITAR  TALE  GERM
```

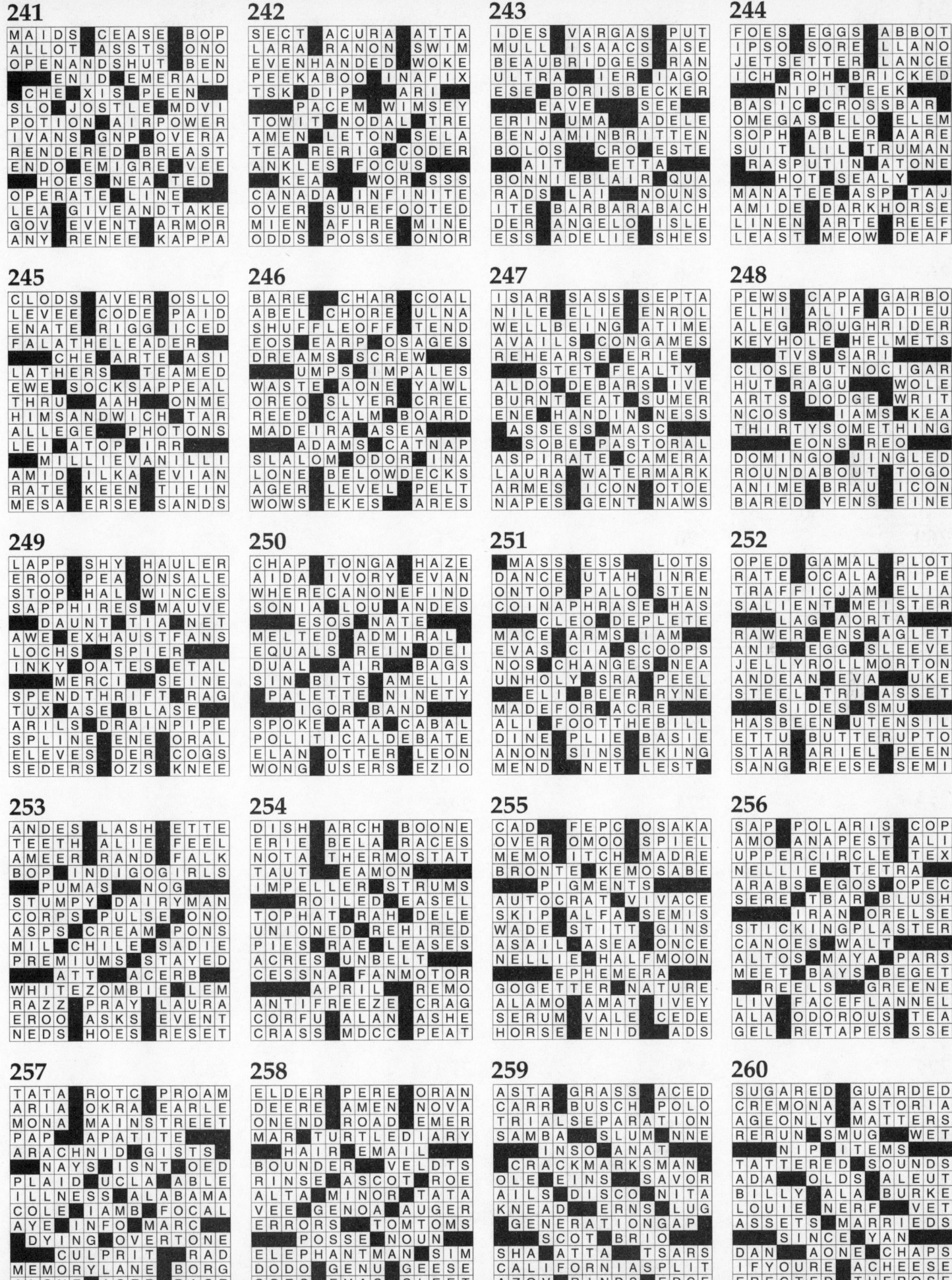

241 242 243 244
245 246 247 248
249 250 251 252
253 254 255 256
257 258 259 260

261

```
ARIA  BALSA  DAFT
LODI  ALIEN  OBOE
BOER  SLEEK  TEEN
 FASHIONPLATES
      PONY  EPI
SETAT  SAD  REHAB
ALICES  ERA  ORA
SATELLITEDISHES
ETA  YON  ASTUTE
SENSE  NAT  AIMED
ALA  EGAL
 FLYINGSAUCERS
CEES  GOOSE  TATA
PENN  LOSES  TIED
ASTO  ODORS  ONTO
```

262

```
SRIS  DALE  PERCE
TENT  EVIL  ALIAS
ALBA  TORA  NESTS
GEORGEWALLACE
SEXIER  OCT
   NORMANTHOMAS
HOT  LEICA  ERASE
AHEM  DRAMA  SLEW
DICOT  EGEST  IAN
JOHNANDERSON
ERE  ARABIA
 STROMTHURMOND
GENII  ORAL  AGRA
AGAZE  PINT  TEEM
LOPED  EGGS  HYDE
```

263

```
WASNT  TRACT  GMC
ICHOR  EARTH  REA
THESUNSHINEBOYS
TYPESETS  OATES
 TEY  SPRIER
EBBED  SHEETS
STAKEACLAIM  QBS
DOCS  AYR  SUET
INK  GARLICBREAD
SCANTY  ALIST
SPARSE  STE
WEARS  STEERAGE
ATCROSSPURPOSES
VIE  NOLAN  EMITS
END  STORK  DENSE
```

264

```
SAV  ADES  CELTIC
ARE  BOTH  ECARTE
LEN  SCHOOLHOUSE
STEP  ERR  OSE
AHEADPLEASE  BAY
ARTIE  GOD  LIE
ARR  AER  FUNT
TAKEITSLOWLET
DEMI  NEA  RAE
ORB  ACT  ADEAL
EMU  THOSELITTLE
LOT  NIL  SLAM
SHAVERSGROW  AMO
PATENT  NONE  SAT
AMENDS  EYED  TSE
```

265

```
ARR  SOS  ROLLS
MAUNALOA  HAWAII
ARBOREAL  OILMEN
ZEBRAORPLATYPUS
ERE  SSE  ART
RHO  DUBS  SOMA
SLOTS  POE  PROS
SPINACHORSQUASH
PEKE  IAN  TURNS
AWED  SLAT  ING
ASE  WAN  ECO
BERYLORFELDSPAR
OLIVER  REPLIERS
NITERS  ADHERETO
YEAST  SAN  LEN
```

266

```
AHOY  SWAP  ZAP
MOVE  MARES  PALE
PRESSAGENT  ISLE
SAN  PRES  ANNUAL
SETS  CROC
SASHAY  HOTSHOTS
CLERK  DOPE  PROW
RAVI  PAPER  ELLE
AMEN  OVID  GNOME
PORKLOIN  BONNET
WORD  GAMY
GEORGE  PERE  ODE
ALMA  SQUEEZEBOX
WEEP  TUSKS  NOWI
KEN  ASST  DENT
```

267

```
EDER  RESEE  BEL
MERE  EVENS  PERE
SELF  TENDS  RENE
DEEPEN  SERENER
REST  NEZ
RESENT  PRECEPTS
ELLEN  FEES  SEEP
EVE  REN  TRE
SEWS  SEPT  MEESE
ESSENCES  FESSED
EER  BENT
SLEDDED  REDEEM
PEPE  EELED  ELEE
EWER  CLEVE  METS
CDE  HEXER  SMEE
```

268

```
LAST  EPEE  PAGAN
ETTA  SATS  AMORE
SHORTSTOP  RATED
LEATHERNECKS
INT  UNI  CLASSES
EAST  ATIE  AGO
ISA  HARDINGS
SILKSTALKINGS
PARTISAN  SEN
ARM  EKES  SLAP
PIASTRE  ASP  ASE
COTTONMOUTHS
POLAR  INTERSECT
ALARM  MEAL  NEAL
TEPEE  ERST  ANNE
```

269

```
PREP  STROM  HARI
LIMO  PRIMA  ODIN
EVIL  IOTAS  BOLT
DELI  CLARKGABLE
ETHEL  AREEL
DOZED  SCRIPT
APOLLO  AIDE  EDD
DALY  DIPPY  CLEO
ALA  BOAR  LOITER
NARNIA  KNOPF
EMAIL  OGDEN
VANCLIBURN  AJOY
ERIK  SENTA  SOLE
NITE  MADAS  THEA
SEAL  SKOSH  ENGR
```

270

```
WAIST  STIFF  QUM
ATTAR  AERIE  ATE
RABBITYEARS  TIA
STEREO  STET  ALL
EDDA  EMIGRES
AAR  ACH  EVE
GROSSYEARNINGS
OCTET  RUE  TRAIT
SCRAMBLEDYEGGS
RNA  SKI  SHE
RUBADUB  SEGA
ONO  BREA  GIVEME
PIX  YEASTOFEDEN
ETE  METOO  TRIAD
RED  ENSUE  STENS
```

271

```
CODA  GRASP  WEST
ODIN  LUGER  RIPE
BORN  ENERO  ORAL
BREADANDBUTTER
AMY  DIE
LILACS  KEEP  SNL
IRISH  IANS  STOA
MEATANDPOTATOES
INRI  ALPS  DARNS
TES  AREA  LAREDO
ERR  SON
MILKANDCOOKIES
ZERO  TAROT  ADZE
ASAP  ETAPE  HERA
PANE  DOMED  NEAT
```

272

```
ROSS  RECAP  SWAB
OGEE  AGATE  PIPE
DRAWINGPAD  ADES
EER  STEP  ARREST
SLED  SLOTS
HASHED  COLLAPSE
ASHES  TOWEL  RCA
LIED  CAVED  SEAS
ODE  LONER  SHALE
SETTINGS  SHADES
MUSTY  CHOW
SHERPA  ERIE  SEE
MATT  COVERSTORY
URAL  TWEET  AFAR
TILE  SENDS  BASE
```

273

```
REVS  SALT  CABAL
EMIT  PLEA  ABASE
AIDA  HEAR  SLAKE
CLOTHESHORSE
TERSER  TAI  DEB
REST  INDIGO
SCARE  CHILIDOGS
ALDA  PAULS  ADOS
BOOKWORMS  HYENA
RUPEES  BABE
ATT  ASP  ERASED
GREASEMONKEY
ROMEO  SOLO  GORE
ADIEU  TUBA  LAIR
FEAST  ARAN  OLES
```

274

```
TEAM  AMAH  SCALA
ANTE  RATE  IAMAT
SCAR  MYOLDFLAME
TORCH  OPIATE
EDISON  UNSNARL
DES  MIASMA  DIRE
MAGMA  MADRE
LIGHTMYFIRE
TOOLE  BURTS
ANEW  STALER  BAA
DEBASER  TETONS
UNEASE  SONGS
SMOKERINGS  TILE
AIRER  TIGE  ETES
PARED  STOA  MOSS
```

275

```
SCENE  EON  ARBOR
PACER  SAY  PAESE
ITHINKTHE  IGLOO
RAIL  NAUT  ATL
OLD  LAT  BRAHMA
ONLYREALLYGOOD
GAUL  ZOO  POE
VEGETABLE
PAS  OLE  EMIR
ISTABASCOSAUCE
CHAPEL  SOP  ETO
POV  IAMA  STAB
BELLI  PJOROURKE
ADELE  SAN  BRAES
MSDOS  ORD  JAYNE
```

276

```
SALE  DARK  SWAP
LRON  ELENA  TONI
AGRI  LODES  ANTE
CURDSANDWHEY
KEY  ENG  AERIE
SNOWS  ARDENS
ASSET  ITAL  PUT
THEWAYTOSANJOSE
PIA  AHAS  OASES
ANTHEM  TERRY
RESET  SAM  VMI
WEIGHSTATION
JIVE  ZEROS  MOPS
OVER  ENERO  ELEE
GETS  ASSN  NAST
```

277

```
PICT  BLAB  TOMB
ECHO  EARL  OPERA
PEAL  ANNO  UTTER
SPLITDECISIONS
RES  SLO
REPLAN  SPLENDOR
ARIOT  TORI  RBI
MATTEROFOPINION
OTO  ENTS  CAVES
SONNYBOY  CHEESE
EAU  ELO
SILENTMAJORITY
ABASK  AGES  NOUS
CANOE  PUCE  COLA
REND  SETS  ALEX
```

278

```
SPASM  ARBS  KAMA
TUTTI  GILT  ASAP
ATALL  ADUE  RIDE
NABOKOV  BLISTER
MOE  BLAH
MAKEUP  BEAM  BCD
ALOES  TAR  TIARA
RIANT  USE  HOTEL
DELTA  SIR  ELITE
INA  CAKE  AWAKES
THEE  CTA
ICEBERG  ATLANTA
TITO  AEON  ROUEN
CAAN  TEUT  UNLAY
HOLD  EURO  SELMA
```

279

```
DUMP  RAHS  SATAN
ESAU  ORAL  ELATE
EARTHSCIENTISTS
TEE  TWIT  TAT
SCH  COSI  SEDERS
THISTLE  EEEE
AIRTOAIRMISSILE
FLEE  NUB  ASIN
FIREOVERENGLAND
PARS  ROOTAGE
ARISTO  ESME  COD
SEN  BOLL  IRK
WATERMELONSEEDS
ADELA  VINE  ERIE
NYLON  ISEE  PANT
```

280

```
SCONE  FINI  DADA
MASUR  EGOS  OLAV
UNITY  WORLDWARI
TEEM  WARDENS
DREAMTEAMII
GLOOMY  EARL
IFS  LOOP  MISCUE
POPEINNOCENTIII
SAYYES  WATT  DNA
ELSE  REROOF
SUPERBOWLLIV
PAROLES  STARTREKV  EXILE
ARIE  KNEE  POOLE
TANS  STYX  ARMED
```

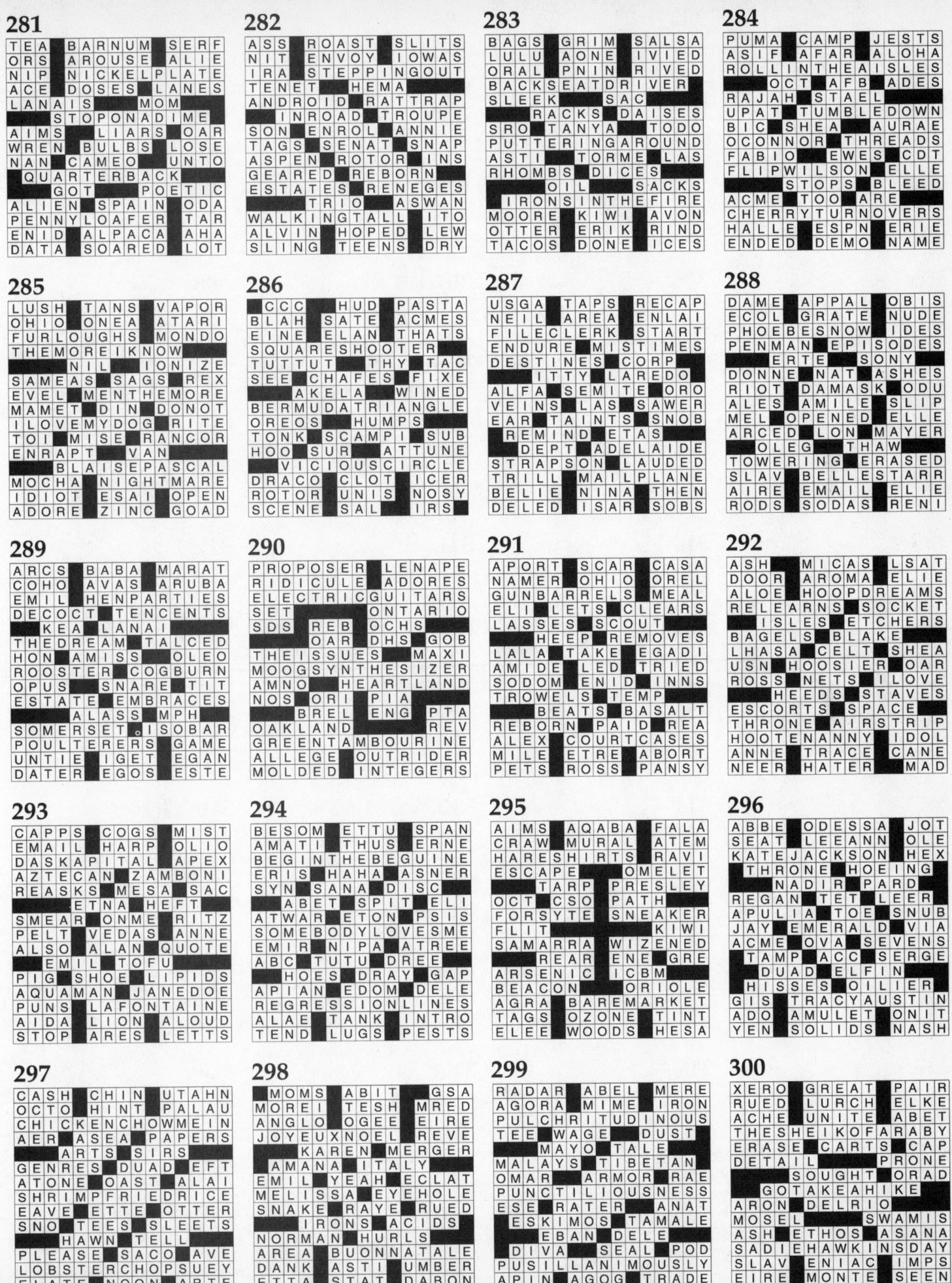

281

```
TEA BARNUM SERF
ORS AROUSE ALIE
NIP NICKELPLATE
ACE DOSES LANES
LANAIS MOM
STOPONADIME
AIMS LIARS OAR
WREN BULBS LOSE
NAN CAMEO UNTO
QUARTERBACK
GOT POETIC
ALIEN SPAIN ODA
PENNYLOAFER TAR
ENID ALPACA AHA
DATA SOARED LOT
```

282

```
ASS ROAST SLITS
NIT ENVOY IOWAS
IRA STEPPINGOUT
TENET HEMA
ANDROID RATTRAP
INROAD TROUPE
SON ENROL ANNIE
TAGS SENAT SNAP
ASPEN ROTOR INS
GEARED REBORN
ESTATES RENEGES
TRIO ASWAN
WALKINGTALL ITO
ALVIN HOPED LEW
SLING TEENS DRY
```

283

```
BAGS GRIM SALSA
LULU AONE IVIED
ORAL PNIN RIVED
BACKSEATDRIVER
SLEEK SAC
RACKS DAISES
SRO TANYA TODO
PUTTERINGAROUND
ASTI TORME LAS
RHOMBS DICES
OIL SACKS
IRONSINTHEFIRE
MOORE KIWI AVON
OTTER ERIK RIND
TACOS DONE ICES
```

284

```
PUMA CAMP JESTS
ASIF AFAR ALOHA
ROLLINTHEAISLES
OCT AFB ADES
RAJAH STAEL
UPAT TUMBLEDOWN
BIC SHEA AURAE
OCONNOR THREADS
FABIO EWES CDT
FLIPWILSON ELLE
STOPS BLEED
ACME TOO ARE
CHERRYTURNOVERS
HALLE ESPN ERIE
ENDED DEMO NAME
```

285

```
LUSH TANS VAPOR
OHIO ONEA ATARI
FURLOUGHS MONDO
THEMOREIKNOW
NIL IONIZE
SAMEAS SAGS REX
EVEL MENTHEMORE
MAMET DIN DONOT
ILOVEMYDOG RITE
TOI MISE RANCOR
ENRAPT VAN
BLAISEPASCAL
MOCHA NIGHTMARE
IDIOT ESAI OPEN
ADORE ZINC GOAD
```

286

```
CCC HUD PASTA
BLAH SATE ACMES
EINE ELAN THATS
SQUARESHOOTER
TUTTUT THY TAC
SEE CHAFES FIXE
AKELA WINED
BERMUDATRIANGLE
OREOS HUMPS
TONK SCAMPI SUB
HOO SUR ATTUNE
VICIOUSCIRCLE
DRACO CLOT ICER
ROTOR UNIS NOSY
SCENE SAL IRS
```

287

```
USGA TAPS RECAP
NEIL AREA ENLAI
FILECLERK START
ENDURE MISTIMES
DESTINES CORP
ITTY LAREDO
ALFA SEMITE ORO
VEINS LAS SAWER
EAR TAINTS SNOB
REMIND ETAS
DEPT ADELAIDE
STRAPSON LAUDED
TRILL MAILPLANE
BELIE NINA THEN
DELED ISAR SOBS
```

288

```
DAME APPAL OBIS
ECOL GRATE NUDE
PHOEBESNOW IDES
PENMAN EPISODES
ERTE SONY
DONNE NAT ASHES
RIOT DAMASK ODU
ALES AMILE SLIP
MEL OPENED ELLE
ARCED LON MAYER
OLEG THAW
TOWERING ERASED
SLAV BELLESTARR
AIRE EMAIL ELIE
RODS SODAS RENI
```

289

```
ARCS BABA MARAT
COHO AVAS ARUBA
EMIL HENPARTIES
DECOCT TENCENTS
KEA LANAI
THEDREAM TALCED
HON AMISS OLEO
ROOSTER COGBURN
OPUS SNARE TIT
ESTATE EMBRACES
ALASS MPH
SOMERSET ISOBAR
POULTERERS GAME
UNTIE IGET EGAN
DATER EGOS ESTE
```

290

```
PROPOSER LENAPE
RIDICULE ADORES
ELECTRICGUITARS
SET ONTARIO
SDS REB OCHS
OAR DHS GOB
THEISSUES MAXI
MOOGSYNTHESIZER
AMNO HEARTLAND
NOS ORI PIA
BREL ENG PTA
OAKLAND REV
GREENTAMBOURINE
ALLEGE OUTRIDER
MOLDED INTEGERS
```

291

```
APORT SCAR CASA
NAMER OHIO OREL
GUNBARRELS MEAL
ELI LETS CLEARS
LASSES SCOUT
HEEP REMOVES
LALA TAKE EGADI
AMIDE LED TRIED
SODOM ENID INNS
TROWELS TEMP
BEATS BASALT
REBORN PAID REA
ALEX COURTCASES
MILE ETRE ABORT
PETS ROSS PANSY
```

292

```
ASH MICAS LSAT
DOOR AROMA ELIE
ALOE HOOPDREAMS
RELEARNS SOCKET
ISLES ETCHERS
BAGELS BLAKE
LHASA CELT SHEA
USN HOOSIER OAR
ROSS NETS ILOVE
HEEDS STAVES
ESCORTS SPACE
THRONE AIRSTRIP
HOOTENANNY IDOL
ANNE TRACE CANE
NEER HATER MAD
```

293

```
CAPPS COGS MIST
EMAIL HARP OLIO
DASKAPITAL APEX
AZTECAN ZAMBONI
REASKS MESA SAC
ETNA HEFT
SMEAR ONME RITZ
PELT VEDAS ANNE
ALSO ALAN QUOTE
EMIL TOFU
PIG SHOE LIPIDS
AQUAMAN JANEDOE
PUNS LAFONTAINE
AIDA LION ALOUD
STOP ARES LETTS
```

294

```
BESOM ETTU SPAN
AMATI THUS ERNE
BEGINTHEBEGUINE
ERIS HAHA ASNER
SYN SANA DISC
ABET SPIT ELI
ATWAR ETON PSIS
SOMEBODYLOVESME
EMIR NIPA ATREE
ABC TUTU DREE
HOES DRAY GAP
APIAN EDOM DELE
REGRESSIONLINES
ALAE TANK INTRO
TEND LUGS PESTS
```

295

```
AIMS AQABA FALA
CRAW MURAL ATEM
HARESHIRTS RAVI
ESCAPE OMELET
TARP PRESLEY
OCT CSO PATH
FORSYTE SNEAKER
FLIT KIWI
SAMARRA WIZENED
REAR ENE GRE
ARSENIC ICBM
BEACON ORIOLE
AGRA BAREMARKET
TAGS OZONE TINT
ELEE WOODS HESA
```

296

```
ABBE ODESSA JOT
SEAT LEEANN OLE
KATEJACKSON HEX
THRONE HOEING
NADIR PARD
REGAN TET LEER
APULIA TOE SNUB
JAY EMERALD VIA
ACME OVA SEVENS
TAMP ACC SERGE
DUAD ELFIN
HISSES OILIER
GIS TRACYAUSTIN
ADO AMULET ONIT
YEN SOLIDS NASH
```

297

```
CASH CHIN UTAHN
OCTO HINT PALAU
CHICKENCHOWMEIN
AER ASEA PAPERS
ARTS SIRS
GENRES DUAD EFT
ATONE OAST ALAI
SHRIMPFRIEDRICE
EAVE ETTE OTTER
SNO TEES SLEETS
HAWN TELL
PLEASE SACO AVE
LOBSTERCHOPSUEY
ELATE NOON ARTE
DANES AWED MASS
```

298

```
MOMS ABIT GSA
MOREI TESH MRED
ANGLO OGEE EIRE
JOYEUXNOEL REVE
KAREN MERGER
AMANA ITALY
EMIL YEAH ECLAT
MELISSA EYEHOLE
SNAKE RAYE RUED
IRONS ACIDS
NORMAN HURLS
AREA BUONNATALE
DANK ASTI UMBER
ETTA STAT DABON
REA EASE ESAI
```

299

```
RADAR ABEL MERE
AGORA MIME IRON
PULCHRITUDINOUS
TEE WAGE DUST
MAYO TALE
MALAYS TIBETAN
OMAR ARMOR RAE
PUNCTILIOUSNESS
ESE RATER ANAT
ESKIMOS TAMALE
EBAN DELE
DIVA SEAL POD
PUSILLANIMOUSLY
APIN AGOG TRADE
LESS PAWN SITES
```

300

```
XERO GREAT PAIR
RUED LURCH ELKE
ACHE UNITE ABET
THESHEIKOFARABY
ERASE CARTS CAP
DETAIL PRONE
SOUGHT ORAD
GOTAKEAHIKE
ARON DELRIO
MOSEL SWAMIS
ASH ETHOS ASANA
SADIEHAWKINSDAY
SLAV ENIAC IMPS
EIRE MONTE SEEN
DENS EIGER INTO
```

301

```
HIHI  RERUN  GOES
ITAL  OMEGA  LILT
PHILOSOPHICALLY
SER  NITS  SUSSEX
     ADEE  AMES
BASKER  AMIS  HAL
OPTIC  SMIT  SOME
THINKSNOTHINGOF
HIES  WARY  LEANT
ADS  GERE  SLANGY
     FLAK  REID
ARMOUR  CAAN  ALA
CHINESEHIBISCUS
TEND  INUSE  KIRK
SEGA  NAMED  IDES
```

302

```
BALD  PARA  GAVIN
AFOR  OMAR  ONICE
CREAMPUFF  BYLAW
HOWWILL  ADAMS
    DIETS  CASEY
  PIEINTHESKY
SOAR  EAST  PTA
SUGARRAYLEONARD
SRO  EARS  BRED
   PIECEOFCAKE
BJORN  HELLO
LURID  DUNGEON
ALINE  JOHNCANDY
SINCE  FLAK  IVES
EAGER  KATY  LYRE
```

303

```
MALTS  ABET  TAPS
APART  SERA  EURO
ROSIETHERIVETER
IRS  PIER  AMOST
ATOMIC  BOONE
   INK  AVOIDING
ALAN  PROPS  MOO
MYWILDIRISHROSE
OLE  OILED  IKES
REDCORAL  OFT
   ONEUP  PLASMA
AMBLE  ODEA  MAD
BYEBYEBLACKBIRD
INDY  SAKI  ELLIE
TASS  PTAS  STEER
```

304

```
AMPS  SEPTA  IOTA
TARA  UNTIL  OMAR
ERIN  PRELL  DENT
SINGAPORESLINGS
TOT  OLEO  TON
    TRY  LABELED
IDIOT  TOOT  AVA
CANVASSTRETCHER
ERR  TATE  HORNE
STELLAR  CUB
   ION  SLAG  SEA
CASTOFTHOUSANDS
OMIT  OREOS  DAIS
DELL  REESE  ERTE
ANTE  DYNES  NESS
```

305

```
BAM  BOOB  ABACI
EGO  ONEA  PAVAN
DONTWORRYABOUT
MENIAL  BICYCLE
EVICT  CREPE  AKA
LIZA  WHERE  ODER
OLE  HEAP  PRODS
   MIDDLEAGE
PALED  IAMA  EBB
OWEN  LUCCI  AMER
PET  DINAH  SNORE
ESTEEMS  COSTAR
YOULLOUTGROWIT
EMCEE  NONO  EVE
DEEMS  GIPP  RED
```

306

```
ITEM  SCARF  AKIN
TELE  LUNAR  DINE
HEADFORTHEHILLS
OTT  ROLE  QUOTAS
THEPIPS  BUNS
   EDS  TREK  CAP
ATSEA  SOON  DULY
BELLYUPTOTHEBAR
LAOS  LOUD  OBESE
EST  STOP  MOI
   GAIN  CAPTIVE
IDREAM  FOUL  LEA
FOOTBALLPLAYERS
ADAM  TEASE  EDGE
TONE  ENTER  SEED
```

307

```
ERAS  WIPER  TASS
ROLE  ASIDE  ALAI
SUPPLYANDDEMAND
TESTIFY  SIAMESE
     UNA  ARY
COMMERCIALPAPER
ATA  ERNS  NICE
SARA  ROTHS  DELI
ARIL  PREP  RAN
SYSTEMSANALYSTS
     RTE  CEO
ASSUAGE  REAGENT
DIGITALCOMPUTER
ANTS  LLAMA  RULE
MOST  OATEN  TILE
```

308

```
SEEM  OLLA  ASIDE
TARA  MEAL  RATON
ASIT  EVIL  ATALE
MECHANICALBULL
PLAIT  HAIR
   STARE  WADERS
NAP  ILOVE  ATOP
EXERCISEBICYCLE
ALOE  AROMA  HEW
TENSED  SNAIL
   OLES  NOLTE
HOLDINGPATTERN
VOGUE  ARON  ITIS
PORTS  FOLD  OGPU
SKEET  UGLY  NOSE
```

309

```
RELATING  RACISM
EXAMINER  ALASKA
CHRISEVERTLLOYD
TAG  EAU  ALT
OLEO  ARTSCHOOLS
RESULT  WHO  UPTO
STRIP  HEM  TEDS
   DECIDED
COAL  ART  OUSTS
CONE  CUE  NOMANS
COUNTESSES  ACOP
  MIA  OHM  TOE
NOBELPEACEPRIZE
OPENLY  REVEALED
MARTYR  KEENNESS
```

310

```
   TLC  CHI  DAG
  SHOO  RAM  ASH
 THEONLYMANWHO
 THINKSIMATENIS
LRON  OTTER  LENT
EARP  FRO  TILDE
ASNAP  UNTIL
KHEDIVE  HALFCUP
   SEDGE  SLOPE
MEDAL  OPP  ALTA
AAAA  LABOR  GLOT
MYSHOESALESMAN
PHYLLISDILLER
LEA  ETA  CION
EMS  GYM  EMB
```

311

```
SAYA  AMIS  MOCHA
ATOM  GEOL  AREAS
MAYOREDWARDKOCH
SNORE  INNER  SKY
   ATTA  GEES
WILLIEMAYS  USNA
ALI  TEEN  EDITOR
TONAL  NTS  ITOLD
EVENED  ITEM  RIO
REND  OSCARMAYER
   COPA  REEL
MOM  HELOT  SOLTI
THEMAYOBROTHERS
SORER  MIEN  ACUT
THETA  EEKS  SHES
```

312

```
LODE  TRIAD  SLOT
EBON  ABOVE  EERO
FOWL  MIDIS  ATNO
TENAM  OVERLOOK
   WINDOW  ROAN
DDE  ORIN  TUNEUP
RON  PULI  TESTY
ANTS  MYNAH  SHUL
MOMMA  GRAB  ARE
ATCOST  SIZE  INS
GOTA  TAYLOR
TRICOLOR  GODOT
MINH  EVERT  OONA
ETTE  SEETO  OWER
NAYS  ENTER  ONAN
```

313

```
TETE  PIVOT  CAIN
OPAL  AMEBA  OLDY
DEMOCRATICSWEEP
DESPOTS  TOPSEED
   ELI  MOM
REPRESENTATIVES
ERR  ALIA  LYLE
CROW  NIXIE  KIEV
AONE  DONT  NNE
PRESIDENTREAGAN
   TBA  URN
ERASERS  ASININE
POLITICALCAUCUS
IBID  NADIA  LAMP
CEDE  GREEN  SLAY
```

314

```
TORO  MAIM  SPADS
OPEC  ERNO  ORNOT
BEDTIMEFORBONZO
EDSON  SONY  DEEP
   POM  PASS
NATURE  MINT  ASE
OCHS  NAIL  EASEL
THESOUNDOFMUSIC
MERYL  NATO  NAZI
ESE  ISIS  UNTIED
   AONE  LEI
BIAS  OHOH  RECUR
ONTHEWATERFRONT
OTTER  LTRS  ODIE
MOANS  LOOT  OATS
```

315

```
SKIT  BIT  STRIP
KIRIS  ISR  PRIMI
IWILL  GHI  LICIT
MISSISSIPPI  KTS
HITIT  PITT
CGT  SIC  TWILIT
CHI  RICH  HIKING
CIRRI  KID  NIGHT
ILLINI  PRIG  HIS
VISITS  SIP  BTS
SITI  FIFIS
BMW  NIGHTLIGHTS
ILIFT  NIS  SHIRT
CITRI  IFI  TIPIN
SITIN  SIN  TSPS
```

316

```
TIFFS  PARIS  DES
ALLAT  AMEBA  AMT
GLADALLOVER  ICE
TIER  ATSEA
CAROLER  RELAYED
ANODES  KAREEM
RISER  FAVRE  IMP
RTES  BARES  CLIO
YAK  HAVEN  POLLS
EDISON  SERENE
HANDLER  CHEERED
ARNEL  PAAR
ILE  MUMSTHEWORD
FED  AMISH  SOFAR
ANY  NASTY  SOFTY
```

317

```
MADE  MIST  FONTS
OPAL  ACME  EMERY
SALESROOM  MAXIM
STICKINGPOINTS
   TEA  INN
RAG  ECHO  SITSIN
ERLE  HARE  SEINE
TOUCHINGREMARKS
ASTRA  DAMA  MEET
RESULT  NARC  DRS
   YES  TOP
ATTACHEDHOUSES
SLYER  EXEMPLARY
HIRED  BALE  SHIN
ETONS  AMEN  ELKE
```

318

```
RAN  CUBISM  MBAS
ILO  ARETHA  OEIL
PUSHBUTTON  LADE
EMIR  VISITED
SNEAKS  REALER
TAR  IOTA  CURIOS
   CRIMP  GECKO
AFT  KEEPING  EAT
BIRDS  DALAI
URIAHS  GETS  VAN
PRANCE  SHEILA
WALKWAY  LEOS
ARAM  KNOCKDOWNS
DINA  EDUCED  ESE
EDEN  SITINS  DOR
```

319

```
ATARI  MAXIM  MBA
CREEM  AMICI  URN
HUSHPUPPIES  MAN
   EARS  LASSO
RESALE  STEALTHY
ELITE  SPANISH
POLES  LIPID  EMU
APED  SIDED  SWAP
YEN  DICER  SPORE
TEETERS  ORRIN
MINDLESS  GUIDED
ANISE  CORN
DUG  THEQUIETMAN
ASH  EATUP  SEINE
TET  SHOES  TRADE
```

320

```
RUSH  MACH  CODES
ONCE  CHOU  ACHES
SCULLCAPS  SHORT
EUBOEA  SKITOW
STATABLE  TRAJAN
   KEA  MAO  OBE
ABASE  GOAL  SNOW
FERRYGODMOTHERS
ILKA  LOEB  HASTY
REL  TON  OAR
EMILIO  ASSASSIN
GOTMAD  SCOTTO
UHHUH  CANOEBIAL
SATIE  IGOR  ELLE
ASSES  DEBT  REYS
```

321
```
ACT  SPEEDS  PERP
LEO  POLLOI  AQUA
LAS  UNSUNG  PUTS
OSCARDELAHOYA
YEAST      TARTAR
   HOOVER  SUITE
GAB  UNITES  SOON
ERE  TONYDOW  NNE
NYES SIMILE  SEW
OAKUM  CADETS
ANEMIC      LIEGE
   EMMYLOUHARRIS
REPO REASON  OJS
OXEN INTEND  DOE
TORS LASSES  EEN
```

322
```
DONHO  NERF  ACTS
ADIOS  OVAL  SHAM
RENTSTRIKE  TAXI
   LIU  LEX  OREL
ACHIEST  REPRISE
CHAN  SRA  DOIT
RICE  LASH  PAYUP
ELK ZEPHYRS  BRO
SEINE  PEPE  WAGS
NEAR  NEV  ALES
HAGGLED  DEWILDE
ALFA  DOC  RAT
ROOT  COUNTYFAIR
SHUE  ANTE  NOISE
HALS  PEST  ERROL
```

323
```
CAMP  CRACK  ESSA
OBIE  AUDIE  SPIC
NELSONEDDY  TINT
STEELERS  STANCE
   TARS  STUDDED
ASSAYS  BOOBOO
MOWS  MAINE  CPA
ELI TWIRLER  TAM
NOV  RAKES  GOGO
ELITES  MOORES
RELATED  BIKE
ACHIER  SELASSIE
JOIN  WHIRLYBIRD
ALPE AIMEE  ALEG
HESS YEATS  DOSE
```

324
```
BAR   BRAN  SMITH
ELOI  LIDO  PASHA
ATOM  INAT  OREOS
MOTOANDMINIVER
     GODS  ALE
OWNERS  LISTLESS
TAUNT  IANA  RCA
HYDEANDMALAPROP
ENE   OLES  MAORI
RESTYLED  HATRED
     REA  CUTE
LEEANDROBINSON
TEXAS  ROAR  TUBA
RAITT  ANTI  SNIP
ANTSY  MASS  GEE
```

325
```
TECH  TAME  JABOT
AGRA  AMOS  IRANI
BRANCHOUT  TUNIC
LEW  AIRE  ATBATS
ATLANTA  OCEAN
BOILOVER  ASH
SABIN  NETS  OOO
TIRE  STENO  LIMA
ONE  ALAN  MILER
PTA  BORDERON
KARTS  LATERAL
SCOPES  JIMI  ARE
POPPA  BOXOFFICE
OPELS  AKIN  USED
TENET  SERA  REDS
```

326
```
MOAT  SCAR  MASH
OPRAH  HOBO  ILKA
MECCA  ACES  GAIN
CHOCOLATECHIPS
   KAT  MAT
GAMEST  AFAR  AHA
OPERA  FAIR  IRON
STRAWBERRYBLOND
EELS  ATOM  ELMER
ERE  SCAN  DESADE
   OAK  EAT
VANILLAEXTRACT
ERIN  ABLE  ETHER
TICK  SOIR  DIANA
ODES  HOST  TROY
```

327
```
HOFFA  OMOO  PABA
ALEAN  WONT  ADAM
TERRYCLOTH  TALE
SONATA  ROENTGEN
DINS  PRAYERS
AMI  MAT  SIC
BOOMERANG  LAYON
CATO  DROOD  KANE
STALK  SNORKELER
LET  FIN  LSD
SAWYERS  SPED
CRABLIKE  PERSIA
ARLO  PENNYCANDY
DOLL  LEDA  AMILE
SWAT  ETON  PATES
```

328
```
PEAL  FLEAS  FETA
RICO  LEASH  RAIN
ONTOPOFTHEWORLD
DESSERTS  EAGLES
ETAS  OPTS
BALERS  GRIT  FIN
ALONE  BIAS  PINA
MIDDLEOFTHEROAD
BEES  SATE  VERNE
INN  MOSS  WEEDER
PUTT  HARM
EFFACE  AIRSPACE
REACHROCKBOTTOM
GATE  IFEEL  ETTU
ORES  CADRE  DYES
```

329
```
ART  LIMIT  SPA
AMAH  INANE  LONI
NINEDOLLARWORDS
NATIONAL  REPEAT
CREW  BIDE
APPEAL  ORBS  MRS
SALAD  ANAL  SOAP
IVEGOTFIVEPENCE
GENE  1000  EATEN
NRA  KERN  INSERT
BECK  ASCH
ISRAEL  AUDIENCE
5MILLIONDOLLARS
OILS  PLAIN  LIAT
TEA  SETTE  SLY
```

330
```
AMP  CAIRO  MAPS
SEES  ONTOP  ASEA
ITSEEMSEVERYTOM
TAKE  MERE  ARS
DIETER  ADAGIO
ACRES  TIS  ALEAN
TEED  MARTINI
ADD  DICKAND  HEM
SALIENT  CAGE
ASNOT  TDS  BORGE
THELAW  DAMASK
TEA  RHEE  USES
HARRYISNAMEDSAM
AVER  STORM  YEAR
TEDS  TASTY  SAT
```

331
```
APAT  DACCA  SPAN
DISH  INOIL  ARMY
ONCEINABLUEMOON
STORMS  RIMA  FRY
STEP  DAUNTS
ORO  MASCARA
MAHARAJA  AHAS
AMONTHOFSUNDAYS
TOOT  TAKESTEN
ASPECTS  YES
DARERS  TOMS
HEM  RENO  AERATE
EVERYNOWANDTHEN
LIME  DREAD  HAVE
PLOD  SARAH  OLES
```

332
```
SAYS  ABES  DRAB
PLEAT  MORE  ROSE
OLLIE  BURR  ACHE
OILSPILL  GAWKER
LEO  ILED  IPSO
WEDS  EFOR  FRO
UPSA  ACRE  ORGAN
TETRA  ACE  NAIVE
ALONG  GOLF  CBER
HEN  NOEL  ICER
EDEN  OPAL  ASI
IMPISH  RETITLED
NEAP  ABAT  MOTEL
MARS  NODE  BLAME
ELKO  DOOR  DRED
```

333
```
BEL  DADA  STEM
ARES  ASIDE  ERTE
SOAP  SHOOK  DICE
IDRATHERBERIGHT
LENTO  EDIT
SPASM  PIECE
LOP  ASTERS  OGRE
IMARRIEDANANGEL
MENU  SPIRAL  YES
ANGST  AEGIS
HEAR  BASTE
HIGHERANDHIGHER
OSLO  ADORE  AREA
BLEU  BANAL  SUNS
SEER  RUMP  BYE
```

334
```
RAHS  MALL  DECAL
EXIT  AREA  ARUBA
FLYINGDOWNTOREO
SEALANE  NEEDLES
EVANS  ODE
WEPT  TUT  SAVE
ELATED  GOOP  BAA
SECONDHANDROLLS
TNT  DEER  DEVOUT
SASH  YEP  EWES
ORA  DEFER
DIORAMA  ROASTER
OLDSVOLKSATHOME
ASIDE  TOOL  ORME
SANER  INNS  TOAD
```

335
```
ELSE  ODETS  DESI
TALL  ROTOR  ONAN
HUEY  DENTALWORK
IRE  PASA  INLAY
CAPTAINSPOST
HINT  OPPOSED
SAFER  ALE  ORE
TRANSITIONMUSIC
OER  DUD  AROCK
PARAPET  AURA
BEAUANDLLOYD
ABASE  DIDO  ZEE
GORENSGAME  ROAM
ERIN  HAGAR  ANTI
SEAT  ABELS  PEST
```

336
```
DIET  CHRIS  SNUG
ANNA  HENNA  TOLL
BACKTOBACK  ASTO
STEERS  HEATERS
SEETHE  RITAS
SOFAS  BOD  LOO
ONA  SPAS  BONNET
BUCO  ARABY  SODA
SPENDS  NOES  SIP
TEE  ONO  ABETS
GOOSE  CABANA
ONFIRST  SYSTEM
LEAD  HANDTOHAND
FACE  ONAIR  EROS
SLED  TEMPO  SASE
```

337
```
ASAN  OPEN  BARK
SOLO  SEAN  RUPEE
FAIRSHARE  IRONY
AVE  TACT  AGREES
RENTA  HOTSHOT
OKAY  ACTS
JETSET  ERRS  DIP
ALAS  ROSSI  TORE
MIX  POST  BARCAR
SAPS  PESO
SKYHIGH  IDOLS
FRAIDY  AIDA  HAM
AETNA  PLAINJANE
SPINY  ELLS  ORAL
TONY  POSH  BAIT
```

338
```
GILA  CDS  RAGTAG
ANAL  CENTIGRADE
SYMBOLFORCARBON
POPUP  TREK  USA
MIS  TESTS
ODS  UHR  AWAKE
PITIMESDIAMETER
IVAN  EVERT  LEAN
NOSHARPSORFLATS
ETHOS  NIL  MST
THEDA  PAS
SOB  VEND  IPASS
THESPEEDOFLIGHT
ONEHUNDRED  LEIA
POTENT  ERR  ESPY
```

339
```
ASTER  MARV  STAR
BOITE  ALIE  ORNO
EATUPTHEPROFITS
SPOILER  SYNAPSE
AREA  GER
ALUMNI  BOOT  CBS
LONE  SHOW  HUA
DOLLARSTODONUTS
ASI  BETA  ARTS
SET  ALAI  ASHLEY
ATO  NAST
MISDEAL  THELADY
INTERNALREVENUE
STEP  ERIE  EATEN
SORT  DALE  SKITS
```

340
```
THAW  SHANA  RPM
REMO  CAROB  ELIS
IRON  ELUDE  MANE
FORTUNATELYANEW
LOA  LES  ENCRE
EFLAT  BAJA  HAL
TREMOLO  TELL
IMAGEISJUST
SANE  ALTOONA
ASS  ONDE  CRIMP
MATZO  MIL  NEE
ARAZORBLADEAWAY
RUNT  OLIVE  CANT
ALTO  TAMES  TRIO
ESP  CHANT  EDEN
```

341

```
TOILS SHOE CAPP
ABOUT TEUT OREO
BOWLEROFTHEYEAR
SEALION RELEASE
   ANTE ALLS
SERB SAG   TOOT
CRAYON NECK XVI
RAY RESIDUE BAR
USO BEAT ZYGOTE
BENE NAH   OWED
ROAM   ASAP
AMERICA REDHEAD
DEMOLITIONDERBY
ICER NELL TRIBE
THUS GOLD OSCAR
```

342

```
TOGAS TOMS AWES
ERASE ARAT CHAT
MOTHERMAYI TOTE
   ISE LAFF SEW
THERES   SLIPON
POOREST   ETON
RAW DEALT SOFAS
ELMO STORE PITA
PLUMP STIES RRS
   COIL ELAPSES
PHONES DEVOTE
MAW TECH   ROT
EROO WHATSUPDOC
STOW AMSO RIOTS
HYDE YOHO SENTA
```

343

```
DABBA COWS MOLD
ALOUD ALOT IDEA
BULLDOGDRUMMOND
MDL DIES AORTA
   FOOL EONS
BEARBRYANT AILS
UNDOES DEBT NAT
STAGY PHD ABABA
ERR SHOO ARENOT
SYNE BUCKROGERS
NOON ACTI
SARAN DORE NED
CROCODILEDUNDEE
AINT ONIN SEEME
MAAS EGOS ERNIE
```

344

```
ZIGS STER FLAKE
AROO LUXE AIRED
SOILFORPLANTING
UNTIL NOIR TATE
   DUPE CAFE
PALS ADDS ORGAN
ABE SITU ORELSE
ROMANGODOFTRADE
TRALEE DUTY DAD
STYLE MYTH KEYS
   ARLO HERA
AMES ORNO ONICE
MICKEYMOUSESDOG
OTHER OSSO ALTO
STOWE NYET SEEN
```

345

```
FRAT DEAR SOFAR
LOCH ENCE HARPO
ISLE NITE ASEAT
THUMBNAILSKETCH
ERIC   HESSES
IRANIS   ALAN
NOLAN VIEW SODA
KNUCKLESANDWICH
SAME EELS YALIE
   BARE DIGSIN
SCARES   JONG
PUTONESFINGERON
ABIDE EAVE RODE
REMIT ATEE EMIT
EDENS LESS DEES
```

346

```
LAB STICH ABCS
COMO TAMPA VIAL
ICESTATIONZEBRA
AIRCADET DORSEY
   SIR GYNT
MICASA TOME VIM
ANOSE TUBA SONY
MCMILLANANDWIFE
BUBS AXED EELER
ORO AYES CLEARS
   ATAD SAR
AVEDON DORISDAY
SENDMENOFLOWERS
PACE GOTTO ABEL
SLED GUEST PIA
```

347

```
SMA SEMI  ELMS
CORSAGES ACQUIT
ROLLCALL BRUISE
AREA DDE HOISTS
PESTO   STOP
   SVC ARCADES
FRO AARON IRANI
REVOLVINGCREDIT
ONENO STOIC ADE
GIRAFFE   ALT
   FARM ERECT
SKIPIT OAR AMOR
PALACE SPINCITY
ANKLES SECRETES
NESS OSHA SST
```

348

```
HIM ARTIS RIPUP
ADE LOUTS AMORE
NIN BANANASPLIT
GOSSAMER STRESS
STAINED   CIAO
   DID PHD VACA
ACURA TREE DOT
SANANDREASFAULT
SST OUST ODEON
THOM RES   GRE
   IRES DESPOTS
SHALOM ROTATION
CAPTAINHOOK LAI
ONEIN BERNE EDD
TAXES CASES DYE
```

349

```
DAR AERIE AMIGA
EXE STAND DENOM
POSTHASTE JAFFA
OLAN LEONA   LON
SOLTI   WILDCARD
ETE NSA CARAMIA
RLS ATMO BERETS
   CHAINMAIL
FAIRER TOMS AND
ALMAATA MAE BOO
STAMPEDE ROOMS
TOR RUBES ALIA
COEDS LETTERING
ANTIS TRUER SEE
RASTA STIRS HES
```

350

```
SOOT FARAD STEM
AGRA RICCI TERI
CHAPTERTEA EATS
RATERS STRAFES
AMERICAS REMO
   GONERIL RAT
DATE TEABYFOUR
OXEN ELSIE INRI
TEATIMERS BEAM
ELF TUREENS
   OREL DRAWBACK
FIREMAN PAELLA
ANTS TEATONECAR
TREE ETHEL COIL
SEAT SHARI HAMS
```

351

```
AMOS BABAS SELA
LISI OVERT PRIG
ASHE BARNEYFIFE
SCARAB GORE KEN
   RUY ELGART
BRIANPICCOLO
EAR TIMOR SOAPS
ETAL NAMES NERO
SENOR MEETS ROB
   WHISTLESTOPS
CURSOR   AGA
UNO DIRE MTHOOD
FLUTEDEDGE IRMA
FIGS INNER TEED
STEP COALS IONS
```

352

```
APEG BLOW GLATT
NOLO RICO PIQUE
DOLLARSTODONUTS
CRAFT TIDE EAST
   LIPS LABS
SPRITE CARR OBS
OLAN PLAN ASSET
HECKLEANDJECKLE
OBESE DOSE AAAA
TED CHIN DARRYL
   RHUE RICE
AHAH RSTU DCLIII
SOCIALDEMOCRATS
PLANE AMOR OUZO
SENOR YARD WEAR
```

353

```
SPAT ASH  SALON
ELLE NEAT PROLE
COLE SALE ARNIE
TWODOWNONETOGO
SSW REC   DREW
   STRESSES IRA
SARAH ETC  IDOL
IHAVENTGOTACLUE
TORE ORE  MEETS
EYE STARTLED
   SHIV RON DIE
PUTINAGOODWORD
CANON IRIS ALEG
ALIVE LAKE LONE
METES BAN  TRES
```

354

```
MASS BART APRES
OVEN OMER TAEGU
BEVERLYHILLSCOP
BREVES   ATEASE
ENRAPT BEAN ISA
DOE REO STUPID
   BORNINEASTLA
OMOO EVE  ESTH
DOCHOLLYWOOD
DEARME TRU  TOR
STR EGAL ATHOME
IOLITE CRIMEA
SUNSETBOULEVARD
ENACT ANNE ETTE
PESOS TEAS SOAR
```

355

```
DAMPS RAFT SWAB
EDICT EROO AURA
POSTOFFICE KNEE
TRE PILES CEDAR
HEROINE   LOOSE
   STICKERS RED
DANA STA STABLE
EVOKE SRA STALE
SERACS ELO ARES
IRT RODLAVER
   HOUSE BOVINES
PAPAS PEALE EVA
ALOT COMMONRAIL
SOLE ASIA TOTAL
SEER DERN STONY
```

356

```
OPALS SACK KATE
RELIT ONOR ELAL
GETSOFFTHETRACK
SKILLET EBONITE
   EARN RST
THIS ESE  ABAR
HEM LISP MALONE
EXPRESSOPINIONS
TEEHEE ORLY NEO
ARLO TKO  SEED
   UTE BABE
SAFFRON ASOCIAL
TRAINSOFTHOUGHT
ARID ERIE BROAD
BARE ESTD SETHS
```

357

```
MAAM MASC BEDS
UCLA PINTO AQUA
STUN ASKER TUTU
MOUNTAINCHAIN
BAIRNS NBA  TEA
ANN CYAN ACCESS
HAUL RIALTO
   MISSINGLINK
SEEDER   SHAM
BEHAVE SALT OWE
ERE ESS  ENAMEL
WASONTHEFENCE
ASTA OATER HIFI
REEK IRONY ENOS
ERRS TEND DIET
```

358

```
SOIT JAVA BOPS
AUDI FIFES TRAP
TRAFALGARSQUARE
   FLAGRANT COW
SETSAIL   SELLS
HIE LEECH  VEE
ERRED   ADOBE
BERMUDATRIANGLE
   PHASE STAIN
CST MANET  SKI
TOKYO   LOATHED
ENA EASTERLY
ANTARCTICCIRCLE
SEEN TENTH OPEN
EDDY SPAS LAOS
```

359

```
WORN SHANE JOAN
ABIE RUBON AXLE
GOOUTOFBUSINESS
SETTO FAGIN NOT
   ERA ALOE
CHURCHATTENDERS
HIM HERR  AVOW
ORBS MAIZE MIRA
MERE COAL  TEM
PRACTICEORIGAMI
   TACO PLO
TVS MIDST AETNA
RECIPEDIRECTION
IRAQ SLAIN HERD
MARS TEMPE ERMA
```

360

```
COPS ABCDE STEP
OVAL HERES NORA
ROUE STANTHEMAN
ELLEN   TISSUE
DITTYBAG   ARCED
   SELES OSCEOLA
FEODOR USE ROSY
ANN NEPTUNE PIA
INGA FOE SPLEEN
TEAPOTS   BOOER
HASPS MERCHANT
   ASKFOR HATER
LIBRARIANS VILA
EDIE UNTIL ROLL
TOOL KESEY ENYA
```

361

```
HONS  ASIF  ITEMS
ERIC  LENA  MIXES
RITE  TACK  BETTE
DOWNTOTHEWIRE
ELITE   DAB   RAF
DET  MOCK  SEANCE
     APRONS  RARE
EMOTIONALOUTLET
RAVI   SCOOTS
SKETCH  KEPT  SHA
EER   LAS   ETHIC
  STAYEDCURRENT
TRIOS  WARP  ERGO
OOZES  EROS  APER
NEEDY  DEWY  DADS
```

362

```
BELT  RISER  ASPS
ARIA  UNCLE  MULE
BASKETCASE  EPEE
ASTER  ARID  LEAK
RESORT   YESSIR
   USED   HABIT
DUCT  NUANCE  ODE
ICH  COPIERS  WEE
ALE  ORELSE  CLAN
LASTS    TACO
  TATTLE  MOLEST
ARCS  HALF  BLAKE
ROOT  RIVERBASIN
IDLE  ONETO  GELS
ZEDS  BESET  ELLE
```

363

```
LECH  SEWUP  DOBY
OCHO  TRINI  IDEA
SLAB  ONTOP  SOAK
EARN  NOH  ICARUS
STOOGE   OATHS
  BIDSUP  UTICA
POT  GETTINGEVEN
AMID  AUFEU  REND
SIDEEFFECTS  STY
STYLI   FAERIE
ANGST   IMPUGN
ANSWER  HEE  INRO
COLA  OCEAN  LION
EVER  WORST  OOZE
SADE  NOSES  GNAT
```

364

```
IANS  TAPED  RAFT
OTOE  ORATE  ERIE
WORLDWITHOUTEND
AZALEA     ROADS
   ERDE  EGO
LABORDAYWEEKEND
ELATE  MEALS  MOR
MAYO  TALUS  SILO
AMO  PATES  ADLAI
YOUVEGOTAFRIEND
   EDS  SUIT
SEDER     CIUDAD
UPAROUNDTHEBEND
RENE  AEIOU  ELIA
FEED  RENTS  RELY
```

365

```
ABLE  APPLE  RITZ
VAIN  CLEAN  ACHE
ITSSOEASYTOMEET
SHAUN  TOSEA  DNA
ESE    ORSO
ENC  EXPENSESYOU
AERATION   SCUPS
THOU  TEARS  AREA
ERODE   CATERING
RUNINTOTHEM  SSE
TERR     WIL
JOB  MAPLE  LOGOS
EVERYWHEREYOUGO
FATE  LAVIE  FARO
FLEX  SNICK  AMEN
```

366

```
ABOMB  ASIA  AGOG
TAUPE  COLD  MIME
ONTHEWHOLE  OVAL
MDS  LION  QUEENS
  TITO  JUMBO
SIMONS  TEAPARTY
CNOTE  MASTS  TIE
AFRO  VERSE  MAMA
LEE  DEERE  CAKES
PROPERTY  PRIEST
  RIFTS  LOUD
PILATE  NINE  GOP
EDEN  BYANDLARGE
ALSO  RAZE  EXILE
TESS  AKIN  REPEL
```

367

```
TABS  TAPIR  BARD
UBET  ABATE  ERIE
BOLA  TARAS  ELLE
BULLFIDDLE  FOLD
STYLI    OAFS
  SLIMS  LATVIA
ATA  EMAIL  NEONS
BALONEYSANDWICH
CLARA  SAMBA  DAY
SCRAMS   LEANT
NEAT    GRUMP
SLUG  BUNKHOUSES
TAXI  ELENA  MESA
AVON  RIVER  PUTT
BARA  SPEED  SPAS
```

368

```
CARE  ZAPPA  LILI
ABAD  ARIES  INON
NEWS  PINTO  ACCT
ATHENS   GUNSMOKE
STILT  LEE  LON
TED  HYENA  ALOUD
ADE  ETO  STARTS
   SUGARFOOT
RISING  MAR  BBS
AMEND  PASTA  ORE
MER  EPA  BENET
MAVERICK  TENANT
ENID  TINGE  ANNE
RICE  CNOTE  CZAR
STER  HOBOS  TANS
```

369

```
CASS  STUD  INFIX
ADAM  TORI  NOONE
TOTE  APIA  CROCS
CRUELLESTMONTH
HER  ILK  RAG  WOO
YENTL  ACID  FEAR
OAK  ABC  LATE
FIERCECREATURES
ANNS  EAT  PAT
INTO  PEER  XENON
LOW  WTS  OPE  ELO
VICIOUSCIRCLES
RANON  RAKE  ALVA
STEED  ALOT  RIEL
TEDDY  ETNA  PELE
```

370

```
CONS  CPAS  CHAKA
OFIT  OUST  LEMON
POOR  MISOGAMIST
SUBURBS   PARI
ARETHINGSTOCOME
ONEROUS   MEL
BLONDE  ANN  BETA
AERIE  SPA  BEGAT
MANX  ETH  REGALE
BRO  STRIDER
INTOTHECITYFROM
IRAN   VILLAGE
ROLLINGPIN  ANDA
AWEEK  TINA  SEEN
GLIDE  HEEL  KENT
```

371

```
AHOY  SWAN   ZAP
MOVE  MARIS  PALE
PRESSAGENT  ISLE
SAN  PRES  ANNUAL
  SETS  CROC
SASHAY  HOTSHOTS
CLERK  DOPE  PROW
RAVI  PAPER  ETRE
AMEN  OVID  GNOME
PORKLOIN  BONNET
  WORD  GAMY
GEORGE  PERE  ODE
ALMA  SQUEEZEBOX
WEEP  TUSKS  NOWI
KEN  ASST  DENT
```

372

```
SHOW  MAME  COBRA
TUNA  AWAY  URIEL
ALIT  YALE  RANGE
RANCHDRESSING
   HEAD   COG
TAWDRY  BRA  SEWN
IDIOM  SLIMS  VIA
LODGEACOMPLAINT
ERE  SPANS  ENACT
DENS  AND  JITNEY
CAR  MAGI
COTTAGECHEESE
ATOLL  LEEK  TIER
PANDA  PASA  AREA
TRESS  OREL  MESS
```

373

```
ETAS  MESS  ELECT
GASP  ONUP  HAVRE
GREATDEPRESSION
STARR  PEW  TOE
KID  LEEGRANT
BUGSPRAY   SAO
UNI  ELAM  INANE
DIVISIONOFLABOR
STEAL  EDNA  EEL
GAM  DANIELLE
RENOVATE   SSR
ANO  RAM  ERASE
INTERCHANGEABLE
DUETO  ONEA  NEER
SISSY  EDDY  DEWY
```

374

```
ABCS  ABE  FRESCA
NAHA  DEL  RETOOK
DRIFTERS  ETALII
SANER  GALESTORM
CROC   SUZI
RAH  TOW  MINDSET
IDI  SLAT  NAILER
TALL  DRANG  GURU
APLOMB  MOOT  SIM
STABILE  RUR  HEP
COLA   TURF
POLAROIDS  NEURO
ISOPOD  HANKSNOW
PHOEBE  ORE  IDOL
SASSED  CAT  TSKS
```

375

```
PEONS  SPOOR  DAB
ELATE  HEIDI  EGO
IFTHEWORLDS  ARA
TEEM   IDLER
LOATHES  DEBITED
ENDUED   CELLS
MEIR  YOUROYSTER
ATEN  LGE  ERMA
YOUCANMAKE  VAIL
ORNOT   NEEDLE
SQUARES  ADDRESS
HASTE   ALOU
ETA  ALOTOFCLAMS
BAG  RENEE  EERIE
ARE  SEEMS  SAMOA
```

376

```
DANA  CEDAR  AFAR
ORES  ADAGE  POPE
FISHINGROD  POSE
FAS  MIEN  DIETED
  SAND  LEGAL
VOYAGE  HONORING
OVATE  RISER  GOA
TIRE  CAKED  THEM
END  GONER  TITLE
DEMURRER  DRESSY
ANISE  BAUD
PESETA  MAIL  ADS
ETTA  GRANNYKNOT
ONES  ECLAT  OKRA
NARY  SALLY  AHAB
```

377

```
FANS  TSAR  DAUBS
OPAL  ITNO  IGLOO
ORSO  MANA  SNEAD
LITTLEIODINE
SLY  ATRY  NEWMAN
SNOW  STY  ONO
ALCOA  ECHO  ANTS
WEEWILLIEWINKIE
ANDS  ELIE  MESSY
ITE  WAS  THAW
TOSSES  SMOG  ASK
PEEWEEHERMAN
DEREK  OPTO  UPTO
ATALL  UTAH  SLOW
MANLY  KILO  HENS
```

378

```
SPF  MISDO  ASCOT
WAR  ESKER  SHULA
AGE  THINGAMAJIG
MAUREEN   AMAZON
INDOOR   INTRA
  AREAS  RAMBLE
TUTSI  RHEA  IAN
WHATCHAMACALLIT
IUM  ALAR  WALDO
THEJOB   ELMAN
UDALL   AKITAS
BUSONI  PLENARY
CONTRAPTION  NIL
OLDIE  IRENE  ESP
BLOND  DARED  YEH
```

379

```
CABS  BOROS  PAAR
AREA  IHEAR  OGRE
FRANZKAFKA  LAIN
EAT  AERO  ILIAD
SUSANSARANDON
DRY   MLIII
PLOT  CASINO  MAD
RAW  PAR  NET  USE
OWN  ORATES  ASAP
GLOBE   BIC
KELLYMCGILLIS
ABETS  POET  EDO
LEES  PAULNEWMAN
MENU  FORTE  HAHA
STEP  CLASS  ONOR
```

380

```
LASHER  ATALANTA
INCOME  BOLIVIAN
ONETOUCHOFVENUS
NENE  PROD  ENTRE
EXALT  ERLE  SHUL
SIR  ITE  EAP  SSS
SNIDER   HORAS
GODDESSOFLOVE
TIBET   UPTIME
TRI  NET  BLU  TUX
HEMA  KATO  SCALP
EVADE  PATE  ALAR
MIGHTYAPHRODITE
ELEONORA  MAIZES
DESCANTS  ASSESS
```

381

R	A	P	T	■	H	E	R	O	D	■	R	A	F	T
U	S	E	R	■	O	L	I	V	E	■	U	L	A	N
N	O	R	A	■	S	E	V	E	N	■	P	I	T	T
F	I	N	N	E	G	A	N	S	W	A	K	E	■	■
■	■	■	Q	U	A	Y	■	■	H	U	E	D	■	■
K	A	P	U	T	■	■	C	I	V	I	L	■	■	■
E	S	A	I	■	A	V	A	T	A	R	■	W	E	E
G	I	L	L	I	G	A	N	S	I	S	L	A	N	D
S	A	M	■	V	E	S	T	A	L	■	A	D	O	G
■	■	■	H	A	D	T	O	■	■	O	B	E	S	E
■	■	S	O	O	N	■	■	C	A	R	R	■	■	■
■	■	M	C	N	A	M	A	R	A	S	B	A	N	D
R	I	T	E	■	A	L	I	B	I	■	D	E	E	P
A	L	E	S	■	T	E	P	I	D	■	O	M	A	R
J	E	T	T	■	S	C	E	N	E	■	R	O	R	Y

382

A	Q	A	B	A	■	B	I	C	S	■	S	H	O	P
L	U	N	A	S	■	A	C	H	E	■	H	A	L	O
L	I	N	T	S	C	R	E	E	N	■	O	L	D	S
■	■	H	E	A	D	S	F	O	R	■	■	L	I	E
R	E	S	E	T	S	■	■	R	A	M	M	E	D	■
E	L	K	S	■	T	E	S	S	■	G	E	O	■	■
A	L	E	■	G	E	N	I	I	■	T	O	N	E	R
M	I	L	E	R	■	A	L	T	■	A	N	I	M	A
S	E	E	T	O	■	C	L	A	N	G	■	T	E	T
■	■	T	A	P	■	T	Y	R	O	■	S	O	N	S
C	H	O	L	E	R	■	■	H	A	I	R	D	O	■
I	A	N	■	D	A	Y	S	H	I	F	T	■	■	■
N	I	K	E	■	P	O	T	A	T	O	C	H	I	P
C	L	E	M	■	I	R	A	N	■	R	O	U	T	E
H	E	Y	S	■	D	E	B	S	■	E	M	B	E	R

383

U	S	M	A	■	S	H	E	A	■	S	C	R	U	B
H	O	O	D	■	P	I	L	L	■	O	H	A	R	A
F	A	R	R	■	O	G	L	E	■	L	U	N	G	S
■	K	E	E	P	T	H	E	C	H	A	N	G	E	■
■	■	■	N	U	T	S	■	■	A	R	K	■	■	■
M	E	A	L	Y	■	C	Y	D	■	W	E	D	■	■
G	I	R	L	S	■	B	O	O	T	■	B	A	L	E
A	N	N	I	E	G	E	T	Y	O	U	R	G	U	N
G	O	I	N	■	U	N	T	O	■	S	E	E	D	Y
A	R	E	■	E	T	A	■	C	H	A	S	E	■	■
■	■	■	A	S	S	■	■	T	R	E	K	■	■	■
■	S	T	E	P	T	O	T	H	E	R	E	A	R	■
T	E	R	S	E	■	B	R	E	D	■	V	I	E	W
O	N	I	O	N	■	J	E	D	I	■	E	D	N	A
A	D	O	P	T	■	S	E	A	T	■	N	E	T	S

384

G	I	L	T	■	A	S	T	I	R	■	I	B	E	T
O	D	O	R	■	S	E	I	N	E	■	R	E	D	O
L	I	R	A	■	H	A	L	V	E	■	E	R	G	O
F	O	R	D	E	E	R	L	I	F	E	■	N	E	T
S	T	E	E	L	■	■	S	T	E	A	M	S	■	■
■	■	■	■	G	A	S	■	■	E	R	R	A	T	A
A	S	S	A	I	L	E	R	■	■	T	E	L	E	■
B	E	A	R	N	E	C	E	S	S	I	T	I	E	S
■	C	A	N	E	■	■	V	I	O	L	E	N	C	E
■	■	L	I	N	D	E	N	■	■	T	W	O	■	■
■	■	T	O	U	R	E	D	■	■	S	P	R	E	E
A	L	I	■	B	O	A	R	T	O	T	E	A	R	S
G	A	Z	A	■	D	R	I	E	R	■	T	W	A	S
E	V	E	N	■	E	A	V	E	S	■	E	L	S	E
E	A	S	Y	■	S	T	E	N	O	■	R	Y	E	S

385

M	I	S	S	T	E	P	■	D	O	L	L	S	U	P
A	S	T	A	I	R	E	■	E	X	A	M	I	N	E
C	A	P	O	R	A	L	■	P	E	N	A	N	C	E
A	D	E	N	O	■	L	L	O	Y	D	■	C	O	P
D	O	T	E	■	E	M	O	T	E	■	R	E	V	E
A	R	E	■	B	L	E	S	S	■	B	A	R	E	R
M	A	R	C	E	L	L	A	■	F	E	V	E	R	S
■	■	■	S	T	I	L	L	L	I	F	E	■	■	■
S	L	O	P	E	S	■	A	L	L	I	N	O	N	E
C	O	R	A	L	■	S	M	A	L	T	■	R	E	Y
O	R	A	N	■	L	O	O	N	Y	■	A	N	G	E
T	E	N	■	D	U	L	S	E	■	A	D	E	A	L
E	L	G	R	E	C	O	■	L	A	N	O	T	T	E
R	E	E	L	S	I	N	■	L	A	E	R	T	E	S
S	I	S	S	I	E	S	■	Y	A	W	N	E	R	S

386

C	R	A	M	■	C	E	D	A	R	■	S	C	A	M
R	O	V	E	■	I	R	A	T	E	■	O	O	P	S
A	G	A	R	■	N	O	M	A	D	■	U	K	E	S
B	U	S	I	N	E	S	S	L	E	T	T	E	R	■
S	E	T	T	E	R	■	■	L	A	S	H	■	■	■
■	■	■	S	T	A	M	P	■	L	A	P	S	E	S
A	N	E	■	M	A	R	S	■	R	A	T	I	O	■
T	A	K	E	S	A	T	O	N	E	S	W	O	R	D
■	O	N	E	T	O	■	A	S	A	N	■	P	E	A
M	U	S	C	L	E	■	E	G	G	O	N	■	■	■
■	■	■	H	O	R	A	■	I	C	E	S	U	P	■
■	P	R	I	S	O	N	S	E	N	T	E	N	C	E
A	L	A	N	■	T	I	L	D	E	■	D	O	O	R
S	A	N	G	■	I	M	A	G	E	■	E	R	N	O
I	N	K	S	■	C	A	P	E	R	■	D	E	N	T

387

E	D	A	M	■	J	E	D	I	■	W	H	E	L	P
L	I	M	A	■	E	X	A	M	■	R	A	D	I	O
H	O	O	K	E	D	O	N	P	H	O	N	I	C	S
I	N	R	E	M	■	G	R	I	T	■	N	I	T	■
■	■	■	M	A	S	K	■	O	V	E	R	A	T	E
■	L	I	N	E	I	T	E	M	V	E	T	O	■	■
A	B	A	■	L	O	N	E	■	O	O	Z	E	S	■
M	A	R	L	■	W	O	L	F	E	■	K	I	L	L
I	■	P	R	Y	O	R	■	T	E	N	S	■	T	I	E
■	■	W	O	R	M	S	E	Y	E	V	I	E	W	■
L	O	R	E	L	E	I	■	D	A	T	A	■	■	■
A	M	I	■	A	I	D	S	■	I	N	A	N	E	■
C	A	S	T	I	N	G	O	U	T	N	I	N	E	S
K	N	E	A	D	■	E	L	M	O	■	S	N	A	P
S	I	N	U	S	■	T	O	A	T	■	H	O	R	N

388

C	E	E	S	■	H	A	D	T	O	■	D	I	G
C	O	B	R	A	■	O	M	A	H	A	■	O	F	A
T	H	E	S	U	L	T	A	N	O	F	S	W	A	P
S	O	N	A	T	A	■	T	E	M	■	A	N	T	E
■	■	■	T	E	C	S	■	■	S	A	S	H	■	■
R	I	T	Z	■	T	I	S	■	S	P	A	D	E	S
I	S	O	■	T	I	T	H	E	■	A	R	E	N	T
N	Y	S	T	O	C	K	E	X	C	H	A	N	G	E
D	E	C	O	Y	■	A	L	C	A	N	■	T	E	E
S	T	A	M	E	N	■	L	O	M	■	D	E	L	L
■	■	■	A	D	E	S	■	■	P	E	T	E	■	■
W	A	F	T	■	T	A	N	■	R	E	P	A	S	T
A	T	O	O	T	H	F	O	R	A	T	O	O	T	H
D	I	X	■	S	E	E	T	O	■	E	R	N	I	E
S	P	Y	■	E	R	R	E	D	■	S	T	E	R

389

■	S	A	N	K	■	W	P	M	■	M	O	M	M	A
L	E	V	E	E	■	A	L	A	■	A	L	E	A	P
O	V	E	R	E	A	T	E	R	■	R	E	T	R	O
V	E	R	O	N	I	C	A	L	O	D	G	E	■	■
E	R	S	■	E	T	H	■	E	P	I	S	O	D	E
R	E	E	F	■	D	I	E	T	■	R	A	Y	■	■
■	■	■	A	B	H	O	R	■	I	M	F	I	N	E
■	S	C	R	O	O	G	E	M	C	D	U	C	K	■
P	A	R	E	N	T	■	N	A	S	A	L	■	■	■
A	G	O	■	B	T	E	N	■	L	I	L	I	■	■
T	A	W	N	I	E	R	■	I	C	E	■	N	I	T
■	■	D	A	D	D	Y	W	A	R	B	U	C	K	S
A	K	I	T	A	■	S	O	C	I	E	T	I	E	S
D	I	N	A	H	■	T	R	A	■	R	A	T	S	O
A	N	G	L	O	■	S	N	L	■	T	H	E	O	■

390

R	E	V	■	P	R	I	C	E	■	D	U	P	E	D
O	L	A	■	R	A	M	O	N	■	E	T	A	G	E
P	E	P	P	E	R	P	O	T	■	C	O	N	A	N
E	V	O	L	V	E	S	■	J	A	P	A	N	S	■
S	E	R	I	A	L	■	P	R	E	L	I	M	■	■
■	■	E	L	Y	S	E	E	S	■	A	A	R	E	■
L	A	P	S	E	■	P	I	N	U	P	S	H	O	T
O	U	R	■	N	F	L	■	A	S	E	■	A	V	A
P	R	E	T	T	I	E	S	T	■	R	A	T	E	S
■	E	A	S	E	■	R	E	P	A	S	T	S	■	■
■	C	R	A	N	N	Y	■	P	I	S	A	N	O	■
S	P	I	E	L	S	■	B	E	N	A	T	A	R	■
A	R	E	N	T	■	P	R	E	C	E	D	E	N	T
F	E	N	C	E	■	B	E	N	I	N	■	A	N	O
E	S	T	E	R	■	A	S	S	E	T	■	M	A	N

391

B	U	Z	Z	■	A	H	S	■	M	O	V	I	E	S
E	P	E	E	■	M	A	I	■	O	R	I	O	L	E
R	O	S	E	B	O	W	L	■	B	O	R	N	I	N
T	N	T	■	B	R	A	E	■	■	T	I	T	O	■
■	■	■	F	L	Y	I	N	G	S	A	U	C	E	R
A	X	E	L	■	■	I	C	I	C	L	E	■	■	■
M	O	R	A	L	E	■	E	L	A	L	■	E	E	S
B	U	R	B	A	N	K	■	D	R	I	P	D	R	Y
I	T	S	■	H	E	E	D	■	F	E	I	G	N	S
■	■	■	S	T	R	E	E	P	■	N	Y	E	T	■
F	A	S	H	I	O	N	P	L	A	T	E	■	■	■
A	L	T	O	■	■	O	A	R	S	■	D	J	S	■
C	A	R	O	M	S	■	R	Y	D	E	R	C	U	P
E	M	A	I	L	S	■	T	A	O	■	Y	O	D	A
T	O	W	N	I	E	■	S	T	R	■	E	N	D	S

392

M	O	J	O	■	F	I	D	O	■	■	F	F	F
A	V	E	R	■	I	N	E	R	T	■	B	O	I	L
M	A	R	B	L	E	C	A	K	E	■	O	G	L	E
E	L	K	■	O	N	A	N	■	A	M	U	S	E	D
■	■	■	R	I	D	S	■	■	A	B	E	L	■	■
F	A	V	O	R	S	■	B	R	A	N	D	I	S	H
A	L	I	C	E	■	H	A	I	G	■	E	D	N	A
N	E	C	K	■	H	I	K	E	S	■	R	I	O	T
G	R	A	B	■	O	D	E	S	■	A	D	O	R	E
S	T	R	O	N	G	E	R	■	P	L	A	T	E	D
■	■	■	T	O	W	S	■	■	P	A	L	M	■	■
M	A	N	T	R	A	■	D	A	T	A	■	K	O	S
O	L	E	O	■	S	T	O	N	E	H	E	N	G	E
S	T	E	M	■	H	A	V	E	N	■	G	O	R	E
H	O	D	■	■	B	E	L	T	■	■	O	W	E	D

393

D	A	S	H	■	E	L	S	A	■	I	S	A	K
O	S	H	A	■	S	T	E	A	D	■	R	O	V	E
S	T	A	G	E	C	O	A	C	H	■	O	L	I	N
E	E	K	■	M	A	N	N	■	E	R	N	E	S	T
D	R	O	V	E	R	■	S	E	R	A	C	■	■	■
■	■	■	O	R	E	G	■	R	E	F	U	G	E	E
N	E	W	L	Y	■	E	A	R	N	■	R	E	E	L
E	R	A	S	■	L	I	M	I	T	■	T	A	R	A
A	L	I	T	■	A	S	S	N	■	A	A	R	O	N
R	E	T	E	A	C	H	■	G	O	B	I	■	■	■
■	■	■	A	R	R	A	S	■	V	E	N	I	C	E
S	T	U	D	I	O	■	H	E	A	T	■	M	A	N
P	A	P	A	■	S	P	O	R	T	S	C	A	S	T
A	C	D	C	■	S	I	N	G	E	■	A	G	E	R
R	O	O	T	■	E	T	E	S	■	M	E	D	E

394

L	I	S	P	■	D	E	L	L	A	■	R	A	I	N
A	C	H	E	■	I	N	E	E	D	■	E	L	S	E
C	A	R	E	L	E	S	S	W	H	I	S	P	E	R
E	M	E	R	I	T	U	S	■	E	R	A	S	E	D
D	E	W	■	A	R	E	■	G	R	I	T	■	■	■
■	■	■	T	R	I	■	D	E	E	S	■	A	F	T
S	O	A	R	■	C	A	E	N	■	E	E	R	I	E
T	H	O	U	G	H	T	L	E	S	S	N	E	S	S
I	N	N	E	R	■	L	A	S	H	■	C	A	T	S
R	O	E	■	O	D	A	Y	■	O	L	E	■	■	■
■	■	■	A	V	O	W	■	A	W	E	■	S	H	E
A	R	I	S	E	N	■	E	L	E	V	A	T	E	D
R	E	C	K	L	E	S	S	D	R	I	V	I	N	G
A	B	E	E	■	E	S	T	E	E	■	I	L	I	E
B	A	R	D	■	S	T	A	N	D	■	S	T	E	R

395

C	A	M	P	■	T	R	E	S	S	■	S	C	A	T
O	M	A	R	■	H	A	B	I	T	■	A	O	N	E
L	A	K	E	S	O	U	R	C	E	■	M	I	N	E
T	H	E	M	E	■	L	O	K	I	■	U	L	A	N
■	■	■	I	R	S	■	■	E	N	E	R	O	■	■
O	N	E	S	E	A	S	O	N	■	G	A	F	F	S
S	O	L	E	■	L	A	M	■	T	A	I	W	A	N
A	L	A	■	P	A	Y	B	A	I	L	■	I	N	E
G	A	S	P	E	D	■	R	A	P	■	S	R	T	A
E	N	T	E	R	■	L	E	A	P	A	H	E	A	D
■	■	■	I	N	T	R	O	■	■	I	R	A	■	■
P	A	C	A	■	O	U	R	S	■	A	D	A	G	E
A	M	I	N	■	S	N	A	P	C	L	O	S	E	D
R	O	T	C	■	E	G	R	E	T	■	W	I	N	G
S	K	Y	E	■	S	E	E	D	S	■	S	A	T	E

396

K	E	W	■	A	B	L	E	R	■	P	E	C	O	S
O	R	R	■	B	R	A	G	A	■	E	X	A	C	T
A	R	E	■	H	A	N	O	I	■	R	E	S	T	S
L	O	S	T	O	N	E	S	S	H	I	R	T	■	■
A	L	T	A	R	■	■	E	A	S	T	■	■	■	■
■	■	B	R	E	A	K	S	T	H	E	T	I	E	■
S	P	A	■	E	R	I	N	■	■	D	U	C	K	■
L	O	X	■	D	E	L	I	G	H	T	■	B	E	E
O	P	E	C	■	■	F	A	R	E	■	A	D	S	■
■	B	E	L	O	W	T	H	E	B	E	L	T	■	■
■	■	■	■	T	H	A	I	■	■	E	R	A	S	E
■	W	E	A	R	S	T	H	E	P	A	N	T	S	■
W	H	I	R	L	■	S	E	E	N	O	■	G	A	S
E	E	R	I	E	■	E	R	R	O	R	■	E	V	E
T	R	E	E	S	■	D	I	D	S	T	■	R	E	X

397

T	H	E	I	R	■	M	A	M	A	■	S	A	N	K
H	O	R	N	E	■	A	V	I	S	■	E	R	I	E
E	P	I	C	S	■	L	E	N	I	E	N	T	L	Y
■	■	S	C	H	O	O	L	R	I	N	G	S	■	■
■	■	■	U	S	E	S	■	■	G	E	N	T	S	■
S	C	O	R	N	S	■	A	S	S	■	E	A	T	■
A	R	M	E	D	■	E	E	R	O	■	R	A	M	A
P	E	A	L	S	O	F	L	A	U	G	H	T	E	R
P	O	N	Y	■	D	O	L	L	■	R	E	E	S	E
■	E	L	I	■	E	E	R	■	H	E	A	R	T	S
■	R	E	S	E	T	■	■	A	M	E	N	■	■	■
■	■	B	R	I	D	G	E	T	O	L	L	S	■	■
B	A	R	B	E	C	U	E	S	■	B	E	A	C	H
E	P	E	E	■	E	D	N	A	■	L	A	N	A	I
L	O	A	D	■	S	E	T	S	■	E	D	A	M	S

398

S	O	C	K	■	K	A	Y	A	K	■	K	I	L	N
O	D	I	N	■	I	N	O	N	E	■	O	T	O	E
N	O	N	E	■	T	I	L	D	E	■	P	A	V	E
G	R	E	E	N	E	■	K	E	N	N	E	L	E	D
■	■	■	H	O	R	A	■	■	S	E	E	K	■	■
S	I	K	O	R	S	K	Y	■	Y	E	S	S	E	S
N	O	E	L	■	■	R	A	T	E	R	■	T	R	I
A	W	E	E	■	P	O	L	E	S	■	K	A	N	T
C	A	N	■	P	A	N	T	S	■	■	I	L	I	E
K	N	E	E	L	S	■	A	T	T	A	C	K	E	D
■	■	L	E	S	T	■	■	Y	O	R	K	■	■	■
K	A	N	K	A	K	E	E	■	D	E	B	A	T	E
A	B	E	T	■	E	N	D	E	D	■	A	R	A	N
L	E	N	O	■	Y	O	D	E	L	■	C	O	M	O
E	D	E	N	■	S	N	A	K	E	■	K	N	E	W

399

R	A	V	I	■	E	V	E	L	■	S	A	L	A	D
I	N	A	C	L	A	I	R	E	■	P	R	O	B	E
P	O	C	K	E	T	P	R	O	T	E	C	T	O	R
E	X	C	E	S	S	■	N	I	A	■	T	I	E	■
■	■	■	I	S	O	■	C	H	A	L	K	T	A	L	K
H	E	N	■	T	Y	R	A	■	E	S	A	■	■	■
A	R	A	■	H	O	A	D	■	■	T	S	A	R	■
W	I	T	H	O	U	T	A	S	C	R	A	T	C	H
K	N	E	E	■	■	F	O	R	A	■	A	M	Y	■
■	S	S	T	■	I	D	O	L	■	L	E	S	■	■
C	U	E	S	H	E	E	T	S	■	E	T	E	■	■
R	I	G	■	E	S	T	■	A	I	R	M	A	N	■
E	N	G	L	I	S	H	L	A	N	G	U	A	G	E
S	T	O	O	L	■	A	E	S	T	H	E	T	E	S
T	A	N	Y	A	■	N	I	K	E	■	R	E	S	T

400

O	T	B	■	R	E	P	A	S	T	■	I	B	A	R
B	O	Y	■	A	V	A	N	T	I	■	D	R	N	O
I	M	P	■	M	A	K	E	I	T	Q	U	I	C	K
S	C	A	U	P	S	■	■	F	L	U	N	G	■	■
P	A	T	N	A	■	M	E	L	E	E	■	H	B	O
O	T	H	E	R	W	I	S	E	■	U	S	T	E	D
■	■	■	A	T	I	L	T	■	D	E	P	O	S	E
E	N	G	R	■	S	L	I	D	E	■	A	N	T	S
T	O	E	T	A	P	■	V	O	L	A	R	■	■	■
O	A	T	H	S	■	S	A	G	E	B	R	U	S	H
N	A	S	■	I	S	T	L	E	■	A	O	R	T	A
■	■	M	I	A	T	A	■	■	I	N	W	A	R	D
L	E	A	R	N	E	D	H	A	N	D	■	N	O	D
A	C	R	E	■	R	I	A	L	T	O	■	U	P	I
P	O	T	S	■	E	A	S	T	O	N	■	S	S	E

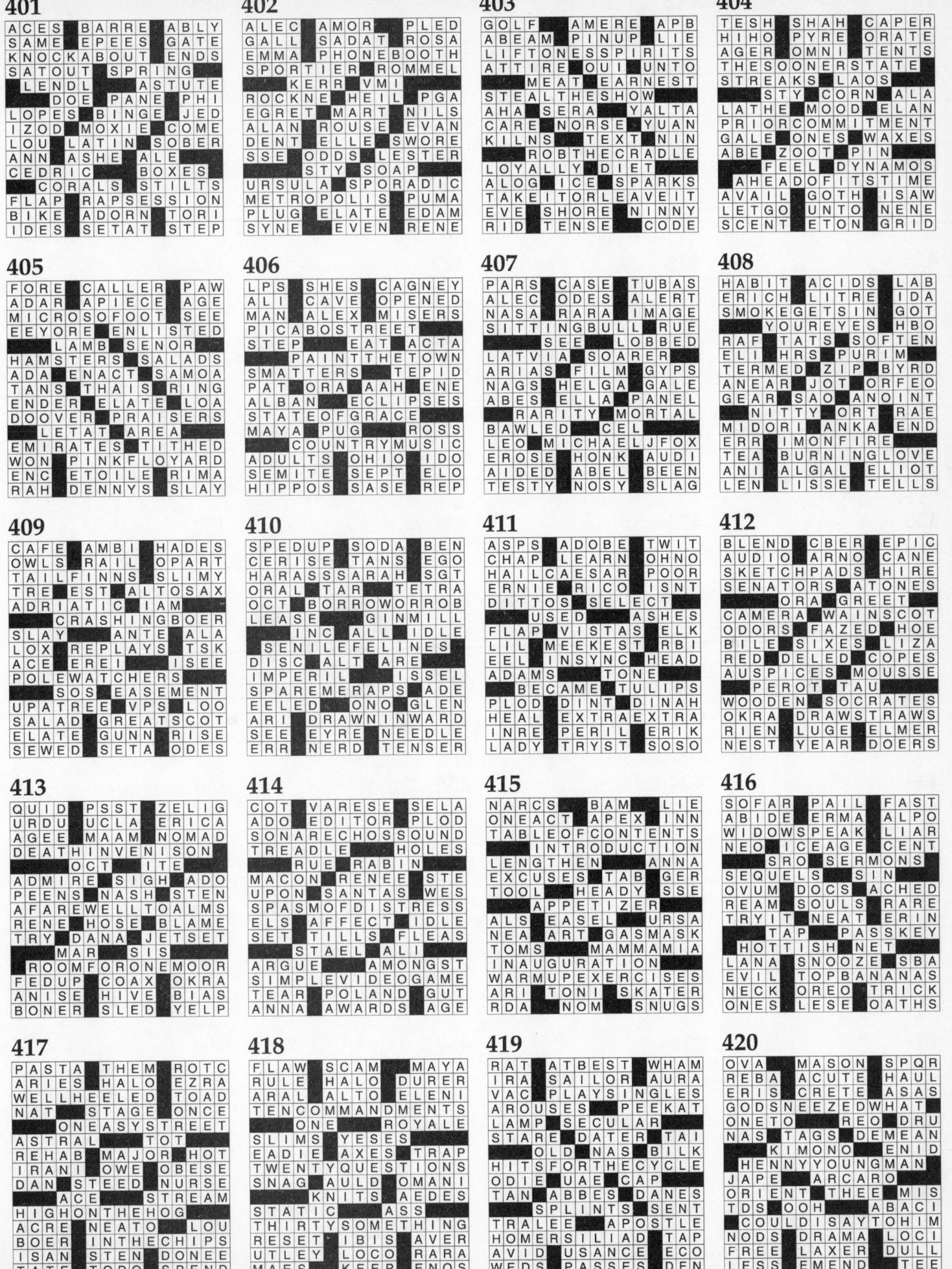

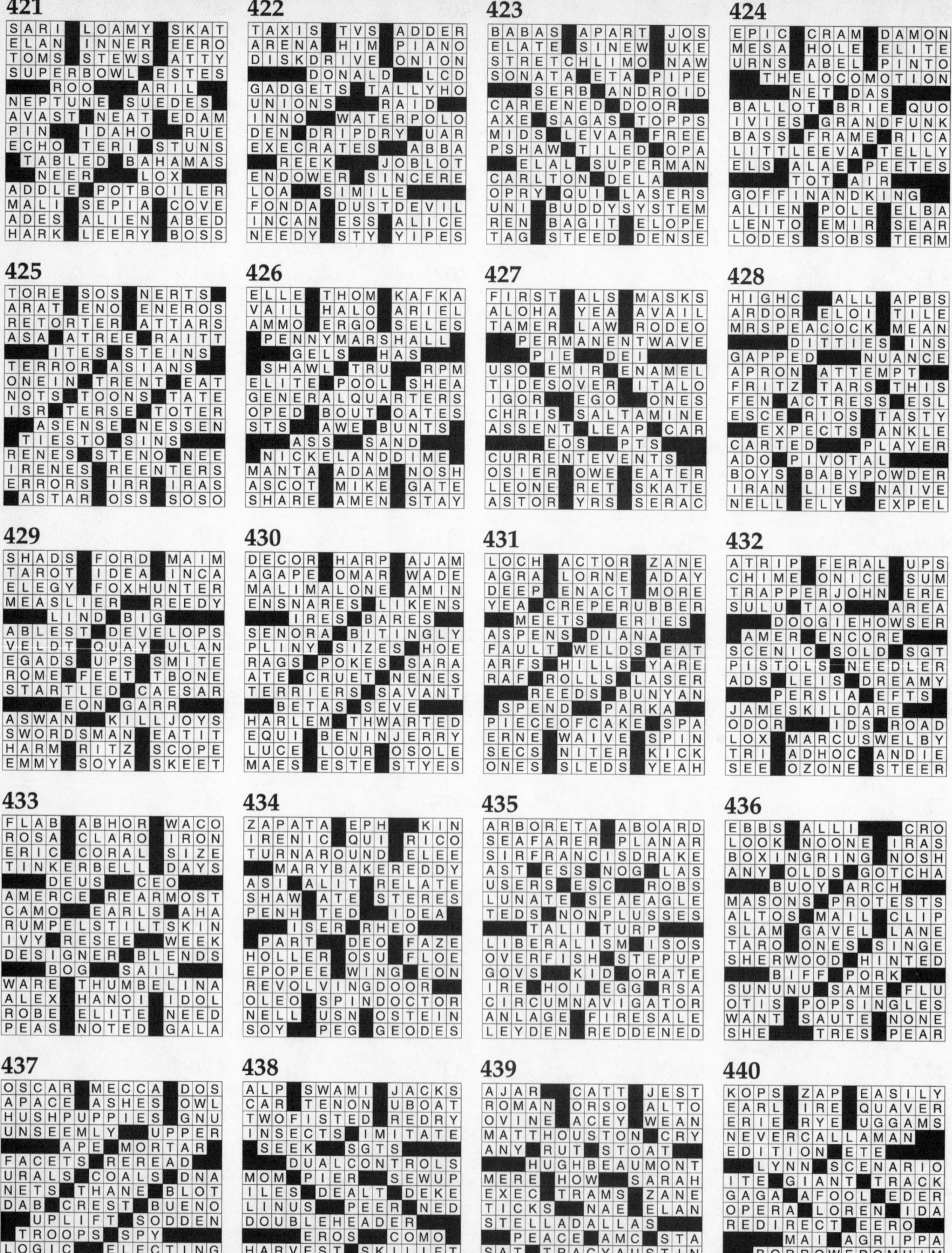

421

S	A	R	I		L	O	A	M	Y		S	K	A	T
E	L	A	N		I	N	N	E	R		E	E	R	O
T	O	M	S		S	T	E	W	S		A	T	T	Y
S	U	P	E	R	B	O	W	L		E	S	T	E	S
			R	O	O			A	R	I	L			
N	E	P	T	U	N	E		S	U	E	D	E	S	
A	V	A	S	T		N	E	A	T		E	D	A	M
P	I	N		I	D	A	H	O		R	U	E		
E	C	H	O		T	E	R	I		S	T	U	N	S
	T	A	B	L	E	D		B	A	H	A	M	A	S
N	E	E	R				L	O	X					
A	D	D	L	E		P	O	T	B	O	I	L	E	R
M	A	L	I		S	E	P	I	A		C	O	V	E
A	D	E	S		A	L	I	E	N		A	B	E	D
H	A	R	K		L	E	E	R	Y		B	O	S	S

422

T	A	X	I	S		T	V	S		A	D	D	E	R
A	R	E	N	A		H	I	M		P	I	A	N	O
D	I	S	K	D	R	I	V	E		O	N	I	O	N
				D	O	N	A	L	D			L	C	D
G	A	D	G	E	T	S		T	A	L	L	Y	H	O
U	N	I	O	N	S				R	A	I	D		
I	N	N	O			W	A	T	E	R	P	O	L	O
D	E	N		D	R	I	P	D	R	Y		U	A	R
E	X	E	C	R	A	T	E	S			A	B	B	A
		R	E	E	K			J	O	B	L	O	T	
E	N	D	O	W	E	R		S	I	N	C	E	R	E
L	O	A			S	I	M	I	L	E				
F	O	N	D	A		D	U	S	T	D	E	V	I	L
I	N	C	A	N		E	S	S		A	L	I	C	E
N	E	E	D	Y		S	T	Y		Y	I	P	E	S

423

B	A	B	A	S		A	P	A	R	T		J	O	S
E	L	A	T	E		S	I	N	E	W		U	K	E
S	T	R	E	T	C	H	L	I	M	O		N	A	W
S	O	N	A	T	A		E	T	A		P	I	P	E
				S	E	R	B		A	N	D	R	O	I	D
C	A	R	E	E	N	E	D			D	O	O	R	
A	X	E		S	A	G	A	S		T	O	P	P	S
M	I	D	S			L	E	V	A	R		F	R	E	E
P	S	H	A	W		T	I	L	E	D		O	P	A
			E	L	A	L		S	U	P	E	R	M	A	N
C	A	R	L	T	O	N			D	E	L	A		
O	P	R	Y		Q	U	I		L	A	S	E	R	S
U	N	I		B	U	D	D	Y	S	Y	S	T	E	M
R	E	N		B	A	G	I	T		E	L	O	P	E
T	A	G		S	T	E	E	D		D	E	N	S	E

424

E	P	I	C		C	R	A	M		D	A	M	O	N
M	E	S	A		H	O	L	E		E	L	I	T	E
U	R	N	S		A	B	E	L		P	I	N	T	O
			T	H	E	L	O	C	O	M	O	T	I	O	N
				N	E	T			D	A	S			
B	A	L	L	O	T		B	R	I	E		Q	U	O
I	V	I	E	S		G	R	A	N	D	F	U	N	K
B	A	S	S		F	R	A	M	E		R	I	C	A
L	I	T	T	L	E	E	V	A		T	E	L	L	Y
E	L	S		A	L	A	E		P	E	E	T	E	S
			T	O	T			A	I	R				
G	O	F	F	I	N	A	N	D	K	I	N	G		
A	L	I	E	N		P	O	L	E		E	L	B	A
L	E	N	T	O		E	M	I	R		S	E	A	R
L	O	D	E	S		S	O	B	S		T	E	R	M

425

T	O	R	E		S	O	S		N	E	R	T	S
A	R	A	T		E	N	O		E	N	E	R	O	S
R	E	T	O	R	T	E	R		A	T	T	A	R	S
A	S	A		A	T	R	E	E		R	A	I	T	T
			I	T	E	S		S	T	E	I	N	S	
T	E	R	R	O	R		A	S	I	A	N	S		
O	N	E	I	N		T	R	E	N	T		E	A	T
N	O	T	S		T	O	O	N	S		T	A	T	E
I	S	R		T	E	R	S	E		T	O	T	E	R
	A	S	E	N	S	E		N	E	S	S	E	N	
T	I	E	S	T	O		S	I	N	S		N	E	E
R	E	N	E	S		S	T	E	N	O		N	E	E
I	R	E	N	E	S		R	E	E	N	T	E	R	S
E	R	R	O	R	S		I	R	R		I	R	A	S
A	S	T	A	R		O	S	S		S	O	S	O	

426

E	L	L	E		T	H	O	M		K	A	F	K	A
V	A	I	L		H	A	L	O		A	R	I	E	L
A	M	M	O		E	R	G	O		S	E	L	E	S
		P	E	N	N	Y	M	A	R	S	H	A	L	L
				G	E	L	S			H	A	S		
S	H	A	W	L			T	R	U			R	P	M
E	L	I	T	E		P	O	O	L		S	H	E	A
G	E	N	E	R	A	L	Q	U	A	R	T	E	R	S
O	P	E	D		B	O	U	T		O	A	T	E	S
	S	T	S		A	W	E		B	U	N	T	S	
				A	S	S		S	A	N	D			
N	I	C	K	E	L	A	N	D	D	I	M	E		
M	A	N	T	A		A	D	A	M		N	O	S	H
A	S	C	O	T		M	I	K	E		G	A	T	E
S	H	A	R	E		A	M	E	N		S	T	A	Y

427

F	I	R	S	T		A	L	S		M	A	S	K	S
A	L	O	H	A		Y	E	A		A	V	A	I	L
T	A	M	E	R		L	A	W		R	O	D	E	O
		P	E	R	M	A	N	E	N	T	W	A	V	E
				P	I	E			D	E	I			
U	S	O		E	M	I	R		E	N	A	M	E	L
T	I	D	E	S	O	V	E	R				I	T	A	L	O
I	G	O	R			E	G	O			O	N	E	S
C	H	R	I	S		S	A	L	T	A	M	I	N	E
A	S	S	E	N	T		L	E	A	P		C	A	R
				E	O	S			P	T	S			
C	U	R	R	E	N	T	E	V	E	N	T	S		
O	S	I	E	R		O	W	E		E	A	T	E	R
L	E	O	N	E		R	E	T		S	K	A	T	E
A	S	T	O	R		Y	R	S			S	E	R	A	C

428

H	I	G	H	C		A	L	L		A	P	B	S
A	R	D	O	R		E	L	O	I		T	I	L	E
M	R	S	P	E	A	C	O	C	K		M	E	A	N
			D	I	T	T	I	E	S			I	N	S
G	A	P	P	E	D			N	U	A	N	C	E	
A	P	R	O	N		A	T	T	E	M	P	T		
F	R	I	T	Z		T	A	R	S		T	H	I	S
F	E	N		A	C	T	R	E	S	S		E	S	L
E	S	C	E		R	I	O	S		T	A	S	T	Y
			E	X	P	E	C	T	S		A	N	K	L	E
C	A	R	T	E	D			P	L	A	Y	E	R	
A	D	O		P	I	V	O	T	A	L				
B	O	Y	S		B	A	B	Y	P	O	W	D	E	R
I	R	A	N		L	I	E	S		N	A	I	V	E
N	E	L	L		E	L	Y		E	X	P	E	L	

429

S	H	A	D	S		F	O	R	D		M	A	I	M
T	A	R	O	T		I	D	E	A		I	N	C	A
E	L	E	G	Y		F	O	X	H	U	N	T	E	R
M	E	A	S	L	I	E	R		R	E	E	D	Y	
			L	I	N	D		B	I	G				
A	B	L	E	S	T		D	E	V	E	L	O	P	S
V	E	L	D	T		Q	U	A	Y		U	L	A	N
E	G	A	D	S		U	P	S		S	M	I	T	E
R	O	M	E		F	E	E	T		T	B	O	N	E
S	T	A	R	T	L	E	D		C	A	E	S	A	R
				E	O	N		G	A	R	R			
A	S	W	A	N		K	I	L	L	J	O	Y	S	
S	W	O	R	D	S	M	A	N		E	A	T	I	T
H	A	R	M		R	I	T	Z		S	C	O	P	E
E	M	M	Y		S	O	Y	A		S	K	E	E	T

430

D	E	C	O	R		H	A	R	P		A	J	A	M
A	G	A	P	E		O	M	A	R		W	A	D	E
M	A	L	I	M	A	L	O	N	E		A	M	I	N
E	N	S	N	A	R	E	S			L	I	K	E	N	S
				I	R	E	S		B	A	R	E	S	
S	E	N	O	R	A		B	I	T	I	N	G	L	Y
P	L	I	N	Y		S	I	Z	E	S		H	O	E
R	A	G	S		P	O	K	E	S		S	A	R	A
A	T	E		C	R	U	E	T		N	E	N	E	S
T	E	R	R	I	E	R	S		S	A	V	A	N	T
			B	E	T	A	S		S	E	V	E		
H	A	R	L	E	M		T	H	W	A	R	T	E	D
E	Q	U	I		B	E	N	I	N	J	E	R	R	Y
L	U	C	E		L	O	U	R		O	S	O	L	E
M	A	E	S		E	S	T	E		S	T	Y	E	S

431

L	O	C	H		A	C	T	O	R		Z	A	N	E
A	G	R	A		L	O	R	N	E		A	D	A	Y
D	E	E	P		E	N	A	C	T		M	O	R	E
Y	E	A		C	R	E	P	E	R	U	B	B	E	R
			M	E	E	T	S		E	R	I	E	S	
A	S	P	E	N	S			D	I	A	N	A		
F	A	U	L	T		W	E	L	D	S		E	A	T
A	R	F	S		H	I	L	L	S		Y	A	R	E
R	A	F		R	O	L	L	S		L	A	S	E	R
			R	E	E	D	S		B	U	N	Y	A	N
S	P	E	N	D		P	A	R	K	A				
P	I	E	C	E	O	F	C	A	K	E		S	P	A
E	R	N	E		W	A	I	V	E		S	P	I	N
S	E	C	S		N	I	T	E	R		K	I	C	K
O	N	E	S		S	L	E	D	S		Y	E	A	H

432

A	T	R	I	P		F	E	R	A	L		U	P	S
C	H	I	M	E		O	N	I	C	E		S	U	M
T	R	A	P	P	E	R	J	O	H	N		E	R	E
S	U	L	U		T	A	O			A	R	E	A	
			D	O	O	G	I	E	H	O	W	S	E	R
A	M	E	R				E	N	C	O	R	E		
S	C	E	N	I	C			S	O	L	D		S	G	T
P	I	S	T	O	L	S		N	E	E	D	L	E	R
A	D	S		L	E	I	S			D	R	E	A	M	Y
			P	E	R	S	I	A			E	F	T	S
J	A	M	E	S	K	I	L	D	A	R	E			
O	D	O	R			I	D	S		R	O	A	D	
L	O	X		M	A	R	C	U	S	W	E	L	B	Y
T	R	I		A	D	H	O	C		A	N	D	I	E
S	E	E		O	Z	O	N	E		S	T	E	E	R

433

F	L	A	B		A	B	H	O	R		W	A	C	O
R	O	S	A		C	L	A	R	O		I	R	O	N
E	R	I	C		C	O	R	A	L		S	I	Z	E
T	I	N	K	E	R	B	E	L	L		D	A	Y	S
			D	E	U	S			C	E	O			
A	M	E	R	C	E		R	E	A	R	M	O	S	T
C	A	M	O			E	A	R	L	S		A	H	A
R	U	M	P	E	L	S	T	I	L	T	S	K	I	N
I	V	Y		R	E	S	E	E			W	E	E	K
D	E	S	I	G	N	E	R		B	L	E	N	D	S
			B	O	G			S	A	I	L			
W	A	R	E		T	H	U	M	B	E	L	I	N	A
A	L	E	X		H	A	N	O	I		I	D	O	L
R	O	B	E		E	L	I	T	E		N	E	E	D
P	E	A	S		N	O	T	E	D		G	A	L	A

434

Z	A	P	A	T	A		E	P	H		K	I	N
I	R	E	N	I	C		Q	U	I		R	I	C	O
T	U	R	N	A	R	O	U	N	D		E	L	E	E
		M	A	R	Y	B	A	K	E	R	E	D	D	Y
A	S	I		A	L	I	T		R	E	L	A	T	E
S	H	A	W		A	T	E		S	T	E	R	E	S
P	E	N	H		T	E	D			I	D	E	A	
			I	S	E	R		R	H	E	O			
P	A	R	T		D	E	O		F	A	Z	E		
H	O	L	L	E	R		O	S	U		F	L	O	E
E	P	O	P	E	E		W	I	N	G		E	O	N
	R	E	V	O	L	V	I	N	G	D	O	O	R	
O	L	E	O		S	P	I	N	D	O	C	T	O	R
N	E	L	L		U	S	N		O	S	T	E	I	N
S	O	Y		P	E	G		G	E	O	D	E	S	

435

A	R	B	O	R	E	T	A		A	B	O	A	R	D
S	E	A	F	A	R	E	R		P	L	A	N	A	R
S	I	R	F	R	A	N	C	I	S	D	R	A	K	E
A	S	T		E	S	S		N	O	G		L	A	S
U	S	E	R	S		E	S	C		R	O	B	S	
L	U	N	A	T	E		S	E	A	E	A	G	L	E
T	E	D	S		N	O	N	P	L	U	S	S	E	S
				T	A	L	I		T	U	R	P		
L	I	B	E	R	A	L	I	S	M		I	S	O	S
O	V	E	R	F	I	S	H		S	T	E	P	U	P
G	O	V	S		K	I	D		O	R	A	T	E	
I	R	E		H	O	I		E	G	G		R	S	A
C	I	R	C	U	M	N	A	V	I	G	A	T	O	R
A	N	L	A	G	E		F	I	R	E	S	A	L	E
L	E	Y	D	E	N		R	E	D	D	E	N	E	D

436

E	B	B	S		A	L	L	I			C	R	O
L	O	O	K		N	O	O	N	E		I	R	A	S
B	O	X	I	N	G	R	I	N	G		N	O	S	H
A	N	Y		O	L	D	S		G	O	T	C	H	A
			B	U	O	Y		A	R	C	H			
M	A	S	O	N	S		P	R	O	T	E	S	T	S
A	L	T	O	S		M	A	I	L			C	L	I	P
S	L	A	M		G	A	V	E	L		L	A	N	E
T	A	R	O		O	N	E	S		S	I	N	G	E
S	H	E	R	W	O	O	D		H	I	N	T	E	D
			B	I	F	F		P	O	R	K			
S	U	N	U	N	U		S	A	M	E		F	L	U
O	T	I	S			P	O	P	S	I	N	G	L	E	S
W	A	N	T		S	A	U	T	E		N	O	N	E
S	H	E			T	R	E	S			P	E	A	R

437

O	S	C	A	R		M	E	C	C	A		D	O	S
A	P	A	C	E		A	S	H	E	S		O	W	L
H	U	S	H	P	U	P	P	I	E	S		G	N	U
U	N	S	E	E	M	L	Y			U	P	P	E	R
				A	P	E		M	O	R	T	A	R	
F	A	C	E	T	S		R	E	R	E	A	D		
U	R	A	L	S		C	O	A	L	S		D	N	A
N	E	T	S		T	H	A	N	E		B	L	O	T
D	A	B		C	R	E	S	T		B	U	E	N	O
	U	P	L	I	F	T		S	O	D	D	E	N	
T	R	O	O	P	S			S	P	Y				
L	O	G	I	C			E	L	E	C	T	I	N	G
A	W	L		K	I	T	T	Y	C	O	R	N	E	R
T	E	A		E	L	A	T	E		T	E	N	S	E
E	R	R		R	A	D	A	R		T	E	S	T	Y

438

A	L	P		S	W	A	M	I		J	A	C	K	S
C	A	R		T	E	N	O	N		U	B	O	A	T
T	W	O	F	I	S	T	E	D		R	E	D	R	Y
I	N	S	E	C	T	S		I	M	I	T	A	T	E
S	E	E	K				S	G	T	S				
			D	U	A	L	C	O	N	T	R	O	L	S
M	O	M		P	I	E	R			S	E	W	U	P
I	L	E	S		D	E	A	L	T		D	E	K	E
L	I	N	U	S			P	E	E	R		N	E	D
D	O	U	B	L	E	H	E	A	D	E	R			
				E	R	O	S		C	O	M	O		
H	A	R	V	E	S	T		S	K	I	L	I	F	T
E	Q	U	I	P			T	W	I	N	P	E	A	K	S
R	U	S	S	O		E	E	R	I	E		M	I	O
E	A	T	E	N		R	E	S	T	S		I	N	S

439

A	J	A	R		C	A	T	T		J	E	S	T
R	O	M	A	N		O	R	S	O		A	L	T	O
O	V	I	N	E		A	C	E	Y		W	E	A	N
M	A	T	T	H	O	U	S	T	O	N		C	R	Y
A	N	Y		R	U	T			S	T	O	A	T	
			H	U	G	H	B	E	A	U	M	O	N	T
M	E	R	E		H	O	W			S	A	R	A	H
E	X	E	C		T	R	A	M	S		Z	A	N	E
T	I	C	K	S			N	A	E		E	L	A	N
S	T	E	L	L	A	D	A	L	L	A	S			
			P	E	A	C	E		A	M	C		S	T	A
S	A	T		T	R	A	C	Y	A	U	S	T	I	N
T	R	I	G		O	R	E	S			F	L	A	T	T
E	N	V	Y		S	I	S	I		F	O	I	L	S
P	O	E	M		S	E	T	A		P	R	E	Y	

440

K	O	P	S		Z	A	P		E	A	S	I	L	Y
E	A	R	L		I	R	E		Q	U	A	V	E	R
E	R	I	E		R	Y	E		U	G	G	A	M	S
N	E	V	E	R	C	A	L	L	A	M	A	N		
				E	D	I	T	I	O	N		E	T	E
L	Y	N	N				S	C	E	N	A	R	I	O
I	T	E		G	I	A	N	T			T	R	A	C	K
G	A	G	A		A	F	O	O	L		E	D	E	R
O	P	E	R	A		L	O	R	E	N		I	D	A
R	E	D	I	R	E	C	T		E	E	R	O		
			M	A	I			A	G	R	I	P	P	A
B	O	R	R	O	W	F	R	O	M	H	I	M		
O	M	E	L	E	T		O	F	A		S	O	L	A
F	E	T	I	S	H		K	I	N		K	N	O	T
T	W	E	N	T	Y		E	X	T		Y	E	T	I

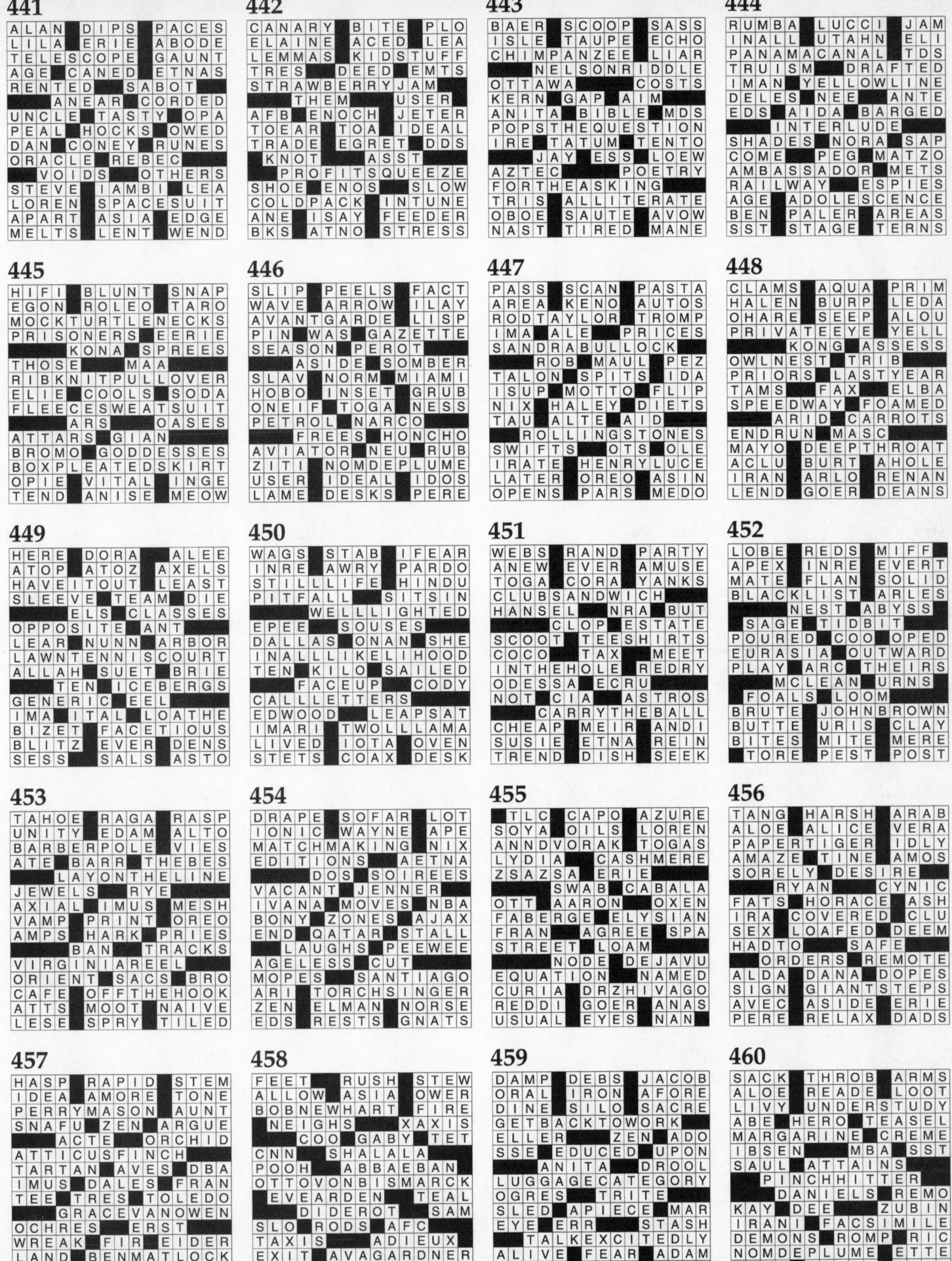

441
```
ALAN DIPS  PACES
LILA ERIE  ABODE
TELESCOPE  GAUNT
AGE  CANED  ETNAS
RENTED   SABOT
   ANEAR CORDED
UNCLE TASTY  OPA
PEAL  HOCKS  OWED
DAN   CONEY RUNES
ORACLE REBEC
  VOIDS   OTHERS
STEVE IAMBI  LEA
LOREN  SPACESUIT
APART ASIA   EDGE
MELTS LENT   WEND
```

442
```
CANARY BITE   PLO
ELAINE ACED   LEA
LEMMAS KIDSTUFF
TRES   DEED  EMTS
STRAWBERRYJAM
     THEM   USER
AFB ENOCH   JETER
TOEAR TOA   IDEAL
TRADE EGRET   DDS
   KNOT   ASST
  PROFITSQUEEZE
SHOE ENOS    SLOW
COLDPACK  INTUNE
ANE  ISAY  FEEDER
BKS  ATNO  STRESS
```

443
```
BAER   SCOOP  SASS
ISLE   TAUPE  ECHO
CHIMPANZEE   LIAR
   NELSONRIDDLE
OTTAWA     COSTS
KERN   GAP    AIM
ANITA BIBLE   MDS
POPSTHEQUESTION
IRE TATUM  TENTO
   JAY ESS LOEW
AZTEC     POETRY
   FORTHEASKING
TRIS  ALLITERATE
OBOE SAUTE   AVOW
NAST TIRED   MANE
```

444
```
RUMBA  LUCCI  JAM
INALL  UTAHN  ELI
PANAMACANAL   TDS
TRUISM   DRAFTED
IMAN   YELLOWLINE
DELES  NEE    ANTE
EDS  AIDA   BARGED
    INTERLUDE
SHADES  NORA   SAP
COME   PEG   MATZO
AMBASSADOR    METS
RAILWAY     ESPIES
AGE ADOLESCENCE
BEN  PALER   AREAS
SST  STAGE   TERNS
```

445
```
HIFI  BLUNT   SNAP
EGON  ROLEO   TARO
MOCKTURTLENECKS
PRISONERS   EERIE
   KONA    SPREES
THOSE      MAA
RIBKNITPULLOVER
ELIE  COOLS   SODA
FLEECESWEATSUIT
   ARS     OASES
ATTARS   GIAN
BROMO   GODDESSES
BOXPLEATEDSKIRT
OPIE  VITAL   INGE
TEND  ANISE   MEOW
```

446
```
SLIP  PEELS   FACT
WAVE  ARROW   ILAY
AVANTGARDE   LISP
PIN WAS    GAZETTE
SEASON      PEROT
    ASIDE  SOMBER
SLAV  NORM   MIAMI
HOBO  INSET   GRUB
ONEIF  TOGA   NESS
PETROL     NARCO
   FREES  HONCHO
AVIATOR  NEU   RUB
ZITI  NOMDEPLUME
USER  IDEAL   IDOS
LAME  DESKS   PERE
```

447
```
PASS  SCAN   PASTA
AREA  KENO   AUTOS
RODTAYLOR   TROMP
IMA  ALE    PRICES
  SANDRABULLOCK
   ROB  MAUL  PEZ
TALON  SPITS   IDA
ISUP  MOTTO   FLIP
NIX  HALEY   DIETS
TAU  ALTE    AID
  ROLLINGSTONES
SWIFTS  OTS    OLE
IRATE  HENRYLUCE
LATER  OREO   ASIN
OPENS  PARS   MEDO
```

448
```
CLAMS  AQUA   PRIM
HALEN  BURP   LEDA
OHARE  SEEP   ALOU
PRIVATEEYE   YELL
   KONG    ASSESS
OWLNEST      TRIB
PRIORS   LASTYEAR
TAMS   FAX    ELBA
SPEEDWAY   FOAMED
   ARID   CARROTS
ENDRUN     MASC
MAYO   DEEPTHROAT
ACLU  BURT   AHOLE
IRAN  ARLO   RENAN
LEND  GOER   DEANS
```

449
```
HERE   DORA   ALEE
ATOP   ATOZ   AXELS
HAVEITOUT   LEAST
SLEEVE  TEAM   DIE
ELS      CLASSES
OPPOSITE     ANT
LEAR  NUNN   ARBOR
LAWNTENNISCOURT
ALLAH  SUET   BRIE
TEN     ICEBERGS
GENERIC     EEL
IMA  ITAL   LOATHE
BIZET  FACETIOUS
BLITZ  EVER   DENS
SESS   SALS   ASTO
```

450
```
WAGS  STAB   IFEAR
INRE  AWRY   PARDO
STILLLIFE   HINDU
PITFALL     SITSIN
   WELLLIGHTED
EPEE     SOUSES
DALLAS  ONAN   SHE
INALLLIKELIHOOD
TEN  KILO   SAILED
FACEUP     CODY
  CALLLETTERS
EDWOOD    LEAPSAT
IMARI  TWOLLLAMA
LIVED  IOTA   OVEN
STETS  COAX   DESK
```

451
```
WEBS  RAND   PARTY
ANEW  EVER   AMUSE
TOGA  CORA   YANKS
   CLUBSANDWICH
HANSEL  NRA    BUT
   CLOP   ESTATE
SCOOT   TEESHIRTS
COCO   TAX    MEET
INTHEHOLE   REDRY
ODESSA     ECRU
NOT  CIA    ASTROS
  CARRYTHEBALL
CHEAP  MEIR   ANDI
SUSIE  ETNA   REIN
TREND  DISH   SEEK
```

452
```
LOBE   REDS   MIFF
APEX   INRE   EVERT
MATE   FLAN   SOLID
BLACKLIST   ARLES
   NEST    ABYSS
SAGE     TIDBIT
POURED  COO    OPED
EURASIA    OUTWARD
PLAY  ARC   THEIRS
MCLEAN     URNS
FOALS      LOOM
BRUTE   JOHNBROWN
BUTTE  URIS   CLAY
BITES  MITE   MERE
TORE   PEST   POST
```

453
```
TAHOE  RAGA   RASP
UNITY  EDAM   ALTO
BARBERPOLE   VIES
ATE  BARR   THEBES
  LAYONTHELINE
JEWELS      RYE
AXIAL  IMUS   MESH
VAMP  PRINT   OREO
AMPS   HARK   PRIES
BAN      TRACKS
VIRGINIAREEL
ORIENT  SACS   BRO
CAFE   OFFTHEHOOK
ATTS   MOOT   NAIVE
LESE   SPRY   TILED
```

454
```
DRAPE  SOFAR   LOT
IONIC  WAYNE   APE
MATCHMAKING   NIX
EDITIONS    AETNA
   DOS    SOIREES
VACANT     JENNER
IVANA  MOVES   NBA
BONY   ZONES   AJAX
END  QATAR   STALL
LAUGHS     PEEWEE
AGELESS     CUT
MOPES    SANTIAGO
ARI  TORCHSINGER
ZEN  ELMAN   NORSE
EDS  RESTS   GNATS
```

455
```
TLC  CAPO    AZURE
SOYA  OILS   LOREN
ANNDVORAK   TOGAS
LYDIA  CASHMERE
ZSAZSA      ERIE
   SWAB   CABALA
OTT  AARON   OXEN
FABERGE   ELYSIAN
FRAN  AGREE   SPA
STREET     LOAM
  NODE   DEJAVU
EQUATION    NAMED
CURIA  DRZHIVAGO
REDDI  GOER   ANAS
USUAL  EYES   NAN
```

456
```
TANG  HARSH   ARAB
ALOE  ALICE   VERA
PAPERTIGER   IDLY
AMAZE  TINE   AMOS
SORELY     DESIRE
   RYAN    CYNIC
FATS  HORACE   ASH
IRA  COVERED   CLU
SEX  LOAFED   DEEM
HADTO      SAFE
ORDERS     REMOTE
ALDA   DANA   DOPES
SIGN  GIANTSTEPS
AVEC   ASIDE   ERIE
PERE   RELAX   DADS
```

457
```
HASP  RAPID   STEM
IDEA  AMORE   TONE
PERRYMASON   AUNT
SNAFU  ZEN   ARGUE
ACTE      ORCHID
ATTICUSFINCH
TARTAN  AVES   DBA
IMUS  DALES   FRAN
TEE  TRES   TOLEDO
GRACEVANOWEN
OCHRES      ERST
WREAK  FIR   EIDER
LAND  BENMATLOCK
ENNE  ASKIN   LOCO
TEAS  STYNE   AMES
```

458
```
FEET   RUSH   STEW
ALLOW  ASIA   OWER
BOBNEWHART   FIRE
NEIGHS     XAXIS
   COO  GABY   TET
CNN    SHALALA
POOH   ABBAEBAN
OTTOVONBISMARCK
EVEARDEN    TEAL
DIDEROT     SAM
SLO  RODS    AFC
TAXIS     ADIEUX
EXIT  AVAGARDNER
ALDA  LIME   SEINE
LYES  PAYS   STOP
```

459
```
DAMP   DEBS   JACOB
ORAL   IRON   AFORE
DINE   SILO   SACRE
GETBACKTOWORK
ELLER   ZEN    ADO
SSE  EDUCED   UPON
   ANITA   DROOL
LUGGAGECATEGORY
OGRES      TRITE
SLED  APIECE   MAR
EYE  ERR    STASH
  TALKEXCITEDLY
ALIVE  FEAR   ADAM
TONIC  ANTI   MINE
ANGST  BASS   SETS
```

460
```
SACK  THROB   ARMS
ALOE  READE   LOOT
LIVY  UNDERSTUDY
ABE  HERO   TEASEL
MARGARINE   CREME
IBSEN   MBA    SST
SAUL    ATTAINS
  PINCHHITTER
DANIELS     REMO
KAY  DEE    ZUBIN
IRANI  FACSIMILE
DEMONS  ROMP   RIC
NOMDEPLUME   ETTE
ALEE   REBEL   SHIN
PARS   YEAST   PSAT
```

461
```
EMIT CRABBE CEL
GARR HELLOS ACE
GRAINOFSALT NAN
    VIP STEWARD
EBSEN CAT ARTE
CANTATAS SOLDER
USA   INSTEAD
  SPLINTERGROUP
  ASTORIA RAE
GRAPHS TELECAST
EELS ASS MALTA
ATTESTS HIT
RIM WINDSORKNOT
ENA ARENAS IRAE
DAN BERATE NATE
```

462
```
WIFE GRIST FIST
HOES RECUR ASTA
AUNTIEMAME TEAM
MSS REIN SPHERE
    SENT SPEE
STAINS CHAIRMAN
LAPSE DUES GONE
ALOT HERES ODDS
TORE OUST COURT
ENTRANCE LASSES
  KNEE RICE
SAFETY MACH OSU
ATAN BROTHERRAT
BORN EERIE YALE
EMMY ELTON ELKS
```

463
```
AMA LESS POKE
MESA ORTHO AREA
ATTN CLAYS MEET
TOOTSIEROLLPOPS
IONIC FOAL
    COMAS GOFOR
ASS PATHOS NAPA
PEPPERMINTPATTY
ERIE MORTAL ESS
SANTO ROBES
  USNA BEALS
PEANUTBUTTERCUP
RANI SONAR GINA
ASEA BUTTE EDAM
YEWS TOES SRS
```

464
```
WARY RABAT JAVA
AREA ELLIE URAL
FILMACTORS JAIL
TOE LOOT TAUTLY
STALER EBB
  ROCKSTARBERRY
BONUS ARISE EOE
AMID TED SPUN
CNN SPINE SIRES
HIGHLANDDANCE
  AIL LESSEN
OPTIMA MITE SRI
FAIR COMMERCIAL
FLED EIDER POSE
SOSO SLITS ONES
```

465
```
MIMI BLISS PLAN
ODOR RECUT YALE
LATE OMEGA RITZ
THENEWSTARWARS
SOLID REAM
  CAMEO RIVAL
HOB MERCHANDISE
EROS DREAM STAN
MAYTHESALES APT
INDIA NEXUS
  REPO EARTH
FORCEBEWITHYOU
PUPU TOXIN ADAR
SLAP ATOLL REST
ILLS LENYA ARTS
```

466
```
BABY THOR BOGIE
AWEE RENO EARLS
RHEA AREA ATILT
KITTYCORNERED
ALLSET VENICE
TEE MIA EAR ROD
  LEONID OOPS
SPINNINGJENNY
JOAD STEAMS
OAR ERE RPI KOS
GREENE ALPINE
NERVOUSNELLIE
INTRO KNEE ATOM
TRAIL ADES TENT
TALES YORE ORSO
```

467
```
TEDS RASP MADAM
IDEA ELLA ALICE
BELL JOANRIVERS
INTL OHM ELATES
ASSYRIA ATE
  FAN APERTURE
GENIE CLASSICAL
OBIE SHIRT GLUM
BALLPOINT SEALS
INEDIBLE CTR
  EEL DRAWERS
SPRIER FOE OREO
PAULYSHORE OREL
ANNIE DRIP DOSE
STEAD LEAS SLED
```

468
```
SHED SEAT TITHE
POGO EXPO UNWED
UPANDATEM STING
REDEEMED SCONCE
  CAN SWANEE
RISEANDSHINE
ALOOF TONY CSA
CLAN COUPE POEM
ESP MOWN JAIME
  TIMETOTURNIN
BARGES ROD
ROBERT PARABOLA
AROMA HITTHEHAY
RADON ALEE AIDE
EXERT MESS TOYS
```

469
```
ARTS UMASS ASIF
LIRA MARLA CURE
TFORMATION UPON
ELUDE EAST MEND
RETIRE SHAKER
  NEXT INBED
SAFE PARTED OVA
ELI RETAINS WIT
NOR ELATED ALLA
TESTS DULL
  TOTALS POLISH
DADA POPE MONTE
EROS POINTAFTER
NEWT ASCII MOVE
SANS LEEDS EWES
```

470
```
WEBB MASKS MOLL
ALLI AHEAP ABOY
SLUG SARNE RICO
IAMNOT AGLUTTON
ODIC ALLY
MASSACRE MARISA
ALLEY OLMAN SAG
JOES IAMAN FINO
ONE INKED TONTO
REPAST RESURGED
  STEP ACRE
EXPLORER OFFOOD
TORO VAUNT OUZO
CROP ASSET ORME
HYPE LETTY TSAR
```

471
```
ABEL ACHE PALS
BOLA SLEET ECOL
AGUN TERRA DENY
FIDDLEAROUND
TEE ERN ELATE
HESSE FEELER
ASTOR ONME TRI
BLOWYOUROWNHORN
NAP ATON EASES
EVILER LONGS
RECON TAE ALA
  GETGOODVIBES
SARA ALONE LEAN
EVEN MINER SAVE
WADS BASS AMER
```

472
```
RIPPLE ONE UGH
AMORAL REVENUE
JASONALEXANDER
AGED TILT DOS
HES PEN TDS SPA
  FIDELIO SWAN
IMAN EMU PONY
VICTORHERBERT
RANT TEA ELKS
ENCS STARHEEL
MAE DOC ALT CPA
MIR TARP ANON
BENEDICTARNOLD
SARDINE SETTLE
ATE MGS OBSESS
```

473
```
MADAM SLUG PHDS
ICOME TORE LIRA
FLOOD ERIN ATEN
FERRIS DAISYMAE
ECHOCHAMBER
JAY OUCH LEI
ALAI STA ALPHA
WILTCHAMBERLAIN
STEEL BEL SURE
RIA EASY LEW
CHAMBERMAID
FOOTBALL SPARSE
LILI COAT PLEAT
ELMO UPIN ELITE
ASSN SENT DYNES
```

474
```
BOWLS DIVA BARB
ARIOT IRIS ALEE
HARRYJAMES LAIR
SLYE ULA AILING
  NERO AURA
DIZZYGILLESPIE
MINOR DAT TACK
ANY ATFIRST TIE
IGOT HOO OPENS
LOUISARMSTRONG
  METE TIER
ZODIAC BAN KWAI
ARID HERBALPERT
CELL EVIL PIANO
HOLY RAGE SENOR
```

475
```
LUKE BELAS SPA
OHNO TRIAGE HIP
BUENOSAIRES ONE
SHE CANED AREAS
  HARD ISME
REAL ONTHELAMB
BERRA EOE ALOE
ONOR EMEND TOTE
DESI PAD MINER
EWESAIDIT YVES
  ONCE HALE
GHENT ODETO LEO
OAR HAVEYOUHERD
INA EVENLY AVID
TDS MERYL TINS
```

476
```
TARP STRIFE DDS
ETUI TAILOR REP
NONETOOSOON INA
  RAP ENDEAVOR
ADORN BRA METE
VINEGAR ALINES
ANT LOURDES
SOMELIKEITHOT
  ABILENE TRA
CANTBE TUMMIES
ADAR ELS EASES
SEMINOLE FAD
BSA ALLFALLDOWN
ATT PLATTE ERIE
HEH SASSED RENE
```

477
```
HOPE GAZER MASK
OXEN OPINE UGLI
MIND VENOM PEAL
EDT JEDCLAMPETT
REAPER ROE
  MAANDPAKETTLE
STERN ROME SHOW
HAT CAWED USE
ACES OPEN HUNTS
MORTIMERSNERD
  ENE ERNEST
LUMANDABNER RAH
ORAL IREAD ABBA
OGLE AGATE WALT
PEER NOTED EYES
```

478
```
HEMEN CAM SCAR
DIANE ODE COPE
STRAW LOT ANISE
HITTHEROADJACK
FETE OREOS RUE
ARI MRI SWAYED
COMEANDGETIT
TREES GUV NEATO
LOVEMETENDER
CESSNA NED HAT
ALA SERTA GEMS
LENDMEYOUREARS
MCCOY DNA STETS
THUS INT TONER
SORT EYE ASTRO
```

479
```
CZAR SHANK ARAB
RUDE TETON NOVA
ALES ELISE DAIS
MUSTARDTHENERVE
APE BEA
STATEOFTHEONION
LATEX IRONS NCO
AMES BRAND RITT
SPA JAMIE SINAI
HAMMERANDPICKLE
ART OME
PLAYKETCHUPBALL
RIND NOLAN OBOE
ONEA DRUID WONT
DEWY STEMS LUIS
```

480
```
SPAYED SAFARI
ORNATE ALAMEDA
JACKOFALLTRADES
OII NEPAL ESTAS
UREA REPOT SATE
RINSE DAWES PER
NETTER ZESTIEST
  ARIP RTES
CARBINES SALTED
UTE EGGED KERRY
BOTS OGRES SEAN
ANILE YIKES ASA
GENERALFACTOTUM
ERUDITE TORERO
SESAME SPADES
```

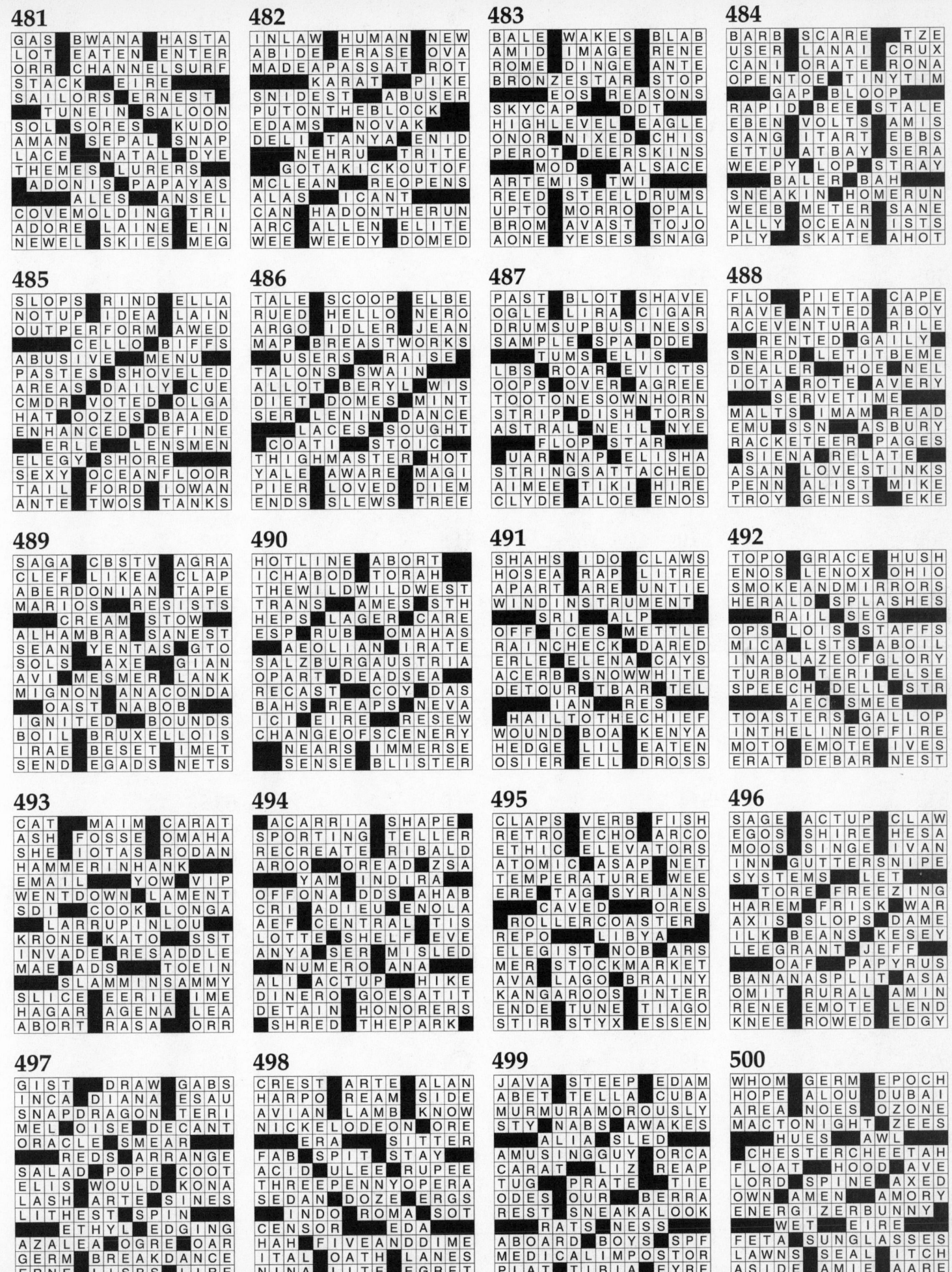

501
```
LOGIC CUM TESLA
ARUBA RNA INCAS
METERMAID MARYS
TWOSTEP BELA
PAR ASH RAILWAY
AGHAST JERKED
TEETH QUAKE ROD
INTO FUNDS RIPE
OTT LEAKY RAVEN
BOVARY GOFERS
TOURIST AIM RAE
ALTI TEARGAS
MILES ROBINCOOK
EVENT ENO CARPI
DARTS DER ERRED
```

502
```
BLIMP CHEF ASPS
AUDIO RAVI RHEA
SPLITLEVEL GONG
KEY HATE TRYONE
OOZE SHELF
WAGGLY CHISELED
ADORE QUIET YAY
LIFE TUBER APSE
LEO PRIED BRIER
SURFEITS CAMELS
BOLAS SOUS
MERITS JINX ODE
IDOL SCATSINGER
LIKE IONE TILES
DEED COED EXERT
```

503
```
FAUNS HIFIS CPR
ADMIT EDEMA ROO
CABCALLOWAY ALS
TREETOPS GOBBLE
ILE RENEGADE
MATEY WIDER KAN
ALAW TILED SEND
ALB VINES MASKS
MACHINES COL
OINKS PALMIST
DELETE AIRLINER
ELL ARABCOUNTRY
AMA GENET SEETO
NOR ERATO KORAN
```

504
```
TASS JUST SCRAP
ABIE IGLU HOOHA
TEXASFLAGSYMBOL
ALOHA IGOR METE
OGRE FOCI
AFAR AROW ATTIC
SAMSON PAIR ERA
SUPERBPERFORMER
ELL DYER ELAPSE
STYNE GATE ITTY
ARAB ALAN
APET COIL DOORS
MOVIERATERSUNIT
OLIVE ROSE TACO
KALEL DRED SNOW
```

505
```
FLUB ASCOTS LST
RATA LOOKAT ITE
IMADEASPARE LED
BAN SPANGLED
ARBOR LEI DAILY
CALYPSO THREES
ENA KEESHAN
THISISTHELIFE
TOPSEED ORE
ABYSMS LABELLE
CREME ALL ORDER
RESETTLE ORA
ONS IMIMPRESSED
STE MANUEL ELLE
SSS ENERGY DOME
```

506
```
WEBS IRMA CARP
ALAI REALM OMOO
RANG KARMA NOTE
ELAND PEAJACKET
NEEDS OLE
NEATER HEROICS
ESS RUMOR ETHER
STEW MINOR SOTO
TEARS MESAS PTA
STEMMED HENSON
CUE ASSET
MILKGLASS SWISH
ODEA ERUPT ECHO
OLEG EERIE SKIP
TYKE SECT TSPS
```

507
```
OTHER RUDER ATM
CHOSE IRISH LIE
HOLLOWVICTORIES
SUE POISE ANDS
CREME DEADEYE
SCANNERS BIASED
HORS NAT BRR
END SAT PIP
PIU ROW BIKE
CARING ROADSTER
HEAVEHO LIRAS
ARNO PASTA TCU
LASTDITCHEFFORT
ETO AFIRE TEPEE
TEM RACED YESES
```

508
```
EPA BIGOT SWORE
TAM ONAIR POLAR
CROCODILEDUNDEE
HORIZON NERDS
ELITE CDS EARS
RES ALAS ORLON
SETS NOR SOFTER
CATBALLOU
RASHES MEA LESS
OTTER SENT LET
BEAD ATL MALTA
BUENO ORATION
BULLDOGDRUMMOND
ANEED IONIA TEE
SASSY ETONS TSE
```

509
```
ZEST SPED SCRAP
ALTO ILSA CHUTE
PLOW GUAM RIPER
SPRINGINGALEAK
OBI OWLETS
JUMPINGBEANS
ARIES RANDY CAM
MATS RAILS COLA
BLT MOIRA AIDAN
BOUNDINGMAIN
FELIPE ORA
LEAPINGLIZARDS
ALBEE RITZ RAND
MEADS OREL OLIO
ERNST GAME NIPS
```

510
```
WRAPS HAND PAL
RECAP ERIE TITO
IAMCALLINGMYCAR
TREK OLD RONALD
QUO GENESES
DISCUS FLAK
ENNUI BOOS JOIN
FLATTERYBECAUSE
TAPE SALE AISLE
APSE TILTED
BESTIRS LON
ELAINE WIG CLUB
ITGETSMENOWHERE
GOES SAVE PINGS
ENS OXEN MAZES
```

511
```
CAVE SALES SHEA
ALAS PROXY EARP
FILEFOLDER AMIE
EVE FREER ACMES
SETTLES CANOE
HAS GIFTWRAP
BEFIT CASTE OBI
AGIN HOMES YULE
BAR DUNES COTES
ADEQUACY AOK
DUNCE ELBOWED
DEREK RATIO OVA
ELIA ONTHELEVEL
AILS HEMEN RENE
RELY ODORS ANTS
```

512
```
COTES SHAMS DAD
ORATE CANOE IRA
BRUCEBANNER CII
DENSE INKER
SOPHIES GANGLY
QUEUES CHOLER
UTTER JOURS AIR
IRES KIRBY DYNE
DER ROVES MISTS
PIECES CAVORT
BLANCH BANANAS
LORNE COOPT
ASK DIANAPRINCE
ZEE EDITS AMOUR
ERR DONOT PADRE
```

513
```
EPIC SPACEK USH
LARA MANILA NCO
FLABBERGAST WHO
ARE ENAMORED
AGANA PRO ADAME
CARAMBA SNIPED
ERA INTENDS
BLABBERMOUTHS
HILLIER OAT
CAROLE RESTORE
ATOLL HAY LETIN
GOODYEAR EAT
ENS JABBERWOCKY
RET ORIONS NILE
SSS ENTREE SAMS
```

514
```
MADRAS ARGO WAG
ATEASE PEAR ERA
HARPSICHORD ALI
TENNISRACKET
ARP SEND IRENE
DURESS IGNORED
STOLE DANA
FISHINGPOLE
ANTE NIXES
BOATING STEALS
ATTIC SHAH MOW
ROLLERSKATES
LOA CELERYSTALK
ELS ANEW READER
YET PEWS STRATA
```

515
```
HONOR GHIA COAT
AMANA RONS OUCH
LATEN INCH ATTA
SNEAKYPEAT LION
LES RIPEN
BREWER BEANO
RESOD POLYGRAPH
INSO WISES TREE
GOODSENSE LEARN
SULKY AIRBUS
METES BUN
PAST HAZARDAGAS
RUSH MEET INANE
IDEO ARNO ETUDE
MENU NOON DELYS
```

516
```
ALMA ICER WADS
WOOF BROKE ATOP
FOOTBRIDGE RENE
USE OISE MOANED
LEDGES STERN
IRKS ERODING
SKINS OLEG PLEA
ANDA GRATE ELAL
SEEN ARCH PASTA
SWADDLE EPIC
TELLA ELECTS
GIGOLO SHEA AWE
AGIN POKERFACED
YOGI EWERS STAG
ERIC REDS PIKE
```

517
```
DECAF ALEC TSAR
OLAND PULL ALIA
OBSERVATIONPOST
RAH IRE SUPPLE
BADAT GENESES
SHOVEL POUND
SAXES HELP KEA
THERITEOFSPRING
SAS AWNS LIBYA
CAPES CAVIAR
RELAXED JANET
EVENED EER ZED
MIDDLEAGESPREAD
UTIL CLAP AORTA
SANE KIDS MESSY
```

518
```
RAJAH JAKE BLOB
OBESE EWER YOKO
ALAIN ROYROGERS
DEN BARKS DOWAH
HEARYE TON
CHANNEL ARRESTS
HERVE ELVES OOH
ELLY TWEAK CUPO
CIO GOING NOPAR
KOWTOWS ANALYZE
ORS WRISTS
SPACE HADNT AKA
ELTONJOHN ADLIB
LOOM OBOE SEETO
LYME BOOR ESSEX
```

519
```
ELSA HADTO EWES
QUIT AIRUP LACE
URGE SLATE ASHE
AIM THEBUNNYHOP
LEASHED WON
IRS SWIVELED
AMINO SKID APE
HAREBRAINEDIDEA
ELK EKED EBSEN
MESSAGES EPA
ALA ENTRUST
RABBITPUNCH SAW
ORAL TONTO JANE
MINE ASTER AGEE
PADS SHORE BERT
```

520
```
SCALE TROT TON
EATIN PIANO HUE
GRANDKENYAN ASS
TOAT DEBITS
STY BET ADUB
OHO TURRET NRA
RENTAL EMERGENT
REGAL SAT TEASE
SNATCHED SEEKER
ANT OWLETS ELM
COST EDE MRS
SCHOOL WWII
TAE FINNISHLINE
ORE ANION OLDEN
WOK REND PEATS
```

521

```
FAZE  TAMP  BALM
OXEN SAFES ISEE
OLDCOUNTRY KANT
LES MAD ECLIPSE
    SEVE HAN
NEWAGEMUSICIANS
ANITA PACE DOT
BEDE POPES ALVA
ORE JADE FLIER
BORROWEDTROUBLE
    INN HARM
STOPGAP ESC APE
ARLO BLUEPENCIL
REEF LANNY ALES
ASOF EYED PURE
```

522

```
CAR  SOLD  TAMPS
ADOS TREE OPART
FASTBREAK MEDIA
ENSILE REF MEET
SOIREE IRE
   RAPIDTRANSIT
BADER ROREM IDO
USED SATED SLOB
SEW RUBEN SILLY
HASTYPUDDING
   WEE CANADA
MALI RAH ERASED
ARENT QUICKLIME
RINGO URSA SAUL
EATEN ATOP NRA
```

523

```
RANI IMPEL SCAR
OXEN MOOLA TORO
BLACKMAGICWOMAN
SET AUTO ERRATA
   ANNS DIEM
AHORSE PENN GBS
LENDA MORT DROP
GREENTAMBOURINE
EVAN ARMY GINZA
REM OKIE CANDOR
   IRES BANK
ODESSA GIRD DOW
YELLOWSUBMARINE
LAME ATALE ANTS
SLOT YEMEN FOOT
```

524

```
ABIE ESTE PHONE
REFLECTED CORAL
CLIFFHANG SLANG
  TORTES INCA
ONBASE CONGER
SOON SHEBANG
CLANG OVINE STU
ATREE RID NICER
RED TASTE DRANG
  MUSTANG ALEE
ACCEPT NONETS
SARA ARAGON
TREND BOOMERANG
ELATE INDELIBLE
RAMON SESS PEEN
```

525

```
BABAR CODE ACME
LIEGE ONUS BOAS
IDROVEMYDOGNUTS
PANG VEX TEEPEE
   VET PEERESS
MOHAIR KIRK
ALAMO ANTI SARA
IDYELLFETCHTHEN
LESS ALAS EASED
  ACAD PARODY
CABINET ROD
USURER JOE CLIO
THROWABOOMERANG
TORN TABS RAZOR
OTOS EAST STYNE
```

526

```
SCRAM SPED CHOP
OHARA HARI HALO
LINER ALIE OWED
ENGAGEMENTRING
   AYE CAR
MATURE POOH UMA
OBESE WINK INON
POPSTHEQUESTION
EVER OPUS ULTRA
DEE ANTE UNLESS
   PIE AND
WILLYOUMARRYME
WADE BONA EIEIO
ELLA UZIS STAIN
BLED NETS SARIS
```

527

```
PAGAN SWAN BASE
ERASE CITE ANKA
TIGHTROPEWALKER
EASY HOE CULLEN
   MET CORSET
PAPAYA TOMA
EXIST KITE LARD
ELEPHANTTRAINER
LESS BOLA JONNY
  ASWE JANETS
MADMEN TUX
WARREN SAD ABBE
HUMANCANNONBALL
AVOW EWOK ALBUM
TERN SEWS PEERS
```

528

```
CASTE STET CHAP
ALLEN POSE LANA
TEARS ADAM OVEN
OXTAILSOUP DRAT
   LAM ETHERS
MINCED RADIO
OVERS BAS SPRIG
MAMA OKS POST
ANOSE ZEN CELLO
  HEROD PUREES
NOODLE ATT
OAHU BARBARYAPE
TRAM ELIA AEGIS
TERM LINT TARPS
ODAY SAGE ERASE
```

529

```
DOTS PLUG MAAM
ONIT MAURA ERST
ZERO ANNAL ACES
ELEVENGALLONHAT
   END SORT
IDO CAT PAIRS
NOW TINA TMEN
NINETEENWHEELER
NEMO DELE IRE
GRITS SAD CDX
   NAPS TOT
FIVELETTERWORDS
INON AROMA PAIL
FDIC RUMMY AREA
EYRE STAY ZEST
```

530

```
PEST ANAXE ACE
ANTI URKEL HOGG
CREDITCARD AMOR
MARINO OED ETA
AGNES TAXRETURN
NESS ARR STOPIT
   RBIS ELOPE
MARRIAGELICENSE
ALIOS NAST
REDSEA INT PLUM
GUESTBOOK SAONE
ITA OOP URSULA
NIBS DEPOSITION
SALE ERODE ESAI
NEW SAWED DADE
```

531

```
MARLA BAR SKATE
AXIOM ORO CORAL
CLIMBINGTHEWALL
HES USE CANTBE
   ESL LEO
MOPTHEFLOORWITH
ASIA RILEY GEO
TAPS WEEDS ALMS
EKE SIETE DOPE
DARKENSONESDOOR
   IAN RES
RANSOM ALL OSS
WINDOWENVELOPES
ASTON LEI ERECT
REEFS TED RENTS
```

532

```
RON ADIPOSE ACT
AMO SELECTS RAE
NOR SWEATYPALMS
DOWSE SLAM MEET
   EON IFONLY
LIGHTFINGERS
OLIO ECOL ATRIA
RIA TRAVELS ERR
DENTS MANO SPAT
  BAREKNUCKLES
BEFORE LII
EARN NANA OSCAR
GREENTHUMBS ARA
ALE RESTORE TEN
TYS CROSSAT EAT
```

533

```
ADAS ODETS ACME
GIRL CURIE THOR
ARGO ELITE TUBA
NEUTRALCORNER
ACETONE ASCOT
TREY DRIVETHRU
   DAD UKE SEEM
ATM LIONESS SOS
SHOO ARI TEE
PARKPLACE GNAT
STATE DANDIES
LOWBROWCOMEDY
CRIB LAMAR OLIN
OOZE ACARE SLUG
DOER BENDS TOME
```

534

```
ANNUL ONTO SAKE
SCONE RUHR CCIV
PAULDUDLEYWHITE
ANE PELE EIDER
   ALTA ABES
CARDIOLOGY TIDE
AMOEBA GLEN NRA
MUDDY SEE AFLAT
ESE ABLE SCRAPE
LEOS EISENHOWER
   CHAP LION
STARE PEAT TAO
THREECENTSTAMPS
URGE ARNE AGATE
BUON DYED MENSA
```

535

```
BASHED OPIE MOE
IMPEDE WHOA ERN
CURRANTNEWS DIT
ELI MIR NATTIER
PETE MILO SHANE
STEAM EMO ETTA
  REGIMENT EAT
PERSIMMONIOUSLY
INE REMNANTS
PATE NED SELMA
EMITS DENS REEL
LORELEI AHA ANA
IRE ORANGEMENTS
NEE TITO BARTOK
EDS HEED ANGORA
```

536

```
ROTS ACED PESTO
AVOW CONE AVAIL
ZUNI THIS JOKED
OLYMPIADUKAKIS
REA RON LIME
   CON ETNA BOA
ASIAN EWOK FRAN
MONTGOMERYCLIFT
ODDS RORY REESE
SAY BATS TUX
  MALI SHE KOS
JACKSONPOLLOCK
PONCE NORM AREA
TENOR ASEA MEAT
SLAYS LYES BANE
```

537

```
APB OSAGE STRIP
SOO FINES TOOLE
TIA FRONTRUNNER
ESTEE TEED
RESENTS SEDATED
KEDGER DERATE
SRI SILOS DEBTS
PUPS FEMUR ALAI
UPPER SADAT ESS
REEVES NAMATH
SERENER NATIONS
   DEAL TEPEE
JUMPERCABLE PEN
INGER EMEER EDS
MAMAS DEEDS RYE
```

538

```
JOEY SASSES BOZ
EGGO EMAILS OHO
FRANKCANNON RAN
FED NUIT WORE
   BARNABYJONES
CROCE LEAR
SHOOK SQUAWKSAT
TOAT UTTER RONA
SORCERERS FOUND
ARIA ELOPE
THOMASMAGNUM
BUMP IRAN PEI
ORE JIMROCKFORD
NON ACCEPT FOIE
ENS GUISES FLEA
```

539

```
TAPS HOOF FOLD
AMOK WALDO ARIA
PUTINORDER LEAR
EST OUTS GALORE
RESTON SEMI
   INDOCTRINATE
SAND NORSE THE
PRAY EVE DOOR
OAR MADEA OPRY
TYCOONARMAND
   FOGY DOODAD
CRINGE BIDS IRA
OHNO LAIDEYESON
MEAT IDLER SCAT
BASE COLA PORE
```

540

```
PEDAL JETS OCHS
ETUDE OLEO PLEA
THEIIIJAKES TINY
RATE ONES DON
INSULIN SEMITE
   VEASYPIECES
ATMO AMA TIPS
THEVIISAMURAI
ARES NES LYND
  XIIANGRYMEN
LATVIA ELAPSED
GEL ERRS EIRE
FAIR XVICANDLES
LARD ERLE TRACK
YALE DYER HOSTS
```

541

```
ADDS  IMAN  TOSCA
DIRE  CART  OLEOS
SPILLEDTHEBEANS
SPLICE   MAGNET
    GAD COGS
COUCHPOTATO  MAS
ONSET ONE  CASK
STUN  TROTS  OMNI
TART  HOT  PLIED
SPY  PEASHOOTERS
   REIN  IRS
ASPENS   RASCAL
THEPUMPKINEATER
TENOR RING  ROVE
NASTY EDGE  EPIC
```

542

```
CZAR  CHAMPS  SCI
OATH  OILERS  TON
OPTIONPLAYS  IRS
INN  ANO   ANTE
STOCKCHARACTER
IOU  EEO   LISZT
DADE  AMASSED
APEX  NICHE  IHAD
  TOUCHER  COVE
ACTOR  LIL   MEW
WARRANTOFFICER
ALIT  OAR   ROM
ILK  BONDSERVANT
TEE  INGEAR  EDIE
SRS  GEORGE  TEXT
```

543

```
BAJA  SIFT  HITME
OLES  TROY  OTHER
SOLIDPROPELLANT
ONLAY   LETSLIDE
XES  ART   ACT
  SNEER  HEISTS
SPAT  EXAM  INTEL
LIQUIDATIONSALE
INURN SINK  EYED
TEAMUP   ODIST
  NUS  SEA  SAP
SALADBAR   SACRA
THEGASHOUSEGANG
ASSET ILKA  OPIE
NOTRE BEET  GEER
```

544

```
PSST  AGHAS  MAMA
ATEE  DEALT  OLEG
WEEDBESTBEGOING
APSE   THERE  GAI
ALI  ASU  ENHANCE
KEN  TORE   RUSES
ARTS  LED   SIT
SOWFARSOWGOOD
  EAR  EVE  SPUR
SPEAK  LEES   PTA
HASTENS  RTE  OCT
IRT  IOTAS   WISH
PLANTTOBEONTIME
TOTO  INBED  STAR
ORES  TEASE  YENS
```

545

```
ASCOT  PAINE  GEL
MOORE  ASSERTIVE
ALGERIATOZAMBIA
SIS  EFREM   SELF
   ESS  REMS
SALSA  ISRAELITE
POUT  ANT  REUNED
ARROWSTOZIPGUNS
STEPIN ZOO  ERSE
MASSMEDIA  CREEL
   PRON  SOS
FEAT  SNAIL  DIM
ANGELHAIRTOZITI
CONCORDAT  NEVER
ELI  THOSE  SNARE
```

546

```
RAM  VOLT  ALANON
AMO  AROO  ROTARY
DUCKSOUP   CRADLE
ASHES   SALADDAYS
REAGAN   ZENO
   RUB  DEVELOP
ECCE  MAP   EVADE
ROLLSBACKPRICES
SMOKE  SIR   LEST
TAGSALE    DOC
  WASP   SHEATH
EASYASPIE  OLLIE
CREATE   CUPOFTEA
HEALER  KRIS  ERR
OATERS  SONY  RST
```

547

```
SPAR  YARD   SUMS
PAREE ELIE  ITAL
ADORN LION  NINA
MEDIABLITZ  CLOP
  AMO   SELLERS
HOLLERED   LOA
ONE  ORES  NISEI
PUTTINONTHERITZ
ESTER SELA   ATO
NAM   BOTTOMED
RIPENER   COS
ADAM  DERSHOWITZ
MITE  IGOT  TAHOE
BORN  CANE  OLAND
OMIT  SLAW  ODDS
```

548

```
SCAM  ORCA  BACKS
URGE  RHOS  INANE
DORA  DONTCRYFOR
SPARTAN  ALT   ETA
  GRIEG   OHM
FADEIN   RUSSIANS
ISING  PETE  SMIT
STAT  SONAR  SAGA
TONI  NOAH  MATER
SPANIARD   SIMILE
  ANR   AGILE
ASK  LET  REAREND
THERESHEIS  ILIE
TAROT  EAST  CANE
AGNES  RUTA  ALES
```

549

```
MAME  NEST  PASTA
IRAN  OMAR  IDLER
SLIDERULE  ROILS
TOSSED   SCARP
  LISA   ATESTS
NEGLECTS   SESTET
ELLER  ESSES  RNA
AMIN  PAINS  TEAK
RID  SALSA  GRACE
ERECTS   TRIREMES
DASHES   SETA
  LOVES  INSEAM
MOORE  COASTLINE
ASPEN  ODIN  ORES
GUESS  WELT  PEWS
```

550

```
PEAS  BALD  CAPRA
RILL  AREA  HURON
OTTO  LIAR  UNITY
WHATAMANWANTS
SEISM  IRK   SOY
ERR  ASLANT  DIME
  AZTEC   ARENA
MOSTOUTOFACARIS
ALAIN    RAITT
KEPT  BONAMI  RAT
OOP  AIR   NAOMI
HISTEENAGESON
HAITI  GREW  SARK
OARED  OGRE  ORAL
THEME  NODS  PYLE
```

551

```
MAAM  PAPA  DAISY
UNDO  EVEN  ORTHO
SNAPTOATTENTION
HEM  URNS   PAINE
  BRIT   ASHE
PASSFAILCOURSES
ESTES  EINE   PCT
ATAD  FAD   FLOE
CRI  DAIS  IRANI
HANDOFFTHEBATON
  ALTO   OUST
BATOR  AONE   RAE
LATERALTHINKING
OUTRE  BRAC  OLEG
AMASS  SASE  DEWY
```

552

```
ANGER  COOP   BEE
MOORE  ADMAN  URN
ELBOWGREASE  TNT
NASSAU   ARTISTE
  ERRS   ATEE
MAC  DUES  SHARP
ECHO  SPEC  EMBED
SHEBA  ALL  REEDY
HEWED  LEAH  DARE
STRAW  SNAG  NOS
  HOPI   GILA
GENTLES   TATTOO
OAF  OILPAINTING
AGA  RELAX  CANER
KAT  RARE  ERASE
```

553

```
CASS  OBAD  NESTS
OMAR  COLA  ULTRA
PAYTHETAB  CLAIR
ASSAULT  SOL  RAG
  MOOS   BEATLE
PROFITMARGIN
SALAD  NAY   DRS
SPEC  ALDEN  ROOF
TOA  BAA   MEARA
DOUBLEHEADER
TALENT   SLOT
ALI  ESS  MORNING
MIMIC  TWOFOOTER
EVITA  YORE  DARE
DETER  EWER  SLOW
```

554

```
MOSES  OPT  TAPED
ECLAT  CEE  AMORE
SAYSUNCLE  KEENE
STET  OUT  TENTED
  MAORI   ORD
TALKSNONSENSE
TREND  GAG   DEAN
OER  ORR  TAN AMI
TARP  EER  ERRED
SPEAKSVOLUMES
  PET   BARON
BERETS  ERG  ELSE
AVERT  CRIESWOLF
REBEL  ATA  SADAT
TRADE  MAT  SLEWS
```

555

```
IFVANNA   WHITE
PIERROT  TOURISM
ABREATH  ROMANCE
NUBS  WILY  SNARL
ELA  HONEST  MOO
MALTA  GOTHEROWN
ASSORT   SERIOUS
  BLYS   DOGS
STOOPTO   WHILST
SHOWWOULD  TEETH
WAH  SMERSH  SAY
IREST  BOAC  BORS
SPANIEL  MUSETTE
HERONRY  ALCOHOL
ITBEA   SPINOFF
```

556

```
TSE  BALES  AFFIX
ELL  AMORE  LAUDE
AIM  SATIE  ORCAS
SPIKETHEPUNCH
EURASIA   NEESON
SPAR  RUMP   SIDE
  ERA  MEAN  ADZ
SLASHPRICES
ALT  FLEE   DOG
MOOT  ENDO  GASP
PUPATE   ROBERTO
CLIPTHEHEDGES
SPOKE  HELMS  YRS
ASCII  ELSIE  LEE
LIKEN  ELECT  EOS
```

557

```
SPEND  THIS  TWAS
ARMOR  HALT  OONA
PICNICAREA  URAL
ICE  VENT  BAREST
DEEDED   SALMI
  ELAL  LEISURE
SPAT  RENT  STRAY
TOROS  SEE  SIGNE
ALEUT  SERB  NETS
TEAROSE   SELF
  ALANS  BOONES
ANTHEM ETON   EDT
LORE  STEEPGRADE
IDEA  OOPS  EERIE
TEED  NEST  DOSED
```

558

```
TAFTS  COLE  JAZZ
STRIP  ORYX  AREA
ARENA  MAROONING
RITACOOLIDGE
ASTER  CUR   CAD
UDDER   SECURE
FARR  EXIT  SARAN
ULAN  RELIC  RIBS
RIMES  CELL  LOSE
ZEBRAS   SEEDY
ENO  BEA  ROSES
GLADYSKNIGHT
THREESOME  AMEER
NOON  ORCA  TOSEE
TWIT  NEAT  ENTRY
```

559

```
OSCAR  RABIN   MDS
NOOSE  AROSE   YET
OWLKINGCOLE  NNE
  EGOS  MAD   ASA
CROWNS   MICHEL
REN  SALAS   EEL
AGE  LINT  REEFS
MAGI  ENDED  SARA
SLOOP  KIRI   GAG
  OUR  SENSE  UNE
REDSEA   ASPECT
OUT  SSH   ORCA
ABE  STORKMARKET
SIR  ERROR  PEEVE
TEN  DONNA  EDGED
```

560

```
CASH  ATTAR  STET
LIKE  SEINE  POPE
ODIN  SENDS  ERIC
PEP  HOMESTRETCH
ODORS    LODES
TRUANT   SEEDY
RETIE  PULSE  KAT
ADOS  WELLS  WISE
MON  BANKS  CACHE
RUINS   DUCKED
CLEFT   OREOS
LEAPFROGGED  TVA
ADZE  EARLS  SAID
PEEN  SHIES  ANNE
PSST  SUDSY  ODES
```

Crossword Solutions

561
```
MAZES RAPT SHIN
ALAMO ETCH TORO
RANSOMNOTE ALMS
TIE TEEM OFFDAY
SHAW GRAF
TERCEL HOEDOWNS
ADIOS TEAM FRAT
LIAR HAILS LIMA
ETTE OURS LITER
SHAKEUPS SAFEST
ELSE MICE
SCHEME SALK AGE
IHOP SINGLESBAR
ZONE ADAM YELLS
EWER TOGA SWEAT
```

562
```
FAWN WASH SNAKE
ODIE AREA EASED
LIZA IRAN CRIES
DEERSTALKERCAP
SUN HEY EWES
TAR BRIT JET
AMOUR GRIN POLO
MAGNIFYINGGLASS
EZRA ARAG LANES
NEE LION COY
CELS MAO LED
MEERSCHAUMPIPE
TEXAN OUTS ETON
ANISE PLEA NEXT
CUTER EARL DRYS
```

563
```
MARS REST PERSE
EPIC ELMO OREOS
ASTA DIAL MALTA
TEALTHEREWASYOU
PRO TRADE
SOVIET AVERAGE
CLINK SATES BOX
RING LAYER PARI
AVE DICED BASEL
MESSIER SERENE
PATIO VAT
ACYANOFTHETIMES
SHORN ITAL COLE
HORSE CELT LAKE
YOKES ERTE ETON
```

564
```
IDTAG NIECE IRS
QUOTA ENDOW BEA
SEAMS GRAPELEAF
HAREMS URGE
RAVIOLI ALIAS
EMERGE EGGPLANT
NANA GROUP
THINGSONESTUFFS
ALOIS TEAK
ENVELOPE POETRY
NOONE PEPPERS
AMIC SALINE
BALLOTBOX RAMBO
LAE RABBI AVAIL
EMS ERASE SEIZE
```

565
```
WAGES KOCH SIPS
EMILY ARLO KNOT
DEFINITEARTICLE
SST DRY DISMAYS
SRO ZAP
SECONDSTORYMAN
STROM ETON ALE
ORATE MIX MAXIS
BUS TONI ARIES
STEERINGCOLUMN
DEP GAT
ATEINTO KEY FAO
PIECEOFONESMIND
SENT EINE IRATE
EDYS STEW ASTER
```

566
```
PACED SHIV TENT
AFREE PICA OLEO
SOURGRAPES ULAN
TUE RAM SUGARY
ALLSET AWASH
PET MOLECULE
FIJI AFAR NONET
ONELANE STOODON
ATALE MUTE KONA
LONESOME MCI
DOPEY PRELIM
ATEMPO SLO ONA
HARI ROTTENEGGS
EVIL TAIL ERIES
MICK ORSO SACRE
```

567
```
RISER MOLL LARK
ERASE ABEE ELEE
PERPLEXING GENE
ONA ILIE REASON
TENSED SPELL
ODES REVELED
AWOL REBA EXILE
TATAR RAY SPAIN
MITRE AGER ERAS
STOPGAP REAR
LASES ARTHUR
ALIENS TETE ONE
JINX ALEXANDRIA
ATTU IONA AESOP
REOS LOOM STENS
```

568
```
LED EMCEE SAID
MILA ROADS USNA
PAINLESSDENTIST
GRAPE HEY AUDIE
ACRED SIRENS
SEETHE YALE
OPEC STRODE GSA
HIGHSPEEDDRILLS
OCS PENPAL NEAP
ARCO EVENTS
BEARIT DARER
ELGIN MEL ATEAM
PLASTICFILLINGS
PETE SIEVE ADES
ONES MIRES LSD
```

569
```
JERK ALAS BIZET
AREA BAIL UTILE
VINE JUDO MANSE
ACOLLEGEGIRLCAN
ACH RAY
BAREST SOAP SEA
ERINS JUAN STAB
BEPOORATHISTORY
ONES ECRU TILLS
PAN ANKA COREYS
AGE QUO
BUTGREATATDATES
ATONE GATE HALO
RAREE ORAL EXAM
SHOWS GARY MINE
```

570
```
EPEES HOIST SST
VOLGA ANDIE PAR
ELBOWGREASE RUE
SEAT OAT SEINE
RUNSOUTOFGAS
BYLINES RAFT
LOOPS HALFSUNK
IDO SCALE VEE
PASSPORT OCEAN
HOYA PTBOATS
VEGETABLEOIL
NERDS ARF LMNO
ERA DRINKFLUIDS
CIV ADAGE ADLAI
KEY MANED PEEKS
```

571
```
LALA BRER AGAPE
ORAN ROTE GOLAN
BESTFOOTFORWARD
EAT RONA TENSES
TAKE SHES
MADAME STES OHS
EMOTE BEER OREL
DUBARRYWASALADY
ISIS ATOM RANGE
CEE ATEN CONGER
ITIS LAUD
PRONTO KISS LES
SINGININTHERAIN
STEER CORE EZRA
TERRE EWES PEEP
```

572
```
MOLD SALK SPA
AGEE IDEA RENEW
CRACKDOWN ELATE
SERIAL DECAMPED
DEEP ANOD
LABEL AGARN REF
IDAS GRABLE AXE
VAN BOOMBOX GIL
EGG ALLIES POLL
DEL LIENS DINES
AMOK SEER
TIDINESS LEASES
IRENE POPARTIST
NASTY IRON ELSA
ASH NEED SLOB
```

573
```
ANGRY SPEC ANKA
SERIO MAYO NOEL
CHOCOLATECHIMPS
HIGH ESS CAMETO
EACH LYRA
KITSCH WAX TWAS
ECU TENOR AORTA
BARBARAMANDRILL
ARIAS KASEM TAU
BEND FEN VILEST
TIED METE
AWAITS SOR ACCT
MARMOSETMAUGHAM
ORME UNUM GUISE
SPYS PONY HEMEN
```

574
```
SCABS ARCS FRAN
ALGAL SWAP RAPA
CARLA LARA ASPS
SWAMPLANDS NCAA
SAND MCCALL
SWAG STAG HALLS
TARMAC NARA
ARMADAS MARACAS
ARAB GSHARP
AWRAP PAST ALTA
CHARTA NCAR
TAMA MADAGASCAR
STAR AFAR CLARA
ALDA NANA KARAT
SLAT ATAB SWANS
```

575
```
RINGS AVID THAT
IDIOM GINA HERO
GOLDILOCKS RAIL
TONES WORSE
BIGOTRY BEATER
ATONED RIALTO
GALEN MERYL FAT
OLDS BANES EGGY
NOD WAITS BROIL
IMELDA GRILLE
FUGARD BOUNDER
ANGLE SPILT
KIEL GOLDFINGER
ETRE ALAD SEEYA
REST PONY HEMEN
```

576
```
SHAH PETS ACTS
PALE ELEE SLEEP
ELLA SPAN PONTI
CLIPBOARD ISSUE
ESSO CREEP
HORA OODLES
TAPIRS MOO HAIG
ALADDIN BALANCE
DELI SEC KAVNER
NASCAR SEED
BAGGY TOUT
FARCE CHOPSTICK
UTURN ROME OSHA
ROBOT ODIN OMIT
NAPS WEED TYPE
```

577
```
PETE SHEAF SHAD
AXED HELLO LINE
LIPSMACKER ATTA
ELI ARKS TONSIL
SEDATE FUNGI
REDEFINE NIP
ASSES VINE AGRA
JOHN SOLES GLEN
AREA EKES SEEDS
RTE EXERTION
PORTS MUTELY
VISHNU STEP QUO
ANKA PEARLSBUCK
STIR LURED BARE
TONE ERIKA SLED
```

578
```
RAN TREAT ASPS
ABEE HARSH STAT
JOHNNYCAKE TELE
AIRTIMES BEAVER
SLURPED HEDGE
EPS RELIEDON
VIJAY DEALT ODO
ERAT JAILS EROS
GAY PENNS ISERE
ASWELLAS INT
AXELS ANTESUP
ILLPAY INCREASE
COKE JACKHAMMER
BREL ADELE SOUR
MERS ROSES SPY
```

579
```
PATHS PYM PANTS
IDEAL LEA ALEUT
TONGUEANDGROOVE
AND IRS EATEN
SIT CUT URI ABE
SOLEPROPRIETOR
ESTOP IVANA
HAHA SNELL ILES
OWENS ROAST
LEATHERANDLACE
EDD RAE GIA APT
ASORT LET VIE
KICKUPONESHEELS
UNHID LEG ELIOT
NEEDS DES RINGS
```

580
```
CHAR TBAR APER
AARON RARE ILSA
SLATE USAF MATS
HOTCROSSBUN YEP
VAT EERIE
TWEET PALLET
SOAR HORN LACKS
PERM SPUDS MOAT
ADMIT ANAT EONS
UNABLE EARLS
SPELL ORD
AHS COLDHEARTED
HAUL NORA GEODE
ERIE DOUR EATEN
METE EMMA LENT
```

581

```
TSP EAVES TIBET
EWE CRACK HOUSE
PARFORTHECOURSE
EMMA ODOR
EPITAPH SANCTUM
SST BOOR TYRANT
OUSTED ELIS
OFFTHESUBJECT
TGIF LINEUP
ALLEGE NEED RPS
JEERING STOREUP
VIAL ETTA
SHOWEDSOMECLASS
HAVEN PROVE KIM
EGADS SEPAL ENS
```

582

```
ALAN LODI ACRE
ROMA IRON STOOL
GOOSENECK HOLES
ONSALE STAND
MASC IRATER
BICKERER DELUGE
ASHER PORED RON
LOIN HAWES SKIT
BBC MELBA REESE
OAKIES ACRONYMS
ARENAS RHOS
NONET LITTLE
ATONE EAGLEEYED
TRUER ELEE ANNE
EATS NEER LEAN
```

583

```
JOG FAIR MAAM
UPAT OPINE EBRO
MAMASFAMILYTIES
PLEXUS TEARGAS
INTHE VMI
COACT ALGA CAT
OSCAR REINS IWO
COMBATMASTERSON
ALE PHONE SOLED
ESS ENOL SUEME
ASI RESIN
AGENT99 TODATE
ROUTE660MINUTES
AGRA OTHER PONS
BOOS SHOW ZOO
```

584

```
JAWS MOORE FAST
EVAN APRIL ASTO
DOYOURECALLWHEN
INN FINAL ENEMY
EROSE IVE
BASE ADINNERWAS
ELBA NIKE ABE
SLOP APTLY STYX
EAR ICER LESE
THOUGHTOUT ARMS
PLY PRIGS
RODEO ATWAR PTA
ANDNOTTHAWEDOUT
MEAD SNARL JUNO
PAYS PONDS STEP
```

585

```
LOSS RAJA PSHAW
INCH APEX AHOLE
NEAR ZEAL RYDER
KIBITZ NEST GEE
VOLTS HOME
SCHEMER INAPIE
COOL DOALL PODS
ALC AVAIL DOT
LOUD ZESTY OGLE
ERSATZ USELESS
PHIL APHID
GTO PEAL ANTEUP
RECAP GILL INGE
INURE EVEL MILL
POSED DENY EDIT
```

586

```
SEWS PACE YORE
CLAM FURLS EMIR
OSLO CLOTH ANTI
WALKS DOORPRIZE
FETA KNEEL
FLYING DROWSY
ILO RILED UNITE
TOWS LEVEL GNAW
CREEL NABOB DRS
HARLEM TORSOS
LEECH MEOW
FLOORSHOW DOSES
LULU AUGER THAI
ABET STALE HOST
KEGS ENDS EPEE
```

587

```
MACAW CHET AGO
ABASE EURO ARID
TURKEYTROT NAVE
ESTE EELS IDLER
YESDEAR IDO
CHADEVERETT
DITTO UNEARTHS
ITHE SEEDS AREA
SCANTEST SNEER
CHINACLOSET
YRS CLEARER
CRUST FOAL COLE
RENO BURMASHAVE
ONIN ASAP PORES
PET GELS FOSSE
```

588

```
CRAB BIDE LUBED
HOSE INON ATONE
IDLE STER RAZOR
LEAFSTHROUGH
LON ORE LGE BBS
STOPORILLSHOOT
ASSES ITALIA
EWOK DIG VOLT
SAMUEL NOTRE
SWIMMINGTRUNKS
EAT PRO AID OER
BRANCHRICKEY
QUEUE ALEE ROSA
USERS MAAM OMAN
EARNS ENDE WOWS
```

589

```
AHAT RAE DAUBS
SENOR ATV ORLOP
NITRO CLEOPATRA
IDO SCIENT BRAT
TINASINATRA AXE
RIGGS ASCI
RANI ACTH TASTE
OLESTRA ADASTRA
KYOTO RARE ESAU
NANS IDLER
RAT INTRAVENOUS
IDEA ARISER ARI
TETRAGONS IOTAS
APRON LGE EVENS
STAND LST OROY
```

590

```
RAMP BROOM LIAR
ULEE AETNA ANTI
NOWANDTHEN ISIS
TELLALIE DONATE
DOE MAVEN
ASHPIT TATI DEE
SHIER PORED OAT
YEGG CANIS HUGH
LAH TOTEN TITLE
ARA ACTS CUSSER
NANKI CAN
UPDIKE ARRESTEE
SOLS YINANDYANG
ECOL EVOKE NITA
ROWE DYNES CLOD
```

591

```
LOBE TOPS ASSET
ATIT RASH PUREE
SHAH URSA IMAGE
SESAMESTREET
IRENE DECODES
ESS THAW RETIES
OASIS ANNE
GASOLINEALLEY
NARC TEMPI
ELMORE DIEM OSS
TASTERS BATHE
FLAMINGOROAD
OPERA EDIE COMA
RILEY LENT ELAN
GAMES LAOS DENS
```

592

```
CHEAT CHAR SLIM
CAPRA HERA TUBE
CRIMINALCHARGES
PEC WASP VESTS
WADE HOES
MANANA TOWNSHIP
ANIN ARRAU ARE
GIVESABADREVIEW
ITE PRICE IGNI
CANAILLE BASSET
ENOL POLE
AWISE PIMA ACT
SHOOTSTHEBREEZE
SOAP SKIT MORAN
TAMS HOLY SNORT
```

593

```
APED CROP PROP
RANUP HIVE LENA
CRAMS AGER ADEN
HOBBITFORMING
ELL OER LEROY
SEESAWS ACETATE
ITE AIL VON
TROLLBRIDGE
ECU EEE NAY
THREADS STYMIED
HINDU BOO MRI
PIXIELANDBAND
EMIT DRAP RIGID
MAKO EIRE STEEL
PEER ACED ERSE
```

594

```
MASH BASH IBID
APPEALSTO OSOLE
CHARGESAT LAXER
HIDDENAGENDA
ODE DYE ASCOTS
ICI ITT PRE
LACONFIDENTIAL
AIRER ORE IONIA
BESTKEPTSECRET
EGO SSS SKY
SENECA ESS ALI
PRIVATELIVES
JESSE ATANYTIME
ALLOW SUCCESSOR
ROOM APIE AONE
```

595

```
TSAR BEAT CEDES
OLGA RARE EMAIL
WARN ERIC RINGO
BAITANDSWITCH
ODE ASSET
BORDERLINE
REREAD ORE STAB
TEENY SPA UTICA
ERGO CEE ORATED
DOWSINGROD
SCRAM STE
HOOKANDLADDER
CANTO EYER UKES
ARGOT ANTI KENT
TIARA PESO EDDY
```

596

```
RAFTS SCALA WAS
EFLAT HOREB IDE
CROCODILEDUNDEE
COWARD TRESS
ASK TESLA ASTI
DESKS ABA TEN
ENTAIL AMASS
TORTOISESHELL
LEFTS HERALD
OAK STA SAMBA
FRAY SLATE ISH
FERAL CAREEN
SNAKEINTHEGRASS
EAT TABOO ALTOS
TSE SNARE DEEDS
```

597

```
PICK CARET SCOT
ERIE ADORE TOME
SONGANDDANCEMAN
ONE BILE OVERT
MAINE GREED
CHASTE BRAD ICH
LUCIE BAITS AAA
ORES CREME SNIT
SOL CLARE FIBRE
EKE RUNS BARONS
BREED CALEB
SCRIP OATS HOE
PAINTINGTHETOWN
ARTS MELEE APED
RAYE PEERS MESS
```

598

```
PECK BALM TSAR
ACRE ASEA BUENO
SHEREKHAN EDENS
TOWNIE DEPLORES
ERRS HORS
TABLE HERON UGH
ERAS SAWING COO
PAR STRIPES KIN
EBB CRONES NENE
EYE HANGS BURGS
ROOF TARA
NAPOLEON RANCID
ALOHA CANDYCANE
TILER HIRE EGGS
SEED ORAN SEEK
```

599

```
GRAZE OLIN FACT
AURAS XENA IDLE
SHOPPINGCENTAUR
PROP RASH ANGER
IGOR SPEEDY
FAUNANDGAMES
LUNGS OSU SHAM
IDI HOSTAGE ECO
PITA BAH YALTA
PEEWEEMERMAN
ASTRAY MOSS
SHOOS TAPA EURO
HARPYWALLBANGER
ELMO OREO HILDA
SEES WAXY SCION
```

600

```
LOSE SHEAF SAGS
ISNT TEASE TRUE
FLICKOFTHEWRIST
TOP ARTS HEATH
ELMS BRIE
HALSEY FAINTED
IDEA BUTTE MIT
SHOULDERHARNESS
SON AISLE INCA
CASTLES CANDOR
PELT CANE
ATHOS SUNK CPA
SHOOTFROMTHEHIP
PARK AUDIO GATE
SWAY DEANS ONYX
```

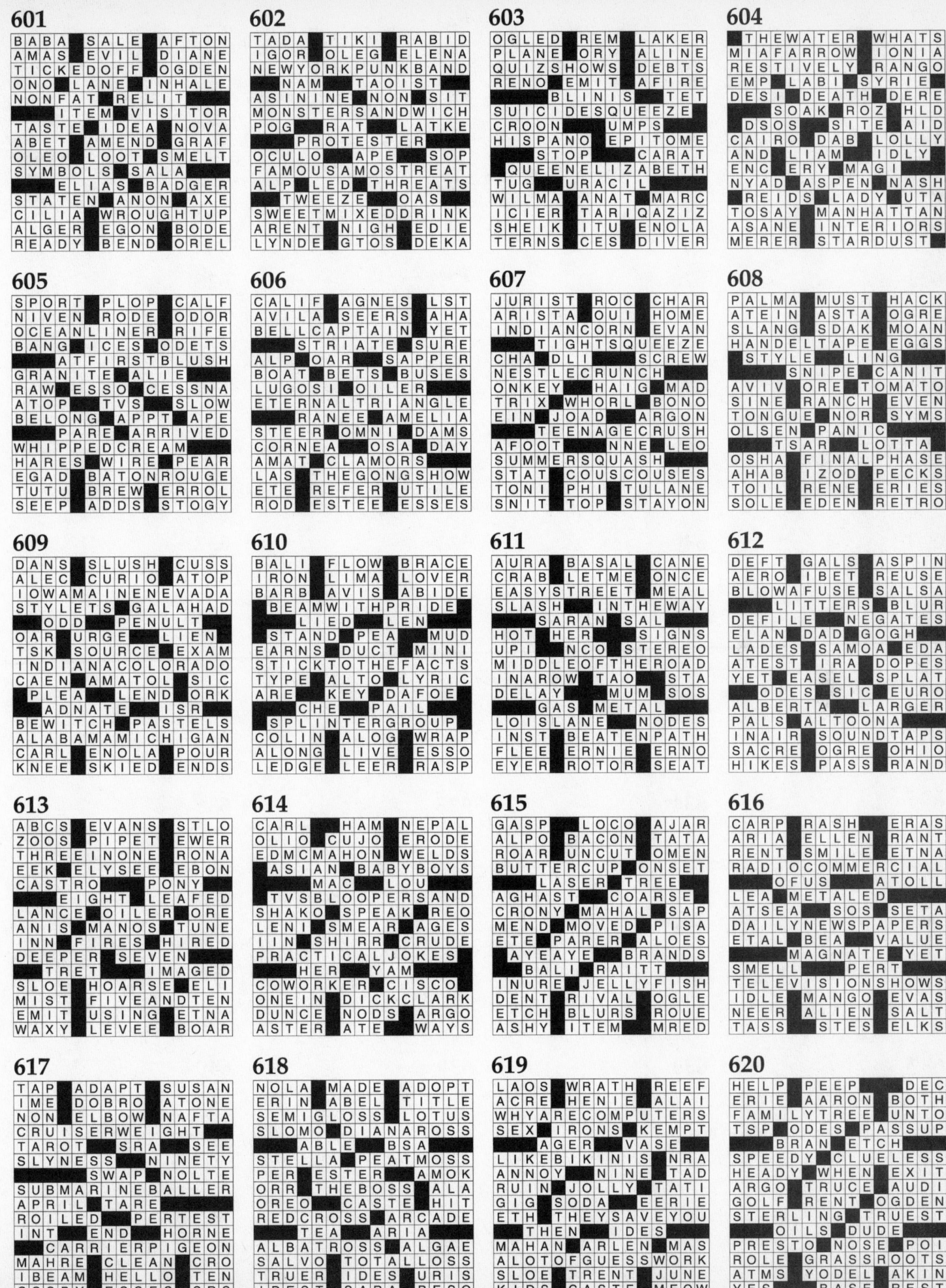

601
BABA SALE AFTON
AMAS EVIL DIANE
TICKEDOFF OGDEN
ONO LANE INHALE
NONFAT RELIT
ITEM VISITOR
TASTE IDEA NOVA
ABET AMEND GRAF
OLEO LOOT SMELT
SYMBOLS SALA
ELIAS BADGER
STATEN ANON AXE
CILIA WROUGHTUP
ALGER EGON BODE
READY BEND OREL

602
TADA TIKI RABID
IGOR OLEG ELENA
NEWYORKPUNKBAND
NAM TAOIST
ASININE NON SIT
MONSTERSANDWICH
POG RAT LATKE
PROTESTER
OCULO APE SOP
FAMOUSAMOSTREAT
ALP LED THREATS
TWEEZE OAS
SWEETMIXEDDRINK
ARENT NIGH EDIE
LYNDE GTOS DEKA

603
OGLED REM LAKER
PLANE ORY ALINE
QUIZSHOWS DEBTS
RENO EMIT AFIRE
BLINIS TET
SUICIDESQUEEZE
CROON UMPS
HISPANO EPITOME
STOP CARAT
QUEENELIZABETH
TUG URACIL
WILMA ANAT MARC
ICIER TARIQAZIZ
SHEIK ITU ENOLA
TERNS CES DIVER

604
THEWATER WHATS
MIAFARROW IONIA
RESTIVELY RANGO
EMP LABI SYRIE
DESI DEATH DERE
SOAK ROZ HLD
DSOS SITE AID
CAIRO DAB LOLLY
AND LIAM IDLY
ENC ERY MAGI
NYAD ASPEN NASH
REIDS LADY UTA
TOSAY MANHATTAN
ASANE INTERIORS
MERER STARDUST

605
SPORT PLOP CALF
NIVEN RODE ODOR
OCEANLINER RIFE
BANG ICES ODETS
ATFIRSTBLUSH
GRANITE ALIE
RAW ESSO CESSNA
ATOP TVS SLOW
BELONG APPT APE
PARE ARRIVED
WHIPPEDCREAM
HARES WIRE PEAR
EGAD BATONROUGE
TUTU BREW ERROL
SEEP ADDS STOGY

606
CALIF AGNES LST
AVILA SEERS AHA
BELLCAPTAIN YET
STRIATE SURE
ALP OAR SAPPER
BOAT BETS BUSES
LUGOSI OILER
ETERNALTRIANGLE
RANEE AMELIA
STEER OMNI DAMS
CORNEA OSA DAY
AMAT CLAMORS
LAS THEGONGSHOW
ETE REFER UTILE
ROD ESTEE ESSES

607
JURIST ROC CHAR
ARISTA OUI HOME
INDIANCORN EVAN
TIGHTSQUEEZE
CHA DLI SCREW
NESTLECRUNCH
ONKEY HAIG MAD
TRIX WHORL BONO
EIN JOAD ARGON
TEENAGECRUSH
AFOOT NNE LEO
SUMMERSQUASH
STAT COUSCOUSES
TONI PHI TULANE
SNIT TOP STAYON

608
PALMA MUST HACK
ATEIN ASTA OGRE
SLANG SDAK MOAN
HANDELTAPE EGGS
STYLE LING
SNIPE CANIT
AVIV ORE TOMATO
SINE RANCH EVEN
TONGUE NOR SYMS
OLSEN PANIC
TSAR LOTTA
OSHA FINALPHASE
AHAB IZOD PECKS
TOIL RENE ERIES
SOLE EDEN RETRO

609
DANS SLUSH CUSS
ALEC CURIO ATOP
IOWAMAINENEVADA
STYLETS GALAHAD
ODD PENULT
OAR URGE LIEN
TSK SOURCE EXAM
INDIANACOLORADO
CAEN AMATOL SIC
PLEA LEND ORK
ADNATE ISR
BEWITCH PASTELS
ALABAMAMICHIGAN
CARL ENOLA POUR
KNEE SKIED ENDS

610
BALI FLOW BRACE
IRON LIMA LOVER
BARB AVIS ABIDE
BEAMWITHPRIDE
LIED LEN
STAND PEA MUD
EARNS DUCT MINI
STICKTOTHEFACTS
TYPE ALTO LYRIC
ARE KEY DAFOE
CHE PAIL
SPLINTERGROUP
COLIN ALOG WRAP
ALONG LIVE ESSO
LEDGE LEER RASP

611
AURA BASAL CANE
CRAB LETME ONCE
EASYSTREET MEAL
SLASH INTHEWAY
SARAN SAL
HOT HER SIGNS
UPI NCO STEREO
MIDDLEOFTHEROAD
INAROW TAO STA
DELAY MUM SOS
GAS METAL
LOISLANE NODES
INST BEATENPATH
FLEE ERNIE ERNO
EYER ROTOR SEAT

612
DEFT GALS ASPIN
AERO IBET REUSE
BLOWAFUSE SALSA
LITTERS BLUR
DEFILE NEGATES
ELAN DAD GOGH
LADES SAMOA EDA
ATEST IRA DOPES
YET EASEL SPLAT
ODES SIC EURO
ALBERTA LARGER
PALS ALTOONA
INAIR SOUNDTAPS
SACRE OGRE OHIO
HIKES PASS RAND

613
ABCS EVANS STLO
ZOOS PIPET EWER
THREEINONE RONA
EEK ELYSEE EBON
CASTRO PONY
EIGHT LEAFED
LANCE OILER ORE
ANIS MANOS TUNE
INN FIRES HIRED
DEEPER SEVEN
TRET IMAGED
SLOE HOARSE ELI
MIST FIVEANDTEN
EMIT USING ETNA
WAXY LEVEE BOAR

614
CARL HAM NEPAL
OLIO CUJO ERODE
EDMCMAHON WELDS
ASIAN BABYBOYS
MAC LOU
TVSBLOOPERSAND
SHAKO SPEAK REO
LENI SMEAR AGES
IIN SHIRR CRUDE
PRACTICALJOKES
HER YAM
COWORKER CISCO
ONEIN DICKCLARK
DUNCE NODS ARGO
ASTER ATE WAYS

615
GASP LOCO AJAR
ALPO BACON TATA
ROAR UNCUT OMEN
BUTTERCUP ONSET
LASER TREE
AGHAST COARSE
CRONY MAHAL SAP
MEND MOVED PISA
ETE PARER ALOES
AYEAYE BRANDS
BALI RAITT
INURE JELLYFISH
DENT RIVAL OGLE
ETCH BLURS ROUE
ASHY ITEM MRED

616
CARP RASH ERAS
ARIA ELLEN RANT
RENT SMILE ETNA
RADIOCOMMERCIAL
OFUS ATOLL
LEA METALED
ATSEA SOS SETA
DAILYNEWSPAPERS
ETAL BEA VALUE
MAGNATE YET
SMELL PERT
TELEVISIONSHOWS
IDLE MANGO EVAS
NEER ALIEN SALT
TASS STES ELKS

617
TAP ADAPT SUSAN
IME DOBRO ATONE
NON ELBOW NAFTA
CRUISERWEIGHT
TAROT SRA SEE
SLYNESS NINETY
SWAP NOLTE
SUBMARINEBALLER
APRIL TARE
ROILED PERTEST
INT END HORNE
CARRIERPIGEON
MAHRE CLEAN CRO
IBEAM HELLO TEN
COSBY ESSES SRS

618
NOLA MADE ADOPT
ERIN ABEL TITLE
SEMIGLOSS LOTUS
SLOMO DIANAROSS
ABLE BSA
STELLA PEATMOSS
PER ESTER AMOK
ORR THEBOSS ALA
OREO CASTE HIT
REDCROSS ARCADE
TEA ARIA
ALBATROSS ALGAE
SALVO TOTALLOSS
TRUER IDES URIS
IDEST SARA PESO

619
LAOS WRATH REEF
ACRE HENIE ALAI
WHYARECOMPUTERS
SEX IRONS KEMPT
AGER VASE
LIKEBIKINIS NRA
ANNOY NINE TAD
RUIN JOLLY TATI
GIG SODA EERIE
ETH THEYSAVEYOU
THEN IDES
MAHAN ARLEN MAS
ALOTOFGUESSWORK
SLOE TRENT JUNE
KIDS CASTE MEOW

620
HELP PEEP DEC
ERIE AARON BOTH
FAMILYTREE UNTO
TSP ODES PASSUP
BRAN ETCH
SPEEDY CLUELESS
HEADY WHEN EXIT
ARGO TRUCE AUDI
GOLF RENT OGDEN
STERLING TRUEST
OILS DUDE
PRESTO NOSE POI
ROLE GRASSROOTS
ATMS YODEL AKIN
YES BASE REST

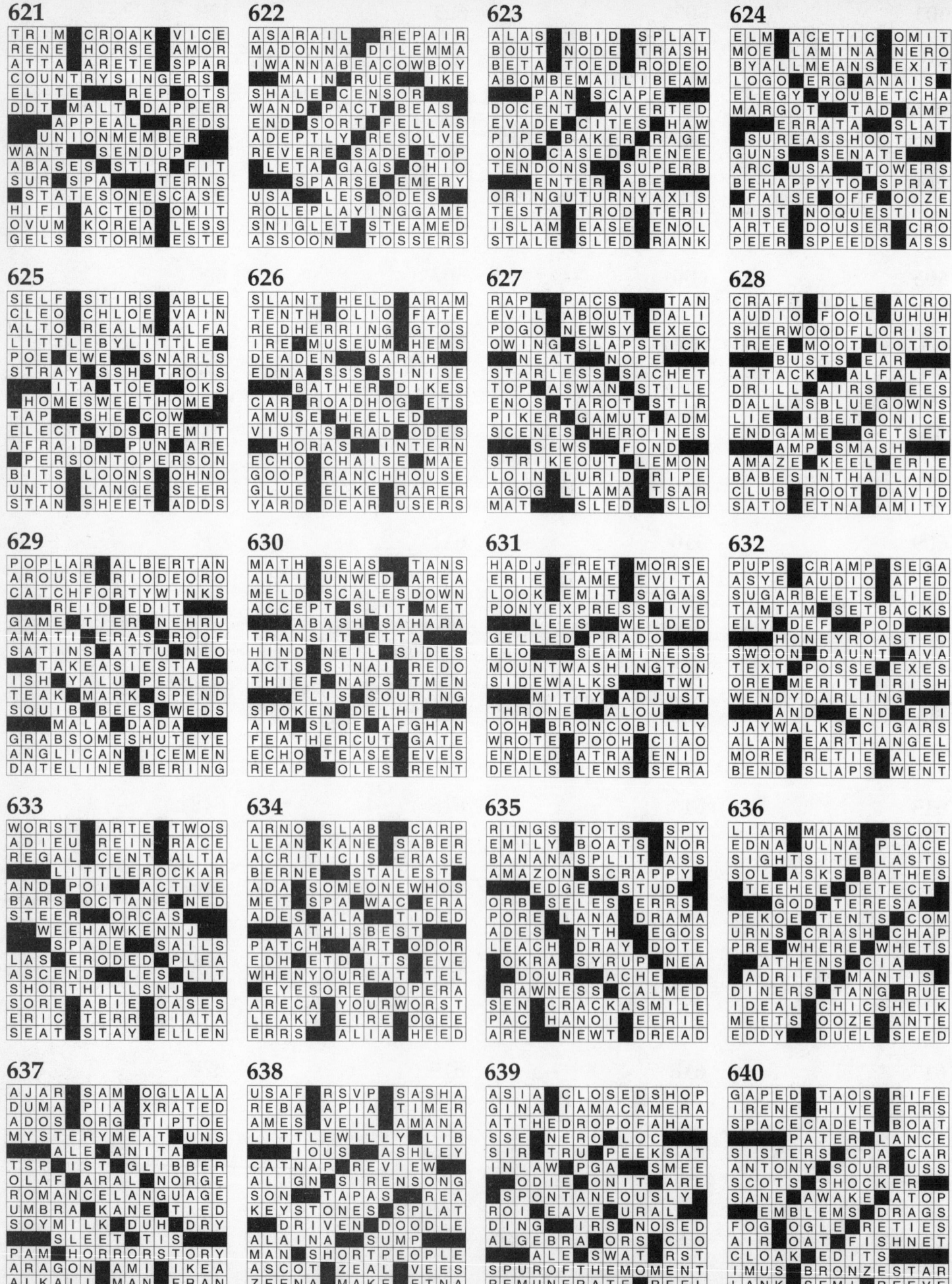

641
SERF SHOP PASHA
AQUA PURE ALAIN
MUSS AFAR STYLE
BUTTERFLIES COW
ASSERT LAUGH
DRAIN SPEECH
ETC INDEBT NERO
LORDS ERA CASES
AREA RADISH EWE
LEANTO STEAM
MEATS CLASPS
LAP THEMILKYWAY
EXULT TUTU HORN
ALFIE TIED ERIC
DEFER ORME MESH

642
DAM HOPED APOD
IRA AMICE TRACY
SCREWBALL RISEN
MAJAS FALSE SLA
ADORES TACKROOM
YER RHO AKINTO
SAS ARP NEL
MOLLYCODDLE
LIE SRI EDA
OPTIMO DUH MUS
BRADPITT MOROSE
LOG ELIOT MANTA
AVERT NAILBITER
DENIS ESTER ORE
INDO STOVE NED

643
ORES FLAG AGED
VENTS IOTA LAVA
ADMIT ROTS SLAM
THEROSETATTOO
EOS PAW CRY SLO
THEBLACKORCHID
LYELL AHEAD
FOCI SLAPS ISMS
ADREM RAHAL
VIOLETSAREBLUE
ANA TAU ORC NIL
THEGILDEDLILY
BAIO ETUI EATEN
IRAN NOTE FREED
ZANE DRED ARNE

644
SCAM STALK MEMO
COLA LATIN AVID
ROLL ERASE GALE
IPUTADOLLARINA
PEDAL LEDA SNO
TRE IRS WATER
FEATURE ROSE
CHANGEMACHINE
GLAD SMASHED
YEMEN HON RIP
PAM ALIA NIECE
NOTHINGCHANGED
ASCH STALE LAMA
PEKE TRIAD ELAN
ERSE SONNY TENT

645
REBA PLOT CART
ACRE HEROD ALOU
TOUR DEERE MOAN
ELSIE SOAPOPERA
HEAD SHOOS
ROASTED THIRST
ELS SLUSH STATE
GLIB ISSUE EZRA
AIDED TELLA OUR
LEERED LIBERTY
KNITS SERB
HONEYCOMB ENACT
EVIL ENOLA ECHO
WANE SETUP SKIN
SLAY DEER TSPS

646
ROVER SASH SOLD
ANITA ELIA CLEO
HONOR MORT ADAM
ONELIFETOLIVE
LIST INDEED
JACLYN WET
ALAI DASH ASSES
GENERALHOSPITAL
SCENE MESH GAVE
TEA RANGED
PAPERS DEER
ALLMYCHILDREN
SLAB RUNT OVERT
TONE OLEO WIRED
EWER WARN SLOPS

647
TEAM LHASA TAG
LUCID EASES OWE
CRAZYEIGHTS PAN
DENY SETAPART
GTE EER RESIZES
REM SLIM ESS
ATIT EPIC ITSME
DRESSTOTHENINES
EASEL NEON LIDS
TOO RISE TIE
OLESTRA RIG CAN
RAKEHELL GASH
AMI FIVEANDTENS
TAN UDINE SYRIA
ERG LANDS ESPN

648
HOOP SAP BIASED
ONUS ULA UNLIKE
LITA RAN SHARES
MOLLYPITCHER
ENAMEL PER BAA
SSW LUCILLEBALL
APSES ERIE
BARBS ELI WANTS
ALOE AWAIT
NEILDIAMOND GPS
GEL END STRAIT
WINSLOWHOMER
MARACA OLE MICE
AVOCET AIR ANEW
DECODE DOS NESS

649
ORALS STINK CTR
PELEE HANOI HIE
THESTLOUISBLUES
IER SAT THISTLE
MATE RAVI TUNIC
ALLTHATJAZZ ENT
SYNE STE RYES
AXED EDIE
CAWS KEG CLOP
AVA BEATSTHERAP
LINDA DOOR TELL
LATIFAH CID SEA
ITSAFREECOUNTRY
NOT LEAVE POEME
SRO EATER ENSOR

650
PIPPI PESCI DUH
AGAIN ORION IRA
DOWNTOEARTH SIN
TERM ETE HAN
DEMAND ARETHA
EMU DEPTH ICH
LAD ROUE THEFT
LIST SUDAN ODOR
ALLAH NOVA IRE
ICE DRESS RCA
ARNOLD SALTED
LOG LIT MAME
ASI CASSIUSCLAY
RIN ANAIS OHARE
MEG TARPS NEWTS

651
SACS LOGE DART
ASHE BONGO IGOR
FEET SHARP RULE
EARTH SWEETTALK
REED STRAY
AYEAYE ARISES
SGT DEGAS ENOLA
PAAR RADAR GUAM
APRON DARES RTE
RETAIN AVENGE
SLURS STIR
BITTEREND SCALE
ODIE SPIRE EPEE
PEER ELDER SEAL
SASS YEWS TSPS

652
FOOLS BEFIT BUT
INDIA ELAND ANE
SMOKYPLACES NBA
HERA LITE AJAR
BLAZEOFGLORY
EVILEYE FIAT
DANES AFFRONTS
GIT DANSE ORE
ENORMOUS CORAL
AINT ALABAMA
HEARTSONFIRE
AXLE CARE RTES
YUL BURNINGLOVE
EDO ISAAC AIMEE
SET LOTSA SNERD

653
BUTTIN JEFF ABA
ATEASE AMIE REN
TAXLAW BOGEYMAN
ALIEN SLOANE
ITS ASTRO UNIX
WATCHTHEBIRDIE
OREO VOLT
PAREXCELLENCE
LIAR BOLT
FLYLIKEANEAGLE
BRIO ESSEN WAX
RANGES HITCH
ACEAWARD GREENE
CAN ELIA HELENA
ESS REDD SELLER

654
SLOPS SLED GAZA
HANOI WORE IBEX
OSHEA ARIA JANE
WHATMAGICDUO
TENSER PREENS
ODD SAO RAG LIT
HELPSONEMAKE
JAPE TUB ANEW
ABANKDEPOSIT
ILL NOD TEM MCV
LESSEN AMPERE
PENANDTELLER
ZERO IGOR RABAT
AMOK NAME STATE
PUCE GREW ESSEX

655
ARCH WEEPY SPEW
BOLO EDGAR HAVE
BLACKBIRDS UVEA
ELY AFTER STORK
OHO TEMPT
SHANNON SKYLARK
HOSE TIP TREMOR
RUFUS BOA ICOME
URANUS PDQ ORES
BIRDMAN SUCCESS
EUGES AOK
CHIRP TWAIN VEE
LOOP WHIRLYBIRD
ANNA HENIE BEDE
DEAR OREAD SWAN

656
BAGS CHEEK BOOK
ELLA HUMAN AXLE
GOODFIGURE LEER
ONO ILE LEBANON
TEMPLE DYLAN
LEAVE SACHET
MENU NATO LEERY
ALAS STAND BARN
PEROT SITE ELSE
SECRET LORCA
MEANS ARMADA
MELISSA TIE RIN
OVEN TOTALWOMAN
LIEU EMILE TONI
ELKS DINED TREE

657
BARD MACY CARPE
ASEA ALOE AMORE
WHAT ROLL TOTER
LOVELYTOLOOKAT
ERODE REN TED
DEW NAP DOTTIER
PIPED IRONY
PRETTYWOMAN
SALON SALEM
CRAFTED GEL HUB
HAT MEA ARENA
BEAUTIFULGIRLS
LIARS COLA SEEK
SAUTE EONS ESSE
UNSER STAT SYST

658
YETI BLAMER MGS
AMAN RELATE ART
PUBCRAWLING GAR
AYN NATALIE
ACCRA LGE CINE
GREENTEA LATEST
TOR RADIATE
WALKINGTHEDOG
LOOSEST VAT
ANNALS TAILPIPE
BEAM SST OLDEN
ASTAIRE ONO
STU RUNNINGWILD
EER ASTUTE ERIE
DDE STATES DELE

659
SLAW ACTI WAVED
HIVE COON OLIVE
AMID ENID RELIC
GADGETFLIES ELK
ELAL AXEL
YEW ELIS UNISON
ALIEN CARR NEMO
NIPSINTHEBUDGET
NOES ASIT RANGE
ITSELF BIBI OAS
NOTA COAT
YUM TARGETHEELS
ATARI RENT ALOE
KAZOO ARCO RIOT
SHEEN SEEM YAMS

660
TOGA MUSES ROW
APED ISTLE AURA
PUTONTHEFEEDBAG
ESS ITEM LOLLS
ONER STARES
REUBEN ELITE
ESNE ATONE FRA
EATYOURHEARTOUT
DUO CRIES HOBO
STAEL ANADEM
DROOLS FRAN
KRUPP TIES SPA
EATHIGHONTHEHOG
ANTS AIMEE GAGA
SKY PEERS ODOR

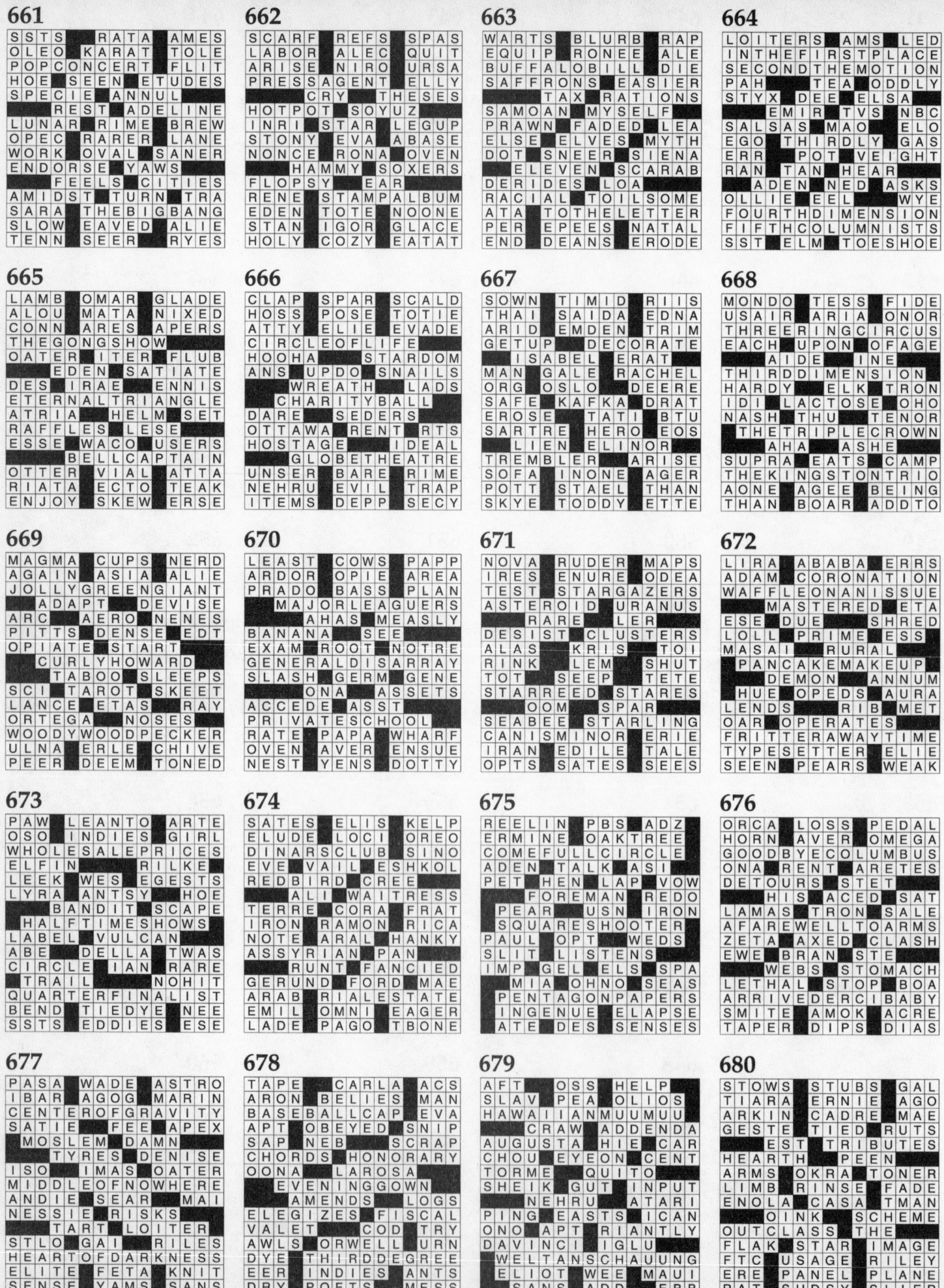

681

```
FUMED TEAR JETT
ATONE WANE ALOE
CARDS IRKS MARX
THESKYSTHELIMIT
      SETH NEE
CRIMEA   STS CAD
HANGTHECOST  OLE
ITEM   VAL  BLOB
LIP  SPENDTHRIFT
DOT  WON  REACTS
      PAL STIR
MONEYISNOOBJECT
IDEA COAT EERIE
ROAR ELIA REINS
ARTY DOLL TREES
```

682

```
PARDS BROS TARA
CHARM RANK ONES
BAZOOKAJOE  RAVI
STEPTOE  REFRIED
      KEN   AISLE
ZITI  AMI  FTD
EVICT ATALL  WBA
ROCKETJSQUIRREL
ORK  MIAOU  PEARL
   DPS KAT DYNA
INTEL    RIM
MAEWEST  SILAGES
PINA  PISTOLPETE
EVER IDEA ELATE
LETS TEXT RERAN
```

683

```
DAM  DAD  NIPIN
RICO SARI ANISE
NEMOWOMEN  VALID
STERILE  KEYNES
     END  SAVE
DADAISM  TALONS
LIL TENAM NYLON
ITT RADAR  DII
STAIR PARIS EST
PORTAL  MACABRE
     ECON ARR
COMETO  TRAIPSE
COLIC REEDSDEER
PLAZA ARNO GERE
REFER DAS  ELF
```

684

```
ANTIC OPAH SAGS
BEIGE RONA ESAI
CAGOLDRUSH  ACRE
STEREO  CAANGELS
      BLAH  CANIT
CAGIRLS  INOLDCA
ALICE  MAMAS
TINY HAPPY  FORE
     AORTA ELBOW
HOTELCA  CASUITE
ENOLA ATIT
CARAISIN  DRAMAS
AJET  CADREAMING
TARE OGRE DONOT
EGOS TOED AKINS
```

685

```
BETH  SASH  PRO
ODOR ARIAS GRIP
NIGHTLIGHT  ROPE
DEA WISH  EVADED
     SANE SWAN
BOWTIE  SCANDALS
ALIEN SEAR SLIT
TIRE THIRD TOBY
EVER RENE PANEL
DESCRIBE  MANGLE
   LISA WELD
FLUENT SAME HOG
RATA ACHYBREAKY
OMAR NOONE BLIP
MPH  BEER BEES
```

686

```
CAWS HERA PRADO
AGIN AWED LALAW
RONA HELL AZURE
ORDINARYINCOME
LAYLA   BEER
     SMOCK ESCAPE
ADS EVENS UPON
GENERALELECTION
ASAP LEARY ARE
RIGHTS STAND
     EIRE IAMBS
COMMONFRACTION
CALEB ERIC ENYA
PADRE METE REEK
ANEAR YEAS SORE
```

687

```
VADER SHOP PATS
OPERA LOVE ERIC
ISAAC USER PITA
DEN KURTRUSSELL
    JEEPS SOILED
GROTTO TEARS
LENO NOODLE DIM
EDENS PIG RHODA
NOS PEELER ONLY
    WAYNE AWAKES
FIERCE SCORN
JODIEFOSTER ORE
ONIT ULNA SATIE
RICH LEAR EXTOL
DATE SOPS NESTS
```

688

```
ADES MARIN CHIN
LAVE ALINE PESO
ELECTRICCURRANT
CARTE HARE  DOE
KIT  RAM  OPAL
    MIMOSA ELIZA
ALDA ATIT NIGER
BERRYTHEHATCHET
BEENE EVER ITSY
ARAIL RENATA
    MELT SMU SAT
GAL ERAS  TAMPA
APEAROFTROUSERS
USSR TRIED WAIT
LOSE HORDE ERLE
```

689

```
SRS FTD REPLATE
PETERII ORIOLES
ANALOGS TSQUARE
AFRAMES  STUD
KRIS REC  EELER
ONTO DRAB  RARE
   ICE ADAM SAX
XCHROMOSOME
BAM STEP EVE
ABET EDEN ENOS
LENAS DIE ORCA
RAMP  CRATION
GFORCES EASTEND
ALBERTS STAINER
BOLDEST TOP TSE
```

690

```
ACCEDE SODA MOC
FOAMED THEO ARR
INSIDETRACK CEE
NEHRU AURA SHOP
ESC COMMANDPOST
ATEAM  TAL
MORE FARM BURRO
ALDA SNOOP RANT
JESTS YENS GNAT
ITE  AIDES
POMMELHORSE ATM
ILIE DESC CACHE
ZED BENCHJOCKEY
ZAG USNA ADHERE
ANE STAR WEEDER
```

691

```
LAMB MAGIC SEAM
ARIA AMANA ALVA
SACREDIBIS TIER
STERN STATUARY
ISIS  BURSTS
DEVOUTCOWARD
RYE ELITE FAZED
URAL LOTTA YALE
MELEE NOTUP NAB
BLESSEDEVENT
AGHAST DIDI
REENACTS ROBOT
SOLE HOLYTOLEDO
ODES ERASE ETON
NENE DOYLE TARS
```

692

```
SCIFI FORM DAVY
ORGAN ONEA ELIA
BIOLOGICALCLOCK
STRAINED  RATES
FLA  STAN
DANE WATCHTOWER
ELAL MARIE AMO
CID SATAN GEL
ABE SATUP BORE
FIRSTTIMER ONYX
HUES  ESL
SPOON TEETOTAL
HOURGLASSFIGURE
ASST IRAS ENLAI
METS ZERO SALTS
```

693

```
SPACER BLOC KLM
TENURE ROLL RAM
ANTLER OBIE EWE
SALVATIONARMY
TIC NHL RELET
OVID REAR DIRE
MEDIACIRCUS NSA
MERL  CHUM
ERA CULTURECLUB
RODS DAHS LENA
RAJAH RAE AAA
SUGARHILLGANG
MTS REEF LANDIS
PET PERT INTENT
HRS OKAY ENERGY
```

694

```
TOMS SPIN SPA
ALEE TOGAS ALEX
NINE OLEIC DOZE
YOUREMYTRILL
ASS NAG OATHS
PESOS SOIREE
AMEER NADA ONE
SYNCOPATEDCLUCK
TRA OLES RITES
ENCASE SIREE
RATIO REP PET
TWEETADELINE
ALEC TRIBE AQUA
FISH SALLE TURK
TVS STEM SEES
```

695

```
MIA ASIMOV TEMP
POL LENORE IVOR
SUBSTATION MAJA
ATALL ONEDAY
ORNERY EMMY EVE
WEEPS PSI ALDER
LAS PATNESS
RESERVECLAUSE
TROLLEY IWO
DEMUR OLD VADER
ELI EAVE LITERS
NOMADS MIATA
ZION SCRUBNURSE
ESSO ERASED MEL
LEAN TOWELS SAL
```

696

```
RAM VAMP CUTER
ERR ELIE SASHAY
VISITING CLEAVE
COTTAGEFRIES
GONE  SUN
ONUS HOUSEORGAN
TED NAPS VERNE
HIGHEST DEACONS
IDEAL SELL PUT
CASTLEWALK BELL
MAL  ESSE
CABINCRUISER
AVENUE TOLLGATE
GIGGLE EWES WRY
EDSEL SADA LYE
```

697

```
DOT LATHS APB
EPOCH ARIEL BAA
EAGLE MENLOPARK
PLAIN PAGE ISLE
PIGS ANOTHER
DIPPER BLEAT
OBIE IOOI FETCH
FACT DONNA ROLE
FRAYS MUGS PLUM
CROPS TRADES
REPLICA TOOT
OLEO THAW ATONE
SLAPHAPPY SEWED
EEK AVAIL TREED
SRS MEHTA DRY
```

698

```
DADA ESS PAGES
AGES NATO ENOLA
MONSIEURVERDOUX
ADO OINK IDO
MRSMINIVER PEEN
EEL VETO ORRS
ANYTIME SLAM
TEEHEE LAMBDA
ERRS USHERED
BOAR ITIS UNA
LOVE MRMAJESTYK
ALI LEAP EVE
MADAMESOUSATZKA
ELLEN SSTS TAIL
SAYSO EEE OPTS
```

699

```
MARC USED RANUP
AROO DALI EVOKE
MAUIMOUSE SARAN
ELENA LAUGHLAST
ATO  LOOSE
DAUGHTERDAWN
ACRE BLEEDS MAD
DIGS ISL SAVE
ODE REHEAT AXES
BEAUTYSBUICK
CROSS PAS
TAUPETOTE BANGS
ALLEN GAUGEGAIN
FLEET ECRU ERGO
TARPS ETON SCOW
```

700

```
APSO TAMP DREW
SLUR COCOA RICE
PASSTHEHAT EIRE
ITA ROSE TOSSUP
CONCUR DOERS
OLES PROCURE
SPRAY TMEN ISAK
LOOT SOARS RENE
OLIO TOGA ACRID
GOLFBAG SOUL
PARES CREAMY
STRAYS TATA LIE
MAUI HORSESHOES
OXEN INAPT ANNE
GIST PEWS MESS
```

701
```
MAST  BASTE MET
ALTAR AREAS AVE
SPARECHANGE  TEN
COSTAR  LOG  RENT
   ALES  REVERTS
CLERMONT  DAH
OUI  LOOS  SANKA
STRIKEUPTHEBAND
TEETH  TERI  NEO
  EAR  DARKAGES
ALUMNUS  PENS
LENS  MIT  RATTLE
AMI  SPLITSCREEN
MOT  ALONE  KARAN
ONE  MESTA  LAKE
```

702
```
ETE  SCALA  BASIS
MIX  PANEL  ELATE
IRE  EVENT  RATED
LITTLEWOMEN  IRA
INERT  ALE  RAT
OGRE  HOSNI  RITE
   MENU  VASES
  SHORTSHRIFT
ARTIE  HOOP
PERT  ASIDE  IMRE
PGA  ART  SNEER
EAT  SMALLCHANGE
ALIAS  PEALE  TAC
RIFLE  LARUE  ALT
SAYIT  ENDER  LES
```

703
```
GOSH  HERE  SAMBA
ALOE  ERIC  PRIED
FEAR  LOCO  AGNES
FORBIDDENFRUIT
   MOE  OAKS
WOODEN  AMIS  OAT
ACCRA  SMIT  ALMA
THEUNTOUCHABLES
CRAM  RUSS  SLINK
HEN  SATE  BREEDS
   BACH  SEE
PROHIBITEDAREA
DIANA  EDIT  SOAP
ICIER  NELL  POSE
SALSA  DALE  STYX
```

704
```
SHAR  MACH  MAZY
IOTA  MARIO  ILIE
CHICKENNAPOLEON
OPERATE  ELLEN
   CALL  PLED
BECAUSETHE  ABUT
ALERT  HIS  MUTI
MIN  JAILS  TIM
BOTH  OSS  RICCI
ITSA  CHICKENHAD
   LAKE  HECK
JAYNE  CANAPES
SOMANYBONYPARTS
USER  ERICA  DIOR
MEND  DANE  SEWS
```

705
```
GOOSE  FLOP  BASH
ARCED  RIDE  UREY
FACTS  ADDRESSED
FLUB  HISS  ABODE
   PAPAL  IRONY
BEACON  HINNY
RANKED  ADV  SOCK
IST  TIZZIES  ULA
MESA  CEE  STATUE
  SPANS  TINSEL
SATUP  DEREK
DOLOR  WOOD  MICE
INPURSUIT  BORAX
LIEN  ISNT  ONTAP
LAND  LAKY  YESNO
```

706
```
BART  SLUMP  APES
AMOS  PERIL  SAVE
SOCK  LANKA  SLAW
INK  RAPSESSIONS
EGOTIST  TIS
  FISH  ELITISTS
FLARE  PLACE  WOW
LOGE  SALTS  MILA
EVE  LUCIE  LINDY
DESSERTS  RUNG
   OAF  BATISTA
ALLTHATJAZZ  HIP
POOH  CAIRO  LIAR
BOCA  ELMER  AFRO
SPOT  SKIDS  STAN
```

707
```
SPUD  ASAP  STS
TIMID  MESAS  CRY
APPLEPOLISH  RON
RESUME  LATITUDE
   TANG  ARAB
ESSENCES  STUNT
AYE  DENTS  SPURN
CRAB  ERA  ERIE
HULAS  SANDS  SEW
PICAS  PERTNESS
   NOLA  RARE
SIGNALED  MIASMA
POW  MOPUPACTION
ATA  INEPT  TENON
MAX  SEES  RENO
```

708
```
ROPER  THIS  SCUD
OPERA  RICH  MONO
OPTIC  ARIA  ALSO
FORCEFIELDS  DER
ESO  ANDY  HAFT
DELTAS  BEGETS
   ONTARIO  HELI
CREWNECKSWEATER
BETE  SCORERS
SECRET  DETERS
MESS  KAAT  DIN
JET  STAFFOFLIFE
ORES  SPIT  RUBLE
AGRA  PURE  ABLER
NEAP  STER  NEEDS
```

709
```
LEVEL  CROC  CHAR
AROMA  HOAR  ROUE
HOITYTOITY  URGE
ROD  SAUL  BOSSED
   GONG  BANTERS
MCCAUGHEYBOYS
REALTY  TOYS  ETA
ELLA  BUB  SNUG
DLI  EGAD  GOESTO
  FRAULEINFREUD
AROUSED  SOFA
MERGES  TOMB  SPA
PANG  SOYBEANOIL
EDIE  ENNA  SIRED
DYAD  DEER  EXTRA
```

710
```
CLOP  AHAB  OBOE
HEAL  SUEDE  RUBY
EASYSTREET  ERIE
EVE  TOAD  TAGGED
PESTER  STENO
   OWED  IRONIES
STABS  RAGE  TRAP
LISA  CEDED  RISE
ALEC  ODOR  TASTE
PLACING  SARI
  OCTET  CULLED
DEGREE  IDOL  ORE
ELMO  MEMORYLANE
FLEA  PREEN  AMID
TEND  TADS  DYES
```

711
```
AUTOS  GAIT  BOSS
STENO  ALSO  LAPP
KEATS  POEM  ASIA
  MOOSEHEADBEER
CCS  ASA  HASSLE
OUTLET  RAN
STEAL  SHAW  COOS
TURTLENECKSHIRT
APSE  VANE  HINDU
   BEG  RENTED
CHASER  STY  MRS
HAWKEYEPIERCE
OBOE  OREL  HANDS
PIKE  NILE  ENTER
STET  EELS  ASSES
```

712
```
HONES  CLUB  CHIP
ADORN  HIRE  LANA
LEAGUEOFNATIONS
ESC  FLOE  MAPLES
   CAFES  BOER
ADOS  MEXICAN
BRUIN  ENOS  PEI
CONFERENCECALLS
SPT  PESO  OCALA
  WHATNOT  HUEY
SERE  RUBES
INLAWS  SIRE  IBM
DIVISIONOFLABOR
EDIT  DEAL  ALLIE
MESH  EDGE  YIELD
```

713
```
CAMP  STLO  SAMAR
OLEO  THIN  ILONA
SAILFROMENGLAND
TIN  AERO  UNITES
   TMEN  SMEE
SPIRIT  SHED  JAN
PENAS  PAAR  SORE
REACHPLYMOUTHMA
ERNE  LUNE  LONER
ESE  MANO  CLOSES
   LOCK  SIMP
SABINE  LAVA  EBB
THANKSGIVINGDAY
AMIDE  ALEC  OGLE
RELAY  PASS  BEES
```

714
```
BORE  FAIL  RADON
APEX  RENE  AFIRE
STEP  ERAS  TAXED
KEVINCOSTNER
DEREK  PAID  SEA
  ELLIOTTGOULD
JAB  LEST  FIDO
ANALYST  SHIFTER
DOLE  ALAN  ERE
EDMONDOBRIEN
DEY  ACTS  REUSE
  JULIEANDREWS
ABZUG  ONME  SNIP
LOATH  SCOT  ETNA
PAGET  EEKS  SAGS
```

715
```
TED  DAZED  FRAME
AXE  INANE  LURID
RAPIDCITY  ECOLE
AMPS  HRS  TEKWAR
   SHOE  BTU
JAGUAR  CROSSBAR
OILER  SAINT  ALA
ILE  DAWDLER  GET
NEA  ABIDE  EVERT
SYNONYMY  REALTY
   DDS  BETS
BRIEFS  JRS  EDGE
LOTSA  QUICKSAND
AMASS  ENNUI  MAD
SPRAT  DEKED  STY
```

716
```
ADOBE  SCI  GRATE
CABAL  TOR  REPOT
THINKTANK  AGENT
SLED  ORC  ACADIA
   SIREE  SIT
  MAANDPAKETTLE
PRAWN  THE  ARIA
LAG  SOO  AWL  ORT
EGIS  FRA  EAVES
BUCKETBRIGADE
   IRE  UNARM
ZOLTAN  GIT  IOTA
EXITS  BUTTERTUB
RENEE  ALI  PATRI
ONERS  MAO  ALONE
```

717
```
AEGIS  REHAB  LPS
BRENT  AROSE  IOU
CANDYHEARTS  ALE
STEELE  SNIT  RED
   NERD  ENMASSE
SECT  BOLD  AMP
ISR  EGO  SNOOTY
LAIC  RENTA  SKYE
TUMULT  ERN  EPA
ETA  ARID  ARES
MIASMAS  ODER
ANN  OUST  ARREAR
RAW  TRUSSBRIDGE
INA  TARAS  EVERY
EER  ALERT  DENIS
```

718
```
SAP  CUPCAKE  ADE
ARE  UNRAVEL  PIN
MYTHREESONS  TAM
BARA  SENT  FILE
ANIMATE  ALTOS
  EIGHTISENOUGH
LEE  NERD  DUE
SHEL  TIGER  GEES
COL  DODO  AWE
ONEDAYATATIME
ROVED  VANILLA
ELAN  NADA  NEER
PUT  HAWAIIFIVEO
ALE  BRAILLE  ERS
DUD  ODYSSEY  NYE
```

719
```
ACTA  SCALD  TASK
PAIR  ARNIE  ASTO
SHEMOVEDACURSER
ENRAGES  MONTANA
   TESSA  RAYON
ESQUE  TATER
SOUR  EPOCHS  JOE
PRIERCOMMITMENT
YEP  ERNIES  CATO
  KLUTZ  TENON
RADII  ESSEN
ALAMEDA  MARTINI
KEYOFAFLATMINER
EVAN  FROZE  ROOM
RENO  TOTED  ENNA
```

720
```
APED  MAMA  PAL
MENU  ERECT  BONE
BEDOFROSES  UNTO
IRS  LISA  HARDEN
   CUTE  RIPE
LATHES  TARRAGON
ALIAS  PACT  URGE
MIMI  ARIES  CEDE
EVER  MOLD  GREED
REDWOODS  GRANNY
   ONUS  WHET
MORMON  SHOE  OFF
IDEA  TIMESTABLE
LOAN  SNORT  POUT
ERR  AGES  BEBE
```

721

```
SHEAF  SHES  DASH
TORSI  TONI  ALPO
DEEPSEATED  NAIL
SSS  CPR  ELAINE
   THICKSKINNED
ELSIE   HIKING
CAMERA  NECK  GEM
OVER  GREEK  BARE
NAE  WRIT  SLOGAN
   POETIC  ORATE
WIDEREACHING
ALASKA  ENG  ALI
FLUE  BROADBASED
TENT  LENT  ONEAL
SRTA  EVES  WACKY
```

722

```
GEAR  PLEAS  PROW
AXLE  TALIA  ROBE
FUDGESWIRL  ICER
FLEAS  NOTE  SKYE
STRIPS   TOMBOY
   NYET   UNRIG
ZAPS  WAITER  ONE
ELI  JETTING  AGO
TIS  ERASED  ODES
ASTIR   ROUX
   ANKLES  WRINGS
SECT  IVES  ADORE
ACHE  NEAPOLITAN
WHIR  UNTIL  ZIPS
SOON  STONE  EPEE
```

723

```
CRAT  PLOT  LAVAL
AIDA  EAVE  ADOBE
PNEUMATICDRILLS
ESP  ENT  HEADSET
RETINUE   BSA
   TUT  ERA  SOPH
OILED  FLIT  NEA
MNEMONICDEVICES
IRA  ERIE  INERT
TIFF  PED  ASI
   RCA  LEATHER
SERIALS  EGG  ELI
KNITTINGNEEDLES
IDIOT  IOTA  RICK
MOSSY  TOON  TOTS
```

724

```
GAB  HOBBLE  PERT
ELI  SHARON  OLEO
NIGHTSTAND  PLAY
EBOAT  EUGENEILL
RATION  NEAR  PTA
ABEGGAR  DRAWSON
LAD  ODE   HERD
   DDAY  RACY
DECO   GUY  STE
INANITY  TRISTAN
STY  COOT  ASKING
THEHYMORS  LINGO
ARNO  THELRANGER
FANS  IONIAN  ENG
FLEE  TOTTED  RTE
```

725

```
PEAT  CLAW  MULE
AMPS  AURA  NASAL
PIPEORGAN  CRAWL
AGE  ARE  GHOSTS
CRAFTY  FLESHOUT
YELL  OREL  DIE
   AMBLE  ESTATE
SKELETONKEY
SCHEME  TWAIN
ORA  WHEN  SACS
BADBLOOD  THEDOT
SILENT  SRI  VIE
AHEAD  BONECHINA
DESKS  EROS  ACED
ESTE  DEBS  HEDY
```

726

```
JOBS  KAPPA  WHIG
OLIO  AIRES  HOSE
HEARTBREAKHOTEL
NOSTRUMS  EYERS
   UKE  DODO
DEVILINDISGUISE
IVORY  ALLY  DIM
NITE  CARLO  TIED
ATE  COLE  SHONE
HARDHEADEDWOMAN
   RIDS  SOO
ORION  ATTRACTS
FOLLOWTHATDREAM
FUEL  IRATE  ELMO
SEXY  GIBED  ALEG
```

727

```
SLAT  MATH  GAMES
LOCI  ALOE  ABASE
ADEN  NAME  REUSE
WIDESTSELECTION
   DAR  LOS
ARE  BASTION  ASS
TAMER  HASP  CLAW
INCREDIBLEVALUE
LEER  ERLE  ABATE
TEE  TAKESON  YET
   POL  CCC
LOWESTPRICEEVER
ASHES  LULU  AERO
SHAVE  ABEL  SNIT
HATES  TEST  EACH
```

728

```
TRACT  SPOUT  HRS
HONOR  HOWSO  YUL
ULTRAVIOLET  PIA
SLEEPIER  AGENT
   END  SPLURGE
LAMAZE  QUILTS
OBESE  GULLY  PAW
BUGS  DRAKE  JAVA
ETA  GEARS  BACON
PARENT  CEMENT
ATHWART  CAD
TOOLS   BALLOONS
OWN  SUPERMARKET
NEE  EGRET  MARIA
ELS  SHORE  PLANT
```

729

```
ACID  MAST  ETHIC
LOVE  ESPY  ARENA
GRAFPAPER  RAIDS
AENEAS  WORD  DYE
   ALUM  SERGE
ESOTERIC  QUANTA
FAR  SERUM  MISER
LURE  RELIC  NEAL
ADDED  STRAW  ESE
TIERED  STRICKEN
   PYLON  HERO
ORO  EGOS  FEASTS
POSIT  STARRSHIP
UNITE  ELLE  TONE
SATED  DOLE  SEED
```

730

```
POMP  RESIN  BABA
OHIO  EAUDE  UFOS
WALLSTREET  YAPS
ERA  HUN  ATWORST
RANCOR  ALLEN
   LENDL  ELMIRA
ALLI  TEAR  LAVIN
HOOF  ORBIT  RAGE
ALOFT  NATO  GNAW
BATHED  MAORI
   ANITA  LANDHO
OCONNOR  MSG  RUB
GROG  DINAHSHORE
RAZE  ECOLE  ILLS
EWER  SEWED  ELSE
```

731

```
LIED  TOFU  SEDGE
ENDO  WALL  POORS
ADIN  ERIC  ANDES
PICKLESPEAR  GEE
SATEEN   RESTERS
   YESES  SEED
REB  TOTO  RAVE
DEEP  STRAP  PRIG
AERO  PART   TAG
   TORE  YAYAS
SALLIES  AGHAST
ALA  BROKENARROW
NINJA  LARK  INRE
DECAL  ANTE  MITE
SNERD  REED  PEAT
```

732

```
MARC  FRAY  ARGON
ONOR  LIDO  TERRE
PAPADOCDUVALIER
STEVE  ORBE  INSO
   ALEC  INRE
CHIT  CHEGUEVARA
LAD  LOEW  SHEKEL
ARISE  TIE  ADEPT
STOWED  NLRB  LAO
PETERROGET  RAYS
   EYES  VETO
ABET  AGUA  DUTCH
MARIAMONTESSORI
IRISH  ODOR  ETAL
DACHA  DORE  DEBT
```

733

```
SOSO  RETAR  ABBA
IDES  ELENA  NERF
NEXT  WAXYZINNIA
KAYE  ATT  ORATOR
   ZAIRE  FRA
POOLED  MASTIFFS
ULM  RECUR  ENOLA
GIBE  DITCH  EXAM
EVICT  TEEUP  YMA
TEETERED  GEEZER
   LED  PEACE
ENAMEL  DAN  HASH
GALAXYZONE  OLIO
ANON  OOZES  EONS
DATE  NOELS  STET
```

734

```
OPTS  ARMOR  SNAG
ALIT  BEANO  TUNA
FAREWELLADDRESS
SSE  ELIA  SIEVES
   TINA  VII  SEALY
TERENCESTAMP
EROS  EDESSA  IWO
RENTAL   HYMNAL
IDS  FLORIO  ETRE
   FLAPONESGUMS
NGAIO  ANN  OARS
EATSAT  DIEM  MUD
PUSHTHEENVELOPE
AGEE  USAGE  BITE
LEAD  SEUSS  SLOP
```

735

```
MAMMA  HALF  SOPH
ATEAM  OMAR  CURE
SAGEADVICE  RTES
STA  SEE  ETUDES
   BASILRATHBONE
SAUTE   SERIES
ARCED  ATMO  FLA
RAKE  SPREE  COAX
ABS  SPEE  BLOKE
   SALONS  RITES
MINTCONDITION
ICIEST  LOG  OAR
CAKE  CLOVEHITCH
AMOR  HIVE  ARETE
HENS  YEAR  MEDIA
```

736

```
AWAY  JACK  DIGIT
RACE  EVAN  ALIVE
OXEN  AIRE  NIGER
MET  ANDREAGASSI
ANIMUS   RED
   CYD  OLDER  APT
COATI  CORN  SNOW
ANCHORAGEALASKA
LEIS  ELIA  OBEYS
LSD  ELAND  REL
   NNE   HERALD
ALLAMERICAN  DER
MIAMI  ORAN  MATE
INLET  AMID  EMUS
STORY  MANY  ASPS
```

737

```
OFA  SCHEMER  APT
RAD  ORINOCO  NEO
BLOODANDTHUNDER
SPRINT  HOTAIR
BETRUE   GRIT
ALE  MSG  PTA  ONS
HYDE   REARRANGE
   SWEATSUIT
PHOTOSTAT  MYRA
CAV  NEA  SCI  OAT
TRIP   ONEDGE
PSEUDO  TOSEED
TEARSONMYPILLOW
ARC  SNEERED  ELK
ESS  RESTORE  RLS
```

738

```
BOP  NAVAJO  CHAP
RUE  OBERON  ROLL
ACT  TENONE  ASIA
THEWILDWILDWEST
ROES  IMLATE
SAXONS  FONZ
ELENA  SORE  CEDE
LONGLONGTRAILER
LEAS  RUGS  IVIES
   ABBY  GREASE
SOMALI  BAHT
THELATELATESHOW
RANT  AGATHA  AXE
URSA  LASHED  LEE
TEAR  SNEERS  END
```

739

```
ATRI  ACES  SERA
THINKTANKS  OPEC
ROCKETSCIENTIST
IRK  NIB  RESTIR
APES  CASHEW  ODE
LEYTE  HMO  AMES
   ELI  ALLURERS
   MASTERMINDS
BROKEOUT  ETE
ROTS  REP  ONSET
APO  AMORAL  TATA
VERILY  SEC  NAG
USINGONESNOODLE
RING  BRAINDRAIN
ANGE  ARMY  GLAD
```

740

```
ARES  MAYA  FJORD
COVE  IRAN  LEMUR
HUEANDCRY  UTILE
YELLOWED  LISTED
   BAD  DADA
JUSTLY  DON  MESS
ABASE  BERG  MCA
COLORCOMMENTARY
KAT  EGOS  ARIAS
STYE  DEN  STELMO
   XRAY  LEI
COOPER  CONVICTS
ORION  SHADETREE
DENSE  MINI  SITE
ASKEW  ASSN  ABED
```

741

```
MOST  BAN     FRO
IDEA  FACTS   SOAP
DOWNFORTHECOUNT
IRS ORTO  ALONG
   ELMER  SANDY
 HELLER  BIN
MARIO  SAD  ISME
THROWINTHETOWEL
VAST  SAY  STARK
   CRY  CREATE
 SAMOA  WAITS
 PROVE  ORGS  LAS
HITBELOWTHEBELT
URIS  IDIOT  UCLA
HOE   DEN   THIN
```

742

```
ATLAS  PTA  BID
COAXER  RAN  AGUE
EMPIRE  OBTAINED
   SANDPAINTING
HAP  OOHS  AETNA
ERIES  NECK  REAR
YELLOWSTONE
  ALLAH   ELTON
   PEBBLEBEACH
SEAL  TREE  ATTAR
INGOT  IVES  HAS
GRAVELGERTIE
MATERIAL  OVERLY
AGER  ADE  WARIER
ESS   RED  NODES
```

743

```
ACHY  WAFTS  FANS
BLUE  AFOOT  EXIT
BART  DIANE  MICA
AWL  FERLINHUSKY
   YOURE   CAR
ARBORS  QUIZSHOW
SOUPY  CURLY  ELI
HORS  DEANS  FADS
ESL  WINDS  JODIE
STYLISTS  PURSER
   AFT  CADET
OLIVERHARDY  ROB
TERI  AILED  MOLE
INKS  CRAWL  ONES
SASH  TENSE  EGGS
```

744

```
GASPED   TRAPP
INHALE  HAGGADAH
STARIS  IDEALIZE
EDDO  TRIES  AIL
AHOOT  OTOS  OLDE
LAWN  DRYS  ADMEN
FLO  MOAN  ASIF
ALFREDHITCHCOCK
AUTO  NATE  ROE
SADIE  VERA  SMUG
ITON  BIST  SLURS
LIU  MARTS  CERT
AMBULATE  FEEDER
SETTLEUP  INVEST
   AEDES  BEERYS
```

745

```
ALAS  RADAR  CAPE
ROLL  OXIDE  ORAL
EDDIEMONEY  BECK
SEAPLANE  AWAKE
   CON  PALE
STRAP  PEARLBUCK
POISE  EDITS  NAN
APSE  PAWNS  ABLE
RAE  ERNIE  EMILE
EZRAPOUND  MEDAL
  KEPT   SIR
ALFIE  REALIZES
CALM  JOHNNYCASH
AHAB  UPEND  ANTE
DRNO  STOAS  NEED
```

746

```
DREAM  PIA  ALLAY
REACT  UNC  BLEND
INREVERSE  OBEYS
PENT  GEE  ERE
GEORGECOSTANZA
EDNA  STAT  NEUT
ESP  SKAT  SLO
CATSPAW  STRATUM
ALA  STAR  EIN
NORA  HIED  ATUB
STATEOFDECLINE
HAS  TAR  HIRT
DEFOG  BAROMETER
BLAME  APT  ORATE
LINER  HEH  BOSSY
```

747

```
DEFT  ASTER  HUGS
OGRE  MAIZE  ANEW
FREDROGERS  IRMA
FEE  ARARAT  REST
STRATA   RODE
  WILMARUDOLPH
CAMEO  ALONE  IOU
OLES  LYING  ANNE
BOA  NIOBE  PIGGY
BETTYFRIEDAN
  BEET  UNTIES
STAN  ALTARS  CLU
CALS  BARNEYFIFE
AXLE  LOOTS  ALID
MISS  ESTES  TYNE
```

748

```
AMPERE  RASH  SAD
VERNAL  ELLA  ADE
GLENCLOTHES  FOB
TEE  ARID  FARO
SHE  RAKER  SIREN
EONS  FLATATTIRE
LUSH  FED  SAT
FREEWAY  SHRIVEL
LEI  RHO  NEVE
SILVERWEAR  GNAT
CREEK  ASSET  TNT
LOGS  ALOT  ACU
ENA  OVERAPPAREL
RET  POST  REVERE
ADO  TWAS  ODESSA
```

749

```
ASTRA  VOW  RIATA
NAHUM  EVA  IDLES
THELIBRETTOISAS
ALOE  EARTH  TART
  DRABS  ABABYS
FRESNO  TONER
EOS  TRAIN  NOBIS
DISCONNECTEDASA
SLAIN  TOEOF  MEN
  RISEN  RIBBED
RASCAL  METOO
ETTU  ADIEU  ROAD
CROSSWORDPUZZLE
AIRES  DOI  MOLAR
PAESE  ONA  PIEIN
```

750

```
CACTI  ACRE  SIAM
ACORN  YEAS  UNDO
LEGIT  ELSA  SNOW
  PEDALPUSHERS
OSPREY   EIRE
CHAINLETTER
LAWN  HALE  PAM
OREG  SHUTS  ARLO
GAD  ATOM  BEGS
  CATBIRDSEAT
SASH   SERENE
SPOKESPERSON
PURE  HERA  OTHER
ANTE  ISLE  PEEVE
SKAT  NOEL  SERAC
```